PARKER AND MELL

THE MODERN LAW OF TRUSTS

AUSTRALIA
LBC Information Services
Sydney

CANADA and USA
Carswell
Toronto, Ontario

NEW ZEALAND
Brooker's
Auckland

SINGAPORE and MALAYSIA
Thomson Information (S.E. Asia)
Singapore

PARKER AND MELLOWS:

THE MODERN LAW OF TRUSTS

Seventh Edition

by

A. J. OAKLEY, M.A., LL.B.,
of Lincoln's Inn, Barrister-at-Law,
Fellow of Trinity Hall, Cambridge

LONDON
SWEET & MAXWELL
1998

First Edition by Profs D. B. Parker & A. R. Mellows	1966
Second Edition "	1970
Third Edition "	1975
Fourth Edition "	1979
Fifth Edition "	1983
Sixth Edition by A. J. Oakley	1994
Second Impression	1995
Third Impression	1997
Seventh Edition by A. J. Oakley	1998

Published in 1998 by
Sweet & Maxwell Ltd of
100 Avenue Road, Swiss Cottage,
London NW3 3PF
http://www.smlawpub.co.uk
Computerset by Interactive Sciences Ltd,
Gloucester
Printed in England by
MPG Books Ltd

A CIP catalogue record for this book is
available from the British Library
ISBN—0 421 630000

No natural forests were destroyed
to make this product;
only farmed timber was used.

PREFACE

In the preface to the first edition of this work in 1966, its authors stated that the law of trusts "is a branch of the law which is developing at a rapid pace and which is highly relevant to modern conditions, not merely to a bygone age". The accuracy of this statement was demonstrated by the fact that four further editions rapidly followed, culminating in the fifth edition in 1983. The unexpected and untimely death of Professor Parker in 1987, just when the authors might have been expected to have been thinking about a further edition, delayed the production of the sixth edition until 1994. Both that edition and this seventh edition have been entrusted to me. However, while it is now fifteen years since an edition was produced by Professor Parker and Professor Mellows, the immense debt which this work owes to their erudition and scholarship will be apparent to anyone familiar with the editions produced by them and will continue to be apparent for many editions to come.

This edition generally follows the same order as its predecessor. I have divided the extremely long Chapter on Express Private Trusts into three Chapters dealing, respectively, with The Formal Requirements for the Creation of a Trust, The Essential Ingredients of a Trust, and The Constitution of a Trust, while I have inserted the extremely short Chapter on Action on Appointment as Trustee into the Chapter on The Appointment, Retirement and Removal of Trustees. Two wholly new Chapters, on Pension Trusts and Trusts in the Conflict of Laws, have been incorporated, the latter having been placed at the end together with the Chapter on Exporting Trusts. The entire text has been updated and reformatted in the hope that each Chapter will now appear to have a similar style.

The principal legislative change since the last edition has been the enactment of The Trusts of Land and Appointment of Trustees Act 1996; its importance is demonstrated by the number of references which it has been necessary to make to its provisions. There have also been significant legislative changes in relation to trustee investment powers and to the taxation of trusts, most of the latter in the most recent Budget. The most important judicial developments have been produced by three decisions of the Law Lords, the decisions of the House of Lords in *Target Holdings v. Redferns* and *Westdeutsche Landesbank Girozentrale v. Islington L.B.C.* and the decision of the Privy Council in *Royal Brunei Airlines v. Tan*. However, many other significant judgments have been handed down at all levels, particularly in the Court of Appeal.

In the prefaces to both the fifth and the sixth editions of this work, reference was made to the Twenty-Third Report of the Law Reform Committee produced in 1982 and the hope was expressed that most of its recommendations would be enacted by the time of the following edition. Some of the ground covered by that Report has now been considered by the Trust Law Committee, established in 1994 under the Chairmanship of Sir John

Vinelott. Its First Working Party, under the Chairmanship of Professor David Hayton, has produced Reports on the Investment Powers of Trustees (which led to the legislative changes in this area already referred to), on Collective Delegation by Trustees (which was incorporated into the Law Commission's subsequent Consultation Paper on Trustees' Powers and Duties) and the Rights of Creditors against Trustees and Trust Funds. Details of most of these proposals for much needed reform of the law of trusts have been incorporated into the text of this edition. This Working Party is also about to produce a Report on the Proper Ambit of Protection of Trustees. A Second Working Party, under the Chairmanship of Mr. John Mowbray, Q.C., has been set up to produce a Report on Apportionment between Capital and Income and the Committee as a whole is to produce what has been described as a new Table A of Trustees' Powers. Legislation to implement some or all of these proposals for reform can be anticipated during the lifetime of this edition.

I would like to thank Professor Mellows for continuing to repose his confidence in me by entrusting me with this further edition, for which I alone am responsible. I would as always like to thank those of my friends and colleagues with whom I have discussed the subject matter of this work over the years for the benefit of their ideas and criticisms and on this occasion I would particularly like to mention Mr Brian Green, Q.C., of Wilberforce Chambers, 8 New Square, Lincoln's Inn, Professor David Hayton, Barrister, Recorder, and Professor of Law in the University of London at King's College London, and Professor Paul Matthews, Solicitor, Coroner, and Visiting Professor of Law at King's College London, from all of whom I have learnt a very great deal in the last two years. I would also like to thank the members of my Chambers for their support and my clerks for their forbearance. Finally, I would like to thank the publishers for producing the Index and the Tables of Cases, Statutes, and Statutory Instruments and for their patience and efficiency.

The law has been stated from the sources which were available to me on April 30, 1998.

June 9, 1998   A. J. Oakley
                                                               11 Old Square
                                                               Lincoln's Inn

CONTENTS

1. INTRODUCTION

2. THE CLASSIFICATION OF TRUSTS

3. THE FORMAL REQUIREMENTS FOR THE CREATION OF A TRUST

4. THE ESSENTIAL INGREDIENTS OF A TRUST

5. THE CONSTITUTION OF A TRUST 124

6. DISCRETIONARY TRUSTS AND POWERS 163

7. LEGALITY OF A TRUST 206

8. PROTECTIVE TRUSTS 231

9. IMPLIED OR RESULTING TRUSTS 238

TABLE OF CASES

TABLE OF STATUTES

xlv

STATUTORY INSTRUMENTS

CHAPTER 1

INTRODUCTION

I. THE TRUST TODAY

THE modern trust is the direct successor of the medieval use. Ever since the use was first invented, it has been impossible for any property lawyer to give a comprehensive service to his client unless he has had a thorough grasp of the law governing the creation, operation and determination of uses and, later on, of trusts. This is as true, arguably more so, today as it has ever been. It is because, throughout their history, lawyers have employed the use and the trust as devices to circumvent inconvenient rules of law that this is the case.

1. *The Historical Background*

It was during the early medieval period that the practice first arose of owners of property transferring it to third parties[1] to the use[2] either of themselves or of some other beneficiary. The effect of such a transfer was that the third parties became the owners of the property in the eyes of the law but held their legal title to the property for the benefit of the transferor and/or any other nominated beneficiary. The fact that the law regarded the third parties as the owners of the property meant that, in the event that they failed to comply with the terms of the use, neither the transferor nor the other beneficiaries had any remedy in the Royal Courts which then existed.[3] However, in such circumstances a complaint could be made by way of

---

[1] Property transferred by way of use was virtually always put in the name of more than one third party so that on the death of any one of them the other(s) would take the property by survivorship; this avoided difficulties, principally in relation to the incidence of taxation but also in relation to enforceability, which would otherwise have arisen if a sole trustee had died. It is still the almost inevitable practice to have more than one trustee, although today the death of a sole trustee will only cause any difficulties in the relatively unlikely event that there is no documentary evidence of the terms on which he is holding the trust property.

[2] The expression comes from the Latin *ad opus*.

[3] By early in the thirteenth century, three courts had been established to deal with specific distinct areas of the Royal jurisdiction. These courts became known as the Court of King's Bench, the Court of Common Pleas, and the Court of Exchequer; they were collectively known as the Courts of Common Law and the body of rules which they enforced was known as the Common Law. They continued in existence until 1875 when they were abolished and their jurisdiction was transferred to the Supreme Court of Judicature.

petition to the King in Council. At first the practice of the Council was to instruct its principal officer, the Chancellor, to investigate the matter and recommend an appropriate remedy, which the Council then put into effect. In due course,[4] however, the quantity of petitions of this and other types which reached the hands of the Chancellor brought about the establishment of what eventually became known as the Court of Chancery, a jurisdiction of the Chancellor quite separate from, although complementary to, that of the original Royal Courts.[5] The Court of Chancery habitually protected those beneficially entitled under uses (and later on those beneficially entitled under trusts). This was one of the first, and remains the best, examples of the Chancellor developing rules of law distinct from those which had been developed by the original Royal Courts. Later on[6] the different rules developed by successive Chancellors were formulated and became known as the rules of Equity, of which the trust has always been the principal institution.

The earliest situations in which uses were employed were generally of a temporary nature. Until 1290, a freeholder who wished to alienate land in the modern sense, that is to say transfer his entire interest therein to the transferee, had to surrender the land in question to his feudal lord so that the latter could make the appropriate feudal grant to the transferee.[7] Between surrender and grant the lord held the land to the use of the transferee.[8] Uses also had to be employed, both before and after 1290, by anyone who wished to transfer his land into the name of himself and another; he had to put the land into the name of a third party who would hold it to his use pending a transfer back into joint names. This was necessary because until as recently as 1926 it was not possible for anyone to convey land to himself.[9] Further,

---

[4] Probably before the end of the fourteenth century.

[5] Initially the jurisdiction of the Chancellor was of an extraordinary nature. However, towards the end of the fifteenth century the numbers of petitions was increasing steadily and the sixteenth century saw such a dramatic increase that the Chancellor could scarcely cope. A substantial part of this increase consisted of petitions from defrauded beneficiaries of uses, making the rise of the use both a cause and an effect of the establishment of this separate jurisdiction. By the end of the Sixteenth Century, what can by then be described as the Court of Chancery had to all intents and purposes ceased to be an extraordinary court. It continued in existence alongside the Courts of Common Law until 1875 when, like them, it was abolished and its jurisdiction was transferred to the Supreme Court of Judicature.

[6] Towards the end of the seventeenth century, principally by Lord Nottingham who was Chancellor from 1675 to 1682.

[7] For this reason such an alienation (technically known as an alienation by substitution) required the consent of the feudal lord. The transferor could alternatively make the appropriate feudal grant himself but this did not transfer his entire interest in the land to the transferee; instead this created a fresh rung in the feudal ladder and the transferor became the feudal lord of the transferee. This did not affect his existing responsibilities to his own feudal lord and, consequently, this form of alienation (technically known as subinfeudation) could be carried out as of right. The Statute Quia Emptores 1290 changed the situation completely by prohibiting subinfeudation and permitting substitution without the consent of the feudal lord, thus establishing the right of free alienability which has been enjoyed by all freeholders from then until the present day.

[8] This remained the method of conveying copyhold land until the abolition of that tenure in 1925.

[9] It is now possible by virtue of Law of Property Act 1925, s.72(3).

there are examples of Crusaders about to depart for the Holy Land[10] transferring their lands to third parties to hold for them until they returned or for their rightful heirs in the event that they did not do so.[11]

However, it soon came to be realised that uses could equally be employed on a permanent basis. An early example is provided by grants of land made to the Franciscan Friars, who were forbidden by their Order from owning land, shortly after they arrived in England in 1224.[12] Other permanent situations quickly followed.

During the thirteenth century the Crown made strenuous attempts to avoid land being given to corporations (the usual donees being the ever increasing number of ecclesiastical foundations). A series of statutes known collectively as the Statutes of Mortmain[13] purported to impose prohibitions on such gifts with a view to preventing land being taken out of circulation more or less indefinitely, something which had the effect of depriving feudal lords of most, if not all, of their revenue therefrom.[14] The effect of these statutes was for over a century able to be avoided by the employment of a use; until 1391,[15] a transfer of the land in question to third parties to the use of the corporation which was the intended donee was effective to circumvent these prohibitions.

More significantly, until 1540,[16] all freehold land automatically descended to the heir; it was simply not possible to make any alternative disposition of such land by will. However, this inability could be circumvented by a landowner transferring any land which he wished to leave away from his heir to third parties during his lifetime; they would hold the land to the use of the transferor for the remainder of his life and thereafter to the use of the intended beneficiary. This enabled the landowner to continue to derive all possible benefits from his land for as long as he lived and, following his death, the third parties would automatically hold the land for and would normally convey it to the intended beneficiary.

However, the reason why uses were most frequently employed in the medieval period was for the purpose of avoiding feudal inheritance taxes; such uses were one of the earliest examples of what are now known as "tax avoidance schemes". On the death of anyone who held land from his feudal lord as a tenant in knight service,[17] any heir who was an adult would, before he could claim his inheritance, have to pay a fixed sum to that feudal lord

---

[10] And others about to embark on hazardous journeys.

[11] Since the odds were substantially against the Crusader returning and he was in any event likely to be absent for many years, such transfers were in practice more likely to be permanent than temporary.

[12] Such a grant was made to the municipal corporation of Oxford to the use of the Friars in 1225.

[13] Culminating in the Statute De Viris Religiosis 1279.

[14] By this time most of the feudal taxes worth collecting were levied on inheritances. Corporations die much more infrequently than natural persons and medieval ecclesiastical foundations never died (at least not until Henry VIII decided to dissolve the Monasteries in the Sixteenth Century)—hence the name Mortmain ("dead hand").

[15] When the device was prohibited by statute (15 Ric. II (1391), c.5).

[16] Prior to the enactment of the Statute of Wills 1540.

[17] Originally the tenure of the aristocractic military class, by the Fourteenth Century this had become and until 1661 remained the basic tenure by means of which land was held by persons other than subsistence farmers and agricultural labourers.

and, if the feudal lord in question was the King,[18] he additionally had to pay a year's profits of the land in question. Any heir who was an infant was in an even worse position. In this event the feudal lord would be entitled to use the land for his own benefit[19] until the infant reached the age of majority[20] and the infant also had either to submit to the feudal lord's choice of a spouse or, if he could not endure the thought of spending a lifetime locked in the arms of the person chosen,[21] to compensate the lord for the value to him of the marriage[22]; further, at the end of the wardship, if the feudal lord in question was the King,[23] the infant had to pay him a half year's profits of the land. All these potential liabilities could be avoided if, before his death, the tenant in knight service conveyed his land to third parties to the use of himself during the remainder of his life and thereafter to the use of his heir. He would continue to derive all possible benefits from his land for as long as he lived and, following his death, the third parties would transfer the land to the heir—in the case of an adult heir, straightaway; in the case of an infant heir, when he came of age. The heir thus received the land as surely as if the tenant in knight service had retained legal title thereto until his death; however, because he had not actually received the land by way of inheritance, the feudal lord was not entitled to any of the payments or other rights mentioned in this paragraph.

Because uses therefore had the effect of depriving feudal lords in general and the King in particular[24] of a substantial proportion of their feudal revenues, uses were understandably unpopular with the Crown. Henry VIII consequently attempted to take away the advantages conferred by the employment of uses by enacting the Statute of Uses 1536.[25] Although the effects of this Statute were draconian,[26] its effects were relatively short-

---

[18] Prior to the Statute of Marlborough 1267, c.16, this additional payment had to be made to all feudal lords.

[19] This right was formally recognised in the Assize of Northampton 1176, c.4. Magna Carta 1215, cc.4, 5 subsequently prohibited feudal lords from destroying the capital value of the inheritance but they remained entitled to the whole of the income which it produced.

[20] 21 for males and 14 for females (unless the death occurred when the female was already over 14 and unmarried, in which case she came of age at 16 or upon earlier marriage).

[21] The lord could not put forward the most unattractive girl he could find in the hope that the infant would refuse and so give the lord a right to compensation. Magna Carta 1215, c.3 contained a list of defects in a potential spouse which prevented her from being put forward.

[22] Prior to Magna Carta 1215, c.3, this payment had to be made to all feudal lords.

[23] Magna Carta 1215, c.3.

[24] Any method of avoiding feudal taxes hit the King harder than any other feudal lord since he alone was always lord and never tenant.

[25] This "executed" the use by transferring the legal title from the third parties to the beneficiary. As a result, none of the devices described in the text, *ante*, continued to work.

[26] Quite apart from reimposing all the feudal taxes discussed in the text, *ante*, the Statute had the effect of preventing anyone from leaving freehold land away from his heir, thus taking away powers which had been common right for more than a century and leaving freeholders unable to meet some of the most serious obligations which morality and natural affection placed on them. This caused a furore and a step back had to be taken almost immediately; the enactment of the Statute of Wills in 1540 enabled two-thirds of land held in knight service and all land held in any other tenures to be left by will. This did not, however, enable the beneficiaries of the will to escape the feudal taxes.

lived[27] and by the eighteenth century the use had returned under the name of the trust.[28] In the meantime the right to leave freehold land by will had been established by Statute[28a] and all the feudal taxes which uses had been employed to avoid had been abolished.[29] However, lawyers found a number of further situations in which trusts could be usefully employed.

In the eighteenth and nineteenth centuries trusts were employed by wealthy landowners in order to tie up their wealth for the benefit of succeeding generations of their families and also in order to make provision for all their dependants; under the traditional form of settlement which developed,[30] the land in question was vested successively in the eldest son of each generation but the trustees were given overriding powers to raise capital for the benefit of all the other members of the family.[31] Trusts were also employed in order to avoid the common law rule, which was in principle of general application, that a married woman could not hold property in her own right during the marriage[31a]; this rule could be overcome by vesting her property in trustees to hold on trust for her. Further, during the nineteenth century, trusts paid a significant role in the development of unincorporated

---

[27] Its most controversial effect was removed by the Statute of Wills (see *ante*, n. 26), the feudal taxes which were reimposed disappeared with the abolition of tenure in knight service in 1661, while the remaining effects of its provisions were rapidly circumvented by the ingenuity of lawyers. Nevertheless the Statute remained in force until 1925 and during this period considerable care had to be taken in drafting in order to avoid its provisions.

[28] The Statute of Uses was held only to "execute" the first of two or more successive uses; second or subsequent uses were neither executed by the Statute nor valid at common law. Consequently, if land was transferred "unto and to the use of" third parties (to the third parties to their own use) to the use of (or on trust for) the intended beneficiary, the third parties retained the legal title and were regarded by the common law as the owners of the property in question. The intended beneficiary under the second use was consequently as unprotected at common law as the beneficiaries of all uses had been before the Statute of Uses. The Chancellor therefore once again intervened to protect the beneficiaries of second or subsequent uses and such uses were renamed trusts. The result of all this was that the third parties held the legal title on trust for the intended beneficiaries just as they had done before the Statute of Uses. The Statute of Uses had thus been avoided by the simple expedient of adding the words "and to the use of". This was acknowledged by Lord Hardwicke L.C. in *Hopkins v. Hopkins* (1738) 1 Atk. 581 at 591, where he said "by this means a Statute made upon great consideration ... has had no other effect than to add at most three words to a conveyance" (a statement which not only overlooks the other very significant consequences of the Statute of Uses but also puts into question the ability of Lord Hardwicke to count).

[28a] See *ante* n. 26.

[29] These were abolished by the Tenures Abolition Act 1661.

[30] A succinct description of settlements of this kind (generally known as "strict settlements") can be found in Megarry & Wade: *The Law of Real Property* (5th ed., 1984), pp. 311–317, 410–416.

[31] This system however prevented the land from being developed since no one person had the power to dispose of or deal with the land in order to do so; the end result was consequently a situation of total sterility. During the Nineteenth Century, it therefore became necessary for the powers of the eldest son (or other beneficiary in possession) for the time being to be very considerably extended and he was finally given full powers of disposal and management by the Settled Land Act 1882.

[31a] This restriction seems to date from the beginning of the Thirteenth Century. In its final form, all the personalty owned by a wife on marriage, or acquired by her thereafter, became the absolute property of her husband; he was also entitled to manage and to take the profits of her freehold land, which by law became vested in both of them. However, the property of the married woman nevertheless passed in accordance with her will or the appropriate intestacy rules on her death. The restriction was finally taken away by the Married Women's Property Act 1882.

associations such as clubs, friendly societies and trade unions; because such bodies are not themselves legal entities and so cannot hold property, they would not have developed in the way that they have had it not been possible for their property to be held by trustees on their behalf.[32] Finally, in the twentieth century, the trust once again came to be used as a means of creating "tax avoidance schemes".[33]

2. *The Principal Uses of the Trust Today*

The many and varied purposes for which trusts are employed today can be summarised as follows:

1. To enable property, particularly land, to be held for persons who cannot themselves hold it. Although the legal title to land cannot be vested in a minor,[34] there is no objection to land being held on trust for such a person. Indeed the legislature has adopted this particular route, providing that a purported conveyance of a legal estate in land to a minor operates as a declaration that the land is held in trust for that person.[35]

2. To enable a person to make provision for dependants privately. The most obvious examples are any provision made by a man for his mistress or his illegitimate child. During his lifetime he can make such provision without publicity but an express testamentary gift in favour of a mistress or an illegitimate child by will may well become public knowledge. Once probate has been obtained, a will becomes a public document and is therefore open to public inspection—indeed tabloid journalists routinely inspect the wills of famous persons in the hope of finding embarrassing information of this type. A trust of property, on the other hand, escapes publicity of this type provided that the person making such provision either settles property on the intended beneficiaries during his lifetime or creates what is known as a secret trust[36] in their favour in his will.

3. To tie up property so that it can benefit persons in succession. It is of course always possible to make an outright gift of property to a parent in the hope and expectation that on the parent's death that property will go to his children but there is no guarantee that it will actually do so. On the other hand, a gift of property to trustees to hold on trust for the parent for life with remainder to the children will ensure[37] that the

---

[32] See *post*, p. 117.
[33] See *post*, pp. 9, 167–173.
[34] Law of Property Act 1925, s.19.
[35] Trusts of Land and Appointment of Trustees Act 1996, Sched. 1, para. 1. Before this Act came into force on January 1, 1997, such a conveyance operated as an agreement for valuable consideration to create a settlement of that land on the minor and in the meantime to hold the land on trust for him (Settled Land Act 1925, s.27); any conveyances so operating on January 1, 1997 thereafter also take effect as declarations of trust.
[36] See *post*, p. 62.
[37] Unless the parent and children agree, after all the children have reached the age of majority, to bring the trust to an end prematurely.

children derive a benefit. It is admittedly not normally possible to ensure that the person ultimately entitled will receive the actual property which is settled, since the trustees will almost always have the power to sell it and re-invest the proceeds. But it is possible to ensure that the person ultimately entitled does at the very least receive whatever assets are derived from that property.

4. To protect family property from wastrels. A person may feel that an outright gift of money to a surviving spouse or child will lead to the money being rapidly dissipated. On the other hand, a gift of that money to trustees to hold on trust to pay either the income or only a limited proportion of the capital to the surviving spouse or child will probably prevent this. Flexibility can be preserved by giving the trustees a discretion as to the amount (if any) of income or capital which they may pay over at any one time; another possibility is for property to be given to trustees to hold on trust for a beneficiary in such a way that the property will be preserved from the beneficiary's creditors in the event that he becomes bankrupt.[38]

5. To make a gift to take effect in the future in the light of circumstances which have not yet arisen and so cannot yet be known. A person who has three young daughters may choose to set up a trust in his will whereby a sum of money is given to trustees for them to distribute among the daughters, either as they think fit or having regard to certain stated factors. They might, for example, in due course decide to give one-quarter each to two of the daughters who had married well and one-half to the poorer unmarried daughter.

6. To make provision, particularly by will, for causes or for non-human objects. By means of a trust money can be donated for the further-ance of education or for the purpose of maintaining a beloved animal such as a favourite dog or cat.

7. To enable two or more persons to own land. One of the more curious features of English land law is that not more than one person can be the absolute legal and beneficial owner of land; if two or more persons wish to own land jointly, they can only do so behind a trust.[39] Since the Second World War, it has become increasingly common for married couples (and for that matter unmarried couples living in a *de facto* relationship) to have the family home vested in their joint names—indeed, building societies and banks normally make any mortgage advance conditional on this being done. Sub-stantially more than half the residential property in the country must now be owned jointly in this way; this means that, technically, well

---

[38] This device is known as a protective trust.

[39] This will be a trust of land under the Trusts of Land and Appointment of Trustees Act 1996. Before this Act came into force on January 1, 1977, the trust in question would either have been a trust for sale or a settlement under the Settled Land Act 1925. All pre-existing trusts for sale have been converted into trusts of land but pre-existing settlements under the Settled Land Act 1925 continue, although no new ones can be created.

over half the houses in the country are now held on trust, a fact which would undoubtedly surprise most of their occupants.[40]

8. To provide pensions for retired persons and their dependants. Since the Second World War pension schemes have become increasingly common and are now regarded as an essential part of virtually every contract of employment and an important factor for the self-employed.[41] Pension schemes for employees are either non-contributory, in which case the whole of the money is provided by the employer, or contributory, in which case both the employer and the employee pay into the fund. Self-employed persons take out personal pension schemes, facilitated by generous tax concessions, which are also available to employees who wish to "top-up" the pension arising out of their employment. In the vast majority of cases, pension funds provided for employees are held by trustees with the objective, usually but sadly not always[42] achieved, of assuring the employee that his pension will in fact be forthcoming and that in the meantime his employer cannot in any way dispose of the money. The funds contributed towards personal pension schemes are typically paid to insurance companies for investment in insurance policies but can also be held in the form of investments by trustees, in such cases usually by trust corporations.

9. To facilitate investment through unit trusts and investment trusts. The objective of such trusts is to enable the small investor to acquire a small stake in a large portfolio of investments and thus to spread his risk across a substantial range of stocks and shares. Further, such portfolios are sufficiently large for their investments to be supervised on a full-time basis. In the case of a unit trust, the promoter, usually the future manager, of the unit trust invites the public to subscribe for units of a fixed initial value. The funds so obtained are invested in the stock market, either entirely generally or with at least the majority of the holdings in a particular nominated sphere, such as in oil companies. The investments so purchased are vested in trustees, usually in a trust corporation. The trustees receive the dividends on the investments which, after payment of their administration expenses and the remuneration of the manager (usually a percentage of the value of the fund), are distributed among the investors in proportion to the number of units held or reinvested to increase the total value of the fund and so of the individual units in it. The

---

[40] This has come to be so much a matter of course that some solicitors are now thought to have given up explaining the provisions of conveyances of land which declare the trusts upon which the property is to be held; if this is indeed the case, the fact that the property is to be held on trust may never even have been mentioned to its purchasers.

[41] In 1995 United Kingdom pension funds were estimated to be worth in excess of £500 billion and growing.

[42] The systematic looting by the late Robert Maxwell of the pension fund established to provide pensions for ex-employees of *The Daily Mirror* caused great concern among employees in general; pension fund administration then became the subject of a Committee of Inquiry, the Pensions Law Reform Committee, which reported in the autumn of 1993 and came down on the side of continuing to utilise the trust vehicle.

manager, who is responsible for selecting the original investments and changing them when he feels this to be appropriate, is obliged to buy back the units at any time at a price fixed by reference to the total value of the fund at any one time. He will offer for sale any units so bought back at a slightly higher price. There are consequently at any one time two different prices at which units are respectively bought back and sold. An investment trust works in a broadly similar way with two important distinctions. First, the fund is not divided into units so that the capital subscribed can be of any amount which the manager is prepared to accept. Secondly, the individual investors can only deal with their investments on the stock exchange (the manager is not under any obligation to buy them back) this consequently means that the price paid will depend on market forces rather than being directly related to the total value of the fund at any one time. The importance of investment vehicles of this kind for the small investor cannot be overestimated.[43]

10. To minimise the incidence of income tax, capital gains tax and inheritance tax. A high proportion of the numerous possible "tax avoidance schemes" which have been devised involve a trust in one way or another.[44] One example will suffice for the moment. At present a person with a high income[45] will pay income tax of 40 per cent on any investment income. If, however, the investment is transferred to trustees to be held on trust for other members of his family who are of more modest means and so pay either no income tax at all or income tax at a lower rate, a substantial tax saving can be made. The minimum saving, without taking into account the administration expenses of the trust, will be 17 per cent of the income (the difference between the 40 per cent tax otherwise payable and the 23 per cent basic rate of tax[46]) and even greater savings will be made if any of the other members of the family does not have enough other income to use up his personal allowance[47] and his 20 per cent tax band.[48]

11. To protect the environment. In other jurisdictions, the trust has developed a role in environmental protection law. In the United States of America, under the so-called "public trust doctrine", each State has a fiduciary obligation to ensure that the public lands which constitute the coastline, the bays of the sea, and the tidal rivers and their beds are made continuously available for the members of the public at large. No such doctrine could operate in this jurisdiction since all

---

[43] Unit trusts and investment trusts are often incorporated in which case they are governed by the Companies Acts 1985 and 1989. All such investment vehicles are in any event subject, in addition to the normal provisions of trust law and company law, to special legislation designed to protect the public against fraud.

[44] Such schemes "involve" trusts because in the majority of cases they will necessitate either the setting up of a trust or the breaking of an existing trust or a combination of the two.

[45] In 1998–99 income tax is payable at 40 per cent on any taxable income (that is the taxpayer's income after the deduction of any personal allowances to which he is entitled) over £27,100.

[46] Payable in 1998–99 on taxable income between £4,301 and £27,100.

[47] £4,195 for a single person in 1998–99.

[48] Payable in 1998–99 on the first £4,300 of taxable income.

such lands are vested in the Crown. However, English law could undoubtedly copy "the 'trusteed' environmental fund" which has been developed in Canada. The purpose of funds of this type is to provide an assurance for the State that, following the termination of some environmentally harmful activity such as mining or logging, the post closure land reclamation will be adequately financed. The party carrying out the activity makes periodic payments to trustees who, like the trustees of a pension fund, invest these payments for return and the accumulated fund is the primary or immediate source for meeting the costs of land reclamation.[49] This interesting use of the trust concept in a field which is today of such enormous international importance and interest could undoubtedly be adopted in this jurisdiction in appropriate circumstances.

All the illustrations which have just been given concern trusts which are deliberately created in order to achieve the objectives in question. However, trusts can also arise in other ways. The court will in certain circumstances infer the existence of a relationship of trustee and beneficiary where the owner of property has intentionally carried out some other transaction (such trusts are known as "resulting trusts"). And the court is able to impose a relationship of trustee and beneficiary as a result of misconduct by the person held to be a trustee (such trusts are known as "constructive trusts").

The multiple purposes for which trusts can be and are employed today emphasise the importance of the trust in modern law and society. They also make it apparent that one of the greatest advantages of trusts is the flexibility of purpose for which they can be used. Another is the fact that the rules which govern trusts are by and large the same whatever the purpose for which they are employed. The remainder of this book attempts to explain those rules.

II. THE DEFINITION OF A TRUST

1. *Suggested Definitions*

Considerable difficulty has been found in providing a comprehensive definition of a trust, but various attempts have been made. The following definitions deserve consideration.

(A) Lord Coke's Definition
Lord Coke defined a trust as "a confidence reposed in some other, not issuing out of the land but as a thing collateral thereto, annexed in privity to the estate of the land, and to the person touching the land, for which *cestui que trust* has no remedy but by subpoena in the Chancery".[50] Some of this language may require elucidation. When Coke says that a trust is collateral to land, not issuing out of it, he means that a trust differs from a legal

---

[49] See D. W. M. Waters in *Equity, Fiduciaries and Trusts 1993* (ed. Waters, 1993), p. 383.
[50] Co. Litt. 272b.

interest: a legal interest continues to subsist even after a purchase for value without notice of that interest, whereas an equitable interest such as that of a beneficiary under a trust does not do so and is, for that reason, collateral. When he says that a trust is annexed in privity to the estate, he means that the trust will only continue so long as the estate continues. And when he says that a trust is annexed in privity to the person, he means that a purchaser for value of the legal estate without notice of the trust takes free from its provisions.

It has to be said, however, that some objections can be made to Coke's formulation. First, what is a "confidence"? This expression does not explain precisely the meaning of "trust". Secondly, the definition imports the idea of a reliance placed by one person on another. This may not be universally correct. The *cestui que trust* (or "beneficiary") may be a babe in arms or unborn or for some other reason wholly ignorant of the trust. The trust in such cases may still be effective (and normally will be) but the *cestui que trust* will place no "reliance" whatever on the trustee. Thirdly, Coke's definition applies only to real property, whereas the subject-matter of a trust has always also been able to be personal property. And, fourthly, it is procedurally out of date; the Court of Chancery no longer exists and the entire Supreme Court of Judicature now has jurisdiction in equity matters.[51] Nevertheless this early definition is undoubtedly worth a mention; subject to the criticisms which have been made, it is at least as useful as most of the modern definitions.

(B) Sir Arthur Underhill's Definition

Sir Arthur Underhill, the original author of the leading practitioners' work which is now known as Underhill and Hayton, *Law of Trusts and Trustees*, described a trust as "an equitable obligation binding a person (who is called a trustee) to deal with property over which he has control (which is called trust property), for the benefit of persons (who are called beneficiaries or *cestuis que trust*[52]), of whom he may himself be one and any one of whom may enforce the obligation".[53]

As a comprehensive definition of all kinds of trusts, it may be objected that this one does not in terms cover charitable trusts and, further, makes no provision for the so-called "trusts of imperfect obligation",[54] such as a trust "for the maintenance and support of my dog Tigger"—this may well amount to a valid trust but is a trust of imperfect obligation because Tigger cannot enforce it. The successive editors of what is now Underhill and Hayton have, however, pointed out that, even though charitable trusts are outside the scope of the work, they are in any event covered by the definition, simply because such a trust is for the benefit of persons, namely the public, on whose behalf the Attorney-General may intervene.[55] They have

---

[51] Supreme Court of Judicature (Consolidation) Act 1925, s.4(4).
[52] This is the plural: "Cestuis que trustent" is "hopelessly wrong": Sweet (1910) 26 L.Q.R. 196.
[53] Underhill & Hayton, *Law of Trusts and Trustees* (15th ed.), p. 1. The definition was approved by Cohen J. in *Re Marshall's Will Trusts* [1945] Ch. 217 at 219 and by Romer L.J. in *Green v. Russell* [1959] 2 Q.B. 226 at 241.
[54] See *post*, p. 110.
[55] See *post*, p. 379.

also stated that trusts of imperfect obligation are not referred to because they are acknowledged to be "anomalous and exceptional".[56]

(C)   The Definition in Lewin on Trusts

Lewin on *Trusts*,[57] the other main practitioners' work, adopts a rather more comprehensive definition, which is based on a definition given by Mayo J. in *Re Scott*.[58] According to this formulation:

"the word 'trust' refers to the duty or aggregate accumulation of obligations that rest upon a person described as trustee. The responsibilities are in relation to property held by him, or under his control. That property he will be compelled by a court in its equitable jurisdiction to administer in the manner lawfully prescribed by the trust instrument, or where there be no specific provision written or oral, or to the extent that such provision is invalid or lacking, in accordance with equitable principles. As a consequence the administration will be in such a manner that the consequential benefits and advantages accrue, not to the trustee, but to the persons called *cestuis que trust*, or beneficiaries, if there be any; if not, for some purpose which the law will recognise and enforce. A trustee may be a beneficiary, in which case advantages will accrue in his favour to the extent of his beneficial interest."[59]

(D)   The Definition in the Recognition of Trusts Act 1987

The Recognition of Trusts Act 1987 incorporates into English law The Hague Convention on the Law Applicable to Trusts and on their Recognition. This international convention contains the following definition of a trust in Article 2:

"For the purposes of this Convention, the term 'trust' refers to the legal relationships created—*inter vivos* or on death—by a person, the settlor, when assets have been placed under the control of a trustee for the benefit of a beneficiary or for a specified purpose. A trust has the following characteristics—

(a)   the assets constitute a separate fund and are not part of the trustee's own estate;

(b)   title to the trust assets stands in the name of the trustee or in the name of another person on behalf of the trustee;

(c)   the trustee has the power and the duty, in respect of which he is accountable, to manage, employ or dispose of the assets in accordance

---

[56] See *post*, p. 110.

[57] (16th ed.), p. 1.

[58] [1948] S.A.S.R. 193 at 196.

[59] For a similar and well-known definition see Keeton *Law of Trusts* (11th ed.), p. 2. For other definitions by text writers, see *Halsbury's Laws of England* (4th ed.), Vol. 48, p. 272; American Law Institute, *Restatement of the Law of Trusts* p. 6, para. 2. For judicial definitions, see *Sturt v. Mellish* (1743) 2 Atk. 610 at 612, *per* Lord Hardwicke L.C.; *Burgess v. Wheate* (1759) 1 Eden 177 at 223, *per* Lord Mansfield C.J.; *Re Williams* [1897] 2 Ch. 12 at 19 (CA), *per* Lindley L.J. As to the meaning of "trust" and "trustee" in Trustee Act 1925, see *ibid*. s.68(17).

with the terms of the trust and the special duties imposed upon him by
law.

The reservation by the settlor of certain rights and powers, and the fact that
the trustee may himself have rights as a beneficiary, are not necessarily
inconsistent with the existence of a trust."

The purpose of the Convention was twofold: first, to provide rules by
which the courts of signatory states can uniformly determine the jurisdiction
by whose rules of trust law trusts with international dimensions are governed (this aspect of the Convention will be considered in detail in Chapter
25); and, secondly, to provide some means of dealing with trusts in jurisdictions where the trust concept is unknown. When property situated in such
jurisdictions becomes the subject matter of a trust, problems potentially arise
because it can be extremely difficult to convince the authorities of the
jurisdiction in question that the trustees are not the beneficial owners of the
trust property.

In commercial terms, the principal potential difficulty relates to the issue
of Eurobonds by United Kingdom financial institutions to raise funds for the
purpose of investment throughout Europe. The funds subscribed and the
assets in which they are invested are held on trust for the subscribers. This
can cause problems where the funds are invested in those jurisdictions in
mainland Europe where the trust concept is unknown. The insolvency of the
trustees may cause the authorities in any of these jurisdictions in which trust
assets are situated to attempt to take the trust assets for the benefit of the
trustees' creditors. Alternatively, where the trustees lend the funds subscribed to organisations situated in any of these jurisdictions, doubts may be
cast on the ability of the trustees to sue those organisations if the latter
default on the loans.

In non-commercial terms, the principal difficulty relates to testamentary
dispositions by the increasingly large number of English people who own
holiday homes in jurisdictions where the trust concept is unknown. Such
owners are quite likely to deal with those homes in the same way as with the
rest of their property and leave them by will to their executors and trustees
on trust for their surviving spouses and/or their children. The immediate
reaction of the authorities of the jurisdiction in question will unquestionably
be to treat the trustees as the beneficial owners of the property, something
which has potentially adverse fiscal consequences; this is because in many of
the jurisdictions of this type the rate of Inheritance Tax payable is determined by how closely the beneficiary is related to the testator[60] and many

---

[60] In Spain, probably the country which contains the largest number of holiday homes owned
by British people, this factor determines both the tax free allowance and the rate of tax
charged. If the tax free sum to which spouses, ascendants and descendants are entitled is
treated as 2X and the rate of tax payable by them is treated as 2Y, then the tax free sum to
which more distant relatives are entitled is X and the rate of tax payable by them is 3Y, while
beneficiaries who are not related in any way to the testator have no tax free sum whatever
and pay tax at the rate of 4Y. The situation is broadly similar, although less extreme, in
France.

trustees will inevitably not be in any way related to their testator. Other difficulties can also arise.[61]

The definition set out above is therefore intended to provide the necessary explanation of the nature of a trust in a form which is capable of being applied to and being comprehensible in a large number of different legal systems. For this reason, its format inevitably not only has to include references to a number of features of a trust which are not mentioned in the definitions already considered but also cannot include specific references to features which apply only to English law, such as the fact that the trustee is compellable by a court acting under its equitable jurisdiction. This definition, like that propounded in Lewin on *Trusts*, does not roll off the tongue as easily as the one propounded by Sir Arthur Underhill. Nevertheless, its comprehensive nature cannot be disputed; no trust recognised by English law falls outside the four corners of this most recent of the many attempts to define a trust.

2. *The Essential Elements of a Trust*

All the definitions which have just been considered point to a number of essential elements, all of which must be present in order for a trust to be effectively constituted.

(A) Property Subject to the Trust
No valid trust can be created unless there is some identifiable property subject to the trust over which the trustees have control. Any property whatever can form the subject matter of a trust, whether that property be tangible, that is to say a chose in possession such as a freehold or leasehold estate, or intangible, that is to say a chose in action such as a share or the benefit of a covenant or simple contract. It is evident from these illustrations that it makes no difference whether the property in question is realty or personalty. Furthermore, it makes no difference whether the interest subject to the trust is a legal estate or an equitable interest. If the legal estate in property is held by trustees on trust, the interests of the beneficiaries are necessarily equitable. If any beneficiary assigns his equitable interest to a third party to hold on quite different trusts, that equitable interest will constitute the subject matter of the second trust (technically a sub-trust and therefore subject to certain special rules which will be considered later[62]); the

---

[61] There may be other adverse fiscal consequences. If the trustees are beneficially entitled to other property in the same jurisdiction, the local Revenue may well try to aggregate the income and capital taxes payable on the trust property with that payable on their own property, thus producing a higher marginal rate of tax (most European countries have many more different rates of tax than the United Kingdom and the top rate is usually substantially higher; in Spain in 1998 it was 58%, which applied to both income tax and capital gains tax). Further, such jurisdictions never recognise the existence of the beneficiaries' equitable interests because there is no way in which they can be protected on the relevant Property Register. This can prejudice the beneficiaries in the event of a dispute between them and the trustees, particularly if the trustees are resident in the jurisdiction in question.

[62] See *post*, p. 49.

legal estate will remain vested in the original trustees.[63] However, property subject to a trust must be capable of being identified. Consequently a liability cannot, without more, be the subject matter of a trust. If a creditor suggests to his debtor and the debtor agrees that, instead of repaying the loan, the debtor should hold the sum in question on trust for a third party, a valid trust will only arise if the debtor segregates the appropriate sum from his other assets by, for example, opening a new bank account for the purpose. If he does so, the trust will then be of the segregated assets, not of the liability. If, on the other hand, he fails to do so, something which in practice is highly likely since if the debtor had the assets to segregate he could equally easily have repaid the loan on the spot, the third party will be unable to point to any property subject to any trust and so will have no remedy.[64]

(B) One or More Trustees

There must be one or more trustees in whom title to the trust property is vested. In principle, any number of persons may be trustees but this basic rule is now subject to a number of statutory restrictions which will be discussed in detail later on.[65] Briefly, there can be no more than four trustees of either a non-charitable trust of land[66] or a trust *mortis causa* of any property for an infant where no trustees are appointed by any will.[67] If a trust is created *inter vivos*, there may well be no trustee other than the person who has created the trust, its settlor; this will be the case where a settlor simply declares that henceforth he is holding the property in question on trust for the objects in question. Alternatively, and necessarily if a trust is created post mortem, the trust may be created by transfer; in this case the trustees will be those persons (normally more than one in order to avoid the problems which might arise if a sole trustee died) to whom the settlor or testator has transferred the property in question; in the case of an *inter vivos* trust, the settlor will frequently be one of the initial trustees. If a settlor attempts to create an *inter vivos* trust by purporting to transfer property to trustees who are neither named nor identified or to persons who are already dead, no valid trust will have been created. If, on the other hand, a testator fails to nominate any trustees in his will, his personal representatives will hold the property as trustees until other trustees are appointed. Once a trust has been validly constituted, it cannot thereafter fail for want of a trustee

---

[63] See *Gilbert v. Overton* (1804) 2 H. & M. 110.

[64] Exactly this situation arose in *M'Fadden v. Jenkyns* (1842) 1 Ph. 153; however, despite the fact that all three parties had clearly intended the debtor to be the trustee, Lord Lyndhurst L.C. generously found that the effect of the agreement was that the creditor held his right to sue the debtor on trust for the third party, thus providing her with a remedy against his personal representatives. The creditor can of course create such a situation intentionally; in *Barclays Bank v. Willowbrook International* (1987) 1 F.T.L.R. 386, a creditor charged to the bank a debt which was due to be repaid and the Court of Appeal held that any repayments made by the debtor were held by the creditor on constructive trust for the bank.

[65] See *post*, p. 468.

[66] Trustee Act 1925, s.34(3).

[67] Administration of Estates Act 1925, s.42.

since anyone in whom the trust property comes to be vested, other than a
bona fide purchaser for value of a legal estate in the property without notice
of the interests of the beneficiaries[68] (or, in the case of registered land, the
statutory equivalent[69]), will be bound by that trust and so will be a trustee
of the property.

(C) An Equitable Obligation

The trustees must be under an equitable obligation, often described as a
fiduciary duty, to deal with the trust property for the persons, purposes or
objects defined by the settlor or testator—if they are not under any duty to
do anything whatever, there cannot be a trust (this does not prevent trustees
being given completely unfettered discretions as to whether and, if so, how
to deal with the trust property; their duty in such cases consists of being
obliged to consider from time to time what, if anything, they should do[70]).
This equitable obligation not only imposes on the trustees potential personal
liabilities to the beneficiaries, liabilities which can be both penal and
extremely stringent[71]; it also binds the trust property itself in the hands of
anyone who has not taken free of the interests of the beneficiaries therein for
the reasons stated in the previous paragraph.

(D) One or More Beneficiaries

No trust can exist without one or more beneficiaries (or *cestuis que trust*) for
whose benefit the property is held. The trustees may also be some or all of
the beneficiaries (most co-owners of land hold the land in question as
trustees on trust for themselves[72]) but a sole trustee cannot also be the sole
beneficiary—in this event, there would simply be no trust.

   The precise nature of the interest of a beneficiary in the trust property has
always been difficult to define.[73] On the one hand, the beneficiary has a
proprietary interest in the subject matter of the trust because he can recover
it from anyone into whose hands it passes other than a bona fide purchaser
for value of a legal estate therein without notice of the interest of the
beneficiary (or, in the case of registered land, the statutory equivalent). On
the other hand, given that if the property does reach the hands of such a
person it cannot be recovered by the beneficiary, whose only option will
then be to bring a personal action against his trustees for breach of trust, his
interest is certainly not a right *in rem*. The best view is that the interest of a

---

[68] The one person whose interests are always preferred to those of the beneficiaries of a trust
(see *Basset v. Nosworthy* (1673) Rep.Temp.Finch 102, where this time honoured rule was laid
down by Lord Nottingham L.C.). For this reason, such a person has traditionally been known
as "equity's darling".
[69] A bona fide purchaser for value claiming under a registered disposition (Land Registration
Act 1925, s.20(1)); some commentators jocularly refer to such a person as "the Registrar's
darling".
[70] See *post*, pp. 163–205.
[71] See *post*, pp. 281–319.
[72] Law of Property Act 1925, ss.34, 36 as amended by Trusts of Land and Appointment of
Trustees Act 1996, Sched. 2, paras 3, 4.
[73] See Latham (1954) 32 Can B.R. 520 on the question generally.

beneficiary is a true hybrid—substantially more than a right *in personam* but substantially less than a right *in rem*. This is reflected by the decided cases, which regard the beneficiary as owner of the trust property for some purposes but not for others. Thus in *Baker v. Archer-Shee*,[74] the beneficiary was held to be the real owner of the trust assets for income tax purposes. On the other hand, in *Schalit v. Joseph Nadler*,[75] a beneficiary was held unable to distrain for rent due under a lease of the trust property granted by the trustee. The Divisional Court stated that "[t]he right of the cestui que trust whose trustee has demised property subject to the trust is not to the rent, but to an account from the trustees of the profits received from the trust".[76] Both these decisions appear to be in accordance with principle.

3. *"Trusts in the Higher Sense" and "Trusts in the Lower Sense"*

As Lord O'Hagan once said,[77] there is no magic in the word "trust", which can mean different things in different contexts. For example, a person may be in a position of trust without being a trustee in the equitable sense and terms such as "anti-trust" or "trust territories" are not intended to relate to a trust enforceable in a court of equity. By the same token, a trust in the conventional legal sense may be created without actually using the word "trust".[78] In each case it is necessary to consider whether the latter type of trust was or was not intended.[79]

This is exactly what had to be decided in *Tito v. Waddell (No. 2)*,[80] a case which Megarry V.-C. aptly described as "litigation on the grand scale".[81] The case involved Ocean Island, a small island in the Pacific, called Banaba by its inhabitants, who were unsurprisingly known as Banabans. The island had formerly been part of the Gilbert and Ellice Islands Protectorate and subsequently became a Crown Colony. At the beginning of the twentieth century, phosphate was discovered on the island and royalties for mining the phosphate were duly paid to the islanders. As time passed, the Banabans understandably sought increases in the royalty payments. Some increases were paid but they were considerably less than what had been claimed. The Banabans continued to make various claims both politically and internationally; but when those claims finally failed, they brought these proceedings, claiming that the rates of royalties payable in respect of certain transactions had been less than the proper rates and that accordingly the Crown, as the responsible authority, was subject to a trust or fiduciary duty for the benefit of the Banabans or their predecessors and was liable for breach thereof.

---

[74] [1927] A.C. 844.
[75] [1933] 2 K.B. 79.
[76] *ibid*. at 83.
[77] In *Kinloch v. Secretary of State for India in Council* (1882) 7 App. Cas. 619 at 630.
[78] *Tito v. Waddell* (No. 2) [1977] Ch. 106 at 211, *per* Megarry V.-C.
[79] See *post*, p. 82.
[80] [1977] Ch. 106.
[81] *ibid*. at 123. The report of the judgment of Megarry V.-C. runs to 241 pages. The Vice-Chancellor also held a view of the *locus in quo*.

The question as to whether there was indeed such a trust or fiduciary duty involved the construction of various agreements and ordinances as well as other documents. In the event, it was held that there was neither a trust nor a fiduciary duty. The essential elements of the decision for the purposes of any definition of a trust[82] appear to be as follows:

1. Although the word "trust" had occasionally been used with reference to the Crown or its agents, that did not create a trust which was enforceable in the courts (what Megarry V.-C. described as a "trust in the lower sense" or "true trust") but rather a trust "in the higher sense", by which was meant a governmental obligation which was not enforceable in the courts.[83]

2. Such a trust "in the higher sense" could only be discharged under the direction of the Crown.[84] There might be many means available of persuading the Crown to honour its governmental obligations, for example of international pressure; but even if its obligations were higher than normal obligations, they were not enforceable by the court.[85]

3. Although some of the ordinances imposed statutory duties on the Crown, they did not also impose fiduciary obligations. As will be seen later on,[86] in some cases a person may be in a fiduciary position even though he is not a trustee in the proper sense of the word (for example, an agent or a company director or a partner) and such a person will be liable if he is in breach of his fiduciary obligations. A relationship giving rise to fiduciary obligations may be either equitable or legal or purely statutory but it must be a relationship with enforceable legal consequences.[87] However, as Megarry V.-C. specifically held, "a trust in the higher sense or governmental obligation lacks this characteristic and where the primary obligation itself is one which the courts will not enforce, then it [cannot] of itself give rise to a secondary obligation which is enforceable by the courts".[88]

4. If a duty is imposed by statute (such as the ordinances in this case) to perform certain functions, that statute will not, as a general rule, also impose fiduciary obligations nor is it to be presumed that it does so. It has to be affirmatively shown that such obligations are indeed imposed.[89]

---

[82] For other aspects of the decision, see *post*, pp. 282, 695.
[83] Adopting the language of Lord Selborne L.C. in *Kinloch v. Secretary of State for India in Council* (1882) 7 App. Cas. 619 at 625.
[84] *Tito v. Waddell* (No. 2) [1977] Ch. 106 at 216.
[85] *ibid.* at 217.
[86] See *post*, pp. 281 *et seq*.
[87] [1997] Ch. 106 at 224.
[88] *ibid.* at 225.
[89] *ibid.* at 235. See also *Swain v. The Law Society* [1983] A.C. 598 (in exercising a statutory power the Law Society was performing not a private duty but a public duty for breach of which there was no remedy in breach of trust or equitable account); see further *post*, p. 282.

Suffice it to say that this book is concerned with "trusts in the lower sense" or "true trusts" and with those situations which give rise to enforceable fiduciary obligations.

III. THE DISTINCTION BETWEEN TRUSTS AND OTHER LEGAL CONCEPTS

1. *Contract*

English law recognises two types of contract, a simple contract (a contract constituted as a result of the existence of offer and acceptance, intention to create legal relations, and consideration) and a specialty contract (a contract constituted by virtue of being in a deed, often also described as a covenant). This section is principally concerned with simple contracts but there is a brief reference to specialty contracts in its final paragraph.

A simple contract is in general not enforceable by a person who is not a party to that contract, whereas a trust can be enforced by a beneficiary who is not a party to the instrument creating the trust (indeed, beneficiaries rarely are parties to such instruments). This rule of contract law is of general application and seems to have been firmly established as a result of the decisions of the House of Lords in *Midland Silicones v. Scruttons*[90] and *Beswick v. Beswick*.[91] There are admittedly some recognised exceptions to the rule which are founded in statute[92] but they have no particular relevance to the law of trusts. However, the rigidity of the general rule has also been mitigated to some limited and rather uncertain extent by the possibility of trusts of the benefit of a contract.

If one of the parties to a simple contract expressly or impliedly contracts as trustee for a third party, the rule that only a person who is a party to a contract can sue upon it remains intact but the third party is nevertheless entitled to the benefit of the contract by virtue of being the beneficiary of a trust. In the event that the other contracting party breaches the contract, there are a number of ways in which the third party may secure the enforcement of the contract against him. The party who contracted as trustee can recover on behalf of the third party beneficiary the damages suffered by

---

[90] [1962] A.C. 446. Compare *New Zealand Shipping Co. v. A. M. Satterthwaite & Co.; The Eurymedon* [1975] A.C. 154, where a stevedore was allowed to claim the benefit of limitation clauses in a bill of lading, and also *Jackson v. Horizon Holidays* [1975] 1 W.L.R. 1468, where the Court of Appeal held that the contract made by the plaintiff was for a family holiday and, although only he could sue for damages for breaches of that contract, he could recover damages not only for his own discomfort and distress but also for that suffered by his wife and children by reason of the defendant's breach of contract to provide them with the holiday contracted for. However, in *Woodar Investment Development v. Wimpey Construction U.K.* [1980] 1 W.L.R. 277, the House of Lords rejected the opinion of Lord Denning M.R. in *Jackson v. Horizon Holidays* in so far as he suggested that a third party was able to sue on a contract.

[91] [1968] A.C. 58.

[92] Such as Married Women's Property Act 1882, s.11; Marine Insurance Act 1906, s.14(2); Law of Property Act 1925, ss.47(1), 56; Occupiers' Liability Act 1957, s.3; Road Traffic Act 1972, s.148(4).

the latter as well as the nominal damages suffered by himself.[93] Alternatively, the third party beneficiary can sue as *cestui que trust* joining the trustee as co-plaintiff and, if the trustee declines to be joined in that capacity, he can be joined with the other party to the contract as a co-defendant. These rules were stated particularly clearly by Lord Wright in *Vandepitte v. Preferred Accident Insurance Corporation of New York*.[94]

No difficulty arises if there is an express declaration of trust or an assignment of the benefit of the contract to trustees. The real difficulty is to know when a trust is to be implied. This is shown by the way in which the case law has developed. One of the earlier cases is *Re Flavell*,[95] where articles of partnership provided that an annuity should be paid by the surviving partner to the widow of his co-partner. It was held that this created a trust of the annuity in favour of the widow which was free from the claims of the co-partner's creditors. A similar decision was reached in *Les Affreteurs Reunis S.A. v. Leopold Walford (London)*,[96] although in this case the position was simplified by the existence of an express agreement enabling the third party to sue.

The principles at stake were subsequently discussed in *Harmer v. Armstrong*,[97] where the plaintiff was seeking specific performance of a contract for the sale of the copyright in certain periodicals which had been entered into for his benefit. The Court of Appeal held that as *cestui que trust* of the contract agreement he was indeed entitled himself to this relief. Lawrence L.J. said that there were two distinct rules as to neither of which there could be any reasonable doubt: first, that the law does not recognise any *jus quaesitum tertio* arising by way of contract and, secondly, that such a right may be conferred by way of a proprietary interest under a trust.[98] The impression given by these dicta that it is an easy matter to discover whether or not a trust in favour of a third party has been created is not, however, borne out by the more recent authorities; on a number of occasions the courts have declined to imply the existence of a trust when they could easily have done so had they been so inclined. In *Vandepitte v. Preferred Accident Insurance Corporation of New York*,[99] a car owner had insured his car in British Columbia with the defendant against third party risks and it had been agreed that the policy should cover all persons driving the car with his consent. His daughter, while so doing, injured the plaintiff, who obtained a

---

[93] See *Gregory and Parker v. Williams* (1871) 3 Mer. 582; *Lloyd's v. Harper* (1880) 16 Ch. D. 290.

[94] [1933] A.C. 70 at 79. In *Bradstock Trustee Services v. Nabarro Nathanson* [1995] 1 W.L.R. 1405 at 1411, Judge Paul Baker, Q.C. declined to extend this principle to an action by trustees in tort for negligence, stating that such a claim could not be regarded as part of the trust property, although any damages which might be recovered would be. The members of a pension scheme were therefore unable to enforce a claim against the defendant solicitors that advice which they had given to the trustees of the scheme had been negligent. Outside the contractual area, the right of a beneficiary to intervene in proceedings is limited to cases where the position of the trustees has been compromised by virtue of a breach of trust, a conflict of interest and duty, or some other exceptional circumstances; see *Hayim v. Citibank* [1987] A.C. 730 at 747–748.

[95] (1883) 25 Ch. D. 89.

[96] [1919] A.C. 801.

[97] [1934] Ch. 65.

[98] *ibid.* at 87–88; compare Romer L.J. at 93–94.

[99] [1933] A.C. 70.

judgment against her in an action of negligence which she did not satisfy. Under the relevant British Columbian legislation, any plaintiff who failed to recover his damages from a motorist upon whom liability had been imposed was entitled to the benefit of any rights which the motorist enjoyed against his insurance company. The question therefore arose as to whether the daughter actually had any rights against her father's insurance company. She was certainly not a party to the contract of insurance; the result therefore depended on whether the agreement that the policy should cover all persons driving the car with the consent of the policy holder had made her the beneficiary of a trust. The Privy Council held that no trust had been proven; the intention to establish such a trust had to be affirmatively shown and this had simply not been done.

A similar result occurred in *Re Schebsman*.[1] A company agreed with one of its employees that, in consideration of his retirement, it would pay certain sums to him during his lifetime and after his death to his wife and child. He subsequently became bankrupt and died soon afterwards. The question then arose as to whether his trustee in bankruptcy could "intercept" the money which the employers were willing to pay to the wife and child. The Court of Appeal held that the employee had not entered into the contract as a trustee for his wife and child. However, although the wife and child could not have enforced the contract against the company, the company was nevertheless free to comply with the terms of the contract and make the required payments. Since the employee would not have been able to intercept the payments, the trustee in bankruptcy could be in no better position. Du Parcq L.J. said that, unless an intention to create a trust was clearly to be collected from the language used and the circumstances of the case, the court ought not to be "astute" to discover implications of any such intention.[2]

A similar reluctance to imply a trust was manifested in *Swain v. The Law Society*.[3] That case concerned the master policy which The Law Society had under its statutory powers arranged for the provision of indemnity insurance, something which was compulsory for all practising solicitors. It had been agreed that a proportion of the commission earned by the insurance brokers in arranging the insurance should be paid to The Law Society, which would apply it for the benefit of the profession as a whole. Two solicitors were dissatisfied with the scheme and claimed that The Law Society was a trustee of the benefit of the master policy contract for the benefit of all individual solicitors and was therefore accountable for the proportion of the commission which it received. Reliance was placed on the fact that the policy contract stated that the policy was being entered into "on behalf of" solicitors and former solicitors, words which, it was claimed, imputed an intention to create a trust. The House of Lords, reversing the Court of Appeal, rejected this argument. It was held that these words were clearly insufficient to express a trust and did not necessarily imply one. As Lord Brightman said,[4] "it would indeed, be surprising if a society of lawyers, who above all might be expected to make their intention clear in a document they

---

[1] [1944] Ch. 83.
[2] *ibid.* at 104.
[3] [1983] A.C. 598.
[4] *ibid.* at 621.

compose, should have failed to express the existence of a trust if that was what they intended to create." Moreover, it was not necessary, as had been argued, to imply a trust in order to secure the commercial viability of the scheme; this was a statutory indemnity scheme, the policy had statutory authority, and accordingly all persons insured had a direct remedy against the insurers if the latter declined to perform their obligations.

The authorities as a whole illustrate the difficulty in practice of establishing any test by means of which it can be determined whether or not a contracting party is entering into a contract as trustee for a third party.[5] One commentator has gone so far as to state that it is virtually impossible to predict the way in which the court will decide a novel case.[6] It has been suggested that one of the reasons for this difficulty is the fact that the concept of trusteeship is too highly charged with magic to admit of an accurate test. "There is a vast deal of magic in words and among the words most highly charged with magic to be found is the word 'trustee'."[7] Whether or not this is the true reason, it appears from decisions such as Re Schebsman and Swain v. The Law Society that the courts have increasingly turned their backs on the earlier authorities and are now most reluctant to interpret a contract as creating a trust in the absence of the clearest possible evidence that a trust was intended. It would therefore now be unwise to place any reliance on the trust concept as a way round the principle of privity of contract.[8]

This view derives further support from the significant fact that no reliance was placed on the trust concept by the members of the House of Lords when they were deciding Beswick v. Beswick,[9] where relief was only granted because of the particular facts of that case. A nephew was employed by his uncle in the latter's business as a coal merchant. An agreement was made between them whereby the uncle assigned the business to the nephew in return for the nephew's promise to pay the uncle £6 10s. 0d. a week for the rest of his life and, after his death, to pay an annuity of £5 a week to his widow. The nephew complied with this agreement during his uncle's lifetime but after his death made only one payment to the widow. She sued him both in her personal capacity and as administratrix of her husband's estate.

---

[5] In addition to the cases mentioned in the text see Tomlinson v. Gill (1756) Amb. 330; Gregory and Parker v. Williams (1817) 3 Mer. 582; Lloyd's v. Harper (1880) 16 Ch.D. 290; Royal Exchange Assurance v. Hope [1928] Ch. 179; Re Gordon [1940] Ch. 851; Re Webb [1941] Ch. 225, in which a trust was held to have been established (this was also held to be the position in respect of a specialty contract in Fletcher v. Fletcher (1844) 4 Hare 67, see post, p. 156). See also Colyear v. Lady Mulgrave (1836) 2 Keen 81; Re Engelbach's Estate [1924] 2 Ch. 348; Re Sinclair's Life Policy [1938] Ch. 799; Re Foster (No.1) [1938] 3 All E.R. 357, in which a trust was held not to have been established.

[6] Williams (1944) 7 M.L.R. 123.

[7] Corbin (1930) 46 L.Q.R. 20.

[8] See also, generally, in addition to the articles mentioned in nn. 6 and 7: Williston (1902) 15 H.L.R. 767; Dowrick (1956) 19 M.L.R. 374; Scamell (1955) 8 C.L.P. 131; Elliott (1956) 20 Conv. (N.S.) 43, 114; Andrews (1959) Conv. (N.S.) 179; Elliott (1960) 76 L.Q.R. 100; Hornby (1962) 79 L.Q.R. 228; Matheson (1966) 29 M.L.R. 397; Lee (1969) 85 L.Q.R. 213; Barton (1975) 91 L.Q.R. 236; Meagher and Lehane (1976) 92 L.Q.R. 427; Friend [1982] Conv. 280.

[9] [1968] A.C. 58. See also Jackson v. Horizon Holidays [1975] 1 W.L.R. 1468, where the Court of Appeal held that the plaintiff was entitled to damages for himself and for his family by reason of the breach of contract. The notion of a trust arising was, however, rejected; see ante, n. 90 and Woodar Investment Development v. Wimpey Construction U.K. [1980] 1 W.L.R. 277.

The House of Lords held that she had no claim in the former capacity because she was not a party to the contract. But because she was administratrix, she could enforce the provisions of the agreement for the benefit of herself in her personal capacity by seeking specific performance. The fact that she would have had no remedy had she had not been the administratrix of the promisee shows up the unsatisfactory state of the law regarding third party beneficiaries.[10] This is precisely why the Law Commission Consultation Paper on Privity of Contract: Contracts for the Benefit of Third Parties[11] has proposed that third parties should be allowed to enforce contractual provisions made in their favour. If these proposals are ever enacted, it will no longer be necessary to imply trusts of the benefit of contracts and most of the law which has been discussed in this section will become obsolete.

Enactment of these proposals would also resolve an allied problem relating to specialty contracts, which will be discussed in detail later on in the context of the constitution of trusts.[12] When a trust has not been completely constituted, the question sometimes arises as to whether a beneficiary of an as yet unconstituted trust can enforce a covenant entered into by the settlor to transfer the intended trust property to the trustees (this question usually arises where the subject matter of the covenant to settle is what is known as after-acquired property, property which had not yet come into existence when the covenant was entered into). While it has always been clear that a beneficiary who is a party to the covenant can enforce that covenant as against the settlor,[13] there has been great controversy as to the rights of a beneficiary who is not such a party. It is at present clearly established that, if there is no completely constituted trust of any type,[14] not only is such a beneficiary unable to compel the trustees to enforce the covenant against the settlor[15] but the trustees will also be directed not to do so if they seek the instructions of the court.[16] Although it has been argued that parties to a covenant should not be restrained from exercising their legal rights thereunder if they wish to do so,[17] the likely consequences of such exercise suggest that the present state of the law should be upheld.[18] Consequently, a third party beneficiary of a specialty contract is in exactly the same position as a third party beneficiary of a simple contract.

2. Debt

It has already been seen that a liability cannot, without more, be the subject matter of a trust and that a debtor will only be able to create a valid trust of the sum owed in favour of his creditor or of a third party if he segregates the appropriate amount from his other assets.[19] Such a trust will clearly come

---

[10] See (1967) 83 L.Q.R. 465.
[11] The Law Commission: Consultation Paper No. 212 (1991).
[12] See *post*, pp. 156–162.
[13] *Cannon v. Hartley* [1949] Ch. 213.
[14] As in *Fletcher v. Fletcher* (1844) 4 Hare 67.
[15] *Re d'Angibau* (1880) 15 Ch.D. 228 (this proposition is of course wholly unobjectionable).
[16] *Re Pryce* [1917] 1 Ch. 234; *Re Kay* [1939] Ch. 329; *Re Cook's Settlement Trusts* [1965] Ch. 92.
[17] Particularly by Elliott (1960) 76 L.Q.R. 100.
[18] See *post*, pp. 160–162.
[19] See *ante*, p. 14.

into existence where the debtor makes an express declaration of trust in respect of duly segregated assets. The effect of the creation of such a trust will be to give its beneficiary an advantage over the other creditors of the debtor in the event of his bankruptcy—this is because the proprietary right of the beneficiary will enjoy priority over the purely personal rights of any unsecured general creditors. For this reason, in the event that the debtor does subsequently become insolvent, such a trust will be vulnerable to challenge under the Insolvency Act 1986[20] on the grounds that it amounts to preferential treatment (technically known as a "preference") of the beneficiary *vis-à-vis* the general creditors. However, if consideration is given to the possibility of the debtor's insolvency at the time when the debt is first created, it is sometimes possible for the creditor to obtain a priority which cannot be successfully challenged.

There is in principle no reason why the same transaction should not give rise to both a trust and a debt; a loan for a specific purpose can be made on terms that the sum advanced will be held on trust for the lender unless and until that purpose is carried out. What is crucial in such circumstances is the intention of the parties. In *Barclays Bank v. Quistclose Investments*[21] a company which was substantially indebted to the bank needed funds in order to pay a dividend on its shares. Quistclose Investments advanced the necessary funds on the basis that they were only to be used for this purpose and they were paid into a separate account at the bank, which was made aware of the arrangement. The company went into liquidation before the dividend had been paid. If Quistclose Investments were no more than a creditor of the company, then the funds in the bank would belong to the company and the bank would be entitled to set off the credit balance of the account against the substantially greater indebtedness of the company.[22] If, on the other hand, the funds were held on trust for Quistclose Investments, its proprietary interest therein would enjoy priority over the rights of the bank. The House of Lords held that arrangements for the payment of a person's creditors by a third person give rise to "a relationship of a fiduciary character or trust, in favour, as a primary trust, of the creditors, and secondarily, if the primary trust fails, of the third person".[23] Once the primary purpose was fulfilled, the third person would be no more than an unsecured creditor. However, there was "no difficulty in recognising the co-existence in one transaction of legal and equitable rights and remedies".[24] Since the purpose for which the funds had been advanced had failed, the funds were still held on trust for Quistclose Investments, whose beneficial interest was binding on the bank because it had been aware of the basis on which the funds had been transferred.

There has been some controversy as to the precise nature of the secondary trust identified by the House of Lords. It has been variously classified as an

---

[20] s.239 in the case of companies, s.340 in the case of individuals. See *post*, pp. 224–230.
[21] [1970] A.C. 567.
[22] Banks have a statutory right to amalgamate the balances of the different accounts held with them.
[23] [1970] A.C. 567 at 580.
[24] *ibid.* at 581.

express trust, a resulting trust and a constructive trust.[25] It is, frankly, difficult to see how a trust which comes into existence because of the express or implied intentions of its trustee and beneficiary can be classified as a constructive trust, since such a trust is imposed by the court as a result of the conduct of the trustee and therefore arises quite independently of the intention of any of the parties.[26] Whether the secondary trust is an express or a resulting trust may well in the end depend on whether the parties have specifically spelt out its terms, in which case it would appear to be an express trust, or whether those terms are implied by the court as a result of a failure by the parties fully to declare the beneficial interests, in which case it would appear to be a resulting trust.[27] The only possible relevant distinction between express and resulting trusts is in relation to formal validity and then only in respect of trusts of land or subsisting equitable interests[28]; it is inconceivable that land could form the subject matter of what has become known as a "*Quistclose* Trust" and it seems highly unlikely, although not actually impossible, that a subsisting equitable interest could do so either. In any event, no matter what the correct classification of the secondary trust actually is, there is no obvious reason to oppose the conclusion reached by the House of Lords in *Barclays Bank v. Quistclose Investments* provided that, as the House of Lords found in that case, it was indeed the common intention of both parties that the funds in question should be held on trust. Such an intention will be clearest where the parties have expressly provided in terms that this should be the case. In *Re Lewis's of Leicester*[29] about half of the floor space of a department store was licensed to independent traders who were operating "shops within a shop". Some of these traders had agreements with the store whereby their takings, which had to pass through the store's till system, should be held by the store on trust for them subject to the deduction of the store's commission. When the store became insolvent, these traders were held able to recover such of their takings as were traceable into the store's bank accounts. But any intention that the funds should be segregated is likely to lead the court to infer that the parties intended to create a trust, even if that word was never actually used by anyone. In *Re Lewis's of Leicester*, other independent traders had agreements which merely provided for the segregation of their takings in a separate bank account and they were held entitled to such funds as had actually been segregated. *Barclays Bank v. Quistclose Investments* has also been applied both where part of the funds advanced had indeed been used for the specific purpose in question, the court holding that the creditor was entitled to recover whatever was left,[30] and where the funds, although advanced for a specific purpose, were paid not by way of loan but rather in satisfaction of a contractual debt.[31] In this latter case Peter Gibson J. stated that:

---

[25] See P. Millett, Q.C. (now Millett L.J.): 101 L.Q.R. (1985) 269 and C. E. F. Rickett: 107 L.Q.R. (1991) 608 and in *Equity, Fiduciaries and Trusts 1993* (ed. Waters), p. 325.
[26] See *post*, p. 266.
[27] See *post*, p. 256.
[28] See *post*, pp. 46 *et seq.*
[29] [1995] 1 B.C.L.C. 428.
[30] *Re EVTR* (1987) B.C.L.C. 647.
[31] *Carreras Rothmans v. Freeman Matthews Treasure* [1985] Ch. 207.

"the principle in all these cases is that equity fastens on the conscience of the person who receives from another property transferred for a specific purpose only and not therefore for the recipient's own purposes, so that such person will not be permitted to treat the property as his own or to use it for other than the stated purpose."[32]

Another reason why the existence of a common intention is important is that in such circumstances it is impossible for the general creditors of an insolvent trustee to contend that the creation of the "*Quistclose* Trust" has deprived them of assets which would otherwise have been divisible between them and so amounts to a preference. In the absence of any common intention, the funds would simply not have been paid over; consequently, there was never any possibility of them becoming part of the general assets of the trustee. This was specifically held in *Re Lewis's of Leicester*. Nor is such a contention feasible where the potential creditor/beneficiary unilaterally specified at the time when he remitted the funds that they were to remain his property in equity unless and until the other party was able to carry out his side of the bargain, for example provide the goods which are being ordered and paid for in advance; such funds could not have become part of the general assets of the trustee either. A reservation of this latter type will clearly bind the potential trustee and his trustee in bankruptcy; however, it will only bind any bank in which the funds have been deposited if they are clearly segregated in what the bank knows to be an account maintained for this particular purpose.

The courts have also held that it is possible for a "*Quistclose* Trust" to be created and the same priority to be conferred as the result of a unilateral act of the potential debtor/trustee. In *Re Kayford*[33] a mail-order company in financial difficulties became concerned as to its ability to provide the goods for which its customers were paying in advance. It consequently opened a "Customers' Trust Deposit Account" into which all purchase moneys received from customers were paid and were withdrawn only as and when their orders could be fulfilled. Shortly afterwards the company went into liquidation. Megarry J. held that the funds in this bank account were held on trust for the customers; by paying the purchase moneys into the trust account, the company had prevented the customers from ever becoming creditors so no question of a preference arose. His decision was followed and applied by the Court of Appeal in *Re Chelsea Cloisters*,[34] where deposits paid to the landlord company by tenants which were to be credited to them at the end of their leases after making good any delapidations and damage caused had also been paid into a separate bank account. However, *Re Kayford* was distinguished in *Re Multi Guarantee Co.*,[35] where, despite the fact that the funds in question had been paid into a separate account in the joint names of the solicitors of the two parties who had been designated, the party to whom the funds had originally been paid had continued to contemplate the possibility of making further drawings therefrom for its own

---

[32] [1985] Ch. 207 at 222.
[33] [1975] 1 W.L.R. 279.
[34] (1981) 41 P. & C.R. 98.
[35] [1987] B.C.L.C. 257.

benefit, and it was not applied in *Re Challoner Club*,[36] where donations were paid into a separate account so that they should not become available to creditors but the circumstances in which the payments would become unconditional had not been adequately defined.[37] The decision in *Re Kayford* has also on occasions been completely overlooked in circumstances where it would have been highly relevant.[38]

It has to be admitted that justifying the existence of a "Quistclose Trust" in cases of this kind is rather more difficult. The persons making the payments never had any intention of becoming anything other than general creditors of the recipient. Consequently, it is not easy to see why the unilateral creation of proprietary rights in their favour does not amount to a preference; if the only reason why they did not become creditors rather than beneficiaries was the same unilateral act of the company, that does not seem to be a sufficient reason for the absence of a preference.[39] In *Re Kayford* itself the answer may be that the mail-order company would undoubtedly have been entitled to reject the orders and return their customers' cheques—it could not conceivably have been contended that that course of conduct amounted to a preference; consequently its acceptance of the orders and segregation of the purchase moneys did not actually make the situation of the general creditors any worse. However, the decision in *Re Chelsea Cloisters* cannot be justified in this way; the company clearly had to go on letting flats and had no realistic option of letting without taking deposits. What is more (and this was a point which clearly troubled Oliver L.J.), sums which had already been received as deposits and paid into the company's normal bank account were drawn out and paid into the segregated fund; the subsequent repayment of these sums to the tenants undoubtedly amounted to a preference of their interests at the expense of those of the general creditors. There can be little doubt that more will be heard of this particular point; it is, however, only relevant where the "*Quistclose* trust" is created by a unilateral act of the recipient/trustee and does not in any way affect the validity of the sort of trust upheld in *Barclays Bank v. Quistclose Investments* itself.

Finally, it must be emphasised that, in the absence of any of the special circumstances considered in the preceding two paragraphs, the liability of a debtor, whether the debt in question is contractual or non-contractual, is a personal liability and does not confer any proprietary rights on the creditor.

---

[36] (1997) *The Times*, November 4, 1997.

[37] The intended trust thus failed for uncertainty of objects (see *post*, p. 92).

[38] In *Customs and Excise Commissioners v. Richmond Theatre Management Limited* [1995] S.T.C. 257 a theatre had sold tickets in advance on the basis of its standard conditions which expressly imposed a trust on the money in favour of the purchasers until the performance in question had taken place. On the face of things, such a trust should have been binding in accordance with *Re Kayford*, indeed possibly in accordance with *Barclays Bank v. Quistclose Investments* as well. However, Dyson J. unexpectedly held that there was no trust because the standard conditions also provided that the theatre was "not accountable for interest or otherwise in respect of the use of the ticket money after its receipt"! As Hanbury & Martin, *Modern Equity* (15th ed., 1997) 51 observes, it is also far from obvious how this conclusion can be reconciled with the decision of the Court of Appeal in *R. v. Clowes (No. 2)* [1994] 2 All E.R. 316, where it was said, in the context of theft, "that the requirement to keep money separately normally indicates a trust, and the absence of such a requirement normally negatives it if there were no other indicators of a trust; the fact that the transaction contemplates the mingling of money is not necessarily fatal to a trust".

[39] See W. Goodhart and G. Jones: 43 M.L.R. (1980) 489.

In *Re Sharpe (a Bankrupt)*[40] the bankrupt purchased a property with the help of a sum lent to him by his aunt as part of an arrangement whereby the aunt was to live in the property for the rest of her life. Browne-Wilkinson J., while finding in her favour on another ground, rejected her claim to a beneficial interest in the property by virtue of her loan advance, holding that where "moneys are advanced by loan there can be no question of the lender being entitled to an interest in the property".[41] He distinguished on the grounds of its "very special" facts the earlier decision in *Hussey v. Palmer*[42] where, in a similar situation, the Court of Appeal had been unable to agree as to whether the payment in question had been made by way of loan or by way of direct contribution to the building of an extension and had, by a majority, imposed a constructive trust on the basis of a principle[43] which is no longer regarded as good law.[44] While it is sometimes difficult to decide, in the context of family arrangements, whether a particular payment has been made by way of loan or by way of contribution to the acquisition of the property in question, once the intention of the parties has actually been established the two possibilities are mutually exclusive.

3. *Estates of Deceased Persons*

(A) Personal Representatives and Trustees Compared
In one sense it can indeed be said that the legal personal representative—an executor in the case of a person nominated as such in a will, otherwise an administrator—of a deceased person is a trustee for the creditors and beneficiaries claiming under the deceased; after all, he holds the real and personal estate for their benefit and not for his own. Further, by virtue of section 69 of the Trustee Act 1925, the provisions of the Act also apply to personal representatives.[45] However, it would be an error to equate the legal position of personal representatives with that of trustees because certain differences still persist, primarily as the result of other statutory provisions.

Thus, while an action by a beneficiary to recover trust property or in respect of any breach of trust cannot, in the absence of fraud or the retention of the property by the trustee,[46] be brought after six years,[47] personal representatives are subject to a different period of limitation, namely twelve years for a claim to personal estate[48] and six years for actions to recover arrears of interest in respect of legacies.[49] However, the exception relating to fraud and to property retained by the trustee applies just as much to personal representatives as it does to trustees.[50] The authority of personal representatives in handling pure personalty is several, whereas that of

---

[40] [1980] 1 W.L.R. 219.
[41] *ibid*. at 223.
[42] [1972] 1 W.L.R. 1286.
[43] That a constructive trust is a general equitable remedy which can be invoked in order to do justice in the individual case. See *post*, pp. 277 & 359.
[44] See *post*, p. 359.
[45] See also Administration of Estates Act 1925, ss.33, 39.
[46] Limitation Act 1980, s.21(1).
[47] *ibid*. s.21(3) and see *post*, p. 694.
[48] *ibid*. s.22.
[49] *ibid*.
[50] *ibid*. See also *post*, p. 694.

trustees is joint.[51] Consequently, one of a number of personal representatives can give a valid title to a purchaser or pledgee of pure personalty whereas one of a number of co-trustees cannot, the intervention of all the trustees being necessary. However, the authority of personal representatives over realty (which since 1925 for this purpose includes leaseholds[52]) is, like that of trustees, joint.[53] Since July 1, 1995, this applies just as much to contracts as to conveyances[54] (previously one of a number of personal representatives could enter into a valid contract for the sale of land).

The functions of personal representatives are also different from those of trustees. The duty of trustees is to administer a trust on behalf of beneficiaries, some of whom may be minors or unborn, and this may be a long continuing process since many years may elapse before a trust is brought to an end. On the other hand, the primary duty of personal representatives is to wind up the estate by, after payment of debts and inheritance tax, transferring the net assets to the persons beneficially entitled to them under the will or intestacy[55] or to any nominated trustees, who more often than not will be themselves, to hold on trust. Furthermore, whereas a beneficiary has an equitable interest in the trust property as soon as a trust takes effect,[56] a legatee or devisee or intestate successor has neither a legal nor an equitable proprietary interest whilst the assets of the estate remain in course of administration. At that stage such persons have only the right to require the deceased's estate to be duly administered by the personal representatives.[57]

It follows that, although a personal representative has, like a trustee, fiduciary duties to perform, those duties are owed to the estate as a whole; it does not, therefore, necessarily follow that the duty of an executor in the course of administering an estate is subject to the trustee's duty to hold an even balance between the different beneficiaries.[58] It was accordingly held in *Re Hayes's Will Trusts*[59] that, where executors had exercised a testamentary power of sale in favour of one of the children of the testator at an estate duty valuation, his other children could not attack the valuation on the ground that the executors did not consider the question of holding an even balance between him and them.

---

[51] *Jacomb v. Harwood* (1751) 2 Ves. Sen. 265; *Attenborough v. Solomon* [1913] A.C. 76. It has been recommended that the power should also be joint in the case of personal representatives (Law Reform Committee on the Powers and Duties of Trustees (23rd Report, Cmnd. 8733 (1982)). For the historical reasons for the existing rule, see 1 Spence's *Equitable Jurisdiction* (1846), p. 578 and *Collier v. Hollinshead* (1984) 272 E.G. 941.

[52] Administration of Estates Act 1925, ss.3(1), 54.

[53] *ibid.* s.2(2).

[54] Law of Property (Miscellaneous Provisions) Act 1994, s.16.

[55] Considered in more detail *post*, p. 469.

[56] At any rate, in the case of a "fixed trust", but not in the case of a "discretionary trust": see *post*, p. 201.

[57] *Commissioner of Stamp Duties (Queensland) v. Livingston* [1965] A.C. 694; *Eastbourne Mutual B.S. v. Hastings Corporation* [1965] 1 W.L.R. 861; *Lall v. Lall* [1965] 1 W.L.R. 1249; *Re Leigh's Will Trusts* [1970] Ch. 277. See further Mellows, *Law of Succession* (5th ed.), p. 411.

[58] *Re Hayes's Will Trusts* [1971] 1 W.L.R. 758 at 764 and see *post*, p. 575 for discussion of trustees' duty in this respect.

[59] [1971] 1 W.L.R. 758.

(B) When Personal Representatives Become Trustees

Personal representatives remain personal representatives indefinitely unless the grant to them is limited or is revoked by the court.[60] However, where a will nominates the persons who are acting as personal representatives as trustees of all or part of the assets comprised in the estate, it is sometimes far from easy to determine the precise moment when, and the circumstances in which, they cease to hold the assets in question as personal representatives and instead hold them as trustees. What has to be determined is whether or not the personal representatives have exhausted all their duties and functions as such and taken on themselves the character of trustees.

Where trusts of land are designed to continue after the administration of an estate has been completed, no problems will arise if the technically correct procedure is followed and the personal representatives vest the land in question in themselves as trustees[61] by means of a document known as an *assent*[62] (the situation is exactly the same where the personal representatives are also beneficially entitled to the property under the will or intestacy in question). Where such a written assent is made, it is clear that the character of the personal representatives changes and they become trustees (or beneficial owners) of the land in question, even though their liability as personal representatives may still persist. However, until 1964 it was generally accepted that such a written assent was not actually necessary in such circumstances and that, when the estate had been fully administered in the sense that all funeral and testamentary expenses and all debts and liabilities had been discharged and the net assets ascertained, the personal representatives became trustees[63] or, alternatively, could exercise their statutory powers to appoint new trustees in their place[64] (or became beneficial owners). However, this generally accepted practice was first doubted[65] and subsequently in 1964 rejected in *Re King's Will Trusts*,[66] where it was held that an express written assent is necessary in every case. Although this decision is a little difficult to reconcile with the wording of the appropriate statutory provision,[67] such an express assent is clearly in practice more desirable because it admits of no doubt as to the precise capacity in which the land in question is being held. However, at the time the decision in *Re King's Will Trusts* was extremely inconvenient since it had the effect of rendering technically defective the title to any land which had been administered in accordance with what had previously been regarded as the accepted practice; consequently, many of these defective titles had to be put in order by the time-consuming and expensive process of obtaining the necessary written assent, sometimes many years after the estate in question had been administered. Now that more than thirty years have passed since 1964, virtually all

---

[60] See *Attenborough v. Solomon* [1913] A.C. 76 and see generally *post, infra*.

[61] *ibid.* at 83.

[62] As in *Re Bowden* (1890) 45 Ch.D. 444; *Re Swain* [1891] 3 Ch. 233; *Re Timmis* [1902] 1 Ch. 176; *Re Oliver* [1927] 2 Ch. 323 (where property was to be held for persons in succession) and as in *Re Claremont* [1923] 2 K.B. 718 (where property was to be held on trust for sale).

[63] *Re Ponder* [1921] 2 Ch. 59; *Re Pitt* (1928) 44 T.L.R. 371.

[64] *Re Cockburn's Will Trusts* [1957] Ch. 438.

[65] *Harvell v. Foster* [1954] 2 Q.B. 367.

[66] [1964] Ch. 542.

[67] Administration of Estates Act 1925, s.36(4).

the defective titles which have not already been rectified must now be hidden behind the present root of title to the land in question[68] and so are in practice completely irrelevant. Whether or not the decision in *Re King's Will Trusts* is actually correct,[69] any assent relating to a legal estate in land is now invariably made in writing. However, the Court of Appeal has since established that an assent to the vesting of an equitable interest need not be in writing but can be inferred by conduct[70] and it has always been clear that assents in writing are not necessary in the case of pure personalty.[71] Assents by the personal representatives to the vesting of both equitable interests in land and pure personalty in themselves, whether as trustees or as beneficial owners, can therefore still be implied and can be taken to have occurred as soon as the administration of the estate in question has been completed.

4. *Agency*

The relationship between principal and agent has some resemblances to the relationship between trustee and beneficiary. For example, agents are liable to their principals, as are trustees to their beneficiaries, for any secret profits made out of the property or business entrusted to them and in such circumstances their respective positions may coincide.[72] The main difference, from which various other consequences follow, is that the relationship between principal and agent is primarily that of creditor and debtor. Consequently, a trustee has full title to the property vested in him,[73] while an agent has not; an agent acts on behalf of his principal and subject to his control, while a trustee does not[74]; and agency is based on agreement, while it is not necessary that there should be—and indeed there rarely is—any agreement between a trustee and his beneficiary.

5. *Equitable Charges*

The distinction here is that a charge merely imposes a liability on the property which is subject to it whereas a trust imposes a fiduciary character on the owner of the property.[75] This has a number of consequences. If property is held subject to a charge and the chargee satisfies the charge, he will hold the property beneficially,[76] whereas a trustee will, on the termination of the trust, hold the property on resulting trust.[77] Again, a chargee is

---

[68] Only where the title to the land in question is still unregistered and where there has been no disposition for value since 1964 is it likely that any technical defect in title created by the decision in *Re King's Will Trusts* will still cause any problems.

[69] The Court of Appeal assumed that *Re King's Will Trusts* had been correctly decided (but in fact distinguished it) in *Re Edwards's Will Trusts* [1982] Ch. 30.

[70] *Re Edwards's Will Trusts* [1982] Ch. 30.

[71] Because Administration of Estates Act 1925, s.36 applies only to realty (which includes, for this purpose, leaseholds).

[72] See *post*, pp. 281, 286.

[73] See *ante*, p. 14.

[74] See *post*, p. 520.

[75] *Cunningham v. Foot* (1878) 3 App. Cas. 974 at 992–993, *per* Lord O'Hagan.

[76] *Re Oliver* (1890) 62 L.T. 533.

[77] See *post*, p. 261.

not accountable for rents and profits during the subsistence of the charge,[78] whereas a trustee is.[79] On the other hand, there is a basic similarity in both a charge and a trust are equitable interests and may therefore be overridden, that is to say destroyed, by a bona fide purchaser for value of the legal estate without notice[80] or, in the case of registered land, the statutory equivalent.[81]

6. Conditions

A condition may, in certain carefully defined circumstances, operate as a trust. Property may be given to a person on condition that he does something or confers a benefit on somebody. But it is only if that condition can, or must necessarily, be fulfilled or satisfied out of the property that it will take effect as a trust.[82] This will not be its effect if the duty is merely collateral.[83]

7. Powers

The basic distinction between a trust and a power is that a trust is imperative whereas a power is discretionary. Almost all trusts involve the exercise of powers or discretions by the trustees. In many cases this does not affect beneficial entitlement. So, depending on the circumstances of the particular trust, the trustees will often have a number of powers of an administrative nature; examples are powers to vary the investments of the trust,[84] to grant a lease of property which is subject to the trust,[85] to settle claims,[86] to apply income for the support of an infant beneficiary or to accumulate it,[87] to apply to the court for guidance as to the execution of the trust,[88] and to insure trust property.[89] Administrative powers are also commonly given to other persons designated in the trust instrument; the power most commonly conferred on persons other than the trustees is the power to remove

---

[78] *Re Oliver* (1890) 62 L.T. 533.
[79] See *post*, p. 540.
[80] *Parker v. Judkin* [1931] 1 Ch. 475.
[81] A bona fide purchaser for value claiming under a registered disposition (Land Registration Act 1925, s.20(1)).
[82] *Att.-Gen. v. Wax Chandlers Co.* (1873) L.R. 6 H.L. 1; *Cunningham v. Foot* (1878) 3 App. Cas. 974 at 995, *per* Lord O'Hagan.
[83] See *Re Brace* [1954] 1 W.L.R. 955 (no trust was held to arises when a house was devised to a daughter on condition that "she provides a home" for another daughter); *Swain v. The Law Society* [1983] A.C. 598 (the words "on behalf of" were held not to express or imply a trust) see *ante*, p. 21 and *post*, p. 282. Compare *Re Frame* [1939] Ch. 700 (a condition in a will that a legatee should adopt the testator's daughter was held to constitute a trust); *Re Niyazi's Will Trusts* [1978] 1 W.L.R. 910 (the words "on condition that" were held apt to create a trust).
[84] See *post*, p. 540.
[85] Trusts of Land and Appointment of Trustees Act 1996, s.6(1).
[86] Trustee Act 1925, s.15.
[87] See *post*, p. 595.
[88] See *post*, p. 501.
[89] Trustee Act 1925, s.19. The position is surprising. Trustees are under no duty to insure (*Re McEacharn* (1911) 103 L.T. 900) and the statutory power is only to insure for a sum up to three quarters of the value of the property. Express powers of insuring usually allow the cover to be effected in the full reinstatement value.

trustees and to appoint new ones in their place[90] (where a trust has a protector, such a power normally extends to him as well). (These, and other, administrative powers which can be conferred by the trust instrument on trustees and other persons will each be the subject of detailed discussion later on.) It cannot be stressed too often that it is fundamental to the nature of a trust that its trustee should not be a puppet dangling at the end of a string pulled by the settlor or the beneficiaries[91] but should instead be a person with the right and the ability to exercise an independent judgment in respect of a wide variety of issues.

The discretions which can be conferred on trustees and other persons are not, however, limited to the type of administrative matters considered in the previous paragraph; they can also extend to beneficial entitlement to the trust property. Trustees can be given powers to select which person or persons will receive the benefit of the capital subject to the trust and/or the income arising therefrom. Such a power can be either wholly unrestricted or restricted to an already defined class of persons.[92] Alternatively, where the trust instrument provides that each member of a class of beneficiaries is to receive some benefit, the trustees may merely be given the power to determine how much each beneficiary will actually receive and, in relation to income, whether it is distributed or accumulated.[93] These powers relating to the existence and extent of beneficial enjoyment can also be conferred on persons who are not themselves trustees; such persons are known as donees of a power. In such circumstances, the trustees hold the property for whatever beneficiaries and to whatever extent the donee of the power in question indicates. The precise nature and interrelation of powers and discretions of this type are discussed fully later on.[94] For present purposes, all that is necessary is an outline of the different categories of trusts and powers relating to beneficial entitlement.

Where a person has a right, but is not under any obligation, to make a selection relating to the beneficial enjoyment of property, he is said to hold a mere power. The traditional view is that, in the event that the person entitled to make the selection fails to do so, the court cannot step in and decide the beneficial enjoyment of the property in question; in other words, when a mere power is not exercised, that power cannot be executed by the court. However, a distinction has recently been drawn between mere powers held by trustees ("fiduciary powers") and mere powers held by anyone else ("non-fiduciary powers" or "personal powers"). It has now been held[95] that in the event that a fiduciary power is not exercised, the court will in appropriate circumstances step in and execute that power. However, the

---

[90] See post, p. 468.

[91] It is in this respect that the position of a trustee differs from that of a nominee, who is often under an express or implied contractual obligation to comply in all respects with the beneficiary's directions.

[92] Such powers are known respectively as general powers and special powers. A third category, the hybrid or intermediate power, has evolved much more recently; such powers are exerciseable in favour of anyone except already defined persons or classes of persons (see Re Manisty's Settlement [1974] Ch. 17).

[93] See post, p. 163.

[94] See post, p. 163.

[95] In Mettoy Pension Trustees v. Evans [1990] 1 W.L.R. 1587.

court is still unable to step in and execute a non-fiduciary or personal power.

Where, on the other hand, a person not only has a right but is also under an obligation to make a selection relating to the beneficial enjoyment of property, he is said to hold a "trust power", an apparently contradictory term which indicates that, contrary to the basic distinction between a trust and power, the power in question is imperative rather than discretionary. A trust power can only arise where the selection is to be made from an already defined class of persons. In this situation, it has always been held that, in the event that the person entitled to make the selection fails to do so, the court can and will step in and decide the beneficial enjoyment of the property in question; in other words, if a trust power is not exercised, the court can and will execute that power.[96] Rather confusingly, two quite distinct situations are described as giving rise to the creation of a trust power. First, where a trustee is under a duty to make a selection relating to the beneficial enjoyment of property vested in him; this situation is more usually described as a discretionary trust. Secondly, where a person who is not a trustee is under a duty to make a selection relating to the beneficial enjoyment of property which is not vested in him; this situation is also described as a "power in the nature of a trust". Given the very considerable differences between trusts and powers, it is most unfortunate that both discretionary trusts and powers in the nature of a trust have been described by the same name; the confusion thus caused has at times extended even to the members of the House of Lords.[97]

Precisely which of the various different kinds of trusts and powers outlined above has been created in any given case is a question of construction of the language of the deed or will in question. Such instruments should ideally be drafted in such a way as to leave no room for doubt. However, in the majority of the cases which have come before the courts, the wording of the instrument in question has given rise to considerable doubt and that doubt has consequently had to be resolved by the application of a number of rules of construction developed for the purpose. These rules and the other important distinctions between trusts and powers, particularly the different rights of the beneficiaries of a trust and the persons in whose favour a power is able to be exercised, will be discussed fully later on.[98]

---

[96] Traditionally, by dividing the property equally among the members of the class; however, other methods of executing a trust power have become established as a result of the decision of the House of Lords in *McPhail v. Doulton* [1991] A.C. 424.

[97] Particularly in *McPhail v. Doulton* [1991] A.C. 424.

[98] See *post*, p. 163.

CHAPTER 2

THE CLASSIFICATION OF TRUSTS

I. STATUTORY, EXPRESS, IMPLIED, RESULTING AND CONSTRUCTIVE TRUSTS

TRUSTS may be created either, first, by statute—these are statutory trusts; or, secondly, where a settlor or testator intentionally creates a relationship of trustee and beneficiary—these are express trusts; or, thirdly, where a settlor or testator carries out some intentional act other than the creation of a relationship of trustee and beneficiary from which the court infers a relationship of trustee and beneficiary—these are implied or resulting trusts; or, fourthly, by operation of law, where a relationship of trustee and beneficiary is imposed by the court as a result of the conduct of the trustee—these are constructive trusts.[1]

1. *Statutory Trusts*

A number of trusts have been created by statute, either expressly or by implication. A large number of these are set out in the Schedules 1 and 2 to the Trusts of Land and Appointment of Trustees Act 1996.[2] Those which are most likely to be relevant for the purposes of this book are as follows:

(a) Under section 34 of the Law of Property Act 1925, as amended by the Trusts of Land and Appointment of Trustees Act 1996,[3] whenever land is conveyed or devised to persons in undivided shares, it vests in the first four persons named in the conveyance or the personal representatives respectively on trust for all the grantees beneficially as tenants in common in equity.

---

[1] For a well-known classification, see *Cook v. Fountain* (1676) 3 Swanst. 585, *per* Lord Nottingham L.C. Compare *Soar v. Ashwell* [1893] 2 Q.B. 390 and *Re Llanover Settled Estates* [1926] Ch. 626.

[2] These Schedules contain the amendments to the various statutes which comprise the Property Legislation of 1925 which are necessary to replace the trusts for sale imposed by that legislation by trusts of land. They also create wholly new statutory trusts, such as the bare trust imposed as the result of a purported grant of an entailed interest. Other statutory trusts may be found in the Settled Land Act 1925 (such as the trust for sale of land imposed by s.36 where undivided shares arise under a settlement subject to the Settled Land Act 1925); however, no new settlements of this kind can now be created.

[3] Sched. 2, para. 3.

(b) Under section 36 of the Law of Property Act 1925, as amended by the Trusts of Land and Appointment of Trustees Act 1996,[4] whenever land is conveyed or devised to persons as joint tenants, it vests in the first four named in the conveyance or the personal representatives respectively on trust for sale for all the grantees beneficially as joint tenants in equity.

(c) Under section 33 of the Administration of Estates Act 1925, as amended by the Trusts of Land and Appointment of Trustees Act 1996,[5] on the death of a person intestate, his property vests in his personal representatives on trust to be divided between his surviving spouse, if any, and his issue or other relatives in the proportions specified by the legislation.[6]

2. *Express Trusts*

Express trusts arise where a settlor or testator intentionally creates a relationship of trustee and beneficiary; this may be done by deed, by writing, by parol or by will.[7] A trust will be regarded as express even where the settlor or testator has expressed himself ambiguously if the court concludes, upon a true construction of the instrument in question, that a trust was what was intended by the settlor; consequently, words of prayer, entreaty or expectation, collectively known as precatory words, may be held to have created an express trust.[8] Further, a power to distribute property among a class of persons may be construed as indicating an intention to create an express trust in favour of that class if there is no gift over in default of appointment. In each case the question is entirely one of construction of the relevant instrument.[9]

3. *Implied or Resulting Trusts*

Implied or resulting trusts arise where a settlor or testator carries out some intentional act other than the creation of a relationship of trustee and beneficiary from which the court infers a relationship of trustee and beneficiary. They consequently arise from the unexpressed but presumed intention of the settlor or testator. The two alternative names stem from the fact that not only are they implied by the court but also often cause the beneficial interest thereunder to "result" to the settlor, to his estate, or to the residuary beneficiaries or intestate successors of the testator. Implied or resulting trusts arise in two sets of circumstances. First, where one person transfers property to another or into the joint names of himself and that other or pays, wholly or in part, for the purchase of property which is vested either in the name of another or in the joint names of himself and that other, there is a presumption that no gift was intended; consequently, the property is held on

---

[4] Sched. 2, para. 4.
[5] Sched. 2, para. 5.
[6] See *post*, p. 469.
[7] See *post*, p. 45 for cases where writing is necessary.
[8] See *post*, p. 82.
[9] See *post*, p. 175.

trust for the payer or, in the case of a joint purchase, for the two of them in proportion to their contributions (this is, however, only a presumption and can be rebutted by the counter-presumption of advancement when the parties are in one of a number of established relationships or by affirmative evidence of the payer's intention to make an outright beneficial transfer). Secondly, where a settlor or testator who creates an express trust fails to exhaust the whole of the beneficial interest in the property in question, the court will imply that so much of the beneficial interest as is undisposed of will be held on trust for the settlor himself, his estate, or the residuary beneficiaries or intestate successors of the testator.[10]

4. *Constructive Trusts*

Constructive trusts arise by operation of law. Unlike all other trusts, a constructive trust is imposed by the court as a result of the conduct of the trustee and therefore arises quite independently of the intention of any of the parties. To give a very well known illustration, where an express trustee of leasehold property used his position to induce the landlord, who had refused to renew the lease to the trust, to renew the lease in his own favour instead, a constructive trust was imposed on him whereby he held the new lease on the same trusts as he had held the old one—his attempt to obtain a personal advantage for himself was regarded as antagonistic to the interests of the beneficiaries and was therefore contrary to the duty of loyalty which he, as an express trustee, owed to them.[11]

II. SIMPLE AND SPECIAL TRUSTS

1. *Simple Trusts*

A simple trust arises where a trustee is simply a repository of the trust property with no active duties to perform.[12] If a settlor or testator vests property in trustees to be held on trust for a nominated beneficiary absolutely, the trust is a simple trust. The only duty which the trustee has to perform is to transfer the whole or some part of the property to the beneficiary if the latter so directs.[13] In such a case, he is known as a bare trustee.

2. *Special Trusts*

A special trust arises where the trustee is appointed to carry out a purpose designated by the settlor or testator and is therefore obliged to exert himself actively in the performance of the trust.[14] Consequently, he is known as an active trustee. Therefore, if the trust created is for the trustee to collect the

---

[10] *Westdeutsche Landesbank Girozentrale v. Islington L.B.C.* [1996] A.C. 669 at 708. See further *post*, p. 238.
[11] *Keech v. Sandford* (1726) Sel.Cas. Ch. 61 and see also generally *post*, p. 307.
[12] Underhill and Hayton, *Law of Trusts and Trustees* (15th ed., 1995), p. 44.
[13] See *Christie v. Ovington* (1875) 1 Ch.D. 279; *Re Cunningham and Frayling* [1891] 2 Ch. 567.
[14] Underhill and Hayton, *op. cit.*, p. 44.

rents and profits of the trust property, to pay the cost of repairs to and insurance of that property out of these rents and profits, to pay whatever is left to a nominated beneficiary for his lifetime and then, on that person's death, to hold the property on trust for someone else absolutely, the trust will be a special one until the death of the life tenant because during that period the trustee has active duties to perform; however, on the death of the life tenant, the trust will become a simple trust and the trustee will become a bare trustee because the only duty still binding on him will be to transfer the trust property to the ultimate beneficiary in the manner and to the extent that he is directed by the latter.

Special trusts are subdivided into ministerial trusts and discretionary trusts. The former require for their performance no more than ordinary business intelligence on the part of the trustees, for example the collection of the rents and profits of the trust property and their distribution in accordance with the instructions of the settlor or testator. The latter require the exercise of a discretion on the part of the trustees. This will be the case and the trust in question will be discretionary where funds are transferred to the trustees for them to divide up at their absolute discretion between a number of local charities such as a Dogs' Home, a Cats' Home, and a Home for Distressed Gentlefolk. A trust will also be discretionary where the trustees have a discretion to determine whether and if so, how much, income should be paid to each of the members of a class of beneficiaries nominated by the settlor or testator.[15]

III. Executed and Executory Trusts

In this context, the terms "executed" and "executory" are used in a particular technical sense. A trust is regarded as executed in this sense when all the terms of the trust are specified in the trust instrument or the declaration which has constituted it. A trust is, on the other hand, regarded as executory in this sense when, although the trust property is vested in the trustees or is the subject matter of an enforceable agreement to vest it in them, that instrument or declaration requires the execution of a further instrument setting out the detailed terms of the trust. The distinction between the two is that, in the case of an executed trust, the settlor has, in the language of the nineteenth century, been his own conveyancer[16] whereas, in the case of an executory trust, he has not. A conventional, if old-fashioned, example of an executory trust is marriage articles from which a formal marriage settlement is later to be prepared.[17] A modern example is a pension scheme established, as most pensions schemes are, by an interim deed of trust which provides for the subsequent execution of a definitive deed of trust. In one such case,[18] the definitive deed of trust was duly executed but its validity was challenged when questions arose as to the entitlement to surplus funds. Scott J. in fact found the definitive deed to be valid but stated that, had he not done

---

[15] See *post*, p. 163.
[16] *Egerton v. Brownlow* (1853) 4 H.L.C. 1 at 210, *per* Lord St Leonards.
[17] For further discussion, see *post*, p. 147.
[18] *Davis v. Richards & Wallington Industries* [1990] 1 W.L.R. 1511.

so, the interim deed would nevertheless have been upheld as a valid executory trust capable of being executed by a court order; this would have had the effect of providing rules corresponding to those in the definitive deed by means of which the questions as to the surplus funds would have been able to have been resolved.

IV. COMPLETELY AND INCOMPLETELY CONSTITUTED TRUSTS

A trust is described as completely constituted when it has been perfectly created by either the settlor declaring himself to be a trustee of the property in question or the settlor or testator vesting that property in the intended trustees by means of the appropriate formalities so that nothing more remains to be done by him. Both executed and executory trusts are inevitably completely constituted trusts. But if, on the other hand, something still remains to be done by the settlor or testator, the trust in question is imperfect and is said to be incompletely constituted; this is another way of saying that, because there is as yet no valid trust, no interest of a proprietary nature has yet vested in the beneficiary. This will be the case where the settlor has undertaken to vest title to the trust property in the intended trustees but has not actually transferred the property in question. In such circumstances, the only conceivable remedies of the beneficiaries will be a direct or indirect contractual action against the settlor; they will have no proprietary remedy against the trustees.[19]

V. FIXED AND DISCRETIONARY TRUSTS

Discretionary trusts have already been mentioned as one of the two types of "special trusts". They must also be contrasted with fixed trusts, which are trusts in favour of pre-determined beneficiaries or classes of beneficiaries. In the case of a fixed trust, each of the beneficiaries is entitled in equity to a fixed pre-determined share of the trust property at the appropriate time and he may enforce his rights thereto against the trustees. In the case of a discretionary trust, on the other hand, the trustees will have to exercise one or more of the discretions vested in them by the settlor or testator before any individual beneficiary has a right to any part of the trust property. The discretion vested in the trustees may merely be that of deciding in what proportions, if any, the trust property is to be divided among the members of a pre-determined class; at the other extreme, the discretion vested in the trustees may be that of deciding the membership of the class itself. Whatever the discretion, unless and until it is exercised, no individual beneficiary or potential beneficiary has any proprietary rights.[20]

---

[19] For further discussion, see *post*, p. 124.
[20] They do, however, have a right to compel the due administration of the trust and can share in the fund on a premature determination. See *post*, p. 201.

VI. PRIVATE AND PUBLIC TRUSTS

A private trust aims to benefit one or more persons who have either been defined by the settlor or testator or are to be determined in the future in the manner which the settlor or testator has provided. A public or charitable trust, on the other hand, aims to bring about or to support some purpose which will be of benefit to society or to some considerable section of society. Because of their public nature, charitable trusts enjoy a number of privileges not shared by private trusts; in particular, they do not have to comply with the requirements of certainty of objects or of the rule against perpetuity and, most important of all today, are exempt from payment of most local and national taxes.[21]

VII. NEW CLASSIFICATIONS?

The traditional classification of implied, resulting and constructive trusts, which has generally been thought to be workable, has been the subject of considerable judicial comment in the last thirty years. The effect of these comments on these types of trusts will be analysed in detail in due course in the appropriate chapters. However, these possible changes to the traditional classification of trusts merit some brief discussion here.

In the first place, it has been contended that the two main sets of circumstances in which implied or resulting trusts arise should respectively be classified as "presumed" and "automatic" resulting trusts. According to this distinction, suggested by Megarry J. in *Re Vandervell's Trusts (No. 2)*,[22] a presumed resulting trust arises when a purchase is made in the name of another person but not on any express trust; in these circumstances, there is a presumption that that other holds the property in question on resulting trust for the real purchaser but this implied or presumed intention can be rebutted either by other legal presumptions or by evidence to the contrary.[23] An automatic resulting trust, on the other hand, arises where a transfer has been made on trusts which have left the whole or some part of the beneficial interest undisposed of (because, for example, those are in some way ineffective or incomplete); in this situation the transferee of the property in question automatically holds it on resulting trust for the transferor to the extent that the beneficial interest has not been disposed of. In such a case, according to Megarry J., the resulting trust "does not depend on any intentions or presumptions, but is the automatic consequence of [the transferor's] failure to dispose of what is vested in him".[24]

The distinction between "presumed" and "automatic" resulting trusts appears at first sight to accord with common sense; however, it is fair to say that, in the same way as a presumed resulting trust is said to be created by implication as the result of a purchase in the name of another, so also an

---

[21] The distinctions are discussed *post*, p. 379.
[22] [1974] Ch. 269, at 294, 295. Megarry J.'s actual decision was reversed by the Court of Appeal at [1974] Ch. 269 but the Court of Appeal made no comment on the judge's formulation.
[23] See *post*, p. 247 for the ways in which it may be rebutted.
[24] [1974] Ch. 269 at 294.

intention could be implied on the part of a settlor or testator that the settled property should result to him in so far as he has failed to dispose of it. The implication of an intention does not appear to be markedly more artificial in the one case than in the other. Precisely this argument was adopted in *Westdeutsche Landesbank Girozentrale v. Islington L.B.C.*[25] by Lord Browne-Wilkinson, who reasserted the traditional view that both types of resulting trusts are examples of trusts giving effect to the common intention of the parties; he said that he was not convinced that Megarry J. had been right to suggest that the second type of resulting trust does not depend on intention but operates automatically.[26] This certainly seems to be preferable to the view of Megarry J.[27] However, a further definition of resulting trusts has now been propounded,[28] namely that such trusts require a transfer of property in circumstances in which the provider of that property did not intend to benefit the recipient. This definition seems highly convincing, at least in so far as the traditional categories of constructive trusts are concerned.[29] However, there can obviously be no doubt whatever that the definition at present recognised by English law is that propounded by Lord Browne-Wilkinson.

In the second place, there have been a number of attempts to bring the concepts of resulting and constructive trusts closer together with a view to changing the basic attitude of English law towards the constructive trust. These attempts were largely initiated by Lord Denning M.R. in a series of cases decided by the Court of Appeal in the years immediately before and after 1970. In *Cooke v. Head*[30] he stated that "whenever two parties by their joint efforts acquire property to be used for their joint benefit, the courts may impose or impute a constructive or resulting trust",[31] while in *Hussey v. Palmer*[32] he said this:

"the plaintiff alleged that there was a resulting trust. I should have thought that the trust in this case, if there was one, was more in the nature of a constructive trust: but this is more a matter of words than anything else. The two run together."[33]

The expressed intention of Lord Denning M.R. was to convert the constructive trust into a remedy for unjust enrichment, as it has long since been in the common law jurisdictions of the United States of America and is now

---

[25] [1996] A.C. 669 at 708
[26] Lord Browne-Wilkinson went on to say that if a settlor or testator has expressly, or by necessary implication, abandoned any beneficial interest in the trust property, there will be no resulting trust; the interest in question will instead vest in the Crown as *bona vacantia*.
[27] Birks, [1996] R.L.R. 3 at 11 regards Lord Browne-Wilkinson's view as "correct", despite the fact that it led to the rejection of his own argument that a resulting trust should arise whenever money is paid under a mistake or under a condition which is not subsequently satisfied.
[28] By R. Chambers: *Resulting Trusts* (1997).
[29] Chambers, *op. cit.*, also classifies as resulting trusts a large number of other situations which most commentators regard as having nothing whatever to do with resulting trusts.
[30] [1972] 1 W.L.R. 518.
[31] *ibid.* at 520.
[32] [1972] 1 W.L.R. 1286.
[33] *ibid.* at 1289.

also in the common law jurisdictions of Canada. Thus in *Hussey v. Palmer*, immediately following the passage which has just been cited, Lord Denning M.R. continued:

"By whatever name it is described, it is a trust imposed by law whenever justice and good conscience require it. It is a liberal process, founded upon large principles of equity. . . It is an equitable remedy by which the court can enable an aggrieved party to obtain restitution."[34]

English law had hitherto regarded the constructive trust as "an institutional obligation attaching to property in certain specified circumstances",[35] one of which was mentioned when constructive trusts were defined at the beginning of this chapter.[36] Despite the efforts of Lord Denning M.R., this remains the situation at present—his approach was and is still being rejected in subsequent decisions in which the traditional approach towards the constructive trust was and is being reasserted.[37] However, there have been some further indications that English law may one day make some further move, probably of a more limited nature than that made in the years immediately before and after 1970, towards a more remedial approach. In 1990 the Court of Appeal stated[38] that "there is a good arguable case" that circumstances may arise in which "the court will be prepared to impose a constructive trust *de novo* as a foundation for the grant of equitable remedy by way of account or otherwise", classifying such a trust as a "remedial constructive trust". And, more recently still in 1996, Lord Browne-Wilkinson said[39] that "the remedial constructive trust, if introduced into English law, may provide a more satisfactory road forward . . . However, whether English law should follow the United States and Canada in adopting the remedial constructive trust will have to be decided in some future case where the point is directly in issue." There can therefore be little doubt that the House of Lords will one day soon be called upon to decide whether to return to the trail blazed by the Court of Appeal immediately before and after 1970 or to retain the more traditional approach adopted before and after that period.

Whatever the fate of this possible new development, however, the series of decisions handed down immediately before and after 1970 has had a lasting influence on the law governing joint enterprises entered into by the members of a family unit. It is in this area of the law that the concepts of resulting and constructive trusts have been brought closer together as a result of the development of what has become known as "the common intention constructive trust", which contains elements of both resulting trusts and constructive trusts. If two or more parties make direct contributions to the acquisition of a property in which they intend to live, the principles of resulting trusts will give each of them a beneficial interest in proportion to his respective contribution, provided that the contrary is not

---

[34] *ibid.* at 1289–1290.
[35] Waters in *Equity and Contemporary Legal Developments* (ed. Goldstein, 1992) 457 at 463.
[36] See *ante*, p. 37.
[37] *Burns v. Burns* [1984] Ch. 317; *Grant v. Edwards* [1986] Ch. 638; *Ashburn Anstalt v. Arnold* [1989] Ch. 1 and, most recently of all, *Halifax Building Society v. Thomas* [1996] Ch. 217.
[38] In *Metall und Rohstoff A.G. v. Donaldson Lufkin & Jenrette* [1989] 1 Q.B. 391 at 473–474.
[39] In *Westdeutsche Landesbank Girozentrale v. Islington L.B.C.* [1996] 669 at 716.

stated in the conveyance by means of which the property is conveyed to one or more of them. However, if one of the parties is subsequently encouraged by the other(s) to believe that he will acquire an enhanced beneficial interest in the property by making contributions of a less direct nature towards the repayment of the mortgage or the subsequent improvement of the property (a straightforward illustration is the payment by one of the parties of all the day to day household expenses so that the other can more easily make the repayments of the mortgage), any attempt subsequently to deprive that party of the enhanced beneficial interest which he or she has been encouraged to expect will be regarded as unconscionable and will lead either to the imposition of a constructive trust or to the invocation of the principle of equitable proprietary estoppel.[40] This development has in no sense undermined the traditional categories of resulting and constructive trusts which have already been mentioned. What it has done is to produce a new type of trust which contains features of both types of trust and it is thought that this may in the end lead to the development of a general principle of unconscionability to replace both the "common intention constructive trust" and the principle of equitable proprietary estoppel. For the moment, however, the "common intention constructive trust" has undoubtedly brought closer together certain aspects of resulting and constructive trusts which are now co-existing in a clearly defined but rather unexpected manner.

---

[40] See particularly *Lloyds Bank v. Rosset* [1991] 1 A.C. 107, discussed *post*, p. 363.

CHAPTER 3

THE FORMAL REQUIREMENTS FOR THE CREATION OF A TRUST

I. CAPACITY TO CREATE A TRUST

ANY person who has a power of disposition over a particular type of property can generally create a trust of it. Accordingly, any person over the age of 18[1] who is not suffering from mental incapacity may create an express trust of any property which is capable of disposition and may also create a trust of certain types of property of which he cannot dispose—an example of the latter type of property is a pension granted by a company to a retired director on the basis that it is non-assignable; the director may nevertheless be able to create a valid trust of the benefit of that agreement. Full capacity is therefore required before a fully binding express trust can be created; however, any property validly transferred under a trust which is subsequently held to be void is generally held by its recipient on resulting trust for the incapable settlor.

The position governing mental incapacity depends on whether a receiver has been appointed under sections 94 and 99 of the Mental Health Act 1983 on the grounds that the settlor is incapable of managing his affairs. Where a receiver has been appointed it is generally thought that any trust purportedly made by the mental patient would be void.[2] The court may, however, order the creation of a trust of a mental patient's property, either on the application of another person or on its own initiative.[3] Further, since January 1, 1970, the court has been able to make a will on behalf of the patient[4] and it is also able to vary any trust which has been made, whether by the patient or by its own order, at any time prior to the patient's death.[5] When exercising these powers, the court must principally consider what the patient would have been likely to have done if he had not been incapable.[6] However, even where no receiver has been appointed, a trust will nevertheless be set aside if it can be shown that the settlor did not understand the nature of the act in which he was engaged.[7] It appears that the burden of proof will,

---

[1] Family Law Reform Act 1969, s.1(1).
[2] There is no authority under the 1983 Act; however, this is the effect of *Re Marshall* [1920] 1 Ch. 284, a decision on the Lunacy Act 1890.
[3] Mental Health Act 1983, s.96(1)(d).
[4] *ibid.* ss.96(1)(e), 97.
[5] *ibid.*
[6] *Re T.B.* [1967] Ch. 247; *Re D.(J.)* [1982] Ch. 237.
[7] *Re Beaney* [1978] 1 W.L.R 770; *Simpson v. Simpson* [1992] 1 F.L.R 601 (both cases in which *inter vivos* gifts which upset the balance of the settlor's estate were held to be void).

at the outset, always lie on the person seeking to set the trust aside; however, where there is a long history of mental illness, this burden will easily be able to be discharged and will then effectively be reversed, since the court will then require evidence that the settlor created the trust during a lucid interval.[8] Where a trust is set aside for this reason, any property transferred will be held by the recipient on a resulting trust for the settlor. It must, however, be emphasised that no trust created for valuable consideration will be set aside where the person providing the consideration was unaware of the mental incapacity of the settlor at the time when the trust was made.[9]

A person under the age of 18 cannot hold land[10] although he can certainly hold an equitable interest in land and will do so in the event of a purported conveyance of a legal estate to him, since this takes effect as a declaration of trust in his favour.[11] Consequently, while a minor cannot create a settlement of a legal estate in land, for no such estate can be vested in him, he can create a trust of such property as he does hold, including a trust of an equitable interest in land. Any trust which he does create is voidable until shortly after he attains the age of 18; if he does not repudiate it then, the trust will become fully binding upon him.[12] However, in order to create even a voidable trust, a minor must be old enough to appreciate the nature of his act. If he is too young to do so, his act is void and property which has been transferred is held by the recipient on a resulting trust[13] for the minor (little does the unsuspecting adult who has a sticky bag of sweets pushed into his hand by a toddler appreciate that thereafter he holds them on resulting trust for him[14]). Finally, it should be noted that it was formerly possible for a minor female aged 17 or over to make a binding settlement (this was at the time when the age of majority was 21)[15]; however, there was no obvious point in preserving this right when the age of majority was reduced to 18 and so it was abolished.[16]

II. THE STATUTORY REQUIREMENT OF WRITING

It has already been seen that an express trust can be constituted *inter vivos* either by declaration, where the settlor declares that specific property vested in him is thereafter the subject matter of a trust, or by transfer, where a settlor transfers specific property to trustees for them to hold on trust, the latter method being the only way of constituting a testamentary trust. The

---

[8] See *Cleare v. Cleare* (1869) 1 P. & D. 655; *Chambers and Yatman v. Queen's Proctor* (1840) 2 Curt. 415.

[9] *Price v. Berrington* (1851) 3 Mac. & G. 486.

[10] Law of Property Act 1925, s.1(6); Family Law Reform Act 1969, s.1.

[11] Trusts of Land and Appointment of Trustees Act 1996, Sched. 1, para. 1 (this replaced Settled Land Act 1925, s.27, under which such a conveyance operated as an agreement for valuable consideration to create a settlement of the land on the minor).

[12] *Edwards v. Carter* [1893] A.C. 360.

[13] See *post*, p. 256.

[14] Presumably he should sell them and convert them into authorised investments: see *post*, p. 540.

[15] Under the Infant Settlements Act 1855.

[16] By the Family Law Reform Act 1969, s.11(a), which repealed the Infant Settlements Act 1855.

creation of trusts by either of these methods is subject to certain statutory rules concerning formalities, *inter vivos* trusts being governed by the Law of Property Act 1925 and testamentary trusts by the Wills Act 1837.

1. *The Statutory Provisions*

The wording of the principal statutory provision governing the creation of *inter vivos* trusts (section 53 of the Law of Property Act 1925) has been the subject of detailed analysis by the courts and therefore needs to be set out in full.

"(1)   Subject to the provisions hereinafter contained with respect to the creation of interests in land by parol—
(a)   no interest in land can be created or disposed of except by writing signed by the person creating or conveying the same, or by his agent thereunto lawfully authorised in writing, or by will, or by operation of law;
(b)   a declaration of trust respecting any land or any interest therein must be manifested and proved by some writing signed by some person who is able to declare such trust or by his will;
(c)   a disposition of an equitable interest or trust subsisting at the time of the disposition, must be in writing signed by the person disposing of the same, or by his agent thereunto lawfully authorised in writing or by will.
(2) This section does not affect the creation or operation of resulting, implied or constructive trusts."

All three of the paragraphs of section 53(1) permit the creation or disposition in question to be made by will.[17] Consequently, testamentary trusts are governed exclusively by the provisions of the Wills Act 1837, section 9 of which (as substituted by section 17 of the Administration of Justice Act 1982) provides that no will is valid unless it satisfies the following conditions: first, it must be in writing and signed by the testator or by some other person in his presence and by his direction; secondly, it must appear that the testator intended by his signature to give effect to the will; thirdly, that signature must be made or acknowledged by the testator in the presence of two or more witnesses present at the same time; and, fourthly, each witness must either attest and sign the will or acknowledge his signature in the presence of the testator (but not necessarily in the presence of any other witness), no particular form of attestation being necessary. The formal validity of any trust whose terms are entirely contained within a will is determined entirely by whether or not that will was executed in accordance with this provision; testamentary trusts of this type therefore do not require any further consideration in this section. It is, however, possible for a will executed in

---

[17] Law of Property Act 1925, s.55 provides, *inter alia*, that nothing in s.53 is to invalidate dispositions by will. It also provides that nothing in that section is to affect any interest validly created before the commencement of the Act, or the acquisition of title by adverse possession, or affect the law relating to part performance (now anyway abolished by the Law of Property (Miscellaneous Provisions) Act 1989).

accordance with this provision to constitute a trust whose existence and/or terms are not revealed on the face of the will; the validity of such trusts is governed by the doctrine of secret trusts, which will be considered in detail right at the end of this section.[18]

Turning now to section 53(1), its different paragraphs require different formalities. Paragraphs a and c require the transaction in question to be in writing; therefore any failure to comply with this requirement makes the transaction in question wholly void. However, the writing need not in all cases contain every detail—if the assignee is to hold subject to some fiduciary duty, the writing need not comprise particulars of the trust.[19] Nor does it seem to be necessary that the writing should all be contained in one document; a number of documents may be joined together for the purpose of satisfying the statute, provided that they are sufficiently connected.[20] On the other hand, paragraph b requires only evidentiary writing so that any failure to comply with this requirement does not make the transaction in question wholly void but merely unenforceable. This has two consequences: first, that the transaction is and remains valid unless and until one of the parties specifically raises the absence of the writing[21]; secondly, the necessary evidentiary writing can take the most diverse forms[22] and be provided at any time and quite unintentionally, provided that it contains all the terms of the trust. A further difference is that the writing required by paragraphs a and c can be signed either by the grantor or by an agent of the grantor who has been duly authorised in writing, while the writing required by paragraph b can be signed only by the grantor.

Nor is the precise scope of section 53(1) entirely clear. Paragraphs a and b are expressed to apply only to interests in land; paragraph c, on the other hand, is not expressly so restricted. However, the definitions section of the Law of Property Act 1925,[23] provides that "equitable interests" means "all the other interests and charges in or over land", unless the context otherwise requires. The question of whether this definition does restrict the scope of paragraph c to interests in land or whether, on the other hand, the context does otherwise require, has not been specifically addressed by an English court (it was considered by the High Court of Australia in *Adamson v.*

---

[18] See *post*, pp. 62–81.

[19] *Re Tyler* [1967] 1 W.L.R. 1269.

[20] *Re Danish Bacon Company Staff Pension Fund Trusts* [1971] 1 W.L.R. 268; Megarry J. stated that this was a novel question on which there appeared to be no previous direct authority.

[21] This can presumably be done at any time, even long after the creation of the trust. In principle, this means that there is nothing to stop the residuary beneficiaries of the estate of a settlor who has created an *inter vivos* trust of land without the necessary formalities from recovering the land in question after the settlor's death, although any beneficiary who had suffered detriment would inevitably be able to resist such a claim by relying on an equitable proprietary estoppel (see *post*, pp. 140–147).

[22] For example, it may be provided by correspondence (*Foster v. Hale* (1798) 3 Ves.Jun. 696), by a recital in an instrument (*Re Hoyle* [1893] 1 Ch. 84), by an answer to interrogatories (*Hampton v. Spencer* (1693) 2 Vern. 288) or even by a telegram (*McBlain v. Cross* (1871) 25 L.T. 804). It remains to be seen whether it would today also be held capable of being provided by a fax, a type of document which it is notoriously easy to forge.

[23] s.201(1)(x).

Hayes,[24] where the members of the court disagreed[25]). It is generally thought that the context does otherwise require; were this not the case, paragraph c would be superfluous since every situation falling within it would already have been caught by paragraph a, something which cannot possibly have been the intention of the legislature. Moreover, the House of Lords applied paragraph c to a relevant disposition of pure personalty in *Grey v. Inland Revenue Commissioners*[26] without any objection being raised, a decision which must resolve the question in this jurisdiction unless and until it is specifically raised.

A further difficulty is the apparent overlaps between paragraphs a, b, and c of section 53(1), which respectively deal with the creation or disposition of any interest in land, any declaration of a trust of land, and any disposition of a subsisting equitable interest or trust. The distinction thus drawn between the creation and the disposition of interests must be applied in the light of the fact that, when property is owned legally and beneficially by the same person, he holds only a legal interest therein, not a separate equitable interest as well.[27] Consequently, when such a person confers an equitable interest in that property on someone else, he is not disposing of an existing equitable interest therein but creating a new one. This is capable of falling within paragraphs a and b but not within paragraph c, which clearly relates only to the disposition of a "subsisting" equitable interest, that is to say one existing separately from the legal estate. This however only rules out any overlap between paragraph b and paragraph c; there may nevertheless be overlaps between, on the one hand, paragraph a and, on the other hand, paragraphs b and c. The fact that, on the face of things, there seems to be a clear overlap between paragraph a and paragraph c, in that a disposition of a subsisting equitable interest in or trust of land is caught by both of them, has no significance in this jurisdiction since the formal requirements of the two paragraphs are identical.[28] Potentially more problematic is the fact that a declaration of trust respecting land appears to fall within both paragraph a and paragraph b, which have different formal requirements; such a trust supported only by evidentiary writing signed by the settlor appears to be void under paragraph a and valid under paragraph b. Once again there is no

---

[24] (1973) 130 C.L.R. 276.
[25] Menzies J. held that the equivalent Western Australian provision was restricted to interests in land, whereas Gibbs J. held that it was not. The remaining judges did not specifically mention this point but, since Walsh and Stephen JJ. agreed with Gibbs J. in other respects, the Australian commentators have concluded that they also rejected the view of Menzies J. and that there was therefore a majority against the provision being so restricted.
[26] [1960] A.C. 1.
[27] *Commissioner of Stamp Duties (Queensland) v. Livingston* [1965] A.C. 694 (Privy Council on appeal from the High Court of Australia).
[28] This is undoubtedly why the question has never been raised. The only way of escaping from this conclusion is to hold that paragraph a is confined to legal interests in land. This was held by Menzies J. in *Adamson v. Hayes* (1973) 130 C.L.R. 276 but the majority of the High Court of Australia (Walsh, Gibbs and Stephen JJ.) took the opposite view. However, none of them specifically mentioned the possible overlap, which would be significant only in Queensland, whose equivalent of paragraph c unusually requires only evidentiary writing—the legislation in the remaining Australian jurisdictions is similar to s.53(1)(c).

English authority and the Australian decisions are mutually inconsistent.[29] If this overlap exists, paragraph b is in effect superfluous, something which again cannot possibly have been the intention of the legislature. It is thought that the potential difficulty could and should be resolved by reading paragraph a as if it said "no interest in land can be created or disposed of *otherwise than by the declaration of a trust* except by writing . . . " (the words emphasised being interpolated). However, unless and until this matter is actually considered by a court, there must be a certain amount of doubt as to whether a declaration of trust of land which is not in writing and is supported only by evidentiary writing signed by the settlor is actually valid.

Finally, the exception contained in section 53(2) qualifies the whole of section 53(1). Consequently, the creation or operation of implied, resulting or constructive trusts does not have to comply with the formal requirements of the section. This provision is applied extremely literally. It clearly exempts such trusts from having to comply with section 53(1)(b). This is illustrated by *Hodgson v. Marks*,[30] where an elderly widow was persuaded by her lodger to convey her house into his name on the spurious grounds that this would prevent him from being turned out of it after her death. He subsequently sold and conveyed the property to third parties without revealing that he had no beneficial interest therein. The Court of Appeal decided that he had held the property on resulting trust for the widow; such a trust arose without any need to comply with the statutory formalities required by section 53(1)(b) and so was capable of binding the third parties.[31] However, although resulting, implied and constructive trusts can come into existence and operate without any need for writing, any disposition of an interest arising under such a trust must comply with section 53(1)(c)—this is demonstrated by the decision of the House of Lords in *Grey v. I.R.C.*,[32] where what was being disposed of by the settlor was an interest arising under a resulting trust.

2. *The Effect of the Statutory Provisions governing Inter Vivos Trusts*

(A) The Creation of a Trust by Declaration in respect of Property Vested in the Settlor

If the interest in the property in question held by the settlor is a legal interest, the effect of the statutory provisions depends on whether it is in land or in pure personalty. If it is an interest in land,[33] section 53(1)(b) applies on any view; consequently, the declaration of trust will require evidentiary writing signed by the settlor, in default of which the declaration

---

[29] In *Adamson v. Hayes* (1973) 130 C.L.R. 276, Gibbs and Stephen JJ. expressly and Walsh J. implicitly but not Menzies J. held that there was such an overlap but the opposite view was subsequently taken at first instance in *Secretary, Department of Social Security v. Jones* (1990) 95 A.J.R. 615 (Supreme Court of Western Australia), where a declaration of trust of land was held only to fall within paragraph b.

[30] [1971] Ch. 892.

[31] It was in fact held to bind the third parties on the grounds that the widow had an overriding interest under s.70(1)(g) of the Land Registration Act 1925.

[32] [1960] A.C. 1. See *post*, p. 52.

[33] This includes freehold and leasehold property: Law of Property Act 1925, s.205(1)(ix).

will be unenforceable. Signature by an agent is insufficient.[34] The appropriate writing will still be required even if the land in question is situated out of the jurisdiction and no writing is necessary according to the *lex situs*; this is because this is a rule of evidence which must be complied with in an English court.[35] If, on the other hand, the property is an interest in pure personalty, none of the statutory provisions applies and so the declaration of trust will be able to be made entirely orally. It is indeed rather surprising that a declaration of trust requires the appropriate writing even if it relates to as little as a square foot of land while a declaration of trust of millions of pounds worth of cash or investments does not; however, that is what the statutory provisions provide.

If, on the other hand, the interest in the property in question held by the settlor is an equitable interest,[36] the result is exactly the same with one further complication. The equitable interest in question must necessarily be taking effect behind an existing trust so that what the settlor will in reality be declaring is a sub-trust. The effect of this may depend on whether the sub-trust declared is passive or active.[37] If it is passive, there is binding authority[38] (although contrary views have been expressed[39]) that the settlor of the sub-trust will "disappear from the picture" and drop out so that his trustees will hold the property directly on trust for the intended beneficiary of the sub-trust; if it is active, there is further authority[40] (and it is generally agreed) that the settlor of the sub-trust will not drop out and will hold his own subsisting interest on trust for the intended beneficiary of the sub-trust. So far as formalities are concerned, the conventional view[41] is that, if the settlor does drop out, his purported declaration of trust will be treated as amounting to a disposition of his subsisting equitable interest under the

---

[34] If, contrary to what was suggested above, there is indeed an overlap between s.53(1)(a) and s.53(1)(b), the former provision will also apply, requiring the declaration of trust to be in writing signed by the settlor or by an agent of the settlor duly authorised in writing, in default of which the declaration will be void.

[35] *Rochefoucauld v. Boustead* [1897] 1 Ch. 196 at 207.

[36] This includes freehold and leasehold property (Law of Property Act 1925, s.205(1)(ix)) and also apparently a share in the proceeds of sale of land (Law of Property (Miscellaneous Provisions) Act 1989, s.2(6)).

[37] It will be regarded as passive where the settlor has declared that his entire interest under the existing trust is to be held for the intended beneficiary of the sub-trust; where, on the other hand, the settlor has either declared that only a part of his interest under the existing trust is to be held for that beneficiary or has reserved some duties which in effect restrict the nature of the interest being given to him (the example which is always given is a declaration of trust to pay the rents and profits of the trust property to the intended beneficiary, thus restricting his rights to call for the capital), it will be regarded as active. It is unclear whether an apparently passive sub-trust for persons by way of succession is passive or active; however, it is suggested that the better view is that of Fry L.J. in *Re Lashmar* [1891] 1 Ch. 258 (by way of dictum) that it is passive.

[38] This was stated in *Grainge v. Wilberforce* (1889) 5 T.L.R. 436 at 437 and held by the Court of Appeal in *Re Lashmar* [1891] 1 Ch. 258.

[39] By B. Green, Q.C. in (1984) 37 M.L.R. 385. This view has also been expressed in some of the common law jurisdictions of the United States of America and seems to be supported in Australia by some remarks of Dixon J. in *Comptroller of Stamps (Victoria) v. Howard Smith* (1936) 54 C.L.R. 614 (High Court of Australia).

[40] *Onslow v. Wallis* (1849) 1 Mac. & G. 506.

[41] See G. Battersby [1979] Conv. 17.

original trust; consequently, section 53(1)(c) will apply, requiring the declaration of sub-trust to be in writing signed by the settlor or by an agent of the settlor duly authorised in writing, in default of which the declaration will be void. According to this view, a declaration of a passive sub-trust (but not an active sub-trust) requires writing under section 53(1)(c). This is not particularly significant in the case of a sub-trust of land, where evidentiary writing under section 53(1)(b) is necessary on any view,[42] but immensely significant in the case of a sub-trust of pure personalty, which would otherwise require no formality whatever. An alternative view has been put forward[43] that all declarations of sub-trust, whether active or passive, have to comply with section 53(1)(c) whether the settlor drops out or not, thus requiring writing in even more cases than the conventional view. However, it is thought that the conventional view should be adopted until such time as the question is considered by a court (it has never had to be considered in relation to the Law of Property Act 1925).

(B) The Creation of a Trust by Transfer in respect of Property Vested in the Settlor

In this case, the settlor must vest the property in question in the trustees on the intended trusts by the appropriate formalities.

If the interest in the property in question held by the settlor is a legal interest, the formalities depend on the nature of the property. Registered land or any interest therein must be transferred by the appropriate land transfer form and duly registered in the name of the trustees in the Land Register,[44] whereas unregistered land must be transferred by deed.[45] The transfer or deed in question will normally set out the trusts on which the interest in land in question is to be held; if it does not do so,[46] those trusts should have been set out in a separate document which complies with section 53(1)(b)[47]—in default, the trustees will hold the property on resulting trust for the settlor. Choses in possession, that is to say personal chattels, can be transferred either by delivery of the chattel with the appropriate intention to give or by deed[48]; the trusts on which they are to be held can be communicated orally. Choses in action must in principle be assigned in accordance with section 136 of the Law of Property Act 1925[49] but the

---

[42] If, contrary to what was suggested above, there is indeed an overlap between s.53(1)(a) and s.53(1)(b), this will make no difference at all.

[43] By B. Green, Q.C. in (1984) 37 M.L.R. 385.

[44] Land Registration Rules 1925, r. 98.

[45] Law of Property Act 1925, s.52.

[46] This will necessarily be the case where the trusts in question are secret (see *post*, pp. 62–81) and was formerly the case where what was being created was a settlement under the Settled Land Act 1925 (no further settlements of this type can now be created).

[47] *Re Baillie* (1886) 2 T.L.R. 660 (half secret trust; the absence of writing has never been raised in respect of a fully secret trust). If there is indeed an overlap between s.53(1)(a) and s.53(1)(b), the writing in question will instead have to comply with s.53(1)(a).

[48] See *Cochrane v. Moore* (1890) 25 Q.B.D. 57. However, if the trust is being constituted pursuant to a contract for the sale of goods, the legal title will pass in accordance with the legislation governing sales of goods.

[49] This provision requires the assignment to be in writing signed by the assignor and for express notice in writing to be given to the debtor or other person from whom the assignor would have been able to claim the debt or other chose in action.

assignment of some specific choses[50] in action is instead governed by their own specific legislative provisions.[51] However, a transfer which has not been made in accordance with these formal requirements may nevertheless take effect in equity by virtue of the Rule in *Re Rose*[52] where the settlor has done everything within his power to bring about the transfer.

If, on the other hand, the interest in the property in question held by the settlor is an equitable interest, then, no matter what the nature of the property, its transfer will constitute a disposition of a subsisting equitable interest; consequently, both the actual transfer and the trusts on which the equitable interest are to be held will have to be in writing complying with section 53(1)(c). An equitable interest can also be assigned under section 136 of the Law of Property Act 1925 on the basis that it is a chose in action.[53]

(C) The Creation of a Trust as a Result of Instructions Given by the Settlor to his Trustees

In all the examples considered so far the settlor in question has himself dealt with property vested in him. It is now necessary to consider the situation where a settlor who is beneficially entitled to property under a trust gives instructions to his trustees to deal with that property in some way in order to vest his interest in a third party.

(1) Where the settlor directs his trustees to hold on trust for a third party

This situation had to be considered by the House of Lords in *Grey v. I.R.C.*[54] Trustees were holding shares as the nominees of the settlor, who was therefore beneficially entitled to them under a resulting trust. The settlor, having made six settlements in favour of his grandchildren, orally directed the trustees to hold the shares on the trusts of those settlements. The trustees then executed six written declarations of trust in similar form, each of which recited their legal ownership of the shares, the settlor's oral direction, and their acceptance of the trust reposed in them by that direction. This apparently pointless manoeuvre was in fact an ingenious scheme to avoid payment of the *ad valorem* stamp duty which was then normally chargeable on a transfer of shares into a settlement.[55] However, the Inland Revenue rejected this scheme and assessed the six written declarations to this duty. The House of Lords held that the directions given by the settlor to the

---

[50] Such as shares, copyrights, certain types of insurance policies, and bills of exchange.

[51] Most shares are transferred simply by filling in the appropriate share transfer form, sometimes printed on the back of the share certificate itself, and sending it to the Registrar of the company in question for entry on the Register of Shareholders.

[52] [1952] Ch. 499. See *post*, p. 131.

[53] This will require the assignment to be in writing signed by the assignor and for express notice in writing to be given to the trustee in question.

[54] [1960] A.C. 1.

[55] Stamp duty is a tax which is payable only on documents so that when a transaction is properly effected orally no duty is payable. A method of avoiding duty had been evolved some considerable time earlier whereby the settlor orally made a declaration of trust and some time later signed a document merely recording what he had done. As long as these two events were separate—see *Cohen and Moore v. I.R.C.* [1933] 2 K.B. 126, no duty was payable because the trust was effected by the oral declaration. *Grey v. I.R.C.* was an attempt to extend this principle by a three stage operation: first, a transfer by the settlor of the shares to the trustees to hold as nominees on his behalf (because this transfer made no change in the

trustees were in fact dispositions by him of his subsisting equitable interest in the shares and so were within section 53(1)(c); because they had not been made in writing as required by that paragraph, they were ineffective at the time but became effective later on the execution of the written declarations of trust by the trustees. The word "disposition" in section 53(1)(c) had to be given the wide meaning which it bears in normal usage and the declarations of trust had accordingly been rightly assessed.

It had been persuasively argued that section 53 was merely a consolidation of three provisions of the Statute of Frauds 1677, sections 3, 7 and 9. There is a general principle that consolidating statutes are not to be interpreted as changing the pre-existing law unless the words are too clear to admit of any other construction. On this basis, the term "disposition" had to be interpreted in the same way as the expression "grants and assignments" found in section 9 which, it was contended, would not cover the directions given by the settlor. It was, as Lord Radcliffe said, a "nice question" whether or not this type of direction would have been caught by section 9; the point had never been decided and perhaps never would be. But the question was only relevant if section 53 was indeed to be treated as a true consolidation of the three sections of the Statute of Frauds. The House of Lords actually held that this was not the case—the section could not be regarded as a consolidating enactment in that sense. The Law of Property Act 1925 was undoubtedly a consolidating statute but what it had consolidated was the Law of Property Act 1922 and the Law of Property (Amendment) Act 1924. While the relevant sections of the Statute of Frauds 1677 were untouched by the 1922 Act, they had been repealed and re-enacted in an altered form by the 1924 Act. Consequently there was no direct link between section 53(1)(c) and section 9 of the Statute of Frauds 1677; the link had been broken by the changes introduced by the 1924 Act and it was those changes, not the previous provisions, which section 53 must be taken as having consolidated. It was therefore inadmissible to allow the construction of the word "disposition" to be limited or controlled by any meaning which could conceivably be attached to "grants and assignments" in section 9 of the Statute of Frauds.[56]

The word "disposition" in section 53(1)(c) must therefore be given the wide meaning which it bears in normal usage; if at the start of a transaction a person has a subsisting equitable interest and at the end of that transaction no longer has that interest, there will have been a disposition and the paragraph will have to be complied with.[57] Only two exceptions to this rule have subsequently emerged. First, it has been established that a disclaimer

---

beneficial interest, this stage unquestionably involved the payment of duty of only 50p); secondly, an oral direction by the settlor to the trustees to hold for a third party (because this direction was oral, this stage equally clearly involved no payment of duty at all); and, thirdly, a subsequent written declaration of trust by the trustees. It was hoped that the oral declaration by the settlor would be sufficient to pass the equitable interest already, in which case no duty would be payable on the subsequent written declaration by the trustees. However the Revenue contended that, by virtue of s.53(1)(c), any disposition by the settlor had to be in writing; consequently, no disposition had taken place until the written declaration of trust had been signed so that stamp duty was payable thereon.

[56] [1960] A.C. 1 at 17–18.

[57] If there is indeed an overlap between s.53(1)(a) and s.53(1)(c), paragraph a will also apply where the subject matter is land but this in practice makes no difference whatever.

of an equitable interest is not caught by section 53(1)(c) and so does not have to be made in writing. This was held in *Re Paradise Motor Company*,[58] where a verbal disclaimer by a person to whom shares had been given in such a way as to give him an equitable interest therein was held to be effective and therefore disentitled him from claiming in the liquidation of the company in question. Secondly, it has been stated that the paragraph does not apply to a right commonly given by pension schemes to employees who are not yet in receipt of their pensions to nominate a person to receive a payment in the event of their death. In *Re Danish Bacon Company Staff Pension Fund*,[59] Megarry J. held that such a right did not amount to a testamentary disposition and so did not have to comply with the formal requirements for wills.[60] He also stated that he "very much doubted" whether the right was caught by section 53(1)(c), doubting not only whether such a nomination could properly be described as a disposition, given that it had no more than a mere possibility of disposing of anything, but also whether the interest of the person at the time of making the nomination could properly be described as "subsisting". This view seems entirely justified; however, given that he was able to hold that there was sufficient writing in any event, he did not actually have to decide the point.

(2) Where the settlor directs his trustees to transfer the trust property to a third party beneficially

This situation occurred in *Vandervell v. I.R.C.*,[61] the first of three cases which arose out of an endowment in favour of the Royal College of Surgeons, whose ramifications were insufficiently investigated.[62] Vandervell had during his lifetime been a very successful businessman. He was beneficially entitled to virtually all the shares in a private products company which he ran and he could declare dividends as and when he pleased. In 1949 he had formed a trust company for the benefit of his children and had transferred money and shares to it to be held on trust for them. In 1958 he decided to respond to an appeal for funds by the Royal College of Surgeons by founding a chair of pharmacology at a cost of £150,000.[63] In the hope of making this endowment in a tax efficient way,[64] he directed a bank, who held shares

---

[58] [1968] 1 W.L.R. 1125.
[59] [1971] 1 W.L.R. 248 at 256.
[60] See *ante*, p. 46. On this point, the decision of Megarry J. was confirmed and applied by the Privy Council in *Baird v. Baird* [1990] 2 A.C. 548.
[61] [1967] 2 A.C. 291.
[62] An incisive statement of the facts can be found in the judgment of Lord Denning M.R. in *Re Vandervell's Trusts (No.2)* [1974] Ch. 269 at 316–318; this decision of the Court of Appeal was the final stage of the third of the three cases.
[63] Just over £2,000,000 when converted to 1998 values using the Retail Prices Index.
[64] Any dividends declared by the company would be subject to deduction at source of the tax payable on company distributions (then 6s.8d. in the pound—33.33 per cent) and would then be subject to surtax (the name then given to what are now known as higher rates of income tax) in the hands of the shareholders (in Vandervell's case at 50 per cent). The total tax payable by Vandervell on any dividends would thus have been 83.33 per cent. The purpose of vesting the shares in the Royal College of Surgeons was to remove any liability of Vandervell to surtax and to enable the College, as a charity, to recover the 33.33 per cent tax already paid on the company distributions. That way a third of the endowment would be being provided out of tax already paid. This scheme would have worked perfectly had Vandervell not failed fully to divest himself of his beneficial interest in the shares.

in his products company as his nominee, to transfer those shares to the College, not however as an outright gift but subject to the College granting to the trust company an option to re-purchase the shares for £5,000 (a figure considerably less than their market value) at any time within five years. It was intended that when sufficient dividends had been declared and paid on the shares to provide £145,000, the trust company would exercise the option, pay the remaining £5,000 and reacquire the shares, which could then be used for other purposes. Between 1958 and 1961 the products company declared dividends on the shares which were more than sufficient to endow the chair at the College.[65] Unfortunately, Vandervell failed to specify the trusts on which the trust company was to hold the option (it appeared that he had not made up his mind whether the option should be held in trust for his children or for the employees of his company). The Revenue therefore argued that Vandervell was liable to surtax on the dividends[66] on the basis that he had throughout retained a beneficial interest in the shares. The House of Lords held, by a majority of three to two, that because no trusts of the option had been declared it was held on resulting trust for Vandervell himself and he had therefore been rightly assessed.

This conclusion, which has nothing to do with formalities, was sufficient to dispose of the case. However, the Revenue also argued that section 53(1)(c) had not been complied with. At the outset Vandervell had held the equitable beneficial interest in the shares which were in the name of his bank; he had never transferred that equitable interest to the College in the manner required by section 53(1)(c); consequently, the beneficial interest was still vested in him and he was for that reason liable to surtax on the dividends declared thereon. The House of Lords rejected this contention, holding that section 53(1)(c) has no application where the holder of the equitable interest also controls the legal interest and intends that both should be transferred to a third party beneficially. In other words, section 53(1)(c) only applies to the disposition of an existing equitable interest when that interest is both before and after the disposition vested in someone other than the holder of the legal interest. The House of Lords had little alternative but to reach this conclusion since otherwise nominees would no longer have been able to pass a beneficial interest to a third party in the absence of a written disposition by or on behalf of the beneficiary.[67] However, the reasons enunciated by the House are less than wholly convincing.

Lord Reid[68] simply declined to give any reasons whatever for his decision on this point. Lord Wilberforce[69] held that Vandervell had done everything in his power to transfer his beneficial interest and so could rely on the Rule

---

[65] The dividends amounted to over £266,000; after tax at source the College received about £175,000 plus the £5,000 payable under the option and it was envisaged that it would also be able to reclaim the tax deducted at source.

[66] Amounting, ultimately, to the whole amount of the dividends; the initial demand was for £250,000 in respect of the first two years of assessment; a further assessment was no doubt made in respect of the third year. The surtax was payable by virtue of the Income Tax Act 1952, s.415.

[67] In particular, the practice whereby brokers who are holding shares on behalf of their clients can and do resell them on the strength of oral instructions would have required some reconsideration in the event that the House of Lords had reached the opposite conclusion.

[68] [1967] 2 A.C. 291 at 307.

[69] *ibid.* at 329–330.

in *Re Rose*[70] which gives effect in equity to transfers which a settlor has done everything within his power to bring about; however, this argument in fact begged the question because Vandervell had only done everything in his power if he did not have to use writing—precisely the question in issue.[71] Lord Upjohn[72] had recourse to the mischief rule of statutory interpretation and held that section 53(1)(c) had been enacted to prevent fraud on those who were truly beneficially entitled; consequently, it could not apply to an absolutely entitled beneficiary like Vandervell, who could control his trustees. Since the only person whom such a person could possibly defraud was himself, there could be no grounds for invoking the section where such an absolute beneficial owner wanted to deal with the legal estate. Lord Pearce agreed with the speech of Lord Upjohn and Lord Donovan[73] reached the same conclusion without specific reference to the rules of statutory interpretation. Lord Upjohn's argument therefore found favour with at least three members of the House and is not wholly unconvincing. However, the mischief rule of statutory interpretation is only supposed to be invoked where there is some ambiguity or lacuna in the provision in question, something which is certainly not the case with section 53(1)(c).[74] It may therefore be that the decision is best regarded as having been taken on policy grounds. But whatever its grounds, it is at least clear and establishes that, where a settlor directs his trustees to transfer the trust property to a third party with the intention that that third party should take both the legal and the beneficial interest in the property, the settlor does not have to comply with section 53(1)(c).

(3) Where the settlor directs his trustees to declare new trusts in favour of a third party

This situation occurred in *Re Vandervell's Trusts (No.2)*,[75] which was itself a consequence of the decision in *Vandervell v. I.R.C.* that the option was held on resulting trust for Vandervell between 1958 and 1961. It will be recalled that during that period the trusts on which the option to repurchase was held had not been specified and the option itself had not been exercised. However, in October 1961 the trust company exercised the option and paid the £5,000 payable thereunder to the Royal College of Surgeons from the funds of the children's settlement. The trust company therefore became the legal owners of the shares themselves, no longer merely of the option to re-purchase them. All subsequent dividends were paid to the trust company and held on the trusts of the children's settlement. But even at this stage Vandervell made no express declaration of the trusts on which the shares or

---

[70] See *post*, p. 131.
[71] See G. H. Jones (1966) 24 C.L.J. 19.
[72] [1967] 2 A.C. 291 at 311.
[73] *ibid.* at 317–318.
[74] Nor is this argument wholly consistent with the decision in *Grey v. I.R.C.* Lord Upjohn admittedly took great pains to confine his argument to the situation where the settlor intended to deal with the legal title and so the *rationes decidendi* of the two decisions are wholly distinct; however, that does not alter the fact that the settlor in *Grey v. I.R.C.* was also absolutely beneficially entitled to the subject matter of the trust and s.53(1)(c) was nevertheless held to apply.
[75] [1974] Ch. 269.

the dividends should be held. It was not until March 1964 (when judgment was given at first instance in *Vandervell v. I.R.C.*[76]) that it occurred to anyone that he might have retained an interest under a resulting trust.[77] Subsequently in January 1965[78] he did execute a deed transferring to the trust company such interest as he might have in the shares or dividends and expressly declaring that the trust company was to hold them on the trusts of the children's settlement. The Revenue accepted that this deed was effective to divest Vandervell of any interest in the shares or dividends. He subsequently died early in 1967, aware of the result of *Vandervell v. I.R.C.*[79] but not of that of the subsequent proceedings which dragged on for more than seven years after his death.[80]

Re Vandervell's Trusts (No.2) concerned the period between October 1961 and January 1965. The Revenue, on the basis that Vandervell had not divested himself of his interest in the shares or the option until January 1965, assessed his estate to surtax in respect of the dividends received by the trust company during this period.[81] In order to be able to pay this tax, his executors therefore had to claim from the trust company all the dividends paid to it during this period (the children were not beneficiaries of the will because Vandervell had thought that he had made sufficient provision for them under their settlement). The Revenue sought and failed to be joined to these proceedings[82] but, pending their conclusion, the executors' appeal against the surtax assessment was stood over.

It has already been seen that the £5,000 payable under the option was provided out of the children's settlement and that thereafter all the dividends received by the trust company were transferred to the children's settlement and treated as part of its funds. Furthermore, the solicitors for the trust company had written a letter to the Revenue stating that the shares which it had purchased would be held on the trusts of the children's settlement. The Revenue admitted that all these dealings, which were done with Vandervell's approval, showed that Vandervell and the trust company intended that the shares should be held on trust for the children's settlement; however, they argued that this intention was in fact unavailing and that, for the following reasons, the shares and dividends had in fact been held on trust for Vandervell until January 1965: first, until October 1961 Vandervell had an equitable interest under a resulting trust—this was indisputable since the House of Lords had so held in *Vandervell v. I.R.C.*[83]; secondly, he himself had never disposed of that interest until January 1965; and, thirdly, and in any event, any disposition prior to January 1965 would

---

[76] [1966] Ch. 261.

[77] Plowman J. so held; the decision of the Special Commissioners had found Vandervell liable on a different ground.

[78] The first day of the hearing of the appeal from the decision of Plowman J. (see [1966] Ch. 261).

[79] The House of Lords handed down its decision on November 24, 1966.

[80] The Court of Appeal gave judgment in *Re Vandervell's Trusts (No.2)* on July 3, 1974.

[81] Amounting to the frivolity of £628,229, at least £8,000,000 when converted to 1998 values using the Retail Prices Index.

[82] *Re Vandervell's Trusts* [1971] A.C. 912. This meant that, paradoxically, the executors had to fight the Revenue's battle on its behalf because they would be liable for the surtax if the Revenue ultimately succeeded.

[83] [1967] 2 A.C. 291. See *ante*, p. 54.

necessarily have been an oral disposition of an equitable interest which, by
virtue of section 53(1)(c), had to be in writing. This argument succeeded
before Megarry J. but the Court of Appeal rejected it as fallacious; the court
held, *inter alia*,[84] that the dealings with the dividends during this period not
only showed an intention to create but actually amounted to the declaration
of a trust of the shares in favour of the children's settlement which, because
its subject matter was pure personalty, could be created without writing.[85]
Section 53(1)(c) was, therefore, irrelevant. Leave to appeal to the House of
Lords was granted but in the end no appeal was in fact made; because the
decision of the Court of Appeal has left the law in some disarray, this was
perhaps unfortunate for legal theory but was presumably a cause of great
relief to the Vandervell trustees.

The decision of the Court of Appeal has in fact given rise to a number of
doubts. As will be seen in the chapter on Constitution of Trusts,[86] it is
questionable whether a valid trust of the shares could have been completely
constituted as a result of the events which had happened. Further, even if a
trust was actually constituted, it is difficult to justify the decision that section
53(1)(c) was not applicable. While there is no doubt that both Vandervell and
the trust company intended that the shares should be held on trust for the
children's settlement, it is difficult to infer that Vandervell could have
intended to dispose or did dispose of his equitable interest under the
resulting trust of the option when he was unaware that he had such an
interest until March 1964 when the first instance decision was handed down
in *Vandervell v. I.R.C.* Further, even if the necessary intention can be inferred
to have existed any time prior to January 1965,[87] why did the decision in
Grey v. I.R.C.,[88] where the settlor had similarly been trying to dispose of an
interest under a resulting trust, not oblige Vandervell to dispose of his
equitable interest in writing in accordance with section 53(1)(c)?[89] The Court
of Appeal actually held that Vandervell's interest under the resulting trust
had been extinguished when the gap in the beneficial ownership which had
given rise to it was filled by the creation or declaration of a valid trust. In
other words, the gap in the beneficial ownership had only existed until the
option was exercised; as soon as this had occurred, a valid trust of the shares
was created in favour of the children's settlement. This proposition can be
interpreted in two ways. It is possible to confine its effect to the situation
where an option is held on trust; in this case *Re Vandervell's Trusts (No. 2)*
merely decides that, where an option is held on resulting trust, a direction
by the beneficiary to the trustees to declare new trusts of the property which
they receive as a result of exercising the option does not require writing

---

[84] Other aspects of their decision are discussed *post*, pp. 129, 144.
[85] Law of Property Act 1925, s.53(1)(b) applies only to trusts of land. See *ante*, p. 47.
[86] See *post*, pp. 129, 144.
[87] When Vandervell executed the deed which the Revenue accepted was effective to deprive
him of any beneficial interest.
[88] [1960] A.C. 1. See *ante*, p. 52.
[89] See the summary of the argument by Stephenson L.J. in *Re Vandervell's Trusts (No.2)* [1974] Ch.
269 at 322–323. This particular point had not been argued before Megarry J. at first
instance.

under section 53(1)(c).[90] However, the formulations of principle in the judgments are not actually restricted to options and so at least suggest that, where any property is held on resulting trust, a direction by the beneficiary to the trustees to declare new trusts of that property does not require writing under section 53(1)(c); if this is indeed the case, then it is not easy to see any satisfactory distinction[91] between *Re Vandervell's Trusts (No.2)* and *Grey v. I.R.C.*, where a similar direction by the beneficiary of a resulting trust to the trustees to hold the property on new trusts was held to require writing.

(D)   The Creation of a Trust as a Result of the Formation of a Specifically Enforceable Contract of Sale

This possibility depends on section 53(2) which provides that section 53 as a whole does not apply to the creation or operation of resulting, implied or constructive trusts.[92] It was contended in *Oughtred v. I.R.C.*[93] that this provision enables equitable interests to be disposed of without any need for writing where the disposition in question is by way of constructive sub-trust arising as the result of the formation of a specifically enforceable contract of sale.

Shares in a private company had been settled on trust for a mother for life and subject thereto for her son. They agreed to exchange other shares in the same company to which the mother was absolutely entitled for the son's equitable remainder, thus enlarging her life interest into absolute ownership. A contract for the sale of shares in a private company, unlike the majority of contracts for the sale of pure personalty, is specifically enforceable; this is because damages would not be an adequate remedy for the loss of the shares. The effect of such a contract is that the vendor holds its subject matter on a constructive trust for the purchaser, who therefore acquires an immediate equitable interest therein.[94] Hence the contract between mother and son automatically gave rise to a constructive trust (strictly speaking, because its subject matter was a subsisting equitable interest, a constructive sub-trust) under which the son held his equitable remainder on trust for his mother. It was argued that as a result of the creation of this passive sub-trust the son had "disappeared from the picture" and dropped out,[95] causing his equitable remainder to pass to his mother; since by virtue of section 53(2) no writing was necessary for the creation of this constructive sub-trust, the mother had therefore acquired an absolute beneficial interest in the shares without the use of any instrument on which stamp duty could be levied. The trustees had admittedly subsequently transferred the legal title to the shares to her but it was argued that this had transferred only a bare legal title, in respect of which only a nominal duty of 50p was payable. The majority of the House of Lords, however, accepted the Revenue's contention that the

---

[90] Where the subject matter is land, s.53(1)(b) (or, in the event of an overlap, s.53(1)(a)) would apply to such a declaration of trust.

[91] Unless there is some forensic difference between telling trustees "to hold on new trusts" and telling them "to declare new trusts".

[92] See *ante*, p. 49.

[93] [1960] A.C. 206.

[94] See *post*, p. 374.

[95] This was stated in *Grainge v. Wilberforce* (1889) 5 T.L.R. 436 at 437 and held by the Court of Appeal in *Re Lashmar* [1891] 1 Ch. 258. See *ante*, p. 50.

latter transfer had to be stamped *ad valorem*. The reasoning behind this decision was stated by Lord Jenkins, who held that, if the subject matter of a sale is such that the full title to it can only be transferred by an instrument, then any instrument executed by way of transfer ranks for the purposes of stamp duty as a conveyance upon sale. He stated that, in the case of a contract for the sale of land, "a constructive trust in favour of the purchaser arises on the conclusion of the contract for sale, but (so far as I know) it has never been held on this account that a conveyance subsequently executed in performance of the contract is not stampable *ad valorem* on a transfer on sale".[96]

The attempt to save stamp duty therefore failed without any need for the majority of the House of Lords to consider the scope of section 53(2). However Lord Radcliffe, who dissented, had to do so; he accepted the contention that the mother had acquired the equitable remainder without any writing having been used.[97] On the other hand, Lord Cohen (also dissenting) and Lord Denning (the only one of the majority to mention the point) both stated by way of dicta[98] that, although the constructive sub-trust had come into existence without any need for writing, the interest arising thereunder could not be transferred without complying with section 53(1)(c). This view, which at first sight appears consistent with *Grey v. I.R.C.*, in fact overlooks the point that authority,[99] admittedly not binding on the House of Lords, establishes that the son, according to that authority, "disappeared from the picture", which must have caused his interest to pass to his mother automatically by operation of law. Consequently, the view of Lord Radcliffe has always seemed preferable and has now been adopted definitively.

The first decision in which this view was subsequently adopted was in *Re Holt's Settlement*,[1] where Megarry J. held that, when beneficiaries of a trust agree for valuable consideration to a variation of the beneficial interests, their existing interests (which are necessarily equitable) are varied without any need for any writing. Further support was provided by the remarks of two members of the Court of Appeal in *D.H.N. Food Distributors v. Tower Hamlets L.B.C.*[2] and of Lord Wilberforce in *Chinn v. Collins*.[3] Lord Radcliffe's view was, however, definitively accepted by the Court of Appeal in *Neville*

---

[96] [1960] A.C. 206 at 240.
[97] *ibid.* at 228.
[98] *ibid.* at 230 at 233.
[99] This was stated in *Grainge v. Wilberforce* (1889) 5 T.L.R. 436 at 437 and held by the Court of Appeal in *Re Lashmar* [1891] 1 Ch. 258.
[1] [1976] 1 Ch. 100 at 116.
[2] [1976] 1 W.L.R. 852. Goff L.J. at 865 and Shaw L.J. at 867 accepted that, where the transaction in question is not a gift, an equitable interest in land could pass without writing.
[3] [1981] A.C. 533 at 548, where he stated that, as soon as there was an agreement for the sale of the equitable interest in shares in a public company held by nominees followed by payment of the price, "the equitable title passed at once to the purchaser". This contract was not even specifically enforceable so that this enunciation of principle is even wider than that of Lord Radcliffe. However, it had the effect of defeating a capital gains tax avoidance scheme and Hanbury & Martin: *Modern Equity* (15th ed., 1997) pp. 86–87 indicates that this may have been an important factor.

v. Wilson.[4] All the shares in a private company were owned beneficially by a second private company but in order to qualify the two directors for office each held the legal title to 60 shares as the second company's nominee. These shares were, as the result of an oral agreement, included in the subject matter of an agreement made by all the shareholders of the second company to distribute all the shares in the first company to them in proportion to their shareholdings; consequently, the two directors had entered into a specifically enforceable contract to assign the subsisting equitable interests in the shares. The Court of Appeal merely had to consider the validity of the contract; no issue arose as to the effect of sub-trusts. Nourse L.J.[5] analysed the speeches in *Oughtred v. I.R.C.* and held that the analysis of Lord Radcliffe was "unquestionably correct". Consequently, the oral contract was not rendered ineffectual by section 53(1)(c) due to the existence of the constructive sub-trust and the effect of section 53(2). This approval of Lord Radcliffe's view must therefore also establish that, where an equitable interest becomes subject to a constructive sub-trust as a result of the creation of a specifically enforceable contract of sale, that equitable interest will, by virtue of section 53(2), immediately vest in the purchaser without any need for writing.[6] However, since only specifically enforceable contracts have this effect, this possibility is now limited to contracts for the sale of shares in private companies and of rare chattels[7]; the only other specifically enforceable contracts, contracts for the sale of land, now have to be in writing anyway.[8]

3. *Equity will not Allow a Statute to be Used as an Instrument of Fraud*

The courts will not allow the statutory provisions which have just been considered (any more than they would allow their predecessor, the relevant sections of the Statute of Frauds 1677), to be applied in such a way as to achieve a fraudulent purpose. A basic equitable maxim is that equity will not allow a statute to be used as a "cloak" or "engine" for fraud. No doubt an important principle behind the statutory provisions already mentioned —this was indeed particularly true of the Statute of Frauds itself—is the prevention of fraud. But it is easy to visualise a situation where an automatic application of the statutory provisions would have the unintended effect of allowing fraud by one party to succeed and in such circumstances the court will intervene for the other party's protection under the umbrella of the equitable maxim. Thus in *Bannister v. Bannister,*[9] the defendant sold and

---

[4] [1997] Ch. 144. A contrary view had earlier been expressed by Chadwick J. by way of dictum in *United Bank of Kuwait v. Habib* [1997] Ch. 107 but the question was not raised on the subsequent appeal which was heard by a differently constituted Court of Appeal after argument but before judgment in *Neville v. Wilson.*

[5] At 157, giving the judgment of the court.

[6] However, this will cease to be the case if a different view is ever taken of the effect of a passive sub-trust. See *ante*, p. 50.

[7] The only type of contracts for the sale of pure personalty which are specifically enforceable; contracts for the sale of property which is readily available on the open market, such as shares in a public company and normal chattels, are not specifically enforceable because damages will always be an adequate remedy for the purchaser.

[8] Under the Law of Property (Miscellaneous Provisions) Act 1989, s.2.

[9] [1948] 2 All E.R. 133; [1948] W.N. 261.

conveyed two adjoining cottages to the plaintiff on the basis that she could continue to occupy one of them rent free for as long as she wished. When he subsequently sought to evict her on the basis that the conveyance did not mention her right of occupation, she successfully counterclaimed for a declaration that the plaintiff held the cottage on trust for her for her lifetime. The Court of Appeal classified as fraudulent the conduct of the plaintiff in attempting to rely on the absence of the writing which section 53(1)(b) of the Law of Property Act 1925 requires for the creation of the interest claimed by the defendant and imposed a constructive trust under which he held the property on trust for her for her lifetime. The relevant authorities will be considered more fully in the chapter on Constructive Trusts.[10]

The principle that equity will not allow a statute to be used as an instrument of fraud has also been relied on by the courts as the justification for the existence of the doctrine of secret trusts. Such trusts arise when an intending settlor makes a gift of property in his will or leaves an existing will unrevoked or dies intestate on the strength of an undertaking by the person entitled under his will or intestacy to hold whatever property he receives on trust for a third party. In such circumstances, the court will enforce performance of the undertaking at the suit of the third party despite the fact that this involves admitting evidence which does not comply with section 9 of the Wills Act 1837. This has been justified on the basis that otherwise the person who made the undertaking would be being allowed to benefit from his own fraud. However, this work adopts the alternative view, which has been relied on by the courts in the majority of the more recent authorities, that the justification for the admission of such evidence is that secret trusts operate outside the will, so that the provisions of the Wills Act have nothing whatever to do with them. Nevertheless, this is a convenient moment to examine the rules governing secret trusts, which are discussed in detail in the next section.[11]

III. SECRET TRUSTS

As was mentioned in the previous section, a secret trust arises when an intending settlor makes a gift of property in his will[12] or leaves an existing will unrevoked[13] or dies intestate[14] on the strength of an undertaking by the person entitled under his will or intestacy to hold whatever property he receives on trust for a third party. In such circumstances the court will enforce performance of the undertaking at the suit of the third party. There

---

[10] See *post*, pp. 358–359.

[11] See *post*, pp. 62–81.

[12] This is what occurs in the overwhelming majority of cases of secret trusts.The earliest cases, *Crook v. Brooking* (1688) 2 Vern. 50 and *Pring v. Pring* (1689) 2 Vern. 99 were cases of this kind, as were *McCormick v. Grogan* (1869) L.R. 4 H.L. 82 and *Blackwell v. Blackwell* [1929] A.C. 318, which are respectively the leading cases on fully secret and half secret trusts.

[13] This occurred in *Tharp v. Tharp* [1916] 1 Ch. 142.

[14] This occurred in *Sellack v. Harris* (1708) 5 Vin.Abr. 512, pl.31. See also *Re Gardner* [1920] 2 Ch. 523, where there was a partial intestacy (a wife made a will which merely left her property to her husband for life; she died possessed only of personalty and he therefore also took the interest in remainder under the intestacy rules; both interests were held to be subject to a fully secret trust communicated and accepted after the date of the will).

are two types of secret trusts, *fully secret trusts* and *half secret trusts*. A trust is fully secret when both the existence of the trust and its terms are concealed; such a trust therefore arises where the property which is the subject matter of the trust is, on the face of the will, left to the recipient absolutely or where the settlor has died intestate. On the other hand, a trust is half secret when the existence of a trust is revealed but its terms are concealed; such a trust therefore arises where the property which is the subject matter of the trust is, on the face of the will, left to the recipient as a trustee. The advantages of a secret trust are that a testator can conceal the true objects of his benevolence from public view—a will is, of course, a public document—and can also, in the case of a fully secret trust, alter those objects at any time before his death simply by communicating with the secret trustee.

Secret trusts depend for their efficacy on the intervention of equity. This intervention is, on the face of things, directly contrary to the important statement of principle contained in section 9 of the Wills Act 1837. This provision, which was summarised at the beginning of the previous section,[15] requires wills to be in writing signed by the testator, or some other person in his presence and by his direction, in the presence of two witnesses both present at the same time, who also sign. It was enacted for an obvious and important reason of policy—to ensure that false claims cannot be generated after the death of a testator when he is in no position to refute them. Such a policy can undoubtedly operate in an extremely harsh way but the courts have, rightly, always been reluctant to admit as evidence in proceedings concerning the administration of an estate any documents which fail to comply with these formal requirements. It is almost inevitable that the existence of secret trusts will only be able to be proved by evidence which does not comply with these requirements; the whole object of the exercise is to exclude the identity of the beneficiary from the formally attested documents admitted to probate. Inevitably, therefore, the evidence of the communication, acceptance and terms of the secret trust in question will be either oral or contained in a document which has not been properly signed and attested. The existence of secret trusts therefore involves a departure both from the letter and the spirit of the Wills Act and consequently, as might be expected, various justifications for their existence have been suggested by the courts. Since several of the rules governing the operation of secret trusts stand or fall depending upon the justification which is adopted, it is necessary to discuss them before considering these rules.

1. *The Theoretical Justification for the Existence of the Doctrine of Secret Trusts*

(A) Fraud

It has often been stated that the justification for the existence of the doctrine of secret trusts is that, if evidence of the terms of the trust were not admitted contrary to the provisions of the Wills Act, the result would be fraud. However, there has been considerable judicial disagreement as to the nature

---

[15] See *ante*, p. 46.

of this fraud. Some judges have found this fraud in the ability of the intended trustee to take the property beneficially if evidence of the terms of the trust is not admitted. Others have instead found it in the consequential failure to observe the intentions of the testator and the consequential destruction of the beneficial interests arising under the trust.

(1) By the legatee

The view that the potential fraud stems from the ability of the intended trustee to take the property beneficially is normally expressed in this way. If evidence of the terms of the trust were not admitted contrary to the provisions of the Wills Act, the person who received the property under the will or intestacy in question would be able to disregard his undertaking to the intending settlor and take the property beneficially. This was the argument adopted by the members of the House of Lords in *McCormick v. Grogan*.[16] The testator made a will leaving all his property to Grogan. When near to death, he summoned Grogan, told him of the will and said that a letter would be found with it. However, he did not seek to obtain any undertaking from him in respect of the letter, which named various persons to whom the testator wished Grogan to give money and the amount of the intended gift to each, concluding with these words: "I do not wish you to act strictly to the foregoing instructions, but leave it entirely to your own good judgment to do as you think I would if living and as the parties are deserving, and as it is not my wish that you should say anything about the document there cannot be any fault found with you by any of the parties should you not act in strict accordance with it." One of the named persons whom Grogan decided to exclude brought an action claiming that Grogan held the property on secret trust to give effect to the provisions of the letter. This action failed on the grounds that the testator had imposed no legally binding obligation upon Grogan. The members of the House of Lords clearly stated that the doctrine of secret trusts was established so as to prevent any possibility of fraud by the secret trustee. Lord Hatherley L.C. said that the doctrine of secret trusts "involves a wide departure from the policy which induced the legislature to pass the Statute of Frauds,[17] and it is only in clear cases of fraud that this doctrine has been applied—cases in which the Court has been persuaded that there has been a fraudulent inducement held out on the part of the apparent beneficiary in order to lead the testator to confide to him the duty which he undertook to perform".[18]

This line of reasoning is a possible justification for the existence of the doctrine when, as in *McCormick v. Grogan*, the trust in question is fully secret. In such a case, unless evidence of the trust is admitted contrary to the provisions of the Wills Act, the intended trustee will be able to take the property beneficially and so will clearly profit from his own misconduct. But this line of reasoning cannot normally justify the existence of half secret trusts. In such a trust, the intended trustee takes the property as a trustee on

---

[16] (1869) L.R. 4 H.L. 82. A similar view had been expressed over a century earlier in *Drakeford v. Wilks* [1747] 3 Atk. 539 and was subsequently repeated by Lord Davey in *Re French* [1902] 1 I.R. 172, 230 (an appeal to the House of Lords from the Court of Appeal of Ireland).

[17] Prior to the enactment of the Wills Act 1837, the formal requirements for wills were contained in the Statute of Frauds 1677.

[18] (1869) L.R. 4 H.L. 82 at 89.

the face of the will. Therefore, if the court declined to admit evidence of the terms of the half-secret trust, he would not take the subject matter beneficially but would clearly hold the property in question on trust for whoever was entitled to the testator's residue or his statutory next-of-kin.[19] On the face of things, therefore, there is no way in which such an intended trustee could profit by failing to carry out his promise to the testator, unless of course he were himself the residuary beneficiary or intestate successor of the testator. It is not entirely clear whether he would in such circumstances be entitled to take the property as residuary beneficiary or intestate successor if the half secret trust failed but it is suggested that in principle he should be able to do so on the grounds that in such a situation he would be claiming the property not as a trustee but in a different capacity of which the testator must necessarily have been aware. On this assumption, an intended trustee holding property under a half secret trust would be enabled to profit by failing to carry out his undertaking to the testator and so the admission of evidence contrary to the terms of the Wills Act could be justified by the fraud argument. But this argument will obviously not apply to the vast majority of half secret trusts simply because the intended trustee will not normally be the appropriate residuary beneficiary or intestate successor. Consequently in such circumstances there would be no possibility whatsoever of the intended trustee taking the subject matter beneficially if evidence of the trust were not admitted contrary to the provisions of the Wills Act. Thus in normal circumstances the fraud argument, while a possible justification for the existence of fully secret trusts, cannot justify the existence of half secret trusts.

(2) On the testator and the beneficiaries

The alternative view is that the fraud in question is committed on the testator and the beneficiaries by reason respectively of the failure to observe the intentions of the former and of the destruction of the beneficial interests of the latter. This view is normally expressed in this way. If evidence of the terms of the trust were not admitted contrary to the provisions of the Wills Act, the testator would be defrauded in that, on the faith of the promise made by the secret trustee, he had either made or left unrevoked a disposition of his property. In the same sort of way, the beneficiaries of the secret trust would be defrauded in that they would be deprived of their beneficial interests. This argument (which of course applies just as much to fully secret trusts as to half secret trusts) emerged as early as 1748 in *Reech v. Kennegal*,[20] where Lord Hardwicke L.C. admitted evidence contrary to the Statute of Frauds "in respect of the promise and of the fraud upon the testator in not performing it". This view was expressed even more clearly in the Irish case of *Riordan v. Banon*[21] in a passage which was subsequently cited with approval by Hall V.-C. in *Re Fleetwood*[22]: "The testator, at least when his purpose is communicated to and accepted by the proposed legatee, makes

---

[19] *Re Pugh's Will Trusts* [1967] 1 W.L.R. 1262.
[20] (1748) 1 Ves. 123. See also the review of the early authorities by Hargrave: *Juridical Arguments and Collections* (1801) Vol. II, p. 912.
[21] (1876) 10 Ir.Eq. 469 (Court of Chancery of Ireland).
[22] (1880) 15 Ch.D. 594 at 606–607.

the disposition to him on the faith of his carrying out his promise and it would be a fraud in him to refuse to perform that promise."

While the authorities so far discussed all emphasised the fraud on the testator, Lord Buckmaster emphasised rather the fraud on the beneficiaries in the leading case of *Blackwell v. Blackwell*.[23] Blackwell left in his will £12,000 to five persons "upon trust ... to apply for the purposes indicated by me to them". In fact the money was to be used to maintain the mistress and illegitimate son of the testator. His deceived wife and child brought an action against the five legatees claiming that no valid trust for these purposes existed. Their counsel raised the argument that fraud could not justify the admission of evidence of the terms of a half secret trust contrary to the provisions of the Wills Act because there was no possibility of a half secret trustee taking the property beneficially. Counsel for the legatees relied not on principle but on the previous practice of the courts manifested in cases such as *Re Fleetwood*. The House of Lords upheld the existence of the doctrine of half secret trusts. Lord Buckmaster (with whose speech Lord Hailsham L.C. concurred) said that "a testator having been induced to make a gift on trust in his will in reliance on the clear promise by the trustee that such trust will be executed in favour of certain named persons, the trustee is not at liberty to suppress the evidence of the trust and thus destroy the whole object of its creation, in fraud of the beneficiaries".[24]

The emphasis placed in the authorities just discussed on the failure to observe the intentions of the testator and the destruction of the beneficial interests is deceptively simple and is, superficially, quite attractive. In fact, however, such arguments are completely circular. To refer to the terms of the secret trust as the "wishes of the testator" and to describe those entitled under the secret trust as "beneficiaries" begs the question; only if evidence of the terms of the trust is admitted contrary to the provisions of the Wills Act is it appropriate to describe the terms of the secret trust as the wishes of the testator and to refer to those entitled thereunder as its beneficiaries. It is not possible to use as a justification for admitting evidence contrary to the provisions of the Wills Act facts which can only be proven if such evidence is admitted. Consequently it is impossible to regard this argument as a valid justification for the existence of the doctrine of either fully secret trusts or half secret trusts.

(B)   That Secret Trusts Operate Outside the Will

Given that fraud can justify only the existence of fully secret trusts, if half secret trusts are to be accepted as valid some other possible justification must be sought. One does indeed exist in the totally different approach adopted by Viscount Sumner in *Blackwell v. Blackwell*. His lordship stated that the provisions of the Wills Act have nothing whatsoever to do with the doctrine of secret trusts and that it is inappropriate to state that evidence of their existence is adduced contrary to the provisions of the Wills Act. He said that it is "communication of the purpose to the legatee, coupled with acquiescence or promise on his part, that removes the matter from the provisions of the Wills Act and brings it within the law of trusts, as applied

---

[23] [1929] A.C. 318.
[24] *ibid.*, at 328–329.

in this instance to trustees, who happen also to be legatees".[25] In other words secret trusts operate wholly outside the will or intestacy in question and so are governed not by the rules of probate but by the rules of the law of trusts, which in no way prevent the introduction of oral evidence. This argument will obviously apply both to fully secret trusts and to half secret trusts. The notion that secret trusts so operate wholly outside the will or intestacy had in fact been referred to many years earlier by Lord Westbury in *Cullen v. Attorney-General for Ireland*.[26] This notion suggests that the enforcement of secret trusts is dependant upon fraud only to the extent that the basic duty of trustees to carry out their obligations as such is dependant on general equitable principles. A similar conclusion may perhaps be drawn from the most recent case on secret trusts, *Re Snowden*,[27] where Megarry V.-C. held that the standard of proof necessary to establish the existence of a secret trust is the ordinary civil standard of proof required to establish an ordinary trust, not the higher standard necessary for rectification claims, on the grounds that "the whole basis of secret trusts . . . is that they operate outside the will, changing nothing that is written in it, and allowing it to operate according to its tenor, but then fastening a trust on to the property in the hands of the recipient".[28] Thus, according to these authorities, the justification for the existence of secret trusts, whether fully secret or half secret, is that such trusts operate wholly outside the will or intestacy in question. This proposition requires close examination.

(1) The problem

Clearly, a secret trust cannot operate completely independently of the will in question simply because the will alone can vest the subject matter of the trust in the secret trustee. To take an extreme example, if the will itself is invalid then the secret trust will fail with it for lack of subject matter. Therefore, the rules of probate clearly have some role to play. The crucial question is at what point the rules of probate cease to operate and are superseded by the rules of the law of trusts.

(2) The crucial situations

This question can only be answered by an examination of the situations where the rules of probate and the rules of the law of trusts are in conflict. There are three such situations: when the secret trustee or secret beneficiary has attested the will, when the secret trustee or secret beneficiary has predeceased the testator or intestate, and where the secret trustee disclaims the gift in his favour. An examination of these situations suggests that the only possible answer is that the rules of probate govern the vesting of the subject matter of the secret trust in the secret trustee, while the rules of the law of trusts govern any matter concerning the operation of the secret trust.

(a) **Attestation.** Section 15 of the Wills Act 1837 provides that a legacy to an attesting witness is ineffective, whereas, as a matter of the law of trusts,

---

[25] [1929] A.C. 318 at 339.
[26] (1866) L.R. 1 H.L. 190 at 198 (on appeal from the Court of Appeal in Chancery of Ireland).
[27] [1979] Ch. 528.
[28] [1979] *ibid.*, at 535.

there is no reason why the trust deed should not be signed by the trustees or beneficiaries. What happens if the secret trustee or the secret beneficiary attests the will?

In *Re Young*[29] one of the beneficiaries under a half secret trust attested the will. Danckwerts J. held that, since the trust arose outside the will, section 15 of the Wills Act 1837 was quite irrelevant and so the beneficiary could take his interest. This conclusion is consistent with the possible principle suggested above and presumably would also apply in the case of a fully secret trust (there is no authority on this point).

No case has yet been reported in which a secret trustee has attested the will. However, if the possible principle suggested above is correct, this matter should be governed by the rules of probate since it concerns the vesting of the legacy. A legatee who takes beneficially on the face of the will is clearly caught by section 15. Therefore, if a fully secret trustee attested the will, the legacy to him would be ineffective and so the secret trust would fail for lack of subject matter (unless, presumably, the property nevertheless vested in the secret trustee under the intestacy rules, in which case he would undoubtedly be bound to perform the trust). On the other hand, a legatee who takes as a trustee on the face of the will is not caught by section 15.[30] Therefore, if a half secret trustee attested the will, the legacy to him would be effective and so the half secret trust would not fail by reason of his attestation. This discrepancy between fully secret and half secret trusts is, admittedly, a little odd; however, there are in fact many examples of discrepancies of this kind.

(b) Predecease. Section 25 of the Wills Act 1837 provides that, subject to certain exceptions which are not here material, a gift in a will lapses if the recipient predeceases the testator. Similarly, no one who predeceases an intestate can possibly take any of his property under the intestacy rules. What therefore happens if the secret trustee or secret beneficiary predeceases the testator or intestate?

If the secret trustee predeceases the testator or intestate, the result once again seems to differ depending on whether the trust in question is fully secret or half secret. In *Re Maddock*[31] Cozens-Hardy L.J. stated, by way of dictum, that if a fully secret trustee predeceases the testator the legacy will lapse and the secret trust will fail for lack of subject matter. This conclusion is another example of probate principles being applied to the vesting of the legacy. On the other hand, it has always been clear that a gift to a person who takes as a trustee on the face of a will will not lapse by reason of his predecease.[32] Thus, if a half secret trustee predeceases the testator, this principle will presumably apply and the secret trust will therefore not fail.

Much more controversy surrounds the situation where the secret beneficiary predeceases the testator or intestate. This occurred in *Re Gardner (No. 2)*.[33]

---

[29] [1951] Ch. 344.
[30] *Cresswell v. Cresswell* (1868) L.R. 6 Eq. 69.
[31] [1902] 2 Ch. 220.
[32] *Re Smirthwaite's Trusts* (1871) L.R. 11 Eq. 251.
[33] [1923] 2 Ch. 230.

Romer J. held that a beneficiary under a secret trust acquires an interest in the trust property as soon as the trust is communicated to and accepted by the secret trustee. Thus, the beneficiary had acquired an interest before his death and that interest naturally passed to his personal representatives for the benefit of those entitled under his will or intestacy. This decision has been rightly criticised on the grounds that a beneficiary under a trust acquires no interest in the trust property until the trust has been completely constituted in accordance with the rules discussed in a later chapter.[34] Since this could not possibly have occurred until the trust property vested in the secret trustee at the death of the testatrix, the beneficiary could not have acquired an interest prior to his death. It is therefore generally accepted that this case was wrongly decided.[35] It is of course quite impossible to justify the reasoning which led Romer J. to his conclusion. If, however, it is accepted that the trust became completely constituted at the death of the testator, what has to be considered is the effect of completely constituting a trust in favour of a person who is already dead—that is, after all, what actually happened in *Re Gardner (No. 2)*. If, as the authorities so far discussed suggest, the rules of probate govern the vesting of the legacy in the secret trustee while the rules of the law of trusts govern any matter concerning the operation of the secret trust, this issue falls to be determined by application of the rules of the law of trusts. Is, therefore, there any rule of the law of trusts which provides that it is not possible to constitute a trust in favour of a dead person? The authorities on the effect of constituting a trust in favour of someone whom the settlor knows to be dead are indecisive.[36] But that is not the situation under discussion; the question is what is the effect of constituting a trust in favour of someone whom the settlor thinks is alive but is in fact dead. This question is totally devoid of authority. If such a trust were valid, it would necessarily have to take effect in favour of those entitled under the dead beneficiary's will or intestacy; if this is the case, for this reason rather than the reasoning adopted by Romer J., *Re Gardner (No. 2)* was correctly decided. However, the overwhelming view of the commentators is that such a trust would be wholly void[37]; if this is the case, then *Re Gardner (No. 2)* was indeed wrongly decided. Whatever view is taken (and in the light of the weight of academic opinion, the second view seems almost inevitable), that view should clearly apply whether the trust in question is fully secret or, as in *Re Gardner (No. 2)*, half secret.

(c) Disclaimer. Where a person who is nominated as a trustee declines to act, the court will appoint another to act in his stead.[38] Thus it seems that

---

[34] See *post*, pp. 124–147.
[35] See, for example, the views of D. J. Hayton in Hayton and Marshall, *Cases and Commentary on the Law of Trusts and Equitable Remedies* (10th ed., 1996), pp. 107–108.
[36] Prior to the enactment of the Property Legislation of 1925, there was some authority that it was not possible to constitute a trust in favour of a dead person (*Re Tilt* (1896) 74 L.T. 163, applying *Re Corbishley's Trusts* (1880) 14 Ch.D 846). However, it is questionable whether these authorities are still good law. Since 1925, a grantee is presumed to take the greatest interest that his grantor was able to give him (Law of Property Act 1925, s.60(1)) and so arguably will take an interest not only for himself but also for those entitled under his will or intestacy.
[37] See *ante*, n. 35.
[38] The power of the court so to appoint trustees stems both from statute (Trustee Act 1925, s.41(1)) and from its inherent jurisdiction (see *Dodkin v. Brunt* (1868) L.R. 6 Eq. 580).

if a half secret trustee declines to act the court will appoint a replacement trustee and the secret trust will therefore not fail.

However, a disclaimer of a testamentary gift by a person who takes beneficially on the face of the will causes the legacy to fail[39]; on this basis a disclaimer by a fully secret trustee will necessarily have this effect. This will not be a problem if the purpose of the disclaimer is to enable the secret trustee to take not under the disclaimed testamentary gift but rather as residuary beneficiary or intestate successor. Such clearly unconscionable conduct will inevitably lead to the imposition of a constructive trust on the basis of the principle enunciated in *Bannister v. Bannister,*[40] which was discussed earlier on. Consequently the secret trustee will hold the property which passes to him under the residuary gift or intestacy on constructive trust to perform the secret trust. But where the disclaiming fully secret trustee takes no other benefit under the will or intestacy of the testator, such a disclaimer will produce a conflict between the rule of probate that a disclaimer of a legacy by a person who takes beneficially on the face of the will causes the legacy to fail and the rule of the law of trusts that equity will not permit a trust to fail for want of a trustee. This conflict has been the subject of opposing dicta: in *Re Maddock,*[41] Cozens-Hardy L.J. suggested that a fully secret trust would fail in such a situation, while in *Blackwell v. Blackwell*[42] Lord Buckmaster said that the court would intervene to prevent such a result. There is something to be said for each view: in favour of the view of Cozens-Hardy L.J. is the proposition that probate principles should govern the vesting of the legacy; on the other hand, in favour of the view of Lord Buckmaster is the fact that a court would undoubtedly be extremely reluctant to permit a trustee who had agreed to act as such to destroy a completely constituted trust by disclaiming his office. It remains to be seen which view is finally adopted.

(3) Conclusion

The discussion of these three difficult areas shows that it is perfectly possible to decide which rule to apply in situations where there is a conflict between the rules of probate and the rules of the law of trusts. It is therefore suggested that this view, as laid down by Viscount Sumner in *Blackwell v. Blackwell,*[43] is both correct and workable. Indeed, nearly all the authorities decided since *Blackwell v. Blackwell* which have just been discussed[44] support the view that secret trusts operate wholly outside the will or intestacy in question. As has already been seen, this view alone is a satisfactory justification for the existence both of fully secret and of half secret trusts. It is therefore suggested that the theoretical justification for the existence of the doctrine of secret trusts is that such trusts operate wholly outside the will or intestacy in question. The enforceability of such trusts in equity is therefore no more dependant upon fraud than is any other type of trust. For these and

---

[39] *Townson v. Tickell* (1819) 3 B. & Ald. 31.
[40] [1948] W.N. 261. See *ante*, p. 61.
[41] [1902] 2 Ch. 220.
[42] [1929] A.C. 318.
[43] [1929] A.C. 318.
[44] The only decision clearly contrary to this conclusion is *Re Gardner (No.2)*, the reasoning of which is on any view clearly incorrect.

other reasons, it will later be suggested that secret trusts are in fact express trusts.

2. *Fully Secret Trusts*

(A) The Prerequisites of a Fully Secret Trust

(1) A beneficial gift of property under the will or intestacy in question
Property must vest beneficially in the intended trustee under the provisions of the will in question or by virtue of the operation of the relevant intestacy rules. In the case of a will, this means that the legatee must take the property as beneficial owner on the face of the will. This requirement is satisfied despite the presence of phrases such as "in the hope that he will use the property for certain purposes which I have communicated to him" or "imposing no trust upon him". Provided that such expressions are, as is highly likely, held to be insufficiently certain to create a trust on the face of the will, any secret trust which is found to exist will, despite their presence, be fully secret.[45]

The effect of attestation or disclaimer by, or the predecease of, a fully secret trustee were considered in the previous part of this section. If, as was suggested there, the theoretical justification for the existence of the doctrine of secret trusts is that such trusts operate wholly outside the will in question, then the effect of the occurrence of any one of these three events will be governed by the rules of probate and will therefore bring about the failure of the gift to the fully secret trustee and, with it, the fully secret trust itself. If, on the other hand, the theoretical justification for the existence of secret trusts is fraud, any secret trust which can be proved to have been the subject of the necessary communication and acceptance will presumably be regarded as taking effect as part of the will in question; if this is indeed the case, the probate rules will still presumably apply with exactly the same

---

[45] An interesting point which has yet to arise in a reported case is whether expressions of this type, although insufficiently certain to create a trust, may nevertheless have an effect upon the rules governing communication of the terms of the trust to the secret trustee. Communication of a fully secret trust may normally be made either before or after the execution of the will provided that it takes place during the lifetime of the testator and may normally be either written or oral. If the will contains some expression such as "in the hope that he will use the property for certain purposes which I have communicated to him in writing", do those words, although imposing no trust upon the face of the will, nevertheless invalidate any communication which is subsequent to the execution of the will and/or any communication which, whether before or after the communication of the will, is oral? (This would undoubtedly be the case if the trust in question were half secret (see *Re Keen* [1937] Ch. 236 and *Re Spence* [1949] W.N. 237, both discussed in the text, *post* p. 76, although such cases are readily distinguishable because in a half secret trust such expressions on the face of the will are necessarily effective to impose a trust and therefore must inevitably limit the trust so imposed). It is clear that a court will admit evidence of a fully secret trust despite the fact that the will in question expressly states that no trust is imposed on the legatee (*Re Spencer* (1887) 57 L.T. 519, where the will contained the words "relying but not by way of trust upon their applying the said sum in or towards the object or objects communicated to them" and a fully secret trust was upheld). In the light of such authorities and the fact that it has been suggested that fully secret trusts operate wholly outside the will in question, it is suggested that in a fully secret trust the presence of such expressions on the face of the will should not have the effect of limiting the permissible ways of communication of the terms of the trust. Nevertheless it would be extremely interesting to see how the courts dealt with this question.

results except where the act of the fully secret trustee in attesting or disclaiming is itself regarded as sufficiently fraudulent to bring about the
enforcement of the trust nevertheless.[46]

(2) Communication and acceptance

The rules governing communication and acceptance emerge from *Moss v.
Cooper*[47] and *Re Boyes*.[48] Before his death, the testator must ask the legatee
and the legatee must agree to hold the legacy on trust for a third party. The
legatee will be deemed to have agreed unless he positively refuses—silence
constitutes assent for this purpose.[49] It does not matter whether the communication of the trust to the legatee takes place before or after the execution of
the will provided that it takes place during the lifetime of the testator—communication by a letter received after the death of the testator is not sufficient
since the legatee then has no opportunity to refuse to act. Nor does it matter
that the legatee does not know the precise terms of the trust—a testator may
hand the legatee a sealed envelope to be opened after his death[50] or reserve
the details of the trusts for future communication provided such communication occurs before his death. These rules equally apply in the case of a
secret trust arising as the result of an intestacy—where no will has been
made because the intestate successor has agreed to hold the property which
he receives on trust for a third party.

Problems sometimes arise where the testator leaves a legacy to two or
more persons jointly and fails to communicate with all of them. Special rules
have been developed to deal with this situation. These rules are generally
stated in the form laid down by Farwell J. in *Re Stead*.[51] If the property is left
to the legatees as tenants in common, only those legatees with whom the
testator has communicated are bound—the others take their shares in the
property beneficially. If the property is left to the legatees as joint tenants,
then if the testator has communicated with any of the legatees prior to the
execution of the will, all the legatees are bound by the trust; on the other
hand, if the testator does not communicate with any of the legatees until
after the execution of the will, only those with whom he does communicate
are bound—the others take their shares beneficially. The cases which are
alleged to establish these peculiar rules have been examined in detail by Mr
Bryn Perrins.[52] He argues convincingly that this formulation of the rules was
based on a misunderstanding of the earlier cases, from which a different rule
in fact emerges. In his view, the only question is whether the gift to all the
legatees was induced by the agreement to act of any of them; if it was, all are
bound but if it was not then only those who have agreed to act are
bound—the others take their shares beneficially. In his opinion, neither the

---

[46] See *ante*, pp. 67, 69.

[47] (1861) 1 J. & H. 352.

[48] (1884) 26 Ch. D. 531.

[49] *Paine v. Hall* (1812) 18 Ves. 475.

[50] *Re Boyes* (1884) 26 Ch.D. 531 (where the letters were not in fact handed to the intended trustee
before the death of the testator and so the communication was held to be unsuccessful); *Re
Keen* [1937] Ch. 236 (actually a case of a half secret trust).

[51] [1900] 1 Ch. 237 at 241.

[52] 88 L.Q.R. (1972) 225.

type of co-ownership nor the time of communication is decisive in determining whether or not the necessary inducement has occurred, although it will obviously be more difficult to show inducement where the legatees are tenants in common and well-nigh impossible to show it where communication is subsequent to the execution of the will. It is not possible to fault Mr. Perrins' analysis of the authorities. However, it remains to be seen whether the courts will adopt his rule in preference to the more traditional ones.

The extent to which the communication and acceptance have to comply with the formal requirements of section 53(1) of the Law of Property Act 1925 will be discussed later on.[53] This depends on the nature of fully secret trusts; the subsection will have to be complied with if they are express trusts but, by virtue of section 53(2) will not apply if fully secret trusts are implied, resulting or constructive trusts.

(3) A beneficiary

No trust can exist without a beneficiary and so it is not possible for the sole trustee of a fully secret trust also to be its sole beneficiary. However, where there is a plurality of fully secret trustees, there is nothing to stop one of them being the sole beneficiary; nor, where there is a plurality of beneficiaries, is there anything to stop a sole fully secret trustee from being included among them. This latter proposition was upheld expressly in *Irvine v. Sullivan*,[54] where a legatee who took absolutely on the face of the will was held to be entitled to take whatever surplus remained after observing the testator's instructions to pay various pecuniary legacies. It also follows from *Ottaway v. Norman*[55] where the question was not raised explicitly but a fully secret trust in favour of the secret trustee for life, with remainder over to the testator's son, was held to be valid.

The effect of attestation by, or the predecease of, the beneficiary of a fully secret trustee was considered in the previous part of this section.[56] If, as was suggested there, the theoretical justification for the existence of the doctrine of secret trusts is that such trusts operate wholly outside the will in question, then the effect of the occurrence of either of these events will be governed by the rules of the law of trusts. Attestation of the will by the beneficiary will therefore be irrelevant but the effect of the predecease of the beneficiary will depend on what the relevant rule of the law of trusts actually is. *Re Gardner (No.2)*[57] decided that in such circumstances the beneficial interest would devolve according to the beneficiary's will or intestacy; this decision undoubtedly constitutes the present law but has been universally condemned by the commentators. If, on the other hand, the theoretical justification for the existence of secret trusts is fraud, any secret trust which can be proved to have been the subject of the necessary communication and acceptance will presumably be regarded as taking effect as part of the will in question; if this is indeed the case, the probate rules will presumably apply rather than the rules of the law of trusts. Attestation of the will by the secret

---

[53] See *post*, p. 79.
[54] (1869) L.R. 8 Eq. 673.
[55] [1972] Ch. 698.
[56] See *ante*, p. 67.
[57] [1923] 2 Ch. 230.

beneficiary will therefore prevent him from taking beneficially under the will while the predecease of the secret beneficiary will unquestionably bring the doctrine of lapse into play; in both cases, the fully secret trustee will therefore presumably hold whatever property he receives on trust for whoever is entitled to the testator's residue or for his statutory next-of-kin.

(B)   The Effect of a Fully Secret Trust
Where all the prerequisites of a fully secret trust are satisfied, the beneficiary will be able to enforce that trust in the same way as any other trust, not only against the fully secret trustee but also against any successor in title to the fully secret trustee who has not taken the property in question free of the equitable interest of the beneficiary. If the first prerequisite is not satisfied because no property vests beneficially in the intended trustee, the fully secret trust will simply fail for want of subject matter. If the third prerequisite is not satisfied because the same person is sole trustee and sole beneficiary, there will simply be no trust and that person will take the property absolutely under the will. However, the situation is less straightforward where the second requirement is not satisfied. If the intended trustee does not hear of the existence of the secret trust until after the death of the testator, he will take the property beneficially even though it can be proved that the testator intended that a secret trust should be imposed upon him. This was held in *Wallgrave v. Tebbs*.[58] However, if the legatee agrees during the lifetime of the testator to hold the property on trust but is not informed of the beneficial interests before the death of the testator, then he will hold the property on trust for whoever is entitled to the testator's residue or for his statutory next-of-kin. This was held in *Re Boyes*.[59] Although the question has never arisen, it is suggested that this would be the case even if the legatee were himself entitled to the residuary estate or were the intestate successor in question.

3. Half Secret Trusts

It is first necessary to distinguish half secret trusts from the cases where the probate doctrine of incorporation by reference arises.[60] If the testator on the face of his will makes a disposition of property for the purposes set out in a named existing and identifiable document, then that document is deemed to be incorporated into the will and is admitted to probate as part of the will even though it does not itself comply with the formal requirements of the

---

[58] (1855) 2 K. & J. 313.
[59] (1884) 26 Ch.D. 531.
[60] This doctrine has on occasions been argued to be the theoretical justification for the doctrine of half secret trusts (see P. Matthews: [1979] Conveyancer 360). Adoption of this argument would indeed explain the otherwise inexplicable and much criticised rule that in a half secret trust communication of the terms of the trust must be made before or contemporaneously with the making of the will in question. However, apart from the fact that there seems to be no authority whatsoever in support of such an argument, its acceptance would involve either extending the probate doctrine of incorporation by reference to oral communications or alternatively requiring communication of the terms of a half secret trust to be in writing (in which case *Blackwell v. Blackwell* was wrongly decided). Neither of these possibilities seems to be consistent either with principle or with precedent and it is therefore suggested that this argument is not an acceptable justification for the doctrine of half secret trusts.

Wills Act.[61] None of the difficulties which surround secret trusts arises in such a case. Where, on the other hand, the testator makes such a disposition but sets out the details of the trust either orally or in a document which is not sufficiently identified by the will, the trust can only take effect, if at all, as a half secret trust.

(A) The Prerequisites of Half Secret Trusts

(1) A non-beneficial gift of property under the will

Property must vest non-beneficially in the intended trustee under the provisions of the will in question. The legatee must therefore take the property as a trustee on the face of the will; in other words, the testator must use an expression which imposes an obligation to hold the property upon trust.

The effect of attestation by, predecease of, and disclaimer by a half secret trustee were considered in a previous part of this section.[62] If, as was suggested there, the theoretical justification for the existence of the doctrine of secret trusts is that such trusts operate wholly outside the will in question, then the effect of the occurrence of any one of these three events will be governed by the rules of probate and will therefore be irrelevant. If, on the other hand, the theoretical justification for the existence of secret trusts is fraud, any secret trust which can be proved to have been the subject of the necessary communication and acceptance will presumably be regarded as taking effect as part of the will in question; if this is indeed the case, the probate rules will still presumably apply with exactly the same results.

(2) Communication and acceptance

Before or contemporaneously with the making of the will, the testator must ask the legatee and the legatee must agree to hold the legacy on trust for a third party. This rule was established by dicta of the members of the House of Lords in *Blackwell v. Blackwell*,[63] was reiterated, also by way of dicta, by the Court of Appeal in *Re Keen*,[64] and was applied, apparently without any contrary argument from counsel, in *Re Bateman's Will Trusts*.[65] It is difficult to see any justification for making this distinction between half secret trusts and fully secret trusts (where, as has already been seen, communication and acceptance may occur at any time prior to the death of the testator). It is therefore suggested that the rule governing fully secret trusts should be applied also to half secret trusts so as to permit communication and acceptance at any time prior to the death of the testator. This has been done in Ireland[66] and in most of the American jurisdictions.[67] However, at present the rule of English law is quite clear—communication and acceptance must occur before or contemporaneously with the making of the will.

As in the case of fully secret trusts, silence constitutes assent and it suffices if the testator hands the legatee a sealed envelope to be opened after his death. However, the communication made must not be contrary to the

---

[61] See for example *In the goods of Smart* [1902] P. 238.
[62] See *ante*, p. 68.
[63] [1929] A.C. 318.
[64] [1937] Ch. 236.
[65] [1970] 1 W.L.R. 1463.
[66] *Re Browne* [1944] Ir.R. 90 (High Court of the Republic of Ireland).
[67] See Scott: *Law of Trusts* (4th ed., 1989), para. 55.8.

express provisions of the will. In *Re Keen*,[68] the testator left £10,000 to two persons "to be held upon trust and disposed of by them among such person, persons or charities as may be notified by me to them or either of them during my lifetime". Before the execution of the will, he had handed a sealed envelope containing the name of the intended beneficiary to one of the legatees. The Court of Appeal held that it did not matter that the testator had given the legatee his instructions in a sealed envelope which was not to be opened until after his death. However, the Court held that the express provisions of the will contemplated only a future communication and so the communication before the date of the will was contrary to the express provisions of the will and consequently ineffective. (Of course, any communication made after the date of the will in accordance with its provisions would also have been ineffective since communication after the date of the will is impermissible in the case of a half secret trust). Similarly, in *Re Spence*,[69] the testator left property to four persons "to be dealt with in accordance with my wishes which I have made known to them". In fact the testator had communicated only with some of the legatees and this communication was held to be contrary to the express provisions of the will and therefore ineffective.

Problems can arise where the testator (without having made an express provision as in *Re Spence*) leaves a legacy to two or more persons jointly and fails to communicate with all of them. Of course all the legatees will quite clearly be trustees and so the only question which arises is whether those with whom the testator failed to communicate hold their share of the property on trust for the communicated purpose or for the residuary beneficiary or intestate successor. There seems to be no reported half secret trust case in which this problem has actually arisen. Presumably the issue would be determined by application of the rules which apply in this situation to fully secret trusts—the nature of these rules is at present uncertain since, as has already been seen,[70] Mr. Perrins has recently challenged the established formulation of the rules.

The extent to which the communication and acceptance have to comply with the formal requirements of section 53(1) of the Law of Property Act 1925 will be discussed later on.[71] This depends on the nature of half secret trusts; the subsection will have to be complied with if they are express trusts but, by virtue of section 53(2) will not apply if half secret trusts are implied, resulting or constructive trusts.

(3) A beneficiary

No trust can exist without a beneficiary and so it is not possible for the sole trustee of a half secret trust also to be the sole beneficiary. This proposition is wholly uncontroversial. In principle it might be thought that, where there is a plurality of half secret trustees, there is nothing to stop one of them being the sole beneficiary and, where there is a plurality of beneficiaries, there is nothing to stop a sole half secret trustee from being included among

---

[68] [1937] Ch. 236.
[69] [1949] W.N. 237.
[70] See *ante*, p. 72.
[71] See *post*, p. 79.

them. However, this does not appear to be the law. According to the decision of the Court of Appeal in *Re Rees' Will Trusts*,[72] a half secret trustee cannot be one of the secret beneficiaries since such a beneficial interest would be contrary to the express provision of the will that he takes the property as a trustee.[73] On the basis that, as has already been suggested, secret trusts operate outside the will, it is not easy to justify this harsh rule, which must undoubtedly lead to the frustration of the intentions of the testator. Considerable doubts as to its validity were expressed by Pennycuick J. in *Re Tyler*,[74] although his lordship conceded that he would have been bound by *Re Rees' Will Trusts* if the point had arisen for decision.

The effect of attestation by, or the predecease of, the beneficiary of a half secret trustee was considered in a previous part of this section.[75] If, as was suggested there, the theoretical justification for the existence of the doctrine of secret trusts is that such trusts operate wholly outside the will in question, then the effect of the occurrence of either of these events will be governed by the rules of the law of trusts. Attestation of the will by the beneficiary will therefore be irrelevant but the effect of the predecease of the beneficiary will depend on what the relevant rule of the law of trusts actually is. *Re Gardner (No. 2)*[76] decided that in such circumstances the beneficial interest would devolve according to the beneficiary's will or intestacy; this decision undoubtedly constitutes the present law but has been universally condemned by the commentators. If, on the other hand, the theoretical justification for the existence of secret trusts is fraud, any secret trust which can be proved to have been the subject of the necessary communication and acceptance will presumably be regarded as taking effect as part of the will in question; if this is indeed the case, the probate rules will presumably apply rather than the rules of the law of trusts. Attestation of the will by the secret beneficiary will therefore prevent him from taking beneficially under the will while the predecease of the secret beneficiary will unquestionably bring the doctrine of lapse into play; in both cases, the fully secret trustee will therefore presumably hold whatever property he receives on trust for whoever is entitled to the testator's residue or for his statutory next of kin.

(B) The Effect of a Half Secret Trust

Where all the prerequisites of a half secret trust are satisfied, the beneficiary will be able to enforce that trust in the same way as any other trust, not only against the half secret trustee but also against any successor in title to the fully secret trustee who has not taken the property in question free of the equitable interest of the beneficiary. However, if the testator asks the intended trustee to hold a particular sum on trust and in fact leaves him a larger sum, only the sum in respect of which the trustee undertook to act will be subject to the secret trust; the residue will be held by him on trust for whoever is entitled to the testator's residue or for his statutory next-of-kin.

---

[72] [1950] Ch. 204.
[73] This rule was also stated by way of dicta in *Irvine v. Sullivan* (1869) L.R. 8 Eq. 673, which actually concerned a fully secret trust.
[74] [1967] 1 W.L.R. 1269 at 1278.
[75] See *ante*, p. 67.
[76] [1923] 2 Ch. 230.

This was held in *Re Cooper*.[77] More generally, if the first prerequisite is not satisfied because no property vests beneficially in the intended trustee under the will, the half secret trust will simply fail for want of subject matter. If either of the other two prerequisites is not satisfied, the trust will obviously not be able to be carried out. In these circumstances, the intended trustee will not take the property beneficially but will hold it on trust for whoever is entitled to the testator's residue or for his statutory next-of-kin. This was held in *Re Pugh's Will Trusts*.[78] It is suggested that the half secret trustee should be able to take the property beneficially if he is himself entitled to the residuary estate or is the intestate successor in question, although this may be contrary to the spirit, if not the letter, of the already criticised decision of the Court of Appeal in *Re Rees' Will Trusts*.[79]

4. *The Property which may be made Subject to a Secret Trust*

In *Ottaway v. Norman*,[80] a testator devised his bungalow to his housekeeper and bequeathed her £1,500 and half his residuary estate. Before the death of the testator, she had agreed to leave the bungalow and whatever money was left at her own death to the testator's son. However, in the event she left all her property away from the son, who brought an action against her executor for a declaration that her estate was subject to a trust in his favour. Brightman J. duly held that the bungalow was subject to a fully secret trust in favour of the son. However, he held that there was no valid secret trust of the residue of the money. His lordship was prepared to assume, without deciding, that it was possible to impose a secret trust under which the secret trustee could deal as he liked with the subject matter during his lifetime and then leave anything that was left to a third party. However, even on that assumption, he held that the terms of the alleged trust were far too unclear. The housekeeper had not been placed under any obligation to keep the money subject to the alleged trust separate from her own funds and, in any event, it was unclear precisely what was meant by money in this context.

This decision has several novel features. It is unusual to find a secret trust where the obligation imposed on the trustee is to enjoy the property left to him for his lifetime, either as in this case by occupying it or by receiving the income therefrom, and then to leave it on in his will to a third party. There is no particular objection to this[81] where the property which is subject to this obligation is clearly ascertainable (as the bungalow in *Ottaway v. Norman* clearly was). However, if a secret trust is also feasible (as Brightman J. was prepared to assume without deciding) where the secret trustee is entitled to dispose of the property at will and need only leave anything that is left to a third party, then secret trusts will necessarily have acquired yet another novel feature—they will have become exempt from complying with the

---

[77] [1939] Ch. 580.
[78] [1967] 1 W.L.R. 1262.
[79] [1950] Ch. 204.
[80] [1972] Ch. 698.
[81] At the time of the decision, objection could have been taken by reason of the fact that such a secret trust evaded the provisions of the Settled Land Act 1925. However, no further settlements subject to this Act can now be created as a result of the Trusts of Land and Appointment of Trustees Act 1996.

rules governing certainty of subject matter which will be considered in the next chapter.[82] The only trusts which at present appear to be exempt from the requirement of certainty of subject matter are the constructive trusts which arise as a result of mutual wills when the first party to die has left a will made in accordance with the agreement between him and the survivor. As will be seen in the chapter on Constructive Trusts,[83] such trusts clearly embrace both the property left to the survivor by the first party to die and whatever property of the survivor is subject to the agreement.[84] Nevertheless, the survivor is entitled, in the absence of any agreement to the contrary,[85] to dispose freely of the property during his lifetime[86]; only whatever remains at his death has to be left to the ultimate beneficiary of the mutual wills.[87] The nature of such trusts has been considered judicially on various occasions[88] but none of the explanations given is really satisfactory; the only answer seems to be to regard such trusts as an entrenched anomaly. The type of secret trust envisaged by Brightman J. would move secret trusts into the murky area which has caused such conceptual difficulties in the case of mutual wills. It is much to be hoped that no such secret trusts will ever be upheld so that the doctrine of secret trusts can be spared this sort of conceptual confusion. That does not alter the fact that the judgment in *Ottaway v. Norman* clearly envisages this possibility.

5. *The Nature of Secret Trusts*

The final question that arises in relation to secret trusts relates to their nature and classification. This is not purely an academic issue. As was seen in the previous section of this chapter,[89] section 53(1) of the Law of Property Act 1925 lays down certain formal requirements for the valid creation of trusts, from which section 53(2) exempts implied, resulting, and constructive trusts. Thus, if secret trusts are express trusts, a secret trust of land must, under section 53(1)(b), be "manifested and proved by some writing signed by some person who is able to declare such trust" while a secret trust of a subsisting equitable interest must, under section 53(1)(c), be "in writing signed by the person disposing of the same, or by his agent thereunto lawfully authorised in writing". On the other hand, if secret trusts are implied, resulting or constructive trusts, no such formalities will be necessary. The authorities are

---

[82] See *post*, pp. 87–92.
[83] See *post*, pp. 367–376. See also *Constructive Trusts* (3rd ed., 1997), pp. 263–272.
[84] *Re Hagger* [1930] 2 Ch. 190.
[85] As in *Re Green* [1951] Ch. 148.
[86] *Birmingham v. Renfrew* (1937) 57 C.L.R. 666 at 689, *per* Dixon J. (High Court of Australia); *Re Goodchild (decd.)* [1996] 1 W.L.R. 694, *per* Carnwath J.
[87] *Birmingham v. Renfrew, ibid.*, does admittedly envisage the possibility of the ultimate beneficiary restraining a disposition by the survivor which is calculated to defeat the mutual wills. However, in practice this will only be feasible where the subject matter of the mutual wills is or includes a specific asset and not where, as is normally the case, it is the residuary estate of both parties.
[88] *Birmingham v. Renfrew* (1937) 57 C.L.R. 666 at 689, *per* Dixon J. (High Court of Australia); *Re Goodchild (decd.)* [1996] 1 W.L.R. 694 at 700, *per* Carnwath J. (not considered on appeal at [1997] 1 W.L.R. 1216).
[89] See *ante*, pp. 45–62.

inconclusive. In *Re Baillie*,[90] a half secret trust of land was held to be ineffective because of the absence of the necessary writing. That decision suggests that half secret trusts, at least, are express trusts. On the other hand, fully secret trusts of land have been upheld in the absence of the necessary writing—most recently in *Ottaway v. Norman*,[91] although neither in this nor in any other of the reported cases has the absence of this writing actually been raised. At first sight, this might be thought to suggest, if only by virtue of the silence of the courts, that fully secret trusts are not express trusts. Any such conclusion would, however, be unsound. The absence of evidentiary writing must be specifically pleaded; if it is not so pleaded, then the absence of the writing will not be a bar to the success of the action.[92] Consequently the fact that fully secret trusts have been upheld in the absence of the evidentiary writing required by section 53(1)(b) is totally irrelevant to the question of whether such writing is actually necessary.

What then is the nature of secret trusts? Most commentators, on the strength of *Re Baillie* and the fact that half secret trusts, unlike fully secret trusts, appear on the face of the will, seem to accept that half secret trusts are express trusts. However, the general view seems to be that no fully secret trust can ever fail for lack of writing, simply because of the maxim that a statute cannot be used as an instrument of fraud; for this reason, many commentators have classified fully secret trusts as constructive trusts.[93] Indeed this classification was assumed by Nourse J. by way of dictum in *Re Cleaver*,[94] a case which actually concerned mutual wills. However, apart from the fact that it seems contrary to principle to distinguish in this way between fully secret and half secret trusts,[95] the proposition that no fully secret trust can ever fail for lack of writing is in fact unsound. Obviously no fully secret trustee would be allowed to profit by raising the absence of the necessary writing as the basis of a claim to take the property beneficially —the clearly unconscionable conduct involved in any attempt to do this would inevitably lead to the imposition of a constructive trust on a quite

---

[90] (1886) 2 T.L.R. 660 (this was of course a decision on the pre-existing provision, Statute of Frauds 1677, s.7).

[91] [1972] Ch. 698.

[92] *North v. Loomes* [1919] 1 Ch. 378 (actually a decision on Statute of Frauds 1677, s.4 (subsequently Law of Property Act 1925, s.40, now repealed by Law of Property (Miscellaneous Provisions) Act 1989, s.2); however s.53(1)(b), like s.40 and Statute of Frauds 1677, s.4, requires only evidentiary writing and is generally thought to be governed by the same principles. A specific decision on the predecessor of s.53(1)(b), Statute of Frauds 1677, s.7, where the point presently under discussion did not arise, is *Foster v. Hale* (1798) 3 Ves.Jun. 696, which concerned the question of what type of writing would satisfy the provision.

[93] See, for example, the view of D. J. Hayton in an earlier edition of Hayton & Marshall, *Cases and Commentary on the Law of Trusts* (8th ed.), pp. 106–107, repeated in the current edition of Underhill and Hayton, *Law of Trusts and Trustees* (15th ed., 1995), p. 228, where he states that it "seems better to regard secret trusts as constructive trusts". This view is also adopted in the current edition of Hayton & Marshall, *Commentary and Cases on the Law of Trusts and Equitable Remedies* (10th ed., 1996), p. 110.

[94] [1981] 1 W.L.R. 939 at 947.

[95] This view was adopted by D. J. Hayton: Hayton and Marshall: *Cases and Commentary on the Law of Trusts* (9th ed.), p. 105, n. 31: "since the court is recognising and enforcing a testator's express trust why not call a spade a spade?"; however, he has since reverted to his previous view (see *ante*, n. 93). A more ambivalent view is expressed by J. E. Martin in Hanbury & Martin: *Modern Equity* (15th ed.), p. 162.

different ground—the principle enunciated in *Bannister v. Bannister*.[96] But there remains the possibility that a fully secret trustee who admits that he is holding the property which he has received under the will or intestacy in question but cannot point to the writing required by section 53(1) will find himself confronted by opposing claims from the beneficiaries of the secret trust and the testator's residuary beneficiary or his statutory next-of-kin. In this situation, the maxim that a statute cannot be used as an instrument of fraud will be of no assistance whatever and the result will be determined by whether fully secret trusts are constructive trusts, in which case the property will go to the beneficiaries of the secret trust, or express trusts, in which case because of the absence of the necessary writing it will go to his residuary beneficiary or the statutory next-of-kin.

It is therefore necessary to decide as a matter of principle whether secret trusts are express trusts or constructive trusts. In the case of both fully secret and half secret trusts the testator clearly intends to create a relationship of trustee and beneficiary. This suggests that, as a matter of definition, both fully secret and half secret trusts should be classified as express trusts. This view is strengthened if, as has already been suggested, the theoretical justification for the existence of the doctrine of secret trusts is not fraud but the fact that such trusts operate wholly outside the will or intestacy in question. It is accordingly suggested that all secret trusts are express trusts and so must comply with section 53(1) of the Law of Property Act 1925. Although, as has already been mentioned, some of the standard texts now appear to be moving towards this view, it has to be admitted that there is as yet no general agreement on this question, which must therefore await definitive resolution by the courts.

---

[96] [1948] 2 All E.R. 133; [1948] W.N. 261; discussed *ante*, pp. 61–62.

CHAPTER 4

THE ESSENTIAL INGREDIENTS OF A TRUST

I. CERTAINTY

IN the leading case of *Knight v. Knight*[1] Lord Langdale laid down that three certainties are required for the creation of a trust: first, the words used must be so couched that, taken as a whole, they may be deemed to be imperative ("certainty of intention"); secondly, the subject matter of the trust must be certain ("certainty of subject matter"); and, thirdly, the persons or objects intended to be benefited must also be certain ("certainty of objects").

1. *Certainty of Intention*

Equity looks to the intent rather than the form. No particular form of words is required for the creation of a trust; the use of the word "trust" is not essential, though, of course, highly desirable. It is possible, therefore, that words expressing desire, belief, recommendation or hope (known as precatory words) may create a trust. And if an intention to create a trust can be clearly deduced from the expressions used by the settlor, even though these are in precatory form, the court will give effect to that intention.

(A) The Changing Attitude of the Courts
An important change in outlook has occurred towards this requirement. Before the middle of the nineteenth century, the courts tended to take the view that any expression of desire or hope or the like on the part of a testator was imperative and therefore created a binding trust. It may indeed be said that it is possible to see in the older cases on precatory trusts an intention attributed to a testator which had the effect of creating an artificial certainty where no such certainty really existed. This practice derived from a rule relating to executors. Until 1858 the estates of deceased persons were administered by the ecclesiastical courts and, until the passing of the Executors Act 1830, an executor was permitted to take the residue of the estate, if any, which had been undisposed of by the will. This was obviously unsatisfactory and so the Court of Chancery endeavoured to make the executor a trustee of any such undisposed-of residue. This had the accidental consequence that the rules relating to certainty of words became confused with the equitable practice in respect of executors. In the same way as the

---

[1] (1840) 3 Beav. 148 at 173. It is not normally possible to introduce extrinsic evidence in order to aid the process of construction (see *Rubin v. Gerson Berger Association* [1986] 1 W.L.R. 526).

Court of Chancery was anxious to make the executor a trustee of the undisposed-of residue for the next-of-kin, that court would also seize on any expression of hope or desire to negative the presumption that the executor was intended to take beneficially. But the court also went further and adopted the policy of regarding any precatory words in the same light; consequently, such words were regarded as sufficiently certain to have created a trust even though the alleged trustee was not an executor and even though there was no undisposed-of residue.

This is apparently how the confusion arose. However, once the Executors Act 1830 had been passed providing for executors to hold any undisposed-of residue for the next-of-kin unless the testator had shown an intention that the executor should take beneficially, it was no longer necessary or desirable to create a trust in cases where precatory words were used. And during the nineteenth century the necessary change in approach was made. Words such as "desire", "wish", "have full confidence" received fresh consideration.[2] One of a number of illustrative decisions is Re Adams and Kensington Vestry,[3] where a testator gave all his real and personal estate to his wife "in full confidence that she would do what was right as to the disposal thereof between my children". The Court of Appeal held that by virtue of these words the widow took an absolute interest in the property unfettered by any trust in favour of the children. The court also stated that some of the previous cases had gone very far and had unjustifiably given words a meaning beyond that which they could possibly bear if looked at in isolation. This well-known authority was by no means the first decision of its type; by the time it was decided, the wind had already changed direction and beneficiaries were no longer being made into trustees unless this was clearly intended by the testator.

(B) The Modern Test

By virtue of the change of approach referred to, the intention of the settlor or testator became all-important. While the use of precatory words can still be held to create a trust in appropriate circumstances, the intention to create a trust has to be established by construction of the instrument. However, the question of what are appropriate circumstances can be peculiarly difficult to establish in practice. This cannot be considered in a vacuum but can only be answered by examining carefully all the words used in the instrument in question,[4] a proposition which indeed might be thought to be self-evident.

---

[2] Perhaps the earliest case which illustrates the new approach was Lambe v. Eames (1871) L.R. 6 Ch. 597 (property to be at disposal of widow "in any way she may think best for the benefit of herself and family").

[3] (1884) 27 Ch.D. 394.

[4] It is now provided by Administration of Justice Act 1982, s.21, that extrinsic evidence, including evidence of the testator's intention, may be admitted to assist in the interpretation of a will (a) in so far as any part of it is meaningless (b) in so far as the language used in any part of it is ambiguous on the face of it (c) in so far as evidence, other than evidence of the testator's intention, shows that the language used in any part of it is ambiguous in the light of the surrounding circumstances. It is also provided (ibid., s.20) that the court has jurisdiction to rectify a will if satisfied that it is so expressed that it fails to carry out the testator's intention in consequence of a clerical error or of a failure to understand his instructions.

It was formulated by Lindley L.J. in *Re Hamilton*[5] in the following way: "You must take the will which you have to construe and see what it means, and if you come to the conclusion that no trust was intended you say so, although previous judges have said the contrary on some wills more or less similar to the one you have to construe."

Some doubt may, however, have been cast on this impeccable principle by *Re Steele's Will Trusts*[6]; the judgment of Wynn-Parry J. is capable of bearing the meaning that, where identical words to those before the court had been held in a previous case to create a trust, that case should be followed unless it was clearly wrongly decided. Such an approach is obviously rather different from construing the instrument on its merits, even when other earlier decisions are taken into account[7]; consequently, if this is indeed what Wynn-Parry J. meant to say, it is not easy to support his view.

(C) Illustrations of the Modern Rule

It would be a difficult, and probably also a fruitless, exercise to consider even a small number of the many decided cases relating to this question. However, at the risk of making the subject seem rather easier than it actually is, two cases, one on each side of the line, may be considered. On the one hand, there is *Re Diggles*[8] where a testatrix gave all her property to her daughter and the latter's heirs and assigns and said "And it is my *desire*[9] that she allows to A.G. an annuity of £25 during her life." The Court of Appeal held that no trust to pay this money had been imposed on the daughter.[10] On the other hand, in *Comiskey v. Bowring-Hanbury*,[11] (which may also be usefully compared with the decision in *Re Adams and Kensington Vestry*[12]) the testator gave all his property to his wife "absolutely *in full confidence*[13] that she will make such use of it as I would have made myself and that at her death she will devise it to such one or more of my nieces as she may think fit". The House of Lords held that, on a true construction of the whole will, the words "in full confidence" created a trust. Whatever doubts there may be about the correctness of the actual decision, the significance of the word "absolutely" perhaps not being fully appreciated and taken into account, as a decision of the highest authority it nevertheless underlines the rule that in

---

[5] [1895] 2 Ch. 370 at 373. See also *Re Williams* [1897] 2 Ch. 12 at 14 and *Comiskey v. Bowring-Hanbury* [1905] A.C. 84 at 89.

[6] [1948] Ch. 603, following *Shelley v. Shelley* (1868) L.R. 6 Eq. 540.

[7] Compare Langan (1968) 32 Conv. (N.S.) 361.

[8] (1888) 39 Ch.D. 253.

[9] Emphasis added.

[10] No trust was held to have been created in the following cases: *Lambe v. Eames* (1871) L.R. 6 Ch. 597 ("in any way she may think best"); *Re Hutchinson and Tenant* (1878) 8 Ch.D. 540 ("have confidence"); *Mussoorie Bank v. Raynor* (1882) 7 App. Cas. 321 ("feeling confident"); *Re Hamilton* [1895] 2 Ch. 370 ("wish"); *Hill v. Hill* [1897] 1 Q.B. 483 ("request"); *Re Williams* [1897] 2 Ch. 12 ("fullest trust and confidence"); *Re Connolly* [1910] 1 Ch. 219 ("specially desire"); *Re Johnson* [1939] 2 All E.R. 458 ("request"); *Swain v. The Law Society* [1983] 1 A.C. 598 ("on behalf of").

[11] [1905] A.C. 84.

[12] (1884) 27 Ch.D. 394; see also *Re Williams* [1897] 2 Ch. 12.

[13] Emphasis added.

the last analysis the question is one of construing the instrument as a whole.[14]

A much more recent illustration of some interest, involving the winding-up of a company, is *Re Kayford*.[15] This case involved rather different considerations. The company carried on a mail order business and its customers paid either the full price or a deposit on account. Difficulties arose over the supply and delivery of goods and so the company opened a separate bank account called a "Customers' Trust Deposit Account" into which all further payments made by customers for goods were paid and subsequently withdrawn only when the goods ordered had been delivered; the idea of this was that if the company had to go into liquidation the money could be refunded to those customers whose goods had not been delivered. When the company did subsequently go into liquidation, the question arose as to whether the money in the bank account was indeed held in trust for those customers or instead formed part of the general assets of the company available for all its creditors. Megarry J. had no doubt that the facts showed that there was a trust so that the sums paid had remained in the beneficial ownership of those who sent them until the goods ordered were delivered.[16]

This first requirement therefore involves certainty of intention to create a trust appearing from the words in the instrument.[17] The words used are, however, relevant not simply for the purpose of deciding whether a trust or a mere moral obligation has been created; there are other possibilities, namely that a power of appointment has been created,[18] or that the Crown may be administering property in its hands in the exercise of its governmental functions without a trust having been created[19] (the mere fact that the word "trust" has been used in relation to the Crown is not decisive[20]).

All the examples referred to so far involved private trusts. Where, on the other hand, the intention discovered in the instrument is to create a charitable trust then, as the House of Lords confirmed in *I.R.C. v. McMullen*,[21] any ambiguity should receive a "benignant" construction if this is at all possible.[22] The House did not, however, find it necessary to resort to such a construction in that case.

---

[14] A trust was held to have been created in the following cases: *Re Steele's Will Trusts* [1948] Ch. 603, ("request"); *Re Endacott* [1960] Ch. 232 ("for the purpose of").

[15] [1975] 1 W.L.R. 279, see *ante*, p. 26.

[16] Megarry J. emphasised that the general rule is that, if money is sent to a company for goods which are not delivered, the sender is merely a creditor of the company unless a trust has been created. In this case, however, he held at 282 that there was a trust whereupon "the obligations in respect of the money are transformed from contract to property, from debt to trust". He also indicated that a trust of this kind might not be effective in favour of trade creditors; however, in the case before him the court was only concerned with the interests of members of the public.

[17] The question whether a trust or a power has been created is considered *post*, pp. 173–183.

[18] *ibid.*

[19] As a "trust in the higher sense". See *Tito v. Waddell (No.2)* [1977] Ch. 106 at 216. See *ante*, p. 17.

[20] *ibid.* at 212. The Crown can be a trustee but only if it deliberately chooses so to do: *ibid.*; *Civilian War Claimants Association v. The King* [1932] A.C. 14 at 27; *Nissan v. Attorney-General* [1970] A.C. 179 at 223.

[21] [1981] A.C. 1. The facts are set out *post*, p. 410.

[22] *ibid.* at 14.

(D)   The Effect of Uncertainty of Intention

If an intention to create a trust cannot be derived from the words used in the instrument but only at most some form of moral obligation, the effect of the consequential uncertainty of intention is that there is no trust. Consequently, the donee will take the property beneficially[23] unless of course the words are construed as having given rise to a power of appointment.[24]

(E)   Sham Trusts

Thus far it has been assumed that a conclusion that an instrument manifests sufficient certainty of intention will be conclusive. However, it is not impossible for the words of the instrument to be held to be a sham in the sense that the settlor never had the slightest intention of parting with his pre-existing beneficial interest in the property in question.[25] In such circumstances his intention will instead have been to prevent some third party, usually his creditors, his estranged spouse or his dependants, from obtaining access to the settled assets. Where a trust is found to be a sham, the settled property will be held still to be vested beneficially in the settlor and therefore available to meet the claims of the creditors or spouse in question.

In *Midland Bank v. Wyatt*,[26] a husband and wife executed a declaration of trust, of whose effect the wife was unaware, in respect of their matrimonial home, which was mortgaged to the bank, whereby the equity therein was held as to one half for the wife and as to the other half for their daughters. The husband subsequently raised further loans from the bank secured on this property on the basis that he was still entitled to one half of the equity and did not reveal the existence of the declaration of trust either to the bank or to his solicitors until the former sought to realise its security. The judge[27] held that the husband had never had any intention of giving an interest in the property to his daughters but had declared the trust in order to safeguard his family from commercial risk; irrelevant of whether his motives were dishonest or fraudulent or simply based on mistaken advice, the declaration of trust was a pretence or sham[28] and was consequently void and unenforceable.[29] In cases of this type the settlor is in effect held to have had no intention to create a trust.

It is however rare for a trust to be held to be a total sham in this way. There is rather more possibility of a trust being held to be a partial sham; this occurs where a trust has been created and duly carried into effect but its provisions and *modus operandi* lead to the conclusion that it is a sham because, for example, the trustees have slavishly followed the directions of the settlor and/or, contrary to the provisions of the trust, have continued to apply some or all of the trust property either directly or indirectly for his

---

[23] See the cases cited *ante*, n. 10.

[24] See *post*, pp. 173–183.

[25] See Brownbill [1992] J.Int.P. 13; Birt (1992) 3 Offshore Tax Planning Review 81.

[26] [1995] 1 F.L.R. 696.

[27] D. E. M. Young, Q.C. sitting as a Deputy Judge of the High Court.

[28] In accordance with the definition of sham propounded by Diplock L.J. in *Snook v. London and West Riding Investments* [1967] 2 Q.B. 786, 802. D. E. M. Young, Q.C. held that there was no requirement that all the parties to the sham should have a common interest and so the unawareness of the wife was irrelevant.

[29] The trust was also held to be voidable under Insolvency Act 1986, s.423. See *post*, p. 225.

benefit. In such circumstances former spouses and dependants have brought claims to the trust property on the basis that it is in reality still vested in the settlor.[30] In cases of this type it is the beneficial interests supposedly vested in persons other than the settlor which are held to be a sham. A decision that a trust is a partial sham therefore casts no doubt on the intention of the settlor to create a trust and consequently has nothing to do with the requirement of certainty of intention at present under discussion; however, it produces exactly the same result as a decision that a trust is a total sham in that it makes the trust property in question available to satisfy the claims of the settlor's creditors or spouse.

2. Certainty of Subject Matter

This is also an essential ingredient for the effectual creation of a trust. The property subject to the trust must either be clearly defined or be capable of ascertainment. This requirement has a number of aspects.

(A) The Property Subject to the Trust

It must be possible to establish exactly what property is subject to the trust. In *Palmer v. Simmonds*,[31] a testatrix left her residuary estate to her husband "for his own use and benefit" but subject to a trust on his death "to leave the bulk of my residuary estate" to four named relatives. This trust was held to fail for uncertainty of subject-matter and so the husband took the property absolutely. A similar result occurred in *Sprange v. Barnard*[32]; the testatrix left stock to her husband "for his sole use, and all that is remaining in the stock, that he has not necessary use for, to be equally divided between" her brothers and sisters. In both of these cases, the husband took the property in question absolutely by virtue of the rule generally known as the Rule in *Hancock v. Watson*[33]; this establishes that, where there is an absolute gift of property in the first instance and the necessary intention subsequently to impose trusts on that property can be established, then in the event that the trusts fail for any reason the property is not held on a resulting trust for the settlor or his estate but will vest absolutely in the person to whom the property was first given absolutely.

In both *Palmer v. Simmonds* and *Sprange v. Barnard* the conclusion was reached that the testator had intended the donee to receive an absolute interest on which the failed trusts were subsequently to be engrafted. However, apparently absolute gifts have sometimes been construed as conferring only a limited interest on the initial beneficiary; such a construction avoids

---

[30] *Rahman v. Chase Bank (CI) Trust Co.* 1991 J.L.R. 103 (Royal Court of Jersey); *Re Marriage of Ashton* (1986) 11 Fam.L.R. 457; *Re Marriage of Goodwin* (1990) 14 Fam.L.R. 801; *Re Marriage of Davidson* (1990) 14 Fam.L.R. 817 (all Family Court of Australia). At least one such claim has also been made in English proceedings in the Family Division heard in Chambers in which the author of this edition was instructed. Similar reported claims relating to sham companies (also known as alter ego companies) have been made in such proceedings; see *Nicholas v. Nicholas* (1984) 5 F.L.R. 285; *Cruttenden v. Cruttenden* [1990] 2 F.L.R. 361; *Green v. Green* [1993] 1 F.L.R. 236.

[31] (1854) 2 Drew 221; compare *Bromley v. Tryon* [1952] A.C. 265.

[32] (1789) 2 Bro.C.C. 585.

[33] [1902] A.C. 14 (formerly known as the Rule in *Lassence v. Tierney* (1849) 1 Mac. & G. 551).

uncertainty of subject matter in respect of the subsequent trusts. In *Re Last*[34] the testatrix left all her property to her brother, providing that "at his death anything that is left, that came from me" was to pass to certain other specified persons. This limitation is very similar to that in *Sprange v. Barnard* but it was in fact construed as conferring merely a life interest on the brother; consequently, on his death, all the property was held on the trusts specified by the testatrix. Similarly, in the earlier case of *Re Thomson's Estate*[35] a testator left all his property to his widow "to be disposed of as she may think proper for her own use and benefit" but "should there be anything remaining of the said property or any part thereof" on her death, it was to be held on various trusts. Hall V.–C. held that the widow had a life interest together with a power to dispose of the property *inter vivos* but no testamentary power so to do; consequently, any property not disposed of during her lifetime was held on the further specified trusts. These decisions are only justifiable on the basis that the intention of the testator was indeed to confer no more than a limited interest on the initial beneficiary.

Another method of avoiding uncertainty of subject matter is for the court to find some way of ascertaining what the subject matter of a potentially uncertain trust actually is. In *Re Golay's Will Trusts*[36] the testator directed his trustees to permit a beneficiary to "enjoy one of my flats during her lifetime and to receive a reasonable income from my other properties". Ungoed-Thomas J. upheld the gift, holding that the yardstick of "reasonable income" indicated by the testator was not what he or some other person subjectively considered to be reasonable but what he identified objectively as "reasonable income", something which the court could therefore quantify. This conclusion was undoubtedly inconsistent with other contemporaneous decisions on certainty[37] but does seem to be consistent with the more recent practice of the courts in trying to avoid, if at all possible, holding dispositions to be void for uncertainty, particularly in respect of expressions such as "reasonable" or "satisfactory".[38]

(B) The Part of the Property Subject to the Trust
Problems have also arisen in connection with attempts to declare trusts of some certain but unidentified part of a larger holding.

(1) Tangible property
The situation with tangible property is relatively clear. In *Re London Wine Company*,[39] wine dealers sent letters to purchasers of wine confirming that they were the sole beneficial owners of the wine which they had bought and paid for; however, no steps were taken to segregate the wine in question from the general mass of stock held by the dealers. It was held that no trust

[34] [1958] P. 137.
[35] (1879) 13 Ch.D. 144.
[36] [1965] 1 W.L.R. 969.
[37] Such as *Re Kolb's Will Trusts* [1962] Ch. 531 (a reference to "blue-chip" securities was held to be uncertain and consequently an investment clause was held to be void for uncertainty).
[38] See particularly *McPhail v. Doulton* [1971] A.C. 424, *post*, pp. 92–95 and, in relation to expressions such as "reasonable" or "satisfactory", *Sudbrook Trading Estates v. Eggleton* [1983] A.C. 444 and *Graham v. Pitkin* [1992] 1 W.L.R. 403.
[39] [1986] Palmer's Company Cases 123.

had arisen so that the purchasers had no proprietary rights in the wine as against the holders of a floating charge which the dealers had granted over their entire assets. This decision remains a useful illustration of the general principle but, because it concerned a sale rather than a gift, its result would now be different because of the Sale of Goods (Amendment) Act 1995, which makes such purchasers tenants in common of the general mass of stock. However, this provision will not avail anyone in the position of the purchasers in *Re Goldcorp Exchange*.[40] They had purchased but had not taken delivery of unascertained bullion; save for a small group whose bullion had indeed been segregated, there was no identifiable property whatever to which any trust could attach and the remaining purchasers thus remained unsecured creditors in the bullion company's insolvency.

(2) Intangible property

The position with intangibles is more controversial. In *Hunter v. Moss*[41] a declaration of trust in respect of 50 shares in a company in which the settlor held 950 shares was upheld on the basis that any identification of the particular 50 shares held on trust was unnecessary and irrelevant. At first instance, the principle enunciated in *Re London Wine Company* was confined to tangible property since "ostensibly similar or identical assets may in fact have characteristics which distinguish them from other assets in the class"[42]—as the judge[43] said, some of the wine might have become corked or might have deteriorated in some other way. He then went on to state that a declaration of trust in respect of £1,000 in a bank account with a current balance superior to £1,000 would also be effectual. Although the principle thus enunciated must clearly be confined to intangible property similar to the choses in action held by the settlor in respect of the shares and the imaginary bank account, it nevertheless caused some surprise. It had hitherto been thought that trusts of such choses in action would only be valid if the settlor declared a trust either of his entire interest in the chose in action or of a fixed proportion thereof[44] (in other words, on the facts of *Hunter v. Moss*, a trust of one-nineteenth of the shares held in the company in question) so that thereafter they would be held on trust for the settlor and the beneficiary in the appropriate proportions.

The settlor appealed to the Court of Appeal where Dillon L.J.[45] simply held that *Re London Wine Company* was "a long way from the present" case and concluded that "[j]ust as a person can give by will a specified number of his shares in a certain company, so equally, in my judgment, he can declare himself a trustee of 50 of his ordinary shares and that is effective to give a beneficial proprietary interest to the beneficiary under the trust". This analogy between a bequest and a declaration of trust has been the subject of

---

[40] [1995] 1 A.C. 74. (Privy Council on appeal from New Zealand).

[41] [1994] 1 W.L.R. 452.

[42] [1993] 1 W.L.R. 934 at 940.

[43] Colin Rimer, Q.C. sitting as a Deputy High Court Judge.

[44] See Underhill & Hayton, *Law of Trusts and Trustees* (14th ed., 1987), p. 105 (now see (15th ed., 1995), p. 61).

[45] [1994] 1 W.L.R. 452 at 458, 459. This was an unreserved judgment with which the other two members of the court simply agreed.

fierce criticism.[46] The effect of a will is to vest the whole estate of the testator in his executors to be administered; consequently, a legatee acquires merely an equitable chose in action until the administration has been completed, at which point he will receive whatever shares are allocated to him by the executors. The effect of a declaration of trust, on the other hand, is to vest an immediate proprietary interest in the beneficiary; this necessitates some immediate means of determining which shares are subject to the trust. How otherwise can it be determined, in the event that the trustee subsequently deals with the shares by, for example, selling 50 of them, with whose shares he has actually dealt—his own, those of the beneficiary, or a rateable proportion of the shares of each of them? Whether or not these criticisms are actually justified, there can be no doubt that the decision in *Hunter v. Moss* is clearly the law at present and it has since been applied in *Holland v. Newbury*[47] by Neuberger J., who upheld a trust where a dealer in securities was holding unidentified shares in identified companies as the nominee of various of its clients. This latter decision made it clear that the crucial distinction is indeed whether the property in question is tangible or intangible (this was the distinction which had been adopted at first instance in *Hunter v. Moss* but Dillon L.J. had made no reference whatever to it in the Court of Appeal). Thus it is apparently now possible to declare a trust of a fixed sum in a bank account with a balance superior to that amount.

Nevertheless it must be emphasised that, even in the case of intangible property, where funds should have been segregated but have not been, there will still be no trust simply because there is no identifiable trust property at all. This occurred in *MacJordan Construction v. Brookmount Frostin*[48] where under the provisions of a building contract 3 per cent of each stage payment was to be retained from but held on trust for the builder; however, the fund which it was envisaged should be constituted to hold these retentions was never set up and so there was nothing to form the subject matter of the intended trust. Similarly, in *Hemmens v. Wilson Browne*,[49] a document purporting to give one party the right to call on the other party for a payment of £110,000 at any time was held not to have created a trust either because there was no identifiable fund which could conceivably form its subject matter.

(C) What Property is Held on Trust for Which Beneficiary

Another aspect of uncertainty of subject matter arises where it is clear what property is intended to be subject to the trust but some or all of the beneficial interests are unascertained in the sense that it is not clear what property is held on trust for which beneficiary.

In *Curtis v. Rippon*[50] the testator left all his property to his wife "trusting that she should, in fear of God, and in love of the children committed to her care, make such use of it as should be for her own and their spiritual and temporal good, remembering always, according to circumstances, the

---

[46] By D. J. Hayton in 110 L.Q.R. (1994) 335.
[47] (1997) *The Times*, July 18, 1997.
[48] (1991) 56 B.L.R. 1.
[49] [1995] Ch. 223.
[50] (1820) 5 Madd. 434.

Church of God and the poor". There was no doubt what property was subject to the trust but the beneficial interest was to be taken by an ascertained beneficiary, subject to the right of others to unascertained portions of it. The rights of the latter were held to fail and the ascertained beneficiary took the entirety under the rule in *Hancock v. Watson*.

Where, on the other hand, all the beneficial interests are unascertained, the trust will fail completely. Thus, in *Boyce v. Boyce*[51] a testator devised two houses to trustees on trust to convey to Maria "whichever house she may think proper to choose or select" and to convey the other house to Charlotte. Maria died in the lifetime of the testator and was thus of course unable to make her choice. The court held that it was impossible to establish which house was held on trust for Charlotte (it is impossible to fault this decision as a matter of construction but it might have been easier to reach the opposite conclusion had there been more than two houses—the consequential direction to convey the "others" to Charlotte could have been construed as "the houses not chosen by Maria"). As a result; the houses were held on resulting trust for the testator's residuary estate (the rule in *Hancock v. Watson* did not apply since there had been no absolute gift of the houses to the trustees in the first instance). In contrast, in *Re Steel*,[52] the testator directed that his residue was to be divided between legatees who had only received "small amounts"; Megarry V.–C. rather generously held that this gift was valid on the basis that the words were merely explaining the testator's motives and ordered the residue to be divided between all the legatees equally whatever the size of their legacies.

(D) The Effect of Uncertainty of Subject Matter
When a trust fails for uncertainty of subject matter then, assuming that there is certainty of intention, a trust will obviously have been intended; consequently, its failure on the grounds of uncertainty of subject matter will not enable the potential trustees to take beneficially unless the Rule in *Hancock v. Watson* applies. As has already been seen,[53] this rule applies where there is an absolute gift of property in the first instance on which trusts are subsequently imposed; if the trusts fail for any reason the property will vest absolutely in the person to whom the property was first given. In every other case, the property is in principle held on resulting trust for the settlor or (if he is dead) for the residuary legatee or devisee under his will, or, if there is no gift of residue, on trust for the persons entitled to his estate under the intestacy rules. There is, however, some authority for the proposition that the court may apply the maxim "equality is equity" and divide the entirety of the beneficial interest equally between the beneficiaries.[54] The best known mode of application of the maxim is to be found in cases involving joint bank accounts held by husband and wife where, after dissolution of the marriage, it is found impracticable to divide the fund meticulously between them.[55] However convenient and "equitable" this may be, it

[51] (1849) 6 Sim. 476.
[52] [1979] 1 Ch. 218.
[53] See *ante*, p. 87.
[54] See *Doyley v. Attorney-General* (1735) 2 Eq.Cas.Abr. 194.
[55] See *Jones v. Maynard* [1951] Ch. 572; *Rimmer v. Rimmer* [1953] 1 Q.B. 63.

is somewhat difficult to justify in principle the application of the maxim in a case involving uncertainty as to the actual beneficial interest taken by the objects of a trust and it is therefore doubtful whether these decisions can actually be justified.

3. *Certainty of Objects*

It is also an essential ingredient for the effectual creation of a trust that its objects should be certain or be capable of being rendered certain. When this is not the case, the consequences are exactly the same as in the case of uncertainty of subject matter: unless the Rule in *Hancock v. Watson* applies, in which case the potential trustees will be entitled to take the trust property beneficially, that property will be held on resulting trust for the settlor or his estate. However, it should be observed that only private trusts are subject to the certainty of objects requirement. A charitable trust will be upheld despite the fact that its objects are uncertain provided that a paramount intention of charity can be upheld[56]; in such circumstances, what is known as a *cy-près* scheme can be made to enable the trust property to be devoted to defined charitable purposes.

(A) The "Complete List" Test

Until the decision of the House of Lords in *McPhail v. Doulton* in 1990,[57] the objects of a trust could only be held to be certain if it was possible to draw up a complete list of those objects. This requirement was originally laid down in *Morice v. Bishop of Durham*[58] early in the nineteenth century. At this time virtually all trusts were fixed trusts, that is to say trusts in favour of pre-determined beneficiaries or classes of beneficiaries, each of whom is entitled to a fixed pre-determined share of the trust property.[59]

However, following the subsequent development of discretionary trusts, whose trustees determine in what proportions, if any, the trust property is to be divided among members of a pre-determined class and sometimes even decide the membership of the class itself, the Court of Appeal confirmed in *I.R.C. v. Broadway Cottages Trust*[60] that such trusts were also subject to the same requirement. In this case the trustees held funds on trust to apply the income for the benefit of all or any of a class of beneficiaries as the trustees might think fit. It was held, as a matter of construction of the trust deed, that a trust had been created in favour of the specified class; that trust was consequently void for uncertainty on the ground that the whole of the class was at any given time unascertainable—the whole range of objects eligible for selection had to be ascertained or be capable of ascertainment at all times. The expressed principle underlying this decision was that the court, if called upon to execute the trust, could only do so on the basis of equal division, something which would not be possible unless the identity of all the members of the class could be ascertained.

---

[56] See *post*, p. 420.
[57] [1971] A.C. 424.
[58] (1804) 9 Ves.Jr. 399, affirmed (1805) 10 Ves.Jr. 522.
[59] See *ante*, p. 39.
[60] [1955] Ch. 20; see also *Re Sayer* [1957] Ch. 423.

This decision had the effect of establishing a crucial difference between, on the one hand, discretionary trusts, and, on the other hand, powers; discretionary trusts were void for uncertainty of objects unless the trustees could at any given time draw up a complete list of all the potential beneficiaries whereas powers, as will be seen shortly,[61] were and still are valid for certainty of objects provided that it can be said with certainty of any given individual whether he is or is not one of the persons in whose favour the power is capable of being exercised.

(B) The "Given Postulant" Test

I.R.C. v. Broadway Cottages Trust was, however, overruled by the majority of the House of Lords in *McPhail v. Doulton*[62] in 1990. The case for rigid requirements for trusts which had been made in the former case, namely that their imperative nature necessarily required that all their objects should be known, was admittedly a persuasive one and had indeed been restated by Lord Upjohn in an intervening decision of the House of Lords concerning powers.[63] But, as Lord Wilberforce indicated in *McPhail v. Doulton*, the law should take account of practicalities, particularly the narrow distinction between discretionary trusts (often also known as trust powers) and mere powers. The theory specifically postulated in *I.R.C. v. Broadway Cottages Trust* that the court can only execute a trust by ordering equal distribution in which every beneficiary shares was rejected as inappropriate: "equal division among all may, probably would, produce a result beneficial to none", being "surely the last thing the settlor ever intended".[64] Lord Wilberforce stated that, if the trustees failed to execute the trust, the court would do so "in the manner best calculated to give effect to the settlor's ... intentions" in one of three ways: either by appointing new trustees, or by directing persons representative of the classes of beneficiaries to prepare a scheme of distribution, or, should the proper basis for distribution be apparent, by directing the trustees how to distribute the fund.[65] (This does not of course mean that equal distribution will never again be ordered; in the case of a small class of beneficiaries whose entire membership is known, it is almost inevitable that equal distribution will still be ordered. It is therefore likely that the novel powers of the court outlined by Lord Wilberforce will only in fact be used where it is not possible to ascertain the entire membership of the class of beneficiaries in question, that is to say in the case of discretionary trusts which would have been void for uncertainty but for the decision in *McPhail v. Doulton*). This fundamental change in judicial attitudes enabled the certainty of objects requirements for discretionary trusts and for powers to be equated; the criterion for both is whether or not it can be said of "any given postulant" that he is a member of the class of potential beneficiaries.

---

[61] See *post*, p. 94.
[62] [1971] A.C. 424.
[63] *Re Gulbenkian's Settlement* [1970] A.C. 508. The point was restated by Lord Hodson in his dissenting speech in *McPhail v. Doulton* [1971] A.C. 424 at 442.
[64] [1971] A.C. 424 at 451.
[65] *ibid.* at 457.

This test had originally been formulated for powers by Harman J. in *Re Gestetner Settlement*.[66] In this case capital was held in trust for such member or members of a specified class as the trustees might think fit. The specified class comprised certain named individuals; any person living or thereafter born who was a descendant of the settlor's father or uncle; any spouse, widow or widower of any such person; five charitable bodies; any former employee of the settlor or his wife and the widow or widower of any such employee; and any director or employee of a named company. Harman J. held that it was unnecessary in a power of this kind to establish that the objects were all capable of ascertainment. It was simply necessary to be able to say of any given person that he was, or was not, an object of the power. The trustees did not have "to worry their heads to survey the world from China to Peru"[67] to find out who was within the designated class. There was no difficulty in ascertaining whether or not any given postulant was a member of the class. Consequently, the power in question was held to be valid.

(C)   The "Given Postulant" Test and the "One Person" Test

Subsequently, there was some uncertainty as to precisely how this test should be applied. Essentially the question was whether or not it should be applied strictly. Under a strict interpretation, if it was impossible to ascertain whether or not a given individual was within the class, the power would fail despite the fact that other classes of persons were clearly within it. The alternative was an even more diluted test, under which any difficulty in saying whether a given individual was or was not within the class would not be fatal, provided that some identifiable person could be shown to be clearly within it. This latter test was admittedly only used on isolated occasions, most notably by Lord Denning M.R.[68] The stricter test was supported by a preponderance of authority[69] and was finally confirmed definitively by the House of Lords in *Re Gulbenkian's Settlement*.[70] This case involved the construction of a clause in a work of precedents then much used by the legal profession. The clause provided that a special power of appointment could be exercised for the maintenance and personal support of all or any one or more of the following persons as the trustees should in

---

[66] [1953] Ch. 673.

[67] *ibid.* at 688–689. This expression was incorrectly attributed by Harman J. to Alexander Pope (see *Re Baden's Trust Deeds* [1969] 2 Ch. 388 at 397, *per* Harman L.J.); the words are in fact those of Samuel Johnson.

[68] In *Re Gulbenkian's Settlement Trusts* [1968] 1 Ch. 126 at 34; see also, *per* Winn L.J. at 138 (the limitation is discussed *post* in the text). It was also used in *Re Gibbard* [1967] 1 W.L.R. 42 at 47–48, where Plowman J. upheld a power to appoint to "any of my old friends", and in *Re Leek* [1967] Ch. 1061 at 1073 where Buckley J. upheld a power to appoint to "such other person as the company may consider to have a moral claim upon you" (the Court of Appeal held ([1969] 1 Ch. 563) that the gift in question was a trust rather than a power and so was void because it was impossible to ascertain all the members of the class. This test still applies to individual gifts subject to the donee satisfying a condition precedent or answering a particular description; see *post*, p. 98.

[69] *Re Coates* [1955] Ch. 495 (for any friends his wife might feel that he had forgotten); *Re Sayer Trust* [1957] Ch. 423 (power in favour of employees, ex-employees, widow, children and "dependants"); in both these cases the power was held to be valid despite the application of the stricter test.

[70] [1970] A.C. 508, applied in *Re Denley's Trust Deed* [1968] Ch. 373.

their absolute discretion think fit: the settlor's son, any wife, children or remoter issue of the son, and any persons in whose house or apartments or in whose company or under whose care and control or by whom the husband might from time to time be employed or residing. The clause had been considered before in *Re Gresham's Settlement*,[71] where Harman J. had held it void for uncertainty on the grounds that there might be a number of persons of whom it could not be determined whether they were or were not within the dragnet of this unusually constructed clause; he had distinguished his own decision in *Re Gestetner Settlement* because there, despite the fact that not all the persons within the specified class were actually known, it could be said whether any given person was or was not within the class. But in *Re Gulbenkian's Settlement* the House of Lords overruled *Re Gresham's Settlement* and held that the clause was sufficiently certain to satisfy the test laid down in *Re Gestetner Settlement*. Lord Upjohn, in affirming the latter test, was unable to accept the more diluted test, which had been put forward by Lord Denning M.R. in the Court of Appeal.[72] It was the requirement thus established for certainty of objects in powers which was subsequently also adopted for discretionary trusts in *McPhail v. Doulton*.

The fact that the test for certainty of objects in powers and discretionary trusts has now been assimilated does not, however, mean that powers and discretionary trusts have themselves been assimilated. As will be seen in a later chapter,[73] the basic distinction between the two remains. In the case of a power, the court will not normally compel its exercise and will only interfere where the trustees exceed their powers or, possibly, where they act capriciously. On the other hand, in the case of a discretionary trust, if the trustees do not exercise their discretion, the court will do so in the manner thought most appropriate to carry out the settlor's intentions. Moreover, as a result of this distinction, "a wider and more comprehensive range of inquiry"[74] as to the range of objects is called for in the case of discretionary trusts than in the case of powers.

(D) Outstanding Uncertainties
There are a number of outstanding uncertainties about the test which now applies both to discretionary trusts and to powers.

(1) The scope of the test
McPhail v. Doulton has established that the "given postulant" test is the appropriate test for certainty of objects of both discretionary trusts and powers. However, in other respects there is some room for debate as to the test's applicability.

(a) Fixed trusts. Does the test laid down in *McPhail v. Doulton* only apply to the type of trust which was under consideration in that case, that is only to discretionary trusts, or does it also apply to fixed trusts?

---

[71] [1956] 1 W.L.R. 573, followed in *Re Allan* [1958] 1 W.L.R. 220, where the same clause had been utilised.

[72] Lord Donovan reserved his opinion on this point.

[73] See *post*, p. 163.

[74] *McPhail v. Doulton* [1971] A.C. 424, *per* Lord Wilberforce at 457.

In the previous editions of this work prepared by Professor Parker and Professor Mellows[75] it was contended that there seems to be no reason in principle why it should not do so. Just as an order for distribution (not necessarily, as has been seen, on the basis of equal division) can be made by the court in the case of a discretionary trust, so also, it might be thought, could such an order be made in the case of a fixed trust where one or more of the beneficiaries are not ascertainable.[76] (The point is conceded to be "more academic than real", arising only in the almost inconceivable case of a trust for objects which could not be fully ascertained also containing a provision for distribution to them in equal or some other definite shares.)

However, the more general view, which is shared by the author of this edition, is that the "given postulant" test does not apply to fixed trusts, in respect of which it is still necessary to be able to draw up a complete list of the objects.[77] It is generally thought, contrary to the view already considered, that if the trust property is to be divided among a class of beneficiaries in fixed shares it would be wholly contrary to the intention of the settlor for the court to order any other form of division; on this basis, it is essential that all the possible beneficiaries should be capable of being ascertained by the time at which any distribution of capital or income has to be made.

The description of the beneficiaries must be both conceptually and evidentially certain. Objects will be conceptually uncertain if the exact meaning of the definition used contains any linguistic or semantic uncertainty. Thus, a trust for the settlor's "old friends" in equal shares would be likely to be conceptually uncertain,[78] simply because the expression used is capable of so many different interpretations.[79] On the other hand, objects will be evidentially uncertain if it is impossible to list all the members of the class at the appropriate time. There is no difficulty about a trust for one person for life followed by a gift in remainder to his children in equal shares since, even if the life tenant has no children at the time at which the trust is constituted, it will become clear whether or not he has any children and, if so, how many not later than nine months after the determination of his life interest upon his death.[80] However, the sort of classes of beneficiaries which were established in *Re Gestetner Settlement*,[81] *Re Gulbenkian's Settlement*[82] and *McPhail v.*

---

[75] See, for example, the fifth edition (1983) at p. 79. See also P. Matthews [1984] Conv. 22.

[76] The authors' reading of Lord Wilberforce's speech was that the new test applies to all trusts. Furthermore, it was contended that it would be regrettable if this were not so, because a discretionary trust is a trust, although having close affinities with powers.

[77] See, for example, Hanbury & Martin, *Modern Equity* (15th ed., 1997), pp. 98–99; Underhill & Hayton, *Law of Trusts and Trustees* (15th ed., 1995), pp. 66–67.

[78] This was stated by Browne-Wilkinson J. in *Re Barlow's Will Trusts* [1970] 1 W.L.R. 278 at 281–282.

[79] However, such an expression would satisfy the more diluted test advocated by Lord Denning M.R. (see *ante*, n. 68), provided that one "old friend" of the settlor could be clearly identified—this was specifically held by Browne-Wilkinson J. in *Re Barlow's Will Trusts* [1979] 1 W.L.R. 278 in respect of a series of individual gifts with a condition precedent or description attached, to which the more diluted test was held to be applicable.

[80] The point at which the children's interest would vest in possession (each child having acquired a vested interest in interest on his birth); the 9 month extension is made so that any posthumous children can be included.

[81] [1953] Ch. 673.

[82] [1970] A.C. 508.

Doulton[83] cannot conceivably be the objects of a fixed trust because of the impossibility of determining between how many persons the capital or income has to be divided. However, provided that it is possible to establish the maximum number of possible beneficiaries, it does not matter that the continued existence or present whereabouts of some of the possible members of the class cannot be discovered since the shares payable to any such beneficiaries can be paid into court to await either their appearance or definitive proof that they did not in fact qualify.[84] All that is necessary is that the list which is able to be drawn up at the appropriate time is, on a balance of probabilities, complete.

(b) **"Powers in the nature of a trust".** It has already been seen that discretionary trusts are today often known as trust powers. However, the same name is also used to denote powers whose donees are under an obligation to exercise them. Such powers are also known as "powers in the nature of a trust".[85] Where such a power is found to exist, the court will execute the power in the event that its donee fails to exercise it. Such a case was *Burrough v. Philcox*.[86] The testator left property on trust for his two children for life and, subject thereto, to their issue but further declared that, if both his children should die without issue, the surviving child should have the power to dispose by will of the property "among my nephews and nieces or their children, either all to one of them or to as many as my surviving child shall think proper". The surviving child died without so appointing. Lord Cottenham L.C. held that, "when there appears a general intention in favour of a class, and a particular intention in favour of individuals of a class to be selected by another person, and the particular intention fails from that selection not being made, the Court will carry into effect the general intention in favour of the class".[87] He held that the words used evinced a general intention of this type; consequently the court could execute the power on behalf of its donee by dividing the property equally among all the members of the class. (Had he not found a general intention of this type, the property would have passed on a resulting trust for those entitled to the residuary estate of the testator.)

With which test for certainty of objects do such powers in the nature of a trust have to comply? If it is still the case that the court would automatically execute such a power by dividing the property equally between all the members of the class, then the test must surely be the same as that for fixed trusts; in this case, according to the general view,[88] it must be possible to draw up a complete list of the members of the class at the appropriate time.

---

[83] [1971] A.C. 424.

[84] See C. T. Emery, (1982) 98 L.Q.R. 551.

[85] The terminological confusion caused by the fact that the expression "trust power" is now used to describe two factually similar but legally quite distinct types of gift has already been mentioned (see *ante*, p. 34). Hanbury & Martin, *Modern Equity* (15th ed., 1997), p. 109 suggests that it may have been the two meanings of "trust power" which caused the discrepancy between the majority and the minority in *McPhail v. Doulton*, the majority having in mind the modern discretionary trust and the minority the old style power in the nature of a trust.

[86] (1840) 5 Myl. & Cr. 72.

[87] *ibid.*

[88] The contrary view has been adopted in previous editions of this work (see *ante*, text to n. 75).

On the other hand, if the remarks of Lord Wilberforce in *McPhail v. Doulton* as to the ways in which the court can now execute a discretionary trust[89] also apply to powers in the nature of a trust, then there will be no need for the "complete list" test to apply and such limitations will presumably also be governed by the "given postulant" test. This question is in fact somewhat academic since powers in the nature of a trust are almost invariably in favour of small groups of beneficiaries, usually, as in *Burrough v. Philcox*, the members of a family. Gifts of this type will inevitably satisfy either test for certainty of objects and in practice, the court would almost inevitably order equal distribution quite irrelevant of whether or not this was actually obligatory. It has been argued that powers in the nature of a trust should be regarded as fixed trusts subject to defeasance by exercise of the power of selection and, as a result, must still be governed by the test appropriate to fixed trusts.[90] However, because of the factual similarity between powers in the nature of a trust and discretionary trusts, it seems as a matter of principle to be more appropriate that such powers should today also be governed by the "given postulant" test on the already mentioned assumption that, whenever the entire membership of the class is known, equal division will in fact be ordered.

(c) **Gifts subject to a condition precedent.** The more diluted test that a formulation will be valid provided that one identifiable person is clearly within it (specifically rejected in respect of powers in *Re Gulbenkian's Settlement*[91]) does undoubtedly apply to individual gifts subject to the donee satisfying a condition precedent or answering a particular description.[92] For these purposes, conceptual certainty is completely irrelevant.

Thus in *Re Allen*[93] a testator left property to the eldest of his nephews "who shall be a member of the Church of England and an adherent to the doctrine of that Church"; this gift was held to be valid on the basis that, whatever the precise meaning of the conditions, it was perfectly possible for a claimant to show that he fell within them. Similarly, in *Re Tuck's Settlement Trusts*[94] what the majority of the Court of Appeal[95] regarded as conditions precedent in a settlement that the principal beneficiary for the time being had to be of the Jewish faith and married to an approved Jewish wife were held to be valid.

The same principle was applied in *Re Barlow's Will Trust*[96] to a limitation which, although not expressed in the form of a condition precedent, amounted to a series of gifts to any individuals who answered a particular specified description. The testatrix provided that "any friends of mine who

---

[89] See *ante*, p. 93.

[90] In Hanbury & Martin, *Modern Equity* (15th ed., 1997), p. 109.

[91] [1970] A.C. 508. See *ante*, p. 95.

[92] Conditions subsequent are subject to a stricter test; the situations in which such a condition will operate must be wholly clear from the outset. For a recent discussion, see *Re Tepper's Will Trusts* [1987] Ch. 49.

[93] [1953] Ch. 810.

[94] [1978] Ch. 49.

[95] Lord Russell of Killowen and Eveleigh L.J. Lord Denning M.R. adopted a different approach, discussed *post*, p. 102.

[96] [1978] 1 W.L.R. 278.

may wish to do so" might purchase any of her paintings at their probate valuation. Browne-Wilkinson J. held that, had this been a gift to a class and therefore had had to satisfy the "given postulant" test, it would have been void for conceptual uncertainty. However, he regarded the limitation as creating a series of individual gifts in the form of options exercisable by any person who qualified as a "friend"; since there might be persons who could, on any conceivable test, prove that they were friends, the limitation was valid.

While the applicability of this "one person" test to conditions precedent and other analogous gifts is clearly established, it would certainly not be easy for the court to decide whether any individual did in fact qualify in such circumstances; any doubts as to qualification would therefore presumably lead to the automatic disqualification of the claimant. However, this is not necessarily an objection to the existence of the test since, as will be seen in the next section, this is now arguably also the case with the "given postulant" test.

(2) Conceptual uncertainty and evidential uncertainty

In *Re Gulbenkian's Settlement*[97] Lord Upjohn posed the already mentioned distinction between conceptual (linguistic or semantic) uncertainty which, if the court cannot resolve it, renders the gift wholly void, and evidential uncertainty, which the court can deal with on an application for directions. This distinction was adopted in *McPhail v. Doulton*[98] and had to be considered in *Re Baden's Deed Trusts (No.2)*,[99] the sequel to *McPhail v. Doulton* in which the test laid down by the House of Lords therein had to be applied to the terms of the trust in question. The trustees were directed to apply the net income of the fund in making at their absolute discretion grants to or for the benefit of any of the officers and employees or ex-officers or ex-employees of a specified company or to any relatives or dependants of any such persons. The Court of Appeal held that this class satisfied the "given postulant" test but the members of the court agreed neither as to the correct interpretation of the test nor, consequently, as to the conceptually certain meaning of the two problematic words, "relatives" and "dependants".

(a) The different views expressed in Re Baden's Deed Trusts (No.2). S-

tamp L.J. interpreted the "given postulant" test strictly, holding that the test would only be satisfied if it was possible to say either "yes" or "no" to any person who could conceivably present himself to the trustees.[1] On the other hand, both Sachs L.J. and Megaw L.J. seemed to broaden the test laid down by the House of Lords. Sachs L.J. held that, provided that the class was conceptually certain, the gift could never fail for evidential uncertainty the burden of proof was on the postulant and, if he could not positively prove that he was within the class, then he was outside it.[2] Megaw L.J. held that, if it could be said with certainty that a substantial number of objects did

---

[97] [1970] A.C. 508 at 524.
[98] [1971] A.C. 424 at 457.
[99] [1973] Ch. 9.
[1] *ibid*. at 28.
[2] *ibid*. at 19.

fall within the class, then it did not matter that, as regards a substantial number of other persons, the answer had to be that "it is not proven whether they are in or out".[3]

All three views are susceptible of criticism. The interpretation advocated by Stamp L.J. in practice does not fall far short of a return to the "complete list" test expressly rejected in *McPhail v. Doulton*; while there is no need for the trustees actually to draw up a list, it has to be admitted that by virtue of this interpretation those otherwise entitled to the property subject to a discretionary trust will be able to upset that trust whenever they can come up with one person whose claim to be a member of the class cannot be proven one way or the other. On the other hand, the interpretations adopted by both Sachs L.J. and Megaw L.J. move some considerable way towards the more diluted test specifically rejected in *Re Gulbenkian's Settlement Trusts* that all that is necessary is to find one identifiable person clearly within the class. The interpretation adopted by Sachs L.J. could clearly lead to there being only one beneficiary within the class but only if the expression used was conceptually certain, something which is not actually required in the case of gifts subject to the "one person" test.[4] The interpretation adopted by Megaw L.J. would require a substantial number of persons rather than just one to fall within the class but it is unclear whether or not conceptual certainty would also be required.

Having expressed these differing views as to the interpretation of the "given postulant" test, the members of the Court of Appeal accepted that, no matter what meaning was given to "dependants", the trust would be both conceptually and evidentially certain.[5] Sachs and Megaw L.JJ. held that the trust would be conceptually certain even if the widest possible meaning, "descendants from a common ancestor", was attributed to "relatives" and that there was no evidential difficulty about ascertaining whether any given postulant was a relative.[6] Stamp L.J., on the other hand, held that, if such a meaning was given to "relatives", the trust would fail because of the impossibility of saying that any given postulant was not a relative of a past or present officer or employee of the company; he consequently interpreted "relatives" as meaning "statutory next-of-kin", an expression which is on any view both conceptually and evidentially certain.[7]

(b) Their effect. It is not easy to determine the precise effect of *Re Baden's Deed Trusts (No.2)* so far as conceptual certainty is concerned. There has been little or no subsequent judicial discussion of this aspect of the interpretation of the test laid down in *Re Gulbenkian's Settlements* and *McPhail v. Doulton*. The limitation in *Re Baden's Deed Trusts (No.2)* was of

---

[3] *ibid.* at 24.
[4] See *ante*, p. 98.
[5] [1973] Ch. 9 at 20, 22, 30.
[6] *ibid.* at 21, 22.
[7] *ibid.* at 28–30. "Relatives" has traditionally been construed as "statutory next-of-kin" if this is necessary to save a gift; however, an appointment by the trustees in favour of relatives who are not statutory next-of-kin is nevertheless valid, which signifies that, in the event that the court is called upon to execute the trust because of a default by the trustees, distribution is necessarily among a narrower class than that available to the trustees (see *Re Poulton's Will Trusts* [1987] 1 W.L.R. 795).

course complex and it must not be thought that problems of this kind will often arise. More straightforward illustrations of conceptual uncertainty are to be found in earlier cases where it was plain that there was, and would still be, conceptual uncertainty of objects. Thus in *Re Astor's Settlement Trusts*,[8] which concerned the *Observer* newspaper, a settlement provided for income to be applied to a number of non-charitable purposes including the "maintenance of good understanding, sympathy and co-operation between nations" and "the preservation of the independence and integrity of newspapers" and other such purposes for the protection of newspapers. Roxburgh J. held the trusts to be void because *inter alia* the objects listed above were void for uncertainty. Purposes must be stated in phrases which embody definite concepts and, moreover, the means by which the trustees are to attain them must be prescribed with a sufficient degree of certainty. Similarly, in *Re Endacott*[9] the Court of Appeal held that a trust which was in essence for "useful" purposes was void for uncertainty because it was not clear what "utility" meant. It is also generally thought that a discretionary trust in favour of "persons having a moral claim" on the settlor would also be void for conceptual uncertainty, although in *Re Leek*[10] a limitation in favour of "such persons as the [donee of the power in question] may consider to have a moral claim" on the settlor was held by Buckley J. to be sufficiently certain, a view which was supported by Harman L.J. in the Court of Appeal by way of dictum.[11]

(c) **Can conceptual uncertainty be cured by delegation?** This last decision raises a question of general importance as to the extent to which conceptual uncertainty can be cured by a provision that the matter is to be settled by the decision of either the trustees or of some third party.

The orthodox view is that a question of fact can be delegated for resolution in this way[12] but not a question of law, since the jurisdiction of the court to decide matters of law cannot be ousted.[13] For present purposes, this suggests that, while an issue of evidential uncertainty could be delegated by the settlor to the trustees[14] or to some third party for resolution, an issue of conceptual uncertainty could not be so delegated.[15] However, in *Dundee*

---

[8] [1952] Ch. 534. See also *post*, p. 106.
[9] [1960] Ch. 232.
[10] [1967] Ch. 1061 (Buckley J.); [1969] 1 Ch. 563, C.A.
[11] As the words in square brackets indicate, Buckley J. actually held that this limitation had created a power; at that time powers alone were subject to the "given postulant" test; on appeal, the Court of Appeal found that the limitation had created a discretionary trust which, under the then law, was void for uncertainty because it was impossible to ascertain all the members of the class (such a trust would of course now also be subject to the "given postulant" test).
[12] *Re Coxen* [1948] Ch. 747.
[13] *Re Wynn* [1952] Ch. 271.
[14] *Re Coxen* [1948] Ch. 747. This case concerned a condition subsequent; a provision that the trustees should be able to determine whether or not the testator's widow had "ceased permanently to reside" at a particular property was upheld. See also *Re Burton* [1955] Ch. 82 at 95.
[15] *Re Jones* [1953] Ch. 125. This case also concerned a condition subsequent; a provision that the "uncontrolled opinion" of the trustees should determine whether or not the testator's daughter had "social or other relationship" with a named person was held to be void for uncertainty.

General Hospital Board of Management v. Walker,[16] the House of Lords held, on a Scottish appeal, that a proviso that a legacy was only to be paid to a hospital if the trustees of the will "were in their sole and absolute discretion" satisfied that the hospital had not been placed under state control made the trustees the sole judges of this question and that there could be no appeal to the courts from their decision unless they had considered the wrong question or failed to consider the right question in a proper manner. This decision suggests that a question of law can now be referred to a third party for decision, in which case there seems no reason why an issue of conceptual uncertainty should not similarly be delegated.

This impression is confirmed by some remarks of Lord Denning M.R. in *Re Tuck's Settlement Trusts,*[17] which concerned conditions precedent in a settlement that the principal beneficiary for the time being had to be of the Jewish faith and married to an approved Jewish wife, it being provided that any dispute was to be referred to the Chief Rabbi for decision. The majority of the Court of Appeal found that these conditions were conditions precedent; consequently, they did not need to be conceptually certain and so were sufficiently certain.[18] Lord Denning M.R., however, held that, in the event that there was any conceptual uncertainty in the conditions, this was cured by the reference to the Chief Rabbi.[19]

This matter cannot yet be regarded as settled, particularly in the light of the fact that Lord Denning's remarks were subsequently overlooked in the rather inadequately reported *Re Wright's Will Trusts.*[20] However, there is clearly considerably more possibility than hitherto that issues of conceptual uncertainty can now be cured in this way.

(3) Administrative unworkability
In *McPhail v. Doulton,*[21] Lord Wilberforce added a third class of potential uncertainty, where "the meaning of the words used is clear but the definition of beneficiaries is so hopelessly wide as not to form 'anything like a class' so that the trust is administratively unworkable" (he gave as an example "all the residents of Greater London"). A discretionary trust was indeed struck down for this reason in *R. v. District Auditor, ex p. West Yorkshire Metropolitan County Council,*[22] where the local authority resolved to create a trust "for the benefit of any or all or some of the inhabitants of the County of West Yorkshire" for various specific purposes.[23] Given that there were 2,500,000 potential beneficiaries, the court, while prepared to assume without deciding that "inhabitant" was sufficiently conceptually certain, held that the trust was void for administrative unworkability on the grounds that the class was much too large.

---

[16] [1952] 1 All E.R. 896. This decision was considered in *Re Jones* [1953] Ch. 125. See *ante*, n. 15; it was distinguished on the grounds that it concerned a condition precedent whereas *Re Jones* concerned a condition subsequent.

[17] [1978] Ch. 49.

[18] *ibid., per* Lord Russell of Killowen at 63–64, *per* Eveleigh L.J. at 64–65.

[19] *ibid.* at 60, 62.

[20] [1981] Law Society Gazette Reports 841.

[21] [1971] A.C. 424 at 457.

[22] (1986) 26 R.V.R. 24. See C. Harpum, (1986) 45 C.L.J. 391.

[23] See *post*, p. 108.

While the concept of administrative unworkability thus clearly applies to discretionary trusts, there has been considerable debate over whether or not it also applies to powers. In *Blausten v. I.R.C.*,[24] the trustees had power to introduce to the class of beneficiaries any person other than the settlor. An argument that this power was void for administrative unworkability was rejected on the ground that although the trustees had this admittedly wide power it could only be exercised with the written consent of the settlor and hence only during his lifetime. Therefore, it could not be said that the settlor had failed to set "metes and bounds" to the beneficial interests which he intended to create or to permit to be created under the settlement. Buckley L.J. clearly assumed, admittedly only by way of dictum, that the concept of administrative unworkability did apply to powers. His reasoning is, however, difficult to reconcile with subsequent decisions.

In *Re Manisty's Settlement*,[25] the trustees had the power to add beneficiaries and to benefit the persons so added and their power was exercisable in favour of anyone in the world except the settlor, his wife and some other persons. Templeman J. held that this power did not fail for administrative unworkability even though there were no expressed restrictions on its operation by the trustees, preferring the view that a power could not be void on the grounds of breadth of numbers but only if its terms were capricious. Megarry V.-C. in *Re Hay's Settlement Trusts*[26] also took the view that a power would not be administratively unworkable on the grounds of mere numbers on the basis that this should not inhibit the trustees in its exercise and would not prevent the courts from controlling them. He did however state that a discretionary trust as broad as the power in that case ("to or for the benefit of any person or persons whatsoever or to any charity" with only the settlor, her husband, and the trustees excluded) would have been void as administratively unworkable. Subsequently, in *Re Beatty's Will Trusts*[27] a power given to trustees in favour of "such person or persons as they think fit" was held valid, this time without any mention of the possibility of it being administratively unworkable.

At this stage, it seemed tolerably clear that the concept of administrative unworkability did not apply to powers. However, as will be seen in a later chapter,[28] the duties of the donee of a power and the remedies available to the objects of a power have now been the subject of an important review in *Mettoy Pensions Trustees v. Evans*[29]; this decision envisages the adaption of the remedies available for the enforcement of discretionary trusts for the purpose of enforcing powers. It has therefore been suggested[30] that this may cause the concept of administrative unworkability to be applied to at least some types of powers. It obviously remains to be seen whether this is yet another consequence of this important decision.

---

[24] [1972] Ch. 256.
[25] [1974] Ch. 17.
[26] [1982] 1 W.L.R. 202.
[27] [1990] 1 W.L.R. 1503.
[28] See *post*, p. 201.
[29] [1990] 1 W.L.R. 1587.
[30] By S. Gardner, (1991) 107 L.Q.R. 214.

(4) Capriciousness

Another possible ground of potential uncertainty is capriciousness, a concept developed by Templeman J. in *Re Manisty's Settlement*,[31] in which he upheld a power of very considerable breadth. He held that the exercise of the process of selection by discretionary trustees and by the donees of powers may be rendered practically impossible if the terms of the discretionary trusts and powers in question are capricious. He gave as an example of a capricious power one in favour of "the residents of Greater London", not because of the number of donees but "because the terms of the power negative any sensible intention on the part of the settlor" and any "sensible consideration by the trustees of the exercise of the power". "If the settlor intended and expected the trustees would have regard to persons with some claim on his bounty or some interest in an institution favoured by the settlor, or if the settlor had any other sensible intention or expectation, he would not have required the trustees to consider only an accidental conglomeration of persons who have no discernible link with the settlor or with any institution."[32]

Because the example given by Templeman J. of a capricious power was exactly the same as the example given by Lord Wilberforce in *McPhail v. Doulton* of an administratively unworkable discretionary trust, it was originally thought that the two concepts were the same,[33] the former being applicable only to powers and the latter being applicable only to discretionary trusts. However, it is now clear that the concept of capriciousness applies both to discretionary trusts and to powers. In *R. v. District Auditor, ex p. West Yorkshire Metropolitan County Council*,[34] the discretionary trust held void for administrative unworkability because the 2,500,000 inhabitants of West Yorkshire constituted too large a class was held not to be capricious since the County Council had every reason for wishing to benefit the inhabitants of West Yorkshire. The concepts of administrative unworkability and capriciousness are therefore apparently distinct, the former but not the latter being limited to breadth of numbers. No discretionary trust or power has yet been set aside on the grounds of capriciousness; it will be interesting to see whether this ever occurs.

(5) Duty to survey the field

Given that, save in the case of a fixed trust, the identity of all the objects of a trust or a power will not necessarily be known, the trustees of a discretionary trust and those entitled to exercise a power in the nature of a trust or a mere power cannot be obliged to consider the claims of every possible object. In *McPhail v. Doulton*[35] Lord Wilberforce stated that the trustees of a discretionary trust "ought to make such a survey of the range of objects or possible beneficiaries as will enable them to carry out their fiduciary duty" and emphasised that a "wider and more comprehensive range of enquiry is called for" in the case of discretionary trusts than in the case of powers.

---

[31] [1974] Ch. 17.
[32] *ibid*. at 27.
[33] See C. T. Emery, (1982) 98 L.Q.R. 551.
[34] (1986) 26 R.V.R. 24.
[35] [1971] A.C. 424.

Where the possible objects number thousands or hundreds of thousands, the trustees must assess "the size of the problem" in a businesslike manner.[36] A more detailed account of the duties of discretionary trustees was provided by Megarry V.-C. in *Re Hay's Settlement Trusts*[37] in the following passage.

"The trustee must not simply proceed to exercise the power in favour of such of the objects as happen to be at hand or claim his attention. He must first consider what persons or classes of persons are objects of the power . . . : what is needed is an appreciation of the width of the field, and thus whether a selection is to be made merely from a dozen or, instead, from thousands or millions. . . . Only when the trustee has applied his mind to the 'size of the problem' should he then consider in individual cases whether, in relation to other possible claimants, a particular grant is appropriate. In doing this, no doubt he should not prefer the undeserving to the deserving but he is not required to make an exact calculation whether, as between deserving claimants, A is more deserving than B."

This duty, considerably broader than had hitherto been thought,[38] has so far been applied only to trustees of discretionary trusts but would presumably also be applied to the donees of powers in the nature of a trust. The duties of a donee of a mere power "cannot be more stringent than those for a discretionary trust".[39] A non-fiduciary donee of a mere power is clearly under no obligation to do anything at all and so cannot possibly have any duty to survey the field. On the other hand, in *Mettoy Pension Trustees v. Evans*,[40] it was stated that a fiduciary donee of a mere power must consider periodically whether or not he should exercise the power, the range of objects of the power, and the appropriateness of individual appointments. As will be seen in a later chapter,[41] a fiduciary donee of a power is consequently "to some extent subject to the control of the courts in relation to its exercise"[42]; as a result, powers held by fiduciaries may well in some respects have been assimilated to discretionary trusts. However, the precise scope of the duties which were enunciated in *Mettoy Pension Trustees v. Evans* must await further clarification.

II. THE BENEFICIARY PRINCIPLE

A further essential ingredient for the effectual creation of a trust is that there should be some beneficiary capable of enforcing it. As Grant M.R. stated in *Morice v. Bishop of Durham*,[43] "there must be someone in whose favour the

---

[36] *Re Baden's Deed Trusts (No.2)* [1973] Ch. 9 at 20, *per* Sachs L.J.
[37] [1982] 1 W.L.R. 202 at 209–210.
[38] In *Re Gestetner* [1953] Ch. 672 at 688 Harman J. had stated that "there is no obligation on the trustees to do more than consider from time to time the merits of such persons of the specified class as are known to them".
[39] *Re Hay's Settlement Trusts* [1982] 1 W.L.R. 202 at 209–210.
[40] [1990] 1 W.L.R. 1587.
[41] See *post*, p. 201.
[42] *Mettoy Pension Trustees v. Evans* [1990] 1 W.L.R. 1587 at 1614.
[43] (1804) 9 Ves. 399 at 405.

court can decree performance". This requirement does not apply to charitable trusts, which can be enforced by the Attorney-General. However, private trusts which do not satisfy the beneficiary requirement will not generally be enforced; "a court of equity does not recognise as valid a trust which it cannot both enforce and control".[44] Nevertheless, there are a number of anomalous cases in which non-charitable purpose trusts have been upheld even though there has been no human beneficiary capable of enforcing them. Such trusts are often described as trusts of imperfect obligation on the grounds that, although they will not be enforced, the courts will not forbid their performance if the trustees wish to carry them out. In *Re Endacott*[45] these cases were said to fall into the following categories: trusts for the erection or maintenance of monuments or graves, trusts for the saying of masses in jurisdictions where such trusts are not regarded as charitable, trusts for the maintenance of particular animals, trusts for the benefit of unincorporated associations, and miscellaneous cases (a few further cases which do not fit into any of the other categories). The decisions which have established these anomalous exceptions have been described as "concessions to human weakness or sentiment"[46] and will not now be extended.[47]

1. *The General Rule*

Trusts for non-charitable purposes are generally void for two different reasons: first, because there is no one who can enforce them and, secondly, because the courts are unable to control the execution of such trusts. This rule was originally established in *Morice v. Bishop of Durham*,[48] which concerned a gift of residue to the Bishop of Durham to be applied by him "for such objects of benevolence and liberality as [he] in his own discretion shall most approve of". Grant M.R. held that this gift failed, saying[49] that "there can be no trust, over the exercise of which this Court will not assume a control, for an uncontrollable power of disposition would be ownership, and not trust". On appeal, Lord Eldon L.C. added[50] that the court had to be in a position both to execute the trust if the trustees for any reason did not do so and to prevent maladministration of the trust. This decision, which was approved by the House of Lords in *Chichester Diocesan Fund and Board of Finance v. Simpson*[51] unquestionably represents English law.

    The first in a line of important decisions which reconsidered the whole question of trusts for non-charitable purposes was *Re Astor's Settlement Trusts*,[52] whose objects included "the establishment, maintenance and improvement of good understanding, sympathy and co-operation between

---

[44] *Re Astor's Settlement Trusts* [1952] Ch. 534 at 549.
[45] [1960] Ch. 232.
[46] *Re Astor's Settlement Trusts* [1952] Ch. 534 at 547.
[47] *Re Endacott* [1960] Ch. 232 at 250–251.
[48] (1804) 9 Ves. 399; (1805) 10 Ves. 522.
[49] (1804) 9 Ves. 399 at 404–405.
[50] (1805) 10 Ves. 522 at 539–540.
[51] [1944] A.C. 341.
[52] [1952] Ch. 534.

nations", "the preservation of the independence and integrity of news-papers" and "the promotion of freedom of the press" (the trust was intended to facilitate the continued independence of the *Observer* news-paper, which had been founded by the Astor family). This case has already been considered in relation to certainty of objects; the conclusion which was reached, that these objects were conceptually uncertain, was however only a secondary ground for the decision that the trusts were ineffectual. The primary question considered by the court was whether, irrelevant of whether or not the objects were certain, the trusts would have been effective as non-charitable purpose trusts. Roxburgh J. concluded that the general principle was that gifts on trust must have a beneficiary or *cestui que trust*, to which principle the anomalous cases already referred to constituted exceptions. He suggested that these cases should, following the view of Underhill,[53] be regarded as concessions to human weakness or sentiment; however, he held that they could not be used to justify the proposition that a court of equity would recognise as an equitable obligation a direction to apply funds in furtherance of enumerated non-charitable purposes in a manner which no court could control.[54]

The views of Roxburgh J. were applied in *Re Shaw*,[55] another decision at first instance, where the main question was whether George Bernard Shaw's testamentary trusts of residue for 21 years for experimentation in the possi-ble reform of the English alphabet of 26 letters by its substitution for a phonetic alphabet of 40 letters were valid charitable trusts. In the event it was held that they were not and the question then arose as to whether they could be valid as non-charitable purpose trusts. Harman J. held that they were invalid since they lacked any *cestui que trust*.

Subsequently, the compass of non-charitable purpose trusts seemed to have been firmly confined by the decision of the Court of Appeal in *Re Endacott*.[56] The testator had given his residuary estate to the North Tawton Parish Council "for the purpose of providing some useful memorial to myself". The court held that this trust did not fall within the "anomalous" class of trusts of imperfect obligation. It was of too wide and uncertain a nature to qualify. Harman L.J. affirmed the views on this type of trusts which had been expressed by Roxburgh J. in *Re Astor's Settlement Trusts*. He said[57]: "I applaud the orthodox sentiments expressed by Roxburgh J. and I think as I think he does, that though one knows there have been decisions which are not satisfactorily classified but are merely occasions when Homer has nodded, yet the cases stand by themselves and ought not to be increased in number nor indeed followed except where the one is exactly like the other." And he added that he could not think that a case of this kind, that of providing outside a church an unspecified and unidentified memorial, was the kind of instance which should be added to these "troublesome, anom-alous and aberrant" cases. Similarly, one of the reasons why the Court of Appeal held in *R v. District Auditor ex p. West Yorkshire Metropolitan Council*[58]

---

[53] See now Underhill & Hayton, *Law of Trusts and Trustees* (15th ed. 1995), pp. 97–102.
[54] [1952] Ch. 534 at 547.
[55] [1957] 1 W.L.R. 729.
[56] [1960] Ch. 232.
[57] *ibid*. at 250–251.
[58] [1986] R.V.R. 24.

that a discretionary trust to apply £400,000 for one of four purposes "for the benefit of any or some of the inhabitants of" West Yorkshire was void was because it was a non-charitable purpose trust.

As will be seen later on,[59] a number of trusts for unincorporated associations, where the subject matter of the gift was to be held on trust for the purposes of the association as a quasi-corporate entity, have been held void on the grounds of perpetuity. Such cases are primarily concerned with perpetuity and are best dealt with under that heading. However, in one of the leading cases, *Leahy v. Attorney-General for New South Wales*,[60] Viscount Simonds, although concluding that the gift in question was indeed void for perpetuity, was clearly of the opinion that such a purpose trust would be void in any event because of the lack of any *cestui que trust* to enforce it. He said[61]:

"If the words 'for the general purposes of the association' were held to import a trust, the question would have to be asked, what is the trust and who are the beneficiaries? A gift can be made to persons (including a corporation) but it cannot be made to a purpose or to an object; so also a trust may be created for the benefit of persons as *cestuis que trust* but not for a purpose or object unless the purpose or object be charitable. For a purpose or object cannot sue but, if it be charitable, the Attorney-General can sue to enforce it."[62]

Thus, the question raised in cases such as *Re Astor's Settlement Trusts* and *Re Shaw*, namely whether the categories of the anomalous trusts of imperfect obligation could be extended to other non-charitable purposes which complied with the requirement for certainty of objects, was clearly answered in the negative both by the Court of Appeal in *Re Endacott* and by the Privy Council in *Leahy v. Attorney-General for New South Wales*. The reasoning adopted, that the lack of a *cestui que trust* to enforce such trusts put their execution outside the control of the courts, appears to be unimpeachable. That of course does not mean that the present position is entirely satisfactory. The present law permits a person to give his property to human beings, whether they are good or bad, to give it to charity, and even to set up trusts for the various anomalous purposes recognised by the law, such as for his dogs and cats or for the promotion of foxhunting. But as a general rule it seems that a person cannot give his property for a social experiment falling outside the confines of the law of charity if that experiment is defined in terms of purposes, no matter how certain those purposes may be[63] (this proposition of course assumes that it is only possible to construe the gift in terms of purposes; if it is possible instead to construe it as an outright gift to

---

[59] See *post*, p. 117.
[60] [1959] A.C. 457.
[61] *ibid.* at 478.
[62] *Re Lipinski's Will Trusts* [1976] Ch. 235, Oliver J. argued (at 246) that this was not intended as an exhaustive statement or to do more than indicate the broad division of trusts into those where there are ascertainable beneficiaries (whether for particular purposes or not) and trusts where there are none.
[63] O.R. Marshall (1953) 6 C.L.P. 151. See also, generally, on the subject: A. Kiralfy (1950) 14 Conv. (N.S.) 374; L. Sheridan (1953) 17 Conv. (N.S.) 46.

a named person or persons, with the purpose merely an expression of the motive for the gift, it will of course be valid[64]).

The qualification "as a general rule" has to be added because, according to the decision of Goff J. in *Re Denley's Trust Deed*,[65] there may in certain circumstances be a way out of this difficulty. He held that the basic rule laid down in *Morice v. Bishop of Durham* was confined to purpose trusts which were "abstract or impersonal"; consequently, he held that a trust, even though expressed as a purpose, which was directly or indirectly for the benefit of one or more ascertainable individuals was nevertheless valid, provided that all its terms satisfied the relevant requirements for certainty. In that case, the expressed purpose of the trust was the maintenance of a sports ground, primarily for the benefit of the employees of a company and secondarily for the benefit of such other persons as the trustees allowed to use it. No question of perpetuity arose since the duration of the trust was restricted in such a way that it could not possibly be void on that ground. Goff J. held the trust to be valid on the basis that it was an express private trust in favour of ascertainable human beneficiaries by whom it could *ex hypothesi* be enforced. Nevertheless, there must be some doubt as to whether this approach, however commendable it may be as an attempt to "liberalise" the law, is actually correct. This is because if a provision is framed as a *purpose* which, as a matter of construction, plainly seems to have been the position in *Re Denley's Trust Deed*, then, despite the fact that the provision is for the benefit of individuals, it is the purpose which is the dominant factor; consequently, if it is non-charitable, it should fail unless it can be brought within the recognised exceptions.

Nevertheless, *Re Denley's Trust Deed* was followed in *Re Lipinski's Will Trusts*,[66] where the testator left his residuary estate to trustees for an unincorporated recreational association, which was not charitable, for the purpose of constructing and improving buildings for that association. Oliver J. held that this was a valid purpose trust, principally because the beneficiaries, the members of the association, were ascertainable and so could enforce the purpose. As a matter of construction, *Re Lipinski's Will Trusts* may well be a stronger case than *Re Denley's Trust Deed* because of the fact that it was a gift to an unincorporated association and thus also able to be upheld on that basis,[67] something which was not the case in *Re Denley's Trust Deed*. The conclusion arrived at in *Re Denley's Trust Deed* was also accepted by Megarry V.-C. in *Re Northern Developments (Holdings)*.[68] Subsequently, however, in *Re Grant's Will Trusts*[69] Vinelott J. expressed the view that *Re Denley's Trust Deed* did not involve a purpose trust at all but rather a discretionary trust. This view is not really consistent either with the lengthy discussion of

---

[64] *Re Sanderson's Trust* (1857) 3 K. & J. 497 at 503; *Re Andrew's Trust* [1905] 2 Ch. 48; *Re Osoba* [1979] 1 W.L.R. 247.

[65] [1969] 1 Ch. 373.

[66] [1976] Ch. 235.

[67] It was held that it was valid as a gift in favour of an unincorporated association with a superadded discretion; see *post*, p. 120.

[68] (1978) unreported; see (1985) 101 L.Q.R. 280.

[69] [1980] 1 W.L.R. 360.

purpose trusts in *Re Denley's Trust Deed* or with the subsequent interpretation of that decision by Oliver J. and Megarry V.-C.; consequently, it
does not appear to be an acceptable explanation of that decision.

If the view expressed in *Re Grant's Will Trusts* is for this reason discounted,
the other three authorities, all first instance decisions, indicate that this type
of non-charitable purpose trust may be treated as a valid express private
trust for the incidental benefit of ascertainable beneficiaries, albeit for a
particular purpose. Such trusts may well, however, have to comply with the
rule against inalienability (discussed in a later part of this section) and so be
limited so that they can take effect only within the perpetuity period. A
distinction has, however, to be drawn between, on the one hand, purpose
trusts of this type which incidentally benefit persons who have no right to
call for the trust property and, on the other hand, trusts by virtue of which
particular persons are to be benefitted in a particular way. An example of the
latter was the trust in *Re Osoba*[70] "for the training of my daughter Abiola up
to university grade", which was construed as an absolute gift made for a
particular motive; such a trust automatically satisfies the beneficiary principle and does not have to comply with the rule against inalienability. It is also
important to emphasise that a valid power cannot be deduced from what is
intended to be a trust, a rule which applies just as much to non-charitable
purpose trusts as to any other trust[71] if a trust is intended, it cannot be
treated as a power.[72] That does not of course prevent the express creation of
powers for non-charitable purposes but such powers impose no obligations
on their donees to exercise them.

Finally, it must be emphasised that, despite the decision in *Re Denley's
Trust Deed*, it is nevertheless from a practical point of view inadvisable to
endeavour to provide expressly for the establishment of a non-charitable
purpose trust, other than one falling within the existing anomalous exceptions, in the hope that it may be declared valid for other reasons. The
simplest solution to the problem has always been and remains the formation
of a company to carry out the non-charitable purpose in question (the
permissible objects of companies are not subject to any of the restrictions
which apply to non-charitable trusts) and the subsequent transfer of the
relevant property to that company.[73]

2. The Anomalous Cases

As has already been mentioned, the situations in which non-charitable
purpose trusts have been upheld even though there has been no human
beneficiary capable of enforcing them have been said[74] to fall into the

---

[70] [1979] 1 W.L.R. 247. See also *Re Sanderson's Trust* (1857) 3 K. & J. 497, *per* Page-Wood V.-C. at 503 and *Re Andrew's Trust* [1905] 2 Ch. 48.
[71] *I.R.C. v. Broadway Cottages Trust* [1955] Ch. 20 at 36; *Re Endacott* [1960] Ch. 232 at 246. This principle is not affected by *McPhail v. Doulton* [1971] A.C. 424 (see *ante*, pp. 92–94).
[72] Compare Morris & Leach, *The Rule Against Perpetuities* (2nd ed.), p. 319.
[73] The Goodman Committee on Charity and Law and Voluntary Organisations (see *post*, p. 387) recommended that trusts for non-charitable purposes should be valid but no steps have been taken to enact this part of their proposals.
[74] *Re Endacott* [1960] Ch. 232; the Court of Appeal adopted the classification put forward in Morris & Leach, The *Rule against Perpetuities* (2nd ed.), p. 306.

following categories: trusts for the erection or maintenance of monuments or graves, trusts for the saying of masses in jurisdictions where such trusts are not regarded as charitable, trusts for the maintenance of particular animals, trusts for the benefit of unincorporated associations, and miscellaneous cases (a few further cases which do not fit into any of the other categories). It also seems that these exceptions will only be upheld if the trust in question is contained in a will. Indeed, it has also been said that the will must be drafted in such a way that any of the property not expended on the non-charitable purpose will fall into residue.[75] This is allegedly because in such circumstances an order can be made whereby the trustees undertake to carry out the non-charitable purpose with the residuary legatees being given leave to apply to the court if the trustees fail to do so; this of course makes the trust in question indirectly enforceable in that the trustees have a choice between carrying out the specified purpose and transferring the property to the residuary legatees. However, the residuary legatees or intestate successors can clearly be given such leave to apply even if the will is not drafted in this way; consequently, there seems no reason in principle why such a provision should be necessary or why the subject matter of the trust should not be the residue itself.[76]

The existence of these anomalous cases, particularly the miscellaneous cases, contrasts markedly with the willingness of the courts to strike down as capricious trusts for the management of property in a manner which confers no obvious benefit on anyone. Such a case was *Brown v. Burdett*[77] where a gift of a house on trust to block up its windows and doors for twenty years was held to be void. There is no possible justification for this difference in attitude; its explanation may be that the anomalous exceptions are regarded as "concessions to human weakness or sentiment".[78] The present state of the authorities really requires a review either by the House of Lords or by the legislature.

These non-charitable purpose trusts are subject to a further requirement, namely that the property subject to the trust must not be rendered inalienable.[79] This principle is one of the aspects of the rule against perpetuities, which will be considered in detail in a later chapter.[80] If at the time when the trust comes into effect there is any possibility that it is capable of continuing for longer than the appropriate perpetuity period, then the trust will be void. The testator may specify a perpetuity period consisting of one or more nominated lives in being plus 21 years or of any fixed period of years up to 21 years.[81] The nominated lives in question can be those of the persons related in some way to the trust or its purposes; alternatively, the testator can use what is known a "royal lives clause", specifying the perpetuity period by reference to the lives of the Royal Family—an example of such a clause is one specifying a period "ending at the expiration of 21 years from the death of the last survivor of all the lineal descendants of his late Majesty

---

[75] *Re Thompson* [1934] Ch. 342 at 344; *Re Astor's Settlement Trusts* [1952] Ch. 534 at 546.
[76] See *Re Endacott* [1960] Ch. 232 at 240.
[77] (1882) 21 Ch.D. 667.
[78] *Re Astor's Settlement Trusts* [1952] Ch. 534 at 547.
[79] *Carne v. Long* (1860) 2 De G.F. & J. 75 at 80.
[80] See *post*, p. 220.
[81] *Re Dean* (1899) 41 Ch.D. 552 at 557.

King George VI[82] who shall be living at the time" when the trust comes into effect. Only human lives can be specified[83]; otherwise it would be open to an eccentric settlor to tie up property indefinitely by settling it on trusts limited by reference to the lives of tortoises or other animals noted for their longevity. Alternatively, the testator may prefer to specify "such period as the law allows" in which case, assuming that there are no relevant lives, the perpetuity period will be 21 years. If no period is specified at all, the trust will be void unless it must necessarily determine before the end of the perpetuity period, which in most cases will mean within 21 years. It is thought that any non-charitable purpose trusts which are upheld in accordance with the decision in *Re Denley's Trust Deed*[84] must also comply with the rule against inalienability but this has not yet actually had to be decided since in *Re Denley's Trust Deed* the trust was expressly limited so that it could only take effect within the perpetuity period.

(A) Trusts for the Erection or Maintenance of Monuments or Graves
A trust for the erection of a particular monument or for the maintenance of a particular grave is not charitable but it has been held that such a trust may nevertheless be valid as a trust of imperfect obligation. Thus in *Trimmer v. Danby*[85] a legacy of £1,000 left by the painter Turner to his executors "to erect a monument to my memory in St Paul's Cathedral" was upheld. There is no requirement that the monument or tombstone be for the testator himself. In *Musset v. Bingle*[86] a somewhat bizarre gift for the erection of a monument to the testator's widow's first husband was also upheld. It does, however, seem that the monument must be of a funerary nature if it is to fall within the scope of this exception.[87] The question of perpetuity has not been raised in any of the cases involving the construction of monuments on the basis that it will inevitably be carried out as soon as is reasonably practicable after the testator's death and thus well within the perpetuity period. Perpetuity is, however, an issue in relation to trusts for the maintenance of monuments and graves. Thus in *Re Hooper*[88] a gift to trustees for the upkeep of graves and monuments "so long as they can legally do so" was held to be valid for 21 years but would clearly have been void for perpetuity if it had not been so restricted. Indeed in *Musset v. Bingle*[89] it had been agreed that a perpetual trust to maintain the monument which was to be erected was void for perpetuity. However, as will be seen in the next part of this section,[90] there

---

[82] The father of the present Queen. Consequently, the royal lives in question are those of HM Queen Elizabeth II, HRH Princess Margaret, and their descendants. It is also probably still possible to use King George V (the grandfather of the present Queen), although the number of his descendants is now very considerable. It is certainly unsafe to specify the descendants of any previous sovereign.
[83] *Re Kelly* [1932] I.R. 255.
[84] [1969] 1 Ch. 373.
[85] (1856) 25 L.J.Ch. 424.
[86] [1876] W.N. 171.
[87] See *Re Endacott* [1960] Ch. 232.
[88] [1932] 1 Ch. 38, following *Pirbright v. Salwey* [1896] W.N. 86 (a gift of consols for application "so long as law permitted" to keep up a burial enclosure was held valid for 21 years).
[89] [1876] W.N. 171.
[90] See *post*, p. 115.

are certain other methods whereby the maintenance of monuments and graves for longer periods can be achieved.

The courts made it clear in these authorities that the trustees could not be compelled to erect the monument or keep up the grave in question but that if they decided to do so they would not be prevented. On the other hand, if the trustees are unwilling to perform the trust, they will hold the trust property on resulting trust for the testator's estate; any surplus left after the purpose has been carried out will be held in the same way. The trust property will also "result" to the testator's estate on the determination of the period stipulated in the instrument for the duration of the trust or of the relevant perpetuity period, as the case may be.

(B) Trusts for the Saying of Masses
It was for a long time uncertain whether or not trusts for the saying of masses were charitable but this point was finally settled in *Re Hetherington*,[91] where such trusts were held to be charitable provided that the masses in question are open to the public. However, in the event that this condition is not satisfied in any individual case, as would be the case where the masses were to be celebrated either for the members of a cloistered and contemplative religious order and/or in a private chapel to which the public are not admitted,[92] the trust in question will clearly be valid as a non-charitable purpose trust provided that it complies with the rule against inalienability by being limited to take effect only within the perpetuity period.[93]

(C) Trusts for the Maintenance of Particular Animals
Gifts for the maintenance of animals in general are charitable.[94] However, gifts for the maintenance of one or more particular animals are not; such gifts can only take effect, if at all, as trusts of imperfect obligation. Thus in *Pettingall v. Pettingall*,[95] the testator bequeathed £50 a year to his executor to provide for the testator's favourite black mare. It was held that the executor could perform the testator's wishes and might keep the surplus for his own purposes. It was also indicated that if the executor failed to look after the mare the beneficiaries could apply to the court to reconsider the arrangement but that, subject to that possibility, the trust was to last for the animal's lifetime. Similarly, in *Re Dean*[96] there was a bequest of an annual sum for the maintenance of the testator's horses and hounds for a period of 50 years, if any of the horses and hounds should so long live. This was also held to be valid; the trustees were clearly at liberty to carry out the terms of the gift although the beneficiaries, being dumb, could not compel them to do so. *Re Dean* is an explicit authority—not all the early cases in this area of the law are particularly explicit—that a trust of imperfect obligation for the upkeep of a given animal may be valid notwithstanding the fact that by its nature it is not enforceable by the beneficiary. Few of the cases on animals deal adequately with the question of perpetuity. Judicial notice is sometimes

[91] [1990] Ch. 1.
[92] Trusts for such orders are not regarded as charitable; *Gilmour v. Coats* [1949] A.C. 426.
[93] *Bourne v. Keane* [1919] A.C. 815 at 874–875.
[94] See *post*, p. 405.
[95] (1842) 11 L.J.Ch. 176.
[96] (1889) 41 Ch.D. 552.

taken of the fact that the expected life of the animal in question is less than the 21 year period.[97] In the large majority of cases, the animals will inevitably survive the testator for a time much shorter than 21 years and it seems convenient and not at all improper that, if a period is not stipulated in the trust instrument, the trust should not fail if the contemplated duration of the life of the animal in question falls short of the 21 year period. However, this does not justify either of the cases mentioned above. Horses can certainly live for more than 21 years and so the decision in *Pettingall v. Pettingall* that the trust was to last for the animal's lifetime could undoubtedly have contravened the rule against inalienability, depending of course on how old the mare was at the time of the testator's death. Further, the fixed period of 50 years established in *Re Dean* certainly does not constitute one of the permissible perpetuity periods and the horses, if not the hounds, could certainly have survived for more than 21 years. The only correct and safe approach to follow with trusts of this kind is therefore to limit the duration of the trust by reference to nominated lives in being or alternatively to use some expression like "for such period as the law allows".

(D)   Trusts for the Benefit of Unincorporated Associations
The existence of this category has always been regarded as somewhat doubtful.[98] The view has been expressed in some quarters that some types of trusts for the benefit of unincorporated associations[99] depend for their validity on the existence of a further anomalous exception to the beneficiary principle. This was thought to be the case where such trusts were held to have been made by way of endowment (one of a number of ways in which gifts in favour of unincorporated associations can be construed); since such an endowment is likely to have been intended to be perpetual, the adoption of this construction will generally lead to the gift being held to be void for perpetuity.[1] But if a trust has been established which satisfies the rule against perpetuities (because, for example, it is held to have been intended to benefit only the existing members[2]), it will also have to satisfy the beneficiary principle. Prior to the decision in *Re Denley's Trust Deed*,[3] it was sometimes thought that such a trust could only do so by virtue of being a further anomalous exception to that principle. However, if the decision in *Re Denley's Trust Deed* is in fact correct, any need for the existence of this particular exception to the beneficiary principle will now have disappeared. Only if that decision is rejected, therefore, will this exception have any further role to play.

(E)   Miscellaneous Cases
From time to time anomalous cases have cropped up which do not fit into any of the other categories. Of these cases, the Court of Appeal in *Re*

---

[97] *Re Haines* (1925), *The Times*, November 7, 1952 (life of cat approximately 16 years) but this may be wrong—see Morris & Leach, *The Rule against Perpetuities* (2nd ed.), p. 323 and compare *Re Kelly* [1932] I.R. 255 at 260–261.

[98] Morris & Leach *op. cit.* in their classification comment that "this group is more doubtful".

[99] Discussed more fully *post*, p. 117.

[1] As in *Leahy v. Attorney-General for New South Wales* [1959] A.C. 457.

[2] As in *Re Drummond* [1914] 2 Ch. 90.

[3] [1969] 1 Ch. 393.

Endacott[4] referred only to *Re Catherall*,[5] where Roxburgh J. had upheld a gift to a vicar and churchwardens for a suitable memorial to the testator's parents and sisters whether or not it was charitable. No doubt was cast on this decision in *Re Endacott* although Lord Evershed M.R. said that the decision could in any event be justified on the grounds that the purposes in question were charitable.[6] However, this certainly cannot be said of the best known of these miscellaneous cases, *Re Thompson*,[7] which concerned a gift of £1,000 to be applied towards the promotion and furtherance of fox-hunting. The residuary legatee, Trinity Hall Cambridge, wished to carry out the testator's wishes in so far as this was legally possible but, as a charity, felt obliged to object to the enforcement of this trust. The gift, which complied with the rule against inalienability, was nevertheless upheld by analogy with *Pettingall v. Pettingall*.[8] Neither this decision nor the other authorities in which trusts of this type have been upheld[9] can be supported. Nor can the apparent preparedness of the courts to allow in principle a number of further trusts of this type which in the event were held void on the grounds of perpetuity.[10] None of these authorities is likely to be followed; in this respect the miscellaneous cases are distinct from those in the other categories, which will be applied but not extended.[11]

3. *Maintenance of Monuments and Tombs for Longer than the Perpetuity Period*

It has already been seen that a trust for the maintenance of monuments and graves will be valid as a trust of imperfect obligation if its duration is limited to the perpetuity period. It may, however, be possible for a testator to ensure that a trust of perpetual duration for this purpose is valid.[12] However, the ways in which this may be achieved are somewhat complex and heavy-handed.

The first possibility is to set up a trust for the maintenance of the whole of the churchyard containing the monument or tomb in question. This is a

---

[4] [1960] Ch. 232.

[5] (June 3, 1959) unreported.

[6] [1960] Ch. 232 at 249.

[7] [1934] Ch. 342.

[8] (1842) 11 L.J.Ch. 176.

[9] *Re Catherall* (June 3, 1959) Unreported but referred to in *Re Endacott* [1960] Ch. 232 at 248–249, (discussed *ante*, p. 107); *Re Gibbons* [1917] 1 I.R. 448, (a trust for property to be disposed of "to [the testator's] best spiritual advantage as conscience and sense of duty may direct", which was upheld where the executors were Roman Catholic priests and were prepared to perform the trust by constructing a church and saying masses in it for the testator's soul).

[10] *Re Nottage* [1895] 2 Ch. 649 (trust to endow an annual cup for yacht racing); *Re Gassiott* (1901) 70 L.J.Ch. 242 (trust to keep a portrait in repair); *Re Lawlor* [1934] V.L.R. 22 (Supreme Court of Victoria, affirmed by the High Court of Australia *sub nom. Roman Catholic Archbishop of Melbourne v. Lawlor* (1934) 51 C.L.R. 1) (trust to found a Catholic newspaper).

[11] *Re Endacott* [1960] Ch. 232 at 250–251, *per* Harman L.J.

[12] It may also be possible to take advantage of Parish Councils and Burial Authorities (Miscellaneous Provisions) Act 1970, s.1, which authorises local authorities and burial authorities to make an agreement to maintain graves and so forth for a period not exceeding 99 years. The text is, however, only concerned with the use of trust machinery for this purpose.

valid charitable trust[13] and so will succeed in bringing about the maintenance of the monument or tomb for ever.

The second possibility is to make a gift to one charity with a gift over to another if the monument or tomb is not kept in repair. This will be successful provided that a trust is actually imposed on the first charity for the upkeep of the monument or tomb. In *Re Tyler*[14] a sum of stock was given to the trustees of the London Missionary Society with a gift over to the Blue Coat School if the Society failed to keep a tomb in repair. Since both the donees were charitable bodies the perpetuity rule did not apply to them[15] but the question still remained whether the condition in question (that is to say, for the maintenance of the tomb) contravened the rule. It was held by the Court of Appeal that, since the testator had not actually required the Society to maintain the tomb, the condition was valid. On the other hand, in *Re Dalzeil*[16] the testator gave to the governors of St. Bartholomew's Hospital the sum of £20,000 "upon and subject to the condition" that they should use the income so far as necessary for the upkeep of a certain mausoleum; if they failed to carry out this purpose, there was a gift over to such other charities as the trustees might select on the same conditions. In this case, the condition, on its true construction, amounted to a positive direction that the income was to be applied in the first instance to the maintenance of the mausoleum; it did not, as in *Re Tyler*, simply impose a moral obligation. Cohen J. accordingly held that the trust failed.

The third possibility, a highly controversial method which probably now no longer works, was to rely on the decision in *Re Chardon*.[17] The testator gave his trustees £200 to invest and to pay the income to a cemetery company "during such period as they shall continue to maintain and keep the graves of my great grandfather and Priscilla Navone in good order and condition". The will further provided that if the graves were not maintained the income was to fall into residue. Romer J. held this gift to be valid. Very great difficulty has been found in ascertaining the meaning of this case; perhaps the best view, even though it does not emerge at all clearly from the judgment, is that the decision could be justified at the time when it was made on the grounds that an interest of the type given to the cemetery company, a determinable interest capable of coming to an end at any time in the future, was not then subject to the rule against perpetuities. *Re Chardon* was followed by Wynn-Parry J. on virtually identical facts in *Re Chambers Will Trusts*[18] but was distinguished by the same judge in *Re Wightwick's Will Trusts*.[19] The distinction drawn in the latter case was that the gift there contained a trust of income for an indefinite period for a non-charitable purpose and was, therefore, void as tending to a perpetuity, whereas in *Re Chardon* there was not actually a trust. In view of the uncertain state of the law, it was extremely risky to rely on *Re Chardon*[20] even before the passing

---

[13] *Re Pardoe* [1906] 2 Ch. 184.
[14] [1891] 3 Ch. 252.
[15] See *post*, p. 380.
[16] [1943] Ch. 277.
[17] [1928] Ch. 464.
[18] [1950] Ch. 267.
[19] [1950] Ch. 260.
[20] See generally W. O. Hart: (1937) 53 L.Q.R. 24; M. J. Albery: (1938) 54 L.Q.R. 258.

of the Perpetuities and Accumulations Act 1964. The enactment of this
legislation appears to have rendered this discussion academic by providing
that a determinable interest is now subject to the perpetuity rule[21] in that the
determining event must now take place no later than the end of the perpetuity period. While this provision would not render the gift void *ab initio*,
any disposition of the income, whether express or implied, to take effect on
the occurrence of the determining event would become void at the end of
the perpetuity period. Consequently, by maintaining the graves until the
end of the perpetuity period, the cemetery company would then acquire an
absolute interest in the fund without any further obligations.[22]

4. *Gifts for the Benefit of Unincorporated Associations*

An unincorporated association has been defined as "two or more persons
bound together for one or more common purposes, not being business
purposes, by mutual undertakings each having mutual duties and obligations, in an organisation which has rules which identify in whom control of
it and its funds rests and on what terms and which can be joined or left at
will".[23] Because an unincorporated association is not a legal person, its
property necessarily has to be vested in some or all of its members as
trustees. Where its purposes are charitable, such trusts do not give rise to
any difficulties. Charitable trusts have to comply neither with the requirement of certainty of objects, nor with the beneficiary principle, nor with the
rule against perpetuities. All these requirements have to be satisfied, however, when the purposes of an unincorporated association are not charitable,
giving rise to very considerable theoretical difficulties.

It was formerly thought that a gift of property to a non-charitable unincorporated association could only be construed in two possible ways. Both
these constructions are still possible but have become uncommon; virtually
all such gifts are now construed in accordance with a third possible construction enunciated by Cross J. in *Neville Estates v. Madden*[24] and considerably developed in subsequent decisions.

The first possibility was and is that the gift may be made to the members
of the association at the date in question. Such a gift may be outright, in that
title to the property in question passes immediately to the members as
tenants in common or joint tenants, or may vest the property in trustees for
the members as beneficial tenants in common or joint tenants. Either way, if
they are tenants in common they can take their share while, if they are joint
tenants, any member can sever his share and then claim it, whether or not

---

[21] Perpetuities and Accumulations Act 1964, s.12.
[22] See Underhill & Hayton, *Law of Trusts and Trustees* (15th ed., 1995), pp. 98–100.
[23] *Conservative and Unionist Central Office v. Burrell* [1982] 1 W.L.R. 522, *per* Lawton L.J. at 525.
    The case was concerned with the meaning of "unincorporated association" for the purposes
    of taxation legislation but this definition seems to be of general application. Underhill &
    Hayton, *Law of Trusts & Trustees* (15th ed., 1995), p. 102 questions whether it is in fact
    necessary that the association should be able to be joined and left at will on the basis that the
    existence of rules restricting membership should not negative the existence of an unin-
    corporated association.
[24] [1962] Ch. 832.

he remains a member. Where such a trust exists, its objects must be sufficiently certain but it will clearly comply with the beneficiary principle and
will not offend the rule against perpetuities.[25] However, this construction is
not without theoretical difficulties; any member who subsequently leaves
will retain his share unless he assigns it to the other members with the
appropriate formalities,[26] no member who subsequently joins will acquire
any interest in the property in question and, where the members are tenants
in common, the share of any member who dies will devolve according to his
will or intestacy. In practice, these theoretical difficulties have generally been
ignored.

The second possibility was and is that the gift is made by way of endowment for the unincorporated association. Such a gift necessarily has to take
effect by way of trust. Any such endowment is likely to have been intended
to be perpetual; consequently, the adoption of this construction will generally lead to the gift being held to be void for perpetuity.[27] However, if a
trust has been established which satisfies the rule against perpetuities, it will
undoubtedly be valid provided that its objects are sufficiently certain; such
a trust will clearly satisfy the beneficiary principle by virtue of the decision
in Re Denley's Trust Deed[28] (prior to that decision, it was sometimes thought
that such trusts constituted one of the anomalous exceptions to the beneficiary principle[29]). Some trusts have been held to satisfy the rule against
perpetuities on the grounds that they were intended to benefit only the
existing members of the unincorporated association.[30] In principle, it must
also be possible to satisfy the rule against perpetuities by expressly providing that the property is to be held on trust for the benefit of the unincorporated association until the end of the perpetuity period and then be
held for some ascertained person (such as the estate of the donor) or some
charitable purpose.

Apart from such exceptional cases, however, prior to the decision in
Neville Estates v. Madden gifts to unincorporated associations were in practice
only valid if the first possible construction was adopted; consequently, there
was a presumption in favour of this construction. Where there was a gift
"for the general purposes of the association", although those words
appeared to seek to impose a perpetual trust which would consequently be
void, they could be disregarded by the court as having virtually no meaning
so as to enable the first construction to be adopted. This was not, however,

---

[25] It is not particularly likely that a trust will be utilised if the intention of the donor is really
only to benefit the existing members. The intention to exclude future members has been far
from clear in some of the decided cases such as Re Drummond [1914] 2 Ch. 90; Re Prevost
[1930] 2 Ch. 383 and Re Turkington [1937] 4 All E.R. 501; such cases would today probably be
regarded as falling within the more recently developed third possible construction.
[26] Where a trust exists, writing will be required by virtue of Law of Property Act 1925,
s.53(1)(c).
[27] Re Macaulay's Estate (1933) [1943] Ch. 435; Leahy v. Att.-Gen. for New South Wales [1959] A.C.
457.
[28] [1969] 1 Ch. 393.
[29] See ante, p. 114.
[30] Re Drummond [1914] 2 Ch. 90 was a case of this kind. These trusts might equally well have
been classified as falling within the first possible construction and, like such trusts, would
today probably be regarded as falling within the third possible construction.

always possible. In *Leahy v. Attorney-General for New South Wales*[31] a ranch was left "upon trust for such order of nuns of the Catholic Church or the Christian Brothers as my executors and trustees shall select". This gift was prima facie valid as a gift to the individual members of the order chosen. However, the Privy Council held that the presumption was rebutted because of the improbability of a beneficial gift to the members of the order who happened to be alive at the date of the death of the testator and because of the nature of the property. As an intended endowment for the benefit of the order as a continuing society, the trust would therefore have been void for perpetuity but for a saving provision in a New South Wales statute.

The absence of any effective method of making gifts for the present and future members of unincorporated associations was hardly satisfactory and was eventually remedied by the enunciation in *Neville Estates v. Madden*[32] of a third possible construction. This is that there may be "a gift to the existing members not as joint tenants, but subject to their respective contractual rights and liabilities towards one another as members of the association. In such a case a member cannot sever his share. It will accrue to the other members on his death or resignation, even though such members include persons who became members after the gift took effect. If this is the effect of the gift, it will not now be open to objection on the score of perpetuity or uncertainty unless there is something in its terms or circumstances or in the rules of the association which precludes the members at any given time from dividing the subject of the gift between them on the footing that they are solely entitled to it in equity".[33] Thus the members of an unincorporated association have the possibility of enjoying rights in property in a new manner distinct from the traditional joint tenancy and tenancy in common (whether this is, strictly speaking, a form of co-ownership is not entirely clear). Where a gift to an unincorporated association is construed in this way, the property in question is held by some or all of the individual members (or, of course, by independent trustees) on trust to be applied in accordance with the contract between the members contained in the rules of the association. This apparently resolves the technical difficulties caused by the adoption of the first possible construction in that any member who leaves or dies will lose his share in the property of the association without any need for any formal disposition and any new member of the association will be able to enjoy the benefit of its property without any need for any transfer thereof (precisely how the statutory formal requirements of the Law of Property Act 1925 and the Wills Act 1837 are actually satisfied has never been made entirely clear; signed acceptance by each member of rules drafted in an appropriate form would presumably satisfy section 53(1)(c) of the Law of Property Act 1925 but certainly would not satisfy the Wills Act 1837—the answer may be that by entering into the contract contained in the rules each member estops himself (and, after his death, his personal representatives) from relying on the absence of the statutory formalities to claim his proportion of the property of the association). The objects of trusts of this type must

---

[31] [1959] A.C. 457.
[32] [1962] Ch. 832.
[33] *ibid.* at 849, *per* Cross J.

of course be sufficiently certain[34] but such trusts will clearly satisfy the beneficiary principle and will satisfy the rule against perpetuities provided that the members are entitled under the rules (if necessary as a result of exercising a power in the rules to change them) to bring the association to an end and to divide its property between themselves.

This construction has been adopted and developed on a number of occasions. In *Re Recher's Will Trusts*,[35] the testatrix left part of her residuary estate to a specified "Anti-Vivisection Society" (a non-charitable unincorporated association). Had the society not ceased to exist before her death, the gift would have been upheld as a non-charitable purpose trust. Brightman J. stated that, where the subscriptions of the members of an unincorporated association are held as an accretion to its funds to be applied in accordance with its rules, any gifts or legacies to the association will, in the absence of any words purporting to impose a trust, be held on the same basis. The rules of the association could be changed by the unanimous agreement of the members; therefore, it was irrelevant that it existed for the promotion of some purpose rather than for the benefit of the members themselves, since they could nevertheless vote to change the rules in order to abandon this purpose and to divide the assets between themselves. *Re Lipinski's Will Trusts*[36] concerned a gift to an unincorporated association "in memory of my late wife to be used solely in the work of constructing the new buildings for the association and/or improvement to the said buildings". The purpose specified was within the powers of the association and, despite the fact that the gift was to be used "solely" for this purpose, Oliver J. held that the members would not thereby be prevented from abandoning the specified purpose and instead dividing the assets between themselves. Consequently, the gift was valid as a non-charitable purpose trust for the benefit of the members of the association. In *News Group Newspapers v. SOGAT 82*[37] the local branches of the union SOGAT 82 were held to be unincorporated associations capable of seceding from the union and dissolving themselves; consequently, a sequestration order issued against the union was held not to apply to funds held by the local branches. Finally, in *Universe Tankships Inc. of Morovia v. International Transport Workers Federation*,[38] the House of Lords held that a payment by shipowners into the Federation fund took effect as an accretion to that fund by way of outright gift rather than a contribution on trust (which would have been void); in the Court of Appeal,[39] Megaw L.J. emphasised that, even if there is no provision for the amendment of the rules of an association, they can nevertheless be "altered at will by the unanimous agreement of the contracting parties". The combined effect of these decisions means that there is now little chance of a gift of this type being void for perpetuity.

There is now a strong presumption that an unincorporated association holds its property in this way; gifts to unincorporated associations will now

---

[34] The trusts in question will almost inevitably be discretionary trusts and so will be governed by *McPhail v. Doulton* [1971] A.C. 424.

[35] [1972] Ch. 526.

[36] [1976] Ch. 235.

[37] [1986] I.C.R. 716.

[38] [1983] 1 A.C. 366.

[39] [1981] I.C.R. 129 at 159.

not normally be construed either as gifts to the members[40] or as gifts for the purposes of endowment. However, this third possible construction is not all-embracing. It can only be applied where there is a set of rules to provide the necessary contract between the members. This was emphasised by Lawton L.J. in *Conservative and Unionist Central Office v. Burrell*.[41] No such contract existed between the members of the religious orders in *Leahy v. Attorney-General for New South Wales*[42]; consequently, this construction could not have been adopted in that case so that the gift would clearly still be held to be an intended endowment and, but for statute, void for perpetuity. Further, the inability of the members to divide the assets between themselves will also prevent this construction from being adopted. In *Re Grant's Will Trusts*,[43] Vinelott J. held that a gift to "the Labour Party Property Committee for the benefit of the Chertsey Headquarters of the Chertsey and Walton Constituency Labour Party" could not be construed as a gift to the members of the Constituency Party. They did not have the power to alter their rules, which were under the control of the National Labour Party. Although this did not of itself give rise to any problems of perpetuity (because the rules provided, in the last resort, for a resulting trust for the original subscribers), the members were clearly unable to dispose of the property among themselves.[44] Vinelott J. held that, consequently and in any event, the gift amounted to a trust for the purposes specified and not, as in *Re Lipinski's Will Trusts*,[45] a gift for the members of the Constituency Party for those purposes and for this reason was void for perpetuity. It has been suggested that the requirement that the members should be able to divide the property between themselves is unnecessary provided that they have the right "to ensure that the funds are used to pay for general expenses benefitting them as members".[46] However, the requirement clearly exists at present.

It should be noted that the way in which a gift to an unincorporated association is construed can have some effect on what happens to the assets of the association in the event of its dissolution. The general rule, clearly established in *Re Bucks Constabulary Fund Friendly Society (No.2)*[47] is that the assets should be divided equally between the existing members at the time of its dissolution (the only exception to this rule is where the association has become moribund in that all or all but one of the members have resigned or died, in which case the assets go to the Crown as *bona vacantia*). Gifts to the association which, in accordance with *Re Recher's Will Trusts*,[48] have become part of the general assets of the association will clearly be treated in the same

---

[40] *Re Grant's Will Trusts* [1980] 1 W.L.R. 360 at 365.
[41] [1982] 1 W.L.R. 522 at 525.
[42] [1959] A.C. 457.
[43] [1980] 1 W.L.R. 360.
[44] The National Labour Party was entitled to alter the rules so as to require the property to be transferred to itself.
[45] [1976] Ch. 235.
[46] Underhill & Hayton, *Law of Trusts and Trustees* (15th ed., 1995), pp. 106–107.
[47] [1979] 1 W.L.R. 936. This view expressed by Walton J. in this case is inconsistent with but generally regarded as preferable to the view expressed by Goff J. in *Re West Sussex Constabulary's Benevolent Fund Trusts* [1971] Ch. 1. It is also inconsistent with the more recent decision of Scott J. in *Davis v. Richards & Wallington Industries* [1990] 1 W.L.R. 1511. These cases are discussed *post*, p. 257.
[48] [1972] Ch. 526.

way. However, in the unlikely event that a gift to the association has taken effect as a valid trust by way of endowment, such a trust will necessarily be limited to take effect only within the perpetuity period and will therefore inevitably contain some provision as to what is to happen to the property thereafter; in such circumstances, this endowment property will presumably devolve in accordance with this provision in the event of the dissolution of the association.

Finally, where a gift is made to bodies which do not satisfy the definition of an unincorporated association because of the absence of the necessary mutual obligations contained in the rules, the gift will take effect by way of mandate or agency. In *Conservative and Unionist Central Office v. Burrell*,[49] where the Court of Appeal held that the Conservative Party was not an unincorporated association for the purposes of taxation legislation because of the absence of any contractual link between a contributor of funds and their recipient, Brightman L.J. characterised the recipient of the funds as the agent of the contributor to deal with the funds in accordance with the purpose or mandate for which the contribution was made. He said this[50]:

"So far as the money is used within the scope of the mandate, the recipient discharges himself *vis-à-vis* the contributor. The contributor can at any time demand the return of his money so far as not spent, unless the mandate is irrevocable, as it might be or become in certain circumstances. But once the money is spent, the contributor can demand nothing back, only an account of the manner of expenditure. No trust arises, except the fiduciary relationship inherent in the relationship of principal and agent. If, however, the recipient were to apply the money for some purpose outside the scope of the mandate, clearly the recipient would not be discharged. The recipient could be restrained, like any other agent, from a threatened misapplication of the money entrusted to him, and like any other agent could be required to replace any money misapplied."

This analysis is not without difficulties. Precisely who is the beneficial owner of the money until it is spent? Presumably the contributor unless and until the mandate becomes irrevocable by, for example, the money being mixed in the larger fund administered by the recipient. What happens if the mandate thereafter cannot be carried out or is carried out leaving a surplus? At first instance[51] Vinelott J. took the view that in such circumstances there would be an implied obligation to return the fund to the subscribers in proportion to their original contributions (anonymous gifts and contributions to raffles would devolve as *bona vacantia*). Do the rights of the contributor survive a change in the identity of the person administering the fund? And, finally, how can testamentary gifts be brought within the framework of mandate or agency when "no agency could be set up at the moment of death between a testator and his chosen agent"?[52] Whatever the answers to these

---

[49] [1982] 1 W.L.R. 522.
[50] *ibid.* at 529.
[51] [1980] 3 All E.R. 42 at 63–64.
[52] [1982] 1 W.L.R. 522 at 530. Brightman L.J. thought that the answer to this problem was not difficult to find but no one else has yet succeeded in finding it (see P. St J. Smart [1987] Conv. 415).

questions, it is clear that there are considerable differences between the mandate or agency analysis and the treatment of gifts to unincorporated associations. It has been suggested that it might be appropriate for the mandate or agency theory to be extended to gifts to unincorporated associations which, according to the rules which have already been discussed, are void.[53] Whether the theory is extended in this, or indeed in any other, way obviously remains to be seen.

---

[53] See P. Creighton [1983] Conv. 15.

CHAPTER 5

THE CONSTITUTION OF A TRUST

I. INTRODUCTION

AN express trust is completely constituted either by an effective transfer of the trust property to trustees or by an effective declaration of trust. The implications of this principle were clearly brought out by Turner L.J. in his classic judgment in *Milroy v. Lord*[1] when he said:

"In order to render a voluntary settlement valid and effectual, the settlor must have done everything which according to the nature of the property comprised in the settlement was necessary to be done in order to render the settlement binding upon him. He may, of course, do this by actually transferring the property to the persons for whom he intends to provide and the provision will then be effectual and it will be equally effectual if he transfers the property to a trustee for the purposes of the settlement, or declares that he himself holds it on trust for those purposes and if the property is personal, the trust may, as I apprehend, be declared either in writing or parol but, in order to render the settlement binding, one or other of these modes must, as I understand the law of this court, be resorted to, for there is no equity in this court to perfect an imperfect gift."

The latter part of this passage emphasises the crucial difference between a completely constituted trust and an incompletely constituted trust. Only when a trust is completely constituted is it binding on the settlor; in other words, only in such circumstances is a trust enforceable by the beneficiaries, whose equitable proprietary interest in the trust property will then be binding not only upon the settlor but also against any third party into whose hands the trust property may come other than a bona fide purchaser of a legal interest therein for value without notice. Trusts which are completely constituted are divided into executed and executory trusts; an executed trust arises when the settlor has defined in the trust instrument precisely what interests are to be taken by the beneficiaries, whereas an executory trust arises where the instrument or declaration requires the subsequent execution of a further instrument whose terms it does not itself define precisely.

When, on the other hand, a trust has not been completely constituted, there is in effect no trust enforceable by the beneficiaries, who therefore have no equitable proprietary interest whatever. Their position is often illustrated by reference to equitable maxims, a recourse which is at best unhelpful and

---

[1] (1862) 4 De G.F. & J. 264 at 274.

at worst potentially confusing. The straightforward proposition that if the settlor has failed to constitute the trust completely equity will not do so for him is often expressed by reference to the maxim that "equity will not perfect an imperfect gift", a maxim which is somewhat imprecise because of the number of exceptions to the basic rule which equity has permitted. In such circumstances, the incompletely constituted trust can only be enforced under the law of contract; the rights of the beneficiaries depend on the existence of a binding contract enforceable by them or on their behalf. In the absence of such a contract, they have no rights whatsoever and, in accordance with the maxim that "equity will not assist a volunteer", they are often described as volunteers; this maxim is positively confusing due to the failure of equity clearly to define precisely who is regarded as a volunteer for this purpose.

This chapter therefore involves the consideration of three questions: first, the circumstances in which a trust will be held to be completely constituted; secondly, the distinction between executed and executory trusts; and, thirdly, the circumstances in which, where a trust is incompletely constituted, the beneficiaries will have a contractual remedy.

II. When Will a Trust Be Completely Constituted?

1. By Transfer of the Trust Property To Trustees

(A) Legal Interests

If the subject matter of the proposed trust is a legal estate or interest, the transfer of the trust property must be effective to vest such estate in the trustees. Consequently the settlor must comply with all the formalities required for a complete transfer of the property in order to give the trustees full legal title thereto. Exactly the same rule applies where the transfer is made with the intention of making a gift; the donor must comply with all the formalities required for a complete transfer of the property in order to give the donee may have full legal title thereto. So if the subject matter of the trust or gift is land, a deed is necessary[2] followed, in the case of registered land, by registration of the transfer on the Land Register[3]; if it is a copyright, then writing is necessary[4]; if it is a bill of exchange or other negotiable instrument, then whether it is payable to the bearer or to the holder, delivery and the appropriate form of indorsement are necessary[5]; if it is shares in a company, the correct form of transfer is necessary followed, in the case of all shares other than bearer shares,[6] by registration of the transfer in the Share Register of the company in question[7]; if it is the benefit of a right of action,

---

[2] Law of Property Act 1925, s.52.
[3] Land Registration Act 1925, s.19.
[4] Copyright Act 1956, s.5(2).
[5] See *Antrobus v. Smith* (1806) 12 Ves. 39; *Jones v. Lock* (1865) 1 Ch. App. 25.
[6] The rights attached to bearer shares vest in whoever has physical possession of the share certificates.
[7] *Milroy v. Lord* (1862) 4 De G.F. & J. 264, see also *post*, p. 127. The relevant Act is the Stock Transfer Act 1963, s.1.

writing is necessary, followed by notice in writing to the other party[8]; and, finally, if it is a chattel, either a deed of gift[9] or an intention to give together with a delivery of possession is necessary, although any such personal delivery must be effectual.[10]

The requirement that the full legal title be transferred to the trustees is illustrated by a number of decisions involving the transfer of shares. In *Milroy v. Lord*[11] itself, the intending settlor had covenanted to transfer bank shares to the defendant on trust for the plaintiff. The defendant already had a general power to transfer the shares into his own name at any time but neither he nor the settlor actually did so prior to the settlor's death, which had the effect of revoking the power of attorney. Since neither the settlor nor the defendant was any longer in a position to make the necessary transfer, the shares therefore remained the settlor's property; consequently, they formed part of his residuary estate and could not successfully be claimed by the plaintiff. Similarly, in *Re Fry*[12] the intending settlor, who was domiciled in the United States of America, executed transfers of shares in a limited company, partly by way of gift to his son and partly to a trust. The company were unable to register the transfers because the consent of the Treasury had not been obtained under the Defence Regulations then operative. The forms required for obtaining this consent were sent to the settlor, who signed and returned them but died before the consent was given. Romer J. held that the trust had not been completely constituted prior to the settlor's death; consequently the shares did not pass either to the son or to the trust but, as in *Milroy v. Lord* formed part of the settlor's residuary estate. In order to perfect the transaction it would apparently have been necessary for the donor to have effected confirmatory transfers after the consent had been given.[13]

These two decisions establish that, for so long as something remains to be done by a settlor in order to render a voluntary transfer effective, that transfer will remain abortive.[14] However, if a settlor has done everything within his power in order to render a transfer effectual but something has yet to be done by a third party, the transfer will be immediately valid in equity; consequently, although it will remain ineffective to pass the legal title unless and until the third party does whatever has to be done by him, the transferor will in the meantime hold the subject matter of the transfer on the trusts of the settlement. This was established by the decision of the Court of

---

[8] Law of Property Act 1925, s.136.

[9] *Jaffa v. Taylor Gallery* (1990), *The Times*, March 21, 1990, where a trust of a painting was held to have been completely constituted without physical delivery to the trustees, one of whom was abroad, on the grounds that the formal declaration of trust contained in the deed transferred title to the painting to the trustees.

[10] See *Re Cole* [1964] Ch. 175, which concerned an alleged delivery of furniture by a husband to his wife when the two were living together in a common establishment. The Court of Appeal held that this did not unequivocally establish either a change in possession or a delivery of the furniture; accordingly there was no effected or perfected gift to her, the court rejecting the contention that a perfect gift of chattels can be constituted simply by showing them to the donee and speaking the appropriate words of gift.

[11] (1862) 4 De G.F. & J. 264. The classic statement of the law made by Turner L.J. at 274 is set out *ante*, p. 124 and *post*, p. 130.

[12] [1946] Ch. 312.

[13] *ibid.* at 316.

[14] See also *Letts v. I.R.C.* [1951] 1 W.L.R. 201, which concerned a direction by a father to a company to allot shares direct to his children.

Appeal in *Re Rose*[15] and as a result is known as the Rule in *Re Rose*; it will be considered in detail later in this section.[16]

It is, however, questionable how far it is possible to reconcile the authorities already discussed with the decision in *Re Vandervell's Trusts (No.2)*,[17] whose facts have already been considered. Lord Denning M.R., as an alternative ground for his decision that the shares in the products company were held on trust for the children's settlement, was of the opinion[18] that Vandervell had made a perfect gift to the trust company of the dividends on the shares "so far as they were handed over or treated by him as belonging to the trust company for the benefit of the children". In reaching this conclusion, his Lordship purported to follow *Milroy v. Lord*[19] itself. It has already been seen that an attempt to create a trust of bank shares was held to have been ineffective because legal title to the shares had never been vested in the intended trust and so the shares finished up in the hands of the settlor's residuary legatees. However, during the settlor's lifetime the dividends payable on the shares had been paid by the bank to the intended trustee by virtue of the power of attorney which he held; he had paid these dividends on to the beneficiary who had in turn used them to purchase other shares in a company. It was held that the settlor should be treated as having made a gift of the dividends to the beneficiary; his residuary legatees therefore had no claim to the shares which had been purchased with the dividends. It is not easy to see how this decision can justify the conclusion reached by Lord Denning M.R. in *Re Vandervell's Trusts (No.2)*. The settlor in *Milroy v. Lord* had given the intended trustee a power of attorney to collect the dividends and so must inevitably have intended them to be held for the beneficiary, whereas Vandervell had not even been aware that he had still retained an equitable interest in the option relating to the shares of his products company at the time when he had made the supposedly perfect gift of the dividends to the trust company; the two decisions thus seem readily distinguishable.

(B) Equitable Interests

The foregoing cases are illustrations of the important principle that if the subject matter of the trust or gift is a legal interest the transferor must do everything which has to be done by him in order to vest the legal title to the property in the trustee or donee. The same principle applies to the transfer of an equitable interest. It is not, of course, necessary for the transferor to procure a conveyance of the legal interest (which will be held by the trustees); all that is necessary is that he should make a perfect assignment of his interest, which in this case will be necessarily and universally required to be in writing by virtue of section 53(1)(c) of the Law of Property Act

---

[15] [1952] Ch. 499. The Court of Appeal applied and followed an earlier first instance decision, coincidentally also bearing the name *Re Rose* [1949] 1 Ch. 78.

[16] See *post*, p. 131.

[17] [1974] Ch. 269. See *ante*, pp. 56–59.

[18] *ibid.* at 321.

[19] (1862) 4 De G.F. & J. 264.

1925.[20] This assignment will, where a trust is being constituted, be followed by a direction to the trustees to hold it for the future upon trust for the assignee.[21] This is as much as the transferor of an equitable interest is able to do. However, the fact that this at least must be done is shown by the decision of the Court of Appeal in *Re McArdle*.[22] In this case, some siblings were entitled under the will of their father to a house after the death of their mother, who lived in the house with one brother and his wife. After the wife had effected various improvements to the house, all the siblings signed a document addressed to her, stating that "in consideration of your carrying out certain alterations to the property we hereby agree that the executors shall repay to you from the estate when distributed the sum of £488" in settlement of the amount spent on improvements. The court held, in effect, that this document was neither one thing nor the other. If it was intended to create a contract, the contract lacked consideration since the only possible consideration was past. If, on the other hand, it was an attempted gift, that gift was imperfect because the donors had not done everything within their power to make the gift complete; it was still necessary for them to authorise the executors to make the necessary payment and unless and until they did so the gift remained ineffectual.

2. *By Declaration of Trust*

By far the most common method of completely constituting a trust is for the settlor to transfer the trust property to trustees in the manner just described. However, it is equally effectual for a settlor to make a declaration of trust that he is henceforth a trustee of the property in question for the intended beneficiaries. Any words which clearly express the intention to create a present and irrevocable trust will give rise to the creation of a completely constituted trust—it is not necessary for an effective declaration of trust that the settlor should say in terms "I hereby declare myself to be a trustee". That does not alter the fact that the necessary intention must be satisfactorily shown. In *Jones v. Lock*[23] a father put a cheque into the hands of his infant son, saying: "Look you here, I give this to baby; it is for himself". He then took back the cheque and put it away but subsequently reiterated his intention of giving the amount of the cheque to his son. Shortly afterwards he died and the cheque was found among his effects. Lord Cranworth L.C. held that there was neither an effective transfer by way of gift nor a valid declaration of trust. It was quite impossible to regard the somewhat theatrical exercise enacted by the father as a delivery of the moneys represented by the cheque. To effect a perfect transfer, he should have paid the cheque into a bank account opened either in the name of his son or in the name of trustees on behalf of his son. Nor had he made a valid declaration of trust since no inference that he had made himself a trustee could be deduced from

---

[20] See *Kekewich v. Manning* (1851) De G.M. & G. 176 (assignment of an equitable reversionary interest in shares); *Gilbert v. Overton* (1864) 2 H. & M. 110 (assignment of an agreement for lease); and *ante*, pp. 50–51.
[21] See *Grey v. I.R.C.* [1960] A.C. 1 (direction to trustees to hold on trust may take effect as an assignment), discussed *ante*, p. 52.
[22] [1951] Ch. 669.
[23] (1865) 1 Ch. App. 25.

his words and actions. In all such cases, it is a question of construction whether the words used, taking into account the surrounding circumstances, amount to a clear declaration of trust. So in *Paul v. Constance*,[24] acknowledged[25] to be a "borderline case", the words used by the deceased were "[T]he money is as much yours as mine", words which he had often repeated to the plaintiff, a woman with whom he had lived for a number of years. He was referring to money in a bank account which had been opened to hold a sum paid to him by way of compensation for an industrial injury; however, the account also contained their joint bingo winnings and the only withdrawal ever made had been used for their joint benefit. The Court of Appeal held, distinguishing *Jones v. Lock*, that the words, taken with the use which had been made of the account during the deceased's lifetime, amounted to a present irrevocable declaration that the plaintiff was entitled to half the balance of the account.

Thus far the law appears reasonably clear. However, the requirements established by the authorities discussed so far seem to have been relaxed materially in *Re Vandervell's Trusts (No.2)*.[26] The Court of Appeal managed to find an effective declaration of trust of the shares in question by the trust company in favour of a settlement for the benefit of Vandervell's children from the following facts: first, that the trust company had used £5,000 from the children's settlement for the purposes of exercising an option to re-purchase the shares; secondly, that thereafter all the dividends received by the trust company had been paid into the bank accounts of the children's settlement and thereafter treated as part of the funds of that settlement; and, thirdly, that the solicitors for the trustee company had written to the Inland Revenue stating that the shares would be held on the trusts of the settlement. None of these facts, least of all the third, seems to indicate a present irrevocable declaration of trust[27]; further, as Stephenson L.J. expressly indicated, it is not easy to see how a limited company like the trust company could have declared a trust by parol or conduct or, for that matter, could have declared a trust at all without a resolution of its board of directors.[28] (This need to find an effectual declaration of trust only of course arose because the Court of Appeal resolved the question of how Vandervell could have disposed of the equitable interest which the House of Lords had held still to be vested in him[29] without using the writing required by section 53(1)(c) of the Law of Property Act 1925 in favour of the trust company in the equally questionable way which has already been considered.[30]) It is not considered that the courts are likely often to be so generous to settlors.

Finally, it should be recalled that if the subject matter of a declaration of trust is land, the requirements of section 53(1) of the Law of Property Act 1925 will need to be complied with. This certainly requires evidentiary writing in accordance with section 53(1)(b), in default of which the trust in question will be valid but unenforceable. Further, if there is indeed an

---

[24] [1977] 1 W.L.R. 527.
[25] *ibid.* at 532, *per* Scarman L.J.
[26] [1974] Ch. 269. The facts are stated in detail *ante*, pp 56–57.
[27] The question was not argued before Megarry J. at first instance.
[28] *ibid.* at 323.
[29] In *Vandervell v. I.R.C.* [1967] 2 A.C. 291. See *ante*, pp. 54–56.
[30] See *ante*, p. 57.

overlap between section 53(1)(b) and section 53(1)(a), the declaration of trust will actually have to be made in writing in accordance with the latter provision, in default of which the trust in question will be wholly void.[31]

3. *By an Ineffective Transfer Taking Effect as a Declaration of Trust*

(A) The General Rule

Where it is clear that the settlor intended to create a trust by transfer but has used an ineffectual method of transfer, the general rule is that this ineffectual transfer will not be interpreted as an effectual declaration of trust. In *Milroy v. Lord*[32] Turner L.J., immediately after the passage from his judgment which has already been cited,[33] continued[34]:

"The cases, I think, go further to this extent: that if the settlement is intended to be effectuated by one of the modes to which I have referred, the court will not give effect to it by applying another of these modes. If it is intended to take effect by transfer, the court will not hold the intended transfer to operate as a declaration of trust, for then every imperfect instrument would be made effectual by being converted into a perfect trust."

This principle was applied in *Richards v. Delbridge*.[35] The deceased, the owner of certain leasehold premises, indorsed and signed on the lease the following memorandum: "This deed and all thereto I give to [the intended transferee] from this time forth, with all the stock-in-trade". The Court of Appeal held that there was no perfected transfer, since the indorsement had not been made with the formalities necessary for a deed and so was ineffective to transfer the leasehold interest. Nor in the circumstances could it take effect as a declaration of trust.

The existence of this principle does not, however, mean that a settlor who intends to create a trust by transfer cannot expressly declare himself to be trustee of the subject matter pending that transfer. If he does so, he will himself be the trustee of a completely constituted trust of the subject matter unless and until he transfers that property to the intended trustees. Thus in *Re Ralli's Will Trusts*,[36] a settlor entered into a covenant to transfer any existing or after-acquired property to the trustees of her marriage settlement; the deed of settlement stated that it was "the intention" of the parties that all such property "shall become subject in equity to the settlement". The settlor failed to transfer to the trustees certain existing property which was caught by the covenant. Buckley J. held that, although no completely constituted trust of the property had arisen by transfer, the settlor had declared herself to be a trustee of any such property pending transfer; consequently this completely constituted trust could be enforced by the beneficiaries of the marriage settlement.

---

[31] See *ante*, pp. 48–49.
[32] (1862) 4 De G.F. & J. 264.
[33] See *ante*, p. 124.
[34] (1862) 4 De G.F. & J. 264 at 275.
[35] (1874) L.R. 18 Eq. 11.
[36] [1964] Ch. 288. See also *Middleton v. Pollock* (1876) 2 Ch.D. 194, where effective declarations of trust were made.

(B) The Rule in Re Rose[37]

As has already been mentioned, where a settlor has done everything within his power in order to render a transfer effectual but something has yet to be done by a third party, the transfer will be immediately valid in equity; consequently, although it will remain ineffective to pass the legal title unless and until the third party does whatever has to be done by him, the transferor will in the meantime hold the subject matter of the transfer on the trusts of the settlement.[38] This was established by the decision of the Court of Appeal in *Re Rose*[39] in which an earlier first instance decision, coincidentally also bearing the name *Re Rose*,[40] was applied and followed. Not surprisingly, the rule so established is known as the Rule in *Re Rose*.

In the first case named *Re Rose*[41] a testator had made a specific bequest of shares but subsequently before his death executed a share transfer in respect of the same shares in favour of the legatee. Because these were shares in a private company, its directors had the right to refuse to register the transfer and did not actually register it until after the death of the testator. The question then arose as to whether the legatee had taken the shares *inter vivos* or could only take them, if at all, post mortem.[42] Jenkins J. held that, because the testator had done everything in his power to transfer the shares *inter vivos*, from that moment he held the shares on trust for the transferee; consequently, the legatee had taken the shares *inter vivos*. This decision was followed and applied by the Court of Appeal in the second case named *Re Rose*.[43] Two transfers of shares in a private company, one by way of gift to the transferor's wife and the other to trustees on trust, were not registered until three months later. The transferor subsequently died at a point when estate duty was payable if the transfers had only been effective on registration but not if they were effective on execution.[44] Were the transfers effective upon execution or upon registration? The Court of Appeal held that, once the transferor had executed the transfers in the appropriate form, the transferor had done everything in his power which was necessary to vest the legal interest in the shares in the transferees. Consequently, from that

---

[37] [1952] Ch. 499.

[38] Since this trust does not arise out of any express or implied intention of the transferor or the beneficiaries, it must therefore necessarily be brought into existence by operation of law and should therefore be classified as a constructive trust (see *post*, p. 337).

[39] [1952] Ch. 499.

[40] [1949] 1 Ch. 78.

[41] [1949] 1 Ch. 78.

[42] This mattered because the bequest was conditional on the shares not having been transferred to the legatee prior to the testator's death; it was therefore possible to argue that the transfer *inter vivos* was ineffective to pass any title but nevertheless sufficient to defeat the testamentary gift, thus preventing the legatee from receiving the shares at all.

[43] [1952] Ch. 499.

[44] A gift made *inter vivos* within a prescribed minimum period prior to death is treated as forming part of the estate of the deceased for the purpose of calculating the tax payable on his estate. Under the present system of Inheritance Tax, a gift is exempt if made *inter vivos* more than seven years before death and if made more than three years before death the tax is progressively reduced. At the time of *Re Rose*, the relevant period for Estate Duty had just been increased to five years without any progressive reductions but the testator's estate was subject to transitional provisions which produced the result stated in the text.

moment the transfers were effective in equity and the transferor consequently held the legal title to the shares on trust for the transferees until they
subsequently acquired legal title thereto upon registration of the transfers.
Therefore no estate duty was payable.

The conclusion reached in these two decisions is not easy to reconcile
either with the passage from the judgment of Turner L.J. in *Milroy v. Lord*[45]
set out above or with the decision in *Re Fry*[46] which has already been
considered.[47] In the second case named *Re Rose*, the Court of Appeal held
that the remarks of Turner L.J. only applied where the transfer in question
had not been carried out in the appropriate way (this was admittedly the
situation under consideration in *Milroy v. Lord*[48] but no such restriction was
actually mentioned by Turner L.J.), while *Re Fry* was distinguished on the
basis that there the transferor had not done all in his power to vest the
property in the transferees, apparently because in order to perfect the transaction he would have had to have effected confirmatory transfers after the
consent had been given. Neither of these distinctions is particularly convincing. Difficulties also arise in relation to the role of the third party. Some third
parties have a merely formal role in that they have no effective discretion to
refuse to act—those responsible for registering a transfer of registered land
or the transfer of shares in a public company clearly fall within this category.
Is the Rule in *Re Rose* limited to situations such as these or does it also
operate where the third party in question is able to decline to act? In both the
cases named *Re Rose* the directors of the companies in question were indeed
entitled to refuse to register the share transfers and in the first case actually
refused to do so for over 18 months. Although the point was not specifically
considered, this must establish that the rule will indeed operate even where
the third party in question is entitled to decline to act. However, in this
respect, it is once again difficult to reconcile the Rule in *Re Rose* with the
decision in *Re Fry*.

Notwithstanding the doubts expressed in the previous paragraph, the
Rule in *Re Rose* is undoubtedly English law at the present time. The rule was
applied by Lord Wilberforce in *Vandervell v. I.R.C.*[49] in order to justify his
conclusion as to the scope of section 53(1)(c) of the Law of Property Act
1925.[50] More recently in *Mascall v. Mascall*[51] it was held that delivery by the
transferor of registered land to the transferee of a duly executed transfer
form and the land certificate will bring the rule into operation so that,
pending the registration of the transferee's title, the transferor will hold the

---

[45] (1862) 4 De G.F. & J. 264 at 274–275.
[46] [1946] Ch. 312.
[47] See *ante*, p. 126.
[48] The settlor had covenanted to transfer bank shares to the defendant on trust for the plaintiff.
The defendant already held a general Power of Attorney to transfer shares of the settlor so
the settlor merely handed over the share certificates to him. However, neither he nor the
settlor ever procured the entry in the books of the bank which was necessary for the transfer
of the legal title.
[49] [1967] 2 A.C. 271. See *ante*, p. 54.
[50] This argument actually begged the question being considered by the House of Lords (see
G. H. Jones (1966) 24 C.L.J. 19) but that does not alter the fact that Lord Wilberforce applied
the Rule in *Re Rose*.
[51] (1984) 50 P. & C.R. 119.

land in question on trust for the transferee.[52] And in *Brown & Root Technology v. Sun Alliance and London Assurance Co.*[53] it was held that an assignment of a lease which had been duly executed with the consent of the landlord but had not even been stamped *ad valorem*, never mind presented to the Land Registry, had taken effect in equity under the rule.[54] There is therefore no doubt that the Rule in *Re Rose* constitutes an exception to the general rule that equity will not regard an ineffective transfer as a declaration of trust.

4. By Virtue of Other Exceptions to the Rule in Milroy v. Lord

(A) The Rule in Strong v. Bird[55]

The decision in *Strong v. Bird* itself had nothing to do with the law of trusts; it established the relatively unobjectionable proposition that an intention to release a debt or to make a gift is manifested and effected by appointing the debtor or the donee as executor of the creditor's will. A complete gift basically involves two elements: intention to make the gift and transfer of legal title to the property in question to the donee. The developed Rule in *Strong v. Bird* establishes that, where a testator maintains up until the time of his death a continuing intention to make a gift, the requirement for the transfer of legal title can be fulfilled by the legal title vesting in the donee as executor by operation of law on the death of the donor. In other words, the appointment of the intended donee as executor perfects the intention of the donor and completes the gift, displacing by virtue of being first in time the equity of anyone else who is otherwise entitled to the property in question under the will.

The rule was originally limited to debts. In *Strong v. Bird* itself, the defendant had borrowed £1,000 from his stepmother who lived in his house, paying him £200 a quarter for board. They agreed that the debt should be paid off by the deduction of £100 from each quarter's payment. Deductions of this amount were duly made for two quarters but on the third quarter-day the stepmother generously refused to hold to the agreement any longer and paid the full £200 board on each subsequent quarter-day until her death four years later. She appointed the defendant as sole executor of her will, which he duly proved. Those otherwise entitled to the stepmother's estate then claimed that the defendant still owed the balance of the debt to her estate. At common law it had long been established that a debt owed to a deceased person was extinguished by the appointment of the debtor as executor.[56] *Strong v. Bird* decided that equity would in this respect follow the common law and deny any claim by the beneficiaries claiming under the will provided that there was evidence that, up until the moment of his death, the creditor had had a continuing intention to release the debt (this

---

[52] Consequently, it was too late for the transferor to revoke his gift of the land in question to his son, who at the time of the purported revocation had had the transfer stamped *ad valorem* but had not yet presented it to the Land Registry.

[53] [1996] Ch. 51. This question did not arise in the subsequent appeal: (1996) 75 P. & C.R. 223.

[54] This prevented the original tenant from exercising a right to bring the lease to an end which could not be exercised following an effective assignment.

[55] (1874) 18 Eq. 315.

[56] At least since *Wankford v. Wankford* (1704) 1 Salk. 299.

was easily demonstrated in *Strong v. Bird* by the fact that the stepmother had continued to pay £200 per quarter).

The rule has since been extended very considerably. In *Re Stewart*[57] it was held that any ineffectual gift, not just the release of a debt, made *inter vivos* to a person who later became the donor's executor would be and was perfected by his appointment as such. However, this will only be the case if it can be shown that after making the ineffectual gift the donor had maintained a continuing intention to make an immediate gift *inter vivos*. In *Re Freeland*[58] a testatrix promised to give the plaintiff a motorcar at a future date but never actually did so. On the testatrix's death the plaintiff became her executrix and claimed that the imperfect gift had thereby been perfected. However, the Court of Appeal refused to apply the Rule in *Strong v. Bird* because no absolute gift had ever been made at all. Similarly, in *Re Wale*,[59] the testatrix, having overlooked the need to transfer part of the intended trust property to the trustees, subsequently forgot all about the trust and treated the part of the property which she had not transferred as her own. It was held that she lacked the necessary continuing intention for the Rule in *Strong v. Bird* to apply. It has also been established that the rule is restricted to specific existing property[60]; thus a continuing unfulfilled intention to make a gift of a sum of money will not be perfected by the intended donee subsequently becoming the donor's executor.

Thus far it is just about possible to justify the existence of the rule. Even though the vast majority of testators will necessarily be unaware of its existence, an executor is at least expressly nominated by his testator. However, it is less easy to justify the subsequent extension of the rule to administrators. This occurred in *Re James*[61] where the deceased had, on the earlier death of his father, handed over the title deeds of his father's house to his father's housekeeper. This was of course insufficient to vest the legal title to the house in the housekeeper—this would have necessitated a deed—but she continued to live there until the son died and it was clear that he had at all times intended her to have the house. When he died intestate, she obtained appointment as his administratrix and so the legal title to the house became vested in her by operation of law. It was held that this fortuitous occurrence brought the rule in *Strong v. Bird* into operation and thus perfected the incomplete gift to her. No administrator is ever nominated by his testator and it is often a matter of pure chance which of the various beneficiaries entitled under a will or intestacy ends up as administrator. It therefore seems highly unreasonable that that person should obtain an advantage over the other beneficiaries by reason of his appointment. This was indeed precisely the reason why the original common law rule relating to the release of debts was never applied to administrators. Precisely these criticisms of *Re James* were forcefully made in *Re Gonin (deceased)*[62] by Walton J. who doubted the decision in that case. However, since both counsel had

---

[57] [1908] 2 Ch. 251.
[58] [1952] Ch. 110.
[59] [1956] 1 W.L.R. 1346. See also *Re Eiser's Will Trusts* [1937] 1 All E.R. 244, where the donor subsequently took security for the debt given.
[60] *Re Innes* [1952] 1 Ch. 188.
[61] [1935] Ch. 449.
[62] [1964] Ch. 288.

accepted its correctness, Walton J. nevertheless applied it to an ineffectual gift *inter vivos* of a house and its furniture by a mother to the daughter who had devoted her life to caring for her parents; however, on the facts he held that sufficient continuing intention had been made out in respect only of the furniture and not of the house.

Other uncertainties remain. It is probable that, like the original common law rule, the rule in *Strong v. Bird* gives the executor or administrator priority only over those beneficially entitled to the estate and not over its creditors but this has never been the subject of judicial comment in this jurisdiction.[63] Nor does it appear to have been expressly decided whether the rule applies where the imperfect gift is in favour of the executor or administrator as trustee rather than beneficially. However in *Re Wale*,[64] where the rule was not in fact applied, no objection was made on the grounds that in that case the executors would have taken as trustees. It consequently appears highly likely that the Rule in *Strong v. Bird* does indeed apply in such circumstances; however, it is only if this is the case that the Rule in *Strong v. Bird* will be capable of operating in such a way as to constitute an otherwise incompletely constituted trust.

(B) The Principle Enunciated in Re Ralli's Will Trusts[65]

In this case, a settlor entered into a covenant to transfer any existing or after-acquired property to the trustees of her marriage settlement. At the time of this settlement she already held existing property caught by the settlement, namely an interest in remainder in the residue of her father's estate subject to the prior life interest of her mother. She never assigned this interest to the trustees of the marriage settlement at any time prior to her death 32 years later. Her mother actually survived her so that it was over four years after her death before her interest in remainder vested in possession. At that point the sole trustee of her father's will was, fortuitously, also the sole trustee of the marriage settlement. He was therefore in one capacity holding on trust for her an interest which she should have assigned to him in a different capacity. Did this have the effect of completely constituting a trust of the interest in favour of the beneficiaries of the marriage settlement? As has already been seen,[66] Buckley J. actually held, as a matter of construction, that the settlor had declared herself to be a trustee for her marriage settlement of any property caught by the covenant pending transfer of that property to the trustees. Thus her interest in remainder had, ever since the date of the marriage settlement, been subject to a completely constituted trust in favour of that settlement. Its beneficiaries could therefore obviously enforce this trust without any need to rely on the fact that the interest had fortuitously vested in their trustee in another capacity. This decision on construction was enough to dispose of the case. However, Buckley J. also held that, since the interest in question had fortuitously reached the hands of the person to whom the settlor should have transferred it, the trust of that property in

---

[63] The question has been considered in Australia; see *Bone v. Stamp Duty Commissioner* (1974) 132 C.L.R. 38 at 53 (High Court of Australia).

[64] [1956] 1 W.L.R. 1346.

[65] [1964] Ch. 288.

[66] See *ante*, p. 130.

favour of the beneficiaries of the marriage settlement had by this means also
become completely constituted, this time by transfer rather than by declaration. He went on to say that it was totally irrelevant how the property had
come into the hands of the person to whom it should have been transferred;
the mere fact, fortuitous though it was, that the property had reached his
hands was sufficient to have completely constituted the trust. Nor was it of
any significance that the result of the case would, on this ground, have been
different had anyone other than the trustee of the marriage settlement been
the trustee of the will.

It seems from the judgment of Buckley J. that these statements were
intended by him to amount to a second *ratio decidendi* rather than merely
obiter dicta. Either way, it does not seem appropriate to regard them merely
as a further extension of the Rule in *Strong v. Bird*. It is admittedly of no great
significance that the person whose hands the property had reached had no
beneficial interest therein—it has never been expressly held that the Rule in
Strong v. Bird is limited to beneficial gifts to executors and administrators
and, as indicated in the previous paragraph, no objection was taken in *Re
Wale*[67] to the applicability of the rule on this ground. It is admittedly rather
more questionable whether the Rule in *Strong v. Bird* is applicable to a
residuary gift, given its restriction to specific existing property.[68] What is
really significant, however, is the fact that the trustee in question does not
appear to have been either the executor or the administrator of the settlor
and that no evidence was either required or given that the settlor had had
any continuing intention of transferring the property in question to the
trustees of her marriage settlement at any time during the 32 years which
had elapsed between the creation of the settlement and her death. Virtually
none of the established requirements of the Rule in *Strong v. Bird* is therefore
actually satisfied by the statements made by Buckley J. in *Re Ralli's Will
Trusts*. It therefore seems more appropriate to regard these statements as
authority for the existence of a wholly distinct principle which can be
formulated in the following way: if property of any type reaches without
impropriety[69] the hands of a person to whom it should already have been
transferred as a trustee *inter vivos*, the trust in question will become completely constituted by transfer whether or not there is any continuing intention on the part of the settlor that this should occur. This principle will
therefore also operate to constitute an otherwise incompletely constituted
trust.

It has to be said that any such rule appears to be inconsistent with the
earlier decision in *Re Brooks's Settlement Trusts*,[70] which was not cited to
Buckley J. In this case, under the terms of a voluntary settlement the settlor
had covenanted to transfer to the trustees any property which he might

---

[67] [1957] 1 W.L.R. 1346.

[68] This restriction was established in *Re Innes* [1952] 1 Ch. 188. The residuary estate in question
was, not surprisingly, in the form of specific investments when the settlor's remainder vested
in possession, which may be the reason why this point did not occur to anyone, but it cannot
possibly have been in this form throughout the existence of her interest.

[69] This point was particularly emphasised by Buckley J. His principle would therefore clearly
not have applied in the event that the property had reached the hands of the trustee as the
result of a disposition of property in breach of trust.

[70] [1939] 1 Ch. 993.

acquire under his parents' marriage settlement. A bank was trustee of both settlements so that, when a sum was subsequently appointed to the settlor as a result of the exercise of the powers contained in the marriage settlement, that sum was already in the hands of the trustees to whom he had covenanted to transfer it. For reasons which will be considered later in this section,[71] neither the trustees nor the beneficiaries of the voluntary settlement could have enforced against the settlor his covenant to transfer that sum. Consequently Farwell J. held that, despite the coincidence of trustees, the settlor was entitled to receive the sum appointed to him. In the light of this decision, it must be questionable whether the novel principle enunciated by Buckley J. in *Re Ralli's Will Trusts* actually represents the law; it remains to be seen whether it is ever followed.

(C) Donationes Mortis Causa

The rules governing *donationes mortis causa*, or death bed gifts, can also have the effect of constituting an otherwise incomplete transfer. In *Cain v. Moon*[72] Lord Russell C.J. provided that an effectual *donatio mortis causa* requires the presence of the following three elements.

(1) The gift must have been made in contemplation of death

All that is necessary is that the donor contemplated death at the time of the gift. Although the point has never been expressly decided in England,[73] the test seems to be subjective and not objective. It is the donor's own state of mind, not the actual circumstances, which is material. Moreover, the title of the donee will not be invalidated if the donor dies from some cause other than the disease from which he knew that he was suffering.[74] In *Wilkes v. Allington*[75] the donor was suffering from an incurable disease and made the gift knowing that he had not long to live. As things turned out, he lived an even shorter time than he thought, because he died two months later from pneumonia. The gift, however, remained valid.

(2) The gift must have been conditional on the death of the donor

The gift must have been made under circumstances indicating that it was conditional on the death of the donor. In this respect it is different from a gift *inter vivos* in that the latter is absolute whereas a *donatio mortis causa* is necessarily conditional on death. The condition is not usually expressed in so many words but an inference to this effect will usually be drawn from the fact of the illness of the donor.[76] This of course means not only that the

---

[71] See *post*, pp. 160–162.

[72] [1896] 2 Q.B. 283.

[73] It appears that an objective test has been adopted in Canada; see the Canadian cases cited *post*, n. 74 and 81 L.Q.R. (1965) 21.

[74] It need not, perhaps, necessarily be illness, though it normally is. Nor apparently need the donor be *in extremis*. The contrary suggestion is made in *Thomson v. Meechan* [1958] D.L.R. 103, but this seems incorrect. For a similar suggestion, see *Canada Trust Co. v. Labrador* [1962] O.R. 151. See also 81 L.Q.R. (1965) 21.

[75] [1931] 2 Ch. 104. See also *Mills v. Shields* [1948] I.R. 367 (death from suicide). *Re Dudman* [1925] Ch. 553 held contemplation by the deceased of suicide to be insufficient but, since this case was decided before the Suicide Act 1961 provided that suicide was and is no longer a crime, it is arguable, but by no means certain, that a *donatio mortis causa* made in such circumstances may now be valid.

[76] *Re Lillingston* [1952] 2 All ER 184.

subject matter of the gift will revert to the donor if he recovers from his illness but also that he can revoke his gift at any time during his lifetime.[77] The donor will be regarded as having expressly revoked his gift if he resumes dominion over it[78] and there is some authority for the proposition that it will also be sufficient if the donor simply informs the donee of his intention to revoke.[79] However, a purported revocation by will will not suffice simply because the will does not take effect until the death of the testator, by which time the donee will have become unconditionally entitled.[80]

However, the fact that the gift is conditional in the sense considered in the previous paragraph does not detract from the basic requirement that for a *donatio mortis causa* to be effective it must, like any other gift, be a present gift and not a gift to take effect at some time in the future.[81]

(3) There must have been some form of delivery from donor to donee
The donor must have delivered to the donee either the subject matter of the gift or the means or part of the means by which the subject matter can be obtained. The nature of this requirement varies according to the nature of the subject matter of the *donatio mortis causa* but it is in all cases a pre-condition that the donor intended to part with dominion,[82] a question which is ultimately a matter of fact.

No difficulties normally arise in the case of personal property which is capable of physical delivery. Handing the chattel itself to the donee will not only constitute delivery[83] but also pass the legal title; sufficient delivery will also occur if the donee is given some means of obtaining the chattel such as the keys of a cupboard in which it is stored.[84] The circumstances of the delivery must also be sufficient to demonstrate that the donor can no longer interfere with the subject matter of the gift.[85]

However, some items of personal property, such as a bank account, are choses in action and so are incapable of physical delivery[86]; in such circumstances, the gift will be ineffective unless the donee can compel the personal representative of the deceased to complete the gift of the chose in action to him. The essential pre-condition which, according to the conventional formulation, must be satisfied is that the donor must have delivered to the donee whatever document constitutes the essential evidence of his title to

---

[77] *Staniland v. Willott* (1850) 3 Mac. & G. 664.
[78] *Bunn v. Markham* (1816) 7 Taunt. 224 at 231.
[79] *Jones v. Selby* (1710) Prec.Ch. 300 at 303. Resuming mere possession for the purpose of ensuring safe custody of the subject matter is not enough; *Re Hawkins* [1924] 2 Ch. 47.
[80] *Jones v. Selby* (1710) Prec.Ch. 300.
[81] *Re Ward* [1946] 2 All E.R. 206.
[82] *Birch v. Treasury Solicitor* [1951] Ch. 298.
[83] See *Re Cole* [1964] Ch. 175.
[84] *Re Mustapha* (1891) 8 T.L.R. 160; see also *Re Lillingston* [1952] 2 All E.R. 184.
[85] *Re Craven's Estates* [1937] Ch. 423 at 427, where the delivery of one of two duplicate keys was held to be insufficient. However, the fact that a donor had possibly retained a second set of car keys which he was too ill to use was held to be insignificant in *Woodard v. Woodard* [1995] 3 All E.R. 980, as was the retention by a donor of a set of keys to a house to which he knew he would not return in *Sen v. Headley* [1991] Ch. 425.
[86] Some choses in action, such as bearer shares and bearer bonds, are transferable by delivery. Delivery of such choses in action will therefore be sufficient to constitute an effective *donatio mortis causa* and so also will delivery of the key of a box containing them; *Re Wasserberg* [1915] 1 Ch. 195.

the chose in action in question. This test was applied in *Re Weston*[87] where a dying man had handed over to his fiancée his Post Office Savings Book; this action was held sufficient to constitute an effective *donatio mortis causa* of the savings recorded in it. In the course of his judgment Byrne J. expressed the view that the document in question must also contain all the essential terms on which the subject matter of the chose in action was held. However, it is easy to visualise circumstances in which a strict application of this rule would work injustice, although it did not do so in *Re Weston*. Consequently, the Court of Appeal was clearly right expressly to disapprove this view in *Birch v. Treasury Solicitor*,[88] which concerned a similar gift of a bank deposit pass-book. The correct approach to be followed is, in the words of Evershed M.R. in that case, that delivery must be made of the "essential *indicia* of title, possession or production of which entitles the possessor to the money or property purported to be given".[89] This principle was applied by the Court of Appeal in *Sen v. Headley*,[90] where the authorities on *donationes mortis causa* of choses in action were reviewed particularly fully.

However, *Sen v. Headley* actually concerned an attempted *donatio mortis causa* of land. In that case, three days before his death the deceased had, with the necessary intention, delivered to the donee the only key to the steel box which contained the title deeds to his unregistered house and land; she already had a set of keys to the house in question and after the deceased's death found the box in a cupboard. Land is, of course, if anything more incapable of physical delivery than a chose in action and in *Duffield v. Elwes*[91] Lord Eldon L.C. had appeared to suggest that land cannot be the subject matter of a *donatio mortis causa*. However, in *Sen v. Headley* the Court of Appeal stated that anomalies do not justify anomalous exceptions, that to make a distinction in the case of land would be to make just such an exception, and that a *donatio mortis causa* of land was "neither more nor less anomalous than any other".[92] Consequently, since the Court of Appeal in *Birch v. Treasury Solicitor* had extended rather than restricted the operation of the doctrine of *donationes mortis causa*, the court held that land is indeed

---

[87] [1902] 1 Ch. 680. A similar conclusion was reached in *Darlow v. Sparks* [1938] 2 All E.R. 235 in respect of national savings certificates and, rather more unexpectedly, in *Re Mead* (1880) 15 Ch.D. 651, in respect of a cheque drawn by a third party in favour of the donor (unexpected because the cheque was capable of being endorsed; the decision would be unexceptionable in respect of a modern cheque stated to be "A/C Payee only" and so not endorsable). However, a cheque drawn by the donor in favour of the donee is not sufficient to take effect as a *donatio mortis causa* because such a cheque is simply a revocable order to the bank to make payment to the payee which will inevitably be revoked by the donor's death (*Re Leaper* [1916] 1 Ch. 579).

[88] [1951] Ch. 298.

[89] ibid. at 311.

[90] [1991] Ch. 425. See M. Halliwell: [1991] Conv. 307.

[91] (1827) 1 Bli. (N.S.) 497.

[92] [1991] Ch. 425 at p. 440. Every *donatio mortis causa* circumvented the Wills Act 1837 and the fact that *inter vivos* transfers of land were subject to statutory formalities not applicable to pure personalty did not constitute a more substantial obstacle since any trust needed to give effect to any *donatio mortis causa* would be a resulting or constructive trust and so exempt from those formalities anyway (the trust would presumably be a resulting trust if the personal representatives of the donor agreed to be bound by the *donatio mortis causa* subject to proof of its constitutent elements but a constructive trust if they sought to rely on the provisions of the Wills Act 1837 to deny its existence).

capable of passing by way of a *donatio mortis causa*. The court then went on to hold that the fact that the donor also had a set of keys to the house and had obviously retained the theoretical ability to deal with the title to it despite the delivery of the key to the donee did not, on the facts, amount to a retention of dominion. The *donatio mortis causa* was therefore upheld. However, it is obviously unlikely that anything less than delivery of the deeds (or, in the case of registered land, the land certificate[93]) or the means of obtaining them will ever be held to constitute an appropriate delivery in respect of land.

Finally, it must be emphasised that, in the case both of choses in action and of land, the legal title to the property in question will not be automatically acquired by the donee as a result of a delivery in the manner prescribed. The gift of whatever property is represented by whatever has been delivered will still be imperfect. The effect of establishing a *donatio mortis causa* is instead that the donor's personal representatives will be compelled to perfect the gift.[94] It is therefore in the case of *donationes mortis causa* of choses in action and of land that equity compels the completion of what would otherwise be an incomplete gift.

(D) The Doctrine of Equitable Proprietary Estoppel[95]

(1) The nature of the doctrine

If the doctrine of estoppel were still limited to the sense in which it has traditionally been generally applied, it would barely be worthy of mention here since the traditional form of the doctrine operated only defensively so as to prevent a party from asserting his rights; as such, it obviously could not operate so as to perfect an imperfect gift or complete an incompletely constituted trust.[96] However, the modern principle of proprietary estoppel can be used offensively, "as a sword" as it is sometimes described, in order that an imperfect gift can be perfected if the donor has stood by and watched the donee improve property or do other acts to his detriment on the supposition that there has been or will be an effective gift. The doctrine appears to

---

[93] This possibility was not specifically envisaged by the Court of Appeal but must follow from their finding that it did not matter that the donor had retained the theoretical ability to deal with his title. In the case of registered land which is mortgaged, the land certificate will of course be held by the Land Registry and all the registered proprietor is likely to have is a copy of the Charge Certificate; if this is indeed all that he has, delivery of such a copy will presumably suffice.

[94] *Re Dillon* (1890) 44 Ch.D. 76 at 82–83.

[95] See K. Gray: *Elements of Land Law* (2nd ed., 1993), chap. 13; M. Pawlowski, *Proprietary Estoppel* (1996).

[96] This is so in a case of so-called promissory estoppel. The traditional distinctions between promissory estoppel and proprietary estoppel have been eroded by recent authorities; see particularly *Taylors Fashions v. Liverpool Victoria Trustees Company* (1976) [1982] Q.B. 133N; *Amalgamated Investment & Property Company v. Texas Commerce International Bank* [1982] Q.B. 84 (leave to appeal to the House of Lords was subsequently not granted [1982] 1 W.L.R. 1); and Halliwell, *Equity & Good Conscience in a Contemporary Context* (1997), pp. 19–38. One distinction which must remain is that promissory estoppel, unlike proprietary estoppel, is not permanent in its effect; the promisor can resile from his position if he gives the promisee notice which provides him with a reasonable opportunity of resuming his former position; see *Re Vandervell's Trusts (No.2)* [1964] Ch. 269 at 301, *per* Megarry J.

be of early origin[97] but until recently has evolved in the form of three separate overlapping categories of cases: first, cases concerning imperfect gifts; secondly, cases concerning common expectations, where parties have consistently dealt with one another in such a way as to cause one of them to rely on a shared supposition that he would acquire rights of some kind in the land of the other; and, thirdly, cases of unilateral mistake, where the owner of land has stood by and allowed another person to act to his detriment on a mistaken belief that he has a legally enforceable interest in the land in question. The principles established by these three groups of authorities have now been synthesised into the modern principle of proprietary estoppel. The key decision in this process seems to have been *Taylor Fashions v. Liverpool Victoria Trustees Company.*[98] In this case Oliver J. rejected the notion that the principle was narrowly confined to the three categories of cases already mentioned. Instead his Lordship found support in these three groups of cases for "a much wider jurisdiction to interfere in cases where the assertion of strict legal rights is found by the courts to be unconscionable".[99] He therefore held that the purchasers of a freehold reversion were estopped from claiming to have taken free for want of registration of options to renew leases which, at the time of their grant, were wrongly thought by conveyancers not to be registrable.

As a result of this synthesis, it is now clear that a successful claim of proprietary estoppel involves three elements: an assurance, a reliance and a detriment. Such an assurance will occur where the owner of land, expressly or by necessary implication, raises in another person an expectation that that person will obtain some interest or entitlement in land which he would not otherwise have. The assurance can range from an express request to incur expenditure through encouragement or incitement so to do, to silent abstention from the assertion of rights, although in the last case the owner of the land obviously has to be shown to have at least some knowledge of the mistaken belief of the other party. Where such an assurance has been made, the other person must then show that he has acted in reliance upon that assurance to his detriment. This involves him showing both that he has changed his position and that this change of position is a direct consequence of the assurance given. Where such a proprietary estoppel has arisen, the court enjoys very considerable flexibility in that a remedy can be provided appropriate to the circumstances of each individual case. Such remedies range from the grant of an unqualified estate in fee simple or lesser interest in or over land such as a lease, or an easement through the grant of a right to occupy the land to the grant of monetary compensation; it is also possible for a grant of a right in or a right to occupy land to be combined with a grant of monetary compensation. The doctrine is of course still developing and, as will be seen later,[1] there is an increasing overlap between the doctrine of proprietary estoppel and the "common intention constructive trust". The terminology employed in the majority of the cases decided prior to *Taylor Fashions v. Liverpool Victoria Trustees Company* would be likely to be very

---

[97] See *Foxcroft v. Lester* (1703) 2 Vern. 456.
[98] (1976) [1982] Q.B. 133N.
[99] ibid. at 147.
[1] See *post*, p. 366.

different if those cases were to recur today. However, there is no doubt whatsoever that all the cases in which proprietary estoppels were upheld would still be decided in the same way and they consequently remain important as illustrations of the situations, formerly quite distinct, which today fall within the doctrine of proprietary estoppel. The difference today is that the enunciation of a broader general jurisdiction means that proprietary estoppels are now likely to be upheld in situations in which this would not formerly have been the case.

For present purposes, what is important is the cases concerning imperfect gifts. A useful starting point is *Dillwyn v. Llewelyn*[2] where a father put his son into possession of land without a conveyance. It was intended that the son should build a house on the land. The son successfully claimed that the land should be formally conveyed to him. Lord Westbury L.C. said: "If A puts B in possession of a piece of land and tells him 'I give it to you that you may build a house on it', and B, on the strength of that promise, with the knowledge of A, expends a large sum of money in building a house accordingly, I cannot doubt that the donee acquires a right from the subsequent transaction to call on the donor to perform that contract, and complete the imperfect donation which was made". In other words, the subsequent acts of the donor gave the donee a right which he did not acquire from the original gift.

As has already been mentioned, what estate or interest the donee takes depends on the circumstances of the case. In *Dillwyn v. Llewelyn* the donee took the fee simple. This was also the result in the much more recent decision in *Pascoe v. Turner*[3] where the parties had lived together in a house as man and wife and the man had encouraged or acquiesced in the woman improving the house in the belief that it belonged to her. He was ordered to execute a conveyance of the house to her. But the facts may indicate a lesser estate or some other right. Thus, in *Inwards v. Baker*[4] the donee was held to be entitled to remain in occupation for as long as he wished. And in *E.R.Ives Investments v. High*[5] the defendant was allowed a right of way for as long as the plaintiff and his successors in title maintained the foundations of a building on the defendant's land; this was because the plaintiff's predecessors in title, by licensing the defendant to use the yard in question, had encouraged him to build a garage on his own adjoining land, something which had created an estoppel in his favour. It was also held that the equitable interest which had arisen as a result of this estoppel was not subject to the rules regarding the registration of land charges,[6] which of course only apply to unregistered land, and so would be governed by the equitable doctrine of notice and bind the whole world other than a bona fide purchaser for value of a legal interest without notice. How such an interest would be treated in relation to registered land has yet to be decided. However, the vast majority of such interests would take effect as overriding interests, either by virtue of the actual occupation of the person entitled to

---

[2] (1862) 4 De G.F. & J. 517.
[3] [1979] 1 W.L.R. 431.
[4] [1965] 2 Q.B. 29. See also *Ward v. Kirkland* [1967] Ch. 194, where a perpetual easement of drainage was granted.
[5] [1967] 2 Q.B. 289.
[6] Under what is now the Land Charges Act 1972.

the beneficial interest[7] or as appurtenant rights,[8] and would consequently bind the whole world. Any other interests would only bind third parties if protected on the Land Register.[9] Other conveyancing implications of proprietary estoppel have not been fully worked out.[10]

Such decisions were applied in *Crabb v. Arun District Council*[11] where there was an agreement "in principle", not amounting to a contract, that the plaintiff should have a right of access, in reliance on which he sold the front portion of his land without reserving a right of way over it giving access to the back portion. The Court of Appeal held that this was a case of proprietary estoppel and that he was therefore entitled to an easement or licence[12]; he had been encouraged to act to his detriment by the defendant's conduct.[13] Similarly, in *Jones v. Jones*[14] a father had led his son to believe that a house would be his home for the rest of his life, on the basis of which expectation the son had given up his job and moved in. It was held that he could pray in aid the doctrine of estoppel and that both the father and his administratrix were estopped from turning the son out during his lifetime. Again in *Re Sharpe*,[15] where an aged aunt had lent money for the purchase of a house by her nephew so that she could live there with him and his wife, it was held that an irrevocable licence to occupy the house had arisen in favour of the aunt until such time as the loan was repaid.

Moreover, the burden of proof is on the plaintiff to show that the defendant has not acted to his detriment or prejudice where the latter is relying

---

[7] Under Land Registration Act 1925, s.70(1)(g). This would have been the case in *Inwards v. Baker* [1965] 2 Q.B. 29.

[8] Under Land Registration Rules, R.258. This would have been the case in *E.R. Ives Investment v. High* [1967] 2 Q.B. 289.

[9] This would have been the case in *Ward v. Kirkland* [1967] Ch. 194.

[10] In *Dodsworth v. Dodsworth* (1973) 228 E.G. 1115 the Court of Appeal held that, if the equity were implemented by giving the claimant the right to occupy a house for his life, the result would be to create a tenancy for life within the Settled Land Act 1925; this would give him more than it had ever been represented that he should have, because he would receive the statutory powers of a tenant for life under that Act, powers which include the rights to sell, lease and mortgage the property in question. However, as Goff L.J. indicated in *Griffiths v. Williams* (1977) 74 Guardian Gazette 1130, the court did not seem to have considered what might in such circumstances be the difficult problem of precisely what constituted the "settlement" within s.1(1) of the Settled Land Act 1925; he observed that it was not easy to see how an equity set up by these means could fall within the terms of the section. The question did not, however, arise for decision and is not likely to do so in the future now that the Trusts of Land and Appointment of Trustees Act 1996 has prohibited the creation of any new settlements subject to the Settled Land Act 1925. If an equity is in future implemented in the way envisaged in *Dodsworth v. Dodsworth*, it will simply take effect as a beneficial interest under a trust of land, by virtue of which the legal title and all the administrative powers will be vested in the person held to be bound by the estoppel. Analogous conveyancing problems arise where a constructive trust is imposed as a result of the unconscionable conduct of the trustee in attempting to go back on an undertaking or agreement. See *post*, p. 359.

[11] [1976] Ch. 179.

[12] An easement according to Lord Denning M.R. and Lawton L.J.; an easement or licence according to Scarman L.J.

[13] One of the acts to his detriment was the sale of land separate from the land over which the access was to be granted. Normally, the acts involve expenditure in relation to the actual land intended to be disposed of.

[14] [1977] 1 W.L.R. 438.

[15] [1980] 1 W.L.R. 219.

upon an estoppel. So, in *Greasley v. Cooke*[16] assurances had been given that the defendant could remain in a house, where not only had she been employed as a maid for more than 40 years but had also lived with one of the children of the family as man and wife. It was held that these assurances raised an equity in her favour and it was to be presumed that she had acted on the faith of those assurances. The plaintiffs failed to rebut the presumption.[17]

The fact that it is essential for a case of proprietary estoppel that a party acted as he did to his detriment in the expectation of acquiring a right to or over somebody else's land is illustrated by *Western Fish Products v. Penwith District Council*.[18] It was held on the facts that, even if the plaintiffs had to their detriment spent money on their land at the encouragement of the Council, they had not done so in the expectation of acquiring any rights over the Council's or any other land and could not therefore rely on proprietary estoppel.[19]

It used to be thought that the conduct of the owner of the property in question could only be held to give rise to the inequitable consequences which are a necessary ingredient of establishing a proprietary estoppel if he was aware of the true facts. This is certainly still a requirement for the type of cases traditionally classified as cases of unilateral mistake. However, it no longer appears to be essential for the type of cases under discussion at present, cases concerning imperfect gifts.[20] Admittedly Megarry J. did uphold the existence of such a requirement at first instance in *Re Vandervell's Trusts (No. 2)*.[21] He refused to find an estoppel, pointing out that, although Vandervell had concurred in the dealings with the moneys and shares carried out by the trust company[22] following the exercise of the option, the company had not been able to show that he even knew that he was the beneficial owner of the option at the time of its exercise. However, the question was not fully argued before him and the opposite view was subsequently taken in the Court of Appeal. The court was of the opinion that if Vandervell had been alive his concurrence in these dealings would have estopped him from denying the existence of a beneficial interest vested in the children's settlement and, consequently, his executors could be in no better position. This was admittedly not the only ground on which the Court of Appeal decided the case[23] and it might therefore be a mistake to read too much into these remarks about proprietary estoppel. Knowledge cannot possibly be, as the Court of Appeal appeared to suggest, totally irrelevant.

---

[16] [1980] 1 W.L.R. 1306.

[17] Lord Denning M.R. said (at 1311) that the incurring of expenditure of money or other prejudice was not a necessary element. However, this appears to be far too wide a generalisation; see at 1313 per Dunn L.J.

[18] [1981] 2 All E.R. 204; see also *Haslemere Estates v. Baker* [1982] 3 All E.R. 525, where there was no legitimate hope or expectation of obtaining any interest in the land.

[19] It was also held that in any event an estoppel could not be raised to prevent a statutory body exercising its statutory discretion or performing a statutory duty; see also *Rootkin v. Kent County Council* [1981] 1 W.L.R. 1186 as to the exercise of a statutory discretion relating to the payment of travelling expenses of a school pupil.

[20] Nor is it for cases concerning common expectation.

[21] [1974] Ch. 269 at 301.

[22] These dealings are referred to *ante*, p. 40.

[23] See *ante*, p. 40.

The better view must be the intermediate position adopted by Oliver J. in *Taylors Fashions v. Liverpool Victoria Trustees Company*[24] when he held that knowledge of the true position by the party alleged to be estopped was merely one of the relevant factors in the overall inquiry. He held that the essential question was whether, in the particular circumstances, it would be unconscionable for a party to be permitted to deny that which, knowingly or unknowingly, he had allowed or encouraged another to assume to his detriment.[25] Accordingly, the principle could apply where, at the time the expectation was encouraged, both parties (not just the representee) were acting under a mistake of law as to their rights. He therefore held that the purchasers of a freehold reversion were estopped from claiming to have taken free for want of registration of options to renew leases which, at the time of their grant, were wrongly thought by conveyancers not to be registrable.[26] This decision which, as has already been seen, set the doctrine of proprietary estoppel on its present course therefore did not involve the law of trusts; however it must nevertheless have had an effect on it.

(2) Its impact on the law of trusts

So far as the law of trusts is concerned, the doctrine may give rise to further difficulties, particularly in relation to cases involving the incidence of taxation such as *Re Rose*.[27] One question that could clearly arise is whether a gift or trust perfected by an estoppel is to be regarded as having been constituted at the time when the gift was made or on the occurrence of the subsequent events which created the estoppel. The latter would certainly seem to be the correct approach.[28] However, in other respects, the position is more doubtful. In *Williams v. Staite*,[29] Cumming-Bruce L.J. considered, without finding it necessary to decide, that the rights of an equitable licensee for life did not necessarily crystallise when his rights came into existence but only when the court came to determine what interest if any he had in the property. Lord Denning M.R. shared the opinion that in an extreme case an equitable licence might be revoked[30] but held that the conduct of the licensees, which involved excessive user and bad behaviour, was not of a kind to bring the equity established in their favour to an end; their behaviour could instead be remedied by an award of damages. While it may be debatable whether an established equity can be forfeited in this way, it does at least seem clear that, when a person is asserting a right to an equity for the first time, his conduct may be taken into account in deciding whether to uphold such a right, thereby applying the basic maxim that "he who comes to equity must come with clean hands".[31] Indeed, virtually everything must depend

---

[24] (1976) [1982] Q.B. 133N.

[25] See also *Amalgamated Investment & Property Company v. Texas Commerce International Bank* [1982] Q.B. 84 (leave to appeal to the House of Lords was subsequently not granted: [1982] 1 W.L.R. 1).

[26] See also *Thomas Bates & Son v. Wyndhams (Lingerie)* [1981] 1 W.L.R. 505; estoppel applied where the mistake was a unilateral rather than a common mistake.

[27] [1952] Ch. 499, discussed *ante*, p. 131.

[28] See generally on the subject Jackson (1965) 81 L.Q.R. 84; Poole (1968) 38 Conv. (N.S.) 96; Sunnucks (1968) 118 New L.J. 769.

[29] [1979] Ch. 291.

[30] ibid. at 297.

[31] Goff L.J. was of this opinion in *Williams v. Staite* [1979] Ch. 291 at 299.

on the facts of the case. In some cases, such as *Re Sharpe*[32] where the licensee was not in any way guilty of misconduct, it is essential that the rights must have arisen at the time of the transaction so that the licensee can have any rights whose breach can be remedied; this of course requires the equity to predate any order of the courts.[33] It therefore seems that there is a distinction between the undeniable existence of an equity prior to any decision of the court which can confer any necessary priority and the manner in which the court may choose, in the exercise of its discretion in the light of all the facts, to implement it.

(3) Conclusion

Many aspects of the scope of the doctrine of proprietary estoppel and the consequences of its utilisation in fiscal and conveyancing terms have still to be clarified. Nevertheless, the doctrine has been described[34] as "one of the most significant movements occurring in the contemporary law of real property". The extent to which its development will increase the extent to which equity will constitute trusts which would otherwise be incompletely constituted remains to be seen. Nevertheless, there can be no doubt that the development of the doctrine has increased both the importance of this particular exception and the possibilities of a trust becoming completely constituted thereby.

(E) Statutory Exceptions

Since January 1, 1997 there has only been one statutory exception to the rule that equity will not constitute a trust which would otherwise be incompletely constituted. A trust will be constituted by statute as a result of a purported conveyance of a legal estate in land to a minor. Because such an estate can only be held by an adult,[35] the conveyance will, by virtue of the Trusts of Land and Appointment of Trustees Act 1996,[36] operate as a declaration that the land is held in trust for the minor in question. Prior to January 1, 1997, there was also a second exception arising out of the fact that it was not possible to create a settlement of a legal estate in land pursuant to the Settled Land Act 1925 without the use of two documents—a trust instrument and a vesting document (either a deed or an assent).[37] The use of only one document did not pass the legal estate but, under section 9 of the Settled Land Act 1925, such a document operated as a trust instrument and therefore took effect as an enforceable trust pending the execution of the vesting deed by the trustees.[38] As a result of the Trusts of Land and Appointment of

---

[32] [1980] 1 W.L.R. 219. The facts are stated *ante*, p. 74.

[33] *ibid*. at 225.

[34] By K. J. Gray in *Elements of Land Law* (2nd ed., 1993), p. 312.

[35] Law of Property Act 1925, s.1(6).

[36] Sched. 1, para.1. Before this Act came into force on January 1, 1997, such a conveyance operated as an agreement for valuable consideration to create a settlement of that land on the minor and in the meantime to hold the land on trust for him (Settled Land Act 1925, s.27); any conveyances so operating on January 1, 1997 thereafter also take effect as declarations of trust.

[37] Settled Land Act 1925, s.4.

[38] The trustees were entitled to execute a vesting deed at any time and could be compelled to do so by the beneficiary who held the estate in possession for the time being (the person described in the Settled Land Act 1925 as the tenant for life).

Trustees Act 1925, no further settlements under the Settled Land Act 1925 can now be created[39] so this exception only survives to the extent that any such settlement created before January 1, 1997 still has no vesting deed, a possibility which will become less and less likely with the passage of time.

III. THE DISTINCTION BETWEEN EXECUTED AND EXECUTORY TRUSTS

Completely constituted trusts may be either executed or executory trusts and it is still in some circumstances important to distinguish not only between these two categories of trusts but also between the two of them and trusts which are incompletely constituted. An executed trust arises when the settlor has defined in the trust instrument precisely what interests are to be taken by the beneficiaries.[40] An executory trust, on the other hand, arises where the instrument or declaration requires the subsequent execution of a further instrument and does not itself precisely define the terms of that instrument.[41]

1. *The Nature of the Distinction*

The practical importance of the distinction between executed and executory trusts relates to their construction although today the position is no longer of as much importance as it used to be.[42] The construction of an executed trust is governed by rules of law, whereas executory trusts are construed more liberally and always with a view to carrying out the true intention of the settlor. This may be illustrated by comparing two cases. In *Re Bostock's Settlement*,[43] the settlor had omitted certain words of limitation which, had they been inserted, would have given an estate in fee simple to the beneficiaries. It was held that, in the absence of those words, the beneficiaries took only a life estate notwithstanding the fact that it was probably intended that they should take an estate in fee simple. This was a case of an executed trust and in the absence of the necessary technical expressions the limitation was construed according to strict rules of law. On the other hand, in *Glenorchy v. Bosville*[44] the testator had devised real property to trustees upon trust to convey the estate, after the marriage of his grand-daughter, to her use for life, remainder to the use of her husband for life, remainder to the use of the issue of her body. Under the rule of construction known as the Rule in *Shelley's Case*[45], the grand-daughter would, if this had been an executed trust, have taken an estate in fee tail. But since this was an executory trust, the court was able to look at the true intention of the testator. His intention

---

[39] Sched. 1, para.1.

[40] See *Egerton v. Brownlow* (1853) 4 H.L.C. 1 at 210, *per* Lord St. Leonards.

[41] Nevertheless the directions as to the trusts to be defined must not be too ambiguous; if they are, there will be no executory trust. See *Re Flavel's Will Trusts* [1969] 1 W.L.R. 444.

[42] See *post*, p. 149.

[43] [1921] 2 Ch. 469.

[44] (1733) Cas. t. Talb. 3; see also *Papillon v. Voice* (1728) P. Wms. 471.

[45] (1581) 1 Co.Rep. 88B. This case does not apply to instruments taking effect after 1925; see *post*, p. 149.

had clearly been to provide for the children of the marriage; consequently it was held that the trustees should, regardless of the Rule in *Shelley's Case,* convey the property to the grand-daughter for life, with remainder to her first and other sons in fee tail and an ultimate remainder to her daughter in fee simple.

These cases illustrate the practical importance of the distinction between executed and executory trusts in matters of construction. Admittedly one case, *Re Arden,*[46] suggests that it could be argued that the distinction is not anything like so clear-cut. It was held, in effect, that the use of an non-technical expression by the creator of an executed trust gave the court a loophole which enabled it to apply a construction which accorded with the real intentions of the settlor. Here the settlor had used the word "absolutely"; Clauson J. held that the use of this word entitled him to decide that the beneficiary in whose favour it had been used took an equitable fee simple although, if that word had been omitted, it was acknowledged that he would only have taken a life interest. If this decision is correct, which is somewhat questionable, a non-technical expression may be given a technical meaning even in an executed trust while the lack of any such expression—as in *Re Bostock's Settlement*[47]—produces the effect prescribed by strict rules of law.

2. *The Special Treatment of Marriage Articles*

One class of executory trusts has been given special treatment. These are executory trusts arising under marriage articles. In such cases the presumption is that the intention of the settlor was to provide for the issue of the marriage so that, despite any technical rules of construction, the husband and wife will normally take life interests,[48] a presumption which will apply unless it is clear that the parties intended to create some other type of interest. This presumption is a strong one and will only be rebutted by the clearest evidence to the contrary. It was particularly significant in the application of the Rule in *Shelley's Case.* In a limitation of land before 1926 for a person for life, remainder to the heirs of his body, that person would have taken an estate in fee tail by virtue of the rule of construction established in that case. But if an executory trust on these lines was contained in marriage articles the court would strive to avoid this construction and would give that person only a life estate; otherwise he would have been able to bar the estate in fee tail, that is to say bar the interest of his successors in title and, by converting his own interest into an estate fee simple, thereby defeat the interests of his issue. However, in the case of other executory trusts, which normally only arise under the provisions of wills, the court, while as always construing the instrument as a whole in order to ascertain the true intention of the settlor, would consider the whole question of construction on its merits. So, in the ancient case of *Sweetapple v. Bindon,*[49] a testator gave £300

---

[46] [1935] Ch. 326.
[47] [1921] Ch. 469.
[48] *Jervoise v. Duke of Northumberland* (1820) 1 Jac. & W. 559 at 574; *Trevor v. Trevor* (1720) 1 P. Wms. 622.
[49] (1706) 2 Vern. 536.

to trustees upon trust to invest it in the purchase of land and settle the land to "the only use of a person and her children" and, in the event that that person died without issue, "the land to be divided between her brothers and sisters then living". Since this was an executory trust under a will, the question of construction was approached on the basis that there was no overriding necessity to give her a life interest; consequently, it was held that she took an estate in fee tail.

3. *The Modern Significance of the Distinction*

What has already been stated is still applicable in principle but, along with the authorities cited, must now be read subject to the effect of the legislation of the twentieth century. The Property Legislation of 1925 had two effects on instruments taking effect on or after January 1, 1926; it, first, abolished the rule in *Shelley's Case*[50] and, secondly, removed any necessity for the use of words of limitation for the purpose of creating an estate in fee simple.[51] The distinction still had to be borne in mind because of the continuing necessity for words of limitation for the creation of entailed interests[52] but this too has ceased to have any relevance since January 1, 1997 given that the Trusts of Land and Appointment of Trustee Act 1996 prevents the creation of any further entailed interests on or after that date.[53]

The modern significance of the distinction is therefore little. Marriage articles are now rare, presumably because, in so far as marriage settlements are still created at all, they are highly likely to have been set up at least partly for the purpose of tax avoidance, something which requires all the documents involved to have been carefully thought out and prepared in advance. Nevertheless, modern examples of executory trusts do still exist. An extremely significant illustration, given the importance of such trusts today, is a pension scheme established, as most pension schemes are, by an interim deed of trust which provides for the subsequent execution of a definitive deed of trust. In *Davis v. Richards & Wallington Industries*,[54] following the execution of an interim deed, the definitive deed was duly executed but its validity was challenged when questions arose as to the entitlement to surplus funds. Scott J. in fact found the definitive deed valid but stated that, had he not done so, he would have upheld the interim deed as a valid executory trust capable of being executed by a court order; this would have had the effect of providing rules corresponding to those in the definitive deed by means of which the questions relating to the surplus funds would have been able to have been resolved. This interesting and highly relevant illustration shows that the distinction between executed and executory trusts can still be important today in the field of construction.

---

[50] Law of Property 1925, s.131.
[51] *ibid.*, s.60.
[52] *ibid.*, s.130.
[53] Sched. 1, para. 5.
[54] [1990] 1 W.L.R. 1511.

IV. WHEN A TRUST IS INCOMPLETELY CONSTITUTED, WHEN WILL THE BENEFICIARIES HAVE A CONTRACTUAL REMEDY?

Where no completely constituted trust has arisen either as a result of the effectual transfer of the intended trust property to the trustees or as a result of a declaration of trust by the settlor and where the beneficiaries are unable to rely on any of the exceptions to the rule that equity will not perfect an imperfect gift, the only possibility open to them will be to rely on the law of contract. There are a number of situations where a contractual remedy will enable the beneficiaries either to bring about the complete constitution of the trust or, in default, obtain common law damages. However, this is obviously not always possible and where no contractual remedy is available to the beneficiaries either, the trust in question is said to be voluntary and the beneficiaries are said to be volunteers. It is a long-established equitable maxim that "equity will not assist a volunteer".[55] Although this maxim is invariably relied on by the courts whenever a beneficiary is denied a remedy, its utilisation adds nothing and is a source of potential confusion. The maxim neither denies a remedy to a beneficiary who already has one nor provides a remedy to a beneficiary who does not have one. Consequently, it does no more than state the obvious, namely that, if a beneficiary can point neither to the existence of a completely constituted trust nor to the existence of any form of contract enforceable either by him or on his behalf, then equity will not assist him. More significantly, the existence of the maxim has hindered the development of the law since, unfortunately but predictably, the courts have tended to utilise it as a substitute for reasoned analysis of whether or not in any particular case any contractual remedy is actually available to the beneficiary.

The contractual remedies available to the beneficiaries of an incompletely constituted trust may arise either under a simple contract (a contract constituted as a result of the existence of offer and acceptance, intention to create legal relations, and consideration) or under a specialty contract (a contract constituted by virtue of being contained in a deed, often also described as a covenant). The contract entered into by the settlor may be a straightforward contract to settle some of his existing property, that is to say property of which he is already able to dispose.[56] However, there is normally little reason for a settlor to enter into such a contract in respect of existing property.[57] Such property can be the subject of a valid assignment, of a valid declaration of a trust, and of a valid contract to assign or declare a trust. Consequently, if the subject matter of a proposed trust is existing property, the settlor can just as easily constitute the trust immediately by transfer to trustees or by declaration as enter into a contract so to do. For this reason,

---

[55] *Ellison v. Ellison* (1802) 6 Ves.Jun. 656 at 662, *per* Lord Eldon L.C.; see also *Jefferys v. Jefferys* (1841) Cr. & Ph. 138.

[56] Such cases were *Williamson v. Codrington* (1750) 1 Ves.Sen. 511 (covenant to settle a plantation); *Fletcher v. Fletcher* (1844) 4 Hare 167 (covenant to settle £60,000) and *Re Cavendish Browne's Settlement Trusts* [1916] W.N. 341 (covenant to settle property to which the settlor was entitled under the wills of persons who had already died).

[57] In both *Williamson v. Codrington* and *Fletcher v. Fletcher*, the reason was undoubtedly the fact that the beneficiaries were the illegitimate children of the settlors, who clearly wished to avoid embarrassing publicity until after their deaths.

most contracts of this type (and most of the cases which have come before the courts) have concerned property which has not yet come into existence, generally known as after-acquired property. Such property cannot be the subject of a valid assignment, which is at law wholly void,[58] although equity will treat the assignment of after-acquired property made in exchange for valuable consideration as a contract to assign or declare a trust if and when the property is acquired.[59] Nor can after-acquired property be the subject of a valid declaration of trust,[60] although equity will enforce this declaration of trust in favour of anyone who has provided valuable consideration if and when the property is acquired.[61] Further, an express contract to assign or declare a trust if and when the property is acquired will be enforced both in equity and at common law[62] if it is a simple contract and is consequently supported by valuable consideration[63] and will be enforced at common law,[64] but not in equity,[65] if it is merely a specialty contract. All this means that, where the subject matter of a proposed trust is after-acquired property, the settlor will have no option but to enter into what either is or is deemed by equity to be a contract to settle the property in question if and when it is acquired.

Because of this significant distinction between existing and after-acquired property, it is important to note that for this purpose existing property is not confined to property which has already vested in possession and is thus available for the immediate enjoyment of the person entitled thereto. Existing property also includes property which has not yet come into possession, either because the interest is vested in interest, in other words awaiting the determination of some prior interest (an example is the interest of a person who is absolutely entitled in remainder during a preceding life tenancy) or contingent (an example is the interest of a person entitled to property at the age of 30 when he has not yet attained that age). Further, existing property includes existing choses in action (an example is the right to recover book-debts arising in the course of a business[66]) and the right to exercise an existing power of appointment only at some future time (an example is an already granted power of appointment which is exerciseable only by will). After-acquired property, on the other hand, is property in respect of which only the future will determine whether or not the person in question ever

---

[58] *Holroyd v. Marshall* (1862) 10 H.L.C. 191 (assignment by way of mortgage of machinery which in the future might be substituted for existing machinery); *Re Tilt* (1896) 40 Sol.Jo. 224 (assignment of an expectancy under the intestacy of a person who was still alive); *Re Ellenborough* [1903] 1 Ch. 697 (assignment of an expectancy under the will of a person who was still alive).

[59] *Holroyd v. Marshall* (1862) 10 H.L.C. 191 at 211, 220.

[60] *Williams v. C.I.R.* [1965] N.Z.L.R. 395 (Court of Appeal of New Zealand) (declaration of trust of the first £500 of the net income arising under a life interest in each of four future years).

[61] *Ellison v. Ellison* (1802) 6 Ves.Jun. 656 at 662; *Williams v. C.I.R.* [1965] N.Z.L.R. 395 (Court of Appeal of New Zealand).

[62] The simple contract will not be enforceable at common law if the valuable consideration in question is marriage, which is not regarded as valuable consideration at law.

[63] *Pullan v. Koe* [1913] 1 Ch. 9. See *post*, p. 154.

[64] *Cannon v. Hartley* [1949] Ch. 213. See *post*, p. 159.

[65] *Jefferys v. Jefferys* (1841) Cr. & P. 138.

[66] As in *Barclays Bank v. Willowbrook International* [1987] 1 F.T.L.R. 386.

acquires any rights at all (examples are the possibility of receiving property (including the right to exercise a power of appointment[67]) under the will[68] or intestacy[69] of someone who is still alive or under an as yet unexercised power of appointment, the possibility of receiving future royalties payable in respect of a copyright or a mining operation,[70] and the possibility of acquiring future book-debts arising in the course of a business[71]). Consequently, while a settlor may assign an equitable remainder to trustees on trust, declare a trust[72] thereof, or enter into either a simple or a specialty contract to make such an assignment or declaration of trust, his possible courses of action in respect of the payments which he hopes to receive as the royalties on a book or a mine are much more restricted; he cannot validly either assign or declare a trust of such payments, although a purported assignment or declaration of trust will be regarded by equity as a contract to assign or declare a trust if and when the property is acquired, but can enter into either a simple contract (enforceable both at law[73] and in equity) or a specialty contract (enforceable only at law) to make such an assignment or declaration of trust.

1. *A Simple Contract to Create the Trust*

If the settlor and the beneficiary have entered into a simple contract for the creation by the settlor of a completely constituted trust in favour of the beneficiary, then both parties to the contract will be entitled to the appropriate contractual remedies.

(A) A Simple Contract Recognised both at Common Law and in Equity

Where the consideration provided by the beneficiary is money or money's worth, then the existence of the contract will be recognised both at common law and in equity. Consequently both settlor and beneficiary will be able to obtain damages for breach of contract or, if the contract in question is capable of being specifically enforced, a decree for specific performance. The availability of specific performance means that in equity the property immediately becomes subject to the trust. Thus, if the settlor contracts with the beneficiary for money or money's worth to transfer land to trustees to hold on trust for him, in equity the land will immediately become subject to the trust and the beneficiary will be able to obtain a decree for specific performance of this contract; thus he will be able to oblige the settlor to transfer the

---

[67] *Re Ellenborough* [1903] 1 Ch. 697.
[68] *Re Tilt* (1896) 40 Sol.Jo. 224.
[69] *Re Parkin* [1892] 3 Ch. 510.
[70] *Coulls v. Bagot's Trustee* [1967] 40 A.L.J.R. 471.
[71] *Tailby v. Official Receiver* (1888) 13 App. Cas. 523. A further example which the author of this edition has recently encountered in practice is any new tenancy or monetary compensation given for the future surrender of a protected tenancy under the Rent Act 1977 (the right to remain in occupation under such a tenancy is not itself a proprietary interest but merely consists of the right to resist eviction and so cannot itself be the subject of an assignment or a declaration of trust).
[72] Strictly speaking, a sub-trust. See *ante*, p. 50.
[73] Provided that the consideration is money or money's worth rather than marriage consideration.

land to the trustees in exchange for the money or money's worth in question. This remedy will also be available to the beneficiary where the subject matter of the intended trust is pure personalty for whose loss equity regards damages as an inadequate remedy; this will be the case where the subject matter is a chattel not readily available on the open market, such as a rare painting, a rare antique, a vintage motor vehicle, or shares in a private company. Where, on the other hand, the contract in question is not capable of being specifically enforced because damages are an adequate remedy for the loss of the subject matter of the intended trust, the beneficiary will be limited to common law damages for breach of contract. These damages will be payable directly to the beneficiary rather than to the intended trustees, although there will obviously be nothing to prevent the beneficiary from himself paying the sum in question on to the trustees and thus creating a completely constituted trust of the money.

These principles apply not only to existing property but also to after-acquired property if and when it is acquired. In *Holroyd v. Marshall*,[74] following the sale of machinery in a mill, the purchaser assigned the machinery to a trustee on trust for the vendor if he should pay £5,000 to the purchaser and if not on trust for the purchaser. The deed of assignment included both the existing machinery and any after-acquired machinery which might be added to or substituted for the original machinery. The House of Lords held that as soon as any further machinery was acquired it vested immediately in equity in the trustee on these trusts and thus could not be the subject of execution by the creditors of the vendor. It has been established by subsequent authorities that this will occur even in the case of property in respect of which specific performance would not normally be decreed provided that the valuable consideration has already been furnished by the beneficiary.[75] Thus in *Re Gillott's Settlement*[76] debtors agreed with their creditors that any income which they received should within 3 days of receipt be paid to a trustee on various trusts for both debtors and creditors. It was held that an equitable interest in each payment received by the debtors vested immediately in the trustee so that the trust of each payment was immediately completely constituted. The majority of the decided cases, however, concern marriage consideration, a type of valuable consideration which is not recognised by the common law, and so will be discussed in the following section.[77]

(B) A Simple Contract Recognised Only in Equity

In one particular situation not recognised by the common law, equity will imply both a contract for the creation by the settlor of a completely constituted trust in favour of the beneficiary and the necessary consideration therefor on the part of the beneficiary. This occurs where the beneficiary can

---

[74] (1862) 10 H.L.C. 191.

[75] Principally by the House of Lords in *Tailby v. Official Receiver* (1888) 13 App. Cas. 523 (a case concerning an assignment by way of mortgage rather than an assignment to trustees on trust).

[76] [1934] Ch. 97. See also *Re Lind* [1915] 2 Ch. 345 and *Re Haynes' Will Trusts* [1949] Ch. 5.

[77] See *post, infra.*

bring himself within a marriage consideration. Where a settlement in consideration of marriage is made either before the marriage or contemporaneously with the celebration of the marriage or subsequent to the marriage pursuant to an agreement made prior to the marriage, equity implies that the settlor, the spouses, and the children and more remote descendants of the marriage are parties to a contract in respect of which they have given consideration. Any of the persons thus deemed to be a party to this implied contract can enforce any of the obligations arising thereunder, not only the original obligation of the settlor to create the settlement in question but also any obligations of the spouses to transfer any of their existing or after-acquired property to the trustees to be held on the trusts of the settlement. Any such obligation is capable of being specifically enforced even where damages would normally be an adequate remedy for the loss of the property in question. In the case of a marriage settlement, common law damages are never an adequate remedy for the simple reason that they are not available in an action by the beneficiaries[78]—the common law does not recognise marriage consideration.

These principles are illustrated by the case of *Pullan v. Koe*.[79] A wife was given a sum of money which was caught by a covenant to settle after-acquired property into which both she and her husband had entered in their marriage settlement. The sum was never transferred to the trustees and part of the money was eventually invested in bonds which were held at a bank in the name of the husband. Following his death, the bonds came into the hands of his executor. Any action by the trustees on the covenants had by then become statute barred. However, it was held that the money received by the wife had been subject to the trusts of the marriage settlement from the moment of its receipt. Consequently, the children of the marriage could specifically enforce the simple contract implied by equity and thus bring about the transfer of the bonds by the executor to the trustees.

Normally the only persons within the marriage consideration are the spouses, the children and the more remote descendants of the marriage.[80] However, there is some authority that, in certain circumstances, illegitimate children and children of an earlier or subsequent marriage of one of the spouses may be brought within the marriage consideration if their interests are so "interwoven" with the interests of the children of the marriage in consideration of which the settlement was made that the interests of the latter cannot be enforced without also enforcing the interests of the former. This was suggested in *Attorney-General v. Jacobs-Smith*[81] and was supported by Buckley J. in *Re Cook's Settlement Trusts*.[82] However, this extension, which is in any case somewhat ambiguous, appears to go only thus far and will apparently not be extended further. In *Re Cook's Settlement Trusts*[83] an

---

[78] Common law damages will of course be available in an action by the trustees to enforce any covenants entered into by either the settlor or the spouses.

[79] [1913] 1 Ch. 9.

[80] *MacDonald v. Scott* [1893] A.C. 642 at 650 establishes that "issue" includes both children and more remote issue such as grandchildren and great-grandchildren.

[81] [1895] 2 Q.B. 341 at 354, *per* Kay L.J.

[82] [1965] Ch. 902. See also *Re D'Avigdor-Goldsmid* [1951] Ch. 1038 at 1053 (overruled on other grounds: [1953] A.C. 347).

[83] [1965] Ch. 902.

attempt was made to establish a similar principle to enable an intended beneficiary who is specially an object of the intended trust or is within the consideration of the deed of settlement to enforce any obligations contained therein. (This alleged principle bears some resemblance to the former doctrine of "meritorious consideration", a principle analogous to marriage consideration which existed at least until the end of the eighteenth century[84]; this principle was based on the natural love and affection between parent and child and consequently could be utilised by the latter to enforce settlements made by the former.) In this case, Sir Francis Cook had entered into a settlement which was not in consideration of marriage in which he had covenanted with his father and with the trustees that, in the event that he sold certain valuable paintings which had been transferred to him by his father, he would pay over the proceeds of sale to the trustees to be held on the trusts of the settlement, ultimately for the benefit of his children. He subsequently purported to give one of the paintings to his then wife who wished to sell it. Buckley J. refused to accept the alleged principle, holding that the equitable exception to the rule that equity will not assist a volunteer is confined to persons within the marriage consideration. Having consequently held that the children could not enforce the covenant against Sir Francis, he then went on to hold, for reasons that will be considered later,[85] that the trustees ought not to enforce the covenant against him either.

Because at the time when a marriage settlement is entered into, it is not normally known whether or not there will actually be any issue of the marriage, it is usual to insert an ultimate remainder in favour of the statutory next-of-kin of one of the spouses. Such persons are not within the marriage consideration and cannot enforce any of the obligations arising under the marriage settlement. This is illustrated by *Re Plumptre's Settlement*.[86] The husband and wife, on the occasion of their marriage, covenanted with their trustees to settle the wife's after-acquired property for the benefit of herself and her husband successively for life, then for the issue of the marriage, and then for the wife's next-of-kin. The husband bought certain stock in the wife's name and the wife afterwards sold it and invested the proceeds of sale in other stock. She then died without issue, leaving her husband as her administrator. It was held that the next-of-kin, because they were volunteers, could not enforce the wife's covenant against her husband as administrator. It was also held that the trustees could not sue for damages for breach of covenant because the claim was statute-barred.[87]

Finally, it should be noted that if the settlement is made after marriage and not in pursuance of an ante-nuptial agreement, it will be wholly voluntary. This is because, although there may be consideration between husband and wife, that consideration would not be their marriage—such being past—but

---

[84] This is generally thought to be the basis on which a covenant to settle a plantation on illegitimate children was enforced in *Williamson v. Codrington* (1750) 1 Ves.Sen. 511 and is one of the possible explanations of the decision in *Fletcher v. Fletcher* (1844) 6 Hare 67 (see G. H. Jones (1965) 24 C.L.J. 46 at 49).

[85] See *post*, p. 160.

[86] [1910] 1 Ch. 609. See also to a like effect *Re D'Angibau* (1880) 15 Ch.D. 228.

[87] Any such action, even if not statute-barred, would probably now be impossible because of the decisions in *Re Pryce* [1917] 1 Ch. 234, *Re Kay's Settlement* [1939] Ch. 329 and *Re Cook's Settlement Trusts* [1965] Ch. 902. See *post*, p. 160.

consideration of some other kind to which their children would be strangers.[88] This was expressly held in *Green v. Paterson*,[89] which was applied in *Re Cook's Settlement Trusts*.

2. A Specialty Contract or Covenant to Create the Trust

Specialty contracts or covenants to settle property on trust have traditionally played an important role in settlements of all types. Not only have settlors commonly entered into covenants to create entirely new trusts by transferring existing or after-acquired property to trustees on trust; trusts which have already been completely constituted have regularly included covenants by the beneficiaries to transfer their existing or after-acquired property to the trustees to be held on the trusts of the settlement. This is illustrated by the cases which have already been discussed in this section. When a covenant to create a trust is entered into in exchange for valuable consideration, it will be enforceable in accordance with the principles which were considered in the immediately preceding part of this section. This part of this section is concerned with the situation where a covenant has been entered into other than for valuable consideration. In such circumstances, the beneficiaries are inevitably in a weaker position. Their only possibilities are as follows: to show that there is a completely constituted trust in their favour of the benefit of the covenant, to show that they are parties to the covenant, and to attempt to enforce the covenant indirectly by means of an action by the trustees on the covenant at common law against the settlor.[90]

(A)   A Completely Constituted Trust of the Benefit of the Covenant
There is no reason in principle why there should not be a completely constituted trust of the benefit of a covenant to settle. Any chose in action can be the subject matter of a trust and so a settlor is certainly capable of declaring that the right which, by means of his covenant, he has conferred upon the trustees to enforce the covenant against him should be held on trust for the beneficiaries of the intended trust. If such a trust can be found to have been created, then, although the trust of the property which the settlor covenanted to settle will remain incompletely constituted unless and until he transfers that property to the trustees, the beneficiaries will nevertheless be entitled to enforce the completely constituted trust of the benefit of the covenant. This trust will be enforceable just like any other trust; the beneficiaries can request the trustee to enforce the covenant against the settlor[91] and, if he declines so to do, they can either bring an action to compel him to do so or sue the settlor directly on the covenant joining the trustees

---

[88] Such as the consideration provided in *Re Cook's Settlement Trusts*.
[89] (1886) 32 Ch.D. 95.
[90] These possibilities have been the subject of an immense body of periodical literature, of which the principal articles are (in chronological order): D. W. Elliott (1960) 76 L.Q.R. 100; J. A. Hornby (1962) 78 L.Q.R. 228; W. A. Lee (1969) 85 L.Q.R. 213; J. L. Barton (1976) 92 L.Q.R. 236; R.P. Meagher & J. R. F. Lehane (1976) 92 L.Q.R. 427; C. E. F. Rickett (1979) 32 C.L.P. 1 and (1981) 34 C.L.P. 189; M. W. Friend [1982] Conv. 280.
[91] *Lloyd's v. Harper* (1880) 16 Ch.D. 290.

as a co-defendant to the action.[92] The principal difficulty lies in determining exactly when such a trust will arise.

In *Fletcher v. Fletcher*[93] a settlor covenanted with trustees that, if either or both of his two illegitimate sons survived him, his executors should, within 12 months of his death, pay to the trustees £60,000 which was to be held on trust for such of the two as reached the age of 21. The existence of the deed was never revealed by the settlor either to the trustees or to his sons; he retained the deed in his possession until his death and it was only discovered some years later among his papers. Only one of the sons both survived the settlor and reached the age of 21; he sought to enforce the covenant against the executors. Wigram V.-C. held that the settlor had clearly vested in the trustees the right to sue his executors for £60,000. He held that this was sufficient to produce a completely constituted trust of the benefit of the covenant, which could be enforced by the son. This decision, which is supported by other contemporaneous authorities,[94] has been interpreted in a variety of ways. However, it has to be seen against the background of the rules which at that time governed certainty of intention (the question of when a settlor will be held to have had sufficient intention to constitute a trust[95]). Until the middle of the nineteenth century, the courts tended to take the view that any expression of desire or hope or the like on the part of the settlor was imperative and therefore created a binding trust. Given that the settlor had clearly intended his sons to receive the benefit of the covenant after his death, it was perhaps not unreasonable, in the light of the view then habitually adopted as to certainty of intention, for Wigram V.-C. to have found a completely constituted trust of the benefit of the covenant. However, following the modification of the rules governing certainty of intention which took place towards the end of the nineteenth century,[96] it is difficult to see how any such intention could today be deduced from the facts of *Fletcher v. Fletcher*. Certainly no such trust has been upheld in any of the cases subsequent to the change in the certainty of intention rule in which arguments based on *Fletcher v. Fletcher* have been raised. Admittedly in one of those cases, *Re Cook's Settlement Trusts*,[97] Buckley J. distinguished *Fletcher v. Fletcher* not on this ground but on the basis that the covenant which he was considering related to after-acquired property, something which was also the case in three other decisions in which *Fletcher v. Fletcher* was not applied.[98] Given that after-acquired property can

---

[92] *Les Affreteurs Reunis v. Leopold Walford* [1919] A.C. 801.

[93] (1844) 4 Hare 67.

[94] None of these authorities contains as clear a statement of principle as that contained in *Fletcher v. Fletcher*; consequently all have been the subject of different explanations. Wigram V.-C. himself relied on *Clough v. Lambert* (1839) 10 Sim. 74 and *Williamson v. Codrington* (1750) 1 Ves.Sen. 511 (although this decision is equally explicable as based on "meritorious consideration" (see *ante*, n. 84)). *Watson v. Barker* (1843) 6 Beav. 283 and *Cox v. Barnard* (1850) 8 Hare 310 have also been described as cases of this type, although the better explanation for the latter, as well as for the much later inadequately reported *Re Cavendish-Browne's Settlement Trusts* [1916] W.N. 341 may well be the presence of a covenant for further assurance.

[95] See *ante*, pp. 82–87.

[96] ibid.

[97] [1965] Ch. 902. The facts were considered *ante*, p. 154.

[98] *Re Plumptre's Settlement* [1910] 1 Ch. 609; *Re Pryce* [1917] 1 Ch. 234; *Re Kay's Settlement* [1939] Ch. 329.

undoubtedly form the subject matter of a covenant,[99] there seems no good reason for this distinction[1] nor is it consistent with other authorities. In *Davenport v. Bishopp*,[2] Knight-Bruce V.-C. indicated that it was possible for there to be a completely constituted trust of the benefit of a covenant to settle after-acquired property, a view which is confirmed by other authorities in which promises to pay uncertain sums on uncertain future dates arising under simple contracts have been held capable of forming the subject matter of a trust.[3] Consequently, the distinction of *Fletcher v. Fletcher* on the grounds of lack of certainty of intention seems clearly preferable to the distinction adopted by Buckley J. in *Re Cook's Settlement Trusts*, which is better explained on the grounds that there was no intention to create a trust of the benefit of Sir Francis Cook's covenant in favour of his children but merely an intention to create a trust if and when its subject matter came into existence and was duly transferred to the trustees. On this basis, a completely constituted trust of the benefit of a covenant to settle either existing or after-acquired property must certainly be capable of being found today if the settlor has clearly manifested the appropriate intention[4] by, for example, stating expressly that, pending transfer of the intended trust property, "the benefit of the covenant to settle shall be held by the trustees on the trusts of the settlement".

While all the commentators would be likely to agree that the use of this wording would give rise to a completely constituted trust of the benefit of the covenant in question, there is no general agreement as to what, if any, other situations should be found to give rise to such a trust. On the one hand, it has been contended that such a trust should never be found in the absence of some clear indication of the type exemplified above that this was indeed the intention of the settlor.[5] This view has the merit of being consistent with the modern rule as to certainty of intention and with all the modern authorities; however, it involves distinguishing *Fletcher v. Fletcher* in one of the ways mentioned above and undoubtedly enables settlors to go back on voluntary covenants to settle.[6] On the other hand, it has been contended that such a trust should be implied into every covenant to settle.[7] This view is clearly inconsistent with the vast majority of the decided cases[8] but does prevent voluntary covenants to settle becoming unenforceable and,

---

[99] See *ante*, p. 152.

[1] See J. L. Barton (1976) 92 L.Q.R. 236 and R. P. Meagher & J. R. F. Lehane (1976) 92 L.Q.R. 427.

[2] (1843) 2 Y. & C.C.C. 451 at 460.

[3] *Lloyd's v. Harper* (1880) 16 Ch.Div. 290 (Lloyd's was held to be entitled to sue as trustee for the benefit of all those with whom an underwriter had entered into contracts of insurance); *Royal Exchange Assurance v. Tomlin* [1928] Ch. 179 (trust of the benefit of a promise to pay a sum only in the event of a person's death before a certain date upheld).

[4] It has been questioned whether the relevant intention should be that of the settlor or of the trustees, since it is the latter who hold the chose in action which is the subject matter of the trust. However, in the case of a covenant to settle other than for value, the better view is that the relevant intention should be that of the settlor (see *The Restatement of Trusts* (2nd ed.), para. 26; C. E. F. Rickett (1979) 32 C.L.P. 1; J. D. Feltham (1982) 98 L.Q.R. 17).

[5] This view has been adopted in successive editions of this work, of Hanbury & Martin, *Modern Equity*, and of Pettit, *Equity and the Law of Trusts*.

[6] See J. D. Feltham (1982) 98 L.Q.R. 17.

[7] See D. W. Elliott (1960) 76 L.Q.R. 100; J. A. Hornby (1962) 78 L.Q.R. 228.

[8] Other than *Fletcher v. Fletcher* and the other cases referred to *ante*, n. 94.

therefore, meaningless.[9] Between these two extreme views, various intermediate positions have been suggested. It has been argued[10] that such a
trust should be implied where the covenant in question gives rise to a debt[11]
but not otherwise.[12] It has also been argued[13] that such a trust should be
implied where the deed in question merely consists of one covenant, on the
basis that, since the deed would otherwise be futile, this must be taken to be
the intention of the settlor, but should not be implied in the case of lengthy
settlements,[14] where the intention of the settlor in relation to individual
covenants is necessarily unclear.[15] However, despite the bewildering variety
of views which have been expressed,[16] there is absolutely no doubt that at
present, for whatever reason, a completely constituted trust of the benefit of
a covenant will not be found in the absence of some clear manifestation of
the appropriate intention of the settlor; it certainly has to be admitted that
only this view seems to be consistent with the modern rule as to certainty of
intention.

(B) A Beneficiary Party to the Covenant

The beneficiaries may be able to maintain an action at common law against
the settlor on the covenant to settle. This will be the case if the covenant to
settle purports to be made with the beneficiaries as covenantees and is either
a deed poll (a deed to which only the settlor is a party) or a deed *inter partes*
(a deed to which the settlor and others are parties) to which the beneficiaries
are either parties or are made parties by section 56 of the Law of Property
Act 1925 (which applies only where the subject matter is land).[17] In *Cannon
v. Hartley*[18] a husband, wife and daughter were all parties to a deed of
separation in which the father covenanted to settle on himself, the wife and
the daughter one half of any property which he might receive under the will
of either of his parents. Having received such property, he refused to settle
it. The daughter was held to be entitled to maintain against him an action for
damages for breach of covenant. Since she had given no value, she was
clearly unable to obtain specific performance. However, the fact that,
because she was a volunteer, equity declined to assist her did not mean that
equity would frustrate her right at common law to enforce a covenant to
which she was a party. She consequently recovered, by way of damages, the
value of the interest which she should have received under the settlement.

---

[9] See *The Restatement of Trusts* (2nd ed.), para. 26 and J. D. Feltham: (1982) 98 L.Q.R. 17.
[10] By M. W. Friend [1982] Conv. 280.
[11] Which will be the case where the subject matter of the covenant is existing money.
[12] In other words, where the subject matter of the covenant is either specific and presently
existing property other than money or after-acquired property.
[13] By D. J. Hayton in Hayton & Marshall: *Cases and Commentary on the Law of Trusts and Equitable
Remedies* (10th ed., 1997) p. 231.
[14] Such as marriage settlements, where covenants to settle are invariably made in favour both
of persons within the marriage consideration and of persons outside it.
[15] The settlor cannot be taken to have intended to create such a trust in favour of persons
outside the marriage consideration.
[16] Those mentioned in the text are only a sample.
[17] See the review of the authorities by Lord Upjohn in *Beswick v. Beswick* [1968] A.C. 98 at
102–105.
[18] [1949] Ch. 213.

Thus, while this remedy will not enable the trust to be completely constituted, the beneficiaries will be able to recover compensation for the loss of
the interest which they would have obtained thereunder.

(C) An Action by the Trustees on the Covenant

Where the beneficiaries are unable to enforce the covenant in either of the
two ways already discussed, either in equity by virtue of the existence of a
completely constituted trust of the benefit of the covenant or at common law
by means of an action on the covenant for damages, they will clearly have
no direct means of enforcing it. This somewhat obvious proposition was
confirmed by the Court of Appeal in Re d'Angibau,[19] where the eventual
beneficiaries under a marriage settlement, the wife's next-of-kin, who were
of course not within the marriage consideration, were held unable to enforce
a covenant by the wife to transfer an equitable remainder to the trustees of
the settlement. In such circumstances, the only remaining option of the
beneficiaries will be to attempt to enforce the covenant indirectly by means
of an action by the trustees on the covenant at law against the settlor.

It is clear that the beneficiaries cannot compel the trusts to bring such an
action. In the absence of any completely constituted trust and of any simple
or specialty contract to which they are parties, they are clearly in no position
to compel anyone to do anything and are undoubtedly volunteers. However, given that the trustees have an undoubted right of action at law against
the settlor, it might be thought that they would be entitled to exercise that
right of action if they so chose and hold any damages recovered from the
settlor on trust for the beneficiaries. This is not in fact the case. It has long
been established that, if the trustees seek the directions of the court,[20] they
will be directed not to sue the settlor on the covenant. Indeed, this rule is so
well established that there is now no need for the trustees to trouble to
obtain any directions—the present authorities provide them with a complete
defence to any action for breach of trust.[21]

In Re Pryce[22] the trustees of a marriage settlement sought directions from
the court as to whether they were bound to enforce in favour of the wife's
next-of-kin (who were the only persons beneficially entitled other than the
wife) a covenant by the wife to settle after-acquired property. Eve J. held that
the next-of-kin could not obtain relief directly[23]; consequently there was no
reason for equity to give them relief indirectly by an order to the trustees to
enforce the covenant. He then went on to hold, without further discussion,
that they were bound not to enforce the covenant.[24] This decision was

---

[19] (1880) 15 Ch.D. 228.
[20] Something which trustees habitually do before embarking on legal proceedings to avoid any
risk of being made personally responsible for the costs in the event that they were subsequently held not to have been properly incurred.
[21] See Re Ralli's Will Trusts [1964] Ch. 288 at 301–302.
[22] [1917] 1 Ch. 234.
[23] His reasons for reaching this conclusion were in fact erroneous, being based on a misunderstanding of the effect of the Judicature Acts of 1873 and 1875, but the conclusion is
nevertheless clearly correct for the reasons already stated in the text.
[24] This conclusion was not in fact necessary, since the negative answer to the question which
Eve J. was asked was, strictly speaking, "the trustees are not bound to sue" rather than "the
trustees are bound not to sue". This is one of the grounds on which the decision has been
criticised; see D. W. Elliott (1960) 76 L.Q.R. 100.

followed and applied in *Re Kay's Settlement*,[25] in which the trustees of a voluntary settlement sought directions whether they should or should not take proceedings in favour of the ultimate beneficiaries against the settlor on her covenant to settle after-acquired property and were directed by Simonds J. not to do so.[26] The same conclusion was reached by Buckley J. in *Re Cook's Settlement Trusts*.[27]

None of these cases contains any reasoned discussion of exactly why the trustees must not enforce the covenant. It has been argued[28] that there is no reason for equity thus to restrain parties to a covenant from exercising their legal rights thereunder if they wish to do so.[29] However, it seems that the consequences of such an action would not ultimately favour the beneficiaries. Even on the assumption that the trustees would be able to obtain substantial damages for breach of covenant (an assumption which, although it has been doubted,[30] is in fact supported both by principle[31] and by precedent[32]), there is no reason why these damages should be held on the trusts of the settlement. In a situation where, *a fortiori*, there is not a completely constituted trust of the benefit of the covenant (if there were, the beneficiaries would of course be able to compel the trustees to enforce the covenant), it appears that any damages arising from any action thereon would be held by the trustees not on trust for the beneficiaries but on resulting trust for the settlor.[33] Since any action brought by the trustees against the settlor would thus result in the damages payable being held on resulting trust for the person paying them, equity is clearly correct to prohibit such a circuitous action. Consequently, for this reason *Re Pryce*, *Re Kay's Settlement* and *Re Cook's Settlement Trusts* were correctly decided.

It thus follows that the beneficiaries will not be able to enforce a covenant to settle indirectly by means of an action by the trustees on the covenant at law against the settlor and thus, in the absence of a completely constituted trust and of any simple or specialty contract to which they are parties, they will have no means either of bringing about the complete constitution of the trust of the benefit of the covenant or of obtaining any compensation for the settlor's failure to comply with his covenant to settle. In this situation, equity indeed declines to assist volunteers. However, it may be that the recent Law Commission Consultation Paper on *Privity of Contract: Contracts for the*

---

[25] [1939] Ch. 329.

[26] The question put to Simonds J. envisaged three possible answers: "the trustees must sue", "the trustees may sue", "the trustees must not sue". Consequently, his direction to the trustees not to sue clearly constitutes his *ratio decidendi*.

[27] [1965] Ch. 902.

[28] Particularly by D. W. Elliott (1960) 76 L.Q.R. 100.

[29] Because of the risk of being held personally liable for the costs, no trustee would be likely to do so unless the beneficiaries were members of his family or had agreed to indemnify him fully.

[30] See O. R. Marshall (1950) 3 C.L.P. 30.

[31] The fact that a party to an action at law is a trustee cannot be a ground for limiting him to nominal damages for the simple reason that the common law does not recognise trusts. For this reason, it should not matter that the trust is in fact incompletely constituted or that the property to be settled is after-acquired.

[32] *Re Cavendish-Browne's Settlement Trusts* [1916] W.N. 341. An analogous authority involving a trust of the benefit of a simple contract is *Lloyd's v. Harper* (1880) 16 Ch.D. 290.

[33] See Underhill & Hayton, *Law of Trusts and Trustees* (15th ed., 1995), pp. 156–159.

Benefit of Third Parties[34] will eventually give such beneficiaries the right to enforce covenants entered into for their benefit. The Consultation Paper proposes that third parties should be allowed to enforce contractual provisions made in their favour. If these proposals are ever enacted, then beneficiaries will have a direct action at common law to enforce covenants to settle property on trust for them and the decisions to this effect (but not otherwise) in *Re Pryce*, *Re Kay's Settlement* and *Re Cook's Settlement Trust* will then become obsolete.

---

[34] The Law Commission, Consultation Paper No.212 (1991).

CHAPTER 6

DISCRETIONARY TRUSTS AND POWERS

I. THE CREATION OF DISCRETIONARY TRUSTS AND POWERS

1. *Generally*

ALMOST all trusts involve the exercise of discretions and powers. Depending on the circumstances of the trust in question, its trustees will generally have a considerable number of powers either conferred expressly by the trust instrument or implied into it by statute. These will normally include powers to deal with the investment of the trust property by making and transposing investments,[1] powers which, if the trust in question is a trust of land, include all the powers of an absolute owner[2]; power to settle claims[3]; power to apply advance capital for the benefit of a beneficiary[4]; power either to advance income for the support of an infant beneficiary or to accumulate it[5]; power to apply to the court for guidance as to the execution of the trust[6]; and power to insure trust property.[7] All these powers, and many more, will be implied by statute into every trust instrument unless they are expressly excluded. Powers of this type are normally conferred only on the trustees. However, equally if not more significant are the powers to replace some or all of the existing trustees and appoint new ones, which the trust instrument may confer on the settlor, on the existing trustees themselves, or indeed on anyone else; these powers are, in the absence of express provision, similarly conferred by statute on the existing trustees although in such circumstances beneficiaries of full age who are between them absolutely entitled to the trust property are now also entitled to exercise them.[8] It must however be stressed that it is fundamental to the nature of a trust that a trustee should

---

[1] See *post*, p. 540.
[2] Trusts of Land and Appointment of Trustees Act 1996, s.6(1). Settlements subject to the Settled Land Act 1925, no more of which can now be created, are however not trusts of land and their position is still governed by Settled Land Act 1925, s.41.
[3] Trustee Act 1925, s.15.
[4] See *post*, p. 616.
[5] See *post*, p. 595.
[6] See *post*, p. 501.
[7] Trustee Act 1925, s.19. The position is surprising. Trustees are under no duty to insure (*Re McEacharn* (1911) 103 L.T. 900) and the statutory power is only to insure for a sum up to three-quarters of the value of the property. However, express powers to insure usually allow cover to be effected for the full reinstatement value.
[8] See *post*, p. 476. These powers were conferred on absolutely entitled beneficiaries by Trusts of Land and Appointment of Trustees Act 1996, ss.19,20 but may be excluded in the trust instrument or, in the case of trusts created prior to the legislation, by a deed executed by the settlor or the surviving settlors of full capacity.

not be a puppet at the end of a string pulled by the settlor or by the beneficiaries[9] but rather a person who can and will exercise an independent judgment over a wide field. This remains the case despite the fact that the trustee in question may have been appointed by someone given an express power so to do or in default by beneficiaries of full age who are between them absolutely entitled to the trust property. The fact that a trustee has been appointed by the settlor or by the beneficiaries does not enable him to escape from liability for breach of trust if he fails to exercise an independent judgment; however, while he will certainly be at risk if he blindly follows the instructions of the settlor, he will admittedly not be at any risk if he follows instructions given to him by beneficiaries of full age who are between them absolutely entitled to the trust property.

Discretions and powers are not, however, limited to the administrative and other matters considered in the previous paragraph. They can and often do extend to the determination of exactly who is to be beneficially entitled to the trust property and in what proportions. Trustees can be given the power to select which of a group of beneficiaries receives benefits from the trust; in such circumstances, they have the right to exclude individual beneficiaries completely. Alternatively, they can be given the power to determine how the trust property should be divided up between a class of beneficiaries, all of whom are to receive something. Trusts of both these types are generally known as discretionary trusts. Exactly the same powers can be given to persons other than the trustees; such persons are technically known as donees of powers. These are not the only ways of achieving these results; trustees may be able to achieve them indirectly by the administrative powers already referred to by, for example, exercising their powers to advance capital or to decide whether to distribute or to accumulate income, although the latter power cannot be exercised after the first 21 years of a trust except during minorities.[10] This chapter is, however, principally concerned with the exercise of discretions and powers to determine beneficial entitlements; needless to say, that does not alter the fact that most of the principles which will be discussed apply equally to all the other discretions and powers which the trust instrument or statute may have conferred.

2. *The Players*

It was seen in Chapter 1[11] that a trust cannot exist unless at least two persons are involved, one or more trustees and one or more beneficiaries (each of the

---

[9] It is in this respect that the position of a trustee differs from that of a nominee, or bare trustee, who is often under an express or implied contractual obligation to comply in all respects with the directions of the beneficiaries. A bare trust is one where property is held directly on trust for a body corporate or one or more beneficiaries of full age absolutely. However, not all trustees whose beneficiaries are of full age and between them absolutely entitled to the trust property are bare trustees. A trustee who holds property by way of succession for persons who are between them absolutely beneficially entitled is certainly not a bare trustee and must act in such a way as to protect the interests both of the tenant for life and of the remainderman. However, both his beneficiaries and the beneficiaries of a bare trust have the right to terminate the trust at any time by calling for the transfer of the trust property to them.

[10] See *post*, p. 616.

[11] See *ante*, p. 15.

two can be and very often is[12] both trustee and beneficiary). Every trust necessarily also has a settlor, who may also be either trustee or beneficiary or both. Discretionary trusts habitually involve further players. Quite apart from the fact that, for reasons which will shortly become apparent, discretionary trusts tend to have a considerable number, sometimes many thousands,[13] of beneficiaries, it is standard practice to vest powers not only in the trustees but also in other donees. There has always been a tendency for such powers to be vested in settlors and in individual beneficiaries; traditional settlements for persons by way of succession have habitually given the settlor or the life tenant a power to choose which of a number of potential remaindermen will take at the end of the life interest—a typical formulation would be a gift "to trustees for my wife for life and subject thereto for such of our children as I the settlor [or she my wife] may by will or by deed appoint and in default of appointment for all our children in equal shares absolutely". Powers of this type are also sometimes given to persons who are otherwise totally unconnected with the settlement. But in recent years it has become increasingly common, particularly in trusts created in off-shore jurisdictions, for much more substantial powers to be given to outsiders. Such powers are generally not limited to the determination of beneficial interests but also include the right to remove the existing trustees and appoint new ones and to direct or alternatively to veto the exercise by the trustees of the administrative powers vested in them. Persons with such powers are just as much donees of powers as persons with more restricted powers. However, as they have proliferated, they have become known as protectors of the settlement in question.[14]

The expression "protector of the settlement" is actually derived from the Fines and Recoveries Act 1833 and originally denoted a person who, in certain circumstances, had to give his approval to a now virtually obsolete estate in land known as an estate in fee tail being converted into an estate in fee simple.[15] However, none of the characteristics of a modern protector is derived from this statute. Further, there is not the slightest need for a person with the sort of substantial powers referred to in the previous paragraph to be described in this way as a protector either in the trust instrument or by anyone else. Such a person can equally be and often is described as an

---

[12] Every property which is jointly owned will, under Law of Property Act 1925, ss.34 & 36 be held by its co-owners as trustees at law on trust for themselves as joint tenants or tenants in common in equity.

[13] As was seen when considering certainty of objects, *ante*, p. 92.

[14] See generally Waters in *Trends in Contemporary Trust Law* (ed. Oakley, 1996), p. 63.

[15] An estate in fee tail devolves on the successive heirs of the body of the original tenant in fee tail; however such an estate can be converted into an estate in fee simple, a process known as barring the entail which has the effect of depriving the next person in line of his inheritance. A tenant in fee tail in possession has since 1833 been able to do this by an *inter vivos* conveyance of the land in fee simple or since 1925 by his will. A tenant in fee tail who does not have an interest in possession has only ever been able to do this *inter vivos* and then only with the consent of the person known as the protector of the settlement. He will now be the holder of the interest in possession for the time being or, in default, the court; until 1926, however, settlors were entitled to nominate up to three persons of their choice to act as protector of the settlement and that possibility is the basis of the modern usage of the expression. (Estates in fee tail do still exist but sadly no more can now be created as a result of the Trusts of Land and Appointment of Trustees Act 1996, Sched. 1, para. 5.)

enforcer, a nominator, a committee or by any other name. All these descriptions are found in the different legislative provisions of those off-shore jurisdictions who have attempted to regulate this new institution.[16] The position of protectors in those jurisdictions is of course governed by the relevant legislation. But in jurisdictions like England and Wales whose legislation contains no reference to protectors, the rights and duties of a protector are governed exclusively by the contents of the trust instrument in question. This was specifically held by the Supreme Court of Bermuda, another jurisdiction which has no relevant legislation, in one of the very few cases which has yet had to consider protectors, *Von Knieriem v. Bermuda Trust Company*, generally known as *The Star Trusts Case*.[17]

No matter what the precise powers conferred on any particular protector actually are, however, his appointment is for one purpose and one purpose only: to direct and control the trustees on behalf of the settlor in the exercise of their discretions. A settlor of a trust *inter vivos* can of course generally fulfil this role himself during his lifetime. He has no formal legal right to any control by virtue of the fact that he was the settlor, not even to have his wishes listened to. However, he will undoubtedly have been responsible for choosing the original trustees and, even if he has not appointed himself to be one of them, they are obviously likely to listen to his views—particularly if, as is usual, he has the power to remove them without having to show cause. Indeed, the fact that settlors are in practice able to use discretionary trusts as a means of divesting themselves of the ownership of property while still retaining control of its ultimate devolution is one of their principal attractions. The object of having a protector is to enable this control to continue after the settlor's death. Where a protector is employed, the settlor will often formalise his own position during his lifetime by appointing himself as the first protector. Even where he does not do so, he will necessarily have appointed the first protector and will normally have the power to remove and replace him. And once the settlor is dead, each Protector is likely to have the power to nominate his successor.

Protectors have not yet become particularly common in trusts subject to English law because the settlors of such trusts are likely to know and, consequently, have confidence in their chosen trustees who are anyway likely to be reasonably susceptible to the influence of the settlor and the beneficiaries. Their frequent utilisation in off-shore trusts is precisely because in practice such trusts have to have locally based trustees whom neither the settlor nor the beneficiaries is even likely to know, never mind trust (it is usually unwise for either the settlor or the beneficiaries of an off-shore trust to be among its trustees)[18]; the presence of a protector throughout the lifetime of the trust is therefore a considerable additional protection for

---

[16] Belize Trusts Act 1992, s.16 ("protector"); British Virgin Islands Trustee Ordinance, s.86 ("protector, nominator, committee or any other name"); Cayman Islands Special Trusts (Alternative Regime) Law 1997, s.2 ("enforcer"); Cook Islands International Trusts Act 1984, s.2 ("protector").

[17] (1994) Unreported but see Butterworths *Offshore Cases and Materials* Vol. 1, pp. 116–125 and Matthews, 9 *Trust Law International* (1995) 108.

[18] This is because the Inland Revenue may then contend that the person in question is in control of the trust and attempt to tax him on its income, thus defeating the whole object of the exercise. This happened in *Inland Revenue Commissioners v. Schroder* [1983] S.T.C. 480, where

the beneficiaries after the settlor's death. However, as the facts of the *Star Trust Case* illustrate, the presence of a protector may not always be helpful to the beneficiaries during the settlor's lifetime, whether the protector is the settlor or someone else. In this case, the trust property comprised a substantial minority holding in a company which was in turn the holding company of a major pharmaceutical group. The settlor was the moving spirit of this holding company but due to a boardroom struggle had to face the possibility that he would be voted off its board of directors. The protector, the settlor's lawyer and personal friend, sought assurances from the trustee, a Bermuda trust company, that it would delegate its votes to him and thus enable him to vote for the settlor. The trust company, apparently under some pressure from the beneficiaries who seem to have been less enthusiastic about the settlor, refused to do so. So the protector simply sacked the trustee and appointed another Bermudan trust company as trustee in its place. The court held that he was perfectly entitled so to do. The position of the settlor was therefore preserved contrary to the wishes of the beneficiaries, who were also deprived of any possibility of recourse against the original trust company.[19] However, as will be seen later on,[20] there are some circumstances in which beneficiaries in this position may well be able to make out a claim against the protector.

3. *Reasons for Creating Discretionary Trusts and Powers*

(A) Flexibility
As was mentioned in Chapter 1,[20a] a settlor or testator often wishes to make a present disposition but to confer a benefit at some time in the future in the light of the circumstances then pertaining, circumstances which have not yet arisen and which therefore necessarily cannot be known. A person who is creating a trust for his children or remoter issue may wish the amount, if any, which each receives to depend on his or her conduct; financial need and/or success. A much larger payment may be justified in the case of a beneficiary who is a student or who is training for entry into a profession or vocation than in the case of a sibling of his who is already well established in business. Alternatively, a person may have definitively decided to devote funds to charitable purposes but may wish the particular recipients of his bounty to be selected according to the social or other needs which seem most pressing at the time in the future when the funds become available. However, it must not be thought that the fact that discretions have been vested in trustees necessarily means that the objects of the trust must be treated unequally. A father who creates a trust for his children or more remote issue leaves the trustees entirely free to treat them all alike if the trustees wish to do; equally, the trustees are free to treat them unequally

---

the Revenue unsuccessfully claimed that this was the result of the settlor having the power to appoint trustees and protectors. Under the present law, a majority of off-shore trustees is necessary even if there was a non-resident settlor and the presence of any on-shore trustee or beneficiary will be fatal if the settlor was resident.

[19] Who could not possibly be held liable for breach of trust if it had been sacked against its will.

[20] See *post*, p. 191.

[20a] See *ante*, p. 7.

whether or not one of the special circumstances which the father may have
had in mind occurs.

(B)   Continuing Control of the Property

It has already been seen that settlors are in practice able to use discretionary
trusts as a means of divesting themselves of the ownership of property
while still retaining control of its ultimate devolution. A settlor who creates
a trust *inter vivos* is likely to be able to exercise control over the exercise of
whatever discretions he confers on the trustees during his lifetime. He can
do this as of right if he chooses to appoint himself either as one of the
trustees or as the first protector of the settlement. Even if he has not done
either of these things, he will usually have appointed the trustees and, if
there is one, the protector. They are obviously likely to listen to his views
particularly if, as is usual, he has the power to remove them without having
to show any cause. Further, the presence of a protector with the power to
nominate his successor will enable this control to be exercised as of right
during the entire lifetime of the trust. Thus the interests of the settlor can be
protected both during and after his lifetime, as can the interests of the
beneficiaries to the extent that they are not in conflict with the interests of the
settlor.

A less direct means by which settlors can control the ultimate devolution
of the trust property is by means of letters of wishes.[21] As their name
suggests, these are documents which exist outside the formal trust documents. They set out the wishes of the settlor but are not binding on the
trustees. The extent to which the beneficiaries are entitled to see them has
not yet been finally established.[22] A genuine letter of wishes, by which the
settlor provides additional guidance for the trustees of a discretionary trust
who have little contact with and may well not know all the members of a
class of beneficiaries, is not only not objectionable; it can be extremely
helpful. Such non-binding guidance can be very useful for both settlor and
trustees, although less so for beneficiaries even in the event that they are
actually allowed to see the document in question. But in off-shore trust
jurisdictions letters of wishes can play a much more sinister role. Deeds of
trust tend to be standard form documents used in hundreds of cases and
often take the form of a declaration of trust by the off-shore trustees stating
that a nominal sum has been transferred to them to be held on the trusts in
question rather than a deed of settlement executed by the settlor. In such
circumstances, letters of wishes are often the only documents which reveal
the identity of the true settlor and the true beneficiaries. They therefore
enable the existence of the settlement and the interests of the beneficiaries
thereunder to be concealed both from their creditors and from the fiscal
authorities of their on-shore jurisdictions. Tailored letters of wishes can also
be used to convince a settlor unfamiliar with the nature of a discretionary
trust that his wishes will in fact be followed when the reality is that they are
not binding. Even worse, letters of wishes are occasionally pure shams,
either because their terms have not been explained to the settlor or because
they have been signed by dummy settlors who request the trustees to take

---

[21] See Matthews [1995] *Offshore Tax Planning Review* 181.
[22] See *post*, p. 498.

into account the wishes of a settlor whose name has not even yet been inserted in the appropriate space on the standard form letter[23]; the latter type of sham letters of wishes obviously often accompany sham trusts.[24] Nevertheless, these abusive uses of letters of wishes should not be allowed to detract from the extremely useful function of a genuine letter of wishes in enabling the settlor to provide non-binding guidance for the trustees and thus control, at least to some extent, the devolution of the trust property.[24a]

(C) Fiscal Considerations

Despite the obvious advantages already discussed, it is nevertheless fiscal considerations which are, at the present time, generally the principal reason for the creation of discretionary trusts. Income tax and capital gains tax are so-called "progressive taxes" in that they are imposed on the "slices" of a person's taxable income or capital gains at a progressively increasing rate. Each person is entitled to receive the first "slice" of his income free of tax.[25] The next "slice" is taxable at 20 per cent, the next "slice" at the so-called basic rate of 23 per cent, and the residue at the higher rate of 40 per cent.[26] Capital gains tax is imposed at the same rate as income tax on such part of a person's taxable capital gains in each year as exceeds his annual exemption.[27] Inheritance tax, on the other hand, is imposed at a fixed rate of 40 per cent on such part of a person's estate (which for this purpose includes any property disposed of other than for value during the seven years immediately prior to his death) as exceeds his lifetime allowance.[28]

In terms of tax planning, a discretionary trust has three main advantages. First, the terms of the trust instrument usually allow the trustees to decide whether to distribute or to withhold income. They can therefore distribute income to a beneficiary in a year when his total income is low, so that his

---

[23] See the facts of *West v. Lazard Brothers & Co. (Jersey)* [1993] Jersey L.R. 165, 201–205.

[24] See *ante*, p. 86.

[24a] See *ante*, p. 7.

[25] The amount of this "slice" is calculated by means of personal allowances, which vary according to the personal circumstances of the individual. For the year 1998–99, a single person is entitled to a personal allowance of £4,195; additional allowances are available to married persons, to single parents, to widows and widowers, and to pensioners, in respect of dependant relatives, and in certain other circumstances. The size of these allowances is reviewed annually in each Budget and listed in the Finance Act by means of which each Budget is brought into effect. Income tax is at present governed by the Income and Corporation Taxes Act 1988.

[26] In 1998–99, the first £4,300 of taxable income (that is the income which exceeds a person's total allowances) was taxed at 20 per cent, taxable income between £4,301 and £27,100 was taxed at 23 per cent, and taxable income in excess of £27,100 was taxed at 40 per cent. The width of the bands and their thresholds are also reviewed annually in each Budget and listed in each Finance Act.

[27] In 1998–99, £6,800. There are many other exemptions, including the taxpayer's main residence, chattels worth less than £6,000, and certain securities. Capital gains tax is at present governed by the Taxation of Chargeable Gains Act 1992.

[28] In 1998–99, £223,000. Further exemptions include all gifts between spouses, small gifts of up to £3,000 per donor and £250 per donee per annum, gifts in consideration of marriage (£5,000 by each parent, £2,500 by each grandparent and £1,000 by anyone else), gifts to charities, and gifts of agricultural or business property. Inheritance Tax is at present governed by the Inheritance Tax Act 1984.

total liability to tax is kept down, and withhold income when the beneficiary's total income is high. Secondly, the trust instrument usually allows the trustees to accumulate income, so that it becomes converted into capital, although this is now only possible for the first 21 years of the trust and during subsequent minorities.[29] Thirdly, a discretionary trust allows income and capital to be spread among members of a family, rather than being bunched in the hands of one member. To take a simple example, suppose that Andrew, Basil and Colin are brothers and suppose, also, that Andrew's top rate of income tax is 40 per cent, that Basil's top rate of income tax is 23 per cent and that Colin, as a student, has no taxable income whatsoever. In principle,[30] if Andrew receives £1,000 of investment income, he would have to pay £400 income tax on it and be left with £600 in his pocket. If, however, the investment income arises in a discretionary trust and the trustees elect to pay £400 to Basil and £600 to Colin, Basil will pay £92 income tax and Colin will pay nothing (assuming in each case, of course, that the investment income does not move his total taxable income into a higher "slice"). The family as a whole, therefore, will now pay only £92 in tax, a reduction of £308.[31]

However, as a result of the widespread use of discretionary trusts in order to preserve income and capital for the benefit of the family, discretionary trusts in general have come under increasing attack from the legislature. Dealing first with income tax, trusts other than discretionary trusts pay income tax at 20 per cent when the tax is withheld at source from income arising from bank deposits and from company distributions and at 23 per cent when the tax is payable by the trustees on income from other sources.[32] However, the income received by a discretionary trust is in general now taxed at a flat rate of 34 per cent (in the case of income arising from bank deposits and from company distributions, the trustees obviously have to pay only the 14 per cent additional to the 20 per cent already withheld at source). However, in the event that income is distributed to the beneficiaries rather than being accumulated, any beneficiary whose top rate of income tax is 23 per cent or less can recover the excess tax paid by the trust. Thus a beneficiary with a top rate of 23 per cent can recover 11 per cent of the income tax paid on the sum distributed to him while a beneficiary with no taxable income at all can recover the whole of the 34 per cent tax paid on the sum distributed to him.[33]

Turning now to capital gains tax, any transfer *inter vivos* of property (other than cash or the settlor's main residence) to any trust is deemed to be a

---

[29] See *post*, p. 595.
[30] This example is only given to illustrate the principle. The result is modified by a number of provisions of the income tax legislation.
[31] However, in practice, the administration expenses of the discretionary trust must also be taken into account.
[32] Income and Corporation Taxes Act 1988, s.686 (as amended by Finance Act 1993).
[33] This will not necessarily enable the recovery of all the income tax paid by the trust because any income expended on administration expenses will not be able to be distributed and so the tax paid in respect of these expenses will not be able to be recovered. However, all administration expenses now have to be set against the 20 per cent tax withheld on company distributions and bank deposit accounts and so bear tax at the lowest possible rate. See *post*, p. 525.

disposal of that property by the settlor.[34] That property is therefore subject to capital gains tax (at whatever rate is payable by the settlor after taking into account his annual exemption) on the difference between its acquisition cost[35] and its market value at the date of the deemed disposal, with appropriate adjustments being made to the capital gain in order to take account of intervening inflation.[36] A settlor of property *inter vivos* can only escape this liability to capital gains tax in certain limited circumstances,[37] in which he can elect to have the capital gain held over; where this is possible, the trust takes over the property at its original acquisition cost, thus obviously increasing the capital gains tax which the trust will itself necessarily have to pay later when it comes to dispose of the property. Such disposals are the other aspect of capital gains tax which affects trusts, this time whether they have been created *inter vivos* or by will; the trustees obviously dispose of the property if they sell it to a third party and are deemed to do so when one or more of the beneficiaries[38] becomes absolutely entitled to the property as against them. In such circumstances, all trusts now (since April 6, 1998) pay capital gains tax at 34 per cent,[39] discretionary trusts being additionally penalised by the fact that their annual exemption is only half that of individuals.[40] Even so, this rate of 34 per cent is still less than the rate of 40 per cent at which most settlors will almost inevitably have to pay capital gains tax; consequently, the transfer of property to a discretionary trust is more likely to reduce than to increase the total capital gains tax payable,[41] which can in fact be reduced even further if the settlor takes full advantage of his annual exemptions.

Turning finally to inheritance tax, any transfer, whether *inter vivos* or testamentary, of any property to a discretionary trust is subject to inheritance tax[42] (paid at 20 per cent in respect of transfers *inter vivos* rather than the usual 40 per cent payable on death) if the total transfers of property in the previous seven years exceed the settlor's current lifetime allowance. A further charge to inheritance tax is made on every tenth anniversary of the

---

[34] Taxation of Chargeable Gains Act 1992, s.70.

[35] Its market value on March 31, 1982 or, if acquired subsequently, its original acquisition cost.

[36] Capital gains made in respect of the period between March 31, 1982 or, if later, the date of acquisition and April 5, 1998 are adjusted by notionally increasing the acquisition cost by reference to the intervening change in the Retail Price Index; capital gains made in respect of periods after April 6, 1998 are adjusted by reducing or "tapering" the gain made by a percentage which increases in accordance with the length of time that the settlor has owned the property being settled.

[37] If the assets settled comprise business property (Taxation of Chargeable Gains Act 1992, s.75) or if the creation of the trust involves a chargeable transfer for the purposes of inheritance tax.

[38] Or, for that matter, the trustees of another settlement.

[39] Taxation of Chargeable Gains Act 1992, s.1AA (previously trusts other than discretionary trusts paid at 23 per cent).

[40] Thus £3,400 in 1998–99. Where the same settlor has created more than one discretionary trust, this exemption is divided between them.

[41] This of course assumes that the value of the property continues to move upwards throughout; if the value of the property falls after it has been transferred to a discretionary trust, the capital gains tax paid at the time of the settlement will obviously be greater than that which would have been paid had the settlor not settled the property.

[42] Inheritance Tax Act 1984, ss.2,3(1).

creation of the discretionary trust at 30 per cent of whatever inheritance tax would have been payable had the property been disposed of at that time[43]; the appropriate proportion of this 10-yearly charge is payable when any property is disposed of during a ten year period.[44] However, no additional inheritance tax will in fact be payable by virtue of these provisions if the settlor settles no more than the total amount of his lifetime allowance in each seven year period.

There is no doubt that discretionary trusts are treated more harshly than other types of trusts but the overall tax payable in respect of a discretionary trust is still less than that payable by a tax payer with a top rate of 40 per cent (and few, if any, settlors are likely to have a lower top rate); further the overall tax will be considerably less if full advantage is taken of the annual capital gains tax exemption and the amount settled is limited to each settlor's lifetime allowance. Moreover, the legislature has given privileged treatment to a special type of discretionary trust, known as an accumulation and maintenance settlement.[45] Such a settlement must be for the benefit of one or more persons under 25, usually but not necessarily the children or grandchildren of the settlor; at least one beneficiary must be alive. The beneficiaries must become entitled to the trust property or to an immediate vested interest in its income upon reaching an age not exceeding 25; in the meantime, the income can either be accumulated or be applied for their maintenance, education or benefit. Such trusts are not liable to any of the additional charges to inheritance tax outlined above; inheritance tax will therefore only be payable in the normal way on the death of the settlor to the extent that his estate (including any property disposed of other than for value in the preceding seven years) exceeds his lifetime allowance. Such trusts also have other fiscal advantages. Although they are liable to income tax and capital gains tax at the higher rate of 34 per cent, no disposal for the purposes of capital gains tax is deemed to occur (as it would in the case of all other types of trusts) when the beneficiaries first become entitled to an absolute interest in the trust property. Further, save in the case of minor children of the settlor, income applied for the maintenance, education or benefit of the beneficiaries is taxed at the top rate applicable to each beneficiary rather than that applicable to his parents; consequently, such a beneficiary will be able to recover the 34 per cent tax already paid by the trustees to the extent that that rate exceeds his own top rate. These advantages are substantial; they are however limited by the fact that accumulation and maintenance trusts can only last for 25 years unless all the beneficiaries have a common grandparent.

Men go to considerable lengths to preserve their wealth and the creation of discretionary trusts remains a popular and successful way of so doing, particularly if full advantage is taken of all the available exemptions and allowances. Further, settlors are not obliged to create their discretionary trusts in this jurisdiction. Consequently, where the property to be settled

---

[43] *ibid.*, ss.61,64.
[44] *ibid.*, s.65.
[45] *ibid.*, s.71.

very greatly exceeds the settlor's lifetime allowance,[46] there has been an increasing tendency to use discretionary trusts set up not here but in other jurisdictions whose trust law was either originally based on English law[47] or has been specifically adapted to embrace the English concept of a trust.[48] Since most of these jurisdictions do not tax discretionary trusts at all, the fiscal advantages of such off-shore settlements are even greater. The legislature has therefore intervened with a view to discouraging the creation of such settlements; the problems which this has produced for a person domiciled and/or resident in some part of the United Kingdom who wishes to create an off-shore trust are discussed in a later Chapter.[49] The same Chapter also considers the increasingly stringent provisions which have been enacted in order to make the beneficial interests of those beneficiaries of off-shore trusts who are or are deemed to be domiciled and/or resident in some part of the United Kingdom liable to United Kingdom taxation.

II. THE BASIC TOOLS: TRUSTS AND POWERS

1. *Generally*

Where it is left to the trustees or indeed to some other person to decide whether a particular individual shall receive a benefit from the trust at all, or to decide the extent of the benefit of any particular beneficiary, the discretion vested in the trustees or other person will be one of two broad types, depending on whether or not they are under an obligation to exercise it.

If they are under an obligation to exercise their discretion, then they are said to hold a trust power, or a power in the nature of a trust. It is important to note that these terms have traditionally been used to denote two quite distinct situations: first, where the person subject to the obligation has the property in question vested in him as a trustee, in which case the term trust power or power in the nature of a trust is virtually indistinguishable from the term discretionary trust—indeed in the leading case of *McPhail v. Doulton*,[50] the two terms were used interchangeably; secondly, where the person subject to the obligation is not himself a trustee of the property in question so that his only role is that of exercising the discretion, in which case, although he may be described as the donee of a trust power or a power in the nature of a trust, he certainly cannot be described as a discretionary trustee since he is not a trustee of anything. If a person is holding property on trust for such of the members of a defined class and in such proportions as he shall in his absolute discretion appoint, then he is likely to be held to

---

[46] In such circumstances, the available exemptions and allowances are much less relevant; further such settlors (and only such settlors) can afford the exorbitant fees normally charged in the off-shore jurisdictions for setting-up and subsequently administering the trusts in question.

[47] Such as the Channel Islands, the Isle of Man, Bermuda, the Bahamas, the Cayman Islands, and a number of other Caribbean and Pacific tax havens.

[48] Such as Liechtenstein.

[49] See *post*, p. 760.

[50] [1971] A.C. 424.

hold a trust power or a power in the nature of a trust in the former sense; he
is in effect a discretionary trustee. If, on the other hand, a person is holding
property on trust for such of the members of a defined class and in such
proportions as a third party shall in his absolute discretion appoint, the third
party is likely to be held to have a trust power or a power in the nature of
a trust in the latter sense; he is not a trustee of anything and no discretion
whatsoever is vested in the person who is holding the property on trust.
There is no practical significance in this distinction. In each of the two cases,
the holder of the trust power is under an obligation to exercise it and, in the
event that he fails to do so, the court will exercise the trust power instead.
All that is important is to remember that there is no requirement that the
holder of a trust power should himself be a trustee of the property in
question.

If the trustees or other person are not under any obligation to exercise the
discretion vested in them, then they are said to hold a mere power or a bare
power or, less commonly, a power collateral.[51] Once again these terms cover
two quite distinct situations, identified much more recently[52]: first, where
the donee of the mere power holds that power in his capacity as a trustee
(either because he is a trustee of the property which is to be appointed or
where this is not the case but it is nevertheless apparent that the power has
been given to him as a trustee[53]), in which case he is said to be a fiduciary
donee; secondly, where the donee of the mere power is not a trustee in any
sense, in which case he is said to be a non-fiduciary donee. If a person is
holding property on trust for such of the members of a class and in such
proportions as he may in his absolute discretion appoint and, in default of
any such appointment, on trust for an identified beneficiary, he is likely to
be held to be a fiduciary donee of a mere power. If, on the other hand, a
person is holding property on trust for such of the members of a class and
in such proportions as a third party may in his absolute discretion appoint
and, in default of any such appointment, on trust for an identified beneficiary, the third party is likely to be held to be a non-fiduciary donee of a mere
power. This distinction is extremely significant. Although a fiduciary donee
of a mere power is under no obligation to exercise it, he does owe certain
obligations towards the objects of the power (as well as a duty to those
entitled in default of appointment not to misuse the power) and is "to some
extent subject to the control of the courts in relation to its exercise".[54] In
particular, he must consider periodically whether or not he should exercise
the power (in default, the court may direct him to do so and, in the last
resort, may remove or replace him), must consider the range of objects of the

---

[51] See *Vestey v. I.R.C. (No.2)* [1979] Ch. 198, *per* Megarry J. at 206 (affirmed on other grounds in
Vestey v. I.R.C. (Nos. 1 & 2) [1979] A.C. 1148) and *Re Hay's Settlement Trusts* [1982] 1 W.L.R. 202,
per Megarry V.-C. at 210.
[52] In *Mettoy Pension Trustees v. Evans* [1990] 1 W.L.R. 1587 at 1614 (not the first enunciation of the
distinction but the first fully developed statement of the remedies available against a fiduciary donee of a mere power). See generally Gardner, 107 LQ.R. (1991) 214.
[53] In *Mettoy Pension Trustees v. Evans* [1990] 1 W.L.R. 1587, a company held a power to appoint
any surplus in its pension fund, which was actually vested in a separate trustee company, in
favour of the pensioners with a gift over in default of appointment to itself. The liquidators
of the company wished to release this power and so enable the surplus to become available
for its creditors. Warner J. held that it was a fiduciary power and so could not be released.
[54] *ibid.*, at 1614.

power, must consider the appropriateness of individual appointments and, above all, is not entitled to release the power so as to cause the property to pass to those entitled in default of appointment. On the other hand, a non-fiduciary donee of a mere power owes no obligations whatever to the objects of the power (his only duty, owed to those entitled in default of appointment, is not to misuse the power); in particular, he does not even have to consider whether to exercise the power and may release it at any time and consequently cause the property to pass to those entitled in default of appointment.

Thus, the first and crucial question is whether the trustees or other person are obliged to exercise the power in question. If the answer to that question is affirmative, then the only remaining matter is in whose favour it should be exercised, either by the donee of the power or, if he fails to do so, by the court. If, on the other hand, the answer to that question is negative, it is necessary to consider whether the donee of the power is a fiduciary or a non-fiduciary; only in the former case is there any possibility of the court intervening in the event that the donee himself fails to exercise his power and even then the role of the court will be limited to ensuring that the fiduciary has complied with his duty to consider periodically whether or not to exercise the power.

2. The Distinction between Trust Powers and Mere Powers

It is now proposed to consider the distinction between trust powers and mere powers more closely. While powers are most frequently found as provisions in trust instruments, they can exist outside a trust and it is therefore necessary to consider a power as a separate concept. A power can be said to be the right to exercise, in respect of property belonging to another, one or more of the rights which are the normal incidents of ownership. Some differences are immediately apparent. For example, a trust is necessarily equitable; a power may or may not be. Thus a power of attorney to convey the legal estate is legal. So is a power of sale of the legal estate exercisable by a mortgagee. On the other hand, a power affecting beneficial entitlement is now necessarily equitable.[55] But, as has been said, the primary basis of the distinction is that a trust is imperative whereas a power is not. The distinction is shown by contrasting a trust for sale and a power of sale. If land is given by will or by deed *inter vivos* to trustees on express trust for sale, then the trustees are under a duty to sell the land, even though statute now implies a power to postpone sale in every case.[56] On the other hand, if

---

[55] LPA 1925, s.1(7).

[56] Trusts of Land and Appointment of Trustees Act 1996, s.4(1). Prior to this legislation, which came into force on January 1, 1997, the existence of a binding obligation to sell converted the land in the eyes of the law (even if not in fact converted) into money as soon as the will or deed took effect, despite the presence of a power to postpone sale in the instrument in question; however, the doctrine of conversion was, in this respect, abolished by Trusts of Land and Appointment of Trusts Act 1996, s.3 except where the trust in question was created by the will of a testator who died before January 1, 1997.

there is merely a power of sale, whether in a will or a deed *inter vivos*, the person in whom the power is vested will not be compelled to exercise it.[57]

The question whether or not a trust or a power has been created is essentially one of construction of the instrument. The distinction may be a fine one in any individual case, because what appears on the face of the trust instrument to be a trust power may in fact be a mere power and vice versa. Further, despite the fact that trust powers often appear in the form of powers, they are nevertheless construed and take effect as trusts. It is important to stress that, when what is in issue is whether a trust power or a mere power has been created, it does not matter whether what has been conferred on the donee of the power is a power of appointment or what is known as a *discretion* (the distinction between the two is considered later on[58]); most of the discussion which follows refers to powers of appointment but is equally applicable to discretions.

The question of construction is best approached by reference to the following three questions. An affirmative answer to either of the first two questions is decisive and establishes that what has been created is a mere power. If both the first two questions are answered in the negative, then the matter is resolved by answering the third question.

(A) Is the Power General?
A general power is by its nature incapable of being a trust power. A power is described as general when it confers on its donee a power to exercise it in favour of whoever he pleases, including the donee himself. Thus, the donee of a general power of appointment can exercise it by appointing the property to himself beneficially. Since he is entitled to do this, the court cannot compel him to appoint to any one else or indeed at all.

On the other hand, a special power is capable of taking effect as a trust power. A power is described as special when it confers on its donee the power to exercise it only in favour of one or more of a number of designated persons or classes of persons. Thus the donee of a special power of appointment can only appoint the property in question to the persons or classes of persons designated by the donor.

The position of the third type of power, the much more recently developed intermediate (or hybrid) power is not entirely clear. Such powers have been described as a power "betwixt and between",[59] neither strictly general nor strictly special. The feature of such a power is that it confers on its donee the power to exercise it in favour of anyone other than one or more designated persons or classes of persons. The person usually excluded is the settlor and his present and future spouses; this is generally done in order to forestall any argument that he has retained a beneficial interest under the

---

[57] In such circumstances, the land was not in the eyes of the law converted into money even prior to the Trusts of Land and Appointment of Trustees Act 1996.
[58] See *post*, p. 183.
[59] *Re Gestetner Settlement* [1953] Ch. 672 at 685.

trust in question, something which could have negative fiscal consequences.[60] It is also common to exclude the donee,[61] whether or not he is also the settlor. Thus the donee of an intermediate power of appointment can appoint the property in question to anyone other than the excluded person or persons. Another common type of intermediate power is the power to add persons to a class of beneficiaries; for the same reasons as above, it is usually crucial to ensure that the settlor and his present and future spouses cannot be so added. Intermediate powers are regarded as general powers for some purposes and as special powers for others.[62] It is, however, difficult to see how an intermediate power could possibly take effect as a trust power because, as in the case of a general power, there is no one in whose favour the court can compel appointment. It is therefore considered that such powers are necessarily mere powers.

(B)   Is there a Gift Over in Default of Exercise?

If the settlor has provided for a gift over, an alternative gift in the event that donee of the power fails to exercise it, then that power cannot be a trust power. The existence of a gift over is incompatible with the imperative nature of a trust and necessarily therefore operates as a denial of one's existence. Thus in *Re Mills*[63] a power was given to appoint among those children and remoter issue who in the opinion of the donee of the power should evidence a desire to maintain the family fortune. This limitation was followed by a gift elsewhere in default of appointment. The Court of Appeal held that because there was a gift over the power did not operate as a trust. It is not easy to think of any example of a gift over in default of exercise other than a gift which, like the gift in *Re Mills*, is a gift over in default of appointment. This second question therefore appears to relate exclusively to powers of appointment.

It is not always easy to decide whether any particular gift is indeed a gift over in default of exercise. Only if it actually is, will a trust power not be able to be upheld. Therefore, if the gift over is to take effect only in the event of a failure of the class in whose favour a power of appointment is to be exercised and/or their non-attainment of a specified age, it will operate only in those circumstances rather than as a result of any failure to make an appointment; consequently, such a power is capable of being held to be a trust power.[64]

However, it is clear that a residuary gift (a gift of that part of the property of a testator which has not been specifically devised or bequeathed) is not a gift over for present purposes; consequently, the presence of a residuary gift

---

[60] As will be seen *post*, p. 530, no inheritance tax is chargeable on the death of any person in respect of any property which he has transferred away more than seven years earlier. The retention of any benefit or potential benefit under the terms of any settlement to which the property has been transferred prevents the seven year period running.

[61] As in *Re Park* [1932] 1 Ch. 580. See also *Re Jones* [1945] Ch. 105 (power to appoint to anybody being a person and not a corporation); *Blausten v. I.R.C.* [1972] Ch. 256; *Re Manisty's Settlement* [1974] Ch. 17; *Re Hay's Settlement Trusts* [1982] 1 W.L.R. 202.

[62] Such a power is a special power for the purposes of the Wills Act 1837, s.21 and the Perpetuities and Accumulations Act 1964, s.7.

[63] [1930] 1 Ch. 654.

[64] *Re Llewellyn's Settlement* [1921] 2 Ch. 281.

will not necessarily deprive a prior power of the character of a trust. Thus in *Re Brierley*[65] a testator gave his wife a life interest in £50,000 with the power to bequeath or appoint that sum among such of her relatives or next-of-kin as she thought proper. She was also given the residue of her husband's estate absolutely. The wife released and thereby purported to extinguish the power of appointment and claimed the whole £50,000 as her own beneficially by virtue of the gift of residue in her favour. The court held that this manoeuvre was not possible; a gift of residue was totally different from a gift over of specific property which is the subject of the power of appointment.

(C)   What was the Real Intention of the Settlor or Testator?
Where the matter has not been resolved by one of the first two questions, then whether or not there is a trust power is entirely a question of construction of the words used in the instrument[66] in order to establish the real intention of the settlor or testator. In *Burrough v. Philcox*,[67] the testator directed that, after certain contingencies had been fulfilled, property was to be held in trust for his two children for life, with remainder to their issue, and declared that, if they should both die without issue, the survivor should have power to dispose by will of the property among his nephews and nieces and their children as he should think fit. The testator's children did in fact die without issue and without any appointment having been made by the survivor of them. It was held that a trust had been created in favour of the testator's nephews and nieces and their children; the trust was simply subject to a power of selection vested in the surviving child. Lord Cottenham stated the principle in these words: "Where there appears a general intention in favour of a class, and a particular intention in favour of individuals of a class to be selected by another person, and the particular intention fails from that selection not having been made, the court will carry into effect the general intention in favour of the class".[68] And, assuming the power is not exercised, if it is in favour of his relations generally and a trust is deduced in their favour, the trust takes effect in favour of the settlor's statutory next-of-kin.[69]

However, it must be emphasised that the fact that there is, as in *Burrough v. Philcox*, no gift over in default of exercise of the power in question does not automatically lead to the conclusion that a trust should be implied. It is apparent from other decisions that a trust will not be implied unless there is, on the true construction of the instrument in question, an indication of a clear intention to benefit the designated person or class in any event with only a mere power of selection conferred on the donee of the power. Thus in *Re Weekes' Settlement*[70] there was a gift of land to the testatrix's husband for life with "power to dispose of all such property by will amongst our

[65] (1894) 43 W.R. 36.
[66] Extrinsic evidence, including that of the testator's intention, may be admitted in certain cases; see Administration of Justice Act 1982, s.21 and see *ante*, p. 83, n. 4.
[67] (1840) 5 Myl. & Cr. 72.
[68] *ibid.* at 92.
[69] *Re Scarisbrick's Will Trusts* [1951] Ch. 622; *Re Baden's Deed Trusts (No.2)* [1973] Ch. 9 at 30, *per* Stamp L.J.
[70] [1897] 1 Ch. 289.

children" but without any gift over in default of appointment. When the power of appointment was not exercised by the husband in favour of the children, Romer J. held that the power had given the husband a mere power, not one coupled with a trust, and accordingly no gift to the children as a whole arose by implication. The judge pointed out that there had been no gift to such of the class as the husband might appoint—as there had been, in effect, in *Burrough v. Philcox*[71]—but only a mere power to appoint among a class. Similarly, in *Re Combe*[72] a life interest in property was given to the son of the testator and, after his death, the property was to be held "in trust for such person or persons as my said son shall appoint but such appointment must be confined to any relation of mine of the whole blood"; there was again no gift over in default of appointment. It was held that the words quoted created a mere power and not a trust; according to Tomlin J., there was nothing in the words of the will to justify importing into it something which was simply not there. The principle laid down in both these decisions was applied in the more recent decision in *Re Perowne*.[73] In this case the testatrix gave all her estate to her husband for life, "knowing that he will make arrangements for the disposal of my estate, according to my wishes, for the benefit of my family". The husband did in fact purport to make an appointment but this turned out to be void; consequently, the question arose as to whether, since the power had not been effectively exercised, what had been created was a trust in favour of the family or a mere power to appoint in their favour. Harman J. declined to spell a trust out of the words which had been used and held they had given the husband a mere power to distribute the testatrix's estate among the large and indefinite class in question.

These decisions illustrate a number of propositions: first, that the question is purely one of construction, namely whether or not the settlor has shown an intention to benefit the objects of the power; secondly that the absence of a gift over in default of appointment does not raise any necessary inference that a trust is intended—it is an argument, and nothing more than an argument, that that was the intention of the settlor or testator; and, thirdly, that because the question is one of construction, the resolution of the problem may depend on "a few words" and "mere straws in the wind".[74]

The fact that this is inevitable in relation to questions of construction is demonstrated by the leading case of *McPhail v. Doulton*.[75] The deed which had to be considered in this case provided that the trustees should apply the net income in making payments at their absolute discretion "to or for the benefit of any of the officers and employees or ex-officers or ex-employees of the company or to any relatives or dependants of any such persons in such amounts or on such conditions (if any) as they think fit". One of the questions which had to be decided was whether the clause had created a trust power or a mere power. At first instance Goff J.[76] held that it had

---

[71] (1840) 5 Myl. & Cr. 72.
[72] [1925] Ch. 210.
[73] [1951] Ch. 785.
[74] *Re Baden's Deed Trusts* [1969] 2 Ch. 388 at 398, *per* Harman L.J. For a formulation of rules for construction, see *Re Leek* [1967] Ch. 1061 at 1073, *per* Buckley J.
[75] [1971] A.C. 424.
[76] [1967] 1 W.L.R. 1457.

created a mere power; the Court of Appeal,[77] by a majority, reached the same conclusion; however, the House of Lords[78] unanimously held that it had created a trust power and therefore took effect as a trust—the clearly expressed scheme of the deed pointed to a mandatory construction. Lord Wilberforce, undoubtedly bearing in mind the differing judicial opinions expressed by the three different tribunals, said[79]:

"It is striking how narrow and in a sense artificial is the distinction, in cases such as the present, between trusts, or as the particular type of trust is called, trust powers, and powers. It is only necessary to read the learned judgments in the Court of Appeal to see that what to one mind may appear as a power of distribution coupled with a trust to dispose of the undistributed surplus, by accumulation or otherwise, may to another appear as a trust for distribution coupled with a power to withhold a portion and accumulate or otherwise dispose of it. A layman and, I suspect, also a logician would find it hard to understand what difference there is."

In the Court of Appeal in *McPhail v. Doulton*,[80] the majority had held that, in cases where the considerations were very evenly balanced in arriving at one or other of the two possible constructions, the court was at liberty to lean towards the construction which would effectuate rather than frustrate the intentions of the settlor or testator.[81] In other words, the court could take account of the legal consequences of any given interpretation; in particular, the consequence that if construed as a trust the gift would be void for uncertainty of objects whereas, if construed as a power, it would be valid, might cause the court to lean in favour of construing it as a power. The House of Lords[82] did not have to consider this particular point because, by a bare majority, they held that the test of certainty of objects for trust powers and mere powers was in fact the same. But because trust powers and mere powers have not been assimilated for all purposes, the view of the Court of Appeal may well still be significant in other circumstances.

3. *The Distinction between Fiduciary and Non-Fiduciary Donees of Mere Powers*

The recently consolidated distinction between fiduciary and non-fiduciary donees of mere powers to which reference has already been made is certainly not new.[83] However, its earlier enunciations did not receive universal judicial approval. As recently as 1969 Lord Upjohn, in *Re Gulbenkian's Settle-*

---

[77] [1969] 2 Ch. 126. Russell L.J. dissented.
[78] [1971] A.C. 424.
[79] *ibid.* at 448.
[80] [1969] 2 Ch. 126 (*sub nom. Re Baden's Deed Trusts*).
[81] On the principle of *ut res magis valeat quam pereat.*
[82] [1971] A.C. 424.
[83] See the authorities cited by Gardner, 107 L.Q.R. (1991) 214.

ment Trusts,[84] felt able to deny that donees of mere powers of appointment ever owed any duties to the objects of those powers. However, in the following year Lord Wilberforce, in *McPhail v. Doulton*[85] foreshadowed the subsequent decision in *Mettoy Pension Trustees v. Evans*[86] by remarking that a "trustee of an employees' benefit fund, whether given a power or a trust power, is still a trustee and he would surely consider in either case that he has a fiduciary duty", adding that it would be "a complete misdescription of his position to say that, if what he has is a power unaccompanied by an imperative trust to distribute, he cannot be controlled by the court unless he exercised it capriciously, or outside the field permitted by the trust".

These remarks set the scene for the authoritative statement of the distinction made by Megarry V.-C. in *Re Hay's Settlement Trusts*.[87] Having stated that a trustee is not normally bound to exercise a mere power and that the court will not compel him to do so, he continued:

"That, however, does not mean that he can simply fold his hands and ignore it, for normally he must from time to time consider whether or not to exercise the power, and the court may direct him to do this. Whereas a person who is not in a fiduciary position is free to exercise the power in any way that he wishes, unhampered by fiduciary duties, a trustee to whom, as such, a power is given is bound by the duties of his office in exercising that power to do so in a responsible manner according to its purpose. It is not enough for him to refrain from acting capriciously; he must do more. He must 'make such a survey of the range of objects or possible beneficiaries' as will enable him to carry out his fiduciary duty. He must find out 'the permissible area of selection and then consider responsibly, in individual cases, whether a contemplated beneficiary was within the power and whether, in relation to the possible claimants, a particular grant was appropriate'."[88]

This statement established a clear distinction between a mere power held by the trustees of the property in question and a mere power held by a third party. It also established that there was some significance in the distinction in that the court could direct the trustees to consider whether or not to exercise their power; this in turn led to the further conclusion, already enunciated in two earlier judgments,[89] that a refusal to follow such a direction from the court might well lead to the replacement of the existing trustees. Further, it has now been established that a donee of a mere power may be classified as a fiduciary even if he is not a trustee of the property in question.

---

[84] [1970] A.C. 508 at 521, 524–525.
[85] [1971] A.C. 424 at 449.
[86] [1990] 1 W.L.R. 1587.
[87] [1982] 1 W.L.R. 202 at 209–210.
[88] The quotations come from the speech of Lord Wilberforce in *McPhail v. Doulton* [1971] A.C. 424 at 449, 457.
[89] *Re Gestetner* [1953] Ch. 672 at 688; *Re Manisty's Settlement* [1974] Ch. 17 at 25.

In *Mettoy Pension Trustees v. Evans*,[90] a company held a power to appoint any surplus in its pension fund, which was actually vested in a quite separate trust company, in favour of its pensioners; in default of appointment, there was a gift over in favour of the company itself. The company became insolvent and its liquidators sought to release this power of appointment so that the gift over in default of appointment could take effect and immediately vest the surplus in the company for the benefit of its general creditors. Warner J. held that the company held this mere power as a fiduciary (he consequently held, as will be seen later in this Chapter,[91] not only that the power could not be released but also that all the remedies available to the court for the purpose of enforcing discretionary trusts were also available to it in the case of mere powers held by fiduciary donees). He adduced two main reasons for concluding that the company held this power as a fiduciary: first, that the inclusion of the power in the rules of the pension fund would have been quite pointless unless its donee were a fiduciary —since the company could have made such payments to its pensioners even if it had been absolutely entitled to the surplus, a non-fiduciary power would have added nothing; secondly, that the pensioners were not volunteers, in that it was unlikely that the surplus had arisen solely as a result of over-contribution on the part of the company and, in any event, the existence of the power and the expectation that its utilisation in their favour would be the subject of proper consideration had undoubtedly formed part of the overall scheme which the employees had contracted to obtain. It is undoubtedly significant that this conclusion was reached in the context of a pension fund, a context in which, as will be seen in a later chapter,[92] a large number of the recent developments in the law of trusts have been enunciated. Thus, one commentator[93] has described the conclusion as "perhaps swayed by a deeper-lying consideration", namely that, if such powers are not held to be fiduciary powers, "the surpluses to which they apply will in practice fall to companies' creditors and successful take-over predators"; whether he is right also to describe the conclusion as "not overwhelming" is rather more questionable.

Whether or not the basis of the classification adopted in *Mettoy Pension Trustees v. Evans* was indeed the special nature of pension funds and the recent public concern about the security of pension schemes, there seems little doubt, particularly in the light of the wholly novel remedies which that decision has made available to the court, that there will be many future attempts to classify as fiduciaries donees of mere powers who are not trustees of the property in question. It remains to be seen whether powers relating to pension funds come to be regarded as a special case or whether the classification and the remedies adopted in *Mettoy Pension Trustees v. Evans* are extended more generally. If they are, the traditional distinctions

---

[90] [1990] 1 W.L.R. 1587.
[91] See *post*, p. 197.
[92] See *post*, Chapter 12.
[93] Gardner, 107 L.Q.R. [1991] 214 at 215–216. He cites in support of this proposition *Re Courage Group's Pension Schemes* [1987] 1 W.L.R. 495 and *Imperial Group Pension Trust v. Imperial Tobacco* [1991] 1 W.L.R. 589 and would now undoubtedly also cite *Re William Makin & Sons* [1993] B.C.C. 435. All these authorities are considered *post*, in Chapter 12.

between trust powers and mere powers may require some reconsideration.

4. *The Requirement of Certainty*

As has already been seen in a previous Chapter,[94] the basic test for certainty of objects is now the same for discretionary trusts, trust powers, powers in the nature of a trust, and mere powers. The only possible continuing distinction relates to the question of the applicability of the requirement of administrative unworkability to mere powers. Prior to the decision in *Mettoy Pension Trustees v. Evans*,[95] it seemed tolerably clear that the concept of administrative unworkability did not apply to mere powers.[96] However, now that that decision has upheld the adaption of the remedies available for the enforcement of discretionary trusts, trust powers and powers in the nature of a trust to mere powers held by fiduciaries, it has been suggested[97] that this may cause the concept of administrative unworkability also to be applied to this type of mere power. It obviously remains to be seen whether this is yet another consequence of this important decision.

III. POWERS OF APPOINTMENT AND OTHER POWERS AND DISCRETIONS

Having considered the conceptual distinction between trusts and powers, it is now possible to consider some of the practical aspects of the distinction. In this section, the distinction between, on the one hand, powers of appointment and, on the other hand, other powers and discretions will be considered.[98]

Where a power has been created for the purpose of enabling its donee to decide which of the members of a class is to derive benefit from a fund, that power may either be a power of appointment or another type of power, usually known as a discretion. (The distinction between the two has nothing to do with the distinction between trust powers and mere powers which has already been considered; as a matter of principle, both powers of appointment and discretions may be either trust powers or mere powers.) Deciding which of the two has been created is often far from straightforward. In *Bond v. Pickford*[99] the trustees were given the power to "apply capital for the benefit of any one or more of the beneficiaries by allocating or appropriating to such beneficiary such sum or sums out of or investments forming part of the capital of the trust fund" as they thought fit. Nourse J held that this power of "allocation or appropriation" was akin to a limited special power of appointment. Such conclusions are important because there are three

---

[94] See *ante*, p. 92.
[95] [1990] 1 W.L.R. 1587.
[96] See *ante*, p. 102.
[97] By Gardner, 107 L.Q.R. (1991) 214 at 218–219.
[98] Both must be distinguished from discretionary trusts, defined *ante*, p. 173; some other aspects of discretionary trusts are considered in the next section *post*, p. 187.
[99] [1982] S.T.C. 403; the subsequent appeal to the Court of Appeal is reported only in *The Times*, May 24, 1983.

significant differences between powers of appointment and other powers
and discretions.

1. *Payments from the Trust Fund*

The first difference relates to payments from the trust fund. Strictly speaking, a power of appointment governs money which will arise or become
payable in the future, whereas a discretion deals with funds which are
already in hand. An analogy can usefully be drawn with the operation of a
railway with each train representing a payment. The exercise of a power of
appointment in favour of a beneficiary amounts to setting the points
towards a particular track. This action does not of course in itself cause a
train to come along and go down that particular track (that is to say, the
exercise of the power of appointment in favour of the beneficiary does not
of itself cause any payment to be made to him). However, whenever a train
comes along (that is to say, whenever funds become available for payment),
that train will go down that track (that is to say, the funds will be paid to that
particular beneficiary) without any further action or decision being taken for
so long as the points remain set in that direction (that is to say, for so long
as the appointment remains unrevoked). On the other hand, the exercise of
a discretion takes place after a train or a number of trains have already
reached the marshalling yard and are under the control of the marshaller
(that is to say, after a payment of funds or a number of payments of funds
have reached the hands of the trustees); in such circumstances, the marshaller has to decide down which of a number of tracks to send the individual
wagons making up the train or trains (that is to say, the trustees have to
decide which of the beneficiaries should receive the whole or some part of
each payment received).

This difference is particularly important when, as is generally the case, the
funds subject to the power are the income of the trust fund. If that income
is subject to a power of appointment, then, once an appointment has been
made, all income arising will go to the beneficiary to whom it has been
appointed without any further decision having to be taken. In the case of a
discretion, on the other hand, a separate decision has to be taken on each
occasion on which any income is available for distribution. This latter point
may be illustrated by *Wilson v. Turner.*[1] In that case the trustees had a power
to pay or apply income arising from the trust fund to or for the maintenance
of an infant beneficiary.[2] They did not make a conscious decision on each
occasion but merely handed over the income to the infant's father. The Court
of Appeal held that the payments so made had to be repaid to the trust fund.
Had the trustees instead from time to time actively considered the merits of
the case and consciously decided to apply the income for the maintenance
of that infant, their decision would have been valid.[3]

The applicability of the distinction to payments of income is of crucial
importance in relation to the incidence of inheritance tax. As will be seen in

---

[1] (1883) 22 Ch.D. 521.
[2] The statutory power of maintenance is considered *post*, p. 595.
[3] A further illustration of the same principle is *Re Greenwood* (1911) 105 L.T. 509, considered
post, p. 494.

a later Chapter,[4] whether or not the death of a person with an interest under a settlement gives rise to a charge to inheritance tax on the value of the settled property depends on whether or not he has an interest in possession in that property. Once there has been an appointment of income in favour of a beneficiary of a settlement, that beneficiary has an interest in possession in the settled property, even if the appointment is revocable; consequently, if he dies without the appointment having been revoked, the whole of the settled property whose income has been appointed to him will be subject to inheritance tax. On the other hand, a beneficiary who is only entitled to any income from a trust in the event that the trustees decide to exercise a discretion in his favour does not have an interest in possession in the trust property and in the event of his death no charge to inheritance tax will arise in respect of the settled property.

2. *Formalities*

The second difference between a power of appointment and a discretion is in relation to formalities. Although in principle no formality is necessary for the exercise of a power of appointment, in practice some formality is almost always prescribed in the instrument by which the power is conferred. Where this is the case, the formal requirements in question have to be strictly complied with. So if a power of appointment is to be exercised by deed, it cannot be exercised by will[5] and a power which is to be exercised by will cannot be exercised by any instrument which is not a will.[6]

However, if the donor of the power not only specifies the type of instrument by which the power is to be exercised, such as a deed or will, but also specifies particular formalities to be observed in the execution of that instrument, such as signature in the presence of witnesses, the requirements stipulated by him are sometimes modified by statute. Section 159 of the Law of Property Act 1925 provides that, in the case of a power which has to be exercised by deed, any exercise of it will be formally valid if the deed in question is executed in the presence of at least two witnesses; similarly, in the case of a power which has to be or is exercised by will, the exercise will be formally valid provided that the will in question complies with the provisions of the Wills Acts.[7]

A possible further exception to the general principle that formal requirements must be strictly observed is that equity has in certain cases perfected the imperfect exercise of a power in a somewhat similar way to that in which it will perfect an imperfect gift.[8] Broadly speaking, equity has done this where the donee of the power intended to exercise it and his exercise of the power was in order to satisfy a moral obligation.[9] There are, however, no

---

[4] See *post*, p. 530.
[5] *Lord Darlington v. Pulteney* (1797) 3 Ves.Jr. 384; *Lady Cavan v. Doe* (1795) 6 Bro.P.C. 175; *Re Phillips* (1884) 41 Ch.D. 417.
[6] *Reid v. Shergold* (1805) 10 Ves.Jr. 370; *Re Evered* [1910] 2 Ch. 147.
[7] Wills Act 1837, s.10; Wills Act 1963, s.2.
[8] See *ante*, p. 133.
[9] *Chapman v. Gibson* (1791) 3 Bro.C.C. 229; *Garth v. Townsend* (1869) L.R. 7 Eq. 220; *Kennard v. Kennard* (1872) L.R. 8 Ch.App. 227.

recent examples of this exception and it cannot be assumed that it would necessarily be applied today.

In contrast, no formality whatever is required for the exercise of a discretion, simply because the discretion is exercised at the moment when those exercising it reach their decision so to do.[10]

It can therefore generally be said that the exercise of a power of appointment requires a physical act by the appointor, whereas the exercise of a discretion requires only a metaphysical act. It should, however, be stressed that questions of formality must not be confused with any requirement that the consent of any person must be obtained prior to exercise. The exercise of both a power of appointment and a discretion can be made subject to consents being obtained and any purported exercise made without those consents will be ineffective.

3. *Revocability*

The third difference between powers of appointment and discretions relates to revocability. It should first be noted that whether a power is actually revocable depends on the terms of the instrument by which it is created. Most modern instruments deal with this question expressly, usually by providing that powers may be exercised either revocably or irrevocably although there is obviously nothing to stop a settlor or testator providing that any particular power can only be exercised irrevocably. In the absence of any express or implied provision dealing with the matter, it seems to be assumed that a power can be exercised in either of the two ways. There does, however, seem to be a presumption that, if nothing is said as to whether a power is being exercised revocably or irrevocably, it is being exercised irrevocably.[11]

A power of appointment looks towards the future. It can therefore clearly be expressed to be revocable, and in this event, subject to the terms of the instrument by which it was conferred, the appointment can be revoked and a new appointment made without limit. On the other hand, when a discretion is exercised, its effect is to confer upon the beneficiary a right to a sum which is in hand. The beneficiary has the right to demand payment, and payment is in fact usually made to him promptly. It is then too late for the person exercising his discretion to seek to change his mind and to recall the money.[12]

It is apparent that a revocable power of appointment and a discretion can both be used to achieve the same general effect. For example, suppose the donor has at his disposal the income of a fund and wishes that for the year 1999 it should go to Charles; for the year 2000 it should go to Douglas; and

---

[10] It is theoretically possible for the donor of the power to prescribe some formal requirement for the exercise of any discretion arising thereunder but it is most unlikely that this would ever be done.

[11] Assuming that this presumption does in fact exist, it must clearly be able to be rebutted by implication in appropriate circumstances.

[12] It is theoretically possible for the donor of the power to provide that the donees of the discretion could change their minds between the exercise of the discretion and the payment over of the sum to the beneficiary in question but it is most unlikely that this would ever be done.

for the year 2001 it should go to Edward. If what the donor has is a revocable power of appointment, at the beginning of 1999 the income can be revocably appointed to Charles; at the beginning of 2000, that appointment can be revoked and a new revocable appointment be made in favour of Douglas; and at the beginning of 2001, the appointment can again be revoked and a new revocable appointment made in favour of Edward. On the other hand, if what the donor has is a discretion, a decision can be made at or after the end of 1999 in favour of Charles; at or after the end of 2000 in favour of Douglas; and at or after the end of 2001 in favour of Edward. The result so far as the beneficiaries in question are concerned is the same in both cases. If, as is likely in the case of modern trust instruments, the donors are trustees and have the option of taking either course of action, they are likely to be influenced in their choice as to how to proceed by fiscal considerations.

IV. Some Provisions of Discretionary Trusts

It should first be noted that the expression "discretionary trust" is used in two senses. The first user is in the sense already considered,[13] the situation where trustees are under an obligation to exercise a discretion of the nature considered previously, where there is an obligation to exercise it. However, the expression is more commonly used to denote the whole of the provisions of a trust instrument by means of which powers are conferred, even though those discretions will inevitably include both of the types of powers described in the previous section, that is to say both powers of appointment and discretions, and are likely to include both trust powers and mere powers. This section considers two specific aspects of such provisions which are commonly found in trust instruments.

1. *The Time during which Powers can be Exercised*

Trustees must exercise any discretion vested in them within a reasonable time. What is reasonable depends on the facts of each case. In *Re Gulbenkian's Settlement Trusts (No.2)*,[14] the trustees learned in April 1957 of a decision[15] which cast doubt on the validity of a provision of the trust instrument relating to the accumulation of income. They therefore retained the income without accumulating it. The doubt raised was not actually resolved until the decision of the House of Lords in *Re Gulbenkian's Settlement Trusts (No. 1)*[16] in October 1968. The question then arose as to whether the trustees were still entitled to exercise their discretion in respect of income which had been accruing ever since 1957. Plowman J. held that in the circumstances the trustees' retention of the income was not unreasonable; consequently, they could still exercise their discretion in respect of the whole of the accrued income. It therefore follows that, provided the surrounding circumstances

---

[13] See *ante*, p. 173.
[14] [1970] Ch. 408.
[15] *Re Gresham's Settlement* [1956] 1 W.L.R. 573, subsequently overruled.
[16] [1970] A.C. 508 and see *ante*, p. 95.

make it reasonable for them so to do, trustees can retain income as income for some time and only then decide whether or not to accumulate it.

On the other hand, if the trustees do not exercise their discretion within a reasonable time, the consequences differ depending on whether or not the discretion in question arose by virtue of a mere power or a trust power. If the discretion arose by virtue of a mere power, which will of course inevitably be of a fiduciary nature, the trustees will have been under a duty to consider whether or not to exercise their discretion but not under any duty actually to exercise it; in such circumstances, any failure to exercise their discretion within a reasonable time will cause it to be lost and, consequently, no longer exercisable.[17] If, on the other hand, the discretion in question arose by virtue of a trust power then the trustees will have been under an obligation to exercise their discretion; consequently, it will not be extinguished by lapse of time. Accordingly, the trustees will be able to exercise it at any time, no matter how much later, and, if they fail to do so, the court will direct them to do so[18] or, in default, execute the trust in one of the ways laid down by Lord Wilberforce in *McPhail v. Doulton*.[19]

2. Modifying the Trusts and the Class of Beneficiaries

In the last few decades, there has been a general tendency to make trusts more and more flexible, which is of course one of the reasons why discretionary trusts have become more popular than fixed trusts. Two of the more recent developments have been to include what are generally known as overriding powers of appointment and powers to alter the class of beneficiaries.

(A)   Overriding Powers of Appointment
Where property is settled on discretionary trusts, it necessarily follows that no one has an immediate interest in possession either as to income or as to capital; this is also the effect of a settlement on fixed trusts for persons who are not *sui juris*. In such circumstances, it has become the normal practice to vest in the trustees a power, exercisable at any time before any beneficiary obtains an absolute interest in the capital of the trust, enabling them, first, to revoke all the existing trusts and declare totally new ones in favour of the same, or sometimes slightly different, beneficiaries and/or, secondly, to transfer the trust property to the trustees of other settlements under which the same, or sometimes slightly different, persons are beneficially entitled. Such powers are generally known as overriding powers of appointment. The first of these powers enables the trusts of a settlement to be modified in the light of subsequent events with a view particularly to avoiding for as long as possible anyone obtaining an interest in possession and so giving rise to the deemed disposal for the purposes of capital gains tax which such an event inevitably brings with it.[20] The second of these powers enables the

---

[17] *Re Gourju's Will Trusts* [1943] Ch. 24; *Re Wise* [1896] 1 Ch. 281; *Re Allen-Meyrick's Will Trusts* [1966] 1 W.L.R. 499.
[18] *Re Locker's Settlement Trusts* [1978] 1 All E.R. 216.
[19] [1971] A.C. 424 at 457; *ante*, p. 93.
[20] See *ante*, p. 170.

trust to be wound up without having to give any of the beneficiaries an interest in possession in the process, although in this case such a deemed disposal cannot be avoided.[21]

Any trust which contains an overriding powers of appointment will inevitably also contain an ultimate absolute beneficial gift in favour of some person or persons who is or are already *sui juris.* No one ever has the slightest intention that these persons, who are generally known as default beneficiaries, should ever obtain an interest in possession save in the unlikely event that all the other beneficiaries are wiped out by some unforeseen disaster such as an air crash or a terrorist bomb. They are there for two purposes: first, to forestall the sort of argument which succeeded in *Vandervell v. I.R.C.*[22] that the ultimate beneficiary is in fact the settlor, something which can affect not only, as in that case, the incidence of income tax but also the incidence of inheritance tax[23] (for the same reason, the settlor and his present and future spouse also have to be excluded from the class of beneficiaries in whose favour the power can be exercised); and, secondly, to forestall any argument that the trustees have for any moment of time in effect, even though not on the face of things, been holding on trust for one of the earlier beneficiaries absolutely, something which would trigger an undesired deemed disposal.

It will be apparent from the contents of the previous two paragraphs that the utilisation of overriding powers of appointment is a complicated affair. The most elaborate precautions have to be taken: first, in order to ensure that what is being done is within the powers which have been conferred on the trustees, which are in turn subject to various overriding rules of law, such as the various rules against perpetuities and accumulations discussed in the next Chapter[24]; and, secondly, to avoid any undesirable or unexpected fiscal consequences. These difficulties multiply when overriding powers of appointment are being used on a second or subsequent occasion because of the need to act in a way which is consistent not only with the provisions of the original settlement but also with the modifications which have already been made. Dealing with such clauses is therefore one of the most difficult and, therefore, one of the most stimulating aspects of modern discretionary trusts.

(B) Powers to Alter the Class of Beneficiaries

It was established in *Re Manisty's Settlement*[25] that in principle there is no objection to the settlor giving powers which permit the trustees to alter the class of beneficiaries, either by addition to or by subtraction from the existing class.

What was actually in issue in that case was a power to add persons to the existing class of beneficiaries. The settlement was a discretionary trust for the benefit of the children and remoter issue of the settlor. The trustees

---

[21] Because the trustees will be holding the property on trust for the trustees of the other settlement absolutely; see *post,* p. 530.

[22] [1967] 2 A.C. 191; see *ante,* p. 54.

[23] See *ante,* p. 185; *post,* p. 530.

[24] See *post,* pp. 208–224.

[25] [1974] Ch. 17 and see *Blausten v. I.R.C.* [1982] Ch. 256 and *Re Hay's Settlement Trusts* [1982] 1 W.L.R. 202, discussed *ante,* p. 103.

purported to exercise a power to bring other persons into that class by
bringing in the settlor's mother and any person who in the future might
become the settlor's widow. Templeman J. held that such a power could
indeed be validly conferred on trustees and that their exercise of it was
therefore valid.[26] Such powers provide a useful means of providing for
people who have been overlooked or whose financial situation suddenly
changes for the worse.

However, the settlement also conferred a power on the trustees to exclude
any individual members of the existing class of beneficiaries. Such a power
is even more useful because it enables the settlor initially to declare a very
wide class of beneficiaries and at the same time give his trustees power to
exclude anyone within that class if this becomes necessary at any later stage
(as it often does, usually as a result of the introduction of new legislation
adversely affecting the fiscal liabilities of the settlor, the trust or the beneficiaries). Templeman J. was equally prepared to accept the validity of this
sort of power.

Needless to say, exactly the same precautions have to be taken in the
exercise of this type of power as in the exercise of overriding powers of
appointment.

V. FACTORS AFFECTING THE EXERCISE OF POWERS AND DISCRETIONS

1. To What Extent can Powers and Discretions be Delegated?

There is no doubt that a settlor or testator can give a power of appointment
to a trustee or indeed to anyone else—even a general power of appointment
given by a testator to his trustees cannot be impugned as a delegation of
testamentary disposition.[27] However, there is some uncertainty as to the
extent to which trustees or others can delegate their powers and discretions.
The basic position is that matters involving a decision on a matter of policy,
or importance, which would include whether a person is to benefit, and, if
so, to what extent, cannot be delegated,[28] but that ancillary decisions taken
in order to give effect to the trustees' decision can be delegated.[29] So, if the
trustees in the exercise of their discretion decide to give a beneficiary £500,
they are entitled to leave to their solicitor the decision as to whether to pay
that sum by cheque or in cash.

The instrument by which a power is conferred can expressly authorise
delegation of its exercise and, occasionally, powers can be delegated by
virtue of express statutory provisions.[30] Where there is no such express

---

[26] The decision is consistent with the approval by the House of Lords in *Pilkington v. I.R.C.*
[1964] A.C. 612 of the exercise of a power of advancement by way of resettlement; see *post*,
p. 624.

[27] *Re Beatty's Will Trusts* [1990] 1 W.L.R. 1503; see Davies, 107 L.Q.R. (1991) 211.

[28] *Re May* [1926] 1 Ch. 136; *Re Mewburn* [1934] Ch. 112; *Re Wills' Will Trusts* [1959] Ch. 1.

[29] *Att.-Gen. v. Scott* (1750) 1 Ves.Sen. 413; *Re Hetling and Merton's Contract* [1893] 3 Ch. 269.

[30] An example of statutory authority to delegate is that conferred by Trusts of Land and
Appointment of Trustees Act 1996, s.9 (replacing Law of Property Act 1925, s.29), which
enables trustees of land to delegate their powers of management; see also *post*, pp. 493,
508.

authority, it seems that delegation can still be made effectively where there is an implied power to this effect in the instrument creating the power but not otherwise.

So far as powers to determine beneficial entitlements are concerned, the question of delegation most often arises where there is a power to appoint a fund among a number of beneficiaries and the donee of the power wishes to make an appointment not in favour of a particular beneficiary absolutely but instead on trust for him. It is clear that the donee of the power cannot appoint the fund on discretionary trusts, even if all the beneficiaries of the discretionary trust in question are beneficiaries of the original settlement, unless this is expressly or impliedly authorised in the trust instrument (most modern overriding powers of appointment contain such express authorisation); this is because an unauthorised appointment on discretionary trusts amounts to the donee of the power delegating to the trustees of the new trust the power to decide what each beneficiary of the discretionary trust will in fact receive.[31] Similarly, if an appointment is made on protective trusts[32] (which has the effect of conferring a life interest which on the life tenant's bankruptcy will determine and be replaced by discretionary trusts), the appointment of the life interest is valid but in the event that it is replaced by the discretionary trusts, the latter will be void.[33] However, it is accepted that any appointment on trust which is validly made in accordance with the terms of the power may also confer a power of advancement on the trustees, even if the trustees of the original settlement did not have one or did not have one as broad, and, to this extent at least, confer a discretion on the trustees of the new settlement.[34]

The different question of the extent to which trustees can delegate their powers of management and administration and appoint agents to act on their behalf is considered in later Chapters.[35]

2. When will the Exercise of Powers and Discretions be Improper?

It will be recalled that the donees of a trust power, whether or not they are also trustees, are obliged to exercise the power in question, whereas the donees of a mere power are not obliged to exercise it, although if they are fiduciaries they must at the very least consider whether or not to do so. Once a power or discretion has been exercised, however, the principles which determine whether or not its exercise was proper are the same whether the power in question was a trust power or a mere power and whether or not it was exercised by a trustee. These principles are as follows.

---

[31] *Re Morris' Settlement* [1951] 2 All E.R. 528; *Re Hay's Settlement Trusts* [1982] 1 W.L.R. 202.
[32] See *post*, p. 231.
[33] *Re Boulton's Settlement Trusts* [1928] Ch. 703; *Re Morris' Settlement* [1951] 2 All E.R. 528; *Re Hunter* [1963] Ch. 72.
[34] This was specifically held in *Re Morris' Settlement* [1951] 2 All E.R. 528, a decision which was excepted to be correct in *Re Wills' Will Trusts* [1959] Ch. 1 and in *Pilkington v. I.R.C.* [1964] A.C. 612.
[35] See *post*, pp. 493, 508.

(A) The Donee of a Power must make a Positive Decision

A power or discretion will only be validly exercised if, as well as complying with whatever formalities are required by the trust instrument,[36] the donee of the power has made a positive mental decision so to do rather than merely allowing a situation to arise as a result of his inaction. Reference has already been made[37] to the decision in *Wilson v. Turner*.[38] In the same sort of way, in *Turner v. Turner*,[39] the exercise of a power of appointment was held to have been invalid when the trustees left all the decisions to the settlor (who was not a trustee) and signed the necessary documents without actually reading them. Further consideration of the way in which this rule is specifically applicable to trustees is made in a later Chapter.[40]

(B) The Donee of a Power does not have to Give Reasons

Unless he chooses to do so, the donee of a power or discretion cannot be compelled to give the reasons which led him to reach his decision as to whether or not to exercise it. In fact, he is best advised not to do so in order to forestall any argument that the reasons are in fact inappropriate. This rule is particularly significant for trustees and its specific applicability to them is considered in greater detail in a later Chapter.[41]

(C) Where the Exercise is Bona Fide

The basic rule is that, where the donee of the power or discretion has exercised it bona fide, the court will not interfere even if it would itself have acted differently. In *Gisborne v. Gisborne*[42] the trustees of a will had discretion to apply the whole or such portion of the income as they should think expedient for the benefit of the testator's wife, who was a person of unsound mind. The trustees refused to apply the whole of the income for her support and proposed to apply only so much of it as would be necessary to maintain her in care when the income from her own property was also taken into account. The House of Lords acknowledged that they would have ordered the trust fund to have been applied primarily for the benefit of the wife; however, in the light of their specific decision that the trustees had acted bona fide, they could not interfere with the exercise of the trustees' discretion.

However, different considerations arise where the exercise of the power or discretion does not have the full effect which its donee intended (this is usually because the effect of some overriding rule of law, such as the various rules against perpetuities and accumulations discussed in the next Chapter).[43] In *Re Hastings-Bass (deceased)*,[44] trustees exercised a power of advancement to resettle property on trust but misunderstood the effect of the rule

---

[36] See *ante*, p. 183.
[37] See *ante*, p. 184.
[38] (1883) 22 Ch.D. 521.
[39] [1984] Ch. 100.
[40] See *post*, p. 493.
[41] See *post*, p. 494.
[42] (1877) 2 App.Cas. 628. See also *R. v. Archbishop of Canterbury and Bishop of London* [1903] 1 K.B. 289.
[43] See *post*, pp. 208–244.
[44] [1975] Ch. 25. See Robert Walker L.J. in *Trends in Contemporary Trust Law* (ed. Oakley, 1996), pp. 123, 125–129.

against perpetuities with the result that, while a valid life interest was conferred on the person principally intended to benefit, all the remainders over were void for perpetuity. The Court of Appeal said this[45]:

"where a trustee is given a discretion as to some matter under which he acts in good faith, the court should not interfere with his action, notwithstanding that it does not have the full effect which he intended, unless (1) what he has achieved is unauthorised by the power conferred on him, or (2) it is clear that he would not have acted as he did (a) had he not taken into account considerations which he should not have taken into account or (b) had he not failed to take into account considerations which he ought to have taken into account."

Given that what had been achieved was sufficient to bring about the saving of tax which was the main objective of the advancement, the court held that, if the trustees had appreciated its true effect, they would have acted broadly as they had done; consequently the advancement was held to be valid.

This principle is not confined to mistakes as to the effect of overriding rules of law but extends to any failure by the donee of a power to take into account any considerations which he should have done. This was specifically held in *Mettoy Pension Trustees v. Evans*[46] by Warner J., who however went on to emphasise that "it is not enough that it should be shown that the trustees did not have a proper understanding of the effect of their act. It must also be clear that, had they had a proper understanding of it, they would not have acted as they did." In circumstances where this is indeed clear, the court will normally declare the purported exercise of the power or discretion wholly void. This is what the Court of Appeal did in *Stannard v. Fisons Pension Trust*,[47] where the trustees of the pension fund had exercised a discretion on the basis of an out of date valuation of the fund. However, it has been stated[48] that, where the court concludes that the donee of the power would have acted in the same way but with the omission of one of the clauses of the deed in question, the court can uphold that deed with the deletion of that clause. It remains to be seen whether and if so how the flexible approach manifested by this statement is carried into effect and in particular whether it will enable trustees who have made an appointment on the strength of advice with which they subsequently become dissatisfied to have the deed which they have executed corrected by the court.

It should also be noted that the beneficiaries of pensions trusts (who, unlike the vast majority of the beneficiaries of family settlements, are not volunteers) also appear to be entitled to attack the exercise of a power or discretion on the grounds that it was in administrative law terms "unreasonable".[49]

---

[45] At 41.
[46] [1990] 1 W.L.R. 1587 at 1624.
[47] [1992] I.R.L.R. 27.
[48] By Warner J. in *Mettoy Pension Trustees v. Evans* [1990] 1 W.L.R. 1587 at 1624–1625.
[49] On the basis of "Wednesbury" unreasonableness (see *Associated Provincial Picture Houses v. Wednesbury Corporation* [1948] 1 K.B. 223); this possibility emerges from *Harris v. Lord Shuttleworth* [1994] I.C.R. 991 and *Wild v. Pensions Ombudsman* [1996] P.L.R. 275.

(D)   Where the Exercise is Not Bona Fide

Where a power or discretion has not been exercised honestly, its purported exercise will be invalid. In such cases, there is said to have been a "fraud on a power". In equity the word "fraud" denotes nothing more than an improper motive and the expression "fraud on a power" is used in connection with the exercise both of a power and of a discretion (in this discussion, "power" includes "discretion"). Various attempts have been made to categorise the circumstances in which there is a fraud on a power,[50] but the most common situations are where a power is exercised in favour of a beneficiary when he has already agreed that he will apply the property in question in whole or in part for the benefit of someone who is not an object of the power[51] and where, even though there has been no such prior agreement, the power is exercised with the intention of benefiting someone outside the scope of the power.[52] Four propositions emerge from the decided cases.

First, the fact that a power is exercised in such a way as to defeat the intention of the donor does not automatically make its exercise void.[53] This rule is comparable to the rule which permits beneficiaries who between them are absolutely beneficially entitled to join together and bring a trust to an end even though the intention of the settlor was that it should continue.[54] Once a power has been conferred, or a trust has been created, the donor or settlor ceases to have any control as such unless he has provided at the time when the power or trust was created that his consent (or the consent of the protector of the settlement) is a necessary pre-condition of any exercise.

Secondly, in every case it is necessary to identify who would be entitled in default of exercise of the power (they may be specified in the trust instrument; alternatively there may be a resulting trust in their favour). Since these are the persons who will lose as a result of any improper exercise of the power, in the event that they agree to it with knowledge of all the relevant facts, the exercise will be valid.[55]

Thirdly, the essential feature which makes the exercise of a power improper is the intention of the person exercising it. If it is exercised with the intention of benefiting some non-object of the power, whether it be the appointor or someone else, the exercise is void. If it is not done with this intention, but the exercise does in fact benefit a non-object, it is valid. Thus, in the situation where a father has a power to appoint in favour of his child, an appointment in favour of that child is basically valid[56]; however, if it is made when the child is very ill, with the intention that the appointor will benefit by taking the child's estate on his or her death, the exercise will be invalid[57] and will strictly be so even if the child subsequently recovers. On the other hand, if a power is exercised with a view to bringing the trust to an end as part of a tax-saving scheme, and the appointment in question is

---

[50] See *Vatcher v. Paull* [1915] A.C. 372.
[51] *ibid.*
[52] *Portland v. Topham* (1867) 11 H.L.Cas. 32; *Vatcher v. Paull* [1915] A.C. 372.
[53] *Lee v. Ferrie* (1839) 1 B. 483.
[54] See *post*, p. 637.
[55] *Re Turner's Settled Estates* [1884] 28 Ch.D. 205; *Re Greaves* [1954] Ch. 434.
[56] *Henty v. Wrey* (1882) 21 Ch.D. 332.
[57] *Lord Hinchinbroke v. Seymour* (1789) 1 Bro.C.C. 395.

made with the intention of benefiting its objects, the appointment is valid even although its confers an incidental benefit on the appointor or on other persons.[58]

Fourthly, where a power is to be exercised in favour of one of its objects but in the hope that the recipient will benefit a non-object, the validity of the exercise will depend upon whether the person in whose favour the power was exercised had legal and moral freedom of action.[59] Suppose that a power is exercisable in favour of a person who makes it known that, if the power is in fact exercised in his favour, he will give part of the fund to his parents, who are not objects. If the intention of the appointment is to benefit the parents, the exercise is invalid under the rule stated in the previous paragraph. If the object of the power is under great pressure to benefit the parents, the exercise is also invalid.[60] However, if the object of the power has genuine freedom of action but wishes to give his parents a benefit, the exercise of the power is good.[61]

3. *The Effect of the Invalid Exercise of a Power or Discretion*

In principle, where the exercise of a power or discretion is improper, its exercise is totally invalid.[62] However, this can in some circumstances work harshly on the objects of the power or discretion. If the appointor reaches an agreement with one of the objects of the power or discretion that the appointor will appoint £1,000 to the object provided that the latter pays £500 to someone who is not an object, then in principle the whole appointment is invalid and the object will receive nothing. Accordingly, in an attempt to help objects, in some cases the court will try to sever the improper element in the appointment from the remainder of that appointment.[63] If there is no intent to benefit the object of the power at all, the exercise is clearly wholly invalid.[64] If, however, there is an intent to benefit the object to some extent, and the improper element is in the form of a condition attached to the appointment, the court will delete the condition to leave the object free to take unconditionally.[65] Further, as has already been seen,[66] where the donee of a power has failed to take into account some consideration which he should have done, if the court concludes that he would have acted in the same way but with the omission of one of the clauses of the deed in question, the court can uphold that deed with the deletion of that clause.[67]

---

[58] *Re Merton* [1953] 1 W.L.R. 1096; *Re Robertson's Will Trusts* [1960] 1 W.L.R. 1050.
[59] *Birley v. Birley* (1858) 25 B. 299.
[60] *Re Crawshay* [1948] Ch. 123; *Re Dick* [1953] Ch. 343.
[61] *Re Marsden's Trusts* (1859) 4 Drew. 594.
[62] *Daubeney v. Cockburn* (1816) 1 Mer. 626.
[63] *Topham v. Duke of Portland* (1858) 1 D.J. & S. 517.
[64] *Re Cohen* [1911] 1 Ch. 37.
[65] *Hay v. Watkins* (1850) 3 Dr. & War. 339.
[66] See *ante*, p. 192.
[67] See *Mettoy Pension Trustees v. Evans* [1990] 1 W.L.R. 1587 at 1624–1625.

4. *The Effect of the Donee's Insolvency*

This question has so far only arisen in the context of pension trusts. Where the employer company is also the trustee of the company's pension fund, its liquidator will find himself facing two directions simultaneously: his basic role is to realise as many assets as possible for the company's creditors whereas the powers held by the company as trustee of the pension fund (which because of the nature of pension schemes are bound to be mere powers) clearly have to be exercised as much for the benefit of the members of the pension scheme as for the company. The authorities decided so far[68] establish that what is crucial is whether the powers vested in the company are fiduciary or personal. If they are fiduciary, then the liquidator of the company is clearly not the appropriate person to exercise them; in such circumstances, the powers will instead have to be exercised by the directors, who will be liable to have any exercise made without taking into account the interests of the members of the scheme set aside. If, on the other hand, the powers are personal (which is admittedly relatively unlikely in the light of *Mettoy Pension Trustees v. Evans*[69]), it would prima facie have been open to the company to exercise those powers for its own benefit anyway and consequently the liquidator will face no conflict of interest if he exercises them in favour of the creditors.

The position of the trustee in bankruptcy of an individual donee of a power has yet to be considered in this jurisdiction.[70] It is not entirely clear whether the power would actually pass to the trustee in bankruptcy anyway; powers are not normally assignable but would this be an objection where the assignment was by operation of law? Assuming that the power did actually pass, there can be no doubt that the trustee in bankruptcy would not be the appropriate person to exercise a fiduciary power; this would have to be done by the court; nor would he be the appropriate person to exercise a non-fiduciary power in favour of persons other than the bankrupt. But what about a non-fiduciary power entitling the bankrupt to appoint to himself, as all general powers of appointment do? Where the will of the donee of a general power of appointment appoints that property to his personal representatives (as most standard form wills automatically do), it is clear that that property is available for the payment of pecuniary legacies if his estate is solvent[71] and is presumably also available for the payment of his creditors if his estate is insolvent. By analogy, therefore, it is possible that such a power may be available to his trustee in bankruptcy for the purpose of appointing the property to the bankrupt for the benefit of his creditors. But this question must clearly await decision.

---

[68] *Simpson Curtis Pension Trustees v. Readson* (1994) 8 Trust Law Intl. 86; *Denny v. Yeldon* [1995] 1 B.C.L.C. 560.

[69] [1990] 1 W.L.R. 1587. See *ante*, p. 182.

[70] It has in Australia in *Re Burton* (1994) 126 A.L.R. 557; however, there the relevant insolvency legislation was held not to pass the power to the trustee in bankruptcy and it was held to be a fiduciary power anyway.

[71] Administration of Estates Act 1925, Sched. I, Pt II, para. 7.

VI. RELEASE OF POWERS

1. *Reasons for the Release of Powers*

Those entitled to exercise powers are sometimes asked to release them. One possible reason for such a request can be the effect of changes in taxation law. An example could be the change in the law which occurred in 1973. Until April 5, 1973, all the income of a trust was taxable in the hands of the trustees at the same rate; however, thereafter an additional charge to tax was (and still is) imposed on income which could be accumulated.[72] In the case of a pre-existing trust under which the trustees had a power to accumulate but, subject thereto, could pay the income to a named person, one possible way of avoiding the additional charge to tax would have been to have asked the trustees to release their power to accumulate so that the named beneficiary became entitled to the whole of the income. However, it is more likely that trustees will be asked to release powers in order to create indefeasible interests. Suppose that trustees hold a fund on trust for such of Michael, Norman and Oliver as they may appoint and, in default of appointment, for all three equally. As long as the power of appointment remains exercisable, none of the beneficiaries can be sure that he will receive any benefit, since the power may be exercised in favour of the other two. Thus, if Michael wishes to raise money by selling or mortgaging his interest, he may ask the trustees to release the power, in order to give him a fixed interest with which he can then deal (this will, however, amount to a deemed disposal for the purposes of capital gains tax). Other reasons for releasing powers are illustrated by the facts of *Re Wills' Trust Deeds*[73]; the trust deeds in question contained a power to appoint the trust property between charitable and non-charitable objects and it was wished to release the latter power in order to convert the trust into one which was entirely charitable.

In considering whether powers can be released, two questions arise: whether a power can properly be released and the extent to which any release made is effective.

2. *The Propriety of a Release*

The circumstances in which a power can be effectively released were considered in *Re Wills' Trust Deeds*[74] where Buckley J. formulated the following general propositions.[75]

   1. If a power is granted to appoint among a class of objects and in default of appointment there is a trust, either express or implied, in favour of the members of that class, the donee cannot defeat the

---

[72] Finance Act 1973, s.16; see *ante*, p. 170.
[73] [1964] Ch. 219.
[74] *ibid.*
[75] *ibid.* at 236, 237. In cases of doubt whether a release should be effected, it seems possible to apply to the court for directions (see *Re Allen-Meyrick's Will Trusts* [1966] 1 W.L.R. 499) alternatively, in cases where a variation of trusts is sought, an application to the court on the question may be made under the Variation of Trusts Act 1958 (see *post*, p. 656).

interest of the members of the class by releasing the power or, which comes to the same thing, by refusing to appoint. (This proposition is self-evident, as Buckley J. himself stated.)

2. A power of the kind just mentioned cannot be released, for the donee is under a duty to exercise it, notwithstanding the fact that the court may not be able to compel him personally to perform that duty. (This proposition seems somewhat debatable in the form in which it is stated; the donee of such a power will not always be under a duty to exercise it and, if he is not, he can surely release it. However, in practice, in view of the trust in default of appointment, any release would in most cases be ineffectual.)

3. Where a power is conferred on trustees *virtute officii* in relation to their trust property, they cannot release it or bind themselves not to exercise it. (This proposition envisages the now established distinction between fiduciary and non-fiduciary donees of mere powers.)

4. The same is true if the power is conferred on persons who are trustees of a settlement but is conferred on them by name and not by reference to their office, if and only if they were on the facts selected as donees of the power because they were trustees. (This proposition also envisages the now established distinction between fiduciary and non-fiduciary donees of mere powers.)

5. Where a power is conferred on someone who is not a trustee of property to which the power relates or, if he be a trustee of it, is not conferred on him in that capacity, then, in the absence of a trust in favour of the object of the power in default of appointment, the donee is not under any duty recognised by the court to exercise the power such as to disable him from releasing it. (This proposition, also described by Buckley J. as self-evident, now requires some reformulation in the light of the fact that it has now been held that a person other than a trustee can be classified as a fiduciary donee of a mere power.)

How do these propositions apply to the different types of powers which have already been discussed?

(A) Trust Powers or Powers in the Nature of a Trust

It is clear that there is no possibility of a trust power or a power in the nature of a trust being released. The very essence of such a power is that the person entitled to exercise it is under an obligation so to do and, if he fails to do so, it will be exercised by the court. Such powers fall within the first two propositions enunciated by Buckley J. (because of the existence, in default of appointment, of an implied trust in favour of the members of the class).

(B) Mere Powers Held by a Fiduciary Donee

Where such powers are held by trustees, they will fall within the third and fourth propositions enunciated by Buckley J. Where a power is conferred upon a trustee *virtute officii*, it is clearly established that he cannot release that power "in the absence of words in the trust deed authorising [him] so to do".[76] Despite the fact that the donee cannot be obliged to exercise the power, he cannot ignore it since, as has already been seen,[77] he must consider periodically whether or not he should exercise the power, the range and objects of the power, and the appropriateness of individual appointments. This is the case both where the power is expressed to be vested in the trustees as such (the third proposition) and where the power is expressed to have been conferred on the trustees by name if they were selected because they were the trustees (the fourth proposition). Thus in *Re Courage Group's Pension Schemes*,[78] it was held that a committee which had been established to manage a pension scheme could not deprive their successors of the right to exercise their powers even if (which was not in fact decided) they were themselves entitled to release, fetter or agree not to exercise those powers.

Where a power is held by a person other than a trustee, the propositions enunciated by Buckley J. would suggest that, save where there is, in default of appointment, an express or implied trust in favour of the members of the class, the power can be released (this follows from the first, second and fifth propositions). However, in *Mettoy Pension Trustees v. Evans*,[79] a mere power held by a person other than the trustee of the property in question was held to be fiduciary and, consequently, incapable of release. Assuming that the donee of the power was correctly classified as a fiduciary (as has already been seen, this conclusion has been described as "not overwhelming"[80]), this decision is clearly correct and therefore necessitates an additional proposition, immediately after the existing fourth one, to the effect that "the same is true if the power is conferred on persons who are not trustees of the property in question but who are nevertheless held to be fiduciary donees of the power" and, additionally, the exclusion from the existing fifth proposition of fiduciary donees.

However, it must be emphasised that a mere power held by a fiduciary donee can be released if the instrument which created it so authorises. The wording of the relevant clause was held to authorise such a release in *Muir v. I.R.C.*[81] This was in effect also the position in *Blausten v. I.R.C.*,[82] where the Court of Appeal came to the conclusion that a resettlement of the trust fund upon trusts identical with the existing trusts, but excluding a particular power vested in the trustees, was a good exercise of the power of appointment (the immediate effect of the appointment was simply to exclude the wife of the settlor from the objects of the discretionary trusts of income and that was held to be within the terms of the power of appointment).

(C) Mere Powers Held by a Non-Fiduciary Donee

Such powers fall within the first, second and fifth propositions enunciated by Buckley J. This suggests that such powers can be released save where there is, in default of appointment, an express or implied trust in favour of the members of the class. There is no doubt that such powers can be released

---

[76] *Muir v. I.R.C.* [1966] 1 W.L.R. 1269, *per* Harman L.J. at 1283 (original emphasis).
[77] See *ante*, p. 180.
[78] [1987] 1 W.L.R. 495.
[79] [1990] 1 W.L.R. 1587.
[80] See *ante*, p. 182.
[81] [1966] 1 W.L.R. 1269.
[82] [1972] Ch. 256.

where this exception does not apply. However, as has already been mentioned, given that the donee of such a power will not be under a duty to exercise it, he should surely be able to release it; such a conclusion was indeed reached in *Re Radcliffe*,[83] where the release by a father of a mere power in order that the shares of his sons (who were entitled in default) might become absolute was upheld even though the release also benefited the father, in that he thereby received the share of a deceased son (this is one of the relatively rare cases where a release in such circumstances served a useful purpose). Another question which is not entirely clear is whether it is still possible, as the fifth proposition states, for a trustee of the property, whose power was not conferred on him in that capacity, to be held to be a non-fiduciary donee. The only other point which should be noted is that it has been held that the doctrine of fraud on a power does not apply to the release of a power, since the release benefits those entitled in default.[84]

3. *The Effectiveness of a Release*

In *Re Wills' Trust Deeds* it was actually held that the power of appointment in question was not coupled with a duty or trust and was accordingly capable of being released. But Buckley J. also raised a fresh point (on which there appeared to be no prior direct authority) in holding that, although the present trustees, by releasing the power, had precluded themselves from exercising it, that would not prevent their successors in title from so doing. He said this:

"A power granted to successive holders of an office is unlike trust property, the entire ownership of which is vested in the trustees for the time being of the settlement and devolves on each change of trustee by succession. Where a power is granted to successive holders of an office all that is vested in the incumbent for the time being of the office is the capacity to exercise the power while he holds that office".[85]

A similar view was taken in *Re Courage Group's Pension Scheme*,[86] although in that case it was not actually decided whether or not the existing donees were entitled to release their power anyway. If this is indeed the law, the purposes already considered for which powers are released may no longer always be achieved because of the possibility of the released power being exercised by later trustees. More is likely to be heard of this particular question.

4. *The Failure to Exercise A Power*

Until such time, if at all, as a power is effectively released, it remains with the trustees and they alone can exercise it. In *Re Allen-Meyrick's Will Trusts*,[87] the trustees of a will held the trust fund upon trust to pay so much of the

---

[83] [1892] 1 Ch. 227.
[84] *Re Somes* [1896] 1 Ch. 250.
[85] [1964] Ch. 219 at 238.
[86] [1987] 1 W.L.R. 495.
[87] [1966] 1 W.L.R. 499.

income as they thought fit to the husband of the testatrix and, subject to the exercise of their discretion in his favour, upon trust for her god-daughters. The husband was an undischarged bankrupt and the trustees had, in the exercise of their discretion, paid the rent of the house in which he lived; however, apart from this, they could not agree as to whether or not to make a further payment to him. They therefore asked the court to accept a surrender of their discretion but Buckley J. refused to do so. It is of course open to the trustees of any trust to seek the directions of the court in any particular circumstances and the court was prepared to give directions as to what should be done with the income which had accrued; however, it would not accept a surrender of the trustees' discretion for the future. This seems to have been largely due to difficulties as to how matters could proceed following surrender; had the court accepted the surrender, there would have been no ready way in which it could have been informed of the actual circumstances of the beneficiaries each time that a decision had to be made. However, the decision actually reached opened up the possibility that, although this would certainly not have been welcomed by the court, the trustees could have sought the directions of the court on a new application each year or so.

VII. The Position of the Potential Beneficiaries

1. *The Potential Beneficiaries Themselves*

What is the position of a person who is one of the objects of a power pending its exercise? Two aspects require consideration.

(A)   The Individual Rights of an Object of a Power

(1)   When can application be made to the court?
A person who is one of the objects of a power can require the donee of the power to consider exercising the power in his favour, or in favour of any of the other objects.[88] Accordingly, if he can show that the donee of the power has refused to consider him as a possible object, he can apply to the court. This is, however, subject to any contrary provision in the instrument by which the power was created (some modern deeds authorise the donees of powers to exercise their discretion in favour of some of the objects of the power without even considering its other objects).

A person who is one of the objects of a power can also apply to the court if, despite giving due consideration to his own position, the donee of the power has acted capriciously in other respects. In *Re Manisty's Settlement*,[89] Templeman J. stated[90] that donees of a power would be acting capriciously if they acted "for reasons which I apprehend could be said to be irrational, perverse or irrelevant to any sensible expectation of the settlor; for example,

---

[88] *Re Gestetner* [1953] Ch. 672, *per* Harman J. at 688; *Re Manisty's Settlement* [1974] Ch. 17, *per* Templeman J. at 25.
[89] [1974] Ch. 17.
[90] *ibid.* at 25.

if they chose a beneficiary by height or complexion or by the irrelevant fact that he was a resident of Greater London".

In other respects, a person who is one of the objects of a power is in a curious position. On the one hand, it seems clear that the donees of the power are not in any way obliged to inform him that he is an object of the power.[91] On the other hand, if he knows that he is an object of the power, it seems that he is entitled to apply to the court in the event that the trustees in whom the property subject to the power is vested are guilty of any acts of improper administration or in the event that the donee of the power either exercises it improperly or purports to release it in circumstances where this is improper. In order to establish whether any such improper activity has occurred, it seems that he is entitled to obtain the same information as a beneficiary under a fixed trust.[92] The existence of these rights obviously provides a good reason for keeping the class of objects of a power as narrow as possible.

The persons entitled to the property in default of appointment are similarly entitled to apply to the court in the event that the trustees in whom the property subject to the power is vested are guilty of any acts of improper administration or in the event that the donee of the power exercises it improperly.

(2) Remedies where the power is not exercised

Where the power in question is a trust power in any of the senses in which this expression is used (whether, in other words, the power is vested in the trustees, in which case it will in effect be a discretionary trust, or in third parties, in which case it will in effect be an old fashioned power in the nature of a trust), the donee of the power will be under an obligation to exercise it; therefore, he can be directed to do so by the court. Where the power is vested in the trustees, the court will additionally have all the powers enunciated by Lord Wilberforce in *McPhail v. Doulton*.[93] Prior to that decision, a trust power was only valid for certainty of objects if a complete list of all its objects could be drawn up; consequently, in the event that the power was not exercised, the court would invariably order that the property should be divided equally between all the objects of the power. However, the new test for certainty of objects established by *McPhail v. Doulton* inevitably means that, in the case of trust powers validated by that decision, not all the objects of the power will be known either to the trustees or to the court. Lord Wilberforce consequently held that, in such circumstances, the court can either appoint new trustees or direct persons representative of the classes of beneficiaries to prepare a scheme of distribution or, should the proper basis for distribution be apparent, direct the trustees how to distribute the fund (this does not, of course, mean that equal distribution will never again be ordered; in the case of a small class of beneficiaries whose entire membership is known, it is almost inevitable that equal distribution will still be ordered). Where, on the other hand, the power is vested in third parties, there does not seem any basis on which the court can replace those third

---

[91] *ibid.*
[92] See *post*, pp. 497, 635.
[93] [1971] A.C. 424 at 457.

parties. Consequently, the court can presumably only either direct persons representative of the classes of beneficiaries to prepare a scheme for distribution or, should the proper basis for distribution be apparent (normally the case in old fashioned powers in the nature of a trust, which tend to be in favour of reduced groups), direct the trustees how to distribute the fund (in the case of a reduced group, inevitably in equal shares).

Where, on the other hand, the power in question is a mere power, the court is unable to direct its exercise. Where that power is held by a non-fiduciary donee, the court can do nothing at all. Where, on the other hand, the power is held by a fiduciary donee, the court can direct the donee to consider whether or not to exercise the power; it has been stated on several occasions[94] that a refusal to follow such a direction from the court might well lead to the replacement of the fiduciary in question. More controversially, it has now been held, in *Mettoy Pension Trustees v. Evans*[95] that all the remedies available to the court to enforce trust powers are also available in the case of mere powers held by fiduciary donees. This was the case in which a company held a power to appoint any surplus in its pension fund, which was actually vested in a separate trustee company, in favour of the pensioners with a gift over in default of appointment to itself. Warner J. held that the company was unable to release the power and thus make the surplus available for its general creditors. It was obviously impossible to leave the liquidators of the company to exercise the power since their duty to the creditors would have conflicted with and presumably prevailed over their duty to consider the claims of the pensioners. No application had been made for the appointment of new fiduciaries (had there been, the obvious remedy would have been to vest the power in the trustee company, which had been the donee of the power at an earlier stage). Warner J. therefore held that he was entitled to approve or dictate a scheme himself and invited further argument as to what scheme was appropriate.[96] This decision has been criticised[97] on the grounds that judicial exercise of fiduciary discretions is inappropriate, even "as regards quasi-public trusts such as pension funds" and that the judge should have confined himself to appointing suitable new fiduciaries. It remains to be seen whether the novel remedies enunciated in *Mettoy Pension Trustees v. Evans* for the non-exercise of a mere power by a fiduciary donee are ever actually put into effect.

(3) Remedies where the power is exercised improperly
Any improper exercise of any power will be set aside, both where the donees "exceed their power, and possibly if they are proved to have exercised it capriciously".[98] Thus in *Turner v. Turner*,[99] where the trustees had left all the decisions to the settlor (who was not a trustee) and had made a series of appointments without reading the necessary documents before signing them, all the appointments were held to be null and void other than one

---

[94] *Re Gestetner* [1953] Ch. 672 at 688; *Re Manisty's Settlement* [1974] Ch. 17 at 25.
[95] [1990] 1 W.L.R. 1587.
[96] This part of the case was adjourned pending an appeal, which seems subsequently to have been settled.
[97] By S. Gardner, 107 L.Q.R. (1991) 214 at 217–218.
[98] *McPhail v. Doulton* [1971] A.C. 424, *per* Lord Wilberforce at 456.
[99] [1984] Ch. 100.

concerning land which had been effective to transfer the legal title, which the appointee therefore held on trust for the settlement. If the person to whom the property was improperly appointed has dealt with it in favour of a third party, save in the relatively unlikely situation in which the third party has acquired the legal title to the property in question (in which case he may be able to claim to be a bona fide purchaser for value without notice or, in the case of registered land, the statutory equivalent), he will not be able to claim to have taken free of the interests of those otherwise entitled under the power and so will be bound by their interests.[1] The only exception to this is the limited defence provided by section 157 of the Law of Property Act 1925, which rather curiously is available only when the appointee was at least 25 years old at the time of the transaction and only to the extent that he was presumptively entitled in default of appointment.

(B)   The Collective Rights of the Objects of a Power
There is one respect in which the objects of a power have a more direct interest in the property subject to the power. It will be seen later that, where a beneficiary of a trust is of full age and *sui juris* and he alone is entitled to the trust fund, he may bring the trust to an end.[2] Somewhat similarly, where all the objects of a trust power combine, then they together may deal with the beneficial interest in the property subject thereto. In *Re Smith*[3] a fund was held on discretionary trust as to income and capital for Lilian and, after her death, for her children. Lilian and her three children, who were between them the only persons entitled to benefit under the trust, together assigned all their interest therein to an insurance company. The assignee was held entitled to demand the whole of the income. Romer J. said that in such a case "you treat all the people put together as though they formed one person, for whose benefit the trustees were directed to apply the whole of a particular fund".[4]

(C)   The Right to Release Interests
Just as a man cannot be forced to accept a gift,[5] so a man cannot be forced to remain an object of a trust power or a mere power and he can, if he so wishes, release his rights thereunder. In that event, the trust power or mere power is administered as if his name did not appear among the class of those entitled to be considered as objects of the exercise of the donee's discretion.[6]

2. *Assignees and Trustees in Bankruptcy*

An assignee or trustee in bankruptcy of a potential beneficiary is, in principle, in the same position as the potential beneficiary himself. Thus in *Re Coleman*[7] the Court of Appeal held that, where the discretionary beneficiary

---

[1] *Cloutte v. Storey* [1911] 1 Ch. 18.
[2] See *post*, p. 637.
[3] [1928] Ch. 915.
[4] See also *Re Nelson* [1928] Ch. 920N.
[5] *Thompson v. Leach* (1690) 2 Vent. 198; *Re Stratton's Deed of Disclaimer* [1958] 2 Ch. 42.
[6] *Re Gulbenkian's Settlement Trusts (No.2)* [1970] Ch. 408.
[7] (1889) 39 Ch.D. 443.

had assigned his beneficial interest, the trustees were compelled to pay to the assignee the amount which they had allotted to the beneficiary. *Re Smith*,[8] which has already been mentioned, is to the same effect. In principle, the position of a trustee in bankruptcy ought to be the same but this is subject to the general principle of bankruptcy law that a bankrupt is entitled to retain sufficient funds for his own support, the trustee in bankruptcy being entitled only to the balance. This principle was applied by Vaughan Williams J. in *Re Ashby*.[9] In that case a discretionary beneficiary became bankrupt and the trustees continued to make payments to him. The beneficiary was held to be entitled to retain what was necessary for his basic support and his trustee in bankruptcy was held to be able to claim the excess.

The terms of the trust instrument may either require payment to be made to the beneficiary personally or entitle the trustees either to pay the beneficiary directly or to make payments to third parties for his benefit. In *Re Bullock*,[10] which was concerned with a discretionary trust containing the latter type of provision, Kekewich J. held that, when a discretionary beneficiary had become bankrupt, the trustees could continue to pay income to third parties for his benefit. The precise scope of this decision is a matter of some doubt and it has been suggested that the power is restricted so that the trustees can only provide the bankrupt with sufficient funds to cover his necessaries. However, this is probably not correct. It seems that, so far as the trustees are concerned, they may continue to apply funds for the benefit of the beneficiary in the same way as they could have done before the bankruptcy. If as a result assets come into the hands of the beneficiary which are not required for his necessaries, as where the trustees apply the money in providing a luxury holiday for the beneficiary, it seems that the trustee in bankruptcy is powerless to intervene. Of course, the trustees must exercise their discretion in good faith and must make the decision with a view to benefiting the beneficiary rather than in order to spite the trustee in bankruptcy.

---

[8] [1928] Ch. 915.
[9] [1892] 1 Q.B. 872.
[10] [1891] 64 L.T. 736.

CHAPTER 7

LEGALITY OF A TRUST

I. GENERALLY

IT is an elementary principle that a trust which is wholly illegal or contrary to public policy will not be enforced. Indeed the court will not only prevent the illegal trust from taking effect but will also generally go so far as to refuse its assistance to the settlor in recovering the property in question. "Those who violate the law", said Lord Truro L.C. "must not apply to the law for protection".[1] The principle will not, however, be stretched to its uttermost limit. A settlor is entitled to recover the property where the illegal purpose is merely contemplated; in these circumstances, there is what is described as a *locus poenitentiae*.[2]

The consequences of a trust which is partially unlawful can be rather different. Strictly speaking, it appears that, if part of the trust funds is to be devoted to an unlawful purpose and the remainder to a lawful purpose, then where the part of the funds to be devoted cannot be ascertained the whole trust will fail because it will be impossible to ascertain the residue.[3] However, it must be truly impossible to ascertain the relevant part and it appears that the court will, if practicable, endeavour to ascertain it in order to uphold the remainder of the gift.[4] Indeed there is some, admittedly indecisive, authority[5] for the proposition that if the lawful purpose is charitable the whole of the property will be devoted to that purpose and the trust for the illegal purpose will be completely disregarded; however, in view of the confused state of the case law, it is not by any means certain that this is indeed the law, notwithstanding the fact that this would be extremely convenient.

This chapter deals principally with the circumstances in which a trust will be void for perpetuity or will be set aside because of the settlor's bankruptcy; both these topics are of the utmost importance in any discussion of the legality of a trust. However, it is beyond the scope of this work to deal exhaustively with the many other types of illegality known to the law, which

---

[1] *Benyon v. Nettlefold* (1850) 3 Mac. & G. 94 at 102. See also *Ayerst v. Jenkins* (1873) L.R. 16 Eq. 275 but *compare Phillips v. Probyn* [1899] 1 Ch. 811.

[2] *Symes v. Hughes* (1870) L.R. 9 Eq. 475.

[3] See *Chapman v. Brown* (1801) 6 Ves. 404.

[4] See *Mitford v. Reynolds* (1842) 1 Ph. 185.

[5] See *Fisk v. A.-G.* (1867) L.R. 4 Eq. 521; *Hunter v. Bullock* (1872) L.R. 14 Eq. 45; *Dawson v Small* (1874) L.R. 18 Eq. 114; *Re Williams* (1877) 5 Ch.D. 735; *Re Birkett* (1878) 9 Ch.D. 576 (all trusts for maintenance of tombs with surplus for a charitable purpose); see also *Re Rogerson* [1901] 1 Ch. 715.

are as capable of vitiating a trust as of vitiating any other transaction; a few examples will be briefly considered.

(1) Restraints on alienation
A restraint on the alienation of property given to a beneficiary absolutely is contrary to public policy and void.[6]

(2) Trusts in favour of illegitimate children
In certain circumstances, trusts which took effect before 1970, whether created by deed[7] or by will,[8] in favour of illegitimate children who were yet to be born were void on the ground that they promoted immorality and so were contrary to public policy. The test of public policy applied to determine validity was whether or not future immorality was in fact being promoted. However, this rule does not apply to trusts contained in deeds *inter vivos* or in the wills of persons dying after 1969.[9]

(3) Restraints on marriage
If a condition and/or a gift over to take effect upon that condition is contained in a settlement and it tends to restrain marriage totally, the condition and gift over are wholly void.[10] However this rule does not apply to conditions or gifts restraining second or later marriages[11]; nor does it apply to a partial restraint operating against designated persons or designated categories of persons such as the members of a particular religious faith or everyone other than the members of a particular religious faith.[12] On the other hand, however, a gift of property until marriage—as opposed to a gift to a person on condition that he does not marry—is perfectly good[13]; validity depends on whether the wording is construed as having given rise to a (valid) determinable interest or a (void) conditional interest (this distinction is perhaps an unnecessarily fine one (some would say unnecessarily perverse) but it is well established). Curiously enough, the same difficulties do not attach to a condition requiring the consent of a particular person to marriage; it is clearly established that such a condition will be valid despite the apparent illogicality that the withholding of consent will bar a marriage just as effectively as the void conditions already referred to.[14]

(4) Trusts separating parent and child
If a trust is designed to separate a parent (even if he or she has been divorced[15]) from his or her child, that will be void as contrary to public policy.[16] Similarly, a trust will fail if it tends to interfere with parental duties;

---

[6] See for example *Floyer v. Bankes* (1869) L.R. 8 Eq. 115.
[7] *Blodwell v. Edwards* (1596) Cro.Eliz. 509; see also *Occleston v. Fullalove* (1874) 9 Ch. App. 147, *per* Mellish L.J.
[8] *Metham v. Duke of Devonshire* (1718) 1 P.Wms. 529.
[9] Family Law Reform Act 1969, s.15(7).
[10] *Lloyd v. Lloyd* (1852) 2 Sim.(N.S.) 255.
[11] *Allen v. Jackson* (1842) 1 Ch.D. 399.
[12] *Jenner v. Turner* (1880) 16 Ch.D. 188.
[13] *Re Lovell* [1920] 1 Ch. 122.
[14] *Re Whiting's Settlement* [1905] 1 Ch. 96.
[15] *Re Piper* [1946] 2 All E.R. 503.
[16] *Re Boulter* [1922] 1 Ch. 75; *Re Sandbrook* [1912] 2 Ch. 471.

such duties should be discharged solely with a view to the moral and spiritual welfare of the child and without being influenced by mercenary considerations.[17]

(5) Name and arms clauses
A number of decisions were overruled by the Court of Appeal in *Re Neeld*[18] so as to produce the unexceptionable principle that a name and arms clause (which may reasonably be regarded as harmless if anachronistic) requiring any husband whom a particular woman or any member of a particular family marries to change his name (usually to hers) on marriage is neither contrary to public policy nor uncertain.

II. PERPETUITIES AND ACCUMULATIONS

Since medieval times, English law has been subjected to the tension between two conflicting influences. Owners of land and of other types of property have generally wished to tie up their property indefinitely, usually for the benefit of their family or for some institution or cause, while the courts and the legislature have always felt that it is in the interest of the nation as a whole that wealth should circulate freely and that property should not be made inalienable. The result has been a compromise. Property may be tied up indefinitely for a purpose which the law wishes to advance, namely a charity.[19] Otherwise property may be tied up only for a comparatively short period. The rule which enforces this restriction is known as the rule against perpetuities.

1. *The Rule Against Remoteness*

The rule against remoteness basically provides that every gift of property must vest in the recipient within the period of a life or lives in being at the time when the gift is made and 21 years thereafter (with allowance being made where appropriate for any period of gestation).[20] (However, any fixed period up to 80 years can be substituted in respect of gifts contained in instruments coming into effect after July 15, 1964 if the settlor or testator so elects in the instrument in question.[21])

The basic rule has, however, been bedeviled by an excess of zeal on the part of the judges. On the basis that property must vest, if at all, within the perpetuity period, the judges have striven to find some possibility, no matter how remote, whereby it might not do so. Whenever they have managed to envisage any such possibility, the gift in question has been held to be void. In the process, common sense has gone out of the window and Alice has walked in the front door. The almost unbelievable nonsense which has

---

[17] *Re Borwick* [1933] Ch. 657.
[18] [1962] Ch. 643.
[19] See *post*, p. 380.
[20] *Cadell v. Palmer* (1833) 1 Cl. & Fin. 372; *Re Wilmer's Trusts* [1903] 2 Ch. 411.
[21] See *post*, p. 211.

ensued is illustrated by *Re Dawson*.[22] There a testator gave property to trustees to hold upon trust for his daughter for life, with remainder to such of her children as should attain the age of 21, with a provision that if any of her children should die under the age of 21, but should themselves leave issue, such issue on attaining the age of 21 would take the share of their parent. When the will came into effect on the death of the testator, his daughter was aged over 60 and all her children were over 21. The court nevertheless managed to hold this gift to be void. With blithe disregard for the principles of biology, it was held that the daughter was still capable of giving birth to a child who might himself subsequently die before reaching the age of 21 leaving issue. Such a future child was obviously not alive at the time of the death of the testator so that the relevant life in being was the testator's daughter. In such circumstances the issue of the after-born child would not attain his vested interest within 21 years from the death of the daughter. Therefore, since it was thus possible that one of the persons entitled in remainder might not obtain a vested interest within the perpetuity period, the entire remainder was therefore void for perpetuity. In the same sort of way, in *Re Gaite*[23] the judicial reasoning solemnly proceeded on the basis that a girl aged less than five could give birth to a child. In the apt expression of Morris and Leach[24] the judicial world would seem to be populated by fertile octogenarians, precocious toddlers and various other freaks.

To order to overcome some of the traps and generally to restore some semblance of sanity, Parliament has intervened on two occasions. Small amendments were made by the Law of Property Act 1925 and large-scale alterations were made by the Perpetuities and Accumulations Act 1964. With only a few exceptions,[25] the latter Act applies only to instruments coming into effect after July 15, 1964.[26]

The modified rule may be stated in the following way: where a gift is made to take effect in the future, it must be seen from the instrument by which it is created that, if it is to vest at all, it must necessarily vest within the period prescribed by law but in the case of instruments governed by the 1964 Act, if it appears that the gift may or may not vest within the prescribed period, the gift is treated as if it does not offend against the rule until such time, if at all, as it becomes clear that it cannot vest within that period. The elements of this definition must now be examined and expanded.

(A) The rule concerns vesting

The rule requires only that gifts must vest within the perpetuity period. The aspect of the rule against perpetuities now being considered—as opposed to the rule against inalienability which will be considered later[27]—has no application to the length of time during which property may be enjoyed. Accordingly, if an outright gift is made to a limited company so that the gift

---

[22] (1888) 39 Ch.D. 155.
[23] [1949] 1 All E.R. 459.
[24] The Rule Against Perpetuities (2nd ed., 1964), p. 89.
[25] See s.8(2).
[26] The date of the Royal Assent (s.15(5)).
[27] See *post*, p. 220.

vests in the company immediately, it may hold the property for more than a thousand years without ever infringing the rule against remoteness.[28]

It is, therefore, essential to know what is meant by "vesting". A future gift may be either vested or contingent. A gift is vested if:

(i) first, the person or persons entitled to the gift are in existence and are ascertained;

(ii) secondly, the size of the beneficiaries' interests is ascertained[29]; and

(iii) thirdly, any conditions attached to the gift are satisfied.

If, therefore, property is left upon trust for Romeo for life, with the remainder to Juliet, the interest of Juliet is vested even if Romeo is still alive. Juliet's interest is vested because she herself is alive and is an ascertained person; the extent of her interest, namely an interest in the whole fund, is ascertained; and no conditions have to be satisfied before she becomes entitled. On the other hand, if the gift were to Romeo for life, with the remainder to Juliet provided she has danced on the moon, her gift does not become vested until that condition is fulfilled.

A vested interest therefore may or may not carry the right to present enjoyment of the property in question.[30] To connotate this distinction, vested interests are classified as being:

(i) either vested in possession, in which case the interest does carry the right to present possession or enjoyment;

(ii) or vested in interest, where the interest carries only the right to future possession or enjoyment of the property in question.

The relevance of this for the purpose of the rule against perpetuities is that the rule is satisfied despite the fact that the gift is only vested in interest. Thus, it was held in *Re Hargreaves*[31] that a gift to a person for life, with remainder to any woman who might become his widow for life, with remainder to his children who attained the age of 21, was good. It is true that the person who might become his wife need not be alive at the date of the settlement, but at the end of the perpetuity period (21 years after the death of the life tenant) it will be possible to say that his widow (if any) and his children who have attained 21 are between them the absolute owners of the property.

(B) The scope of the rule

The general principle is that the rule applies to all future gifts. In particular, for the purposes of the law of trusts, it applies to future gifts arising under

---

[28] See, however, *post*, p. 220.

[29] *Pearks v. Moseley* (1880) 5 App. Cas. 714. This requirement for vesting applies only to the rule against perpetuities.

[30] It is a question of construction whether an interest is contingent or is vested liable to be divested: *Brotherton v. I.R.C.* [1978] 1 W.L.R. 610.

[31] (1889) 43 Ch.D. 401.

an *inter vivos* settlement or trust, and to trusts created by will. To this general principle there are three exceptions:

(i) first, a gift to charity is exempt from the rule if the prior interests are also given to charity; this is considered in further detail in a later Chapter[32];

(ii) secondly, rights of redemption under mortgages are not within the rule, so that a mortgagor's right to redeem can be exercised outside the perpetuity period.[33] Similarly, certain provisions of leases, such as options to renew the lease[34] and options to purchase the freehold or leasehold reversion[35] are not within the rule against remoteness; and

(iii) thirdly, future personal obligations are not within the rule; thus a covenant to pay future mining royalties would not be within the rule against remoteness.[36]

(C) The perpetuity period
The maximum period for which vesting may be postponed is:

(i) either the period of a life or lives in being, and a further period of 21 years;

(ii) or, where there is no life in being, a period of 21 years;

(iii) or, in the gifts governed by the 1964 Act in this respect, a fixed period up to and not exceeding 80 years provided that that period is specified in the instrument creating the gift as the perpetuity period.

However, it should be noted that, in certain circumstances, the statutory period of 80 years may actually turn out to be shorter than the common law period; nevertheless, the use of the statutory period has the advantage of simplicity and certainty.

One of the more difficult questions affecting perpetuities is how to identify the life or lives in being. It is clear that the life or lives chosen do not need to take any benefit under the gift. Consequently, the use of what is known as a "royal lives clause" is not uncommon; this is a clause which specifies the perpetuity period by reference to the Royal Family. One of the forms of royal lives clauses in use at the present time is "the period ending at the expiration of 21 years from the death of the last survivor of all the lineal descendants of his late Majesty King George VI[37] who shall be living

---

[32] See *post*, p. 380.
[33] *Knightsbridge Estates Trust v. Byrne* [1939] Ch. 441.
[34] *Woodall v. Clifton* [1905] 2 Ch. 257 at 265, 268.
[35] Perpetuities and Accumulations Act 1964, s.9(1).
[36] *Witham v. Vane* (1883) Challis R.P. 440.
[37] The father of the present Queen. Consequently, the royal lives in question are those of H.M. Queen Elizabeth II, HRH Princess Margaret, and their descendants. It is also probably still possible to use King George V (the grandfather of the present Queen), although the number of his descendants is now very considerable. It is certainly unsafe to specify the descendants of any previous sovereign (see the doubts cast, as early as 1901, on the validity of using the lives of descendants of Queen Victoria (then still alive) in *Re Moore* [1901] 1 Ch. 936).

at the time when the gift comes into effect". There is in principle no reason why other persons should not be used provided that their lifespan and that of their children is sufficiently well documented; however, in practice, this would only be likely to work if the person in question was still alive, something which would substantially shorten the period. Nor is there in principle any limit to the number of lives which may be selected, provided they can all be identified. In *Re Moore*[38] the settlor specified as the lives in being all persons then living; however, the gift was void on the ground that it was impossible to identify which of them was the survivor.

In the case of royal lives clauses and their like, it is apparent from the wording of the instrument in question that they are intended to be the lives in being for the purposes of the rule against perpetuities. However, in other cases it may be far more difficult to decide whether or not a person is to be taken as a life in being. The basic principle (or a basic principle) is that every person who is living at the date of the gift and is mentioned in it or whose existence is implied by it is a life in being. Thus, a gift by a testator to "my grandchildren" necessarily presupposes the existence of his children; therefore those of his children who are alive at the date of his death will be taken to be lives in being in respect of this gift for the purpose of this Rule against Perpetuities.

It should also be noted that a child *en ventre sa mère* is treated as a child who is alive if this is necessary to save a gift. Accordingly, a gift to the children of a child *en ventre sa mère* will necessarily be valid, for the unborn child will by implication be regarded as a life in being and his or her own children must necessarily be born within his or her own lifetime or within nine months thereafter.[39] Similarly, the perpetuity period itself may be extended in the case of a pregnancy. If a period of 80 years is prescribed and at the end of that time a woman is pregnant with a child who would, if alive, take the gift, then that child will in fact take provided he or she is born alive.[40] The last two examples can in fact be combined so that a perpetuity period includes two periods of gestation. A gift to the children of a child *en ventre sa mère* at the age of 21 is necessarily valid because, even if the unborn child is male and he dies leaving a child *en ventre sa mère*, the latter child will reach the age of 21, if at all, within 21 years and nine months of the death of his father, who must himself be born, if at all, within nine months of the gift taking effect—in such a case, the perpetuity period is up to nine months plus a life in being plus a further nine months plus 21 years.

The obvious and amusing proposition that any life selected must be human should also be noted; it is apparently not permissible to choose either a specified animal (because some animals, such as tortoises, are extremely long-lived) or a specified long-lived tree such as a Californian pine. Only in an Irish case has this point actually been pronounced upon; this was in *Re Kelly*[41] where it was stated by way of dictum that the life chosen must be that of a human and not of an animal. A similar pronouncement on the subject of trees is awaited.

---

[38] [1901] 1 Ch. 936.
[39] *Long v. Blackall* (1797) 7 T.R. 100.
[40] See *Cadell v. Palmer* (1833) 1 Cl. & F. 372, especially at 421, 422.
[41] [1932] I.R. 255 at 260, 261.

In the case of instruments governed by the 1964 Act in which advantage has not been taken of the possibility of specifying a fixed period of up to 80 years, section 3(4) of the 1964 Act prescribes rules for identifying the lives in being. The Act provides that such of the following as are alive and ascertainable at the date of the gift, and no other persons, shall constitute the lives in being:

(i) the person who made the disposition (only relevant in a gift *inter vivos*);

(ii) in the case of a contingent gift to an individual or individuals, any person who may in time satisfy the conditions and that person's parents and grandparents;

(iii) in the case of a class gift, any member or potential member of the class and that person's parents and grandparents;

(iv) any person who is given any power, option, or other right in connection with the gift; and

(v) where the interest is to arise only in the event that the prior interest of some person determines, the person having that prior interest.

Further provisions apply where there is a special power of appointment.[42] The lives of persons in the second, third and fourth categories are disregarded if the number of those persons is so large as to render it impossible to ascertain the date of death of the survivor.

(D) "Possibilities not probabilities"

The general principle is that any possibility of the gift not vesting within the perpetuity period will make it void. This principle can be expressed by saying that the rule is concerned with "possibilities not probabilities", subject in the case of gifts governed by the 1964 Act to the "wait and see" rule considered below.[43] Illustrations of this principle are provided by the decisions in *Re Dawson* and *Re Gaite* which have already been mentioned above. However, the advances in biological knowledge made this century now enable the court, when considering gifts governed by the 1964 Act, to make certain presumptions,[44] namely that a male cannot have a child at an age of less than 14 and that a female can have a child between the ages of 12 and 55 but not outside that age-span.

(E) "Wait and see"

In relation to gifts which came into effect prior to the 1964 Act, it is necessary to construe the instrument creating the gift at the date when it comes into operation. Therefore if a gift is made to a person for life, with remainder to the first of his sons who goes to Canada, and at the date when the gift comes into effect that person has no children, the gift to the son will be void for perpetuity; the life tenant is the only life in being and no son of his may not

---

[42] See *post*, p. 218.
[43] See *post*, *infra*.
[44] Perpetuities and Accumulations Act 1964.

go to Canada within 21 years of his death. In relation to gifts from this era (a large number of which are still operating despite the 34 years which have passed since 1964), it is not possible to wait and see whether he does in fact have a son who goes to Canada within 21 years from his death.

However, section 3 of the 1964 Act provides that, in relation to gifts which are subject thereto, the court may in some cases "wait and see" whether or not any particular gift in fact offends against the rule. The first and most important case is that, where a gift may or may not become vested within the perpetuity period (which means whichever of the common law perpetuity period or the statutory period of up to 80 years is relevant), the gift is to be treated as if it does not offend against the rule until it can be definitely shown that the gift will necessarily vest, if at all, after the end of the appropriate period. Thus, if an instrument coming into operation after July 15, 1964 contains a gift to a person who does not as yet have any children for life, with remainder to the first of his sons who goes to Canada, then it is possible to wait and see first whether he has any sons and, secondly, whether any of his sons goes to Canada within 21 years of the death of the survivor of him and his parents.[45] If any does, the gift is valid. Otherwise, the gift becomes void for perpetuity (and the following remainder vests) as soon as it is clear that it cannot vest; this will be at the earliest of the following times: his death without sons, the death of all his sons, or the expiry of 21 years from the death of him and his parents.

(F) Age-reducing provisions

Section 163(1) of the Law of Property Act 1925 provides that, where the vesting of property is made to depend on the attainment by the beneficiary of an age greater than 21 and by virtue of that condition the gift is void for perpetuity, the age of 21 is to be substituted for the age stated in the instrument. The section applies only when the gift would otherwise have been void for perpetuity and only to instruments coming into effect between January 1, 1926 and July 15, 1964 (both inclusive).

This provision is replaced by section 4 of the 1964 Act for instruments coming into effect after July 15, 1964. By this section the age substituted is not 21 but the age nearest to the age which would have prevented the disposition from being void. Under the 1964 Act, therefore, the instrument is altered only to the extent necessary to save the disposition from offending against the rule. Further, before applying this section, it is first necessary to apply the "wait and see" rule. Suppose, therefore, that there is a gift to the first child of William to attain the age of 30 and that William has no children when the testator dies. As William is a life in being, it is necessary to wait until the death of the survivor of him and his parents and assess the position then. At that point there will still be 21 years to go. If by then all his children have reached the age of 10, the gift will necessarily vest, if at all, within the period. If, however, his only child is then five, the vesting age will have to be reduced to save the gift and it will be reduced to 25 so that the vesting

---

[45] For the purposes of wait and see, the life tenant's parents are also lives in being (under s.3) so it is possible to wait and see until 21 years after the death of the survivor of him and his parents.

takes place within the 21 years still left after the death of William and his parents.[46]

(G) Gifts after the death of a surviving spouse

A similar provision of the 1964 Act which has no equivalent in the Law of Property Act 1925 enables gifts to children to be saved in other situations. Suppose that there is a gift to such of the children of Andrew as are living at the date of death of the survivor of Andrew and his spouse. This gift is void at common law, because Andrew may subsequently marry a woman who was not born at the date of the gift. Accordingly only Andrew, and not his wife, will be a life in being and, as his wife may survive him for more than 21 years, the interest of the children may vest outside the perpetuity period. Again the "wait and see" rule has to be applied first. If Andrew has no surviving spouse or his surviving spouse turns out to have been alive at the date of the gift or survives him and his parents for less than 21 years, the gift will have been saved by "wait and see". If this does not save the gift, which will mean that a surviving spouse of Andrew who was not alive at the date of the gift survives him and his parents for 21 years, then by virtue of section 5 of the Act the gift vests in interest immediately before the end of the perpetuity period; thus the children alive then qualify and the gift will have vested in interest exactly 21 years after the death of Andrew and his parents.[46a] However, it should be noted that this does not terminate any interest held in possession at that time; the effect of section 5 is to vest the gift in interest not in possession. So if, as is quite likely, the surviving spouse has a prior life interest (so that the original gift was to Andrew for life, remainder to any surviving spouse of Andrew for life, remainder to the children of Andrew living at the death of Andrew and his spouse), her interest will continue until her death and only then will the interest of the children vest in possession.

(H) Class gifts

Special provisions relate to gifts to the members of a class. For this purpose, a class is a number of persons who "come within a certain category or description defined by a general or collective formula, and who, if they take at all, are to take one divisible subject in certain proportionate shares".[47] The problem that such gifts pose is that it is possible that some of the potential members of the class may not yet have been born or may not yet have satisfied some other condition at the moment when the gift takes effect. Although for the purposes of the general law any member of the class who has fulfilled all necessary conditions is regarded as having a vested interest while those who have not yet qualified obviously only have contingent interests, for the purposes of the Rule against Perpetuities the gift is not regarded as vesting in any member of the class until all the members of the class are definitely known. In other words, the Rule against Perpetuities demands that all the members of the class must qualify if at all within the

---

[46] Who are also lives in being for the purposes of wait and see.
[46a] Who are also lives in being for the purposes of wait and see.
[47] *per* Lord Selborne L.C. in *Pearkes v. Mosely* (1880) 5 App.Cas. 714 at 723.

perpetuity period.[48] A gift to the children of Brian who attain the age of 21 is clearly valid for perpetuity since all the members of the class will necessarily attain that age if at all within 21 years of Brian's death and therefore within the perpetuity period. A gift to the children of Brian who marry is potentially void for perpetuity since one or more of Brian's children may not marry within 21 years of Brian's death in which case that child or children may not have qualified by the end of the perpetuity period.

Class gifts are further complicated by the existence of certain rules of construction known as the *class-closing rules*.[49] These rules, which can be excluded by contrary intention,[50] provide that a class whose size is not yet fixed will close when any member of the class becomes entitled to claim a vested interest in possession; the closed class includes any potential members of the class who have been born by then but excludes all potential unborn persons.[51] The fact that these rules reduce the size of classes means that they can operate to save a gift which would otherwise be void for perpetuity. Thus the gift to the children of Brian who marry will be saved from being void for perpetuity if any child of Brian has married when the gift takes effect since the class will immediately close on the children born by then, who can only marry in their own lifetimes and therefore will necessarily qualify if at all within the perpetuity period. But the class-closing rules operate in exactly the same way in respect of gifts which are entirely valid for perpetuity. Thus in the case of the gift to the children of Brian who attain the age of 21, the class will close when the first child reaches 21 on the children born by then even though the presence of the excluded children would not cause the gift to be void for perpetuity.

For a class gift in a instrument not governed by the 1964 Act to be valid, it had to be possible to establish at the moment when the gift took effect that every single member of the class would necessarily fulfil any necessary conditions, if at all, within the perpetuity period; the possibility that any member of the class to do so rendered the entire gift void.[52] Thus a gift to the children of Brian who marry which was contained in such an instrument would be wholly void for perpetuity unless saved by the class-closing rules in the manner already described.

Where the 1964 Act applies, however, the vast majority of class gifts will be saved by the wait and see provisions. In the case of the gift to the children of Brian who marry, if any child marries during the wait and see period the class-closing rules will operate to exclude any children born thereafter and by the end of that period all possible members of the class may either have

---

[48] *Leake v. Robinson* (1817) 2 Mer. 363.

[49] These are often also known, not wholly accurately, as the Rule in *Andrews v. Partington* (1791) 3 Bro.C.C. 401. Recent illustrations of the working of these rules can be found in *Re Chapman's Settlement Trusts* [1977] 1 W.L.R. 1163 and *Re Clifford's Settlement Trusts* [1981] Ch. 63.

[50] However, the contrary intention must be extremely clear; a gift "to the children of Brian who attain the age of 21 whenever born" would certainly contain a contrary intention but a gift "to all the children of Brian who attain the age of 21" would not.

[51] However, where the only requirement for membership of the class is birth, the class will close only if any member of the class has qualified when the gift vests in possession; if no member of the class has been born by then, the class can never close thereafter for the somewhat obvious reason that otherwise the first member's birth would cause the class to close on himself alone.

[52] *Pearks v. Moseley* (1880) 5 App.Cas. 714; *Re Hooper's Settlement Trust* [1948] Ch. 586.

married or died unmarried. The wait and see provisions will not, however, have saved the gift if at that point one or more members of the class have qualified but one or more other members of the closed class have not yet done so but are still capable of so doing so. At that point if the reason for the failure to qualify is an age requirement over 21, that age can be reduced to the extent necessary to save the gift under section 4(1) of the Act in the manner already described.[53] Where there is some other reason for the failure to qualify, recourse can instead be had to section 4(4) of the Act to save the gift. Under this subsection, any members of the closed class who have not qualified by the end of the perpetuity period are simply excluded. In the case of the gift to the children of Brian who marry, the wait and see period will end 21 years after the death of the last survivor of Brian, Brain's parents, and any wife or children of Brian who were ascertainable when the instrument in question took effect. If at that point any of the children of Brian who were alive when the first child married have not yet themselves married, they will simply be excluded from membership of the class.[54]

(J) Dependent limitations

Prior to the 1964 Act, where a gift followed and was dependent upon prior limitations which were void, that gift was necessarily also void.[55] Vested gifts are of course not subject to the Rule against Perpetuities at all and so could not possibly be affected by the fact that they followed a prior void gift. Contingent gifts were, however, void if they not only followed but were also dependent upon a prior void gift.[56] The distinction between gifts which merely followed and gifts which both followed and were dependent on a prior void gift was not particularly easy to draw in practice[57]; in broad terms, a gift had to have its own independent date of vesting if it was not to be regarded as dependent.[58] Thus a gift for life to the first child of Charles who marries but if none does to the first child of David who attains the age of 21 for life was wholly void unless a child of Charles has already married—the gift to David's child, although it would have been valid if it had stood alone, is wholly dependent on the prior void gift. On the other hand, in the case of a gift to the first child of Charles who marries for life and subject thereto to the first child of David who attains the age of 21, the gift to David's child is in no sense dependent on the prior gift and so was valid at common law. This distinction is still important for gifts not governed by the 1964 Act. However, section 6 of that Act provides that no gift governed by it can fail merely because it is dependent upon a prior void gift. This

---

[53] See *ante*, p. 214.
[54] Where a class gift contains a double contingency, one of which is an age contingency, such as a gift to the children of Brian who marry and attain the age of 40, then it is possible under s.4(3) of the Act both to age-reduce and to exclude if that will cause fewer members to be excluded. Thus, if at the end of the wait and see period, some members have married but are not yet 40, some members are 40 but have not yet married, and some are neither married nor 40, the first group can be saved by age reduction but the other two groups will have to be excluded.
[55] *Re Hubbard* [1963] Ch. 275; *Re Buckton* [1964] Ch. 497; compare *Re Robinson* [1963] 1 W.L.R. 628.
[56] *Re Coleman* [1936] Ch. 528.
[57] *Re Backhouse* [1921] 2 Ch. 51.
[58] *Re Coleman* [1936] Ch. 528.

means that where the Act applies both the gifts to David's child are now valid for perpetuity; the gifts to Charles' child both remain void at common law unless a child of his has already married but both are obviously now highly likely to be saved by the wait and see provisions.

(K)   Powers of appointment

(1)   Classification of powers

The classification of powers has already been discussed.[59] It is doubtful whether at common law intermediate powers should for the purposes of the Rule against Perpetuities be classified as general or special powers but it is suggested that the rules prescribed by the 1964 Act for instruments governed by that Act should be followed for common law purposes. In any event, by virtue of section 7 of the 1964 Act a general power is a power exercisable by one person only, which can be exercised by the donee of that power to transfer property to himself without the consent of any other person.[60] A power may be general even if it is exercisable only by will and not *inter vivos*.[61] For the purposes of the perpetuity rule, it therefore follows that, depending on its terms, an intermediate power may be either general or special. Thus a power to appoint to anyone except Eric will, for the purposes of the Rule against Perpetuities, be a general power unless the donee of the power is Eric himself.

(2)   Validity of powers

Two questions have to be considered: first, whether the power is itself valid and, secondly, whether the appointment made under the power is valid.

(a)   Whether the power is itself valid

(i)   *Special powers*. A special power is void at common law if it is capable of being exercised outside the perpetuity period.[62] However, for instruments governed by the 1964 Act, the wait and see provisions may be applied in order to establish whether the power is in fact fully exercised during the perpetuity period. Where it is exercised only partially within the period, the power is only void to the extent that it was not exercised during the perpetuity period.[63]

(ii)   *General powers*. Because the donee of the power may appoint to himself, property subject to a general power is regarded for most purposes as property belonging to the donee. Therefore, so far as the validity of the power is concerned, it is necessary only that the power should be acquired by the donee within the perpetuity period; it is not necessary for it to be

---

[59] See *ante*, p. 173.
[60] Except where consent is required as to the mode of exercise of the power.
[61] This is also the position at common law; see *Rous v. Jackson* (1885) 29 Ch.D. 521.
[62] *Re Abbot* [1893] 1 Ch. 54.
[63] Perpetuities and Accumulations Act 1964, s.3.

exercised within that period.[64] However, where the general power in question is exercisable by will, it is governed by the same rules as special powers.[65]

(b) Whether the appointment is valid

(i) *Special powers.* Because the disposition of property subject to a special power is restricted, the perpetuity period commences at the date when the power is created, not when it is exercised. In principle, therefore, at common law it is necessary to consider the position as at the date of creation of the power, assume that the appointment is then made, and then see whether the gift made by virtue of the appointment necessarily vests, if at all, within the perpetuity period. Even at common law, however, it is permissible to take into account the circumstances prevailing at the time when the power is exercised. Therefore, despite the fact that the terms of the appointment might theoretically enable the gift to vest outside the perpetuity period, if the circumstances existing at the time of the appointment establish that the gift must vest, if at all, within the period, the appointment will be valid. This can be illustrated by considering a gift by will by Charles to Desmond for life with power to appoint that property to his children and Desmond appoints that property to his son Fergus, who was born after the death of Charles but has attained the age of 10, "as and when he attains the age of 30". If this situation is examined only as at the time when the power was created, that is to say on the death of Charles, the gift and appointment have to be read together as if they provided: "to Desmond for life, with remainder to Fergus as and when he attains the age of 30"; since Fergus was not alive at that point, he could clearly take more than 21 years after the death of Desmond and so the gift would *prima facie* be void at common law. However, since it is permissible to take into account the circumstances existing when the power was exercised, it can be seen that, since Fergus is already 10, the gift will necessarily vest, if at all, within 20 years of the death of Desmond and consequently the appointment is valid.

Quite apart from the limited form of wait and see which is therefore permissible at common law, the general wait and see provisions of the 1964 Act also apply to powers which are both created and exercised after July 15, 1964.[66]

(ii) *General powers.* In the case of general powers, the perpetuity period runs from the date of the exercise of the power, not from the date of its creation. Therefore rules in respect of property comprised in a general power are the same as for property comprised in an absolute gift. However, if a power is general in its terms but is only exercisable by more than one donee, it is treated as a special power for the purposes of the Rule against Perpetuities.[67]

---

[64] *Re Fane* [1913] 1 Ch. 404.
[65] *Woolaston v. King* (1868) L.R. 8 Eq. 165.
[66] Perpetuities and Accumulations Act 1964, s.3 (compare s.8, which relates only to administrative powers of trustees).
[67] *Re the Earl of Coventry's Indentures* [1974] Ch. 77.

(L) The general effect of the Act

The 1964 Act which, it is repeated, applies only to gifts coming into force after July 15, 1964[68] clearly contains provisions which in the long term are most welcome[69] but in the short term has had the effect of creating a dual system.

(M) The effect of failure to comply with the Rule against Remoteness

If a limitation in a trust instrument infringes the Rule against Perpetuities, the interest in question will be held on resulting trust[70] for the settlor. Where the void limitation is contained in a will, that means that the property in question will fall into residue or, if it is itself the residuary gift or there is no residuary gift, will be distributed according to the intestacy rules.

2. *The Rule Against Inalienability*

(A) Generally

The corollary to the rule that a gift must vest, if at all, within the perpetuity period is the principle that property must not be rendered inalienable.[71] The basis of this principle is that land and, for that matter, all other property should be kept freely marketable and in circulation among the members of the community. A gift is inalienable if there is some provision which prevents the property being disposed of. This provision may be either a term of the gift itself,[72] or, in the case of a gift to a club or association, a rule of that club or association.[73]

To this general principle there are two exceptions: first, by analogy with the rule against remoteness, it seems that property may validly be made inalienable during the lifetime or lifetimes of persons in being at the time of the gift and for 21 years thereafter[74]; and, secondly, property may be made inalienable in the hands of a charity.[75]

A gift to a body corporate which is not a charity is not in general capable of falling foul of the rule against inalienability. Even though the company may, if it so wishes, retain the property indefinitely for the benefit of its shareholders, it will not be under any obligation to retain the property if the gift is absolute. It is only where some condition is imposed on the gift prohibiting the company from disposing of the property that the gift will offend against the rule and be void.[76]

---

[68] With the minor exception of s.8, which relates only to the administrative powers of trustees.

[69] Apart from s.10, they represent the recommendations of the Law Reform Committee, Cmnd.18 (1956).

[70] See *post*, p. 256.

[71] *Carne v. Long* (1860) 2 De G.F. & J. 75 at 80.

[72] *Re Patten* [1929] 2 Ch. 276.

[73] *Rickard v. Robson* (1862) 31 Beav. 244; *Re Nottage* [1895] 2 Ch. 649; *Re Drummond* [1914] 2 Ch. 90.

[74] *Carne v. Long* (1860) 2 De G.F. & J. 75; *Re Dean* (1889) 41 Ch.D. 552 at 557.

[75] *Chamberlayne v. Brockett* (1872) 8 Ch.App. 206 at 211.

[76] A further reason for it being void was that no person could enforce the trust. *Morice v. Bishop of Durham* (1805) 10 Ves. 521 at 539; *Bowman v. Secular Society Ltd* [1917] A.C. 406 at 441; *Re Wood* [1949] Ch. 498.

The rule is principally applicable to non-charitable purpose trusts and to gifts to unincorporated associations. These have already been considered in Chapter 4.[77] It should be noted that section 15(4) of the 1964 Act provides that a donor of property for these purposes cannot opt to use for the purposes of the rule against inalienability the statutory period of up to 80 years which section 1 makes available for the purposes of the rule against remoteness; and in this respect, therefore, the position remains the same as it was before that Act.[78]

As will be seen later on,[79] a gift to a charity is not void even if the property in question is made inalienable and a gift over from one charity to another charity is not void either even though the property may vest in the second charity at some wholly remote time in the future.[80] The normal provisions of the Rule against Perpetuities do however apply in the case of a gift from a non-charity to a charity and a gift from a charity to a non-charity.

3. *The Rule Against Accumulations*

Another consequence of the principle that property and wealth should generally be free to circulate has been the statutory control of accumulations. This resulted from the decision in *Thellusson v. Woodford*[81] where the court upheld a direction from Thellusson that the income from his property should be accumulated for the whole of the perpetuity period, which in his case turned out to be somewhat in excess of 70 years. This decision led Parliament to intervene by enacting in 1800 what is often known as the Thellusson Act to restrict accumulations to a much shorter period. The position is now governed by sections 164 to 166 of the Law of Property Act 1925, as amended by section 13 of the Perpetuities and Accumulations Act 1964.[82]

Section 164 of the Law of Property Act 1925 lays down the general rule that income may not be accumulated for longer than any one of the following periods:

(i) the life of the settlor (this is the period adopted in the case of gifts *inter vivos* where no other period is specified);

(ii) 21 years from the death of the testator or settlor (this is the period adopted in the case of gifts by will where no other period is specified);

(iii) the duration of the minority or minorities of any persons living at the death of the testator or settlor (this period begins from the death of the settlor or testator);

---

[77] See *ante*, pp. 105 *et seq.*
[78] The provision appears to be clearly to this effect, but see R. H. Maudsley, *The Modern Law of Perpetuities*, p. 177, in which the opposite view is argued.
[79] See *post*, p. 380.
[80] *Re Tyler* [1891] 3 Ch. 252 and see *post*, p. 380.
[81] (1798) 4 Ves.Jun. 227.
[82] As further amended by Family Law Reform Act 1969, Sched. 3, para. 7.

    (iv) the duration of the minority or minorities of any persons entitled under the settlement (in this case the beneficiary need not be alive at the death of the testator or settlor and the accumulation period will commence at the birth of that beneficiary).

The 1964 Act added two further possible periods in respect of instruments coming into operation after July 15, 1964:

    (v) the period of 21 years from the date of making the disposition; and

    (vi) the duration of the minority or minorities of any person in being at the date of making an *inter vivos* disposition.

Any direction to accumulate for a period longer than one of the foregoing makes the whole gift void if it is directed that the accumulation is to continue for longer than the perpetuity period but is invalid only as to the excess over the longest authorised period if it is not so directed.[83]

Section 165 of the Law of Property Act 1925 expressly upholds the validity of successive periods of accumulation where a direction is given for income to be accumulated for one of the authorised periods and at the end of that period, or indeed at some time thereafter, the income has to be accumulated under the general law or under some other statutory provision. As will be seen later on,[84] where property is held on trust for an infant, by virtue of section 31 of the Trustee Act 1925 any income which is not applied for the maintenance of the infant has to be accumulated until he reaches the age of majority. So if a testator gives property to a person for life, with remainder to his eldest son, the testator can direct that the income be accumulated for a period of 21 years from his death and, in the event that the eldest son is still an infant at the death of his father, the income can be accumulated pursuant to the will for the first 21 years and thereafter during any later period in which the eldest son is entitled to an interest in possession but is an infant pursuant to section 31 of the Trustee Act 1925.[85] The existence of this rule is particularly important for one type of discretionary trust, known as an Accumulation and Maintenance Trust, which will be considered later on.[86]

There are certain exceptions from the general restrictions on accumulations and in these cases any period of accumulation may be specified. These are:

    (i) accumulations for the payment of the debts of any person;

    (ii) accumulations for the purpose of raising portions[87] for the children or more remote issue of the settlor, or any person entitled under the settlement; and

---

[83] *Re Jefferies* [1936] 2 All E.R. 626.
[84] See *post*, p. 595.
[85] See also *Re Maber* [1928] Ch. 88.
[86] See *post*, p. 539.
[87] *Re Bourne* (1946) 115 L.J.Ch. 152.

(iii) accumulations of the produce of timber or wood.[88]

4. *Possible Future Reforms*

In 1993 the Law Commission issued a Consultation Paper on Perpetuities and Accumulations.[89] This Paper contains a detailed examination of the present law, which is criticised on a number of grounds, including complexity, uncertainty and inconsistency.

So far as concerns the Rule against Remoteness, the Law Commission suggested four options: first, to do nothing; secondly, to abolish the rule without replacement; thirdly, to replace the rule with a new rule, either a general rule limiting the duration of trusts or the conferral on the courts of a wide discretion to vary trusts; and, fourthly, to reform the rule in one or more of five possible ways: removing the need to apply the common law before applying the "wait and see" provisions, making a fixed period of years the only perpetuity period, introducing a *cy-près* power for the court to reform dispositions, making provisions for advancements in reproductive technology, and introducing new exceptions to the rule. Their provisional choice was between abolishing the rule without replacement and reforming the rule in one or more of the five ways mentioned.

There were no proposals concerning the Rule against Inalienability.

So far as concerns the Rule against Accumulations, the Law Commission suggested three options: first, to do nothing; secondly, to abolish the rule without replacement; and, thirdly, to reform the rule in one of the following possible ways: changing the accumulation period to a fixed period of, say, 80 years, reducing all existing periods of 21 years to 18 years, codifying all the relevant law in one statute, or introducing new exceptions to the rule. Their provisional choice was between abolishing the rule without replacement and reforming the rule in one of the ways mentioned.

This Consultation Paper produced a certain amount of initial comment, both from a technical[90] and from a comparative[91] point of view. In the last edition of this work,[92] it was stated that it was obviously premature to speculate on the likely contents of the future Law Commission Report which was expected to follow the consultation process. However, as this edition went to press, the Law Commission produced a Report advocating two totally different reforms: first, the introduction of a straight 125-year period for the purposes of the Rule against Perpetuities and the Rule against Inalienability on the basis that, in view of increasing life-expectancy, this period would often not be that much longer than the effect of a Royal Lives Clause; and, secondly, the complete abandonment of the present Rule against Accumulations and its replacement by a similar straight 125-year period, thus abandoning completely the policy behind the Thellusson Act and reverting to the pre-existing law. It remains to be seen if, and if so when,

---

[88] Law of Property Act, s.164(2).
[89] "The Law of Trusts. The Rules against Perpetuities and Excessive Accumulations". Consultation Paper No.133, (1993).
[90] See H. W. Wilkinson, [1994] Conv. 92; C. T. Emery, 57 M.L.R. (1994) 602.
[91] See D. Brownbill, [1994] 1 J.Int.P.1.
[92] (6th ed., 1994), p. 175.

these proposals are brought into effect; if they are, this section of this Chapter will be considerably shorter in future editions of this work!

III. Safeguarding Property from Creditors

Ever since uses, the forerunners of trusts, were first invented, attempts have repeatedly been made by those who contemplate the actual or potential threat of financial ruin to employ uses and trusts in order to put their property beyond the reach of their creditors. Prima facie a transfer of property by a settlor to trustees on trust for his wife or some other relative or friend has the effect of removing that property from his assets and consequently of preventing his trustee in bankruptcy from claiming it on behalf of his creditors. Where the beneficiary of the trust is the settlor's wife, the effect and usually the objective is that the settlor can continue to enjoy the benefit of the settled property indirectly by living with her in property belonging to the trust and having his living expenses provided by her out of the income to which she is entitled. And even where a settlor does not act so blatantly as to derive indirect benefit from the property himself, there is no doubt whatever that he will inevitably prefer his property to be enjoyed by his relatives and friends rather than by his creditors. It is not surprising that both these results are looked on with disapproval by the legislature which has long placed statutory restrictions on the use of trusts for these purposes. These statutory restrictions are what will be considered in this section; where they do not apply, trusts remain an effective means of preventing creditors from laying their hands on a person's property.[93]

Until relatively recently this area of the law was governed by two distinct statutory provisions: section 172 of the Law of Property Act 1925, which enabled dispositions of property made with intent to defraud creditors to be set aside, whether or not the person who made the disposition was bankrupt, and section 42 of the Bankruptcy Act 1914, which enabled various dispositions to be set aside when the person who had made them had become bankrupt. Both were, however, repealed by the Insolvency Act 1985. The present law is contained in the Insolvency Act 1986.

1. *Transactions Defrauding Creditors*

Section 423 of the Insolvency Act 1986 enables the court to intervene where it is satisfied that any person, whether a natural person or a body corporate,[94] has entered into a transaction at an undervalue for the purpose of putting assets beyond the reach of anyone who is making or may at some time make a claim against him or of otherwise prejudicing the interests of such a person in relation to the claim which he is making or may make.

As in the case of all previous provisions of this type, there is no requirement that the person entering into the transaction should be bankrupt or even that he should be in debt. As Jessel M.R. said in *Re Butterworth, ex parte*

---

[93] See *post*, p. 231.
[94] See also Insolvency Act 1986 s.207.

Russell,[95] where a settlement made by a prosperous baker immediately before purchasing a different type of business (that of a grocer) of which he had no experience was set aside under the predecessor of section 172 of the Law of Property Act 1925: "a man is not entitled to go into a hazardous business, and immediately before doing so, settle all his property voluntarily, the object being this: 'If I succeed in business, I make a fortune for myself. If I fail, I leave my creditors unpaid. They will bear the loss.' That is the very thing which the Statute of Elizabeth was meant to prevent." It is admittedly somewhat ironic that, at about the time when this observation was made, legislation was being introduced permitting for the first time the incorporation of companies with limited liability, which makes it entirely legitimate, subject to certain minimum requirements as to membership, for the shareholders to adopt exactly the policy so stringently condemned by Jessel M.R. But, despite the fact that the legislature has accepted that an appropriate way for an investor to limit his possible losses in hazardous ventures is to carry them out in the name of a limited company, it has continued to prohibit the use of trusts and settlements for the same purpose. Consequently, a transaction which has been entered into at an undervalue can still be impeached whenever the court is satisfied that it was entered into for one of the purposes mentioned above; it is only necessary that this purpose was a substantial and not necessarily its sole motive[96] nor is there any requirement for dishonesty.[97] Hence, section 423 was successfully invoked in *Moon v. Franklin*[98] when a husband used the substantial proceeds of sale of his practice to make substantial gifts to his wife at a time when he was threatened with legal proceedings which he knew might not be covered by sufficient insurance. Similarly, the Court of Appeal held in *Barclays Bank v. Eustice*[99] that there was a strong prima facie case for the applicability of the section when a debtor had transferred his assets to various members of his family at an undervalue, retaining insufficient assets to meet an expected action by the bank.

A person enters into a transaction at an undervalue in the following circumstances: first, if he makes a gift or enters into a transaction on terms which provide for him to receive no consideration; secondly, if he enters into a transaction in consideration of marriage; or, thirdly, if he enters into a transaction for a consideration whose value, in money or money's worth, is significantly less than the value, in money or money's worth, of the consideration provided by himself. The only reported case actually concerning the declaration of a trust is *Midland Bank v. Wyatt*,[1] where a husband and wife declared that their matrimonial home was held on trust for the wife and their children; however, since the trust was held to be a sham and consequently void, the property had at all times remained vested in the husband anyway. However, these requirements were clearly satisfied both

---

[95] (1882) 19 Ch.D. 588 at 598.
[96] *Chohan v. Saggar* [1992] B.C.C. 306. See also the authorities cited in the text.
[97] Hence the section can apply even where the transferor's legal advisers considered it proper; see *Arbuthnot Leasing International v. Havalet Leasing (No.2)* [1990] B.C.C. 636.
[98] (1990) *The Independent*, June 22, 1990.
[99] [1995] 1 W.L.R. 1238.
[1] [1995] 1 F.L.R. 696. See *ante*, p. 86.

in *Moon v. Franklin*,[2] where a husband purchased property in the joint names of himself and his wife without any financial contribution from her, transferred to her his interest in their matrimonial home, and gave her a sum of money, and in *Barclays Bank v. Eustice*,[3] where a father granted an agricultural tenancy and sold agricultural assets to his sons on unusual terms as to payment.[4] On the other hand, a transaction made for full value cannot be impeached under this section even where there was a clear intention to prejudice creditors.[5] The precise meaning of undervalue has had to be considered on a number of occasions. In *Agricultural Mortgage Corporation v. Woodhead*,[6] a mortgagor who was a farmer granted an agricultural tenancy to his wife at the full market rent, which if binding on the mortgagee would have more than halved the value of its security. The Court of Appeal held that the wife had acquired not just the tenancy but also a number of additional benefits, the safeguarding of the family home, the ability to acquire and carry on the family business and a substantial surrender value, all of which enabled her to hold the mortgagee to ransom and for none of which she had given any value at all. On the other hand, in *Re M.C. Bacon*[7] a company which created a floating charge over its assets in favour of a bank to secure its overdraft in consideration of the bank making further advances, continuing to honour cheques and, consequently, not calling in the overdraft was held not to have entered into a transaction at an undervalue. The assets of the company had not been reduced by the creation of the floating charge and so it had not provided any consideration in money or money's worth. Since no value in money or money's worth could be attributed to the consideration provided by the bank either, there was no imbalance between the consideration provided by the two parties.

Under section 424, an application to the court can be made by anyone prejudiced by the transaction; however, where the person entering into the transaction has become insolvent (bankrupt, in the case of a natural person, wound up or the subject of an administration order[8] in the case of a body corporate), any such application requires the leave of the court—in such circumstances, it is the official receiver, the trustee in bankruptcy, or the liquidator who has the primary right to apply. Where a voluntary arrangement has been approved,[9] the supervisor of the voluntary arrangement can also apply. Any application made is treated as having been made on behalf of everyone prejudiced by the transaction.

On application, the court can, under section 423(2), make such order as it thinks fit for restoring the position to what it would have been if the transaction had not been entered into and protecting the interests of the

---

[2] (1990) *The Independent*, June 22, 1990.
[3] [1995] 1 W.L.R. 1238.
[4] The rent was payable substantially in arrears and the payment of the purchase price was deferred.
[5] This was not the case under Law of Property Act 1925, s.172; see *Lloyds Bank v. Marcan* [1973] 1 W.L.R. 1387.
[6] (1995) 70 P. & C.R. 53.
[7] [1991] Ch. 127 (actually a decision on s.239 (preferences); see *post*, p. 229). See also *Re Kumar (a Bankrupt)* [1993] 1 W.L.R. 224.
[8] Under Pt II of the Insolvency Act 1986.
[9] Under Pt I of the Insolvency Act 1986 in the case of bodies corporate and under Pt VIII in the case of natural persons.

persons prejudiced by the transaction. More specifically, section 425(1) enables the court to require the vesting in whoever it may direct, for the benefit of everyone in respect of whom the application is treated to be made, of the following: any property transferred, any property representing the application of the proceeds of sale of the property transferred or of any money transferred, and any sum which the court decides should be payable in respect of any benefit received as a result of the transaction. Thus, in *Moon v. Franklin*[10] an order was made restraining any dealing with the land and requiring the return of the unspent part of the monetary gift and in *Agricultural Mortgage Corporation v. Woodward*[11] the tenancy granted was set aside. Such orders are obviously capable of prejudicing third parties; however, section 425(2) provides that no such order shall prejudice any interest in property acquired from a person other than the original transferor in good faith for value without notice nor require any person who was not a party to the original transaction to pay any sum in respect of any benefit received in good faith for value without notice.

2. *Transactions Capable of being Impeached on Bankruptcy*

The Insolvency Act 1986 has replaced section 42 of the Bankruptcy Act 1914 with a series of provisions which enable transactions at an undervalue and by way of preference entered into by natural persons and by bodies corporate to be set aside in the event that they occurred during stipulated periods of time prior to their bankruptcy.

(A) Transactions entered into by natural persons

(1) Transactions at an undervalue
Section 339 enables the trustee in bankruptcy to apply to the court for an order where a natural person has entered into a transaction at an undervalue (which has the same meaning as in section 423)[12] within the periods of time set out in section 341. The court may make such order as it thinks fit to restore the position to what it would have been if the transaction had not been entered into. The available orders, set out in section 342, are similar to those which may be made under section 425[13]; no order may either prejudice any interest in property which was acquired from a person other than the bankrupt in good faith for value without notice of the relevant circumstances or require a person who was not a party to the transaction to make any payment in respect of any benefit which he received as a result of the transaction in good faith for value without notice of the relevant circumstances.

A trustee in bankruptcy can therefore claim a spouse's share in the matrimonial home to the extent that the beneficial interest held exceeds the contributions made to its acquisition during the appropriate period. The fact that that beneficial interest has been acquired as the result of a property

---

[10] (1990) *The Independent*, June 22, 1990.
[11] (1995) 70 P. & C.R. 53.
[12] See *ante*, p. 225.
[13] See *ante*, p. 226.

adjustment order on divorce makes no difference since the order can be set aside[14]; particular problems may arise where the matrimonial proceedings were compromised since if the compromise reached cannot be assessed in terms of money or money's worth the section will apply.[15]

Section 341 provides that the basic period is two years prior to the date of the presentation of the bankruptcy petition but this period is increased to five years if the person later to become bankrupt was insolvent at the time of the transaction or became insolvent as a result of carrying it out. A person is insolvent for this purpose if at the time of the transaction he was unable to pay his debts as they fell due or if the value of his assets was less than the value of his liabilities, taking into account both contingent and prospective liabilities. There is a rebuttable presumption that a person was insolvent in this sense in the event that the other party to the transaction was an associate of his, defined by section 435 as including relatives of the bankrupt or of his spouse, his partners, his employers, his employees and any companies with which he was at the time related.

The length of this period, the rebuttable presumption of insolvency in the case of transactions between associates, and the very wide definition of associate pose very considerable potential problems, not only because of the difficulty of rebutting the presumption of insolvency but also because of the difficulty of proving five years after the event that the transaction was not at an undervalue. Consequently, the only safe way to proceed when entering into a transaction between persons who fall within the definition of associates is to obtain affidavit evidence at the time from suitably qualified persons that the transaction was not at an undervalue and/or from the accountants of the parties that neither of them was insolvent at the time of or in consequence of the transaction. This will obviously involve a certain amount of expense but will avoid any possibility of future problems if any of the parties becomes bankrupt in the next five years.

At one time, even greater problems arose in the case of gifts of unregistered land. Since any subsequent purchaser will see the deed of gift in the course of his investigation of title, he will necessarily have notice of the relevant circumstance that the land was acquired at an undervalue. Thus, the enactment of section 339 had the effect of rendering the title of any donee of unregistered land bad for two years because of the possibility of the transferor becoming bankrupt during that period; the donee was thus effectively prevented from disposing of the land for value for that period. Matters were even worse in the highly likely event that the donor and donee fell within the definition of associates; in such circumstances, the period increased to five years unless the donee could affirmatively prove, presumably by affidavit evidence from the donor's accountants, that the donor was not insolvent either at the time of or in consequence of the transaction. However, following the making of representations,[16] it was provided by the Insolvency (No. 2) Act 1994 that a transaction can be set aside against a purchaser of unregistered land only if he has notice both of the surrounding circumstances and of relevant bankruptcy proceedings. Consequently, a

---

[14] Insolvency Act 1986, 14th Sched.
[15] *Re Kumar (a Bankrupt)* [1993] 1 W.L.R. 224.
[16] See (1992) 89/5 L.S.Gaz., p. 13.

purchaser who knows, as he necessarily will, of a transaction at an under-value will be protected provided first that he makes the normal convey-ancing searches and enquiries and, secondly, that these do not reveal any bankruptcy proceedings being brought against the donor.

(2) Transactions by way of preference

Section 340 enables the trustee in bankruptcy to apply to the court for an order where a natural person has given a preference to any person within the periods of time set out in section 341. The court may make such order as it thinks fit to restore the position to what it would have been if the preference had not been given—the available orders are set out in section 342.[17] Such a preference will have been given if the effect of the transaction is to improve the position of a creditor, surety or guarantor in the event of bankruptcy. An order can only be made if the transaction was influenced by a desire to bring about this result, although such a desire will be presumed where the other person is an associate. However, it has been held that, where the transaction has been entered into as a matter of commercial necessity, it was not influenced by any desire to give a preference.[18]

Section 341 provides that the basic period is six months prior to the date of presentation of the bankruptcy petition but this period is increased to two years if the person to whom the preference was given was an associate. However, if the transaction was not only by way of preference but also at an undervalue, the longer periods which apply to transactions at an under-value will be applicable instead.

(B) Transactions entered into by bodies corporate

The provisions of the Insolvency Act 1986 which govern transactions entered into by bodies corporate are broadly similar to those which apply to natural persons; only the differences will be mentioned here.

Section 238 deals with transactions at an undervalue (defined in the same way but without any reference to marriage consideration); no order will be made if the court is satisfied that the company entered into the transaction in good faith for the purpose of carrying on its business and there were at the time reasonable grounds for believing that the company would be benefited thereby. The period of time is two years prior to the onset of insolvency but a transaction will only be set aside if the company was unable to pay its debts at the time of the transaction or became unable to do so as a result of it.

Section 239 deals with transactions by way of preference. In *Re M.C. Bacon*,[19] a company which could not have continued trading without its bank's support created a floating charge over its assets in favour of the bank to secure its overdraft shortly before becoming insolvent; it was held that, since the granting of the floating charge had been made for reasons of commercial necessity and not with any desire to improve the position of the

---

[17] See *ante*, p. 227.
[18] *Re M. C. Bacon* [1990] B.C.L.C. 324.
[19] [1990] B.C.L.C. 324.

bank in the event of insolvency, no preference had been given. The basic period is six months prior to the onset of insolvency but this period is increased to two years if the transaction by way of preference is in favour of a person connected with the company or at an undervalue. Once again, a transaction will only be set aside if the company was unable to pay its debts at the time of the transaction or became unable to do so as a result of it.

IV. Safeguarding Property from Claims by Dependants

The development of statutory obligations to maintain dependants has inevitably led to attempts being made to avoid these obligations by the use of trusts and, equally inevitably, to the introduction of statutory restrictions on the use of trusts to defeat claims for maintenance and for financial provision out of estates.

1. *Claims made in the Course of Matrimonial Proceedings*

Section 37 of the Matrimonial Causes Act 1973 enables a spouse to apply to the court for an order where the other spouse is about to make or has made some disposition of property with the intention of reducing the assets available for the provision of financial relief in matrimonial proceedings. Such an intention is presumed if the disposition was made within the three-year period prior to the date of the application for financial relief; otherwise, intention must be proved affirmatively. If the disposition has not yet been made, the court may make such order as it thinks fit; if the disposition has already been made, it may be set aside.

2. *Claims for Financial Provision out of Estates*

Under the Inheritance (Provision for Family and Dependants) Act 1975, the ability of a testator freely to dispose of his assets is made subject to an obligation to provide for his surviving spouse and other dependants, who can apply to the court for a share of the estate if reasonable financial provision for them has not been made. In order to prevent a testator from defeating such claims by disposing of all his property *inter vivos*, sections 10–13 of the Act provide that any person who, during the last six years of the deceased's life, has benefited from a disposition made other than for value "with the intention of defeating an application for financial provision under this Act" can be required to provide sums of money up to but not exceeding the value of the property received so that appropriate financial provision can be made. It should be noted that the necessary intention has to be determined on a balance of probabilities and does not have to constitute the only motive of the deceased for the making of the disposition.

CHAPTER 8

PROTECTIVE TRUSTS

It has already been seen that a trust which contravenes the policy of the insolvency laws can be set aside.[1] This chapter discusses some indirect means by which this result can be avoided. However, before considering them, two overriding fundamental points must be emphasised.

First, a proviso or condition contained in a trust of property in favour of a third party that that property is not to be subject to the claims of his creditors will be void.[2]

Secondly, a trust set up by a person in favour of himself until bankruptcy, with remainders over, may also be ineffective. This is the well known Rule in *Re Burroughs-Fowler*[3] and it prevents the type of trusts considered in this Chapter from being created by the potential bankrupt, as distinct from any one else. Where a trust is created in contravention of this rule and the person in question duly becomes bankrupt, the settled property will generally vest in his trustee in bankruptcy as if the settlement had never been created. However, this will not be the case if the interest which the potential bankrupt has conferred upon himself in fact determines prior to his bankruptcy. In *Re Detmold*,[4] a husband had settled his own property on trust for himself for life or until alienation, whether voluntary or involuntary by operation of law in favour of a particular creditor, and subject thereto on trust for his wife and children. His interest was the subject of an involuntary alienation as the result of a judicial charge created by a judgment. He subsequently became bankrupt and his trustee in bankruptcy sought to set the settlement aside. North J. held that the gift over in favour of the wife and children was in such circumstances valid and effective; consequently, his trustee in bankruptcy could take nothing. This decision shows that a provision for determination will be effective if the determining event which first occurs is one other than the bankruptcy of the settlor.

Nevertheless, it is true to say that a settlor who wishes to achieve the objective of protecting the settled property against a spendthrift or reckless beneficiary by guarding against alienation or bankruptcy will need to use more sophisticated machinery than that already described. Essentially he will instead have to create a determinable interest in favour of a third party coupled, if necessary, with protective and discretionary trusts.

---

[1] See *ante*, p. 224.
[2] *Younghusband v. Gisborne* (1844) 1 Coll.C.C. 400, affirmed (1846) 15 L.J. Ch. 355; *Re Sanderson's Trust* (1857) 3 Kay & J. 497.
[3] [1916] 2 Ch. 251.
[4] (1889) 40 Ch.D. 585; see also *Re Johnson* [1904] 1 K.B. 134.

I. DETERMINABLE INTERESTS

It has long been established that a settlor can validly grant an interest to any beneficiary (other, of course, than himself) which is determinable in the event of his bankruptcy.[5] At first sight it appears somewhat surprising that such a grant is effective to whisk the property away from the beneficiary's creditors in the event of his bankruptcy when the same settlor cannot settle property on the same beneficiary subject to a condition or proviso that it will not be available to the latter's creditors in the event of his bankruptcy. The different result follows from the basic distinction between the nature of determinable interests and conditional interests, a distinction which, no matter how outmoded, is nevertheless fundamentally logical. A provision for a determining event does not deprive the beneficiary, or his creditors, of anything; it merely sets the limits of the interest which is being granted; on the other hand, a condition of this nature, like all other conditions, technically operates so as to cut down an interest which has already been granted. However, the existence of this admittedly fine distinction means that a draftsman must take special care not to create a conditional interest by accident and thereby defeat the intentions of the settlor.

II. PROTECTIVE TRUSTS[6]

Protective trusts provide a highly effective means of restraining spendthrift beneficiaries. They combine a determinable life interest with a series of discretionary trusts. The beneficiary's life interest is normally made determinable in the event of alienation or bankruptcy and in this event will be replaced by a discretionary trust in favour of the former life tenant and/or members of his family.

1. Section 33 of the Trustee Act 1925

At one time the normal practice was to set out the provisions of trusts of this kind *in extenso*. However, with the objective of shortening the length of settlements, section 33 of the Trustee Act 1925 provides that the mere reference in a settlement to the fact that property is held "on protective trusts" will be sufficient to bring into play the protective trusts specifically set out in that section.

Section 33 provides that, where income, including an annuity or other periodical payment, is directed to be held on protective trusts for the benefit of any person for his life or for any less period[7] (such person being described in the section as "the principal beneficiary"), then during that period the income will be held on the following trusts (this is of course necessarily

---

[5] *Billson v. Crofts* (1873) L.R. 15 Eq. 314; *Re Aylwin's Trusts* (1873) L.R. 16 Eq. 585.

[6] See Sheridan (1957) 21 Conv. (N.S.) 110.

[7] For an illustration of protective trusts designed to last until remarriage and the effect of a nullity decree on the second marriage, see *D'Altroy's Will Trusts* [1968] 1 W.L.R. 120. See also Matrimonial Causes Act 1973, ss.11, 12, 16.

without prejudice to any prior interests arising under the settlement in question):

1. upon trust for the principal beneficiary during the trust period or until he does or attempts to do any act or thing, or any event happens (other than an advancement made under any statutory or express power) whereby, if the income were payable during the trust period to the principal beneficiary absolutely during that period, he would be deprived of the right to receive the same or any part thereof;

2. in the event that the trust fails or determines during the trust period, then for the residue of that period the income is to be held upon trust to be applied as the trustees in their absolute discretion (without being liable to account for the exercise of such discretion) think fit for the maintenance or support or otherwise for the benefit of all or any of the following persons, either for the principal beneficiary and his or her wife or husband, if any, and his or her children or more remote issue[8] if any or, if there are no such persons other than the principal beneficiary, for him or her and the persons who would, if he or she were dead, be entitled to the trust property or to its income.[9]

Section 33 does not apply to trusts coming into operation before January 1, 1926 (hardly likely to be a problem any longer) and, more importantly, is subject to any variation of its provisions which may be made in the trust instrument in question.[10] The section also provides that nothing therein operates to validate any trust which, if contained in the trust instrument, would be liable to be set aside.[11]

2. "On Protective Trusts"

The purpose of the section is merely to avoid any need for the trusts in question to be set out expressly in the trust instrument. Quite apart from the provision just referred to whereby the statutory provisions can be modified[12] to suit the circumstances of any individual settlement, protective trusts can also be (and often still are) expressly created by being set out *in extenso*. Furthermore, irrelevant of whether the statutory form is used or its essence is set out in terms, its effect is confined to engrafting the trusts in question on the life interest granted. For this reason it was held by Vaisey J. in *Re Allsopp's Marriage Settlement*[13] that, if the life interest is ever totally extinguished, as it was in that case by an order made by the court in divorce proceedings, the engrafted protective trusts are also extinguished on the basis that they are incapable of any separate existence.

---

[8] Including illegitimate children and issue; Family Law Reform Act 1969, s.15(3).

[9] s.33(1).

[10] s.33(2).

[11] s.33(3). Accordingly, a settlement made on the settlor himself until bankruptcy and then on discretionary trusts may be ineffective; *Re Burroughs-Fowler* [1916] 2 Ch. 251. See *ante*, p. 231.

[12] See *ante*, n. 10.

[13] [1959] Ch. 81.

3. *Determining Events*

The question of what events will be sufficient to produce a forfeiture of a protected life interest (as the interest of the principal beneficiary is described) and bring the discretionary trusts into operation has been considered in a large number of cases. This point is of importance not only where the trusts contained in section 33 have been employed but also where there is an express protective trust. Indeed many of the cases which are about to be considered involved express protective trusts; the general view is, however, that the principles laid down therein are equally applicable to the statutory trusts.

It is self-evident that the bankruptcy of or any alienation by the principal beneficiary will bring about the forfeiture of the protected life interest. But it is less obvious (although it was nevertheless so held by Luxmoore L.J. in *Re Walker*[14] to be the case) that the protected life interest will also be forfeited if the bankruptcy of the principal beneficiary has already occurred by the time the protective trust first comes into operation. However, as the following illustrations show, determining events have taken the most diverse forms.

In *Re Balfour's Settlement,*[15] various sums had in breach of trust been advanced by the trustees to the principal beneficiary. The trustees then asserted their right to retain the income of the fund in order to make good their own breach of trust. The principal beneficiary subsequently went bankrupt. Farwell J. held that, since the trustees had asserted their right to the income before the date of bankruptcy, the life interest had determined and the discretionary trust in question had come into operation; nothing therefore passed to the trustee in bankruptcy. Similarly, in *Re Baring's Settlement Trusts,*[16] the principal beneficiary had failed to comply with a court order to bring her children within the jurisdiction and a writ of sequestration was therefore issued empowering the sequestrators to take possession of all her real and personal estate until she did so. The sequestrators gave the trustees notice not to pay any further money to the principal beneficiary and required that all future income should be paid to them. Morton J. held that, since the trusts were designed to confer continuous enjoyment of the income on the principal beneficiary, the sequestration was effective to determine her life interest and bring the discretionary trusts into operation; the payment of income was therefore at the discretion of the trustees and could not be demanded by the sequestrators. And again, in *Re Dennis' Settlement Trusts,*[17] Farwell J. held that the execution of a deed of variation of the protective trusts set out in the principal deed of settlement which had the effect of providing for the payment of part of the income to another person, equally brought the forfeiture clause into operation.

On the other hand, a wide variety of other events have been held not to have the effect of determining a protected life interest. In *Re Tancred's*

---

[14] [1939] Ch. 974.
[15] [1938] Ch. 928.
[16] [1940] Ch. 737.
[17] [1942] Ch. 283.

Settlement,[18] the principal beneficiary appointed the trustees of the settlement as his attorneys to receive the income of the settled funds; not surprisingly Buckley J. held that this did not cause his life interest to be forfeited. The same conclusion was reached in *Re Oppenheim's Will Trusts*[19] where a receiver had been appointed to a principal beneficiary who had been certified as a person of unsound mind. Similarly, it was held by the Court of Appeal in *Re Westby's Settlement*[20] that a statutory charge on the settled property to secure the expenses incurred by a receiver appointed in such circumstances was not the kind of charge at which forfeiture clauses were intended to be directed. All these decisions show that, in the words of Farwell J., "we must bear in mind that the courts do not construe gifts on forfeitures so as to extend their limits beyond the fair meaning of the words unless they are actually driven to it. Forfeitures are not regarded with favour."[21]

Consideration has also had to be given as to the effect of a court order on a forfeiture clause. In *Re Mair*[22] Farwell J. held that an order of the court under section 57 of the Trustee Act 1925[23] giving the trustees power to raise capital moneys for the benefit of life tenants would not cause a forfeiture of the protected life interests of those tenants; this was because he held section 57 to be an overriding provision which is deemed to be read into every single settlement. This decision must, however, be compared with that of Eve J. in *Re Salting*,[24] where the scheme sanctioned by the court under section 57 involved an agreement by the life tenant to pay the premiums on insurance policies on the basis of a promise that the trustees would pay them out of income if he failed to do so; the conclusion reached was that any failure by the life tenant to pay the premiums would produce a forfeiture. In cases of this type it is clear that what has produced the forfeiture is an act or omission of the life tenant, rather than the exercise by the court of its overriding power.

While the principles established by these two decisions discussed are perfectly clear enough, the position is otherwise by no means straightforward. Particular difficulty arises from cases involving orders in matrimonial proceedings varying protective trusts. In *General Accident, Fire and Life Assurance Corporation v. I.R.C.*,[25] the Court of Appeal had no doubt that an order in matrimonial proceedings for the principal beneficiary to pay an annual sum of money to his wife during her lifetime had not brought about a forfeiture of the protected life interest which he had under section 33;

---

[18] [1903] 1 Ch. 715.
[19] [1950] Ch. 633.
[20] [1950] Ch. 296.
[21] *Re Greenwood* [1901] 1 Ch. 887, 891 (assignment of income accrued due in the hands of trustees: no forfeiture). See also *Re Longman* [1955] 1 W.L.R. 197 (authority given by beneficiary for payment of debts out of a future dividend; where no dividend was ever declared, there was no forfeiture). For other cases involving the application of the Trading with the Enemy Act 1939, see *Re Gourju's Will Trusts* [1943] Ch. 24; *Re Hall* [1944] Ch. 46; *Re Wittke* [1944] 1 All E.R. 383; *Re Furness* [1944] 1 All E.R. 575; *Re Harris* [1945] Ch. 316; *Re Pozot's Settlement Trusts* [1952] Ch. 427.
[22] [1935] Ch. 562.
[23] See *post*, p. 657.
[24] [1932] 2 Ch. 57.
[25] [1963] 1 W.L.R. 1207.

accordingly, the discretionary trusts set out in that section did not come into operation. This conclusion was reached because the court order in question overrode the trusts of the settlement. Not only was this an event to which both the life tenant and the trustee had to bow; it was moreover not an event of the type contemplated by the section, whose provisions were instead intended to protect spendthrift, improvident or weak life tenants.[26] However, if the principle thus enunciated by the Court of Appeal is of general application, it is by no means easy to reconcile their decision with the earlier decision of Danckwerts J. in *Re Richardson's Will Trusts*.[27] In that case an order had been made in matrimonial proceedings for the payment of an annual sum to the wife of the protected life tenant to be charged on the principal beneficiary's life interest and it was also ordered that a deed be settled to give effect to the charge. Danckwerts J. held that, because the order for the execution of a deed had not been complied with, the effect of that order was to create an equitable charge over the interest of the principal beneficiary; this in turn involved the forfeiture of his protected life interest and so the discretionary trusts set out in section 33 came into operation. This was undoubtedly in some ways a highly convenient result; the life tenant had subsequently been adjudicated bankrupt and the decision that a prior forfeiture had occurred meant that the income of the settlement did not fall into the hands of his trustee in bankruptcy. However, it does seem rather strange that a failure by the principal beneficiary to comply with an order of the court to settle a deed of variation will result in a forfeiture of his protected life interest while compliance with such an order will not do so.

While the policy behind the decision of the Court of Appeal in *General Accident, Fire and Life Assurance Corporation v. I.R.C.*[28] is considered to have been desirable, it is somewhat doubtful whether the principle which the court applied was actually the correct one. The effect of an order of the Family Division—whether or not that order has to be implemented by a deed—is to deprive the life tenant of some or all of his income, an event which must surely constitute a forfeiture under section 33 and would probably also do so under the terms of most express protective trusts. On the other hand, quite different considerations may well be regarded as applying to an order of the court under section 57 of the Trustee Act 1925 simply because, as has already been seen, that provision is to be read into every settlement.

4. *Advances*

Section 33 expressly provides that advances under any express or statutory[29] power of advancement do not produce a forfeiture and bring the discretionary trusts set out therein into play.[30] This leaves open the question of whether the absence of words of exemption of this type in an express

---

[26] *ibid., per* Donovan L.J. at 1218.
[27] [1958] Ch. 504.
[28] [1963] 1 W.L.R. 1207.
[29] Under Trustee Act 1925, s.32; see *post*, p. 618.
[30] s.33(1).

protective trust will necessarily mean that the protected life interest granted thereby will determine if any advancement is in fact made.

The relevant authorities are not unanimous; however, they are only in slight disarray and the general consensus of judicial opinion is that no advancement made either under an express power or a statutory power will bring about a forfeiture. In *Re Hodgson*[31] Neville J. specifically held that an advancement made under an express power did not bring about a forfeiture. His lordship found to be attractive and decisive an argument that the provision for forfeiture "should be read as though there had been inserted at the end of the clause 'But this provision is not to affect any steps taken by the husband to enable the advances by the trustees hereinafter provided for to take effect'." In *Re Shaw's Settlement*[32] Harman J. came to exactly the same conclusion on similar facts. Further in *Re Rees*,[33] Upjohn J. held that this conclusion also applied to the statutory power of advancement which is contained in section 32 of the Trustee Act 1925. It was only in *Re Stimpson's Trusts*,[34] where once again there was no express advancement clause so that reliance had to be put on the statutory power, that it was held that the principal beneficiary had forfeited his interest by consenting to an advancement under section 32. There is, however, a factual distinction between the last two cases. In *Re Stimpson's Trusts* the will in question had been made in 1906, although it did not come into effect until 1929, and so its draftsman obviously could not have had in mind the provisions of section 32 of the Trustee Act 1925 not enacted until nearly 20 years later; in *Re Rees*, on the other hand, the will in question had been made in 1935 and so its draftsman had necessarily to be taken to have been aware of that provision.

It is therefore a possibility, although admittedly a somewhat remote one, that in the almost inconceivable event that a case like *Re Stimpson's Trusts* came before the courts today, the court would view in the same way a situation where a will made before 1926 had contained no express advancement clause but the life tenant had after 1925 consented to an advancement being made under the statutory power. Consequently, although the validity of that decision has been doubted,[35] it does appear to have applied the correct principle. The statutory power of advancement can undoubtedly be ousted by a contrary intention[36] and the fact that the will in question had been made before 1926 might well be held to constitute a sufficient contrary intention for this purpose.

---

[31] [1913] 1 Ch. 34 at 40.
[32] [1951] Ch. 833.
[33] [1954] Ch. 202.
[34] [1931] 2 Ch. 77.
[35] See *Re Rees* [1954] Ch. 202, *per* Upjohn J. at 209.
[36] Trustee Act 1925, s.69.

CHAPTER 9

IMPLIED OR RESULTING TRUSTS

I. INTRODUCTION

IMPLIED or resulting trusts arise where a settlor or testator carries out some intentional act other than the creation of a relationship of trustee and beneficiary from which the court infers a relationship of trustee and beneficiary. They consequently arise from the unexpressed but presumed intention of the settlor or testator. The two alternative names stem from the fact that not only are they implied by the court but also often cause the beneficial interest thereunder to "result" to the settlor, to his estate, or to the residuary beneficiaries or intestate successors of the testator. Implied or resulting trusts arise in two main sets of circumstances. First, where one person transfers property to another or into the joint names of himself and another or pays, wholly or in part, for the purchase of property which is vested either in the name of another or in the joint names of himself and that other, there is a presumption that no gift was intended; consequently, the property is held on trust for the payer or, in the case of a joint purchase, for the two of them in proportion to their contributions (this is, however, only a presumption and can be rebutted by the counter-presumption of advancement when the parties are in one of a number of established relationships or by affirmative evidence of the payer's intention to make an outright beneficial transfer). Secondly, where a settlor or testator who creates an express trust fails to exhaust the whole of the beneficial interest in the property in question, the court will imply that so much of the beneficial interest as is undisposed of will be held on trust for the settlor himself, his estate, or the residuary beneficiaries or intestate successors of the testator.[1]

It has been contended the two main sets of circumstances set out in the preceding paragraph should respectively be classified as "presumed" and "automatic" resulting trusts. According to this distinction, suggested by Megarry J. in *Re Vandervell's Trusts (No. 2)*,[2] a presumed resulting trust arises when a purchase is made in the name of another person but not on any express trust; in these circumstances, there is a presumption that that other holds the property in question on resulting trust for the real purchaser but this implied or presumed intention can be rebutted either by other legal presumptions or by evidence to the contrary.[3] An automatic resulting trust, on the other hand, arises where a transfer has been made on trusts which

---

[1] *Westdeustche Landesbank Girozentrale v. Islington L.B.C.* [1996] A.C. 669 at 708.

[2] [1974] Ch. 269 at 294, 295. Megarry J.'s actual decision was reversed by the Court of Appeal at [1974] Ch. 269 but the Court of Appeal made no comment on the judge's formulation.

[3] See *post*, p. 242.

have left the whole or some part of the beneficial interest undisposed of (because, for example, those are in some way ineffective or incomplete); in this situation the transferee of the property in question automatically holds it on resulting trust for the transferor to the extent that the beneficial interest has not been disposed of. In such a case, according to Megarry J., the resulting trust "does not depend on any intentions or presumptions, but is the automatic consequence of [the transferor's] failure to dispose of what is vested in him".[4]

The distinction between "presumed" and "automatic" resulting trusts appears at first sight to accord with common sense; however, it is fair to say that, in the same way as a presumed resulting trust is said to be created by implication as the result of a purchase in the name of another, so also an intention could be implied on the part of a settlor or testator that the settled property should result to him in so far as he has failed to dispose of it. The implication of an intention does not appear to be markedly more artificial in the one case than in the other. Precisely this argument was adopted in *Westdeutsche Landesbank Girozentrale v. Islington L.B.C.*[5] by Lord Browne-Wilkinson, who reasserted the traditional view that both types of resulting trusts are examples of trusts giving effect to the common intention of the parties; he said that he was not convinced that Megarry J. had been right to suggest that the second type of resulting trust does not depend on intention but operates automatically.[6] This certainly seems to be preferable to the view of Megarry J.[7] However, a further definition of resulting trusts has now been propounded,[8] namely that such trusts require a transfer of property in circumstances in which the provider of that property did not intend to benefit the recipient. This definition seems highly convincing, at least in so far as the traditional categories of constructive trusts are concerned.[9] However, there can obviously be no doubt whatever that the definition at present recognised by English law is that propounded by Lord Browne-Wilkinson.

II. PURCHASE IN THE NAME OF ANOTHER

1. *The Presumption of Resulting Trust*

One of the most important and the most common situations in which the presumption of resulting trust arises is where real[10] or personal[11] property is

---

[4] [1974] Ch. 269 at 294.

[5] [1996] A.C. 669 at 708

[6] Lord Browne-Wilkinson went on to say that if a settlor or testator has expressly, or by necessary implication, abandoned any beneficial interest in the trust property, there will be no resulting trust; the interest in question will instead vest in the Crown as *bona vacantia*.

[7] Birks, [1996] R.L.R. 3 at 11 regards Lord Browne-Wilkinson's view as "correct", despite the fact that it led to the rejection of his own argument that a resulting trust should arise whenever money is paid under a mistake or under a condition which is not subsequently satisfied.

[8] By R. Chambers: *Resulting Trusts* (1997).

[9] Chambers, *op. cit.*, also classifies as resulting trusts a large number of other situations which most commentators regard as having nothing whatever to do with resulting trusts.

[10] *Dyer v. Dyer* (1788) 2 Cox Eq. 92.

[11] *Re Scottish Equitable Life Assurance Society* [1902] Ch. 282, in respect of personal property.

purchased in the name of another or in the name of the purchaser and another. In such circumstances, a resulting trust will be presumed to arise in favour of the person who is proved to have paid the purchase money; in other words, the beneficial interest in the property "results" to the true purchaser. This general principle was established as long ago as 1788 by Eyre C.B. in *Dyer v. Dyer*.[12] At one time it was particularly significant in establishing the ownership of matrimonial property, particularly the matrimonial home, on the breakdown of marriage; however, now that the courts have an unfettered discretion to reallocate property interests on divorce, this is no longer the case. However, it remains relevant in establishing the ownership of matrimonial property during marriage and is particularly important in relation to joint enterprises by members of a family unit, especially residential property occupied by unmarried partners.

The latter situation emphasises that there are many variations on this basic theme. If the purchase money is paid partly by the person in whose favour the property is vested and partly by someone else (or, for that matter, by two persons in neither of whom the property is vested), they will clearly both have a beneficial interest in the property. In such circumstances, the question will obviously arise as to the nature of their beneficial ownership, namely whether they are beneficial joint tenants, in which case, in the absence of any subsequent severance, the survivor will take the property absolutely, or beneficial tenants in common, in which case the share of each will devolve in accordance with his will or intestacy; in the latter case, the size of their respective shares will also have to be established.

The answer to these questions will essentially depend on whether the purchase money has been contributed in equal or unequal shares. If the purchase has been made in unequal shares, then irrelevant of the identity of the person in whom the property is vested, the beneficial interests will be held in common and will devolve in accordance with the will or intestacy of each beneficial owner in accordance with his respective contributions.[13] This is simply because, in many cases, equity leans against a joint tenancy because of the potential unfairness of its attendant consequence that the survivor is entitled to the whole of the property. Inequality in contributions to the purchase price is the clearest possible example of a situation which equity considers to be incompatible with the right of survivorship; consequently, even if the person in whom the legal title is vested happens to be the survivor, he will continue to hold the property on trust for himself and for those entitled to the estate of his co-proprietor in the same proportions as before.

However, no such considerations will come into play if the purchase money is contributed equally; prima facie the purchasers will be deemed to have purchased with a view to taking as joint tenants with the consequential applicability of the principle of survivorship.[14] However, equity regards the existence of a business relationship between the contributors as inconsistent with the existence of a right of survivorship, even if the contributions have

---

[12] (1788) 2 Cox Eq. 92 at 93.
[13] *Wray v. Steele* (1814) 2 V. & B. 388.
[14] *Lake v. Gibson* (1732) 1 Eq.Cas.Abr. 290; *Lake v. Craddock* (1732) 3 P.Wms. 158 (seemingly reports of the same case under different names).

been equal.[15] It is not enough that both parties happen to be in business with one another; the property must be acquired in the course of that business.[16] However, the matter is treated broadly. In *Malayan Credit v. Jack-Chia MPH*,[17] the parties had separate businesses and were not in any sense partners; they leased business premises as joint tenants on the basis that each would occupy a particular part of the premises and contribute towards the rent and outgoings in proportion to the area each occupied. The Privy Council held that the equitable presumptions should not be treated rigidly as closed categories; holding premises for separate business purposes was sufficient to give rise to a tenancy in common in equity.

The position with joint mortgages is, however, much more straightforward. If two persons advance money on the security of a mortgage and take the mortgage in the name of only one of them or in the names of both of them jointly, then, quite irrelevant of the proportions in which the money was advanced, there is no right of survivorship and the interest of each mortgagee will devolve according to his will or intestacy. This is because a mortgage advance cannot possibly be regarded as anything other than a commercial undertaking; therefore there cannot conceivably have been any intention that an interest therein should be subject to any right of survivorship.[18] This is the case even if the mortgage in question incorporates, as it will in the absence of contrary intention, a statutory term[19] that the money is lent on a joint account,[20] the courts taking the view that the purpose of this clause is to permit repayment to a surviving mortgagee rather than to affect the rights of the mortgagees *inter se*.

However, it must be emphasised that the general principle laid down in *Dyer v. Dyer* will not be applied arbitrarily. It is essential that a purchase actually be made. So if a payment is made at the request of and by way of loan to the person in whose name the property is vested, there will be no resulting trust simply because in such circumstances the lender will not have advanced the purchase money as purchaser but merely as lender.[21] Further, there will be never be a resulting trust if it would be contrary to the law or to public policy to allow the presumption to arise. So, in an early case, it was decided that, if a person purchased an estate in the name of another so as to give the latter a vote at a parliamentary election, he will take beneficially even if there was no intention whatever to give the estate to him.[22]

---

[15] *Lake v. Gibson* (1729) 1 Eq.Cas.Abr.290; *Lake v. Craddock* (1732) 3 P.Wms. 158; *Malayan Credit v. Jack Chia-MPH* [1986] A.C. 549.
[16] *Tan Chew Hoe Noe v. Chee Swee Cheng* (1928) L.R. 56 Ind.App. 112.
[17] [1986] A.C. 549.
[18] *Morley v. Bird* (1798) 3 Ves. 628.
[19] Implied by Law of Property Act 1925, s.111.
[20] (1887) 34 Ch.D. 732.
[21] *Aveling v. Knipe* (1815) 19 Ves. 441. The opinion of Phillimore L.J. in *Hussey v. Palmer* [1972] 1 W.L.R. 1286 at 1291, which appears to be to the opposite effect, appears erroneous. Of course, completely different considerations apply where money is lent for a particular purpose which fails; in such circumstances, the borrower holds the money on trust for the lender: see *Barclays Bank v. Quistclose Investments* [1970] A.C. 567; *ante*, p. 24; *post*, p. 256.
[22] *Groves v. Groves* (1829) 3 Y. & J. 163 at 175; see also *Gascoigne v. Gascoigne* [1918] 1 K.B. 223; *Re Emery's Investment Trusts* [1959] Ch. 410; *Chettiar v. Chettiar (No. 2)* [1962] A.C. 294.

It must also be noted that, given that on any view this kind of resulting trust is based upon some form of presumed intention, no trust will arise where no such intention can be implied. Thus in *Savage v. Dunningham*[23] it was held that, where there had been an informal flat-sharing arrangement under which the occupiers made contributions to the rent, the purchase of the flat by one of the flat-sharers did not give rise to a resulting trust in favour of the others. Plowman J. held that an income payment such as rent did not indicate any intention whatever in respect of the subsequent acquisition of the capital asset. However, the opposite result was reached in *Dewar v. Dewar*,[24] where the facts were admittedly very different. The plaintiff and the defendant, who were brothers, bought a house with their mother. The plaintiff and the mother each provided £500 and the defendant raised the remaining £3,250 on mortgage. The house was conveyed into the name of the defendant, as it presumably had to be in order to secure the mortgage advance. Goff J. held that the plaintiff's £500 had not been a loan; the presumption of a resulting trust applied and he was therefore entitled to a proportional share in the house. However, the mother's £500 was held on the facts to have been a gift and so there was no resulting trust in her favour.

2. *The Rebuttable Nature of the Presumption*

The presumption which arises on a purchase in the name of another is rebuttable by parol or, for that matter, any other evidence that the purchaser intended to confer a benefit on that other. Further, in certain circumstances, the presumption is actually reversed and it is instead presumed that there is no resulting trust. This is the case where the person in whom the property is vested is the lawful wife or child of the purchaser or is a person to whom he stood *in loco parentis* at the time of the purchase. In these cases, the donor is presumed to have intended to make an "advancement" to the donee and the presumption of resulting trusts is therefore said to have been rebutted by the presumption of advancement. It should also be remembered in this connection that section 53(1)(b) of the Law of Property Act 1925 (which provides that a declaration of trust as to land must be manifested and proved by writing) does not apply to implied, resulting or constructive trusts; consequently, oral evidence is admissible to show what the true nature of the transaction actually was.[25]

(A)   Intention to confer a benefit

This is entirely a matter of evidence. If it can be shown that there was an intention to confer a benefit on the donee, no resulting trust can arise. In *Standing v. Bowring*[26] the plaintiff transferred £6,000 Consols into the joint names of herself and her godson. She did this with the express intention that the godson, in the event that he survived her, should take the Consols but that she herself should retain the right to the dividends during her lifetime;

---

[23] [1974] Ch. 181.
[24] [1975] 1 W.L.R. 1532.
[25] Law of Property Act 1925, s.53(2).
[26] (1885) 31 Ch.D. 282.

she had also been told that her act was irrevocable. The Court of Appeal held that the presumption of a resulting trust had been rebutted; there was ample evidence that at the time of the transfer and for some time previously the plaintiff had intended to confer a benefit on her godson by making the transfer. Similarly, in *Dewar v. Dewar*[27] the presumption of a resulting trust in favour of a mother who had made a contribution to the purchase of property in her son's name was rebutted by evidence that she had intended to make a gift.

(1) Joint banking accounts

An intention to confer a benefit has been presumed in cases where a balance of a bank account has been put into joint names.[28] While this is generally accepted to be the law, there is a potential difficulty where the donor subsequently maintains the right to use the substance of the gift during his lifetime; in such circumstances, the gift of the balance of the account to the other appears to be in the nature of a testamentary provision and, having not been made in accordance with the Wills Act 1837,[29] could be argued to be ineffective. This argument indeed appealed to Romer J. in *Young v. Sealey*[30] but he declined to apply it because of the disturbing effect it would have on existing titles. The point remains open for adjudication by the Court of Appeal.

(2) Joint banking accounts of husband and wife

A variant of the previous situation is where spouses have maintained a joint bank account in which their mutual resources have been pooled. In such circumstances it will be at the very least difficult, and in many cases quite impossible, to divide up the balance by ascertaining how much was paid in by each spouse. It has therefore been held that, in the event of dissolution of the marriage, each will be entitled to one half. The same principle will apply to investments which have been made by the husband in his own name out of money held in such a joint banking account.[31] However, it should be noted that, where such investments are instead made in the name of the wife, the situation may well be governed by the presumption of advancement, in which case she will prima facie take the investments beneficially.[32]

(B) The presumption of advancement

The second situation where the presumption of a resulting trust does not operate is where it is reversed by the presumption of advancement. This is,

---

[27] [1975] 1 W.L.R. 1532.

[28] See *Marshal v. Crutwell* (1875) L.R. 20 Eq. 328 at 330, *per* Jessel M.R. In that case the presumption (of advancement) was rebutted on the ground that the joint account had been merely for convenience. However, in *Re Figgis* [1969] 1 Ch. 123 it was held that the presumption was not rebutted by the available evidence: the "convenience" principle did not apply.

[29] s.9 (as substituted by Administration of Justice Act 1982, s.17).

[30] [1949] Ch. 278.

[31] *Jones v. Maynard* [1951] Ch. 572; *Rimmer v. Rimmer* [1953] 1 Q.B. 63. Compare *Re Cohen* [1953] Ch. 88, where a bundle of notes found hidden in the matrimonial home after the death of both spouses, who died within a few months of each other, was held to be the property of the wife to whom the residue belonged.

[32] See *post, infra.*

however, only the case where the real purchaser is the husband or father of or a person standing *in loco parentis* to the nominal purchaser. In these cases the presumption is that the purchaser intended to advance the property to the nominal purchaser, in other words to give it to him; consequently, there is no resulting trust. Once the presumption has arisen (it is of course capable of being rebutted by contrary evidence), it cannot be upset by any subsequent event unless evidence of that event is admissible under the rules which will be discussed in the next section. This can be illustrated by the old case of *Crabb v. Crabb*,[33] where a father transferred stock from his own name into the name of his son and a broker. He also told the broker to carry the dividends to the son's account. Later, by a subsequent codicil to his will, the father bequeathed the stock to another person. It was held that the son had taken an absolute beneficial interest in the stock at the time of the transfer and so the father had nothing left to bequeath.

(1) Husband and wife

The presumption of advancement by a husband in favour of his wife now has an extremely limited application, particularly when the marriage has broken down. This is a result of the following restatement of the law elaborated by Lord Diplock in *Pettitt v. Pettitt*.[34]

"The consensus of judicial opinion which gave rise to the presumptions of 'advancement' and 'resulting trust' in transactions between husband and wife is to be found in cases relating to the propertied classes of the nineteenth century and the first quarter of the twentieth century among whom marriage settlements were common, and it was unusual for the wife to contribute her earnings to the family income. It was not until after World War II that the courts were required to consider the proprietary rights in family assets of a different social class. The advent of legal aid, the wider employment of married women in industry, commerce and the professions, and the emergence of a property-owning, particularly a real-property-mortgaged-to-a-building-society-owning democracy has compelled the courts to direct their attention to this during the last 20 years. It would, in my view, be an abuse of the legal technique for ascertaining or imputing intention to apply to transactions between the post-war generations of married couples 'presumptions' which are based on inferences of fact which an earlier generation of judges drew as to the most likely intentions of earlier generations of spouses belonging to the propertied classes of a different social era."

Notwithstanding these remarks of Lord Diplock, the doctrine of advancement can still have some application where for some reason, such as death, the evidence of one or both of the parties is unavailable. Where, on the other hand, both parties are available to give evidence, the court much prefers to hear them and to form its own view of their intention. Where this is done, it is highly unlikely that the presumption of advancement will ever have any effect.

---

[33] (1834) 1 Myl. & K. 511.
[34] [1970] A.C. 777 at 783.

In so far, if at all, as the presumption may still be operative, it is immaterial that the marriage is later dissolved or is the subject matter of a decree of nullity on the grounds that the marriage was voidable.[35] However, if a marriage is held to have been void *ab initio*, the presumption of advancement does not appear to apply—this is simply because the marriage is treated as never having existed at all.[36] The essential requirement of the presumption is for the property to be purchased in the name of the lawful wife of the purchaser. For this reason the presumption does not apply in favour of a purchaser's *de facto* wife or his mistress.[37]

Nor does the presumption of advancement apply where a wife purchases property in the name of her husband; in such circumstances, what is presumed to arise is a resulting trust in favour of the wife.[38] This used to be the case only where the property was purchased with the wife's capital, not where it was purchased with her income. However, in *Mercier v. Mercier*[39] the Court of Appeal held that there was no fundamental distinction between capital and income except in degree, although Romer L.J. made it clear that the fact could be of importance when he said[40]: "No doubt in certain cases, in considering whether a gift was intended, the fact of the money having been income received by him with her consent may be material in respect of the weight of evidence but there is no other distinction, so far as I am aware, between capital and income." There is no doubt whatever that the effect of this decision was to upset the pre-existing law; consequently, the fact that income rather than capital has been applied will now only be material evidentially in deciding whether or not there was an intention to benefit the husband and thereby rebut the presumption of a resulting trust in favour of the wife.

(2) Parent and child

"Child" here means "legitimate child". It is absolutely clear that if a father purchases property in the name of his child the presumption of advancement will apply.[41]

The traditional view is that if a mother does the same thing the presumption will not apply.[42] However, the authorities are not unanimous. In *Sayre v. Hughes*,[43] Stuart V.-C. appears to have held that what was most material

---

[35] *Dunbar v. Dunbar* [1909] 2 Ch. 639. A nullity decree in respect of a voidable marriage now has a prospective, not a retrospective effect. Accordingly the marriage is to be treated as if it had existed until the decree; Matrimonial Causes Act 1973, s.16. For the grounds on which a marriage is regarded as void or voidable, see *ibid*. ss.11, 12.

[36] See *Re Ames' Settlement* [1946] Ch. 217. See also *Re D'Altroy's Will Trusts* [1968] 1 W.L.R. 120.

[37] *Soar v. Foster* (1858) 4 K. & J. 152.

[38] Although if the property is part of the matrimonial assets the court may apply the maxim that equality is equity: see, for example, *Jones v. Maynard* [1951] Ch. 572; *Rimmer v. Rimmer* [1953] 1 Q.B. 63; and *ante*, p. 243; *post*, p. 361.

[39] [1903] 2 Ch. 98.

[40] *ibid*. at 101.

[41] *Dyer v. Dyer* (1788) 2 Cox Eq. 92.

[42] *Re De Visme* (1863) 2 De G.J. & S. 17; *Bennet v. Bennet* (1879) 10 Ch.D. 474. The same view was adopted much more recently in *Sekhon v. Alissa* [1989] 2 F.L.R. 94.

[43] (1868) L.R. 5 Eq. 376. See also *Garrett v. Wilkinson* (1848) 2 De G. & Sm. 244 at 246. The High Court of Australia upheld the existence of a presumption of advancement between mother and child in *Nelson v. Nelson* (1995) 132 A.L.R. 133.

was whether the mother's motivation was to confer a benefit on her child—a view which, if accepted, could clearly lead to the opposite conclusion and work an advancement in favour of the child, although Stuart V.-C. was specifically considering only the case of a widowed mother. Nor do the authorities in support of the traditional view agree as to the justification for it. In *Re De Visme*[44] it was held that the presumption of advancement would not arise as between mother and child because a married woman was under no obligation to maintain her children. On the other hand, in *Bennet v. Bennet*[45] Jessel M.R. held that the presumption of advancement essentially applied only to the father not because the mother was under no liability to maintain her children but because the father alone was under a moral obligation to make provision for his child, no such obligation being imposed on the mother. A quite different reason for rejecting *Re De Visme* in modern conditions is the fact that the National Assistance Act 1948[46] imposes a statutory duty on a mother to care for her children. However, in *Sekhon v. Alissa*,[47] the most recent case in which the traditional view was adopted, Hoffmann J. chose simply to apply the older authorities without distinguishing between the different views expressed therein and therefore held that the presumption of resulting trust and not the presumption of advancement applied where a mother provided the majority of the price of a property purchased in the name of her daughter. Nor can any assistance be drawn from the rather earlier decision in *Gross v. French*,[48] where the Court of Appeal merely held that, even if the presumption of advancement did apply, there was sufficient evidence to rebut it.

The traditional position is frankly unsatisfactory. It is particularly difficult to see why a mother, especially if she has money, is not under the same moral obligation to maintain her children as their father is said to be. Having said that, however, it may not matter all that much in practice. If there is indeed no presumption of advancement between mother and child, the presumption of resulting trust in favour of the mother which consequently arises can be rebutted by any evidence of an intention on her part to benefit the child[49] and it is improbable that children will find this particularly difficult to achieve. The failure of the daughter to do so in *Sekhon v. Alissa*[50] admittedly shows that this cannot be assumed; however, that decision is perhaps best explained on the grounds explained in the next section, namely that the daughter could anyway only have rebutted the presumption by introducing evidence of an unlawful purpose which should not in fact have been admissible.

(3) Person in loco parentis and child

A person *in loco parentis* is a person standing in the position of a parent, that is to say in the situation of the lawful father of the child. According to Jessel

---

[44] (1863) 2 De G.J. & S. 17.
[45] (1879) 10 Ch.D. 474.
[46] ss.42(1), 64(1).
[47] [1989] 2 F.L.R. 94.
[48] (1976) 238 E.G. 376.
[49] See *Beecher v. Major* (1865) 2 Drew. & Sm. 431.
[50] [1989] 2 F.L.R. 94.

M.R. in *Bennet v. Bennet*,[51] such a person is one who takes upon himself the duty of the father of a child to make provision for that child. For example, an uncle or grandfather may, in the particular circumstances of the case, put himself *in loco parentis* to a child after, for example, the death of the latter's father.[52] Again, a father of an illegitimate child may, in the circumstances, be *in loco parentis* to that child.[53] However, for a person to be *in loco parentis* he must actually place himself in the situation of the father; simply to pay an illegitimate child's school fees would not of itself be enough in itself to raise the presumption.[54]

(4) The rebuttable nature of the presumption
When a presumption of advancement does arise, it is just as capable of being rebutted by evidence of actual intention as is a presumption of resulting trust. Thus in *McGrath v. Wallis*,[55] a father contributed about four-fifths of the purchase price of a house which was acquired for the occupation of father, mother, son and daughter but the property was put in the name of the son so that the balance of price could be raised by way of mortgage (the father was unemployed). A declaration of trust was indeed drawn up by means of which the beneficial interests were to be four-fifths to the father and one-fifth to the son but for some reason this was never executed. Following the death of his parents, the son claimed to be absolutely beneficially entitled. However, the need for an acceptable mortgagor, the absence of any evidence that the father had instructed the solicitors not to proceed with the declaration of trust, and the absence of any reason why the father should have wished to give the property to his son absolutely, were held sufficient to rebut any presumption of advancement. The presumption will also be rebutted if the mental state of the purchaser is such that he is incapable of any intention at all.[56]

3. *The Admissibility of Evidence to Rebut the Presumptions*

(A) What sort of evidence is admissible?
It is obviously important to determine exactly what sort of evidence is admissible for the purpose of rebutting the presumptions of resulting trust and advancement. The leading case on admissibility is *Shephard v. Cartwright*.[57]

The deceased had been a successful businessman. He had at various times formed a number of private companies which had been so successful that he had amalgamated them and turned them into a public company. At varying times he had shares in this company allotted to his three children but there was no evidence that any share certificates had been issued in their favour. In any case, the father continued to deal in these shares; at various times he

---

[51] (1879) 10 Ch.D. 474 at 477.
[52] *Ebrand v. Dancer* (1680) 2 Ch. Cas. 26 (grandchild whose father was dead); *Currant v. Jago* (1844) 1 Coll.C.C. 261 (nephew of wife maintained by her husband).
[53] *Beckford v. Beckford* (1774) Lofft 490.
[54] *Tucker v. Burrow* (1865) 2 Hem. & M. 515.
[55] [1995] 2 F.L.R. 114.
[56] *Simpson v. Simpson* [1992] 1 F.L.R. 601.
[57] [1955] A.C. 431.

sold them and received the proceeds of sale. However, at a later stage, he did place to the credit of the children in separate deposit accounts the exact amount of the cash consideration for the shares which he had sold. Later still, he obtained the children's signatures to documents (as to the contents of which they were wholly ignorant) authorising him to withdraw money from these deposit accounts and indeed in due course, unknown to them, his drawings exhausted those accounts. When he died, some 13 years after the accounts had been exhausted, his children brought an action against his executors claiming an account of money due to them. The executors contended that the presumption of advancement in favour of the children had been rebutted by the control which the father had continuously exercised over the shares. This argument succeeded in the Court of Appeal but the House of Lords held that the registration of the shares in the names of the children gave rise to a presumption of advancement and that nothing had happened which was capable of rebutting that presumption. The law on the admissibility of evidence for the purposes of rebuttal was stated explicitly by Viscount Simonds. He adopted[58] the following passage from Snell's *Principles of Equity.*[59]

"The acts and declarations of the parties before or at the time of the purchase, or so immediately after it as to constitute a part of the transaction, are admissible in evidence either for or against the party who did the act or made the declaration; subsequent acts and declarations are only admissible as evidence against the party who made them, and not in his favour."

As Viscount Simonds said, there are numerous cases of high authority[60] on which this passage is founded. The applicable law, having been somewhat disturbed by the Court of Appeal, which appeared to hold that subsequent acts were admissible in favour of the parties who did them, is therefore no longer in doubt.[61] It is not too difficult to state its principles in the abstract. They establish, in the context of the presumption of advancement between father and child, first that a father's declaration at the date of the transaction will be admissible in his favour to rebut the presumption, secondly, that a father's declaration made after that date will not be admissible in his favour but will only be admissible against him in favour of his child in order to support the presumption of advancement[62] and, thirdly, that subsequent acts and declarations by the child will be admissible against him by the father in order to rebut the presumption.[63] However, difficulties may well be found in applying these general rules in practice.

First, the question of whether or not a subsequent act is part of the same transaction as the original purchase or transfer is a potential cause of considerable difficulty—there is no universal criterion by which a link can,

---

[58] *ibid.* at 445.
[59] (28th ed.) at p. 185.
[60] See, for example, the cases cited *post*, nn. 62, 63.
[61] Evidence of subsequent declarations may now be admissible as a result of the Civil Evidence Act 1968, s.2, which relates to hearsay evidence.
[62] *Stock v. McAvoy* (1872) L.R. 15 Eq. 55; *Redington v. Redington* (1794) 3 Ridg.P.R. 106 at 177; *Sidmouth v. Sidmouth* (1840) 2 Beav. 447.
[63] *Scawin v. Scawin* (1841) 1 Y. & C.C.C. 65.

for this purpose, be found between one event and another but it is nevertheless essential that a link is able to be found.[64] In *Shephard v. Cartwright* itself, Viscount Simonds pointed out that the events which happened after the allotment of shares to the children did not form part of the original transaction, that is to say the allotment. All subsequent events were independent of that original transaction and, far from flowing inevitably from it, they would never have happened but for the phenomenal success of the testator's business.

Secondly, difficulties arise as to whether, and if so what, subsequent acts and declarations will rebut the relevant presumption. An early case which shows the difficulties that there may be in rebutting the presumption on this basis is *Lord Grey v. Lady Grey*[65]; Lord Finch L.C., having considered the fact that the son had permitted his father to continue to receive the profits of the property in question, said that that fact was insufficient to rebut the presumption because it was an "act of reverence and good manners"![66] Of course, there are some circumstances which will go to rebut the presumption. Thus, it was held in *Warren v. Gurney*[67] that the fact that the father had retained the title deeds was, although not in itself conclusive, of great significance when coupled with certain contemporaneous declarations by the father. Another circumstance which assists in rebutting the presumption is the fact that the son is the father's solicitor.[68]

Yet, as Viscount Simonds said in *Shephard v. Cartwright*,[69] any such evidence of subsequent acts is regarded jealously. A question which arose in that case was whether, if the events which happened after the allotments of the shares could not be admitted in evidence as forming part of the original transaction, they could nevertheless be admitted as constituting an admission against the acquisition by the children of any interest. However, it is an indispensable condition of such conduct being admissible that it should have been performed with knowledge of the material facts. It was undisputed that in *Shephard v. Cartwright* the children had, under their father's guidance, done what they had been told to do without inquiry or knowledge. This fact precluded the admission in evidence of their conduct as constituting an admission against their own interest and, had it been admitted, would have deprived it of all probative value.

(B) Illegal and fraudulent conduct

There is a further restriction on the ability to adduce evidence in rebuttal of the presumptions of resulting trust and advancement. This is that neither presumption can be rebutted by evidence that the property was put into the name in question for a fraudulent or illegal purpose and that the purchaser nevertheless really intended to retain the beneficial interest. This basic rule has never been doubted. However, it is now subject to two qualifications: first, the existence of a fraudulent or illegal purpose will not prevent a property right from being claimed if the claimant can demonstrate his right

---

[64] [1955] A.C. 431 at 448–449, *per* Viscount Simonds.
[65] (1677) 2 Swans. 594.
[66] *ibid.* at 600.
[67] [1944] 2 All E.R. 472.
[68] *Garrett v. Wilkinson* (1848) 2 De G. & Sm. 244.
[69] [1955] A.C. 431 at 449.

thereto without having to rely on evidence of that purpose; secondly, that the evidence of a fraudulent or illegal purpose is admissible if the claimant subsequently withdrew from that purpose before it had been in any way carried out.[70]

The basic rule may be illustrated by *Gascoigne v. Gascoigne*[71] where a husband who had put property into the name of his wife was held unable to adduce evidence to show that he had done so for the purpose of defeating his creditors; consequently, she was beneficially entitled to it. A similar result occurred in *Tinker v. Tinker*,[72] although in that case the husband's intention was apparently honest. In the words of Lord Denning M.R., he simply found himself on the horns of a dilemma in that, as between himself and his wife, he wanted to say that the property belonged to him whereas, as between himself and his creditors, he wished to say that it belonged to her. In such circumstances, the effect of the presumption of advancement was decisive. This was also the case in *Chettiar v. Chettiar (No. 2)*,[73] where a father sought to evade regulations governing the holding of rubber plantations in Malaya which differed depending on whether more or less than 100 acres were held (in the former but not the latter case, the permissible production was controlled by an assessment committee). He acquired 40 acres at a time when he already owned 99 acres and, in order to avoid having to disclose to the authorities that he held more than 100 acres, had the 40 acres put into the name of his son. He had not the slightest intention of making a gift of them and therefore subsequently claimed that the son held them on trust for him. The Privy Council, in an opinion delivered by Lord Denning, held that the father could only rebut the presumption of advancement by disclosing his intention to deceive the authorities. The court was bound to take notice of this illegality and therefore would not lend him its aid; the legal and beneficial estate consequently lay where it had fallen.

In all three of these decisions, evidence of the illegal or fraudulent conduct in question was necessary in order to rebut the presumption in question. Prior to the decision of the House of Lords in *Tinsley v. Milligan*,[74] it was thought that the court would equally decline to intervene in favour of a participant in an illegal or fraudulent purpose even where no such evidence was actually necessary.[75] This was indeed the view adopted by the minority in that case but the majority qualified the basic rule by holding that the existence of a fraudulent or illegal purpose will not prevent a property right from being claimed if the claimant can demonstrate his right thereto without

---

[70] See Davies in *Trends in Contemporary Trust Law* (ed. Oakley, 1996), p. 31; Virgo [1996] C.L.J. 23.

[71] [1918] 1 K.B. 223; see also *Re Emery's Investment Trusts* [1959] Ch. 410 (avoiding payment of taxes).

[72] [1970] P. 136. *Gascoigne v. Gascoigne* and *Tinker v. Tinker* were distinguished in *Griffiths v. Griffiths* [1973] 1 W.L.R. 1454, where a husband's false representation as to ownership formed no part of the legal proceedings between him and his wife (this decision was varied by the Court of Appeal on other grounds at [1974] 1 All E.R. 932).

[73] [1962] A.C. 294.

[74] [1994] 1 A.C. 340.

[75] On the basis of the "clean hands" policy laid down by Lord Eldon L.C. in *Muckleston v. Brown* (1801) 6 Ves. 52.

having to rely on evidence of that purpose.[76] In that case, two female lovers agreed to put a house which they were purchasing into the sole name of the plaintiff in order to enable the defendant to make fraudulent claims for housing benefit. After this fraud had been practiced for a number of years, the two quarrelled and the plaintiff left. Subsequently, at a time when the defendant had discontinued her fraudulent claims and "made her peace" with the authorities, the plaintiff sought her eviction; the defendant counter-claimed for a declaration that the property was held on trust for both of them in equal shares. The Court of Appeal[77] held that a more flexible approach should be adopted in cases of fraudulent or illegal conduct on the basis that "the underlying principle is the so-called public conscience test. The court must weigh, or balance, the adverse consequences of granting relief against the adverse consequences of refusing relief. The ultimate decision calls for a value judgment."[78] However, this new principle was unanimously rejected by the House of Lords, who confirmed the basic rule that evidence of a fraudulent or illegal purpose is not admissible to rebut a presumption of resulting trust or of advancement. But the majority held[79] that the defendant did not need to rely on any such evidence to assert her claim. On its face, the transaction between the parties had given rise to a presumption of resulting trust in her favour; she was therefore presumed to have an equitable proprietary interest in the property unless that presumption could be rebutted. She could therefore assert her claim to that interest without having to produce any evidence as to why the property had been conveyed into the sole name of the plaintiff and was consequently entitled to her beneficial interest therein.

Tinsley v. Milligan was subsequently applied by the Court of Appeal in *Silverwood v. Silverwood*,[80] where the majority of the testatrix's assets were placed in the names of two of her grandchildren and not declared to the Department of Social Security when she subsequently applied for income support. Her executor was held to be entitled to recover them on the basis that there was a presumption of resulting trust in her favour; even on the

---

[76] This has been the subject of considerable criticism; see Halliwell [1994] Conv. 62; Stowe 57 M.L.R. (1994) 441. Council in 143 N.L.J. (1993) 1577 says that the effect of the decision is that "He who comes to equity should keep unclean hands in his pockets", an amusing addition to the list of equitable maxims which will no doubt in due course prove to be as misleading as most of the others.

[77] [1992] Ch. 310.

[78] *ibid.* at 319, *per* Nicholls L.J. A different flexible public policy approach was subsequently adopted by the High Court of Australia in *Nelson v. Nelson* (1995) 132 A.L.R. 133, in which *Tinsley v. Milligan* was rejected. A mother was held able to rebut the presumption of advancement in favour of her children (which would probably not have arisen here anyway) by adducing evidence that she had purchased the property in their name in order to obtain housing subsidies which would not have been available had she purchased in her own name; she was therefore entitled to the property under a resulting trust but the majority went on to hold that as a condition of relief she was herself obliged to do equity by reimbursing the housing subsidies.

[79] It had long been established that the legal owner of property can rely on his title despite the fact that it was acquired as a result of an illegal transaction (*Bowmakers v. Barnet Instruments* [1945] K.B. 65). The disagreement between the members of the House of Lords was as to whether the "clean hands" policy to which courts of equity have always subscribed prevented this principle from also being applicable to an equitable owner.

[80] (1997) 74 P. & C.R. 453.

assumption that the testatrix had been party to the unlawful purpose (which was not held), evidence of it was only necessary to rebut any argument by the grandchildren that the assets had been given to them. Nourse L.J.,[81] while repeating his preference for the flexible approach rejected by the House of Lords in *Tinsley v. Milligan*, emphasised that, by virtue of that decision, a claimant is entitled to recover provided that he is not forced either to plead or to rely on any fraudulent or illegal conduct.

The principle thus enunciated and the second qualification to the basic rule that evidence of a fraudulent or illegal purpose is admissible if the claimant subsequently withdrew from that purpose before it had been in any way carried out provide alternative explanations for the earlier decision in *Sekhon v. Alissa*.[82] Property purchased by a mother and daughter was conveyed into the sole name of the daughter with a view to evading capital gains tax; however, the property was never actually sold so this objective was not in fact realised. Hoffmann J., having concluded that there was no presumption of advancement between mother and daughter, held that, since the illegal purpose had not been carried out, the mother could introduce evidence of it in support of the presumption of resulting trust. However, if the facts are instead considered in the light of the principle enunciated by the majority of the House of Lords in *Tinsley v. Milligan*, it can be seen that the absence of any presumption of advancement meant that there was a presumption of resulting trust in favour of the mother, on which she could rely without having to adduce evidence of her illegal purpose. Any attempt by the daughter to rebut the presumption of resulting trust would have required evidence of the illegal purpose, which would not have been admissible. Had, on the other hand, the parties instead been father and daughter, the father would not have been able to rebut the consequential presumption of advancement because the necessary evidence of the illegal purpose would have been inadmissible and the daughter would have been entitled to the property absolutely.

The fact that the effect of the decision in *Tinsley v. Milligan* is that the result of any particular case thus depends entirely on what the relationship between the parties actually is has been the subject of considerable criticism.[83] However, this seems an entirely logical consequence of the continued existence of the presumption of advancement, even if it has "fallen into disfavour". It is of course feasible to criticise (as these critics admittedly do) the decision in *Tinsley v. Milligan* as such. It would however be somewhat unreasonable to criticise the decision in *Tinsley v. Milligan* merely because of the effect produced on the rule laid down therein by the presumption of advancement, which was not relevant in that case and which the House of Lords could hardly have derogated even if it had been.

The second qualification to the basic rule, on which Hoffmann J. relied in *Sekhon v. Alissa*, has since been applied by the Court of Appeal in *Tribe v. Tribe*.[84] A father transferred shares in a family company to his son for a

---

[81] *ibid.* at 758–759.
[82] [1989] 2 F.L.R. 94.
[83] *Tribe v. Tribe* [1996] Ch. 107 at 118 *per* Nourse L.J.; *Silverwood v. Silverwood* (1997) 74 P. & C.R. 453 at 458, *per* Nourse L.J.; Hanbury & Martin, *Modern Equity* (15th ed., 1997), p. 251.
[84] [1996] Ch. 107.

consideration which was not in fact paid in order to be able to deceive his landlord, to whom he was potentially liable for the cost of substantial works to the leased premises, as to his assets and consequently safeguard them. In the event, the issue of the repairs was resolved without resort to any deception.[85] The son subsequently claimed to be absolutely entitled to the shares by virtue of the presumption of advancement. The Court of Appeal held that, since the father's illegal purpose had not in any way been carried out, he could introduce evidence of it in order to rebut the presumption of advancement. The precise scope of this qualification to the basic rule was also very considerably clarified. Earlier authorities had required "repentance" from the unlawful or fraudulent purpose, although it was far from clear whether this "repentance" had to be genuine (which it would have been in *Sekhon v. Alissa* because the house had never been sold but would not have been in *Tribe v. Tribe* because the father had not "repented" until the danger to his assets was past). The Court of Appeal rejected the requirement completely and held that evidence of an unlawful or fraudulent purpose can be introduced by anyone who has withdrawn from the transaction in question before the unlawful or fraudulent purpose has been carried out. Although this undoubtedly broadens the scope of this second qualification, the Court of Appeal felt that it was not inconsistent with the policy underlining the basic rule: "if the policy which underlines the [basic] rule is to discourage fraud, the policy which underlines the [qualification] must be taken to be to encourage withdrawal from fraud before it is implemented, an end which is no less desirable".[86]

The decisions actually reached in *Tinsley v. Milligan* and *Tribe v. Tribe* are certainly compatible and there is no doubt that the respective qualifications to the basic rule which they establish are mutually consistent. However, in *Tribe v. Tribe* Millett L.J. said that a transferee cannot be prevented from rebutting a presumption by leading evidence of the transferor's subsequent conduct to show that it was inconsistent with any intention to retain a beneficial interest, giving the example of a transfer of property from uncle to nephew in order to conceal it from his creditors, with whom he subsequently settles on the basis that he has no interest therein.[87] How can the admission of evidence of this illegal purpose in order to rebut the presumption of resulting trust possibly be consistent with the principles laid down in *Tinsley v. Milligan* and subsequently applied in *Silverwood v. Silverwood*[88] (in which *Tribe v. Tribe* was not cited), by virtue of which the uncle would undoubtedly be able to rely on the presumption of resulting trust? These observations and the comments of Nourse L.J., both in *Tribe v. Tribe*[89] and in *Silverwood v. Silverwood*,[90] as to the arbitrariness of the rule laid down by the House of Lords suggest that the last word has yet to be spoken on both these qualifications to the basic rule that evidence of an unlawful or fraudulent purpose is inadmissible.

---

[85] The landlord agreed to take a surrender of one of the two leases and sold the father the reversion on the other one.
[86] [1996] Ch. 107, *per* Millett L.J. at 133.
[87] *ibid.* at 130.
[88] (1997) 74 P. & C.R. 453.
[89] [1996] Ch. 107 at 118.
[90] (1997) 74 P. & C.R. 453 at 458.

III. VOLUNTARY CONVEYANCE OR TRANSFER

This situation envisages a direct transfer of property without consideration; in order to answer the question of whether the presumption of a resulting trust applies it is necessary to consider separately a transfer of land and a transfer of pure personalty.

1. *Land*

It has already been seen[91] that between 1536 and 1925 the Statute of Uses 1536 would execute any use or trust by transferring the legal title to the beneficiary of the use or trust; thus, during this period a transfer of property to A on trust for B had the effect of vesting both legal and beneficial title in B. Consequently, the only way of creating a trust was to transfer the property "unto and to the use of" A on trust for B; the Statute of Uses executed the use in favour of A, passing legal title to him but did not affect the trust in favour of B, which took effect in equity. Where, on the other hand, a transfer of property was intended to be voluntary and pass both legal and beneficial title to the transferee, the transfer would usually be expressed to be made "to the use of" or "for the benefit of" the grantee; in the absence of words such as these, the property would have finished up vested in the grantor both at law and in equity, the equitable interest therein being the subject matter of a resulting trust in his favour which would then be executed by the Statute of Uses 1536 so as to carry the legal estate back to him as well. The presence of these words undoubtedly passed legal title to the transferee in just the same way as a transfer "unto and to the use of" an intended trustee vested legal title in him; their presence was clearly also intended to pass the equitable title to him as well but, despite dicta that this was indeed their effect,[92] some commentators[93] thought that as a matter of principle the absence of any further express beneficial gift meant that the transferee held the property on resulting trust for the transferor.

The Statute of Uses was repealed by the Property Legislation of 1925 with effect from January 1, 1926; consequently formulae such as those set out above were no longer necessary. An express trust can now be created simply by transferring property to A on trust for B. The Law of Property Act 1925 purported to deal with voluntary transfers by enacting section 60(3): "In a voluntary conveyance a resulting trust for the grantor shall not be implied merely by reason that the property is not expressed to be conveyed for the use or benefit of the grantee." The definitions section of the Law of Property Act 1925 (s.205) provides that, unless the context otherwise requires, "property" means "any interest in real or personal property"; however, it is generally thought and will be assumed hereafter that the context (and in particular the references to "conveyance" and "conveyed") does otherwise require and that the effect of this provision is confined to land—it has

---

[91] See *ante*, p. 4.
[92] *Young v. Peachey* (1742) 2 Atk. 254 at 257; *Lloyd & Johnson v. Spillet* (1741) 2 Atk. 148 at 150; *Fowkes v. Pascoe* (1875) 10 Ch.App. 343, 348.
[93] Maitland, *Equity* (2nd ed.), p. 77; White and Tudor, *Leading Cases in Equity* (9th ed.), Vol. II, p. 762.

certainly never been referred to in any case concerning pure personalty. Even so, the effect of the provision has been described as "debatable" by Russell L.J. in *Hodgson v. Marks*[94] and different views have been expressed as to what it actually means.

Most commentators take the view that, "in the absence of evidence to the contrary, there will be no resulting trust on a voluntary conveyance to another, unless it has been expressly conveyed upon trusts which fail to dispose of the entire equitable interest".[95] However, this view goes far further than the provision, which restricts itself to stating that no resulting trust will arise merely because of the absence of the words in question; it is also far from clear what words in the provision justify a resulting trust where there is evidence to the contrary and nowhere else.[96] Consequently, this work has consistently adopted the contrary view that there appears to be nothing in section 60(3) which prevents a resulting trust from being implied for reasons other than the absence of the words in question and, in particular by the operation of general equitable principles. The matter has yet to be finally decided. In practice the issue is avoided by the almost invariable insertion into voluntary conveyances of express words of gift sufficient to rebut any equitable presumption which may still arise.

Curiously enough, some of the commentators who adopt the view that, in the absence of contrary intention, there will be no resulting trust on a voluntary conveyance to another, take a different view when the conveyance is into the joint names of the transferor and the transferee.[97] Since there is nothing in the provision to justify such a distinction, this seems a further argument against their view. Needless to say, this work takes the view that the result is identical whether the transferor conveys the land into the name of the transferee or into the joint names of the two of them; a resulting trust will arise whenever general equitable principles so dictate.

2. *Pure Personalty*

It appears that a transferee of pure personalty under a voluntary transfer is presumed to hold the property upon a resulting trust for the transferor. This was certainly the case before 1926[98] and none of the authorities since 1925 has made any reference to section 60(3) of the Law of Property Act 1925, which must therefore be presumed not to apply to pure personalty. Thus, in

---

[94] [1971] Ch. 892 at 933 (his Lordship did not make specific reference to the provision but there is no doubt whatever that he was referring to its effect).

[95] Pettit, *Equity and the Law of Trusts* (8th ed., 1997), p. 161, citing Snell's *Principles of Equity* (29th ed.), p. 183. See also Hayton & Marshall, *Commentary and Cases on the Law of Trusts and Equitable Remedies* (10th ed., 1996), p. 307 and Underhill & Hayton, *Law of Trusts and Trustees* (15th ed., 1995), p. 334.

[96] These commentators have to introduce this qualification in order to deal with the decision in *Hodgson v. Marks* [1971] Ch. 892, where there was evidence to the contrary and a resulting trust of land was upheld. However, if s.60(3) permits there to be a resulting trust in that situation, there is no obvious reason why there should not also be one in other appropriate situations.

[97] Hayton & Marshall and Underhill & Hayton, *op. cit.* make no reference whatever to s.60(3) in relation to such a conveyance. Pettit, *op. cit.* says that "there is here a stronger argument for a resulting trust".

[98] See also *Fowkes v. Pascoe* (1875) 10 Ch.App. 343 at 345–348.

Re Vinogradoff[99] war loan stock was transferred into the joint names of the transferor and her granddaughter, who was then four years of age but to whom she was not *in loco parentis*. Farwell J. held that a resulting trust had arisen.

3. *Rebuttal of the Presumption*

Whenever there is a voluntary transfer capable of giving rise to a presumption of resulting trust, the counter-presumption of advancement will, where applicable, arise if the transferor is the husband or father of, or *in loco parentis* to, the transferee. Further, both the presumption of resulting trust and the presumption of advancement are, as usual, capable of being rebutted by contrary evidence.

IV. FAILURE OF THE TRUST OR BENEFICIAL INTEREST

1. *Failure of the Trust*

Whenever the trusts of a settlement fail, there is a resulting trust of the trust property for the settlor or his estate. Thus in *Re Ames' Settlement*,[1] the funds of a marriage settlement were held on a resulting trust for the settlor's estate once the marriage had been declared void by a decree of nullity made by a Kenyan court. The settlement for which the marriage had constituted the consideration failed completely because, in that case, the legal effect of the decree was that the parties not only were no longer married to one another but never had been at all.[2] Similarly, if property is given to a person to hold on trust and therefore not beneficially but no effective trusts are ever established, the property will be held on a resulting trust for the grantor.[3]

The same basic principle applies if a loan is made for a particular purpose which fails; in such circumstances, the money is held on a secondary trust for the lender. The leading case is *Barclays Bank v. Quistclose Investments*,[4] which concerned the collapse of a company known as Rolls Razor. Quistclose Investments had agreed to lend money to the company but only for the purpose of paying a dividend on the company's shares. Before the dividend became due for payment, Rolls Razor went into liquidation, which had the effect of preventing its payment. The House of Lords held that Quistclose Investments was entitled to the repayment of the money on the basis of a secondary trust, the purpose for which it was lent having failed. It was

---

[99] [1935] W.N. 68.

[1] [1946] Ch. 217.

[2] In this case the marriage was merely voidable but the effect of the nullity decree was that the marriage was void *ab initio*. Since the Nullity of Marriage Act 1971, s.5 (now Matrimonial Causes Act 1973, s.16), this is no longer the position under English law; this section provides that a nullity decree in respect of a voidable marriage has only a prospective and not any retrospective effect. However, if the marriage is "void", it is treated as never having taken place. For a list of the grounds on which a marriage will be void or voidable, see Matrimonial Causes Act 1973, ss.11, 12.

[3] *Re Vandervell's Trusts (No. 2)* [1974] Ch. 269.

[4] [1970] A.C. 567.

further held that the money, which had been paid into an account at Barclays Bank, who were Rolls Razor's bankers, could be recovered from the bank because it had notice of the facts giving rise to the trust; consequently, the bank could not as against Quistclose Investments retain the funds in order to reduce Rolls Razor's liability to it under its overdrafts in other accounts. There has been considerable controversy as to the precise nature of this secondary trust, which has variously been classified as an express trust, a resulting trust, and a constructive trust[5] but the opinion of the author of this edition is that it is an express trust. For this reason, a detailed discussion of the decision in *Barclays Bank v. Quistclose Investments* and of the authorities in which it has been applied is found in an earlier chapter.[6]

2. Unexhausted Beneficial Interests

(A) Failure wholly to dispose of the beneficial interest
The same principle will be applied where the beneficial interest has not been wholly disposed of. However, it is not applied in all cases. A relatively recent decision in which it was applied is *Re Gillingham Bus Disaster Fund*.[7] In 1951 24 Cadets in the Royal Marines were killed when a motor vehicle ran into them. The mayors of several boroughs in the area wrote the following letter to the *Daily Telegraph*: "The Mayors have decided to promote a Royal Marine Cadet Memorial Fund to be devoted to defraying funeral expenses, caring for the boys who may be disabled and then to such worthy cause or causes in memory of the boys who lost their lives as the Mayors may determine." This appeal resulted in subscriptions amounting to the then very substantial sum of nearly £9,000, contributed partly by identifiable persons but mainly anonymously as a result of street collections and the like. The trustees spent about £2,500 in fulfilling the objectives set out in the letter and then took out a summons for guidance as to what to do with the surplus. Harman J. held that the trust could not be classified as charitable; consequently, the surplus had to be held on resulting trust for the donors, even though many of them were in fact anonymous. This conclusion followed naturally from the principle that where money was held upon trust and the trust declared did not exhaust the fund it would revert to the donor or settlor upon a resulting trust. The reasoning behind the application of the principle to these particular facts was that a donor did not part with the money out and out but only to a certain extent, namely with the intention that the wishes contained in his declaration of trust should be carried into effect. It must be emphasised, as Harman J. duly observed, that this doctrine does not rest on any evidence of the state of mind of the donor who in the vast majority of cases of this type will certainly not expect to get his money back under any circumstances. A resulting trust arises even where the donor's expectation has been cheated of fruition for some reason which was totally unknown at the time of the gift; this was indeed the case in *Re*

[5] See *ante*, p. 25, n. 25.
[6] See *ante*, p. 23.
[7] [1958] Ch. 300 (affirmed on points not affecting this aspect of the decision by the Court of Appeal at [1959] Ch. 62; see also *post*, p. 418; Atiyah (1958) 74 L.Q.R. 190. For charitable gifts the position is otherwise; see *post*, p. 430.

Gillingham Bus Disaster Fund, where the donors' expectations failed because of an an inference of law drawn only in the light of the knowledge of events which occurred after they had made their contributions to the fund.

It must be emphasised that the basis of the decision in *Re Gillingham Bus Disaster Fund* was that there was no intention on the part of the donors to part with their money out and out when they contributed it; in particular, such an intention could no more be attributed to the anonymous contributor who had made his gift in response to a street collection than it could to a contributor who was identifiable. As Harman J. said,[8] "I see no reason myself to suppose that the small giver who is anonymous has any wider intention than the large giver who is named. They all give for the one object. If they can be found by inquiry the resulting trust can be executed in their favour. If they cannot I do not see how the money could then change its destination and become *bona vacantia*."[9] Such part of the surplus whose donors could not be identified therefore had to be paid into court to await claims by them under the consequential resulting trusts[10]; most of it is probably still there today!

On the other hand, as the remarks of Harman J. indicate, if it could have been shown that each donor made his gift out and out with no intention of reclaiming it whatever the fate of the appeal might be, the surplus would have belonged to the Crown as *bona vacantia*. There is no doubt that this is a more practicable solution so far as the proceeds of collecting boxes are concerned because it is obviously likely to be a wholly fruitless exercise to try to establish who in fact contributed how many pounds or pence to the collection and is therefore entitled to have his contribution returned—this is of course precisely why most of the surplus had to be paid into court. Doubts have subsequently been expressed as to whether the decision of Harman J. in this respect was correct as a matter of law. In *Re West Sussex Constabulary's Benevolent Fund Trusts*[11] Goff J. declined to follow *Re Gillingham Bus Disaster Fund*, at any rate so far as concerned the proceeds of collecting boxes. He held that persons who put money into collecting boxes should be taken to have intended to part with the money out and out absolutely in all circumstances; consequently, the Crown was entitled to that money as *bona vacantia* on later failure of the trusts. There are admittedly some dicta which support this view[12] but they are not particularly weighty because they concerned a rather different question, namely whether the fact that contributions were made by unidentifiable donors to an appeal for charitable purposes indicated an intention to make the gifts outright so as to enable the funds to be applied *cy-près*, that is to say to other analogous

---

[8] [1958] Ch. 300 at 314.

[9] In similar circumstances a resulting trust was held to arise in *Re Holbourn Aero Components Air Raid Distress Fund* [1946] Ch. 86 but in that case there was no argument about *bona vacantia*. Compare *Re Hillier's Trusts* [1954] 1 W.L.R. 9, where Upjohn J. held in these circumstances in favour of *bona vacantia* (when the Court of Appeal affirmed this decision at [1954] 1 W.L.R. 700, Denning L.J. approved the formulation of Upjohn J.).

[10] Under Trustee Act 1925, s.63.

[11] [1971] Ch. 1.

[12] *Re Hillier's Trusts* [1954] 1 W.L.R. 700 at 715, *per* Denning L.J.; *Re Welsh Hospital (Netley) Fund* [1921] 1 Ch. 655 at 659, 660, *per* P.O. Lawrence J.; *Re North Devon and Somerset Relief Fund Trusts* [1953] 1 W.L.R. 260 at 1266, 1267, *per* Wynn-Parry J.

charitable purposes.[13] Neither of these decisions can therefore be regarded as decisive and so the question of whether the proceeds of collecting boxes for non-charitable purposes which fail are held on resulting trust or are *bona vacantia* remains to be settled; while, on the one hand, it seems highly artificial to make a distinction between the intention of unidentified donors and that of identified donors, it is on the other hand equally true that the consequences of the existence of a resulting trust are highly inconvenient.

There is, in any event, another essential distinction between the facts of the two decisions. *Re Gillingham Bus Disaster Fund* concerned a fund raised to deal with one particular tragedy, a fund in which none of the contributors had any direct or indirect financial interest (other, of course, than the possibility of recovering any unspent surplus in the event that that surplus was indeed held on resulting trust); the contributors paid their money on an outward looking basis. *Re West Sussex Constabulary's Benevolent Fund Trusts*, on the other hand, concerned a fund for the benefit of the dependants of the members of an unincorporated association and the contributors therefore largely paid their money on an inward looking basis. Further, the fund included not only the proceeds of collecting boxes, the proceeds of entertainments, raffles and sweepstakes, and donations and legacies but also the contributions of past and present members. Goff J. therefore had to deal with many types of contribution which were not present in *Re Gillingham Bus Disaster Fund*.

It has already been seen that he rejected the applicability of the doctrine of resulting trusts to the proceeds of street collections. He took a similar view in respect of the proceeds of entertainments, raffles and sweepstakes, holding that it was not appropriate to apply the doctrine of resulting trusts for two reasons: first, because the relationship was one of contract, not of trust (a contributor paid his money as the price of being entertained or of having his ticket put into the draw and that was precisely what he received); and, secondly, because there was no direct contribution to the fund at all—only the profit, if any, made out of the entertainment or the draw was ultimately received. The distinction thus made between trust and contract certainly seems sound in respect of these sources of funds. Goff J. consequently held that, since it was not appropriate to apply the doctrine of resulting trusts, the proceeds of these sources of funds must also be held for the Crown as *bona vacantia*. However, he held that the donations and legacies were indeed held on resulting trust.

That left the question of the contributions of past and present members, a question which arises whenever the funds of an unincorporated association contain a surplus on its dissolution. Such a surplus can clearly be dealt with in a number of ways. First, it can be regarded as being held on resulting trust for the members of the association in proportion to their contributions to its funds. This was the view taken in *Re Printers' and Transferrers' Society*,[14] where the surplus of the funds of a society which had collected weekly contributions from its members to provide defence and support, and in particular strike and lock-out benefits, for them was divided between those who were members at the time of its dissolution in proportion to their

---

[13] See *post*, p. 420.
[14] [1899] 2 Ch. 184.

contributions. Similarly, in *Re Holbourn Aero Components Air Raid Distress Fund*,[15] a fund established for employees who were on war service or who suffered loss in air raids which was financed by voluntary subscriptions from the employees was divided up between all contributors in proportion to the amount contributed. Secondly, and alternatively, the funds can be regarded as being subject to the contractual rights and liabilities of the members towards one another as members of the association. This was the view taken in *Cunnack v. Edwards*,[16] where it was held that the personal representatives of members of a society founded to provide funds for the widows of the members could not claim a share when the purposes of the society came to an end. The members, in making their contributions to the society, had received all that they had contracted for in the form of pensions for the widows. Consequently, the Crown took the surplus as *bona vacantia*. This was the decision which Goff J. chose to follow and apply in *Re West Sussex Constabulary's Benevolent Fund Trusts*; he therefore held that the contributions of the past and present members were also held for the Crown as *bona vacantia*.

However, it is now generally accepted that the resulting trust approach is normally no longer appropriate in respect of surpluses of the funds of unincorporated associations on their dissolution. It has already been seen[17] that there is now a strong presumption that the funds of an unincorporated association should be regarded as being subject to the contractual rights and liabilities of the members towards one another as members of the association. Consequently, in *Re Bucks Constabulary Fund Friendly Society (No. 2)*,[18] Walton J. held that only where the association has become moribund, in that all or all but one of the members have resigned or died, will the assets of the association be held as *bona vacantia* and that in all other circumstances they will be divided equally between the existing members at the time of its dissolution, save where the rules of the association provide for division in some other way. He therefore divided equally between the members alive at the date of dissolution the surplus of a fund established to provide benefits for the members and the dependants of the members of a police force which had been amalgamated with other constabularies. Given that the association in question was a friendly society, this decision can technically be distinguished from that in *Re West Sussex Constabulary's Benevolent Fund Trusts*. However, Walton J. criticised that case and it is tolerably clear that he would have decided it differently, dividing all the funds held by Goff J. to be *bona vacantia* equally between the members of the association; indeed it is possible that he might also have done the same with the donations and legacies which Goff J. had held to be subject to resulting trusts.

It is generally thought that the view adopted by Walton J. in *Re Bucks Constabulary Fund Friendly Society (No. 2)* (which has been followed[19]) is the most appropriate of the various possibilities which have been discussed, principally because it is the view which fits most easily with the modern

[15] [1946] Ch. 86 & 194.
[16] [1896] 2 Ch. 679.
[17] See *ante*, pp. 117–123.
[18] [1979] 1 W.L.R. 936.
[19] In *Re G.K.N. Bolts & Nuts (Automotive Division) Birmingham Works, Sports and Social Club* [1982] 1 W.L.R. 774.

attitude to unincorporated associations in general.[20] However, this approach is not yet universal. In *Davis v. Richards & Wallington Industries*[21] Scott J. took a different view in relation to a hypothetical surplus in a pension fund, opining that such part of the surplus as represented the employer's contributions would be held on resulting trust while such part as represented the employees' contributions would be held as *bona vacantia*. He reached this latter conclusion only because no intention could be imputed to the employees that they should receive any surplus and because a resulting trust of their contributions would have been unworkable; had this not been the case, neither the contractual relationship between employer and employees nor the fact that they had obtained everything for which they had contracted would necessarily have prevented a resulting trust in their favour as well. As will be seen in the Chapter on Pensions Trusts, such trusts are subject to many special rules and the treatment of surplus has been and remains a particular problem; it is also questionable to what extent statutorily regulated pensions trusts can really be regarded as unincorporated associations in the normal sense of that expression. That may be the explanation for this decision. If it is not, then all that can be said is that the decision seems to be out of line with the other modern authorities (*Re Bucks Constabulary Fund Friendly Society (No. 2)* was cited but not discussed). What is clear is that this question of how surpluses in the funds of unincorporated associations should be treated is unlikely to be finally settled until the matter is considered by the Court of Appeal.

Two principal questions thus remain outstanding and both await review at appellate level. First, the question of whether surplus funds of the type considered in *Re Gillingham Bus Disaster Fund*, where no unincorporated association was involved, are held on resulting trust or as *bona vacantia* has still to be clarified in the light of the opposing attitudes adopted in that case and in *Re West Sussex Constabulary's Benevolent Fund Trusts* in this respect. And, secondly, the question of how surpluses in the funds of unincorporated associations on their dissolution should be treated awaits a final decision as to whether or not the resulting trust analysis preferred in the earlier authorities has been finally discredited by the decision in *Re Bucks Constabulary Fund Friendly Society (No. 2)*.

(B) Incomplete trusts

A resulting trust solution will generally be adopted where the instrument is silent as to the way in which the beneficial interest is to be applied. Thus, if property is settled upon trust to pay the income to a life tenant and the instrument makes no provision for the destination of the property on the death of the life tenant, the trustee will prima facie hold the property on a resulting trust for the settlor or his estate. This occurred in *Re Cochrane*[22] where, apparently as a result of a blunder by the draftsman, a provision was left out of the instrument so that the funds were not effectively disposed of. In such situations, there is no doubt that the nominated trustee cannot take beneficially; moreover, it has been held that he cannot even adduce evidence

[20] See *ante*, pp. 117–123; see also Gardner, [1992] Conv. 41.
[21] [1990] 1 W.L.R. 1511; see Gardner, *op. cit.*
[22] [1955] Ch. 309.

to that effect.[23] However, it must be emphasised that the implication of a resulting trust is merely the prima facie solution and may well be over-ridden as a matter of construction of the instrument; the court may be still able to construe the instrument in such a way that the trustee takes benefi-cially subject to the fulfilment of the trust in favour of the life tenant. So, in Re Foord[24] property was given by will to the testator's sister absolutely on trust to pay his wife an annuity. The income was more than sufficient to meet the annuity and, upon a true construction of the will, the sister was held entitled to the balance. A similar conclusion was arrived at in Re Andrew's Trust[25] where a fund had been subscribed for the education of the children of a distressed clergyman and "not for equal division between them". Kekewich J. held that there was no resulting trust; consequently, after their education had been completed the children were entitled to the balance equally. However, this latter decision is not particularly easy to reconcile with the decision in Re The Trusts of the Abbott Fund.[26] There a fund had been subscribed for the maintenance of two distressed ladies and Stirling J. held that on the death of the survivor the balance was held on a resulting trust for the donors. Kekewich J. justified his decision in Re Andrew's Trust on the ground that the subscribers parted with their money once and for all when they gave it, the education of the children being merely the motive for their gifts. While the distinction between these two cases is a very fine one, ultimately the question is one of construction in each case; it is therefore certainly possible that both Re Andrew's Trust and Re The Trusts of the Abbott Fund may have been right on their particular facts. Precisely this point was made in Re Osoba,[27] where gifts had been made to the mother, wife, and daughter of the testator for various purposes which had failed or become exhausted. The Court of Appeal held, on a construction of the will, that these created trusts for the benefit of the beneficiaries and the respective purposes were to be disregarded as no more than expressions of the testator's motives in making the gifts.

(C) Failure of a common purpose

In most cases the parties to a transaction have the same purpose but this is not necessarily so. The question therefore arises as to whether, when two or more persons acquire property each for a separate purpose and one of those purposes, previously uncommunicated to the other person(s) fails, a result-ing trust arises. The answer appears to be that it does not. The question was considered in Burgess v. Rawnsley.[28] An elderly widowed couple met and became friendly.[29] The man was the tenant of a house in which he lived in

---

[23] Re Rees' Will Trusts [1949] Ch. 541.

[24] [1922] 2 Ch. 519.

[25] [1905] 2 Ch. 48.

[26] [1900] 2 Ch. 326. In Re West Sussex Constabulary's Benevolent Fund Trusts [1971] Ch. 1, it was held that Re The Trusts of the Abbott Fund was indistinguishable with regard to funds derived from donations and legacies from identified persons. For discussion of other aspects of Re West Sussex Constabulary's Benevolent Fund Trusts, see ante, p. 259.

[27] [1979] 1 W.L.R. 247.

[28] [1975] Ch. 429.

[29] Apparently despite the fact that, according to her evidence, "he looked like a tramp" and "had been picking up fag-ends".

the downstairs flat, the upstairs flat being vacant. Subsequently, they agreed to purchase the house, each of them providing half of the purchase price, and it was conveyed to them as joint tenants. The man bought the house as a matrimonial home in contemplation of marriage, but the woman said that she had intended to live in the upstairs flat and that he had never mentioned marriage to her. They did not in fact marry and she never moved into the house. Later she orally agreed to sell her share in the house to him but then refused to do so. Following his death, his daughter, as administratrix of his estate, claimed that there was a resulting trust of his share in favour of his estate or, alternatively, that the joint tenancy had been severed by the oral agreement to sell. The woman claimed that the house was hers by survivorship. The Court of Appeal unanimously held that the joint tenancy had been severed. That was of course sufficient to dispose of the case but there was a difference of opinion as to whether there was also a resulting trust. Browne L.J. and Sir John Pennycuick held that, since the man alone had entered into the conveyance in contemplation of marriage and he had not communicated that purpose to the woman, there was no common purpose which could fail so as to give rise to a resulting trust. On the other hand, Lord Denning M.R. considered that where parties contemplate different objects both of which fail, the position is the same as where their common object fails; consequently, the property is held on resulting trust for them in proportion to their payments. The view of the majority seems to be the more logical.

(D) Termination
It has been seen that a resulting trust comes into existence whenever there is a gap in the beneficial ownership. Accordingly, as was held in *Re Vandervell's Trusts (No. 2)*,[30] when that gap is filled by someone becoming beneficially entitled, or where a trust is expressly declared, the resulting trust comes to an end.[31]

3. *Bona Vacantia*

It has already been seen[32] that, where a beneficial interest has not been wholly disposed of, the property in question will in some circumstances be applied as *bona vacantia* rather than subject to a resulting trust. The doctrine of *bona vacantia* is also relevant where a beneficiary who is entitled to property dies wholly or partially intestate without any intestate successors. In these circumstances, it used to be necessary to distinguish between two classes of case: first, where the property is vested in trustees and, secondly, where it is vested in executors.

(A) Trustees
If property is vested in trustees upon trust absolutely for a beneficiary who is living when the interest takes effect and the beneficiary then dies intestate

---

[30] [1974] Ch. 269. The facts are stated *ante*, p. 54.
[31] *ibid.* at 320. No consideration was given as to the question of whether the equitable interest under the resulting trust should have been disposed of by writing in accordance with Law of Property Act 1925, s.53(1)(c); see *ante*, p. 45.
[32] See *ante*, pp. 257–261.

leaving no one entitled to take as his intestate successor, there cannot possibly be a resulting trust because the beneficial interest will have effectively vested in the beneficiary during his lifetime.

Where the property in question is personalty, it is clearly established that in such circumstances the beneficial interest belongs to the Crown as *bona vacantia*; it has no owner and must devolve accordingly. This has always been the law.

Where, on the other hand, the property in question is realty, the position was at one time different. The law used to be that the trustee took it beneficially because the Court of Chancery did not apply the law of escheat to interests in real property. However, the law was changed first by the Intestates Estates Act 1884[33] and then by the Administration of Estates Act 1925; consequently, if a person dies after 1925 without testate or intestate successors, his real estate, like his personal estate, will go as *bona vacantia* to the Crown.[34]

(B) Executors

So far as vesting of property in executors is concerned, the position at law at one time was that, if a testator died without having disposed of his residuary estate, his executors were entitled to it if the residue was personal estate or to the extent to which it consisted of personalty. Further, equity followed the rule of common law unless it was shown, on a true construction of the will, that the testator intended to exclude the executors from taking a benefit; if such an intention could be shown, they would of course hold as trustees for the testator's statutory next-of-kin.[35]

However, the law was changed by the Executors Act 1830, which provided that executors should hold as trustees for the next-of-kin unless it could be shown from the will that it was intended they should take beneficially. This statute had the effect of shifting the burden of proof from the next-of-kin to the executors. However, the executors nevertheless remained entitled to the residuary personalty beneficially if there were no next-of-kin. This last loophole was eventually closed by the Administration of Estates Act 1925, which provided that, even in the absence of persons entitled on intestacy, the executors will hold all the undisposed of property of their testator as *bona vacantia*; this rule will only be overridden if the will clearly shows that the executors are to take beneficially.[36]

V. OTHER POSSIBLE TYPES OF IMPLIED OR RESULTING TRUSTS

It has on occasions been contended[37] that resulting trusts can also arise as a result of an ineffective transfer, where for example property has been transferred under a transaction which is void *ab initio*, under a transaction which

---

[33] ss.4, 7.
[34] Administration of Estates Act 1925, ss.45, 46.
[35] See *ante*, p. 82.
[36] ss.46, 49.
[37] By Chambers, *Resulting Trusts* (1997) *passim*. See also the authorities discussed *post*, pp. 721–725.

is voidable, or as the result of a mistake. The objective of such contentions is to enable the transferor to assert that he has retained a sufficient equitable proprietary interest in the property transferred to be able to bring an equitable proprietary claim against the transferee, usually in order to obtain priority over the latter's general creditors[38] but sometimes, when the property transferred is money, in order to obtain compound rather than simple interest thereon.[39] The possibility of such a resulting trust arising where the transaction under which the property was transferred is void *ab initio* was rejected by the House of Lords in *Westdeutsche Landesbank Girozentrale v. Islington L.B.C.*,[40] in which doubt was also cast on the possibility of such a resulting trust arising as a result of a mistaken transfer. However, considerable doubt remains about both the latter situation and the situation where property has been transferred under a transaction which is voidable. The authorities are discussed in detail later on in the context of the rules governing equitable proprietary claims.[41] In so far as there is indeed any authority for the existence of a resulting trust in any of these situations, it is considered that that authority cannot be supported as a matter of principle and should not be followed.

---

[38] As in *Chase Manhattan Bank v. Israel-British Bank (London)* [1981] Ch. 105.
[39] As in *Westdeutsche Landesbank Girozentrale v. Islington L.B.C.* [1996] A.C. 669.
[40] [1996] A.C. 669.
[41] See *post*, pp. 721–725.

CHAPTER 10

CONSTRUCTIVE TRUSTS

I. INTRODUCTION[1]

1. The Nature of Constructive Trusts

CONSTRUCTIVE trusts arise by operation of law. Unlike all other trusts, a constructive trust is imposed by the court as a result of the conduct of the trustee and therefore arises quite independently of the intention of any of the parties. Exactly which trusts fall within this definition cannot be stated with the same precision. As Edmund Davies L.J. remarked in *Carl-Zeiss Stiftung v. Herbert Smith (No. 2)*,[2] "English law provides no clear and all-embracing definition of a constructive trust. Its boundaries have been left perhaps deliberately vague, so as not to restrict the court by technicalities in deciding what the justice of a particular case may demand." Judges have preferred to describe constructive trusts rather than to define them; thus Deane J. in *Muschinski v. Dodds*[3] described the constructive trust as "a remedial institution which equity imposes regardless of actual or presumed agreement or intention (and subsequently protects) to preclude the retention or assertion of beneficial ownership to property to the extent that such retention or assertion would be contrary to equitable principle".

The lack of a precise definition makes it difficult to determine precisely what trusts may properly be classified as constructive trusts. The line of distinction between express and constructive trusts has been blurred by the fact that, until the enactment of the Limitation Act 1939, express trustees were unable to rely on the Statutes of Limitation as against the beneficiaries whereas the limitation period ran in favour of potential constructive trustees; this encouraged the courts to classify as express trusts certain trusts which were clearly nothing of the sort.[4] There has also been, historically, some confusion between resulting trusts and constructive trusts and, as has already been seen,[5] some judges have continued to use the terms almost

---

[1] This topic is considered in much greater detail in Oakley, *Constructive Trusts* (3rd ed., 1997), the 2nd edition of which formed the basis of this chapter in the previous (6th) edition of this work. See also A. W. Scott: (1955) 71 L.Q.R. 39; Waters, *The Constructive Trust* (1965); Elias, *Explaining Constructive Trusts* (1990); Cope, *Constructive Trusts* (1992); Goff & Jones, *The Law of Restitution* (4th ed., 1993), Chap. 2; Ford & Lee, *Principles of the Law of Trusts* (3rd ed.), Chap. 22; Hayton & Marshall: *Commentary and Cases on the Law of Trusts and Equitable Remedies* (10th ed., 1996), Chap. 7.

[2] [1969] 2 Ch. 276 at 300.

[3] (1985) 62 A.L.R. 429 at 451 (High Court of Australia).

[4] See *Soar v. Ashwell* (1893) 2 Q.B. 390.

[5] See *ante*, p. 41.

interchangeably when endeavouring to establish the existence and extent of beneficial ownership of residential family property.[6] However, some classifications are well established, long settled, and generally agreed. All the commentators accept that the following three situations give rise to the imposition of a constructive trust: first, where advantages have been obtained by fiduciaries breaching their duty of loyalty[7]; secondly, where strangers have intermeddled with property subject to a trust[8]; and, thirdly, where advantages have been obtained by fraudulent or unconscionable conduct.[9] However, there are certain other types of trust whose classification is more controversial. Such trusts include secret trusts,[10] mutual wills,[11] and the trusts which arise as a result of the creation of contracts of sale which are specifically enforceable,[12] as a result of the exercise by mortgagees of their powers under their mortgage,[13] and in order to give effect in equity to transfers of property which are at law incomplete.[14] These types of trust are extremely difficult to classify and have been classified in many different ways by different commentators. It is, however, suggested that all these trusts other than secret trusts should in fact properly be classified as constructive trusts.

The imposition of a constructive trust potentially produces liabilities both of a proprietary and of a personal nature for the constructive trustee. Given the inherent nature of a trust as a relationship in respect of property, the imposition of a constructive trust necessarily confers on the beneficiary proprietary rights in the subject matter of the constructive trust, while the constructive trustee is necessarily subject to the liability which is imposed on every trustee to account personally to his beneficiary for his actions as trustee. However, the court is able to specify the precise moment at which the constructive trust takes effect and, consequently, the moment at which these proprietary rights and fiduciary obligations come into existence. As Millett J. observed in *Lonhro Plc v. Fayed (No. 2)*,[15] "it is a mistake to suppose that in every situation in which a constructive trust arises the legal owner is necessarily subject to all the fiduciary obligations and disabilities of an express trustee".

It might be expected to follow from the inherent nature of a trust that a constructive trust can only be imposed if there is some identifiable property upon which to impose it, in other words that the property which is the subject matter of the trust must be able to be identified in the hands of the constructive trustee, either at the time when the matter is brought before the courts or at some earlier stage. There is indeed authority for this proposition.[16] However, there are a number of decided cases in which constructive

---

[6] See *Hussey v. Palmer* [1972] 1 W.L.R. 1286 at 289.
[7] See Section II of this Chapter, *post*, p. 281.
[8] See Section III of this Chapter, *post*, p. 319.
[9] See Section IV of this Chapter, *post*, p. 350.
[10] See *ante*, p. 62.
[11] See Section V of this Chapter, *post*, p. 367.
[12] See Section VI of this Chapter, *post*, p. 374.
[13] See Section VII of this Chapter, *post*, p. 376.
[14] See ante, p. 131 and Section VIII of this Chapter, *post*, p. 377.
[15] [1992] 1 W.L.R. 1 at 12.
[16] *Re Barney* [1892] 2 Ch. 265 at 273.

trusts have been imposed where there has been no obviously identifiable property subject to the trust; in all of these cases, the person upon whom the constructive trust was imposed had in one way or another dishonestly assisted in bringing about a disposition of trust property in breach of trust.[17] The existence of these authorities has led some commentators to contend that there is a second type of constructive trust which can arise without any necessity for there to be any identifiable trust property,[18] a view which has recently received powerful support from Lord Browne-Wilkinson in *Westdeutsche Landesbank Girozentrale v. Islington L.B.C.*[19] This alleged second type of constructive trust obviously does not confer any proprietary rights on the beneficiary thereunder but merely imposes on the constructive trustee a personal liability to account to the beneficiary for his actions. For this reason, the constructive trust so imposed has been described as "a fiction which provides a useful remedy where no remedy is available in contract or in tort".[20] It has to be admitted that it is virtually impossible to justify some of the existing authorities without accepting the argument that there is indeed such a second kind of constructive trust; nevertheless, it is not easy to see how an obligation which is not imposed in respect of any identifiable property can properly be classified as a trust. Indeed Ungoed-Thomas J. stated in *Selangor United Rubber Estates v. Cradock (No. 3)*[21] that this type of constructive trust "is nothing more than a formula for equitable relief. The court of equity says that the defendant shall be liable in equity, as though he were a trustee". In accordance with this reasoning, it seems more appropriate to regard these decisions not as examples of the imposition of a constructive trust but rather as examples of equity imposing a quite distinct remedy—a personal liability to account in the same manner as a trustee. This view was confirmed in *Agip (Africa) v. Jackson*[22] by Millett J., who adopted this terminology.[23] However, it has to be admitted that, as Lord Browne-Wilkinson's remarks clearly demonstrate, most of the judges have continued to describe those guilty of dishonest assistance of this type as constructive trustees.

2. *The Effect of the Imposition of a Constructive Trust*[24]

(A) When and How Does a Constructive Trust Take Effect?

It is important to know at precisely what moment a constructive trust takes effect for a number of reasons. The moment at which the constructive trust takes effect will determine the extent to which the rights of the constructive beneficiary will be binding upon third parties, whether the general creditors

---

[17] See Section III of this Chapter, *post*, p. 319.
[18] See Ford & Lee: *op.cit.*, para. 22020 and previous editions of Hayton & Marshall: *op.cit.* (*e.g.* the 9th ed., 1991, pp. 440–441).
[19] [1996] A.C. 669 at 705. "The only apparent exception to this rule [that there must be identifiable trust property] is a constructive trust imposed on a person who dishonestly assists in a breach of trust."
[20] D. J. Hayton (1985) 27 Malaya Law Review 313, 314.
[21] [1968] 1 W.L.R. 1555 at 1582.
[22] [1990] Ch. 265 at 291.
[23] It has also been adopted by some Commonwealth judges.
[24] See *Equity and Contemporary Legal Developments* (ed. Goldstein, 1992) p. 427.

of the constructive trustee or any person to whom the property which forms the subject matter of the constructive trust has been transferred. Further, as from the moment at which the constructive trust takes effect, the constructive beneficiary will be entitled to any income or other fruits produced by the property which forms the subject matter of the constructive trust. It seems to be generally accepted that, in the absence of any judicial order to the contrary, a constructive trust will take effect from the moment at which the conduct which has given rise to its imposition occurs. This was specifically held by Browne-Wilkinson J. in *Re Sharpe (a Bankrupt)*[25] and has been assumed without discussion on many other occasions. It is for this reason that the interest of a beneficiary under a constructive trust is binding on the trustee in bankruptcy of the constructive trustee and takes priority over the claims of his general creditors[26]; such an interest is also capable of taking priority over third party purchasers of the property or interests therein[27] provided that the third party in question has not taken free of the beneficial interest in question.[28] Further, any order that the constructive trustee should account for income or profits has effect as from the date upon which the constructive trust took effect.[29] Since the vast majority of constructive trusts are imposed because of the circumstances in which the constructive trustee has acquired the property which forms the subject matter of the constructive trust, that trust will therefore normally take effect from the moment at which the constructive trustee acquires the property in question. However, this is not an absolute rule; there are circumstances in which the conduct which has given rise to the imposition of a constructive trust occurs only some time after the acquisition of the property by the constructive trustee.[30] In this case, consistent with the general rule, the constructive trust will obviously only take effect from the moment at which that conduct occurred.

It is, however, clear that the general rule is capable of being varied by the court in any individual case. The court is free to specify the precise moment at which the constructive trust takes effect and can therefore modify the effect of its imposition both on third parties and on the constructive trustee himself. Thus, in *Muschinski v. Dodds*[31] the High Court of Australia imposed a constructive trust to give effect to a variation in the beneficial interests in property purchased by an unmarried couple but expressly held that, in order to avoid any possible prejudice to third parties, the constructive trust imposed in that case would take effect only as from the date of the publication of the judgments. In the same sort of way, in *Lonhro v. Fayed (No. 2)*[32] Millett J. stated that, in the event that the victim of a fraudulent misrepresentation elects to avoid the contract, the representor thereafter holds its subject matter on constructive trust for him but is not retrospectively

---

[25] [1980] 1 W.L.R. 219 at 225.
[26] As was held in *Re Sharpe (a Bankrupt)* [1980] 1 W.L.R. 219 at 225.
[27] As in *Belmont Finance Corporation v. Williams Furniture (No. 2)* [1980] 1 All E.R. 393.
[28] As in *Thompson's Trustee v. Heaton* [1974] 1 W.L.R. 605.
[29] As in *Boardman v. Phipps* [1967] 2 A.C. 46.
[30] As in *Bannister v. Bannister* [1948] W.N. 261; *Lyus v. Prowsa Developments* [1982] 2 All E.R. 953 and *Ungurian v. Lesnoff* [1989] 3 W.L.R. 840.
[31] (1986) 160 C.L.R. 583.
[32] [1992] 1 W.L.R. 1 at 11–12.

subject to all the fiduciary obligations of an express trustee in respect of the period before the contract was avoided. These statements merely re-emphasise the universality of the general rule.

Where there is some disagreement between the commentators, on the other hand, is over the question of whether or not a constructive trust can only take effect as the result of a court order providing for its imposition.[33] This question was considered in *Chase Manhattan Bank v. Israel (British) Bank*[34] by Goulding J., who held that, at least under the law of the State of New York (with which the case was primarily concerned), a court order is not necessary. This view was also adopted by a bare majority of the Supreme Court of Canada in *Rawluk v. Rawluk*.[35] As will be seen later in this section, the common law jurisdictions of both Canada and the United States of America recognise the constructive trust as a general equitable remedy, something which English law has so far declined to do. Consequently, it is suggested that, at least in this jurisdiction, the better view is that a constructive trust should be able to take effect only as the result of a court order. The manner in which this question is resolved does not in any way affect priorities as between the beneficiary and third parties but may affect the fiscal position of the beneficiary; if a constructive trust can take effect without any need for a court order, the beneficiary may find himself liable to income tax and capital gains tax on an interest arising under a constructive trust which he has never claimed and never enjoyed. It is therefore very much to the advantage of the beneficiary that a constructive trust should not be able to take effect without a court order.

(B) The Position of the Constructive Beneficiary

(1) The distinct proprietary and personal liabilities of the constructive trustee

The position of the constructive beneficiary who chooses to rely on his proprietary rights will obviously primarily depend on the precise nature of the constructive trust which has been imposed; he will clearly have the rights appropriate to the interest in the trust property to which he has been held to be entitled. In the event that the beneficiary is held to have an absolute interest in the property which forms the subject matter of the constructive trust, he will obviously be entitled to call for the transfer of the property to him together with any income or other fruits which the property has produced since the moment at which the constructive trust took effect.[36] In the event that the beneficiary is held to have some lesser interest in the

---

[33] The disagreement is between the two principal American practitioners works, Scott on Trusts and Bogert: *Trusts* and *Trustees*.

[34] [1981] Ch. 105 *passim*.

[35] (1990) 65 D.L.R. (4th) 161.

[36] See *Re Duke of Marlborough* [1894] 2 Ch. 133; *Re Macadam* [1946] Ch. 73, discussed *post*, p. 652; *Williams v. Barton* [1927] 2 Ch. 9, discussed *post*, p. 292; *Lyell v. Kennedy* (1889) 14 App.Cas. 437, discussed *post*, p. 323; *Belmont Finance Corporation v. Williams Furniture (No. 2)* [1980] 1 All E.R. 393, discussed *post*, p. 343.

subject-matter of the constructive trust, his position, at least in relation to the property, will be exactly the same as if the interest in question had been expressly created. Thus, where the beneficiary of a constructive trust is held to have a concurrent interest in the property which forms its subject matter,[37] his rights to enforce that interest against a third party or to obtain an order for sale of the property will be determined by exactly the same criteria as apply to a co-ownership which has arisen as the result of an express or statutory trust of land.[38] The position is similar where the beneficiary is held to have a limited interest in the subject-matter of the constructive trust; thus when a constructive trust is imposed to enforce lifetime occupancy rights, the life interest thus conferred on the beneficiary will take effect as if it had been expressly created.[39] It is also possible, although much less common in practice, for the constructive beneficiary to be given an interest in the subject-matter of the constructive trust by way of lien or charge in order to secure his right to a payment; this has been done[40] to secure a profit made by agents of a trust who utilised confidential income acquired in the course of representing the trust to acquire with their own funds a majority share-holding in a private company of which the trust was a substantial minority shareholder—had the profit not been paid over, the beneficiary, like the holder of any other charge, could have forced a sale of the shares.

If the beneficiary chooses instead to rely on the personal liability of the constructive trustee to account, he will in effect be claiming equitable compensation for breach of trust from the constructive trustee. He will thus recover the value of whatever interest he is held to have in the subject matter of the constructive trust, valued as at the moment at which the constructive trust took effect, together with interest thereon. (This is also the measure of recovery in the alleged second type of constructive trusts, better regarded as examples of equity imposing a personal liability to account in the same manner as a trustee.[41]) Since such reliance on the personal liability of the constructive trustee to account is normally[42] alternative to reliance on the proprietary rights held by the beneficiary in the subject matter of the con-structive trust, payment by the constructive trustee of the appropriate sum will have the effect of discharging those proprietary rights; consequently, the

---

[37] By virtue of having made direct or indirect financial or other contributions towards its acquisition. See *Burns v. Burns* [1984] Ch. 317 and *Grant v. Edwards* [1986] Ch. 638, discussed *post*, p. 363.

[38] These criteria are now contained in the Trusts of Land and Appointment of Trustees Act 1996.

[39] Under a trust of land pursuant to the Trusts of Land and Appointment of Trustees Act 1996. Prior to this legislation, such a beneficiary would usually become a tenant for life under the Settled Land Act 1925 which had the inconvenient result of conferring on him full admin-istrative powers to deal with the property (see *Ungurian v. Lesnoff* [1990] Ch. 206 and *Costello v. Costello* [1996] 1 F.L.R. 805). However, under the new legislation, these powers remain vested in the constructive trustee.

[40] In *Phipps v. Boardman* [1964] 1 W.L.R 993 (Ch. Div.)—this decision was subsequently affirmed by both appellate courts without any comments being made as to the nature of the con-structive trust imposed.

[41] See *ante*, p. 267 and *post*, p. 323.

[42] Save in the unusual situation where the beneficiary seeks to rely on both the remedies available to him. See the next paragraph.

constructive trustee will thereafter be absolutely beneficially entitled to the
property upon which the constructive trust was imposed.[43]

(2) The choice of remedy when the property is still in the hands of the constructive trustee

When the property upon which the constructive trust is imposed is still
identifiable in the hands of the constructive trustee, the beneficiary will be
able to choose either to exercise his proprietary rights in the subject matter
of the constructive trust, or to rely on the personal liability of the constructive trustee to account or, in rare circumstances, to exercise both of these
remedies. Where the constructive trustee is solvent, the election between
these two remedies will not normally have any particularly significant
effects on the measure of the recovery of the beneficiary. As has already been
seen, reliance on his proprietary rights will entitle the beneficiary to recover
the appropriate interest in the property together with any income or other
fruits which the property has produced since the moment at which the constructive trust took effect, while reliance on the personal liability of the
constructive trustee to account will entitle the beneficiary to recover the
value of the appropriate interest at the moment at which the constructive
trust took effect together with interest thereon. Consequently, if any increase
in the value of the property plus the value of any income or other fruits
which it has produced is more or less the same as the interest payable on the
value of the property since the moment at which the constructive trust took
effect, there will be no financial advantage in the beneficiary electing for one
remedy rather than for the other. This is only likely not to be the case in the
event of a substantial rise or a substantial fall in the value of the property,
when it will obviously be to the advantage of the beneficiary to opt respectively for his proprietary rights or for the personal liability of the constructive trustee to account. The only exception to this will be where it can
be shown that any fall in the value of the property was the responsibility of
the constructive trustee. In this event, there seems no reason why the
beneficiary should not alternatively seek to rely on both the remedies available to him; if this is indeed possible, he will be able both to claim the
appropriate interest in the property in question and, by relying on the
personal liability of the constructive trustee to account, to obtain damages
for the fall in value of the property. While this will not of course increase the
total measure of recovery, it will enable the beneficiary to recover the
property itself. There seems no reason whatsoever why such a process
should not be possible in an appropriate case.

Where, on the other hand, the constructive trustee is insolvent, the election between the two remedies will be immensely significant. If the beneficiary chooses to rely on his proprietary rights, he will take priority over the
general creditors of the insolvent constructive trustee, whereas if he instead
chooses to rely on the personal liability of the constructive trustee to

---

[43] Thus, once the agents of the trust referred to in the previous paragraph had paid their profit
to the constructive beneficiary, they would have once again become absolute owners of the
shares which they had purchased and could have retained them indefinitely. However, in
such circumstances prudence would normally dictate an immediate sale of the shares at that
point in order to forestall any possibility of the beneficiary coming back with a claim for
future income or capital profits.

account, he will rank with, rather than ahead of, the general creditors. Consequently, the only situation in which the beneficiary is likely to choose to rely on the personal liability of the constructive trustee to account will be where the property which is the subject matter of the constructive trust has fallen in value to a percentage of its original value smaller than the percentage which is likely to be paid out by the trustee in bankruptcy to the general creditors. In such circumstances, in the event that it can be shown that the constructive trustee was responsible for the fall in value of the property, it will always be in the interest of the beneficiary to take advantage of the possibility of relying on both the remedies available to him in order both to recover the appropriate interest in the property in question and to claim damages for the fall in its value; this is because such a double claim will give him both the property and the same percentage of the claim for damages as is paid out to the general creditors. However, except in the extremely unlikely situation which has just been considered, the beneficiary will, in the event of the insolvency of the constructive trustee, inevitably choose to rely on his proprietary rights so as to obtain priority over the general creditors. This will in turn diminish the mass of general assets available for distribution among the general creditors of the insolvent trustee so that each general creditor will therefore obtain a smaller proportion of the sum owed to him. Thus, the imposition of a constructive trust upon a person who is, or subsequently becomes, bankrupt will almost inevitably prejudice the interests of his general creditors, who will *ex hypothesi* not be before the court to object to the imposition of the constructive trust in question. In such circumstances, the only possibility of avoiding the consequent prejudice to the interests of the general creditors will be for the trustee in bankruptcy of the constructive trustee to go to the court under section 340 of the Insolvency Act 1986[44] in order to seek an order setting aside the constructive trust on the grounds that its imposition has given a preference to the beneficiary. Such a claim was successfully made in *Re Densham (A Bankrupt)*[45] but, as that case demonstrates, it is often a matter of pure chance whether the legislation is applicable and so this possibility cannot be regarded as a substantial safeguard for the interests of the general creditors.

(3) The choice of remedy when the property is no longer in the hands of the constructive trustee

When the property upon which the constructive trust is imposed is no longer identifiable in the hands of the constructive trustee, the property may nevertheless still be identifiable in the hands of a third party. In such circumstances, it will be possible to recover the property by tracing it in equity into the hands of that third party, unless the latter is able to establish one of the accepted defences to the beneficiary's equitable proprietary claims; these include bona fide purchase for value of a legal interest in the property without notice of the adverse claim of the beneficiary under the constructive trust (or, in the case of property not subject to the equitable doctrine of notice, the statutory equivalent thereof) and change of position.

---

[44] See *ante*, p. 227.
[45] [1975] 1 W.L.R. 1519 (this case concerned the previous statutory provision, Bankruptcy Act 1914, s.42).

Such an equitable proprietary claim is possible because the imposition of a constructive trust gives rise to the relationship of trustee and beneficiary which, on any view, is sufficient to satisfy the prerequisites of such a claim.[46] Where the trust property can be followed in this way into the hands of a third party, the situation will differ very little from that which has already been discussed. The beneficiary will have a choice between, on the one hand, exercising his proprietary rights in the subject matter of the constructive trust by following that property into the hands of the third party and, on the other hand, relying on the personal liability of the constructive trustee to account. The election between the two remedies will be dependant on exactly the same factors as have already been discussed. Where both the third party and the constructive trustee are solvent, the only relevant factors will be any changes in the value of the property, the presence or absence of income and other fruits, and the amount of interest payable by the constructive trustee. Where, on the other hand, the constructive trustee is insolvent, the beneficiary will almost always choose to rely on his proprietary rights and pursue his equitable proprietary claim against the third party.

It may, on the other hand, not be possible to recover the property upon which the constructive trust has been imposed. This will be the case where the property either has disappeared as the result of casual expenditure or dissipation by the constructive trustee or a third party, or has reached the hands of a third party against whom it is not possible to maintain an equitable proprietary claim because he is able to establish one of the accepted defences to such claims. In such circumstances, the only remedy available to the beneficiary will be to rely on the personal liability of the constructive trustee to account. Where the constructive trustee is solvent, this will not normally produce any particularly significant disadvantage. Where, on the other hand, the constructive trustee is insolvent, the absence of any proprietary rights will prevent the beneficiary from being able to claim priority over the general creditors of the constructive trustee since the liability of the constructive trustee to account will rank with, rather than ahead of, the claims of the general creditors.[47]

(4) The remedy where there has never been any identifiable property
It has already been seen[48] that some commentators have contended that there is a second kind of constructive trust, which can arise without any necessity for there to be any identifiable trust property, and that this view has recently received the powerful support of Lord Browne-Wilkinson.[49] Constructive trusts of this type allegedly arise where liability is imposed for dishonestly assisting in a disposition of trust property in breach of trust. It has already been suggested that it is preferable to regard this situation as an example of equity imposing a quite different remedy—a personal liability to account in the same manner as a trustee. No matter how this liability is classified, there is however no doubt at all about its nature. The absence of

[46] See *post*, p. 718.
[47] See *Selangor United Rubber Estates v. Cradock (No. 3)* [1968] 1 W.L.R. 1555.
[48] See *ante*, p. 267.
[49] In *Westdeutsche Landesbank Girozentrale v. Islington L.B.C.* [1996] A.C. 669 at 705.

any identifiable property prevents any proprietary claim from being available. Consequently, the person in whose favour liability for dishonest assistance is imposed has no choice of remedy; all that he can do is to rely on the personal rights thus conferred upon him. His rights will enjoy no priority over the general creditors of the person on whom liability has been imposed and will therefore rank with, rather than ahead of, the claims of those creditors in the event of insolvency.

3. *When and on what Grounds will a Constructive Trust be Imposed?*

The most important single factor that will determine when, and on what grounds, a constructive trust will be imposed is the role which the courts consider that the constructive trust occupies in the legal system as a whole. Their perception of this role must inevitably take into account the various possible consequences of the imposition of a constructive trust which have just been considered. In this respect, the different common law jurisdictions adopt different attitudes.

(A) The Attitude of the American Jurisdictions

All the common law jurisdictions of the United States of America have long adopted the attitude that the constructive trust is an instrument for remedying unjust enrichment. Thus a constructive trust may be imposed whenever the constructive trustee has been unjustly enriched by receiving some item of property at the expense of the constructive beneficiary. In other words, all that has to be shown is that the constructive trustee has received some item of property which, as against the constructive beneficiary, he cannot justly retain. This does not mean that a constructive trust will be imposed whenever unjust enrichment is found to exist; a constructive trust is merely one of a number of remedies available to the court and will be imposed when the court feels that it is appropriate to give the victim of the unjust enrichment a proprietary remedy.

The origin of this view of the constructive trust was the Restatement of the Law of Restitution published by the American Law Institute in 1937; paragraph 160 provides: "Where a person holding title to property is subject to an equitable duty to convey it to another on the ground that he would be unjustly enriched if he were permitted to retain it, a constructive trust arises." This provision unquestionably represents the attitude of American judges. As Cardozo J. has remarked[50]: "A constructive trust is the formula through which the conscience of equity finds expression. When property has been acquired in such circumstances that the holder of the legal title may not in good conscience retain the beneficial interest, equity converts him into a trustee." The principle of unjust enrichment is, in America, the underlying basis of the "principal types of situations in which a constructive trust is imposed"[51]; whether a constructive trust is imposed therefore depends on the presence or absence of unjust enrichment, not on whether the case can

---

[50] In *Beatty v. Guggenheim Exploration Co.* (1919) 225 N.Y. 380 at 386, 122 N.E. 378 (New York Court of Appeals).
[51] W. A. Seavey and A. W. Scott (1938) 54 L.Q.R. 29, 42.

be brought within one of the distinct situations which English law recognises as giving rise to the imposition of a constructive trust. However, the
principle of unjust enrichment is not applied rigidly; the American courts
will also impose constructive trusts where property is obtained by mistake
or by fraud or other wrong, whether or not the constructive trustee has been
unjustly enriched.[52] The extent to which the constructive trust is a remedy[53]
and the extent to which it is distinguished from both express and resulting
trusts is demonstrated by the fact that the constructive trust is not even
included within the definition of a trust in the Restatement of Trusts; indeed
constructive trusts are considered in the Restatement of Restitution rather
than in the Restatement of Trusts.

(B) The Attitude of the Canadian Jurisdictions

The Supreme Court of Canada recognised the principle of unjust enrichment
as a basis for the imposition of a constructive trust much more recently.[54]
The remedial constructive trust which thus became part of the law of the
common law jurisdictions of Canada has so far principally, but not exclusively,[55] been deployed in relation to joint enterprises by members of a
family unit.[56] However, the Supreme Court of Canada has specifically
declined to hold that unjust enrichment is a prerequisite of the imposition of
a constructive trust, instead holding that the remedial constructive trust
based on unjust enrichment exists side by side with the more traditional
situations in which constructive trusts have been imposed, which it has
classified as cases of wrongful conduct.[57] The court held that the principle
which underlies both types of constructive trust is the principle of "good
conscience", in other words that "a constructive trust may be imposed
where good conscience so requires".[58] The Supreme Court has also laid
down two series of criteria which determine whether a constructive trust
should be imposed on the grounds of, respectively, unjust enrichment[59] and
wrongful conduct.[60]

(C) The Attitude of the Remaining Common Law Jurisdictions

The remaining common law jurisdictions have not as yet accepted that the
unjust enrichment of the constructive trustee is, without more, a sufficient
ground for the imposition of a constructive trust. This has recently been

---

[52] Scott on *Trusts* (4th ed., 1989 with 1994 Appendix), para. 461.
[53] The remedial theory of the constructive trust is considered in Cope: *op.cit.*, pp. 24–49. See also
P. B. H. Birks and S. Gardner in *Frontiers of Liability* (ed. Birks, 1994), Vol. II, pp. 214, 186.
[54] In *Pettkus v. Becker* (1980) 117 D.L.R. (3d) 257.
[55] See *Lac Minerals v. International Corona Resources* (1989) 61 D.L.R. (4th) 14 (Supreme Court of
Canada).
[56] See *Pettkus v. Becker* (1980) 117 D.L.R. (3d) 257; *Sorochan v. Sorochan* (1986) 29 D.L.R. (4th) 1 and
Peter v. Beblow (1993) 101 D.L.R. (4th) 621 (all decisions of the Supreme Court of Canada). The
present Canadian law is considered by D. W. M. Waters in *Equity and Contemporary Legal
Developments* (ed. Goldstein, 1992), p. 457 and in *Frontiers of Liability*, (ed. Birks, 1994) Vol. II,
p. 165.
[57] *Korkontzilas v. Soulos* (1997) 146 D.L.R. (4th) 214.
[58] *ibid.* at p. 227, *per* McLachlin J., who cited some rather unrepresentative statements to this
effect in English and New Zealand authorities.
[59] In *Pettkus v. Becker* (1980) 117 D.L.R. (3d) 257 at 273–274.
[60] *In Korkantzilas v. Soulas* (1997) 146 D.L.R. (4th) 214 at 231.

illustrated in this jurisdiction by the decision of the Court of Appeal in *Halifax Building Society v. Thomas*.[61] The defendant obtained a mortgage advance from the plaintiff by fraudulently misrepresenting his identity and earnings. The plaintiff, having satisfied all sums due to it under the mortgage out of the proceeds of sale, sought to retain the surplus on the basis, *inter alia*, that it was beneficially entitled under a constructive trust imposed on the defendant in accordance with the American Restatement of Restitution to prevent what would otherwise be his unjust enrichment. The Court of Appeal specifically held that "English law has not followed other jurisdictions where the constructive trust has become a remedy for unjust enrichment" and declined "to extend the law of constructive trusts in order to prevent a fraudster benefitting from his wrong".[62]

This is not to say that there have never been any other attempts to introduce the principles adopted in North America into English law. In the years immediately before and after 1970, it did appear that English law might be moving towards an approach similar to that which was subsequently adopted in Canada. At that time, a number of decisions emanating from the Court of Appeal suggested that a constructive trust "is a trust imposed by law whenever justice and good conscience require it . . . it is an equitable remedy by which the court can enable an aggrieved party to obtain restitution".[63] However, subsequent decisions[64] rejected the approach manifested in this series of cases and English law seems for the moment to have reverted to its traditional attitude towards the constructive trust, an attitude which has perhaps been most accurately described by the statement that in England "the constructive trust continues to be seen as an institutional obligation attaching to property in certain specified circumstances".[65]

Although the constructive trust is therefore not at present a remedy for unjust enrichment, there have, however, been some indications in the last few years of the possibility of a move towards a more remedial approach. In *Metall und Rohstoff A.G. v. Donaldson Lufkin & Jenrette*[66] the Court of Appeal accepted that "there is a good arguable case" that circumstances may arise in which "the court will be prepared to impose a constructive trust *de novo* as a foundation for the grant of equitable remedy by way of account or otherwise", classifying such a trust as a "remedial constructive trust". Subsequently, in *Westdeutsche Landesbank Girozentrale v. Islington L.B.C.*,[67] these

---

[61] [1996] Ch. 217.

[62] At 229. The surplus had anyway been the subject of a confiscation order under Criminal Justice Act 1988, Pt. 6 in favour of the Crown Prosecution Service so the case was effectively between the plaintiff and the Crown Prosecution Service.

[63] *Hussey v. Palmer* [1972] 1 W.L.R. 1286 at 1290, *per* Lord Denning M.R., who was the principal advocate of this particular development.

[64] See *Burns v. Burns* [1984] Ch. 317; *Grant v. Edwards* [1986] Ch. 638; *Ashburn Anstalt v. Arnold* [1989] Ch. 1. This followed earlier rejections by the Court of Appeal of New South Wales in *Allen v. Snyder* [1977] 2 N.S.W.L.R. 685 and by the High Court of New Zealand in *Avondale Printers and Stationers v. Haggie* [1979] 2 N.Z.L.R. 124.

[65] D. W. M. Waters in *Equity and Contemporary Legal Developments* (ed. Goldstein, 1992), pp. 457, 463.

[66] [1990] 1 Q.B. 391 at 473–474.

[67] [1996] A.C. 669 at 715.

remarks were seized on by Lord Browne-Wilkinson as a possible justification for the decision of Goulding J. in *Chase Manhattan Bank v. Israel-British Bank (London)*[68] that a bank which had mistakenly paid the same sum twice rather than once to another bank could maintain an equitable proprietary claim against it. Lord Browne-Wilkinson took the view that "the retention of the moneys after the recipient bank learned of the mistake may well have given rise to a constructive trust"[69] and opined that "the remedial constructive trust, if introduced into English law, may provide a more satisfactory road forward".[70] Similar sentiments have been voiced in Australia and in New Zealand.[71] However, Lord Browne-Wilkinson clearly stated that "whether English law should follow the United States and Canada in adopting the remedial constructive trust will have to be decided in some future case when the point is directly in issue".[72] There can therefore be little doubt that the House of Lords will one day soon be called upon to decide whether to return to the trail blazed by the Court of Appeal immediately before and after 1970 or to retain the more traditional approach adopted before and after that period. However, despite the apparent enthusiasm of Lord Browne-Wilkinson for the remedial constructive trust, other senior judges have expressed very different sentiments. Sir Peter Millett, writing extra-judicially,[73] has described the remedial constructive trust as "a counsel of despair which too readily concedes the impossibility of propounding a general rationale for the availability of proprietary remedies". In the light of such observations, the outcome of the future deliberations of the House of Lords is certainly not a foregone conclusion.

Pending any such decision, the English courts, like those in Australia and in New Zealand, continue to see the constructive trust "as an institutional obligation attaching to property in certain specified circumstances"[74]; they have, generally speaking, only been prepared to impose a constructive trust when some cause of action against the constructive trustee has arisen independently. It is not enough to say, as in America, that a constructive trustee "is not compelled to convey the property because he is a constructive trustee; it is because he can be compelled to convey that he is a constructive trustee".[75] In order to obtain the imposition of a constructive trust, the beneficiary must be able to demonstrate some legal or equitable wrong by the constructive trustee, be it breach of fiduciary duty, participation in a breach of trust, or fraudulent or unconscionable conduct. Such developments in the law as have occurred have been brought about by the enlargement of the concepts of fiduciary relationship[76] and unconscionable

---

[68] [1981] Ch. 105. See *post*, p. 723.
[69] [1996] A.C. 669, 714. His lordship doubted the conclusion of Goulding J. that a mistaken payment is of itself sufficient to make the recipient a constructive trustee thereof.
[70] *ibid.* at 716.
[71] *Muschinski v. Dodds* (1985) 160 C.L.R. 583 at 615 (Deane J. in the High Court of Australia); *Gillies v. Keogh* [1989] 1 N.Z.L.R. 327 at 330 (Turner P. in the Court of Appeal of New Zealand).
[72] [1996] A.C. 669 at 716.
[73] (1995–96) 6 King's College L.J. 1.
[74] D. W. M. Waters in *Equity and Contemporary Legal Developments* (ed. Goldstein, 1992), pp. 457, 463. See also *Re Polly Peck International (No. 4)* (1998) *The Times*, May 18, 1998.
[75] Scott on *Trusts* (4th ed., 1987 with 1994 Appendix), para. 462.
[76] See section II of this Chapter, *post*, p. 281.

conduct[77] rather than by recourse to the principle of unjust enrichment. For the moment, therefore, the unjust enrichment of the constructive trustee is still not in itself sufficient.

(D) What Should Be the Attitude of English Law?

It has long been argued that the English courts should adopt the American approach, now also adopted in Canada, and also impose constructive trusts in order to prevent unjust enrichment. "What English law needs," wrote Professor Donovan Waters in 1964, "is a practical, down to earth remedy, as vivid as specific performance and injunction, and within which the courts are brought immediately face to face with the policy decisions or the equities that the courts must and do already make or weigh."[78] The principle of unjust enrichment has, however, been rejected by other commentators.[79] As is implicit in the recent judicial observations already considered,[80] there is in principle no reason why the categories of situations in which English courts will impose a constructive trust should be regarded as closed. However, the liabilities which arise as the result of the imposition of a constructive trust provide a strong argument against its use as a general equitable remedy to do justice in the instant case in the way in which it is used in North America.

The proprietary nature of the liabilities which arise as the result of the imposition of a constructive trust affects the existing property rights both of the constructive trustee and, in the event of his bankruptcy, of his general creditors. As a matter of principle, such alterations of existing property rights should not be able to ensue merely from the desire of a court to do justice in the instant case. It has never been the practice of English courts to alter existing property rights merely in order to do justice *inter partes*. The House of Lords has repeatedly stated that rights of property are not to be determined according to what is reasonable and fair or just in all the circumstances,[81] a principle which is crucial for the maintenance of that certainty which should be the hallmark of every system of law. The imposition of a constructive trust in order to bring a dispute to a conclusion which appears to be just and equitable in the way that the Court of Appeal did immediately before and immediately after 1970 is inevitably contrary to such a principle. The consequences of the imposition of a constructive trust thus constitute powerful arguments against the use of the constructive trust as a means of doing justice *inter partes*. These important considerations bear no weight in North America simply because the courts of the common law jurisdictions of the United States of America have for many decades been much more ready than the English courts to interfere with existing third party rights; there a claimant is permitted to bring an equitable proprietary

---

[77] See section IV of this Chapter, *post*, p. 350.
[78] *The Constructive Trust* (1964), p. 73.
[79] Cope, *op.cit.*, (1992), p. 48 (who is, however, prepared to accept that the constructive trust is remedial in nature); P. B. H. Birks in *Frontiers of Liability* (ed. Birks, 1994), Vol. II, pp. 214, 223 (who rejects the remedial constructive trust outright as "an object of suspicion").
[80] See *ante*, p. 266.
[81] *Pettitt v. Pettitt* [1970] A.C. 777; *Gissing v. Gissing* [1971] A.C. 886; *Lloyds Bank v. Rosset* [1991] 1 A.C. 107.

claim whenever he can show that that property has been wrongfully disposed of with knowledge of the wrongful nature of the disposition[82] (the existence of a pre-existing trust is not, as in English law, a prerequisite of such a claim[83]). A litigant thus permitted to bring an equitable proprietary claim will inevitably obtain priority over the third party creditors of the other party. (Canada seems to have adopted the same attitude in respect of remedial constructive trusts imposed in order to prevent unjust enrichment; however, the Supreme Court has specifically held[84] that for a constructive trust to be imposed on the grounds of wrongful conduct a legitimate reason must be shown for seeking a proprietary remedy[85] and there must be no factors such as the interests of intervening creditors which would render the imposition of a constructive trust unjust in all the circumstances.) Since the rights of third party creditors can thus so readily be altered, the fact that the imposition of a constructive trust brings about such an alteration of priorities is not a particularly significant consideration; there is therefore no reason why this should be specifically taken into account in deciding whether or not a constructive trust should be imposed. In England, on the other hand, the courts are extremely reluctant either to interfere with existing property rights or to grant priority over the general creditors of a bankrupt. Therefore, the fact that the imposition of a constructive trust has both these effects should be a much more significant consideration in England than in North America.

Since the imposition of a constructive trust has far-reaching ramifications not only for the person upon whom it is imposed but also for third parties, its indiscriminate invocation and imposition is, at least in England, therefore highly undesirable. The constructive trust should not be invoked in the way that the Court of Appeal did immediately before and immediately after 1970 as some sort of instant remedy to prevent what the court regards as an unjust result in an individual case. Thus, in this sense at least, constructive trusts should not be imposed merely in order to prevent unjust enrichment. This does not mean that the present process whereby the principle of unjust enrichment is gradually being incorporated into English law[86] should not continue, merely that the constructive trust is not an appropriate instrument for dealing out justice inter partes. Although the categories of situations in which English courts will impose constructive trusts should not be regarded as closed, these categories should be extended only where the courts are prepared to lay down some new principle which will apply generally, as the House of Lords has done on occasions in the past.[87] No such principle should be established without the fullest consideration of its probable effects

---

[82] American Restatement of the Law of Restitution, para. 202. See also A. W. Scott (1955) 71 L.Q.R. 39, 48.

[83] See post, p. 718.

[84] Korkontzilas v. Soulos (1997) 146 D.L.R. (4th) 214 at 231.

[85] A reason which is either personal or related to the need to ensure that others like the defendant remain faithful to their duties. ibid.

[86] Most recently in Lipkin Gorman v. Karpnale [1991] 2 A.C. 548 (in relation to the defence of change of position) see post p. 738 and in Woolwich Equitable Building Society v. I.R.C. [1993] A.C. 70 (in relation to the recovery of overpayments of taxes made under statutory instruments subsequently held to be ultra vires).

[87] As in Pettitt v. Pettitt [1970] A.C. 777; Gissing v. Gissing [1971] A.C. 886 and Lloyds Bank v. Rosset [1991] 1 A.C. 107.

on the interests of third parties and of the possibility of reducing these effects by varying the normal consequences of the imposition of a constructive trust in the way which was done in *Muschinski v. Dodds*[88] and envisaged in *Lonhro v. Fayed (No. 2)*.[89] Finally, any principle laid down must above all be capable of being applied with sufficient certainty to enable litigants to be safely advised as to the probable outcome of legal proceedings.

II. Advantages Obtained by Fiduciaries Breaching their Duty of Loyalty

One of the best known situations in which constructive trusts are imposed is where a fiduciary has obtained a benefit as a result of a breach of the duty of loyalty which he owes to his principal.[90]

1. *What Relationships will be Classified as Fiduciary?*

A fiduciary "is, simply, someone who undertakes to act for or on behalf of another in some particular matter or matters. That undertaking may be of a general character. It may be specific and limited. It is immaterial whether the undertaking is gratuitous. And the undertaking may be officiously assumed without request".[91] A fiduciary is expected "to act in the interests of the other—to act selflessly and with undivided loyalty".[92] This obligation to act selflessly is what distinguishes a person who owes fiduciary obligations from a person who owes merely contractual obligations; the latter is permitted to act in his own self interest, provided that he does not engage in conduct which the courts are prepared to classify as unconscionable.[93]

The "category of cases in which fiduciary obligations and duties arise from the circumstances of the case and the relationship of the parties is no more closed than the categories of negligence at common law".[94] Certain relationships are always classified as fiduciary. Traditionally there have been four: trustee and beneficiary, agent and principal, director and company, and partner and co-partner—the relationship in question may either have been expressly created or have arisen as a result of the officious conduct of the alleged fiduciary. It has also long been clear that the relationship between solicitor and client is fiduciary[95] and in recent years the existence of two further fiduciary relationships, between senior management employee and

---

[88] (1985) 160 C.L.R. 583; see *ante*, p. 269.

[89] [1992] 1 W.L.R. 1.

[90] Of the vast literature on this subject, the most relevant work for present purposes is Goff & Jones, *op.cit.* pp. 643–673. See also Finn: *Fiduciary Obligations* (1977) and in *Equity, Fiduciaries and Trusts* (ed. Youdan, 1989), pp. 1; Shepherd: *The Law of Fiduciaries* (1981) and Glover: *Commercial Equity: Fiduciary Relationships* (1995). A list of relevant articles can be found in *Constructive Trusts* (3rd ed., 1997), p. 85, nn. 1, 2.

[91] Finn: *Fiduciary Obligations* (1977), p. 201.

[92] Finn in *Equity, Fiduciaries and Trusts* (ed. Youdan, 1989), pp. 1, 4.

[93] *ibid.*

[94] *ibid.*

[95] This was implicit in *Nocton v. Lord Ashburton* [1914] A.C. 14 and was specifically held in *Brown v. I.R.C.* [1965] A.C. 244.

company[96] and between member of the Security Services and the Crown,[97] has been confirmed. Other jurisdictions have also added the relationships between doctor and patient[98] and between parent child-abuser and victim child[99] and are confidently expected to do the same in respect of the relationship between priest and parishioner.[1] The full range of fiduciary obligations and prohibitions is normally imposed on fiduciaries within these categories, although this does not mean that the position of each is actually the same.[2] The relationships between accountant and client, broker and client, promoter and company, and guardian and ward have also been held, in certain circumstances and in respect of specific transactions, to be fiduciary and a member of the armed forces of the Crown has even been held to be a fiduciary in respect of his uniform and the opportunities and facilities attached to it.[3] On the other hand, it has been held that a duty imposed by statute to perform certain functions does not, as a general rule, impose fiduciary obligations and that the presumption is, in the absence of indications to the contrary in the statute, that no such obligations are imposed[4]; it has also been held that the Crown will not become a fiduciary unless it deliberately chooses so to do.[5]

Whether the traditional categories of fiduciary relationships should be enlarged and whether fiduciary obligations should be imposed outside the traditional categories should in principle depend on whether the situation in question falls within the definition of a fiduciary relationship. In fact, however, few comprehensive definitions have ever been suggested and none of those suggested has ever received any general approval. Consequently, whether a relationship is classified as fiduciary has, in practice, depended on the extent to which it has satisfied the characteristics of a fiduciary relationship. These are generally recognised to be: the existence of an undertaking by the alleged fiduciary to the other party to the relationship; reliance placed on the alleged fiduciary by the other party to the relationship; property of the other party under the control of the alleged fiduciary; and vulnerability of the other party to the alleged fiduciary in that some power or discretion is vested in the latter which is capable of being used to affect the legal or practical interests of the former. None of these four characteristics is accepted to be of universal application (although the existence of an undertaking and, in particular, the existence of vulnerability are undoubtedly the most significant); however, each of them has, at one time or another, been

---

[96] *Sybron Corporation v. Rochem* [1984] Ch. 112 at 127.

[97] *Att.-Gen. v. Guardian Newspapers (No. 2)* [1990] 1 A.C. 109.

[98] *McInerney v. MacDonald* (1992) 93 D.L.R. (4th) 415 (Supreme Court of Canada); *S.E.C. v. Willis* (1992) 787 Fed.Supp. 58 (U.S. District Court, New York) and the other authorities cited by T. Frankel in *Equity, Fiduciaries and Trusts* 1993 (ed. Waters, 1993), p. 173.

[99] *M.(K.) v. M.(H.)* (1993) 96 D.L.R. (4th) 449 (Supreme Court of Canada). The courts have so far declined to classify non-parental child abusers as fiduciaries: *H. v. R.* [1996] 1 N.Z.L.R. 299 (New Zealand High Court).

[1] T. Frankel, *op.cit.*

[2] *Henderson v. Merrett Syndicates* [1995] 2 A.C. 145 at 205.

[3] *Reading v. Att.-Gen.* [1951] A.C. 507.

[4] *Tito v. Waddell (No. 2)* [1977] Ch. 106 at 235. See also *Swain v. The Law Society* [1983] A.C. 598, where the Law Society was held not to be in a fiduciary relationship with the members of the solicitors' profession.

[5] *Tito v. Waddell (No. 2)* [1977] Ch. 106 at 212.

held to be sufficient for the imposition of fiduciary obligations. Detailed consideration of these characteristics and the way in which they have been applied by the courts is outside the scope of a book on the law of trusts.[6] For present purposes, it is only necessary to consider the extent, if at all, to which fiduciary obligations should be upheld in commercial transactions.

The effect of imposing fiduciary duties on the parties to a commercial transaction is to expose those parties to the equitable remedies to which fiduciaries are potentially subject. Proceedings instituted in order to establish the existence of fiduciary obligations in a commercial transaction generally have as their primary objective the imposition on one of the parties of a constructive trust in favour of the other in respect of the benefits which the alleged fiduciary has obtained by entering into some related transaction on his own behalf.[7] The proprietary claim which such a trust automatically makes available to the other party is obviously capable of stripping away a substantial proportion of the assets of the fiduciary, particularly if the constructive trust is imposed in such a way as to deprive him of both the past and future profits of the transaction in question. These will be profits to which the fiduciary will have appeared to be entitled and whose disappearance is capable of reducing very considerably the assets available for his general creditors,[8] who will necessarily not be before the court to defend their interests. This is why the extent to which commercial relationships entered into at arm's length and on an equal footing should be held to give rise to fiduciary obligations has been the subject of so much discussion in recent years.

Many commercial transactions expressly create fiduciary relationships; this will be the case where it is expressly provided that one or more of the parties is subject to fiduciary obligations or where the transaction has expressly created a relationship which is always classified as fiduciary. Where this is not the case, the English courts have, generally speaking, been "mindful of the stern warnings uttered by Lindley L.J.[9] and Atkin L.J.[10] of the dangers of applying equitable doctrines to commercial transactions. To do so would paralyse the trade of the country and fundamentally affect the security of business transactions."[11] These warnings were specifically heeded by the Court of Appeal in *Polly Peck International v. Nadir (No. 2)*[12] in 1992. "There has been a natural reluctance to impose upon parties in a commercial relationship who are in a relatively equal position of strength the higher standards of conduct which equity prescribes. One manifestation of this reluctance is the disinclination of judges to find a fiduciary relationship when the arrangement between the parties is of a purely commercial

---

[6] These questions are considered in detail in *Constructive Trusts* (3rd ed., 1997), pp. 85–110.

[7] This is the principal motive but not the only one. Others include more favourable limitation periods and more favourable rules governing the assessment of damages.

[8] Indeed in *Re Goldcorp Exchange* [1995] 1 A.C. 74 (discussed *post*, p. 285), the objective was to obtain priority not only over the general creditors but also over a secured creditor, the holder of a floating charge (a charge over whatever assets a company may have at any one time).

[9] In *Manchester Trust v. Furness* [1895] 2 Q.B. 539 at 545.

[10] In *Re Wait* [1927] 1 Ch. 606 at 634 *et seq.*, especially 639–640.

[11] Sir Anthony Mason (when Chief Justice of Australia) extra-judicially, 110 L.Q.R. (1994) 238, 245.

[12] [1992] 4 All E.R. 769 at 782, *per* Scott L.J.

kind and they have dealt with each other at arm's length and on an equal footing."[13] This was undoubtedly the attitude adopted by the Privy Council on an appeal from Bermuda in *Kelly v. Cooper*,[14] also in 1992, in relation to an estate agency contract. The Privy Council held that, despite the fact that it is normally a breach of an agent's duty to act for competing principals, it is the business of estate agents to act for numerous principals and to acquire information which is confidential to each principal; that being so, the fiduciary duties owed by them to each principal were to be defined by the terms of the contract of agency. A similar view was adopted by Judge Paul Baker, Q.C. in *Re Stapylton Fletcher.*[15]

This attitude has also persisted in other jurisdictions[16]; however, the courts there now appear to be much more ready to hold that the parties have not been dealing on an equal footing. In such cases, the "fiduciary relationship has been the spearhead of equity's incursions into the area of commerce".[17] In Australia and in New Zealand, joint venture arrangements have very readily been held to give rise to fiduciary obligations[18] and in 1994 the then Chief Justice of Australia stated, extra-judicially, that "a fiduciary relationship will arise out of a commercial arrangement when one party undertakes to act in the interests of the other party rather than in his or her own interests in relation to a particular matter or aspect of their arrangement and that other party, being unable to look after his or her interests in that matter or aspect of the arrangement, is basically dependent upon the first party acting in conformity with his or her undertaking".[19] However, his views have yet to be carried into effect by the Australian courts. In Canada, the courts have expressed a willingness to impose fiduciary obligations in favour of any party to a commercial transaction who is vulnerable to the other, even where the vulnerability has arisen only by virtue of the relative sizes and resources of the two commercial enterprises involved, but have emphasised that it is only rarely that such vulnerability will be found to exist.[20]

What are the possibilities of English law adopting similar attitudes? The consequences of the imposition of fiduciary obligations both for the fiduciary himself and for his general creditors constitute strong arguments against the adoption in England of the approach advocated in the Commonwealth and any thoughts that English law might have been about to develop along those lines were rapidly disabused by the opinion of the Privy Council in *Re*

---

[13] Sir Anthony Mason, *op.cit.*, 245.

[14] [1993] A.C. 205.

[15] [1994] 1 W.L.R. 1181.

[16] *Jirna v. Master Donut of Canada* (1973) 40 D.L.R. (3d) 303 (Supreme Court of Canada); *United States Surgical Corporation v. Hospital Products International* (1984) 156 C.L.R. 41 (High Court of Australia).

[17] Sir Anthony Mason, *op.cit.*, 245.

[18] *United Dominion Corporation v. Brian* (1985) 157 C.L.R. 1.

[19] Sir Anthony Mason, *op.cit.*, 245–246, citing *Liggett v. Kensington* [1993] 3 N.Z.L.R. 257, where the Court of Appeal of New Zealand imposed fiduciary obligations upon a gold trader who had offered purchasers the option of leaving their bullion in the custody of the trader on the purchasers' behalf as "non-allocated bullion". This decision was subsequently reversed by the Privy Council *sub. nom. Re Goldcorp Exchange* [1995] 1 A.C. 74—see *post*, p. 285.

[20] *Lac Minerals v. International Corona Resources* (1989) 61 D.L.R.(4th) 14; *Hodgkinson v. Simms* (1994) 117 D.L.R.(4th) 161 (both Supreme Court of Canada).

Goldcorp Exchange in 1994.[21] This, curiously enough, was an appeal from the decision which constituted the principal authority cited by the Chief Justice of Australia in support of the proposition set out in the previous paragraph. The Court of Appeal of New Zealand[22] had imposed fiduciary obligations on a gold-dealer which had offered its purchasers the option of leaving their bullion in its custody on the purchasers' behalf as "non-allocated bullion". Purchasers who did so were issued with a certificate of ownership and were entitled to take physical possession of their bullion on seven days' notice. The Court of Appeal's conclusion that the company was a fiduciary was based on two propositions: first, that it was bound to protect the interests of the purchasers and, secondly, that it was, for all practical purposes, free from control and supervision by them.[23] The Privy Council, however, heeded the warnings of Lindley L.J. and Atkin L.J. to which reference has already been made. Lord Mustill said this:

"But what kind of fiduciary duties did the company owe to the customer? None have been suggested beyond those which the company assumed under the contracts of sale read with the collateral promises; ... No doubt the fact that one person is placed in a particular position *vis-a-vis* another through the medium of a contract does not necessarily mean that he does not also owe fiduciary duties to that other by virtue of being in that position. But the essence of a fiduciary relationship is that it creates obligations of a different character from those deriving from the contract itself. ... Many commercial relationships involve just such a reliance by one party on the other, and to introduce the whole new dimension into such relationships which would flow from giving them a fiduciary character would (as it seems to their Lordships) have adverse consequences far exceeding those foreseen by Atkin L.J. in *Re Wait*.[24] It is possible without misuse of language to say that the customers put faith in the company, and that their trust has not been repaid. But the vocabulary is misleading; high expectations do not necessarily lead to equitable remedies."

These observations seem to rule out, at least for the present, any possibility of English law developing along the lines of the Australian and New Zealand decisions even in respect of joint venture arrangements, never mind in accordance with the wider principles enunciated in the various Commonwealth jurisdictions. The attitude manifested by the Privy Council does have the great advantage that the interests of third parties cannot be prejudiced by the conversion of a general creditor into a preferential creditor as the result of the imposition of fiduciary obligations on a bankrupt. For this reason, it is hoped that, in the event that English law does one day develop along the lines advocated in the Commonwealth, the courts will not lose sight of the interests of third parties but will take them into account in the manner envisaged in the introductory section of this Chapter.

---

[21] [1995] 1 A.C. 74.
[22] [1993] 1 N.Z.L.R. 257.
[23] *ibid.* at 583, 584, *per* Cooke P.; at 596, 597, *per* Gault J. Compare the view of the dissentient, McKay J. at pp. 604, 605.
[24] [1927] 1 Ch. 606 at 634 *et seq.*, especially at 639–640.

2. The Nature of the Liability of Fiduciaries

In *Bray v. Ford*[25] Lord Herschell laid down two overlapping principles: a fiduciary cannot be permitted to profit from his fiduciary position and a fiduciary must not allow his personal interest to prevail over his duty of loyalty to his principal. The precise relationship between these two rules has been expressed in a number of ways. In *Swain v. The Law Society*[26] Stephenson L.J. regarded the first of these principles as merely one of the many examples of the second principle. However, it is clear that a fiduciary cannot profit from his fiduciary position even when there is no real conflict of interest and duty. Consequently, it is perhaps preferable to adopt the view of Deane J.[27] that the two principles "while overlapping, are distinct".

Within these principles, the attitude of English law towards fiduciaries is relatively consistent. Of course, as is only to be expected, the law differs from fiduciary relationship to fiduciary relationship.[28] This is the case even as between the traditional categories of fiduciary relationships; thus a director is in a more favourable position with regard to property transactions with his company than is a trustee with regard to property transactions with his trust. This apart, however, the attitude of English law towards fiduciaries is, generally speaking, a harsh one. As James L.J. remarked in *Parker v. McKenna*,[29] the rule that a fiduciary may not profit from his position without the knowledge and consent of his principal "is an inexorable rule, and must be applied inexorably by this court, which is not entitled, in my judgment, to receive evidence, or suggestion, or argument as to whether the principal did or did not suffer any injury in fact by reason of the dealing of the [fiduciary]". Not only is it thus irrelevant that the principal has suffered no loss; it is also irrelevant that the fiduciary acted in the utmost good faith and that his actions in fact benefitted his principal. This inexorable rule exists for reasons of policy, namely to avoid the remotest risk of a fiduciary being swayed from his duty of loyalty to his principal by his own self interest. However, the decided cases provide innumerable examples of courts penalising fiduciaries (particularly trustees) totally irrespective of whether there was any serious conflict between their duty of loyalty and their self interest. Only where the making of the profit in question has been authorised in advance in the instrument by which the fiduciary obligation was created or has received the fully informed prior consent or subsequent ratification of the principal is the fiduciary allowed to retain it.[30]

Lord Herschell remarked in *Bray v. Ford*[31] that this harsh rule "might be departed from in many cases, without any breach of morality, without any wrong being inflicted, and without any consciousness of wrongdoing". However, until very recently English law has shown few signs of being disposed to relax its strict penal rule in favour of a more flexible rule that fiduciaries should only be penalised where there has been a serious conflict

---

[25] [1896] A.C. 44 at 51–52.
[26] [1982] 1 W.L.R. 17 at 29.
[27] In *Chan v. Zacharia* (1984) 53 A.L.R. 417 at 433 (High Court of Australia).
[28] See Millett J. in *Lonrho v. Fayed (No. 2)* [1992] 1 W.L.R. 1 at 11–12.
[29] (1874) L.R. 10 Ch. 96.
[30] *Sergeant v. National Westminster Bank* (1990) 61 P. & C.R. 518.
[31] [1896] A.C. 44 at 51.

of interest and duty. A rare example of flexibility some 30 years ago were the remarks of Danckwerts and Sachs L.JJ. in *Holder v. Holder*[32] to the effect that whether or not a transaction should be set aside because of an alleged conflict of interest and duty was a matter for the discretion of the judge. Much more recently, there have been considerably greater signs of flexibility in the area of pension trusts. In *Re Drexel Lambert UK Pension Plan*[33] Lindsay J., while acknowledging that the remarks of Lord Herschell were "not a licence for the rule to departed from when it can be seen that no breach of morality or wrongdoing would ensue", did however hold that that "the rule does not apply with such force as to deny the court even the jurisdiction to give directions"[34]; he therefore approved an application made by the trustees of a pension scheme, all of whom were by virtue of being members of the scheme also beneficiaries and therefore had a conflict of interest and duty, for the distribution of the actuarial surplus of the pension fund in question. Subsequently Scott V.-C. went even further in *Edge v. Pensions Ombudsman*,[35] where the trustees had amended the rules of a pension scheme in order to make a necessary elimination of its surplus by reducing employee contributions and enhancing pensions in payment. He held that, given that statute[35a] now requires pension schemes to have member-nominated trustees, it was "quite simply ridiculous" to contend that the member trustees had to be excluded from any new or enhanced benefits obtained by the exercise of their powers.

It remains to be seen whether this understandable, but nevertheless highly desirable, relaxation of the traditional position in the area of pension trusts is also applied outside that area. If it is and the strict rule is consequently relaxed, as it has been in other jurisdictions, it will have to be decided whether the conflict of interest and duty is to be measured prospectively or retrospectively, whether, in other words, the question of whether there was a real sensible possibility of conflict has to be considered in the light of the facts existing at the time when the course of conduct complained of commenced or in the light of the facts existing at the time when that course of conduct ended. No clear answer to this question has been given in any of the decided cases, perhaps because the adoption of the strict penal rule has rendered it irrelevant. It is, however, suggested that the retrospective approach is preferable.

3. *Remedies for Breach of Fiduciary Duty*

The first and most significant remedy for breach of fiduciary duty, the one which is most favourable to the principal, and also the one with which this chapter is obviously mainly concerned, is the imposition of a constructive trust. It has already been seen[35b] that this requires the identification of some

---

[32] [1968] Ch. 353; see *post*, pp. 298–299.
[33] [1995] 1 W.L.R. 32.
[34] *ibid.* at 41.
[35] (1997), *The Times*, December 13, 1997.
[35a] Pensions Act 1995, ss.16–21.
[35b] See *ante*, p. 267.

specific property which either is or has been in the hands of the fiduciary on which the trust can be imposed and that the precise position of the principal depends on the nature of the constructive trust which has been imposed. When a constructive trust is not available, the principal can have recourse only to some form of personal remedy.

The second possible remedy is for the principal to seek an account. This remedy will be sought where the principal wishes to recover assets which have passed through the hands of a fiduciary who has committed a breach of fiduciary duty but cannot identify any specific property which either is or has been in the hands of the fiduciary which represents those assets or their product. In these circumstances, he will seek an account of whatever assets have reached the hands of the fiduciary. This involves the fiduciary rendering an account of what he has done with the property which has been in his hands. If the principal is dissatisfied with what the fiduciary has done, then he has the right to "surcharge" or "falsify" the account rendered. The effect of him opting to take either of these courses of action is considered later on in Chapter 24.[35c] Any compensation which the principal recovers will be equitable compensation of the type which courts of equity have always been able to award; its continued availability was confirmed by the decision of the House of Lords in *Nocton v. Lord Ashburton*.[35d] However, such an award will give him no priority over the fiduciary's general creditors—an account remains a personal remedy despite the fact that the person against whom it is sought is a fiduciary.

The third possible remedy, which is available only as an alternative and not in addition to the first two,[36] is for the principal to seek equitable compensation for breach of fiduciary duty; the availability of this type of compensation was established by the decision of the House of Lords in *Nocton v. Lord Ashburton*.[37] The purpose of such an award is basically, to restore the principal to the position which he occupied prior to the breach of fiduciary duty in question. A number of examples of awards of equitable compensation of this type will be seen hereafter: first, where a fiduciary has failed to disclose a conflict of interest and duty and, in particular, has entered into some form of transaction with his principal without adequate disclosure[38]; secondly, where there has been a breach of an equitable obligation of confidence[39]; and, thirdly, where a fiduciary has disposed of trust property in breach of trust.[40] The precise measure of recovery is a matter of some controversy but the general view seems to be that common law principles of remoteness of damages should be applied to the assessment of equitable compensation.[41]

[35c] See *post*, pp. 679–681.
[35d] [1914] A.C. 932.
[36] *Tang Man Sit v. Capacious Investments* [1996] 1 A.C. 514 (Privy Council on Appeal from Hong Kong).
[37] [1914] A.C. 932.
[38] See *post*, pp. 300–302.
[39] See *post*, p. 317.
[40] See *post*, pp. 679–681.
[41] See *Constructive Trusts* (3rd ed., 1997), pp. 117–121 and the authorities there cited.

The fourth possible remedy, which is available only where the fiduciary has entered into some form of transaction with his principal without adequate disclosure, is for that transaction to be rescinded *ab initio*.[42] However, this is only possible for so long as *restitutio in integrum* is still possible. This remedy is available only as an alternative to the three remedies already discussed.

Finally, there is obviously nothing to prevent the principal from seeking injunctive relief as a supplement to any of the remedies already discussed (usually in order to prevent a fiduciary from disposing of property which is claimed to be subject to a constructive trust or susceptible of *restitutio in integrum*); injunctive relief is also often sought independently in cases involving a breach of the equitable obligation of confidence. In theory, it is also possible for the principal to seek damages in lieu or in addition to an injunction under Lord Cairns' Act[43] but in practice it is now almost inevitable that any monetary award for breach of fiduciary duty will instead be made pursuant to *Nocton v. Lord Ashburton.*

4. *The Classification of the Authorities*

The many authorities have been classified in a number of different ways. It is proposed to consider them in this order: first, cases where a fiduciary has as a result of his position obtained unauthorised remuneration; secondly, cases where a fiduciary has entered into a transaction in a double capacity in that he has purported to represent the interests both of his principal and himself and, thirdly, cases where a fiduciary has as a result of his position obtained a benefit to the exclusion of his principal.

5. *Unauthorised Remuneration Obtained by a Fiduciary as a Result of his Position*

(A) When is a Fiduciary Entitled to Claim Remuneration?
The detailed rules governing the extent to which a trustee is entitled to claim and retain remuneration and benefits are discussed in a later chapter.[44] For present purposes, it is merely necessary to state that a trustee is, prima facie, under a duty to act without remuneration, even where he devotes a considerable amount of time and trouble to managing the trust business. Further, if by virtue of his position as trustee, he holds an office of profit, such as a directorship in a company in which the trust has a shareholding, he will prima facie be liable to account to the trust for any remuneration which he receives as a result of holding that office. The position of other express fiduciaries is more favourable; while they are in principle, like trustees, expected to act without remuneration,[45] it is in practice highly unlikely that

---

[42] See *post*, pp. 300–302.
[43] The name usually given to the Chancery Amendment Act 1858. This Act has long since been repealed but the jurisdiction conferred thereby is now contained in the Supreme Court Act 1981, s.50.
[44] See *post*, p. 640.
[45] *Guinness v. Saunders* [1990] 2 A.C. 663 at 689–690.

they will have agreed to do so without first having provided for the payment of the appropriate remuneration. Thus the Articles of Association of a company generally provide for the payment of remuneration to its directors,[46] a Partnership Deed will normally provide for the payment of remuneration to the partners, and a contract of agency will normally make provision for the payment of the appropriate remuneration to the agent. Thus, in normal circumstances, a director of a company who is appointed by the board to a directorship of a subsidiary may undoubtedly retain both sets of directors' fees and a partner who is appointed by his partners to a directorship in a company in which the partnership holds shares may similarly retain his director's fees. However, in the event that the payment of remuneration has not been authorised, or the formula by which authorisation has to be obtained has not been complied with,[47] the fiduciary will not be entitled either to remuneration or to the benefits of any other office to which he has been appointed by virtue of his fiduciary position and will be liable to account to his principal for any sums received.[48] Further, the House of Lords has held that, where the formula by which authorisation has to be obtained has not been complied with, the court has no inherent jurisdiction to award remuneration to the fiduciary in question.[49]

(B)   Liability in respect of Unauthorised Remuneration

Where a fiduciary is liable to account for remuneration received as such, he will in principle clearly be liable as a constructive trustee in respect of the remuneration so obtained. However, only where the remuneration in question is still identifiable at the date of action (as will be the case where the remuneration takes the form of shares or, as is not uncommon today, share options) will there be any purpose in imposing such a trust. Where the remuneration has already passed into the general funds of the fiduciary (as will obviously be more usual), then the fiduciary will be liable merely to account to his principal for its value. In this situation there will obviously be no need for the imposition of a constructive trust, since any fiduciary liable to account for remuneration of this kind will inevitably be an express fiduciary.

(C)   Liability in respect of Secret Profits

A fiduciary will also be liable to account for any other payments which he may receive as a result of his position. Such payments are generally known as secret profits. It is clearly established that no fiduciary who receives a secret profit may retain it as against his principal unless its retention was either authorised in advance or subsequently ratified by the principal with full knowledge of all relevant facts.

---

[46] The Table A Articles of Association recommended by statute reserve to the company in general meeting the right to determine the remuneration of the directors of the company.
[47] In *Guinness v. Saunders* [1990] 2 A.C. 663, the remuneration of the director in question had not, as required by the Articles of Association, been approved by the board of directors.
[48] *ibid.*
[49] *ibid.*, at 693–694, 700–702.

(1) Who is regarded as a fiduciary for these purposes?

For the purposes of the application of this principle, the courts take a particularly broad view of what constitutes a fiduciary relationship. In *Attorney-General v. Goddard*[50] the principle was applied to a police officer who had been bribed not to report brothel keepers; in *Reading v. Attorney-General*[51] it was applied to an ex-R.A.M.C Sergeant who had obtained large sums from smugglers for riding in his uniform through Cairo in lorries in which smuggled goods were being transported, thus enabling the lorries to pass the civil police without search; and in modern conditions it would presumably be applied to a security guard who was bribed to switch off the alarm system, thus facilitating the entrance of thieves.[52] It is arguable whether it is appropriate for relationships of this kind to be classified as fiduciary. In *Reading v. Attorney-General*, the Sergeant was claiming by petition of right the return of some £19,000 which had been found in his possession and confiscated when he was eventually apprehended. For this action to fail, some basis for the Crown's right to confiscate the money had to be found. At first instance[53] Denning J. held that there was no fiduciary relationship between the suppliant and the Crown but that no such relationship was in fact necessary. However, in the Court of Appeal[54] Asquith L.J. took a different view, holding that, assuming a fiduciary relationship to be necessary, such a relationship arose from the use by the suppliant of his uniform and the opportunities attached to it. He admitted that this was using the concept of fiduciary relationship "in a very loose sense" but this did not stop the House of Lords from confirming his view. It is possible to criticise his reasoning on the grounds that the relationship between Sergeant Reading and the Crown does not appear to satisfy any of the criteria for the existence of a fiduciary relationship other than (possibly) the existence of property of the other party under the control of the alleged fiduciary property; in particular, it is not easy to see how the Crown was in any way vulnerable by virtue of some power or discretion vested in him which was capable of being used to affect its legal or practical interests. That is not to say that *Reading v. Attorney-General* was wrongly decided since its result can certainly be justified on other grounds.[55] However, the decision undoubtedly demonstrates how widely the courts are prepared to construe the concept of fiduciary relationship in order to permit the recovery of secret profits.[56]

---

[50] [1929] L.J.(K.B.) 743.

[51] [1951] A.C. 507.

[52] This illustration was provided by Sir Peter Millett extra-judicially in [1993] R.L.R. 7. In *Brinks v. Abu-Saleh (No. 3)* (1995), *The Times*, October 23, 1995, a security guard who provided both a key to and information about the security of a Heathrow warehouse was held to be a fiduciary but this was for the purposes of imposing liability on third parties rather than on him.

[53] [1948] 2 K.B. 268.

[54] [1949] 2 K.B. 232.

[55] By virtue of the principle that no criminal may benefit from his crime. See Section IV of this Chapter, *post*, p. 350.

[56] *Reading v. Att.-Gen.* was approved and applied in the equally extreme case of *Jersey City v. Hague* (1955) 155 At.(2d) 8, which concerned a successful attempt to recover from the Mayor of Jersey City the percentages of the salaries of each employee of the city which he had extorted over a period of 30 years in consideration of continued employment.

(2)   For what profits will a fiduciary be liable?

It has already been stated that a fiduciary will be liable for any payments which he may receive as a result of his position. The vast majority of the reported cases have concerned bribes and commissions received by fiduciary in order either to induce him to take a particular course of action or to reward him for having done so. A bribe may be defined as an undisclosed payment made to a person known by the payer to be a fiduciary in circumstances in which it could induce the fiduciary to favour the payer in some way in his dealings with the fiduciary or with the fiduciary's principal.[57] In such circumstances, the principal has a choice of remedies. He can rescind any transaction entered into as a result of the bribe,[58] provided of course that he can still make *restitutio in integrum*, and, additionally or alternatively, sue either the briber[59] or the fiduciary[60] for the amount of the bribe. It is the last of these remedies which is relevant for present purposes. In the two leading cases, *Lister & Co. v. Stubbs*[61] and *Attorney-General for Hong Kong v. Reid*,[62] liability of this type was imposed on the recipients of bribes. Such persons necessarily act in bad faith but liability is imposed on the recipients of commissions even if they are in good faith, something which is wholly inconsistent with normal commercial practices. In *Williams v. Barton*[63] a trustee used a firm of which he was a member to value trust securities. His action was completely bona fide but he was nevertheless held liable to account to the trust as a constructive trustee for the commission which he had made out of the introduction of the trust business. This decision means that a solicitor who receives a commission for introducing a client to a broker will be liable to account to the client for this commission unless the latter has expressly authorised the retention of the payment in question.

In normal circumstances, it will be virtually impossible for a fiduciary successfully to contend that any particular payment by way of secret profit was not in fact received as a result of his position. However, it has recently been held that the law will not go so far as to impose unreasonable restraints either on the freedom of speech of a former fiduciary or on his ability to earn his living by exploiting expertise acquired during the fiduciary relationship. This was in *Attorney-General v. Blake*,[64] which concerned an attempt by the Crown to intercept the royalties payable in respect of the autobiography of George Blake, a former member of the Secret Intelligence Service who had become a spy for the Soviet Union, to which he managed to escape after having been imprisoned. The Attorney-General contended that Blake owed the Crown a fiduciary duty first not to use his position as a former member of the Security Intelligence Service so as to make himself a profit and,

---

[57] *Hovenden and Sons v. Milhoff* (1900) 83 L.T. 41 at 43; *Industries and General Mortgage Co. v. Lewis* [1949] 2 All E.R. 573 at 575.

[58] *Logicrose v. Southend United F.C.* [1988] 1 W.L.R. 1256.

[59] *Hovenden and Sons v. Milhoff* (1900) 83 L.T. 41; *Mahesan v. Malaysian Government Officers' Co-operative Housing Society* [1979] A.C. 374 at 383.

[60] These claims were held to be alternative rather than cumulative in *Mahesan v. Malaysian Government Officers' Co-operative Housing Society* [1979] A.C. 374.

[61] (1890) 45 Ch.D. 1.

[62] [1994] 1 A.C. 324 (Privy Council on appeal from New Zealand).

[63] [1927] 2 Ch. 9.

[64] [1997] Ch. 84.

secondly, not to use the Crown's property, including intangible property such as originally confidential information, for his profit. Only the first of these alleged duties is relevant for present purposes. Scott V.-C. held that both were formulated in terms too wide to be acceptable and went on to dismiss the Crown's claim for the reasons stated above, both of which appear to relate principally to the second duty. This decision was affirmed on appeal,[65] where the Crown succeeded on public law grounds not argued at first instance. However, there seems little likelihood that the principles which commended themselves to Scott V.-C. will often be invoked successfully; it is hardly likely that the courts would look very charitably on a trustee who deferred the receipt of bribes and commissions until after his retirement and then sought to retain them on that ground.

(3) The nature of the liability

In principle, a fiduciary who is liable to account for secret profits will be liable as a constructive trustee in respect of the secret profit in question. This remedy was imposed in *Williams v. Barton*,[66] which of course meant that the principal was therefore entitled to follow the payment into its product in the admittedly unlikely event that it could be shown to have been invested in assets which had appreciated in value. However, until the decision of the Privy Council in *Attorney-General for Hong Kong v. Reid*,[67] the decided cases appeared to draw a distinction between bribes and other secret profits. In *Lister & Co. v. Stubbs*[68] the defendant was the plaintiff's foreman and was responsible for buying in whatever was needed in his employer's business. He regularly gave orders to a third party in return for a large commission. In an action to recover this bribe, the plaintiff sought an order restraining the defendant from dealing with certain investments purchased with the money received on the basis that the defendant was a constructive trustee of the bribes and so the plaintiff would be entitled to follow the money into its product and recover the investments. However, the Court of Appeal declined to grant this order, holding that the only obligation of the defendant was to pay over the sums received to the plaintiff the relationship between them was held to be that of debtor-creditor rather than trustee-beneficiary. Although this decision was consistently followed,[69] it seemed quite extraordinary that the defendant in *Williams v. Barton* should have

---

[65] [1998] 2 W.L.R. 805.

[66] [1927] 2 Ch. 9.

[67] [1994] 1 A.C. 324.

[68] (1890) 45 Ch.D. 1.

[69] In *Att.-Gen. Ref. (No. 1 of 1985)* [1986] 2 All E.R. 219 and in *Islamic Republic of Iran Shipping Line v. Denby* [1987] 1 F.T.L.R. 30. In Australia, the view had been expressed that the decision in *Lister & Co. v. Stubbs* was anomalous and should be confined to its own facts (*Consul Development v. D.P.C. Estates* [1974] 1 N.S.W.L.R. 443 (New South Wales Court of Appeal); the question was left open on the further appeal to the High Court of Australia ((1975) 132 C.L.R. 373)). Subsequently, the reasoning in *Lister & Co. v. Stubbs* was described as impeccable when applied to cases in which the person claiming the money had simply made what was described as an outright loan to the fiduciary (*Daly v. The Sydney Stock Exchange* (1986) 160 C.L.R. 371 (High Court of Australia)). This restricted the effect of *Lister & Co. v. Stubbs* in Australia to cases where a bribe was paid over to a fiduciary in the form of money.

been held to have been a constructive trustee of a commission which he had earned in good faith if the defendant in *Lister & Co. v. Stubbs* was held not to have been a constructive trustee of an illicitly earned bribe. All the commentators agreed that both cases should have been decided in the same way. Some thought that a constructive trust should not have been imposed in either case on the grounds that proprietary remedies should be limited to situations where the claimant can show that he has lost property which, but for the conduct of the fiduciary, he would have obtained.[70] Others thought that a constructive trust should have been imposed in both cases on the grounds that a fiduciary should never be allowed to retain any advantage from the violation of his fiduciary obligations, something which can only be achieved by the imposition of a proprietary remedy.[71] This issue was resolved by the Privy Council in *Attorney-General for Hong Kong v. Reid*.[72]

This case concerned a Hong Kong Public Prosecutor, who was convicted of having accepted bribes as an inducement to him to exploit his official position to obstruct the prosecution of certain criminals. He was ordered to pay the Crown the sum of HK$12,400,000, the value of assets then controlled by him which could only have been derived from the bribes. No payments having been made, the Attorney-General for Hong Kong brought proceedings in New Zealand claiming that three freehold houses which the bribes had been used to purchase were held on constructive trust for the Crown. The Court of Appeal of New Zealand applied *Lister & Co v. Stubbs* and dismissed this claim.[73] The Privy Council reversed this decision, holding that *Lister & Co. v. Stubbs* had been wrongly decided. Lord Templeman's opinion did not directly consider the important issue of policy on which the commentators were divided. He held that, as soon as any bribe is received, the fiduciary becomes in equity the debtor of his principal for the amount of the bribe, which should immediately be transferred to his principal. Because equity considers as done that which ought to have been done, the bribe therefore becomes subject to a constructive trust in favour of the principal as soon as it is received. Although this analysis is questionable in a number of respects,[74] it provided a basis for an examination of the case law, from which Lord Templeman concluded that *Lister & Co. v. Stubbs* was consistent neither with prior authority nor "with the principles that a fiduciary must not be allowed to benefit from his own breach of duty, that the fiduciary should account for the bribe as soon as he receives it and that equity regards as done that which ought to be done".[75] Although this decision is not, of course,

[70] P. B. H. Birks, *An Introduction to the Law of Restitution* (1989) 388; R. M. Goode: (1987) 103 L.Q.R. 433, 422–445 and in *Essays on the Law of Restitution* (1991), p. 216.
[71] Sir Peter Millett, extra-judicially, in [1993] Restitution L.R. 7, citing Underhill & Hayton: *Law of Trusts and Trustees* (14th ed.), p. 305; *Constructive Trusts* (2nd ed.), p. 56; Goff & Jones: *op.cit.*, p. 657; Pettit: *Equity and the Law of Trusts* (6th ed.), p. 152; Meagher, Gummow & Lehane: *Equity—Doctrines and Remedies* (2nd ed.), para. 1323; Finn, *Fiduciary Obligations* (1977), para. 513; Sir Anthony Mason extra-judicially in *Essays in Equity* (ed. Finn, 1985), p. 246.
[72] [1994] 1 A.C. 324.
[73] [1992] 2 N.Z.L.R. 385.
[74] See [1994] C.L.J. 31.
[75] [1994] 1 A.C. 324 at 336.

formally binding on English courts, it will presumably be followed.[76] Whatever its shortcomings, it has removed a glaring inconsistency in the treatment of secret profits and has established that the liability of a fiduciary who receives a bribe will be exactly the same as that of a fiduciary who receives any other type of secret profit.

6. *Transactions into which a Fiduciary has Entered in a Double Capacity*

This second group of cases concerns transactions in which a fiduciary has purported to represent the interests of both his principal and himself. Such situations produce an obvious conflict between the personal interest of the fiduciary in the transaction and his duty of loyalty towards his principal. Consequently, no matter how fair the transaction, the principal has the right to have the transaction set aside unless he was fully aware of the facts.

(A) Purchases of Property by a Fiduciary from his Principal

Such purchases are regulated by two rules, which Megarry V.-C. in *Tito v. Waddell (No. 2)*[77] described as the self-dealing rule and the fair-dealing rule, names which have been in general use ever since. The self-dealing rule applies to purchases by trustees from their trusts[78] and, at least in theory, to purchases by directors from their companies[79] (although in practice the Articles of Association of virtually all companies expressly permit such purchases provided that appropriate disclosure is made). The fair-dealing rule applies to purchases by trustees of the interests of their beneficiaries[80] and to purchases by other fiduciaries (such as agents) from their principals.[81]

(1) The self-dealing rule

In *Tito v. Waddell (No. 2)*,[82] Megarry V.-C. said that "if a trustee purchases trust property from himself, any beneficiary may have the sale set aside *ex debito justitiae*, however fair the transaction". The rationale of the self-dealing rule was laid down by Lord Eldon L.C. in *Ex parte Lacey*.[83] He applied the principle that a trustee must not place himself in a position where his interest and duty conflict, holding that, since in a purchase by a trustee from his trust he is both vendor and purchaser, the sale is necessarily bad. In such circumstances it is impossible to determine from the evidence whether or not the purchase has been made on advantageous terms and so the court has no option but to set aside the sale at the instance of any beneficiary.

Although *Lister & Co. v. Stubbs* was said to be still binding on the High Court by Scott V.-C. in *Att.-Gen. v. Blake* [1997] Ch. 84 at 96.

See *Tito v. Waddell (No. 2)* [1977] Ch. 106 at 224–225 (Megarry V.-C.).

Ex parte Lacey (1802) 6 Ves. 625.

Aberdeen Railway Co. v. Blaikie Brothers (1854) 1 Macq. 461 at 472; *Movitex v. Bullfield* [1988] B.C.L.C. 104.

Chalmer v. Bradley (1819) 1 J. & W. 51.

Edwards v. Meyrick [1842] 2 Hare 60.

[1977] Ch. 106 at 224–225.

(1802) 6 Ves. 625.

While most purchases which fall foul of these authorities are indeed not wholly void but merely voidable at the instance of any beneficiary, this is however not always the case. Formulations such as that of Megarry V.-C. overlook the fact that it is impossible for a person to contract with himself or for a trustee to exercise his power of sale in favour of himself.[84] Any transaction which falls foul of either of these rules is not merely voidable but wholly void. Since 1925[85] this will admittedly only be the case when the same person is, or the same persons are, both vendor and purchaser. Therefore a sole trustee cannot sell to himself and a plurality of trustees cannot sell to themselves (validity depends on there being at least one party who is not both vendor and purchaser) unless such a transaction is authorised by the trust instrument. But any breach of this rule will render both contract and conveyance wholly void[86]; the only way out of such a situation is for the trustee either to try to acquire the equitable interests of the beneficiaries[87] (a transaction which will be governed by the fair-dealing rule) principal or to seek the leave of the court.

However, where there is one party to a transaction who is not both vendor and purchaser, it will indeed not be void but merely voidable at the instance of any beneficiary. The many cases in which this rule has been applied have illustrated that it is quite irrelevant that the fiduciary was honest, the sale open and the price fair. In *Wright v. Morgan*[88] property was devised to two trustees on trust for sale for one of them. The will stated that the trustees were required to offer the trustee-beneficiary the land at a price to be fixed by independent valuers. The trustee-beneficiary assigned his beneficial interest to the other trustee, who bought the property at the price fixed by the independent valuers in accordance with the terms of the will. The Privy Council held that this sale had to be set aside, since only a sale to the trustee-beneficiary had been authorised by the will. The fact that the price was to be fixed independently was not sufficient, for the trustees could themselves fix the time at which the property was to be sold and this could clearly have had a substantial effect on the price ultimately received. This does seem to be a somewhat artificial conflict of interest. However, a similar attitude was taken in an eighteenth-century case,[89] in which it was held that a trustee must not purchase trust property which is put up for auction as he is in a position to discourage bidders.

Wright v. Morgan of course demonstrates that, just as in the case of potentially void transactions, the trust instrument can specifically authorise

---

[84] See Mr. Justice B. H. McPherson, extra-judicially, in *Trends in Contemporary Trust Law* (ed. Oakley, 1996), p. 135.

[85] Until 1926, prior to the enactment of Law of Property Act 1925, s.82, the rule applied if anyone either contracted with or conveyed to himself, even if someone else was also a party on one side or the other.

[86] Hence the decision in *Franks v. Bollans* (1868) 3 Ch.App. 717, where a trustee sold to himself, would still be the same today.

[87] This would have worked in *Williams v. Scott* [1900] A.C. 499 (Privy Council on appeal from New South Wales) had there been sufficient disclosure by the trustees to the beneficiaries.

[88] [1926] A.C. 788.

[89] *Whelpdale v. Cookson* (1747) 1 Ves.Sen. 9.

a transaction which is potentially voidable. This has recently been specifically held in *Sargeant v. National Westminster Bank*.[90] As has already been mentioned, the Articles of Association of virtually all companies also expressly permit purchases by directors provided that disclosure of their interest is made in whatever way is required by the provision in question.[91] In the absence of such a provision, the trustee will again have to do the same as in the case of a potentially void transaction, either try to acquire the equitable interests of the beneficiaries in the property in question (a transaction which will be governed by the fair-dealing rule) or seek the leave of the court to purchase. The court requires to be satisfied that the sale is in the interests of all the beneficiaries before it will grant its approval and the evidence on this point must be very clear.[92] Such leave is obviously necessary in cases where some of the beneficiaries are not *sui juris* or are unborn or unascertained and, for the reasons set out below, is highly prudent in almost all other cases. However, in principle, there seems no reason why a trustee should not purchase trust property without such authorisation if all the beneficiaries agree, provided of course that they are all *sui juris* and are between them absolutely entitled to the whole of the beneficial interest in the property; there is no reason for the court to upset a sale where the beneficiaries have genuinely agreed to it, although such an agreement would only be effective if the trustees had disclosed to the beneficiaries all the information which they possessed relating to the property. Nevertheless, despite the theoretical possibility of such an unimpeachable sale taking place in this way, there are two serious practical objections to it. First, the onus on the trustee-purchaser of demonstrating that the beneficiaries were given all the relevant information and that they all freely gave their consent is an extremely difficult burden of proof to discharge. Secondly, despite the fact that a valid title will have been acquired, the property will often be as unmarketable thereafter as if the transaction had been potentially voidable. A liability to have a sale set aside affects subsequent purchasers with notice; consequently, where some information acquired by the purchaser shows that the vendor formerly held the property as a trustee, it will be almost impossible to sell. Even where the trustee is able to produce a written agreement showing that the beneficiaries did indeed consent, a subsequent purchaser will not be able to be sure that the trustee gave to the beneficiaries all the information in his possession before they entered into the agreement; consequently, only in quite exceptional circumstances will a subsequent purchaser complete his purchase.

---

[90] (1990) 61 P. & C.R. 518.

[91] The Companies Acts have long contained a provision requiring directors who are in any way, whether directly or indirectly, interested in a contract or proposed contract with the company to declare the nature of their interest at a meeting of the directors of the company. The present provision is Companies Act 1985, s.317. The Table A Articles of Association recommended by statute provide that directors will not be liable to account for benefits resulting from transactions with the company which have been duly disclosed in accordance with the section. Many Articles of Association additionally provide that such directors should neither vote nor be counted in the quorum on any matter in which they are interested. See *Movitex v. Bullfield* [1988] B.C.L.C. 625.

[92] *Farmer v. Dean* (1863) 32 Beav. 327; *Campbell v. Walker* (1800) 5 Ves. 678.

Where a potentially voidable transaction has been entered into without any of these kinds of authorisation, it is only in most extraordinary circumstances will the court refuse to set aside a purchase of trust property by a trustee at the instance of the beneficiary, other of course than in the event that the trustee can successfully raise against the beneficiary a defence of delay, or laches.[93] However, the court did exceptionally refuse to upset a transaction in *Holder v. Holder*.[94] One of the executors of a will renounced his executorship after carrying out certain acts which, it was conceded, amounted to intermeddling. He was the tenant of certain farms which the other executors offered for sale by auction subject to his tenancy. At the auction he purchased the farms at a good price, probably higher than would have been paid by anyone other than a sitting tenant and well above the reserve price (which had been fixed by an independent valuer). One of the beneficiaries subsequently sought to have the sale set aside. The Court of Appeal refused to do so. Harman L.J. held that the rule in *Ex parte Lacey* was based on the principle that no man may be both vendor and purchaser. Here the purchaser had played no real part in the administration of the estate and had renounced his executorship long before the sale. All the beneficiaries were aware of this and so could not have been looking to him to protect their interests. Thus the mischief which the rule was intended to prevent did not arise and there was no reason to set aside the sale. Such an attitude, while quite different from that adopted in *Wright v. Morgan*, does not in any way affect the principle in *Ex parte Lacey*. But both the other members of the court declined to accept the principle of that decision. Danckwerts L.J. said that Chancery judges were daily engaged in ascertaining the knowledge and intentions of parties to proceedings the court could unquestionably sanction such a purchase and so the rule in *Ex parte Lacey* could be no more than a rule of practice. So, he held, this type of issue was a matter for the discretion of the judge. Sachs L.J. took very much the same view. All three members of the court then went on to hold that, in any event, the beneficiaries had acquiesced in the purchase and could not now seek to set it aside.

The approach taken in this case by Danckwerts and Sachs L.JJ. suggested that the courts might be about to move away from the automatic application of the self-dealing rule and instead apply the fair-dealing rule to purchases of property by a trustee from his trust. This would have meant that such purchases would be set aside only where the trustee was unable to convince the court that he had obtained no advantage by virtue of his position, a flexible approach which would undoubtedly have been preferable. However, *Holder v. Holder* has not in fact been interpreted in this way. In *Re Thompson's Settlement*,[95] Vinelott J. took the view that the decision in *Holder v. Holder* had been reached for the reasons enunciated by Harman L.J. and held that the self-dealing rule "is applied stringently in cases where a trustee concurs in a transaction which cannot be carried into effect without his concurrence and who also has an interest in or holds a fiduciary duty to another in relation to the same transaction".[96] He therefore held that two

---

[93] See *Tito v. Waddell* (No. 2) [1977] Ch. 106 at 249–250.
[94] [1968] Ch. 353.
[95] [1986] Ch. 99.
[96] *ibid.* at p.115.

leases in favour of a company and a partnership of which the two trustees were respectively a shareholder and a partner were not valid. Thus, at least for the moment, the self-dealing rule appears to retain its full force.

(2) The fair-dealing rule

This rule, which is less stringent, applies to purchases by trustees of the interests of their beneficiaries and to purchases by other fiduciaries (such as agents) from their principals. Where a trustee purchases the beneficial interest of one of the beneficiaries under the trust, the mischief which the rule in *Ex parte Lacey* was intended to solve does not arise since the trustee is not both vendor and purchaser. Hence the courts have always been prepared to uphold such purchases provided that the trustee is able to establish that he obtained no advantage by reason of his position[97]; in particular, he must be able to show that he did not abuse his position as trustee, that he concealed no material facts, that the price was fair, and that the beneficiary did not rely solely on his advice.[98] This will be an almost impossible burden of proof to discharge when the beneficiary is an infant[99]; in such circumstances, the trustee will need to seek the leave of the court.

Similarly, where a fiduciary such as an agent purchases property from his principal, he is in practice unlikely to be both sole vendor and purchaser and, even if he is, in comparison with the position of a trustee or a director who is purchasing the property of his principal, he will have far fewer possibilities of taking unfair advantage of his principal. Consequently, such purchases will similarly be upheld provided that the fiduciary is able to show that he did not abuse his position in any way, that he paid a fair price, and that he has made full disclosure of his interest and of any information which he possesses about the property.[1]

(3) The precise limits of the rules

The self-dealing rule and the fair-dealing rule cannot be evaded by selling to an associate of the fiduciary rather than to the fiduciary himself; the rules have proved strong enough to prevent evasion. Most of the decided cases concern purchases by associates of trustees. In the first place, although a sale to a relative of the trustee is not necessarily bad,[2] a purchase taken in the name of the trustee's children will usually be upset[3] and it is very risky to take a purchase in the name of the trustee's spouse,[4] at least if at the time the two "were living in perfect amity" rather than "separate and in emnity for a dozen years".[5] Nor can the rules be overcome by selling to a limited company of which the trustee is the majority shareholder[6] or of which he has

---

[97] *Chalmer v. Bradley* (1819) 1 J. & W. 51.
[98] *Coles v. Trecothick* (1804) 9 Ves. 234.
[99] See *Sanderson v. Walker* (1807) 13 Ves. 601.
[1] *Edwards v. Meyrick* (1842) 2 Hare 60.
[2] *Coles v. Trecothick* (1804) 9 Ves. 234.
[3] *Gregory v. Gregory* (1821) Jac. 631.
[4] *Ferraby v. Hobson* (1847) 2 Ph. 255; *Burrell v. Burrell's Trustee* 1915 S.C. 333.
[5] *Tito v. Waddell* (No. 2) [1977] Ch. 106 at 240.
[6] *Silkstone and Haigh Moor Coal Co. v. Edey* [1900] 1 Ch. 167; *Movitex v. Bullfield* [1988] B.C.L.C. 104.

control.[7] It seems that a sale by a trustee to a company of which he is a member, but which he does not control, which is necessarily not void, is not *ipso facto* voidable either; however, if the beneficiaries seek to upset the transaction, the company may have to show that the trustee had taken all reasonable steps to find a purchaser and that the price paid by the company was at the time adequate.[8]

Similar rules presumably apply to partnerships; certainly, a sale to a partnership comprising the trustee and his family will not be valid.[9] It is equally offensive to the rules to sell the property to a third person, with an agreement or understanding for its repurchase.[10] However, it has been held that, where there was no agreement or understanding for repurchase at the time of the sale to the third person, the fact that the trustee had sold the property to that person with the hope of being able to repurchase was not a sufficient ground for setting the sale aside.[11] Finally, a sale may be upset if a trustee retires with the intention that the property will be conveyed to him after his retirement.[12] If, however, a sufficient length of time has elapsed between the retirement and the sale for the court to be satisfied that the ex-trustee has not taken any advantage of knowledge about the property gained while he was a trustee, the sale will be upheld. Such a transaction has been upheld where there was an interval of 12 years between retirement and purchase.[13]

(4) The consequences of liability

When a transaction is void under the principles discussed above, it will simply have no effect. Thus in *Franks v. Bollans*,[14] a trustee contrived, by means of an extremely intricate deed, to sell to himself part of the land which he was holding on trust. One of the beneficiaries was subsequently held still to be beneficially entitled to it on the grounds that both contract and conveyance were wholly void. She was, however, fortunate that the trustee still held the property which he had purchased. Where this is not the case, the property will only be able to be recovered from a third party if the latter has not taken free of the beneficiary's interest.[15] If he has, then the only recourse of the beneficiary will be to attempt to follow the property into its product in the way which will be discussed in a later Chapter[16] or to attempt to obtain compensation for breach of trust.[17]

---

[7] *Re Thompson's Settlement* [1986] Ch. 99; *Movitex v. Bullfield* [1988] B.C.L.C. 104.
[8] *Farrar v. Farrar's* (1888) 40 Ch.D. 395.
[9] *Re Thompson's Settlement* [1986] Ch. 99.
[10] *Williams v. Scott* [1900] A.C. 499.
[11] *Re Postlethwaite* (1888) 37 W.R. 200; 60 L.T. 514.
[12] *Wright v. Morgan* [1926] A.C. 788; *Re Mullholland's Will Trusts* [1949] 1 All E.R. 460.
[13] *Re Boles and the British Land Company's Contract* [1902] 1 Ch. 244.
[14] (1868) 3 Ch.App. 717.
[15] Only likely if the third party has not purchased for value or if the property is unregistered land. A purchaser for value of registered land or pure personalty will almost inevitably have taken free.
[16] See *post*, pp. 716 *et seq.*
[17] This will only be possible if a breach of the self-dealing rule is itself a breach of trust, something which is not at present entirely clear. See *Constructive Trusts* (3rd ed., 1997), p. 147, n. 70.

When on the other hand a transaction is not void but merely voidable at the instance of the principal, he must avoid it within a reasonable time, otherwise his failure to do so will entitle the fiduciary to invoke the defence of laches.[18] If the sale is so avoided, the consequences will be as follows.

If the property is still in the hands of the fiduciary, then the principal will have a choice. He will be able to recover the property together with any income produced in the meantime provided that he is in a position to make *restitutio in integrum* by returning to the fiduciary the price which he paid therefor. (In the case of beneficiaries under a trust, this option will require the consent of all of them because of the risk that the property may not be able subsequently to be resold at a higher value, in which case "the beneficiaries would be worse off than if the claim had never been made".[19]) Alternatively, the principal can require the property to be put up for sale again under the direction of the court[20]; the fiduciary will not be allowed to bid at this resale if any of his principals objects to him so doing.[21] The reserve price will normally be the price originally paid by the fiduciary with interest thereon, plus the value of any improvements which he has made to the property and interest thereon, less any income produced by the property or, if the fiduciary has himself been in occupation, the appropriate occupation rent.[22] If the sale "realises more than the reserve fixed by the court, the surplus belongs to the [principal], whereas if it realises less [the fiduciary] will be held to his bargain"[23] and so will lose the difference. It will only be in the interests of the principal to use either of these remedies where the property is worth at least as much as the fiduciary paid for it. If it has fallen in value, avoiding the transaction will give the principal a property worth less than the sum which he has to return to the fiduciary; consequently, it will be in his interests to affirm the transaction.

If, on the other hand, the property is no longer in the hands of the principal, any third party to whom it has been transferred will have acquired legal title thereto because of the fact that the transaction was voidable rather than void. If the third party has not taken free of the right of the principal to have the purchase set aside (a mere equity), he will be in exactly the same position as the fiduciary. If, however, he has taken free of this mere equity because he is a bona fide purchaser for value without notice or a statutory equivalent, then the property will not be able to be recovered by the principal, whose position will be as follows. He will be entitled to recover any profit made by the fiduciary on the resale[24] with interest

---

[18] See *Tito v. Waddell (No. 2)* [1977] Ch. 106 at 249–250.
[19] *Holder v. Holder* [1968] Ch. 353 at 370–371 (Cross J.).
[20] This was what was ordered at first instance in *Holder v. Holder, ibid.*, where the purchase was set aside.
[21] *Tennant v. Trenchard* (1869) 4 Ch.App. 537.
[22] This was the form of order made in *Holder v. Holder* at first instance; although the right to add to the reserve price the value of any improvements was conceded in that case, the existence of the right to do so emerges clearly from *O'Sullivan v. Management Agency and Music* [1985] Q.B. 428 at 466.
[23] *Holder v. Holder* [1968] Ch. 353 at 371 (Cross J.).
[24] *Hall v. Hallett* (1784) 1 Cox 134; *Ex parte James* (1803) 8 Ves. 337 at 351; *Silkstone and Haigh Moor Coal Co. v. Edey* [1900] 1 Ch. 167.

thereon.[25] In the event of a resale at less than the true value, he will also be able to claim the difference between the price paid and the true value with interest thereon[26]; this will be recoverable by way of compensation for breach of fiduciary duty under *Nocton v. Lord Ashburton*[27] (such compensation is also available as an alternative to an account of profits[28]). If, on the other hand, the price paid by the third party was less than the price paid by the fiduciary because the property had fallen in value, the fiduciary will have made no profit and the principal will have suffered no loss; consequently, in such circumstances, the principal will neither have nor be entitled to any remedy.

(B) Sales of Property by a Fiduciary to his Principal

Such sales will be set aside at the instance of the principal, unless the fiduciary has fully disclosed the nature of his interest in the transaction, no matter how honest the fiduciary or fair the price.[29] Such a sale may be set aside even where the fiduciary purchased the property in question before he entered into the fiduciary relationship. Thus, in *Armstrong v. Jackson*[30] a stockbroker did not disclose to his client that ever since the formation of a company he had owned the shares which he was encouraging the client to buy. Five years later, by which time the shares had fallen in value to less than a fifth of the purchase price, the client discovered the true facts and successfully sought rescission of the sale. If, on the other hand, the property has increased in value, it will not be in the interests of the principal to set aside the transaction. In the event that, for this or any other reason, the principal seeks not to set aside the sale but to recover the profit made by the fiduciary out of the transaction, his right to do so will clearly depend on when the fiduciary purchased the property.

In *Bentley v. Craven*[31] the defendant was responsible for the purchase of sugar for a partnership of sugar refiners of which he was a member but also carried on an independent business as a sugar dealer. He purchased a quantity of sugar which he later resold to the partnership at a price which, although resulting in a profit to him, was the fair market price of the day. He was held liable to account for his profit to the partnership since he had been a fiduciary at the date of purchase and so should have purchased for the partnership rather than for himself. A similar decision was reached where an investment adviser purchased a property of a type which he knew that his client wished to purchase and subsequently sold it on to her at a

---

[25] Formerly 4% but, following *Bartlett v. Barclays Bank Trust Co.* [1980] Ch. 515 at 547, it seems that the rate will now be that of the court's short-term investment account (established under the Administration of Justice Act 1965, s.6 (1)).

[26] *Lord Hardwicke v. Vernon* (1800) 4 Ves. 411.

[27] [1914] A.C. 932. See I. E. Davidson: (1982) 13 Melbourne U.L.R. 349.

[28] *McKenzie v. McDonald* [1927] V.L.R. 134 (Court of Appeal of Victoria). This is one of the possible explanations of *Coleman v. Myers* [1977] 2 N.Z.L.R. 225 (Court of Appeal of New Zealand), where minority shareholders recovered compensation from the directors of the company (held, unusually, to owe them fiduciary duties because of the family nature of the company) who had recommended the acceptance of an under-valued takeover bid without disclosing that the offeror was a company controlled by one of them.

[29] *Gillett v. Peppercone* (1840) 3 Beav. 78.

[30] [1917] 2 K.B. 822.

[31] (1853) 18 Beav. 75.

substantial profit.[32] On the other hand, in *Re Cape Breton Co.*[33] a director acquiesced in the sale to his company of certain mining claims in which he had a beneficial interest. After discovering the facts, the company elected not to set aside the sale. Subsequently, after the property had been sold on at a loss, the company tried to claim the profit made by the director. This action failed because the director had acquired the property more than two years before the company in question had been formed. This conclusion is clearly correct when the fiduciary has sold at the market value. The Court of Appeal actually held, by a majority, that it made no difference that the director had sold above the market value. However, the House of Lords[34] held that there was no evidence that the sale price was above market value. This point therefore did not have to be decided but Lord Herschell considered that an agent employed to purchase non-specific goods in the market would be liable for the excess if he sold his own goods to the company above market value.[35] Therefore, although the decision of the Court of Appeal clearly constitutes the law at present, this particular point cannot be regarded as finally settled.

These authorities show that, when the principal does not seek to rescind the sale or cannot do so because rescission is barred on the grounds of affirmation, laches or bona fide purchase, he will only have a remedy where the fiduciary acquired the property after he entered into the fiduciary relationship in question or, possibly, where the sale price was above the market value. All the authorities discussed deal with fiduciary relationships other than that of trustee and beneficiary. There appears to be no English authority dealing with a purchase by a trustee of his own property for his trust but an American decision[36] and dicta in *Bentley v. Craven* suggest that the same rules will apply to such transactions.

(C) Regular Trading between Fiduciary and Principal

Where a fiduciary engages in regular trading between his own business and a business which he is managing in a fiduciary capacity, the situation will be governed by exactly the same principles as where a fiduciary sells his own property to his principal.[37]

(D) Loans from a Fiduciary to his Principal

This situation recently occurred in *Swindle v. Harrison*,[38] where a solicitor made a loan to his client to enable her to complete the purchase of a property and avoid the loss of the 20 per cent deposit which she had already paid. No other source of finance was available to her. The transaction did not ultimately prove profitable and she was unable to repay the advance, which was secured on the property. She had obviously been aware of the source of the funds but sought to resist realisation of the security on the grounds that

---

[32] *Cook v. Evatt (No.2)* [1992] 1 N.Z.L.R. 676 (High Court of New Zealand).
[33] (1885) 29 Ch.D. 795.
[34] *Cavendish Bentinck v. Fenn* (1887) 12 App.Cas. 652.
[35] *ibid.* at 659. The remedy would presumably have been either an account of profits or compensation under *Nocton v. Lord Ashburton*.
[36] *Cornet v. Cornet* (1916) 269 No. 298.
[37] This situation is discussed by Finn, *Fiduciary Obligations* (1977), pp. 228–231.
[38] [1997] 4 All E.R. 705.

the solicitor had not explained to her exactly how much interest he would be making. The Court of Appeal accepted that this amounted to a breach of fiduciary duty. However, since *restitutio in integrum* was obviously impossible because of her inability to repay the loan, her only conceivable remedy was equitable compensation under *Nocton v. Lord Ashburton*.[39] This was in fact denied because her position would have been even worse had the loan not been made.[40]

7. Benefits obtained by a Fiduciary as a result of his Position to the Exclusion of his Principal

This third group of cases has emerged as the result of the rigorous application by the courts of a decision in 1726[41] which established what was, in the light of the prevailing legal rules and financial circumstances, a wholly understandable prohibition on trustees renewing for their own benefit leases formerly held by their trusts. This decision has had two quite distinct effects. First, it has produced a line of authority concerning the extent to which this prohibition also applies to other fiduciaries and the associated question of whether a fiduciary may purchase for his own benefit the freehold reversion in property of which his principal is lessee. Secondly, and totally unconnected with any question of the renewal of leases or the purchase of reversions, the decision has also had a profound effect on the general question of what opportunities a fiduciary is entitled to utilise for his own benefit.

(A) Speculation by a Fiduciary with the Property of his Principal

This is almost the only situation within this third group of cases which is wholly uncontroversial. Where a fiduciary engages in speculation with the property of his principal, the latter will be entitled to all the profits made by the fiduciary under a constructive trust.[42]

A somewhat extreme example of the operation of this principle is *Reid-Newfoundland Co. v. Anglo-American Telegraph Co.*[43] Under the terms of a contract, a telegraph company had erected a special telegraph wire for use in the operation of a railway. The contract provided that no commercial messages should be passed over this wire except for the account of the telegraph company. When this prohibition was directly contravened, the telegraph company successfully claimed that the profits made thereby were held subject to a constructive trust in its favour. The Privy Council appear to have regarded the company operating the railway as the agent of the telegraph company in respect of its use of the latter's telegraph wire. Thus, the former had in breach of fiduciary duty made a profit out of the use of the latter's property and so was clearly bound to account for that profit under a constructive trust.

---

[39] [1914] A.C. 932.
[40] See *post*, pp. 679 *et seq*.
[41] *Keech v. Sandford* (1726) Sel.Cas.Ch. 61.
[42] *Brown v. I.R.C.* [1965] A.C. 264.
[43] [1912] A.C. 555.

However, a similar claim failed in *Attorney-General v. Blake*.[44] It has already been seen[45] that the Attorney-General contended that the Soviet spy Blake owed the Crown a fiduciary duty not to use the Crown's property, including intangible property such as originally confidential information, for his profit. Scott V.-C. held that this duty was formulated in terms too wide to be acceptable and went on to dismiss the Crown's claim on the grounds that the law will not go so far as to impose unreasonable restraints either on the freedom of speech of a former fiduciary or on his ability to earn his living by exploiting expertise acquired during the fiduciary relationship. This decision was affirmed on appeal,[46] where the Crown succeeded on public law grounds not argued at first instance, but it is certainly not easy to see how the principles enunciated by Scott V.-C. could be applied to fiduciaries such as trustees.

When liability is imposed in this type of case, the situation will be as follows. Where the principal has been owner of the property throughout, and also in cases where the fiduciary is already holding the property in question on trust for his principal, the constructive trust will be imposed merely on the profit. But if the property has instead reached the hands of the fiduciary in some other way, both the property and the fiduciary's profit will be subject to a constructive trust. If there is no profit, because the speculation has resulted in a loss, a constructive trust may still be imposed, if necessary, upon any of the property remaining in the hands of the fiduciary and, in the event that the value of the property has fallen as a result of the breach by the fiduciary of his duty of loyalty, the principal will be able to recover compensation for that loss under *Nocton v. Lord Ashburton*.[47] The latter actually occurred in *Tang Man Sit v. Capacious Investments*.[48] The defendant had made secret profits from letting certain houses on his land which he had agreed to assign to the plaintiff, who had financed their construction pursuant to a joint venture agreement. The plaintiff recovered not only those profits but also compensation for their diminution in value as a result of their wrongful occupation.

(B) Competition between a Fiduciary and the Business of his Principal
There are certain circumstances in which a fiduciary will not be able to compete with the business of his principal. Different rules apply to the different fiduciary relationships.

Where the trust property includes a business, or the trustees carry on any income earning activity, a trustee must not commence a business or activity on his own account which will compete with that of the trust. Thus, in *Re Thomson*[49] one of the assets of a trust was a yachtbroker's business, which was being carried on by the trustees. One of them sought to set up on his own a similar business in the same town, which would have competed with the trust business, but the court granted an injunction restraining him from doing so. The decision in *Re Thomson* appears to be at variance with that in

---

[44] [1997] Ch. 84.
[45] See *ante*, p. 292.
[46] [1998] 2 W.L.R. 805.
[47] [1914] A.C. 932.
[48] [1996] 1 A.C. 514 (Privy Council on appeal from Hong Kong)
[49] [1930] 1 Ch. 203.

the earlier Irish case of *Moore v. M'Glynn*.[50] There the court had refused an injunction, although it was thought that the setting up of a competing business would be a good ground for removing the trustee from his trusteeship. It was said that a breach of trust would only be committed if in carrying on the new business the trustee practised deception, or solicited the customers from the old shop. It is sometimes suggested that this decision can be reconciled with that in *Re Thomson* on the basis that the yachtbroker's business was so specialised that any other yachtbroking business in the town was bound to compete with the trust business, even if the customers were not solicited. This is a possible solution, but it does not appear to have been the basis of the decision in *Re Thomson*. *Re Thomson* seems clearly right in principle and it may well be that *Moore v. M'Glynn* would not now be followed. As has been shown, in other circumstances the court has been so astute to find a conflict of interest that it is doubtful if it would stop itself from finding a conflict where the same business was being carried on, at least if it were serving the same locality. Where, however, a person who is carrying on a business is then appointed to be a trustee, the position seems to depend on whether the person making the appointment knew of that business. If he did, the trustee will be entitled to continue his business, but if it then appears that there is an actual conflict of interest, he may be required to resign, or be removed.[51]

It might be expected that, if an unpaid trustee may thus in appropriate circumstances be prevented from competing, the paid director and partner would necessarily be prohibited from so doing. Partners are indeed under a statutory duty not to compete with the partnership business[52] but the position of directors is both obscure and anomalous. At common law, a director is not under any obligation not to compete with his company; this emerges from *London and Mashonaland Exploration Co. v. New Mashonaland Exploration Co.*,[53] where it was held that a director cannot be restrained from acting as a director of a rival company, a decision which was approved in *Bell v. Lever Bros*[54] by Lord Blanesburgh, who added that "[w]hat he could do for a rival company he could, of course, do for himself". However, in the light of authority that an employee may not compete with the business of his employer,[55] it seems likely that an executive director will be under a similar duty not to compete with his company—this seems to have been recognised by Lord Denning in *Scottish Co-operative Wholesale Society v. Meyer*,[56] which concerned an application under what is now section 459 of the Companies Act 1985 to wind a company up on the grounds that the manner in which its affairs were being conducted was unfairly prejudicial to the applicant. In practice, the matter must often be dealt with in the Articles of Association or in the service contract of any individual director. Thus, in *Thomas Marshall*

---

[50] [1894] 1 Ir.R. 74.
[51] See, by analogy, *Peyton v. Robinson* (1823) 1 L.J.(O.S.)Ch. 191; *Moore v. M'Glynn* [1894] 1 Ir.R. 74.
[52] By virtue of the Partnership Act 1890, s.30.
[53] [1891] 1 W.N. 165.
[54] [1932] A.C. 161 at 165.
[55] *Hivac v. Park Royal Scientific Instruments* [1946] Ch. 169.
[56] [1959] A.C. 324 at 366–367.

Exports v. Guinle,[57] a managing director had specifically agreed in his service contract not to engage in any other business without the company's consent or to disclose confidential information. It was alleged that he had done both as a means of diverting the company's business to himself and that, subsequently, he had repudiated his service contract by resigning half way through a fixed 10 year contract. Interim injunctions were granted restraining him from dealing with the company's customers and from disclosing any confidential information. This decision was based primarily on the express contractual stipulation but also, to a lesser extent, on his fiduciary obligations as a director. This suggests that, at least in the case of executive directors, competing with the business of the company will constitute a breach of fiduciary duty. However, it appears that merely to accept directorships in competing companies does not constitute a breach of the duty of loyalty owed by the director to the first company.

The authorities discussed establish that, where a fiduciary has breached his duty of loyalty by competing with the business of his principal, the latter can obtain an injunction restraining such competition. Further, although there does not seem to be any case in which this has actually been held,[58] the fiduciary should be liable to account to his principal for any profits which he has made out of this competition under a constructive trust.

(C) Renewal by a Fiduciary for his own Benefit of a Lease Formerly Held by his Principal

In *Keech v. Sandford*[59] a lease of a market was held on trust for an infant. The trustee sought, unsuccessfully, to renew the lease for the benefit of the trust. However, the landlord, although not prepared to renew the lease to the trust, was prepared to grant a renewal to the trustee in his personal capacity and the trustee duly took up the lease in his own right. Lord King L.C. held that any trustee who abuses his position by entering into a transaction with a third party must account for the benefit of the transaction as a constructive trustee. Consequently the trustee held the benefit of the lease on constructive trust for the infant. The rationale of the rule was stated both simply and cynically: if a trustee on the refusal of a lessor to renew a lease to the trust were permitted to take a lease himself, few leases would ever be renewed in favour of trusts. This prohibition was wholly understandable at that time. Many ecclesiastical, charitable and public bodies were by law restricted as to the length of leases which they were able to grant and leases were therefore renewed more or less as a matter of right. By taking a renewal of a lease for himself, a trustee was therefore in practice depriving the trust of a grant which it had a right to expect. This was also the time of the South Sea Bubble, a period of extravagant financial speculation and even more extravagant financial collapses, when the existence of stringent controls on the activities of fiduciaries was unquestionably necessary. However, the rule laid down in *Keech v. Sandford* has continued to be applied despite the relaxation of the rules as to the length of leases and the greater financial

---

[57] [1979] Ch. 227.
[58] Such a claim was made, unsuccessfully, in *Moore v. M'Glynn* [1894] 1 Ir.R. 74, where the trustee was held to have been entitled to compete with the trust business.
[59] (1726) Sel.Cas.Ch. 61.

stability of the nineteenth and twentieth centuries indeed it has been extended so as to apply also to other fiduciaries.

The precise limits of the rule were discussed very fully in *Re Biss.*[60] The Court of Appeal held that the rule applies with all its stringency to persons clearly occupying a fiduciary position such as trustees or agents; there is an irrebuttable presumption that such persons cannot retain the benefit of transactions entered into in their personal capacity. On the other hand, persons owing a special but non-fiduciary duty are subject only to a rebuttable presumption. Thus if such a person can show that he did not abuse his position, he can retain the benefit of the transaction. The court considered mortgagees, tenants for life, joint tenants, tenants in common and (rather unexpectedly) partners to be in this category. There seems no good reason why partners, who are quite clearly fiduciaries for all other purposes, should be in the latter rather than the former category and *Thompson's Trustee v. Heaton*[61] and *Popat v. Shonchintra*[62] (which actually concerned purchases of freehold reversions) may well have changed the law in this respect, although this question cannot yet be regarded as finally settled. On the other hand, it is clear that the rule in *Keech v. Sandford* does not apply to a person who owes neither fiduciary obligations nor a special non-fiduciary duty. Thus in *Savage v. Dunningham*,[63] where three persons were sharing an unfurnished flat and the rack rent payable therefor, it was held that one of them was perfectly entitled to purchase a long leasehold interest therein for his own benefit.

While the rule in *Keech v. Sandford* is certainly a stringent penal rule which it is impossible to justify in modern conditions, there is absolutely no doubt that it remains English law.

(D) Purchase by a Fiduciary of the Reversion on a Lease Held by his Principal

The rule in *Keech v. Sandford* has been extended to cases where the fiduciary has acquired the reversion, normally but obviously not necessarily the freehold reversion, in property of which his principal is lessee. When the fiduciary has acquired the reversion by means of an abuse of his fiduciary position or has only obtained the opportunity to purchase because, as fiduciary, he is the nominal lessee, it is clearly in accordance with principle for a constructive trust to be imposed.[64] Similarly, where the lease in question is renewable by custom, the fiduciary will also hold the reversion on constructive trust for his principal since, otherwise, he would be able to prejudice the interests of his principal by declining to renew the lease.[65] On the other hand, where the lease in question is not renewable by custom or by right, the acquisition of the reversion by the fiduciary can hardly be said to prejudice his principal and until relatively recently it was held that in such

---

[60] [1903] 2 Ch. 40.
[61] [1974] 1 W.L.R. 605. See *post*, p. 309.
[62] [1995] 1 W.L.R. 908. See *post*, p. 309.
[63] [1974] Ch. 181.
[64] *Griffith v. Owen* [1907] 1 Ch. 105.
[65] *Phillips v. Phillips* (1885) 29 Ch.D. 673.

circumstances a fiduciary who had not abused his position was entitled to retain the reversion for his own benefit.[66]

Thus far, the law was both clear and in accordance with principle. More recent cases have, however, raised some doubt as to whether a fiduciary can ever purchase a reversion for his own benefit. In *Protheroe v. Protheroe*[67] a husband held a leasehold on trust for himself and his wife in equal shares. After they had separated, he acquired the freehold reversion. The Court of Appeal, in a short extempore judgment which did not refer to any of the authorities just discussed, held that a trustee of leasehold property can never acquire the freehold for himself and imposed a constructive trust. It seems highly likely that the husband only obtained the opportunity to acquire the reversion because he was, as trustee, the nominal lessee. If this was the case, discussion and application of the earlier authorities would have made no difference. However, the broad principle thus enunciated was subsequently applied in *Thompson's Trustee v. Heaton*.[68] After the dissolution of a partnership, one of the partners remained in possession of land of which the partners had been and remained joint lessees. After that partner's death 14 years later, his executors acquired the freehold reversion and subsequently resold the land. The trustee in bankruptcy of the other partner successfully claimed to be entitled to one half of the profit so obtained, Pennycuick V.-C, holding that on the facts the leasehold interest remained an undistributed asset of the partnership and thus, by virtue of *Protheroe v. Protheroe*, neither partner could acquire the reversion for his sole benefit.

This decision obviously casts doubt on the statement by the Court of Appeal in *Re Biss*[69] that partners were only to be caught by the rule in *Keech v. Sandford* if it could be shown that an advantage had actually been obtained by virtue of their position (this dictum has admittedly already been criticised[70] but should it not at the very least have been discussed?). More significantly, the broad statement in *Protheroe v. Protheroe* was applied without reference to the earlier authorities, the application of which might well have led to a different result. This would not, however, have been the case in *Popat v. Shonchintra*,[71] in which *Thompson's Trustee v. Heaton* was subsequently applied, where another former partner had only acquired the opportunity to purchase the freehold because he had continued to run the business and was so clearly a trustee thereof. This decision also establishes that the beneficial interests in such reversions are divided in proportion to each partner's capital injections—an entirely justifiable extrapolation of the rule in *Keech v. Sandford*.

It may therefore well be that *Protheroe v. Protheroe* has swept away all the earlier distinctions and has established that a fiduciary may never purchase for his own benefit a reversion in property of which his principal is lessee.

---

[66] *Randall v. Russell* (1817) 3 Mer. 190; *Bevan v. Webb* [1905] 1 Ch. 620.
[67] [1968] 1 W.L.R. 519.
[68] [1974] 1 W.L.R. 605.
[69] [1903] 2 Ch. 40.
[70] See *ante*, p. 308.
[71] [1995] 1 W.L.R. 908. On appeal ([1997] 1 W.L.R 1367), the case was decided on the basis of technical partnership rules.

If this is indeed the case, then only where, as in *Savage v. Dunningham,*[72] a purchaser of a reversion is not a fiduciary at all will he be able to acquire it for his own benefit. The principle enunciated in *Protheroe v. Protheroe* seems unnecessarily harsh and it is therefore suggested that the approach of the earlier authorities was preferable.

(E)   Utilisation by a Fiduciary for his own Benefit of an Opportunity of Profit

A fiduciary is obviously entitled to utilise for his own benefit opportunities which have nothing whatever to do with the fiduciary relationship in question. The mere fact that a person is a trustee of an investment fund does not prevent him from purchasing shares in his private capacity—were this not the case, it would be impossible to find anyone prepared to accept a trusteeship. Equally obviously, if such a trustee obtains the opportunity to take up a rights issue by virtue of the fact that the trust is a shareholder in the company in question, then he is not entitled to take up that rights issue in his personal capacity and if he does so the shares in question will be subject to a constructive trust in favour of the fund. A fiduciary will only be in breach of his duty of loyalty to his principal if the transactions into which he enters in his personal capacity fall within the scope of his fiduciary obligations. As Oliver L.J. stated in *Swain v. The Law Society*[73]:

"What one has to do is ascertain first of all whether there was a fiduciary relationship and, if there was, from what it arose and what, if there was any, was the trust property and then to inquire whether that of which an account is claimed either arose, directly or indirectly, from the trust property itself or was acquired not only in the course of, but by reason of, the fiduciary relationship."

The question of whether a transaction falls within the scope of a fiduciary relationship will sometimes be capable of being resolved by reference to the terms of the agreement between the fiduciary and principal in question. Thus in *Aas v. Benham*[74] a member of a ship-broking partnership utilised information which he had received in his capacity as partner to help form a ship-building company of which he became a director. An action by his partners for an account of the benefits received from the company failed on the grounds that the business of the company was quite different from the business of the partnership, the Court of Appeal holding that there was nothing to prevent a partner utilising information obtained in his fiduciary capacity provided that he was not competing with the partnership business.[75] However, it is not often that the scope of a fiduciary obligation is

---

[72] [1974] Ch. 181.
[73] [1982] 1 W.L.R. 17, CA at 37. This approach was approved by Lord Brightman in the House of Lords at [1983] 1 A.C. 598 at 619.
[74] [1891] 2 Ch. 244.
[75] See also *British American Oil Producing Co. v. Midway Oil Company* (1938) 82 P. (2d) 1049 (Supreme Court of Oklahoma).

closely defined by the parties thereto and when it is not rather more difficulties can be encountered.

(1) Clear misconduct by the fiduciary

Cases of clear misconduct by a fiduciary are of course quite straightforward. In *Cook v. Deeks*[76] three of the four directors and shareholders of a company, with the intention of excluding the fourth member, arranged for a contract which they had negotiated on behalf of the company to be made with them in their private capacities. The excluded member claimed successfully that the company was entitled to the benefit of this contract. The Privy Council held that the whole reputation of the three had been obtained with the company; they could have excluded the plaintiff quite legitimately by using their majority shareholding to wind up the company but instead had used their position as directors to deprive the company of any chance of obtaining the contract. This was a clear case of abuse of fiduciary position. However, an identical attitude has been adopted where the misconduct of the fiduciary has been much more questionable. The decided cases of this type have generally arisen when the principal in question has been unable or unwilling to utilise an opportunity and the fiduciary has subsequently utilised that opportunity for his own benefit.

(2) Opportunities unutilised by the principal

(a) *The approach of the English authorities.* In *Regal (Hastings) v. Gulliver*[77] the plaintiff company owned a cinema in Hastings and wished to acquire two other local cinemas with the intention of selling the whole enterprise as a package. A subsidiary, with a capital of 5,000 £1 shares, was formed to take leases of these two cinemas. The original scheme was for only 2,000 of these shares to be paid up but the owner of the cinemas declined to grant the leases on this basis. Since the company could not afford to put more than £2,000 into the subsidiary, four of the directors and the company solicitor each subscribed for 500 shares and the fifth director found some outsiders to take up the remaining 500. The combined concern was then sold not as a whole but by way of takeover and each holder of shares in the subsidiary obviously made a profit. The purchasers then brought an action against all five directors and the company solicitor claiming that this profit had been made out of a breach of their fiduciary duty and therefore had to be accounted for to the company (this claim was wholly unmeritorious; its only objective was to recover part of the price which the purchasers had freely agreed to pay). The action against the director who had not subscribed for any shares obviously failed, for he had made no profit.[78] So too did the action against the company solicitor, for he had subscribed for his shares with the consent of the board of directors as then constituted. But the actions against the other four directors succeeded in the House of Lords, whose

---

[76] [1916] A.C. 554.

[77] [1942] 1 All E.R. 378; [1967] 2 A.C. 134N.

[78] No claim was brought against the outsiders for their profit. Any such claim would have been governed by the principles to be discussed in the next section of this Chapter (see *post*, p. 319).

decision was based fairly and squarely on *Keech v. Sandford*. Lord Russell of Killowen stated that the directors had unquestionably acquired their shares by virtue of their fiduciary position. It made no difference that the company could not itself have subscribed for the shares—the trust in *Keech v. Sandford* could not itself have obtained a new lease and that had made no difference. Thus the four directors had to surrender a profit which they would have been able to retain had the transaction been carried out in a different way and so were deprived of any return on their investment, while the purchasers finished up paying less for the cinemas than they had originally bargained to pay.

Given that the company could not afford to put more than £2,000 into the subsidiary, what alternative did the directors have? Lord Russell of Killowen thought that they should have obtained a resolution of the shareholders in general meeting approving the transaction.[79] This view seems to conflict with the decision in *Cook v. Deeks*,[80] where such a resolution had been obtained and was held to be ineffective. It was suggested in *Prudential Assurance Co. v. Newman Industries (No. 2)*[81] that a ratification by a company in general meeting will only be effective if the directors in question do not control the majority of the votes. It is not clear whether or not the directors of Regal (Hastings) did in fact control the majority[82]; only if they did not is this a valid distinction between *Cook v. Deeks* and *Regal (Hastings) v. Gulliver*. However, a very much more generous attitude to ratification was subsequently demonstrated by the Privy Council in *Queensland Mines v. Hudson*,[83] where the board of the plaintiff company, being fully informed of all relevant facts, decided to renounce all interest in the exploitation of certain mining exploration licences which it had obtained and assented to the venture being taken over by the defendant, a director of the company who had been its managing director until a shortage of finance had prevented the plaintiff from exploiting the licences itself. When the plaintiff subsequently claimed to be entitled to the profit obtained by the defendant, the Privy Council held that the defendant had obtained the opportunity to make this profit by virtue of his position as managing director of the plaintiff and was therefore in principle liable under *Regal (Hastings) v. Gulliver* to account for his profit; however, the fully-informed decision of the board amounted to sufficient consent to enable him to retain the profit. This conclusion is clearly inconsistent with the decision in *Regal (Hastings) v. Gulliver*, where all the members of the board had taken part in the impeached transaction and so must necessarily have consented to it. The approach taken by the Privy Council may be able to be justified on the grounds that the plaintiff had only two shareholders, both of whom were represented on the board, and the shareholder represented by the defendant held only 49 per cent of the shares the decision of the board can thus be regarded as a decision of the shareholders where the majority was not controlled by the defendant, which satisfies the test suggested in *Prudential Assurance Co. v. Newman Industries*

---

[79] [1942] 1 All E.R. 378 at 389; [1967] 2 A.C. 134N at 150.
[80] [1916] A.C. 554.
[81] [1981] Ch. 257 at 308 (Vinelott J.).
[82] The Editorial Note in [1942] 1 All E.R. 378 at 379 assumed that they did; Vinelott J. in *Prudential Assurance Co. v. Newman Industries (No. 2)* [1981] Ch. 257 at 308 disagreed.
[83] (1977) 18 A.L.R. 1.

(No. 2). In any event, one commentator has argued that the approach of the Privy Council should now be followed so that "if the board has taken a bona fide decision that the company should reject the opportunity on its merits, it may then permit one (or more) of its members to take it up".[84] It is clear that "a court is likely to take a deal of persuading that the board's decision to reject the opportunity was taken bona fide in the interests of the company rather than in that of their fellow director—especially if he has a powerful personality".[85] In practice, for the moment the only safe option seems to be a decision of the shareholders in general meeting and even this can only be guaranteed to work if the directors in question do not control the majority of the votes.

Leaving on one side the question of ratification, there is no doubt whatsoever that the decisions in *Regal (Hastings) v. Gulliver* and *Queensland Mines v. Hudson* are entirely consistent on the question of the liability of the directors in question to account and certainly represent English law at present. In both cases it was assumed that, in the absence of the appropriate consent, any director who obtained an opportunity by virtue of his fiduciary position was liable to account to the company for this profit. Thus it is clear that the courts are not prepared to countenance a fiduciary exploiting an opportunity for his own benefit and are more concerned to penalise him for having taken up an opportunity of entering into a profitable transaction on his own behalf than to ascertain whether or not there has been a conflict between his duty of loyalty to his principal and his own self-interest.

(b) *The approach of other jurisdictions.* Other jurisdictions have felt able to adopt a more flexible approach and have permitted directors to take up opportunities for their own benefit without the prior consent or subsequent ratification of their companies where there was no serious conflict of duty and interest.

In *Peso Silvermines v. Cropper*,[86] the defendant was on the board of the plaintiff company at a time when the company geologist invited and advised that board to purchase certain mining claims, some of which were contiguous to claims already owned by the company. The board rejected this offer partly for financial reasons and partly because some of the directors considered the claims to be an uninviting business risk. Subsequently, the geologist, with the defendant and two other directors of the plaintiff, formed a company to purchase and exploit these claims. In due course, the plaintiff was taken over and its new board claimed that the defendant held his shares in the new company on constructive trust for the plaintiff. This claim failed. The Court of Appeal of British Columbia rejected *Regal (Hastings) v. Gulliver* and held, by a majority, that the strict penal rules of equity had been carried far enough and were not appropriate for a modern country in a modern era. The Supreme Court of Canada took a rather narrower view and merely distinguished *Regal (Hastings) v. Gulliver* on the grounds that the defendant had acted entirely in good faith in participating in the initial decision of the

---

[84] Gower, *Principles of Modern Company Law* (5th Ed., 1992), p. 570.
[85] *ibid*.
[86] (1966) 56 D.L.R.(2d) 1 (British Columbia Court of Appeal); 58 D.L.R.(2d) 1 (Supreme Court of Canada).

board not to purchase the claims. He had not obtained any advantage at all as a result of participating in this decision and was therefore entitled to take up a subsequent offer in his private capacity without being liable to account for his profit. Even this narrower view seems preferable in every way to the approach adopted in *Regal (Hastings) v. Gulliver*. It is undoubtedly possible to criticise *Peso Silvermines v. Cropper* on the grounds that "[t]o allow directors to decide that the company shall not accept the opportunity and then to accept the opportunity themselves might impose too great a strain on their impartiality".[87] However, the sort of attitude adopted by the House of Lords in *Regal (Hastings) v. Gulliver* prevents such matters of policy being raised at all; this in itself is an argument for the adoption of a more flexible attitude, even if its adoption does not in the end alter the conclusion actually reached by the courts.

In *Consul Development v. D.P.C. Estates*[88] the High Court of Australia adopted an attitude similar to that of the Supreme Court of Canada. The plaintiff was one of a group of property companies which employed a manager to find properties for purchase. He was under an express duty of confidentiality in respect of all group business and had undertaken not to engage in real estate business other than for the group. However, in breach of these obligations, he collaborated with another employee of the group, who was also the managing director of the defendant, by providing him with information about a number of properties which the defendant then acquired, telling him, for reasons which were entirely plausible, that the group was not interested in their acquisition. The plaintiff succeeded in recovering the manager's own profit on the grounds that he had breached his duty of loyalty but failed in its claim that the properties were subject to a constructive trust. A majority of the High Court held that the manager would have been entitled to purchase the properties for himself if the group had really declined to buy them. The defendant was entitled to believe that this was in fact the case and so was clearly entitled to purchase them for its own benefit and retain its entire profit. This approach also seems preferable to that adopted in *Regal (Hastings) v. Gulliver*.

(c)   *The two approaches contrasted in Boardman v. Phipps.*[89] The contrast between the two approaches emerges extremely clearly from the majority and minority speeches handed down in the controversial decision of the House of Lords in *Boardman v. Phipps*.

A testator established a trust for the benefit of his widow and children. Some 12 years after his death, the trust solicitor, Boardman, became concerned about one of the principal assets of the fund—a 27 per cent holding in a private company. After an unsuccessful attempt to bring about the election of one of the testator's sons to the board of the company, Boardman reached the conclusion that the only way of protecting the trust investment was to acquire a majority holding in the company. He suggested this to the

---

[87] Gower, *op.cit.*, 567. Similar sentiments have been expressed by D. D. Prentice in (1967) 30 M.L.R. 450 and by Swan J. in *Irving Trust Co. v. Deutsch* (1934) 73 Fed. (2d) 121, 124 (United States Circuit Court of Appeals).

[88] (1975) 132 C.L.R. 373.

[89] [1967] 2 A.C. 46.

managing trustee, who said that it was entirely out of the question for the trust to acquire such a holding. Boardman and the son then decided to purchase the outstanding shares themselves. They duly obtained control of the company and by capitalising some of the assets, were able to make a distribution of capital without reducing the value of the shares. The trust benefitted by this distribution to the tune of £47,000 and Boardman and his colleague made a profit of about £75,000. However, in the course of negotiations leading up to the takeover, Boardman had purported to represent the trust and thereby had incontrovertibly obtained information which would not have been made available to the general public. One of the other sons of the testator, who had not been particularly fully consulted, therefore claimed that this profit of £75,000 had been made by the utilisation of information which had reached Boardman while acting on behalf of the trust and so in a fiduciary capacity. This claim was upheld by the House of Lords, who held that the shares which had been acquired were subject to a constructive trust in favour of the trust. Thus, in effect, the trust obtained the whole of the profit made on the takeover, less an allowance which the House awarded to Boardman under its inherent jurisdiction by way of remuneration for the work which he had done.[90]

All the members of the House of Lords agreed that the defendants had placed themselves in a fiduciary relationship by acting as representatives of the trust for a number of years and that out of this fiduciary relationship they had obtained the opportunity to make a profit and the knowledge that a profit was there to be made (this was clearly the case).

The majority adduced two inter-connected reasons for going on to hold that the defendants were therefore liable as constructive trustees to account for their profit to the trust. Lord Hodson and Lord Guest both clearly held that, since the only basis on which the defendants had obtained their information was the fact that they had been purporting to represent the trust, this information was trust property. Therefore, the defendants had, in effect, made a profit out of speculating with trust property and thus were clearly liable. Lord Cohen reached the same conclusion by a slightly different route. He held that information was not property in the strict sense of the word and that it did not necessarily follow that a fiduciary must account for any profit obtained by the use of information acquired in his fiduciary capacity. In this case, however, the information had been acquired while the defendants had been purporting to represent the trust. Thus, the defendants were liable to account for their profit under the principle in *Regal (Hastings) v. Gulliver*. Further, all three members of the majority felt that Boardman had placed himself in a position where his duty and interest might conflict (such a conflict would have arisen, for example, had the trustees sought his advice as to the merits of the trust acquiring a majority holding in the company). No matter how remote the possibility of such a conflict arising, a fiduciary who placed himself in this position was bound to account to his principal for any profit he had made. Since the defendants had accepted that their positions were the same, both were thus liable to account for their profit. In the opinion of the majority, it was quite immaterial that the defendants had acted honestly and openly in a manner highly beneficial to the trust in a

---

[90] This aspect of the decision will be discussed, see *post*, p. 647.

situation where the trust itself could not have utilised the information which they had received.

The dissentients (Viscount Dilhorne and Lord Upjohn) took the view that the remoteness of the possibility of any conflict of interest arising and the various factors just referred to which the majority had found irrelevant led inescapably to the conclusion that the defendants had not breached their duty of loyalty to the trust. Lord Upjohn said that a conflict of interest only arose where the reasonable man looking at all the relevant circumstances would think that there was a real sensible possibility of conflict and not where the only possibility of conflict arose from events not contemplated as real sensible probabilities by any reasonable person. Boardman knew when he decided to proceed on his own behalf that there was no possibility of the trustees seeking his advice as to the merits of a purchase by the trust—the managing trustee had already told him that this was quite out of the question. Further, Lord Upjohn doubted the classification of the information as trust property. He said that information was not in any sense property; equity would merely restrain its transmission to another in breach of confidence. This was not such a case.

If the information was indeed properly classifiable as trust property, then the defendants had of course made a profit out of speculating with property of the trust and were therefore clearly liable as constructive trustees under the principle laid down in *Reid-Newfoundland Co. v. Anglo-American Telegraph Co.*,[91] which was discussed at the beginning of this section.[92] However, it is clear that information cannot be trust property in any normal sense; if it were, it could presumably be followed into the hands of the whole world other than a bona fide purchaser thereof for value without notice. Given the essential nature of information, which can be divulged in its entirety to any number of persons, such a conclusion could lead to quite absurd results.[93]

That is not to say that a fiduciary should automatically be entitled to utilise for his own benefit information which has come to him in his fiduciary capacity. A fiduciary who by the utilisation of such information abuses his fiduciary position should clearly be liable as a constructive trustee, but as a result of the application of the principles which have already been discussed, not by the automatic classification of the information as the property of his principal. Such a case was *Industrial Development Consultants v. Cooley*.[94] The defendant, who was managing director of the plaintiff company, had been attempting, on behalf of the plaintiff, to obtain a contract to design certain depots for the Eastern Gas Board. These attempts failed because the Gas Board did not like the plaintiff's organisation and were not prepared to deal with the plaintiff in any capacity. The following year, a representative of the Gas Board sought a meeting with the defendant in his private capacity and intimated to him that if he could free himself from his ties with the plaintiff he had a very good chance of obtaining the contract for himself. The defendant therefore secured his release from his contract with the plaintiff by a totally false representation that he was on the verge of a

---

[91] [1891] 2 Ch. 244.
[92] See *ante*, p. 304.
[93] See G. H. Jones: (1968) 84 L.Q.R. 472.
[94] [1972] 1 W.L.R. 443.

nervous breakdown and accepted an offer from the Gas Board to do substantially the same work which he had unsuccessfully attempted to obtain for the plaintiff the year before. The plaintiff claimed that the defendant was a trustee of that contract for the benefit of the plaintiff and successfully sought an account of the defendant's profits. At the time when the defendant first realised that he had an opportunity of obtaining the contract for himself, the only capacity in which he was carrying on business was as managing director of the plaintiff and as such he was under a fiduciary duty to pass on to the plaintiff any information which reached him while carrying on business in that capacity. His failure to do so and subsequent utilisation of the information for his own benefit was a clear breach of fiduciary duty which made him a trustee of the contract for the plaintiff, who was entitled to all the profit thereunder. Similar decisions have been reached in other jurisdictions.[95] It is thus clear that a constructive trust can be imposed on a fiduciary who has abused his position whether or not the information which he has utilised is classified as the property of his principal.[96] Therefore, given the absurd consequences of such a classification, there is no good reason why it should ever be adopted.

There has also been considerable criticism of the majority decision in *Boardman v. Phipps* that the fiduciaries were not entitled to exploit for their own benefit the opportunity of purchasing a controlling interest in the company.[97] Not only has reference been made to the fact that other jurisdictions have felt able to adopt a more flexible approach.[98] It has also been demonstrated that the conflict of interest found to exist by the House of Lords is in fact wholly illusory; given that it arose out of the mere possibility that Boardman might in the future have been asked to advise the trustees, in this eventuality he could, like any other solicitor, have declined to advise them or, if they insisted, have declared his interest.[99] There is much to be said for these criticisms but that does not alter the fact that the approach adopted by the majority in *Boardman v. Phipps* in relation to the rights of

---

[95] *Pre-Cam Exploration Co. v. McTavish* [1966] S.C.R. 551; *Canadian Aero Services v. O'Malley* (1973) 40 D.L.R.(3d) 371 (both decisions of the Supreme Court of Canada); *Consul Development v. D.P.C. Estates* (1975) 49 A.L.J.R. 74 (High Court of Australia).

[96] Quite apart from any question of the imposition of a constructive trust for breach of fiduciary duty, both fiduciaries and non-fiduciaries may be held liable for breach of the equitable obligation of confidence; where a person who has received information in confidence takes unfair advantage of it to the prejudice of the person who disclosed it to him, the courts will consider the whole gamut of remedies open to them and award that which is most appropriate to the situation. See Goff & Jones, *op.cit.*, pp. 679–702 and F. Gurry, *Breach of Confidence* (1984).

[97] See particularly G. H. Jones: (1968) 84 L.Q.R. 472 and Finn, *Fiduciary Obligations, op.cit.*, pp. 244–246.

[98] In the authorities discussed *ante*, p. 313 and also in *Manufacturers Trust Co. v. Becker* (1949) 338 U.S. 304, where the Supreme Court of the United States of America held that directors of a company had been entitled to encourage their associates to purchase its debentures at a time when their market value was a fraction of their face value; not only had the directors acted in the best interests of the company, their associates' profits had been made at the expense not of the company but of the selling bond-holders, who had in no way been misled or deceived.

[99] If it is indeed the law that a person cannot benefit himself in any matter in which he might in the future be asked to advise, it is difficult to see how any professional person can ever safely enter into a transaction on his own behalf in any area in which he habitually advises.

fiduciaries to utilise for their own benefit opportunities of profit is entirely consistent with the earlier authorities such as *Regal (Hastings) v. Gulliver* and is undoubtedly representative of the present state of English law.

(d)   *Possible ways forward.* By way of conclusion, mention should be made of two possible means by which the harsh attitude at present adopted under English law might conceivably be alleviated.

The first relates to remedies. All the decisions adverse to fiduciaries which have been discussed in this section have given rise to the imposition of a constructive trust. This fact is in itself an aspect of the penal attitude displayed by the authorities. However, the relatively recent decision of the High Court of Australia in *Warman International v. Dwyer*[1] has demonstrated that the other remedies available for breach of fiduciary duty which have already been discussed[2] can also be utilised in cases of this type. The plaintiffs had declined an opportunity to participate in a joint venture with a manufacturer whose products they distributed. The manufacturer therefore terminated the distributorship, as it was entitled to do at any time, and instead carried out the joint venture with the defendant, the employee of the plaintiffs most closely connected with the distributorship. He had clearly committed a technical breach of fiduciary duty[3] but the court declined to hold that the goodwill of the joint venture was held on constructive trust for the plaintiffs, awarding instead an account of the first two years' profits of the joint venture less an appropriate allowance for the expenses, skill expertise, effort and resources contributed by the joint venturers. The High Court specifically distinguished between cases in which a fiduciary acquires an asset which was within the scope and ambit of his fiduciary responsibilities, where it will be appropriate to impose a constructive trust, and cases in which a business is acquired and operated, where it may well not be. Adoption of this approach by the English courts would not necessarily alter the result of either *Regal (Hastings) v. Gulliver* or *Boardman v. Phipps*[4] but would have a profound effect on the liability of fiduciaries who acquire and operate businesses as a result of a purely technical breach of fiduciary duty.

Secondly, in *Target Holdings v. Redferns*[5] Lord Browne-Wilkinson, in an entirely different context,[6] said that it is "wrong to lift wholesale the detailed rules developed in the context of traditional trusts and then seek to apply them to trusts of quite a different kind". No better example of this practice can be found than the utilisation by Lord Russell of Killowen in *Regal*

---

[1] (1995) 128 A.L.R. 201.

[2] See *ante*, p. 287.

[3] Although he had not participated in the plaintiffs' decision to reject the manufacturer's proposal, his conduct had probably caused the manufacturer to terminate its agency earlier than it might otherwise have done.

[4] This would only be the case if the shares acquired in those cases by the respective fiduciaries could be held not to fall within the scope and ambit of their fiduciary responsibilities; it is somewhat improbable that such a conclusion would ever be reached on the facts of *Regal (Hastings) v. Gulliver* although it has already been argued that it should have been in *Boardman v. Phipps*.

[5] [1996] 1 A.C. 421, see *post*, p. 683.

[6] That of the liability of trustees who have paid away trust property in breach of trust to reconstitute the trust fund.

(Hastings) v. Gulliver of the decision in *Keech v. Sandford* more than two centuries earlier: it made no difference in *Regal (Hastings) v. Gulliver* that the company could not itself have subscribed for the shares—the trust in *Keech v. Sandford* could not itself have obtained a new lease and that had made no difference there. If Lord Browne-Wilkinson's remarks cause judges to think twice before automatically applying conclusions reached in totally different legal and economic contexts to modern conditions, English law may indeed one day adopt the more flexible attitudes already manifested in other jurisdictions.

III. Dispositions of Trust Property in Breach of Trust[7]

When trust property has been disposed of in breach of trust, the courts will, in certain circumstances, impose the obligations of trusteeship on those responsible for the wrongful disposition. Equity has always been prepared to impose on any person who has officiously chosen to act as a fiduciary the appropriate fiduciary obligations, by virtue of which he will hold any property which he has received in his assumed capacity on constructive trust for the person on whose behalf he has chosen to act. Such a person has obviously intermeddled with property which is subject to a trust but this is merely the most obvious example of a constructive trust being imposed as a result of a disposition of trust property in breach of trust. However, equity is also prepared, in appropriate circumstances, to impose the obligations of trusteeship on strangers in three other situations: first, on anyone who has dishonestly been accessory to, or assisted in, a disposition of property in breach of trust (this type of liability is now generally known as liability for "dishonest assistance", although until a change in the law in 1995 it was instead generally known as liability for "knowing assistance"); secondly, on anyone who, with the requisite level of knowledge, has received for this own benefit property which has been disposed of in breach of trust (this type of liability is generally known as liability for "knowing receipt"); and, thirdly, on anyone who has received lawfully and not for his own benefit property subject to a trust but who has subsequently either misappropriated it or dealt with it in some other manner which is inconsistent with the trust (this type of liability is generally known as liability for "inconsistent dealing").

It is important to distinguish between these different types of liability. If solicitors or accountants invest trust funds in their hands without any instructions from the trustees, they will be potentially liable to be treated as

---

[7] Virtually every legal periodical has contained a recent article on this subject. See particularly: C. Harpum: (1986) 102 L.Q.R. 114 & 267 and in *Frontiers of Liability* (ed. Birks, 1994), p. 9; D. J. Hayton: (1985) 27 Malaya Law Review 313; R. P. Austin in *Essays in Equity* (ed. Finn, 1985), p. 196; P. L. Loughlin: (1989) 9 O.J.L.S. 260, P. B. H. Birks: [1989] L.M.C.L.Q. 378 & [1993] L.C.M.L.Q. 218; E. McKendrick: [1991] L.M.C.L.Q. 378; P. D. Finn in *Equity, Fiduciaries and Trusts* 1993 (ed. Waters, 1993), p. 195; Lord Nicholls of Birkenhead, extra-judicially, in *Restitution—Past, Present and Future* (ed. Cornish, 1998), p. 231.

trustees of the investments because of their officious conduct; if, in accordance with directions from the trustees, they transfer trust funds to a third party in breach of trust, they will be potentially liable for "dishonest assistance"; if, in accordance with directions from the trustees, they use trust funds to settle their professional fees, they will be potentially liable for "knowing receipt"; and, if they themselves debit the trust funds to settle their professional fees, they will be potentially liable for "inconsistent dealing".

Similarly, if a bank deals with funds in an account which it knows to be a trust account without any instructions from the trustees, it will be potentially liable to be treated as a trustee of those funds because of its officious conduct; if it permits a cheque drawn on that account to be credited in breach of trust to the account of a third party but acts merely as the conduit by means of which the funds are transferred from one account to the other, it will be potentially liable for "dishonest assistance"; if the account of the third party is overdrawn at the time of the transfer, the bank may additionally be potentially liable for "knowing receipt" to the extent that it has utilised the funds in reduction of the overdraft; and, if the bank itself debits the balance of the account to cover an overdraft created in another account held by the same person, it will potentially be liable for "inconsistent dealing". However, in the case of banks, it is not always particularly easy to distinguish between liability for "dishonest assistance" and liability for "knowing receipt" in relation to the fees and commissions which banks commonly charge for carrying out certain types of transactions. Fees are normally charged for transactions such as issuing banker's drafts while commissions are normally charged for bank transfers, particularly those to other jurisdictions in the same or in a different currency. In the event that such a transaction amounts to a breach of trust, the potential liability of the bank in respect of the amount of the banker's draft or transfer will clearly be for "dishonest assistance"; however, in principle the bank should also be potentially liable for "knowing receipt" in respect of any fees or commissions which it has charged. Not only has this latter liability generally been ignored by the courts; a quite different distinction was adopted in *Polly Peck International v. Nadir (No. 2)*.[8] In this case a bank effectively controlled by the plaintiff company made a number of transfers of the plaintiff's funds totalling about £45,000,000 to the London branch of the Central Bank of Northern Cyprus in exchange for a corresponding amount of either sterling or Turkish lire being credited to its account with the Central Bank in Northern Cyprus. Scott L.J. held[9] that the potential liability of the Central Bank to the liquidators of the plaintiff company in respect of the sterling transfers was for "dishonest assistance" since it had "received the funds transferred not in its own right but as banker and, as a banker, credited the funds . . . in Northern Cyprus" but that its potential liability in respect of the Turkish lire transfers was for "knowing receipt" because "it was exchanging Turkish lire for sterling and became entitled to the sterling not as banker . . . but in its own right". Apart from any fees or commissions which the Central Bank may

---

[8] [1992] 4 All E.R. 769.
[9] *ibid.* at 777.

have charged, to which no reference was made, the bank became no more beneficially entitled to the Turkish lire than it did to the sterling. It is therefore difficult to justify the distinction made by Scott L.J.[10] and it is suggested that it should not be followed.

The growth of discovered corporate fraud in recent years has ensured that the courts have had to consider the availability and scope of these remedies on an ever-increasing number of occasions. The proceedings which have been brought have, however, generally involved not only claims for the imposition of the obligations of trusteeship but also a considerable number of other claims arising out of the same disposition of property in breach of trust; the possibilities include proprietary claims, both at law and in equity, to trace the property into the hands of its recipients, personal claims at law for money had and received, and personal claims in equity against whoever was responsible for initiating the disposition in question. (Indeed the inter-relation of all these different claims has made some of the recent proceedings extremely complex and commentators have begun to question whether so many different remedies should continue to be available for the same dis-position of property.[11]) However, there is no doubt at all that by far the most effective way to proceed is to seek the imposition of the obligations of trusteeship, particularly if anyone can be found who is potentially liable for "dishonest assistance" given that potential defendants of this type tend to be either members of the professions with insurance against liability for pro-fessional negligence or financial institutions of virtually guaranteed sol-vency.[12] Such persons are far more likely to be able to satisfy any unfavourable judgment than the other potential defendants—the initiators of the offending disposition and the recipients of the property in question. Indeed the presumed solvency of persons who have been accessory to or dishonestly assisted in a disposition of property in breach of trust is the basic reason why this particular area of the law has become so important in recent years.

---

[10] It has not been followed in New Zealand; see *Nimmo v. Westpac Banking Corporation* [1993] 3 N.Z.L.R. 218 and *Cigna Life Insurance New Zealand v. Westpac Securities* [1996] 1 N.Z.L.R. 80.

[11] See particularly Sir Peter Millett, writing extra-judicially: (1991) 107 L.Q.R. 71; Lord Hoff-mann, writing extra-judicially, in *Frontiers of Liability* (ed. Birks, 1994), p. 27; C. Harpum: *ibid.*, at p. 9; P. D. Finn, *op.cit.*, p. 195; Lord Nicholls of Birkenhead, writing extra-judicially, in *Restitution—Past, Present and Future* (ed. Cornish, 1998), p. 231.

[12] Liability for "dishonest assistance" is potentially much more onerous than liability for "knowing receipt" or "inconsistent dealing". The latter will generally merely restore the status quo; any order for repayment of the trust funds utilised will normally simply recon-stitute the original potential loss in respect of the professional fees or overdraft in question. The only situation in which the position will be any worse than it was at the outset will be if the use of the trust funds to discharge the fees or overdraft has given a false impression of the financial position of the client and thus caused further fees to be run up or further advances to be made. The imposition of liability for "dishonest assistance" will, on the other hand, necessarily involve the payment of funds which have never been beneficially received by the member of the professions or advanced by the financial institution in question; what is more, the quantum of potential liability is not in any way restricted to the value of the fees and commissions which the services rendered could reasonably have been expected to bring in.

1. *Officiously Acting as a Fiduciary*[13]

Any person who takes it upon himself to act as a fiduciary without having been appointed as such will in every respect be treated as if he had been expressly appointed to the office in question and will be held to be a constructive trustee of any property acquired by him in the course of his intervention.

In *Mara v. Browne*[14] A. L. Smith L.J. stated that "if one, not being a trustee and not having authority from a trustee, takes upon himself to intermeddle with trust matters or to do acts characteristic of the office of trustee, he may therefore make himself what is called in law a trustee of his own wrong—*i.e.* a trustee *de son tort*, or, as it is also termed, a constructive trustee". Control of the property is a prerequisite of liability. In *Re Barney*,[15] Kekewich J., referring specifically to this type of liability, stated particularly clearly that "it is essential to the character of a trustee that he should have trust property actually vested in him or so far under his control that he has nothing to do but require that, perhaps by one process, perhaps by another, it should be vested in him".

A good illustration of the imposition of this type of liability is provided by *Blyth v. Fladgate*.[16] Trust funds were, by direction of the sole trustee, paid to a firm of solicitors and invested in Exchequer Bills, which were deposited in the name of the firm. Subsequently, following the death of the sole trustee and before any new trustees had been appointed, the Exchequer Bills were sold and the proceeds of sale invested in a mortgage, the security for which proved to be insufficient. The partners of the firm were held liable to account to the trust for the sums so lost on the basis that they themselves had been carrying out the functions of the trustees; they were clearly constructive trustees of the proceeds of sale and, as such, responsible for any improper investment. It is entirely proper that the law should impose the office of trustee upon a person who purports to act as such without authority. Such a person should clearly be burdened with all the same responsibilities and liabilities as an express trustee.[17] Thus, in addition to being a constructive trustee of any property which he receives, he will also be responsible for any diminution in its value and will be subject to all the rules discussed in the previous section of this Chapter; if an intermeddler obtains a secret profit, he will be in exactly the same position as if he had been an express trustee.

Similar principles apply to fiduciaries other than trustees. Most of the cases have concerned persons who have taken it upon themselves to act as agents. In *Lyell v. Kennedy*,[18] during the 22 years which it took to determine the identity of the heir at law of a landowner, his manager continued to collect the rents from the tenants without telling them of the death of their landlord. The House of Lords held that, since he had taken it upon himself

---

[13] C. Harpum in *Frontiers of Liability* (ed. Birks, 1994), p. 9 describes this as "Primary Liability".
[14] [1896] 1 Ch. 199 at 209.
[15] [1982] 2 Ch. 265 at 273.
[16] [1891] 1 Ch. 337. The explanation of the decision given in the text is that adopted by Vinelott J. in *Re Bell's Indenture* [1980] 1 W.L.R. 1217.
[17] *Soar v. Ashwell* [1893] 2 Q.B. 390 at 394, *per* Lord Esher M.R.
[18] (1889) 14 App.Cas. 437.

to receive the rents of property which he knew to belong to another, he held these sums (which had been placed in a separate bank account) on constructive trust for the heir. Lord Selborne emphasised that the motives which induce a person to intermeddle in the administration of a trust or other fiduciary relationship are totally irrelevant to the imposition of a constructive trust; thus it made no difference whether the manager had intervened with the intention of protecting the interests of the heir at law or with the intention of taking the benefit for himself. The latter was clearly the intention of the prospective purchaser in *English v. Dedham Vale Properties*[19] who, purporting without authority to act as agent for the prospective vendors, submitted an application for planning permission in respect of part of the subject matter of the proposed sale and was held liable to account to the vendors for the profits made thereby.[20]

2. Dishonestly Assisting in a Disposition of Property in Breach of Trust[21]

(A) Terminology

This first situation in which the obligations of trusteeship have been imposed, on persons who have dishonestly been accessory to or assisted in a disposition of property in breach of trust, is now generally known as liability for "dishonest assistance", although until a change in the law in 1995 it was instead generally known as liability for "knowing assistance". The vast majority of the judgments describe those persons on whom this type of liability is imposed as constructive trustees. It will however be apparent from the preceding paragraphs that the essential feature of this type of liability is the fact that property subject to a trust has by virtue of the assistance provided reached the hands of a third party who may or may not himself be under some proprietary or personal obligation to restore it. Indeed, it is only ever necessary to attempt to impose this head of liability upon persons who have not beneficially received the property in question (anyone who has actually taken the property beneficially will be subject to the different, and probably more stringent, heads of liability for "knowing receipt" or "inconsistent dealing" which will be discussed later on in this section). The classification of such persons as constructive trustees, although clearly established by the authorities, is as a matter of principle somewhat difficult to reconcile with the inherent nature of a trust. As has already been mentioned in the introductory section of this Chapter,[22] given that a trust is a relationship in respect of property, it might be expected to follow that a constructive trust can only be imposed if there is some identifiable property upon which to impose it. However, in the cases in which the obligations of trusteeship have been imposed on persons who have dishonestly been accessory to or assisted in a disposition of property in breach of trust, there has often been no obviously identifiable property subject to the trust.

---

[19] [1978] 1 W.L.R. 93.
[20] Had he waited until after exchange of contracts, the equitable interest thereby acquired would have entitled him to make the application for his own benefit.
[21] C. Harpum in *Frontiers of Liability* (ed. Birks, 1993) describes this as "Secondary Liability".
[22] See *ante*, p. 267.

Where the person upon whom the obligations of trusteeship have been imposed has played an active part in the disposition of the property in question, as in the case of a solicitor or bank who, following the instructions of trustees, has actually made the disposition in question, it is just about possible to identify property subject to the trust. This is because the fact that the property in question passed through the hands of the person upon whom the obligations of trusteeship were imposed makes it possible to argue that a constructive trust in fact arose at the moment when the property was actually in the hands of the constructive trustee. However, quite apart from the fact that none of the judges has ever seemed to have regarded as important the question of what property was subject to the constructive trust said to be being imposed, there are other decisions in which it is, on any view, totally impossible to identify any such property. This is because in these cases the obligations of trusteeship were imposed on persons who had never received or in any way controlled the property in question. Thus in *Eaves v. Hickson*[23] the obligations of trusteeship were imposed on a father who produced a forged marriage certificate to the trustees of a settlement in order to convince them that his children were legitimate and so entitled to the trust property, which was duly distributed to them. Liability was imposed on the basis that he had dishonestly induced the disposition in question and so was accessory to it.

As has already been seen, the existence of these authorities has led some commentators[24] to contend that there are in fact two types of constructive trust. This view recently received powerful support from Lord Browne-Wilkinson in *Westdeutsche Landesbank Girozentrale v. Islington L.B.C.*,[25] where he said: "The only apparent exception to this rule [that there must be identifiable trust property] is a constructive trust imposed on a person who dishonestly assists in a breach of trust who may come under fiduciary duties even if he does not receive identifiable trust property." This view acknowledges that the type of constructive trust imposed in *Eaves v. Hickson* does not confer any proprietary rights on the constructive beneficiary (obviously the case since none of the trust property had ever been in the hands of the father at any stage) but merely imposes on the constructive trustee a personal liability to account to that beneficiary for his actions. For this reason the constructive trusteeship so imposed has been described as "a fiction which provides a useful remedy where no remedy is available in contract or in tort."[26]

Nevertheless, while there is no doubt that it was entirely appropriate for the defendants in *Eaves v. Hickson*, and in at least some of the other cases in which the courts have purported to impose constructive trusts, to have been held liable, it is not easy to see any point in classifying an obligation as a trust if no proprietary rights can be conferred thereby—why create an exception to the general requirements for the existence of a trust if that exception will not enjoy the main consequence of the existence of a trust?

---

[23] (1861) 30 Beav. 136.
[24] See Ford & Lee: *op.cit.*, para. 22020 and previous editions of Hayton & Marshall: *op.cit.* (*e.g.* the 9th ed., 1991, pp. 440–441)
[25] [1996] A.C. 669 at 705.
[26] D. J. Hayton (1985) 27 Mal.L.R. 313 at 314.

Ungoed-Thomas J. stated in *Selangor United Rubber Estates v. Cradock (No. 3)*[27] that this type of constructive trust "is nothing more than a formula for equitable relief. The court of equity says that the defendant shall be liable in equity, as though he were a trustee." In accordance with this reasoning, it seems more appropriate to regard decisions of this type not as examples of the imposition of a constructive trust but rather as examples of equity imposing a quite distinct remedy—a personal liability to account in the same manner as a trustee. This view was confirmed by Millett J. in *Agip (Africa) v. Jackson*,[28] who adopted this terminology.[29] Nevertheless, it has to be admitted, as Lord Browne-Wilkinson's remarks clearly demonstrate, that most of the judges have continued to describe persons on whom such liability is imposed as constructive trustees.[30]

(B) The Elements of Liability for "Dishonest Assistance"

In *Barnes v. Addy*[31] Lord Selborne L.C. stated that "strangers are not to be made constructive trustees merely because they act as the agents of trustees in transactions within their legal powers, transactions, perhaps, of which a Court of Equity may disapprove, unless those agents receive and become chargeable with some part of the trust property, or unless they assist with knowledge in a dishonest and fraudulent design on the part of the trustees". In this passage Lord Selborne was concerned to protect not agents who have exceeded the scope of their authority—such agents will be liable either for breach of their obligations as such[32] or for officiously acting as fiduciaries under the authorities which have already been considered[33]—but agents who have followed the instructions of the trustees. He held that if, as a result of so doing, they have assisted in bringing about a disposition of property in breach of trust, they are only to be liable to the beneficiaries if they have assisted with knowledge in a dishonest and fraudulent design on the part of the trustees.

Even though it has been demonstrated that this classic statement of the law was not wholly consistent with the pre-existing authorities,[34] it has been used as the starting point in almost every subsequent decision. What conduct will give rise to this form of liability? In *Baden v. Société Générale*[35] Peter Gibson J. isolated four distinct elements: the existence of a trust; the existence of a dishonest and fraudulent design on the part of the trustee of the trust; the assistance by the stranger in that design; and the knowledge of the

---

[27] [1968] 1 W.L.R. 1555 at 1582.

[28] [1990] Ch. 265 at 292.

[29] It has also been adopted by some Commonwealth judges.

[30] Particularly by the Court of Appeal in *Agip (Africa) v. Jackson* [1991] Ch. 547 and in *Polly Peck International v. Nadir (No. 2)* [1992] 3 All E.R. 769.

[31] (1874) 9 Ch. App. 244 at 251–252.

[32] As in *Lee v. Sankey* (1873) L.R. 15 Eq. 204, where solicitors employed to receive the proceeds of sale of part of the trust property paid it to only one rather than both of the trustees. He misinvested it and died insolvent. The solicitors were held liable to account to the beneficiaries for the sums paid to him.

[33] See *ante*, p. 322.

[34] See C. Harpum in *Frontiers of Liability* (ed. Birks, 1993).

[35] (1983) [1993] 1 W.L.R. 509N at 573. The full name of this case is *Baden v. Société Générale pour Favoriser le Développement du Commerce et de l'Industrie en France S.A.*

stranger. However, the second and fourth of these requirements were sub-stantially modified in two important respects by the decision of the Privy Council in *Royal Brunei Airlines v. Tan.*[36] In the light of this, it now seems preferable to isolate the following four distinct elements: the existence of a trust; the existence of a misfeasance or breach of trust on the part of the trustee of the trust; being accessory to or assisting in the misfeasance or breach of trust; and dishonesty by the accessory or person assisting.

(1) The existence of a trust

Most of the older cases concerned the situation expressly envisaged by Lord Selborne, where agents of trustees have assisted in bringing about a mis-application of the trust property by following the instructions of the trus-tees.[37] Many modern cases have equally concerned express trusts, frequently the situation where a failure to segregate funds held on trust from the other funds of the trustee has permitted the funds to be taken in discharge of the trustee's overdraft.[38] However, it is clear that "the trust need not be a formal trust. It is sufficient that there should be a fiduciary relationship between the 'trustee' and the property of another person."[39] Consequently, this first requirement is equally satisfied where the mis-application of property occurs as a result of agents following the instructions of any other express fiduciary. The "directors of a company are treated as if they were the trustees of the company's property under their control"[40] and many modern cases have concerned illegal or unauthorised transactions carried out in accordance with the instructions of company directors. There has been a whole series of cases resulting from successful attempts to use the funds of a company to finance its own acquisition,[41] while a number of cases have resulted from directors misapplying a company's funds for their own personal benefit.[42] It is also sufficient if the trust in question is constructive rather than express,[43] even if the constructive trust only arose as a result of the misapplication of the property. Millett J. emphasised in *Agip (Africa) v. Jackson*[44] that "the embezzlement of a company's funds almost inevitably involves a breach of fiduciary duty on the part of one of the company's employees or agents" and he went on to hold that "there is a receipt of trust property when a company's funds are misapplied by a director and, in my judgment, this is equally the case where a company's funds are misapplied by any person whose fiduciary position gave him control of them or enabled

---

[36] [1995] 2 A.C. 378.
[37] As in *Barnes v. Addy* (1874) 9 Ch.App. 214; *Williams v. Williams* (1881) 17 Ch.D. 437; *Williams-Ashman v. Price & Williams* [1942] 1 Ch. 219.
[38] As in *Royal Brunei Airlines v. Tan* [1995] 2 A.C. 378.
[39] *Baden v. Société Générale* (1983) [1993] 1 W.L.R. 509N at 573.
[40] *ibid.*
[41] As in *Selangor United Rubber Estates v. Cradock (No. 3)* [1968] 1 W.L.R. 1555; *Karak Rubber Company v. Burden (No. 2)* [1972] 1 W.L.R. 602; *Belmont Finance Corporation v. Williams Furniture* [1979] Ch. 250 *(No. 2)* [1980] 1 All E.R. 393; *Eagle Trust Co. v. S.B.C. Securities* (1991) [1993] 1 W.L.R. 484.
[42] *Baden v. Société Générale* (1983) [1993] 1 W.L.R. 509N; *Eagle Trust Co. v. S.B.C. Securities* (1991) [1993] 1 W.L.R. 484; *Cowan de Groot Properties v. Eagle Trust* (1991) [1992] 4 All E.R. 700; *Polly Peck International v. Nadir (No. 2)* [1992] 4 All E.R. 769.
[43] *Competitive Insurance Company v. Davies Investments* [1975] 1 W.L.R. 1240.
[44] [1990] Ch. 265 at 290.

him to misapply them". This principle is not of course confined to funds but applies to property of any type.[45] A glance at some of the authorities cited in the footnotes will emphasise the substantial sums which were at stake in them and the extent to which the victims of corporate fraud are increasingly looking towards members of the professions and financial institutions to compensate them for their losses.

Only rarely has there been any dispute as to whether or not this first requirement has been satisfied. However the unusual facts of *Brinks v. Abu-Saleh (No. 3)*[46] did produce a contention that the claim brought in that case failed because of the lack of any trust. The theft of over £26,000,000 from the plaintiff's Heathrow warehouse had been facilitated by one of the plaintiff's employees, a security guard who had provided both a key to the premises and information about its security arrangements to the other persons involved in the robbery. The plaintiffs subsequently sought recovery of the stolen property or damages in respect of its loss from no fewer than 57 defendants. In these particular proceedings, the plaintiff was contending that, because the robbery had taken place as a result of the actions of a dishonest fiduciary (the security guard), it "had an equity to trace into [the proceeds of the robbery], which were in the nature of trust moneys". It therefore sought the imposition of liability for "dishonest assistance" on one of the defendants who had accompanied her husband on various trips by car in the course of which he had transported to Zurich over £3,000,000 of the proceeds of the robbery for one of the convicted robbers, thereby enabling this sum to be laundered. It was conceded that the security guard was a fiduciary but it was argued that he did not owe a fiduciary duty which was sufficient to impress the proceeds of the robbery with a trust. Rimer J. predictably rejected this argument so the claim satisfied this first requirement. However, he went on to hold that it satisfied neither the third nor the fourth requirements.

(2) The existence of a misfeasance or breach of trust

In *Barnes v. Addy* Lord Selborne held that liability would only be imposed on persons who "assist with knowledge in a dishonest and fraudulent design on the part of the trustees". Although it has since been demonstrated that requirement "leapt forth fully formed from the brow of Lord Selborne",[47] all subsequent authorities prior to the decision of the Privy Council in *Royal Brunei Airlines v. Tan*[48] regarded it as an essential prerequisite of liability. After a certain amount of debate,[49] the Court of Appeal eventually decided in *Belmont Finance Corporation v. Williams Furniture*[50] that "dishonest" and "fraudulent" had the same meaning and signified something more than

---

[45] Information in respect of which a manager owed a fiduciary duty to his company would have sufficed in *Consul Development v. D.P.C. Estates* (1975) 132 C.L.R. 373.

[46] (1995), *The Times*, October 23, 1995. Transcript available from The New Law Publishing Co.

[47] C. Harpum in *Frontiers of Liability* (ed. Birks, 1993). The requirement did not exist earlier in the nineteenth century: see *Fyler v. Fyler* (1841) 3 Beav. 550; *Att.-Gen. v. The Corporation of Leicester* (1844) 7 Beav. 176.

[48] [1995] 2 A.C. 378.

[49] Largely provoked by the controversial remarks of Ungoed-Thomas J. in *Selangor United Rubber Estates v. Cradock (No. 3)* [1968] 1 W.L.R. 1555 at 1582, 1590.

[50] [1979] Ch. 250 at 267.

mere misfeasance or breach of trust. In *Baden v. Société Générale*[51] Peter
Gibson J. applied these statements of the Court of Appeal and held, quoting
R. v. Sinclair,[52] that what was required was "the taking of a risk to the
prejudice of another's rights, which risk is known to be one which there is
no right to take".

However, this view was rejected in *Royal Brunei Airlines v. Tan*.[53] The
airline was seeking to impose liability for "dishonest assistance" on the
managing director and principal shareholder of an insolvent travel agency
which had paid into its ordinary current account the ticket moneys which,
according to I.A.T.A. regulations, it held on trust for the airline. The Court
of Appeal of Brunei Darussalam had applied *Belmont Finance Corporation v.
Williams Furniture* and rejected this claim on the grounds that, while the
evidence revealed what Lord Nicholls described[54] as "a sorry tale of mismanagement and broken promises, . . . it was not established that [the travel
agent] was guilty of fraud or dishonesty". However, the Privy Council
rejected *Belmont Finance Corporation v. Williams Furniture* and reversed the
decision of the Court of Appeal of Brunei Darussalam, concluding that

"what matters is the state of mind of the third party sought to be made
liable, not the state of mind of the trustee. . . . his state of mind is essentially
irrelevant to the question whether the third party should be made liable to
the beneficiaries for the breach of trust. If the liability of the third party is
fault-based, what matters is the nature of his fault, not that of the trustee. In
this regard dishonesty on the part of the third party would seem to be a
sufficient basis for his liability, irrespective of the state of mind of the trustee
who is in breach of trust".[55]

The conclusion of the Privy Council as to the law, set out in a paragraph
headed "The accessory liability principle",[56] therefore establishes that "[i]t is
not necessary that . . . the trustee or fiduciary was acting dishonestly,
although this will usually be so where the third party who is assisting him
is acting dishonestly".

The Privy Council has therefore reduced the pre-existing requirement for
the existence of a dishonest and fraudulent design on the part of the trustee
of the trust to a requirement for a misfeasance or breach of trust on his part,
which will in practice be automatically satisfied whenever there has been a
disposition of property in breach of trust. This has resolved the problem of
the status of the nineteenth century authorities prior to *Barnes v. Addy*, in
particular the decision in *Eaves v. Hickson*,[57] where a father who produced a
forged marriage certificate to the trustees of a settlement in order to convince them that his children were legitimate[58] and so entitled to the trust

---

[51] (1993) [1993] 1 W.L.R. 509N at 574.
[52] [1968] 1 W.L.R. 1246 at 1249.
[53] [1995] 2 A.C. 378.
[54] *ibid.* at 383.
[55] *ibid.* at 385.
[56] *ibid.* at 392.
[57] (1861) 30 Beav. 136.
[58] He had married the mother of the children after their birth but at that time there was no
doctrine of legitimation by subsequent marriage.

property was held personally liable to account as a trustee to those otherwise entitled to the property to the extent that it could not be recovered from the children. Because the trustees had clearly not been either dishonest and fraudulent, it was unclear prior to *Royal Brunei Airlines v. Tan* whether this decision was an example of a quite distinct head of liability for "knowing inducement" of a breach of trust or whether it had simply been overtaken by *Barnes v. Addy* and would thereafter have had to have been decided differently; the Privy Council has now established that it is an unusual but straightforward example of liability for "dishonest assistance".

The change in the pre-existing law made by the Privy Council is therefore both important and welcome; it unquestionably forms part of the *ratio decidendi* of the Board and, although technically constituting the law only of Brunei Darussalam, is obviously bound to be adopted by the English courts.[59]

(3) Being accessory to or assisting in the misfeasance or breach of trust

It is "a simple question of fact"[60] whether someone has been accessory to, or assisted in, the misfeasance or breach of trust in question. It makes no difference whether the agent has previously advised against the course of conduct in question,[61] whether he has made the appropriate enquiries and reasonably come to what was in fact an incorrect conclusion,[62] or whether he has simply relied on the instructions given without checking relevant documents in his possession.[63] All that matters is the fact of having been accessory to or assisted in a misfeasance or breach of trust in a significant way.

In this connection, it should be noted that, although the vast majority of cases of this type inevitably involve agents of trustees or other fiduciaries, liability also extends to persons who have been in some other way accessory to a disposition of property in breach of trust. Thus, in *Eaves v. Hickson*[64] liability was imposed on the person who had induced the disposition in question while in *Royal Brunei Airlines v. Tan*[65] liability was imposed on the managing director of the company which had misapplied the trust moneys. There is nothing particularly surprising about the imposition of liability for "dishonest assistance" on the persons who, like the defendant in that case, are in physical control of a corporate trustee. Although such persons are not "strangers" to the defaulting trustee in the way that its solicitors and bankers are, they are nevertheless its agents. They have immunity from direct liability as insiders (directors owe fiduciary duties only to their company, not to either its shareholders or beneficiaries) and it would be absurd if they could also claim immunity from liability for "dishonest assistance" on the grounds that they were not "outsiders".

---

[59] *Royal Brunei Airlines v. Tan* has already been referred to with approval in the Chancery Division at least twice (in *Brinks v. Abu-Saleh (No. 3)* (1995), *The Times*, October 23, 1995 and in *H. v. J.A.P.T.* [1997] P.L.R. 99) but not in relation to this particular requirement.

[60] *Baden v. Société Générale* (1983) [1993] 1 W.L.R. 509N at 574–575.

[61] As in *Barnes v. Addy* (1874) 9 Ch.App. 214.

[62] As in *Williams v. Williams* (1881) 17 Ch.D. 437.

[63] As in *Williams-Ashman v. Price & Williams* [1942] 1 Ch. 219.

[64] (1861) 30 Beav. 136.

[65] [1995] 2 A.C. 378.

The possibility of imposing liability for "dishonest assistance" on the directors of a corporate trustee has since been expressly confirmed by Lindsay J. in *H. v. J.A.P.T.*,[66] in which the members of a pension scheme were trying to bring proceedings as a result of the corporate trustee investing a large proportion of the assets of the scheme in purchases of properties from the employer company at excessively high prices. This was of course a breach of trust by the corporate trustee but the latter was, as so often in this type of case, a company without any assets. The availability of proceedings for "dishonest assistance" against the directors of the corporate trustee, who were, as is also often the case, also the directors of the employer company, meant that they would be liable to the members in the event that their conduct could be shown to be dishonest and so bring them within the fourth requirement to be discussed in the next section. However, *H. v. J.A.P.T.* also threw up a possible alternative means of imposing liability on these directors without any need to show dishonesty on their part. The making of these purchases was arguably a breach of the fiduciary duty which they owed to the corporate trustee as its directors, a duty of strict liability not dependant on them having been dishonest or even negligent. It was contended, and Lindsay J. accepted as arguable and so declined to strike out a claim, that the members of the scheme were entitled to argue that such rights of action as the corporate trustee had against its directors were themselves part of the property of the pension trust, thus enabling the members of the scheme to force the trustee company to sue the directors and hold the fruits of that action on trust for them.[67] Although this claim (described by Lindsay J. as a "dog-leg claim") is in itself nothing to do with liability for "dishonest assistance", it is potentially an even more effective way of attacking the directors of corporate trustees. However, an appeal against his decision was subsequently compromised so it remains to be seen whether such a claim is indeed feasible.

It is rare for the significance of the conduct of the person potentially liable for "dishonest assistance" to be challenged as a matter of fact but this was done successfully in *Brinks v. Abu-Saleh (No. 3)*,[68] the facts of which have already been considered.[69] Rimer J. held that the defendant in question had accompanied her husband on the various trips by car to Zurich (in the course of which he had transported for one of the convicted robbers and thereby enabled the latter to launder over £3,000,000 of the proceeds of the robbery of the plaintiff's Heathrow warehouse) merely in her spousal capacity; her presence therefore had not constituted relevant "assistance" in furtherance of the breach of trust complained of. Therefore, although the plaintiff's claim satisfied the first two requirements (the existence of a trust and a misfeasance on the part of the trustee of the trust), this rather generous finding of fact meant that the plaintiff's claim failed to satisfy the third requirement (as will be seen later on,[70] Rimer J. then went on to hold that the fourth requirement was not satisfied either). However, the facts of this case

---

[66] [1997] P.L.R. 99.
[67] By analogy with the decision in *Fletcher v. Fletcher* (1844) 4 Hare 67: see *ante*, pp. 156–159.
[68] (1995), *The Times*, October 23, 1995.
[69] See *ante*, p. 327.
[70] See *post*, p. 334.

were extremely unusual and it is obviously unlikely that the presence or absence of this requirement will often be the subject of dispute.

(4) Dishonesty by the accessory or person assisting

This is the aspect of liability for "dishonest assistance" which has produced most judicial disagreement. In *Barnes v. Addy*[71] Lord Selborne held that liability would only be imposed on persons who assisted "with knowledge". This caused Peter Gibson J. in *Baden v. Société Générale*[72] both to regard knowledge as the last of his four distinct elements and to identify five different categories of knowledge. These were: "(i) actual knowledge; (ii) wilfully shutting one's eyes to the obvious; (iii) wilfully and recklessly failing to make such inquiries as an honest and reasonable man would make; (iv) knowledge of circumstances which would indicate the facts to an honest and reasonable man; (v) knowledge of circumstances which would put an honest and reasonable man on inquiry". Although these categories have been justifiably described as "unhelpful"[73] and "unrememberable",[74] they were referred to in every single subsequent case in which liability for "dishonest assistance", "knowing receipt" and "inconsistent dealing" was in issue. They remain relevant, at least for the moment, for the imposition of the latter two types of liability. However, in *Royal Brunei Airlines v. Tan*,[75] the Privy Council specifically rejected their applicability to liability for "dishonest assistance" in favour of the requirement for dishonesty by the accessory or person assisting (indeed, it is precisely for this reason that what used to be known as liability for "knowing assistance" has now had to be renamed liability for "dishonest assistance").

In the light of the fact that the decision in *Royal Brunei Airlines v. Tan*, although technically constituting the law only of Brunei Darussalam, is obviously bound to be adopted by the English courts,[76] the pre-existing law will merely be summarised. Consistent with the expressed primary concern of Lord Selborne in *Barnes v. Addy*[77] to protect agents of a trust, the older cases[78] restricted liability to strangers whose knowledge fell within what Peter Gibson J. would later classify as categories (i), (ii) and (iii). However, a different view was taken by Ungoed-Thomas J. in *Selangor United Rubber Estates v. Cradock (No.3)*,[79] the first of a number of cases resulting from successful attempts to use the funds of a company unlawfully to finance its own acquisition. He there held that an agent who had assisted in bringing about a misapplication of property subject to a trust would be liable for "knowing assistance" if he either knew or ought to have known of the

---

[71] (1874) 9 Ch.App. 214.

[72] (1983) [1993] 1 W.L.R. 509N at 575–576.

[73] *per* Millett J. in *Agip (Africa) v. Jackson* [1990] Ch. 265 at 293.

[74] By Blanchard J. in *Nimmo v. Westpac Banking Corporation* [1993] 3 N.Z.L.R. 218 at 228 (High Court of New Zealand).

[75] [1995] 2 A.C. 378.

[76] *Royal Brunei Airlines v. Tan* has already been referred to with approval in the Chancery Division at least twice (in *Brinks v. Abu-Saleh (No. 3)* (1995), *The Times*, October 23, 1995 and in *H. v. J.A.P.T.* [1997] P.L.R. 99) in relation to this particular requirement.

[77] (1874) 9 Ch.App. 244.

[78] *Barnes v. Addy* itself; *Williams v. Williams* (1881) 17 Ch.D. 437; and *Williams-Ashman v. Price & Williams* [1942] 1 Ch. 219.

[79] [1968] 1 W.L.R. 1555.

misapplication in question consequently, the bank was liable for "knowing assistance". This decision was subsequently followed,[80] most significantly in *Baden v. Société Générale*,[81] where Peter Gibson J. accepted a concession by counsel that its effect was that strangers falling within all five of the categories of knowledge which he had identified would be liable for what was then generally known as "knowing assistance". On the other hand, the more traditional approach was adopted in a number of other decisions,[82] most significantly by the Court of Appeal in *Carl-Zeiss Stiftung v. Herbert Smith (No. 2)*[83] and in *Belmont Finance Corporation v. Williams Furniture*.[84] Despite the continued existence of these conflicting authorities, it eventually came to be generally accepted that the more traditional approach was correct and liability would only be imposed on persons whose knowledge fell within the first three of the categories of knowledge identified by Peter Gibson J. in *Baden v. Société Générale*. This was stated particularly clearly by Millett J. in *Agip (Africa) v. Jackson*[85] and, despite some alarums and excursions when that case went to the Court of Appeal,[86] his view was confirmed by Scott L.J. in *Polly Peck International v. Nadir (No. 2)*.[87] There is consequently no doubt whatever that that was the position when the Privy Council came to decide *Royal Brunei Airlines v. Tan*.[88]

It has already been seen[89] that the airline was seeking to impose liability for what was then known as "knowing assistance" on the managing director and principal shareholder of an insolvent travel agency which had paid into its ordinary current account the ticket moneys which, according to I.A.T.A. regulations, it held on trust for the airline. The Court of Appeal of Brunei Darussalam had rejected this claim on the grounds that it had not been established that there had been a fraudulent and dishonest design on the part of the travel agent. However the Privy Council held that there was no such requirement and that it was only necessary to show a misfeasance or a

---

[80] In cases such as *Karak Rubber Company v. Burden (No. 2)* [1972] 1 W.L.R. 602 and *Rowlandson v. National Westminster Bank* [1978] 3 All E.R. 370.

[81] (1983) [1993] 1 W.L.R. 509N at 575–582.

[82] Such as *Competitive Insurance Company v. Davies Investments* [1975] 1 W.L.R. 1240; *Re Montagu's Settlement Trusts* [1987] Ch. 264; *Lipkin Gorman v. Karpnale* [1987] 1 W.L.R. 987 (Alliott J.) (the question did not have to be decided in the Court of Appeal ([1989] 1 W.L.R. 1340) and did not arise in the House of Lords ([1991] 2 A.C. 548); this decision is discussed in detail *post*, p. 346.

[83] [1969] 2 Ch. 276. This case principally concerned "knowing receipt" but both Sachs and Edmund Davies L.JJ. stated that an agent could not be liable for "knowing assistance" unless he had actual knowledge of the misapplication in question.

[84] [1979] 1 All E.R. 118; *(No. 2)* 1 All E.R. 393. This case resulted from another successful attempt to purchase a company with its own money. The Court of Appeal first held, on a pleading issue, that liability for "knowing assistance" was restricted to the first three categories of knowledge later identified by Peter Gibson J. and subsequently held, on the merits, that the agents had throughout genuinely believed that the transaction was a good commercial proposition.

[85] [1990] Ch. 265.

[86] [1991] Ch. 547. This was because Fox L.J., while affirming the decision of Millett J., stated that the degree of knowledge required had been described in two authorities which Millett J. had expressly rejected, *Selangor United Rubber Estates v. Cradock (No. 3)* and *Baden v. Société Générale*.

[87] [1992] 4 All E.R. 769.

[88] [1995] 2 A.C. 378.

[89] See *ante*, p. 328.

breach of trust. This conclusion would in itself have been sufficient to dispose of the appeal; since it had been conceded that there had been a breach of trust in which the managing director had assisted with actual knowledge, all the requirements for the imposition of liability were clearly satisfied. However, the Privy Council did not restrict its observations to this particular aspect of accessory liability, holding that "[a] conclusion cannot be reached on the nature of the breach of trust which may trigger accessory liability without at the same time considering the other ingredients including, in particular, the state of mind of the third party".[90] Lord Nicholls considered and rejected the two extreme possibilities of imposing either no liability whatever or alternatively strict liability on a third party who assists a trustee to commit a breach of trust but does not himself receive any trust property. Having thus necessarily opted for the imposition of some form of fault-based liability, he reviewed the existing authorities and the opinions of the commentators and concluded[91]:

"Drawing the threads together, their Lordships' overall conclusion is that dishonesty is a necessary ingredient of accessory liability. It is also a sufficient ingredient. A liability in equity to make good resulting loss attaches to a person who dishonestly procures or assists in a breach of trust or fiduciary obligation. It is not necessary that, in addition, the trustee or fiduciary was acting dishonestly, although this will usually be so where the third party who is assisting him is acting dishonestly. 'Knowingly' is better avoided as a defining ingredient of the principle, and in the context of this principle the *Baden* scale of knowledge is best forgotten."

Because of the concession that the managing director had had actual knowledge of the breach of trust, it is technically possible to argue that these observations of the Board relating to the requirement at present under discussion are no more than dicta. However, in the light of the fact that the Board itself not only made no distinction of this kind but also referred to the necessity of taking "an overall look at the accessory liability principle", these observations are likely to be equally influential. The five categories of knowledge identified by Peter Gibson J. in *Baden v. Société Générale* were clearly rejected in favour of the principle that liability should be imposed on third parties who have dishonestly, but not negligently, assisted in a disposition of property in breach of trust. Although this principle is quite distinct in approach, the results of its application are in practice unlikely to be significantly different from that of the pre-existing law. Its great advantage is its simplicity and clarity in comparison with the difficulty of applying the categories of knowledge identified by Peter Gibson J. It remains to be seen whether the courts will adopt a wholly objective standard when considering whether or not any particular third party has been dishonest or also take into account more subjective factors applicable only to the specific third party so as to impose either a higher or a lower standard of behaviour on him. It has been persuasively suggested[92] that the burden of establishing

---

[90] [1995] 2 A.C. 378 at 386.
[91] *ibid.* at 392.
[92] By R. Nolan [1995] C.L.J. 507.

any such higher or lower standard of behaviour should be on the party alleging its applicability.

Finally, although dishonesty has thus replaced knowledge as the barometer of the conduct of the accessory or person assisting, there may nevertheless be a continuing requirement that that person know of the existence of a trust. It has already been seen[93] that in *Brinks v. Abu-Saleh (No. 3)*[94] the attempt to impose liability for "dishonest assistance" on the defendant in question for having accompanied her husband on various trips by car to Zurich (in the course of which he had transported for one of the convicted robbers and thereby enabled the latter to launder over £3,000,000 of the proceeds of the robbery of the plaintiff's Heathrow warehouse) failed because the claim against her did not satisfy the third requirement. Rimer J. nevertheless went on to consider whether or not it satisfied the fourth requirement. She was clearly unaware of the source of the funds being transported and so necessarily also unaware of the existence of any trust. Rimer J. stated that he did not consider that the Privy Council had "intended to suggest that an accessory could be made liable regardless of whether he had any knowledge of the existence of the trust" in question. Consequently, even if she had been guilty of assistance, "accessory liability" would not have been imposed upon her.

Should knowledge of the existence of a trust or other fiduciary relationship indeed be a prerequisite of the imposition of "accessory liability"? In the vast majority of reported cases, claims for the imposition of liability for "dishonest assistance" have been brought against persons who were at all times necessarily fully aware of the existence of a trust or other fiduciary relationship; prior to the decision in *Royal Brunei Airlines v. Tan* the crucial question was usually whether or not they knew or ought to have known of the wrongful disposition of some property subject thereto. However, in what seems to be the only other reported case in which knowledge of the existence of such a relationship has been relevant, Millett J. reached the opposite conclusion from that of Rimer J. In *Agip (Africa) v. Jackson*[95] he held, most persuasively, that: "it is no answer for a man charged with having knowingly assisted in a fraudulent and dishonest scheme to say that he thought that it was 'only' a breach of exchange control or 'only' a case of tax evasion. . . . A man who consciously assists others by making arrangements which he knows are calculated to conceal what is happening from a third party, takes the risk that they are part of a fraud practised on that party." Further, any continued existence of a requirement of knowledge would be extremely difficult to reconcile with the de-emphasis on the requirement of knowledge which formed such an important part of the advice of the Privy Council. It is therefore suggested that in this respect the judgment of Rimer J. should not be followed.

(C) The Liability of Agents of Invalidly Appointed Trustees

In *Barnes v. Addy* Lord Selborne was primarily concerned to protect agents of a trust who act in accordance with the instructions of the trustees. Is this

---

[93] See *ante*, p. 330.
[94] (1995), *The Times*, October 23, 1995.
[95] [1990] Ch. 265 at 295.

protection available to an agent even if the trustee by whom he is instructed has not himself been validly appointed? This issue arose in *Mara v. Browne*[96] where it was argued that an agent appointed by such a trustee must act as a principal and so would be deprived of the protection of *Barnes v. Addy* —this would of course mean that the agent in question would be treated as if he were officiously acting as a fiduciary and so, under the principles which have already been discussed,[97] would inevitably be liable no matter what his motives and his honesty. This argument succeeded at first instance before North J.[98] but the Court of Appeal found that the trustee in question had been validly appointed and so the issue did not have to be decided. However, Lord Herschell stated that the protection of *Barnes v. Addy* would be available to such an agent. It is suggested that this latter view, although not clearly established, is preferable since it is unreasonable to expect an agent to carry out a detailed investigation into the status of his principal.

(D)   The Liability of Partners of Persons Liable for "Dishonest Assistance"

When an agent is held personally liable to account in the same manner as a trustee on the grounds that he has assisted in bringing about a misapplication of property subject to a trust, are his partners subject to the same liability? In *Re Bell's Indenture*[99] liability for "dishonest assistance" was imposed on a solicitor who had assisted the trustees of a settlement who were also life tenants thereof to distribute the whole of the trust property to themselves in breach of trust. The remaindermen sought to impose a similar liability on his partners, relying on *Blythe v. Fladgate*[1] where, as has already been seen,[2] all the partners of a firm of solicitors who had officiously been acting as trustees were held liable to account to the trust. *Blythe v. Fladgate* had been followed at first instance in *Mara v. Browne*,[3] where North J. had imposed liability both on the agent employed by the invalidly appointed trustee and on his partner. However, in the Court of Appeal in *Mara v. Browne*[4] (where the issue did not arise) all three members of the court had indicated that they would have held the opposite on the grounds that it is not part of the implied authority of a partner to make his co-partners liable for "dishonest assistance". In *Re Bell's Indenture* Vinelott J. followed and applied these statements of the Court of Appeal in *Mara v. Browne* and exonerated the partners, distinguishing *Blythe v. Fladgate* on the grounds that in that case the solicitors had been acting officiously as trustees. However, in *Agip (Africa) v. Jackson*[5] both Millett J. and the Court of Appeal, without citation or discussion of any of the previous authorities, imposed liability for "dishonest assistance" both on an accountant who had been dishonestly carrying out money-laundering and on his partner. This decision of the

---

[96] [1896] 1 Ch. 199.
[97] See *ante*, p. 322.
[98] [1895] 2 Ch. 69.
[99] [1980] 3 All E.R. 425.
[1] [1891] 1 Q.B. 337.
[2] See *ante*, p. 322.
[3] [1895] 2 Ch. 69.
[4] [1896] 1 Ch. 199.
[5] [1990] Ch. 265 (Millett J.); [1991] Ch. 547, CA.

Court of Appeal must obviously represent the law at present but the matter cannot be regarded as finally settled until the conflicting authorities have been the subject of a reasoned judgment.

(E) What Should a Suspicious Agent Do?

If an agent suspects that he may be assisting in a misapplication of property subject to a trust and it is too late for him to withdraw from the transaction (this would be the position of a solicitor or a bank who became suspicious about the provenance of funds being held to the order of a client), he is entitled to apply by originating summons to the High Court under Order 85 of the Rules of the Supreme Court for administration directions. In the event that there are sufficient grounds for his suspicions, any directions given by the court can, if necessary, override any legal or other professional privilege of confidentiality to which the client would normally have been entitled.[6] What an agent cannot safely do, however, is to refuse to comply with his client's instructions merely because he has become suspicious; this can only safely be done where he has positive evidence of a misfeasance or breach of trust on the part of the client. In *T.T.S. International v. Cantrade Private Bank*,[6a] the Royal Court of Jersey went so far as to enter summary judgment against a bank who had refused to comply with instructions to transfer the balance of an account out of the jurisdiction; the court found, first, that at the relevant time there was no evidence of a dishonest and fraudulent design (still necessary at that time); secondly, that there was no evidence that the funds would be paid to anyone other than their true owners; and, thirdly, that the bank had taken an overly cautious view of its duties, appearing more concerned to protect itself against possible claims than to look after the interests of its account holders. Refusing to comply with the instructions of clients therefore appears only to be feasible in extreme cases.

3. Receiving Property Disposed of in Breach of Trust

(A) The Different Remedies Available Against the Recipient

The imposition of the obligations of trusteeship on the recipient of property disposed of in breach of trust is generally known as liability for "knowing receipt".[7] The imposition of such liability is, however, only one of a number of claims which may be available to the person from whom the property has been abstracted. If the property or its product is still identifiable in the hands of the recipient or of any third party to whom it has been subsequently transferred, he will also have the possibility of bringing a proprietary claim, either at law or in equity, to enable him to follow the property into the hands of its present holder.[8] Additionally he may be able to bring a personal action at law for money had and received against the recipient, a personal action in equity against whoever was responsible for initiating the misapplication, and a claim for the imposition of the obligations of trusteeship against

---

[6] *Finers v. Miro* [1991] 1 All E.R. 182.

[6a] (1995), unreported but see (1995) 4 J.Int.Tr. 60.

[7] C. Harpum in *Frontiers of Liability* (ed. Birks, 1993) describes this as "Restitutionary Liability".

[8] See *post*, p. 716.

anyone who has been guilty of "dishonest assistance".[9] For example, in *Agip (Africa) v. Jackson*,[10] where an employee of the plaintiff company fraudulently altered the names of the payees on a number of payment orders to make them payable to one of a series of dummy companies operated by the defendant firm of accountants who, as soon as the funds were received, transferred the funds on to third parties and wound up the company in question, the plaintiff, having already obtained an unsatisfied judgment against the dummy company in question, sought the following relief against the defendants: at law, a proprietary claim to follow the funds into the hands of the defendants and a personal claim for money had and received and, in equity, a proprietary claim to follow the funds into the hands of the defendants and the imposition of the obligations of trusteeship for "knowing receipt" and "dishonest assistance". In *Lipkin Gorman v. Karpnale*,[11] where a member of a firm of solicitors had drawn from the firm's client accounts funds which he subsequently gambled away at a casino, the solicitors claimed that its bank was liable for conversion of cheques, for conversion of a draft, for breach of contract and for "dishonest assistance" and that the casino was liable for money had and received, for negligence, for conversion of cheques, for conversion of a draft, and for "knowing receipt" and, additionally, was liable in equity to both proprietary and personal claims as a result of its receipt of the solicitors' funds.

It has already been observed[12] that the interrelation of these different claims makes proceedings of this type extremely complex. The principal difficulty is the existence of what have been described[13] as "arbitrary and anomalous distinctions" between the claims at law and the claims in equity. It is perhaps inevitable that, as will be seen in a later Chapter,[14] the prerequisites of and defences to proprietary claims differ depending on whether the claim is being brought at law or in equity. But there are also distinctions between the different personal claims. An action at law for money had and received will succeed quite irrelevant of the state of mind of the recipient of the money; the only defences available to him will be bona fide purchase for value without notice and change of position.[15] On the other hand, liability in equity for "knowing receipt" depends on whether the recipient falls within the appropriate[16] categories of knowledge identified by Peter Gibson J. in *Baden v. Société Générale*[17] (as used also to be true of liability for "knowing assistance"). In other words, liability at law is strict, subject to defences, while liability in equity depends on the state of mind of the recipient. This (and other) distinctions have led commentators to question whether so many different remedies should continue to be available for

---

[9] See *ante*, p. 323.
[10] [1990] Ch. 265 (Millett J.); [1991] Ch. 547 (Court of Appeal).
[11] [1987] 1 W.L.R. 987 (Alliott J.); [1989] 1 W.L.R. 1340, CA; [1991] 2 A.C. 548, HL.
[12] See *ante*, p. 321.
[13] By Millett J. in *El Ajou v. Dollar Land Holdings* [1993] B.C.L.C. 735 at 757. Millett J. contended that these distinctions should not be insisted upon.
[14] See *post*, p. 710.
[15] *Lipkin Gorman v. Karpnale* [1989] 1 W.L.R. 1340, CA; [1991] 2 A.C. 548, HL. See P. B. H. Birks [1991] L.M.C.L.Q. 473.
[16] There is disagreement as to precisely which of the five categories suffice for this purpose.
[17] See *ante*, p. 331.

the same misapplication of property.[18] Indeed Millett J. once commented[19] that he did not see "how it would be possible to develop any logical and coherent system of restitution if there were different requirements in respect of knowledge for the common law claim for money had and received, the personal claim for an account in equity against a knowing recipient and the equitable proprietary claim". As a result of observations of this type, the Law Commission is at present considering this whole area of the law with a view to rationalising all the available remedies and the majority view seems to be that the best way forward is to introduce a universal principle of strict liability subject to clearly defined defences.[20] For the moment, however, the existing distinctions between the different claims obviously continue.

For present purposes, it is important only to distinguish between, on the one hand, the possibility of following the property disposed of in breach of trust into the hands of its recipient by means of an equitable proprietary claim and, on the other hand, the imposition of the obligations of trusteeship upon him. Where property has been disposed of in breach of trust, the interests of the beneficiaries in that property are, in accordance with the basic principles of property law, enforceable against the whole world unless and until the property in question reaches the hands of someone who takes it free of their equitable proprietary interests therein. When the property or its product is pure personalty or unregistered land, the interests of the beneficiaries will be enforceable against the whole world other than a bona fide purchaser for value of a legal interest therein without notice of those interests. When, on the other hand, it is registered land, their interests will be enforceable against the whole world if they either are overriding or have been protected as minor interests on the Land Register but otherwise will not be enforceable against any bona fide purchaser for value claiming under a registered disposition. Further, whatever the nature of the property, any claim of the beneficiaries to enforce their interests will additionally be subject to the established defences to equitable proprietary claims which will be considered in a latter chapter.[21] Any recipient of property disposed of in breach of trust who is liable to an equitable proprietary claim will of course be a trustee of such property as is in his hands—this is simply because the equitable interests of the beneficiaries therein must necessarily take effect behind a trust of the legal interest. However, the fact that it is possible to bring an equitable proprietary claim against the recipient does not necessarily mean that the obligations of trusteeship will be imposed upon him in respect of all the property which he originally received. This was stated particularly clearly by Megarry V.-C. in *Re Montagu's Settlement*.[22]

In fact in only three situations is it actually necessary to seek the imposition of liability for "knowing receipt": first, where the recipient has dealt with some or all of the property in such a way that it can no longer be the

---

[18] See the articles cited *ante*, p. 321, n. 9.
[19] By Millett J. in *El Ajou v. Dollar Land Holdings* [1993] B.C.L.C. 735 at 759.
[20] See the articles cited *ante*, p. 321, n. 9.
[21] See *post*, pp. 737–743.
[22] [1987] Ch. 264 at 272–273.

subject of an equitable proprietary claim; secondly, where the property has depreciated in value while in the hands of the recipient; and, thirdly, where the recipient has obtained some incidental profit from the property.[23] In these circumstances, the equitable proprietary claim will enable the beneficiaries to recover only such property, if any, as remains in the hands of the recipient; the loss caused by any dealing with or reduction in the value of the property and any incidental profit obtained will only be recoverable if the recipient is held to have been a constructive trustee of the whole of the property originally transferred to him. In the overwhelming majority of the cases in which the imposition of liability for "knowing receipt" has been sought, the recipient has dealt with some or all of the property in such a way that it can no longer be the subject of an equitable proprietary claim.

(B) The Elements of Liability for "Knowing Receipt"
Liability for "knowing receipt" has never been dependent on the existence of any dishonest or fraudulent design on the part of the person who disposed of the property in breach of trust; consequently the decision of the Privy Council in *Royal Brunei Airlines v. Tan*[24] to replace this requirement for the imposition of liability for "dishonest assistance" does not in any way affect liability for "knowing receipt", which has never required more than the misfeasance or breach of trust preferred by the Privy Council. In *El Ajou v. Dollar Land Holdings*,[25] Hoffmann L.J. isolated three distinct elements of this type of liability: a disposition of property in breach of trust, beneficial receipt of the property disposed of in breach of trust or of its traceable product, and knowledge by the recipient.

(1) A disposition of property in breach of trust
This requirement must be exactly the same as the first and second requirements for the imposition of liability for "dishonest assistance". Thus, "the trust need not be a formal trust. It is sufficient that there should be a fiduciary relationship between the "trustee" and the property of another person",[26] which can be either express or constructive, and that there should have been a disposition of property in breach of the appropriate fiduciary duty. In practice this requirement is likely to cause as few problems as the equivalent requirements for the imposition of liability for "dishonest assistance".

(2) Beneficial receipt of the property disposed of in breach of trust or of its traceable product
It is merely a question of fact whether the property disposed of in breach of trust or its traceable product has been beneficially received by the person on whom it is sought to impose liability for "knowing receipt". However, when property disposed of in breach of trust is received by persons for them to

---

[23] Such as one of the types of secret profits discussed in the previous section of this Chapter.
[24] [1995] 2 A.C. 378.
[25] [1994] 2 All E.R. 685.
[26] Peter Gibson J. in *Baden v. Société Générale* (1983) [1993] 1 W.L.R. 509N at 573, referring to liability for "dishonest assistance".

hold on trust, the recipient trustees are for these purposes regarded as receiving it beneficially.

Establishing this question of fact is, however, sometimes far from simple and in such circumstances is determined in the same way as in legal and equitable proprietary claims.[27] In *El Ajou v. Dollar Land Holdings*,[28] a claim for the imposition of liability for "knowing receipt" was brought by and on behalf of the victims of a fraudulent share dealing operation carried out from Amsterdam on behalf of three Canadians. The fraudsters had subsequently, through a Panamanian company, entered into a joint venture for the development of property in England with an English company which had not been involved in the fraud. The plaintiff claimed that the Canadians' investment in the joint venture had been made with funds of which he and the other victims had been defrauded. These funds had, prior to their investment, been moved through several civil law jurisdictions which did not recognise the existence of trusts and at one point a substantial sum had been sent from Geneva to Panama, where it had disappeared for a short time prior to the reappearance of a roughly similar sum in Geneva. Millett J. held that the property could be followed despite the passage of the funds through the civil law jurisdictions and that, notwithstanding their brief disappearance in Panama, there was sufficient evidence to conclude that the victims' funds had indeed been used to make this investment. The mere fact that the victims' funds had been invested in the joint venture did not make the English company liable in any way; at that stage the plaintiff's only conceivable claim would have been to attempt to attach the 50 per cent interest in the joint venture held by the Canadians' Panamanian company. However, the Canadians subsequently decided to withdraw from the joint venture and the English company duly purchased their interest. The plaintiff then claimed that as a result of this purchase the funds of which he and the other victims had been defrauded had reached the hands of the English company, which was therefore liable for "knowing receipt". The mere receipt of the funds was not of course sufficient for the imposition of liability; it was also necessary to establish that the English company had had the requisite knowledge of the fraud. Its chairman, who had originally brought the joint venturers together, had had dealings with the Canadians prior to the joint venture and was unquestionably aware of the manner in which they had acquired their funds. The case therefore turned on whether or not knowledge acquired by him in a quite different capacity prior to any involvement with the English company could be attributed to it once he became its chairman. Millett J. actually held that it could not be. However, on this point he was reversed by the Court of Appeal who duly imposed liability for "knowing receipt" on the English company; they were therefore obliged to pay a second time for the 50 per cent interest for which they had already paid the Canadians. To make matters still worse, they were held liable in subsequent proceedings[29] to account not for the sum which they had actually paid to the Canadians but for 50 per cent of the substantially higher amount for which they had sold on the joint venture property.

---

[27] See *post*, p. 716.
[28] [1993] B.C.L.C. 735 (Millett J.); [1994] 2 All E.R. 685, CA.
[29] *El Ajou v. Dollar Land Holdings (No. 2)* [1995] 2 All E.R. 213.

(3) Knowledge by the recipient

The knowledge of the recipient is assessed by reference to the five categories of knowledge identified by Peter Gibson J. in *Baden v. Société Générale*[30]: "(i) actual knowledge; (ii) wilfully shutting one's eyes to the obvious; (iii) wilfully and recklessly failing to make such inquiries as an honest and reasonable man would make; (iv) knowledge of circumstances which would indicate the facts to an honest and reasonable man; (v) knowledge of circumstances which would put an honest and reasonable man on inquiry". A person in category (i) obviously has actual knowledge and "[a]ccording to Peter Gibson J., a person in categories (ii) or (iii) will be taken to have actual knowledge, while a person in categories (iv) or (v) has constructive notice only".[31] These categories have been justifiably described as "unhelpful" and "unrememberable"[32] and warnings have been given "against over refinement or a too ready assumption that categories (iv) and (v) are necessarily cases of constructive notice only. The true distinction is between honesty and dishonesty".[33] Further, as has already been seen,[34] they were specifically rejected by the Privy Council in *Royal Brunei Airlines v. Tan*[35] as the barometer of liability for "dishonest assistance". However, at least for the moment, they remain relevant in relation to liability for "knowing receipt".

The existence of the requisite level of knowledge has to be proved by the claimant, not disproved by the recipient.[36] Where this burden of proof cannot be discharged, a recipient of property disposed of in breach of trust will obviously not be liable for "knowing receipt". This is the case whether or not that recipient has given value.[37]

Carl-Zeiss Stiftung v. Herbert Smith (No. 2)[38] was a subsidiary action to a claim brought by an East German Company against a West Germany Company. Each claimed to be the original Zeiss Foundation and hence to be entitled to use the Zeiss trademark (the company had become divided due to the division of Germany after the Second World War). In the main action, the East German Company was claiming that the property and the assets of the West German Company either belonged to or were held on trust for them. In this subsidiary action, the East German Company claimed that the solicitors acting for the West German Company in the main action held their legal fees on constructive trust for them, in other words that the solicitors were liable for "knowing receipt". The basis of this claim was that the solicitors had actual notice that the East German Company claimed to be entitled to all the assets of the West German Company including, obviously

---

[30] (1983) [1993] 1 W.L.R. 509N at 575–576.
[31] *Agip (Africa) v. Jackson* [1990] Ch. 265 at 293, *per* Millett J.
[32] *Nimmo v. Westpac Banking Corporation* [1993] 3 N.Z.L.R. 218 at 228, *per* Blanchard J. (High Court of New Zealand).
[33] *Agip (Africa) v. Jackson* [1990] Ch. 265 at 293, *per* Millett J.
[34] See *ante*, p. 332.
[35] [1995] 2 A.C. 378.
[36] *Polly Peck International v. Nadir (No. 2)* [1992] 4 All E.R. 769 at 777.
[37] Whether or not he has given value will of course be highly relevant in relation to an equitable proprietary claim, since only if he has will he be able to make out the defence of bona fide purchase for value without notice.
[38] [1969] 2 Ch. 276.

enough, any legal fees paid to their solicitors. The Court of Appeal dismissed this claim on the somewhat controversial ground[39] that notice of an adverse claim to the property of the West German Company had not amounted to notice of a trust since difficult questions both of fact and law were involved in the claim; the solicitors therefore had had no effective knowledge of any adverse claim to the funds which they had received and therefore were, in effect, bona fide purchasers for value without notice of the fees which they had received. Similarly, in *Cowan de Groot Properties v. Eagle Trust*[40] directors of a company which lacked liquid funds sold five properties at a gross undervalue in order to make an urgent payment needed to keep an important company project in existence. Subsequently the company repudiated the sale and claimed that the purchaser was liable for "knowing receipt". Knox J. held that the purchaser did not fall within any of the five categories of knowledge identified by Peter Gibson J. in *Baden v. Société Générale* and so was consequently not liable for "knowing receipt".

The courts have also declined to impose "the heavy obligations of trusteeship"[41] upon recipients of property disposed of in breach of trust who received that property in good faith without any knowledge of the breach of trust in question. In *Re Diplock*,[42] under the provisions of a will subsequently declared to be void for uncertainty, executors distributed large sums of money to various charities who received the property in good faith without the slightest idea that the House of Lords would at a later stage hold that the will was void.[43] The next of kin of the testator (who were entitled under the resulting intestacy) brought an action against the charities to recover the money. They were obviously entitled to bring an equitable proprietary claim in order to follow the sums so paid into their product.[44] But the Court of Appeal held that the charities were not liable for "knowing receipt" and so the sums which could not be recovered by means of the equitable proprietary claim could not be recovered by the imposition of a constructive trust. This decision was expressly approved by the House of Lords in *Westdeutsche Landesbank Girozentrale v. Islington L.B.C.*[45]

However, it is far from clear which of the five categories of knowledge identified by Peter Gibson J. in *Baden v. Société Générale* suffice for the imposition of liability for "knowing receipt". In this respect, the authorities are in considerable disarray.

A recipient of property disposed of in breach of trust who has actual knowledge of the breach of trust will obviously be liable for "knowing receipt". In *Belmont Finance Corporation v. Williams Furniture (No. 2)*,[46] the directors of a company had had actual knowledge of a transaction whereby that company had permitted its wholly owned subsidiary to be purchased with its own money, a transaction which amounted to a breach of trust by

---

[39] See D. M. Gordon (1970) 44 A.L.J. 261.
[40] [1992] 4 All E.R. 700.
[41] This was the description utilised by Lord Greene M.R. in *Re Diplock* [1948] Ch. 465.
[42] [1948] Ch. 465.
[43] In *Chichester Diocesan Fund v. Simpson* [1944] A.C. 341.
[44] See *post*, p. 710.
[45] [1996] A.C. 669.
[46] [1980] 1 All E.R. 393.

the directors of the subsidiary. The purchase price for the subsidiary had of course been paid to the parent company which had therefore received property with actual knowledge that it had been disposed of in breach of trust. The Court of Appeal held that the parent company was therefore liable for "knowing receipt" and so was a constructive trustee of the purchase moneys received. Similarly, in *El Ajou v. Dollar Land Holdings*,[47] the Court of Appeal imposed liability for "knowing receipt" on a company because it had acquired the interest of a co-venturer at a time when, through its chairman, it was aware that the co-venturer had originally acquired its interest with the proceeds of fraud.

Liability for "knowing receipt" is clearly not confined to cases of actual knowledge. In *Nelson v. Larholt*[48] one of the executors of a will drew eight cheques on the estate's bank account, all of which were signed by him as executor of the testator, in favour of the defendant who cashed the cheques in good faith. The other executor and the beneficiaries claimed that the defendant held the proceeds of the cheques on constructive trust for the estate. Denning J. held that the defendant must be taken to know what any reasonable man would have known. Eight successive requests to cash cheques clearly drawn on the bank account of an estate would have placed a reasonable man on enquiry. Thus the defendant must be taken to have known of the executor's breach of trust and so, although he had obtained the cheques for value in good faith, he was held to be liable for "knowing receipt" and was a constructive trustee of their proceeds. The category of knowledge relied on by Denning J. as the basis for the imposition of this constructive trust appears to fall within the fifth category of knowledge which would later be identified by Peter Gibson J. (knowledge of circumstances which would put an honest and reasonable man on inquiry). Consequently, *Nelson v. Larholt*, together with dicta both in *Belmont Finance Corporation v. Williams Furniture (No. 2)*[49] and in a number of first instance decisions,[50] was subsequently cited in *Cowan de Groot Properties v. Eagle Trust*[51] as authority for the proposition that liability for "knowing receipt" will be imposed if the recipient has any of the five categories of knowledge identified by Peter Gibson J.

However, *Nelson v. Larholt* was explained in a different way in *Carl-Zeiss Stiftung v. Herbert Smith (No. 2)*,[52] where Sachs L.J. described *Nelson v. Larholt* as a case where there had been an obvious shutting of eyes as opposed to a mere lack of prudence and suggested that a negligent, if innocent, failure to make inquiry was not sufficient to attract liability for "knowing receipt". This interpretation of the decision appears to place the defendant in *Nelson v. Larholt* within the second category of knowledge which would later be

---

[47] [1994] 2 All E.R. 685.
[48] [1948] 1 K.B. 339.
[49] *International Sales and Agencies v. Marcus* [1982] 3 All E.R. 551 at 558; *Agip (Africa) v. Jackson* [1990] Ch. 265 at 290; *Westpac Banking Corp v. Savin* [1985] 2 N.Z.L.R. 41 at 71 (High Court of New Zealand).
[50] In *Cowan de Groot Properties v. Eagle Trust* [1992] 4 All E.R. 700.
[51] [1969] 2 Ch. 276.
[52] [1969] 2 Ch. 276 at 298.

identified by Peter Gibson J. (knowledge that he would have obtained but for wilfully shutting his eyes to the obvious). This narrower view of liability for "knowing receipt" was adopted by Megarry V.-C. in *Re Montagu's Settlement*,[53] where he held that only the first three of the five categories of knowledge identified by Peter Gibson J. would give rise to liability for "knowing receipt". This case concerned a settlement made in 1923 under one of the clauses of which certain chattels, largely comprising the furniture, plate, pictures and other heirlooms of the Montagu family, were assigned to the trustees who, in the events which happened, were under a fiduciary duty, after the death in 1947 of the ninth Duke of Manchester, to select and make an inventory of such of the chattels as they considered suitable for inclusion in the settlement and to hold the residue of the chattels on trust for the tenth Duke of Manchester absolutely. However, the trustees in fact made no such selection or inventory but instead treated all the chattels as being the absolute property of the tenth Duke. Many of the chattels were therefore sold by him in 1949 and the remainder were taken by him to Kenya where he was then living. Following his death in 1977, the eleventh Duke of Manchester sought to recover the chattels or their value from his stepmother, the tenth Duke's executrix. Megarry V.-C. ordered an inquiry in order to establish which of the chattels would have been selected had the trustees complied with their obligations in 1947 and held that such of the selected chattels as were still in the hands of the executrix could be recovered from her by means of an equitable proprietary claim. However, recovery of the value of such of the selected chattels as had been sold and would therefore would not be able to be recovered in this way required the imposition of liability for "knowing receipt". Megarry V.-C. held that the tenth Duke did not fall into any of the first three categories of knowledge identified by Peter Gibson J. in *Baden v. Société Générale* and so his executrix was not liable for "knowing receipt". He held that the mistake as to the interpretation of the settlement had occurred as a result of what his lordship described as "an honest muddle". Admittedly the tenth Duke's solicitor, and possibly also the tenth Duke himself as one of the settlers of the 1923 settlement, had at one stage been aware of the true position. However, his lordship held that "a person is not to be taken to have knowledge of a fact that he once knew but has genuinely forgotten: the test (or a test) is whether the knowledge continues to operate on that person's mind at the time in question".[54] He also held that, where a person has received property as a result of a disposition in breach of trust, any knowledge which may be possessed by his solicitor will not be imputed to him "at all events if the donee or beneficiary has not employed the solicitor to investigate his right

---

[53] [1987] Ch. 264.

[54] *ibid.* at 285. In *El Ajou v. Dollar Land Holdings* [1993] B.C.L.C. 735 at 762, Millett J. held that, in the same way, "where the knowledge of a director is attributed to a company, but is not actually imparted to it, the company should not be treated as continuing to possess that knowledge after the director in question has died or left its service. In such circumstances, the company can properly be said to have 'lost its memory'." Although the Court of Appeal reversed Millett J., Nourse L.J. stated ([1994] 2 All E.R. 685) that, while this proposition did not assist the defendant, he "might agree" with it.

to the bounty, and has done nothing else that can be treated as accepting that the solicitor's knowledge should be treated as his own." This narrower view of liability for "knowing receipt" was subsequently applied by Alliott J. at first instance in *Lipkin Gorman v. Karpnale*[55] and by Steyn J. in *Barclays Bank v. Quincecare*.[56]

At this stage there were consequently two conflicting lines of authority based on the two different interpretations of the decision in *Nelson v. Larholt*. A further refinement was subsequently introduced by Vinelott J. in *Eagle Trust v. S.B.C. Securities*.[57] He held that the question of whether the fourth and fifth categories of knowledge identified by Peter Gibson J. in *Baden v. Société Générale* suffice for the imposition of liability for "knowing assistance" only arises in non-commercial transactions.[58] In commercial transactions, on the other hand, "if, in the ordinary course of business, a payment is made in discharge of a liability to the [recipient], the [recipient] cannot be made liable as a constructive trustee merely upon the ground that he knew or had reason to suspect that there had been a breach of trust disentitling the trustee to make the payment. It must be shown that the circumstances are such that knowledge that the payment was improper can be imputed to him."[59] Thus in commercial transactions, liability for "knowing receipt" will be imposed if the recipient has any of the first three categories of knowledge identified by Peter Gibson J. in *Baden v. Société Générale* or "if the circumstances are such that, in the absence of any evidence or explanation by the [recipient], that knowledge can be inferred"—it being inferred "if the circumstances are such that an honest and reasonable man would have inferred that the moneys were probably trust moneys and were being misapplied".[60] This case concerned an attempt to impose liability for "knowing receipt" on the underwriter of a rights issue made by the plaintiff company in connection with a share exchange takeover; the underwriter had received in discharge of the sub-underwriting obligations of the plaintiff's chief executive what turned out to be the plaintiff's own funds. Because these funds had been received in a commercial context to discharge a debt, Vinelott J. struck out a claim alleging only knowledge within the fourth and fifth categories identified by Peter Gibson J. The Court of Appeal subsequently granted the plaintiff leave to amend the pleadings so as to allege knowledge within the first three categories as well. When the case came on

---

[55] [1987] 1 W.L.R. 987 (the question did not have to be decided in the Court of Appeal ([1989] 1 W.L.R. 1340) and did not arise in the House of Lords ([1991] 2 A.C. 548); see *post*, p. 346.
[56] (1988) [1992] 4 All E.R. 363.
[57] (1991) [1993] 1 W.L.R. 484.
[58] For such transactions, Vinelott J. appeared to favour the broader view of liability for "knowing receipt" rather than the view expressed in *Re Montagu's Settlement*. A similar view was taken by Millett J. in *El Ajou v. Dollar Land Holdings* [1993] B.C.L.C. 735 at 758–759, who was "content to assume, without deciding, that dishonesty or want of probity involving actual knowledge (whether proved or inferred) is not a precondition of liability but that a recipient is not expected to be unduly suspicious and is not to be held liable unless he went ahead without further inquiry in circumstances in which an honest and reasonable man would have realised that the money was probably trust money and was being misapplied".
[59] (1991) [1993] 1 W.L.R. 484 at 506.
[60] *ibid.*

for trial,[61] Arden J. followed and applied the statement of principle enunciated by Vinelott J. She held[62] that "in a "knowing receipt" case, where the receipt occurs in the discharge of a lawful debt (at least one arising out of a transaction which does not itself constitute a breach of trust[63]), actual knowledge within categories (i), (ii) and (iii) in the Baden case is required". The underwriter was held to have had no such knowledge so the action failed. The principle enunciated by Vinelott J. had in the meantime also been applied with exactly the same consequences by Knox J. in *Cowan de Groot Properties v. Eagle Trust*.[64] While the further refinement introduced by these authorities is certainly consistent with the traditional reluctance of equity to extend the doctrine of constructive notice to commercial transactions,[65] to have distinct tests for different types of transactions may well only succeed in confusing the situation even further.

The conflicting lines of authority which have been discussed urgently require a considered review by an appellate court. The matter was raised in the Court of Appeal in *Polly Peck International v. Nadir (No. 2)*[66] but Scott L.J. did not consider an interlocutory appeal to be "the right occasion for settling the issue"; however, he left the question open by accepting that the third category of knowledge identified by Peter Gibson J. in *Baden v. Société Générale* would lead to liability for "knowing receipt" while admitting to "some doubts" as to whether the fifth category of knowledge would also do so. It is to be hoped that at least one of the proceedings presently pending in which it is being sought to impose liability for "knowing receipt" reaches the Court of Appeal since any clearly expressed statement of the law would be preferable to the existing confusion.

(C) The Way Forward

In *Lipkin Gorman v. Karpnale*[67] a member of a firm of solicitors had drawn from the firm's client accounts funds which he subsequently gambled away at a casino. Liability for "dishonest assistance" and "knowing receipt" was considered only at first instance, where Alliott J. held, *inter alia*,[68] that the bank was liable for "dishonest assistance" in respect of some of the funds drawn from the client accounts[69] and that the casino was not liable for

---

[61] *Eagle Trust v. S.B.C. Securities (No. 2)* (1994) [1996] 1 B.C.L.C. 121.

[62] *ibid.* at 152.

[63] Such as the transaction in *Belmont Finance Corporation v. Williams Furniture (No. 2)* [1980] 1 All E.R. 393; this was the ground on which Arden J. distinguished this decision.

[64] (1991) [1992] 4 All E.R. 700. However, both Arden J. and Knox J. went on to state that, in the event that they were wrong as to the law, the respective recipients had had no knowledge within the fourth or fifth categories either, so both claims would actually have failed on any view of the law.

[65] See *Manchester Trust v. Furness* [1895] 2 Q.B. 539 at 545, discussed *ante*, p. 283.

[66] [1992] 4 All E.R. 769 at 777.

[67] [1987] 1 W.L.R. 987 (Alliott J.); [1989] 1 W.L.R. 1340, CA; [1991] 2 A.C. 548 (House of Lords).

[68] Alliott J. also held the casino liable for conversion of a draft (this liability was affirmed by both appellate courts) and not liable in an action for money had and received.

[69] For those drawn after the bank manager became aware of the uncontrolled nature of the solicitor's gambling.

"knowing receipt". However, the Court of Appeal considered only the potential liability of the bank for breach of contract and the potential liability of the casino principally for money had and received. Both these claims failed and only the liability of the casino was considered (and upheld) in the House of Lords. It has already been observed[70] that an action for money had and received does not depend on the state of mind of the recipient of the money; he will be strictly liable unless he can make out an established defence. The disagreement between the Court of Appeal and the House of Lords was as to whether a casino is a bona fide purchaser for value without notice.[71] The House of Lords denied this defence to the casino but permitted it to invoke a wholly new defence of change of position, under which its liability was restricted to its net winnings from the solicitor. This defence, which will be discussed in detail in a later Chapter,[72] is clearly not restricted to actions for money had and received and is likely to be generally available. It is therefore almost inevitable that any future imposition of liability for "knowing receipt" will be subject to this new defence of change of position.

The availability of this defence will clearly influence the desperately needed review of the conflicting lines of authorities which at present exist in English law, whether it is carried out by the courts in the same way that liability for "dishonest assistance" was reviewed by the Privy Council in *Royal Brunei Airlines v. Tan*[73] or by the Law Commission. If the only question which had to be considered in such a review were which of the existing lines of authority should be preferred, it would be suggested that the view expressed by Megarry V.-C. in *Re Montagu's Settlement*[74] should be adopted on the grounds that it achieved a much needed consistency between the circumstances in which a personal liability to account would be imposed upon a person who had assisted in bringing about a disposition of trust property in breach of trust and the circumstances in which a constructive trust would be imposed on a person who had received property disposed of in breach of trust; on this basis only the first three categories of knowledge identified by Peter Gibson J. in *Baden v. Société Générale* would give rise to the imposition of liability for "knowing receipt". However, not only has the Privy Council specifically rejected these categories of knowledge in relation to "accessory liability". The present law has also increasingly been the subject of considerable criticisms as a whole, principally because of the variety of different claims which can be brought as a result of a disposition of property in breach of trust and of what have been described[75] as the "arbitrary and anomalous distinctions" between them. This suggests that it is now more likely that a review of the law will lead to the rejection of all the conflicting authorities which have been discussed in favour of one of the

---

[70] See *ante*, p. 337.
[71] This depended on the interpretation of the Gaming Act 1845.
[72] See *post*, p. 738.
[73] [1995] 2 A.C. 378.
[74] [1987] Ch. 264.
[75] *El Ajou v. Dollar Land Holdings* [1993] B.C.L.C. 735 at 757, *per* Millett J.

more radical solutions which have been proposed by the commentators. The majority view[76] seems to be in favour of a rationalisation of all the existing remedies by the introduction of a universal principle of some form of strict liability subject only to the defences of bona fide purchase for value without notice and change of position; liability for "knowing receipt'" would then no longer depend on the state of mind of the recipient, which would be relevant only in respect of the availability of the defences. Whether and, if so, when such a principle is introduced remains to be seen. For the moment liability for "knowing receipt" clearly still depends on the state of mind of the recipient; what at present remains undecided is the level of knowledge which is necessary.

4. Inconsistent Dealing with Property Subject to a Trust

Any person who has received lawfully and not for his own benefit property subject to a trust will be liable to account for that property as a constructive trustee if he subsequently either misappropriates it or deals with it in some other manner which is inconsistent with the trust. The decided cases on what is generally known as liability for "inconsistent dealing"[77] fall into two groups.

The first group of cases concerns agents. It has already been seen[78] that banks enjoy a right of set off between different accounts held by the same customer. If a bank manager has been duly notified that an account held at his branch in the name of an individual is in fact a trust account, the bank will be holding the credit balance of that account wholly lawfully and in no sense for its own benefit. If, however, the bank seeks to debit the credit balance of the trust account by way of set off against an overdraft created in another account held in the name of the same individual, it will potentially be liable for "inconsistent dealing". In *Barclays Bank v. Quistclose Investments*,[79] Quistclose Investments made a loan to Rolls Razor for the specific purpose of paying a dividend and the funds were paid into a new account at Barclays Bank opened by Rolls Razor specifically for the purpose. When Rolls Razor went into liquidation prior to the date on which the dividend

---

[76] Advocated by P. B. H. Birks: [1993] L.M.C.L.Q. 218, by C. Harpum (the Law Commissioner charged with the review) in *Frontiers of Liability* (ed. Birks, 1994), p. 9, and by Lord Nicholls of Birkenhead, writing extra-judicially, in *Restitution—Past, Present and Future* (ed. Cornish, 1998), p. 231. This result was also clearly envisaged by Millett J. in *El Ajou v. Dollar Land Holdings* [1993] B.C.L.C. 735 at 759. Two other views deserve attention: Lord Hoffmann, writing extra-judicially in *Frontiers of Liability* (ed. Birks, 1994), p. 27, has advocated that liability for "knowing receipt" should arise, if at all, under the law of tort and in particular the torts of negligence and deceit, and that all the forms of equitable liability should be abolished; and P. D. Finn in *Equity, Fiduciaries and Trusts* 1993 (ed. Waters, 1993), p. 195, has argued for the abandonment of much, if not all, of the existing law and its replacement by the following three questions, all of which need to be answered in the affirmative before what he denominates "participatory liability" can be imposed: (1) Has a fiduciary committed a breach of fiduciary duty or breach of trust? (2) Has the third party participated in the manner in which the breach has occurred? (3) In so doing, did that party know or have reason to know that a wrong was being committed by the fiduciary on his or her beneficiaries?

[77] C. Harpum in *Frontiers of Liability* (ed. Birks, 1993), p. 9 describes this (along with liability for "knowing receipt") as "Restitutionary Liability".

[78] See *ante*, p. 24, n. 22.

[79] [1970] A.C. 567.

was due to be paid, Barclays Bank claimed to offset the balance of this new account against the indebtedness of Rolls Razor in other accounts. The House of Lords held that Rolls Razor had been holding the funds in question on trust to pay the dividend and, subject thereto, for Quistclose Investments since the bank had been made aware of the situation but had failed to draw the appropriate inference from facts known to it, it held the funds which it had sought to misapply on trust for Quistclose Investments. Similarly in *Neste Oy v. Lloyds Bank*[80] the plaintiff shipowner was accustomed whenever one of its vessels entered a United Kingdom port to transfer to the bank account of its agent at Lloyds Bank sufficient funds to enable the agent to discharge all liabilities incurred by the vessel. A number of such payments were made immediately before and immediately after the agent appointed a receiver. Lloyds Bank set off all the payments so made against the indebtedness of the agent. Bingham J. held that there was no express trust of any of the payments and that, even if there had been a trust in respect of any of the payments made before the appointment of the receiver, the bank would have taken free of that trust on the grounds that it did not fall within any of the categories of knowledge identified by Peter Gibson J. in *Baden v. Société Générale*. However, he held that the agent had become a trustee of the payment received after the appointment of the receiver; at the time of its arrival, the bank had already known of the appointment of the receiver and had therefore been placed upon enquiry. The bank was consequently bound by this trust and was not subsequently entitled to set off the payment. An agent will thus clearly be liable for "inconsistent dealing" if he knowingly misapplies property subject to a trust; the categories of knowledge which suffice for the imposition of liability for "knowing receipt" should also apply to the imposition of liability for "inconsistent dealing".

The second group of cases concerns strangers who receive property subject to a trust which has been misapplied without sufficient knowledge to be held liable for "knowing receipt". If such a stranger subsequently acquires the necessary knowledge of the misapplication of the property in breach of trust, he will nevertheless be liable as a constructive trustee if he subsequently deals with the property in a manner inconsistent with the trust. In *Sheridan v. Joyce*[81] a trustee lent out trust funds in breach of trust. The borrower originally had no knowledge whatever of this breach of trust and so was clearly not liable for "knowing receipt". He subsequently discovered the true facts and thereafter made all the payments of interest to the beneficiary rather than to the trustee. Nevertheless, when the trustee subsequently sought repayment of part of the principal, the borrower made the repayment to him despite the contrary requests of the beneficiary and the money so repaid was lost. The borrower was held liable to repay the sum a second time on the grounds that he had dealt inconsistently with property which he knew to be subject to a trust. Once again the categories of knowledge which suffice for the imposition of liability for "knowing receipt" should also apply to the imposition of liability for "inconsistent dealing".

---

[80] [1983] 2 Lloyd's Rep. 658.
[81] [1844] 1 Jo. & Lat. 41 (Court of Chancery of Ireland).

IV. ADVANTAGES OBTAINED BY FRAUDULENT OR UNCONSCIONABLE CONDUCT

From its earliest days, equity has always been prepared to grant relief against fraudulent and unconscionable conduct and one aspect of this relief is the imposition of a constructive trust on any person who has obtained an advantage as the result of such conduct.

1. The Doctrine of Undue Influence[82]

Since the eighteenth century, it has been a rule of equity that a person who obtains a manifest and unfair disadvantage as a result of undue influence will be unable to retain the benefit of the transaction in question. The equitable doctrine of undue influence which has been developed in the subsequent two centuries applies only to *inter vivos* transactions.[83] The specific situations in which the doctrine is applicable were set out by the House of Lords in *Barclays Bank v. O'Brien*.[84]

(A) The Scope of the Doctrine

In *Barclays Bank v. O'Brien*,[85] Lord Browne-Wilkinson said: "A person who has been induced to enter into a transaction by the undue influence of another ("the wrongdoer") is entitled to set that transaction aside as against the wrongdoer. Such undue influence is either actual or presumed." His lordship went on to approve the following classification.[86]

Cases of actual undue influence fall into Class 1. A claimant who alleges this type of undue influence has "to prove affirmatively that the wrongdoer exerted undue influence on the complainant to enter into the particular transaction which is impugned."[87] If he can discharge this burden of proof, the wrongdoer will be unable to retain the benefit of the transaction in question whether or not it was to the manifest disadvantage of the claimant. This was held by the House of Lords in *C.I.B.C. Mortgages v. Pitt*.[88] A husband exerted actual undue influence on his wife in order to induce her to join with him in mortgaging their matrimonial home, ostensibly to raise funds for the purchase of a holiday home but in fact to enable the husband to raise funds for the purchase of shares. Although the transaction was not manifestly disadvantageous to her, she was held entitled to set aside the transaction as against him, although not as against the mortgagee. "Actual undue influence is a species of fraud. Like any other victim of fraud, a person who has been induced by undue influence to carry out a transaction

---

[82] See generally Goff & Jones, *op.cit.*, Chap. 10.
[83] The analogous probate doctrine is much more rigid.
[84] [1994] 1 A.C. 180.
[85] *ibid.* at 196–197.
[86] Originally laid down by the Court of Appeal in *Bank of Credit and Commerce International v. Aboody* [1990] 1 Q.B. 923 at 953.
[87] [1994] 1 A.C. 180 at 196–197.
[88] [1994] 1 A.C. 200, overruling on this point the decision of the Court of Appeal in *Bank of Credit and Commerce International v. Aboody* [1990] 1 Q.B. 923 at 953.

which he did not freely and knowingly enter into is entitled to have that transaction set aside as of right."[89]

On the other hand, cases of presumed undue influence fall into Class 2. In the words of Lord Browne-Wilkinson in *Barclays Bank v. O'Brien*[90]:

"In these cases the complainant only has to show, in the first instance, that there was a relationship of trust and confidence between the complainant and the wrongdoer of such a nature that it is fair to presume that the wrongdoer abused that relationship in procuring the complainant to enter into the impugned transaction. In Class 2 cases therefore there is no need to procure evidence that actual undue influence was exerted in relation to the particular transaction impugned: once a confidential relationship has been proved, the burden then shifts to the wrongdoer to prove that the complainant entered into the impugned transaction freely, for example by showing that the complainant had independent advice."[91]

He went on to hold that such a confidential relationship can be established in two ways, which are described as Class 2(A) and Class 2(B) cases. Class 2(A) comprises "[c]ertain relationships (for example solicitor and client, medical advisor and patient) [which] as a matter of law raise the presumption that undue influence has been exercised." Other relationships of this kind include parent-child, trustee-beneficiary and, particularly, spiritual adviser-religious devotee.[92] However, he specifically held that the relationship between husband and wife and between cohabitees does not fall within Class 2(A). He then went on to define Class 2(B) cases as follows:

"Even if there is no relationship falling within Class 2(A), if the complainant proves the *de facto* existence of a relationship under which the complainant generally reposed trust and confidence in the wrongdoer, the existence of such relationship raises the presumption of undue influence. In a Class 2(B) case therefore, in the absence of evidence disproving undue influence, the complainant will succeed in setting aside the impugned transaction merely by proof that the complainant reposed trust and confidence in the wrongdoer without having to prove that the wrongdoer exerted actual undue influence or otherwise abused such trust and confidence in relation to the particular transaction impugned."

The many cases in recent years in which the doctrine of undue influence has been relied on by spouses, or *de facto* partners, in order to challenge the validity of mortgages of their homes made in order to secure financial support for the business of the other spouse or partner are all examples of

---

[89] *ibid.* at 808.
[90] [1994] 1 A.C. 180 at 189.
[91] This was done in *Inche Noriah v. Shaik Allie Bin Omar* [1929] A.C. 127 at 135, PC. See also *Banco Exterior Internacional v. Thomas* [1997] 1 W.L.R. 221.
[92] In *Allcard v. Skinner* (1887) 36 Ch.D. 145 at 183 Lindley L.J. stated that "the influence of one mind over another is very subtle, and of all influences religious influence is the most dangerous and the most powerful".

conduct falling within Class 2(B). So was a relationship between son-in-law and trusting father-in-law in *Mahoney v. Purnell*.[93]

However, in cases of presumed undue influence, the person who exerted the undue influence will nevertheless be able to retain the benefit of the transaction unless it can be shown to have been wrongful in that, as the House of Lords held in *National Westminster Bank v. Morgan*,[94] it constituted "a disadvantage sufficiently serious to require evidence to rebut the presumption that in the circumstances of the relationship between the parties it was procured by the exercise of undue influence". In the case of a gift, this requirement will be satisfied "if the gift is so large as not to be reasonably accounted for on the ground of friendship, relationship, charity or other ordinary motives on which ordinary men act".[95] In the case of a bilateral transaction, this requirement will be satisfied by any inadequacy of consideration in favour of the person who has exerted the undue influence; a sale at an undervalue will satisfy this requirement[96] but the transaction which was challenged in *National Westminster Bank v. Morgan*,[97] a short term loan made at a commercial rate of interest to enable the borrower to prevent a mortgagee from going into possession of her home, did not.

(B)   The Effect of the Application of the Doctrine

Where the doctrine of undue influence applies, it is normally sufficient for the courts simply to set aside the transaction. If property has actually been transferred to the person who exerted the undue influence, the court will order its return; if, on the other hand, as is usually the case in bilateral transactions of the type which have been before the courts so often in recent years, the person who exerted the undue influence has obtained some mortgage or charge by way of security for the liabilities of himself, the chargor or a third party, that security will be unenforceable. However, where the property in question has reached the hands of third parties who have taken it free of the right of the victim of the undue influence to set the transaction aside, it will obviously no longer be able to be set aside; in this situation the courts have power to award the victim fair compensation in equity[97a] under *Nocton v. Lord Ashburton*.[98]

In none of these circumstances is it necessary to classify the nature of the interest retained by the person upon whom the undue influence was exerted in any property which he has transferred away. Such a classification does however become necessary as soon as any third party becomes involved. It is clear that the right to have a transaction set aside on the grounds of undue influence is capable of being assigned both *inter vivos*[99] and upon death[1] and so may be enforced by the successors of the person upon whom the undue influence was exerted. It also seems clear that, in the event of the death or

---

[93] [1996] 3 All E.R. 61.
[94] [1985] A.C. 686 at p. 704.
[95] *Allcard v. Skinner* (1887) 36 Ch.D. 145 at 185.
[96] *Possathurai v. Kannappa Chettiar* (1919) L.R. 47 I.A. 1 at 3–4, PC.
[97] *National Westminster Bank v. Morgan* [1985] A.C. 686 at 703.
[97a] *Mahoney v. Purnell* [1996] 3 All E.R. 61.
[98] [1914] A.C. 932; see *ante*, p. 288.
[99] *Dickinson v. Burrell* (1866) L.R. 1 Eq. 337.
[1] *Stump v. Gaby* (1852) 2 De G.M. & G. 623.

insolvency of the person who exerted the undue influence, the interest of the person whom he influenced is regarded as analogous to an interest arising under a trust; thus in effect the person who exerted the undue influence holds any property transferred to him as a result of that undue influence on constructive trust. His personal representatives or trustee in bankruptcy will therefore obviously be bound by this constructive trust so that the person who transferred the property will be able to trace it in equity into their hands and, if necessary, claim priority over the general creditors of the transferee. But where, on the other hand, the person exerting the undue influence transfers property which he has received on to a third party or causes property to be transferred directly to a third party in the first place, the interest of the transferor seems to be regarded as a mere equity rather than a full equitable interest. Such a mere equity clearly binds a volunteer[2] and any third party who has notice of the undue influence, even if he has purchased the property for value.[3] Further it seems to follow from the authorities that the transferor will be able to trace the property in equity into the hands of persons who are so bound by his interest.[4] However, it will not bind any bona fide purchaser for value of a legal or equitable interest in the property who has no notice of the undue influence.

(C) Mortgages of Homes in order to Secure Business Debts

In recent years the doctrine of undue influence has been invoked on many occasions in relation to mortgages granted by married couples or *de facto* partners over their homes in order to secure financial support for the business of one of the mortgagors; the other mortgagor subsequently attempts to resist the mortgagee's action for possession by claiming that the mortgage was obtained by undue influence. The facts of the leading case, *Barclays Bank v. O'Brien,*[5] are typical. The husband's company's bank manager agreed to an increased overdraft facility on the basis that the husband would guarantee the company's indebtedness and that this guarantee would be secured by a charge on the matrimonial home. The documents were sent by the bank to a branch near the matrimonial home with instructions fully to explain the transaction and the nature of the documentation and to advise the O'Briens that if they were "in any doubt they should contact their solicitors before signing". Mrs O'Brien was in fact given neither explanation nor advice and signed the documents without reading them. Cases of this type where the mortgage has been granted by way of surety predominate. A variant is for an advance actually to be obtained on the security of the residential property ostensibly for the benefit of both co-owners when it is in fact to be used for the purposes of only one of them. Thus in *C.I.B.C. Mortgages v. Pitt,*[6] Mr and Mrs Pitt obtained an advance on the security of their matrimonial home on the basis that its proceeds were to be used for the purchase of a holiday home. In fact the husband wished to purchase shares and had pressured his wife into signing the application and

---

[2] *Goddard v. Carlisle* (1821) 9 Price 169.
[3] *Lancashire Looms v. Black* [1934] 1 K.B. 380.
[4] *ibid.* at 417, *per* Lawrence L.J.
[5] [1994] 1 A.C. 180.
[6] [1994] 1 A.C. 200.

the charge, neither of which she read. In all such cases the question which arises is in what circumstances the mortgagee will be affected by any undue influence which is found to have been exerted.

The mortgagee will clearly be affected by any undue influence exerted by a person whom it has used as its agent for the purposes of obtaining the signature of his victim. However, as Lord Browne-Wilkinson held in *Barclays Bank v. O'Brien*,[7] reliance on this agency argument is highly artificial since, in obtaining the signature of the victim, "[the principal debtor] is acting for himself not for the creditor". Therefore it is only in very unusual circumstances that mortgagees will now be adversely affected by this argument.[8] It is also theoretically possible, where mortgagee and victim have used the same solicitor, for information communicated to the solicitor to be imputed to the mortgagee but this is highly unlikely in practice.[9] Consequently, in the normal case, a mortgagee will only be affected by any undue influence if it is held to have notice of it, a question which will be determined by the application of the following principle laid down by Lord Browne-Wilkinson in *Barclays Bank v. O'Brien*.[10]

"[I]n my judgment a creditor is put on inquiry when a wife offers to stand surety for her husband's debts by the combination of two factors: (a) the transaction is on its face not to the financial advantage of the wife; and (b) there is a substantial risk in transactions of that kind that, in procuring the wife to act as surety, the husband has committed a legal or equitable wrong that entitles the wife to set aside the transaction.

Normally the reasonable steps necessary to avoid being fixed with constructive notice consist of making inquiry of the person who may have the earlier right (*i.e.* the wife) to see whether such right is asserted. It is plainly impossible to require of banks and other financial institutions that they should inquire of one spouse whether he or she has been unduly influenced or misled by the other. But in my judgment the creditor, in order to avoid being fixed with constructive notice, can reasonably be expected to take steps to bring home to the wife the risk she is running by standing as surety and to advise her to take independent advice. As to past transactions, it will depend on the facts of each case whether the steps taken by the creditor satisfy this test. However for the future in my judgment a creditor will have satisfied these requirements if it insists that the wife attend a private meeting (in the absence of the husband) with a representative of the creditor at which she is told of the extent of her liability as surety, warned of the risk she is running and urged to take independent legal advice."

---

[7] [1994] 1 A.C. 180.

[8] This did however occur in *Shams v. United Bank* (1994), unreported, where the bank gave its indebted client confidential information about the financial status of the victim and he, with the help of two of the employees of the bank, persuaded her to guarantee his debts by using his position of influence in a religious sect to which they all belonged.

[9] As a result of *Halifax Mortgage Services v. Stepsky* [1996] Ch. 1 (E. G. Nugee, Q.C.), [1996] Ch. 207, CA, in practice the information is likely to have been acquired before the solicitor began to represent the mortgagee and cannot in any event be divulged without the mortgagor's consent.

[10] [1994] 1 A.C. 180 at 196–197.

The operation of this principle is not confined to husbands and wives but is "applicable to all other cases where there is an emotional relationship between cohabitees" and to cases "where the creditor is aware that the surety reposes trust and confidence in the principal debtor in relation to his financial affairs".[11]

There is no doubt at all as to what a mortgagee has to do in transactions entered into after *Barclays Bank v. O'Brien* in order to avoid being affected by any undue influence which may have occurred. However, the numerous cases which have had to be decided since *Barclays Bank v. O'Brien* have all concerned transactions entered into prior to that decision. Consequently, the principal problem which has exercised the courts has been to decide whether the steps taken by creditors who did not have the benefit of the observations of Lord Browne-Wilkinson do or do not satisfy his principle. The two cases whose facts have already been discussed caused no difficulty whatsoever. In *Barclays Bank v. O'Brien* itself, the wife had received no advice whatsoever and so the bank was obviously unable to rely on its security as against her. On the other hand, in *C.I.B.C. Mortgages v. Pitt*[12] the fact that the transaction was ostensibly for the purchase of a holiday home and so as much for the benefit of the wife as the husband meant that the finance company was not even placed on inquiry and could equally obviously enforce its security against her. The principal difficulty has arisen where the creditor has required the debtor to arrange for the potential victim to be independently advised by a solicitor and the advice has been given in the debtor's presence by the debtor's solicitor (or another member of the same firm). In a number of first instance decisions,[13] advice by the debtor's own solicitor has been held to be insufficient but the Court of Appeal has subsequently held, on at least three occasions but not always unanimously,[14] that the creditor is entitled to rely on the confirmation of the solicitor that independent advice has been given both where it was given in the presence of the debtor and where it was given by the debtor's own solicitor. The House of Lords may well at some stage be called upon to resolve this difference of interpretation, which will also be relevant to transactions entered into after *Barclays Bank v. O'Brien* in the exceptional circumstances where the creditor is obliged to insist on independent legal advice. There has also been some controversy as to what remedies are available when the creditor has in some way failed to comply with these requirements. Is the right of the victim to have the transaction set aside *in toto* or only subject to such of the terms of the transaction as he or she was aware of at the time it was entered into? The situation at present seems to be that the victim is entitled to have the transaction set aside *in toto*[15] unless he or she received a direct financial benefit from it.[16] This question also requires definitive resolution.

[11] *ibid.* Nor is it confined to cohabitees. See *Massey v. Midland Bank* [1995] 1 All E.R. 929.
[12] [1994] 1 A.C. 200.
[13] See, for example, *TSB Bank v. Camfield* [1995] 1 W.L.R. 430.
[14] *Massey v. Midland Bank* [1995] 1 All E.R. 929; *Banco Exterior International v. Mann* [1995] 1 All E.R. 936; *Bank of Baroda v. Rayarel* [1995] 2 F.L.R. 376; *Barclays Bank v. Thomson* [1997] 4 All E.R. 816.
[15] *TSB Bank v. Camfield* [1995] 1 W.L.R. 430.
[16] *Midland Bank v. Greene* [1994] 2 F.L.R. 827.

2. *The Benefits of Crime*[17]

It has long[18] been clear that "no system of jurisprudence can with reason include among the rights which it enforces rights directly resulting to the person asserting them from the crime of that person".[19] Of the two obvious areas where this principle might be expected to operate, where property has been acquired by means of theft or as a result of an unlawful killing, there is in fact little scope[20] for the operation of the principle in the former area since a thief acquires no title to the property which he steals and so is normally[21] unable to pass any title to any third party. There is, however, very considerable scope for the operation of the principle in the latter area. This is well illustrated by *In the Estate of Crippen*[22] where the residuary legatee of the hanged Dr Crippen (his mistress) was held not to be entitled to the property which Crippen would normally have received as the intestate successor of the wife whom he had murdered.

Some difficulties have arisen as to the precise scope of the operation of the principle. It clearly applies to anyone found to have committed murder, even unsuccessfully[23]; it is not necessary for a conviction to have been secured in criminal proceedings[24] nor are the results of any criminal proceedings decisive.[25] On the other hand, the principle does not apply to an insane killer (a person found not guilty of murder by reason of insanity or subsequently held by a civil court to have been insane[26]), since a finding of insanity constitutes an acquittal.[27] The extent to which the principle should operate between these two extremes, in particular in relation to manslaughter and to the offence of causing death by reckless driving,[28] is a matter of some controversy. It has been contended[29] that the operation of the principle should be limited to intentional killing and should therefore not apply to a person convicted either of unintentional manslaughter (involuntary manslaughter or voluntary manslaughter on the ground of diminished responsibility) or of causing death by reckless driving. However, although it has

---

[17] See Goff & Jones, *op.cit.*, Chap. 37, T. G. Youdan (1973) 89 L.Q.R. 235; T. K. Earnshaw & P. J. Pace (1974) 37 M.L.R. 481.

[18] At least since *Bridgman v. Green* (1755) 2 Ves.Sen. 627.

[19] *Cleaver v. Mutual Reserve Fund Life Association* [1892] 1 Q.B. 147 at 156.

[20] Although the principle might have been a preferable ground for the conclusion reached in *Reading v. Att.-Gen.* [1951] A.C. 507. (See *ante* p. 291).

[21] Except where the purchaser is protected by the Sale of Goods Act 1979 or the Consumer Credit Act 1974.

[22] [1911] P. 108.

[23] In *Evans v. Evans* [1989] 1 F.L.R. 351, a wife convicted of inciting others to murder her former husband, who survived, was deprived of benefits payable under the divorce settlement.

[24] In *Re Sigsworth* [1935] 1 Ch. 89, the murderer committed suicide and so no criminal proceedings could be brought.

[25] *Gray v. Barr* [1971] 2 Q.B. 554 (principle applied where the defendant was acquitted of both murder and manslaughter); this is possible because of the different standards of proof, although according to *Halford v. Brookes* (1991), *The Times*, October 10, 1991 a finding of murder in civil proceedings requires the criminal standard of proof.

[26] *Re Holgate* (1971) (discussed by T. K. Earnshaw & P. J. Pace: *op.cit.*).

[27] Criminal Procedure (Insanity) Act 1964, s.1.

[28] Synonymous with involuntary manslaughter except in name and maximum sentence (*R. v. Seymour (Edward)* [1983] A.C. 493).

[29] By T. Youdan: *op.cit.*, pp. 237–238; T. K. Earnshaw & P. J. Pace: *op.cit.*, pp. 492–496.

been stated that there may be some types of unlawful killing to which the principle does not apply,[30] the courts have so far taken the view that it is not appropriate to draw any distinction between voluntary and involuntary manslaughter and have applied the principle to both[31] (it seems to follow from this approach that the principle would also be applied to the offence of causing death by reckless driving—rather surprisingly, this question does not yet seem to have been considered).

When applicable, the principle will deprive the unlawful killer of benefits received under his victim's will,[32] his victim's intestacy,[33] the proceeds of a life insurance policy maintained on the life of his victim,[34] and enhanced social security benefits arising out of the death of his victim.[35] In the unlikely event that the property has already reached his hands (normally it will be intercepted), a constructive trust will be imposed for the benefit of those otherwise entitled. In *Re Sigsworth*[36] a murderer was absolutely entitled under the will of his victim, his mother, and was also, with his brother, her intestate successor; her entire estate passed to her other intestate successor, her other son. The courts have never had to decide whether those claiming through an unlawful killer are also disqualified or whether he is treated as having predeceased his victim. This question would have arisen in *Re Sigsworth* had the murderer left issue, who under the intestacy rules would have stood in his shoes and he predeceased his victim. It has been suggested[37] that an unlawful killer should be treated as having predeceased his victim; this view would entitle the notional issue of the murderer in *Re Sigsworth* to take jointly with the other intestate successor. Similar problems arise where the unlawful killer and his victim hold joint or successive interests. Where one of two joint tenants unlawfully kills the other, it has been held that the killer acquires the entire legal title to the property by virtue of the principle of survivorship but holds that legal title on constructive trust for himself and the representatives of his victim in equal shares as tenants in common.[38] Where a person entitled to property in remainder unlawfully kills the life tenant,[39] it has been suggested[40] that the killer's enjoyment should be postponed for as long as mortality tables predict that the victim would have lived, the latter's representatives receiving the income in the meantime under a constructive trust.

---

[30] In *Gray v. Barr* [1971] 2 Q.B. 554 at 581.

[31] *Re Giles* [1972] Ch. 544; *R. v. Chief National Insurance Commissioner, ex parte Connor* [1981] 1 Q.B. 758; *Re Royse (deceased)* [1985] Fam. 22; *Re K. (deceased)* [1986] Fam. 180.

[32] *Re Sigsworth* [1935] 1 Ch. 89.

[33] *In the Estate of Crippen* [1911] P. 108; *Re Sigsworth* [1935] 1 Ch. 89.

[34] *Cleaver v. Mutual Reserve Fund Life Association* [1892] 1 Q.B. 147; *Davitt v. Titcumb* [1990] Ch. 110.

[35] *R. v. Chief National Insurance Commissioner, ex parte Connor* [1981] 1 Q.B. 758 (murderess of husband deprived of widow's pension).

[36] [1935] 1 Ch. 89.

[37] In Goff & Jones, *op.cit.*, p. 707.

[38] *Re K. (deceased)* [1986] Fam. 180. This conclusion, although supported by Commonwealth authority, is not of course consistent with the view that the unlawful killer is treated as having predeceased his victim since on this hypothesis the representatives of the victim would be entitled to the property absolutely.

[39] The problem has not as yet arisen, although it was postulated in *Re Calloway* [1956] Ch. 559.

[40] By Youdan: *op.cit.*, pp. 250–251.

The court now has a discretion under the Forfeiture Act 1982 to grant relief against forfeiture to a person guilty of unlawful killing other than murder.[41] Where a court has determined that the principle has operated to bring about a forfeiture, it can modify the effect of the principle where it "is satisfied that, having regard to the conduct of the offender and of the deceased and to such other circumstances as appear to the court to be material, the justice of the case requires the effect of the rule to be so modified in that case".[42] Such an order was made in *Re K (deceased)*[43] wholly relieving from forfeiture a wife convicted of the manslaughter of her husband, who had for years been violently attacking her; during one such attack, with the intention of frightening him and deterring him from following her out of the room, she picked up a loaded shot gun which went off and killed him. Although the extreme facts of this case made this decision to exercise the discretion wholly uncontroversial, it is questionable whether it is entirely appropriate for judges to be obliged to make moral judgments of the type envisaged by this legislation.

3. *Other Fraudulent and Unconscionable Conduct*

The courts have always been prepared to impose a constructive trust upon a person who has acquired property by other types of fraudulent or unconscionable conduct. The vast majority of such constructive trusts have been imposed in order to prevent a transferee of property from going back on an undertaking or agreement made at the time of acquisition to respect an interest therein which has not been created or protected in the manner required by the law. Such cases are manifestations of the principle that equity will not permit the provisions of a statute to be used as an instrument of fraud.[44]

Of course it is not always fraudulent to rely on a failure to comply with the requirements of the law. Equity will not prevent a party to an oral contract for the sale of land from repudiating it on the grounds that it does not comply with the Law of Property (Miscellaneous Provisions) Act 1989[45] nor prevent a settlor who has made an oral declaration of trust respecting land from raising the absence of the writing required by the Law of Property Act 1925.[46] Similarly, if an incumbrancer has neglected to protect his interest by the appropriate registration, equity will not prevent a third party purchaser of the land from relying on a statutory right to take free of the interest in question.[47] Equity will only intervene in the event of an attempt to renege on an undertaking or agreement. Thus in *Bannister v. Bannister*[48] the defendant sold and conveyed two adjoining cottages to the plaintiff on the basis that she could continue to occupy one of them rent free for as long as she

---

[41] Excluded by Forfeiture Act 1982, s.5.

[42] Forfeiture Act 1982, s.2(2).

[43] [1985] 1 W.L.R. 262 (Vinelott J.); [1986] Ch. 180 (Court of Appeal).

[44] *Rochefoucauld v. Boustead* [1897] 1 Ch. 196 at 206.

[45] s.2 requires that all the terms of such a contract must be in writing and signed by all the parties.

[46] s.53(1)(b). See *ante*, p. 46.

[47] *Midland Bank Trust Company v. Green* [1981] A.C. 513.

[48] [1948] W.N. 261.

wished. When he subsequently sought to evict her on the basis that the conveyance did not mention her right of occupation, she successfully counterclaimed for a declaration that the plaintiff held the cottage on trust for her for her lifetime. The Court of Appeal classified as fraudulent the conduct of the plaintiff in attempting to rely on the absence of the writing which the Law of Property Act 1925 requires for the creation of the interest claimed by the defendant and imposed a constructive trust under which he held the property on trust for her for her lifetime.[49] In this case, the informal agreement in question was being enforced by the person in whose favour it had originally been made; however, equity is equally prepared to enforce agreements made for the benefit of third parties. Thus in *Binions v. Evans*[50] a cottage was sold at a reduced price on the basis that the purchasers would honour the right of a widow of a former employee of the vendor to occupy the property rent-free for the rest of her life. When they sought to evict her, the majority of the Court of Appeal classified the conduct of the purchasers as unconscionable, applied *Bannister v. Bannister* and imposed a constructive trust on the purchasers to give effect to the interest of the widow.[51] Similarly, in *Lyus v. Prowsa Developments*[52] a building plot was sold by mortgagees subject to and with the benefit of a building contract between the mortgagor and the plaintiffs. The purchaser subsequently claimed to have taken the land free of this contract because the plaintiffs had failed to protect it in the manner required by the Land Registration Act 1925. It was held that the provision in the contract of sale relating to the building contract had conferred new rights on the plaintiffs, which the purchaser had expressly agreed to honour. Consequently, because of the subsequent attempt to renege on this agreement, the purchaser held the plot on constructive trust to complete the house thereon and convey the plot to the plaintiffs for the price agreed in the original contract.

4. The Legacy of the "New Model" Constructive Trust[53]

Until relatively recently the courts limited the imposition of constructive trusts for the purpose of granting relief against fraudulent and unconscionable conduct to the extreme situations which have been considered so far. However, in the years immediately before and after 1970, a series of decisions emanating from the Court of Appeal imposed constructive trusts of this type not only as a result of fraudulent or unconscionable conduct but

---

[49] This caused the imposition of a settlement under the Settled Land Act 1925 and thus potentially involved the reconveyance of the cottage to the defendant, an admittedly odd result but one of which the plaintiff could hardly complain. However, this would no longer be the case today since no more settlements of this type can be created following the Trusts of Land and Appointment of Trustees Act 1996; the defendant would now simply hold the cottage in question on trust for the plaintiff.

[50] [1972] Ch. 359. See also *Neale v. Willis* (1968) 19 P. & C.R. 839.

[51] Lord Denning M.R. reached the same conclusion by a different route: see *post*, p. 361.

[52] [1982] 1 W.L.R. 1044. This decision has been criticised on the grounds that it casts doubt on the ability of a purchaser to rely on his statutory right to take free of incumbrances of which he is aware but which have not been protected in the appropriate way. However, the statements of the Court of Appeal in *IDC Group v. Clark* [1992] 1 E.G.L.R. 187 at 190 confirmed that the decision is explicable for the reasons stated in the text.

[53] This expression was coined by Lord Denning M.R. in *Eves v. Eves* [1975] 1 W.L.R. 1338.

also as a result of conduct which the individual judges were prepared to classify merely as inequitable. The underlying and indeed often expressed objective of the judges in question was to prevent results which would otherwise have been inequitable. If application of the basic principles of property law led to a result which, in the view of the court in question, was contrary to good conscience, that court acted upon the conscience of the party who would otherwise have obtained this unjust benefit and imposed a constructive trust upon him to bring the result into line with the requirements of justice. This approach was, of course, much closer to the American attitude to the constructive trust[54] and was thought to be symptomatic of a general change of attitude towards the constructive trust. Even though subsequent decisions rejected the approach manifested in this series of cases and English law consequently appeared to have reverted to its traditional position, indications of a more remedial approach have continued to make their appearance. In 1990 the Court of Appeal accepted that "there is a good arguable case" for the existence of a "remedial constructive trust",[55] while in 1996 Lord Browne-Wilkinson stated[56] that "the remedial constructive trust, if introduced into English law, may provide a more satisfactory road forward" for developing proprietary restitutionary remedies. These remarks leave room for little doubt that the House of Lords will one day soon be called upon to decide "whether English law should follow the United States and Canada by adopting the remedial constructive trust".[57] Admittedly, any form of remedial constructive trust adopted is likely to be of a much more limited nature than what was envisaged in the years immediately before and after 1970 when attempts were being made to convert the constructive trust into a general equitable remedy capable of doing justice in any individual case. In any event, the series of decisions handed down at that time has never been able to be wholly ignored. While their influence on the law governing contractual licences has, admittedly, been almost wholly negated, their influence on the law governing joint enterprises entered into by the members of a family unit has undoubtedly played some part in the development of what some commentators now call "the common intention constructive trust".[58]

(A) Contractual Licences

Contractual licences have traditionally been regarded more as creatures of the law of contract than of the law of property. While it has long[59] been recognised that a contractual licensee may, in appropriate circumstances, be able to obtain the assistance of equity to force the licensor to perform his contract,[60] until 1952 it had never been suggested that he had any proprietary right in the subject matter of his licence capable of binding a third party,

---

[54] See *ante*, p. 275.
[55] In *Metall und Rohstoff A.G. v. Donaldson Lufkin & Jenrette* [1990] 1 Q.B. 391 at 473–474.
[56] In *Westdeutsche Landesbank Girozentrale v. Islington L.B.C.* [1996] A.C. 669 at 716.
[57] *ibid.*
[58] See, particularly, D. J. Hayton in [1990] Conv. 370 and in Hayton & Marshall, *op.cit.*, pp. 497–510.
[59] Since *Winter Garden Theatre (London) v. Millenium Productions* [1948] A.C. 173.
[60] *Foster v. Robinson* [1951] 1 K.B. 149 (injunction); *Verrall v. Great Yarmouth Borough Council* [1981] Q.B. 202 (specific performance).

unless the latter had in some way estopped himself from revoking the licence.[61] However, in *Errington v. Errington and Woods*,[62] despite the existence of clear House of Lords authority to the contrary,[63] the Court of Appeal held that a contractual licence which could be enforced in this way against the licensor created an interest in land capable of binding third parties. Despite subsequent doubts,[64] Lord Denning M.R. carried this novel proposition a stage further in *Binions v. Evans*[65] by holding that such a licence could be enforced by the imposition of a constructive trust if it was just and equitable so to do, a view which was subsequently ratified by the whole of the Court of Appeal in *D.H.N. Food Distributors v. Tower Hamlets L.B.C.*[66] However, the Court of Appeal subsequently "put the quietus to the heresy that a mere licence creates an interest in land"[67] in *Ashburn Anstalt v. Arnold*.[68] The court accepted that a third party who attempted to renege on an agreement or undertaking to honour a contractual licence would be liable as a constructive trustee in the manner which has already been discussed.[69] However, in the absence of any such agreement or undertaking, the court held that a contractual licence could bind no third party and that in such circumstances it would not be appropriate for a constructive trust to be imposed. Although the court obviously could not overrule *Errington v. Errington and Woods*, it stated that that decision had been made *per incuriam*, which makes it unlikely that anything further will be heard either of the principle enunciated therein or of its subsequent extension in *Binions v. Evans*. This legacy of the "new model" constructive trust thus appears to have been nullified.

(B) Joint Enterprises by Members of a Family Unit

It has already been seen[70] that where property has been purchased in the name of another it will be presumed to result to whoever actually provided the purchase moneys, including if appropriate the person into whose name the property has been put, in proportion to their respective contributions. Such resulting trusts are just as applicable to joint enterprises by members of a family unit as to any other situation. However, during the last 30 years, the courts have had to grapple with an increasing variety of less direct contributions to the acquisition of property made by members of family units, whose

---

[61] *Inwards v. Baker* [1965] 2 Q.B. 29; *Greasley v. Cooke* [1980] 1 W.L.R. 1306; *Hopgood v. Brown* [1955] 1 All E.R. 550; *E.R. Ives Investment v. High* [1967] 2 Q.B. 379. In *Re Basham* [1986] 1 W.L.R. 1498 the existence of a proprietary estoppel was held to give rise to the existence of a "floating" constructive trust similar to that which arises in the case of Mutual Wills (see *post*, p. 367) but this view is generally held to be misconceived.

[62] [1952] 1 K.B. 290.

[63] *King v. David Allen and Sons, Billposting* [1916] 2 A.C. 54.

[64] As a result of *National Provincial Bank v. Hastings Car Mart* [1965] A.C. 1175 at 1239, 1251 (matter left open for future discussion) and *Re Solomon (A Bankrupt)* [1967] Ch. 573 at 583 (contrary view preferred).

[65] [1972] Ch. 359; see *ante* p. 359.

[66] [1976] 1 W.L.R. 852.

[67] *I.D.C. Group v. Clark* [1992] 1 E.G.L.R. 187 at 190.

[68] [1988] Ch. 1.

[69] See *ante*, p. 358.

[70] See *ante*, p. 239.

interests have often been protected by what have been described[71] as "common intention constructive trusts" and, more recently, by the principle of equitable proprietary estoppel.

The first cases of this type concerned the devolution of matrimonial property on the breakdown of marriage. The law contained in these cases no longer applies where the marriage has been terminated since the courts have now acquired an absolute discretion to vary matrimonial property rights at the termination of marriage[72]; it is however still applicable to disputes that arise during marriage concerning the property rights of the spouses, to analogous situations involving unmarried couples and to other types of joint enterprises. The underlying principle applicable to cases of this type was laid down by the House of Lords in *Pettitt v. Pettitt*[73] and *Gissing v. Gissing*,[74] namely that property rights have to be determined in the light of the intentions of the parties at the time of acquisition of the property. However, in *Gissing v. Gissing* Lord Diplock said this[75]:

"A resulting, implied or constructive trust—and it is unnecessary for present purposes to distinguish between these three classes of trust—is created by a transaction between the trustee and the *cestui que trust* in connection with the acquisition by the trustee of a legal estate in land, whenever the trustee has so conducted himself that it would be inequitable to deny to the *cestui que trust* a beneficial interest in the land acquired. And he will be held so to have conducted himself if by his words or conduct he has induced the *cestui que trust* to act to his own detriment in the reasonable belief that by so acting he was acquiring a beneficial interest in the land."

The first sentence of this passage, when isolated from the qualification subsequently placed thereon, appears to suggest that the courts may impose a constructive trust to do justice *inter partes* whenever the result would, otherwise, be inequitable and it was indeed cited as authority for that proposition in several subsequent cases in the Court of Appeal,[76] in one of which[77] Lord Denning M.R. stated that "whenever two parties by their joint efforts acquire property to be used for their joint benefit, the courts may impose or impute a constructive or resulting trust".

The two different approaches can be seen side by side in *Eves v. Eves*.[78] The parties, who were living together as man and wife, purchased a delapidated house as a home for themselves and their children, which was conveyed into the sole name of the man because he pretended to the woman that she was too young to acquire the legal title. All the purchase price was found by the

---

[71] See, particularly, D. J. Hayton in [1990] Conv. 370 and in Hayton & Marshall: *op.cit.* pp. 364–378.

[72] Under what is now Matrimonial Causes Act 1973, s.25.

[73] [1970] A.C. 777.

[74] [1971] A.C. 886.

[75] *ibid.* at 905.

[76] *Heseltine v. Heseltine* [1971] 1 W.L.R. 342 (dispute during marriage concerning the property rights of the spouses); *Cooke v. Head* [1972] 1 W.L.R. 518 (unmarried couple); *Hussey v. Palmer* [1972] 1 W.L.R. 1286 (joint enterprise between married couple and parent).

[77] *Cooke v. Head* [1972] 1 W.L.R. 518 at 520.

[78] [1975] 1 W.L.R. 1338.

man but the woman did a very considerable amount of work on the house. In the Court of Appeal she was granted a one-quarter share therein under a constructive trust. Lord Denning M.R. imposed a "new model" constructive trust on the strength of the first sentence of the passage cited above. But the majority applied *Pettitt v. Pettitt* and *Gissing v. Gissing* correctly, holding that it could be inferred from the circumstances that there had been an arrangement between the parties whereby the woman was to acquire a beneficial interest in the house in return for her labour in contributing to its repair and improvement; this entitled her to an interest under what has subsequently been called a "common intention constructive trust". Subsequent cases have preferred this latter approach[79] and the scope of the "common intention constructive trust" has now been restated, if anything more narrowly, by the House of Lords in *Lloyds Bank v. Rosset*.[80]

In this case Lord Bridge, speaking for the House of Lords, said this[81]:

"The first and fundamental question which must always be resolved is whether, independently of any inference to be drawn from the conduct of the parties in the course of sharing the house as their home and managing their joint affairs, there has at any time prior to acquisition, or exceptionally at some later date, been any agreement, arrangement or understanding reached between them that the property is to be shared beneficially. The finding of an agreement or arrangement to share in this sense can only, I think, be based on evidence of express discussions between the partners, however, imperfectly remembered and however imprecise their terms may have been. Once a finding to this effect is made it will only be necessary for the partner asserting a claim to a beneficial interest against the partner entitled to the legal estate to show that he or she has acted to his or her detriment or significantly altered his or her position in reliance on the agreement in order to give rise to a constructive trust or a proprietary estoppel.

In sharp contrast with this situation is the very different one where there is no evidence to support a finding of an agreement or an arrangement to share, however reasonable it might have been for the parties to reach such an agreement if they had applied their minds to the question, and where the court must rely entirely on the conduct of the parties both as the basis from which to infer a common intention to share the property beneficially and as the conduct relied on to give rise to a constructive trust. In this situation direct contributions to the purchase price by the partner who is not the legal owner, whether initially or by payment of mortgage instalments, will readily justify the inference necessary to the creation of a constructive trust. But, as I read the authorities, it is at least extremely doubtful whether anything less will do."

---

[79] *Midland Bank v. Dobson* [1986] 1 F.L.R. 171 (dispute during marriage concerning the property rights of the spouses); *Burns v. Burns* [1984] Ch. 317; *Grant v. Edwards* [1986] Ch. 638 (unmarried couples); *Re Sharpe (a Bankrupt)* [1980] 1 W.L.R. 219 (joint enterprise between nephew and aunt).

[80] [1991] 1 A.C. 107.

[81] *ibid.* at 132–133.

This admirably succinct statement of the present law establishes that, provided that there has been some express agreement, arrangement or understanding that the property is to be shared beneficially, then any act of detriment, whether or not actually envisaged by the agreement, will be sufficient to give rise to a constructive trust; on the other hand, where an agreement between the parties can only be inferred, only direct financial contributions to the purchase price will justify the inference necessary to give rise to a constructive trust.

The first limb of this test is, if anything, broader than the pre-existing law; where some express agreement can be found, not only the contribution envisaged in that agreement but also any other act of detriment, even if none was envisaged, will give rise to a constructive trust. Thus, if *Eves v. Eves* recurred, provided that there had indeed been an express agreement that the woman was to have an interest, it would now be irrelevant whether or not the parties had envisaged that she would do her very considerable amount of work on the house; all that would matter would be that she had actually done so.

On the other hand, the second limb of this test is considerably narrower than the pre-existing law. In the absence of an express agreement, no matter how much work the woman in *Eves v. Eves* had done she would not now obtain a beneficial interest simply because she had not made any direct financial contribution to the purchase price. Thus in *Lloyds Bank v. Rosset* itself, the wife had supervised builders who were renovating a delapidated building and had herself done a certain amount of preparatory cleaning and some painting and decorating but had made no direct contribution to the purchase price; this was held to be insufficient to justify the inference of any common intention that she should have a beneficial interest. It is of course highly desirable that unsolicited work on the property of another should not, in the absence of express subsequent ratification, lead to the creation of an interest therein. However, the requirement for a direct financial contribution to the purchase price may cause difficulties when substantial indirect financial contributions to, for example, household expenses have been necessary to enable the holder of the legal title to repay the mortgage. There will obviously be no difficulty where there is direct evidence of an express common intention that the contributor is to have a beneficial interest,[82] since this situation will fall within the first limb of the test. In the absence of any such express agreement, prior to *Lloyds Bank v. Rosset* such contributions would have caused such a common intention to be inferred.[83] However, it appears that such contributions will now be insufficient to justify the inference necessary to give rise to a constructive trust; the contributor will therefore presumably be limited to claiming what is likely to be a much smaller beneficial interest under a resulting trust proportional to the contributions actually made. This aspect of the decision in *Lloyds Bank v. Rosset* is clearly less than satisfactory.

---

[82] This was the situation in *Grant v. Edwards* [1986] Ch. 638, a decision which was expressly approved by Lord Bridge in *Lloyds Bank v. Rosset*.
[83] As in *Burns v. Burns* [1984] Ch. 317.

The position in this respect has been to some extent ameliorated by the decision of the Court of Appeal in *Midland Bank v. Cooke*,[84] although this decision has also somewhat obscured the clear distinctions established by *Lloyds Bank v. Rosset*. The matrimonial home had been purchased, in part, with a sum provided by the husband's parents. This was held to have been a gift to both spouses so the wife had to this extent made a direct contribution to the purchase price and therefore had a beneficial interest of at least 6.47 per cent. She had subsequently discharged household outgoings out of her earnings and contributed both physically and financially to the improvement of the house and garden. However, both spouses testified that there had been no discussion or agreement at the time of acquisition as to the beneficial ownership of the property. According to *Lloyds Bank v. Rosset*, the absence of any common intention meant that the wife's subsequent contributions could not be taken into account and the County Court Judge so held. Unexpectedly, however, the Court of Appeal took a wholly different view. Waite L.J. referred to the speech of Lord Diplock in *Gissing v. Gissing*[85] and held[86]:

"When the court is proceeding, in cases like the present where the partner without legal title has successfully asserted an equitable interest through direct contribution, to determine (in the absence of express evidence of intention) what proportions the parties must be assumed to have intended for their beneficial ownership, the duty of the judge is to undertake a survey of the whole course of dealing between the parties relevant to their ownership and occupation of the property and their sharing of its burdens and advantages. That scrutiny will not confine itself to the limited range of acts of direct contribution of the sort that are needed to found a beneficial interest in the first place. It will take into consideration all conduct which throws light on the question what shares were intended. Only if that search proves inconclusive does the court fall back on the maxim that 'equality is equity'."

He then assessed the wife's beneficial interest at 50 per cent on the basis that "[o]ne could hardly have a clearer example of a couple who had agreed to share everything",[87] a conclusion which it is not particularly easy to square with the spouses' own evidence that they had never considered the beneficial ownership of the house at all! Leave to appeal to the House of Lords was refused.

Where does this decision leave the law? The speech of Lord Diplock in *Gissing v. Gissing* does indeed provide support for the propositions enunciated by Waite L.J. in the passage cited. The difficulty is that this is precisely the respect in which *Lloyds Bank v. Rosset* narrowed the pre-existing law, a

---

[84] [1995] 2 F.L.R. 915.
[85] [1971] A.C. 886 at 908: set out *ante*, p. 362.
[86] [1995] 2 F.L.R. 915 at 926.
[87] *ibid.* at 928. A similar "broad brush" approach to the quantification of beneficial interests was subsequently taken by the Court of Appeal in *Drake v. Whipp* [1996] 1 F.L.R. 826 although, in the light of concessions made by counsel at first instance, it might be a mistake to read too much into this decision.

point which Waite L.J. does not appear to have taken into account. Consequently it now appears that, whenever some direct contribution to the purchase price can be shown, no matter how small provided, presumably, that it is not *de minimis*, the court can infer from the conduct of the parties not only a common intention that indirect contributions were to enhance that interest but also the amount by which that interest is to be enhanced. In contrast, the position of the indirect contributor who cannot show any direct contribution to the purchase price will still be wholly governed by *Lloyds Bank v. Rosset* and such a person will consequently be unable to establish any beneficial interest whatever. This revival, for some but not for all purposes, of those aspects of *Gissing v. Gissing* which were thought to have been abrogated by *Lloyds Bank v. Rosset* is scarcely satisfactory either; it is therefore almost inevitable that further changes in the law will follow, as the result either of another case reaching the House of Lords or of the review of the property rights of home-sharers which is to be undertaken by the Law Commission.[88]

Further difficulties[89] may arise in quantifying the beneficial interests. Where the express common intention of the parties envisaged that the beneficial interest should be held in specific proportions, then this common intention should clearly be upheld provided that the parties have duly made whatever contribution was envisaged. But what is to happen where one of the parties has failed to provide the whole of the contribution which was envisaged?[90] The difficulties are even greater where a common intention envisaging a beneficial interest but no contribution is followed by acts of detriment in reliance on the existence of the beneficial interest. Are the beneficial interests to be quantified in the proportions envisaged quite irrelevant of the scale of the acts of detrimental reliance? These questions have yet to be considered by the courts but it has been suggested[91] that the courts should adopt the flexible approach already utilised in the area of equitable proprietary estoppel and provide a remedy appropriate to the circumstances of each individual case.[92] There is no doubt that in this area of the law there is an increasing overlap between the "common intention constructive trust" and the doctrine of equitable proprietary estoppel[93]; indeed it has been suggested[94] that the distinction between the two is now quite illusory and that it is "time that the courts and counsel moved beyond pigeon-holing circumstances into common intention constructive trusts and equitable estoppels and concentrated upon the basic principle of unconscionability underlying both doctrines".[95] The principle of unconscionability certainly

---

[88] Announced in the Programme published in July 1995 and welcomed in both *Midland Bank v. Cooke* and *Drake v. Whipp*.

[89] Highlighted by D. J. Hayton in [1990] Conv. 370 and in Hayton & Marshall: *op.cit.*, pp. 364–378.

[90] Hayton & Marshall: *op.cit.*, p. 370 envisages the situation where half of the potential contribution is withheld.

[91] *ibid.*

[92] Following suggestions made by Browne-Wilkinson V.-C. in *Grant v. Edwards* [1986] Ch. 638 at 656.

[93] See particularly, *per* Browne-Wilkinson V.-C. in *Grant v. Edwards* [1986] Ch. 638 at 656 and, *per* Lord Bridge in *Lloyds Bank v. Rosset* [1991] 1 A.C. 107 at 132.

[94] In Hayton & Marshall: *op.cit.*, p. 373.

[95] *ibid.*

underlies "common intention constructive trusts"; it is only appropriate to classify them as constructive trusts at all because of the fact that in cases of this type the holder of the legal title will almost inevitably have attempted to go back on an express agreement or common intention. Indeed it is precisely for this reason that, when there is no such express agreement or common intention, only direct contributions to the purchase price will do, a proposition which is only another way of saying that in such circumstances the trust which arises is resulting rather than constructive. It is clear that this area of the law has yet to find its final form; however, unless and until the House of Lords chooses to go back on *Lloyds Bank v. Rosset*, the principles enunciated in that decision constitute the framework within which the profession and the lower courts must attempt to operate. However, the decision of the Court of Appeal in *Midland Bank v. Cooke* demonstrates that this framework may be rather more flexible than the House of Lords (or anyone else) originally thought.

The legacy of the "new model" constructive trust in this area of the law has therefore been to produce a line of authority culminating, at least in terms of the doctrine of precedent, in *Lloyds Bank v. Rosset*; ironically, this has produced at least some narrowing of the circumstances in which this type of constructive trust will be held to arise—the extent of the narrowing of course depends on the long term effect of *Midland Bank v. Cooke*. All this has in turn thrown into sharper relief the principle of unconscionability which now underlies much more clearly the new "common intention constructive trusts". The short existence of the "new model" constructive trust may therefore in the end lead to the development of a general principle of unconscionability to replace both the "common intention constructive trusts" and the doctrine of equitable proprietary estoppel.

V. MUTUAL WILLS

Mutual wills arise where two or more persons enter into a legally binding agreement to make wills in a particular form with the intention that the provisions of such wills will be irrevocably binding. As soon as the first of the parties dies leaving a will made in accordance with the agreement, equity regards that agreement as irrevocable so far as the survivor is concerned and gives effect to it by the imposition of a trust. Thus if the survivor ultimately leaves his property other than in accordance with the agreement, his personal representatives will be deemed to hold it on trust for the agreed beneficiary.

This intervention of equity is, on the face of things, directly contrary to the Wills Act 1837 in that the agreement between the parties will normally[96] have to be proved by evidence which does not comply with the formal requirements for wills contained in section 9 thereof. This provision was enacted for an obvious and important reason of policy—to ensure that false claims cannot be generated after the death of a testator when he is in no

---

[96] The agreement between the parties may be recited in one or both of the wills in question although this is not usually the case. It will certainly not be mentioned in any will executed in breach of the agreement.

position to refute them. However, it has long been accepted that the intervention of equity can be justified by the fact that the survivor would otherwise be enabled to benefit by his own fraud.[97] As soon as one of the parties dies leaving a will made in accordance with the agreement, he will irrevocably have disposed of his property in reliance upon the agreement. Therefore any revocation of the mutual will at this stage will be a blatant fraud in that it will enable the survivor to take the benefit for which he contracted—the disposition by the other party of his property in accordance with that agreement—without the corresponding burden. This will be the case not only where the survivor takes some material benefit under the will but also where he disclaims any such benefit and where the agreement gave him no such benefit since in all three situations he will have obtained the benefit which he sought—the disposition of the property under the will. Consequently, equity imposes a trust to prevent the survivor from benefiting by his own fraud.

1. *The Prerequisites of Mutual Wills*

(A)   A Legally Binding Agreement Between the Parties

Evidence must be adduced that the parties intended that the provisions of their wills should be irrevocably binding. The best conceivable evidence is obviously recitals in the wills themselves. In *Re Hagger*[98] a husband and wife made a joint will[99] which expressly stated that the parties had agreed to dispose of their property by that will and that there was to be no alteration or revocation except by agreement. Although the mere fact that the parties had made a joint will did not necessarily make it a mutual will, this recital clearly showed that the parties had agreed to bind themselves to make a mutual will. Equally convincing proof will be recitals of this type in the separate wills of the parties to the agreement. However, cases only tend to reach the courts where the survivor has revoked his mutual will in breach of the agreement and in such a situation his will will obviously contain no such recital. A recital in the sole will of the first party to die will be no more than prima facie evidence of an agreement.[1] In such a case and also in situations where there is no mention of any agreement in either will, the agreement will have to be proved by other forms of evidence. No agreement will be inferred merely because two parties make wills in substantially similar forms. In *Re Oldham*[2] a husband and wife both made wills leaving their property to the other absolutely with the same alternative provisions in the event of the other's predecease. Although it was clear that they had agreed to make substantially identical wills, no evidence could be adduced of any agreement not to revoke and so the judge declined to infer such an agreement, particularly since both had left their property to the other absolutely

---

[97] *Dufour v. Pereira* (1769) Dick 419, 421 (better reported in 2 Hargrave, *Jurisconsult Exercitations* 100, 104).

[98] [1930] 2 Ch. 190.

[99] Such a document takes effect not as one will but as the separate wills of each party and is admitted to probate successively as the will of each testator.

[1] If it is finally found that there is insufficient evidence to prove the existence of mutual wills, it is possible that the equitable doctrine of election may apply.

[2] [1925] Ch. 75.

(although this will clearly be a factor against the implication of such an agreement, there is nothing to prevent parties expressly agreeing to make mutual wills in this form, something which occurred both in *Re Green*[3] and in *Re Cleaver*[4]). Even the fact that both parties clearly intended that their assets should eventually go to the same third party in any event will not be enough, unless it can also be shown that they intended to enter into a legally binding obligation. Thus in *Re Goodchild (deceased),*[5] a husband and wife, as part of a wider scheme dealing with the disposal of their business, each made wills in favour of the other absolutely and subject thereto in favour of their son. Evidence from their solicitor as to the advice which he habitually gave[6] led the court to conclude that the fact that the wife had understood that her intentions would be binding on the husband after her death, something which he would at that stage have taken for granted, did not mean that he had thought it necessary to bind himself so to do; the wills were therefore not mutual.[7]

(B) A Disposition of Property in Accordance with the Agreement

Equity will only intervene once one of the parties has died leaving a will made in accordance with the agreement. The vast majority of mutual wills involve the parties making a disposition in favour of the other with the same ultimate or substitutionary beneficiary; thus each party may leave property to the other for life and subject thereto to the same third party[8] or to the other absolutely with the same substitutionary provisions in the event of predecease.[9] The property in question is most commonly the residuary estate of each but there is no reason why the agreement should not be for each to leave a specific sum of money or specific assets in this way with no restriction whatever on the disposition of the residue. Even where the agreement in question is for each party to dispose of his residue in this manner, it is common for each to make individual specific bequests or pecuniary legacies.[10] Until recently it has been unclear whether or not it is a prerequisite of the doctrine of mutual wills that the will of the first to die should, as in all the examples discussed so far, contain some disposition in favour of the survivor; however, it has now been established that this is not actually necessary. In *Re Dale*[11] spouses both made wills which they had agreed should be irrevocable in favour of their two children in equal shares. It was contended that the doctrine of mutual wills could only operate where the survivor obtained a personal financial benefit under the will of the first to die. Morritt J. rejected this argument, holding that it would be no less a

---

[3] [1951] Ch. 148.

[4] [1981] 1 W.L.R. 939.

[5] [1996] 1 W.L.R. 694 (Carnwath J.); [1998] 1 W.L.R. 1216, CA.

[6] He had never advised any of his clients to make mutual wills and had never had occasion to look into how such wills were drafted.

[7] However, the son was held entitled to make a claim under the Inheritance (Provision for Family and Dependants) Act 1975 in respect of the will of the wife (who had died first) on the grounds that it did not make reasonable provision for him, although only her sole property was available for this purpose.

[8] As in *Re Haggar* [1930] 2 Ch. 190.

[9] As in *Re Green* [1951] Ch. 148 and *Re Cleaver* [1981] 1 W.L.R. 939.

[10] As in *Re Cleaver* [1981] 1 W.L.R. 939.

[11] [1994] Ch. 31.

fraud on the first to die if the agreement was that each party should leave his property to third parties rather than to the other; in both cases the survivor would have obtained the benefit for which he had contracted—the agreed disposition of property in the will of the first to die. It must follow from this decision that the survivor will be equally bound to dispose of his property in accordance with the agreement if he disclaims any benefit to which he is entitled under the will of the first to die; in this case also he will have obtained the benefit for which he has contracted but will have freely chosen to renounce it.[12] A further question, which has not yet been considered by the courts, is whether the doctrine of mutual wills is limited to agreements which, as in all the examples discussed so far, are in substantially similar form. Will the doctrine also operate if the agreement is that, if the first party leaves property to the second party, the latter will leave that property and other property of his own on to a third party? Such an agreement is obviously subject to two conditions precedent: the first party must die before the second party and must leave the property in question to him; equally obviously, if either of these pre-conditions is not fulfilled, the second party will clearly be under no obligation whatsoever to leave his own property to the third party. On the assumption that the necessary legally binding agreement in this form can be proved, there seems no reason why this situation should not be regarded as falling within the doctrine of mutual wills; if so, once the first party has predeceased the second party having made the appropriate disposition of property in his favour, equity will intervene to prevent the second party from going back on the agreement.

2. The Effect of Mutual Wills

(A) Before Either Party has Died

Equity will not intervene until one of the parties has died leaving a will made in accordance with the agreement. Consequently the position before either party has died will be governed by contractual principles. Like any other contract, the agreement between the parties can of course be revoked at any time by mutual agreement. If on the other hand, one party uni-laterally revokes his mutual will in breach of the agreement during the lifetime of the other, the latter will be able to recover damages for breach of contract. However, since the only possible loss is loss of the right to receive an unascertained amount at an unascertained time in the future and since the other party still has unrestricted powers to dispose of his own property, it is relatively unlikely that any substantial damages could be recovered. A further bar to any successful action for damages in these circumstances is the fact that it seems that no such action will be available if the mutual will was revoked not by the act of the party but by operation of law (for example by his marriage, divorce or remarriage[13]); it appears that only intentional revocation will ground an action for damages.[14] Thus, while it is clear that

---

[12] This was stated *obiter* in *Re Haggar* [1930] 2 Ch. 190 and must now clearly have been confirmed by *Re Dale* [1994] Ch. 31.

[13] Wills Act 1837, ss.18, 18A.

[14] *Robinson v. Ommanney* (1883) 23 Ch.D. 285. See also *Re Marsland* [1939] Ch. 820, where the Court of Appeal reached a similar conclusion in respect of a covenant not to revoke a will contained in a deed of separation.

revocation of the mutual will during the joint lives of the parties will determine the agreement and release the other party from his obligations thereunder,[15] no effective remedy is likely to result to the other party.

(B) Where the First Party to Die Does Not Leave a Will Made in Accordance with the Agreement

If the other party does not discover that the first party to die has revoked his will until after the latter has died without leaving a will in accordance with the agreement, he will be able to claim damages from the latter's estate. However, although the loss suffered will certainly be able to be quantified in such a case, the other party will not have relinquished his powers over his own property and so may still find difficulty in obtaining substantial damages. The only exception to this seems to be the situation where he himself dies so soon after the first party to die that he does not have any opportunity of changing his own will and so dies leaving a will made in accordance with the agreement; in these circumstances, there seems no reason why his estate should not successfully bring an action for damages for breach of contract against the estate of the first to die for the value of the property which, according to the agreement, should have been disposed of in the will of the first to die. Save in this exceptional situation, however, where the first party to die does not leave a will made in accordance with the agreement, while it is clear that the survivor will be released from his own obligations under the agreement, he is unlikely to have any effective remedy against the estate of the first to die.

(C) Where the First Party to Die Leaves a Will Made in Accordance with the Agreement[16]

Once the first party to die has made the disposition of property envisaged by the agreement, a trust is immediately imposed upon the survivor for the benefit of those entitled under the agreement. This emerges most clearly from *Re Hagger*[17] where one of the ultimate beneficiaries under the joint mutual will of a husband and wife survived the wife but predeceased the husband. Clauson J. held that her interest under the trust imposed by equity arose on the death of the first to die, the wife, and therefore did not lapse when she predeceased the husband.

The purpose of the imposition of the trust is to prevent the survivor from revoking his will in breach of the agreement. However, equity does not interfere with the fundamental probate principle that no will is irrevocable. If the survivor revokes his mutual will in breach of the agreement, his property will pass under his new will or his intestacy to his personal representatives, who will hold it on trust to give effect to the agreement.[18] This will be the case even if the will is revoked by operation of law upon a subsequent marriage, divorce or remarriage.[19]

---

[15] *Stone v. Hoskins* [1905] P. 194.
[16] See J. D. B. Mitchell: (1951) 14 M.L.R. 137.
[17] [1930] 2 Ch. 190.
[18] *In the Estate of Heys* [1914] P. 192.
[19] *Re Green* [1951] Ch. 148.

However, whether or not the survivor revokes his will, difficulties arise in determining precisely what property is subject to the trust. Of course this will primarily be determined by the agreement. In *Re Green*[20] the agreement specifically provided that each party would leave his property to the other absolutely and, at the death of the survivor, half his residuary estate was to be treated as his property and the other half as property received under the will of the first to die. Vaisey J. held that only the property which was to be treated as the property of the first to die was subject to the trust. This decision is justifiable as a matter of construction of the agreement in question but certainly cannot apply where an agreement contains no such provision. In such a case, there is absolutely no doubt that the property received by the survivor under the mutual will is subject to a trust. If the survivor receives a limited interest, such as a life interest, the property will already be held on an express trust and so there is no scope for the trust imposed by equity. If, on the other hand, he receives an absolute interest, a trust will clearly be imposed but its precise nature is far from clear. In one sense, the survivor will be holding the property on trust for himself for his lifetime and then for the benefit of the ultimate beneficiary of the mutual will. But it is most unclear whether the interest of the survivor is a life interest in the technical sense (in which case he will have no right to resort to the capital) or whether the survivor has the right to dispose of the capital for his own benefit. This problem becomes even more acute when the survivor's own property is considered. Is this property subject to a trust from the time the first party dies and, if so, what is the nature of this trust?

It seems fairly clear from the decision in *Re Hagger*[21] that the survivor's own property is subject to a trust from the death of the first party since in that case the beneficiary was held to have an interest in property which was quite clearly vested in the survivor until his death. But if all the property owned by the survivor at the death of the first party becomes subject to a trust in favour of himself for life and thereafter for the ultimate beneficiary of the mutual will, the survivor will not be able to dispose of his own property for his own benefit without committing a breach of trust. Further, what happens to any property acquired by the survivor after the death of the first party? Does it immediately become subject to the same trust? If so, the effect of the death of the first party will be to make the survivor a life tenant not only of the property which he receives under the will but also of his own property, whether then existing or after acquired. The survivor will therefore have no power during the rest of his life to apply any capital for his own benefit. It could of course on the other hand be argued that the intention of the parties could reasonably be assumed to be that the survivor has the right to deal as he wishes with his own property and perhaps also with the property left to him absolutely under the terms of the agreement. The difficulty about this view is that the trust imposed by equity then becomes so uncertain as to be virtually useless since the survivor can destroy the subject matter of the agreement by alienation or dissipation.

This problem has only rarely had to be considered by the courts because most litigation involving mutual wills does not commence until after the

---

[20] [1951] Ch. 148.
[21] [1930] 2 Ch. 190.

death of the survivor—only then will the ultimate beneficiary discover whether or not the survivor has honoured his agreement. Where the subject matter of the agreement is a specific property,[22] the beneficiaries of the mutual will can clearly recover it or, if the survivor has in breach of trust sold it during his lifetime, its proceeds of sale. But where the subject matter is, as is more usual, each party's residue, litigation commenced after the death of the survivor can in practice only be concerned with the property owned by the survivor at his death; consequently, the English courts have generally been content to apply the terms of the agreement to this property. However, in the Australian case of *Birmingham v. Renfrew*,[23] Dixon J. considered the nature of the trust imposed during the life of the survivor and said this[24]:

"The purpose of an arrangement for corresponding wills must often be, as in this case, to enable the survivor during his life to deal as absolute owner with the property passing under the will of the party first dying. That is to say, the object of the transaction is to put the survivor in a position to enjoy for his own benefit the full ownership so that, for instance, he may convert it and expend the proceeds if he choose. But when he dies he is to bequeath what is left in the manner agreed upon. It is only by the special doctrines of equity that such a floating obligation, suspended, so to speak, during the lifetime of the survivor can descend upon the assets at his death and crystallise into a trust. No doubt gifts and settlements, *inter vivos*, if calculated to defeat the intention of the compact, could not be made by the survivor and his right of disposition, *inter vivos*, is, therefore, not unqualified. But, substantially, the purpose of the arrangement will often be to allow full enjoyment for the survivor's own benefit and advantage upon condition that at his death the residue shall pass as arranged."

This decision was cited with approval by Carnwath J. in *Re Goodchild (deceased)*,[25] where he held that:

"the trust which is held binding in equity... is an unusual form of trust, since it does not prevent the surviving testator using the assets during his lifetime. It is 'a kind of floating trust which finally attaches to such property as he leaves upon his death.'[26]"

A somewhat similar view was expressed by Brightman J. in *Ottaway v. Norman*,[27] a case concerning secret trusts, where he said:

"I am content to assume for present purposes but without so deciding that if property is given to the primary donee on the understanding that the primary donee will dispose by will of such assets, if any, as he may have at

---

[22] As it was in *Re Newey (deceased)* [1994] 2 N.Z.L.R. 590 (High Court of New Zealand).
[23] (1937) 57 C.L.R. 666 (High Court of Australia).
[24] *ibid.* at 689.
[25] [1996] 1 W.L.R. 694 at 700.
[26] Citing *Birmingham v. Renfrew* (1937) 57 C.L.R. 666, *per* Latham C.J. at 675 (High Court of Australia).
[27] [1972] Ch. 698 at 713.

his command at his death in favour of the secondary donee, a valid trust is created in favour of the secondary donee which is in suspense during the lifetime of the primary donee, but attaches to the estate of the primary donee at the moment of the latter's death."

These views undoubtedly recognise what actually happens in most mutual will cases. However, the passages from *Birmingham v. Renfrew* cited with approval by Carnwath J. seem to envisage the possibility of the ultimate beneficiary restraining an *inter vivos* disposition by the survivor (this would certainly be possible where the subject matter of the mutual will is a specific property and the beneficiaries of the will discover that the survivor intends to sell it). On the other hand, Brightman J. instead limits the scope of the trust to the property available to the survivor at this death (this difference may be because Brightman J. was actually dealing with a secret trust rather than with mutual wills). It would be extremely interesting to see how, where the subject matter of mutual wills was each party's residue, a court reacted to such an attempt to restrain an *inter vivos* disposition by the survivor and, in particular, whether any relief given was limited to the property received under the will of the first to die or extended to the survivor's own property. In any event, it seems hardly satisfactory to describe the suspended obligation referred to by both judges as a trust, since such an obligation lacks the element of certainty of subject matter which is one of the principal requirements of a trust. Perhaps the only answer is to regard the trust imposed to give effect to mutual wills as an entrenched anomaly.

3. *The Nature of the Trust Imposed by Equity*

It is quite clear that the trust imposed to give effect to mutual wills is not an express trust. However, there is a difference of opinion as to whether this trust is an implied or resulting trust or a constructive trust. Nothing turns on the classification adopted. Earlier editions of this work have suggested that it should be classified as an "implied, though not a resulting" trust.[28] However, in *Re Cleaver*[29] Nourse J. took the view that it should be classified as a constructive trust. Both views are referred to with apparent approval in different sections of the judgment in *Re Dale*.[30] However, since this trust is imposed to prevent the survivor obtaining a benefit by his own fraudulent conduct, it seems to the author of the present edition that it is akin to the types of constructive trust described in the previous section of this Chapter and so should be classified as a constructive trust.

VI. THE VENDOR AS CONSTRUCTIVE TRUSTEE

When a vendor has entered into a contract of sale which is capable of being specifically enforced, equity in accordance with one of its earliest maxims

---

[28] (5th ed.), p. 154.
[29] [1981] 1 W.L.R. 939.
[30] [1994] Ch. 31.

regards as done that which ought to be done. Consequently, the equitable doctrine of conversion operates and equity regards the purchaser as owner of the subject matter of the contract and the vendor as owner of the purchase money. The operation of this equitable doctrine does not, of course, affect the legal title to the subject matter of the contract, which remains in the vendor pending performance of the contract. Thus the effect of the operation of the doctrine is to separate the legal and beneficial ownership of the property and it is only to be expected that equity therefore regards the vendor as a constructive trustee of the property pending performance of the contract. No corresponding trust of the purchase money will arise simply because such a trust would lack the necessary certainty of subject matter but the vendor acquires a lien or charge on the property for the unpaid purchase money.

The operation of the equitable doctrine of conversion and the consequent constructive trust are important because of the effect that can be produced both upon the devolution of property and upon the liabilities of the parties. Where a party to a contract dies after the equitable doctrine has operated, his property will devolve as if the contract has been performed. Thus, if a vendor or purchaser of freehold land dies after the doctrine of conversion has operated, the interest of the vendor devolves with his personalty and the interest of the purchaser devolves with his realty. However today[31] this is important only in the relatively unlikely case of a testator leaving his realty and his personalty (or his land and pure personalty) to different persons. However, the effect of the operation of the doctrine of conversion on the liabilities of the parties remains as important today as it has ever been because of the fact that the vendor becomes a trustee of the subject matter of the contract. His liability to deal with the property as a trustee can be relied on by the purchaser not only in the event that the vendor fails to take reasonable care to preserve the property in a reasonable state of preservation[32] but also to recover secret profits[33] and to follow the subject matter of the trust into its product[34]; the corollary of this, however, is that the purchaser becomes liable for all the risks attendant upon ownership, in particular that of accidental destruction.[35] Of course, this trusteeship of the vendor is of an extremely unusual nature; the vendor himself retains a substantial interest in the property for the simple reason that, in the event that the contract is not in the end completed, he will once again become absolute legal and beneficial owner; further, he is entitled to receive and retain any income produced by the property until the completion of the sale.[36] However, as soon as the purchase price has been paid in full, the qualified nature of the vendor's trusteeship will disappear since he no longer has any

---

[31] Before 1926, when real and personal property devolved in different ways on intestacy, this effect was of much greater importance.

[32] *Clarke v. Ramuz* [1891] 2 Q.B. 456 at 459–460.

[33] *English v. Dedham Vale Properties* [1978] 1 W.L.R. 95.

[34] *Lake v. Bayliss* [1974] 1 W.L.R. 1075.

[35] The Law Commission has proposed that this risk should pass only on completion (Law Commission No. 191 (1990), para. 2.25) and a provision to this effect has been inserted in the Standard Conditions of Sale (3rd ed., 1995) Cond. 5.1.1.

[36] *Cuddon v. Tite* (1858) 1 Giff. 395.

interest to protect and from that moment onwards he will be a bare trustee of the property for the purchaser.

Since the doctrine of conversion will only operate when a contract of sale is capable of being specifically enforced, it is a prerequisite that the failure of the vendor to transfer the subject matter of the contract to the purchaser is incapable of being adequately compensated by an award of damages. Little or no difficulties have been encountered in applying the equitable doctrine to the relatively few contracts for the sale of chattels which satisfy this requirement[37]; such contracts are capable of being specifically enforced from the moment at which they are entered into and so the vendor under such a contract will hold its subject matter on trust for the purchaser from the moment of contract. However, the vast majority of contracts which are capable of being specifically enforced are contracts for the sale of land and the application of the equitable doctrine to contracts of this type has encountered difficulties caused by the nature of title to land and, in particular, by the fact that a contract for the sale of land is not specifically enforceable until the vendor has made title in accordance with the contract or the purchaser has agreed to accept such other title as the vendor actually has. The constructive trusteeship of the vendor does not therefore arise until title has been so made or accepted,[38] when it is generally thought to have retrospective effect to the date of the contract. This is not an appropriate place to consider the various ways in which this basic principle has been developed in the light of the many different situations which can arise under the various types of contracts for the sale of land; these matters are fully discussed elsewhere.[39]

It has to be admitted that the inevitable self-interest of the vendor in the successful conclusion of the transaction does not sit very easily with his classification as a trustee. For this reason, many doubts have been expressed[40] as to whether it is appropriate for the relationship of vendor and purchaser to be classified as that of trustee and beneficiary. There is no doubt that the classification has led to the development of some anomalous rules but it is by no means certain that different anomalies would not have resulted from basing the relationship entirely on the law of contract. In any event, for the moment there seems little justification for or likelihood of any attempt to recast the relationship between vendor and purchaser on any other basis than that of constructive trustee and beneficiary.

VII. THE MORTGAGEE AS CONSTRUCTIVE TRUSTEE

At the time[41] when the majority of mortgages of land were effected by means of transfer of the subject matter of the mortgage to the mortgagee subject to a proviso for retransfer upon discharge of the mortgage debt,

---

[37] Such as contracts to sell a rare antique, a rare book, or shares in a private company.
[38] *Lysaght v. Edwards* (1876) 2 Ch.D. 499 at 506–507, 510, 518.
[39] See *Constructive Trusts* (3rd ed., 1997), pp. 282–292 and J. T. Farrand, *Contract & Conveyance* (4th ed., 1983), pp. 167–173.
[40] Notably by D. W. M. Waters, *The Constructive Trust* (1964), pp. 141–142.
[41] Prior to the enactment of the Property Legislation of 1925.

many judges saw fit to describe the mortgagee as a constructive trustee of the mortgaged property. Even when the courts came to recognise that the mortgagee, as such, was not a trustee at all,[42] it was nevertheless still clearly established that a mortgagee might be held to have become a constructive trustee as a result of the exercise of his powers under the mortgage and that, once the mortgage debt had been fully repaid, the mortgagee became a constructive trustee of the mortgaged property pending its retransfer to the mortgagor. Now[43] that mortgages of land cannot be created by way of transfer of the subject matter, a mortgagee cannot possibly become a constructive trustee of the mortgaged property, which cannot now be vested in him, but only of property which reaches his hands as a result of the exercise of his powers under the mortgage. After some initial uncertainty, it became clear that the mortgagee was not a trustee of his power of sale and therefore could exercise his contractual right quite irrespective of the interests of the mortgagor[44]; however, any surplus produced by the exercise of this power of sale was held by the mortgagee on a constructive trust for the mortgagor.[45] This old constructive trust of the proceeds of sale seems now to have been totally superseded by the creation of a statutory trust.[46] Further, the better view is that a mortgagee in possession is not a constructive trustee of any rents and profits which he has or should have received but is merely under an obligation to account for them to the mortgagor.[47] It thus seems that, so far as the mortgagee is concerned, the constructive trust no longer has any role to play.

VIII. TRANSFERS OF PROPERTY WHICH ARE AT LAW INCOMPLETE

As has already been seen,[48] the formalities necessary for the transfer of the legal title to certain kinds of property cannot all be carried out by the parties themselves. A transfer of registered land is not effective to pass the legal title to that land until the duly executed transfer form is presented to the Land Registry and registered in the Register of Titles. Similarly, a transfer of shares is not effective to pass the legal title to those shares until the transferor has complied with the procedure required by the Articles of Association of the company in question and the transfer is duly registered in the Register of Shareholders. In both these cases, the intervention of a third party is necessary to enable legal title to pass; consequently the transfer will not be effective at law until the third party in question acts. However, it has been held that once the parties have complied with all the formal requirements capable of being carried out by themselves, the transfer will become effective in equity and the transferor will hold the property in question on trust for the transferee pending the intervention of the third party. This rule was

---

[42] See *Marquis Cholmondeley v. Lord Clinton* (1820) 2 Jac. & W. 1.
[43] Law of Property Act 1925, s.85.
[44] *Warner v. Jacob* (1882) 20 Ch.D. 220.
[45] *Banner v. Berridge* (1881) 18 Ch.D. 254.
[46] Law of Property Act 1925, s.105 (originally Conveyancing Act 1881, s.21(3)).
[47] *Kirkwood v. Thompson* (1865) 2 De G.J. & S. 613.
[48] See *ante*, p. 125.

established in two unconnected cases both named *Re Rose*[49] and for this reason is generally known as the Rule in *Re Rose*.

The precise scope of this Rule, which is clearly English law at the present time, has already been considered.[50] It is also clear that the trust which arises as a result of the operation of the Rule in *Re Rose* does not arise out of any intention of the parties thereto; it must therefore necessarily be brought into existence by operation of law and should therefore be classified as a constructive trust.

---

[49] [1949] Ch. 78; [1952] Ch. 499.
[50] See *ante*, p. 131.

CHAPTER 11

CHARITABLE TRUSTS

I. THE CHARITIES ACT 1993

THE law and practice of charitable trusts was radically reformed by the Charities Act 1960.[1] This Act achieved the arduous task of renovating the appalling mass of statute law relating to charitable trusts. It cleared a great deal of dead wood from the Statute Book, especially that body of statutes known as the Charitable Trusts Acts 1853–1939. What was not obsolete was extracted from them and conveniently contained in the new statute. It is true to say that this Act contained the whole of the statute law relating to charitable trusts from the sixteenth century to the present day, and also added new provisions in keeping with modern circumstances, although, as will be seen, the Act was not primarily concerned with the legal nature of charity which continues to be governed by the case law. The Act implemented, wholly or in part, many of the recommendations of the Nathan Committee on such trusts which published its report in 1952.[2] Subsequently, further reforms, intended to increase the powers of the Charity Commissioners to control abuse and maladministration by charitable trustees, were enacted in the Charities Act 1992 as a result of the Woodfield Report.[3] The Charities Act 1960 and much of the Charities Act 1992 have now been consolidated in the Charities Act 1993. Its effect and scope, where of general interest, is considered in the succeeding pages.

II. DISTINCTIONS FROM PRIVATE TRUSTS

A charitable trust is aimed to benefit society at large or an appreciable part of it. A private trust is aimed to benefit defined persons or defined classes of persons. In general, charitable trusts are subject to the same rules as private trusts, but because of their public nature they enjoy a number of advantages which are not shared by private trusts.

---

[1] For accounts of the Act, see Nathan, *Charities Act* 1960; Maurice, *Charities Act* 1960.
[2] Cmd. 9538. (Its full title is the "Committee on the Law and Practice relating to Charitable Trusts.")
[3] Efficiency Scrutiny of the Supervision of Charities, 1987; National Audit Office Report. House of Commons Paper 380. 1986–87; Annual Report 1987.

1. *Perpetuity*[4]

Charitable trusts are not subject to that aspect of the perpetuity rule commonly called the Rule against Inalienability. The objects of the charity may last for ever, but a gift for such purpose will still be valid.[5] But they are, generally, subject to the perpetuity rule in the sense that the interest must vest in the charity within the perpetuity period. Thus, in *Re Lord Stratheden and Campbell*[6] an annuity of £100 was bequeathed for provision "for the Central London Rangers on the appointment of the next lieutenant-colonel". Since the next lieutenant-colonel might not be appointed within the perpetuity period, the limitation transgressed the rule and the gift was held by Romer J. to be invalid. However, even here there is an exception; provided that the trust in favour of one charity takes effect within the period, a gift over from that charity to another on the happening of an event which may be too remote will still be valid.[7] But this exception will not apply to a gift over to a charity after a gift to a non-charity[8] in such a case the normal rules as to vesting in the second charity within the perpetuity period must be observed. It is as if for this purpose the law regards "charity" as a unity—thus a gift from one charity to another charity is from or to this "unity" so that there is no scope for the operation of the perpetuity rule, while a gift from or to this unity is subject to it in the usual way.

2. *Certainty*

A charity will not fail for uncertainty of objects provided that the settlor clearly intended the fund to go exclusively to charity.[9] If this is satisfied the trust will not fail if he omits to specify the objects with particularity. In such circumstances a *cy-près* scheme[10] will be made to render the objects more precise. Again, for this purpose, it seems that the law regards charity as a unity, so that once the gift to this unity is established, it cannot fail.

3. *Construction*

In construing instruments the intention of which is to set up a charitable trust but where there is an ambiguity, a "benignant" construction should be given if possible.[11] This was confirmed by the House of Lords in *I.R.C. v.*

---

[4] See *ante*, p. 208.

[5] *Chamberlayne v. Brockett* (1872) L.R. 8 Ch.App. 206.

[6] [1894] 3 Ch. 265, applying *Chamberlayne v. Brockett* (1872) L.R. 8 Ch.App. 206. It is now possible to take advantage of the "wait and see" rule introduced by the Perpetuities and Accumulations Act 1964, s.3, in respect of instruments taking effect after the commencement of the Act.

[7] *Re Tyler* [1891] 3 Ch. 252 but compare *Re Dalziel* [1943] Ch. 277; these cases are discussed *ante*, p. 116.

[8] *Re Bowen* [1893] 2 Ch. 491 at 494; *Re Peel's Release* [1921] 2 Ch. 218; *Re Wightwick's Will Trusts* [1950] Ch. 260; *Re Spensley's Will Trusts* [1954] Ch. 233.

[9] See *Moggridge v. Thackwell* (1803) 7 Ves. 36, affirmed (1807) 13 Ves. 416. Provided that the gift has a charitable object, it does not matter that the precise purposes specified are too vague and uncertain to be charitable themselves; *Re Koeppler's Will Trusts* [1986] Ch. 423.

[10] See *post*, p. 420.

[11] See *ante*, p. 85 in relation to construction of private trusts.

McMullen[12] (although it was not necessary to resort to such a construction in that case) and such a construction was adopted by the House of Lords in *Guild v. I.R.C.*[13]

4. *Taxation*

For taxation purposes, the distinction between a charitable trust and a private trust is seen both in the special taxation privileges which are afforded to a charitable trust, and to the taxation inducements which are offered to individuals for them to confer benefits on charitable trusts.

(A) Income Tax and Corporation Tax

With regard to income tax, it is necessary to distinguish between the investment income and the trading income of the charity. Its investment income is exempt from income tax provided that it is applied for charitable purposes only.[14] If the charity carries on trade, its profits from the trade are exempt from income tax only if they are applied solely for its purpose and either the purpose or one of the primary purposes of the charity is to carry on that particular trade or the work in connection with the trade is mainly carried out by the beneficiaries of the charity.[15] Where the charity is incorporated, the same principles as for income tax apply to corporation tax.[16]

The question whether a body is established for charitable purposes is a question of law to be decided in accordance with the usual principles, but the question whether or to what extent income is applied to charitable purposes is one of fact.[17] However, in *I.R.C. v. Helen Slater Charitable Trust*[18] the Court of Appeal held that one charity "applies" its income for charitable purposes if it pays that income to another charity, albeit that the terms of the instrument governing the second charity are almost identical to those of the instrument governing the first charity.

(B) Deeds of Covenant

If a person executes a deed of covenant by which he covenants to pay a part of his income to a charity for a four-year period that part of his income is treated as the income of the charity for the purposes of the basic rate of income tax.[19] In practice, the covenantor deducts income tax at the basic rate from his payment, and the charity is entitled to claim a refund of the tax. In 1998/99 the basic rate of income tax is 23 per cent. Accordingly, where an individual is liable to income tax at this rate, the net cost, after income tax, of paying £5,000 per annum to charity is £3,850.

The same general principles apply to the case of a company which enters into a deed of covenant. It may deduct the gross amount of the payments

---

[12] [1981] A.C. 1 at 16. The facts are stated *post*, p. 410. See also *Re Hetherington (deceased)* [1990] Ch. 1.
[13] [1992] 2 A.C. 310.
[14] Income and Corporation Taxes Act 1988, s.505.
[15] *ibid.*
[16] *ibid.* ss.505(1), 506(1).
[17] See *Williams' Trustees v. I.R.C.* [1947] A.C. 447.
[18] [1982] Ch. 49.
[19] Income and Corporation Taxes Act 1988, s.660. Finance Act 1989, s.56.

from its profits before these are assessed for corporation tax, provided that it deducts income tax at the basic rate from the gross amount before making the payment to the charity and accounts to the Revenue for the tax so deducted.[20]

(C) Capital Gains Tax

A capital gain accruing to a charity will not attract capital gains tax provided that it is both applicable and is in fact applied to the charitable purposes.[21] If the charity is incorporated, then it is entitled to exemption from corporation tax on its capital gains on the same basis.[22]

There is also a substantial inducement to make gifts to a charity. Normally, when a person makes a gift, capital gains tax is payable by him on, broadly, the difference between the value of the asset at the time of the gift, and its value at the time of acquisition.[23] However, no capital gains tax is payable where the disposal is to a charity.[24]

(D) Inheritance Tax

Compared with other private persons or bodies, charities enjoy important privileges with regard to inheritance tax:

(i) gifts made to charities, whether by will or *inter vivos*, are wholly exempt from the tax[25];

(ii) gifts made to nationally important institutions, such as the National Gallery, the British Museum or the National Trust, are wholly exempt from the tax, whether the gift takes effect on death or *inter vivos*[26];

(iii) gifts made to a charity by way of a payment from a discretionary trust are entitled to unlimited exemption[27];

(iv) the Treasury is empowered to exempt, for example, a gift of land of outstanding scenic or historical or scientific interest, gifts of buildings of outstanding historical or architectural or aesthetic interest, property given as a source of income for the upkeep of such land or buildings, and pictures, books, manuscripts, works of art, and so forth, of national or historic or scientific interest.[28]

It is, however, important to emphasise that, as a general rule, the exemptions apply only to gifts to charities which are immediate and absolute.[29] To this general rule there is the qualification that if the donor wishes a charity to

---

[20] Income and Corporation Taxes Act 1988, s.683. Finance Act 1989, s.59.
[21] Taxation of Chargeable Gains Act 1992, s.256.
[22] Capital gains tax applies only to capital gains made by individuals. Capital gains made by corporations are subject to corporation tax.
[23] *ibid.* s.35.
[24] *ibid.* s.257.
[25] Inheritance Tax Act 1984, s.23.
[26] *ibid.*
[27] *ibid.* s.76.
[28] *ibid.* s.27.
[29] *ibid.* s.23.

benefit only after the death of himself and his spouse, he can leave a life interest in the property to the spouse, and on the latter's death, to the charity absolutely. Inheritance tax is not payable on the death either of the donor or his spouse.[30]

In addition to taking advantage of these immunities which are peculiar to charity, a donor may also take advantage of another exemption which applies generally, namely, that gifts to a total value of £3,000 in any one year are exempt.[31]

There is, therefore, considerable encouragement to make gifts to charity. Moreover, from the charity's point of view, any capital distributions made by it are also exempt.[32]

(E) Stamp Duty[33]
Charities are exempt from stamp duty in relation to any conveyance, transfer or letting made or agreed to be made to them.[34]

(F) Value Added Tax
Although there is no general exemption for charities from value added tax, certain medical charities are, in effect, exempt from the tax[35] and supplies to such charities are also exempt.[36]

(G) Rating
The general law of rating is governed by the Local Government Finance Act 1933, section 43 of which provides for the rating relief (both mandatory and discretionary) given to charities.

Mandatory relief to the extent of 80 per cent[37] of the non-domestic rates which would otherwise be chargeable is available in respect of land occupied by or used by trustees for a charity and wholly or mainly used for charitable purposes. With regard to occupation, it is in most cases clear that the charity or the trustees of the charity are in occupation. More difficult questions may arise where the charity has provided a house or accommodation for servants or staff and whether mandatory relief can be claimed in respect of it. The test appears to be whether the occupation of the servant is required with a view to the more efficient performance of his duties so as to constitute occupation by the charity.[38] Secondly, with regard to the requirement that the land be wholly or mainly used for charitable purposes, it appears to be required that the charity's use of the property be wholly "ancillary to" or "directly facilitates" the carrying out of its main charitable

---

[30] Inheritance Tax Act 1984, s.18.
[31] *ibid*. s.57.
[32] *ibid*. s.58(1)(a).
[33] See *post*, p. 517.
[34] Finance Act 1982, s.129.
[35] Value Added Tax Act 1983 Scheds. 5, 6.
[36] *ibid*.
[37] Special mandatory relief in the form of total exemption from rates is available in respect of places of public religious worship and buildings ancillary thereto; Local Government Finance Act 1988, Sched. 5, para. 11 and see *Broxtowe Borough Council v. Birch* [1983] 1 W.L.R. 314 for the meaning of "public religious worship".
[38] *Glasgow Corporation v. Johnstone* [1965] A.C. 609; *Northern Ireland Valuation Court v. Fermanagh Protestant Board of Education* [1969] 1 W.L.R. 1708.

purposes.[39] The meaning of these expressions was considered by the House of Lords in *Oxfam v. Birmingham City District Council*,[40] where Oxfam claimed relief from rates in respect of gift shops which it used for the sale of articles, mostly clothing, which had been donated to it, the profits being applied to Oxfam's objects. It was held that the charity gift shops did not "directly facilitate" the main object of the charity, and rating relief could not be claimed. Lord Cross held[41] that there was a distinction between user for the purpose of getting in, raising or earning money for the charity, as opposed to user for purposes directly related to the achievement of the objects of the charity. The charity gift shops simply raised money for Oxfam and were accordingly excluded from relief.[42]

In addition to this relief, which is obtainable as of right, the rating authority has a discretion to reduce further, or remit entirely, the rates payable by a charity.[43]

III. DEFINITION OF A CHARITY

What is a charity?[44] For the reasons implicit in the distinctions already made between charitable and private trusts, it is essential to know when a trust is charitable and when it is not. The answer to this question is to be found, if at all, almost entirely in the case law. But the answer—in borderline cases, at any rate—may be difficult to find. In fact the whole subject has been condemned in the words of one writer as the "wilderness of legal charity".[45] There is a vast number of cases, and they certainly do not present an orderly picture.

In borderline cases, it may still be necessary to go back to a statute of Elizabeth I (43 Eliz. I, c.4, 1601) commonly called the Charitable Uses Act 1601, in the preamble of which certain objects are listed. These are as follows:

"The relief of aged, impotent and poor people, the maintenance of sick and maimed soldiers and mariners, schools of learning, free schools and schools in universities the repair of bridges, ports, havens, causeways, churches, sea-banks and highways, the education and preferment of orphans, the relief, stock or maintenance for houses of correction, the marriage of poor maids, the supportation, aid and help of young tradesmen, handicraftsmen and persons decayed, the relief or redemption of prisoners or captives and the aid or ease of any poor inhabitants concerning payment of fifteens, setting out of soldiers and other taxes."

---

[39] *Glasgow Corporation v. Johnstone* [1965] A.C. 609 at 622, *per* Lord Reid.
[40] [1976] A.C. 126. Compare *Aldous v. Southwark L.B.C.* [1968] 1 W.L.R. 1671.
[41] *ibid.* at 146.
[42] The Rating (Charity Shops) Act 1976 remedied the effect of this decision with regard to charity shops so as to make them eligible for relief, but otherwise the decision remains intact.
[43] Local Government Finance Act 1988, s.47.
[44] See, for general surveys, Brunyate (1945) 61 L.Q.R. 268; Cross (1956) 72 L.Q.R. 187.
[45] Bentwich (1936) 49 L.Q.R. 520.

The statute itself was repealed by the Mortmain and Charitable Uses Act 1888, but in effect the preamble remained alive.[46] Admittedly, the purposes listed in this ancient statute have never been treated as sacrosanct. In many cases they have been extended by the addition of a multitude of analogous objects, analogy upon analogy, and in some cases the analogies are perhaps rather far-fetched. In others, the decision has been based on a more general question whether the purpose is or is not within the "spirit and intendment" or the "equity" or the "mischief" of the statute—with analogy used only as "handmade".[47] Even so, it is still possible to find a number of cases based on a detailed examination of the words of the statute in recent years.[48]

It was commonly thought that section 13(2) of the Mortmain and Charitable Uses Act 1888, although repealing the Statute of Elizabeth I, had expressly preserved the preamble and that when this subsection was itself repealed by the Charities Act 1960[49] the preamble had been thereby destroyed. However, if section 13(2) is actually considered it seems to fall short of providing that in all cases the court must continue to refer to the preamble; it refers specifically only to enactments and documents in which a reference to charity is made and these do not prima facie include the reported judgments of superior courts. But the main point is that, even if section 13(2) had been omitted altogether from the 1888 Act, the court would still have been bound to decide a case with the preamble in mind, because the practice of the courts had developed into a rule of law. And this rule of law—having, as it were, an independent existence irrespective of statute—could not be extinguished without an express statutory provision to that effect. Indeed the Charities Act 1960 made it reasonably clear that no change in the law was intended. The Act repealed section 13(2) but in substitution provided that a reference in any enactment or document to a charity within the preamble should be construed as a reference to charity in the meaning it bears as a legal term according to the law of England and Wales.[50] Thus the Charities Act 1960 itself seemed to make it clear that the law of England and Wales, based on the preamble over a period of 380 years, should remain intact. In other words, the repeal of section 13(2) with the substitution of new provisions does not affect the edifice of law built on the foundations of the preamble.[51]

This approach, based on a construction of the relevant statutory provisions, seems reasonably conclusive on its own. The relevance of the preamble has, however, also been affirmed by subsequent authoritative judicial decisions. Thus in *Scottish Burial Reform and Cremation Society v. Glasgow City Corporation*,[52] where cremation was held to be a charitable purpose, the

---

[46] See post, infra.

[47] *Incorporated Council of Law Reporting for England and Wales v. Att.-Gen.* [1972] Ch. 73 at 88, per Russell L.J.

[48] See for recent examples: *Re Cole* [1958] Ch. 877; *Re Sahal's Will Trusts* [1958] 1 W.L.R. 1243.

[49] s.38(1).

[50] s.38(4). See also the definition of "charity" in s.45(1) (now Charities Act 1993, s.96 as amended by Charities (Amendment) Act 1996) and "charitable purposes" in s.46(1) (now Charities Act 1993, s.97). For the purposes of the former provision the charity must be subject to control by the High Court in the exercise of the court's jurisdiction with respect to charities; see *Construction Training Board v. Att.-Gen.* [1973] Ch. 173 and see post, p. 433.

[51] See Tudor on *Charities* (8th ed.), pp. 2 et seq.

[52] [1968] A.C. 138.

House of Lords acknowledged that this was undoubtedly the accepted test, though, as Lord Upjohn said, "in only a very wide and broad sense",[53] meaning, as Lord Wilberforce put it, "that what must be regarded is not the wording of the preamble, but the effect of decisions given by the courts as to its scope, decisions which have endeavoured to keep the law as to charities moving according as new social needs arise or old ones become obsolete or satisfied".[54] Likewise, in *Incorporated Council of Law Reporting for England and Wales v. Attorney-General*,[55] the Court of Appeal, in affirming the charitable status of the Council, specifically held that the publication or dissemination of law reports was a purpose beneficial to the community, being within the spirit and intendment of the preamble to the Statute of Elizabeth.

In short, it is still technically necessary today to decide whether a case falls within "the letter or the spirit and intendment" of the preamble. In practice, in most cases, it will be sufficient to refer to the relevant prior case law to dispose of the problem whether a particular trust is charitable or not. Only in a novel case may the court be compelled to refer back to the basic principles or indeed the letter of the preamble.

The preamble was not, of course, a definition of charity. It was simply a catalogue of purposes which in 1601 were regarded as charitable. Indeed at no time has there been a statutory definition, except for the limited one provided for in section 1 of the Recreational Charities Act 1958.[56] Suggestions were made before the Charities Act 1960 was passed that there ought to be a definition of charity in the Act.[57] A similar discussion is contained in the 1989 White Paper "Charities: A Framework For the Future".[58] But these suggestions have so far been resisted because it was thought to be almost impossible to provide a foolproof definition applicable to all the cases that might arise.[59] If any had been provided it might have proved an erratic or insufficient yardstick. The question is debatable. Many laymen and some lawyers find it extraordinary that the question whether a trust is charitable—with all the fiscal and other privileges enjoyed by legal charity—should depend at the present day on a statutory provision of the early seventeenth century and the welter of case law which has grown up around it.

The point has been judicially recognised. For example, Lord Upjohn once said that the preamble had been "stretched almost to breaking-point".[60] The difficulties are undoubtedly exacerbated by the immunity from taxation which all English charities enjoy. In the words of Lord Cross in *Dingle v.*

---

[53] [1968] A.C. 138 at 151.

[54] *ibid.* at 154.

[55] [1972] Ch. 73.

[56] See *post*, p. 406.

[57] See for example the Nathan Report.

[58] Cmd. 694.

[59] "There is no limit to the number and diversity of the ways in which man will seek to benefit his fellow men"; *I.R.C. v. Baddeley* [1955] A.C. 572 at 583, *per* Viscount Simonds.

[60] *Scottish Burial Reform and Cremation Society v. Glasgow City Corporation* [1968] A.C. 138 at 153 but compare *Incorporated Council of Law Reporting for England and Wales v. Att.-Gen.* [1972] Ch. 73 at 94, *per* Sachs L.J.: "I appreciate the wisdom of the legislature in refraining from providing a detailed definition of charitable purposes in the 1960 Act. Any statutory definition might well produce a fresh spate of litigation and provide a set of undesirable artificial distinctions".

Turner,[61] validity and fiscal immunity march hand in hand. He suggested that one possible solution would be to separate them and say that only some charities should enjoy fiscal privileges. No doubt this would cause a great deal of contention but might prove to be a practical proposition. Perhaps the membership of this country of the European Union—as well as the growing number of transnational charities—may provide the necessary impulse for a statutory rationalisation of the law.[62]

The problems of definition should not, however, be underestimated and it may be noteworthy that the Goodman Committee[63] was unable to devise one; it instead recommended that the categories of charity should be re-stated in simple and modern language replacing that of the Act of 1601 and extending these to include objects now considered to be within the scope of charity (so called "guide-lines").[64] The case law would not be irrelevant but the court would have more freedom to reconsider it in the light of the new categorisation. On the other hand, the Expenditure Committee of the House of Commons[65] has recommended that a statutory definition of charity is needed. They do not, however, provide one; they simply emphasise that all charities should be required to satisfy the test of benefit to the community.[66] On this it may be observed that one of the difficulties in this area of the law is to define what is, and what is not, for the "public benefit".[67]

Legislation embodying the Goodman Committee's "guide-lines" would be helpful in modernising the law.

IV. CLASSIFICATION OF CHARITABLE TRUSTS

A leading case in which a classification of charitable trusts was made and on which many succeeding cases have been based is *Commissioners for Special Purposes of Income Tax v. Pemsel*.[68] Here Lord Macnaghten classified the trusts which have been held to be charitable under four heads: first, trusts for the relief of poverty; secondly, trusts for the advancement of education; thirdly,

---

[61] [1972] A.C. 601 at 624 (a case involving the relief of poverty, discussed *post*, p. 392).

[62] See Official Report of Debates of the Council of Europe, 1972, Vol. 3, p. 598; Doc. 3052, 1972, of the Council of Europe, Vol. 11. See also *Trusts and Foundations in Europe* (ed. Neuhoff and Pavel); Pomey, *Traite des Fondations D'Utilité Publique*; Boúúaert, *Tax Problems of Cultural Foundations and of Patronage in the European Community*; S. Bright, [1989] Conv. 28; N. Gravells, 40 M.L.R. (1977) 397.

[63] An independent committee on Charity Law and Voluntary Organisations set up by the National Council of Social Service under the chairmanship of Lord Goodman which reported in 1976.

[64] At p. 16. These "guide-lines" are set out in Appendix 1 to the Report (p. 123).

[65] 10th Report Session 1974–75.

[66] At p. xiii.

[67] See *post*, p. 388.

[68] [1891] A.C. 531 at 583. Compare the classification in the American *Restatement of Trusts* which specifically refers also to two other purposes: (1) promotion of health and (2) governmental and municipal purposes (Vol. II. p. 1140).

trusts for the advancement of religion; and, fourthly, trusts for other purposes beneficial to the community not falling under any of the other three heads.[69]

This is the nearest that there is to a definition in English law. The first three heads do not, generally, present too much difficulty. A case falling within any of those heads will *prima facie* be assumed to be charitable as being for the benefit of the community, unless the contrary is shown. The fourth head presents, as will be seen, greater difficulty but it seems that the courts prefer the vague and undefined approach based on the "equity" or the "mischief" of the preamble, rather than the stepping-stones approach based on analogy, in determining the question whether a trust falling under this head is charitable.[70]

Before each head is considered, it is necessary to emphasise the requirement, which applies generally, that a charitable trust must have a public character.[71]

1. *The Public Element in Charity*

It does not follow from the requirement of a public character that all public trusts are charitable. What it means is that a trust is incapable of being charitable in the legal sense unless it is for the benefit of the public, or some section of the public, with the exception only of trusts for the relief of poverty[72]—and whether or not the test is satisfied is decided by the court on the evidence[73] and not on the opinion of the settlor. A number of illustrations, from the many cases on the topic, may be taken. Thus in *Re Compton*[74] a trust for the education of the descendants of three named persons was held not to be a valid charitable trust, because the beneficiaries were defined by reference to a personal relationship and it, therefore, lacked the quality of a public trust. The trust was indeed a family trust and not one for the benefit of a section of the public. Again, in *Re Holbourn Aero Components Air Raid Distress Fund*[75] an emergency fund which had been built up during the last war had been used partly for comforts for ex-employees serving in the Forces, and later for employees who had suffered distress from air-raids. It was held that because of the absence of a public element no charitable trust had been created and the surplus funds, over which the application had been made to the court, should be returned to the contributors.[76]

---

[69] The classification was based on the argument of Sir Samuel Romilly in *Morice v. Bishop of Durham* (1805) 10 Ves. 522 at 532.

[70] The House of Lords preferred it in *Scottish Burial Reform and Cremation Society v. Glasgow City Corporation* [1968] A.C. 138 and the Court of Appeal preferred it in *Incorporated Council of Law Reporting for England and Wales v. Att.-Gen.* [1972] Ch. 73.

[71] Another requirement to be satisfied is that the trust be exclusively charitable; see *post*, p. 415.

[72] See *post*, p. 392.

[73] *Re Hummeltenberg* [1923] 1 Ch. 237; *National Anti-Vivisection Society v. I.R.C.* [1948] A.C. 31; *Re Wootton* [1968] 1 W.L.R. 681.

[74] [1945] Ch. 123.

[75] [1946] Ch. 194.

[76] On the basis that they were the members of an unincorporated association (see *ante*, p. 260).

But perhaps the most important illustration is to be found in *Oppenheim v. Tobacco Securities Trust Co.*,[77] where *Re Compton*[78] was applied. Here, trustees were directed under a settlement to apply moneys in providing for the education of children of employees or ex-employees of British American Tobacco or any of its subsidiary or allied companies. The employees numbered over 110,000. The House of Lords held (Lord MacDermott dissenting) that, although the group of persons indicated was numerous, the nexus between them was employment by a particular employer and it therefore followed that the trust did not satisfy the test of public benefit which was required to establish it as charitable. It was argued that the court should take into account the number of employees, but this was rejected by the majority. As Lord Normand said,[79] if there is no public element to be found in the bare nexus of common employment all attempts to build up the public element out of circumstances which had no necessary relation with it but were adventitious, accidental or variable must be unavailing where the settlor has chosen to define the selected class solely by the attribute of common employment. Putting this more generally, an aggregate of individuals ascertained by reference to some personal tie, for example blood or contract, such as the relations of a particular individual, the members of a particular family, the members of a particular association, does not amount to the public or a section thereof for the purpose of the general rule and will not, accordingly, rank as legally charitable.[80]

Lord MacDermott dissented, saying[81] that he saw "much difficulty in dividing the qualities or attributes, which may serve to bind human beings into classes, into two mutually exclusive groups, the one involving individual status and purely personal, the other disregarding such status and quite impersonal. As a task this seems to me no less baffling and elusive than the problem to which it is directed, namely the determination of what is and what is not a section of the public for the purposes of this branch of the law." More recently, in *Dingle v. Turner*[82] Lord Cross was of the same opinion. Moreover, he felt that whether or not the potential beneficiaries of a trust could fairly be said to constitute a section of the public was "a question of degree" and depended on the purpose of the trust. This sort of formulation, however, seems to be no more helpful, perhaps less helpful, in the present state of the law than the old formulation based on the distinction between personal and impersonal relationship.

However, if the trust is construed so as to grant a mere preference to a limited class, such as employees or relations, the trust will succeed as a charity. It succeeded, for example, in *Re Koettgen's Will Trusts*,[83] where a trust was established for the furtherance of the commercial education of British-

---

[77] [1951] A.C. 297, applied in *I.R.C. v. Educational Grants Association* [1967] Ch. 993 (up to 85 per cent of the income of an educational trust was paid to children of employees of Metal Box Ltd; income tax was not recoverable because the income was not applied for charitable purposes only).
[78] [1945] Ch. 123.
[79] *ibid.* at 310–311.
[80] *Re Scarisbrick* [1951] Ch. 622 at 649, *per* Jenkins L.J. See also *Re Compton* [1945] Ch. 123.
[81] [1951] A.C. 297 at 317.
[82] [1972] A.C. 601 at 621.
[83] [1954] Ch. 252.

born persons, with a direction that preference be given to employees of a particular firm. The essential question is whether or not it is a mere expression of preference. If it goes beyond that and amounts to a positive obligation the trust will not be regarded as charitable because the obligation will vitiate the public character of the trust. And it is certainly possible to argue on this basis, as it has been argued,[84] that *Re Koettgen's Will Trusts* was wrongly decided. Its validity was indeed doubted by Lord Radcliffe in *Caffoor v. Commission of Income Tax, Colombo*,[85] where the Privy Council held that the trust in question was a family trust and not of a public character for charitable purposes. The doubts were repeated by Walton J. in *Re Martin*[86] where a trust to establish a home for old people, with a right for either or both of the testator's daughters to reside there, was held not to be charitable. In essence the question will always be reduced to one of construction.[87]

A number of major charities carry on part of their activities in foreign countries, and a question which is still not finally settled is whether or how the requirement of public benefit is satisfied in such a case. The essential question is what is meant by the public or a section thereof. The Charity Commissioners appear to have no doubt that the advancement of religion, the advancement of education and the relief of poverty (the first three heads mentioned in *Pemsel's Case*)[88] are charitable purposes in whatever part of the world they are carried out but, with regard to the fourth head of that classification, for other purposes beneficial to the community, such purposes will only be charitable if of benefit to the community of the United Kingdom.[89] The Commissioners concede that benefit to the United Kingdom, when derived from charities carried out overseas, need not be material or direct; accordingly, charities with general humanitarian objects, such as cancer research, can benefit the community of the United Kingdom even if carried on in foreign countries but where the purposes are for the local provision of public works or development projects such as roads and irrigation, these will only be charitable "if they are a reasonably direct means to the end of relieving poverty in observable cases". Where there is a benefit to the community of the United Kingdom, the court will not ignore the probable results of the trust on the community of the country in question which may well have a wholly distinct history and social structure. One of the reasons why a trust to bring about the abolition of torture and other inhuman punishments was held not to be charitable in *McGovern v. Attorney-General*[90] was that the court could not judge the probable effects on the local community of the necessary legislation.

There is ample authority of long standing that overseas charities falling within the first three heads of Lord Macnaghten's classification will be

---

[84] See, for example, *I.R.C. v. Educational Grants Association* [1967] Ch. 123.
[85] [1961] A.C. 584 at 604. Compare *Re George Drexler Ofrex Foundation Trustees v. I.R.C.* [1966] Ch. 675.
[86] (1977), *The Times* November 16, 1977.
[87] For other aspects of "public benefit", particularly in relation to trusts for the advancement of religion and for other purposes beneficial to the community, see *post*, pp. 404, 405.
[88] [1891] A.C. 531 at 583.
[89] Report of the Charity Commissioners for England and Wales for 1963, p. 24.
[90] [1982] Ch. 321.

charitable[91]; there is little authority, and that conflicting, as to the fourth head. In *Camille and Henry Dreyfus Foundation Inc. v. I.R.C.*,[92] Lord Evershed M.R. expressed the opinion, *obiter*, that there should be a benefit to the United Kingdom, whereas in *Re Jacobs*[93] it was held by Foster J. that a gift for the planting of a grove of trees in Israel was a valid charitable gift.[94] The latter decision is plainly in conflict with the views of the Charity Commissioners but is not necessarily wrong. It is not easy to distinguish the fourth head of charity from the other preceding heads in this context. Why, for example, should a missionary trust be charitable but not a trust for public works which will raise standards of living? It should be added that a case like *Keren Kayemeth Le Jisroel v. I.R.C.*,[95] which might seem to support the Commissioners' opinion,[96] is not directly in point. In this case a company had been formed with the main object of purchasing land in Palestine, Syria and other parts of Turkey in Asia, and the peninsula of Sinai, for the purpose of settling Jews in such lands. The House of Lords held that the company's objects were not charitable within Lord Macnaghten's fourth head. The reasons, however, for so holding was that the court could not identify the community either as the community of all Jews throughout the world or as the community of the Jews in the regions prescribed for the settlement. It was on the ground of lack of "identifiability" and not on grounds of overseas benefit that the case was decided.[97]

The Goodman Committee recommended that no distinction should be drawn between charitable activity by English charities at home or abroad; any object which is charitable at home should also be considered as charitable when carried out abroad.[98]

A separate question concerns the status of foreign charities. These cannot acquire charitable status here, for the simple reason that the law of charity in the foreign country may be different from ours.[99]

---

[91] See, for example, *New v. Bonaker* (1867) L.R. 4 Eq. 655 (education); *Re Norman* [1947] Ch. 349 (religion); *Re Robinson* [1931] Ch. 122 (relief of disabled foreign soldiers; to be equated for this purpose with the relief of poverty); *Re Niyazi's Will Trusts* [1978] 1 W.L.R. 910 (relief of poverty in Cyprus).

[92] [1954] Ch. 672 at 684.

[93] (1970) 114 S.J. 515.

[94] As promoting agriculture; see *I.R.C. v. Yorkshire Agricultural Society* [1928] 1 K.B. 61, applied in *Brisbane City Council v. Att.-Gen. for Queensland* [1979] A.C. 411 (show-ground) and see *Re Hadden* [1932] 1 Ch. 133.

[95] [1932] A.C. 650.

[96] The Commissioners do not, however, cite any authorities for their views.

[97] See also *Williams' Trustees v. I.R.C.* [1947] A.C. 447, which involved an institute for the moral, social and spiritual welfare of Welsh people in London. Lord Simonds held that the difficulty of finding the community of Welsh people was not less than the difficulty of finding the community of Jews in *Keren Kayemeth Le Jisroel v. I.R.C* [1932] A.C. 650.

[98] The Goodman Committee, however, stated that if the overseas activities of the charity are contrary to the public interest of the U.K., there should be a procedure whereby the Foreign Office could make an order requiring the charity to stop that activity (p. 36).

[99] The Goodman Committee recommended (p. 37) that the law governing foreign charities should remain as it is, but consideration should be given to allowing such charities to register in this country if certain conditions (for example satisfying the Charity Commissioners that the objects are charitable in English law and filing accounts here) are satisfied and mutual arrangements can be made by international convention. See also the works cited *ante*, p. 387 n.62.

2. *The Poverty Exception*

The principle that a trust should have a public element is not of absolutely universal application. There is, as indicated above, one important exception to it. This is that trusts for the relief of poverty have been held to be charitable even though they are not for the benefit of the public or a section of it. The exception may arise where the personal tie is one of blood or contract. In the case of blood, there are the so-called "poor relations" cases. The case of contract may be exemplified by a trust for the relief of poverty amongst employees of a particular firm or company.

This particular exception cannot be accounted for by reference to any principle,[1] but it was established by authorities of long standing which were binding on the Court of Appeal, and were reaffirmed by the House of Lords in *Dingle v. Turner.*[2] In that case there was a trust to apply income in paying pensions to poor employees of a company. It was held that the trust was charitable.

The class of persons within the expression "poor relations" is self-evident; however, while the older cases of this type[3] seem to have been approved more or less as a matter of course, some consideration has been given in the more recent cases as to the nature of the relief granted and the size of the class in question. Trusts for such of the testator's relatives as shall be "in needy circumstances" and "in special need" were upheld in, respectively, *Re Scarisbrick*[4] and *Re Cohen,*[5] while in *Re Segelman*[6] a gift to "poor and needy" members of a class of six named relatives and their issue, totalling 26 persons at the date of the testator's death and likely to increase substantially in the future, was also upheld.

Cases such as *Dingle v. Turner* and *Gibson v. South American Stores (Gath & Chaves)*[7] where a gift to employees of a particular company to whom a poverty qualification was attached was upheld as a valid charitable gift illustrate the contractual tie. And the principle was applied in *Re Young*[8] to members of a club and in *Spiller v. Maude*[9] to members of a society.

It was argued in *Dingle v. Turner* that the tests postulated in *Re Compton*[10] and *Oppenheim v. Tobacco Securities Trust*[11] ought, in principle, to apply to all charitable trusts and that the "poor relations" cases, the "poor members" cases and the "poor employees" cases were all anomalous and should be

---

[1] It has been tentatively suggested that "the relief of poverty is of so altruistic a character that the public benefit may necessarily be inferred"; see *Re Scarisbrick* [1951] Ch. 622 at 639, *per* Evershed M.R. But this is not the basis of the case law and in any event seems highly debatable. In *Dingle v. Turner* [1972] A.C. 601 it was assumed that the law was anomalous.

[2] [1972] A.C. 601.

[3] See, for example, *Isaac v. Defriez* (1754) Amb. 595; *White v. White* (1802) 7 Ves. 423; *Att.-Gen. v. Price* (1810) 17 Ves. 371.

[4] [1951] Ch. 622. It was also held in this case that it does not matter that the trust fund can be distributed to the "poor relations" in such a way as to exhaust the capital.

[5] [1973] 1 W.L.R. 415

[6] [1996] Ch. 171.

[7] [1950] Ch. 177. See also *Re Coulthurst* [1951] Ch. 661 (officers and ex-officers of bank).

[8] [1955] 1 W.L.R. 1269.

[9] (1881) 32 Ch.D. 158N.

[10] [1945] Ch. 123.

[11] [1951] A.C. 297.

overruled; alternatively, that if it was not practicable to overrule the "poor relations" cases because of their antiquity, the same could not be said of the "poor employees" cases which dated only from 1900.[12] However, it was held that the "poor members" and "poor employees" decisions were a natural development of the "poor relations" cases and to draw a distinction between them would be quite illogical; moreover, although not as old as "poor relations" trusts, "poor employees" trusts had been recognised for many years and there would be a large number of such trusts in operation today.[13] The exception will not, however, be extended to other classes of trusts.[14]

It was also decided by the Court of Appeal in *Re Scarisbrick*[15]—and this did not appear to have been expressly decided before—that the exception was not restricted to perpetual or continuing trusts (to which it will normally apply) but even covered a trust for immediate distribution. Here a gift for poor members of the class of relations of three children of the testatrix was upheld as a valid charitable trust, although the distribution of the property had to be made within the perpetuity period.

3. *Limits of Public Benefit*

It is important to notice that, although the general rule is (subject to trusts for the relief of poverty) that every charitable trust should have a public element, it is not essential that everybody should be able to avail himself of its benefits. As Viscount Simonds said in *I.R.C. v. Baddeley*,[16] there is a distinction "between a form of relief extended to the whole community, yet by its very nature advantageous only to the few and a form of relief accorded to a selected few out of a larger number equally willing and able to take advantage of it". Thus, to illustrate the first class cited by Viscount Simonds—which will create a valid charitable trust—a gift for the benefit of New South Wales soldiers returning after the 1914–18 war was held by the Privy Council in *Verge v. Somerville*[17] to be valid; so also will a trust for the erection of a sea wall even though this is perhaps of benefit primarily to persons whose houses front the sea.

In illustration of Viscount Simonds' second class—which will fail as a charity—a gift to Presbyterians who could claim a particular descent was held by the Privy Council to fail for this reason in *Davies v. Perpetual Trustee Co.*[18] A trust in favour of the Methodists in West Ham and Leyton was also held to fail in *I.R.C. v. Baddeley*.[19]

---

[12] *Re Gosling* [1900] 2 W.R. 300.
[13] The Goodman Committee considered that "poor relations" and "poor employees" trusts are not justifiable and should no longer qualify as charitable (p. 17).
[14] *Re Compton* [1945] Ch. 123 (education); *Oppenheim v. Tobacco Securities Trust* [1951] A.C. 297, *supra* (education); *Davies v. Perpetual Trustee Co.* [1959] A.C. 439 (religion).
[15] [1951] Ch. 622.
[16] [1955] A.C. 572 at 592. The case is considered *post*, p. 406.
[17] [1924] A.C. 496.
[18] [1959] A.C. 439.
[19] [1955] A.C. 572.

4. *Lord Macnaghten's Classification*

(A) Trusts for the Relief of Poverty
The Act of 1601 included among its objects the relief of "the aged, impotent
and poor". But although the word "and" was used it became well-settled
that the expression should be read disjunctively.[20] This rule was confirmed
in *Re Robinson*,[21] where there was a gift to the old over 65 years of a certain
district, and in *Re Lewis*,[22] where there was a gift for 20 blind children of
another district. Both gifts were upheld. The question was most recently
considered in *Joseph Rowntree Memorial Trust Housing Association v. Attorney-
General*[23] where Peter Gibson J., although confirming the disjunctive reading, added a significant rider, which did not appear from the cases
previously cited, namely, that in order to be charitable, the gift to the
beneficiaries (the aged or the impotent) had to have as its purpose the relief
of a need attributable to their condition. (It is hoped that this approach will
finally scotch the theory that a trust for the relief of "aged peers" or
"impotent millionaires" will be charitable[24]; a gift of money to such persons
would not relieve a need of theirs as aged or impotent persons.) In the case
itself, a charitable housing association wished to build small self-contained
dwellings for sale to elderly people on long leases in consideration of a
capital payment. It was held that since the provision of special accommodation relieved a particular need of the elderly, whether poor or not, attributable to their aged condition, the proposed housing schemes were charitable.
Peter Gibson J., in reaching this conclusion, applied the reasoning of Lord
Wilberforce in *Re Resch's Will Trusts*,[25] which concerned a private hospital
which charged substantial fees but was not run for the profit of individuals.
A gift to the hospital was held to be charitable.

The next question is, what is meant by the words "aged", "impotent" and
"poor" in this context? First, what is meant by "poverty"? It is clear that the
degree of poverty need not be acute. It is unnecessary to show destitution.
Accordingly gifts for such objects as "ladies of limited means"[26] or "decayed
actors"[27] and similar purposes are well recognised as being charitable. All
that seems to be required is that the individuals in question be in straitened
circumstances and unable to maintain a modest standard of living.[28] But it
is essential that all the objects fall within the designation "poor" if a trust for
the relief of poverty is to be upheld. If someone who is not poor is able to
benefit, the gift will fail as a gift for the relief of poverty. Thus, in *Re Gwyon*[29]
a fund was directed to be set aside to provide "knickers" (by which was

---

[20] *Re Fraser* (1883) 22 Ch.D. 827; *Re Elliott* (1910) 102 LT. 528; *Re Glyn* (1950) 66 T.L.R. (Pt. 2) 510; *Re Cottam* [1955] 1 W.L.R. 1299 and the cases cited in the text.
[21] [1951] Ch. 198.
[22] [1955] Ch. 104.
[23] [1983] Ch. 159.
[24] (1955) 71 L.Q.R. 16 (R.E.M.).
[25] [1969] 1 A.C. 514 and see *Re Neal* (1966) 110 Sol. Jo. 549.
[26] *Re Gardom* [1914] 1 Ch. 662.
[27] *Spiller v. Maude* (1881) 32 Ch.D. 158N.
[28] See *Re Mary Clark Homes* [1904] 2 K.B. 645; *Re Gardom* [1914] 1 Ch. 662; *Shaw v. Halifax Corporation* [1915] 2 K.B. 170; *Re Clarke* [1923] 2 Ch. 407; *Re De Carteret* [1933] Ch. 103. See also Cross (1956) 72 L.Q.R. 182 at 206.
[29] [1930] 1 Ch. 225.

meant a type of short trouser) for the boys of Farnham. The garments were unusual not only in their name but also because there were to be embroidered on the waistband the words "Gwyon's Present". Successful applicants were to be entitled to a new pair of knickers each year provided that on the subsequent application the legend "Gwyon's Present" was still decipherable on the old ones. Whatever may have been the testator's intention, none of these conditions necessarily imported poverty and the trust failed as a charity. Moreover it was held in *Re Sanders' Will Trusts*[30] that a gift for the "working classes" was not a gift for the relief of poverty because this expression did not necessarily indicate poor persons. It is possible, as Harman J. said—and indeed it has been so held[31]—that if the gift had been made to members of the "working classes" who were aged or widows, then the object of relieving poverty might be implied. But in *Re Sanders*, as Harman J. made plain, there was nothing of this kind. The members of the working class were not old persons, they were not widows, they were simply men working in the docks and their families. It was, therefore, impossible to infer any element of poverty. This case was, however, distinguished in *Re Niyazi's Will Trusts*[32] where a trust for a working men's hostel in Famagusta, Cyprus, providing modest accommodation for persons of the lower income group, was upheld as charitable, although, in the words of Megarry V.-C., the case was "desperately near the border-line".[33]

There is also no decisive definition of the terms "aged" or "impotent". It has been held that people who are not under the age of 50 are aged.[34] But in view of the advance in medical science this now seems very doubtful. If the settlor wishes to specify an age he may be taking a risk today if the age is lower than 60. The word "impotent" has been generously construed, although never precisely defined. It includes permanent disability,[35] the seriously ill or wounded,[36] and also covers the prevention of cruelty to children.[37]

It is, of course, essential to establish that in the case of relief of poverty there is a trust for the relief of poverty in the proper sense of that expression. The point is that a trust for poor persons may take effect as a private rather than a charitable trust. The distinction is—and this is a matter of construction—whether the gift is for the relief of poverty amongst a particular description of poor people or is merely a gift to particular poor persons, the relief of poverty among them being the motive of the gift. In the former case the trust is charitable, in the latter it is private.[38]

---

[30] [1954] Ch. 265 (appeal settled, *The Times* July 22, 1954).
[31] *Re Glyn* (1950) 66 T.L.R. (Pt. 2) 510; see also *Re Cottam* [1955] 1 W.L.R. 1299 (provision of flats for aged).
[32] [1978] 1 W.L.R. 910.
[33] *ibid.* at 915.
[34] *Re Wall* (1889) 42 Ch.D. 510. See also *Re Payling's Will Trusts* [1969] 1 W.L.R. 1595; *Re Armitage* [1972] Ch. 438.
[35] *Re Fraser* (1883) 22 Ch.D. 827; *Re Lewis* [1955] Ch. 104.
[36] *Re Hillier* [1944] 1 All E.R. 486.
[37] *C.I.R. v. Pemsel* [1891] A.C. 531 at 572; compare *Re Cole* [1958] Ch. 477; *Re Sahal's Will Trusts* [1958] 1 W.L.R. 1243.
[38] *Re Scarisbrick* [1951] Ch. 622 at 650, 651, *per* Jenkins L.J.; *Dingle v. Turner* [1972] A.C. 601 at 617, *per* Lord Cross; *Re Cohen* [1973] 1 W.L.R. 415 at 423, *per* Templeman J.

A related question involves housing associations, which provide housing for the "aged, impotent and poor" and which enjoy charitable status because they are within the preamble to the Act of 1601. But it is common to find associations feeling the need to adopt a particular policy of tenant selection, for example, selecting tenants who earn less than the average wage, so as to preserve charitable status. Such a policy may be inconvenient and indeed fail if one or more of the residents are not in fact poor.[39] The Goodman Committee recommended[40] that housing trusts should be charitable even though the trustees take account of the housing need, not merely of the income of the tenant, provided that, to avoid abuse, the association is registered with the Housing Corporation under the Housing Acts and registered with the Charity Commission. Such difficulties now appear to have been alleviated in some degree by the decision in *Joseph Rowntree Memorial Trust Housing Association v. Attorney-General.*[41] It was held that it was not essential that a charitable gift be made solely by way of bounty and, accordingly, the beneficiaries could be required to contribute to its cost. The fact that the housing schemes concerned made provision for special housing for the elderly on a contractual basis did not therefore prevent the schemes from being charitable. It was also held that the possibility that a beneficiary might profit by an increase in value of the property on a subsequent sale by him did not alter the fact that the trusts were charitable.

(B) Trusts for the Advancement of Education

The general rule is conventionally stated to be that there must be an intention that learning should be imparted, not simply that it should be accumulated. This may now be a somewhat misleading yardstick, because the tendency in many of the cases is to widen the field of "education" in this context. But the conventional meaning appears to have been adopted by Harman J. in *Re Shaw.*[42] Here George Bernard Shaw by his will directed his trustees to use his residuary estate for a number of designated purposes. These included, first, inquiries into how much time per individual scribe would be saved by substituting for the established English alphabet one containing at least 40 letters; secondly, to inquire how many persons were speaking and writing English in the usual form at any moment in the world; thirdly, to ascertain the time and labour wasted by the lack of at least 14 unequivocal syllables and estimate the loss of income in British and American currency; and, fourthly, to employ a phonetic expert to transliterate the testator's play Androcles and the Lion into the proposed English alphabet. It was held that the trusts were not charitable for they merely tended to an increase of public knowledge in the advantages of the proposed alternative alphabet; the research and propaganda enjoined by the testator merely tended to the increase of public knowledge in a particular respect, namely, the saving of time and money by the use of the proposed alphabet. There

---

[39] *Over-Seventies Housing Association v. Westminster L.B.C.* (1974) 230 E.G. 1593.
[40] At p. 32.
[41] [1983] Ch. 159. The facts are stated *ante*, p. 394.
[42] [1957] 1 W.L.R. 729 (appeal dismissed by consent on terms that a sum of money should be devoted to these inquiries; [1958] 1 All E.R. 245N).

was "no element of teaching or education" combined with this. It was also argued that the trusts were charitable as being in some way beneficial to the community (within the fourth head of Lord Macnaghten's classification). This argument was also rejected because it was highly controversial whether the proposals were in fact beneficial.

The question of the ambit of "education" was given fresh consideration by Wilberforce J. in *Re Hopkins' Will Trusts*.[43] The testatrix had given part of her residuary estate to the "Francis Bacon Society" to be applied towards finding the "Bacon-Shakespeare" manuscripts. One of the main objects of the society was "to encourage the general study of the evidence of Francis Bacon's authorship of plays commonly ascribed to Shakespeare". The terms of the will were, therefore, held to mean that the money was to be used to search for manuscripts of plays commonly ascribed to Shakespeare but believed by the testatrix and the society to have been written by Bacon. The judge held that the purposes of search or research for original manuscripts of England's greatest dramatist were within the law's conception of a charitable purpose on two grounds; first, as being for education and, secondly, as being for other purposes beneficial to the community within the fourth head of Lord Macnaghten's classification, because it was a gift for the improvement of this country's literary heritage. He had something to say about the dictum of Harman J. in *Re Shaw* that if the object was merely the increase of knowledge that in itself was not a charitable object unless combined with teaching or education. Wilberforce J. was unwilling to treat these words as meaning that the promotion of academic research was not a charitable purpose unless the researchers were engaged in teaching or education in the conventional sense. Many people would agree with the judge's conclusion that the term "education" should be used in a wide sense, certainly as extending beyond teaching.[44] Wilberforce J. also performed the valuable service of spelling out the requirements that must be satisfied by "research" in order to be charitable, though even this formulation was not expressed to be exhaustive: first, it must be of educational value to the researcher; or, secondly, it must be so directed so as to lead to something which will pass into the store of educational material; or, thirdly, so as to improve the sum of communicable knowledge in an area which education may cover, education in this last context extending to the formation of literary taste and appreciation.[45]

This decision might be said to be part of a trend which has broadened the field of "education", from which *Re Shaw* is arguably an aberration. Among many cases which demonstrate how widely the idea of education has

---

[43] [1965] Ch. 669. See also *Re Shakespeare Memorial Trust* [1923] 2 Ch. 398 (erection and endowment of a Shakespeare Memorial National Theatre with the object of performing Shakespeare's plays, reviving English classical drama and stimulating the art of acting; held to be a good charitable trust).

[44] *ibid* at 680.

[45] At p. 680. The Goodman Committee recommended that "research" should be a charitable object in its own right.

been considered,[46] *Re Dupree's Deed Trusts*[47] where a trust for the encouragement of chess playing among the boys and youths of Portsmouth was upheld as charitable might be instanced. Again, in *Re Delius*[48] the wife of the composer Delius gave her residuary estate for the advancement of her late husband's musical work by means of gramophone recordings, publication of his works and financing of public performances of his work. It was held that the purpose of the trust was to spread the knowledge and appreciation of Delius' work throughout the world and constituted an effective educational charity. It seems rather curious that it was found necessary to point out that the fact that pleasure was an incident of that appreciation or that the effect of the trust was to enhance the reputation of Delius did not prevent this result. More conventionally, the promotion of "art" has also been held to be charitable.[49] But perhaps one of the most striking, if not startling, cases in which education was given an extremely and perhaps unjustifiably wide connotation was *Re Shaw's Will Trusts*[50] where the testatrix, who was the wife of George Bernard Shaw and (it is necessary to add) herself of Irish origin bequeathed the residue of her estate upon trusts for, among other things, the teaching, promotion and encouragement in Ireland of self-control, elocution, oratory, deportment, the arts of personal contact, of social intercourse and the other arts of public and private life. It was held that these somewhat eccentric trusts were wholly educational in character and constituted valid charitable trusts. Much less controversial was *Re South Place Ethical Society*[51] where it was held that the cultivation of a rational religious sentiment was for the advancement of education because a rational sentiment could only be cultivated by educational methods.

As might be expected, trusts for the establishment and support of professorships and lectureships are educational in character[52] but it should also be noticed that satellite purposes such as increasing the stipends of university teachers and fellows of colleges will also be upheld.[53] The same

---

[46] See also *Re Mellody* [1918] 1 Ch. 228 (annual school treat); *Re Cranstoun* [1932] 1 Ch. 537 (preservation of ancient buildings); *Re Spence* [1938] Ch. 96 (collection of arms and antiques); *Re Webber* [1954] 1 W.L.R. 1500 (Boy Scouts); *Re Levien* [1955] 1 W.L.R. 964 (raising musical standards); *Re Koettgen's Will Trusts* [1954] Ch. 252 (commercial education); *Royal Choral Society v. I.R.C.* (1943) 112 L.J.K.B. 648 (choral society); *Re Royce* [1940] Ch. 514 (church choir).

[47] [1945] Ch. 16.

[48] [1957] Ch. 299.

[49] *Re The Town and Country Planning Act 1947* [1951] Ch. 132. But "artistic" is too vague to be charitable; see *Associated Artists v. I.R.C.* [1956] 1 W.L.R. 752. With regard to "the arts" the Goodman Committee recommended that their promotion should be a proper charitable object in its own right, not merely as a sub-branch of education.

[50] [1952] Ch. 163.

[51] [1980] 1 W.L.R. 1565. For other aspects of the case see *post*, pp. 402, 419.

[52] *Attorney-General v. Margaret and Regius Professors at Cambridge* (1682) 1 Vern. 55.

[53] *Case of Christ's College, Cambridge* (1751) 1 W.B.I. 90.

principles apply to schools,[54] colleges and universities,[55] and learned societies and institutions.[56]

It was also held in *Incorporated Council of Law Reporting for England and Wales v. Attorney-General*[57] that the Council was an educational charity[58]; the preparation of law reports was for the advancement of education because their purpose was to record accurately the development and application of judge-made law and thereby disseminate knowledge of that law. The law, it was held by the Court of Appeal, was properly to be regarded as a science and therefore books which were produced for the purpose of enabling it to be studied were published for the advancement of education. It was also held that the fact that the reports were used by the legal profession for the purpose of earning fees did not make the purposes non-charitable. It may be observed that, despite the fact that the Council was carrying on a business, its profits could only be applied in the pursuit of the Council's objects. If the profits could have enured for the benefit of its individual members, it would not have achieved charitable status.[59]

Another case, which may be thought to have given an equally robust interpretation to educational charity, is *London Hospital Medical College v. I.R.C.*,[60] which involved the students' union of the London Hospital. The union was under the control of the medical college, an educational charity, and its objects were to "promote social, cultural and athletic activities amongst the members and to add to the comfort and enjoyment of the students". The question was whether the predominant object of the union was the furtherance of the purposes of the medical college as a school of learning (in which case it was charitable) or whether its objects were the private and personal benefit of those students who were members of the union (in which case it would not be).[61] Brightman J. held that it had no *raison d'être* except to further the educational purposes of the medical college and it was accordingly charitable. He said that what it did and was intended to do was to assist the teaching of medicine by providing those physical,

---

[54] See *The Abbey Malvern Wells v. Ministry of Local Government and Planning* [1951] Ch. 728, where a girls' school was carried on by a private company but under a trust deed all dividends were applied for school purposes. The school was held charitable. Danckwerts J. said (at 737) that all schools of learning are treated as charitable unless they exist purely as profit-making ventures. Compare *Re Girls Public Day School Trust* [1951] Ch. 400 where the school in question was not charitable because shareholders were beneficially interested. See also *post*, p. 406.

[55] *Case of Christ's College, Cambridge* (1751) 1 W.B.I. 90.

[56] For example, the Royal College of Surgeons: see *Royal College of Surgeons v. National Provincial Bank* [1952] A.C. 631.

[57] [1972] Ch. 73.

[58] Russell L.J. dissented, so far as the educational aspect was concerned, but all the members of the Court of Appeal agreed that it was also charitable as being for the benefit of the community within the fourth head of Lord Macnaghten's classification: see *post*, p. 405.

[59] Compare the cases cited *ante*, n. 54.

[60] [1976] 1 W.L.R. 613; compare *Re Bushnell* [1975] 1 W.L.R. 1596 in which a trust for the advancement of "socialised medicine" was held not to be educational; see *post*, p. 413. In certain cases trusts for sport may be upheld as educational trusts; see *post*, p. 409.

[61] This was the result in *I.R.C. v. City of Glasgow Police Athletic Association* [1953] A.C. 380, discussed *post*, p. 410.

cultural and social outlets which were needed, or at any rate highly desirable, if the art of teaching was to be efficiently performed at the College.[62]

But although, generally speaking, education has been regarded as a conception of some width for the purposes of charity, there are limits beyond which the courts will not go. There is, in the end, a question of degree to be determined, and it might be argued that the alphabet trust in *Re Shaw* fell on the wrong side of the line. But a case where the trusts were clearly out of order was *Re Pinion*.[63] A testator gave his studio and pictures, one of which he attributed to Lely and some of which were painted by himself, his antique furniture, silver, china and other things to be offered to the National Trust to be kept intact in the studio and maintained as a collection. If the National Trust declined the trust, as in fact it did, he authorised the appointment of trustees to carry out the trust. It was acknowledged that a gift to found a public museum may be assumed to be charitable if no one questions it. But if the utility of the gift was brought in question, as it was here, it was essential to know something of the quality of the exhibits and for this purpose expert evidence was admissible to assist the court in judging the educational value of the gift.[64] The evidence was to the effect that the collection was of low quality—the Lely was bogus and the testator's own paintings were bad. Among the furniture there were some genuine English and Continental pieces of the seventeenth and eighteenth centuries which might be acceptable as a gift to a minor provincial museum. But, according to the terms of the will, everything had to be exhibited together, and the good things would be stifled by the large number of absolutely valueless pictures and objects. Harman L.J. could conceive of no useful purpose in "foisting on the public this mass of junk".[65] The Court of Appeal, reversing Wilberforce J., held that the trust had neither public utility nor educational value and therefore failed as a charity.

It is, it might be thought, an elementary proposition that if an institution is devoted to educational purposes (or indeed any other specific charitable purposes) its funds can only be applied to those purposes. Nevertheless the question arose for decision in *Baldry v. Feintuck*.[66] In this case the University of Sussex Students Union, which was conceded in argument[67] to be an educational charity, voted to authorise payments to "War on Want", a charitable (but non-educational) organisation and to a campaign of protest against the Government's policy of ending the supply of free milk to schoolchildren, this being political and therefore non-charitable.[68] Brightman J. held that the moneys could not be applied for such purposes. A similar

---

[62] *London Hospital Medical College v. I.R.C.* [1976] 1 W.L.R. 613 at 623, 624. It was apparently thought relevant that the London Hospital is on a site adjoining the Whitechapel and Commercial Roads in the East End of London; this was described as a "somewhat remote part of London"; *ibid.* at 621.

[63] [1965] Ch. 85.

[64] For another example of expert evidence being admitted, see *Gilmour v. Coats* [1949] A.C. 426 and see *post*, p. 404.

[65] [1965] Ch. 85 at 107.

[66] [1972] 1 W.L.R. 552.

[67] See, *per* Brightman J. in *London Hospital Medical College v. I.R.C.* [1976] 1 W.L.R. 613 at 624.

[68] See *post*, p. 412.

decision was reached in *Webb v. O'Doherty*,[69] where expenditure of student union funds on a campaign to end the Gulf War was restrained.

One of the current controversial questions in the field of education concerns the charitable status of independent schools[70]; there is no doubt whatever that many of them are registered charities. The Expenditure Committee recommended that in order to be charitable, schools should "manifestly devote the education they provide towards meeting a range of clear educational needs throughout the whole community",[71] thereby indicating that many independent schools should lose their charitable status. The Goodman Committee considered, however, that any decision to curtail independent education would be a political one; that any such policy should be implemented by political decision; and that, while independent education continues to exist, it should, as a general proposition, remain within the ambit of charity.[72]

(C) Trusts for the Advancement of Religion

As in the criminal law, so in equity there is a large measure of tolerance. Indeed a high degree of tolerance was recognised over a hundred years ago in *Thornton v. Howe*,[73] where Romilly M.R. recognised as charitable a trust for the publication of the work of Joanna Southcott even though he evidently thought her doctrines to be ridiculous. It would also appear from this case that the advancement of all religions which are "not subversive of all morality"[74] will be held to be charitable. As it happens, there is not a great deal of authority on non-Christian religions,[75] but there seems no reason why all of them should not be recognised. Yet there may be limits to the court's liberality, for the court appears in this context to have taken account only of monotheistic religion. Thus in *Yeap Cheah Neo v. Ong Cheng Neo*[76] the Privy Council held that a trust requiring ancestor worship was not charitable. This case is not, however, decisive and it could be distinguished on the ground that the religious observances enjoined were not for the public

---

[69] (1991), *The Times*, February 11, 1991.

[70] See *ante*, p. 399.

[71] *op. cit.* at p. xvi.

[72] Making the point that the present system makes a very considerable contribution to the field of education, p. 25.

[73] (1862) 31 Beav. 14.

[74] *ibid.* at 20. This principle was applied by Plowman J. in *Re Watson* [1973] 1 W.L.R. 1472 in upholding a trust for the publication and distribution of religious writings of no intrinsic merit but which displayed a religious tendency, and by Walton J. in *Holmes v.Att.-Gen.* [1981] Ch. Com. Rep. 10 in upholding a trust for the Exclusive Brethren. The correctness of Romilly M.R.'s statement of principle in *Thornton v. Howe* however still remains open to review by the court. See also *Bowman v. Secular Society Ltd* [1917] A.C. 406.

[75] But see *Straus v. Goldsmid* (1837) 8 Sim. 614 (trust for practice of Jewish religion valid); *Neville Estates v. Madden* [1962] Ch. 832 (trust for Catford synagogue valid); *Dawkins v. Gown Suppliers (PSA)* (1993), *The Times*, February 4, 1993 (Rastafarians).

[76] (1875) L.R. 381. See also *Re Hummeltenberg* [1923] 1 Ch. 237 (gift to college for training spiritualistic mediums); *Re Price* [1943] Ch. 422 (gift to the "Anthroposophical Society"). Neither of the cases fell within trusts for the advancement of religion and could only be considered under the fourth head of Lord Macnaghten's classification. The former was held invalid; the latter valid. On the other hand, in *Funnell v. Stewart* [1996] 1 W.L.R. 288, a gift to a group which engaged in faith healing but also held religious services some of which were open to the public was held to be charitable on the basis that the religious element contained sufficient public benefit.

benefit, merely for the alleged advantage of the deceased and his family. It would appear that the time has come to recognise formally the major religions of the world, whatever their forms, although in certain cases a line has to be drawn. Increasingly today "fringe" religious organisations have come into being.[77] Some are so fanciful or freakish that public benefit can justly be said to be lacking and charitable status should not be accorded to them.[78]

Clearly, however, a gift for rationalist purposes—designed to demonstrate that religious belief is erroneous—would not fall within the ambit of a trust for the advancement of religion.[79] Likewise, gifts for ethical or moral societies not founded on belief in a deity are not for the advancement of religion. Nevertheless, they may be held to be charitable on other grounds. The question arose in *Re South Place Ethical Society*[80] which was established for the study and dissemination of "ethical principles" and the cultivation of a rational religious sentiment eschewing all supernatural belief. "Ethical principles" were described by Dillon J. as belief in the excellence of truth, love and beauty, but not belief in anything supernatural. It was held that the Society was not founded for the advancement of religion because, in the words of the judge, "religion is concerned with man's relations with God, and ethics are concerned with man's relations with man."[81] The objects of the Society were, however, upheld as charitable on other grounds; first, they were for the mental and moral improvement of man and were, therefore, beneficial to the community within the fourth head of Lord Macnaghten's classification[82] and, secondly, they were for the advancement of education.[83]

Quite apart from gifts for the advancement of a religion or a religious sect as such, a number of satellite purposes have been recognised as charitable under this head, notably gifts for mission work. Thus in *Re Moon's Will Trusts*[84] a bequest for "mission work" was made. The expression was held on the evidence to connote "Christian mission work" and that was held to be charitable. Similarly, trusts for the maintenance and repair of a church, a stained glass window,[85] or a vault[86] within a church have been held to be charitable; this will also apply to the churchyard and burial ground even if restricted to a particular religious sect[87] and also to the graves in it, provided

---

[77] The Unification Church (The "Moonies") has been registered as a Charity (Annual Report 1982, paras 36–38).
[78] The Goodman Committee considered that religious organisations detrimental to the moral welfare of the community should be excluded (p. 23).
[79] *Bowman v. Secular Society Ltd* [1917] A.C. 406.
[80] [1981] 1 W.L.R. 1565.
[81] *ibid.* at 571. It was noted (at 573) that Buddhism was accepted as a religion although there was no belief in a god, but that question was not explored further.
[82] See *post*, p. 419.
[83] See *ante*, p. 402. The Goodman Committee recommended that ethical and moral societies not founded on belief in a deity should be recognised as charitable on the basis that they promote the moral improvement of the community.
[84] [1948] 1 All E.R. 300.
[85] *Re King* [1923] 1 Ch. 243. See also *Re Royce* [1940] Ch. 514.
[86] *Hoare v. Osborne* (1886) L.R. 1 Eq. 585.
[87] *Re Manser* [1905] 1 Ch. 68 (Society of Friends).

that the object of the gift is the maintenance of all the graves.[88] Indeed, even cremation has also been held to be a charitable purpose.[89]

It is essential that the purpose of a trust should be exclusively charitable, a rule of general application subject to the Charitable Trusts (Validation) Act 1954.[90] In this context, therefore, the purpose of the trust should be exclusively religious. A draftsman may easily quite unwittingly say far too much—even by only a word or two—in the trust instrument. The cases on the question of whether a trust is exclusively religious are difficult and present several fine distinctions. Normally, a gift will be made to a person holding a religious office, such as a bishop, and the additional words that may permissibly be used to create a valid charitable trust appear to fall into two groups.

First, they may give an absolute discretion to the donee. In *Re Garrard*,[91] a gift was made "to the vicar and churchwardens of Kingston to be applied by them in such manner as they shall in their sole discretion think fit". Similarly, in *Re Rumball*[92] a gift was made "to the bishop for the time being of the Windward Islands to be applied by him as he thinks fit in his diocese". In both cases, as in several others,[93] where an absolute discretion was conferred, the gift was upheld as charitable. The reason was that the gift was made to a person by his official name whose official status required charitable duties to be performed. Accordingly, the gift was assumed to be made for the charitable purposes inherent in that official status. This principle which arises *virtute officii* applies not merely to religious persons but to the holders of other offices.

Secondly, the words used may confine the object of the gift within the ambit of the donee's religious function. For example, in *Re Eastes*[94] there was a gift "to the vicar and churchwardens, to be used by them for *any purpose in connection with the Church*[95] which they shall select". This gift was upheld. But if the testator goes on to invite the donee to take into account the social as well as the religious functions of his office, the gift will fail. Here the settlor may unconsciously say too much. This principle—though it may be no more than apparent—is illustrated by the leading case of *Dunne v. Byrne*[96] where a gift was made to the Roman Catholic Archbishop of Brisbane and

---

[88] *Re Pardoe* [1906] 2 Ch. 184; in this case a gift for a peal of bells on the anniversary of the restoration of the monarchy also held to be charitable but this is questionable. Compare Brunyate (1946) 61 L.Q.R. 268, 274; *Re Eighmie* [1935] Ch. 524 (keeping in repair burial ground and monument to testator's late husband) and see *ante*, p. 115.

[89] *Scottish Burial Reform and Cremation Society v. Glasgow Corporation* [1968] A.C. 138.

[90] See *post*, p. 417.

[91] [1907] 1 Ch. 382.

[92] [1956] Ch. 105. The judgment of Jenkins L.J. is a notable exposition of the law.

[93] See *Re Simson* [1946] Ch. 299 ("to the Vicar of St. Luke's Ramsgate, to be used for work in the parish"; valid). Compare *Farley v. Westminster Bank* [1939] A.C. 430, ("for parish work"; bad); *Re Flinn* [1948] Ch. 241 (to the Archbishop of Westminster Cathedral to be used by him "for such purposes as he shall in his absolute discretion think fit"; valid). See also *Re Norman* [1947] Ch. 349 (to the editors of a missionary periodical who were also trustees of a missionary church, to be applied "for such objects as they may think fit"; valid).

[94] [1948] Ch. 257. See also *Re Bain* [1930] 1 Ch. 224 (to a vicar "for such objects connected with the church as he shall think fit"); *Re Norton's Will Trusts* [1948] 2 All E.R. 842 ("for the benefit of the parish"). Compare *Farley v. Westminster Bank* [1939] A.C. 430.

[95] Emphasis added.

[96] [1912] A.C. 407.

his successors to be used as they "may judge most conducive to the good of religion in the diocese". The words in inverted commas were held by the Privy Council to be too wide and the gift failed. Perhaps the most notorious words to induce fatality are "parish work"; a gift failed for this reason in the well known decision of the House of Lords in *Farley v. Westminster Bank*.[97]

What has been said so far represents an attempt to rationalise some of the case law. But it should be noted that these cases are not easy to reconcile and depend on an extremely close reading of the gift or trust. And at times recognising the distinction between any two cases decided differently requires hair-splitting to an extent which seems excessive.[98]

Like other charitable trusts—with the exception of trusts for the relief of poverty—a religious trust must be for the benefit of the public.[99] Although it can be difficult to assess public benefit in a religious trust, the test nevertheless has to be satisfied. Thus, in the controversial decision in *Gilmour v. Coats*,[1] the trust fund was to be applied for the purposes of a Carmelite convent. The convent comprised an association of strictly cloistered and purely contemplative nuns who did not engage in any activities for the benefit of people outside the convent. The House of Lords held, first, that the benefit of intercessory prayer could not be proved in law and, secondly, that the element of edification was too vague and intangible. It might be thought that far too stringent a test of public benefit was applied in this case.[2] However, whether this is so or not, it is distinguishable from a case like *Neville Estates v. Madden*,[3] which concerned Catford synagogue which was not open to the public as of right; Cross J. nevertheless held that a trust in favour of the synagogue was charitable. The distinction was that the enclosed nuns lived apart from the world, whereas the members of the synagogue lived in the world and a public benefit accrued as a result of their attendance at a place of religious worship.

Rather different considerations have been applied to trusts for masses for the dead.[4] Luxmoore J. in *Re Caus*[5] held that a gift for such purposes was charitable. There was no provision in the testator's will that the masses

---

[97] [1939] A.C. 430. The words "parochial institutions or purposes" were also fatal in *Re Stratton* [1931] 1 Ch. 197.

[98] See cases cited *ante*, nn. 93, 94.

[99] See Newark (1946) 62 L.Q.R. 234.

[1] [1949] A.C. 426. Likewise see *Cocks v. Manners* (1871) L.R. 12 Eq. 574 (enclosed Roman Catholic convent); *Hoare v. Hoare* (1886) 56 L.T. 147 (private chapel); *Re Joy* (1889) 60 L.T. 175 (to suppress cruelty to animals by prayer); *Re Warre's Will Trusts* [1953] 1 W.L.R. 725 (retreat house but this case seems to have been wrongly decided; retreatants do mix in the world since they go into retreat only for a few days' contemplation and prayer). Compare *Neville Estates v. Madden* [1962] Ch. 832 discussed in the text and *Re Banfield* [1968] 1 W.L.R. 846, where the gift was to a religious community ("Pilsdon Community House") and was held to be a charitable trust because of its primarily religious character and also because it was for the general public benefit in providing a temporary home of rest for those who needed it.

[2] The Goodman Committee suggested that contemplative communities do not normally have proper charitable objects, but a value judgment has to be made in each case.

[3] [1962] Ch. 832 and see *Holmes v. Att.-Gen.* (1981) Ch. Com. Rep. 10 (Exclusive Brethren).

[4] It is established that a gift for masses is not void as being for superstitious uses; *Bourne v. Keane* [1919] A.C. 815. The question remains however whether it is charitable.

[5] [1934] Ch. 162.

should be said in public and the judge did not distinguish between masses said in public and those said in private; indeed he appeared to indicate that a gift for masses was in all cases charitable. This appeared erroneous in the light of *Gilmour v. Coats* and this was duly confirmed in *Re Hetherington (deceased)*,[6] where a gift of £2,000 to the Roman Catholic Bishop of Westminster for "masses for the repose of the souls of my husband and my parents and my sisters and also myself when I die" was held to be charitable only on the grounds that sufficient public benefit was conferred by the public celebration of a religious rite and that the provision of stipends for the celebrants endowed the priesthood. It does not, however, seem likely that the latter reason would be sufficient to cause a gift for masses to be said in private to be charitable. Such trusts can however take effect as non-charitable purpose trusts.[7]

(D) Trusts for Other Purposes Beneficial to the Community

This is the residuary class in Lord Macnaghten's classification in *Pemsel's Case*. It has been seen that the modern trend appears to be to look to the "equity" or the "mischief" of the preamble to the Statute of Elizabeth I in order to decide whether a given purpose falls within it, rather than rely on the approach based upon analogy.[8] The class certainly presents a most variegated collection of decisions and the following does not profess to be an exhaustive account but merely illustrations of a number of the purposes which have been allowed admission into this class.[9]

(1) Animals

It is clearly established that a trust for the protection of animals generally is a valid charitable trust.[10] This is the case, it has been held, because it benefits humanity by promoting morality and curbing an inborn tendency to cruelty[11]—a somewhat surprising process of reasoning even in an animal-loving country. But, however surprising, it indicates that the reason for the recognition of these trusts is that they promote the moral or spiritual welfare of the community whereas the basis of most of the other examples of Lord Macnaghten's fourth head is "public utility".[12]

---

[6] [1990] Ch. 1.

[7] See *ante*, p. 113.

[8] See, for example, *Scottish Burial Reform and Cremation Society v. Glasgow City Corporation* [1968] A.C. 138; *Incorporated Council of Law Reporting for England and Wales v. Att.-Gen.* [1972] Ch. 73; see *ante*, p. 399.

[9] For a detailed treatment, see Tudor on *Charities* (8th ed.), pp. 88 *et seq.*

[10] *Re Wedgwood* [1915] 1 Ch. 113 (secret trust for protection and benefit of animals).

[11] *Re Wedgwood, ibid.* at 117, per Lord Cozens-Hardy M.R.; *Re Moss* [1949] 1 All E.R. 415 at 497–498, *per* Romer J. (cats and kittens). Compare earlier cases: *London University v. Yarrow* (1857) 1 De G. & J. 72 (animal hospital) and *Re Douglas* (1887) 35 Ch.D. 472 (Home for Lost Dogs), where the court emphasised public utility but this is not the modern trend. See *ante*, p. 113.

[12] For other examples of "moral or spiritual improvement" see *Re Price* [1943] Ch. 422 (gift to the "Anthroposophical Society"); *Re South Place Ethical Society* [1980] 1 W.L.R. 1565 (society for the study and dissemination of "ethical principles" and the cultivation of a rational religious sentiment; see *ante*, p. 402).

A second proposition, which arises from the decision of a particular case, *Re Grove-Grady*,[13] is that if the settlor establishes a trust to provide a sanctuary for all kinds of animals from human molestation with no safeguards against the destruction of the weaker animals by the stronger, the trust is not charitable. As Lord Hanworth M.R. pointed out,[14] the one characteristic of the trust was that the sanctuary was to be free from molestation by man, while all the fauna within it were to be free to molest and harry one another. And such a purpose did not afford any advantage to animals or any protection from cruelty to animals nor did it afford any elevating lesson to mankind.[15]

Thirdly, there is the principle established by the House of Lords in *National Anti-Vivisection Society v. I.R.C.*[16] that a trust to abolish vivisection is not charitable. It was so held in this case for two reasons; first, the advantages accruing from the abolition of vivisection did not equal those derived from its retention; and, secondly, anti-vivisection could not be achieved except by legislation and (so it was said) the law could not stultify itself by holding that it was for the public benefit that the law itself should be changed.[17]

Finally, it should be noticed that, although an animal hospital is *prima facie* charitable,[18] it will not be if it is carried on for private profit as a profession, occupation or trade.[19]

(2) Recreational trusts

The Recreational Charities Act 1958, which came into force on March 3, 1958, regulates recreational trusts. The Act was passed because of the highly inconvenient decision of the House of Lords in *I.R.C. v. Baddeley*[20] which concerned certain trusts "for the promotion of the moral, social and physical well-being of persons resident in West Ham and Leyton who for the time being are members or likely to become members of the Methodist Church by the provision of facilities for moral, social and physical training and recreation". It was decided, by a majority, that the trusts failed because they were expressed in language so vague as to permit the property to be used for purposes which the law did not recognise as charitable and also because they did not satisfy the necessary test of public benefit. This case produced a situation where legislation of some kind was essential because, as a result

---

[13] [1929] 1 Ch. 557, compromised on appeal *sub nom. Att.-Gen. v. Plowden* [1931] W.N. 89.
[14] [1929] 1 Ch. 557 at 573–574.
[15] The main reason for citing this case is to emphasise the importance of careful drafting of the trust instrument so that the "public benefit" requirement is satisfied. There is no doubt that a competently drawn trust for the preservation of wild life, taking due account of public benefit, will be charitable.
[16] [1948] A.C. 31, reversing *Re Foveaux* [1895] 2 Ch. 501. See also *Re Jenkins's Will Trusts* [1966] Ch. 249 (gift to the British Union for the Abolition of Vivisection).
[17] Adopting Tyssen on *Charitable Bequests* (1st ed., 1898), p. 176. See also *Bowman v. Secular Society Ltd* [1917] A.C. 406 at 442, *per* Lord Parker (political purposes) and see *post*, p. 412.
[18] *London University v. Yarrow* (1857) 1 De G. & J. 72.
[19] See *Re Satterthwaite's Will Trusts* [1966] 1 W.L.R. 277 at 284, *per* Russell L.J.
[20] [1955] A.C. 572.

of the decision, it appeared that there might be grave doubts as to the charitable status of many organisations and trusts, including women's institutes, boys' clubs, miners' welfare trusts and village halls which had for a very long time been assumed to enjoy charitable status. The Recreational Charities Act 1958 was therefore enacted extremely promptly. It provides that it shall be and shall be deemed always to have been charitable to provide, or assist in providing, facilities for recreation or other leisure-time occupations if the facilities are provided in the interest of social welfare.[21] This is subject to the overriding proviso that the trust will not be charitable unless it is for the public benefit.[22] Furthermore the requirement that facilities must be provided in the interest of social welfare is not satisfied unless, first, it is provided with the object of improving the conditions of life for the persons for whom the facilities are primarily intended,[23] and, secondly, either those persons have need of such facilities by reason of their youth, age, infirmity or disablement, poverty or social and economic circumstances[24] or the facilities are to be available to the members or female members of the public at large.[25]

The composition of this part of the Act seems to be somewhat curious. It will be noted in particular that the two final ingredients are alternative to one another. Accordingly, it appears that a recreational trust in favour of a limited class of the public will be within the Act if the beneficiaries are youthful, aged, infirm, disabled, or their "social and economic circumstances" are such that they have need of the facilities provided. But if the beneficiaries do not fall into these prescribed classes, the facilities must be available to the whole of the public and a trust in favour of a limited class will fail. There may well be a case for confining the objectives of the Act in this way. However, it is a little unfortunate that the position is not formulated with more precision.

The effect of these provisions (in particular the terms "social welfare" and "conditions of life") was considered by the Court of Appeal in *I.R.C. v. McMullen*,[26] which concerned the Football Association Youth Trust. The majority held, among other things, that the recreational facilities provided were primarily intended for pupils in schools and universities but that they were not provided with the object of improving the conditions of life of such pupils; they were instead provided for those of them who were persuaded to, or did, play football or some other game or sport irrespective of their conditions of life. Consequently, the trusts did not fall within the Act. Bridge L.J. dissented on the ground that the provision of recreational facilities for pupils unquestionably improved the pupils' conditions of life and met a social need of youth. This decision was reversed by the House of Lords on other grounds,[27] so the question of the effect of the Act did not fall to be

---

[21] s.1.(1). The expression "social welfare" is used in the Local Government Finance Act 1988.
[22] s.1(1) proviso.
[23] s.1(2)(a).
[24] s.1(2)(b)(i).
[25] s.1(2)(b)(ii).
[26] [1979] 1 W.L.R. 130; for another aspect of the decision and the facts, see *post*, p. 410. See also Warburton (1980) Conv. 173.
[27] [1981] A.C. 1; see *post*, p. 410.

considered. However, as a matter of statutory interpretation, the view of Bridge L.J. appeared highly persuasive and has now duly been approved by the House of Lords in *Guild v. I.R.C.*[28] This case concerned a gift of residue "to the town council of North Berwick for the use in connection with the sports centre in North Berwick or some similar purpose in connection with sport". This gift was held to fall within the Act on the grounds that "persons in all walks of life and all kinds of social circumstances may have their condition of life improved by the provision of recreational facilities of suitable character"[29] and the facilities of the centre would have this effect.

Subject to the facilities being provided in the interests of social welfare, the Act is specifically applied, in particular, to the "provision of facilities at village halls, community centres and women's institutes and to the provision and maintenance of grounds and buildings to be used for purposes of recreation or leisure-time occupation and extends to the provision of facilities for those purposes by the organising of any activity".[30] But these are simply well-known examples of recreational charities so this provision will not affect the generality of the statutory powers.

Miners' welfare trusts are specially provided for[31]; such trusts as had been declared before December 17, 1957,[32] were validated retrospectively, although there were certain savings as to past transactions.[33] The provision indeed seems entirely retrospective and so all new miners' trusts must fall within the statutory provisions already discussed.[34]

The Act leaves untouched the existing law as to the meaning of charity.[35] It also seems to have left untouched the other point—that the trusts must be for the public benefit—which came under consideration in *I.R.C. v. Baddeley*. It seemed, certainly from the opinion of Viscount Simonds,[36] that the membership, actual or potential, of the Methodist Church, at least in a defined area, did not amount to a class sufficient to satisfy the test of public benefit, although Lord Reid, who dissented, took a different view.[37] If the opinion of Viscount Simonds is to be adopted, trusts such as those in this case would still fail. Of course it was the other aspect of the decision, that the trusts were too uncertain, which aroused apprehension among the women's institutes and other bodies which the Act was designed to cure. This limited objective may have been successfully achieved, even though the material provisions are somewhat clumsily and ambiguously expressed. It was thought at the time that it would be difficult to apply and probably create more difficulties

---

[28] [1992] 2 A.C. 310 (a Scottish Appeal but the English definition of charity is incorporated into Scots law for tax purposes).

[29] *ibid.*

[30] s.1(3).

[31] s.2.

[32] This was the day of the first reading of the Bill in the House of Lords.

[33] s.3(2), (3), (4), (5).

[34] s.1.

[35] s.3(1).

[36] [1955] A.C. 572 at 589–593.

[37] *ibid.* at 606. Lord Somervell seemed to agree with Lord Simonds; Lord Porter and Lord Tucker expressed no opinion on the point.

than it solved[38]; however, it has only occasionally had to be considered in reported decisions.[39]

(3) National and local defence

All trusts which promote the armed forces of the Crown are charitable[40] and this rule will apply even if the means to the end are indirect.[41] Likewise a trust for the Mercantile Marine, though not strictly part of the armed forces of the Crown, is charitable.[42] A more general purpose of promoting the defence of the United Kingdom from the attack of hostile aircraft has also been upheld.[43]

The same applies to more mundane, but equally important, domestic protection. Thus in *Re Wokingham Fire Brigade Trusts*,[44] Danckwerts J. held that the provision and maintenance of a public fire brigade was a charitable purpose because it was designed to prevent damage to property and loss of life. The promotion of the efficiency of the police is also self-evidently charitable. This was stated in *I.R.C. v. City of Glasgow Police Athletic Association*,[45] but in that case the question was whether the association itself was charitable and it was held not to be because it was simply a sports club for the benefit of the members.

(4) Trusts for sport

It appears to be settled that a gift for the promotion of any given sport is not as such charitable. Accordingly, in *Re Nottage*,[46] where a trust was established to provide annually a cup for the most successful yacht of the season, with the expressed object of encouraging the sport of yacht racing, the Court of Appeal held that that was a gift for the encouragement of a mere sport which, though it might be beneficial to the public, was not charitable.[47] However, trusts for this purpose which are drawn so as to fall within the Recreational Charities Act 1958[48] will now be effective. In any case, the provision of prizes for sport in a school was held in *Re Mariette*[49] to be valid as advancing that part of the education of students which had to do with their bodily and physical development. And the same result occurred in *Re*

---

[38] See Maurice (1959) 23 Conv. (N.S.) 15.
[39] See *Wynn v. Skegness U.D.C.* [1967] 1 W.L.R. 52 where a seaside holiday home for Derbyshire miners was assumed to fall within the 1958 Act as a recreational charity; *I.R.C. v. McMullen* [1979] 1 W.L.R. 130, reversed on other grounds [1981] A.C. 1, see *post*, p. 410.
[40] *Re Stratheden and Campbell* [1894] 3 Ch. 265 (benefit of volunteer corps); *Re Stephens* (1892) 8 T.L.R. 792 (for teaching shooting); *Re Barker* (1909) 25 T.L.R. 753 (for prizes to be competed for by cadets).
[41] *Re Good* [1905] 2 Ch. 60 (providing a library for the officers' mess and providing plates for the mess); *Re Donald* [1909] 2 Ch. 410 (for the mess of the regiment and the poor of the regiment); *Re Gray* [1925] Ch. 362 (regimental fund for the promotion of sport).
[42] *Re Corbyn* [1941] Ch. 400.
[43] *Re Driffill* [1950] Ch. 92.
[44] [1951] Ch. 373.
[45] [1953] A.C. 380 at 391.
[46] [1895] 2 Ch. 649.
[47] See also to the same effect *Re Clifford* (1911) 106 L.T. 14 (angling); *Re Patten* [1929] 2 Ch. 276 at 289, 290 (cricket); *Re King* [1931] W.N. 232 (general sport); *I.R.C. v. City of Glasgow Police Athletic Association* [1953] A.C. 380 (athletic sports and general pastimes).
[48] See *ante*, p. 406.
[49] [1915] 2 Ch. 284. See also *Re Dupree's Deed Trusts* [1945] Ch. 16 (chess; see *ante* p. 398).

Gray,[50] where there was a gift for the promotion of a sport in an army regiment and it was held to be charitable because it increased the army's efficiency; however, the validity of this last decision was doubted in *I.R.C. v. City of Glasgow Police Athletic Association*.[51] The doubts appear to be unfounded because the army's efficiency will indeed be promoted if its soldiers are physically fit.[52]

It is clear that the trust instrument in question has to be construed in order to decide whether a particular charitable purpose is in fact promoted by the prescribed sporting activity. In *I.R.C. v. McMullen*[53] the legal status of the Football Association Youth Trust had to be decided. Its object was to organise or provide or assist in the organisation and provision of facilities which would enable and encourage students at schools and universities to play Association Football or other games and sports and thereby to assist in ensuring that due attention was given to the physical education and development of such pupils as well as the occupation of their minds and, with a view to furthering this object, to provide such facilities as playing fields, equipment, and so forth. The House of Lords held, unanimously reversing Walton J. and the Court of Appeal, that the purpose of the deed was not merely to organise the playing of Association Football in schools and universities but also to promote the physical education and development of students as an addition to their formal education; therefore, it created a valid charitable trust for the advancement of education,[54] the sporting activities contributing to a balanced education. Lord Hailsham of St Marylebone L.C.[55] was at pains to reject any idea which would cramp the education of the young within schools or university campuses, limit it to formal instruction; or render it devoid of pleasure in the exercise of skill.[56] The principle in *Re Mariette*[57] was held to apply.

(5) Locality trusts

A gift to a locality, such as a town or village, will be charitable even if no charitable purposes are specified.[58] A scheme[59] will be made so that the funds can be devoted to such purposes within the locality as are charitable. It has also been decided that the same principle applies to a gift to "my country, England".[60] That such trusts should be valid as charities seems

---

[50] [1925] Ch. 362.

[51] [1953] A.C. 380 at 391, 401.

[52] The Goodman Committee recommended that the encouragement of sport and recreation should be recognised as an independent charitable object, provided that the necessary element of benefit to the community is present, and in so far as the Recreational Charities Act 1958 (see *ante*, p. 398) does not make this clear, then it should be amended.

[53] [1981] A.C. 1.

[54] For consideration of the Recreational Charities Act 1958, see *ante*, p. 398.

[55] A former Secretary of State for Education and Science.

[56] *ibid.* at p. 18.

[57] [1915] 2 Ch. 284.

[58] See *Goodman v. Saltash Corpn* (1882) 7 App.Cas. 633; *Re Allen* [1905] 2 Ch. 400; *Re Norton's Will Trusts* [1948] 2 All E.R. 842.

[59] See *post*, p. 420.

[60] *Re Smith* [1932] 1 Ch. 153. See also *Nightingale v. Goulbourne* (1847) 5 Hare 484 (gift to "the Queen's Chancellor of the Exchequer for the time being" to be used by him for the benefit of "my beloved country, Great Britain"; valid. The case can also be justified on the ground that it was made *virtute officii*, see *ante*, p. 403).

curious[61] but is now established beyond all possible doubt.[62] But it is most important if a locality trust is to be upheld to ensure that either exclusively charitable purposes within the locality are specified in the trust instrument, or, alternatively, that no purposes whatsoever are specified. If the settlor uses words which demonstrate in terms that the subject-matter of the gift may be used for non-charitable purposes, it will fail. Such a gift failed in *Houston v. Burns*,[63] where the trust was for "public, benevolent or charitable purposes" in a Scottish parish. If, therefore, the purposes are not charitable *per se*, the localisation of them will not of itself make them charitable.[64]

(6) Institutional and other charities

A trust which is designed for a village hall, community centre, or other similar institutional purposes will, if drawn so as to fall within the Recreational Charities Act 1958,[65] create a valid charitable trust. Trusts for hospitals and other kindred purposes have been upheld as charitable as a matter of general law.[66]

The refinements which are all too evident in the law of charity were brought to the fore in the controversial and unfortunate decision of the Court of Appeal in *Re Cole*,[67] where the majority held that a gift for "the general benefit and general welfare" of the children for the time being in a children's home maintained by a local authority was not charitable. Romer L.J. in particular based his decision to this effect on a close reading of the preamble to the Charitable Uses Act 1601 and concluded that the conceivable provision of benefits, which could include such "new-fangled devices" as television sets, for the children in question, who might well be juvenile

---

[61] See Tudor on *Charities* (8th ed.), pp. 105 *et seq*; *Williams' Trustees v. I.R.C.* [1947] A.C. 447 at 459, *per* Lord Simonds.

[62] The Goodman Committee considered that local and denominational charities should be permitted to continue and be encouraged, and the same general principles should apply to analogous trusts for ethnic or national groups. With regard to the latter, there is a limited exception in favour of charities; in the Race Relations Act 1976 it is provided (s.34) that any discrimination necessary to comply with the terms of the governing instrument of a charity which is established to confer a benefit on persons of a particular racial group shall not be unlawful, but it specifically excludes from the exception any provision which restricts the benefits by reference to race or colour. Accordingly, a school for the education of Pakistanis or Spaniards could lawfully be confined to such persons but any provision excepting persons on racial grounds would be in breach of the Act. There is also an exception in favour of charity under the Sex Discrimination Act 1975. It is provided (s.43) that where the trusts contain a provision for conferring benefits on one sex only, anything done by the charity trustees to comply with that provision is not unlawful. This safeguards the position of single sex charities, like the Y.M.C.A., Y.W.C.A., Boy Scouts and Girl Guides and many small parochial charities restricted to one sex (such as elderly widows). See further the Reports of the Charity Commissioners for 1975 and 1976.

[63] [1918] A.C. 337; see also *Att.-Gen. v. National Provincial and Union Bank of England* [1924] A.C. 262 (patriotic purposes in the British Empire); *Re Strakosch* [1949] Ch. 529. The matter is discussed generally *post*, p. 415.

[64] *Williams' Trustees v. I.R.C.* [1947] A.C. 447 at 459–460, *per* Lord Simonds. This case involved an Institute of Welshmen in London which was not charitable because they were not an identifiable section of the community.

[65] See *ante*, p. 398.

[66] See, *Re Dean's Will Trusts* [1950] 1 All E.R. 882; *Re White's Will Trusts* [1951] 1 All E.R. 528; *Re Smith's Will Trusts* [1962] 2 All E.R. 563; *Re Adams* [1967] 1 W.L.R. 162; *Le Cras v. Perpetual Trustee Co.* [1967] 1 All E.R. 915; *Re Resch's Will Trusts* [1969] A.C. 514.

[67] [1958] Ch. 877.

delinquents, were not within the express terms of the preamble or within its spirit and intendment. The decision was followed by Danckwerts J. in *Re Sahal's Will Trusts*[68] on similar facts. But the dissenting view of Lord Evershed M.R. in *Re Cole* seems the more commendable, by reason of its wider outlook "that the inference to be drawn from the preamble is that the care and upbringing of children who for any reason have not got the advantage or opportunity of being looked after and brought up by responsible and competent persons, or who could by these or other reasons, properly be regarded as defenceless or 'deprived' are matters which prima facie qualify as charitable purposes".[69]

(7) Political trusts

In *Bowman v. Secular Society*[70] Lord Parker of Waddington stated the general position as follows:

"A trust for the attainment of political objects has always been held invalid, not because it is illegal, for everyone is at liberty to advocate or promote by any lawful means a change in the law, but because the court has no means of judging whether a proposed change in the law will or will not be for the public benefit, and therefore cannot say that a gift to secure the change is a charitable gift."

This basic principle, as has been already seen,[71] was applied by the House of Lords in *National Anti-Vivisection Society v. I.R.C.*[72] in rejecting as charitable a trust to abolish vivisection as it would involve legislation to change the law; it was reaffirmed more recently by Slade J. in *McGovern v. Attorney-General*[73] which concerned the legal status of Amnesty International. The general object of this unincorporated non-profit making body was expressed to be to secure throughout the world the observance of the provisions of the Universal Declaration of Human Rights in regard to various categories of persons referred to in its constitution as "prisoners of conscience", namely persons who were imprisoned, detained or restricted because of their political, religious or conscientiously held beliefs or their ethnic origin, sex, colour or language. There were also various specific objects of the association whose legal effect had to be considered: first, the release of prisoners of conscience—this was held to be for political purposes and therefore not charitable because it involved putting pressure on foreign governments to change their policies; secondly, the abolition of torture or inhumane treatment or punishment—this was held not to be charitable because it would involve legislation requiring the abolition of corporal or capital punishment; and, thirdly, providing research into the observance of human rights and the dissemination of that research—this would, if it had stood alone, have been charitable but it did not. The trusts were required to be exclusively charitable, they were not, and accordingly they all failed. This decision is an

---

[68] [1958] 1 W.L.R. 1243.
[69] [1958] Ch. 877 at 892.
[70] [1917] A.C. 406.
[71] See *ante*, p. 406.
[72] [1948] A.C. 31.
[73] [1982] Ch. 321.

important illustration of the principle that, although a trust for the relief of human suffering or distress may well be capable of being of a charitable nature, it will not qualify if the main object is to secure an alteration in the law or government policy of the United Kingdom and/or of a foreign country. It is therefore established that a trust to advance a political purpose will fail as a charity. Such trusts are often disguised as educational trusts but such educational character as they may have will not enable them to succeed as charities if the primary object is political.[74] This was in effect the position in *McGovern v. Attorney-General*. The trusts also failed for this reason in *Bonar Law Memorial Trust v. I.R.C.*[75] and in *Re Hopkinson*,[76] trusts in favour respectively of the Conservative Party and the Labour Party.

These last two decisions were applied in *Re Bushnell*,[77] where the testator had directed a fund to be used "for the advancement and propagation of the teaching of socialised medicine", with directions as to how the managers of the fund should carry out and foster this purpose. Goulding J. held that the trust could not be supported as an educational trust; the directions with regard to the principles of "socialised medicine" dominated the whole of the trust. It was also held that the trust was not beneficial to the community within the fourth head of Lord Macnaghten's classification in *Pemsel's Case* since validity or otherwise had to be tested at the date of the testator's death in 1941, a date at which the court could not have decided the question because it would have involved considering the desirability or otherwise of legislation to bring into being a state health service, which would have been a political question. The fact that a state health service had subsequently been introduced was irrelevant; the trust had to stand or fall by the character of its objects as at the date of the testator's death.

It should however be stressed that the mere existence of some political motive is not necessarily fatal to a charitable trust. Thus in *Re Koeppler's Will Trust*[78] the organisation of conferences with political themes but without any intention of furthering the interests of any particular political party was held to be an educational charitable purpose. The question is whether a trust's leading purpose is political, by for example promoting legislation with a view to changing the law, in which case it will fail, or whether that purpose is subsidiary. This point was made by Lord Normand in *I.R.C. v. National Anti-Vivisection Society*[79]; there the primary purpose of the Society was political—as were the objects of Amnesty International in *McGovern v. Attorney-General*. It is, however, by no means easy to distinguish the earlier decision of Stirling J. in *Re Scowcroft*,[80] where it was held that a gift for the maintenance of a village club and reading-room "to be used for the furtherance of Conservative principles and religious and mental improvement, and to be kept free from intoxicants and dancing" was good. It may perhaps be distinguishable by virtue of the ground on which the case was apparently decided, namely that all the purposes prescribed were to be carried out

---

[74] See *Bowman v. Secular Society Ltd* [1917] A.C. 406.
[75] (1933) 49 T.L.R. 220.
[76] [1949] 1 All E.R. 346.
[77] [1975] 1 W.L.R. 1596.
[78] [1986] Ch. 423.
[79] [1948] A.C. 31 at 76; see *ante*, p. 406.
[80] [1898] 2 Ch. 638.

simultaneously so that the clearly political purpose was not, in the event, predominant.

A recent development in charity law and administration is, as the Charity Commissioners have pointed out,[81] the increasing desire of charities for "involvement" in the causes with which their work is connected, such as housing and other services for the under-privileged in society. *McGovern v. Attorney-General* was an example of this problem in the international arena but many charities operating in this country also feel that merely to relieve distress in particular cases is not enough. They wish to go further: to draw the attention of the public as forcefully as they can to the need for action to remedy certain social conditions. The result has been that pressure groups, action groups and lobbies have come into being, giving rise to the problem of whether such activities are of such a "political" nature as to vitiate the charitable status of the organisation in question. The Charity Commissioners in their Report for 1981 suggested fairly detailed guidelines for charity trustees in these circumstances. These include[82]: first, a charity should undertake only those activities which can reasonably be said to be directed to achieving its purposes and which are within the powers conferred by its governing instrument; secondly, the governing instrument should not include powers to exert political pressure except in a way that is merely ancillary to a charitable purpose; thirdly, the powers and purposes of a charity should not include power to bring pressure to bear on the Government to adopt, alter or maintain a particular line of action; fourthly, the charity should spend its money on the promotion of public general legislation only if in doing so it is exercising a power which is ancillary to and in furtherance of its charitable purposes; fifthly, if the objects include the advancement of education, care should be taken not to overstep the boundary between education and propaganda; sixthly, if the objects include research, the charity must aim for objectivity and balance; and, seventhly, charities whether operating in this country or overseas, must avoid both seeking to influence or remedy those causes of poverty which lie in the social, economic and political structures of countries or communities,[83] and bringing pressure to bear on a government to procure a change in policies or administrative practices, and seeking to eliminate social, economic, political or other injustice.

(8) Trusts for the environment

Trusts for the protection of the environment and the conservation of the national heritage have become increasingly active. Such trusts are analogous to the public works referred to in the preamble to the Act of Elizabeth I.[84] They often appear to be involved in the political arena but, provided that the

---

[81] Report of the Charity Commissioners for England and Wales for 1969, p. 5; see also Report for 1981, p. 19.

[82] For further details, see the Report for 1981, pp. 19–22 and the Annual Report 1986, App. A. Guidelines had been suggested earlier; see the Report for 1969.

[83] See the Report for 1981, pp. 22–23 for the Commissioners' criticism of the "political" activities of "War on Want".

[84] The preamble refers to the repair of bridges, ports, havens, causeways, sea banks and highways.

political activity carried on by the trustees is ancillary to and not the main object of the trust, they would appear to be unobjectionable.[85]

V. THE EXCLUSIVE NATURE OF CHARITY

It is essential, subject to the Charitable Trusts (Validation) Act 1954 when it applies, that the trustees be bound to devote the funds to charitable purposes, even if these are expressed not specifically but in a general way. For example, the settlor may join the word "charitable" with another adjective, such as "benevolent", "patriotic", "philanthropic". It might be thought that if the word "and" is used, for example "for charitable and benevolent purposes", the gift will succeed because it can only be applied to such benevolent purposes as are charitable. It might also be thought that if the word "or" is used, for example "for charitable or benevolent purposes", the gift will fail because the property can be applied to benevolent purposes which are not charitable. This may well turn out to be the case but cannot actually be assumed with any confidence; it is entirely a question of construction. The word "and" may have been used disjunctively and the word "or" conjunctively.[86] There is also a great deal of authority on "and/or".[87] Two leading decisions of the House of Lords must be mentioned briefly to emphasise the rule that a trust fund must be capable of being devoted exclusively to charitable purposes, in both of which the word "or" was given its normal disjunctive meaning. In *Houston v. Burns*[88] the gift was made for "public benevolent or charitable" purposes in a Scottish parish. The gift failed as not being charitable because the words were wide enough to justify the trustees in disposing of the fund for non-charitable purposes. But the case which brought home the effect of this rule with a vengeance was *Chichester Diocesan Fund and Board of Finance v. Simpson*.[89] The words used there were "charitable or benevolent" and the same conclusion was reached as in *Houston v. Burns*. Executors had paid the money in question, which was a very substantial sum, to some 139 charities, not anticipating litigation by the next-of-kin, which in fact occurred. The latter's case to

---

[85] The Goodman Committee (p. 34) recommended that environmental trusts should continue to enjoy charitable status and that their scope should be widened (e.g. so as to deal with the method of development of the environment).
[86] See *Re Sutton* (1885) 28 Ch.D. 464; *Re Best* [1904] 2 Ch. 354 ("charitable and deserving" and "charitable and benevolent" objects respectively were upheld). Contrast *Att.-Gen. of the Bahamas v. Royal Trust Co.* [1986] 1 W.L.R. 1001, where a gift for "education and welfare" was interpreted disjunctively and was held void.
[87] See, in addition to the cases mentioned in the text, *Morice v. Bishop of Durham* (1805) 10 Ves. 522; *Hunter v. Att.-Gen.* [1899] A.C. 309; *Blair v. Duncan* [1902] A.C. 37; *Re Davidson* [1909] 1 Ch. 567; *Re Da Costa* [1912] 1 Ch. 337; *Att.-Gen. for New Zealand v. Brown* [1917] A.C. 393; *Re Chapman* [1922] 2 Ch. 479; *Re Davis* [1923] 1 Ch. 225; *Att.-Gen. v. National Provincial and Union Bank of England* [1924] A.C. 262; *Att.-Gen. for New Zealand v. New Zealand Insurance Co.* [1936] 3 All E.R. 888; *Re Atkinson's Will Trusts* [1978] 1 W.L.R. 586 (evidence inadmissible to show that by "worthy" the testator meant "charitable").
[88] [1918] A.C. 337.
[89] [1944] A.C. 341.

recover the money from the charities themselves also went to the House of Lords as the leading case of *Re Diplock*.[90]

1. *Apportionment*

It should be remembered, however, that a settlor may direct an apportionment of the funds between charitable and non-charitable purposes. This class of gift will not fail, even if the trustees fail to make the appointment, because the court will in the last resort apportion the funds equally between the objects. Therefore, if the non-charitable purposes are void, for example, for uncertainty, only that part of the funds devoted to them will fail.[91]

2. *Incidental Non-Charitable Purposes*

It is also important to notice that the fact that a non-charitable purpose is incidental or ancillary to the achievement of a purpose which is, in fact, charitable will not destroy the gift. Thus, in *Royal College of Surgeons v. National Provincial Bank*[92] the House of Lords held that the College was in law a charity, since its object, as recited in the Charter, was "the due promotion and encouragement of the study and practice of surgery", the professional protection of its members provided for in its by-laws being merely ancillary to that object. Likewise, in *Incorporated Council of Law Reporting for England and Wales v. Attorney-General*,[93] it was held that the fact that legal practitioners used law reports in order to earn their professional fees did not have the result that the objects of the Council were not charitable. The same result occurred in *Re Coxen*,[94] where a sum of money was given by the testator to the Court of Aldermen of the City for an annual dinner to be held after their meeting to consider the business of managing a trust in favour of orthopaedic hospitals which the testator had also set up. The dinner was held by Jenkins J. to be purely ancillary to the primary charitable trust and for its better administration. And in *London Hospital Medical College v. I.R.C.* [95] it was held that, if the students' union existed to further the educational purposes of the College,[96] then it was immaterial that the union also provided a personal benefit for the individual students who were elected members of the union and chose to make use of its facilities.[97]

---

[90] [1948] Ch. 465 (affirmed *sub nom. Ministry of Health v. Simpson* [1951] A.C. 251); see *post*, p. 705.
[91] *Salusbury v. Denton* (1857) 3 K. & J. 529; *Re Clarke* [1923] 2 Ch. 407.
[92] [1952] A.C. 631.
[93] [1972] Ch. 73.
[94] [1948] Ch. 747.
[95] [1976] 1 W.L.R. 613.
[96] This was held to be the position; see *ante*, p. 399.
[97] See also, to a similar effect, *Neville Estates v. Madden* [1962] Ch. 852, in which it was held that the social activities of a synagogue were merely ancillary to the strictly religious activities of the synagogue; see *ante*, p. 404.

3. Subsidiary Purposes

Incidental purposes such as those just mentioned must be carefully distinguished from purposes which are subsidiary but not merely incidental. A well-known illustration is *Oxford Group v. I.R.C.*,[98] where the Court of Appeal held that one of the objects set out in the Group's memorandum of association, namely to support "any charitable or benevolent" associations, actually conferred powers which were so wide that they could not be regarded as charitable; they were not merely ancillary to the main, admittedly charitable, objects set out elsewhere in the memorandum. The Group did not therefore constitute a charity.

4. Charitable Trusts (Validation) Act 1954

It was as a result of the decision in *Oxford Group v. I.R.C.* that the Nathan Committee recommended some amendment of the law on the grounds that the decision was thought to affect a large number of charities.[99] However, they did not go so far as to recommend its complete reversal. The legislative result was the Charitable Trusts (Validation) Act 1954,[1] a brief but, as it has turned out, exceptionally difficult, statute to interpret for the following reasons.

First, the Act defines, in section 1(1), as an "imperfect trust provision", any provision declaring the objects and so describing them that consistently with the terms of the provision of the property could be used exclusively for charitable purposes but could nevertheless be used for purposes which are not charitable. Secondly, the instrument in which the "imperfect trust provision" is contained must have taken effect before December 16, 1952,[2] the date of the publication of the Nathan Report. Thirdly, the Act is to apply, by virtue of section 2(1), to any disposition or covenant to make such a disposition where, apart from the Act, the disposition or covenant would have been invalid[3] under the law of England and Wales, but would have been valid if the objects were exclusively charitable. Fourthly, the Act will not apply if the property or income from the trust has been paid or distributed on the basis that the imperfect trust provision was void.[4] Finally, and this emphasises the limited applicability of the Act, the imperfect trust provision takes effect, as to the period before the Act came into force on July 30, 1954, as if the whole of the declared objects were charitable and, as to the period after the Act came into force, as if the provision required the property to be applied for the declared objects only so far as they are charitable.[5]

Very real difficulty, as already indicated, has been found in the interpretation of these provisions; indeed one Lord Justice of Appeal confessed

---

[98] [1949] 2 All E.R. 537. See also *Ellis v. I.R.C.* (1949) 31 Tax Cas. 178.

[99] 1952 Cmd. 8710, Chap. 12.

[1] Compare the Conveyancing Act 1919–1954 (New South Wales), discussed in *Leahy v. Att.-Gen. for New South Wales* [1959] A.C. 457.

[2] s.1(2).

[3] For example, for perpetuity, uncertainty or other similar reason: *Vernon v. I.R.C.* [1956] 1 W.L.R. 1169.

[4] s.2(2).

[5] s.1(2)(a), (b).

that he was "floored" by them on two occasions.[6] Especial difficulty has been found in reconciling section 1(1) and section 2(1). The definition of an imperfect trust provision is limited to a provision declaring the objects for which the property is held and "objects" is synonymous in section 1(1) with purposes. How then should section 2(1) be interpreted? It can be argued, most forcibly, that the definition in section 1(1) includes certain gifts which are already valid, for example a gift to certain named purposes for a period limited to the perpetuity period, some purposes being charitable and others (for example a gift "for my dog Fido") not charitable but nevertheless valid. Section 2(1), according to this line of argument, then takes this class of bequest outside the mischief of the Act into which section 1 has put it. It is hard to disagree that it is "an odd state of things if Acts of Parliament are passed in such a form that it is necessary to amend the effect of the first section by putting in a second".[7]

Apart from this problem, other difficulties have arisen. A leading case on one of them is *Re Gillingham Bus Disaster Fund*,[8] some features of which have had a somewhat mixed reception in later first instance decisions. One question was whether the appeal launched in the *Daily Telegraph* was validated by the Act. This appeal was launched by the mayors of several boroughs, after a number of cadets had been killed and injured in a road accident, "to promote a Royal Marine Cadet Memorial Fund to be devoted to defraying funeral expenses, caring for the boys who may be disabled and then to such worthy cause or causes in memory of the boys who lost their lives as the Mayors may determine". A majority of the Court of Appeal held that an imperfect trust provision was not validated unless the contributions to the fund were dispositions to which the Act applied, namely dispositions creating more than one interest in the same property.[9] A contribution was admittedly a disposition but, in view of the terms of the appeal, it did not create separate interests in the same property, one for funeral expenses, the second for the care of the disabled and the third for worthy causes; accordingly, it was held not to be validated by the Act.[10]

This is also what Harman J. had held at first instance and seems to be correct.[11] However, he also stated by way of dicta that section 1(1) should be construed as applying only to trusts framed in such terms that the objects referred to included some express reference to charitable purposes as well as including other non-charitable purposes. It did not apply to purposes stated in a general way, for example for public purposes, which could embrace charitable purposes but contained no express reference to charity or any charitable purpose. The Court of Appeal, by a majority, decided the point on the different ground already mentioned; this rendered this question irrelevant and, although they expressed some sympathy with the view of Harman J., they abstained from expressing any opinion on it. Ormerod L.J., who dissented and to whose decision alone the point was relevant, decided that

---

[6] *Re Harpur's Will Trusts* [1962] Ch. 78 at 95, *per* Harman L.J. See also *Re Gillingham Bus Disaster Fund* [1958] 1 Ch. 300 (Harman J.).
[7] *Re Harpur's Will Trusts* [1962] Ch. 78 at 96, *per* Harman L.J.
[8] [1959] Ch. 62.
[9] s.2(3).
[10] Compare *Re Chitty's Will Trusts* [1970] Ch. 254.
[11] Although dissented from by Ormerod L.J. [1959] Ch. 62.

section 1(1) should not be construed in the restricted manner favoured by Harman J. but in accordance with its language which he considered to be unambiguous.

In these circumstances, Buckley J. in *Re Wykes' Will Trusts*[12] felt himself free to adopt the view on this point favoured by Ormerod L.J. and declared that a trust for "benevolent or welfare" purposes was an imperfect trust provision to which the Act applied. This last decision was considered by Cross J. in *Re Mead's Trust Deed*.[13] He said that a benevolent or welfare fund "is closely akin to a trust for the relief of poverty".[14] He therefore held that a trust to provide a convalescent home for members of a trade union and a home for its poor retired members was validated by the Act and as from the date of the Act the property should be held for those members of the union who were poor persons and, in the case of the home for the aged, for poor retired members. *Re Wykes' Will Trusts* was further considered, again by Cross J., in *Re Saxone Shoe Co. Ltd's Trust Deed*[15] and assumed to have been correctly decided; however, it was held on the facts that this particular trust was essentially a discretionary private trust and was not therefore validated. However, the judge set certain clear limits to the doctrine enunciated by Buckley J. in *Re Wykes' Will Trusts*. He said:

"In such a phrase as 'welfare purposes' there is at least some flavour of charity which may justify one in saying that the testator was seeking to benefit the public through the relief of a limited class. Here there is nothing of that kind, and if such a trust as this is validated by the Act, I do not see why one should stop short of turning any such invalid private trust into a trust for the relief of such beneficiaries as may from time to time be poor."[16]

Nevertheless this problem, which is essentially one of construction of the Act, remains open; it has not been directly adjudicated upon by the Court of Appeal. There seems, however, to be no overriding reason why the restrictive application favoured by Harman J. should be adopted; all that seems to be essential is that the expression used has a charitable connotation. Indeed, in *Re South Place Ethical Society*[17] Dillon J. held that the words "for such purposes either religious or civil" as the trustees might appoint constituted an imperfect trust provision within the meaning of the Act; they were to be construed as "such purposes, either religious or civil, being charitable" and the provision was accordingly validated.

The vexed question of the effect of the Act also arose for decision on another matter in *Re Harpur's Will Trusts*.[18] The Court of Appeal had to consider the question of whether a trust to divide a trust fund "between such institutions and associations having for their main objects the assistance and care of soldiers, sailors, airmen and other members of HM Forces

---

[12] [1961] Ch. 229.
[13] [1961] 1 W.L.R. 1244.
[14] *ibid*. at 1251.
[15] [1962] 1 W.L.R. 943.
[16] *ibid*. at 958–959.
[17] [1980] 1 W.L.R. 1565.
[18] [1962] Ch. 78.

who have been wounded or incapacitated during the recent world war" as the trustees thought fit had been validated by the Act. It was held that this provision was not within the scope of section 1(1) because that was limited to provisions declaring the objects and so describing them as to enable effect to be given to them by an application for purposes which are exclusively charitable. This has the somewhat surprising result that a gift to institutions, whose objects are not described in the trust instrument, will not be comprehended within the subsection.

It has been seen that the Act can only apply to instruments taking effect before December 16, 1952. However, since the validity of a provision may also arise for consideration on the determination of a life or other limited interest which is still in being, the Act cannot be regarded as merely of academic interest.[19] By now, however, its importance must have substantially diminished and in due course it will no doubt be able to be omitted from this work.

VI. THE CY-PRÈS DOCTRINE

A settlor may select a particular object of charity which fails, or may be or become impossible or impracticable[20] to carry out, or may become illegal,[21] or may not exhaust the whole fund. What happens to the trust in such circumstances? It will not necessarily fail because the *cy-près* doctrine[22] may apply, in which case the funds will be applied to objects as near as possible to the settlor's intention.

1. *Conditions for Application of the Doctrine*

Two conditions must be satisfied, first, the existence of a "general charitable intention", and, secondly, "impossibility" in the light, where applicable, of section 13 of the Charities Act 1993.[23]

(A) General Charitable Intention
The settlor must, as a general rule, have manifested a general charitable intention. However, this requirement is not of universal application. It will only apply where the original trust has failed *ab initio*. The absence of a general charitable intention will not be fatal to those trusts which have taken effect but fail later; in such a case (and also in that of unidentified donors,

---

[19] If a person has a future interest in property the subject of the provision, he may challenge its validity within one year of the interest vesting in possession: s.3. *Re Chitty's Will Trusts* [1970] Ch. 254.

[20] See the cases cited in the text and also *Att.-Gen. v. City of London* (1790) 3 Bro.C.C. 171 (promotion of Christianity among the infidels of Virginia); *Ironmongers Co. v. Att.-Gen.* (1844) 10 Cl. & F. 908 (redemption of British slaves in Turkey or Barbary).

[21] For example exceeding the rules of accumulation; *Re Monk* [1927] 2 Ch. 197; *Re Bradwell* [1952] Ch. 575 (income settled on trusts exceeding accumulation periods).

[22] For a full survey of the subject, see Sheridan and Delaney, *The Cy-près Doctrine*; Tudor on *Charities* (8th ed.), pp. 391 *et seq.*

[23] Formerly Charities Act 1960, s.13.

which is considered later on)[24] the funds will be applicable *cy-près*. Once money has been effectively and absolutely dedicated to charity, whether in pursuance of a general or a particular charitable intent, the testator's residuary legatees or next-of-kin are excluded forever.[25] The Court of Appeal held in *Re Wright*[26] that this be the case even if the failure occurs during the existence of a prior life interest before the charity is entitled in possession to the funds. The material date for the purpose of deciding whether the *cy-près* doctrine is applicable is therefore the date when the trust came into existence (in the case of a will, the death of the testator). It is only if it has failed by then that the question of whether a general charitable intention has been shown becomes relevant.

However, this will only be the case if an absolute gift has been made. This is a question of construction of the instrument as to whether an absolute and perpetual gift has been made to charity with a gift over which has failed for remoteness or for some other reason leaving the original gift intact or whether the gift is to charity for a limited period, in which case any interest which is undisposed of results to the grantor.[27]

(1) Gifts to charitable purposes

In cases of initial failure, the question whether or not a general charitable intention has been shown is entirely one of construction of the instrument. It is necessary to consider, as in all matters of construction, the whole scope and intent of that instrument. The essential question which has to be decided in this process is whether the paramount object of the settlor was to benefit a particular object *simpliciter* or whether it was instead to effect a particular mode of charity independently of the given object even though an object was specifically indicated.[28]

Subject to the warning that the cases do not by any means present a consistent picture, the authorities may perhaps be divided into two classes.

The first class of case is where the gift is in form made for a particular charitable purpose but it is possible, taking the instrument as a whole, to say that, notwithstanding the form of the gift, the paramount intention is to give the property in the first instance for a general charitable purpose rather than a specified purpose; a direction has thus been engrafted onto the general gift as to the intention of the settlor relating to the manner in which the general gift is to be carried into effect. In this sort of case, even though it may be impossible to carry out the specified directions, the gift for the general

---

[24] See *post*, p. 423.
[25] *Re Wright* [1954] Ch. 347 at 363, *per* Romer L.J. See also *Re Wokingham Fire Brigade* [1951] Ch. 373.
[26] [1954] Ch. 347. See also to the same effect *Re Moon's Will Trusts* [1948] 1 All E.R. 300.
[27] See *Re Cooper's Conveyance Trusts* [1956] 1 W.L.R. 1096 at 1102, *per* Upjohn J. Compare *Re Peel's Release* [1921] Ch. 218; *Re Bawden's Settlement* [1954] 1 W.L.R. 33N. The Rule in *Hancock v. Watson* [1902] A.C. 14, which was formerly known as the Rule in *Lassence v. Tierney* (1849) 1 Mac. & G., whereby a gift to donee with further directions which do not exhaust the funds is taken by the donee absolutely, also applies to charitable gifts; *Re Monk* [1927] 2 Ch. 197 at 211.
[28] See *Re Taylor* (1888) 58 L.T. 538 at 543.

charitable purpose will remain perfectly good and the court or the Charity Commissioners will direct a scheme as to how it is to be carried out *cy-près*.

The second class of case is where, on the true construction of the instrument, the gift is not only in form but also in substance one for a particular purpose only; in such circumstances, if it proves impossible to carry out that particular purpose, the whole gift will fail; there is no room for the application of *cy-près*.[29]

The question as to the class in which a gift falls often raises serious problems of construction. The way in which the court sets about its task may be illustrated by the following cases. In *Biscoe v. Jackson*[30] money was to be applied towards the establishment of a soup kitchen in Shoreditch and a cottage hospital there. It was not in fact possible to apply the fund in the manner indicated. The Court of Appeal held that there was a sufficient general intention of charity for the benefit of the poor of Shoreditch to entitle the court to execute the trust *cy-près*. It was in effect therefore decided that the direction to establish a soup kitchen and a cottage hospital was only two ways of benefiting the poor of Shoreditch whom there was a general intention to benefit. A more difficult example is *Re Lysaght*.[31] The testatrix gave a fund to the Royal College of Surgeons, for the establishment of studentships but provided that Jews and Roman Catholics should be excluded from them. Buckley J. held, first, that this discriminatory provision did not form an essential part of the testatrix's intention; secondly, that her paramount intention was that the College should be the trustee of the fund and, thirdly, that the impracticability of giving effect to this inessential part of her intention by virtue of the fact that the College had refused to accept her gift subject to it would not be allowed to defeat her paramount intention. Accordingly a scheme was directed under which the offending provision was deleted. Although the principle behind the decision is entirely clear, it is not however at all easy, as a matter of construction of the will, to accept the judge's conclusion that this discrimination did not form part of the testatrix's paramount intention.

Another illustration, probably more straightforward from the point of view of construction, is *Re Woodhams*,[32] where the testator gave the residue of his estate to two colleges of music to found scholarships which were to be restricted to boys who were orphans from named children's homes. The colleges refused to accept the gift on these conditions, partly because of the decrease in the number of orphans and partly because of the adequacy of public grants for education, but was prepared to accept it if the restrictions were deleted. Vinelott J. held that the testator had chosen orphans from these homes as those most likely to need assistance but that it was not an essential part of the scheme that the scholarships should be so restricted; accordingly that the trusts could be modified without frustrating his intention.

---

[29] The substance of this formulation is borrowed from *Re Wilson* [1913] 1 Ch. 314 at 320. For another formulation, see *Re Lysaght* [1966] Ch. 191 at 201, 202, *per* Buckley J.

[30] (1887) 35 Ch.D. 460.

[31] [1966] Ch. 191, applying *Re Robinson* [1923] 2 Ch. 332 (requirement of wearing a black gown in church held impracticable).

[32] [1981] 1 W.L.R. 493.

A case on the other side of the line is *Re Good*,[33] where there was a trust to provide rest homes in Hull. There was a detailed scheme of the types of home to be provided, the types of inmates to be admitted, and the management powers of the trustees. The scheme was in fact impracticable because the funds were insufficient. Wynn-Parry J. held that the language of the will and in particular the detailed instructions were inconsistent with the implication of a general charitable intention; therefore the *cy-près* doctrine did not apply. Similarly in *Re Spence*,[34] Megarry V.-C. held that on the construction of the will a gift to a specified old folk's home was one for a specific charitable purpose which, although possible when the will was made, had become impossible; it was not a gift to the old people of a particular district. Accordingly there was no general charitable intention and the gift failed.

(2)   Gifts to charitable institutions[35]
The above illustrations generally concerned trusts for charitable purposes rather than trusts for charitable institutions. It seems necessary to deal with the latter separately since the circumstances of such institutions may vary considerably. The existence of a general charitable intention is not necessarily decisive of the matter.[36]

(a)   Non-existent institutions. It appears to be relatively easy to infer a general charitable intention where the charity named by the testator has never existed. In *Re Harwood*[37] it was held that a gift to a "peace society" which had never existed indicated a general charitable intention; thus the fund could be applied *cy-près* to other existing similar organisations. Such a construction may, however, be rebutted by the circumstances of the gift. Thus, in *Re Goldschmidt*[38] Harman J. held that the presence in the will of a residuary gift in favour of other charitable purposes into which lapsed funds would fall was a factor against deducing a general charitable intention.

(b)   Institutions ceasing to exist. Real difficulty is encountered in reconciling some of the cases in this category; much depends on the wording of the gift and the circumstances of the institution. The main question is whether the institution has actually ceased to exist or whether it has merely changed its form so that the original charity may be identified in its new form.

---

[33] [1950] 2 All E.R. 653. See also to the same effect *Re Packe* [1918] 1 Ch. 437 (holiday home for clergymen of Church of England and their wives); *Re White's Trusts* (1886) 33 Ch.D. 449 (almshouses); *Re Wilson* [1913] 1 Ch. 314 (school); *Re Harwood* [1936] Ch. 285. Compare *Re Finger's Will Trusts* [1972] Ch. 286.
[34] [1979] Ch. 483; another gift in the same will to a Blind Home was held to be identifiable with a home for the blind of a different name and address and so was valid.
[35] Compare the discussion by Hutton (1969) 32 M.L.R. 283.
[36] Compare *Re Spence* [1978] [1979] Ch. 483 at 491, *per* Megarry V.-C. to the effect that the distinction is between particularity and generality but this is not exhaustive.
[37] [1936] Ch. 285. See also *Re Davis* [1902] 1 Ch. 876 ("Homes for the Homeless"). See also *Re Satterthwaite's Will Trusts* [1966] 1 W.L.R. 277.
[38] [1957] 1 W.L.R. 524 (gift to "Fund for Relief of Distressed German Jews" and no fund of that name existed; failed).

In *Re Rymer*[39] there was a gift by will to the Rector for the time being of St Thomas' Seminary for the education of priests in the diocese of Westminster for the purposes of such a seminary. The seminary ceased to exist during the testator's lifetime. It was held that the gift had been made to a particular institution and so it lapsed. Although the case could have been treated as a purpose trust for the purpose of training priests (which in fact it was not), it would presumably still have failed because a particular, rather than a general, charitable intention had been shown. In some cases, however, the gift may instead be construed as one for the purposes of the institution. If so, the gift will not necessarily lapse if the institution ceases to exist. Thus, in *Re Roberts*,[40] there was a gift of residue for division among six named charitable institutions including the Sheffield Boys Working Home. That home was not in existence at the testator's death; it had been sold. Wilberforce J. held that the bequest in favour of the home was validly given on charitable trusts because, although the bequest was a gift for the purposes of the institution, it was not so correlated with the physical entity of the institution that the charity ended when the trusts of the Home ceased to exist; the funds of the Home remained subject to charitable trusts. A scheme was therefore appropriate and the gift was applied in accordance with that scheme.

The question is not, however, merely one of deducing a continuation of the charitable purposes in this way; it appears that there is an additional requirement to be satisfied, namely that on the closing down of the institution there are still funds or endowments available for carrying on its work. This requirement was insisted on by Plowman J. in *Re Slatter's Will Trusts*[41] where the gift had been made to a hospital which had closed down; it was held that its work had not been transferred elsewhere because the need for it had gone and because it had no funds available for carrying out that work.

(c) **Amalgamated, absorbed or re-organised institutions.** The point made in *Re Slatter's Will Trusts* is also relevant in cases where an institution has been amalgamated with, or absorbed in, other institutions, or otherwise re-organised. Such changes may be effected in various ways, most commonly by a scheme made by the court or the Charity Commissioners. Thus, in *Re Faraker*[42] a scheme had been made by the Commissioners consolidating the endowments of a number of charities with the general purpose of relief of the poor of Rotherhithe. A gift was subsequently made to one of these charities, "Hannah Bayley's Charity", whose original object was rather more limited. It was held that the gift did not lapse. The principle to be derived from this case is that an endowed charity cannot be destroyed by alterations made by scheme of the court or the Charity Commissioners so that any subsequent accretion to its funds takes effect on the trusts as altered. The case was subsequently applied in similar circumstances in *Re Lucas*.[43]

---

[39] [1895] 1 Ch. 19. See, for a similar result, *Re Goldney* (1946) 115 L.J.Ch. 337.
[40] [1963] 1 W.L.R. 406.
[41] [1964] Ch. 512.
[42] [1912] 2 Ch. 488.
[43] [1948] Ch. 424, distinguished in *Re Spence* [1979] Ch. 483.

Alterations to the constitution or objects of the institution in this way may have been made not only by scheme but also by statute,[44] or improperly under the terms of the trust deed without the sanction of the court or the Charity Commissioners.[45] Subsequent gifts to that endowed institution will not lapse. Informal changes are sometimes made by trustees, even more improperly, without reference to the terms of the trust deed. The essence of the matter in the case of informal changes of this kind is that, just as the court or the Charity Commissioners cannot destroy an endowed charity, neither can the trustees or the governing body destroy it, again with the result that gifts to the original institution will not lapse.[46]

There is, however, a complicating factor; if an institution has power to dissolve itself and formally does so, it appears that a subsequent gift to the institution will lapse unless a general charitable intention can be shown on the part of the donor. This is the effect of *Re Stemson's Will Trusts*,[47] where Plowman J. held that a gift to an incorporated institution lapsed when it had previously been dissolved and its funds had been disposed of in accordance with its constitution. It therefore appears that a charity which no one has any power to terminate retains its existence despite such vicissitudes as schemes, amalgamations or changes of name for so long as it has funds. But if the charity is founded, not as a perpetual charity, but as one liable to termination and its constitution provides for disposal of its funds in that event, then any gift made to the charity after it has ceased to exist will lapse in the absence of a general charitable intention.[48]

(d) Distinction between incorporated and unincorporated institutions. If the law were not already sufficiently complicated, it appears that a distinction must also be drawn between bodies which are incorporated and those which are unincorporated. This distinction was made by Buckley J. in *Re Vernon's Will Trusts*[49] and applied by Goff J. in *Re Finger's Will Trusts*,[50] which was in turn applied by the Court of Appeal in *Re Koeppler's Will Trust*.[51] The reasoning is that in the case of an unincorporated body the gift is in itself a purpose trust; provided that the work is still being carried on, the gift will be given effect to by a scheme notwithstanding the disappearance of the donee during the lifetime of the testator unless there is something positive to show that the continued existence of the donee was essential to the gift. In the case of a corporation, however, the position is different, as there has to be something positive in the will to create a purpose

---

[44] Many of the cases involved re-organisation of hospitals nationalised and re-organised under the National Health Services Act 1946; see *Re Morgan's Will Trusts* [1950] Ch. 137; *Re Glass* [1950] Ch. 643N; *Re Hutchinson's Will Trusts* [1953] Ch. 387.

[45] See *Re Bagshawe* [1954] 1 W.L.R. 238, where a scheme was made simply in accordance with the trust machinery, not by an outside body.

[46] See, to this effect, *Re Watt* [1932] Ch. 243N; *Re Withall* [1932] Ch. 236; see also *Re Hutchinson's Will Trusts* [1953] Ch. 387. A scheme is necessary or at any rate desirable where an informal change has been effected; see *Re Roberts* [1963] 1 W.L.R. 406.

[47] [1970] Ch. 16.

[48] *ibid.* at 26.

[49] [1972] Ch. 300N.

[50] [1972] Ch. 286.

[51] [1986] Ch. 423.

trust at all[52]; this is because a gift to a corporate body *prima facie* takes effect as a gift to that body beneficially.[53]

The distinction is in fact somewhat debatable, for it is arguable that a gift or trust made in favour of an incorporated body is not for that body *simpliciter*, but for its purposes; companies do have objects. *Re Finger's Will Trusts*[54] illustrates the difficulties. There were gifts by will both to an unincorporated association, the National Radium Commission, and to an incorporated body, the National Council for Maternity and Child Welfare. Both had been dissolved before the testator's death. The gift to the Commission was held to be a purpose trust for the work of the Commission which was not dependent on its continuing existence; consequently, the fund could be applied under a scheme.[55] The gift to the Council, however, failed because the testator could not be taken to have intended that the gift could be applied for its purposes. Goff J., however, managed to avoid this potentially anomalous result by holding that, although the gift to the Council had failed, the share of the fund applicable to the Council could nevertheless be applied *cy-près* because the will as a whole showed a general charitable intention.[56]

(e) **Institutions ceasing to exist after the gift takes effect.** The above illustrations concerned cases where the institution had ceased to exist or been otherwise re-organised before the gift took effect. If the charity ceases to exist after the testator's death it is however clear, as has already been mentioned and as the Court of Appeal held in *Re Slevin*,[57] that it is unnecessary to show a general charitable intention for the gift to be upheld. The subject-matter of the gift will have already vested in the recipient and, since the latter has ceased to exist, it will devolve on the Crown with the rest of the institution's property. The Crown will in practice allow it to be disposed of in favour of charity.

(3) **Gifts to a mixture of charitable and non-charitable purposes or institutions**

The fact that one gift for a non-charitable purpose is found among a number of gifts for charitable purposes does not permit the inference that the testator intended the non-charitable gift to take effect as a charitable gift when in terms it is not charitable. This is so even though the non-charitable gift may have a close relation to the purposes for which the charitable gifts were made. This was held to be the position in *Re Jenkins's Will Trusts*[58] where a gift made to an non-charitable anti-vivisection association was coupled with gifts for the charitable purpose of preventing cruelty to animals. As Buckley J. said, in rejecting an application for a *cy-près* scheme: "If you meet seven

---

[52] [1972] Ch. 286 at 295.
[53] See *Re Stemson's Will Trusts* [1970] Ch. 16.
[54] [1972] Ch. 423.
[55] See also *ante*, p. 424 in respect of the re-organisation of charitable institutions.
[56] See also *Re Stemson's Will Trusts* [1970] Ch. 16.
[57] [1891] 2 Ch. 236.
[58] [1966] Ch. 249.

men with black hair and one with red hair you are not entitled to say that there are eight men with black hair".[59]

It has been argued[60] that the previous case of *Re Satterthwaite's Will Trusts*[61] is inconsistent with this decision. In this case a human-hating testatrix gave money to the "London Animal Hospital". No hospital of this name could be identified but, because of other gifts in favour of established animal charities, the gift was held by the Court of Appeal to be applicable *cy-près*. The case is, however, probably distinguishable on the ground that a gift to an admittedly unidentified animal hospital had a sufficient charitable "flavour" about it to justify this result.

(B) "Impossibility" and Section 13 of the Charities Act 1993[62]

The second condition for the application of the *cy-près* doctrine used to be that it was or had become "impossible"[63] to carry out the settlor's intention or, alternatively, that a surplus remained after fulfilment of the purpose[64]; indeed, it has been held[65] that any surplus which is directed to be accumulated in excess of the statutory rules for accumulation is in the same position.

What then is the meaning of "impossibility"? It was not, and indeed is still not, possible simply to disregard the wishes of a settlor because they are unpopular or because the moneys could be applied for a more beneficial purpose. Nevertheless the word "impossible" was in general widely construed. Thus in *Re Dominion Students Hall Trust*,[66] the charity in question was restricted to Dominion students of European origin, yet the objects were stated to be the promotion of community interest in the Empire. An application was made to the court to delete the words "of European origin". Evershed J. held that the retention of these words amounted to a "colour bar" which would defeat the object of the charity; the word "impossible" should be construed widely and covered the case.

In view of this dilution of the term "impossible", it was clearly desirable to provide a new test to clarify it. Section 13 of the Charities Act 1960, now section 13 of the Charities Act 1993, provided a comprehensive treatment of the subject. It is sufficient if the matter can be brought under one of the following heads:

(1) Under Paragraph A, where the original purposes[67] in whole or in part, have been as far as may be fulfilled, or cannot be carried out,

[59] [1966] Ch. 249 at 256.
[60] See Pettit, *Equity and the Law of Trusts* (8th ed.), p. 308.
[61] [1966] 1 W.L.R. 277.
[62] Formerly Charities Act 1960, s.13.
[63] See cases cited in the text and also *Att.-Gen. v. City of London* (1790) 3 Bro.C.C. 171 (the promotion of Christianity among the infidels of Virginia); *Re Ironmongers Co. v. Att.-Gen.* (1844) 10 Cl. & F. 908 (redemption of British slaves in Turkey and Barbary).
[64] *Re King* [1923] 1 Ch. 243; *Re North Devon and West Somerset Relief Fund* [1953] 1 W.L.R. 1260; *Re Raine* [1956] Ch. 417.
[65] *Re Monk* [1927] 2 Ch. 197; *Re Bradwell* [1952] Ch. 575.
[66] [1947] Ch. 183.
[67] The words "original purposes" appear in all five paragraphs. They are applicable to the trusts of the disposition as a whole, and not severally in relation to its respective parts; *Re Lepton's Charity* [1972] Ch. 276 at 285.

or not according to the directions given and to the spirit of the gift.[68] This expression "spirit of the gift" appears in four of the five paragraphs. It is not a new phrase, being apparently borrowed from the Education (Scotland) Act 1946.[69] Although doubts about its meaning have been expressed,[70] it should not create any real difficulties. It has been said that "it is equivalent in meaning to the basic intention underlying the gift, as ascertained from its terms in the light of the admissible evidence".[71] The working of Paragraph A is illustrated by *Re Lepton's Charity.*[72] This case concerned a gift by will in 1715 of land to be held on trust to pay out of the rents a sum of £3 a year to the minister of a chapel and the net surplus to the poor and aged of the town. The evidence was to the effect that at the date of the will the total income was £5 a year. The land had been sold and was represented by investments yielding £791 a year. Pennycuick V.-C. held that the basic intention had plainly been defeated when, in modern conditions, the minister took a derisory £3 out of the total of £791; he made an order by way of scheme to provide for the payment to the minister to be raised from £3 to £100 per annum.

(2) Under Paragraph B, where the original purposes provide a use for only part of the property.[73] This can be illustrated by the facts of *Re North Devon and West Somerset Relief Fund,*[74] where a surplus remained out of funds subscribed for the relief of a flood disaster at Lynmouth.

(3) Under Paragraph C, where the property given and other property applicable for similar purposes can be more effectively used in conjunction and to that end can suitably, regard being had to the spirit of the gift, be made applicable for common purposes.[75] Strictly speaking, this is not a *cy-près* scheme at all since it has never been necessary to show "impossibility" to order to effect a consolidation of a number of charities.[76]

(4) Under Paragraph D, where the original purposes were laid down by reference to an area which was then, but has since ceased to be, a unit for some other purpose or by reference to a class of persons or to an area which has for any reason since ceased to be suitable, regard being had to the spirit of the gift, or practical for the purposes of administering the gift.[77] Common examples of the application of this paragraph are where the area in which the charity was originally to operate is, because of changes in local government

---

[68] Charities Act 1993, s.13(1)(a).
[69] s.116(2).
[70] Viscount Simonds, 221 HL Official Report 601 (March 1, 1960).
[71] *Re Lepton's Charity* [1972] 276 at 285, *per* Pennycuick V.-C. See also *Re Lysaght* [1966] Ch. 191; see *ante*, p. 422.
[72] See also *post*, p. 430.
[73] s.13(1)(b).
[74] [1953] 1 W.L.R. 1260; see also *Re King* [1923] 1 Ch. 243; *Re Raine* [1956] Ch. 417.
[75] s.13(1)(c).
[76] See *Re Faraker* [1912] 2 Ch. 488.
[77] s.13(1)(d).

boundaries or the class of beneficiaries, hard to identify or where the area or class of beneficiaries has dwindled or is otherwise provided for, so that no substantial public benefit is being conferred by the fulfilment of the original purposes. Thus in *Peggs v. Lamb*[78] this paragraph was applied to a gift for the benefit of the freemen of the borough of Huntingdon, whose numbers had become substantially reduced; a scheme was directed so as to enlarge the class to cover the inhabitants of the borough as a whole.

(5) Under Paragraph E, where the original purposes have, in whole or in part, in the period since they were originally laid down either (i) been adequately provided for by other means, or (ii) ceased as being useless or harmful to the community or, for other reasons, to be in law charitable, or (iii) ceased in any other way to provide a suitable and effective method of using the property given, regard being had to the spirit of the gift.[79] The jurisdiction created by this paragraph, and in particular by sub-paragraphs (i) and (iii), affords the most important relaxation of the old *cy-près* rule and will probably be of the most practical use in enabling funds to be utilised for the maximum benefit of the public. Sub-paragraph (i) may be illustrated by the situation where the original benefits of the charity are now provided for by the statutory services of public or local authorities. This would apply, for example, to a charity for the upkeep of a road or bridge[80]; if the original purpose were kept on foot, its only real purpose would be to relieve the rates or the exchequer and it is therefore now possible to apply the funds *cy-près*. Sub-paragraph (ii) will not often arise; indeed, there does not seem to have been a single reported case where a valid charitable trust has ceased to be charitable. But the principle may well in the future be applied more often than has hitherto been thought. This is because an institution registered by the Charity Commissioners is conclusively presumed to be a charity while on the register for all purposes other than rectification of the register.[81] If a charity is removed[82] from the register on the ground that its purposes are not in fact or, more improbably, no longer charitable, this sub-paragraph will clearly be applicable. It will therefore be applicable to the endowments of independent schools if their charitable status is ever withdrawn.[83] However, it is sub-paragraph (iii) which provides the widest relaxation of all. However, although its words are very general, it does not have a completely unlimited effect. It is still necessary to take into account the spirit of the gift, something which will prevent a *cy-près* scheme being made simply because the original purpose selected by the donor is less effective than some other application of the funds. It is still essential to establish that the mode of application which the

---

[78] [1994] Ch. 172.
[79] s.13(1)(e).
[80] See Charitable Uses Act 1601; *ante*, p. 384.
[81] Charities Act 1993, s.4(1).
[82] s.4(2).
[83] See J. Jaconelli, [1996] Conv. 24.

donor selected has ceased to be suitable or effective.[84] In *Re Lepton's Charity*,[85] it was held that the court had jurisdiction under this sub-paragraph (as well as under the wider terms of Paragraph A, where the original purposes, in whole or in part cannot be carried out, or not according to the directions given and to the spirit of the gift,[86]) to direct an application of the property *cy-près*.

These provisions of section 13 of the Charities Act 1993 alter the law only so far as it previously required a failure of the original purposes of a charity before a *cy-près* application could be ordered.[87] This therefore means that it is still necessary that a general charitable intention, on the lines already discussed, should be manifested, subject to the modifications provided for in respect of unidentified donors.[88] It must also be emphasised that the section applies only to alterations of the "original purposes"; only then is a scheme necessary. Proposals which do not involve any such alteration are governed by different principles.[89]

The jurisdiction to make a scheme is exercisable by the court or, almost invariably in practice, by the Charity Commissioners.[90]

2. *Unidentified Donors*

Section 14 of the Charities Act 1960, now section 14 of the Charities Act 1993, introduced reforms which were long overdue. This section provides that property given for specific charitable purposes which fail is to be applicable *cy-près* as though it had been given for charitable purposes generally, pro-vided that it belongs either to donors who, after such advertisements and inquiries as are prescribed by regulations made by the Charity Commis-sioners,[91] cannot be identified or found or to a donor who has executed a written disclaimer of his right to have the property returned.[92] It is further provided that, for these purposes, property is to be conclusively presumed, without the necessity for advertisements or inquiries, to belong to donors who cannot be identified if it consists either of the proceeds of cash collec-tions made by means of collecting boxes or other means not adapted for distinguishing one gift from another or of the proceeds of any lottery, competition, entertainment, sale or other such money-raising activity, although, as regards the latter, allowance must be made for prizes or articles for sale to enable the activity to be undertaken.[93] Donors who can be identified or who apply within six months of the making of a scheme are

---

[84] The Goodman Committee recommended (p. 95) that the *cy-près* doctrine should be amended or clarified to make it clear in appropriate cases that a fundamental change in the objects of the charity can be allowed.

[85] [1972] Ch. 276.

[86] See *ante*, p. 427. Pennycuick V.-C. was of opinion that this sub-paragraph was no more than "a final writing out at large" of paragraph [A]; *ibid.* at 285.

[87] s.13(2).

[88] See *post, infra.*

[89] *Oldham Borough Council v. Att.-Gen.* [1993] Ch. 210.

[90] See *post*, p. 350.

[91] Charities Act 1993, s.14(8).

[92] Charities Act 1993, s.14(1).

[93] s.14(3).

entitled to the return of their property or its proceeds of sale.[94] The court may, by order, direct that property be treated, without advertisement or inquiry, as belonging to donors who cannot be identified whenever it appears to the court either that it would be unreasonable, having regard to the amounts likely to be returned to the donor, to incur expense with a view to returning the property, or that it would be unreasonable, having regard to the nature, circumstances and amount of the gifts, and to the lapse of time since they were made, for the donors to expect the property to be returned.[95] Finally, the section is retrospective; it therefore applies to property given for charitable purposes before the commencement of the Charities Act 1960.[96]

These provisions reversed the previous law. Formerly the law was that, unless a general charitable intention could be shown in the usual way, the trustees were bound to refund the money and, if the donors could not be found, the money had to be paid into court to await the usually remote possibility that they would reclaim it. This was indeed the result in Re Ulverston,[97] where an appeal was launched for the building of a new hospital and insufficient funds were given for the purpose. The Court of Appeal held that a specific, not a general, charitable intention had been manifested and the funds were therefore to be held on a resulting trust for the contributors. As has been seen, the Charities Act 1960 reversed the previous law by the simple expedient of providing that donors in the circumstances indicated, but only in those circumstances, shall be deemed to have a general charitable intention.[98] Moreover, the fact that the section is retrospective enabled money lodged in court before the commencement of the Charities Act 1960 to be applied cy-près thereafter.

VII. THE ADMINISTRATION OF CHARITIES

1. Central Authorities

There is now only one central authority exercising jurisdiction over charities,[99] the Charity Commissioners for England and Wales.[1] Formerly, the Secretary of State for Education and Science and the Secretary of State for Wales had concurrent jurisdiction with the Charity Commissioners and exercised it in relation to charities of an educational nature.[2] The reason for conferring the exercise of functions under the Charities Act 1993 exclusively

---

[94] s.14(5),(6), (10).
[95] s.14(4).
[96] Charities Act 1993, s.14(10); Charities Act 1960, s.14(7).
[97] [1956] Ch. 622.
[98] The fact that contributions are from anonymous sources may, however, still be relevant in cases where the trust is not charitable; see ante, p. 257.
[99] This has been the case since the Education Act 1973, s.1(1)(a), which came into force on February 4, 1974.
[1] Charities Act 1993, s1(1) and Sched. 1. The Goodman Committee recommended (p. 120) that in addition an independent Charities Board should be created with a chairman and members independent of the Charity Commission. Its members would come from a wide background and from different parts of the country. Its function would include being consulted by the Charity Commissioners and to advise them on matters of policy and administration.
[2] Charities Act 1960, s.2(1), repealed by Education Act 1973, s.1(1)(a).

upon the Commissioners is that these functions are primarily judicial and not, therefore, appropriately to be exercised by Ministers of the Crown. As to the constitution of the Commission, it is provided that there are to be a Chief Charity Commissioner and from two to four other Commissioners,[3] at least two of whom must be barristers or solicitors.[4] They are appointed by the Home Secretary[5] but are quite independent of him in their day-to-day administration[6]; they cannot even be compelled to follow any general guidance which he may care to give.[7]

2. *The Official Custodian for Charities*

Before the Charities Act 1960 there were two officers, the Official Trustee of Charity Lands and the Official Trustee of Charitable Funds. They existed so that the legal title to charity lands and to charity funds respectively could be vested in them. There seemed to be no good reason why there should be two such offices[8] and the Charities Act 1960 combined them into one under the title of the Official Custodian for Charities.[9] There are advantages in vesting property in him as custodian trustee. First, it may make the title to that property more straightforward and, secondly and more importantly, it makes it unnecessary to appoint new trustees on deaths or retirements, thereby saving the expense of new appointments. The Official Custodian for Charities is an officer of the Charity Commissioners and ranks as a corporation sole, having perpetual succession and an official seal. Because he is simply a custodian trustee, the actual management and control of the property in question remains in the charity trustees. However, by virtue of the Charities Act 1992 the future role of the Official Custodian is to be limited to land[10] and he is to progressively divest himself of other property by transferring it to the trustees, or to such other persons as they nominate. This reform, which involves the divesting of holdings in excess of £1.25 billion, was carried out in order to increase the responsibility of the trustees. The Official Custodian for Charities nevertheless may retain any property vested in him by virtue of an order of the Commissioners made under section 18 of the 1993 Act where they feel that this is necessary for the protection of the charity in question.[11]

---

[3] Charities Act 1993, Sched. 1., paras 1(1), (5). At present there are four other Commissioners.

[4] Sched. 1, para.1(2).

[5] *ibid.*, para. 1(3).

[6] s.1(3),(4).

[7] *ibid.* The Expenditure Committee recommended (p. 31) that the Home Secretary should answer questions on charities and on the Charity Commissioners (such questions are at the present time referred to the Commissioners who reply in writing), and that the Home Secretary should have more flexibility where amendments to the law are required and wider powers to make orders and statutory instruments affecting the Commissioners and their work, subject to affirmative resolution of the House of Commons. The Goodman Committee, however, considered (p. 122) that the Commissioners should have the same degree of self-regulation as many other public bodies.

[8] See Nathan Report, para. 228.

[9] Charities Act 1960, s.3(1), now Charities Act 1993, s.2(1). See also Charities Act 1993, ss.21–22 for the vesting of property in the Official Custodian.

[10] s.29.

[11] See (1992) 142 N.L.J. 541.

3. Registration

Sections 3 and 4 of the Charities Act 1993[12] provide for a central register of charities. Before the Charities Act 1960 was passed, the alarming fact was that neither the actual number of charities nor the amount of money devoted to charitable purposes had ever been known with any sort of precision. These registration provisions must, since 1960, have gone a long way towards curing this palpable defect of charity administration. There is now a positive duty on all charity trustees to apply for registration enforceable by order of the Commissioners.[13] All charities are registrable[14] unless they are expressly relieved from the requirement.[15] One example of the latter is to be found in the so-called "exempt charities"; these are not subject to any of the supervisory powers of the Commissioners because satisfactory arrangements have already been made for carrying out the objects of such trusts and safeguarding the trust property. Examples of exempt charities are certain universities and colleges, the Church Commissioners, industrial and provident societies and friendly societies.[16] Some charities are also entitled to relief from registration in addition to the so-called "exempt charities". These are charities without any permanent endowment, that is to say no property which must be retained as capital, without property bringing in an income of more than £1,000 a year, and without land in its use and occupation.[17] Furthermore, any charity excepted by order or regulation is not required to be registered[18]; a number of regulations to this effect covering, for example, voluntary schools,[19] boy scouts and girl guides[20] have been made. A further exemption[21] operates in favour of registered places of worship.[22]

Registration raises a conclusive presumption that the institution is a charity at any time while it is on the register.[23] This accordingly removes a

---

[12] These provisions were in 1960 almost entirely new in their effect. Although a statutory obligation to register was imposed by the Charitable Donations Act 1812, this was not observed in practice.

[13] On December 31, 1997, over 184,000 charities were on the register; Report of the Charity Commissioners for England and Wales for 1997.

[14] It is necessary that, in order to be a charity, the organisation in question be subject to control by the High Court in the exercise of the court's jurisdiction with respect to charities. If that jurisdiction is wholly ousted by statute in relation to the organisation, then the organisation is not a charity and cannot be registered; see *Construction Training Board v. Att.-Gen.* [1973] Ch. 173 (where, however, the Board was held to be a charity because the provisions of the Industrial Training Act 1964 did not oust the jurisdiction of the court; the court still had control over the Board's functions).

[15] Charities Act 1993, s.3.

[16] See Charities Act 1993, s.3(5)(a), Sched. 2.

[17] s.3(5)(c).

[18] s.3(5)(b).

[19] The Charities (Exception of Voluntary Schools from Registration) Regulations 1960 (S.I. 1960 No. 2366).

[20] The Charities (Exception of Certain Charities for Boy Scouts and Girl Guides from Registration) Regulations 1961 (S.I. 1961 No. 1044).

[21] The Goodman Committee recommended (p. 75) that the Home Secretary should re-examine regularly the validity of exemptions and exceptions.

[22] Charities Act 1993, s.3(5)(c) and for definition of "Registered Place of Worship", see Places of Worship Registration Act 1855, s.9.

[23] s.4(1).

great deal of uncertainty about the status of certain institutions. But provision is necessarily made for a person who is or may be affected by the registration of an institution or trust as a charity to object to its entry on the register or apply for its removal on the ground that it is not in fact a charity, something which is of course a question for the general law.[24] This provision is intended for the benefit of anyone, especially a donor's residuary legatees or next-of-kin, whose interests will be affected by the answer to the question of whether the institutions or trusts should be classified as charities. An appeal against any decision of the Commissioners may be brought in the High Court.[25] The Commissioners also themselves have the positive duty to remove from the register any institution which no longer appears to them to be a charity and also to remove any charity because it has ceased to exist or is not operating.[26]

Any registered charity with a gross income of over £5,000 in its last financial year must state the fact of its registration in all documents soliciting donations and on all bills, invoices and receipts.

4. Accounts

The Charities Act 1993[27] also imposed much more rigorous duties on the trustees of unincorporated charities (the duties in this respect of incorporated charities are the usual ones imposed on all companies by the Companies Act 1985) to keep proper accounts and to prepare annual accounts. These must be audited if income exceeds £100,000; on the other hand, if income is less than £25,000, all that is required is statements of income and expenditure and a balance sheet. The trustees must also send to the Charity Commissioners annual reports of their activities, enclosing the accounts and, where appropriate, their auditors' report.

5. Co-ordination of Charitable Activities

Sections 76 to 78 of the 1993 Act, which were entirely new in 1960,[28] have as their aim the formation of a basis for co-operation between charities and the statutory welfare services. They authorise local authorities to review the working of those charities with that of the statutory services.[29] However, no obligation is put on a charity actually to co-operate. The Act requires mutual

---

[24] s.4(2).
[25] s.4(3),(4). The Goodman Committee recommended that appeals from administrative decisions of the Charity Commissioners should be made to an appellate tribunal, that there should be a right of appeal to the court from the decision of that tribunal on a point of law and that legal aid should be available for appeals on points of law.
[26] s.3(4). The Goodman Committee recommended (p. 69) that the Charity Commissioners should have power to require such information as they think fit about the proposed activities of the charity with power to refuse registration if it appears appropriate or, alternatively, to grant registration subject to review after three years. A charitable company incorporated under the Companies Acts may also be wound up on an application made by the Attorney-General under Charities Act 1993, s.63(1); see *Liverpool and District Hospital for Diseases of the Heart v. Att.-Gen.* [1981] Ch. 193.
[27] Charities Act 1993, s.5(1).
[28] As Charities Act 1960, ss.10–12.
[29] ss.41–49 and Charities (Accounts and Reports) Regulations (S.I. 1995 No. 2724).

agreement between the local authority and the charity.[30] It was obviously hoped that it would lead to rationalisation of charitable activities over the country as a whole but few reviews seem yet to have been put in hand.[31] Moreover, the review powers relate only to local charities. There are no powers to ensure reviews or co-ordination of national charities.[32]

6. Scheme-Making and Other Powers

Section 16 of the 1993 Act empowers the Commissioners to exercise a jurisdiction concurrent with that of the High Court to make schemes relating to the administration of the charity, or orders for the appointment and removal of trustees and with regard to the vesting or transfer of property.[33] Although the court has a scheme-making power, it should be emphasised that in practice the vast majority of such schemes will be made by the Commissioners.[34] A scheme will obviously take a wide diversity of forms; it may, for example, take the drastic form of rewriting the original user trusts or management trusts of the charity or both. Appointments and removals of trustees will not normally require a scheme; they will be made simply by order of the Commissioners. And the same will apply to vesting the property in the Official Custodian for Charities.[35]

In the usual way, jurisdiction can only be exercised by the Commissioners on an application made by the charity or on a reference by the court[36] or, save in the case of an exempt charity, on the application of the Attorney-General. However, in the case of a non-exempt charity with an annual income of less than £500, they may exercise their jurisdiction on the application of any trustee, of any person interested in the charity, or of any two inhabitants in the locality where it operates.[37]

Power is also specifically given to the Commissioners to act for the protection of charities where there has been misconduct or mismanagement and where the property of the charity needs to be protected and properly applied.[38] In these circumstances they are empowered to remove or appoint trustees and to prevent the operation of any banking account.[39]

---

[30] s.78(2).
[31] The Goodman Committee recommended (p. 82) that the review process should be proceeded with as speedily as possible, and that responsibility should be taken from the local authorities and given to the Charity Commissioners. It is also recommended that "neighbourhood trusts", catering for not too large an area, should be set up whenever practicable so as to retain the local character of the trusts. The Expenditure Committee recommended (p. 21) compulsory powers of "municipalisation" of local charities; this was rejected by the Goodman Committee.
[32] The Goodman Committee recommended (p. 99) that co-operation between national charities should be developed and encouraged by persuasion, not by legal means, and that the Charity Commissioners should initiate a review or reviews to determine how this can be done.
[33] s.16(1).
[34] s.16(1), (4).
[35] s.18.
[36] s.16(4).
[37] s.16(5).
[38] s.18(1).
[39] s.18(1). For the procedure on appeal against removal (see s.18(7)), see *Jones v. Att.-Gen.* [1974] Ch. 148.

A number of miscellaneous powers are also conferred on the Commissioners. Most important perhaps of all is the power to make an order where it appears that the proposed action is in the interests of the charity, authorising dealings or other action to be made or taken, whether or not it is within the administrative powers of the trustees.[40] This power, which is primarily administrative, is akin to the powers conferred by section 57 of the Trustee Act 1925[41] and by section 64 of the Settled Land Act 1925.[42] It may, for example, authorise any given transaction, compromise or application of property or may, more specifically, authorise a charity to use common premises, or employ a common staff or otherwise combine, for any administrative purposes, with any other charity, although these are purely examples and do not limit the generality of the statutory power.[43]

Other powers include that of advising charity trustees if the latter apply for advice[44]—a most convenient facility in practice—and powers to preserve charity documents.[45]

7. Investment

The powers and duties of trustees of a charity, with regard to investment of trust funds, are governed, in general, in the same manner as in the case of non-charitable trusts, by the terms of the trust instrument, if any, and by the general law of trusts relating to investments.[46]

The Trustee Investments Act 1961[47] enables trustees, subject to a number of safeguards, to invest a proportion, not exceeding three-quarters[48] of the trust fund, in a wide range of investments including stocks and shares in public companies. But in order to make effective use of the provisions of this Act a substantial fund is necessary so that risk can be spread and management expenses assimilated without difficulty. However, many charities have extremely small trust funds and, if special provision had not been made, a large number would not have been able to get effectual benefits from the Act. It was therefore thought desirable to make general provision, by way of common investment schemes, for the joint administration of a number of charitable trust funds for the purposes of investment. Common investment

---

[40] s.26(1).
[41] See *post*, pp. 502, 657.
[42] See *post*, p. 658.
[43] s.26(2).
[44] s.29.
[45] s.30.
[46] See *post*, p. 540 and see also *Soldiers', Sailors' and Airmen's Families Association v. Att.-Gen.* [1968] 1 W.L.R. 313, where it was held that a corporation incorporated by royal charter cannot, by the making of rules, confer upon itself powers wider than those conferred upon it by the general law or the royal charter.
[47] See *post*, p. 554.
[48] Until recently the proportion was only one-half. The Charities (Trustee Investments Act 1961) Order 1995 (S.I. 1995 No. 1092) first increased the percentage for charitable trusts alone but this was superseded by the current provision, the Trustee Investments (Division of Trust Fund) Order (S.I. 1996 No. 845), which applied this increase to all trusts.

schemes had been made before, but only in particular cases, by statute[49] and by the court,[50] and the Charity Commissioners have always had the power to make schemes of a similar nature. However, no general provisions for the establishment of common investment funds were available until the passing of the Charities Act 1960.

Section 22 of the Charities Act 1960, now section 24 of the Charities Act 1993, enables the court and the Charity Commissioners to make schemes, known as "common investment schemes", for the establishment of common investment funds, providing first for property transferred to the fund by or on behalf of a charity participating in the scheme to be invested under the control of trustees appointed to manage the fund and, secondly, for the participating charities to be entitled, subject to the provisions of the scheme, to the capital and income of the fund in shares determined by reference to the amount or value of the property transferred to it by or on behalf of each of them and to the value of the fund at the time of the transfers.[51]

It is expressly provided that the court or the Charity Commissioners may make a common investment scheme on the application of two or more charities.[52] In *Re University of London Charitable Trusts*[53] Wilberforce J. held that this provision enabled an application to be made by the trustees of any two or more charitable trusts, notwithstanding the fact that, as in this case, the trustees of such trusts are the same. More recently, the creation of common deposit funds has been authorised so as to still any doubts as to whether funds could merely be deposited at interest under the earlier schemes. These are now governed by section 25 of the Charities Act 1993.

Initially, a scheme was made by the Commissioners, known as the Charities Official Investment Fund, in which all charities may participate[54] and in 1976 two further schemes were made.[55]

8. Dealings with Charity Property

Here an important reform was effected by section 29 of the Charities Act 1960. It abolished the old restrictions on dealings in charity property, which were fraught with excessive complexity. It was necessary in the past to decide for this purpose whether a charity was, in the language employed, a plain or an endowed or a mixed charity. But these distinctions—and their attendant difficulties—can now be forgotten except in the increasingly unlikely event that a past transaction appears on the title to property and

---

[49] See Universities and Colleges (Trusts) Act 1943, which enabled the Universities of Oxford and Cambridge and the Colleges in those universities and also Winchester College to make schemes providing for funds to be administered as a single fund. (See *Re Freeston's Charity* [1978] 1 W.L.R. 741.) Private Acts have established common investment schemes for other universities; see, *e.g.* Liverpool University Act 1931; Birmingham University Act 1948.

[50] See *Royal Society's Charitable Trusts* [1956] Ch. 87; *Re University of London Charitable Trusts* [1964] Ch. 282.

[51] s.24(1).

[52] s.24(2).

[53] [1964] Ch. 282.

[54] It was made on December 4, 1962.

[55] Charinco Charities Narrower-Range Common Investment Fund, and Charibond Charities Narrower-Range Common Investment Fund; see the Report of the Charity Commissioners for 1976.

requires investigation.[56] Under section 29, the question which had to be considered was what the class of land in the ownership of the charity actually was. It may be of three kinds. First, it may be part of the "permanent endowment", which means property held subject to a restriction which prevents its being spent in the same way as income.[57] It is necessary for this purpose, therefore, that a distinction be made in the trust instrument between the expenditure of capital and the expenditure of income. Secondly, it may be "functional land", land which may or may not be part of the permanent endowment but is or has been in the use and occupation of the charity.[58] Thirdly, it may be neither of these but instead bought as an investment with funds expendable without distinction between capital and income. In the first two cases, the sanction of the court or the Charity Commissioners was required. In the third case, it was not[59]; in this case, which is probably the least common of all, a sale would not indicate a radical change in the character of the charity as a sale under the first two heads would, and for this reason, presumably, no consent was required.

Section 29 has now been replaced by what is now section 36 of the Charities Act 1993 (originally section 32 of the Charities Act 1992). No land may be sold, leased or otherwise disposed of without an order of the court or of the Charity Commissioners unless the trustees have obtained and considered a written report on the proposed disposition from a qualified surveyor, advertised the proposed disposition for such period and in such manner as the surveyor has advised, and are satisfied that the terms are the best reasonably obtainable. Leases for seven years are subject to less stringent requirements.[60] Where the land in question is expressly held on trust for the purposes of the charity, it is also required that public notice be given and any representations received within one month duly considered, unless the purpose of the transaction is to acquire replacement property. The instrument by which any disposition is effected must certify that these provisions have been complied with; the certificate is conclusive in favour of a purchaser for money or money's worth.[61]

9. *Ex Gratia Payments*

The court and the Attorney-General have the power to authorise charity trustees to make *ex gratia* payments out of funds held on charitable trusts,[62] for example, in pursuance of a moral obligation in favour of relatives of the deceased. This jurisdiction is not, however, exercised lightly; it is necessary to show that, if the charity were an individual, it would be morally wrong of him not to make the payment.[63]

---

[56] See Tudor on *Charities* (8th ed.), pp. 239–244.
[57] s.45(3).
[58] s.29(2).
[59] *ibid.*
[60] Comparable provisions apply to mortgages; see s.38.
[61] s.37.
[62] *Re Snowden* [1970] Ch. 700.
[63] *ibid.* at 710.

10. *The Appointment of Charity Trustees*[64]

Generally the rules which apply to private trusts govern appointment of charity trustees.[65] A major general exception is that the restriction on the number of trustees imposed by section 34 of the Trustee Act 1925,[66] does not apply. But there were and still are certain other specific provisions. Under the Trustees Appointment Acts 1850, 1869 and 1890, a convenient mode of appointment was provided. The Acts related to land held on religious or educational trusts where the method of appointment was not prescribed in the trust instrument or had lapsed. All that was required was that the appointment should be made under the hand and seal of the chairman of a meeting of the charity at which the appointment could be made; it was simply to be executed in the presence of the meeting and attested by two witnesses. This was a "conclusive" act of appointment and also operated to vest the property in the new trustees together with the continuing trustees. These Acts were repealed by the Charities Act 1960,[67] but the provisions were nevertheless preserved in relation to land acquired before January 1, 1961.

Apart from this, the Charities Act 1960 also provided in what is now section 83 of the Charities Act 1993 that new trustees may be appointed at a meeting, if a memorandum of the appointment is signed at the meeting by the person presiding or in some other manner prescribed by the meeting, and attested by two witnesses; that is then "sufficient" evidence of the appointment. This provision applies to all charities (unlike the Trustees Appointment Acts of last century) but it can be made use of only when the trusts permit it and, most importantly, it is only "sufficient" (as opposed to "conclusive") evidence of appointment, thus enabling its sufficiency to be checked on investigation of title by a purchaser.

The Charities Act 1992 in what is now section 73 of the Charities Act 1993 provided for the disqualification from holding the office of charitable trustee of anyone convicted of an offence involving dishonesty or deception, of undischarged bankrupts, and of those previously removed from such an office on the grounds of misconduct or mismanagement. Any one who acts while so disqualified is guilty of an offence carrying a maximum sentence of two years imprisonment and/or a fine. The Charity Commissioners may remove any trustee if satisfied that there has been misconduct or misman-agement and that this is necessary or desirable for the purpose of protecting the property of the charity or if a trustee has been discharged from bank-ruptcy during the last five years, is a corporation in liquidation, is mentally

---

[64] The Goodman Committee recommended (p. 77): first, that all charities should normally have a provision for rotation of trustees other than *ex officio* trustees; secondly, that there should be an age limit of 70 for trustees other than *ex officio* trustees; and, thirdly, that charity executives should not be trustees as a general rule. These recommendations were welcome on the grounds that too many charities appear to provide employment (albeit often unpaid) for the very aged members of the community; however, they have not been enacted. For the powers of a receiver and manager appointed for a charity, see *Att.-Gen. v. Schonfeld* [1980] 1 W.L.R. 1182.
[65] See *post*, p. 462.
[66] See *post*, p. 479.
[67] s.35(6).

incapable, has not acted, is outside England and Wales, or cannot be found.[68]

11. *Mortmain*

The law of mortmain was belatedly repealed by the Charities Act 1960.[69] This law, going back as far as the thirteenth century, prevented corporations holding land without a licence from the Crown. Its purpose was to prevent land being tied up in the dead hand (mortmain) of such artificial persons and it was aimed particularly at ecclesiastical corporations. It had as its underlying purpose the protection of the feudal revenues of the Crown and other feudal lords. The law was extended to gifts to charity by the Charitable Uses Act 1735. This Act, as well as the old law, was re-enacted by the Mortmain and Charitable Uses Act 1888. One of the principal provisions relating to charity in this Act was to require enrolment of every assurance of land in the Central Office of the Supreme Court. This Act was later replaced by section 29(4) of the Settled Land Act 1925, which required, in place of this, the recording of any such assurance with the Charity Commissioners. This subsection was in turn repealed and replaced, so far as educational charities were concerned, by section 87(2) of the Education Act 1944, which required assurances of land to be recorded with the Minister of Education.

The registration provisions of what is now the Charities Act 1993 have rendered recording unnecessary. But since the whole of the law of mortmain has been abolished, it is not only the field of charity that is affected but the law generally. Moreover, the repeal is retrospective so that the title to property will not be defeated by failure to comply with the Mortmain Acts in the past.[70]

12. *Enforcement of Charitable Trusts*[71]

The Crown has the function of enforcing charitable trusts as *parens patriae*, and the Attorney-General, on behalf of the Crown, will be joined as a party to any proceedings involving charity. However, proceedings may be taken with reference to a charity, not only by the Attorney-General, but also by the charity, by any of the charity trustees, or by any persons interested in the charity, or, if it is a local charity, by any two or more inhabitants of the area of the charity,[72] but not where there is a *bona fide* dispute as to the existence of a charity; if there is such a dispute the Attorney-General should bring the action.[73] All such persons, other than the Attorney-General, must first obtain an order from the Charity Commissioners or the court authorising the institution of proceedings.[74]

---

[68] Charities Act 1993, s.18.
[69] s.38 & Sched. 7, Pt II.
[70] That is before July 29, 1960; s.38(2).
[71] For personal liability of charity trustees, see Hawkins (1979) 75 L.Q.R. 99.
[72] Charities Act 1993, s.33(1).
[73] *Re Belling* [1967] Ch. 425; *Hauxwell v. Barton-upon-Humber U.D.C.* [1974] Ch. 432; *Childs v. Att.-Gen.* [1973] 1 W.L.R. 497.
[74] Charities Act 1993, s.33(2).

CHAPTER 12[1]

PENSION TRUSTS[2]

ONE of the most important purposes for which trusts are employed today is to provide pensions for retired persons and their dependants. Since the Second World War, pension schemes have become increasingly important and are now regarded as an essential part of virtually every contract of employment and an important factor for the self-employed. At the end of 1995, about 11 million employed persons, almost half the national work force, were members of pensions schemes by virtue of their employment; additionally, personal pension schemes had been taken out by about 5 million persons, either the self-employed or employees "topping-up" the pension arising out of their employment. Quite apart from the social significance of pension provision, which is likely to become even more important in the light of the declared policy of the present government to move towards an increasing dependance on private rather than state pensions, the net value of the investment assets of pension schemes was at that time of the order of £500 billion and growing, thus constituting a substantial proportion of the available investment capital of the country.

Pension funds provided for employees are, in the vast majority of cases, held by trustees with the objective, usually but sadly not always[3] achieved, of assuring the employee that his pension will in fact be forthcoming on his retirement and that in the meantime his employer cannot in any way dispose of the pension contributions which have been made; this objective

---

[1] The author of this edition would like to acknowledge the great assistance which he has derived in the preparation of this new Chapter from the unpublished papers presented to the Chancery Bar Association in January 1998 by Sir Robert Walker, Dr Julian Farrand (the Pensions Ombudsman), Mark Herbert, Q.C., Christopher Nugee, Q.C. and John Stephens.

[2] Pensions law is considered in detail in Tolley's *Pensions Handbook* (2nd ed., 1995). More detailed still are the two looseleaf practitioner works: Ellison, *Pensions Law & Practice* and Inglis-Jones and Hand, *The Law of Occupational Pension Schemes*. The immense quantity of Statutes, Statutory Instruments, and announcements by the Inland Revenue and the Occupational Pensions Regulatory Authority may be found in the looseleaf *NAPF Pensions Legislation Service*. A useful summary of pensions law as it existed prior to the Pensions Act 1995 and the recommendations which led to that legislation may be found in Pension Law Reform: Pension Law Review Committee Report (1993) Cmnd. 2342.

[3] The systematic looting by the late Robert Maxwell of about £450 million from the pension fund established to provide pensions for ex-employees of *The Daily Mirror* caused great concern among employees in general; pension fund administration then became the subject of a Committee of Inquiry, the Pensions Law Reform Committee, which reported in the autumn of 1993 (Pension Law Reform: [1993] Cmnd. 2342, generally known as "the Goode Report") and came down on the side of continuing to utilise the trust vehicle. However, the Committee proposed a substantial number of reforms, some of which were enacted in the Pensions Act 1995 (see R. Nobles (1996) 59 M.L.R. 241).

has, at least in principle, been considerably enhanced by the recently enacted requirement that one-third of the trustees (or, where the trustee is a trust company, its directors) must be nominated by the employees.[4] The funds contributed to personal pension schemes by both the self-employed and by employees are typically paid to insurance companies for investment in insurance policies but can also be held in the form of investments by trustees, in such cases usually trust corporations. The fact that virtually every single leading decision in the last decade on the basic principles of trust law has involved a pension fund in one way or another demonstrates that litigation involving pension trusts has proliferated; it also means that a basic knowledge of the working of pension trusts is now essential for every trust lawyer.

I. THE NATURE OF PENSION SCHEMES

This Chapter is entirely concerned with pension schemes provided as part of a contract of employment, technically known as *occupational pension schemes* and, more specifically, with those schemes in which payments are made to trustees to be invested and in due course used for the provision of benefits for the employees; such schemes may be either contributory, in which case both employer and employee pay into the fund, or non-contributory, in which case the whole of the necessary funding is provided by the employer. Only occupational pension schemes are likely to give rise to litigation between the members and the trustees susceptible of affecting the basic principles of trust law. Even where the funds invested in a personal pension scheme are vested in trustees rather than, as is more usual, in insurance policies, there is no likelihood of any litigation of this type simply because the membership of the scheme is confined to the contributor and his dependants. Both occupational pension schemes and personal pension schemes are, of course, superimposed on the basic old age pension provided by the State, although the relative importance of the latter is likely to diminish in the light of the declared policy of the present government to decrease dependence thereon. The way in which the State pension is calculated is relevant to the way in which occupational pension schemes work (and in particular the terminology employed in its calculation is often utilised in judgments); a brief consideration of this question is therefore necessary.

1. *The State Pension*

The provision made by the State pension scheme for employees (Category A pensions) comprises a basic pension[5] and an additional element, related to the employee's earnings (this is generally described by reference to the acronym SERPS). SERPS apply only to earnings between the lower and

---

[4] Pensions Act 1995, ss.16–21. Unfortunately, this rule only operates where the employer cannot persuade the members to accept alternative arrangements more favourable to himself.
[5] In the year 1998–1999, £103.40 per week for married couples, £64.70 per week for single persons.

upper limits in respect of which National Insurance Contributions are pay-able[5a]; these earnings are revalued each year to take account of inflation during the period prior to retirement.[6] For a person retiring before the end of the tax year 1998–99, his earnings during his 20 best years are averaged and 25 per cent of that amount is taken into account; for a person retiring thereafter, his earnings are averaged over his entire working life and the percentage taken into account will be reduced by $\frac{1}{2}$ per cent each year until it reaches 20 per cent (these two changes[7] have of course substantially reduced the value of the SERPS element). In all cases, a pension of one-eightieth of the amount taken into account is paid for each year of the person's working life up to a maximum of forty-eightieths. The State also provides the same two elements by way of pension to the widow or wid-ower of a deceased employee (Category B pensions) if the former's own State pension entitlement is lower.[8] All these pensions are increased annually in line with the Retail Prices Index.

The two elements of the State pension are payable whether or not the person in question is a member of a private pension scheme. However, it is possible for an occupational pension scheme to contract out of SERPS; this means that its members agree not to take the SERPS element of their pension from the State and the private pension scheme then has to meet that liability instead. Financial incentives are provided to encourage contracting out in the form of reduced National Insurance Contributions by both employers and employees. Where the members of a scheme have elected to contract out, it is obviously essential that the pension provided to each member on retirement is at least as much as he would have obtained by way of the SERPS element. For service prior to the tax year 1997–98, this amount was known as the guaranteed minimum pension (GMP) and was calculated by a formula similar, but not actually identical, to that by which the SERPS element itself is calculated. During this period, it was possible for schemes to cease to be contracted out, in which case its members had to be bought back into the SERPS scheme by the payment of what were known as "state scheme premiums".[9] Schemes which contracted out in or after the tax year 1997–98 (schemes which had already done so were obliged to re-elect so to

---

[5a] In the year 1998–1999, the lower limit was £3,228 per annum and the upper limit was £25,220 per annum.
[6] Until the Pensions Act 1995, the revaluation was of all earnings below the upper limit and, when the entire income was totalled and averaged on retirement, the amount of the lower limit in the last complete tax year prior to retirement was deducted. Now only the earnings between the lower and upper limits are revalued, totalled and averaged so there is no need for any deduction; because changes in the lower limit are based on prices not earnings, this change provides a reduction in the value of the SERPS element additional to those already brought into effect (see the text to the next footnote).
[7] Made by the Social Security Act 1986, s.18. A further reduction in the value of the SERPS element has been made by the Pensions Act 1995 (see the previous footnote).
[8] The State also provides non-contributory pensions to persons who retired before the State scheme started (Category C pensions) or are over 80, satisfy certain residence conditions, and have no other category of State pension (Category D pensions).
[9] Where a member leaves a contracted out scheme prior to retirement, the pension to which he remains entitled to obtain on his retirement will include his GMP element, which will continue to grow by virtue of the process of revaluation. Originally only the GMP element of his pension was revalued (thereby gradually consuming any additional pension to which he was entitled) but by what is known as "anti-franking legislation", any excess in his pension

do) have instead to meet a statutory standard (accumulated GMPs survive) and it is no longer possible to contract back into the SERPS scheme. The statutory benefits in respect of each year worked are basically one-eightieth of 90 per cent of the average earnings between the lower and upper limits in respect of which National Insurance Contributions are payable during the three years prior to termination of service, together with a spouse's pension of one-half, revaluation of the pension payable during any further period up to actual retirement, and limited indexation of pensions in payment.

2. *Occupational Pension Schemes*

It should first be noted that no employer is under any legal obligation whatever to make any provision for his employees by way of pension.[10] Employers who provide no pension benefits simply pay National Insurance Contributions at the higher contracted in rate so that the employees will receive both the basic and the SERPS elements of the State pension when they retire (at present at 65 in the case of a male and at 60 in the case of a female but the latter age is to be raised to 65 gradually over a 10 year period commencing on April 6, 2010). Given the low level of pension produced by SERPS, most employees in this position need to give serious consideration to taking out a private pension scheme.

(A) Types of Schemes
Of the various types of occupational pension schemes which exist, this Chapter is only concerned with those occupational pension schemes in which employees and/or employers make payments to trustees to be invested in assets which will provide the payment of the benefits for which the scheme provides as they fall due. Brief mention should, however, be made of some of the other types of schemes.

The majority of schemes for employees in the public sector (the best example is the civil service) are established by legislation and are therefore backed by the revenue of the Government rather than by a segregated trust fund; in such circumstances, the employees have to rely on the certainty of the continuity of Government revenue to meet its statutory obligations rather than the performance of any fund.

Some non-statutory schemes are also, in the same sense, unfunded in that the employer does not segregate any assets for the purpose of providing for

---

over his GMP element was first preserved and eventually made subject to revaluation itself (see Pension Schemes Act 1993, ss.87–92, 83–86 respectively). However, a member who leaves an occupational pension scheme is now entitled to transfer his pension rights to any other approved pension scheme which he joins (Pension Schemes Act 1993, Pt IV; Pensions Act 1995, s.95); if he chooses to do so, the sum transferred to his new scheme in respect of his accrued pension entitlements must include the GMP (or current equivalent) element of that entitlement.

[10] In *Warrener v. Walden Engineering* (1993) Employment Appeal Tribunal Case No. 104/92 this was even held to be the case where an employer took over both a business and employees of its former owner who were previously provided with pension benefits which he had not specifically contracted to continue to provide; however, it is thought that, if this question is referred to the European Court of Justice, that court may well revert to the previous view that the Protection of Employment (Transfer of Undertakings) Regulations 1981 require the employer to continue to provide the same benefits.

the payment of the benefits as they fall due (such schemes are known as "pay-as-you-go" schemes and are necessarily non-contributory). Employer and employees have to rely on the employer still having sufficient assets to fund the appropriate benefits at the appropriate time. The employees would certainly be most ill-advised so to rely in the case of a trading company, which could simply become insolvent or sell its business to a third party who was not bound by the contracts of employment in question; and the employer could find himself with the need to make a substantial payment before he expected to have to do so if any employee who left before retirement exercised his statutory right to an immediate cash transfer of the value of his accrued benefits to another pension scheme.[11] Further, such schemes do not enjoy any of the taxation benefits of funded schemes so the employer will need to be satisfied that the net return which he can receive by leaving in his business the funds which would otherwise have provided the pension contributions will be at least as much as the gross returns which would be obtained by investing them in a funded scheme. However, employers such as the owners of large historic landed estates which they are in practice incapable of selling could certainly run "pay-as-you-go" schemes; their employees would presumably be content to rely on the underlying value of the estates in question while the benefits payable by way of pensions and lump sums in any one year could be charged by the employer as trading expenses against the income of the estate.

Even within the vast majority of private pension schemes which are funded by the segregation of assets in the hands of trustees, many of the smaller schemes operate as insured schemes, under which the trustees take out a contract with an insurance company in respect of each employee to provide the benefits which he has contracted to receive and use the pension contributions merely to pay the premiums on the policy; in such schemes, assuming that the policies in question provide whatever cover is appropriate from time to time, the only question which the trustees ever have to consider is whether the contributions are sufficient to pay the premiums.

(B) Funded Schemes

The remaining schemes, where the trustees place the contributions paid to them in a fund which they then invest in order to provide in advance for the payment of pensions as they fall due, are known as funded schemes. They pose rather more problems.

Most schemes of this type are associated with groups of trading companies or a single trading company, where membership is dependent on being an employee of a company within the scheme. However, there are also what are known as "industry-wide" schemes, in which the definition of membership is by reference to employment in the industry, rather than by any particular employee—an example is the Merchant Navy Pension Scheme. One of the many ways in which schemes are classified is into

---

[11] Pension Schemes Act 1993, Pt IV; Pensions Act 1995, s.95. The sum transferred to the new scheme in respect of any member's accrued pension entitlements must include the GMP (or current equivalent) element of that entitlement.

"defined benefit" and "defined contribution" schemes. Both may be either contributory or non-contributory.

(1) "Defined benefit" schemes

A "defined benefit" scheme provides benefit in accordance with length of service and salary. Such schemes are normally now contributory (except in the case of relatively low paid employment) and are usually on a "balance of cost" basis; the employee makes a fixed contribution of an established percentage of his salary and the employer has to make whatever contributions are from time to time actuarially necessary to provide the benefits for which the scheme is potentially liable as they fall due. In this type of scheme, it is the employer rather than the employee who runs the risk of a poor investment performance. The Pensions Act 1995 introduced a "minimum funding requirement" (MFR)[12] by virtue of which periodic actuarial valuations must be obtained in order to determine whether the assets are sufficient to fund the minimum liabilities of the scheme; if they are not, the employer must eliminate the shortfall, within one year if it is greater than 10 per cent, within five years if it is less. On the other hand, a good investment performance may enable the employer to take what is known as a "contributions holiday" by ceasing to pay any contributions whatever until an established surplus in the fund has been used up.

The most usual type of scheme is a "final salary" scheme but there are variants, of which the most common is the highest salary in the last three (or five) years of employment prior to retirement (however, not all the payments received by the employee will necessarily qualify; allowances and bonuses are generally not pensionable, which means that they are excluded). The benefits provided by the scheme are determined, subject to limits imposed by the Inland Revenue as a condition of approval of the scheme, by length of service; a fairly standard percentage is one-sixtieth for each year of service, although many quasi-public employees, such as university lecturers, who have their own separately funded schemes, only receive a much more miserly one-eightieth for each year of service.

The benefits provided always include an annuity of the appropriate percentage of the relevant salary, usually guaranteed for five years (which means that the balance is payable to the pensioner's estate if he dies during this period). They also have to include (since 1973)[13] preservation rights, that is to say the right to what is known as a "deferred pension" by means of which the accumulated pension rights of any employee who leaves prior to retirement age are preserved and enhanced by revaluation and (since 1978),[14] in the case of contracted-out schemes, provision for the payment in priority to all other liabilities of the scheme of whatever is from time to time regarded as the equivalent of the SERPS element of the State pension. The package of benefits usually also includes some or all of the following: an option to commute part of the annuity for the immediate payment of a lump

---

[12] ss.56–59.
[13] By virtue of Social Security Act 1973, now Pension Schemes Act 1993, ss.93–101.
[14] Social Security Pensions Act 1975, introducing SERPS and (for "defined benefit" schemes) contracting-out of SERPS with effect from April 1978; now Pensions Schemes Act 1993, s.14.

sum—the annuity is then reduced by reference to a formula; an annuity, usually between a half and two-thirds of the pensioner's annuity, for a surviving widow (sometimes also extended to widowers) and/or any dependent children; and a death in service benefit, a lump sum which the trustees have the discretion to distribute, sometimes with a right of nomination for the member.[15] All pensions in payment are now subject to "limited prices indexation" (LPI), in that they are required to increase in line with the retail prices index or (if less) by 5 per cent per annum.[16]

(2) "Defined contribution" schemes

A "defined contribution" scheme is also known as a "money purchase" scheme. Such schemes are, usually, but not necessarily, contributory. The contributions made to the scheme are invested by the trustees and held by them for each member of the scheme and his dependants. Each member has in effect his own notional sub-fund comprising the contributions made by or on his behalf and the value of his benefits depends entirely on his share of the net return made by the investments in which the trustees invest the fund; his position is not unlike that of the holder of units in a unit trust. In such schemes, it is consequently the employee, not the employer, who assumes the risk of a poor investment performance. For this reason, the minimum funding requirement introduced by the Pensions Act 1995 does not apply to "defined contribution" schemes. Schemes of this type have therefore become rather more popular for new schemes than they were prior to this legislation, when "final salary" schemes predominated.

On retirement, or death in service, the notional sub-fund is realised and used to purchase an annuity, usually index linked, for the benefit of the member and his dependants and to provide whatever other benefits are envisaged by the scheme (such as the right to commutation of part of the annuity for the payment of an immediate lump sum). The payments of the annuity are also now subject to limited price indexation and so must increase in line with the retail prices index or (if less) by 5 per cent per annum; the difference, of course, is that the employer is not obliged to pay for these increases which must therefore be borne in mind when the annuity is being purchased.

(C) Fiscal Regulation

Substantial fiscal benefits are available to schemes which the Inland Revenue recognises as "exempt approved schemes"[17]; such recognition and all other matters relating to the taxation of pension schemes are dealt with by a branch of the Inland Revenue now called the Pension Schemes Office. The main criteria are the Inland Revenue limits on benefits and, to a lesser extent, on contributions. Pension payments are limited to two-thirds of

---

[15] See Inheritance Tax Act 1984, s.151(5); in *Wild v. Smith* [1996] O.P.L.R. 129, Carnwath J. upheld the ruling of the Pensions Ombudsman that the member in question had not validly nominated his mistress as a dependant.

[16] Pensions Act 1995, s.51. The introduction of this requirement obviously makes more onerous the minimum funding requirement introduced by the same legislation.

[17] Under Income and Corporation Taxes Act 1988, ss.590–612. Approval is mandatory if the scheme fulfils the conditions in s.590, while discretionary approval can be granted under s.591 (the criteria are set out in the Inland Revenue "Practice Notes" IR12 (1991)).

"final salary"; in the case of employees joining after March 1987, only after 20 years' service (with the appropriate number of thirtieths until then),[18] with an upper index linked limit for those joining after May 1989 of (in 1998) £84,000 per annum. Lump sum payments are limited to 150 per cent of "final salary" (or, for those joining after March 1987, £100,000 if less) and only then after 20 years' service (with the appropriate number of three-eightieths until then) with further restrictions to 225 per cent of the initial annuity for those joining after May 1989. Death in service lump sum benefits are limited to four times the amount of remuneration at the time of death plus the return of all contributions paid with interest. A widow's (or, where relevant, widower's) pension is limited to two-thirds of the maximum pension payable. Finally, an employee's total contributions are limited to 15 per cent of his pensionable earnings.

Under an "exempt approved scheme", the contributions of the employer are treated as trading expenses and thus are exempt from both income and corporation tax, while the employee is exempt from income tax both on his own contributions and on those of the employer. Lump sum payments are tax free in the hands of a pensioner, although his pension payments will be subject to income tax at his marginal rate. An approved funded scheme is liable neither to income tax nor to capital gains tax on its investments; however, the benefit of the income tax exemption was substantially reduced in 1998 when the exemption from the 20 per cent tax retained by companies on their dividends was removed. An approved insured scheme is entitled to equivalent benefits.

Approval is available both to all types of funded schemes and to insured schemes. There also seems no reason why the Inland Revenue should not in its discretion approve "pay-as-you-go" schemes if satisfied with their underlying assets and their limits on benefits; this would enable lump sum payments made under such schemes to be tax free in the hands of their beneficiaries.

However, approval will be withdrawn, with extremely adverse retrospective fiscal consequences, in the event that an approved scheme is found to have an excessive surplus of assets over liabilities which is not brought within the statutory limit of 105 per cent.[19] All schemes must have an actuarial valuation at least every three years. However, in calculating the "statutory surplus", assets and liabilities have to be valued using prescribed actuarial assumptions which are generally regarded as rather "conservative". Consequently, it is perfectly possible for there to be a substantial surplus in the fund when it is valued in accordance with the actuary's normal assumptions and criteria but no statutory surplus at all. The way in which surpluses are eradicated is one of the most conflictive questions and consequently the most litigated issue in contemporary pension law and will be the subject of specific consideration later in this Chapter.[20]

---

[18] Employees who joined before March 1987 reached the two-thirds limit after 10 years service but until then could have only the appropriate number of sixtieths.

[19] Income and Corporation Taxes Act 1988, Sched. 22; Pension Scheme Surpluses (Valuation) Regulations 1987 (S.I. 1987 No. 412), referring to the previous legislation in Finance Act 1986, Sched. 12.

[20] See *post*, p. 458.

(D) Non-Fiscal Regulation

A considerable quantity of non-fiscal regulation is provided by the statutory provisions which have already been considered relating to preservation values, transfer values, contracting out, limited pricing indexation, and the minimum funding requirement. Further regulation has been provided by the decisions of the European Court of Justice relating to aspects of sex discrimination, where it has been held to be discriminatory to confer pension entitlements on women at any earlier age than on men,[21] and relating to part-time employees.[22] A number of the other provisions of the Pensions Act 1995 which are discussed in the course of this Chapter have also provided such regulation.

A quite different form of non-fiscal regulation is provided by tribunals. There are two tribunals specifically dealing with pension schemes: first, the Occupational Pensions Regulatory Authority (OPRA), set up by the Pensions Act 1995[23] in substitution for the previous Occupational Pensions Board; and, secondly, the Pensions Ombudsman, a one man tribunal originally created in 1990 which is now regulated by the Pension Services Act 1993[24] as amended by the Pensions Act 1995.[25] Additionally, there are a number of investment and financial regulatory bodies which are the appropriate tribunals for the investigation of matters such as complaints about the selling of personal pension schemes, which have been very frequent in recent years; such complaints should in the first instance be made to The Personal Investment Authority.

OPRA is the body primarily charged with the investigation of any complaint or dispute concerning non-compliance with the statutory rules relating to the requirement for member nominated trustees, the payment of surplus or excess assets to the employer, the restrictions on employer related investments, the requirements to appoint professional advisers and to keep books and records, the minimum funding requirements and schedules of contributions thereto, and the requirement for "money purchase schemes" to keep schedules of payment. Once called in, OPRA has considerable powers, including the power to remove trustees from office, to impose fines and civil penalties for breach of statutory duty, and to wind up a scheme where it feels that this is in the interests of the members as a whole; however, it cannot otherwise order the payment of compensation for the benefit of the members of the scheme. Nor is it authorised to investigate breaches of the equal treatment or indexation provisions or breaches of the general law of trusts. These excluded matters can only be dealt with by a complaint to the Pensions Ombudsman or by proceedings in the High Court.

The Pensions Ombudsman has no jurisdiction to deal with any of the matters with whose investigation OPRA is primarily charged. His jurisdiction is instead to investigate complaints made against past or present trustees, managers and employers that maladministration of their pension

---

[21] *Barber v. Royal Exchange Assurance Group* [1991] 1 Q.B. 344; *Coloroll Pension Trustees v. Russell* [1995] I.C.R. 179.

[22] A decision on this question is awaited at the time of writing.

[23] ss.1–15.

[24] ss.145–152.

[25] Which amends the relevant sections of the 1993 Act.

scheme has caused injustice to a member or deferred member[26] of that scheme or the widow, widower or surviving dependant of such a person. This original jurisdiction has now been extended to cover complaints by trustees of one pension scheme about the trustees of another scheme and complaints by the employers and trustees of a scheme about one another. Maladministration for this purpose has been said to involve "bias, neglect, inattention, delay, incompetence, ineptitude, perversity, turpitude, arbitrariness and so on".[27] Only this will do; it was held in *Hillsdown Holdings v. Pensions Ombudsman*[28] that he cannot investigate breaches of trust unless they involve one of these types of act or omission. The essence of the complaint has to be that the complainant not only disagrees with the decision which has been made but also has reason to believe that it was not properly made or implemented. The Pensions Ombudsman also has jurisdiction to investigate and determine disputes of fact of law which arise incidentally to a complaint of maladministration. Appeal from his determinations on a point of law now lies to the Chancery Division of the High Court.[29] There have been a large number of such appeals[30] and a number of doubts still remain as to the extent of his jurisdiction. He can clearly direct apologies, order the holding of another meeting or election, and award compensation for financial loss. On the other hand, it was held in *Edge v. Pensions Ombudsman*[31] that, where the act of maladministration consists of a breach of trust, he cannot order any remedy which could not have been ordered by the High Court. Whether he can order compensation of types which could not have been ordered by the High Court is less clear, having been in issue but not finally decided in *Westminster City Council v. Hayward*.[32] Doubts have also been expressed[33] as to whether his jurisdiction extends to claims in tort. These and other aspects of the jurisdiction of the Pensions Ombudsman will doubtless be clarified in due course; in the meantime, both

---

[26] A former member of the scheme who left his employment before reaching retirement age and has still not done so.

[27] This is the famous "[Richard] Crossman Catalogue" of what constitutes maladministration.

[28] [1997] 1 All E.R. 862 at 884.

[29] Formerly it was to the Crown Office List of the Queen's Bench Division.

[30] 83 at the time of writing, all except two against the Pensions Ombudsman. He is an automatic party to appeals against his own adjudications; his right to appear if he so chooses to defend his own adjudication as a kind of *amicus curiae* was confirmed by Turner J. in the first appeal brought against an adjudication, *Dolphin Packaging Materials v. Pensions Ombudsman* (1993), unreported. He also appears to be entitled to appeal to the Court of Appeal against any reversal of his original adjudication by the High Court; his right to do so was challenged unsuccessfully in an unreported interlocutory hearing in the Court of Appeal in *Miller v. Stapleton* (1996) (the decision at first instance is reported at [1996] 2 All E.R. 449—the substantive appeal was later abandoned) but in view of the comments made by Peter Gibson L.J. on that occasion is likely to be the subject of further challenge in the future.

[31] (1997), *The Times*, December 12, 1997.

[32] A jurisdiction to award compensation for distress was upheld in the High Court by Robert Walker J. at [1996] 3 W.L.R. 563 (his decision was subsequently followed by Carnwath J. in *Wild v. Smith* [1996] O.P.L.R. 129 contrary to the latter's own earlier decision in *Miller v. Stapleton* [1996] 2 All E.R. 449). However, this specific issue was not considered by the Court of Appeal at [1997] 3 W.L.R. 641 although Millett L.J. made some general observations about the jurisdiction of the Pensions Ombudsman. Also in issue is his jurisdiction to award compensation for delay and for inconvenience.

[33] In *NHS Pensions Agency v. Beechier* [1997] P.L.R. 95.

the outcome of proceedings before him and the fate of his adjudications on appeal remain somewhat uncertain.

II. SPECIAL FEATURES OF PENSION TRUSTS[34]

A pension trust has all the characteristics of a private trust, the employer being the settlor, the trustees being the trustees, and the members of the scheme and their dependants being the beneficiaries. There are further parallels with private trusts in that the remedies of a member are those of a beneficiary enforceable in equity against the trustees—there is no need for privity of contract—and in that the trustees have duties in relation to matters such as investment and discretionary powers which they can exercise. However, these similarities with private trusts are in many ways less important than the differences; there is almost invariably an underlying contract of employment whose existence affects the construction of the trust documents and almost every aspect of the parallels between employer as settlor and member as beneficiary needs qualification. These differences are revealed, above all, when any question arises as to the destination of surplus.

1. *The Position of the Employer*

Because of the absence of any obligation on employers to make any provision for their employees by way of pension, the decision to set up a pension scheme is necessarily that of the employer. It will initiate the necessary discussions with its employees and give instructions and provide the finance for the preparation of the necessary documentation.[35] It will also provide the (usually nominal) initial trust property. This clearly makes it the settlor. However, unlike the settlor of a private trust, the employer will inevitably have a continuing obligation to make financial contributions to the scheme for so long as it continues to have employees who are members.

The employer may well also be the trustee of the scheme or appoint the members of its board of directors as the trustees or, in the not infrequent case

---

[34] See Sir Robert Walker, writing extra-judicially, in *Trends in Contemporary Trust Law* (ed. Oakley, 1996), p. 123.

[35] Pension scheme documentation tends to be bulky. Because of the need for Inland Revenue approval, schemes tend to be created by an Interim Deed, which identifies the employer(s), the trustees, and the criteria for membership and also deals with contracting-out and priorities on the winding-up of the scheme. Following approval, this Interim Deed is replaced by a Definitive Deed, often containing little more than the appointment of the trustees and a power of amendment, to which extremely detailed Rules are appended; these set out the nature of the benefits provided, the rules as to contributions and transfers into and out of the scheme, and provisions relating to contracting-out, administrative powers, and the events which will trigger and the priorities on winding-up. The Deed and the Rules tend to be the subject of frequent amendment, usually in the form of an updated version of both incorporating all the amendments to date. An important role can also be played by the announcements and booklets issued to the members by the employer or the trustees; these have been known to give rise to an estoppel by convention even when they are not actually consistent with the Deed and Rules—see *Icarus (Hertford) v. Driscoll* [1990] P.L.R. 1; *ITN v. Ward* [1997] P.L.R. 131. Other scheme documentation includes the scheme accounts and the actuarial reports and three-yearly valuations.

where the trustee is a separate company, appoint its own directors as directors of the trustee company—small schemes almost invariably follow one of these practices, although it is now in principle necessary for at least one-third of the trustees to be nominated by the members of the scheme.[36] In any event the scheme will unquestionably vest powers in the employer. Some of these powers will clearly be fiduciary in the full sense of the term—an example is powers of the type considered in *Mettoy Pension Trustees v. Evans*[37] to appoint any surplus in the pension fund, which in that case was vested in a separate trustee company. Even where such powers are not actually fiduciary, the employer will nevertheless be subject to what has become known as the *"Imperial"* obligation of good faith,[38] by virtue of which a power cannot be exercised in such a way that it seriously damages the relationship of good faith between the employer and its employees and ex-employees.

Further, the employer will almost certainly also be a beneficiary of the scheme in that it is virtually bound to have a claim to at least some part of any surplus which arises while the scheme is still on-going or as a result of its being wound up.

2. The Position of the Trustees

(A) The Composition of the Trustees
As has already been seen, the employer may well also be the trustee of the scheme or appoint the members of its board of directors as the trustees or, in the not infrequent case where the trustee is a separate company, appoint its own directors as directors of the trustee company—small schemes almost invariably follow one of these practices, although it is now in principle necessary for at least one-third of the trustees to be nominated by the members of the scheme.[39] However, in the case of small self-administered schemes containing 12 or fewer members, Inland Revenue approval is dependent on there being what is known as a "pensioneer trustee",[40] a non-member of the scheme, usually a body corporate, there to protect Inland Revenue interests and to prevent the disappearance of the assets if anything goes wrong.

Further, where the employer becomes insolvent, it is the responsibility of its liquidator to ensure that there is at least one "independent trustee" and, if there is not, to appoint one[41]; this is in order to deal with conflicts of

---

[36] Pensions Act 1995, ss.16–21. Unfortunately, this rule only operates where the employer cannot persuade the members to accept alternative arrangements more favourable to himself.
[37] [1990] 1 W.L.R. 1587; see *ante*, p. 182.
[38] Because it was laid down in *Imperial Group Pension Trust v. Imperial Tobacco* [1991] 1 W.L.R. 589.
[39] Pensions Act 1995, ss.16–21. Unfortunately, this rule only operates where the employer cannot persuade the members to accept alternative arrangements more favourable to himself.
[40] Income and Corporation Taxes Act 1988, s.591(6).
[41] Pensions Act 1995, ss.22–26.

interest which can become particularly acute on insolvency.[42] The appointment of an independent trustee does not displace the other trustees (unless the insolvent employer was the sole trustee) but all the discretionary powers conferred on the trustees (and all fiduciary powers conferred on the employer) become exercisable only by him.[43]

(B) Duties and Powers

The duties of the trustees are in principle the same as those of the trustees of any other private trust, namely to protect the trust funds and to administer them in accordance with the trusts on which they are held. In the pension trust context, the former duty is straightforward, merely obliging the trustees to ensure that the employer pays whatever contributions it is obliged to make and to inform OPRA and the members in the event of any failure to comply with the minimum funding requirement. The latter duty is complicated by a number of special factors.

The most important of these is the endemic conflicts of interest arising out of the fact that a majority of the trustees are likely to be representatives of the employer and the remainder are likely to be members (or at the very least representatives of the members) of the scheme. These conflicts of interest become particularly acute whenever it is necessary to deal with surplus, whether on the winding-up of the scheme or while it is on-going. Indeed, it has been held that no member trustee can take any benefit under any augmentation of benefits arising out of the exercise of a discretion vested in him or which he has helped to negotiate.[44] However, it does not seem that this view can possibly survive the remarks of Scott V.-C. in *Edge v. Pensions Ombudsman*,[45] where he held that it was "quite simply ridiculous" to contend that the member trustees had to be excluded from an augmentation of benefits made as the result of the exercise of their discretion as to how to deal with a surplus.

Other special factors include the fact that pension trusts are very long lasting—"exempt approved schemes" (and some others) are specifically exempted from the rule against perpetuities[46]—and the fact that pensions trusts are often extremely flexible and confer on the trustees considerable powers of amendment and augmentation of benefits. In exercising these powers, which are often exercisable by the trustees only with the prior consent of the employer, it appears that the trustees are not under any obligation to be impartial as between the different classes of beneficiaries or to adopt a starkly confrontational role with the employer or to ignore the latter's interests; all this was specifically held by Scott V.-C. in *Edge v.*

---

[42] See *Icarus (Hertford) v. Driscoll* [1990] P.L.R. 1 and *Mettoy Pensions Trustees v. Evans* [1990] 1 W.L.R. 1587, *ante*, p. 182.

[43] An independent trustee can automatically lose his independence, in which case, unless he is the sole trustee, he equally automatically ceases to be trustee even if he is unaware of the fact. See *Clark v. Hicks* [1992] P.L.R. 213.

[44] By Vinelott J. in *Re William Makin & Sons* [1993] O.P.L.R. 171 at 179 and in *British Coal Corporation v. British Coal Staff Superannuation Scheme Trustees* [1994] O.P.L.R. 51 at 62.

[45] (1997), *The Times*, December 13, 1997. See *ante*, p. 287.

[46] Pension Schemes Act 1993, s.163.

Pensions Ombudsman.[47] However, the way in which the powers are exercised must be consistent with the purposes for which they were conferred and must of course not infringe any express or implied restrictions in the trust deed or affect any accrued rights of any class of beneficiaries.[48] Further, their exercise must be in the interests of the beneficiaries when all relevant considerations, including any corresponding benefits validly demanded by the employer as a condition of its consent,[49] are taken into account.

Other standard powers of trustees are also considerably modified in the case of pension trustees. In particular, the Pensions Act 1995[50] modifies the normal investment powers of trustees.[51] The Act both confers on the trustees unrestricted powers of investment and entitles them to delegate those powers to fund managers. It requires them to have a formal statement of investment principles and puts on a statutory basis their duties to diversify, to take advice, to select suitable investments, and to consider whether to retain them. Employer-related investments are limited by statute to 5 per cent of the assets of the scheme and loans to the employer are totally prohibited.[52] Liability for any breach of the trustees' duty of care or skill in the performance of any investment function cannot be excluded.

Finally, the trustees are now required themselves to appoint their advisers, such as auditors and solicitors, in writing.[53]

(C) Recovery of Lost Funds

Where pension funds have been lost, the trustees also have a duty to seek to recover them. This is sometimes necessary because of some fairly blatant intentional breach of trust, such as over-investment in the employer or the excessive augmentation of the benefits of its directors. However, this is more likely to be necessary when a scheme is being wound up because at this point the liabilities of the scheme will for the first and only time be able to be assessed exactly. In any of these circumstances, recovery can potentially be sought from three groups of defendants: first, from past trustees; secondly, from those who have already received benefits under or from the scheme; and, thirdly, from professional advisers such as solicitors and actuaries. A case where recovery is being sought from members of all three of these groups because of alleged payments to the employer for inadequate consideration and excessive augmentation of benefits for its chairman is *H. v. J.A.P.T.*,[54] which has so far only been the subject of interlocutory proceedings.

---

[47] (1997), *The Times*, December 13, 1997. On the other hand, in *Re Courage Group's Pension Schemes* [1987] 1 W.L.R. 495, Millett J. suggested that the trustees' duty was to represent the members in any negotiation with the employer.

[48] If it does, Pensions Act 1995, s.67 will have to be complied with.

[49] Some threats by employers not to consent other than on certain terms are quite legitimate; others fall foul of the "Imperial" duty of good faith; see *ante*, n. 38.

[50] Pensions Act 1995, ss.33–36.

[51] See *post*, pp. 540 *et seq*.

[52] Pensions Act 1995, s.40.

[53] Pensions Act 1995, s.47. Previously actuaries and solicitors were generally appointed by the employer prior to the scheme being set up. Trustees now at the very least have to confirm these appointments; however, whether this will make any difference depends on the effect of the provisions of the Act relating to the appointment of trustees already considered.

[54] [1997] P.L.R. 99 (an appeal was compromised).

There are a number of difficulties about seeking recovery from past trustees. First, in the absence of fraud they are, like any other trustee,[55] likely to be protected by the trustee exemption clauses which are absolutely standard in pension trusts deeds (although, as has just been seen, these cannot cover any breach in their duty of care or skill in the performance of any investment function). Secondly, save in the case of small pension schemes, there is little likelihood that any individual trustee will be able to make up a sufficient amount of any loss to be worth suing. And, thirdly, where (as is more often than not the case) the trustee is a £100 company without a single asset, its own directors will not owe direct fiduciary duties to the members of the scheme[56] and so cannot be sued directly unless they have actually acted dishonestly and so can be held liable for "dishonest assistance".[57] However, a possibility has now been found of suing them indirectly where the conduct complained of is not dishonest but is nevertheless a breach of the fiduciary duty which as directors they owe to the corporate trustee. In *H. v. J.A.P.T.*[58] it was contended, and Lindsay J. accepted as arguable and so declined to strike out a claim, that in such circumstances the members of the scheme were entitled to argue that such rights of action as the corporate trustee had against its directors were themselves part of the property of the pension trust, thus enabling the members of the scheme to force the trustee company to sue the directors and hold the fruits of that action on trust for them. However, an appeal against his decision was compromised so it remains to be seen whether this type of claim (which Lindsay J. described as a "dog-leg claim") is indeed feasible.

Seeking recovery from a pensioner who has simply received an over-payment of his pension is in principle relatively straightforward; the over-payment can either simply be recouped out of future payments or be the subject of an action for money paid under a mistake of fact. However, the payment of a pension must amount to at least some form of representation that the recipient is entitled to it and a series of overpayments may well therefore give rise to an estoppel. Sums paid away to outsiders in breach of trust are potentially recoverable by means of either an equitable proprietary claim[59] or a claim for "knowing receipt".[60] Neither type of claim is likely to be particularly straightforward. Equitable proprietary claims depend on the ability to identify the sums paid and, quite apart from the fact that it is far from clear what categories of knowledge will actually lead to the imposition of liability for "knowing receipt", it is doubtful whether anyone other than a former trustee or the employer or their associates could be held to have any knowledge of any breach of trust at all. However, liability for "knowing receipt" was duly imposed in *Hillsdown Holdings v. Pensions Ombudsman*[61] on

---

[55] See *Armitage v. Nurse* [1998] 1 Ch. 241; see *post*, p. 699.
[56] *Bath v. Standard Land Co.* [1911] 1 Ch. 618.
[57] See *ante*, pp. 323 *et seq.*
[58] [1997] P.L.R. 99.
[59] See *post*, pp. 718 *et seq.*
[60] See *ante*, pp. 336 *et seq.*
[61] [1997] 1 All E.R. 862. An equitable proprietary claim was also held to lie against the employer as a matter of principle but no findings of fact had been made below as to what assets were still identifiable when it acquired notice of the members' adverse claim.

an employer to whom a surplus of £11 million[62] had been paid as a result of the improper use of a power.

Finally, the difficulties of successfully maintaining proceedings for professional negligence against solicitors and actuaries are well known. Where pension funds have been lost, the principal problem is usually that of showing that the advice which the scheme's professional advisers either gave or failed to give actually caused the breach of trust complained of—paradoxically, the more blatant the breach of trust, the more difficult it becomes to demonstrate a causal connection with whatever professional advice was given.

Because of these difficulties, before bringing any such proceedings the trustees will inevitably take out a summons seeking the approval of the court in advance for their expenditure of the trust funds on the costs involved; this is in order to avoid any risk of them having to pay the costs themselves if they lose. Representative beneficiaries will be joined to any such summons, which is generally known as a *Beddoe* Summons,[63] so that they can express their view as to whether the likelihood of success in the proceedings justifies the expenditure of part of what is left of the trust fund on an attempt to recover what has been lost.

3. *The Position of the Beneficiaries*

The beneficiaries of a pension trust always include at least three classes: those persons at present in pensionable employment with the employer ("members"); those persons who have been but are no longer in pensionable employment with the employer but are not yet in receipt of pensions from the scheme ("deferred members"); and those persons who have retired and are in receipt of pensions from the scheme ("pensioners"). The interests of these classes of beneficiaries are often quite different, particularly on a winding up where there is a shortfall in assets; in such circumstances, the trust deed normally provides that the pensioners are to be paid in full before the members and deferred members receive anything. Further, as has already been seen, the employer will almost certainly also be a beneficiary in that it is virtually bound to have a claim to at least some part of any surplus which arises while the scheme is still on-going or as a result of its being wound up.

The essential difference[64] between the beneficiaries of a pension scheme and the beneficiaries of a family trust is that the former will inevitably have provided consideration for their beneficial interests by virtue of the contributions paid to the scheme on their behalf. This is as much the case in a non-contributory scheme as a contributory scheme since either way the payment of the contributions will be a term of their contract of employment.

---

[62] The actual surplus disposed of was over £18 million but 40% thereof was payable (and had been paid) in tax.

[63] After the decision in *Re Beddoe* [1893] 1 Ch. 547. Such proceedings were considered in *McDonald v. Horn* [1995] 1 All E.R. 961 and *Alsop Wilkinson v. Neary* [1996] 1 W.L.R. 1220 (which did not involve a pension trust).

[64] See *Imperial Group Pension Trust v. Imperial Tobacco* [1991] 1 W.L.R. 589; *Thrells v. Lomas* [1993] 1 W.L.R. 456; *McDonald v. Horn* [1995] 1 All E.R. 961.

Thus, in the unlikely event that the pension trust does not become completely constituted, its beneficiaries will have a contractual remedy against the employer.[65] This is also the reason for the existence of the "Imperial" obligation of good faith to which reference has already been made,[66] by virtue of which the employer cannot exercise a power in such a way that it seriously damages the relationship of good faith between the employer and its employees and ex-employees.

However, this does not mean that the beneficiaries of a pension trust have any more rights than the beneficiaries of a family trust to be informed about the reasons for decisions made by the trustees as to the exercise of the discretions vested in them; this was specifically held in *Wilson v. Law Debenture Corporation*,[67] where the general rule laid down in *Re Londonderry's Settlement*[68] was applied to a pension trust. However, the beneficiaries (and prospective beneficiaries such as their spouses and dependants) do have a statutory right to see all the scheme documentation, including in particular accounts, actuarial reports and valuations, and documents relating to the minimum funding requirement.[69]

The remedies available to the beneficiaries of a pension trust against the trustees are exactly the same as those available to the beneficiaries of a family trust. Where the only dispute is as to the proper construction of the trust deed, this will normally be resolved by the trustees taking out a construction summons, effectively "friendly" litigation in which all parties' costs will be paid out of the trust fund in any event.[70] "Hostile" litigation, on the other hand, is likely to be one of two kinds of dispute: either an individual dispute, where a particular beneficiary claims not to have been properly treated, or a collective dispute, where a complaint is made on behalf of the beneficiaries as a whole or of one of the classes of beneficiaries. In the event that an individual dispute of this type comes to court (as distinct from being dealt with by whatever internal dispute resolution procedure the pension scheme in question has[71] or as a result of the intervention of the Occupational Pensions Advisory Service[72] or, where appropriate, of the Pensions Ombudsman), costs will follow the event and do not come out of the assets of the pension trust.[73] Collective disputes pose rather greater problems of costs in the event that they come to court; this is because it is likely that the employer, the trustees, and the beneficiaries, either as a whole or in distinct classes where their interests are different, will need to be separately represented and expert evidence may well be necessary as well.

---

[65] See *ante*, pp. 150 *et seq.* Such a claim was made in *Davis v. Richards & Wallington Industries* [1990] 1 W.L.R. 1511 but the trust was in fact held to be a valid executory trust (see *ante*, p. 149).

[66] Because it was laid down in *Imperial Group Pension Trust v. Imperial Tobacco* [1991] 1 W.L.R. 589.

[67] [1995] 2 All E.R. 337.

[68] [1965] Ch. 918; see *post*, p. 496.

[69] Pensions Act 1995, s.41.

[70] *Re Buckton* [1907] 2 Ch. 406.

[71] Some such procedure is now obligatory under Pensions Act 1995, s.50(1).

[72] An independent voluntary organistaion giving free help and advice to members of the public; since 1991, it has been a company limited by guarantee and is funded by grants from the Occupational Pensions Board.

[73] *McDonald v. Horn* [1995] 1 All E.R. 961 (followed in *Alsop Wilkinson v. Neary* [1996] 1 W.L.R. 1220, which did not involve a pension trust).

In such circumstances, a representative beneficiary will be appointed to represent each class of beneficiaries which has a distinct interest; such representative beneficiaries will generally be able to obtain a "pre-emptive costs order", whereby their own costs, and any costs which they may eventually be ordered to pay to any other party, will be paid out of the trust fund in any event.[74]

4. The Treatment of Surplus

It has already been seen that Inland Revenue approval of a pension scheme will be withdrawn, with extremely adverse retrospective fiscal consequences, in the event that an approved scheme is found to have an excessive surplus of assets over liabilities which is not brought within the statutory limit of 105 per cent.[75] Consequently, whenever an actuarial valuation of the fund, which has to be made at least every three years, shows a surplus in excess of this limit, steps have to be taken to eradicate it. There are basically three ways of doing so: permitting the employer to stop contributing to the scheme until the surplus is eradicated (this is known as a "contributions holiday"); transferring the whole or part of the surplus directly to the employer; and enhancing the present benefits of the pensioners and the future benefits of the members and deferred members. Only the last two of these methods are feasible in the other situation in which surplus has to be dealt with, namely when it arises as a result of winding up the scheme.

In the latter situation, trust documents which are well drawn will provide expressly what is to happen to any surplus, the possibilities being either an obligation or a power to augment benefits up to Inland Revenue limits and/or a transfer to the employer. However, since 1993, the surplus cannot be transferred to the employer until provision has been made for limited price indexation of all benefits.[76] Where the trust documents are silent, the courts have resorted to the principles of resulting trusts which have already been discussed.[77] Thus in *Davis v. Richards & Wallington Industries*[78] Scott J. envisaged[79] that such part of the surplus as was derived from the employer's contributions should be subject to a resulting trust in its favour while such part of the surplus as was derived from the employee's contributions should be held for the Crown as *bona vacantia*. However, the Pensions Act 1995 has now greatly reduced the possibility of anything passing as *bona vacantia* to the Crown by providing[80] that surplus can be returned to the employer after augmentation of all benefits up to Inland Revenue limits

---

[74] Orders of this type were made in *McDonald v. Horn* [1995] 1 All E.R. 961.

[75] Income and Corporation Taxes Act 1988, Sched. 22; Pension Scheme Surpluses (Valuation) Regulations 1987 (S.I. 1987 No. 412), referring to the previous legislation in Finance Act 1986, Sched. 12.

[76] Pension Schemes Act 1993, s.108.

[77] See *ante*, pp. 257–261.

[78] [1990] 1 W.L.R. 1511.

[79] He was considering a hypothetical surplus which would have had to be distributed had he not held the scheme in question to have been validly constituted.

[80] Pensions Act 1995, s.77.

both where the trust documents are silent in this respect and where they contain a prohibition on so doing (something which the Inland Revenue formerly required as a condition of approval).

Surpluses which arise while a scheme is still on-going have caused rather more difficulties.[81] In such circumstances, both the employer and the beneficiaries of the scheme are likely to take the view that the surplus belongs to them, the employer on the basis that the pension fund is a security provided for the protection of the beneficiaries and that it is therefore entitled to any equity in that fund, the beneficiaries on the basis that the fund constitutes part of their pay. Neither of these views constitutes the whole truth but each has a point: on the one hand, the open-ended commitment in which the employer has to make up any deficit while the scheme is on-going must give him at least some rights to any surplus; on the other hand, the beneficiaries are entitled not only to their fixed rights under the scheme but also to unquantifiable expectations of enhanced benefits. In reality, as Vinelott J. said in *Taylor v. Lucas Pensions Trust*,[82] the surplus of an occupational pension trust "does not in any intelligible sense belong to anyone".

Resolution of these necessarily conflicting points of view depends primarily on the terms of the pension trust in question. As Knox J. said in *L.R.T. Pension Fund Trustee Co. v. Hatt*,[83] quoting the words of Cooke P. in a New Zealand decision,[84] "Considerations of the merits are of little importance. What must be decisive are the terms of the trusts constituted by the particular scheme." Consequently, in any individual case what is necessary is to establish which of the possible methods of dealing with a surplus is permitted by the Definitive Deed and the Rules and, in so far as any of them is not, what is the nature and scope of any power to amend the Deed and Rules. Everything therefore depends on the terms of the scheme, properly construed, and on any statutory provisions which override them. In the latter respect, OPRA has a statutory power to override the prohibitions on the return of any surplus to the employer which are found in many older schemes because the Inland Revenue at one time required such prohibitions as a condition of approval,[85] while the Pensions Act 1995 provides that any power to return assets to the employer must be controlled by the trustees and can be exercised only if they are satisfied that this is in the interests of the beneficiaries and there has been limited price indexation of all benefits under the scheme.[86] The combination of these last two requirements means that it may still be appropriate, in the light of the facts of any particular case, for the trustees to negotiate further benefits on top of limited price indexation. But the "bottom line" provided for the first time by the Pensions Act 1995 ensures that much more intelligible advice can be given to trustees than was previously the case.

---

[81] The substantial surpluses produced during the 1980s became an important element in takeovers of the employers in question. See *Re Courage Pension Schemes* [1987] 1 W.L.R. 498.
[82] [1994] O.P.L.R. 29.
[83] [1993] P.L.R. 227.
[84] *U.E.B. Industries v. Brabant* [1991] P.L.R. 109 (Court of Appeal of New Zealand).
[85] Now in Pensions Act 1995, s.69 (first introduced in 1973).
[86] Pensions Act 1995, s.37.

III. INTERESTS UNDER PENSION TRUSTS AND THIRD PARTIES

Because the purpose of a pension scheme is to provide an income on retirement, the Pensions Act 1995 provides that accrued rights thereunder cannot, generally speaking, be dealt with by the beneficiary by way of assignment, surrender or charge[87]; this does not of course affect assignments or surrenders in favour of the beneficiary's surviving spouse and dependants after his death. However, in two situations, on bankruptcy and on divorce, third parties may wish to assert a claim to the interest of a beneficiary under a pension trust.

(A) Bankruptcy

It is not the policy of the insolvency legislation to deprive a bankrupt beneficiary of a pension scheme of the provision which he has made for his retirement and consequently the basic rule is that his accrued rights are not available to his creditors.[88] However, it would be wholly inappropriate if a beneficiary who anticipated that he was in some danger of becoming bankrupt was allowed to deprive his creditors of assets by making additional voluntary contributions to an existing occupational pension scheme. The Pensions Act 1995[89] therefore inserts into the Insolvency Act 1986 provisions[90] relating to the setting aside of contributions made within the five years immediately prior to the bankruptcy similar to the provisions which have already been considered[91] relating to the setting aside of dispositions made during the same period; the criteria is whether the contributions were excessive and unfairly prejudicial to the creditors, a question to which the intentions of the beneficiary in making them will clearly be particularly relevant.

(B) Divorce

The two most valuable assets of most married couples are likely to be their matrimonial home and their pension rights. The courts have long had an absolute discretion to vary matrimonial property rights at the termination of marriage.[92] However, accrued rights under a pension trust have only been capable of being varied by means of this discretion in the relatively rare situation where the trust in question can be held to constitute a marriage settlement. This is only likely where a private pension scheme has been set up for both spouses by one of them or by a company of which the latter is the alter ego. This was indeed what had happened in *Brooks v. Brooks*,[93] where such a settlement was found to have been created by virtue of the fact that the husband had power under a pension scheme set up for him by his company to elect to provide a pension for a spouse out of the fund; the pension trust was therefore varied to provide his wife with both an immediate pension and a deferred pension payable from the husband's death.

---

[87] Pensions Act 1995, s.91.
[88] Pensions Act 1995, s.91(3).
[89] Pensions Act 1995, s.95.
[90] Insolvency Act 1986, ss.342A, 342B, 342C.
[91] See *ante*, pp. 224–227.
[92] Under what is now Matrimonial Causes Act 1973, s.25.
[93] [1996] A.C. 375.

However, Lord Nicholls emphasised in his speech that this procedure would not work where persons other than the spouses were beneficiaries of the pension trust in question and specifically stated that legislation would be necessary to enable the courts "to split pension rights on divorce in the more usual case of a multi-member scheme where the wife has no earnings of her own from the same employer".[94] The Pensions Act 1995[95] has now inserted provisions[96] into the Matrimonial Causes Act 1973 to enable the court, when making a financial provision order, to divert all or part of the benefits (whether lump sum or periodical payments) payable to one of the former spouses under an occupational or a private pension scheme to the other former spouse as and when they become payable under the scheme. This process is known as earmarking. The Family Law Act 1996 also contains provisions envisaging a rather different process, the splitting of pensions, on divorce but their content is not yet finally determined[97] and they are unlikely to be implemented until April 2000. Precisely how these two sets of provisions will interrelate remains to be seen.

---

[94] [1996] A.C. 375 at 396.
[95] Pensions Act 1995, s.166.
[96] Matrimonial Causes Act 1973, ss.25B, 25C, 25D.
[97] The issues were set out in a White Paper published in February 1997.

CHAPTER 13

THE APPOINTMENT, RETIREMENT AND REMOVAL OF TRUSTEES

THE appointment and retirement of trustees is a matter of prime concern for everyone connected with the trust. Once the trust has been set up, the settlor, unless he has specially reserved powers to himself, will have handed to his trustees complete control over the property subject to the trust. The interest of the beneficiaries will only be adequately protected if the trustees are scrupulously honest, are prepared to give adequate time to the administration of the trust, have enough common sense and business acumen to do well with the trust property and are able to treat fairly beneficiaries whose interests possibly conflict, such as a tenant for life and his remainderman.[1] So far as the trustee himself is concerned, his appointment is not to be considered lightly. Unless there is a provision in the trust instrument to the contrary,[2] he will have to devote his time to the administration of the trust entirely without payment or other benefit. In return for his efforts, he may well receive from the beneficiaries not gratitude but bitterness[3] and, if he is not as careful as he might be and consequently makes a mistake, he may find himself liable to make good any loss out of his own pocket.[4]

I. TYPES OF TRUSTEE

1. *Ordinary Trustees*

In general, any individual, limited company or other corporation may be appointed a trustee,[5] and a limited company may act as a trustee jointly with an individual,[6] as well as with another limited company or other corpora-

---

[1] The conflict of interest between tenant for life and remainderman is explained in connection with investments, see *post*, pp. 540 *et seq.*

[2] See *post*, pp. 640 *et seq.*

[3] In *Re Londonderry's Settlement* [1965] Ch. 918, a discretionary beneficiary to whom and to whose family a total of £165,000 had been paid showed anything but gratitude to the trustees.

[4] See *post*, p. 676.

[5] See *ante*, p. 44.

[6] The Bodies Corporate (Joint Tenancy) Act 1889. See *Re Thompson's Settlement Trusts* [1905] 1 Ch. 229.

tion.[7] Except in the case of infants,[8] there is no statutory prohibition upon the appointment of any person as a trustee; however, there are some persons who, while they have the legal capacity to be trustees, may nevertheless be so undesirable as trustees that the court will remove them if they are ever appointed. A person may be undesirable in this sense either because of a defect in his character involving financial irresponsibility, as manifested by some circumstances leading to bankruptcy,[9] or by conviction of crimes involving dishonesty,[10] or because by being appointed a trustee he would be placed in a position where his interest as a beneficiary under the trust would conflict with his duty as a trustee. It appears, however, that there has been a change in attitude with regard to the appointment of a beneficiary as a trustee. In *Forster v. Abraham*,[11] in 1874, where the court upheld the appointment of the life tenant as a trustee, the general undesirability of making such appointments was stressed. By contrast, one of the fundamental bases of the Settled Land Act 1925[12] is to make the beneficiary who is a tenant for life also a trustee; Parliament has therefore given the lie to the old notions. While the appointment of a beneficiary as a sole trustee may well be undesirable, the appointment of a beneficiary as one of two or more trustees will often be advantageous, because the beneficiary will be induced to do the best he can for the trust by his financial interest in the property as well as by his duty as trustee.

Infants are in a curious position. It is clear that an infant may be a trustee. Thus in *Re Vinogradoff*[13] a woman transferred a holding of War Stock into the joint names of herself and her granddaughter, then aged four. There was no presumption of advancement[14] and the court decided that the granddaughter held that stock as a trustee on resulting trust.[15] But although an infant may be a trustee by implication or by operation of law, he cannot be expressly appointed as a trustee; section 20 of the Law of Property Act 1925 declares void the appointment of an infant as a trustee. If an infant is to be a trustee, he will therefore have to become a trustee otherwise than by express appointment.

The general principle is that an ordinary trustee is not entitled to remuneration for his services. This is considered in detail in a later Chapter.[16]

---

[7] While it has always been possible for all the original trustees to be limited companies or other corporations and for a trust corporation to be sole trustee, it is only since January 1, 1997 that it has been possible for individual trustees to retire leaving as trustees only limited companies and/or other corporations (Trusts of Land and Appointment of Trustees Act 1996, Sched. 3, para. 3(12), (13) amending Trustee Act 1925, ss.37(1)(c), 39(1)).

[8] See *post, infra*.

[9] *Re Barker's Trusts* (1875) 1 Ch.D. 43.

[10] *Coombe v. Brookes* (1871) L.R. 12 Eq. 61; *Re Forster* (1886) 55 L.T. 479; *Re Henderson* [1940] Ch. 764; see *post*, p. 475.

[11] (1874) L.R. 17 Eq. 351.

[12] s.16. No further settlements under the Settled Land Act 1925 can now be created (although existing ones continue) but that does not affect the validity of the point in the text.

[13] [1935] W.N. 68.

[14] The woman did not stand *in loco parentis* to her granddaughter.

[15] See *ante*, p. 255.

[16] See *post*, p. 640.

2. *Judicial Trustees*

A judicial trustee is a person or corporation appointed by the court to act as a trustee where it is desired that the administration of the trust shall be subject to close supervision by the court. The appointment is made under the provisions of the Judicial Trustees Act 1896 and is not to be confused with the appointment of a private trustee by the court. The appointment of a judicial trustee is generally made on the application of an existing trustee or beneficiary, but the appointment can also be made at the instance of a person who is intending to create a trust.[17] It is also possible to appoint a judicial trustee in respect of the administration of an estate. At one time, when there was no machinery by means of which a personal representative could retire, this provided a means of replacing one who was no longer able to act. However, the court can now appoint a replacement under section 50 of the Administration of Justice Act 1985. In an application under the 1985 Act, the court may proceed as if it were an application under the 1896 Act and vice versa.[18]

The distinctive feature of a judicial trustee is that the beneficiaries are protected in the event of his default by virtue of the fact that he is usually required to give security to the court for the proper performance of his duties.[19] He is subject to close supervision by the court, and special provisions govern the auditing of his accounts.[20] As a result, a judicial trustee becomes an officer of the court, so that he is able to obtain the directions of the court informally at any time.

In practice it is rare for a judicial trustee to be appointed save where complex litigation is in prospect,[21] where there has been gross mismanagement of a trust in the past, or where its admininstration involves problems of extraordinary complexity or difficulty.[22]

A judicial trustee may always charge for his services[23] and is paid from the trust funds.

3. *Trust Corporations*

(A) Definition
It has already been seen[24] that, in principle, any company as well as any individual can be appointed as a trustee. However, a company which is appointed a trustee is not necessarily a trust corporation. This term is applied to a body corporate, such as a bank or insurance company, which

---

[17] Judicial Trustees Act 1896, s.1(1).
[18] Administration of Justice Act 1985, s.50(4); Judicial Trustees Act 1896, s.1(7).
[19] Judicial Trustees Act 1896, s.4(1); Judicial Trustee Rules 1983, r.6.
[20] Judicial Trustees Act 1896, ss.1(6), 4(1); Administration of Justice Act 1982, s.57; *Re Ridsdel* [1947] Ch. 597.
[21] See *Re Diplock* [1948] Ch. 465; affirmed *sub nom. Minister of Health v. Simpson* [1951] A.C. 251.
[22] *Re Chisholm* (1898) 43 S.J. 43.
[23] Judicial Trustees Act, ss.1(5), 4(1); Judicial Trustee Rules 1983, r.11.
[24] See *ante*, p. 462.

undertakes the business of acting as a trustee and which fulfils certain conditions.[25] The basic conditions are[26]:

(i) Its constitution must authorise it to undertake the business of acting as a trustee and of acting as a personal representative.

(ii) It must have an issued capital of not less than £250,000, of which not less than £100,000 must have been paid up in cash.

(iii) The company must be incorporated either in the United Kingdom or some other European Union country.

(iv) The company must have a place of business in the United Kingdom, no matter where it is incorporated.

The second of these conditions, which was intended to afford a considerable measure of protection to beneficiaries, is now totally inadequate so to do. The value of assets in any one trust may exceed several times over the amount of the minimum required paid up capital. Furthermore, the test relates to the amount of the issued share capital of the company, not its asset value. Thus, provided that a company had actually issued shares to the extent of £250,000, it would still be eligible to be a trust corporation even if it had by some act of imprudence managed to lose all its shareholders' funds.

In addition to commercial companies which carry on the business of acting as trustees, a number of other bodies also rank as trust corporations. They are given this status so that they can take advantage of the privileges given to trust corporations.[27] The following persons and bodies are included in the definition of trust corporation:

(i) Any body corporate which is appointed by the court to be a trustee in any particular case.[28]

(ii) Certain bodies which are incorporated to act as trustees of charitable trusts.[29]

(iii) Certain public officers, such as the Public Trustee,[30] the Treasury Solicitor, and the Official Solicitor.[31]

---

[25] The path to the definition is tortuous: first, certain bodies are entitled to act as custodian trustee (see *post*, p. 467) by virtue of the Public Trustee Rules 1912, as amended; secondly, the Public Trustee Rules 1912 were made under the power conferred by the Public Trustee Act 1906; and, thirdly, s.68(18) of the Trustee Act 1925, provides that the definition of a "trust corporation" for the purposes of the Act includes any corporation entitled to act as a custodian trustee under the rules made under the Public Trustee Act 1906.

[26] The Public Trustee (Custodian Trustee) Rules 1975 (S.I. 1975 No. 1189). The rules were made to implement the EEC Council Directive 73/183/EEC.

[27] See *post*, p. 466.

[28] Trustee Act 1925, s.68(18).

[29] The incorporation must be by Special Act, or Royal Charter, or under the Charitable Trustees Incorporation Act 1872; Public Trustee Rules 1912, r.30(c), (d), as substituted.

[30] Trustee Act 1925, s.68(18). See also the Public Trustee and Administration of Funds Act 1986, which confers on the Public Trustee all the functions of the Judge of the Court of Protection under the Mental Health Act 1983, Part VII.

[31] Law of Property (Amendment) Act 1926, s.3(1).

(iv) Major local authorities[32] and certain public authorities, such as the Gas Council and Regional Hospital Boards.[33]

(B)   Ability to Act
A trust corporation can act in the administration of any trust[34] unless the trust instrument forbids its employment.

(C)   Privileges
The general principle is that, whenever statutory provisions require an act to be done by two private trustees, that act can be done by a sole trustee where that trustee is a trust corporation. It follows that the main privileges of a trust corporation are as follows:

(i) A trust corporation can by itself give a good receipt for capital money under a trust of land[35] or a settlement under the Settled Land Act 1925.[36]

(ii) A trust corporation can by itself exercise various powers of management, such as the apportionment of blended funds, accepting compositions and effecting compromises.[37]

(iii) Where a private trustee acts jointly with a trust corporation and the private trustee wishes to delegate the performance of his duties, he may delegate them to the trust corporation.[38] He cannot, however, delegate his powers to his co-trustee if the co-trustee is a private trustee.

(iv) A private trustee may be discharged without a fresh trustee being appointed in his place where a trust corporation will be left to perform the trusts.[39]

As a result of these provisions, it is common to find a trust corporation acting as the sole trustee of a trust, despite the fact that it can act jointly with a private trustee.

(D)   Remuneration
A trust corporation is generally in the same position as a private trustee[40] and is only entitled to remuneration where there is a provision to that effect in the trust instrument. In practice, therefore, a commercial body which is a trust corporation will not agree to act until arrangements are made for its

---

[32] The Public Trustee Rules 1912, r.30(g); Local Government Act 1972, s.241.
[33] The Public Trustee Rules 1912, r.30(e), (f).
[34] *Re Cherry's Trusts* [1914] 1 Ch. 83.
[35] Trustee Act 1925, s.14(2), as amended by Trusts of Land and Appointment of Trustees Act 1996 Sched. 3, para. 3(3).
[36] Settled Land Act 1925, ss.94, 95.
[37] Trustee Act 1925, s.19.
[38] Trustee Act 1925, s.25(1)(2), substituted by the Powers of Attorney Act 1971. See *post*, p. 513.
[39] See *post*, p. 484.
[40] See *post*, p. 640.

remuneration. However, where the court appoints a trust corporation to be a trustee, it may fix its remuneration.[41]

4. *The Public Trustee*

The Public Trustee is a corporation sole and was established by the Public Trustee Act 1906. His main function is to administer private trusts, particularly small trusts, although he may also be appointed a judicial[42] or custodian trustee,[43] and be appointed to administer the property of a convict.[44] His functions were extended by the Public Trustee and Administration of Funds Act 1986, which confers on him all the functions of the Judge of the Court of Protection in relation to the property and affairs of mental patients under Part VII of the Mental Health Act 1983.[45] He may not act as the trustee of a religious or charitable trust[46] and may only carry on a business owned by a trust for the purpose of winding it up.[47] Although the Public Trustee is a public officer, he can only act in the administration of any trust if he has been appointed to do so in the same way as a private individual. Also, he may refuse to accept any trust for any reason other than the smallness of the trust property. He may act either alone or jointly with other trustees. However, he is able to act alone notwithstanding any normal requirement for a plurality of trustees to act in, for example, the case of an overreaching conveyance.[48]

As he is a corporation sole, the Public Trustee never dies. This means that where he is the sole trustee, it is never necessary for there to be an appointment of new trustees. A further advantage is that if he acts improperly and loss occurs, the State makes good that loss.[49]

The Public Trustee may always charge for his services,[50] his fees being calculated not on the amount of work done but on the value of the property administered. This provision is particularly important where persons are trustees of a trust instrument which contains no charging clause. They themselves cannot derive any benefit from the trust and so may find it difficult to persuade private trustees to accept office in their stead but they can always hand their trusteeship over to the Public Trustee.

5. *Custodian Trustees*

The function of a custodian trustee, who may be the Public Trustee or any other trust corporation, is to hold the trust property, leaving the administration of the trust in the hands of managing trustees. A custodian trustee is usually appointed so that once the trust property is vested in his name, it

---

[41] Trustee Act 1925, s.42.
[42] See *ante*, p. 464.
[43] See *post, infra*.
[44] Public Trustee Act 1906, s.5.
[45] s.3.
[46] *Re Hampton* (1918) 88 L.J.Ch. 103.
[47] Public Trustee Rules 1912, r.7(1),(2).
[48] *Re Duxbury* [1995] 1 W.L.R. 425.
[49] Public Trustee Act 1906, s.7.
[50] *ibid.*, s.9, as amended by the Public Trustee (Fees) Act 1957.

will not be necessary to have any further appointment of new trustees, and so that he may have custody of the trust deeds and securities.

A custodian trustee may always charge for the services which he performs in that capacity.[51]

II. THE APPOINTMENT OF TRUSTEES

Trustees may be appointed, first, on the creation of a new trust and, secondly, during the continuance of an existing trust, whether in substitution for a trustee who is retiring or who has died, or in addition to the existing trustees. In both cases, the appointment is almost always made by deed without the court becoming involved in any way but, in exceptional cases, when there is no one else able to do so, the court can make the appointment itself. Thus both appointments made outside the court and appointments made by the court itself must be considered. In some circumstances, there are restrictions on the maximum number of trustees. It is also possible for a trustee to assume office as a result of his own conduct.

1. *Appointing the Original Trustees*

When a settlor creates a trust *inter vivos*, he will usually appoint the first trustees of the settlement himself. If he wishes to appoint people other than himself to be the trustees, he will include a clause appointing them in the original settlement or trust deed. On the other hand, he may wish to appoint himself. He may make a declaration of trust—that is, he may declare that from the time of that declaration he will hold specified property on certain trusts—and he will then be the only trustee of the trust. Or he may appoint himself and another to be the first trustees. But as soon as the trust has come into existence, the settlor will have lost his right as settlor to appoint the trustees of the settlement. He may in the trust instrument have given someone the power to nominate future trustees or he may have nominated himself[52] to do so; however, if he makes any future appointment under that power, he will do so because he is the person named in the trust instrument, not because he was the settlor.

Occasionally, there will be no trustees of a new trust. The trustees named in the settlement may be dead, or may refuse to act or the settlor may have forgotten to name any. If the trust instrument nominates someone to appoint new trustees, that power can then be used; otherwise the appointment will have to be made by the court.[53] In doing so, the court will be giving effect to the equitable maxim that "the court will not allow a trust to fail for want of a trustee".

In practice trusts arise most frequently as the result of a death. Where the deceased left a will, he may have expressly set up a trust thereby. Alternatively, a trust may arise by operation of law. Thus, if he left a legacy to a child, the money cannot actually be paid to that child until he reaches the

---

[51] Public Trustee Act 1906, s.2; see *post*, p. 648.
[52] See *post*, p. 470.
[53] *Dodkin v. Brunt* (1868) L.R. 6 Eq. 580.

age of 18 because an infant cannot give a good receipt for capital money. Until then the money will have to be held upon trust for the child. If, on the other hand, the deceased died intestate, the devolution of his property will be governed by the Administration of Estates Act 1925, as varied by subsequent statutes and statutory instruments.[54] In some circumstances, the intestate's property will have to be held on statutory trusts. For example, if the deceased was worth £200,000 and left a wife and son, the wife will be entitled to £125,000. The remaining £75,000 will be divided into two parts; one part goes to the son, and the other part is held upon trust for the wife for life, with remainder after her death to the son.[55]

It is possible where a trust is created by will to designate different persons as trustees and executors but normally the same persons are both executors and trustees. In particular, where there is no appointment of a different person as a trustee, the executor may automatically become the trustee. Whether he will in fact do so depends on the function which he is discharging at the point in time being considered. The rules which govern the time at which an executor becomes a trustee are not considered here,[56] but it is sufficient to say that the functions of an executor (or, in the case of an intestacy, an administrator) are:

(i) in the case of an executor, obtaining probate of the deceased's will or, in the case of an administrator, obtaining letters of administration of the deceased's estate;

(ii) getting in the deceased's property and the debts due to him;

(iii) paying any inheritance tax, and the deceased's debts;

(iv) paying the legacies;

(v) agreeing the distribution account with the beneficiaries; and

(vi) distributing all the property which can be immediately distributed, that is to say all the property remaining after the payment of debts and legacies, other than that which is governed by a trust or which is not immediately payable to a beneficiary because he is under 18.

When all this has been done, in general the executor or administrator ceases to be a personal representative; if there is still any of the deceased's property in his name, thenceforth he holds it as a trustee, not as a personal representative. In the case of land, however, an executor or administrator will continue to hold the property as personal representative until he assents to its vesting in himself as trustee.[57]In this case, therefore, the test is not one of function, but whether there has been the formal act of making an assent.

---

[54] Such as the Intestates Estates Act 1952, the Family Provision Act 1966, and the Inheritance (Provision for Family and Dependents) Act 1975.

[55] The wife would in addition receive the personal chattels of the deceased.

[56] See further Mellows, *The Law of Succession* (5th ed.), p. 321.

[57] *Re King's Will Trusts* [1964] Ch. 542; see *ante*, p. 28.

2. *Appointing New Trustees*

It is necessary to distinguish, on the one hand, the persons who are able to appoint new trustees and, on the other hand, the occasions on which they are able to do so.

(A) The Persons who can Appoint New Trustees

The rules relating to the appointment of new trustees are the same whether the trust was set up *inter vivos* or arose as the result of a death.

(1) The order in which the rules are applied

Where the trust instrument makes provision for the appointment of new trustees, either generally or in the specific situation which has arisen, the person or persons nominated clearly have the primary right to make any appointment. However, if reliance is placed on that power, then its terms must be strictly followed.

Where, on the other hand, the trust instrument does not make any provision for whatever situation has arisen, then new trustees may be appointed in two distinct ways which exist alongside one another. First, by virtue of the statutory power contained in section 36 of the Trustee Act 1925 (if there is a conflict between the provisions of the trust instrument and the statutory power, the statutory power prevails), the following persons in the following order have the right to appoint new trustees: the person or persons nominated in the trust instrument; the existing trustees; and the personal representatives of the last or only surviving trustees (only if there is no person in any one group or if the persons in that group refuse to appoint can an appointment be made by a person in the subsequent group). Secondly, by virtue of section 19 of the Trusts of Land and Appointment of Trustees Act 1996, where all the beneficiaries are of full age and capacity and between them absolutely entitled to the trust property, they can direct the appointment of new trustees.

Additionally, in one particular situation, where a trustee is incapable by reason of mental disorder of exercising his functions as such and there is no one able and willing to exercise the statutory power contained in section 36 of the Trustee Act 1925, then by virtue of section 20 of the Trusts of Land and Appointment of Trustees Act 1996, where all the beneficiaries are of full age and capacity and between them absolutely entitled to the trust property, they can direct his replacement.

Finally, failing all else, new trustees can be appointed by the court.

(2) Observations about the rules

The rules are applied strictly in the order set out above; thus in *Re Higginbottom*[58] the existing trustee had the power to appoint new trustees and her right to do so was held to prevail against the wishes of a large majority of the beneficiaries who sought to appoint others.[59]

---

[58] [1892] 3 Ch. 132.
[59] See also *Re Brockbank* [1948] Ch. 206.

Where an appointment is made in good faith by the person entitled, the court will not interfere with the appointment even if it would have preferred someone else to have been appointed.[60]

Where two or more persons have the power of appointing new trustees, they must exercise the power jointly unless there is a provision in the trust instrument to the contrary. If they cannot agree who the new trustee shall be, they are treated as refusing to exercise their power and so that the power to appoint becomes exercisable by the persons in the next category. Thus in *Re Sheppard's Settlement Trusts*[61] the trust instrument gave the power of appointing trustees to two persons. When they could not agree on the appointee, it was held that the power could be exercised by the continuing trustees. The position is the same if the person having the power to appoint cannot be found[62] or is incapable of making the appointment.[63]

The person who has the power of appointing new trustees may appoint a separate set of trustees for any part of the trust property which is held on trusts distinct from those on which the remainder of the trust property is held.[64] If, therefore, trustees hold three quarters of the trust fund upon trust for Andrew and his family, and one quarter for Bernard and his family, separate trustees can be appointed for the quarter held for Bernard. While, however, the appointment is valid for all purposes connected with the administration of the trust, for certain tax purposes the original trustees will continue to be regarded as trustees.[65]

(B) The Occasions on which Trustees may be Appointed

(1) By the exercise of an express power in the trust instrument

Where a person is nominated in the trust instrument,[66] whether it is the settlor, the protector of the settlement (if there is one), or anyone else, he is usually given the power to appoint new trustees in all circumstances; he may even be given power at any time to replace all the existing trustees without having to show cause. Such a power was conferred on a protector in *Von Knieriem v. Bermuda Trust Co. (the Star Trusts Case)*[67] and his exercise of it was held to have been valid even though he had apparently acted more in the interests of the settlor than of the beneficiaries; he was not obliged to state any reasons nor did there have to be any.

Where, however, a power is able to be exercised only in limited circumstances, that power is strictly construed. In *Re Wheeler*,[68] a person was nominated to appoint a new trustee in the place of any trustee who was "incapable" of acting. One trustee became bankrupt, and so became "unfit" to act[69] but not "incapable" of acting. It was held that the nominated person

---

[60] *Re Gadd* (1883) 23 Ch.D. 134; *Re Norris* (1884) 27 Ch.D. 333; *Re Sales* (1911) 55 S.J. 838.
[61] [1888] W.N. 234.
[62] *Craddock v. Witham* [1895] W.N. 75.
[63] *Re Blake* [1887] W.N. 75.
[64] Trustee Act 1925, s.37(1)(b).
[65] *Roome v. Edwards* [1982] A.C. 279.
[66] See *Re Walker and Hughes* (1883) 24 Ch.D. 698 and *Re Sheppard's Settlement Trusts* [1888] W.N. 234.
[67] (1994) Butterworths Offshore Cases and Material Vol. 1, 116. See *ante*, p. 166.
[68] [1896] 1 Ch. 315 (a case on Trustee Act 1893, s.10(1), re-enacted in Trustee Act 1925, s.36(1).
[69] As to the distinction, see *post*, p. 475.

did not have a power to appoint in those circumstances because the condition was not fulfilled.[70] Further, where a power to appoint is given jointly to two or more persons, it can only be exercised by those persons. Unless, therefore, there is evidence of a contrary intention, the power will not be exercisable at all where one of the donees of the power dies, or becomes incapable of making the appointment.[71]

Where a beneficiary is nominated in the trust instrument as having power to appoint new trustees, the power of appointment is generally treated as being detached from the beneficial interest. Thus, if the beneficiary disposes of his interest then, unless there is a provision in the trust instrument to the contrary, he will still be entitled to appoint new trustees.[72]

An illogical difference exists in respect of the appointment of a new trustee between the position where an existing trustee is retiring, and where an additional trustee is to be appointed without the retirement of an existing trustee. If he is acting solely under the statutory power,[73] a person who is nominated in the trust instrument to appoint new trustees may appoint himself to be a trustee in the place of a retiring trustee but not as an additional trustee. This results from a difference of wording in the Trustee Act. Section 36(1), which applies where a new trustee is being appointed in the place of an outgoing trustee, gives the power to the nominated person to "appoint one or more other persons (whether or not being the persons exercising the power) to be a trustee", while section 36(6), which confers the power to appoint additional trustees, gives the nominated person a power to appoint "another person or other persons to be the trustee". It is hard to imagine that this difference was intended by the legislature.

(2) By exercise of the statutory power

Section 36(1) of the Trustee Act 1925 sets out a number of circumstances in which new trustees can be appointed by anyone nominated in the trust instrument for this purpose[74] and, in default, by the surviving or continuing trustees or the personal representatives of the last surviving trustee.[75] However, it must be emphasised that this provision gives rise only to a power to appoint a new trustee and does not impose any duty so to do.

The right of a surviving or continuing trustee so to appoint under section 36(1) is, rather surprisingly, extended by virtue of section 36(8) to a trustee who has refused to act or wishes to retire if he is willing to act in exercising the powers of the section. The curious result of this is that, despite the fact that a trustee refuses to act as a trustee, or wishes to retire, he must be allowed to join in the appointment of a new trustee if he wishes to do so.

---

[70] See also *Turner v. Maule* (1850) 15 Jur. 761; *Re Watts' Settlement* (1851) 9 Hare 106; *Re May's Will Trusts* [1941] Ch. 109.

[71] *Re Harding* [1923] 1 Ch. 182.

[72] *Hardaker v. Moorhouse* (1884) 26 Ch.D. 417.

[73] *Re Power's Settlement Trust* [1951] Ch. 1074. The Law Reform Committee (23rd Report, 1982) recommended that the person having power to appoint trustees should be able to appoint himself. However, this recommendation was not put into effect by the Trusts of Land and Appointment of Trustees Act 1996.

[74] Such a person will not need to rely on the statutory power where he has been given express power to appoint in the situation which has arisen but only in other situations not expressly envisaged by his power.

[75] *Re Shafto's Trusts* (1885) 29 Ch.D. 247.

However, for the purposes of this provision, the expression "refusing or retiring trustee" is narrowly construed. In *Re Stoneham's Settlement Trusts*[76] a new trustee was appointed in the place of another trustee who had remained out of the United Kingdom for longer than 12 months, something which justifies compulsory removal from office. On his return, the displaced trustee applied to the court to upset the appointment on the ground that he had not participated in it. However, Danckwerts J. held that a trustee who is removed compulsorily from the trust is not a "refusing or retiring" trustee but a "removed" trustee, so that his participation is not necessary.

Where there are no surviving or continuing trustees and the appointment can instead be made by the personal representative of the last surviving trustee, it is necessary to distinguish, on the one hand, the power of appointment itself and, on the other hand, the method of proving entitlement to exercise that power. The executor of the last surviving trustee has the power to appoint new trustees as soon as that last trustee dies. Accordingly, it is not necessary for him to obtain a grant of probate before exercising his power to do so.[77] However, a personal representative can only actually prove his entitlement to exercise the power by producing a grant of probate or letters of administration in respect of the estate in question. This can cause problems in respect of overseas grants.

It is the general practice of the English court only to recognise grants of probate or letters of administration which have been issued in the United Kingdom or, if issued by a court overseas, have been re-sealed by a court in the United Kingdom. The point arose in *Re Crowhurst Park*.[78] In that case, the deceased was the sole trustee of various tenancies of land in England. His widow obtained a grant of probate of his will in Jersey, but she did not obtain a grant in the United Kingdom. The widow executed a deed by which, in her capacity as the personal representative of the deceased, she purported to appoint herself as the new trustee of that trust. It was held that while she was entitled to exercise the power of appointment, she could only prove that entitlement by a grant of probate or letters of administration granted in the United Kingdom. Accordingly, the widow could not take action in respect of the tenancies until she obtained a United Kingdom grant.

Although personal representatives of the last surviving trustee may therefore appoint new trustees, this is a mere power and they cannot be compelled to do so.[79] They are, however, given statutory encouragement to exercise their power. Thus, even if they intend to renounce their office as personal representatives, they are still entitled to appoint new trustees before they renounce.[80] Without the express statutory provision, the exercise of the power would be sufficient to show an acceptance of the office of personal representative.

The statutory power makes provision for the appointment of new trustees both in place of an outgoing trustee and as an additional trustee, where all

---

[76] [1953] Ch. 59.
[77] *Re Parker's Trusts* [1894] 1 Ch. 707; *Re Crowhurst Park* [1974] 1 All E.R. 991 at 1001.
[78] [1974] 1 All E.R. 991.
[79] *Re Knight's Will* (1883) 26 Ch.D. 82.
[80] Trustee Act 1925, s.36(5).

existing trustees are remaining. In both cases the appointment must be made *inter vivos*; it cannot be made by will.[81] The only formal requirement is that it should be made in writing but it is in most cases desirable that it should be made by deed.[82]

(a) Appointing a replacement for an outgoing trustee. Where an appointment is being made of a replacement for an outgoing trustee, the section applies in the case of any outgoing trustee, whether or not he was the original trustee of the trust, and whether or not he was appointed by the court. The statutory power applies in the following situations:

(i) *Where a trustee is dead.* This includes the position where a person nominated as a trustee dies without ever having taken up his office. This would be the case, for example, where a person who is nominated as the trustee of a will trust dies before the death of the testator.

(ii) *Where a trustee remains out of the United Kingdom for more than twelve months.* The residence abroad must be a continuous residence and a break for even a very short time, such as a week, will prevent this provision operating.[83] The motive for the residence is irrelevant,[84] so that even if the trustee has been imprisoned abroad, he can still be removed from his trusteeship.

In some circumstances the trust instrument modifies the statutory provision, and seeks to achieve the same broad effect by different wording. Where this is done, the provision must be carefully construed, but the courts lean towards an interpretation that the period abroad must have an element of permanence. This was satisfied in *Re Earl of Stamford*[85] where the power arose if a trustee should "be abroad", and a trustee lived in France, making only occasional visits to England.[86]

The provision can now be totally inappropriate where a foreign trust is to be established, or where an English trust is to be "exported".[87] In such cases, it is prudent to provide expressly that a trustee shall not be capable of being replaced merely because he is resident abroad.

(iii) *Where a trustee desires to be discharged.* This statutory provision is wide enough to include the position where the trustee desires to be discharged from only part of the trust.[88] This might occur where part of a trust fund is set aside to provide a life interest for a beneficiary and the trustee wishes to retire as a trustee of the main fund, while remaining a trustee of the appropriated fund.

---

[81] See *Re Parker's Trust* [1894] 1 Ch. 707.
[82] So that Trustee Act 1925, s.40 may operate; see *post*, p. 483.
[83] *Re Walker* [1910] 1 Ch. 259.
[84] *Re Stoneham* [1953] Ch. 59.
[85] [1896] 1 Ch. 288.
[86] See also *Re Moravian Society* (1858) 26 Beav. 101.
[87] See *post*, p. 760.
[88] If this statutory power is excluded, a trustee cannot be discharged from part only of the fund without the intervention of the court; *Savile v. Couper* (1887) 36 Ch.D. 520; *Re Moss's Trusts* (1888) 37 Ch.D. 513.

(iv) *Where a trustee refuses to act.* Logically, this provision should apply only to a person who has accepted the trusteeship and refuses to act after accepting office. Until that time, it is difficult to see how he could be a "trustee". However, there is old authority on the predecessor of the section to the effect that it also includes a trustee who disclaims.[89]

(v) *Where a trustee is unfit to act.* There is little authority as to the meaning of "unfitness" for the purposes of this provision but it seems clear that "unfitness" here refers not to medical infirmity but to defects of character. In the absence of authority, it is only possible to deduce the meaning of the expression from some of the circumstances in which the court will remove trustees.[90] These cases include conviction of a crime involving dishonesty[91] and in certain circumstances bankruptcy. In the case of bankruptcy the court will generally remove a trustee who has become bankrupt,[92] particularly if the beneficiaries request this to be done, if only on the ground that a person who has lost all his own money ought not to be in charge of other people's money. But as an exception to this, the court has refused to remove a trustee whose bankruptcy was due to misfortune and who was entirely free of moral blame.[93]

(vi) *Where a trustee is incapable of acting.* Incapacity here refers to physical or mental incapacity to attend, or to attend properly, to the administration of the trust.[94] Special provisions affect mental incapacity where the trustee also has a beneficial interest in the property if he is a person whose mental illness makes him subject to the provisions of the Mental Health Act 1983. In this case, no appointment of a new trustee in his place may be made without the consent of the authority having jurisdiction over him under Part VII of the Mental Health Act 1983.[95]

A person is also incapable of acting if there is any legislation in force which expressly prohibits persons in specified circumstances from holding property or acting as trustees. Such a prohibition has applied to enemy aliens in time of war.[96]

(vii) *Where a trustee is a minor.* As has been seen,[97] a minor cannot validly be expressly appointed a trustee and the provisions will only apply where the minor is a trustee under a resulting or constructive trust.

---

[89] *Noble v. Meymott* (1841) 14 Beav. 471; *Re Hadley* (1851) 5 De G. & Sm. 67; *Viscountess D'Adhemar v. Bertrand* (1865) 35 Beav. 19; *Re Birchall* (1889) 40 Ch.D. 436.

[90] See *post,* p. 486.

[91] *Turner v. Maule* (1850) 15 Jur. 761; *Re Wheeler and De Rochow* [1896] 1 Ch. 315; *Re Sichel's Settlements* [1916] 1 Ch. 358.

[92] *Re Barker's Trusts* (1875) 1 Ch.D. 43.

[93] *Re Bridgman* (1860) 1 Drew. & Sm. 164.

[94] *Re Moravian Society* (1858) 26 Beav. 101; *Re Watt's Settlement* (1872) L.R. 7 Ch. 223; *Turner v. Maule* (1850) 15 Jur. 761; *Re East* (1873) 8 Ch.App. 735; *Re Lemann's Trusts* (1883) 22 Ch.D. 633; *Re Blake* [1887] W.N. 173; *Re Weston's Trusts* [1898] W.N. 151.

[95] Mental Health Act 1983, s.148, Sched. IV, para. 4(a), replacing Mental Health Act 1959, ss.149(1), 153 & Sched. VII, which in turn replaced Trustee Act 1925, s.36(9).

[96] *Re Sichel's Settlements* [1916] 1 Ch. 358.

[97] See *ante,* p. 463.

(viii)   *Where section 36(3) applies.* The statutory power can also be utilised where a corporation which has been acting as a trustee is dissolved.

(b)   Appointing an additional trustee. The statutory power to appoint additional trustees is contained in section 36(6). This provision only permits the appointment of an additional trustee where there are not more than three existing trustees. Although more than one additional trustee may be appointed at the same time, the total number of trustees must not be increased beyond four, and this restriction applies to all trusts, not only to trusts affecting land.[98] The former rule that additional trustees could not be appointed under this section if any existing trustee was a trust corporation has now been abrogated.[99]

(3)   By the beneficiaries
Where the trust instrument does not make any provision for the appointment of new trustees,[1] then in two situations the beneficiaries of the trust will have a power of appointment unless it is excluded by the settlor.[2]

The first situation exists alongside the statutory power of appointment conferred by section 36 of the Trustee Act 1925. Where all the beneficiaries of the trust are of full age and capacity and between them absolutely entitled to the trust property,[3] they have at any time and in any circumstances the power to give a written direction to the existing trustee(s), or if there are none to the personal representatives of the last surviving trustee, to appoint as trustee(s) whatever person or persons they specify. This is a new power contained in section 19 of the Trusts of Land and Appointment of Trustees Act 1996. It can be coupled with a direction to some or all of the existing trustees to retire[4] and will have to be so coupled if its effect is that the permissible number of trustees[5] is exceeded. It is important to stress that,

---

[98] See *post*, p. 479.
[99] Trusts of Land and Appointment of Trustees Act 1996, Sched. 3, para. 3(11).
[1] The relevant legislation (Trusts of Land and Appointment of Trustees Act 1996) refers throughout to "trusts created by a disposition" and, although this must presumably include trusts created orally because of the incorporation (by virtue of s.23(2)) of the non-inclusive definition of "disposition" in the Law of Property Act 1925, s.205(1)(ii), the wording of the 1996 legislation does not always fit very easily with trusts so created.
[2] Trusts of Land and Appointment of Trustees Act 1996, s.21(5) provides that the two provisions conferring this power on the beneficiaries (ss.19 & 20) can be excluded by the trust instrument; in respect of trusts created before January 1, 1997, the provisions can be excluded by a deed executed by the settlor (or the survivor of joint settlors) but if this is not done the provisions apply to such trusts (which of course means that they necessarily apply to all trusts created by will before that date).
[3] "Absolutely entitled to the trust property" would normally include the beneficiaries of a discretionary trust as a whole. However, "beneficiary" is defined in s.22(1) of the Act as "a person who under the trust has an interest in property subject to the trust". Barraclough & Matthews: *The Trusts of Land and Appointment of Trustees Act 1996* (1997) take the view that, because the House of Lords held, in *Gartside v. I.R.C.* [1968] A.C. 553 that, at least for tax purposes, an object of a discretionary trust has no interest in any part of the property, discretionary beneficiaries may not be able to utilise these powers. However, this decision does not necessarily have any effect other than for tax purposes and so the author of this edition of this work does not agree with this view; the matter obviously awaits judicial resolution.
[4] See *post*, p. 486.
[5] See *post*, p. 479.

whereas the power given by section 36 of the Trustee Act 1925 is limited to the circumstances listed in that section, the power given by section 19 of the Trusts of Land and Appointment of Trustees Act 1996 can be exercised whenever the beneficiaries fulfil its sole precondition and as often as they like; where this provision applies, they can therefore completely frustrate the power conferred by the Trustee Act 1925.

The second situation, however, has not one but a number of preconditions. The beneficiaries must still all be of full age and capacity and between them absolutely entitled to the trust property. But they only have a power of appointment where a trustee is incapable by reason of mental disorder of exercising his functions as such and where, further, neither anyone with a power of appointment under the trust instrument nor the surviving trustees nor any personal representative of the last surviving trustee is able and willing to appoint a trustee in his place. If all three of these preconditions are satisfied, then by virtue of section 20 of the Trusts of Land and the Appointment of Trustees Act 1996 the beneficiaries may give a written direction to an appropriate representative of the incapable trustee (his receiver, or holder of his enduring power of attorney or person authorised for the purpose under the Mental Health Act 1983) to appoint whoever they specify in his place.

(4) By the court

If all else fails, the new trustees may be appointed by the court. Whenever it is desirable that a new trustee should be appointed, and it is "inexpedient, difficult or impracticable so to do without the assistance of the court" the court may appoint a new trustee either as an additional trustee, or in substitution for an existing trustee.[6] The court will not, in the absence of exceptional circumstances, exercise its power if advantage can be taken of a provision in the trust instrument or of the statutory power.[7] Further, there appears to be no reported decision in which the court has appointed a trustee against the wishes of a person who has the power to appoint and who is prepared to exercise it in good faith. This is so even if the court would prefer to see someone else appointed.[8] Where the court proposes to appoint a new trustee in substitution for an existing trustee, it may do so even against the wishes of the existing trustee.[9]

In practice this power is used mainly first where there is doubt whether the statutory power can be exercised, for example, as to whether a trustee is in fact "unfit" to act; secondly, where there is no person capable of making an appointment; and, thirdly, where it is wished to increase the number of trustees and the statutory power under section 36 does not apply.

Occasionally an application is made to the court for the appointment of a new trustee simply because if a new trustee is so appointed it cannot afterwards be alleged that the trustee was appointed in circumstances which were improper or in order to facilitate a breach of trust.[10] The court will,

---

[6] Trustee Act 1925, s.41. See also *Re Hodson's Settlement* (1851) 9 Hare 118; *Finlay v. Howard* (1842) 2 Dru. & War. 490.

[7] *Re Gibbon* (1882) 45 L.T. 756; 30 W.R. 287.

[8] *Re Higginbottom* [1892] 3 Ch. 132, see *ante*, p. 470; *Re Brockbank* [1948] Ch. 206, see *ante*, p. 470.

[9] *Re Henderson* [1940] Ch. 764.

[10] See *post*, p. 676.

therefore, only exercise its power where it is clearly in the interest of the beneficiaries for it to make the appointment. An example of a case where the court refused to exercise its power is *Re Weston's Settlement*,[11] which is discussed in a later Chapter.[12]

The court has a discretion as to whom it will appoint as a trustee, but the principles upon which this discretion will be exercised are as follows:

    (i) If the settlor has expressly or by clear implication made known his wishes, the court will have regard to his wishes. This is particularly so if the settlor has indicated whom he does not wish to be appointed.

    (ii) A trustee will not be appointed to promote the interest of some of the beneficiaries in opposition to the interest of other beneficiaries.[13] The attitude of the courts has, however, changed over the last century or so in two important respects. First, it used to be that the court would not appoint a beneficiary to be a trustee.[14] The reason was the fear that the trustee-beneficiary would be tempted to act more in his own interest than that of the other beneficiaries. However, more recently, following the statutory examples,[15] it has been realised that in some circumstances a person who has a beneficial interest may put a greater effort and enthusiasm into the administration of the trust than someone else, and that the appointment of such a person as a trustee may be appropriate, particularly where there is also an independent trustee. The second respect in which the attitude of the courts has changed is with regard to professional advisers. In the middle of the nineteenth century the courts would almost never appoint the family solicitor to be a trustee,[16] but with perhaps greater confidence in the integrity of professional advisers, and realisation of the advantage which detailed knowledge of the family circumstances brings, such persons may now be appointed, particularly where this is desired by the beneficiaries.

    (iii) The court will have regard to whether the proposed appointment will promote the execution of the trust, or whether it will impede it.[17]

An interesting situation arises where the existing trustees make it known that they will refuse to act with the person whom the court proposes to

---

[11] [1969] 1 Ch. 223.
[12] See *post*, p. 777.
[13] *Re Parsons* [1940] Ch. 973.
[14] For example *Re Harrop's Trusts* (1883) 24 Ch.D. 717; *Re Knowles' Settled Estates* (1884) 27 Ch.D. 707.
[15] See *ante*, p. 463.
[16] *Re Kemp's Settled Estates* (1883) 24 Ch.D. 485; *Re Earl of Stamford* [1896] 1 Ch. 288; *Re Spencer's Settled Estates* [1903] 1 Ch. 75.
[17] *Re Tempest* (1866) 1 Ch.App. 485.

appoint. On the one hand the court's dignity is involved. In *Re Tempest*[18] Turner L.J. said[19]:

"I think it would be going too far to say that the court ought, on that ground alone, to refuse to appoint the proposed trustee: for this would, as suggested in the argument, be to give the continuing or surviving trustee a veto upon the appointment of the new trustee. In such a case I think it must be the duty of the court to inquire and ascertain whether the objection of the surviving or continuing trustee is well founded or not, and to act or refuse to act upon it accordingly."

On the other hand, the basic object of the court's power is to promote the interests of the beneficiaries, and these are not protected if there is serious friction between the trustees. Indeed, on this ground alone the court will sometimes remove a trustee.[20]

Unless, presumably, a trustee has been guilty of serious malpractice, so that his removal is a matter of urgency, the court is reluctant to appoint new trustees in the place of existing trustees if to do so would place the existing trustees in a worse financial position. In *Re Pauling's Settlement (No.2)*,[21] it was sought to remove trustees against whom an action had been brought for breach of trust.[22] But this was resisted because they might have been able to have impounded the beneficiaries' interests[23] if they were successful in an appeal in the other action. Wilberforce J. held that even if they were removed they could still exercise their right to impound. As it happened the court refused to appoint new trustees in the place of the existing trustees, because, *inter alia*, to have done so would have deprived them of security for the costs which would be payable to them if the appeal were successful.

3. Restrictions on the Numbers of Trustees

The general principle is that any number of persons may be trustees, and the determining factor is not a legal one, but the practical one of having enough trustees to be able to take advantage of various skills and experience, but not too many to make the working of the trust unwieldy. Nevertheless, there are certain restrictions on the numbers of trustees:

(i) The maximum number of trustees of a trust of land or of a settlement subject to the Settled Land Act 1925 is four, and if more than four persons are named, the first four named who are able and willing to act are the trustees; this is provided by section 34 of the Trustee Act 1925. This limitation does not apply in the case of land held upon trust for charitable, ecclesiastical or public purposes.[24]

---

[18] (1866) L.R. 1 Ch.App. 485.
[19] (1866) L.R. 1 Ch.App. 485 at 490.
[20] *Re Henderson* [1940] Ch. 764.
[21] [1963] Ch. 576.
[22] This case is discussed at pp. 621 and 702.
[23] As to the circumstances in which a beneficiary's interest can be impounded, see *post*, p. 703.
[24] Trustee Act 1925, s.34(3).

(ii) There need only be one trustee to hold land but, unless that trustee is a trust corporation two or more trustees are needed to give a valid receipt for capital money,[25] so that two or more trustees are in fact needed to sell land.

(iii) Where under a will or on intestacy property is to be held for an infant and no trustees are appointed by any will, the personal representatives of the deceased may appoint trustees to hold that property on trust for the infant, but the number of those trustees must not exceed four.[26] This applies whatever the nature of the property.

(iv) Where an additional trustee is being appointed under the power in section 36 of the Trustee Act 1925 referred to above and all the existing trustees are remaining, the number of trustees must not be increased to more than four in any case.

(v) Where a trustee wishes to retire but it is not proposed to appoint a new trustee in his place, he can only do so if a minimum of two persons or a trust corporation will remain as trustees thereafter; this is provided by section 39 of the Trustee Act 1925.[27]

In any event, a minimum of two trustees is usually desirable, in order to give the beneficiaries adequate protection. One of the basic safeguards for beneficiaries is that property must usually be under the control of at least two persons, so that it is very much more difficult for one to misappropriate the money.

4. Assumption of Office by Conduct

Acceptance of the office of trustee of an *inter vivos trust* is usually signified by the trustee executing the trust deed. But in any case, where a trustee does any act in carrying out the trust, he will be presumed from his conduct to have accepted the office. Any act, even though slight, in carrying out the terms of the trust is sufficient.[28]

5. Actions which Trustees should Carry Out on their Appointment

(A) Disclosure Prior to Appointment
It has already been seen in Chapter 10 that a trustee should not, except with the express consent of the person setting up the trust, or of all the beneficiaries, put himself in a position in which his own interests might conflict with his duties of impartiality as a trustee. As a result of this rule, it has been decided that a person who is asked to become a trustee ought before being

---

[25] Trustee Act 1925, s.14(2).
[26] Administration of Estates Act 1925, s.42.
[27] As amended by Trusts of Land and Appointment of Trustees Act 1996, Sched. 3, para. 3(13). See *post*, p. 484.
[28] *Lord Montfort v. Lord Cadogan* (1816) 19 Ves. 635; *James v. Frearson* (1842) 1 Y. & C.C.C. 370. Thus a person designated a trustee should expressly announce if he does not wish to act.

appointed to disclose any circumstances unknown to the persons appointing him which might bring his interest and duty into conflict. In *Peyton v. Robinson*,[29] for example, a beneficiary under a trust was indebted to the trustee personally, but this fact was not known to the settlor. The terms of the trust instrument gave the trustee a discretion to make payments to this beneficiary. In exercise of this discretion, the trustee made payments, but it was held that he could not accept repayment of his debt from the amount paid to the beneficiary. The trustee was placed in a position where his interest, to pay trust money to the beneficiary with a view to being repaid his debt, conflicted with his duty, to exercise his discretion entirely without thought for his own personal advantage.

(B) Following Appointment
When a person accepts a trusteeship, he should do four things: first, acquaint himself with the terms of the trust; secondly, inspect the trust instrument and any other trust deeds; thirdly, procure that all the property subject to the trust is vested in the joint names of himself and his co-trustees, and that all title deeds are placed under their joint control; and, fourthly, in the case of an appointment as a new trustee of an existing trust, to investigate any suspicious circumstances which indicate a prior breach of trust, and to take action to recoup the trust fund if any breach has in fact taken place. If he fails to do these things, he may make himself liable in an action for breach of trust.

(1) Acquainting himself with the terms of the trust
The first duty of a trustee on appointment is to ensure that he knows and understands the terms of the trust instrument because, as is explained elsewhere,[30] if a trustee pays money to a wrong beneficiary, or pays the right beneficiary too little money, or departs in any other way without authority from the terms of the trust instrument, he thereby commits a breach of trust, however honestly he may act. In certain circumstances he may apply to the court for relief from liability,[31] but even if the court grants total or partial relief, a breach of trust will still have been committed. In *Nestle v. National Westminster Bank*[32] the trustee bank had doubts as to the precise nature of its investment powers. The Court of Appeal described these doubts as "understandable" but held that it was "inexcusable that the bank took no step at any time to obtain legal advice as to the scope of its powers".[33] (In fact, however, the plaintiff beneficiary was unable to show that she had suffered any loss thereby so no liability was actually imposed.)

(2) Inspection of the trust documents
The second duty of a trustee on appointment is to inspect the trust instrument in order to ascertain whether any notices have previously been given to the trustees of dealings by beneficiaries with their interests in the trust

---

[29] (1823) 1 L.J. (O.S.) Ch. 191.
[30] See *post*, p. 676.
[31] Under Trustee Act 1925, s.61, discussed *post*, p. 700.
[32] [1993] 1 W.L.R. 1260.
[33] *ibid*. at 1265, *per* Dillon L.J.

fund. A beneficiary who has an interest under a trust is usually entitled to sell, mortgage, give away or in some other manner deal with his interest in the trust fund, just as he may deal with any other property. As far as the trustees are concerned, this disposition is complete when the assignee gives notice of the disposition to the trustees.[34] Once such notice has been given, the trustees must pay to the assignee the trust money to which the beneficiary named in the trust instrument would otherwise have been entitled. If a memorandum of the transaction is endorsed on the trust instrument, this is sufficient to give the persons who are the trustees for the time being notice of the dealing by the beneficiary with his equitable interest.[35]

Furthermore, if a beneficiary should attempt to assign or charge his interest more than once, the assignee or chargee who is the first to give notice of the dealing to the trustees takes priority.[36] If, therefore, a newly appointed trustee finds on inspection of the trust instrument more than one notice of assignment, he must ascertain carefully the order in which such notices were received.

(3) Placing the trust property under joint control

The third duty of a trustee on appointment is to ensure that all the trust property is placed in the joint names of himself and his co-trustees. As soon as he is appointed he becomes responsible with his co-trustees for what happens to the trust property, and if he negligently allows property to remain in the names of others and loss occurs, he may be liable to make good the loss to the beneficiaries out of his own pocket.[37] The property may be placed in the name of the new trustee, jointly with the continuing trustees, by the mode of transfer appropriate to the type of property.[38] The appropriate mode of transfer in respect of the major types of property is:

(a)	freehold land, where title not registered by H.M. Land Registry	Conveyance
(b)	leasehold land, where title not registered by H.M. Land Registry	Assignment
(c)	freehold or leasehold land where title is registered by H.M. Land Registry	Transfer, and registration of transfer at Land Registry
(d)	stocks and shares	Transfer, and registration of transfer by company or authority concerned
(e)	debts, and other choses in action	Assignment (plus notice to the other party to secure priority)
(f)	negotiable instruments payable to bearer	Delivery and indorsement
(g)	personal chattels	Either assignment or physical delivery

[34] By virtue of the rule in *Dearle v. Hall* (1828) 3 Russ. 1.
[35] Law of Property Act 1925, s.137.
[36] *Dearle v. Hall* (1828) 3 Russ. 1.
[37] See *post*, p. 676.
[38] The use of the appropriate mode of transfer is also discussed in connection with whether a trust is completely constituted; see *ante*, p. 125.

These formalities can sometimes be avoided, however, by virtue of section 40 of the Trustee Act 1925, when a person is appointed a new trustee, or retires from trusteeship, and the appointment or retirement, as the case may be, is effected by deed (the section does not, however, apply where property is held by a personal representative[39] because, in this case, there is not an existing trust). Section 40 provides that unless the deed contains a provision to the contrary, it automatically vests the trust property in the new or remaining trustees as joint tenants. The section applies to all types of trust property except, first, mortgages of land, when a formal transfer of mortgage is required; secondly, leasehold land, where the lease provides that before any assignment the permission of the landlord must be obtained, and the landlord's permission has not been obtained before the deed of appointment or retirement has been executed (the reason for this exception is to prevent an unwitting breach of covenant under the lease, so giving rise to a possible claim for forfeiture); thirdly, stocks and shares, where a formal transfer has to be registered by the company; fourthly, land title to which is registered in the Land Registry, in respect of which, although no transfer is actually necessary,[40] the deed of appointment or retirement has to be registered so that the proprietorship register is brought up to date. The first three exceptions arise by virtue of section 40(4) of the Trustee Act 1925 and the fourth arises by virtue of by section 47 of the Land Registration Act 1925.

Further, section 40 obviously cannot apply to "bearer" securities, in respect of which difficulties sometimes arise. "Bearer" securities are issued securities which are not registered in the name of anyone. The issuing company pays dividends to whoever at the time when the dividend is payable is able to produce to the company the bearer certificate, or any coupons attached to it. By definition bearer securities cannot be placed in the names of the trustees. Section 7 of the Trustee Act 1925, however, provides that bearer securities shall be deposited by the trustees for safe custody and collection of income with a bank and that the trustees are not responsible for any loss which may result from such deposit. Provided the bank holds the securities to the order of all the trustees, they are absolutely protected. But in *Lewis v. Nobbs*,[41] where one trustee allowed bearer securities to remain in the hands of his co-trustee, who misappropriated them, it was held that the trustee was guilty of a breach of trust in having allowed the securities to remain under the control of the other so that they could be so misappropriated. Similarly, all title deeds to trust property should be deposited with a bank or agent to be held to the order of all trustees.[42]

(4) Investigating previous breaches of trust

The final duty on a trustee on appointment is to consider the possibility that there have been previous breaches of trust. A new trustee is not expected to act like a bloodhound straining to sniff out some breach of trust; in the

---

[39] See *ante*, p. 30.

[40] Although a transfer is not essential, for practical purposes it is desirable, as if a transfer is not executed, HM Land Registry may insist on retaining the deed of appointment or retirement, or on being supplied with a certified copy of it.

[41] (1878) 8 Ch.D. 591.

[42] See also *Underwood v. Stevens* (1816) 1 Mer. 712; see *post*, p. 679.

absence of suspicious circumstances he may assume that the previous trustees have properly discharged their duties.[43] But the new trustee must inquire into any circumstances which might suggest that a breach of trust has been committed, for if, through not inquiring into such circumstances, the trust fund suffers, he may find himself liable. In such circumstances, he will be liable not because he participated in the original breach of trust but because he himself has committed a breach of trust in not making sufficient inquiry.[44] The most obvious circumstances which would put a new trustee on inquiry is if the trust fund is materially less when he is appointed than it has been at some previous time. There may be many bona fide explanations of this but the new trustee must inquire and, if appropriate, take action.

III. THE RETIREMENT OF TRUSTEES

1. The Circumstances in which Trustees Must Retire

A trustee must retire from his office if the beneficiaries are able to give him and do give him a direction so to do under section 19 of the Trusts of Land and Appointment 1996. Where a trust instrument does not make any provision for the appointment of new trustees and all the beneficiaries of the trust are of full age and capacity and between them absolutely entitled to the trust property,[45] then, unless their power so to do has been excluded by the settlor,[46] they have at any time and in any circumstances the power to give a written direction to any existing trustee requiring him to retire. However, he is only obliged to execute the necessary deed of retirement if three further conditions are satisfied: first, there will be a sufficient number of trustees left thereafter[47]; secondly, either a replacement is to be appointed[48] or the continuing trustees consent; and, thirdly, "reasonable arrangements have been made for the protection of any rights of his in connection with the trust".[49]

2. The Circumstances in Which Trustees May Retire

A trustee may retire from his office in any of four ways:

  (i) by taking advantage of any power in the trust instrument;

---

[43] Re Straham (1856) 8 De G.M. & G. 291.
[44] Harvey v. Olliver (1887) 57 L.T. 239.
[45] See ante, n.3.
[46] See ante, n.2.
[47] Two persons or a trust corporation.
[48] Such a trustee will obviously normally be appointed by the beneficiaries, also pursuant to the section; see ante, p. 476. However, this is not actually necessary so he could equally be appointed by whoever has the statutory power of appointment under Trustee Act 1925, s.36.
[49] It is not entirely clear what this means. The "reasonable arrangements" can hardly be intended to replace the indemnity and the lien on the trust property which Trustee Act 1925, s.30(2) confers on any retiring trustee (see post, p. 505); presumably they therefore enable a trustee who is forced to retire to claim more security than he would otherwise have been able to.

    (ii) by taking advantage of the powers in the Trustee Act 1925, namely

        (a) section 36, where a new trustee is being appointed in his place, or

        (b) section 39, where no new trustee is being appointed;

    (iii) by obtaining the consent of all beneficiaries, who must be *sui juris* and between them absolutely entitled to the whole beneficial interest;

    (iv) by obtaining the consent of the court.

If there is provision in the trust instrument for a trustee to retire, then a trustee can take advantage of this power, even though it is wider than the statutory power. In fact, however, the statutory power in sections 36 and 39 of the Trustee Act 1925 is so wide that specific provisions are not now normally included in trust instruments. Retirement when coupled with the appointment of a new trustee has already been considered but by section 39 a trustee can retire even where no new trustee is being appointed in his place. Under this section,[50] a trustee may retire if;

    (i) after his retirement there will remain as trustees a minimum of two persons or a trust corporation; and

    (ii) he obtains the consent to his retirement of the remaining trustees; and

    (iii) he obtains the consent of anyone named in the trust instrument as having the power to appoint new trustees; and

    (iv) the retirement is by deed.

None of these conditions applies, however, if one of the remaining trustees is the Public Trustee.[51] The requirement that two persons or a trust corporation shall remain as trustees applies to all trusts; it has no connection with the fact that the presence of at least two trustees or a trust corporation is necessary in order for a valid receipt to be given for capital payments arising under a trust of land or settlement under the Settled Land Act 1925.[52]

Provided the conditions of section 39 are fulfilled, the retirement will be effective, but if the trustee has retired in order to procure or facilitate a breach of trust, he may nevertheless remain liable for such breach.[53]

As a last resort, if none of these cases applies, a trustee may apply to the court to be discharged as a trustee. The court will usually discharge a trustee provided that there is at least one other trustee who continues or some suitable new trustee can be found; however, the trustee who wishes to retire will usually be ordered to pay the costs of the application unless he can

---

[50] As amended by Trusts of Land and Appointment of Trustees Act 1996, Sched. 3, para. 3(13).
[51] Public Trustee Act 1906, s.6.
[52] See *ante*, p. 479.
[53] See *post*, p. 677.

show that the circumstances have materially altered since he accepted the trusteeship.[54]

There is one important difference between the scope of section 36 and that of section 39. As has been seen,[55] under section 36 a trustee can retire from part only of the trusts, but under section 39 the trustee can retire only from the whole of the trusts.

Whether these conditions can be overridden by the express provisions of the settlement is not entirely clear. It is questionable as a matter of principle whether a statutory power of this type should be able to be ousted, a view which appeared to be confirmed by Warner J. in *Mettoy Pension Trustees v. Evans*[56] when he stated that there was a doubt as to whether the purported retirement of two individual trustees had left the remaining trustee company as sole trustee of the scheme. However, in *L.R.T. Pension Trust Co. v. Hatt*[57] Knox J. in effect decided that it was possible to exclude the now abrogated requirement for either two individuals or a trust corporation to continue as trustees[58]; although his specific decision is no longer of any relevance, his approach must constitute the law at present. It remains to be seen which of the two approaches will be adopted in future decisions.

There is, however, no doubt at all that a retirement which does not comply with these requirements is invalid and that the trustee in question will consequently remain in office.[59]

3. *Release of Retiring Trustees*

When trustees retire they sometimes request a formal release of any liability arising from the trusteeship. If trustees retire in favour of new trustees, they are not entitled to such a release unless the trust instrument contains a provision to that effect, something which trusts instruments in many tax havens habitually do. However, it seems that if trustees retire upon the winding up of the trust they are entitled to such a release.[60] Either way, however, a release is only effective to the extent that the beneficiaries are in possession of all the relevant facts.

IV. THE REMOVAL OF TRUSTEES

A trustee may be removed from his office:

   (i) under a power contained in the trust instrument;

---

[54] The court has expressed its disapproval of applications being made to the court for the appointment of a new trustee where advantage could be taken of the statutory power, and doubtless it would be equally disapproving if applications were made to it for retirement when advantage could be taken of the statutory power.

[55] See *ante*, p. 485.

[56] [1990] 1 W.L.R. 1587 at 1607; see M. Jacob: (1986) 1 Trust Law & Practice 95.

[57] [1993] P.L.R. 227.

[58] As a result of Trusts of Land and Appointment of Trustees Act 1996, Sched. 3, para. 3(13), the requirement is now only for two "persons" or a trust corporation.

[59] *Mettoy Pension Trustees v. Evans* [1990] 1 W.L.R. 1587.

[60] *Tiger v. Barclays Bank* [1951] 2 K.B. 556.

(ii) under the statutory power contained in section 36 of the Trustee Act 1925;

(iii) in effect, as a result of the beneficiaries directing him to retire under section 19 of the Trusts of Land and Appointment of Trustees Act 1996 in the way which has already been considered, although this is technically retirement rather than removal; or

(iv) by the court.

Powers of removing trustees contained in the trust instrument are strictly construed, so that if it is desired to take advantage of any such power, it must be clear that the circumstances envisaged by such power have actually arisen.[61] The power of removal of trustees under section 36 when a new trustee is being appointed, has been dealt with above. The circumstances are, it will be recalled:

(i) where the trustee remains out of the United Kingdom for more than 12 months consecutively;

(ii) where he refuses to act;

(iii) where he is unfit to act;

(iv) where he is incapable of acting.[62]

Removal by the court presents some difficulty. The court's primary concern is to protect and enhance the interests of the beneficiaries. Thus where the trustee is convicted of dishonesty or by becoming bankrupt or otherwise[63] shows that he is not fit to be in charge of other people's property, the court will remove him.[64] Nevertheless, removal by the court does involve, at least to the outside world, some degree of moral stigma and difficulties arise where an application is made to remove a trustee, not because he has done anything wrong, but because he cannot agree with or work with his co-trustees.

The position was considered by the Privy Council in *Letterstedt v. Broers*,[65] where Lord Blackburn observed:

"In exercising so delicate a jurisdiction as that of removing trustees, their Lordships do not venture to lay down any general rule beyond the very broad principle that their main guide must be the welfare of the beneficiaries. Probably it is not possible to lay down any more definite rule in a matter so essentially dependent on details often of great nicety."[66]

---

[61] *London and County Banking Co. v. Goddard* [1897] 1 Ch. 642. Such a power was of course exercised in *Von Knieriem v. Bermuda Trust Co. (the Star Trusts Case)* (1994) Butterworths Offshore Cases and Material, Vol. 1, 116. See *ante*, pp. 166, 471.

[62] *Re Lemann's Trust* (1883) 22 Ch.D. 633.

[63] *ibid.*; *Re Phelps' Settlement Trust* (1885) 55 L.J.Ch. 465 (intellectual decay).

[64] See the cases discussed *ante*, p. 474.

[65] (1884) 9 App.Cas. 371. See also *Earl of Portsmouth v. Fellows* (1820) 5 Madd. 450.

[66] (1884) 9 App.Cas. 371 at 382.

Mere friction between trustee and beneficiary is not an adequate ground but if there were a permanent condition of hostility between one trustee and the other trustees, the court would probably remove him. In *Re Wrightson*[67] Warrington J. said: "You must find something which induces the court to think either that the trust property will not be safe or that the trust will not be properly executed in the interests of the beneficiaries." A permanent condition of hostility between trustees would probably be a sufficient deterrent to efficient administration of the trust for the court to exercise its powers.

It is difficult to appeal successfully against an order by an inferior court ordering the removal of a trustee. Thus, in *Re Edwards Will Trusts*,[68] where Megarry V.-C. had removed a trustee without giving any reasons for so doing, the Court of Appeal refused to interfere with his decision.

V. THE DELEGATION OF TRUSTEESHIP

In limited circumstances, a person can delegate his powers as trustee without ceasing to be a trustee. These circumstances are considered later on.[69]

VI. THE PROTECTION OF PURCHASERS

A useful provision for the protection of purchasers is contained in section 38 of the Trustee Act 1925. It will be remembered that under section 36 some of the grounds for the removal of a trustee and the appointment of a new one are that the trustee has remained out of the United Kingdom for more than 12 months, that he refuses to act, or that he is unfit to act. Some of these grounds can give rise to dispute. Thus a displaced trustee could argue that he was not in fact unfit to act so that his purported removal was ineffective. In the absence of a provision to the contrary, in the event of the purported removal being ineffective a purchaser would not obtain a good title if he bought from the new trustees. However, section 38 provides that a statement in a deed of appointment that a trustee

    (i) has remained out of the United Kingdom for more than 12 months or

    (ii) refuses to act or

    (iii) is incapable of acting or

    (iv) is unfit to act

"shall, in favour of a purchaser of a legal estate, be conclusive evidence of the matter stated". Because it is "conclusive", a purchaser need not look

---

[67] [1908] 1 Ch. 789 at 803.
[68] [1981] 2 All E.R. 941.
[69] See *post*, p. 513.

behind the statement.[70] Further, in favour of a purchaser, an appointment of trustees which depends on such a statement being true is valid, and any express or implied vesting declaration is also valid.[71]

However, section 38 only applies in the case of land and no protection is conferred by the inclusion of such a statement in other circumstances.

Although the section gives protection to purchasers, it does not affect the position of a person who has not in fact ceased to be a trustee. If, therefore, a person is purportedly removed as a trustee on the ground that he is unfit to act and another person is purportedly appointed in his stead, the person purportedly removed could apply to the court for a declaration that he continues to be a trustee. Even if such a declaration were to be made, however, it would not prejudice a purchaser of land who had relied on the statement in the instrument of appointment.

---

[70] Contrast the position where enactments provide only for "sufficient" evidence. See, for example, Administration of Estates Act 1925, s.36(7), and *Re Duce and Boots Cash Chemists (Southern) Ltd's Contract* [1937] Ch. 642.

[71] Trustee Act 1925, s.38(2).

CHAPTER 14

THE ADMINISTRATION OF TRUSTS

THIS Chapter is concerned with the general obligations of the trustees with regard to the trust property and various specific powers which they are given to facilitate its administration.

I. THE TRUSTEES' STANDARD OF CARE

In the management of a trust, one of the most frequent decisions which trustees are likely to take is in respect of investments and their duties in this respect are dealt with fully in Chapter 17. What will be dealt with in this Chapter is the standard of care which trustees are bound to exercise over the whole field of administration of a trust. In a series of cases[1] the rule has been laid down that unpaid trustees are bound to use only such due diligence and care in the management of the trust as an ordinary prudent man of business would use in the management of his own affairs. There is no doubt about the rule but its application to particular circumstances can cause great difficulty. No doubt this is due, at least in part, to the fact, as Lord Blackburn pointed out in *Speight v. Gaunt*,[2] that judges and lawyers who see only the cases in which losses have been incurred and do not see the infinitely more numerous cases in which expense and trouble and inconvenience have been avoided, are apt to think that men of business are rash.

Each case will of course be decided on its own facts but several decisions should be considered. Thus, with regard to debts payable to the trust, trustees should obtain payment with all reasonable speed and, if payment is not made within a reasonable time, proceedings should be instituted[3] for this is the manner in which an ordinary prudent man of business would deal with debts due to him. But in *Ward v. Ward*[4] the House of Lords held that a trustee exercised his discretion reasonably in not suing immediately a beneficiary who was also a debtor to the trust since, had proceedings been taken, that beneficiary would have been ruined and his children, who were also beneficiaries, placed in difficult circumstances.

Where trustees hold shares in a private company, they must exercise reasonable care to obtain information about the affairs of the company and,

---

[1] *Brice v. Stokes* (1805) 11 Ves. 319; *Massey v. Banner* (1820) 1 Jac. & W. 241; *Bullock v. Bullock* (1886) 56 L.J.Ch. 221; *Speight v. Gaunt* (1883) 9 App.Cas. 1.
[2] (1883) 9 App.Cas. 1.
[3] *Re Brogden* (1888) 38 Ch.D. 546; *Millar's Trustees v. Polson* (1897) 34 Sc.L.R. 798; *Fenwick v. Greenwell* (1847) 10 Beav. 412; *Grove v. Price* (1858) 26 Beav. 103.
[4] (1843) 2 H.L.Cas. 777.

where a trustee is also a director, he may be held liable in an action by a
beneficiary as a result of his conduct of the management of the company. In
Re Lucking' Will Trusts[5] a trustee was a director of a private company, in
which the trust held a majority shareholding. The trustee-director allowed
another director to overdraw heavily from the company until he was eventually dismissed. This overdrawing was largely possible because that other
director sent blank cheques to the trustee-director, which he duly signed and
returned. In due course the dismissed director was adjudicated bankrupt,
owing the company about £16,000. The trustee-director was held liable for
the reduction in the value of the trust shares as a result of that defalca-
tion.[6]

A trustee will do well to bear in mind continually that at some time in the
future a disgruntled beneficiary may well seek to question his actions. Thus
where, for example, trustees wish to sell or lease property, they should
normally ascertain the true value of the property by employing a valuer and
sell or lease with regard to his figures.[7] By so doing they both comply with
the test of the ordinary prudent man of business and also give themselves
protection against subsequent accusations by the beneficiaries that the property was dealt with at too low a figure.[8]

Many of the clearest examples of trustees acting but not complying with
the standard of the ordinary prudent man of business are cases of failure to
take action. Therefore, if a trustee allows rent to fall into arrears, he may be
ordered to make good the loss[9] and a trustee will also be liable if he fails to
register any transaction which needs to be registered, such as a transfer of
registered land, or of shares, and as a result of his failure to do so enables
someone else to obtain priority.[10]

Occasionally, however, the rule that a trustee must act like an ordinary
prudent man of business conflicts with another rule, that a trustee must do
the best he can for the beneficiaries. Suppose, for example, that trustees who
wish to sell a house have received and provisionally accepted an offer for
£100,000 and subsequently receive an offer for £110,000. The trustees are
under an obligation to consider the second offer, even if, had they been
dealing with their own property, they would not have entertained it if only
for considerations of ordinary commercial morality. They still retain their
discretion and if there is some reason which genuinely leads them to conclude that the first offer should be accepted, for example, if the sale to the
first proposed purchaser would be completed materially earlier, they may
conclude that the first offer should be accepted. But their discretion must be
exercised generally in the interests of the beneficiaries[11] and, in the example
given, they should accept the second offer unless there is some good reason
for accepting the first.

The courts appear to recognise that an ordinary prudent man of business
does not make a wise decision on every occasion. A trustee is not, therefore,

---

[5] [1968] 1 W.L.R. 866.
[6] See also *Re Miller's Deed Trusts* (1978) L.S. Gaz. May 3, 1978.
[7] *Oliver v. Court* (1820) 8 Pr. 127.
[8] *Grove v. Search* (1906) 22 T.L.R. 290.
[9] *Tebbs v. Carpenter* (1816) 1 Madd. 290.
[10] *Macnamara v. Carey* (1867) Ir.R. 1 Eq. 9.
[11] *Buttle v. Saunders* [1950] 2 All E.R. 193.

liable merely because he makes an error of judgment. In *Buxton v. Buxton*[12] a trustee was directed to sell bonds with all reasonable speed. He decided to delay sale but the bonds fell in price. It was held that he was not liable to make good the loss. He had actively exercised his discretion and acted in complete good faith; so he was not made liable merely because his decision, as events turned out, was wrong.

What has been said so far applies to the unpaid trustee. Where the trustee is a paid trustee, a higher standard of diligence is required. As Harman J. said in *Re Waterman's Will Trusts*,[13] "I do not forget that a paid trustee is expected to exercise a higher standard of diligence and knowledge than an unpaid trustee". The test for the paid trustee can probably be stated to be that he must exercise the degree of diligence and show the degree of knowledge that a specialist in trust administration could be expected to show.

II. JOINT ACTS

Except in rare circumstances, any act or decision to be effective must be the act or decision of all the trustees. There is no question here of a decision of the majority binding all the trustees.[14] The settlor or testator has reposed his trust in all the trustees; the liabilities and responsibilities are those of all the trustees. Actions taken and decisions made in the administration of the trust must therefore be those of all the trustees. It may often happen that one trustee who is more enthusiastic in his duties than his co-trustee will come to be spoken of as the "acting trustee", whose decisions are merely endorsed by his co-trustee(s). But in this context "acting trustee" is not a concept recognised by law. The trustees must each exercise his discretion and each is equally liable.[15]

Should a dispute arise, a trustee may be justified in concurring in an action of his co-trustee with which he is not in favour, either because he considers his co-trustee to be more experienced in, or to be more knowledgeable about, the type of transaction in hand[16] or in order to prevent a complete deadlock in the administration of the trust. Whether he is being reasonable in deferring to his co-trustee, or whether he should have stood firm and if necessary made an application to the court, will depend on the circumstances of the particular case.

To this general rule that all the trustees must act jointly there are certain exceptions. First, the trust instrument can of course authorise individual action. Secondly, one trustee alone often has power to give a receipt for income, whether rent or dividends from shares. The latter is a necessary provision, because the articles of association of most companies provide that dividends are to be paid to the first-named registered holder of those shares.

---

[12] (1835) 1 Myl. & Cr. 80.
[13] *Re Waterman's Will Trusts* [1952] 2 All E.R. 1054. See also *Re Pauling* [1964] Ch. 303.
[14] *Boardman v. Phipps* [1967] 2 A.C. 46.
[15] *Munch v. Cockerell* (1840) 5 Myl. & Cr. 178.
[16] *Re Schneider* (1906) 22 T.L.R.

Thirdly, just as some acts can be delegated to an agent, so most of those acts can be delegated by all the trustees to one of their number. Lastly, in the case of trustees of a private trust, a majority of trustees can pay money into court[17] even if the minority objects.

Although it is not an exception to the basic principle, it is possible to achieve the practical result that not all the trustees need agree on a certain course of action if a provision to this effect is contained in the trust instrument. This can be done by imposing a primary duty on the trustees to follow a particular course of conduct but also giving them a secondary power not to do so, or to follow some other course, if they all agree. This method is adopted by the Trusts of Land and Appointment of Trustees Act 1996 in respect of land which is subject to an express trust for sale; despite the primary duty imposed on the trustees to sell the land, section 4 of that Act gives the trustees an express power to exercise a discretion to postpone sale indefinitely without being responsible for so doing. However, the trustees can only exercise their power to postpone sale if they all agree so to do; consequently, if only one of them wishes to sell, all the trustees have to comply with their duty so to do.[18] Prior to the enactment of the 1996 Act, the Law of Property Act 1925 both imposed such a duty and conferred such a power on the trustees of all jointly owned land[19]; however, such land is now instead subject to a trust of land,[20] which while equally conferring on the trustees the same power to postpone sale,[21] imposes no specific duty to sell.

It should also be noted that, in some circumstances, the decision of the majority of trustees of a charity can bind all its trustees.[22]

III. THE TRUSTEES' DISCRETION

It is an inherent part of the position of every trustee that he give due consideration to the exercise of any discretions vested in him[23]; there are a wide variety of circumstances in which he will need to do so. The trustee can of course only exercise the discretions vested in him within the limits prescribed by law or by the trust instrument; consequently, if trustees are given a discretion to do certain acts only with the consent of some person, they must ensure that that consent is duly obtained. In *Re Massingberd's Settlement*[24] trustees were given power to vary investments with the consent of the tenant for life. They sold Consols, which were an authorised security, and with the consent of the tenant for life invested the proceeds in an

---

[17] Trustee Act 1925, s.63.
[18] *Re Mayo* [1943] Ch. 302.
[19] By virtue of ss.34–36 and s.25 respectively.
[20] ss.25 & 35 are repealed by Trusts of Land and Appointment of Trustees Act 1996, Sched. 4 and the effect of ss.34 & 36 is amended by Trusts of Land and Appointment of Trustees Act 1996, s.1.
[21] Trusts of Land and Appointment of Trustees Act 1996, s.4.
[22] *Re Whiteley* [1910] 1 Ch. 600.
[23] Generally with regard to the trustee's discretion, see *ante*, Chap. 6.
[24] *Re Massingberd's Settlement* (1890) 63 L.T. 296.

unauthorised mortgage. Subsequently they realised that unauthorised mortgage, and reinvested in an authorised mortgage, but this time without the
consent of the tenant for life. As his consent had not been obtained, it was
held that the trustees had committed a breach of trust and so were liable to
purchase for the trust the same number of Consols as had originally been
held, credit being given for the investment which they had made in the
authorised security.

Assuming that all such limits on the trustee's discretion are observed, it is
of paramount importance that the trustees should exercise their discretion as
the result of an active mental process and not allow a situation to arise
merely as a result of their inaction. An illustrative decision is *Wilson v.
Turner*[25] where the trustees had a power to pay or apply income arising from
the trusts to or for the maintenance of an infant beneficiary. They did not
make any conscious decision whether or not to do so but merely handed
over the income to the infant's father; the Court of Appeal duly held that the
money should be repaid to the trust fund. However, had the trustees
actively considered the merits of the case and consciously decided to apply
the income for the maintenance of the infant, their decision would have been
valid and would have been upheld. A similar decision was reached in *Re
Greenwood*.[26] Section 15 of the Trustee Act 1925 gives trustees a power to
compound liabilities, and, provided they act in good faith, they are protected against loss. Eve J. however held that this section only protects
trustees if they have actively exercised their discretion so that they will not
be protected if loss results merely through inaction on the part of the
trustees. The test is therefore not the consequences of the trustees' action or
inaction, but the nature of their own mental processes.[27]

However, where the trustees do consciously exercise their discretion, they
derive a large measure of support from the courts. Trustees are not obliged
to give reasons for their decisions and, if they do not do so, the court will not
interfere with their decision unless they have acted dishonestly; the court
will not interfere even if it would itself have come to a different decision. In
Re Beloved Wilkes' Charity,[28] trustees had a duty from time to time to select a
candidate to be sent to the University of Oxford to be trained as a minister
of the Church of England; they were obliged to select any suitable candidate
who came forward from certain nominated parishes but in default had a
more general discretion. They decided to nominate a candidate from outside
those parishes rather than one from within them. Lord Truro L.C. declined
to interfere with this decision, saying:

"It is to the discretion of the trustees that the execution of the trust is
confided, that discretion being exercised with an entire absence of indirect
motive, with honesty of intention, and with a fair consideration of the
subject. The duty of supervision on the part of this court will thus be
confined to the question of the honesty, integrity and fairness with which the

---

[25] (1883) 22 Ch. D. 521.
[26] (1911) 105 L.T. 509.
[27] Trustee Act, 1925, s.15 does not make it necessary for all the beneficiaries to consent before the
trustees accept the compromise; *Re Earl of Stafford* [1978] 3 W.L.R. 223.
[28] (1851) 3 Mac. & G. 440.

deliberation has been conducted, and will not be extended to the accuracy of the conclusion arrived at."

However, although it has thus been established that trustees need not give reasons for their decisions,[29] if they do choose to state those reasons, the court will examine their reasons in order to ascertain whether or not the trustees have acted in error. In *Klug v. Klug*,[30] a mother who was one of a number of trustees declined to concur in the exercise of a power in favour of her daughter on the grounds that she disapproved of the latter's marriage. The court held that this was an impermissible reason and overruled her. Decisions can also be reviewed if the trustees ask themselves the wrong question or, while considering the right question, do not approach it in good faith, do not properly apply their minds to it or close their eyes to the facts.[31]

What is the position of trustees who have a discretion and fail to exercise it? The answer depends on whether their discretion arises under a power which is merely permissive or is obligatory. If the power is merely permissive in that they are not under any obligation to exercise it, their discretion will lapse after a reasonable period and cannot later be revived.[32] If on the other hand the discretion is obligatory, it will never lapse, but will instead be enforced. In *Re Locker's Settlement Trusts*[33] the trustees of a discretionary trust held income subject to a positive obligation to distribute the income among such of the beneficiaries as they should determine. They failed to distribute income which had arisen during a three year period but some years later wished to distribute it then. On their application to the court for a declaration as to whether the discretion was still exercisable, the court held that it indeed was because it was of an obligatory nature.

IV. THE DUTY TO PROVIDE INFORMATION

A trustee must be prepared at all times to give any beneficiary who so requires information as to the state of the trust property and to dealings; he must therefore provide him any relevant accounts and, within certain limits, with documents relating to actions taken in the administration of a trust.[34] However, beneficiaries can obviously only require such information if they are actually aware that they are beneficiaries under the trust in question so this in turn raises the question of the extent to which beneficiaries are entitled to be informed of that fact.

---

[29] *R. v. Archbishop of Canterbury and Bishop of London* [1903] 1 K.B. 298 and see post, *infra*.
[30] [1918] 2 Ch. 67.
[31] *Dundee General Hospital v. Walker* [1952] 1 All E.R. 986.
[32] *Re Allen-Mayrick's Will Trusts* [1966] 1 W.L.R. 499; *Re Gulbenkian's Settlement Trusts (No. 2)* [1970] Ch. 408.
[33] [1978] 1 All E.R. 216.
[34] *Tiger v. Barclays Bank* [1952] 1 All E.R. 85.

1. *The Duty to Provide Accounts*

A trustee must maintain accurate accounts of the trust property. He must allow a beneficiary, or his solicitor, to inspect those accounts and the vouchers supporting them and he must be prepared to give full information as to the amount of the trust fund. He is not obliged to supply copies of the accounts, or settlements of account, to the beneficiaries unless the beneficiaries themselves pay for those copies. In one case[35] it was held that a trustee who was illiterate, and so could not keep accounts, was justified in employing an agent simply for the purpose of keeping those accounts. Under the modern law, trustees, whether illiterate or not, will be entitled to employ agents for this purpose.[36]

Where trust money is invested, the trustees must on request supply a beneficiary with details of the investments, and even produce to the beneficiary the stock or share certificates, or other deeds and documents, representing that investment. Where, however, a beneficiary requires information as to his position under a trust, and this information cannot be supplied by the trustees without incurring expense, the trustees can pass on the expense to the beneficiary. Trustees who do not keep proper accounts may be ordered to do so by the court, and may be forced to bear personally the costs of the application to the court.[37] As the trustees may at any time be called upon to give information as to the administration of a trust, it is advisable for them to keep in addition to the trust accounts a trust diary. This is a type of minute book in which decisions taken in the administration of a trust are recorded. In view of the fact that a beneficiary is usually entitled to access to the trust diary and that, as has just been said, if trustees give reasons for their decisions, the court will inquire into the accuracy of their decision but not otherwise, trustees may choose to record their decision but not their reasons.

2. *The Duty to Provide Other Documents*

A beneficiary is also entitled to inspect most other documents relating to the trust. This is because, just as the beneficiaries are the equitable owners of the trust property, they are also the equitable owners of the documents which have arisen in the course of the trust administration, and often at the expense of the trust. In *O'Rourke v. Darbishire*,[38] Lord Wrenbury observed:

"A beneficiary has a right of access to the documents which he desires to inspect upon what has been called in the judgments in this case a proprietary right. The beneficiary is entitled to see all trust documents, because they are trust documents, and because he is a beneficiary. They are, in this sense, his own."

---

[35] *Wroe v. Seed* (1863) 4 Giff. 425.
[36] See post, p. 508.
[37] See (1936) 52 L.Q.R. 365.
[38] [1920] A.C. 581.

This right of access is clearly not confined to the beneficiaries of fixed trusts since in *Re Londonderry's Settlement*[39] it was regarded as basically applicable to a discretionary trust whose beneficiaries were the members of a family, although, as will be seen below, in that case different considerations determined the non-availability of the documents which the beneficiary wanted to see. This was confirmed by the recent decision of Neuberger J. in *Murphy v. Murphy*.[40] However, doubts have been expressed as to whether such access is or should be available to every single potential member of the enormous classes of beneficiaries which many modern discretionary trusts now have.[41] This question awaits decision.

Whatever the scope of the basic right of access, it is at least clearly established that it will not be allowed to impinge on the rule that trustees are not obliged to give reasons for their decisions. This was the issue which *Re Londonderry's Settlement*[42] actually had to resolve. The trustees of a settlement were to distribute the trust fund in such proportions as they thought fit among certain named persons. One of them considered that she had received too little[43] and, in order to launch an attack upon the trustees, sought to inspect numerous trust documents which would probably have indicated the reasons which led the trustees to make the distributions that they had made. The disgruntled beneficiary claimed that she had a right to inspect the documents. The trustees claimed that she had not; they could not to be compelled to give reasons for their decisions and, if the court ordered that the beneficiary was able to see the documents which she wished to see, the rule which enabled the trustees to keep their reasons to themselves would be defeated. The Court of Appeal held, in effect, that the rule enabling a beneficiary to inspect trust documents did not extend to documents which gave reasons for the trustees' decisions; indeed the court went so far as to order that, where a document is basically in the category of those which the beneficiary is entitled to see but also contains details of the trustees' reasons, the latter passages should be covered up when the document is produced to the beneficiary.

Although this decision is unquestionably welcome, the reasons given by the court are far from clear. The court clearly had sympathy with the trustees' contention that family strife would result if the beneficiary were given access to documents which gave their reasons for their dealings with the trust property. It may well be that the court first decided what conclusions they wanted to reach and then tried to find some reasons with which to support it. Harman L.J. considered, but did not decide, whether the documents were "trust documents" at all, thereby implying that if they were not the beneficiary would not have a right of access to them. He could not make up his mind about this but said[44]:

---

[39] [1965] Ch. 918.

[40] (1998), *The Times* May 2, 1998.

[41] See J. D. Davies: (1995) 7 Bond Law Review 5, referring to the remarks of Mahoney J.A. in *Hartingan Nominees v. Rydge* (1992) 29 N.S.W.L.R. 405 at 425 & 432 (Court of Appeal of New South Wales).

[42] [1965] Ch. 918.

[43] She and her family had in fact received £165,000. The total amount of the trust fund is not recorded.

[44] [1965] Ch. 918 at 933.

"I would hold that, even if documents of this type ought properly to be described as trust documents, they are protected for the special reason which protects the trustees' deliberations on a discretionary matter from disclosure. If necessary, I hold that this principle overrides the ordinary rule."

Danckwerts L.J. based his decision firmly on the practical ground that, if the trustees' reasons were not protected from disclosure, it would be impossible for them to do their job. The third member of the Court of Appeal, Salmon L.J., also toyed with the idea of declaring that the documents were not trust documents but had to admit defeat[44a]:

"The category of trust documents has never been comprehensively defined. Nor could it be—certainly not by me."

There are thus several possible reasons for the conclusion reached; however, the decision does at least clearly establish that beneficiaries do not have a right of access to documents which the trustees intend to be private and which record the reasons for their decisions. This proposition has recently been reviewed in *Wilson v. The Law Debenture Trust Corp.*[45] in the context of the discretions vested in the trustees of a pension trust, specifically in respect of a decision not to transfer a surplus in the fund to another pension scheme to which its member employees had been transferred. Despite the fact that, as has already been seen,[46] the beneficiaries of a pension fund are not volunteers, Rattee J. affirmed the applicability of the decision in *Re Londonderry's Settlement* and refused to order the trustees to reveal their reasons.[47]

All the questions considered so far had to be considered in a slightly different context, that of whether beneficiaries are entitled to see letters of wishes, in *Hartingan Nominees v. Rydge*,[48] a decision of the Court of Appeal of New South Wales. As has already been seen,[49] letters of wishes are documents which exist outside the formal trust documents; they set out the wishes of the settlor but are not binding on the trustees. Access was, by a majority, denied but each of the three members of court took a different view; one of the members of the majority held that letters of wishes are not trust documents and so do not fall within the basic right of access; the other member of the majority held that letters of wishes are trust documents but do not have to be disclosed because they provide insight into the trustees' reasons; and the dissentient held that letters of wishes are trust documents but should be disclosed even if they do provide insight into the trustees' reasons (in effect, therefore, rejecting *Re Londonderry's Settlement*). Different majorities therefore held that letters of wishes are trust documents and that

---

[44a] *ibid.* at 938.

[45] [1995] 2 All E.R. 337.

[46] See *ante*, p. 456.

[47] The decision has been criticised by D. Schaffer: (1994) 8 Trust law International 118. It may anyway in practice be indirectly undermined by the fact that the Pensions Act 1995 now requires that, at least in principle, every pension trust must have member trustees; see *ante*, p. 452.

[48] (1992) 29 N.S.W.L.R. 405.

[49] See *ante*, p. 168.

they do not have to be disclosed. The author of this edition favours the view that they are not trust documents and for that reason do not have to be disclosed.

The fact that documents which are, like those in *Re Londonderry's Settlement*, clearly trust documents do not have to be disclosed for the reasons stated in that case is, however, not necessarily the end of the matter. In that case, the beneficiary had made a direct application to inspect the documents in question. The Court of Appeal made it clear that their decision did not govern the question of whether such documents were disclosable in pending proceedings brought upon some other ground. If, for example, a beneficiary brings proceedings against the trustees for breaches of trust which involve an allegation of improper motive on the part of the trustees, it may well be that in the course of discovery the beneficiary will be entitled to see all the trustees' documents, including those which reveal the reasons for their decisions. There is as yet no direct English authority on this point; if the question ever arises, the courts will have to try to decide whether there is a genuine need for discovery in the other proceedings or whether the latter have been brought mainly in order to try to flush out the documents in question.[50] However, dicta in *Hartigan Nominees v. Rydge*[51] suggest that the principle of non-disclosure of reasons is paramount and may not be circumvented even by the process of discovery.

3. *The Duty to Inform Beneficiaries of their Rights*

A settlor of an *inter vivos* trust is not obliged to notify either the trustees or the beneficiaries of its existence. Thus in *Fletcher v. Fletcher*[52] a settlor entered into a covenant with trustees that, if either or both of his two illegitimate sons survived him, his executors should, within 12 months of his death, pay to the trustees £60,000 which was to be held on trust for such of the two as reached the age of 21. He never revealed the existence of the deed either to the trustees or to his sons; he retained the deed in his possession until his death and it was only discovered some years later among his papers. As has already been seen,[53] this did not prevent the one son who survived him and reached the age of 21 from enforcing what was held to be a completely constituted trust of the benefit of that covenant. This was of course a most unusual case and in such circumstances the trustees are under no obligation to act. However, save where an *inter vivos* trust is created by declaration, it will only be validly constituted once the trust property has been vested in the trustees[54]; this will in practice require the trustees to be parties to the trust instrument, in which case they will necessarily be aware of the trust's existence.

It is much more common for testamentary trusts to be created without either trustees or beneficiaries being aware of their existence. A testator is under no obligation whatever to inform his executors and testamentary

---

[50] A unpermissible tactic which is generally known as a "fishing expedition".
[51] (1992) 29 N.S.W.L.R. 405, *per* Mahoney J.A. at 437.
[52] (1844) 4 Hare 67.
[53] See *ante*, p. 157.
[54] See *ante*, p. 124.

trustees that he has nominated them to act as such and there is certainly no reason to suppose that he will inform the beneficiaries of his will of their possible future interests thereunder. Executors and testamentary trustees are under no obligation to act even if they have been informed of their appointment, never mind if they have not. If an executor agrees to act, in practice one of the first things which he will do is to send a copy of the will to each beneficiary who has rights thereunder. However, it has been held that executors are under no duty so to do,[55] although their position will clearly change once the administration of the estate is concluded if they continue to hold assets of the estate as trustees.

This is because it is clear that trustees who have agreed to act are under a duty to inform the beneficiaries of the existence and nature of their interests under the trust. This was held in *Hawkesley v. May*,[56] where the plaintiff was jointly entitled with his sister to the income and capital of the trust fund at 21. When he reached that age, the trustees failed to inform him of his rights and continued accumulating the income until his sister also reached that age. Havers J. held that they had been under a duty to inform him of his interest and of his immediate entitlement to call for his share of the income. This was a fixed trust but the same principle presumably applies to discretionary trusts in favour of relatively small groups of beneficiaries. However, the position of potential members of the enormous classes of beneficiaries in favour of whom many modern discretionary trusts are created is more problematical. It is clearly impracticable to oblige or to expect trustees of this type of discretionary trust to notify every single potential member of his potential rights thereunder[57]; the most that they could conceivably be expected to do would be to advertise for potential beneficiaries to present themselves so that the trustees can comply with the duty to survey the field which, as has already been seen,[58] is imposed on them by *McPhail v. Doulton*[59] and *Re Hay's Settlement Trusts*.[60] However, it cannot seriously be doubted that the need to compel the proper administration of trusts dictates that trustees should be obliged to give a truthful answer to any potential beneficiary who actually enquires.

A different aspect of the right of a beneficiary to know of the existence of his interest had to be considered in *Murphy v. Murphy*.[61] The plaintiff was aware that he was a beneficiary of two discretionary trusts, one set up by his father, who had reserved the power to appoint its trustees, and one set up by his deceased mother, who had not reserved any such power but whose estate had been administered by the father. The plaintiff issued a summons to compel his father to reveal to him the identity of the current trustees of

---

[55] *Re Lewis* (1868) 5 L.R. Eq. 545. This was a particularly strong case since the executor was entitled to the subject matter of a legacy in the event that the beneficiary in question failed to claim it and the failure to inform the latter of the existence of the legacy meant that he failed to do so prior to his death.

[56] [1956] 1 Q.B. 304.

[57] See J. D. Davies: (1995) 7 Bond Law Review 5, referring to the remarks of Mahoney J.A. in *Hartingan Nominees v. Rydge* (1992) 29 N.S.W.L.R. 405 at 425 & 432 (Court of Appeal of New South Wales).

[58] See *ante*, p. 104.

[59] [1971] A.C. 424.

[60] [1982] 1 W.L.R. 202, *per* Megarry V.-C. at 209–210.

[61] (1998), *The Times*, May 2, 1998.

these trusts. Neuberger J. held that no principle of equity had been invoked to suggest that the court had no power to grant such relief; the fact that the plaintiff was merely a discretionary beneficiary was irrelevant and did not affect the court's discretion to order discovery.

V. DIRECTIONS OF THE COURT

Where trustees are in doubt as to the manner in which they should act, they may apply by way of summons to the court to seek its directions. If the trustees place before the court all the relevant facts and subsequently act in accordance with the court's directions, it is an established principle that they will be absolutely protected. The trustees made such an application in *Re Londonderry's Settlement*.[62] At first instance Plowman J. decided that the documents ought to have been disclosed. The trustees appealed, successfully as it turned out, but the Court of Appeal nearly refused to hear the appeal. Harman L.J. observed:

"This appeal, as it seems to me, is an irregularity. Trustees seeking the protection of the court are protected by the court's order and it is not for them to appeal."[63]

There is little doubt that if the trustees had acted under the (erroneous) decision of Plowman J. they would have been protected. But if, as they did, they considered the decision both wrong and adverse to the interests of the beneficiaries, why should they not have been entitled to appeal? It is particularly ironic that this statement[64] on the part of Harman L.J., which tends to reflect a narrow outlook all too often encountered in the Chancery Division, should have been made in a case where, because the trustees did appeal, the law was patently improved—for all trustees. Fortunately Salmon L.J. took a different view:

"However, in my view the trustees were fully justified in bringing this appeal. Indeed it was their duty to bring it since they believed, rightly, that an appeal was essential for the protection of the general body of beneficiaries."[63a]

What is remarkable is not that Salmon L.J. made this statement but that he had to make it.

Unfortunately, however, Salmon L.J. introduced a further difficulty. It might have been thought that the rule should have been that if trustees apply to the court and are given a decision which is wrong, then they may appeal. According to Salmon L.J. they must appeal; in other words, they have a duty to do so. One day it may have to be decided how far trustees are protected if they act in accordance with the decision of the court when they believe that decision to be wrong.

---

[62] [1965] Ch. 918.
[63] *ibid.* at 930.
[63a] *ibid.* at 936.
[64] See also (1965) 29 Conv. (N.S.) 81.

An application was also made to the court in *Barker v. Peile,*[65] where several actions had arisen as a result of uncertainty as to who were proper beneficiaries and the court acceded to the wish of the trustee to be relieved of the liability and annoyance of being a trustee. Special circumstances must, however, exist before the court will release a trustee from his obligations in this way.

Trustees may also make an application to the court for the construction of words in a will or settlement whose meaning is uncertain; such applications are known as construction summons and require all those persons who could be beneficiaries according to any of the possible constructions to be joined as defendants.

In administration proceedings, the courts have a useful power contained in section 57 of the Trustee Act 1925. This section will be considered in detail later on[66]; for present purposes it is sufficient to note that, by virtue of this provision, where the trustees wish to effect any sale, letting, charge, or any other disposition of trust property, or wish to purchase property or make an investment with trust money and have no power to do so either under the trust instrument or under the general law, the court may sanction the transaction in question. The court has jurisdiction to impose any conditions which it thinks fit when approving such a transaction but can only authorise a transaction which is made "in the management or administration" of the trust property. However, the court has power to give authority under this section only where:

(i) the trustees propose to do an act not authorised by the general law or by the trust instrument;

(ii) that act is in the management or administration of the trust property and

(iii) the court thinks that it is expedient to sanction it.

Section 57 is designed to ensure that the property is administered as advantageously as possible in the interests of the beneficiaries. However, the provision must be considered in conjunction with the general principle that the court will not rewrite a trust; consequently, the power will only be exercised to authorise specific dealings with trust property. In *Boardman v. Phipps*[67] the trustees held shares in a private company and had the opportunity to acquire further shares, although such acquisition was not authorised by the trust instrument. In litigation in which one of the beneficiaries successfully impugned the subsequent purchase of the same shares by another beneficiary and the trust solicitor, Lord Denning M.R. said in the Court of Appeal that the acquisition of these shares was so clearly in the interest of the beneficiaries that the proper course would have been for the trustees to have applied to the court under section 57 for power to make the purchase.[68] However, only the briefest reference was made to this point

---

[65] (1865) 2 Dr. & Sm. 340.
[66] See post, p. 657.
[67] [1967] 2 A.C. 46.
[68] [1965] Ch. 992 at 1020.

in the subsequent appeal to the House of Lords because it had formed no part of the pleaded case and had not been mentioned in the argument at any stage.[69]

Finally, it should be noted that section 57 does not authorise rearrangement of beneficial interests but this can effected in other ways, principally under the Variation of Trusts Act 1958; this possibility is considered in a later Chapter.[70]

VI. ADMINISTRATIVE POWERS RELATING TO TRUST PROPERTY

Part II of the Trustee Act 1925 confers general powers on trustees, particularly with regard to the administration of property. Under these powers, trustees may where appropriate raise money by sale or mortgage, sell trust property at auction and insure the property. Although this is not actually mentioned by the statute, trustees are bound to see that trust property does not fall into decay through want of repair.[71] However, the provisions of the Trustee Act 1925 relating to insurance seem less than wholly satisfactory. Section 19 gives the trustees power if they so wish to insure the property but only for an amount not exceeding three-quarters of the full value of the property. This section seems to envisage a standard of conduct considerably lower than that with which trustees are generally supposed to comply, that of the reasonably prudent man of business, who would at least at the present day invariably not just insure the property but insure it for its full re-building cost.[72] It is therefore not surprising that the Law Commission proposed the replacement of this provision in a Consultation paper published in July 1997.[73] Their provisional recommendation is that all trustees should have the same power to insure the trust property as they would if they were its absolute owners[74] and should be under a duty[75] to insure the trust property in circumstances when, against such risks as, and for such amount as a reasonably prudent person would have insured the property.[76] It is much to be hoped that these proposals[77] are enacted.

Section 15 confers upon trustees the power to

"(a) accept any property, real or personal, before the time at which it is made transferable or payable; or
(b) sever and apportion any blended trust funds or property; or
(c) pay or allow any debt or claim on any evidence that he or they think sufficient; or

---

[69] [1967] 2 A.C. 46. Their controversial decision is analysed in detail: see *ante*, p. 314.
[70] See *post*, p. 656.
[71] *Re Hotchkys* (1886) 32 Ch.D. 408.
[72] See further Kenny, "The Underinsured Beneficiary" (1982) 79 L.S.G. 755.
[73] Law Commission Consultation Paper No. 146, Trustees' Powers and Duties.
[74] *ibid.* at para. 9.18.
[75] Save where absolutely entitled beneficiaries of full age direct them not to insure.
[76] Law Commission Consultation Paper No. 146 at para. 9.21.
[77] Which also confer a discretion to enable the trustees to apportion the premiums as between capital and income.

(d) accept any composition or any security, real or personal, for any debt or for any property, real or personal, claimed; or

(e) allow any time for payment of any debt; or

(f) compromise, compound, abandon, submit to arbitration, or otherwise settle any debt, account, claim, or thing whatever relating to the testator's or intestate's estate or to the trust."

A trustee will not be liable for any loss which occurs from the exercise of any of these powers, provided that he has acted in good faith.[78] The consent of the beneficiaries is not necessary.[79] These rules are illustrated by Re The Earl of Strafford.[80] The settlor had settled valuable chattels and his wife owned similar chattels. When the wife died, the beneficiaries of her will took her chattels but the beneficiaries of the trust claimed that those chattels were trust property. A compromise was proposed under which, broadly, the beneficiaries under the wife's will would take some chattels outright, would take a life interest in others and would give up the remainder. The trustees were minded to accept the proposed compromise but one of the beneficiaries under the trust objected. The Court of Appeal held that it was for the trustees to decide whether they considered the compromise was in the interest of all beneficiaries taken together and that, if they did, they had power to accept it despite the opposition of one of the beneficiaries.

Some powers over property can only be exercised on proof of legal ownership and in respect of trust property these powers can only be exercised by the trustees. In Schalit v. Nadler[81] a beneficiary who was solely entitled to trust property which was leased levied distress for arrears of rent. It was held that only the trustee as legal owner could levy distress; consequently, the distress actually levied was wrongful. Similarly, only the legal owner can serve a notice to quit on a tenant.

VII. MORTGAGING THE TRUST PROPERTY

Section 16 of the Trustee Act 1925 applies where trustees are authorised either by the general law or by the trust instrument "to pay or apply capital money subject to the trust for any purpose or in any manner". In these circumstances, the section gives the trustees power to raise the requisite money either by mortgaging or selling the trust assets. However, the section is construed narrowly and is confined to the cases where money is required either to preserve assets or to advance capital. In Re Suenson-Taylor's Settlement[82] the trustees, who had very wide powers of investment and who, in accordance with these powers, properly held a large area of land for investment purposes, wished to borrow upon the security of that land in order to buy further land. It was held that this would be outside the power conferred by section 16. The court however observed that there could be cases where

[78] per Eve J. in Re Greenwood (1911) 105 L.T. 509.
[79] Re Earl of Strafford [1979] 1 All E.R. 513.
[80] ibid.
[81] [1933] 2 K.B. 79 and see ante, p. 17.
[82] Re Suenson-Taylor's Settlement [1974] 3 All E.R. 397.

it was necessary to purchase further land in order to protect existing investments. For example, if trustees own a house, it may be appropriate to buy land which the house overlooks, in order to prevent anyone else building upon it. Such a purchase is now clearly permissible under the Trusts of Land and Appointment of Trustees Act 1996 since trustees of land now have all the powers of an absolute owner.[83] However, that does not necessarily mean that the purchase price can be raised on mortgage.

VIII. EXPENSES

It will be seen later on[84] that, except in special circumstances, a trustee is not entitled to be paid for his services. He is, however, entitled to be reimbursed all his expenses which have been properly incurred (however, he is not normally entitled to interest thereon). This right of reimbursement is in respect both of money actually spent by the trustee and of liabilities which he has incurred. Thus in *Benett v. Wyndham*[85] a trustee of an estate directed woodcutters employed on the estate to fell some trees. The woodcutters were negligent and allowed a bough to fall on a passer-by who was injured. The trustee, as legal owner of the estate, was sued and he was allowed to reimburse himself the damages out of the trust fund. However, it does not follow that a trustee will be allowed all his expenses; they must be reasonable and proper in all the circumstances. In *Malcolm v. O'Callaghan*[86] an ingenious trustee made a number of journeys to Paris to be present at the hearing of a case in the French courts which concerned the trust, but which turned solely on a question of French law and for which the trustee's presence was in no way necessary. He was not allowed his expenses against the trust.

A trustee is obviously entitled to be reimbursed the expenses of properly taking or defending legal proceedings on behalf of the trust in the same way as other expenses. But before taking or defending proceedings a trustee can apply to the court for its approval; therefore if he does not do so the proceedings are unsuccessful, it will be up to him to prove that he had reasonable grounds for taking or defending proceedings. If he cannot prove this, he will be deprived of his costs.

The trustee's right of indemnity is generally against the trust property,[87] not against the beneficiaries. If, therefore, the trustee's right of indemnity exceeds the value of the trust property, he will not normally be able to claim the balance from the beneficiaries personally. The right of indemnity can, however, be enforced against a beneficiary personally in three circumstances: first, where the beneficiary in question was the creator of the trust[88];

---

[83] s.6(1).
[84] See post, p. 640.
[85] (1862) 4 De G. 7. & J. 259.
[86] (1835) 3 Myl. & Cr. 52.
[87] Trustee Act 1925, s.30(2).
[88] *Matthews v. Ruggles-Brise* [1911] 1 Ch. 194.

secondly, where the trustee accepted the trust at the request of that beneficiary[89]; and, thirdly, where the trustee is a bare trustee.[90]

IX. PAYMENTS TO BENEFICIARIES

The general principle is that a trustee is absolutely responsible for ensuring
that the right amount is paid to the right beneficiary. In *Eaves v. Hickson*[91]
trustees were provided with a forged marriage certificate which led them to
believe that certain children were legitimate and consequently beneficiaries;
they therefore paid the trust funds out to them. The trustees were nevertheless held liable to make good to the rightful beneficiary so much of these
funds as could not be recovered either from the children or from their father,
who had provided the forged certificate. Similarly, where trustees paid trust
money to a wrongful beneficiary, on an erroneous but bona fide construction
of the trust instrument, they were held liable to make good the loss.[92] Where
the trustees have in the particular circumstances acted honestly and reasonably and ought fairly to be excused, the court has a discretion to grant them
relief,[93] but this does not alter the trustees' primary obligation of ensuring
payment to the rightful beneficiary.

Where there is any doubt as to who is entitled to trust property, the
trustees should apply to the court for directions and will then be protected
if those directions are complied with. If the beneficiary entitled cannot be
traced, the trustees may pay the money into court, and so obtain a good
discharge for it. And where one of several beneficiaries cannot be traced, the
court may authorise the trustees to distribute the trust fund as if the beneficiary who cannot be traced were dead.[94] Nevertheless, the court will discourage trustees from making payment into court of trust money where
there is no good reason for doing so by making the trustees personally liable
for the costs of the application for payment in. The power of payment into
court is one of the exceptional cases in which the wishes of the majority of
the trustees binds them all.

The court equally discourages applications by trustees for protection
where they incur no practical risk at all. Thus, in *Re Pettifor*[95] Pennycuick J.
said that in normal circumstances the court would consider it an unnecessary waste of money for trustees to come to court and ask for liberty to
distribute a trust fund on the basis that a woman of 70 would not have a
further child.

In most cases of long-standing trusts, there cannot be any debts due from
the trust of which the trustees are unaware. However, where there is a
possibility of outstanding debts, advantage should be taken of section 27 of
the Trustee Act 1925. Under this section, the trustees may advertise in the
London Gazette, and usually also in another newspaper, their intention of

---

[89] *Jervis v. Wolferstan* (1874) L.R. 18 Eq. 18 at 24.
[90] *Hardoon v. Belilios* [1901] A.C. 118.
[91] *Eaves v. Hickson* (1861) 30 Beav. 136.
[92] *Hilliard v. Fulford* (1876) 4 Ch.D. 389.
[93] Trustee Act 1925, s.61; see *post*, p. 700.
[94] The so-called "Benjamin Order"; *Re Benjamin* [1902] 1 Ch. 723.
[95] [1966] Ch. 257.

distributing the trust fund to the beneficiaries and requiring persons interested in the trust fund to send them notice of their claim. Any such claims must be sent in within the time fixed by the notice, which must not be less than two months after it is published. At the expiration of that time, the trustees can safely distribute the trust fund after discharging only those claims of which they have notice. If a creditor subsequently comes forward, he may be able to follow the trust property into the hands of the beneficiaries to whom it has been distributed but will have no remedy against the trustees themselves.

Trustees must, of course, remember that beneficial interests under the trust can be assigned or charged. Where an assignee makes a claim to trust property, the trustees will, before making payment, have to investigate his title to the interest assigned, and they will be obliged to give effect to effective assignments.

Finally, when a trusteeship comes to an end, the trustee is entitled to put himself into the position in which no further disputes can be raised about payments to the beneficiaries. To achieve this he is entitled to present his final accounts to the beneficiaries and to require them to give him a formal discharge from his trusteeship. If they refuse, he may have the accounts taken in court, that is, examined by an official of the Chancery Division, at the expense of the trust fund and in that way obtain confirmation that they are in order.

CHAPTER 15

DELEGATION: THE EMPLOYMENT OF AGENTS

THE trustees may wish to engage others to assist them in the execution of the trust or the administration of trust property. This may the case where the trustees consider it appropriate for the trust accounts and records to be kept by a solicitor or accountant or where particular action requires special skills, such as advising with regard to changes of investment or where there are particular difficulties in administration, as where trust property is situated abroad.

Where the trustees appoint any person to act on their behalf in the execution of the trust, he is known as their "agent".

Whenever an agent is appointed there are six questions to be asked:

(i) What powers do trustees have for the appointment of agents?

(ii) Should the power be exercised?

(iii) In what manner is it to be exercised?

(iv) What is the extent of the agent's authority?

(v) Can agents be paid from the trust fund?

(vi) If an agent defaults, and loss is occasioned to the trust fund, to what extent are the trustees themselves liable for that loss?

I. THE TRUSTEES' POWERS TO APPOINT AGENTS

The trust instrument itself may confer an effective power for the appointment of agents.

Section 23(1) of the Trustee Act 1925 confers the principal power for the appointment of agents. It empowers trustees to appoint a solicitor, banker, stockbroker, or any other person to transact any business, or to do any act which is necessary in the execution of the trust, or the administration of the trust property. It will be appreciated that what must be necessary is the doing of the act, or the transaction of the business, not the appointment of the agent. Accordingly, trustees have the power to appoint an agent to do an act even if they could have done it themselves.[1] In practice, almost all agents are appointed under this power.

Other narrower powers are:

---

[1] However, see *post*, p. 510.

(i) The power to appoint agents to deal with property situated abroad.[2]

(ii) The power to permit a solicitor to have a deed incorporating a receipt for money signed by the trustees.[3] This is required for an ordinary sale of trust property where a conveyance or transfer incorporating such a receipt will be handed over by the trustees' solicitor in exchange for the purchase money.

(iii) The power to permit a solicitor or banker to have a receipt for insurance monies signed by the trustees, so that the solicitor or banker can obtain the policy monies from the insurers.[4]

(iv) The power to employ a valuer in connection with a proposed loan of trust money which is to be secured by mortgage.[5]

(v) The power for trustees for the sale of land to delegate revocably their powers as absolute owners of the land to the person who is entitled in possession to the land.[6]

II. Should the Power be Exercised?

The general rule is that trustees must consider the exercise of any power,[7] and, if they do decide to exercise it, that exercise is only good if the trustees consider that it is in the interest of the trust.[8] The power to appoint agents is subject to this general rule. There will usually be no difficulty where the agent is appointed to transact business which requires some special skill which the trustees do not themselves have. Even if an agent is appointed to do an act which the trustees could have done themselves, the appointment will be good if the trustees consider it to be in the interest of the trust.

III. The Manner in which the Power is to be Exercised

Subject to any provision in the trust instrument to the contrary, all agents must be personally appointed by the trustees, and they must exercise reasonable care in deciding whether to make the appointment. Thus in *Fry v. Tapson*,[9] trustees were prepared to lend trust money on mortgage, as they were entitled to do. The trustees did not exercise their own judgment as to the valuer to be appointed but relied on the advice of their solicitors. The surveyor chosen in fact was the agent of a mortgagor and had a financial interest in the transaction being completed. The money was lent and, when loss occurred, it was held that the trustees were bound to make good the

---

[2] Trustee Act 1925, s.23(2).
[3] *ibid.* s.23(3)(a).
[4] *ibid.* s.23(3)(c).
[5] *ibid.* s.8.
[6] Trusts of Land and Appointment of Trustees Act 1996, s.9(1).
[7] *Klug v. Klug* [1918] 2 Ch. 67.
[8] *Re Lofthouse* (1885) 29 Ch.D. 921 at 930.
[9] (1884) 28 Ch.D. 268.

loss. They would not have been made liable if they had made an independent choice of the agent themselves. This is an example of a decision which the trustees ought themselves to have made, and not an act which could properly be delegated.

IV. THE EXTENT OF THE AGENT'S AUTHORITY

The general principle is clear. Trustees have to take the basic decisions themselves. For example, if there is a discretionary class of beneficiaries under the trust, the trustees must themselves decide the proportions in which the beneficiaries are to receive the trust property or, if the trust has capital money, how it is to be invested. On the other hand they can employ agents to implement their decisions and to carry out most of the routine administration of the trust. Thus the trustees must make the decisions; they may employ agents to carry them out.[10] And they may employ agents whether or not they could have done the acts themselves.[11] This represents a marked change from the pre–1926 position, when a trustee could not properly appoint an agent unless it was reasonably necessary to do so or the circumstances were such that a reasonably prudent businessman would have appointed an agent had he been dealing with his own affairs.[12] If the trustees purported to delegate to an agent a function that they ought personally to have discharged, such as that relating to the distribution of a discretionary trust fund, the agent's decision was ineffective.[13] Thus any funds distributed would have been distributed without a proper decision being made and the trustees could be called upon to make good the sum in question to the trust fund out of their own pockets.

There can often be difficulty in determining whether an agent is to be appointed to do a ministerial act, where the appointment is proper, or an act which requires the trustees' own decisions. This is particularly so with regard to investment. Is it necessary for the trustees to take the decision on each sale and purchase or, provided that they have laid down guidelines, can they leave it to investment advisors to make the particular decisions? An actively-managed portfolio of stock exchange investments may require rapid decisions to be made, often within the day, and sometimes within the hour. Accordingly, private individuals may give stockbrokers or merchant bankers authority to deal with investments in whatever way they think fit. The interests of the trust fund may require such agents to have similar powers.

---

[10] It follows that, in making the basic decisions, a trustee should not allow someone who is not a trustee to join in making those decisions; *Salway v. Salway* (1831) 2 Russ. & Myl. 215; *White v. Baugh* (1835) 3 Cl. & Fin. 44. But although the trustees must themselves make the decision, there is no objection to them consulting the beneficiaries; *Fraser v. Murdoch* (1881) 6 App.Cas. 855.

[11] *Re Vickery* [1931] 1 Ch. 572.

[12] *Re Weall* (1889) 42 Ch.D. 674; *Ex parte Belchier* (1754) Amb. 218; *Speight v. Gaunt* (1883) 22 Ch.D. 727.

[13] See, for example, *Wilson v. Turner* (1883) 22 Ch.D. 521; see *post*, p. 607.

V. THE REMUNERATION OF AGENTS

An agent will have been properly appointed if the trustees had power to appoint him to carry out the particular matter for which he has been appointed, they considered that the appointment was in the interest of the trust and the trustees themselves decided to make the appointment. Where these conditions are satisfied, the trustees are entitled to pay agents their proper remuneration from the trust fund.[14]

VI. THE TRUSTEES' LIABILITY FOR THE DEFAULT OF THEIR AGENT

It might have been expected that if an agent is properly appointed,[15] trustees would not be liable for any loss which occurs if the agent defaults. However, because of inconsistencies in the wording of two provisions of the Trustee Act 1925, sections 23(1) and 30, there is some uncertainty as to the extent of the trustees' liability in such circumstances. Section 23(1), which confers the general power to appoint agents, concludes by providing that trustees "shall not be responsible for the default of any such agent if employed in good faith". Section 30 provides that a trustee shall be answerable and accountable only for his own acts, receipts, neglects or defaults, and not for those of any other person with whom any trust money or securities may be deposited, or for any other loss "unless the same happens through his own wilful default".

Under the law prior to the enactment of the Trustee Act 1925 it had been held in *Re Brier*[16] that, where there was a provision exempting a trustee from liability for loss caused by an act of an agent unless the loss occurred through the "wilful default" of the trustee, the trustee was nevertheless liable for the loss because he failed to exercise reasonable supervision over the agent. At first sight, section 23(1) therefore appears to be inconsistent with section 30. Suppose that an agent is appointed in good faith but the trustee fails to exercise reasonable supervision over him and a loss occurs. If section 23(1) is applied, the trustee is not liable, because the test of liability is the appointment of the agent, and in this example the agent was appointed in good faith. But if section 30 applies and the old law is followed, the trustee is liable, because he has been guilty of wilful default in not exercising adequate supervision.

It was against this background that *Re Vickery*[17] had to be decided in 1931. The executor of a will employed a solicitor to wind up the estate. At the time when he appointed him, he knew nothing about the solicitor which could have suggested that he should not have been appointed. However, three months after this appointment, one of the beneficiaries of the will told the executor that the solicitor had previously been suspended from practice, and that he had nevertheless subsequently been allowed to practice again. The beneficiary asked the executor to employ another solicitor and objected to

[14] Trustee Act 1925, s.23(1).
[15] See *ante*, p. 508.
[16] (1884) 26 Ch.D. 238.
[17] [1931] 1 Ch. 572.

the executor giving to the solicitor (in accordance with the usual practice) a signed authority so that he could obtain money on behalf of the estate from the Post Office Savings Department. The executor refused to take the matter away from that solicitor, who was then promising to settle it; however, the solicitor did not do so and ultimately absconded with the money. The beneficiary sued the executor. Maugham J. observed:

"It is hardly too much to say that [section 23] revolutionises the position of a trustee or an executor so far as regards the employment of agents. He is no longer required to do any actual work himself, but he may employ a solicitor or other agent to do it, whether there is any real necessity for the employment or not."[18]

To this extent there is no quarrel with the decision. However, the judge went on to find that the solicitor was undoubtedly appointed in good faith and that the executor was not himself guilty of "wilful default". As the agent had been appointed in good faith and the executor had not himself been guilty of wilful default, he was not liable for the money, either under section 23 or under section 30.

The judge held that "wilful default" means either "a consciousness of negligence or breach of duty, or recklessness".[19] In coming to this conclusion, the judge purported to follow two decisions of the Court of Appeal, *Re Trusts of Leeds City Brewery Ltd's Deed*[20] and *Re City Equitable Fire Insurance Co.*[21] In so doing, Maugham J. appears to have altered the previous position as laid down in *Re Brier*.[22]

The decision has been criticised[23] in so far as it appears to decide that a trustee is no longer under an obligation to exercise supervision over his agent. It is possible to criticise the decision on several grounds. In the first place, the Trustee Act 1925 is generally a consolidating Act, and section 30 is a re-enactment of the substance of section 31 of the Law of Property Amendment Act 1859, the provision under which *Re Brier* was decided. The decision in *Re Vickery* is therefore contrary to the presumption that a consolidating Act does not change the law. Secondly, the case of *Re City Equitable Fire Insurance Co.*, which contained the definition of wilful default which Maugham J. followed, was not a case on the law of trusts; while this may be adequate for cases outside the law of trusts, it is alleged by some that this case ought not to apply to the employment of agents by trustees, because in connection with trusts "wilful default" has had the wider meaning, as in *Re Brier*, of including lack of reasonable care. Thirdly, it is difficult to reconcile this interpretation of section 23(1) with other parts of section 23; on that basis, subsections (2) and (3) of section 23, which deal with the power to appoint agents in specific circumstances, appear to be unnecessary.

---

[18] [1931] 1 Ch. 572 at 581.
[19] And see *Wyman v. Paterson* [1900] A.C. 271; *Re Sheppard* [1911] 1 Ch. 50; *Robinson v. Harkin* [1896] 2 Ch. 415.
[20] [1925] Ch. 532.
[21] [1925] Ch. 407.
[22] (1884) 26 Ch.D. 238.
[23] See H. Potter: (1931) 47 L.Q.R. 330–332; W. Holdsworth: (1931) 47 L.Q.R. 463–465; G. H. Jones: (1959) 22 M.L.R. 381.

For example, section 23(3)(a) expressly empowers a trustee to appoint a solicitor to be his agent to receive trust money while, in the light of the interpretation of section 23(1) adopted by Maugham J., there appears to be no need for this provision.

More importantly, *Re Vickery* does not resolve the apparent inconsistency between section 23(1) and section 30, and their tests of appointment in good faith and wilful default, respectively. Perhaps they are to be reconciled on the basis that a trustee will be liable for any loss which arises through the default of an agent who is not appointed in good faith, but that if he is appointed in good faith, the trustee will nevertheless be liable if he is guilty of wilful default in the sense mentioned.[24] It is also possible to argue that section 23(1) excludes only the trustee's vicarious liability for the acts of an agent while his personal liability is governed by section 30.[25]

The force of the other criticisms remains. There seems little doubt that the decision in *Re Vickery* was technically incorrect on the legal principles previously established. It can, however, be argued that the result of the case is desirable. Due regard must indeed be paid to the fact that a trustee is looking after someone else's money, and must certainly not be flippant in so doing. But regard must also be had to the fact that the trustees may be acting without remuneration and may derive no benefit whatever from their trusteeship, no matter how much time and trouble they devote to the trust. Surely Maugham J., while admittedly changing the law, introduced a measure of equity where little existed before. A trustee is still plainly liable if he is consciously negligent or reckless; why should he be liable for more?[26]

VII. THE DELEGATION OF TRUSTEESHIP

So far this Chapter has been concerned with the delegation by a trustee of ministerial acts, while retaining his responsibility to take the fundamental decision himself. In one case, however, a trustee may delegate the power to take the basic decisions. Under section 25 of the Trustee Act 1925[27] a trustee can by power of attorney delegate all or any of his trusts, powers and discretions. The delegation cannot be for a period exceeding one year, although there appears to be no restriction on the number of times on which a delegation can be made.

This type of delegation has to be made by power of attorney and the donor must give written notice of the delegation to each of the other trustees and to any other person who has a power of appointing new trustees.[28] This

---

[24] *Re Vickery* was distinguished by Cross J. in *Re Lucking's Will Trusts* [1968] 1 W.L.R. 866, on the basis that a person employed by a trustee as managing director of a business owned by the trust was not a person with whom trust money or securities were deposited within the meaning of s.30 and accordingly the test of "wilful default" was irrelevant. The trustee was held liable for the loss caused by the managing director's defalcations on the ground that he had failed in his duty to conduct the business of the trust with the same care that an ordinary prudent businessman would apply to his own affairs. See also *post*, p. 678.

[25] See G. H. Jones: (1959) 22 M.L.R. 381.

[26] *Underwood v. Stevens* (1816) 1 Mer. 712, discussed *post*, p. 679, is an example of the injustice of the pre-1926 position.

[27] Substituted by Powers of Attorney Act 1971, s.9.

[28] Trustee Act 1925, s.25(4).

notice must specify the date when the power comes into operation, its duration, the donee, the reason why the power is being given, and which of the trusts, powers and discretions are being delegated. However, even if this notice is not given, a person dealing with the donee of the power is not prejudiced.[29] The donee of the power stands in the same position as the donor, except that the donee cannot himself delegate.[30]

The delegation can in principle be to anyone but where there are only two trustees, one trustee cannot delegate to the other, except where that other is a trust corporation.[31]

The section is in practice rarely used. While it is useful in enabling a delegation of discretions, it has a disadvantage for the donor of the power in that the donor is liable for every act or default of the donee. Thus, even if the donee is only doing an act which could have been the subject of a section 23 delegation, the donor will nevertheless be fully liable. The section could work completely unjustly, particularly as the donor may have no control over the acts of the donee.

Since the enactment of the Enduring Powers of Attorney Act 1985, it has been possible to create a power of attorney which will survive the incapacity of the donor. Powers of attorney under section 25 of the Trustee Act cannot be enduring powers of attorney—this is expressly provided by section 2(8) of the 1985 Act. However, section 3(3) provides that the donee of an enduring power of attorney may "execute or exercise all, or any of the trusts, powers or discretions vested in the donor as trustee" and may also give a valid receipt for capital money. On the face of things, this provision seems to have given trustees a quite separate right to delegate their powers by enduring power of attorney not subject either to any time limit or to any obligation to notify anyone. To make matters worse, the execution of any enduring power of attorney will presumably constitute such a delegation, whether or not the donor trustee has considered the matter and so intends. This goes way beyond the intended purpose of the subsection, which was to enable one of two trustees for sale to permit the other to deal with jointly owned property vested in them in the event of his incapacity. Assuming that the subsection is not at present so limited,[32] it certainly should be.

This matter has been under consideration by the Law Commission who have proposed[33] that section 3(3) should be repealed and be replaced by two different sets of rules applying respectively to trustees who are also beneficiaries (such as co-owners of land) and to all other trustees. Trustees who are also beneficiaries should be able to utilise enduring powers of attorney without limit of time, those dealing with the attorney being able to rely on the statement in the power that the donor has a beneficial interest; they should also continue to be able to delegate by power of attorney under section 25 of the Trustee Act 1925 with the usual 12 month time limit. Other trustees should only be able to delegate under this provision with this time limit but their power to delegate should include the power to grant an

---

[29] *ibid.*
[30] Trustee Act 1925, s.25(6).
[31] Trustee Act 1925, s.25(2).
[32] D. J. Hayton argues that it already is in (1990) 106 L.Q.R. 87 at 89.
[33] See Law Com. No. 220 (1994) Delegation by Individual Trustees.

enduring power of attorney but only for 12 months. In all cases delegation to a sole co-trustee would be permitted but such a trustee would have to appoint a co-trustee in order to be able to give a valid receipt for capital money. It should also be made clear that there is no need for an incapacitated trustee of land to be discharged prior to any dealing with the legal estate[34] where an enduring power of attorney has been granted. Enactment of these proposals would not only clarify the present uncertainty but would also substantially improve the present law.

VIII. PROPOSALS FOR REFORM

This area of the law has recently been reviewed by the Law Commission in conjunction with the independent Trust Law Committee and a Consultation Paper[35] was issued in June 1997. It is of course too early to say whether the provisional proposals of the Law Commission either as formulated in the Consultation Paper or as varied in the light of the consultation process will be carried into effect; if they are, a considerable part of the contents of this Chapter will require amendment. The principal provisional conclusions are as follows.

The Consultation Paper proposes that "subject to any expression of contrary intention in the trust instrument, trustees—(1) should have authority to delegate to agents their powers to administer the trust, including their powers of investment and management; but (2) should have no authority to delegate their powers to distribute the income or capital of the trust for the benefit of its objects, except in relation to trust property abroad", the power being able to be exercised either generally or in relation to specific acts.[36] (This proposal is without prejudice to the existing powers of individual trustees to delegate which were considered in the previous section of this Chapter, some of which are of course the subject of separate proposals by the Law Commission.) This proposed power is intended to be subject to the imposition of obligations on the trustees regularly to review any delegation and, in the case of the delegation of powers to select investments, to sell, lease or charge trust property, to grant options or rights of pre-emption over trust property and to acquire property for the benefit of the trust, to draw up and at reasonable intervals review a written statement of their policy as to the exercise of these powers and take reasonable steps to ensure that the agent complies with it.[37] Further proposals relate to the payment of agents,[38] to sub-delegation[39] and to the ability of the trustees to sanction conflicts of interest.[40]

---

[34] This is normally necessary under Law of Property Act 1925, s.22(2); the Law Commission propose that this provision should be amended to clarify its non-applicability where an enduring power of attorney has been granted.
[35] Law Commission Consultation Paper No. 146: "Trustees' Powers and Duties".
[36] *ibid.* at para. 6.26.
[37] *ibid.* at paras. 6.31, 6.32.
[38] *ibid.* at para. 6.34.
[39] *ibid.* at para. 6.37.
[40] *ibid.* at para. 6.39.

The Consultation Paper also proposes that there should be one standard of care expected of trustees in relation to the proposed power which should apply both to the selection of any agent and to the terms of his employment and to their supervision of the agent once appointed. The preferred standard of care is one lying between requiring trustees to act with the care of the ordinary prudent businessman and requiring them to "act with the care and diligence that may reasonably be expected having regard to the nature, composition and purposes of the particular trust, the skills which the trustees actually have, or if they are employed as professional trustees, those which they either ought to have or hold themselves out as having."[41] However, these are only two of the five possible standards of care reviewed in the Consultation Paper[42] and those consulted are particularly asked to choose from among all five. It can therefore be anticipated that this is the aspect of the present proposals most likely to change as a result of the consultation process.

Any version of these proposals which is eventually adopted will undoubtedly both clarify and improve the existing law.

---

[41] *ibid.* at para. 6.55.
[42] The others are to act in good faith, to be vicariously liable for all the acts and defaults of their agents and to be required to satisfy a series of specified criteria, compliance with which would be a defence to any proceedings.

CHAPTER 16

THE TAXATION OF A TRUST

In order to appreciate the contemporary significance of a trust, it is necessary to understand the basic principles of taxation which affect trusts. On the one hand, the prime motive for the creation of the trust may be the mitigation of the family's taxation liability.[1] On the other hand, when the trust is in being, taxation considerations will weigh heavily with the trustees. These considerations may influence the way in which the trust fund is invested,[2] how the trustees deal with income,[3] and the manner in which they exercise their discretion in respect of capital in favour of beneficiaries.[4] Trustees are concerned with four main taxes[5]:

(i) Stamp Duty;

(ii) Income Tax;

(iii) Capital Gains Tax; and

(iv) Inheritance Tax.

In particular circumstances they are also concerned with other types of taxation. For example, if they own land, they may be subject to council tax, but these other types of taxation are not considered in this Chapter.

I. Stamp Duty

Stamp duty is a once-and-for-all tax payable on a variety of different transactions. Where the transaction is one which gives rise to liability to stamp duty, the duty is paid at a stamping office of the Inland Revenue and upon payment of the duty a stamp is impressed on the document showing the amount of the duty paid. It follows that if a transaction can be effected without any document, such as a purely oral declaration of trust,[6] no question of stamp duty can arise.

---

[1] See *ante*, p. 9.
[2] See, generally, p. 540.
[3] See *post*, p. 595.
[4] See *post*, p. 616.
[5] For charitable trusts see *ante*, p. 379. For a more detailed treatment of the problems raised in this chapter, see Mellows, *Taxation for Executors and Trustees*.
[6] See, however, *ante*, p. 52 *et seq.*

The main inducement to pay stamp duty is that a document which ought to be stamped but is not stamped cannot be admitted in evidence in any legal proceedings.[7] Further no registrar will register a stampable document which is unstamped because, if he does so, he renders himself liable to a fine.[8] Trustees will insist that a trust deed is properly stamped, because they may at any time have to justify their position, or their acts as trustees, by production in court of the trust deed.

Technically an instrument should be stamped before execution but in practice the Revenue permit stamping within 30 days of its execution without imposing any penalty.[9] Where it is not stamped within that period, the Revenue are entitled to charge as a condition for stamping the document out of time the amount of the duty, a penalty of up to £10, and interest at 5 per cent on the unpaid duty up to a maximum of the unpaid duty.[10] In some cases, even though no duty is actually payable, the legislation nevertheless requires the document to be presented for adjudication and in these cases the document is deemed not to have been properly stamped unless it contains a stamp to the effect that it has been adjudicated.[11]

There is no general principle that every document by which every transaction is effected attracts stamp duty; a document is only stampable if it comes within one of the classes of documents specifically mentioned in the Stamp Act 1891. The amount of stamp duty to be paid depends on the class of documents within which it falls; however, the sum payable will be either a fixed duty (usually 50p)[12] or an *ad valorem* duty (usually a percentage of the value of the transaction). Where *ad valorem* duty is payable, in the case of shares and securities it will be charged at 50p per £100 or part of £100 (in effect a rate of 0.5 per cent); in the case of all other property, it will be charged at variable rates: in 1998–99, transactions up to £60,000 were exempt[13]; transactions between £60,001 and £250,000 were charged at £1 per £100 or part of £100; transactions between £250,001 and £500,000 at £2 per £100 or part of £100; and transactions above £500,000 were charged at £3 per £100 or part of £100. Any instrument relating to any transaction chargeable at less than the maximum rate must contain a certificate of value, stating that the transaction effected by the instrument does not form part of a larger transaction or series of transactions in respect of which the amount or value or the aggregate amount or value of the consideration exceeds the relevant limit.[14]

It is appropriate to consider liability to stamp duty on the inception of a trust, during the continuance of a trust, and upon its termination.

---

[7] Stamp Act 1891, s.14(4). *Ram Rattam v. Parma Nand* (1945) L.R. 73 Ind.App. 28.
[8] Stamp Act 1891, s.17.
[9] *ibid*. s.15.
[10] *ibid*. s.15(1).
[11] *ibid*. s.12.
[12] *ibid*. s.62.
[13] Finance Act 1986 *passim*.
[14] The initial £60,000 exemption below which no stamp duty is payable does not apply to shares and securities because it would be too easy to split larger transactions into £60,000 slices (Finance Act 1963, s.55 (2)).

1. *On the Inception of a Trust*

A conveyance or transfer on sale is subject to *ad valorem* duty.[15] A voluntary disposition executed before March 26, 1985, was also subject to *ad valorem* duty "as if" it were a conveyance or transfer on sale.[16] A declaration of trust which, while not voluntary, was not for full consideration was stated to fall within this provision[17] and a voluntary declaration of trust was held to do so[18]; however, a declaration of trust in consideration of marriage was exempt.[19] Consequently, the creation *inter vivos*[20] in writing of a trust of property which could only be transferred by an instrument, such as land, shares and securities, was subject to *ad valorem* duty, although such a transfer of cash was subject only to the fixed 50p duty. However, this charge to *ad valorem* duty was abolished by the Finance Act 1985.[21] The fixed 50p duty and an adjudication stamp continued to be required until 1987 when these requirements were also removed.[22] The effect of these reforms is that a transfer of property to trustees on trust no longer attracts stamp duty of any kind save in the relatively unlikely case that consideration in money or money's worth is furnished, in which case the transaction will be a transfer on sale and will be subject to the appropriate *ad valorem* duty. However, a declaration in writing by a settlor that he is himself holding property on trust is still subject to the fixed 50p duty. No stamp duty is ever payable in the case of conveyances, transfers or lettings to a charity.[23]

When a transfer *inter vivos* of property to trustees on trust was prima facie subject to *ad valorem* duty, the duty was chargeable on the document by which the beneficial interest was transferred. Many *inter vivos* settlements are created by means of two instruments, one being the trust instrument declaring the terms of the trust and the other being the conveyance or transfer transferring the legal title. In such a case, the former document was chargeable with the *ad valorem* duty and the latter with the fixed 50p duty. If, therefore, the owner of shares wished to create a settlement of them, he might execute a transfer of the shares to the proposed trustees and then execute the trust instrument only on the execution of the latter instrument was the *ad valorem* duty payable.

This fact caused a number of attempts to be made to avoid the *ad valorem* duty by creating the trust merely by means of an oral declaration. In a trust of any size, however, this was not convenient because a record of the exact terms of any trust is highly desirable. Accordingly, it became common for a settlor to make an oral declaration of trust in his solicitor's office, with one of the solicitor's secretaries taking a shorthand note of what was said. This

---

[15] Stamp Act 1891, Sched. I.

[16] Finance (1909–10) Act 1910, s.74(1).

[17] s.74(5).

[18] *Martin v. I.R.C.* (1930) 15 A.T.C. 631.

[19] Finance Act 1963, s.64.

[20] No stamp duty is payable on either a will or a grant of representation so that no duty has ever been payable in respect of the creation of testamentary trusts.

[21] s.82.

[22] Stamp Duty (Exempt Instruments) Regulations 1987.

[23] Finance Act 1982, s.129.

would provide a permanent record. Although this device was theoretically justifiable, its efficacy became open to some doubt in view of *Cohen and Moore v. I.R.C.*[24] In that case settlors orally declared that they would hold certain securities upon the trusts declared by a draft deed. Five weeks later, the draft deed was executed. It was held that the verbal declaration and the later deed formed one transaction, so that duty was payable.

A similar device, less open to this sort of objection, would be for the settlor to make his declaration of trust by recording it with its complicated provisions on tape and for the tape not to be transcribed for a considerable period. A tape would almost certainly not rank as a document and so *ad valorem* duty would not be exigible.

An extension of the device first described was for the settlor first to transfer the property to the trustees to hold as his nominees, then orally to direct them to hold the property on the trusts of the settlement, and finally for the trustees to execute declarations of their acceptance of the settlor's directions. However, as has already been seen,[25] this device was struck down by the House of Lords in *Grey v. I.R.C.*[26] on the grounds that the oral direction amounted to a disposition of a subsisting equitable interest and so was void under section 53(1)(c) of the Law of Property Act 1925; consequently, the written declarations of trust transferred the beneficial interests and so were subject to *ad valorem* duty.

Of course, at present none of these devices is necessary but if *ad valorem* duty is ever reimposed on voluntary dispositions they will once again become extremely important. However, it is questionable whether these devices would in fact survive in the light of the intervening evolution of the much more stringent attitude towards tax avoidance enunciated in *Craven v. White*,[27] where Lord Oliver stated that, if any pre-ordained series of transactions is in practice always likely to and in fact does take place in its pre-ordained order for the sole purpose of tax mitigation, the court can be justified in treating the series as a single composite whole.

Finally, it should be noted that no stamp duty is payable on either a will or a grant of representation so that no duty has ever been payable in respect of the creation of testamentary trusts.

Any stamp duty which is payable on the creation of a trust is the responsibility of the settlor and it is not properly payable out of the trust fund unless the trust instrument contains an express authority for the duty to be paid by the trustees.

2. *During the Administration of a Trust*

Where a conveyance or transfer is made without causing any change in the beneficial interests, that document prima facie attracts only the fixed 50p

---

[24] [1933] 2 K.B. 126.
[25] See *ante*, p. 52.
[26] [1960] A.C. 1.
[27] [1989] A.C. 398.

duty.[28] Accordingly a deed of retirement or appointment of new trustees, or some other instrument executed in connection with such retirement or appointment, such as a transfer of shares from an old to a new trustee,[29] formerly attracted the payment of this fixed duty.[30] However, by virtue of the Stamp Duty (Exempt) Regulations 1987, the vesting of property subject to a trust in the trustees on the appointment of a new trustee or in the continuing trustees on the retirement of a trustee is exempted from the fixed 50p duty and does not have to be presented for adjudication; however a certificate should be included in, endorsed on, or attached to the instrument to the effect that the instrument falls within the appropriate category (in the illustration given, category A) of the Schedule to the Regulations.

If the trustees in the course of administration of the trust rearrange the assets, they will be liable to stamp duty on the purchase of assets at the same rate as on a purchase by any individual. This is so notwithstanding that the value of the trust fund is not increased, for stamp duty is payable on each transaction, in this case on the purchase of shares. Stamp duty paid on such purchase documents ranks as part of the cost of the asset for capital gains tax purposes.[31]

One apparent anomaly is that, by virtue of a Practice Direction,[32] when an order is made under the Variation of Trusts Act 1958,[33] an undertaking is given to submit a duplicate of the order for adjudication. At the time when the Practice Direction was made, voluntary dispositions were subject to *ad valorem* duty. Now that this is no longer the case, there seems no good reason for the continuing requirement of adjudication, which should be declared to be redundant.

3. On the Termination of a Trust

In normal circumstances no *ad valorem* duty is payable on the termination of a trust, for by that time the beneficiary has become absolutely entitled beneficially with the result that the termination of the trust produces no change in the beneficial interests. The fixed 50p duty is prima facie payable but this requirement is in fact removed by the Stamp Duty (Exempt Instruments) Regulations 1987. If, however, the termination comes about as the result of a rearrangement of beneficial interests, the rearrangement formerly constituted a voluntary disposition of a beneficial interest and so was subject to *ad valorem* duty. This in *Platt's Trustees v. I.R.C.*,[34] where a life tenant executed a deed releasing his life interest, thereby accelerating the interest in remainder and enabling distribution of the trust fund, *ad valorem* duty was held to be payable on the deed of release. However, this will clearly no

---

[28] Stamp Act 1891, s.62.
[29] Stock exchange securities are excluded from the automatic vesting provisions of Trustee Act, s.40; see *ante*, p. 482.
[30] Stamp Act 1891, ss.23(1), 62.
[31] See *post*, p. 526.
[32] [1966] 1 W.L.R. 345.
[33] See *post*, p. 674.
[34] (1953) 34 A.T.C. 292.

longer be the case unless *ad valorem* duty is reimposed on voluntary dispositions.

II. INCOME TAX

For the purposes of income tax, and for that matter of capital gains tax and of inheritance tax, trustees are treated as a separate and continuing body of persons.[35] Because trustees constitute a separate body, the liability of the trust to tax is computed without taking into account the trustees' personal tax position. Because trustees constitute a continuing body, the tax liability of the trust is unaffected by any changes in the persons who are from time to time the trustees. For most taxation purposes, therefore, a trust is treated almost as if it had its own separate legal personality.

The taxation of the income of trusts is in many ways more simple than the taxation of income of private individuals, because the various allowances and reliefs which affect the computation of an individual's liability do not apply.

The taxation of the income of a trust is based on these principles:

(i) The whole of the income of the trust is taxable, irrespective of its ultimate disposal.[36] Thus, the income of the trust is taxable whether it is paid to beneficiaries, absorbed in administration expenses, or accumulated.

(ii) Trust income is generally taxable at the basic rate of income tax. This varies from time to time, but at present[37] it is 23 per cent,[38] save in the case of company distributions, such as dividends on shares, and interest on bank deposits which are taxable only at 20 per cent.[39] In the case of a private individual, on the other hand, the effect of personal allowances is to exempt from income tax the first "slice" of his income.[40] The next "slice" is taxable at 20 per cent, the next slice at the basic rate of 23 per cent, and the residue at the higher rate of 40 per cent[41] (company distributions and bank interest are taxed at 20 per cent unless the individual is liable to tax at the higher rate of 40 per cent, in which case they are treated as the

---

[35] The principle is assumed but not expressly enacted for the purposes of income tax.

[36] The rate at which income tax is paid will vary according to the nature of the income and to whether the trust is discretionary or not see *infra*.

[37] In 1998–99.

[38] This has been the case since 1988–89.

[39] Income and Corporation Taxes Act 1988, s.207A (inserted by Finance Act 1993).

[40] In 1998–99, a single person was entitled to a personal allowance of £4,300; additional allowances are available to married persons, to single parents, to widows and widowers and pensioners, in respect of dependant relatives and in certain other circumstances. The amounts of these allowances are reviewed annually in each budget.

[41] In 1998–99, the first £4,300 of taxable income was taxed at 20 per cent, taxable income between £4,301 and £27,100 was taxed at 23 per cent and taxable income in excess of £27,100 at 40 per cent. The width of the bands and their thresholds are also reviewed annually in each Budget.

top slice of his income and are therefore taxable at 40 per cent).[42] None of these complications generally applies to trust income. Whether the income is £1 per annum or £100,000 per annum that income is chargeable at the basic rate of 23 per cent (or, in the case of company distributions and bank interest, at 20 per cent).

(iii) There is one exception to the above principles. Accumulation and discretionary settlements have long been used as devices to take income away from taxpayers who are liable to pay income tax at the higher rate. In an attempt to counteract this, it is provided that income which is to be accumulated, or which is payable under a discretion,[43] is chargeable at a flat rate of 34 per cent rather than at the basic rate of 23 per cent or, in the case of company distributions and bank interest, 20 per cent.[44] Consequently, the trustees have to pay a further 11 per cent tax (14 per cent in the case of company distributions and bank interest). This does not apply, however, to the extent that the income arises under a charitable trust, or is properly applied in the administration of the trust.[45] The beneficiary is in no worse position where the income is distributed to him as income,[46] for he can make a repayment claim if he is not liable to pay tax at the higher rate of 40 per cent on the top slice of his income.

It follows from these principles that all payments of income from the trust to the beneficiaries are paid from a fund which has been taxed. Accordingly, with each payment of income, the trustees are bound to issue to the beneficiary a certificate of the tax notionally deducted from that payment.

The gross equivalent of the net payment made to the beneficiary is then regarded as part of the beneficiary's total income, and he may then obtain any repayment which is appropriate having regard to his total income.

An example may illustrate these principles. Suppose that a trust fund has an income of £4,000 per annum gross, £2,000 of which proceeds from company dividends or bank interest and £2,000 from other sources. The administration expenses are £400 and the trustees are obliged by the trust instrument to accumulate one half of the income and to distribute the other half to a beneficiary who has a fixed interest. The 20 per cent tax payable on the company dividends and bank interest will be the subject of a tax credit received from the company or bank in question; consequently, the trustees will not need to take any action in respect of this income except in the case of the part of the settlement which is an accumulation and discretionary settlement, where they will have to pay the further 14 per cent tax. However, the trustees will be responsible for all the tax payable in respect of the income from other sources, whether it is taxable at 23 per cent or at 34 per

---

[42] Assuming that the taxpayer is liable to pay 40 per cent tax even if the company distributions are disregarded if he still has some part of his 23 per cent band unutilised, the distributions will be taxed at 23 per cent until the threshold of the higher rate is reached.
[43] Income and Corporation Taxes Act 1988, s.686 (as amended by Finance Act 1993).
[44] *ibid.* s.207A.
[45] *ibid.* s.686(2).
[46] If the income is accumulated and the beneficiary receives a sum from the accumulation, he receives a capital, and not an income sum, and no repayment claim can be made.

cent. The gross figures of course determine the tax liability of any beneficiary to whom income is distributed.[47] The tax payable is calculated as
follows:

Gross income		£4,000
Less: tax at 20% on dividends and interest of £2,000	£400	
tax at 23% on other income of £2,000	£460	
administration expenses[48]	£400	
	£1,260	£1,260
		£2,740
Net income available for distribution (50%)		£1,370
Gross income available for accumulation (50%)	£1,370	
Less: additional tax to raise to 34%: 34% x £1,800 (income susceptible to 34% rate) less 50% of tax already paid (50% x £860)[49]	£193.80	
Net income available for accumulation	£1,176.20	

The beneficiary who receives £1,370 net is treated as having received
£1,800[50] from which tax of £387 is treated as having been deducted.[51]
Suppose that he has no significant income from other sources and, even with
the trust income, his income is insufficient to absorb his personal reliefs so
that he will not be liable to income tax, not even at the lower rate of 20 per
cent. In these circumstances, he can make a repayment claim and recover
from the Inland Revenue the £387 tax which he has suffered (in order to do
this, he will need to produce a certificate of deduction of tax issued by the
trustees). The net benefit to him will therefore be £1,757.[52] If, on the other
hand, the beneficiary is already paying income tax at the higher rate of 40
per cent, he will be treated as having received £1,800 from which tax of £387
has been deducted. He is, however, liable to pay tax at the higher rate of 40
per cent. Therefore, his overall tax liability is £720 (40 per cent of £1,800) and
he will consequently have to pay a further £333 (£720 less the £387 treated
as having been paid by the trust). The net benefit to him will therefore only
be £1,037.

---

[47] For the purposes of the example, the gross figure for dividend income will be used.
[48] Administration expenses are not liable to the flat rate of 34 per cent.
[49] The total income available for accumulation before tax is £2,000 (half the total) from which
half the administration expenses (£200) has to be deducted because these expenses are not
liable to the flat rate of 34 per cent. Half the tax already paid is attributable to each half of the
fund.
[50] Grossed up by 23 per cent (the basic rate of tax).
[51] The tax credit is of 20 per cent in respect of the half of the income from the dividends and
bank deposits and of 23 per cent in respect of the half of the income from other sources; hence
20 per cent x £900 (£180) and 23 per cent x £900 (£207).
[52] This figure does not equal the total income attributable to this half of the fund (£2,000) less
its half share of the administration expenses (£200) because the tax payable on the administration expenses cannot be recovered.

These principles lead to three general results which trustees will wish to bear in mind. First, as the whole income of the trust is taxable, liability to tax can only be avoided if non-income-producing assets are held by the trust. An example is for trusts to purchase pieces of silver or works of art.[53] A more prosaic example is the purchase of National Savings Certificates, which produce no income but are repayable on maturity with a capital bonus.[54] However, such increments will be of a capital nature for all purposes, so that a life tenant will not, in general, be entitled to any part of the bonus.[55] While a trustee must keep tax considerations in mind, he must also keep in mind his general obligation to balance the interests of tenant for life and remainderman.[56]

The second result of the basic principles is that, where trustees have a discretion to accumulate income, they can only accumulate out of taxed income. Accordingly, accumulation is not a method of avoiding income tax completely but, as is shown in a later Chapter,[57] in some circumstances it may be appropriate to accumulate income as capital and then to make an advancement of capital.

The third result is that trustees will wish to consider the likely taxation result of a distribution of income upon the tax position of the beneficiary. If, as in the example given above, the personal tax position of the beneficiary is such that he can make a repayment claim, a distribution of income to him will be clearly advantageous. If, however, the beneficiary is already paying income tax at the higher rate of 40 per cent, the trustees will know that the beneficiary will also have to pay higher rate income tax on any income paid to him by the trust.

If, instead, the trustees have a discretion as to the payment of income, all the income will be taxable at a flat rate of 34 per cent. Consequently, most tax will be recoverable if the trustees pay as much as possible of the income to the beneficiaries with the lowest personal rate of taxation since they will be able to reclaim at least some of the tax paid by the trust on the sum actually distributed to them.[58] If, on the other hand, all the beneficiaries are paying tax at the higher rate of 40 per cent, no tax will be able to be recovered and the trustees will have to choose between accumulating the income, which will at least restrict their tax liability to the 34 per cent already paid, with a view to a subsequent capital distribution, or paying the income to one or more of the beneficiaries on the basis that they will then be responsible for paying a further 6 per cent tax on the sum actually distributed to them.

---

[53] Provided that the pieces of silver are sold for a figure not in excess of £6,000, no capital gains tax is payable. Trustees hope, therefore, to dispose of the silver at a profit which will attract liability neither to income tax, because the profit is not of an income nature, nor to capital gains tax.

[54] See post, p. 546.

[55] Re Holder (1953) Ch. 468. See, however, post, p. 593.

[56] In Nestle v. National Westminster Bank [1993] 1 W.L.R. 1260, the remainderman accused the trustees of allowing the tax interests of the tenant for life to influence unduly their choice of investments. The judgments contain an important discussion of the criteria which trustees should follow (see post, p. 540).

[57] See post, p. 616.

[58] The tax paid on any administration expenses will not be able to be recovered since the right of recovery is limited to the income actually received by the beneficiary.

III. CAPITAL GAINS TAX

The object of capital gains tax is to make a charge on capital gains made either by private individuals or by any body of persons such as trustees as a result of any actual or deemed disposal of an asset *inter vivos*, whether by way of sale, exchange or gift; no charge is made on disposals *mortis causa*.[59] Capital gains tax is imposed on any increase in the value of an asset between the date of its acquisition and the date of its disposal; any decrease in the value of an asset can be set off against future capital gains. The value of the asset at the date of its acquisition is adjusted to take account of whatever inflation occurred prior to April 6, 1998; however, in the case of an asset acquired before March 31, 1982, its acquisition value is deemed to be its market value on that date[60] so that gains made prior to that date escape tax. Capital gains made after April 5, 1998 are "tapered", that is to say reduced by a percentage in accordance with the period thereafter during which the asset in question has been owned. Capital gains tax is payable at the same rate as income tax[61] on that part of a private individual's capital gains in each year as exceeds his annual exemption of, in 1998–99, £6,800 in the case of private individuals and[62] (there are many other exemptions, including a private individual's main residence,[63] chattels worth less than £6,000,[64] and certain securities).[65] However, trusts enjoy an annual exemption of only half that of a private individual (£3,400 in 1998–99) and from April 6, 1998 pay capital gains tax at the flat rate of 34 per cent.[65a]

1. *Trusts to which the Capital Gains Tax Legislation Applies*

The trust provisions of the capital gains tax legislation only apply where there are not one or more beneficiaries absolutely and concurrently entitled to the whole of the trust property as against the trustees. The basic rule is that property is regarded as "settled property" for the purposes of the capital gains tax legislation whenever it is held on trust.[66] However, there are three situations in which the trust property is treated as if it were vested

---

[59] The property of a deceased person is deemed to be acquired by his personal representatives for its market value on the date of his death, thus giving the beneficiaries a "tax-free uplift" in the event that this value is superior to its acquisition value. However, the property of the deceased will of course be liable to Inheritance Tax and any Inheritance Tax payable in respect of the settled assets will, in the event that it is chargable on those assets, have the effect of reducing the "tax-free uplift".

[60] Taxation of Chargeable Gains Act 1992, s.35. From that date, there is a published indexation allowance in respect of the period until April 5, 1998. Thereafter, indexation is irrelevant, any reduction in the apparent capital gain being made by means of the "tapering" relief referred to in the text. The latter was introduced by Finance (No. 2) Act 1998, s.119, Sched. A1.

[61] *ibid.* s.4. Hence the rate is either 20 per cent, 23 per cent or 40 per cent for private individuals and 25 per cent for trusts other than accumulation and discretionary trusts, whose rate is 34 per cent.

[62] *ibid.* s.3, Sched. I (these exemptions are index-linked).

[63] *ibid.* s.222.

[64] *ibid.* s.262.

[65] *ibid.* s.115.

[65a] *ibid.* s.1AA inserted by Finance Act 1998, s.120.

[66] *ibid.* s.68.

in the beneficiary[67]: first, where the beneficiary is absolutely entitled to the property as against the trustee; secondly, where the beneficiary would be absolutely entitled to the property as against the trustee were he not an infant; and, thirdly, where the property is held for two or more persons who jointly are or would be absolutely entitled to the property as against the trustee. Such a situation was claimed to arise in *Tomlinson v. Glyns Executor and Trustee Company*[68] where trustees held property in trust for such of four infant beneficiaries as attained the age of 21 or married under that age. When the trustees disposed of certain investments at a profit, they claimed that the infant beneficiaries were together absolutely entitled to the investments as against the trustees.[69] The Court of Appeal held that infancy was not the only reason which, at the time of the disposal of the investments, prevented the beneficiaries from being absolutely entitled because they had only a contingent interest until they reached the age of 21 or married under that age.

2. *Capital Gains on the Creation of a Settlement*

The creation of a settlement constitutes a disposal of the trust property by the settlor at its market value, even if the settlement is revocable, and whether or not he or his spouse is a beneficiary.[70] If chargeable assets are settled, any chargeable gain will be made by the settlor and capital gains tax will be payable by him thereon at the same rate as that at which he pays income tax; any chargeable loss[71] will also be made by the settlor but, because he and the trustees are connected persons,[72] that loss will be deductible only from future chargeable gains arising out of subsequent disposals by the settlor to the same settlement. It used to be possible to postpone the payment of the tax until the property was eventually sold[73] but this is now only possible if the assets settled comprise business property[74] or if the creation of the trust involves a chargeable transfer for the purposes of inheritance tax.[75]

3. *Capital Gains on the Disposal of Assets by the Trustees*

When a trust is created, the trustees are deemed to acquire the trust property at its market value (or, if acquired before March 31, 1982, at its market value then). When an asset is purchased in a transaction at arm's length, the consideration, together with the expenses associated with the purchase, constitutes the acquisition value.

---

[67] *ibid.* s.60.
[68] [1970] Ch. 112.
[69] If the trustees had succeeded in their contention, there would still have been a capital gains tax liability. However, it would have been calculated according to a special basis then in force which was open only to private individuals; see Finance Act 1965, s.21.
[70] Taxation of Chargeable Gains Act 1992, s.70.
[71] For disposals after November 29, 1993 the indexation allowance cannot create or increase an allowable loss. Consequently losses will be only chargeable if genuinely incurred.
[72] By virtue of Taxation of Chargeable Gains Act 1992, s.18(3).
[73] Under Finance Act 1980, s.79 (repealed in 1989).
[74] Taxation of Chargeable Gains Act 1992, s.165.
[75] See *post*, p. 530.

Apart from assets which are exempt from capital gains tax, not many of which are likely to be held by trustees, any disposition of an asset for a consideration in excess of its acquisition value gives rise to a chargeable gain in respect of the difference. Where the trustees incur expense such as stamp duty, legal costs and registration fees in acquiring an asset and in arranging for its disposal, the total of these costs is added to the acquisition value and only the difference is chargeable. Capital gains made by trusts are taxable at 34 per cent (until April 5, 1998, capital gains made by trusts other than accumulation and discretionary trusts were taxable only at 23 per cent).

A simple transaction, without taking account of any adjustment to the acquisition cost by virtue of inflation, would be:

Proceeds of sale of shares		£10,100
Less: purchase price	£8,000	
broker's commission on purchase	£100	
stamp duty on purchase	£40	
	£8,140	£8,140
		£1,960
Less: expenses of sale		£160
Chargeable gain		£1,800
Capital gains tax payable:		
34% of £1,800:		£612

Of course, if this was the only chargeable gain made by the trust during the year in question, it would be within the annual exemption of, at present, £3,400. The tax shown above would therefore only be payable in full if the annual exemption had already been completely used up.

Clearly, the most usual situation in which trustees will incur this type of liability is where they switch assets in the course of the administration of the trust. Equally clearly, the existence of capital gains tax will have an inhibiting effect on changing assets.

4. *The Exit Charge*

When a beneficiary becomes absolutely entitled to the whole or any part of the trust property, the trustees are deemed to have disposed of the assets in question to him at their market value at that date and he is deemed to have acquired them for their market value at that date.[76] A beneficiary will become absolutely entitled in this sense on fulfilling some contingency, such as attaining the age of 21, or on the determination of a prior interest, or when in other circumstances the trustees make a decision to pay or to transfer the

---

[76] Taxation of Chargeable Gains Act 1992, s.71(1).

asset to him. An immediate liability to capital gains tax will arise which is payable by the trustees; payment of the tax can only be postponed in the limited circumstances already discussed. If after this time the trustees continue to hold the assets in their name, they do so as nominees for the beneficiary. In this case, the trust will no longer be a settlement for the purposes of the capital gains tax legislation; the property will be deemed to be held by the beneficiary so that any future liability for capital gains tax will fall on the beneficiary and not on the trustees.

Thus if shares worth £100,000 were settled on trust for the settlor's daughter contingent on her reaching the age of 21, a deemed disposal will take place when she attains that age. If the shares are then worth £120,000, capital gains tax of £6,800 (34 per cent of £20,000) will be payable by the trustees. This will also be the case if instead the shares were held on trust for such of the settlor's children as the trustees might in their absolute discretion determine and if the trustees decided to allocate these shares to the settlor's daughter absolutely (since April 6, 1998, 34 per cent is payable whatever the type of trust; previously only 23 per cent would have been payable in the former case). If the shares are subsequently sold for £130,000, then, whether they have in the meantime been retained by the trustees or transferred to the daughter, the further capital gain of £10,000 will be attributable to the daughter and she will pay capital gains tax thereon at the same rate as that at which she pays income tax.

In principle, one beneficiary can become absolutely entitled as against the trustees even though there are other beneficiaries who do not. If, therefore, property is held on trust for such of the settlor's three children as attain the age of 25 and, if more than one of them, in equal shares, when the eldest child attains the age of 25 the membership of the class will become fixed.[77] If there are then three children, the eldest child will immediately become absolutely entitled to a one third share in the property even though the younger children are still under 25.[78] If the second child dies under the age of 25, the eldest child will then become absolutely entitled to a further one sixth share (one half of the deceased child's presumptive share) and, when the youngest child attains the age of 25, the latter will become absolutely entitled to the remaining half share of the property.[79] However, where the settled property consists of land, it seems that one beneficiary cannot become absolutely entitled if the other beneficiaries do not also do so.[80]

Special rules apply when a beneficiary becomes absolutely entitled as the result of the determination of a prior life interest because of the death of the life tenant. Although there is still a deemed disposal by the trust and a deemed acquisition by the beneficiary, no capital gains tax will be payable because of the basic principle that no charge to capital gains tax is made on disposals *mortis causa*.[81] The absolutely entitled beneficiary will therefore acquire the trust property at its market value on the date of the death of the

---

[77] Under the class closing rules mentioned *ante*, p. 216, n. 50.
[78] *ibid.*
[79] *Stephenson v. Barclays Bank Trust Company* [1975] S.T.C. 151; *Pexton v. Bell* [1976] 1 W.L.R. 885.
[80] *Crowe v. Appleby* [1976] 1 W.L.R. 885.
[81] Taxation of Chargeable Gains Act 1992, s.73.

life tenant. There may, however, be inheritance tax liability.[82] The only exception to this rule is where the settlor has postponed the payment of the capital gains tax payable on the creation of the settlement; in this case, the capital gains tax becomes payable on the death of the life tenant.[83]

5. Where a Settlement Continues

Where on the determination of a prior interest a settlement continues without any beneficiary becoming absolutely entitled, there are no capital gains tax consequences unless the prior interest has determined because of the death of the life tenant, in which case the rules discussed immediately above apply; there will be a deemed disposal and a deemed reacquisition by the trustees but no capital gains tax will be payable unless the settlor has postponed payment of his own capital gains tax.[84] Thus, if property is settled on the settlor's daughter until her marriage and subject thereto to his son if he attains the age of 25, the marriage of the daughter before the son has attained the age of 25 will determine her interest but the son is still not absolutely entitled and so there will be no deemed disposal until he reaches the age of 25, when capital gains tax will be payable. If, on the other hand, the trust is to the daughter for life and subject thereto to the son if he attains the age of 25, the death of the daughter before the son has attained the age of 25 will produce a deemed disposal and reacquisition of the property by the trustees at its market value on the date of the daughter's death but no capital gains tax will be payable.

6. Resettlements

When property is transferred from one settlement to another, the trustees of the second settlement (even if they are the same persons as the trustees of the original settlement) become absolutely entitled as against the original trustees and a charge to capital gains tax will normally arise.[85] If the resettlement occurs only as the result of the exercise by the trustees of their powers under the original settlement, it seems that the exercise of a special power of appointment will not amount to a resettlement and a consequential deemed disposal of the property in question[86]; on the other hand, while the exercise of a wider power, such as a power of advancement, will not necessarily amount to a resettlement, it will have this effect if the new settlement is complete in itself and is sufficiently separate to require no further reference back for any purpose to the original settlement.[87]

IV. INHERITANCE TAX

Inheritance tax is imposed at a fixed rate of 40 per cent on such part of a person's estate (which for this purpose includes any property disposed of by

---

[82] See post, p. infra.
[83] Taxation of Chargeable Gains Act 1992, s.74.
[84] ibid. s.72.
[85] Hoare Trustees v. Gardner [1979] Ch. 1.
[86] Roome v. Edwards [1981] S.T.C. 96; Bond v. Pickford [1983] S.T.C. 517.
[87] Swires v. Renton [1991] S.T.C. 490.

him other than for value during the seven years immediately prior to his death) as exceeds his lifetime allowance of, at present,[88] £223,000.[89] His estate includes any property in which he has an interest in possession.[90] Inheritance tax is governed by what is now known as the Inheritance Tax Act 1984,[91] which was subsequently substantially modified by the Finance Act 1986.

1. *Exempt, Potentially Exempt, and Chargeable Transfers*

Inheritance tax focuses around the transfer of value, something which occurs whenever a person makes a disposition as a result of which the value of his estate immediately after the disposition is less than it would have been but for the transfer, the amount by which it is less being the value transferred by the transfer.[92] A transfer of value may be exempt, potentially exempt, or chargeable.

The principal example of an exempt transfer is any transfer of any amount between spouses, whether *inter vivos* or *mortis causa*.[93-94] There are a number of further exemptions. Some are personal, such as gifts of up to £3,000 per donor and £250 per donee per annum, gifts in consideration of marriage of varying amounts up to £5,000, and payments for the maintenance of dependants. Others are institutional, including gifts to charities, to certain bodies concerned with the preservation of the national heritage or of a public nature, and to political parties, and gifts of works of art, of agricultural or business property, and of woodlands.

A potentially exempt transfer is any transfer made *inter vivos* by a private individual after March 17, 1986.[95] If the transferor dies within three years of making the transfer, the rate of inheritance tax payable is the same as that chargeable on death; the tax is payable on the value of the property at the time of transfer or the value of the property at the date of death, whichever is the lower. If he dies more than three years but less than seven years after making the transfer, the rate of inheritance tax payable is a proportion of that chargeable on death (there is a reduction of 20 per cent of the tax for each year or part of a year after the first three that the transferor has survived); as before, the tax is payable on the value of the property at the time of transfer or the value of the property at the date of death, whichever is the lower. If the transferor survives for seven years after making the transfer, it becomes exempt from inheritance tax. However, in certain exceptional circumstances, a transfer made *inter vivos* by a private individual is immediately liable to inheritance tax, at half the rate applicable on death (such a transfer is known as an initially chargeable transfer). The tax so paid

---

[88] In 1998–99.

[89] There are also a number of further exemptions, including small gifts of up to £3,000 per annum, gifts between spouses, gifts in consideration of marriage, gifts to charities, and gifts of agricultural or business property.

[90] See *ante*, p. 184.

[91] It was originally called the Capital Transfer Tax Act 1984 (the tax was rechristened in 1986) and the Act may be cited in either form herein it will be cited as the Inheritance Tax Act 1984.

[92] Inheritance Tax Act 1984, s.3.

[93-94] *ibid.* s.18.

[95] *ibid.* s.3A (introduced by Finance Act 1986, s.101).

forms part of the property transferred; consequently, if the transferor pays the tax himself, the transfer must be "grossed up" for this purpose.[96] In the event that the transferor dies within seven years, additional inheritance tax is payable in the manner already described. The principal example of a transfer of this type is the creation of an accumulation or discretionary trust.

A chargeable transfer is any transfer made *inter vivos* by a private individual which is either initially chargeable or subsequently becomes chargeable by reason of his failure to survive seven years and any transfer *mortis causa*. Inheritance tax is payable on the value of all chargeable transfers after the first £223,000[97] at 40 per cent in respect of transfers on death or within three years of death, at the appropriate proportion of 40 per cent in respect of transfers made within seven years of but more than three years before death, and at 20 per cent in respect of initially chargeable lifetime transfers. It is therefore necessary to keep a lifetime record of all transfers *inter vivos*; first, because if any potentially exempt transfer becomes chargeable any transfers made during the seven year period preceding that transfer will have to be aggregated with it in order to decide the inheritance tax ultimately payable thereon; and, secondly, because any transfers made within the seven years preceding death will have to be aggregated with the estate of the transferor to determine the amount of inheritance tax payable in respect of his estate. The presence of potentially exempt transfers makes the calculation of the inheritance tax payable far from straightforward.

A potentially exempt transfer will take effect as a chargeable transfer in the event that the transferor has reserved a benefit thereunder; this is for the somewhat obvious reason that he cannot be permitted to enjoy the advantages of making a potentially exempt transfer if he has retained enjoyment of the property in question. Where there is such a reservation of benefit, the property will be regarded as continuing to form part of the transferor's estate unless and until such time as the benefit in question ceases (from which time the seven year period will start to run) and will be taxed accordingly on his death. The transferor will be treated as having reserved a benefit in two cases[98]: first, where the donee has not, prior to the seven year period preceding the donor's death (or, if the donor has died within seven years of the gift, at the date of the gift), bona fide assumed the possession and enjoyment of the property; and, secondly, where, at any time during the seven years prior to the donor's death (or, if he dies within seven years of the gift, at any time after the gift), the property is not enjoyed "to the entire exclusion, or virtually to the entire exclusion, of the donor and of any benefit to him by contract or otherwise".

2. How Inheritance Tax is Calculated

Suppose that a person who has just died, leaving an estate, other than that part which he has left to his spouse and which is therefore exempt from

---

[96] *ibid.* s.7. Where the transferor pays the inheritance tax on an immediately chargeable transfer of £100,000, the "grossed up" figure will be £125,000 (because 80 per cent of this amount is £100,000), thus producing a tax liability of £25,000.
[97] In 1998–99.
[98] Inheritance Tax Act 1984, ss.38, 39.

inheritance tax, of £250,000, made the following *inter vivos* transfers: eight years ago, a transfer of £100,000 to his son (a potentially exempt transfer); six and a half years ago, a transfer of £150,000 to trustees on trust for such of his grandchildren as attain the age of 21 (a potentially exempt transfer); four and a half years ago, a transfer of £300,000 to trustees on discretionary trust for all his descendants (an initially chargeable transfer); and two years ago, a transfer of £100,000 to his daughter (a potentially exempt transfer). Suppose also that throughout this period and at the time of his death the lifetime allowance was £223,000 and the only rate of inheritance tax was 40 per cent (this is of course totally unrealistic, since the lifetime allowance is raised in line with inflation, but it is the only way to make the example comprehensible). It is necessary to calculate the inheritance tax payable twice: first, transfer by transfer during the deceased's lifetime and, secondly, on his death.

The transfers made eight years ago and six and a half years ago were both potentially exempt so no inheritance tax was payable on either occasion. The transfer made four and a half years ago was, however, initially chargeable so inheritance tax was payable. At that time, the deceased had not used up any of his lifetime allowance of £223,000 (the potentially exempt transfers were assumed not to be chargeable and therefore did not have to be aggregated for that purpose) consequently, the first £223,000 of the £300,000 used up the deceased's lifetime allowance of £223,000 so that inheritance tax was payable at 20 per cent (half the death rate) on the remaining £77,000, thus requiring the immediate payment of £15,400 (it will be presumed that the tax was paid by the trustees of the settlement—had it been paid by the deceased, the total amount of the transfer would have had to be "grossed up" to take account of the tax). The transfer made two years ago was also potentially exempt so no inheritance tax was payable then either. Thus the total inheritance tax payable during the deceased's lifetime was £15,400.

By the time of the deceased's death, the potentially exempt transfer of £100,000 made eight years ago had become exempt. However, all of the other three transfers and the deceased's estate give rise to inheritance tax liabilities which need to be calculated individually in chronological order. The personal representatives are liable to pay any inheritance tax due in respect of the estate; any liability in respect of the *inter vivos* transfers falls primarily on the individual transferees but in default also passes to the personal representatives.

(i) The potentially exempt transfer of £150,000 made six and a half years ago is not in fact exempt. During the seven years preceding that transfer, the deceased had made one previous transfer, that of £100,000 eight years ago. That used up £100,000 of his lifetime allowance of £223,000. Thus, £123,000 of this allowance remained at that time to offset against the transfer of £150,000. The £27,000 balance is thus liable to inheritance tax. The death rate is 40 per cent but because the deceased survived for six and a half further years, there is a reduction of 80 per cent (20 per cent for each year or part of a year after the first three). Consequently, the inheritance tax payable is 20 per cent of 40 per cent of £27,000, thus £2,160.

(ii) The initially chargeable transfer of £300,000 made four and a half years ago has already suffered inheritance tax of £15,400. During the seven years preceding that transfer, the deceased had made two previous transfers, that of £100,000 eight years ago and that of £150,000 six and a half years ago. These used up all his lifetime allowance of £223,000. Thus, the whole of the £200,000 is liable to inheritance tax. The death rate is 40 per cent but because the deceased survived for four and half further years, there is a reduction of 40 per cent (20 per cent for each year or part of a year after the first three). Consequently, the inheritance tax payable is 60 per cent of 40 per cent of £300,000 less the £15,400 already paid, thus £56,600.

(iii) The potentially exempt transfer of £100,000 made two years ago is not in fact exempt. During the seven years preceding that transfer, the deceased had made three previous transfers, that of £100,000 eight years ago, that of £150,000 six and a half years ago, and that of £300,000 four and a half years ago. These used up all his lifetime allowance of £223,000. Thus, the whole of the £100,000 is liable to inheritance tax. The death rate is 40 per cent and there is no reduction because the deceased did not survive for three years. Consequently, the inheritance tax payable is 40 per cent of £100,000, thus £40,000.

(iv) The deceased's estate of £250,000, other than the part which he left to his spouse, which is therefore exempt from inheritance tax, is liable to inheritance tax. During the seven years preceding his death, the deceased has made three previous transfers, that of £150,000 six and a half years ago, that of £300,000 four and a half years ago, and that of £100,000 two years ago. These used up all his lifetime allowance of £223,000. Thus, the whole of the £250,000 is liable to inheritance tax. The death rate is 40 per cent. Consequently, the inheritance tax payable is 40 per cent of £250,000, thus £100,000.

As the amount of inheritance tax payable illustrates, this is of course a splendid illustration of how not to do it! In general, the potentially exempt transfers and, preferably, also the initially chargeable transfers during any seven year period should be restricted to the amount of the lifetime allowance because of the risk that the transferor may die before they have become exempt, thus producing the sort of countback and the level of inheritance tax liability evidenced in the example.

3. *The Liability to Inheritance Tax of Settlements*

When potentially exempt transfers were introduced,[99] only one specific type of trust, an accumulation and maintenance trust, was able to take effect as such a transfer. However, potentially exempt transfers were subsequently

[99] By Finance Act 1986.

enlarged to include settlements in which there is an interest in possession[1]; consequently, when such a settlement is created *inter vivos*, it is capable of taking effect as a potentially exempt transfer, subject of course to the rules about reservation of benefit by the settlor which have already been discussed. However, discretionary trusts (other than accumulation and maintenance trusts) can still not take effect as potentially exempt transfers and, if created *inter vivos*, are consequently still initially chargeable transfers.

(A) Settlements in which there is an Interest in Possession

A settlement contains an interest in possession for the purposes of the inheritance tax legislation if the beneficiary whose interest is in possession has the right to receive the income of the settlement as it arises. It does not matter that the trustees have power to revoke his entitlement or to appoint the income to someone else; however, the existence of a power to accumulate, whether or not it is being exercised, prevents the settlement from having an interest in possession for this purpose.[2]

A settlement in which there is an interest in possession for the purposes of the inheritance tax legislation can take effect as a potentially exempt transfer, provided that there is no reservation of benefit by the settlor. Consequently, there is no liability to inheritance tax on the creation of the settlement although, in the event that the settlor does not survive for a further seven years, inheritance tax may nevertheless be payable on his death for the reasons and upon the bases illustrated in the previous section.

A beneficiary who has an interest in possession for the purposes of the inheritance tax legislation is regarded as being beneficially entitled to the property which forms the subject matter of the settlement—the fact that he may have no more than a life interest therein is irrelevant for this purpose.[3] Consequently, when an interest in possession comes to an end, its beneficiary is regarded as having made a transfer of the value of his interest whether its determination was the result of his own positive act, such as a disposition or surrender, or the result of reaching its natural limit, such as the occurrence of a determining event or the death of a life tenant.[4] Such a transfer may be exempt, potentially exempt, or chargeable. It will be exempt if it falls within any of the general exemptions already mentioned (other than the small gifts exemption of £250, which does not apply to settlements).[5] (Consequently, if a husband has an interest in possession under a settlement for his life time and the beneficiary next entitled under the settlement is his wife, no inheritance tax will be payable whether it passes to her as a result of a surrender *inter vivos* or as a result of his death.) Such a transfer will be potentially exempt if it occurs *inter vivos*. Consequently, a disposition or surrender of the interest *inter vivos* and a determination as a result of the interest reaching its natural limit will all be potentially exempt transfers. If the beneficiary survives a further seven years, the transfer will become exempt. If he does

---

[1] By Finance (No.2) Act 1987.
[2] The authorities all concern capital transfer tax, where the same criteria applied. See particularly *Pearson v. I.R.C.* [1981] A.C. 753.
[3] Inheritance Tax Act 1984, s.49.
[4] *ibid.* ss.51, 52.
[5] *ibid.* s.57.

not do so, the transfer will become chargeable, as will any non-exempt transfer occurring as a result of the death of the beneficiary. In these cases, the inheritance tax payable is assessed on the basis of the lifetime transfers made by the beneficiary, not those made by the settlor.[6] However, the tax due is actually payable out of the settled property and the trustees and the beneficiary are jointly responsible for its payment.

There are certain special reliefs. Where the settled property reverts to the settlor or his spouse, there is, subject to certain qualifications, total relief[7]; where as a result of the transfer the beneficiary becomes entitled to some other interest in the settled property, there will be partial relief if and to the extent to which his new interest is worth less than his previous interest (there being a potentially exempt transfer to this extent), while if he becomes entitled to the settled property absolutely, there will be a potentially exempt transfer of the amount of any purchase moneys he has paid for the outstanding interests[8]; finally, where tax is payable within five years of a previous chargeable transfer, quick succession relief reduces the rate of tax.[9]

(B) Discretionary Trusts

For the purposes of the inheritance tax legislation, a discretionary trust is any settlement in which there is no interest in possession,[10] with the exception of accumulation and maintenance trusts, which will be considered in the next section, and certain other trusts which are given special treatment (including charitable trusts, newspaper trusts, maintenance funds for historic buildings, superannuation schemes, trusts for the benefit of employees and disabled persons, and protective trusts).[11]

As has already been seen, the creation *inter vivos* of a discretionary trust is an initially chargeable transfer and consequently is subject to an immediate payment of inheritance tax, charged at half the death rate (thus at present[12] charged at 20 per cent rather than 40 per cent) if and to the extent that the total of transfers which are neither exempt nor potentially exempt during the seven years preceding the transfer exceed the settlor's lifetime allowance. Further, in the event that the settlor dies within seven years of the transfer, the amount of inheritance tax payable may have to be reassessed if any transfer which was potentially exempt at the time of the original assessment turns out in the end not to be exempt from inheritance tax (see the example discussed in the previous section).

A further charge to inheritance tax is made on every tenth anniversary of the creation of the discretionary trust at 30 per cent of the inheritance tax which would have been payable if the property subject to the settlement on the day before the tenth anniversary in question had been transferred to the settlement at that time[13]; calculation of the inheritance tax due takes into

---

[6] *ibid.* s.52.
[7] *ibid.* s.54.
[8] *ibid.* s.53(2).
[9] *ibid.* s.141.
[10] *ibid.* s.58.
[11] *ibid.* ss.58, 86, 87, 88 & 89.
[12] In 1998–99.
[13] Inheritance Tax Act 1984, ss.64, 66.

account the state of the settlor's lifetime allowance at the time when the settlement was originally made and any transfers made during the seven years immediately preceding the creation of the settlement. Account is also taken of any settled property which has ceased to be subject to the discretionary trust during the preceding ten years (as will be seen in the next paragraph, inheritance tax will have been payable when that property ceased to be subject to the trust).

If any of the settled property ceases to be subject to the discretionary trust, a further charge to inheritance tax is made.[14] This charge arises not only where a capital payment is made to a beneficiary but also where, in accordance with their discretionary powers, the trustees create a settlement with an interest in possession or an accumulation and maintenance trust. The intention of this charge is to produce the appropriate proportion of the inheritance tax which would have been payable on the next tenth anniversary of the creation of the discretionary trust. If the discretionary trust has already lasted for more than 10 years, the further charge is the appropriate fraction of the tax paid on the last 10 year anniversary, taking into account the number of quarters which have passed in the current 10 year period.[15] (Consequently, if two years have passed since the last 10 year anniversary, the appropriate fraction is eight-fortieths so the tax payable on the value of the property taken out is eight-fortieths of the rate of tax payable on the last 10 year anniversary, which was of course itself 30 per cent of the inheritance tax which would have been payable had the property been settled then.) If, on the other hand, the discretionary trust has not yet lasted for 10 years, the rate of tax payable is 30 per cent of the appropriate fraction (calculated in the same way on the basis of the number of quarters in the first 10 year period which have already passed) of the rate of tax which would have been payable on a hypothetical chargeable transfer, at the time when the property is taken out of the settlement, of the property originally settled, taking into account as before the state of the settlor's lifetime allowance at the date of the creation of the settlement.[16] A simple illustration of these formulae follows; more complex illustrations are provided in specialist works on taxation.

Suppose that £100,000 is settled on discretionary trust by a settlor who, at the date of the settlement, has already used up all his lifetime allowance in the preceding seven years. Exactly five years after the creation of the settlement, the trustees appoint an interest in possession in £10,000 to one of the beneficiaries. Exactly 12 years after the creation of the settlement, they make a similar appointment of £10,000 to another beneficiary. Suppose also that the only rate of inheritance tax is at all times 40 per cent. Inheritance tax will be payable on the creation of the settlement, on each appointment of £10,000, and on the tenth anniversary of the creation of the settlement (if the settlor fails to survive for seven years after the date of the creation of the settlement, further inheritance tax may also be payable on his death This possibility is illustrated by the example discussed earlier on pages 532–534).

---

[14] *ibid*. s.65.
[15] *ibid*. s.69.
[16] *ibid*. s.68.

(i) On the creation of the settlement, inheritance tax is payable charged at half the death rate (therefore at 20 per cent). Since the settlor has at the date of the settlement already used up all his lifetime allowance in the preceding seven years, this tax is payable in full. Consequently, £20,000 tax is payable. It will be assumed that this is paid by the trustees (were it to be paid by the settlor, the sum settled would have to be "grossed up"). Thus only £80,000 is actually held on discretionary trust.

(ii) On the appointment of £10,000 exactly five years after the creation of the settlement, twenty quarters have passed. Consequently, the inheritance tax payable is twenty-fortieths (50 per cent) of 30 per cent of the rate of tax payable on a hypothetical chargeable transfer of the property originally settled taking into account the state of the settlor's lifetime allowance at the date of the creation of the settlement. The latter rate is once again 20 per cent, since the settlor had already used up all his lifetime allowance at the date of the creation of the settlement. Consequently, the overall rate of tax is 50 per cent of 30 per cent of 20 per cent, which is 3 per cent. Therefore the tax payable is 3 per cent of £10,000, thus £300. It will be assumed that this is paid by the beneficiary (were it to be paid by the trustees, the sum appointed would have to be "grossed up").

(iii) On the tenth anniversary of the creation of the settlement, suppose that the property subject to the settlement is now worth, due to capital appreciation and some accumulation of income, £110,000. The hypothetical chargeable transfer is thus of £120,000 (the £110,000 still settled and the £10,000 paid out during the preceding 10 year period). The tax payable on such a hypothetical transfer would once again be 20 per cent, the settlor having used up all his lifetime allowance at the date of the creation of the settlement. Consequently, the overall rate of tax is 30 per cent of 20 per cent, which is 6 per cent. Therefore, the tax payable is 6 per cent of £120,000, thus £7,200 (this will have to be paid out of the settled property).

(iv) On the appointment of £10,000 exactly 12 years after the creation of the settlement, eight quarters have passed since the tenth anniversary of the creation of the settlement. Consequently, the inheritance tax payable is eight-fortieths (20 per cent) of the rate of tax paid on the tenth anniversary of the creation of the settlement, which was 6 per cent. Therefore, the tax payable is 20 per cent of 6 per cent, that is 1.2 per cent, of £10,000, thus £120. It will once again be assumed that this is paid by the beneficiary (were it to be paid by the trustees, the sum appointed would have to be "grossed up").

It will be seen from this example that, apart from the inheritance tax payable on the creation of the settlement, which will be avoided if the property settled falls within the settlor's lifetime allowance, the incidence of inheritance tax is not substantial. This type of trust therefore retains some attraction for a settlor, particularly if it is limited to the settlor's lifetime allowance.

(C)   Accumulation and Maintenance Trusts

An accumulation and maintenance settlement must be for the benefit of one or more persons under 25, usually but not necessarily the children or grandchildren of the settlor. At least one beneficiary must be alive at the date of the settlement. The beneficiaries must be entitled to the trust property or to an immediate vested interest in its income upon reaching an age not exceeding 25; in the meantime, the income can either be accumulated or be applied for the maintenance education or benefit of the children.[17] However, such trusts can only last for 25 years unless all the beneficiaries have a common grandparent. (If the trust ceases to qualify, inheritance tax becomes payable as if it were a normal discretionary trust).

There are no particular fiscal advantages in respect of income tax; the income of the trust is taxed at the flat rate of 34 per cent and any income applied for the maintenance or education of a beneficiary is, provided that the trust is irrevocable, taxed as the income of the beneficiary (unless he is a minor unmarried child of the settlor, in which case it is aggregated with the income of the latter).[18] So far as capital gains tax is concerned, there is no deemed disposal when the beneficiaries obtain vested interests (however, this only postpones capital gains tax; it does not eliminate it). The principal fiscal advantages of such trusts relate to inheritance tax. Accumulation and maintenance trusts are potentially exempt transfers[19]; consequently, such trusts are not liable to any of the additional charges to inheritance tax outlined in the previous section (this is why inheritance tax is payable if a discretionary trust is converted into an accumulation and maintenance trust). Consequently, no inheritance tax will be payable at all if the settlor survives a further seven years; even if he fails to do so, inheritance tax will only be payable to the extent that his estate and the transfers made during the last seven years of his life exceed his lifetime allowance.

---

[17] *ibid.* s.71. For a detailed discussion of the conditions, see *Inglewood (Lord) v. I.R.C.* [1983] 1 W.L.R. 366.

[18] Income and Corporation Taxes Act 1988, ss.663–665.

[19] Inheritance Tax Act 1984, s.3A.

CHAPTER 17

INVESTMENT

I. THE GENERAL STANDARD OF CARE

THE duty of a trustee in investing trust funds is to take such care as an ordinary prudent man would take if he were under a duty to make the investment for the benefit of other persons for whom he felt morally bound to provide.[1] Lord Watson in *Learoyd v. Whiteley*[2] specified the requirement as follows:

"As a general rule the law requires of a trustee no higher degree of diligence in the execution of his office than a man of ordinary prudence would exercise in the management of his own private affairs. Yet he is not allowed the same discretion in investing the moneys of the trust as if he were a person *sui juris* dealing with his own estate. Business men of prudence may, and frequently do, select investments which are more or less of a speculative character but it is the duty of a trustee to confine himself to the class of investments which are permitted by the trust and likewise to avoid all investments of that class which are attended with hazard. So long as he acts in the honest observance of these limitations the general rule already stated will apply."

In addition to adhering to this general standard of care, a trustee is also bound to make his investments in such a way that those entitled in possession will obtain a reasonable income and yet the capital will be preserved for those entitled to it in remainder.[3] High income investments are likely to produce little, if any, capital appreciation and thus will generally benefit the tenant for life at the expense of the remaindermen, while low income investments are likely to produce more substantial capital appreciation and thus will generally benefit the remaindermen at the expense of the tenant for life. A balance must be secured so that all beneficiaries are treated equally and fairly. In *Nestlé v. National Westminster Bank*,[4] the remainderman complained that the fund to which she became entitled when her interest vested in possession would have been worth almost four times as much had it been properly invested. The trustees had erroneously regarded their investment powers as more limited than they actually were and, as a result, had

---

[1] *Re Whiteley* (1886) 33 Ch.D. 347 at 355, *per* Lindley L.J. affirmed *sub nom. Learoyd v. Whiteley* (1887) 12 App. Cas. 727.
[2] *ibid*. at 733.
[3] *Re Whiteley* (1886) 33 Ch.D. 347 at 350, *per* Cotton L.J.
[4] [1993] 1 W.L.R. 1260.

invested in a more restricted range of investments than they were actually obliged to. Further, they had failed to make sufficiently regular reviews of the fund. However, since the remainderman was unable to prove that any loss had been suffered thereby, the Court of Appeal held that she was not entitled to any compensation. The Court also emphasised that trustees are entitled to take into account the taxation position of the beneficiaries; consequently, they had been entitled, where the tenant for life was non-resident, to purchase investments which would not be subject to deduction of income tax at source or to what is now inheritance tax on his death; further, they could take into account the relative wealth of the tenant for life and the remainderman in deciding whether to purchase high income or low income investments. However, the Court did hold that at least half of a trust fund held for persons by way of succession should be invested in "equities", ordinary shares issued by commercial companies which tend to keep pace with inflation.[5]

It therefore follows that, even if the trustee invests in securities authorised by statute[6] or by the trust instrument itself,[7] he will not necessarily be protected from attack by the beneficiaries. Even an authorised investment may in the particular circumstances of the case be unjustified and amount to a breach of the trustees' general duties of care and impartiality. But in circumstances such as these the onus would be on the beneficiaries to establish that the investment was imprudent and not for the trustees to show the converse.[8] As Hoffmann J. said at first instance in *Nestlé v. National Westminster Bank*[9]:

"Trustees like the Bank act for reward and therefore owe duties of professional skill, but the engagement into which they enter is not one of insurance. They do not guarantee results. Possibly for a suitable premium such a guarantee could be obtained, but I very much doubt it and the transaction would be very different from that which the Bank undertook for modest reward."

Having said that, however, certain positive duties in relation to investment are now expressly imposed by the Trustee Investments Act 1961,[10] and these will apply to any power of investment, whether it is exercised under or outside the Act; breach of these duties is obviously capable of grounding a claim.

All the same principles apply to the variation and continuation of investments. The trustees have, as might be expected, the power to vary investments already made,[11] and also to continue these investments even if they have since ceased to be authorised.[12] But these powers are, of course, subject

---

[5] See *post*, pp. 549–550.
[6] See *post*, p. 554.
[7] See *post*, p. 561.
[8] *Shaw v. Cates* [1909] 1 Ch. 389 at 395, *per* Parker J.
[9] (1988), unreported except in 10 Trust Law International 112.
[10] s.6(1)(a),(b); see *post*, p. 564.
[11] *Hume v. Lopes* [1892] A.C. 112.
[12] Trustee Act 1925, s.4, as modified by the Trustee Investments Act 1961, s.3(4), Sched. 3, para. 2; see *post*, p. 562.

to the general and statutory[13] duties of care and impartiality incumbent on a trustee. However, in this respect, Hoffmann J. made it clear at first instance in *Nestlé v. National Westminster Bank*[14] that "modern trustees acting within their investment powers are entitled to be judged by the standards of current portfolio theory, which emphasises the risk level of the entire portfolio rather than the risk attaching to each investment taken in isolation". This view was also adopted by the Treasury in the Consultation Paper on the Investment Powers of Trustees published in May 1996[15] and must therefore now be regarded as part of the general law.

There has recently been some discussion of whether trustees, in reaching their decisions as to the selection and retention of particular investments, are entitled to take into account non-financial considerations. In *Cowan v. Scargill*,[16] five of the ten trustees of a mineworkers' pension fund were appointed by the National Union of Miners. They refused to accept an investment plan submitted to the trustees by an advisory panel of experts in so far as it envisaged new or continuing investment overseas and in energies which were in direct competition with coal. Such investments were contrary to the policy of the National Union of Miners, which was understandably primarily interested in preserving the prosperity and, consequently, in ensuring the continued existence of the British coal mining industry. Their arguments were thus ideological in nature. There can be little doubt that most pension funds would indeed be benefited by the maintenance of the prosperity of the industry in question but, as Megarry V.–C. commented, the mineworkers' pension fund was in this respect unusual because of the declining nature of the coal mining industry, there being substantially more pensioners than miners so that the assets of the fund far exceeded the value of the industry. Further, overseas investments can be substantially more risky than home investments because of the possibility of exchange rate variations. However, Megarry V.-C. held that the trustees would be in breach of trust unless they accepted the investment plan submitted. Their duty was to act in the best interests of their beneficiaries[17] and, if the purpose of the trust was the provision of financial benefits, a power of investment had to be exercised so that the funds yielded the best return by way of income and capital appreciation.

"Trustees may have strongly held social or political views. They may be firmly opposed to any investment in South Africa or other countries, or they may object to any form of investment in companies concerned with alcohol, tobacco, armaments or many other things. In the conduct of their own affairs, of course, they are free to abstain from making any such investments. Yet under a trust, if investments of this type would be more beneficial to the

---

[13] Trustee Investments Act 1961, s.6(1)(a),(b); see *post*, p. 564.

[14] (1988), unreported except in 10 Trust Law International 112.

[15] See *post*, p. 556.

[16] [1985] Ch. 270. See generally R.Ellison: (1991) 5 Trust Law International 157; L.Irish & A.Kent: (1994) 8 Trust Law International 10; Lord Nicholls of Birkenhead, extra-judicially: (1995) 9 Trust Law International 10.

[17] The Uniform Prudent Investor Act 1994, s.5 (United States of America) now similarly requires investment solely in the interest of the beneficiaries.

beneficiaries than other investments, the trustees must not refrain from making the investments by reason of the views that they hold."[18]

In exceptional cases, account could be taken of the particular inclinations of the beneficiaries but this was not relevant in the case in hand since many of the beneficiaries no longer had any financial interest in the welfare of the coal industry. The trustees were therefore pursuing union policy at the potential expense of the beneficiaries and, in the last resort, would have to be removed from office.

It is possible that the fact that the trustees so overtly based their case on ideological grounds did not favour their case. There seems no reason why trustees should not limit themselves to investments which they regard as politically and ethically "sound" provided that they have satisfied themselves that these investments are no less financially sound than those which they have rejected. What *Cowan v. Scargill* decides is that they must not fetter their discretion by deciding to exclude any particular class of investments irrelevant of their financial merits. This is confirmed by *Martin v. City of Edinburgh District Council*,[19] where a Scottish court held that a breach of duty had been committed by a local authority which, in order to oppose apartheid, had adopted a policy of disinvesting in companies which had interests in South Africa without considering whether this was in the best financial interests of the beneficiaries. It is therefore clear that no investment policy, whether to prefer or whether to avoid particular classes of investments, can be adopted unless the trustees have paid the necessary attention to the financial interests of the beneficiaries.

It has also been contended that trusts for charitable purposes should not make investments in undertakings whose operations are incompatible with those purposes. In *Harris v. Church Commissioners*[20] the Bishop of Oxford sought a declaration that in the management of their assets the Church Commissioners were obliged to have regard to the object of promoting the Christian faith through the established Church of England and were not entitled to act in a manner which would be incompatible with that object. This declaration was denied. Nicholls V.-C. held that, where charitable trustees held assets as investments, the discharge of their duty of furthering the purposes of the trust would normally require them to seek the maximum return which was consistent with commercial prudence and they could not properly use such assets for non-investment purposes. The Commissioners already had a policy of excluding investments in certain business activities which might be offensive to the Church of England, such as armaments, gambling, tobacco, newspapers and the then apartheid-ridden South Africa. This was entirely proper but it would not be right for them to adopt a still more restrictive policy which would entail taking into account non-financial considerations to an extent which would give rise to a risk of significant financial detriment to the proper object of the trusts.

All the cases which have been discussed concerned trusts of a public nature. While the considerations expressed therein clearly also apply to

---

[18] [1985] Ch. 270 at 287–288.
[19] [1988] S.L.T. 329.
[20] [1992] 1 W.L.R. 1241.

private trusts, there is of course nothing to stop any settlor, or indeed the totality of the beneficiaries if they are all *sui juris*, from prescribing that the trustees either must make or must refrain from making investments of any particular type.

II. TYPES OF INVESTMENT

It has just been indicated that, when any investment is contemplated, the trustee will have to give due consideration to the interest of all the beneficiaries, and he will have to hold the balance equally between them. Further, as will be shown later in this Chapter, before deciding on an investment, a trustee must generally consider advice—and consider is the operative word; he must not unthinkingly follow such advice—on whether the contemplated investment will be satisfactory. Again, he must diversify the trust investments, which means not merely that the trust fund must be held in different investments but, so far as is appropriate to the circumstances of the trust, that it must be held in different types of investment.

Before he can adequately do any of these things, a trustee must have some knowledge of the characteristics of different types of investment. (Investments are colloquially termed "securities" but that term is somewhat dangerous; a "security" in this sense is not necessarily "secure".) The points to consider with any investment are, *inter alia*:

(i) whether or not that investment is a "fixed-interest" security;

(ii) whether or not the capital value will fluctuate; and

(iii) if the capital value will fluctuate, in what way such fluctuation is likely.

If a security is a "fixed-interest" security, the amount of interest or dividend which is produced will never alter. The trustee who buys £1,000 Treasury 8.5 per cent Stock 2005 knows that, whatever happens to the economic state of the nation, he will receive £85 per annum income. On the other hand, if he invests in ordinary shares of commercial companies, known as "equities", he does not know what he will receive, for this will depend entirely on the amount of the dividend which the companies in each year decide to pay. In bad years they may pay nothing, but in other years they may pay a larger amount than any fixed-interest security.

As regards capital value, there are only a few types of security where there will be no fluctuation. This will only occur where such securities are purchasable solely from the Government or other persons issuing them and are not bought and sold among private individuals. The best-known examples are National Savings Certificates, which may be bought over the counter of the Post Office or Trustee Savings Bank, and some bonds issued by local authorities.

By contrast, the capital value of all other securities, whether of the Government, local authorities, or commercial undertakings dealt with on a stock exchange, will fluctuate. To understand the terminology used in connection with this fluctuation, it is necessary to distinguish between the *nominal price* of an investment and its *market price*. The nominal price is the value of the investment as named on its face and at which, usually, it was originally issued. The market price is the price at which that security can for the time being be purchased. Suppose that the Government issued in 1950 a new stock which carries interest at £4 per cent and that a person purchased from the Government a holding of £100 of the stock for £100 cash. Suppose also that in 1999 someone buys on the Stock Exchange that holding for £80 cash. The purchaser would be described as buying that holding of £100 nominal stock for a market price of £80. The interest, of course, is always calculated on the nominal value and so, however much the market price alters, the amount of interest will always be the same. When a security is bought for the same amount of cash as its nominal value—in the example just given, the purchase in 1950 of £100 nominal stock for £100—that security is said to be bought at "par".

The other term which is used in this context is "yield". This is the amount of income from a security expressed as a percentage of the market price paid for it and not of its nominal price. So if £80 cash is paid for £100 nominal £4 per cent stock, as the interest is fixed at £4 per annum the yield is

$$\frac{£4}{80} \times 100 = £5 \text{ per annum}$$

More precisely, the "yield" as just described is the "interest only" or "flat" yield. Where an investment is purchased at less than its nominal value but will be redeemed at its nominal value, its "redemption yield" may also be calculated. Very broadly, the redemption yield measures the gain to be expected on the redemption of the security together with the income which will be derived.[21]

It must be stressed that there are many factors which will govern fluctuations of market price, but in the case of Government securities, there are two in particular. First, there is the general level of interest rates obtainable elsewhere. If the normal yield at any time is £10 per cent from investments which are considered "safe", the market price of Government securities is likely to be adjusted so that that security will produce a yield of about £10 per cent. If the market price were substantially higher, no one would buy the Government securities, a safe £10 per cent yield could be obtained elsewhere. The second factor is whether and at what pace inflation (and so, depreciation in the purchasing power of money) is likely to occur. If a period of rapid inflation is forecast, most investors will not favour fixed-interest securities, but will choose investments from which the return is likely to increase as inflation occurs; thus lack of demand will force down the market value of the fixed-interest securities. The most notorious example is 3.5 per cent War Loan, which during the last period at which inflation was relatively high (during 1993) had a market value in the region of £38 for each £100 nominal of stock. By the time the last edition of this work was published in 1994, inflation had fallen and so the market value had risen to £58.

---

[21] The redemption yield is, strictly, the amount by which the eventual capital sum which will be obtained on the redemption of the security, together with the income which will arise until redemption, has to be discounted to reduce the security to its present value.

It has been relatively constant ever since, its value during 1998 having at the time of writing[22] fluctuated between a low of £55 and a high of £60.

In the case of ordinary shares in commercial companies, the yield will also be important and this may be expected to be rather higher than from Government securities; a commercial undertaking cannot give the capital guarantee which the Government does and the yield is greater to compensate for this. Companies of national standing can become insolvent. But there are two other important factors which influence the capital value of ordinary shares. First, the anticipated ability of the company to pay dividends in the future at least at the rate which it has paid for them in the past. Secondly, the company's prospects for any increased profits and growth in the future.

With these principles in mind, the major types of investment can be considered as follows.

1. *Fixed-Interest Securities*

(A) National Savings Income Bonds
The capital value of these securities issued by the Government never changes and the investor is guaranteed that he will receive back the amount which he originally invested. These bonds are not, strictly speaking, fixed interest securities because the rate of interest paid is adjusted from time to time in line with general changes in sterling interest levels. The interest is paid monthly.

(B) National Savings Certificates
These are also Government securities but differ from National Savings Income Bonds because the interest is not paid as it accrues but is added to capital. When the certificates are repaid, the investor therefore receives back the exact amount of his investment, together with the accumulated interest in the form of an addition to capital.[23]

(C) Building Society Investments
Investments in building societies are of two main kinds: on deposit accounts and on share accounts. The difference is that, should the building society be wound up, the depositors are paid out in full before the shareholders. For this reason, the shareholders receive a slightly larger income than that paid to the depositors but in practice investments both in deposit accounts and in share accounts in building societies which are recognised as suitable for trustee investments[24] are regarded as absolutely safe, although only investments on deposit account are within the narrower range of "trustee investments".[25] The interest is usually payable twice yearly or can be added to capital.

---

[22] May 1998.
[23] As to the entitlement to the increment; see *post*, p. 593.
[24] Under the provisions of House Purchase and Housing Act 1959, s.1. See also Trustee Investment Act 1961, Sched. 1, Pt II, para. 12.
[25] See *post*, p. 557.

Although dealt with here under the heading of fixed-interest securities, building society investments are not, strictly speaking, fixed-interest ones because the rate of interest does fluctuate slightly but not usually by a large amount. There is, however, no variation at all in the capital value of building society investments.

(D) "Gilt-edged" Securities

This term, often abbreviated to "gilts", is a hark-back to days when securities of the United Kingdom Government were thought of more highly than they are today; it denotes stocks issued or guaranteed by the Government, by the nationalised industries, and by some Commonwealth governments. They are fixed-interest securities but as they are dealt with on the Stock Exchange[26] their capital value does fluctuate.

There are two categories of gilt-edged securities: dated and undated stock. When stock is dated—for example 3.5 per cent Funding Stock 2004—the investor knows that at the stated date the security will be redeemed at its nominal value. If, therefore, trustees buy £100 3.5 per cent Funding Stock 2004 in 1998 for £92.50 (its actual price at the time of writing[27]), they know that in 2004 the Government will in effect buy back the stock from them for £100.

Undated stocks, such as the War Loan stock to which reference has already been made,[28] are often never redeemed and the holders of them can never know how much their holdings will realise on the market at any future time.

Some British Government securities are "index-linked". These are considered later.[29]

(E) Debentures

A "debenture" is an acknowledgment of indebtedness by a company supported by a mortgage or charge created by the company over its assets, or a bond issued by a company unsupported by such a charge.[30] A private individual can only mortgage or charge property which he has at the time when that mortgage or charge is created and a debenture may likewise be secured by a charge on a specific item of a company's property. But a company has an advantage over individuals in that it may create a "floating charge" which is a general charge over all its assets. Such a charge does not restrict the company from dealing with its assets but, should any liquidation occur, the charge which until then has been "floating" above the company's

---

[26] Persons who have National Savings Bank accounts may purchase "gilts" through the Post Office and at their option have the dividends, credited to their National Savings Bank account. In this case the Post Office acts as intermediary and it purchases the security on the Stock Exchange. Thus, although in this case the securities may be purchased through the Post Office, the principle is not altered.

[27] In May 1998. The price is relatively low because the income is so poor; the purchaser obtains a yield of 3.79% and a gross redemption yield of 4.96%. On the other hand, a purchaser of £100 8.5%. Treasury Stock 2005 has, because of the much higher income, to purchase the stock at the over par figure of £114.75, giving a yield of 7.41% and a gross redemption yield of 6.04%.

[28] See *ante*, p. 545.

[29] See *post*, p. 549.

[30] Companies Act 1985, s.744; Trustee Investment Act 1961, Sched. 1, Pt. IV, para. 4.

assets suddenly "descends" upon them and converts itself into a fixed charge over those assets. This is a convenient way for a company to support its borrowing with security without impeding its dealings with its assets. But there is no need for a debenture to be supported by any security. If it is not, it operates in the same way as an unsecured loan to a private individual. For investment purposes, debentures are frequently equated with preference shares, with which they will be considered further.

(F) Preference Shares

Preference shares are shares issued by commercial companies carrying a fixed rate of interest and in this respect they are similar to debentures. The rate of interest is usually but not necessarily indicated in the title, for example 6 per cent Preference Shares. The 6 per cent is the rate of interest calculated by reference to the nominal value of the stock and not to its market value. As long as the company makes a profit, or, usually, has reserves of profits from previous years, the holder is paid his dividend.

Debenture holders stand in the position of lenders to the company and they are entitled to have their interest paid first. Preference shareholders are in the position of investors in the company and they rank next after the debenture holders. It is only after the debenture and the preference shareholders have been paid that the company can declare a dividend on its ordinary shares.

There is a risk, in some cases more theoretical than real, that the company will not have any money and in this case, of course, the debenture holder or preference shareholder will receive nothing. To compensate for this risk, the yield on debentures and preference shares is usually higher than on gilt-edged securities. Frequently both debentures and preference shares are redeemable at a given date in the same way as dated gilt-edged stocks and sometimes the holder has the option to convert the shares into ordinary shares at a stated time. Both debentures and preference shares may be dealt with on the Stock Exchange,[31] so that their capital value fluctuates.

There are two special classes of preference shares. The first is the *cumulative preference share*. The significance of the word "cumulative" is that, if in any year the company does not pay a dividend, the dividend for that year will be paid out of any profits for future years. The other special type of preference share is the *participating preference share*. This type of share combines the characteristics of preference and ordinary shares. The company first pays the shareholders a dividend up to the amount of their preference—say, 6 per cent; it then pays the ordinary shareholders a dividend of the same amount and, if there is still any money available for distribution, it is divided equally between holders of the participating preference and ordinary shares. Participating preference shares are, therefore, preference shares which are capable, subject to certain conditions, of participating in profits normally reserved for ordinary shareholders. Preference shares which are non-participating do not carry this right.

---

[31] "May" be dealt with on the Stock Exchange, because private companies, whose securities are not handled by the Stock Exchange, may nevertheless issue debentures and shares. When these securities change hands, the price is a matter for direct negotiation between buyer and seller, unless some provision is made in the articles of association to govern the price.

2. *Inflation-Adjusted Securities*

A relatively recent development has been the issue of British Government securities which carry a low rate of interest but whose capital value is adjusted in accordance with increases in the Retail Prices Index. Most of these securities are dealt in on the Stock Exchange but there are also some index-linked National Savings Certificates.

Index-linked stocks which are dealt in on the Stock Exchange have a base figure determined by the Retail Prices Index in force eight months[32] before the stock was issued. The amount of interest payable, and the amount payable on the redemption of the stock are then both adjusted for movements in the Retail Prices Index.

The amount payable on the redemption of index-linked National Savings Certificates is similarly calculated. In addition, certain bonuses are also payable.

3. *Ordinary Shares*

Ordinary shares, or "equities", are the basic type of share issued by commercial companies. In each year the company decides the amount available for distribution after paying its expenses and making provision for future requirements. The holders of debentures and preference shares are then paid out and however much is left is distributed between the ordinary shareholders (with, sometimes, the participating preference shareholders also benefiting). The dividend on ordinary shares therefore fluctuates with the trading profits of the company. If the company is flourishing, as its trading profits go up, so will its ordinary dividends and, as the dividend increases, so people will be prepared to pay more for the shares, which of course means that the capital value of those shares goes up as well. But the reverse is the case when the company does badly.

Equities have a distinct advantage in times of inflation for, as inflation progresses, so the price of the company's products will increase and this should lead to more money being available for dividends. The purchasing power of these dividends may well be no more than before but at least the investment stands the chance of keeping pace with inflation and so preserving its purchasing power.

Generally speaking, equities are the least safe of the various types of investment. For this reason their capital value fluctuates more than that of the other types.

Some equity shares produce a fairly small income, because rather than distribute its profits the company may prefer to plough back much of its profits into its business. In this case, although the dividends are small, the value of the company itself may be growing, and this will lead to an increase in the value of the shares. On the other hand, some shares will pay a high dividend but the prospects of the company may be precarious or the profitability of the company may be unlikely to increase, in which case there is not

---

[32] The 8 month lag is for administrative convenience in making the calculations.

likely to be much capital appreciation of the shares. And it must be remembered that capital appreciation is likely to benefit the remainderman more than the life-tenant.[33]

4. *Unit and Investment Trusts*[34]

The managers of these trusts buy other Stock Exchange securities and invite the public to invest in the fund. The managers then receive the dividends from the securities, pay the expenses, and themselves a salary, and distribute the remainder to the investors. Such an investor has, therefore, a minimal stake in numerous companies and thus spreads the risk. But at the same time he receives less than he would have done had he invested directly in the most profitable companies in which the managers invest and it must be remembered that the managers take out their remuneration before any money is available for the unit holders. One advantage of investing these trusts is that the managers are in a position to keep a day-to-day eye on the investments, and they have the ready opportunity for altering investments at the appropriate time.

Unit and investment trusts are often organised to cope for special needs, for example low income and high capital appreciation, or high income and low capital appreciation, or something between the two.

5. *Non-Income Producing Investments*

The traditional meaning of the word "investment" is an asset which produces income[35] with the connotation that it is likely to produce a surplus on revenue account over the anticipated period of holding of the asset.[36] This is still the legal meaning of the word. However, as a result of fiscal legislation, it has become more and more prudent in many situations to reduce or eliminate income and to seek capital appreciation. Consequently, in general and financial usage, the word now implies any asset which will produce a good return even if that is entirely in the form of capital appreciation.

The fiscal legislation has produced the following results:

     (i) Income, when paid to a beneficiary, is taxable in his hands up to a maximum effective rate of 40 per cent.[37] Capital gains realised by trustees are taxable at the rate of 34 per cent, by beneficiaries at the maximum rate of 40 per cent.

     (ii) Where trustees receive income in the first instance and accumulate it, that income is subject to income tax at 23 per cent or, in the case

---

[33] Although, of course, if the capital appreciation occurs because the dividends are being increased, the tenant for life will benefit by virtue of this increase in the dividends.

[34] See *ante,* p. 8.

[35] See *post,* p. 552.

[36] See the reasoning in *Cooke v. Haddock* (1960) 39 T.C. 64; *Johnston v. Heath* [1970] 1 W.L.R. 1567.

[37] See *ante,* p. 522.

of accumulation and discretionary settlements, 34 per cent.[38] If they hold an asset which never produces income, their liability is to capital gains tax only and this is payable only when the asset is disposed of.[39]

As a result, trustees have increasingly sought to lay out trust funds in the acquisition of non-income, or low-income, producing assets. It must be stressed that this can only be done where there is an express power in the trust instrument[40] but, given this power, the following are some of the possibilities which have recently found favour.

(A) Split-Level Shares and Units
In principle these are either equity shares or units in unit trusts. The device depends on there being two classes of shares or units. One class carries the entitlement to all income, but no capital appreciation. The other class carries entitlement to all capital appreciation, but no income. Shares and units in the former class are usually taken up by bodies which are exempt or partially exempt from income tax, such as charities and pension funds. Shares and units in the latter class are usually taken up by private individuals and trustees. It will be appreciated that in normal circumstances shares and units in the latter class, although paying no dividends, will steadily increase in value, and that value will be realised on disposal.

(B) Single-Premium Bonds
The essence of this arrangement is that a policy of assurance is effected with an insurance company for the payment of one premium only, which is paid at the outset. The insurance company invests the funds in an agreed manner, such as in equities or in property. At an agreed date, often after the expiry of 10 years, or on the earlier death of the life assured, the policy matures, and the payee receives a sum equivalent to the original premium paid, together with a profit which depends on the success which the insurance company has had in the investment of its funds. In principle, the total proceeds of the policy are received as capital.[41]

(C) Chattels
A wide variety of chattels have been purchased by trustees as growth investments. Over the last few years trustees have invested in works of art, antique furniture, silver, silver bullion and oriental carpets. Almost invariably these are unsuitable as investments unless one has considerable freedom of choice as to the time of disposal; due to the volatility of the various markets, a period of some years may have to elapse before it becomes a good time to sell.

---

[38] See *ante*, p. 522.
[39] See *ante*, p. 526.
[40] *Re Power* [1947] Ch. 572.
[41] Although, so far as the trustees are concerned, the total proceeds rank as a capital receipt, a charge to income tax may arise.

(D) Loans to Beneficiaries

In some circumstances, it may be thought desirable that capital appreciation should accrue to a beneficiary rather than to the trustees. In such circumstances, the trustees may wish to lend trust funds to the beneficiary, interest free, perhaps securing the loan by taking a charge over the assets which the beneficiary purchases with them. On the death of the beneficiary, the loan is repaid from his estate. However, where this is done, the whole of the capital appreciation accrues to the beneficiary and not to the fund as a whole, so that this could only be proper where it is expressly authorised by the trust instrument or all other beneficiaries affected agree.

6. *Foreign Currency Securities*

As well as considering the type of investment to be made, trustees will wish to consider the currency of the investment. For example, trustees may wish to invest part of the fund in the stocks of foreign governments or companies, such as United States Treasury Bills, denominated in United States dollars, or Australian equity shares. Most of the types of investment which have so far been described have their counterparts in other countries. In addition, it is possible to invest in "currency funds". In essence, these are shares in companies[42] who apply the whole of their funds in making deposits in the various leading currencies of the world. By this spread, some protection is obtained against a fall in the exchange rate of sterling and those other currencies.

7. *Land*

Trustees have long been entitled to invest in a mortgage of land, that is to say lend money on the security of a mortgage. However, their right to do so is fenced around by a considerable number of statutory restrictions and it is therefore more appropriate to discuss the nature of this right in the context of the legislation which is generally applicable to trustee investments.[43]

However, until recently, trustees had no power to purchase land by way of investment in the absence of an express power in the trust instrument so to do. Further, even if the purchase of land was expressly authorised, it did not necessarily authorise purchase for residence only. Thus in *Re Power*[44] the clause was to the effect that "all moneys required to be invested under this my will may be invested by the trustee in any manner in which he may in his absolute discretion think fit including the purchase of freehold property in England and Wales". Jenkins J. held that the trustees were not entitled to purchase a dwelling-house with vacant possession for occupation by a

---

[42] For taxation reasons, the companies are incorporated outside the U.K., most frequently in Jersey.

[43] See *post*, pp. 565–569.

[44] [1947] Ch. 572; *Re Wragg* [1919] 2 Ch. 58, where the land in question was to yield income, was distinguished.

beneficiary; this was on the basis that "investment" entails an income yield and the purchase of a home for occupation by a beneficiary does not yield income.[45]

However, the position was radically changed by the enactment of Trusts of Land and Appointment of Trustees Act 1996. This legislation applies to any trust of land as defined therein,[46] namely any trust of property which consists of or includes land[47] and any trust of the proceeds of sale of land.[48] Section 6(3) confers on the trustees of any such trust the power to purchase a legal estate in any land in England and Wales, whether for investment, for occupation by a beneficiary or for any other reason.[49] Further, section 12(1) confers on any beneficiary who is entitled to an interest in possession in land subject to a trust of land the right to occupy it at any time if either the purposes of the trust include making the land available for his occupation or the land is held by the trustees so as to be so available.[50] However, where a trust is not a trust of land, which will be the case where its initial trust property is entirely pure personalty, the basic prohibition on the purchase of land in the absence of an express power in the trust instrument continues to apply. But where such an express power exists and is exercised, the trust will then become a trust of land, presumably for ever after,[51] and any land

---

[45] Trustees could only purchase land in two cases. First, if they had an express power for this purpose under the trust instrument (a number of precedents commonly used in practice enable this to be done and use is also made of a clause specifically designed to circumvent the decision in *Re Power* [1947] Ch. 572 by giving an absolute discretion to the trustees to invest as they think fit including the purchase of land for occupation by a beneficiary). Secondly, if they were able to rely on a special statutory power appropriate to the circumstances of the case (such a statutory power still exists under Settled Land Act 1925, s.73(1)(xi) (although no new settlements subject to this legislation can now be created), under which capital money can be used to purchase land; further, under the now repealed Law of Property Act 1925, s.28(1), trustees for sale of land could purchase land with the proceeds of sale provided that they had not ceased to be trustees for sale within the statutory definition contained in s.205 of the same Act (*Re Wakeman* [1945] Ch. 177) by having parted with all the land held on trust for sale).

[46] This excludes settlements under the Settled Land Act 1925, which continue to be governed by s.73(1)(xi) of that Act under which capital money can be used to purchase land; such settlements irrevocably cease to be governed by that Act once all land and heirlooms held thereunder have been sold (Trusts of Land and Appointment of Trustees Act 1996, s.2(4)).

[47] s.1(1)(a).

[48] s.17(1), referring to s.17(3) under which "trust of proceeds of sale of land" means any trust of property which consists of or includes any proceeds of a disposition of land held in trust (which includes a settlement formerly subject to the Settled Land Act 1925) or any property representing such proceeds.

[49] s.6(4). s.6(1) gives trustees of land all the powers of an absolute owner for the purpose of exercising their functions as trustees although in relation to investment this can hardly add anything to s.6(3), (4).

[50] This right does not extend to any land which is unavailable or unsuitable for his occupation (s.12(2)). Detailed provisions (in s.13) govern the trustees' rights to exclude and restrict beneficiaries' rights of occupation.

[51] Because even if at some later stage it holds no land, it is virtually certain still to be a trust of the proceeds of sale of land (the only situation in which this might not be the case is if the trustees had apportioned all the land to one beneficiary and transferred it to him; in such circumstances, they would hold neither land nor the proceeds of sale of land on trust and might be held to have lost their powers to purchase land by analogy with *Re Wakeman* [1945] Ch. 177—despite the fact that the actual decision in that case has been reversed).

purchased will be able to be used for occupation by any qualified benefi-ciary.[52]

III. THE TRUSTEE INVESTMENTS ACT 1961

Under the general law trustees are entitled to invest funds only in invest-ments authorised *either* by express terms of their trust instrument *or* by statute. Until the Trustee Investments Act 1961 was passed, the investments authorised by statute were extremely limited. They were largely governed by section 1 of the Trustee Act 1925, which contained what was usually known as the "Statutory List" of permitted trust investments. These were basically restricted to: stock issued by the British Government and govern-ments of Commonwealth countries and colonies; stock guaranteed by the British Government; stock and mortgages issued by British local authorities; and mortgages of land in Great Britain. The essential point, on which criticism tended principally to focus, was the restricted nature of these investments. Practically all of them carry interest at a fixed rate and are repayable at par so that both income and capital beneficiaries were inevita-bly prejudiced by the subsequent progressive decline in the value of the pound. First, each eventual repayment of invested capital at its nominal par value would in real terms involve a capital loss. Secondly, the income received by a life-tenant would remain nominally the same but would in real terms also become worth progressively less each year. The longer a trust had been running, the more acute these difficulties became as the trust itself became older. Of course, this was only the case if the trustees were indeed restricted to the Statutory List but they would be unless a wider power of investment was conferred by the trust instrument, something which was relatively unusual in the period before the Second World War. The majority of long-term trusts constituted during this period therefore suffered cumu-lative income and capital losses on the lines already mentioned.

The striking omission from the Statutory List—understandable in 1925—was the absence of a power to invest in equities. In the short-term, this was actually fortunate, for in the economic depression which the United Kingdom suffered in the decade after the Trustee Act 1925 came into force, gilt-edged securities generally proved to be far better investments than equities. But in the longer term, trusts which contained an unrestricted power of investment and thus enabled the trustees to invest in equities generally fared a great deal better than those whose investments were restricted to the Statutory List. This came to be realised following the Second World War and settlors were accordingly advised to give their trustees very much wider investment powers than those contained in the Statutory List. But there was no such possibility for the many trusts already created which conferred, expressly or by implication, only the statutory investment powers.

Not surprisingly, many voices were raised against the continuation of this state of affairs. Reform was advocated by, among others, the Nathan Com-mittee in 1952 and in 1955 a White Paper stated that the Government

---

[52] The decision in *Re Power* [1947] Ch. 572 has therefore on any view been reversed.

intended to introduce a reform of the law. During the rather lengthy period before the resulting legislation actually came into force, some relaxations did occur. As a result of the decision in *Re Royal Society's Charitable Trusts*,[53] it became generally realised that charitable trustees had the power to apply to the court for an extension of their investment powers. The enactment of the Variation of Trusts Act 1958[54] subsequently extended the power to apply to the court to all trusts, whether charitable or non-charitable, and many applications were made under that Act for an extension of investment powers as well as for a variation of beneficial interests. Such applications, however, cost time and money and were no substitute for a general reform of the law as stated in section 1 of the Trustee Act 1925 so that it could be taken advantage of by all trustees without any need first to apply to the court. The reform was at length achieved, admittedly in a form which was perhaps unnecessarily complex linguistically, by the enactment of the Trustee Investments Act 1961, which came into force on August 3, 1961.

As will be seen,[55] the Act permitted up to a maximum of 50 per cent of the trust property to be invested in the ordinary shares of companies who fulfilled specified criteria; investment in what the Act classified as "wider-range investments" of this type was only possible if the fund was divided into two halves and the whole of the other half invested in what the Act classified as "narrower-range investments", investments whose income and capital performance was likely to be more predictable. Inevitably these new powers were principally utilised by trusts which had already been running for several years—most trusts created since the Second World War already had investment powers which were wider than those contained in the Act. But this resolved the difficulties which had led to the legislation and its initial success was indicated by the fact that the courts became unwilling save in special circumstances to sanction applications under the Variation of Trusts Act 1958 for powers of investment more extensive than those conferred by the Act of 1961.[56]

However, the provisions of the Act inevitably became out of date as new investment vehicles emerged and, although the lists of permissible investments of the various different types envisaged by the Act can be and have been augmented by statutory instrument,[57] the restriction to 50 per cent investment in equities has again progressively caused trusts governed by the Act to underperform trusts with wider investment powers. As long ago as 1982 the Law Reform Committee recommended that authorised investments should be divided into those which can be made without advice and those which can only be made with advice and that the trustees should be free to invest in such proportions as they choose.[58] However, despite the intervening emergence of even more new investment vehicles since 1982, for a long time no notice was taken of this recommendation and the courts were again faced with and began to sanction applications under the Variation of

---

[53] [1956] Ch. 87.
[54] See *post*, p. 656.
[55] See *post*, *infra*.
[56] *Re Kolb's Will Trusts* [1962] Ch. 531.
[57] See *post*, nn. 66–67.
[58] (23rd Report) The Powers and Duties of Trustees (1982) Cmnd. 8733.

Trusts Act 1958 for more extensive powers.[59] Finally, following a further review by the Trust Law Committee[60], in 1996 the maximum proportion of the trust property which could be invested in equities was by statutory instrument increased to 75 per cent for all trusts[61] (the same increase having been given to charitable trusts in the previous year[62]). Pension trusts had already been the subject of separate statutory provisions in the Pensions Act 1995,[63] although these did not actually come into force until later on, on April 7, 1997.

The Treasury has since made further proposals for reform in a Consultation Document issued in May 1996,[64] which envisaged the outright repeal of the Trustee Investment Act 1961 by means of an Order under the Deregulation and Contracting Out Act 1994. Some doubts were in fact expressed as to whether such an order would be effective so to do.[65] In any event, the draft order which was subsequently laid before Parliament did not actually purport to repeal the Act of 1961. It merely removed any need to divide the fund, thus giving trustees a free choice of trust investments, which were to be extended by a separate order. The restrictions on those equities in which trustees could invest were to be lifted and trustees were no longer to be obliged to obtain advice in all cases. However, the trustees were to remain subject to the general standards and duties imposed by the law of trusts with specific obligations to consider diversification and the suitability to the trust of proposed investments. In the end, however, the draft order was never approved due to the proroguing of Parliament prior to the General Election of 1996. It remains to be seen whether it or some other equivalent proposal is introduced during the present Parliament. In the meantime the Trustee Investment Act 1961 remains in force with the sole difference that up to 75 per cent of the trust property can now be invested in equities. Its replacement of the old Statutory List by two categories of "narrower-range investments" listed in Parts I and II of its First Schedule and the "wider-

---

[59] *Trustees of the British Museum v. Att.-Gen.* [1984] 1 W.L.R. 418. However, it has since been made clear that, unless such applications are combined with an application to vary the beneficial interests, they should instead be brought under Trustee Act 1925, s.57 (*Anker-Peterson v. Anker-Peterson* (1991) 88/16 L.S.Gaz. 32).

[60] Press Release of November 23, 1995.

[61] The Trustee Investment (Division of Trust Fund) Order 1996 (S.I. 1996 No. 845). The possibility of such an order being made changing the percentages to this extent (but no further) was expressly envisaged by Trustee Investments Act 1961, s.13; trustees who have already made a division in the previous proportions can choose whether or not to make a further one in the new proportions.

[62] The Charity Trustee Investments Act 1961 Order 1995 (S.I. 1995 No. 1092).

[63] ss.33–36, see *ante*, p. 454. Trustees of all pension funds which are trust schemes are given the same power to make investments as if they were absolutely entitled to the assets of the fund, subject to the need for diversification and, save in the case of investments classified by the Trustee Investments Act 1961 as "narrower-range investments requiring advice", to obtaining and considering proper advice.

[64] Investment Powers of Trustees.

[65] See [1996] Conv. 406. It was far from clear that the scheme established by the Trustee Investments Act 1961 constituted a "restriction" "affecting any person in the carrying on of any trade, business or profession or otherwise". If it did not, the Order would not have fallen within the wording of the Deregulation and Contracting Out Act 1994 at all. Even if it did, this was hardly the sort of exercise which was envisaged when the legislation was enacted.

range investments" listed in Part III of that Schedule therefore remains operative for the moment.

1. *Narrower-Range Investments*

The investments specified in Part I are Narrower-Range Investments not requiring advice. They include Defence Bonds, National Savings Certificates and National Savings Bank deposits, which are conveniently described as "small savings" investments. In general terms, they are the type of investment which can be made over the counter at a Post Office or Trustee Savings Bank. It is unnecessary for a trustee to seek expert advice before investing in this type of investments[66] because there can be no fluctuation in their capital value.

The investments specified in Part II are Narrower-Range Investments requiring advice. As their name suggests, a trustee has to take expert advice before investing in this type of investments. They approximate to those in the old Statutory List. But they also include certain securities which did not previously rank as trustee investments:

    (i) fixed-interest securities[67] registered in the United Kingdom issued by local or public authorities[68] in the Commonwealth, in the European Union, or by the World Bank and regional Development Banks[69]

    (ii) debentures[70] of United Kingdom companies which comply with certain prescribed conditions as to paid-up capital and dividend records[71];

    (iii) any units of a gilt unit trust scheme[72]; and

---

[66] s.6(2). The narrower-range investments specified in Pt I also now include Ulster Development Bonds (Trustee Investments (Additional Powers) (No.2) Order 1962 (S.I. 1962 No. 2611)); National Development Bonds (Trustee Investments (Additional Powers) Order 1964 (S.I. 1964 No. 703)); British Savings Bonds (Trustee Investment (Additional Powers) Order 1968 (S.I. 1968 No. 470)); National Savings Income Bonds (Trustee Investments (Additional Powers) Order 1982 (S.I. 1982 No. 1086)); National Savings Deposit Bonds (Trustee Investments (Additional Powers) (No. 2) Order 1983 (S.I. 1983 No. 1525)); National Savings Indexed-Income Bonds (Trustee Investments (Additional Powers) Order 1985 (S.I. 1985 No. 1780); National Savings Capital Bonds (Trustee Investments (Additional Powers) Order 1988 (S.I. 1988 No. 2554)); National Savings FIRST Option Bonds (Trustee Investments (Additional Powers) Order 1992 (S.I. 1992 No. 1738)); and National Savings Pensioners Guaranteed Income Bonds (Trustee Investments (Additional Powers) Order 1994 (S.I. 1994 No. 265)).

[67] That is securities which under the terms of issue bear a fixed rate of interest: Sched. 1, Pt IV, para. 4. "Securities" includes "shares, debentures, Treasury Bills and Tax Reserve Certificates"; *ibid*. Variable-interest securities have been added by Trustee Investment (Additional Powers) Order 1977 (S.I. 1977 No. 831).

[68] Sched. 1, Pt V, para. 4.

[69] *ibid*., paras 5, 5A, 5B. Approved issuers are specified by Statutory Instrument from time to time; a recent list can be found in Trustee Investments (Additional Powers) (No.2) Order (S.I. 1994 No. 1908).

[70] "Debenture" includes for this purpose debenture stock and bonds whether containing a charge on the assets or not, and loan stock and notes (Sched. 1, Pt IV, para. 4).

[71] Sched. 1, Pt II, para. 4; *ibid*. Pt IV, para. 3. These requirements are the same as for Pt III investments.

[72] Sched. 1, Pt II, para. 10A (added by Trustee Investments (Additional Powers) (No. 2) Order (S.I. 1994 No. 1908)).

(iv) deposits with most building societies.[73]

2. *Wider-Range Investments*

The investments specified in Part III of the First Schedule are Wider-Range Investments, which also require expert advice. It was this wholly new category of trustee investments which raised the most attention in 1961. They include:

(i) shares, stock and debentures of certain United Kingdom companies[74];

(ii) shares of certain designated building societies[75]; and,

(iii) units of authorised unit trusts.[76] The striking feature was the inclusion of equities and other securities of United Kingdom companies are included; however, such investments in United Kingdom companies are hedged round with restrictions.

3. *Companies Eligible for Investment*

A number of restrictions apply to investment in debentures (which are within Part II of the First Schedule) and in stocks and shares (which are within Part III of that Schedule).

First, they will not constitute trustee investments unless they are quoted on a recognised stock exchange.[77] Secondly, shares and debenture stock must be fully paid up or issued on terms that they are to be fully paid up within nine months from the date of issue.[78] And, thirdly, the company in question must have a total issued or paid-up capital of at least £1 million[79] and must also have paid in each of the immediately preceding five years a dividend on all its shares.[80] This third requirement was quite stringent in 1961. However, the capital requirement has obviously been very considerably watered down by inflation since then and it has been realised that there is no statutory requirement as to the amount of the dividend which has to be paid. A company which is experiencing bad trading conditions will therefore nevertheless often pay a minute dividend on its shares, even if it is as little as 0.01p a share, simply in order to ensure that its shares continue to be approved trust investments.

4. *Division of the Fund*

The trustees cannot make or retain any wider-range investments unless the trust fund is divided into two parts, a narrower-range part and a wider-

---

[73] Building Societies Act 1986, s.120(1), Sched. 18, Pt I, para. 4.
[74] Sched. 1, Pt II, para. 1; *ibid*. Pt IV, para. 3.
[75] Sched. 1, Pt III, para. 2.
[76] *ibid*., para. 3.
[77] Sched. 1, Pt IV, para. 2(a).
[78] Sched. 1, Pt IV, para. 2(b).
[79] *ibid*., para. 3(a).
[80] *ibid*., para. 3(b).

range part.[81] Only the wider-range part can be used for investment in the wider-range investments specified in Part III.[82] This division, which is perhaps the most important general feature of the Act, originally had to be made into two equal parts (the "50:50").[83] Since 1996 it has had to be made into unequal parts, 25 per cent for the narrower-range part and 75 per cent for the wider-range part[84] (funds divided before 1996 can be redivided in the new proportions, which of course involves a transfer of assets from one part to the other, if the trustees so wish). Once made the division is permanent and the two parts of the fund have to be kept separate.[85] While the wider-range part can be invested in wider-range investments, although there is nothing to prevent the trustee from investing some or all of it in narrower-range investments if he chooses. On the other hand, the narrower-range part must all be invested in narrower-range investments.

Moreover, in order to make sure that the division is permanent, provision is made for "compensating transfers" if property is transferred from the narrower range to the wider range.[86] Thus, if property in the narrower-range part is invested in a wider-range investment, there must be a compensating transfer from the wider-range part in the opposite direction; if this is not possible because the wider-range part consists only of wider-range investments, the necessary amount of them must be sold and the proceeds of sale transferred and reinvested in narrower-range investments as soon as possible.[87]

Having said this, however, the two parts of the fund will obviously not appreciate at exactly the same rate. When the economy is buoyant, the wider-range part can be expected to appreciate faster than the narrower-range part; in such circumstances, the protection superficially given by the division of the fund progressively reduces. When, on the other hand, the economy is in recession, the narrower-range part is likely to appreciate faster than the wider-range part, particularly if any of the companies in which wider-range investments have been made encounter serious difficulties.

5. Accruals

Property may accrue to the trust fund after the division. In this respect, a distinction has to be made between various classes of accrual. If property accrues to a trust fund by virtue of the ownership of property that is already held (*e.g.* on a bonus issue of shares or on the foreclosure of a mortgage) or was previously in their hands (*e.g.* where trustees have sold shares but retained their right to a bonus issue), then that property will accrue to that

---

[81] s.2(1).
[82] s.2(1), (2).
[83] s.2(1).
[84] The Trustee Investment (Division of Trust Fund) Order 1996 (S.I. 1996 No. 845). The possibility of the Treasury making such an order up to, but not exceeding, this particular percentage in the wider-range part was expressly envisaged by s.13, which also contains the provisions for redivision of funds already divided.
[85] s.2(1).
[86] *ibid.*
[87] s.2(2).

part of the fund which contains or contained the investment which gen-erated it.[88] But in every other case the trustees must ensure that the value of each part of the fund is increased proportionately by the same amount; this may involve a compensating transfer being made from one part of the fund to the other.[89] This would prove to be necessary where, for example, div-idends or income are received as capital, where an expectancy falls in or the proceeds of sale of an expectancy are received, or where a gift is made to trustees on the trusts of the settlement.

6. *Withdrawals*

Although compensating transfers may be necessary in the event of the withdrawal of property from the trust fund, special provision is made for one class of withdrawal. It is provided that withdrawals from a trust fund in the exercise of any power or duty[90] of the trustees may be made from either part of the fund at their discretion[91]; therefore in this case there is no need for any compensating transfers. For example, if there is £1,000 in the nar-rower range and £1,000 in the wider range and the trustees have to raise £500 to pay taxes or to pay an absolutely entitled beneficially or to make an appropriation to a separate trust fund or any other purpose, the £500 can be taken from either part of the fund at the trustees' discretion. This may well mean that the envisaged percentages of the two parts of the fund will be partially abrogated unless, of course, £250 is taken from each part. This breach in the rule is presumably justified by the advantage of giving a certain latitude to trustees in the performance of their powers and duties in this respect.[92]

Moreover, there are certain ancillary provisions governing the trustees' power to appropriate part of the fund to form a separate trust fund. If at the time of appropriation the original fund was divided into a wider-range part and a narrower-range part, it will be necessary to make a division of the new fund if it is intended to make use of the statutory investment powers as to that fund. But this division need not necessarily be in the percentages laid down in the Act. It is provided that the wider-range part and narrower-range part of the appropriated fund may be constituted either in the statu-tory proportions or so as to bear the same proportion to each other as the two corresponding parts of the original fund bore at the date of appropria-tion or "in some intermediate proportion".[93] This third alternative may require elucidation. It will presumably apply to a case where at the date of appropriation the 75:25 rule applies to the original fund but the wider-range part has increased in value beyond 75 per cent to, say, 85 per cent of the whole so that the proportions are 85:15 and not 75:25. In this case the wider-range part and the narrower-range part of the appropriated funds may be constituted in any proportion between 85:15 and 75:25. It could legitimately,

---

[88] s.2(3)(a).
[89] s.2(3)(b).
[90] See Trustee Act 1925, s.10(4).
[91] s.2(4).
[92] See 234 HL Official Report 13, 14.
[93] s.4(3).

for example, be in the proportion of 80 per cent for the wider-range part and 20 per cent for the narrower-range part.

It should also be noticed that no provision is made for compensating transfers between the assets in the two parts of the original fund which are not appropriated to form a separate trust fund. Thus if at the date of appropriation £16,000 is comprised in wider-range investments and £4,000 in narrower-range investments and £2,000 is appropriated out of the narrower-range funds, the proportion to which the original fund will now be constituted will be altered to 8:1.

These rules governing appropriations constitute a further potential weakening of the protection superficially given by the division of the fund.

7. *Special-Range Investments*

The statutory powers of investment are additional to any special powers conferred on the trustees by the will or settlement in question, by the court,[94] or by Parliament.[95] As a result, the Trustee Investment Act 1961 also had to make provision for cases where trustees wished to combine their special powers of investment with the powers conferred by the Act. Accordingly, it is provided that any property (not including narrower-range investments but including wider-range investments) which trustees are entitled to hold pursuant to such special powers must be carried to a separate "special-range" part of the fund.[96] So if the statutory powers are utilised in cases where the trustees are also utilising special powers of investment of some sort, then the fund will be divided into three parts—a special-range part, a wider-range part and a narrower-range part.

Difficulties of administration may, however, arise if "special-range" property is converted into investments authorised by the Act. In these circumstances, the trustees must ensure these investments are divided in such a way that the value of both the narrower-range part and the wider-range part is increased by the appropriate proportion (if necessary, by compensating transfers).[97] For example, trustees who hold gold pursuant to a special power of investment and also hold gilt-edged securities may wish to take advantage of the Act and invest in equities. If the trustees wish to retain the gold, it will be carried to a separate part of the fund, namely the special-range part. The gilts will be divided into a narrower-range part and a wider-range part in the appropriate proportions and the trustees may then sell as much of the gilts in the wider-range part as they wish to invest in equities. If further gold accrues to the trust, it will also have to be carried to the special-range part. But if some of the gold is sold and converted into

---

[94] For example, under the Variation of Trusts Act 1958 or Trustee Act 1925, s.57; see *post*, p. 542. See also s.15, which preserves the power of the court to confer investment powers wider than those given by the 1961 Act; also *Re Cooper's Settlement* [1962] Ch. 826; *Re Kolb's Will Trusts* [1962] Ch. 531; *Re Clarke's Will Trusts* [1961] 1 W.L.R. 1471; *Re University of London Charitable Trusts* [1964] Ch. 282; *Trustees of the British Museum v. Att.-Gen.* [1984] 1 W.L.R. 418 (all cases on the Variation of Trusts Act 1958); *Anker-Petersen v. Anker-Petersen* (1991) 88/16 L.S.Gaz. 32 (Trustee Act 1925, s.57).

[95] s.3(1).

[96] s.3(3), Sched. 2.

[97] *ibid.*, para. 3.

securities authorised by the Act, the proceeds of the conversion will have to be dealt with in such a way that the appropriate percentage of them is transferred to the wider-range part and the narrower range part.

Where the trustees have power to purchase gold pursuant to such a special power, there is no doubt that the property in the wider-range part of the fund can at any time be realised and used to purchase more gold under the special power. Whether the narrower-range part of the investments can be used for this purpose is not at all clear. If this is indeed possible, the surprising result is that the narrower-range investments could be exhausted in exercising the special power so that the trust fund would consist only of wider-range investments and of the gold acquired under the special power. This would seem to be contrary to the basic principle of proportionality as between gilts and equities which in general underlies the Act but there does not actually appear to be anything in the Act to prevent it happening. If this is so, then the Act contains an unexpected lacuna. However, it might be dangerous for trustees to take advantage of this possibility for their conduct in so doing could possibly be impugned as a breach of the trustees' general duties of care and of their statutory duty to ensure diversification.[98]

These provisions relating to special-range property do not apply where the trustees' special powers of investment were conferred or varied by an order of the court made within the period of 10 years ending on August 3, 1961 or by an enactment or statutory instrument made within the like period or by a local Act passed within the Parliamentary Session 9 & 10 Eliz.2 (1960–61).[99] If any of these things occurred and the trustees subsequently wish to make use of the powers contained in the Trustee Investment Act 1961, the normal rules as to the division of the fund into a narrower-range part and a wider-range part apply; however, the trustees cannot make use of the Act so as to make or hold wider-range investments whilst any wider-range investments are comprised in the narrower-range part of the fund.[1] The rule of general law that a trustee may retain an investment which has ceased to be authorised[2] is thereby overridden for this purpose.[3] To take an example, the trusts may have been varied within the prescribed period by the court to enable the trustees to invest 80 per cent of the fund in what the Act subsequently classified as wider-range investments (such as units in a unit trust). If the trust fund is subsequently divided under the Act, certain wider-range investments will inevitably be comprised in the narrower-range part of the fund; unless and until these had been sold for reinvestment in the narrower-range investments, the trustees would not be able to make any further investment in units of a unit trust. They would thus be unable to make use of the statutory powers until a true division had been effected. Because of this situation, it is obviously much more likely in practice that in such circumstances, rather than relying on the Act, an application would be made to the court to seek whatever further extension of investment powers was required.[4]

---

[98] See *post*, p. 563.
[99] s.3(4).
[1] Sched. 3, para. 1.
[2] Trustee Act 1925, s.4; see *ante*, p. 541.
[3] Sched. 3, para. 2.
[4] Under Variation of Trusts Act 1958 or Trustee Act 1925, s.57. See *ante*, n. 94.

8. *The Duties of Trustees*

Trustees naturally have, as a matter of general law, a duty of care and impartiality in making investments, and this is so whether these are made under the Act or under a special power of investment.[5] But the Act itself imposes certain positive statutory duties in addition. First, the trustees must have regard to the need for securing diversification in so far as is appropriate to the circumstances of the trust.[6] No doubt circumstances legitimately to be taken into account would be the smallness of the fund or the life-tenant's paramount need of income. Secondly, they must have regard to the suitability to the trust of investments of the class proposed and of the particular investment as an investment of that class.[7] The sort of problem with which trustees will be faced here is whether, and to what extent, for instance, present income should be sacrificed to future growth and much will depend on arriving at a decision on the actual needs of the beneficiaries, the expected duration of the trust and, most important today, the beneficiaries' tax position.

The way in which these factors have to be considered is shown by taking three examples:

(i) If trustees are holding funds on trust for an infant beneficiary at the age of 18 in, say, 2004, they might invest not merely in any gilt, nor merely in any dated gilt, but in 9.5 per cent Conversion Stock 2004. This particular stock will be redeemed in 2004 at its highest value, just in time for the proceeds to be paid to the beneficiary, and it has the added attraction that the increase in its capital value will be exempt from capital gains tax,[8] whereas increases in the capital value of most other investments will be subject to that tax when the beneficiary reaches the age of 18 and becomes absolutely entitled as against the trustees.

(ii) If a very small sum is to be held for a fairly short period—say, between five and 10 years—but the beneficiary has adequate income from other sources, National Savings Certificates might be a suitable investment; although the rate of interest is small, this interest is free of tax[9] and the certificates are also exempt from capital gains tax.[10]

(iii) If the beneficiary currently entitled to the income of the trust has a small total income, the trustees might endeavour to invest at least part of the fund in a security which produces a high income, so far as they consider this consistent with their duties to the remainderman. But they should not select just any security which produces a high income, or even just any security which produces a high

---

[5] See *ante*, p. 540.
[6] s.6(1)(a).
[7] s.6(1)(b).
[8] Taxation of Chargeable Gains Act 1992, s.115.
[9] Income and Corporation Taxes Act 1988, s.326.
[10] Taxation of Chargeable Gains Act 1992, s.121.

income and is considered particularly safe. Where a beneficiary's total income is small, he is able to reclaim the tax paid on the trust income; in respect of company distributions, this claim is limited to the 20 per cent "tax credit" which the company in question has retained out of dividend. However, no such claim can be made where the income is derived from abroad. Accordingly, where the beneficiary is potentially able to make a repayment claim, the trustees must look for a company which has virtually the whole of its activities in England so that a full tax credit will be available to be reclaimed.

It is in the light of considerations of this type that the full significance of the requirement for trustees to have regard to the suitability both of the class of investment proposed, and of the particular investment as an investment of that class, becomes apparent.

Furthermore, with the exception of the small savings investments listed in Part I of the First Schedule of the Act, the trustee must, before deciding on an investment, obtain and consider proper written advice from an expert, who since the enactment of the Financial Services Act 1986 has had to be authorised under that legislation. Advice must be given as to whether the investment is satisfactory in the light of the statutory and other requirements which have already been considered. The operative words are "obtain and consider"; the trustee is not therefore bound to follow the advice. (As will be seen later on, different considerations apply to a mortgage investment. In this case the advice is not required to extend to the suitability of the loan in question; that matter depends on the valuation required by section 8 of the Trustee Act 1925.[11])

It is also provided that a trustee who is retaining any investment made by the settlor or testator must decide at what intervals the circumstances and particularly the true nature of the investment make it desirable to "obtain and consider" proper written advice as to whether it should still be being retained; having so decided, he must then duly obtain and consider the advice.[12]

"Proper advice" is the advice of a person whom the trustee reasonably believes to be qualified to give it by reason of his financial ability and experience[13]; since the enactment of the Financial Services Act 1986 the adviser must anyway be licensed thereunder although the trustee must bear in mind that not everyone licensed thereunder will necessarily be qualified to advise as to the particular circumstances of his trust. However, these requirements will not apply where one of two or more trustees is himself so qualified; he may well be qualified as a stockbroker or solicitor to give advice and if so he may properly give it.[14] He is not under a duty to obtain and consider advice from another source. The position is the same where one of the trustees is a trust corporation, such as a bank. If an officer of the corporation gives advice, it will be unnecessary to take further advice.[15]

---

[11] See *post*, p. 565.
[12] s.6(3), (5).
[13] s.6(4).
[14] s.6(6).
[15] s.6(4), (6).

9. *Saving for Powers of the Court*

It is expressly enacted that the extension of investment powers provided for in the Act is not to lessen the court's power to confer wider powers on trustees.[16] This refers both to the Variation of Trusts Act 1958 and to section 57 of the Trustee Act 1925. The interaction between these provisions and the 1961 Act will be dealt with when the subject of variation of trusts is considered.[17]

IV. MORTGAGES OF LAND

1. *General Principles*

Investment in a mortgage of land, that is to say lending money on the security of land, will be an authorised investment within the meaning of the Trustee Investments Act 1961 falling within the narrower-range of investments requiring advice if made on a mortgage of property in the United Kingdom if it is freehold property or leasehold property where the unexpired term is not less than 60 years.[18] This kind of investment, whether within or outside the statutory limits, may also be expressly authorised by the trust instrument.

But a trustee is not always justified in investing the trust funds on mortgage. He must naturally act in good faith and with reasonable care and impartiality. He should not therefore make this sort of investment simply for the benefit of one of the beneficiaries and certainly not for the benefit of a person who is not even a beneficiary.[19] The rule that a trustee is not necessarily free from responsibility because he invests in an authorised security[20] applies with considerable force to investment on mortgage and the limitations on the trustee's powers imposed both by statute and by general principles such as these show this clearly.

Certain general propositions have been established by the case law. Accordingly a trustee should, in the absence of express authority to do otherwise, invest only in first legal mortgages of freehold or leasehold land within the limits prescribed. The security should be a first mortgage because it is desirable that the mortgage should enjoy priority. He should therefore avoid second mortgages since a first mortgagee may exercise the power of

---

[16] s.15.

[17] See *ante*, n. 60 and *post*, p. 656.

[18] Sched. 1, Pt II, para. 13. Technically, trustees of land may no longer be bound by the 60 year restriction in relation to land in England and Wales because of the power conferred on them by Trusts of Land and Appointment of Trustees Act 1996, s.6(3) to purchase any legal estate in such land (both "purchase" and "estate" are defined (in s.23(1), (2)) in the same way as in the Law of Property Act 1925 and so clearly include an advance by way of legal mortgage on the security of a legal charge. However, in practice, any mortgage advance on the security of a shorter lease would be highly imprudent.

[19] See *Whitney v. Smith* (1869) L.R. 4 Ch. 513 at 521; *Re Walker* (1890) 62 L.T. 449.

[20] See *ante*, p. 540.

sale in such circumstances as to leave nothing for the second mortgagee.[21] He should obtain a legal interest and, in theory, avoid equitable mortgages because otherwise he might be postponed to a subsequent legal mortgage. In practice, however, the possibility of protecting equitable mortgages[22] under the provisions of the Land Registration Act 1925 and the Land Charges Act 1972 will prevent an equitable mortgage which has been protected in the appropriate way from being postponed to any subsequent mortgage; in practice, therefore, this would seem to constitute sufficient protection. A trustee should also avoid what is called a *contributory mortgage* (that is to say, a joint loan by the trustee and other persons) because in such a case the trustee would not possess complete control.[23] On the other hand, a sub-mortgage, provided that it confers a legal estate, may be quite proper, for here the mortgagee will mortgage to the trustee and the latter will obtain a legal estate.[24]

However, the Trustee Investments Act 1961 may anyway now have modified the necessity for a first legal mortgage because, having declared that mortgages of freehold property and certain leasehold property are narrower-range investments requiring advice,[25] it defines "mortgage" in the same way as in the Trustee Act 1925.[26] This definition includes "every estate and interest regarded in equity as merely a security for money",[27] which will include an equitable mortgage. Lewin on Trusts suggests that the effect of the Act is to sweep away the old prohibitions on inferior types of mortgage.[28] This is arguably also the effect of the Trusts of Land and Appointment of Trustees Act 1996 in so far as concerns the ability of trustees of land to advance money on the security of second legal mortgages.[29] In both cases it is highly doubtful whether this was the legislative intention and it seems safer for trustees to assume that the old restrictions still apply.

2. *Statutory Duties*

A trustee should also observe the statutory rules relating to the value of the property.

Various conditions in relation to value expressly imposed by the Trustee Act 1925 are unaffected by the Trustee Investments Act 1961. These should be fulfilled before investment is made in this class of security. It must be

---

[21] *Norris v. Wright* (1851) 14 Beav. 291; *Lockhart v. Reilly* (1857) 1 De G. & J. 464. The Law Reform Committee (23rd Report, 1982) recommended that trustees should have power to lend on the security of second mortgages and trustees of land probably technically now have the power to lend on the security of second legal mortgages for the reasons stated: see *ante*, n. 18.

[22] *Swaffield v. Nelson* [1876] W.N. 255.

[23] *Webb v. Jonas* (1888) 39 Ch.D. 660.

[24] *Smethurst v. Hastings* (1885) 30 Ch.D. 490.

[25] s.1(1), Sched. 1, Pt II, para. 13.

[26] s.17(4).

[27] Trustee Act 1925, s.68(7).

[28] (16th ed.), pp. 370, 371.

[29] Because of the power conferred on them by Trusts of Land and Appointment of Trustees Act 1996, s.6(3) to purchase any legal estate in such land (both "purchase" and "estate" are defined (in s.23(1), (2)) in the same way as in the Law of Property Act 1925 and so clearly include an advance by way of legal mortgage on the security of any legal charge.

emphasised that the rule is that the trustee "should", as a matter of prudence, fulfil these conditions; he is not bound to do so.[30] But a trustee would certainly be unwise in ignoring them because compliance with them provides cogent evidence of the existence of care.[31] The material provisions are found in section 8 of the Trustee Act 1925. This section provides that a trustee lending money on the security of any property will not be chargeable with breach of trust by reason only of the proportion borne by the amount of the loan to the value of the property at the time when the loan was made if it appears to the court that the trustee acted in accordance with the criteria set out below.

(i) In making the loan the trustee must have been acting upon a report as to the value of the property made by a person whom he reasonably believed to be an able practical surveyor or valuer instructed and employed independently of any owner of the property, whether such surveyor or valuer carries on business in the locality where the property is situated or elsewhere.[32] In interpreting this provision in *Re Walker*,[33] Kekewich J. held that the trustee need only believe the surveyor or valuer to be able but that the latter must in fact be employed independently of the owner of the property. The point about employment was doubted by Warrington J. in *Re Solomon*,[34] where he seemed to think that a belief of independent employment would be sufficient. But the view of Kekewich J. seems to be in accordance with the natural meaning of the words in the section. In deciding whether the surveyor or valuer is an able practical man, it would appear that the trustee must still exercise his own judgment; he cannot, for example, trust blindly in the nomination of his solicitor and certainly cannot trust in any way that of the mortgagor's solicitor.[35] The surveyor or valuer need not, however, necessarily be a local man, nor have specialised local knowledge.[36]

(ii) The amount of the loan must not exceed two-thirds of the value of the property as stated in the report.[37] This is the utmost limit and a trustee ought not to lend more even if the surveyor actually advises that a greater proportion may be advanced; indeed in many cases, in order to leave a margin for depreciation and unpaid interest, it will be advisable to lend less. Everything depends on the particular property. If it is liable to deteriorate or is specially

---

[30] *Palmer v. Emerson* [1911] 1 Ch. 758.

[31] *Re Stuart* [1897] 2 Ch. 583 at 592; *Palmer v. Emerson* [1911] 1 Ch. 758 at 769. See also *Chapman v. Brown* [1902] 1 Ch. 785.

[32] s.8(1)(a).

[33] (1890) 62 L.T. 449 at 452; see also *Re Somerset* [1894] 1 Ch. 231 at 253, *per* Kekewich J.

[34] [1912] 1 Ch. 261 at 281 (compromised on appeal [1913] 1 Ch. 200). See also *Shaw v. Cates* [1909] 1 Ch. 389.

[35] *Shaw v. Cates* [1909] 1 Ch. 389 at 404, *per* Parker J.

[36] There is no such requirement in the Act. However, the trustee should not ignore the importance of local knowledge in arriving at a correct valuation; see *Fry v. Tapson* (1884) 28 Ch.D. 268.

[37] s.8(1)(b).

subject to fluctuations in value then a prudent trustee will, assuming that the investment is itself a proper one, require a larger margin for protection.[38] What is the position of a trustee who lends more than two-thirds? Section 9 provides that if a trustee makes such a loan but the security is otherwise a proper investment (in other words, if the only breach is the percentage), then the mortgage will be deemed to be an authorised investment for the sum which could properly have been lent and the trustee will only be liable in respect of the excess (with interest). Thus in *Shaw v. Cates*[39] the trustees had advanced £4,400 on the security of land. This was held to be a proper investment only for £3,400. The trustees were therefore liable only to make good the excess of £1,000 with interest.

(iii) The loan must be made under the advice of the surveyor or valuer expressed in the report.[40] This means, of course, that the latter must actually advise the trustee that the investment is a proper one.

3. *Limitations to the Statutory Provisions*

It will be observed that section 8 of the Trustee Act 1925 provides relief from liability "by reason *only of the proportion*[41] borne by the amount of the loan to the value of the property". The section also refers to lendings on the security of property "on which he can properly lend". Section 9 refers to a security which is "otherwise proper", the only excess being in the amount lent. These words would appear clearly to provide protection only in matters of value and will not be of assistance where the nature of the security itself comes into question. The trustee must therefore establish in the first instance the propriety of the investment independently of value.[42] It seems to follow that a trustee would be liable in any case for advancing money on the security of speculative property and particularly of wasting property; in such cases his liability would be based on the fact that he should never have lent the money on such a security at all, not because he had lent too much, even if that was the case. Yet curiously enough, Warrington J. held in *Re Solomon*[43]—and the general approach of Parker J. in *Shaw v. Cates*[44] could also be considered as being to the same effect—that, if the property is of a speculative character and the trustee acts on a valuer's report made in the prescribed manner, the trustee will be entitled to protection. However, this approach, even though perhaps commendable as a matter of policy in

---

[38] See *Shaw v. Cates* [1909] 1 Ch. 389 at 398, 399. See also *Palmer v. Emerson* [1911] 1 Ch. 758 at 765, 766.
[39] *Shaw v. Cates, ibid.*
[40] s.8(1)(c).
[41] *Re Walker* (1890) 62 L.T. 449, *per* Kekewich J.; *Blyth v. Fladgate* [1891] 1 Ch. 337, *per* Stirling J.
[42] Emphasis added.
[43] [1912] 1 Ch. 261.
[44] [1909] 1 Ch. 389.

enabling a trustee to rely on an expert's advice, seems contrary to principle.

4. *Purchase of Land*

Despite the fact that investments on the security of mortgages are, at least according to most statutory definitions,[45] purchases of interests in land, the rules governing purchases of interests in land other than mortgages are quite different. These have of course already been discussed.[46]

V. INVESTMENT CLAUSES

The general rule is conventionally stated to be that clauses in trust deeds enlarging the trustee's powers of investment beyond the scope authorised by law are construed strictly.[47] To what extent, however, this rule is in practice followed today is debatable. Indeed it is arguable that nowadays investment clauses should be given a liberal interpretation. But this is, of course, a generalisation which cannot dogmatically be said to be either right or wrong. A number of illustrations from the case law on each side of the line—one from the late nineteenth century and the others from the present day—will be considered. In *Bethell v. Abraham*[48] trustees were empowered to "continue or change securities from time to time as to the majority shall seem meet". This clause was strictly construed by Jessel M.R., who held that the words related merely to determining the time at which a change of securities was to be made; they did not authorise a substantive change of investment outside the authorised range. This case may be compared with the more recent decision in *Re Harari's Settlement Trusts*[49] where the clause empowered the trustees to invest "in or upon such investments as to them may seem fit", Jenkins J. held that there was no justification for implying any restriction on these words and that the trustees were consequently able to makes investments outside the authorised range. A similarly liberal result was arrived at in *Re Peczenic's Settlement Trusts*,[50] where the trustees were authorised to make such investments in "any shares stocks property or property holding company as the trustees in their discretion shall consider to be in the best interest of" the beneficiary. Buckley J. held that the trustees were authorised to invest in anything of these types which was properly able to be treated as an investment but not to invest merely on personal security, which was clearly not within the list. These illustrations appear to

---

[45] Such as those in the Law of Property Act 1925, s.205(1)(x), (xxi), which are incorporated into the Trusts of Land and Appointment of Trustees Act 1996 by s.23(1), (2).

[46] See *ante*, p. 552.

[47] *Re Peczenic's Settlement Trusts* [1964] 1 W.L.R. 720 at 722, *per* Buckley J.

[48] (1873) L.R. 17 Eq. 24.

[49] [1949] 1 All E.R. 430.

[50] [1964] 1 W.L.R. 720.

manifest different attitudes to investment clauses in the modern law; however, the true position seems to be that it is entirely a question of construction of the particular investment clause before the court and that, although previous cases may be helpful, they will not necessarily be decisive.[51]

Use of one of the well-known model clauses which clearly give to the trustees unrestricted investment powers, including powers to purchase property for residential purposes (although this is not now actually necessary)[52] and also to invest on personal credit,[53] will of course avoid any difficulties of construction. The use of such a power is generally advised today. At the same time, it will be appreciated that, even if the trustees have such a power, they must still act with reasonable care and impartiality in deciding on their investments.[54]

VI. ANCILLARY STATUTORY POWERS

1. Redeemable Stock

The trustees are entitled to invest in authorised securities,[55] notwithstanding the fact that they are redeemable and even if the price paid exceeds the redemption value[56]; if they do, they are entitled to retain them until redemption.[57]

2. Bearer Securities

A trustee is entitled, unless expressly prohibited by the instrument creating the trust, to retain or invest in securities payable to their bearer which, if they had not been made thus payable, would have been authorised investments.[58] But it is required that, until they are sold, the bearer securities should be deposited by the trustee with a bank for safe custody and for the collection of any income arising.[59] If they are accordingly deposited, the trustee will not be liable for any loss incurred[60]; moreover, it is provided that any fees paid in respect of the deposit itself or the collection of income is to be paid out of the income of the trust property.[61]

---

[51] See also, in addition to the cases cited in the text, *Re Maryon-Wilson's Estate* [1912] 1 Ch. 55; *Re McEacharn's Settlement Trusts* [1939] Ch. 858; *Re Hart's Will Trusts* [1943] 2 All E.R. 557; *Re Douglas' Will Trusts* [1959] 1 W.L.R. 744 (affirmed on another point [1959] 1 W.L.R. 1212); *Re Kob's Will Trusts* [1962] Ch. 531 (interpretation of various investment clauses).

[52] Due to the overruling of *Re Power* [1947] Ch. 572 by the enactment of the Trusts of Land and Appointment of Trustees Act 1996; see *ante*, p. 552.

[53] Only an express power to lend on personal security will enable such a loan to be made: see *Khoo Tek Kong v. Ching Joo Tuan Neoh* [1934] A.C. 529; *Re Peczenic's Settlement Trusts* [1964] 1 W.L.R. 720. Compare *Re Laing's Settlement* [1899] 1 Ch. 593. See also *Tucker v. Tucker* [1894] 1 Ch. 724.

[54] See *ante*, p. 540.

[55] That is under the Trustee Investment Act 1961.

[56] Trustee Act 1925, s.2(1).

[57] *ibid.*, s.2(2).

[58] *ibid.*, s.7(1).

[59] *ibid.*, s.7(1), proviso.

[60] *ibid.*, s.7(2).

[61] *ibid.*

3. *Lending on Mortgage*

A supplementary power is conferred on trustees properly lending money on the security of trust property[62] to contract that the money will not be called in for a fixed period not exceeding seven years provided that interest is paid within a specified time not exceeding 30 days after it becomes due and provided also that the mortgagor is not in breach of any covenant contained in the mortgage for the maintenance and protection of the trust property.[63]

4. *Sale of Land*

If land is sold by trustees for an estate in fee simple or for a term of years having at least 500 years to run, they may contract that the payment of any part of the purchase-money not exceeding two-thirds be left on mortgage.[64] But it is essential that the mortgage contains a covenant by the mortgagor to keep any buildings insured to their full value.[65] In this situation, it is not necessary for the trustees to obtain a report as to value and they are not liable for any loss incurred by reason of the security being insufficient.[66]

5. *Capital Reorganisations and Bonus Issues*

Where any securities[67] of a company are subject to a trust, the trustees may concur in any scheme or arrangement for any of the following purposes:

(i) for the reconstruction of the company;

(ii) for the sale of all or any part of its property or undertaking to another company;

(iii) for the acquisition of the securities of the company, or of control thereof, by another company[68];

(iv) for its amalgamation with another company; and

(v) for the release, modification or variation of any rights, privileges or liabilities attached to the securities. They are also entitled to take up any new securities in lieu of the old securities and furthermore are not responsible for any loss if they act in good faith. They can also retain any new securities for any period for which they could properly have retained the original ones.[69]

If any conditional or preferential right to subscribe for any securities in a company is offered to trustees in respect of their holdings in the company,

---

[62] See *ante*, p. 565.
[63] Trustee Act 1925, s.10(1).
[64] *ibid.*, s.10(2).
[65] *ibid.*
[66] *ibid.*
[67] This term includes shares and stock; *ibid.* s.68(13).
[68] (iii) was added by Trustee Investment Act 1961, s.9(1).
[69] Trustee Investment Act 1961, ss.10(3), 9(1).

they may either exercise the right and apply capital money subject to the trust in payment of the consideration, or renounce such right, or sell it for the best consideration that can be reasonably obtained to any person including a beneficiary. They are not liable for any loss, provided they act in good faith. If the right is sold, the consideration will be capital money.[70] The power to subscribe for securities includes a power to retain them as if they were the original holding, but subject to any conditions which attach to that holding.[71]

6. *Consents*

The supplementary powers of investment considered in the last three subsections are exercisable subject to the consent of any person whose consent to a change of investment is required by law or by the trust instrument.[72]

7. *Deposits and Payment of Calls*

Pending the negotiation and preparation of any mortgage or during any time when an investment is being sought, the trustees may deposit the trust money in a bank. Any interest payable is applicable as income.[73] They may also apply capital money subject to a trust in payment of the calls on any shares subject to the same trust.[74]

VII. CONTINUING SUPERVISION

In addition to making investments, trustees are under a duty to keep them under review to the same extent as would a prudent businessman when dealing with his own affairs. In the case of holdings in large quoted public companies, a periodic review will usually be sufficient. However, where the trustees have a majority holding or some other special position of influence, they will be expected to take advantage of it. If a reasonably prudent businessman would require information about the company's affairs which is not generally available, trustees will need to obtain it. If a reasonably prudent businessman would insist on board representation, or board control, trustees will themselves need to insist on it.

In *Bartlett v. Barclays Bank Trust Co. (No.1)*,[75] a person incorporated a company to manage his properties. He then settled almost the whole of the shares in the company upon trust for his wife and issue. Initially the board included members of the settlor's family but that gradually changed. However, the trustees, while sending a representative to statutory meetings of the company, did not seek representation on the board. The company purchased a property opposite the Old Bailey in the City of London, at a price well in

---

[70] Trustee Act 1925, s.10(4).
[71] Trustee Investment Act 1961, s.9(2).
[72] Trustee Act 1925, s.10(5).
[73] s.11(1).
[74] s.11(2).
[75] [1980] Ch. 515.

excess of its investment value, in the hope that permission would be obtained for its development. Permission was not forthcoming and the company later disposed of the property at a loss. Brightman J. held that the trustees were in breach of their duty to obtain the information which, as they were majority shareholders, was available to them.

Information is not, however, an end in itself[76] and must be used to protect the interest of the beneficiaries. If necessary, a trustee must intervene to remove directors[77] and procure the appointment of his own nominees.[78]

Some professional trustees and trust corporations are reluctant to assume this responsibility and look for a provision in a trust instrument which negatives what would otherwise be their duty to interfere in the management of companies in which they are shareholders.

VIII. INSIDER DEALING

A particular problem arises with regard to "insider dealing". Part V of the Criminal Justice Act 1993, which came into force on March 1, 1994, repealing the previous legislation (the Insider Dealing Act 1985), imposes wide-ranging prohibitions on insider dealing. Section 52 provides that a person will be guilty of insider dealing in three situations:

(i) if he deals in securities about which he has unpublished price-sensitive information (a person is defined as dealing in securities if he acquires or disposes of them or procures, directly or indirectly, an acquisition or disposal of the securities by an agent, nominee or other person acting at his direction);

(ii) if he encourages another person to deal with the securities, knowing or having reasonable cause to believe that the acquisition or disposal would take place on a regulated market; and,

(iii) if he discloses the information, other than in the course of his employment or profession, to another person.

If a person who is a director or other officer of a company and thereby obtains unpublished price-sensitive information about the company, is also a trustee of a trust which holds shares in the company he is immediately placed in a position of conflict of duty. On the one hand, he must not contravene the Criminal Justice Act 1993, which creates criminal offences. On the other hand, he must do the best he can for the trust.

The previous legislation contained an express provision dealing with the position of such a trustee. Section 7 of the Insider Dealing Act 1985 provided that a trustee who, in that capacity, dealt in securities was presumed to have done so otherwise than with a view to financial advantage (and so not to have committed an offence) if he acted on the advice of a person who

---

[76] See, *e.g. Re Lucking's Will Trust* [1968] 1 W.L.R. 866, discussed *ante*, p. 513, where the trustees had information but did not use it.
[77] [1980] Ch. 515 at 530.
[78] Criminal Justice Act 1993, Pt V.

appeared to him to be an appropriate person from whom to seek such advice and did not appear to him to be prohibited by the legislation from dealing in the securities. However, there was no corresponding presumption in relation to the disclosure of the information. The legislation thus appeared to suggest that, where a trustee had obtained inside information, he should obtain advice from the trust's investment advisers about that investment in question, without arousing their suspicions and without disclosing his own information, and that subsequently to act, or to join with his co-trustees in acting, on that advice would not amount to an offence.

There is no provision in the Criminal Justice Act 1993 expressly dealing with the position of trustees. However, section 53 provides that a person will not be guilty of either dealing or encouraging dealing if he shows that he would have done what he did even if he had not had the information (as in the previous legislation, the defence does not apply to disclosure). The Economic Secretary to the Treasury[79] explained in Standing Committee that this defence "allows a trustee who possesses insider information to deal in price-affected securities on the basis of independent investment advice".[80] This suggests that the protection expressly given to trustees by the Insider Dealing Act 1985 has survived, although not explicitly, in the Criminal Justice Act 1993. While the advice to a trustee in this difficult position must therefore remain the same, the fact is that, in many cases where a trustee is known to be in a position in which he is likely to be able to obtain inside information, it will be impossible for him to seek advice from the trust's investment advisers without arousing suspicion by so doing. In such circumstances, the only prudent course may well be for him to resign his trusteeship.

---

[79] Mr Anthony Nelson.
[80] *Hansard*, June 10, 1993, Standing Committee B, Col. 175.

CHAPTER 18

APPORTIONMENTS

It has already been seen[1] that a fundamental rule is that a trustee must not allow a conflict of interest to arise between his own personal position and his duties to the beneficiaries. The sister rule is that, where there is a conflict between the interests of different beneficiaries, a trustee must hold a balance between them. This is not so much because this is what the settlor actually did intend, for he may well never have given the matter any thought, but rather because equity presumes that this is what the settlor would have intended had he directed his mind to the point. It is therefore not necessary to find any actual evidence of intention on the part of the settlor for this principle to apply, yet on the other hand he is able to provide expressly or by implication that the principle shall not operate. Avoidance of a conflict of interest is of particular importance in relation to investments: it is also this principle which underlies the rules governing apportionments.[2] These formal rules apply as between tenants for life and remaindermen. However, other conflicts of interest can arise. In *Lloyds Bank v. Duker*,[3] the conflict of interest was between majority and minority beneficiaries. The testator who owned 999 of the 1,000 shares of a private company, left 46/80ths of the 999 shares to his wife. It was held that the 574 shares which represented this proportion could not be transferred to her because such a majority holding would give her the control of the company and, in relation to the remaining minority shares, would be worth more than her due proportion. Consequently, the trustees were directed to sell all 999 shares and distribute the proceeds of sale in the appropriate proportions.

I. APPORTIONMENTS BETWEEN CAPITAL AND INCOME

1. *The Principle*

Suppose that Basil settles property upon trust for Clare for life, remainder to Priscilla absolutely, and the trust property consists of: £5,000 3.5 per cent War Stock; the cow Buttercup; and the right under his grandfather's will to

---

[1] See *ante*, p. 281.
[2] The Law Reform Committee (23rd Report, 1982) has recommended that the rules of conversion and apportionment referred to in the first part of this Chapter should be replaced by a new statutory duty to hold a fair balance between beneficiaries with different interests. The Trust Law Committee is also proposing to produce a Consultation Paper dealing with the subject matter of this Chapter.
[3] [1987] 1 W.L.R. 1324.

receive £15,000 on the death of his father, Bert, who is still alive (this right is known as a reversionary interest).

If these assets are retained in their present form, the holding of War Stock will produce a steady income, and a capital sum will be available to Priscilla on the death of Clare. Buttercup, a fine milk-yielding cow, may produce at first a high income but, as she grows old and her milk production decreases, she will become less and less valuable. She may well die before Clare and, if this is the case, Clare will have derived the whole of the benefit from her and Priscilla will have had none. The case of the reversionary interest is precisely the opposite. Until Bert dies, income is paid to neither Clare nor Priscilla and, if Clare dies before Bert, she will have received no benefit at all from this asset. Equity presumes that it was not Basil's intention that the beneficiaries should be treated so haphazardly and their fortunes left so much to chance. The basic solution is, therefore, for Buttercup and the reversionary interest to be sold and the proceeds invested in authorised securities so that the income may be paid to Clare and a capital sum preserved intact for Priscilla. The rules which follow prescribe how this is to be done. However, once any necessary apportionment between capital and income according to these rules has been made, the trustees are apparently entitled to make investments which produce either high or low income depending on the relative wealth of the tenant for life and the remainder-man.[4]

The rules governing the necessary sale are not, however, always easy to apply. There are three questions to consider:

(i) Is there a duty to convert a particular asset into an authorised investment?

(ii) If so, does the income have to be apportioned between the date when the duty arises and the date when the conversion actually takes place?

(iii) If so, how is such apportionment calculated?

These questions are progressive so that, if the answer to any one is "no", there is no need to consider the remaining questions.

2. Is There a Duty to Convert?

The duty to convert the trust property into authorised investments may arise in two circumstances.

First, if the trust instrument so directs. The most frequent case of an express direction to convert occurs when there is an express trust for sale but any direction to convert is for this purpose equally adequate.

Secondly, as a result of the operation of the rule in *Howe v. Lord Dartmouth*,[5] which directs conversion of an asset to take place where there is no express direction in the trust instrument, but only where all the following conditions are satisfied:

---

[4] *Nestlé v. National Westminster Bank* [1993] 1 W.L.R. 1260.

[5] (1802) 7 Ves. 137. For a relatively up-to-date account of the rule, see L. A. Sheridan: *"Howe v. Lord Dartmouth* Re-examined" (1952) 16 Conv. (N.S.) 349.

(i) the trust was created by will;

(ii) there are at least two beneficiaries, and they are entitled in succession;

(iii) the property consists of residuary personalty;

(iv) the asset is wasting, reversionary or of an unauthorised character; and

(v) there is no contrary intention in the will.

The rule does not apply to a settlement *inter vivos*; the terms of such settlements must be observed strictly because, so it is said, the settlor knew exactly the state of the assets when the settlement was created.[6]

The only one of the five conditions listed which is likely to cause any difficulty is the question of whether or not there is a contrary intention. In *Re Sewell's Estate*[7] the trustees were given a discretion as to what part of the testator's estate should be converted. This was held to have excluded the rule in *Howe v. Lord Dartmouth* because a discretion to convert was inconsistent with the duty to convert which the rule would impose. However, in order to exclude the rule, the power must be consciously exercised.[8] In *Alcock v. Sloper*[9] property was left upon trust for a life tenant and, after his death, upon trust for it to be sold and the proceeds divided between various named beneficiaries. Here too it was held that the rule in *Howe v. Lord Dartmouth* had been excluded, because the express duty to convert on the death of the life tenant was inconsistent with an implied duty to convert on the death of the testator, which is what the rule would have imposed.

The decision in *Alcock v. Sloper*[10] must be contrasted with that in *Re Evans*,[11] where property was given to trustees upon trust for a life tenant and, after her death, upon trust to be divided into three equal shares and distributed to three other members of the family. It was held that *Howe v. Lord Dartmouth* did apply, because the division on the death of the life tenant could be of property in either its converted or unconverted form and consequently the directions in the will were not inconsistent with a duty to convert implied by *Howe v. Lord Dartmouth*.

Where the settlor shows an intention that the property should be enjoyed *in specie*, this clearly negatives the rule.[12] Bennett J. took this proposition a stage further in *Re Fisher*[13] by saying that, where there is a trust for conversion with a power to postpone, the settlor thereby shows that he intends that the property may be enjoyed *in specie*, and that this also is inconsistent with the duty to convert which would be imposed by *Howe v. Lord Dartmouth*. However, in the later case of *Re Berry*,[14] Pennycuick J. refused to follow *Re*

[6] *Re Van Straubenzee* [1901] 2 Ch. 779, *per* Cozens-Hardy J. and see *Milford v. Peile* (1854) 2 W.N. 181; *Hope v. Hope* (1855) 1 Jur. (N.S.) 770.
[7] (1870) L.R. 11 Eq. 80; see also *Simpson v. Earles* (1847) 11 Jur. 921.
[8] *Re Guinness* [1966] 1 W.L.R. 1355.
[9] (1833) 2 My. & K. 699; *Daniel v. Warren* (1843) 2 Y. & Coll. C.C. 290.
[10] (1833) 2 My. & K. 699.
[11] [1920] 2 Ch. 309.
[12] *Macdonald v. Irvine* (1878) 8 Ch.D. 101.
[13] [1943] Ch. 377.
[14] [1962] Ch. 97.

Fisher. Although the logical basis of the latter decision is clear, Pennycuick J. commented that that decision was "contrary to the whole current of authority"; it was an attempt to extend the scope of the exceptions from *Howe v. Lord Dartmouth* too far.

The cases turn on fine differences in wording and, while it may be very difficult to say on any particular set of facts whether *Howe v. Lord Dartmouth* is excluded, the rule itself is clear: has the testator made any provision which is expressly or impliedly inconsistent with a duty to convert at the date of death? If he has not done so and the other conditions listed above are fulfilled, *Howe v. Lord Dartmouth* will apply.

3. Whether There is a Need to Apportion Income

If there is a duty to convert, it will be seen below that conversion should take place either at the date of death, or as at one year from the date of death.[15] It will be obvious that, in the former case, there is no conceivable way of effecting actual conversion at that date while, even in the latter case, actual conversion will often be delayed. The question therefore arises whether, in the event of conversion being delayed, the tenant for life is entitled to the actual income produced by the asset until it is converted or whether he is entitled only to an apportioned part of it. The primary rule is that if the testator has provided, expressly or by implication, that the tenant for life is to enjoy the actual income which the property produces, then that intention will prevail. Where it cannot be shown that the testator expressed any such intention, then the following rules apply.

First, where the trustees improperly postpone conversion, an apportionment will be ordered. Thus in *Wentworth v. Wentworth*[16] the trustees had a power to postpone conversion until a certain date. The trustees improperly postponed conversion beyond that date and the Privy Council held that apportionment should be made as from that date.

Secondly, where the property in question is realty, the tenant for life is entitled to the actual income which the property produces. It will be remembered that *Howe v. Lord Dartmouth* never operates to impose a duty to convert realty so that such a duty in respect of realty can only have come into existence as the result of an express trust for conversion.

Thirdly, in the case of personalty, the tenant for life is entitled only to an apportioned part of the income, unless there is an intention that he shall enjoy the asset *in specie.*[17] Thus the presumption is in favour of the enjoyment of actual income in the case of realty and of only an apportioned part of the income in the case of personalty.

4. How is the Apportionment Calculated?

If there is a duty to convert and if, because the property has not been converted by the due date, the income has to be apportioned until conversion takes place, how is such apportionment calculated? Where the asset

---

[15] See *post, infra.*

[16] [1900] A.C. 163.

[17] *Re Chaytor* [1965] 1 Ch. 233. Where there is a trust for conversion with a power to postpone, the beneficiary will only receive an apportioned part of the income; *Re Berry* [1962] Ch. 97.

concerned is a reversionary interest, the rule in *Re Earl of Chesterfield's Trusts*[18] applies. This is dealt with below. As regards other property which has to be converted, it is necessary first to ascertain the valuation date. At common law there was a presumption that the executor's functions in administering the estate ought to be completed within one year from the death of the testator. From this the rule evolved that, where there is no power to postpone sale, conversion ought to be effected within one year from the date of death; in this case, in order to be able to calculate the apportionment, the asset has to be valued as at one year from the date of death.[19] If, however, there is a power to postpone, this negatives the intention that the property should be valued as at one year from the date of death, and, because a better date could not be thought of, in this case the property is valued at the date of death.[20]

Thus

(a) if there is no power to postpone, the valuation date is one year from the date of death, but

(b) if there is a power to postpone, the valuation date is the date of death.

Whichever the valuation date, the tenant for life is entitled to interest on the value of the asset as at the valuation date from the date of death until the date of actual conversion. Traditionally, the rate of interest applied has been 4 per cent.[21] but, as this is unrealistically low, it may be that the court would now adopt the rate which is equivalent to that paid on the court's short-term investment account.[22] If the actual income is larger than the apportioned figure, the balance is added to capital. If the actual income is smaller than the appropriate rate, the tenant for life receives that actual income, and is entitled to have it made up from future surpluses of income or, if there are none, from capital when the asset is sold. The deficiency cannot be made good from previous surpluses of income because these have already been notionally added to capital.

An example may help. Suppose that the copyright to a book is left upon trust for Angela for life, with remainder to Mary, and that the copyright is worth £1,200 at the date of death and £1,000 one year from the date of death. The copyright is eventually sold three years after the date of death and during the intervening three years the royalties actually received are: Year 1: £70; Year 2: £32; and Year 3: £48.

It is necessary first to ascertain the valuation date. Where there is a power to postpone, this will be the date of death. At this date the copyright is worth

---

[18] (1883) 24 Ch.D. 643.

[19] *Re Eaton* (1894) 70 L.T. 761.

[20] *Re Owen* [1912] 1 Ch. 519; *Re Parry* [1947] Ch. 23.

[21] The actual rate of interest is in the discretion of the court, but 4 per cent is usually taken as the appropriate figure; see *Re Lucas* [1947] Ch. 558; *Re Parry* [1947] Ch. 23; *Re Berry* [1962] Ch. 97.

[22] See *Bartlett v. Barclays Bank Trust Co. (No.2)* [1980] Ch. 515 and *Jaffray v. Marshall* [1993] 1 W.L.R. 1285 (overruled on other grounds by the House of Lords in *Target Holdings v. Redferns* [1996] 1 A.C. 421): see *post*, p. 690. See also *Re Fawcett* [1940] Ch. 402; *Re Parry* [1947] Ch. 23.

£1,200 so that, if the appropriate rate of interest is 4 per cent, Angela is entitled to 4 per cent × £1,200 = £48 per annum. In Year 1 she will receive £48, the balance of £22 being added to capital. In Year 2 she will receive £32, with the right to make good the deficiency of £16 in the future. In Year 3 she will receive £48, and will be entitled to a further £16 from the proceeds of the sale of the copyright to make good the deficiency in Year 2. If, however, there is no power to postpone, the valuation date is one year from the date of death. Angela is therefore entitled to receive 4 per cent × £1,000 = £40 per annum. In Year 1 she will receive £40, with £30 being added to capital. In Year 2 she will receive £32. In Year 3 she will receive £40, plus £8 to make good the shortfall in Year 2. She will therefore need to receive no part of the proceeds of sale of the copyright.

At this point it must again be stressed that the questions posed at the beginning of this discussion (is there a duty to convert; if so, does the income have to be apportioned; if so, how is such apportionment calculated) are progressive. Therefore it is only if there is a duty to convert that it is necessary to consider whether the income has to be apportioned and it is only if there is a duty to convert and if the income does have to be apportioned that it is necessary to make the type of calculation just considered.

5. *Re Earl of Chesterfield's Trusts*[23]

A special method is necessary for calculating the apportionment of reversionary interests because these do not actually produce any income until they fall into possession.

At the outset it should be noted that reversionary interests are saleable. Thus, going back to the example on pages 575–576, one of the assets which Basil left upon trust for Clare for life, remainder to Priscilla absolutely, was the right to receive £15,000 on the death of his father, Bert, who was still alive. At Basil's death the trustees could have sold that reversionary interest. The price which would be obtained would be largely governed by Bert's age at the date of Basil's death but whatever was obtained would have been invested in authorised securities, the income paid to Clare for life, and the capital held for Priscilla.

However, it is usually economically better not to sell but rather to retain the reversionary interest until it falls into possession. If this is done, before the money that is eventually received is invested it is clearly equitable to pay part of the amount received to Clare as compensation for the fact that she has had no income from the asset since the trust came into operation. The rule in *Re Earl of Chesterfield's Trusts* provides that, where a reversionary interest which ought to be converted is retained until it falls into possession, part of it is to be treated as arrears of income and paid to the tenant for life and only the balance is to be regarded as capital.

The rule itself says that the proportion of the amount actually received which is to be regarded as capital is that which, if invested at 4 per cent compound interest with yearly rests, would, after allowing for the deduction of income tax at the basic rate for the time being in force, have produced

---

[23] (1883) 24 Ch.D. 643.

the sum actually received. It remains to be decided whether 4 per cent is still the appropriate rate of interest to be applied.[24] "Yearly rests" are the intervals at which the interest is compounded.[25]

Returning to the example, suppose that Bert lived for three-and-a-quarter years after the trust came into operation and, assuming that the basic rate of tax throughout that period was 25 per cent, the trustees would find that £13,625.22 invested when the trust came into operation at 4 per cent compound interest with yearly rests would, after allowing for the deduction of tax at 25 per cent have produced £15,000 at the date when this sum was actually received.[26] The £13,625.22 would therefore be invested by the trustees as capital, and the remaining £1,374.78 would be paid to Clare as income for the preceding three-and-a-quarter years.

---

[24] See *ante*, p. 579.

[25] The calculation can be complicated, but, for those who do not have super mathematical skills, the most straightforward method of making the calculation will be to follow these steps:

1. Determine the gross rate of interest to be applied. Traditionally this has been 4% but, as has been noted, a higher rate may be appropriate.
2. Deduct the basic rate of income tax, to give a net rate of interest.
3. Calculate the amount which £100 would produce if invested for the period between the date of death and the date when the reversionary interest falls in at the net rate of interest compounded annually.
4. Multiply the amount received when the reversionary interest falls in by the following fraction:

$$\frac{100}{\text{the sum calculated by 3}}$$

5. The product is the capital element.
6. The balance is the income element.

[26] Following the steps outlined in n. 25, the calculation is as follows (although in 1998–99 the basic rate was 23%, a basic rate of 25% is being utilised because it makes the mathematical calculations considerably easier and therefore more comprehensible):

1. Gross rate: taken as 4 per cent
2. Basic rate of income tax: 25 per cent. The net rate is, therefore,

$$4 \text{ per cent} \times \frac{75}{100} = 3 \text{ per cent}$$

3. The compounded amount £110.09 is calculated as follows:

Period	Amount on which calculated	Rate	Interest for period	Total at end of period
Year 1	£100.00	3%	£3.00	£103.00
Year 2	£103.00	3%	£3.09	£106.09
Year 3	£106.09	3%	£3.18	£109.27
Last 3 months	£109.27	3%	£0.82	£110.09

4. The capital element of the amount received, £15,000 is:

$$£15,000 \times \frac{100}{110.09} = £13,625.22 = 5$$

5. The income element is (£15,000 − £13,625.22) = £1,374.78

The same rule applies to any other property which does not produce any income. Thus it applied in *Re Duke of Cleveland's Equity*[27] to a debt which bore no interest and was not receivable immediately. And in *Re Chance*[28] compensation for the refusal of planning permission under Part I of the Town and Country Planning Act 1954[29] was held to be apportionable.

6. *Leaseholds*

It used to be necessary to give special consideration to leaseholds. Before 1926, a residuary gift of leaseholds was treated in the same way as any other gift of residuary personalty. From 1926 to 1996, leases with over 60 years to run were authorised investments so there was no question of any apportionment in respect of them.[30] So far as leases with less than 60 years to run, which were not authorised investments, were concerned, it was clear that, by virtue of the now repealed section 28(2) of the Law of Property Act 1925, the tenant for life was entitled to the actual income where there was an express trust for the conversion of leaseholds,[31] but it was thought in some quarters[32] that the pre–1926 position still applied where the duty to convert the leaseholds in question arose only by virtue of the Rule in *Howe v. Lord Dartmouth*.[33] Since 1997 all leaseholds have been authorised investments by virtue of section 6(3) of the Trusts of Land and Appointment of Trustees Act 1996.[34] Consequently, there is now no question of any apportionment in respect of any leasehold.

---

[27] [1895] 2 Ch. 542.
[28] [1962] Ch. 593.
[29] The Town and Country Planning Act 1947 provided, in general terms, that an owner of land could not carry out any building or other works on his land without obtaining the permission of the local authority, and without paying a "development charge". The value of land was often less after the passing of this Act than before it, and in an effort to give to the landowner compensation, it was proposed that a £300 million fund would be established, on which landowners could make a claim for the depreciation in the value of their land. The fund was, in fact, never set up and the system was changed under the Town and Country Planning Act 1954, whereby the amount of the landowner's claim, plus one-seventh of it for interest (less payments for certain events made before the 1954 Act came into force), formed what is known as an "unexpended balance of established development value". Where such a balance exists, in certain cases compensation is payable up to the amount of that balance where an application for planning permission is refused. This was the situation in *Re Chance* [1962] Ch. 593. Part of the interest of the decision lies in the fact that an unexpended balance of established development value and so of money paid under the system, represents interest and the amount of that interest could be determined. Wilberforce J. however, took the whole amount of the compensation received and apportioned that.
[30] *Re Gough* [1957] Ch. 323.
[31] *Re Brooker* [1926] W.N. 93.
[32] S. J. Bailey: (1930–32) 4 C.L.J. 357.
[33] (1867) L.R. 4 Eq. 295.
[34] See *ante*, p. 552.

II. OTHER APPORTIONMENTS

1. *The rule in Allhusen v. Whittell*[35]

There will always be an interval of time between the date of death and the date when an asset is realised. Where a person creates a trust by will in favour of persons in succession and there are debts and liabilities to be paid, it would appear that the tenant for life will gain increasingly as that delay increases. Suppose that the gross assets of an estate held on trust for persons by way of succession amount to £20,000 and that the debts amount to £5,000. If the debts are paid forthwith, the tenant for life will have the income from the remaining £15,000. If, however, the debts are not paid for a year, the tenant for life will receive the income for that year on £20,000. The essence of the rule of apportionment laid down in *Allhusen v. Whittell* is to charge the tenant for life with interest on the amount subsequently used for the payment of debts so that, broadly, the tenant for life is placed in the same position as if the debts had been paid on death.

In its modern form[36] the rule requires a calculation of the average income of the estate from the date of death to the date of payment, taken net after deduction of income tax at the basic rate.[37] The tenant for life is charged with interest at the rate of the net average income, so that the debt once paid is regarded as being paid partly from income and partly from capital. Suppose that a debt of £500 is paid one year from the date of death, that the average income of the estate taken throughout that period is 4 per cent and that the basic rate of income tax during that year is 23 per cent. The calculation is therefore:

Take a basic unit of		£100.00
Add		
Average income for one year at £4 per cent	£4.00	
Less tax	£0.92	
	—	£3.08
		£103.08

Each debt paid one year from death is therefore regarded as being paid in the proportion:

$$\frac{100.00}{103.08} \text{ from capital; and}$$

$$\frac{3.08}{103.00} \text{ from income.}$$

Thus, the debt of £500 will be paid:

---

[35] (1867) L.R. 4 Eq. 295.
[36] *Re McEwen* [1913] 2 Ch. 704; *Re Wills* [1915] 1 Ch. 769; *Corbett v. C.I.R.* [1938] 1 K.B. 567.
[37] *Re Oldham* (1927) 71 S.J. 491.

$$\frac{100.00}{£103.08} \times £500 = £485.06 \text{ from capital; and}$$

$$\frac{3.00}{£103.08} \times £500 = £14.94$$

This £14.94 will be charged to the tenant for life.

It is easy to appreciate the theoretical justification for this rule and it is also easy to see its practical defects. In particular, a separate calculation is necessary for each debt paid at a different time. Further, where payments are to be made a considerable time after death, as where the testator in his lifetime entered into a covenant to pay an annuity and the annuity was charged on the residue of his estate, the proportion borne by income steadily increases.[38] Except where very large debts are involved or where a very long delay occurs in payment, the trouble of making the calculation does not justify the small adjustment between tenant for life and remainderman; consequently it is now very common to exclude the operation of the rule.

2. *The Rule in Re Atkinson*[39]

Where an authorised mortgage forms part of the estate and, upon realisation of the security by sale, the proceeds of sale are insufficient to pay the outstanding principal and interest in full, the proceeds of sale are apportioned between the tenant for life and remainderman in the proportion which the amount due for arrears bears to the amount due in respect of principal. This is the rule in *Re Atkinson*[40] and it applies to any mortgage which forms part of the assets derived from the testator or settlor and also to any authorised mortgage taken by the trustee himself.

Suppose that during his lifetime a testator made a mortgage advance of £25,000 upon the security of a house at £12 per cent interest. Suppose also that the mortgagor pays a total of only £1,200 interest in respect of the period after the death of the testator and that the property is sold for £23,000 three years after death, no part of the capital secured by the mortgage having been repaid at any point. The apportionment of the £23,000 is as follows:

---

[38] *Re Dawson* [1906] 2 Ch. 211; *Re Perkins* [1907] 2 Ch. 596; *Re Poyser* [1910] 2 Ch. 444.
[39] [1904] 2 Ch. 160.
[40] *ibid.*

Capital outstanding		£25,000
Interest outstanding:		
3 Years at £12 per cent		
on £25,000	£9,000	
less: actually paid	£1,200	
		£ 7,800
Total capital and interest due		£32,800

$$\text{Capital element of proceeds of sale} = \frac{£25,000}{£32,800} \times £23,000 = £17,530$$

$$\text{Income element of proceeds of sale} = \frac{£7,800}{£32,800} \times £23,000 = £5,470$$

Total proceeds of sale	£23,000

The scope of the rule is in doubt. In principle it ought to apply whenever an asset carrying both capital and interest at a fixed rate is realised at a loss and it has been held to apply to an amount received in a liquidation on account of principal and arrears of interest due under a holding of debenture stock.[41] However, the rule is not applied where preference dividends are in arrears.[42]

The rule in *Re Atkinson* is applied only to a capital sum realised on the sale of a security and not to income received from the asset. Thus, if under a power contained in a mortgage the trustees take possession of the property and let it, the net rents are applied entirely in the discharge of arrears of interest and only when those arrears have been paid in full is the surplus applied as capital.[43] If there are arrears of interest outstanding at the date of death, those are paid in full in priority to the interest due to the estate from the period from the date of death to the date of extinction of the mortgage.[44]

Where trustees foreclose under a mortgage, the mortgagor then loses all title to the property and the property itself becomes an asset of the estate. Accordingly, from the date of foreclosure the tenant for life is entitled to the whole of the net rents and profits until sale[45] but, if there are arrears of interest before foreclosure, it seems that a *Re Atkinson* apportionment will be made when the property is ultimately sold.[46]

There is no authority as to whether income tax should be deducted in making a calculation for the purposes of the rule in *Re Atkinson*. It is suggested that the appropriate method of applying the rule is first to ascertain the arrears of interest and the proportion due to income without

---

[41] *Re Walker* [1936] Ch. 280; compare *Re Taylor* [1905] 1 Ch. 734.
[42] *Re Sale* [1913] 2 Ch. 697; *Re Wakley* [1920] 2 Ch. 205.
[43] *Re Coaks* [1911] 1 Ch. 171.
[44] *ibid.*
[45] Law of Property Act 1925, s.31; *Re Horn* [1924] 2 Ch. 222.
[46] *Re Horn, ibid.* at 226.

taking into account income tax. When that proportion has been calculated, the tenant for life's entitlement should be reduced by an amount equal to income tax at the basic rate on that sum.

III. APPORTIONMENTS RELATING TO STOCKS AND SHARES

In contrast to the Rule in *Howe v. Lord Dartmouth*, which applies to unauthorised investments, apportionments of a different type are sometimes necessary in the case of authorised investments.

1. *Dividends*

The first case is of apportionment of dividends received for shares. Thus, if shares are left on trust for Peter for life, with remainder to Paul for life, it may be necessary, on the death of Peter, to apportion dividends between Peter's estate and Paul. The Apportionment Act 1870 applies to most types of periodical payment and deems them to accrue from day to day. If, therefore, Peter dies on the fifty-ninth day of a year, and the company declares a dividend amounting to £150 for that calendar year, 59/365ths of £150 will belong to Peter's estate and the balance will be payable to Paul. The period in respect of which the company in question states it is paying the dividend necessarily governs the rights of all the beneficiaries. This can produce superficially rather strange results. If a company pays no dividend in 1998 and 1999 but pays a dividend in 2000 which is three times as large as normal but which is stated by the company to be in respect of 1996. If Peter as before dies on the fifty-ninth day of 1996, he will only be entitled to 59/365ths. It might have been thought more equitable in these circumstances for Peter to have received 789/1095ths (being the fraction of days for the period 1998, 1999 and 2000 for which Peter has lived) but this is not the rule.[47]

It is also necessary to make a time apportionment when there is an alteration in the class of income beneficiaries. In *Re Joel*[48] a fund was held upon trust for the testator's grandchildren contingently on attaining the age of 21. The gift carried the intermediate income, which could accordingly be utilised for the benefit of the grandchildren.[49] Goff J. held that, each time a member of the class died under 21 or a new grandchild was born, the income of the trust ought to be apportioned; that way each member of the class enjoyed only that part of the income attributable to the period during which he was alive.

However, for the purposes of taxation the rules differ from those laid down by the Apportionment Act 1870; the whole of the dividend is treated as the income of the person who is entitled to the income of the trust on the

---

[47] *Re Wakley* [1920] 1 Ch. 205. The Law Reform Committee (23rd Report, 1982) recommended that the statutory rule should not apply on the death of a testator by whose will a trust is created.

[48] [1967] Ch. 14. The Law Reform Committee (23rd Report, 1982) recommended that the rule in this case should be abrogated.

[49] See *post*, p. 595.

day on which the income in question is payable.[50] Suppose that one of the assets of a fund held on trust for Roger for life, with remainder to Susan for life, is a holding of shares in a company which pays dividends in respect of years ending on March 31, and that in June 1999 the company declares a dividend for the year which ended on March 31, 1999. If Roger dies on February 15, 1999, his estate will be entitled to almost all the dividend by virtue of the Apportionment Act 1870; however, the whole of the dividend will form part of Susan's taxable income for the year of assessment 1999/2000.

2. Scrip Dividends

Companies sometimes give shareholders a choice between receiving their dividends in cash and receiving additional shares. Dividends paid in the form of shares are known as scrip dividends. This choice does not pose any particular problems for the trustees if the value of the scrip offered is more or less the same as the cash dividend. In both cases the dividend will belong to the tenant for life and in such circumstances trustees have traditionally opted to take the dividend in cash. However, in the last few years there have been a large number of enhanced scrip dividends, under which the value of the scrip on offer can be as much as 50 per cent more than the cash dividend with, sometimes, the possibility of converting the scrip into cash by selling it on at a pre-arranged price, never as high as the value of the scrip but still substantially more than the cash dividend. Trustees are clearly under an obligation to consider whether to take up such an offer. If they do, the question arises as to whether the tenant for life is entitled to the whole of the scrip or the pre-arranged purchase price for which it is sold. It has been held that in these circumstances an apportionment is necessary as between income and capital.[51] If this is indeed the case, the tenant for life will be entitled to no more than the amount of the cash dividend: the additional value of the scrip or the pre-arranged price for which it is sold will therefore have to be added to the capital of the trust. If enhanced scrip dividends continue to be popular, it is likely that a test case will at some stage be necessary to establish definitively whether or not such an apportionment is indeed necessary.

3. Purchases and Sales Cum and Ex Dividend

On the face of things, an apportionment would appear to be appropriate where stocks and shares are bought and sold. There are obviously a number of factors which affect the price of stock exchange investments, such as the yield which is obtained,[52] the stability of the company concerned, the general economic condition of the country as a whole, and the future prospects of the company; however, an important short-term factor is the date when the dividend is to be paid. Any example is obviously artificial but, assuming

---

[50] *I.R.C. v. Henderson's Executors* (1931) 16 T.C. 282; *Bryan v. Cassin* [1942] 2 All E.R. 262; *Wood v. Owen* [1941] 1 K.B. 92; *Potel v. I.R.C.* [1971] 2 All E.R. 504.

[51] *Re Malam* [1894] 3 Ch. 578.

[52] See *ante*, p. 544.

all other factors remain constant, if a dividend of £500 is payable on January 1, and July 1, on a holding of stock worth £20,000, on January 2, the stock is worth £20,000 but its value on June 30, the day before the payment of the next dividend, will be £20,000 plus £500, therefore £20,500.[53] If trustees purchase that stock on January 2, for £20,000 and sell it for £20,500 on June 30, does the whole of that £20,500 belong to capital or is the sum apportioned so as to attribute £20,000 to capital and £500 to income? After all, had the holding been kept for one day longer, the £500 would have been received as a dividend and treated as income. Somewhat surprisingly, there is in this case no rule providing for any apportionment and the whole amount received is deemed to be capital. The explanation for this apparently inequitable rule is that there are in practice so many factors which affect the value of shares that it is thought too difficult to lay down any set rules to govern how the apportionment is to be calculated. It has, however, been said that if the rule of non-apportionment leads to a "glaring injustice" apportionment will be ordered.[54]

4. Bonus Shares

Considerable difficulty has been caused where a company issues bonus shares. Suppose the capital of a company consists of 10,000 £1 ordinary shares and that the company has prospered and has retained accumulated profits of £5,000. If the company distributes the £5,000 to its shareholders, this sum is clearly income in the hands of any trustee shareholders. But the company may alternatively decide to retain the £5,000 permanently by using it to fund for the issue of 5,000 additional shares to be distributed free to the existing shareholders in the company on the basis of one new share for each two shares already held. Are these new shares equally to be treated as income in the hands of any trustee shareholders?

The general rule is that the new shares are capital and must be held by the trustees as such; however, the tenant for life will of course obtain some benefit from them by virtue of the fact that he will be entitled to the dividends which they produce.[55]

However, where the company has no power under its articles of association to create new shares in this way and therefore ought to have distributed the accumulated profit in cash, the shares distributed are regarded as income—this was decided in Bouch v. Sproule.[56] That decision was considered by the Privy Council in Hill v. Permanent Trustee Co. of New South Wales,[57] where Lord Russell of Killowen laid down the following principles.[58]

> (i) Where a company makes a distribution of money among its shareholders, it is not concerned at all with the way in which the

---

[53] In fact the holder of the stock will pay income tax on the dividend, so that the additional worth is £500 less tax.
[54] Re MacLaren's Settlement Trusts [1951] 2 All E.R. 414 at 420, per Harman J.
[55] I.R.C. v. Blott [1921] 2 A.C. 171.
[56] (1887) 12 App.Cas. 385.
[57] [1930] A.C. 720.
[58] ibid. at 730–732.

shareholders deal with that money. Thus, where the shareholder is a trustee, the company is not itself concerned with whether the money is treated as capital or income.

(ii) Unless a company is in liquidation, it can only make a payment by way of a return of capital under a scheme for the reduction of capital approved by the court.[59] (Restrictions are placed on a reduction of capital by a company so that creditors of the company shall not be prejudiced.) In any other case, apart from liquidation, it follows that, if the company is able to distribute money, that money must be profit so far as the company is concerned.

(iii) Where the shareholder is a trustee, he will therefore generally receive the money as income which as such will be payable to the tenant for life. This will not be the case, however, if there is some provision in the trust instrument to the contrary, or if the following principle applies.

(iv) Where the company has power under its articles of association to utilise its profits by adding them to capital and issuing bonus shares representing the amount of that additional capital to its shareholders, those shares are capital.

(v) Where the company's capital is increased in this way, its assets are undiminished (for the cash never leaves its hands), whereas if a distribution of profits is made the company's assets are consequently diminished.[60]

To these five principles a sixth was, in effect, added by Plowman J. in *Re Outen*,[61] namely that, where under a power in its articles of association a company capitalises profits, not by using the profits to issue new shares but by issuing some other investment in the company, that other investment is capital in the hands of a shareholder who is a trustee. This case arose out of a takeover bid made in 1962 by I.C.I. for Courtaulds. The bid was resisted by the directors of Courtaulds who, in order to persuade their stockholders not to sell their stock to I.C.I., capitalised £40 million of reserves, which represented capital profits, in accordance with the company's articles of association and used this sum to make a free issue of new loan stock to their stockholders. Before the takeover battle had commenced, a testatrix had left her holding of stock to trustees upon trust and in due course they, along with all the other stockholders in Courtaulds, were issued with a holding of the new loan stock. Was this to be treated as capital or as income? Plowman J. held that, although Courtauld's actions had not involved the creation of any new shares, that company had effected a capitalisation under which the assets which were its subject matter ceased to have the character of divisible profits. The company's decision to this effect was binding on its stockholders; consequently the loan stock was capital.

---

[59] See now Companies Act 1985, s.135.
[60] Though why this should be relevant to a trustee is difficult to understand.
[61] [1963] Ch. 291.

A further complication arises where a company gives its shareholders the option either to have bonus shares or cash. In such circumstances what is crucial is whether the company intends to make a capital distribution or whether it really intends to distribute income.[62] If the intention of the company is to make a capital distribution then, whether the trustees take the bonus shares or the cash, what is received by them will be capital (in fact the cash offer is usually inferior in value to the offer of bonus shares and so the trustees should normally take the bonus shares). If, on the other hand, the intention of the company is to distribute income, then what is received by the trustees will be income; if the trustees take the cash, this will obviously be payable to the tenant for life but, if they take the bonus shares (which is what they should normally do), it has been held that the tenant for life will still receive only the value of the cash offer, the remainder of the value of the shares being regarded as capital.[63]

In summary, in the ordinary case where a company issues bonus shares, the reserves or profits which are used within the company to back the bonus shares are retained by the company as long-term capital. Consequently, bonus shares are in general received by trustees as capital. Where, on the other hand, the company has no power under its articles of association to create new shares in this way, the shares distributed are received by trustees as income. This is also the case where the intention of the company was to distribute income.

5. *Capital Profits Dividends*

All forms of distribution by a company by way of money or money's worth other than the issue of bonus shares or stock consist of the company passing on to its shareholders a profit which it has received without the company itself retaining any long-term benefit from the distribution. Therefore in the ordinary case, such dividends are received by the trustees as income.

The best illustration of this is provided by capital profits dividends—the distribution by a company of capital profits either in cash or in some other valuable form. A series of cases were decided around 1951 in relation to a capital profit dividend declared by Thomas Tilling & Co. A substantial part of the business of this company consisted of operating buses and coaches. When this part of its business was nationalised, the company received in compensation some British Transport stock, which it in turn distributed among its shareholders as a capital profits dividend. Was this stock to be regarded as capital or as income for the purposes of a trust? In *Re Sechiari*[64] and *Re Kleinwort*[65] it was held that trustees received the stock as income and so it belonged to the tenant for life. The position was not the same as that of bonus shares in the company making the distribution, where the increase in the number of shares entitles the holders to participate in future dividends; this was an isolated payment, complete in itself, from which no future benefit would accrue directly from the company.

---

[62] *I.R.C. v. Fisher's Executors* [1926] A.C. 395.
[63] *Re Malam* [1894] 3 Ch. 578.
[64] [1950] 1 All E.R. 417.
[65] [1951] Ch. 860.

Nevertheless, in *Re Kleinwort* Vaisey J. considered that, in special circumstances, the sum received was properly apportionable between capital and income. Such circumstances would arise where the trustees had committed a breach of trust, particularly in not maintaining a balance between the conflicting interests of different beneficiaries. Thus if the trustees acted solely with the intention of benefiting the tenant for life at the expense of the remainderman by investing in shares in a company in the expectation of a capital profits distribution, they would have committed a breach of trust and the court would undoubtedly apportion the capital profits dividend between income and capital. However, in *Re Rudd*,[66] it was held that a breach of trust had not been committed merely by virtue of the fact that trustees, who foresaw the capital dividend and so could have sold the stock with a large profit for capital, did not do so; consequently, the court refused to apportion the capital profit dividend received. This decision seems to be based entirely on the motive of the trustees which involved no intention of prejudicing the remainderman. Special circumstances were, however, found to exist in *Re MacLaren*.[67] The tenant for life consented to the purchase of stock in Thomas Tilling & Co. as a capital investment after it became known that that company intended to distribute the British Transport stock among its shareholders. It was held that he had to be regarded as having consented to the British Transport stock being regarded as capital and that it therefore was to be treated as capital.

The principle just illustrated by reference to the Thomas Tilling & Co. cases applies to any case where a company makes a capital profit and distributes it either in cash or in some other valuable form. That profit will therefore in normal circumstances be received by the trustees as income and so will be payable to the tenant for life. Where the distribution is as substantial as that made by Thomas Tilling & Co., the capital value of the fund will thereby be substantially reduced—in that case, the price of the shares fell by as much as 77 per cent; an enormous windfall for the tenant for life and a substantial loss for the remaindermen.

6. *Demergers*

Similar potential difficulties are caused by the recently fashionable practice of demerging companies, that is to say hiving off some composite part of the businesses of a company into a new company and issuing all the shareholders of the original company with fully paid up shares in the new demerged company. This is done by the original company transferring the part of its assets which relate to the businesses which are to be demerged to a new subsidiary company and then declaring a dividend out of distributable profits. There are two ways of proceeding thereafter: the "direct" method is for the original company to satisfy the dividend directly by allocating to its shareholders shares in the subsidiary company, which then becomes the demerged company; the "indirect" method is for the shares in the subsidiary company to be transferred to a quite separate company, which then satisfies the dividend indirectly by allocating its own shares to

---

[66] [1952] 1 All E.R. 254.
[67] [1951] 2 All E.R. 414.

the shareholders of the original company. Both of these methods appear to amount to a capital distribution which, in accordance with the principles just discussed, appears to be received as income for the purposes of a trust and will therefore be payable to the tenant for life. In one of the largest demergers to date, that of the bioscience activities of I.C.I. into a new company, Zeneca Group, this potentially had the effect of halving the value of the capital of any trust which held shares in I.C.I. and providing the tenant for life with a windfall of half the capital value of the shares.

The companies involved were sufficiently anxious about this question to arrange for a test case, *Sinclair v. Lee*,[68] to be brought to establish how the shares allocated in the new company would be treated for the purposes of a trust. This demerger was to be carried out by the "indirect" method. Nicholls V.-C. stated that:

"no one, unversed in the arcane mysteries I shall be mentioning shortly, would have any doubt over the answer. Nobody would think that the Zeneca Group shares could sensibly be regarded as income."[69]

His Lordship relied on the fact that, since this demerger was to be carried out by the "indirect" method, the shares of the demerged company, Zeneca Group, would never be held or received by I.C.I.; this enabled him to distinguish the authorities discussed in the previous two sections of this Chapter and he therefore held that the distribution of Zeneca Group shares would indeed be capital for the purposes of a trust.

This decision establishes that shares in a company which is demerged by the "indirect" method will be capital for the purposes of a trust. However, the decision leaves completely open the position of shares in a company which is demerged by the "direct" method. Since the ground on which Nicholls V.-C. was able to distinguish the earlier authorities applies only to "indirect" demergers, it may well be that the opposite conclusion will be reached in respect of "direct" demergers. It may be that another test case will have to be brought in order to resolve this question.

7. Taxation Considerations

The treatment of the various types of dividends, distributions, and shares which have just been considered for the general purposes of trust administration has to be distinguished from their treatment for the purposes of taxation.

Company distributions are normally paid with a tax credit of 20 per cent so that the sum actually received has in effect suffered tax of 20 per cent. Trustees need take no further action in respect of distributions paid over to a beneficiary who has a fixed interest: the distributions are taxed as his income so, if he is a higher rate taxpayer, he has to pay a further 20 per cent tax. However, accumulation and discretionary settlements pay tax at a flat rate of 34 per cent and so a further 14 per cent tax will be payable by the trustees of these settlements.

---

[68] [1993] Ch. 497.
[69] *ibid.* at 504.

Where trustees elect to take scrip dividends rather than cash and where shares are held which carry with them the right to receive bonus shares,[70] then, if the company is resident in the United Kingdom,[71] the shares received are treated as income. The usual 20 per cent tax credit will not be forthcoming from the company and so tax is payable as if a dividend had been paid of an amount which, after deducting income tax at the basic rate in force, equals the value of the scrip dividend or other shares at the date of issue.[72] If the scrip dividend or shares are passed to an income beneficiary, the notional amount of the dividend is treated as part of his income for income tax purposes. If the scrip dividend or shares are retained by the trustees as an accretion to capital for a remainderman there will be no further tax liability[73]; however, if the dividend or shares are retained by the trustees of a discretionary or accumulation settlement, they will have to pay a further 11 per cent tax to bring the tax paid up to the flat rate of 34 per cent.[74] Bonus shares and capital profits dividends are treated in the same way. Where, on the other hand, the company which pays the scrip dividend or in which the shares are held which carry with them the right to receive bonus shares is resident outside the United Kingdom, the shares which are received are treated as capital for taxation purposes if they would be so treated for the purposes of trust administration.[75]

The transfer of shares in demerged companies is not a distribution and so does not give rise to any payment of income tax. However, there are potential difficulties as to precisely what the base cost of the shares is for the purposes of capital gains tax where the shares are treated as the property of a fixed interest beneficiary; this particular question awaits resolution.

IV. APPORTIONMENTS IN RESPECT OF NATIONAL SAVINGS CERTIFICATES

It has been seen[76] that, by virtue of the Apportionment Act 1870, it may be necessary to apportion by time dividends or other income between the person entitled to the income before an event, such as death, and the person entitled after that event. It is, however, first necessary to establish that the amount in question is of an income nature. This problem arises in particular with the increment over the purchase price which is payable on the encashment of National Savings Certificates. In *Re Holder*[77] the testator in his

---

[70] That is, the terms upon which the shares are issued gives the shareholders the right to call for bonus shares.

[71] Income and Corporation Taxes Act 1988, s.349.

[72] If, therefore, the basic rate of income tax is 23% and an issue of scrip is made which is worth £100, the company will be treated as if it paid a dividend of £129.87 from which income tax had been deducted (£129.87 less £29.87 tax = £100).

[73] Because, in general, income received by trustees subject to deduction of tax at source is not further taxable in their hands; see *ante*, p. 522.

[74] Trustees of this type of settlement are liable for income tax at a flat rate of 34%. See *ante*, p. 523. In the example given *ante*, n. 72, the trustees would therefore be liable to pay an additional 11% of £129.87 = £14.29.

[75] *I.R.C. v. Wright* (1926) 11 T.C. 181.

[76] See *ante*, p. 586.

[77] [1953] Ch. 468.

lifetime purchased National Savings Certificates for £375, which were encashed after his death for £534. Roxburgh J. held that, by virtue of the terms on which the certificates were issued by the Government, the increment up to the date of death was capital. It was conceded that the increment which arose between the date of death and the date of encashment was to be treated as income, but the point was not argued. Although the basis for the concession does not appear from the report of the case, it would appear to be a correct concession, following the rule in *Re Earl of Chesterfield's Trusts*.[78]

V. APPORTIONMENT OF OUTGOINGS

Subject to contrary directions in the trust instrument, expenses which relate solely to the income of a trust, such as the cost of making an income tax return, are primarily payable out of income, and other expenses, such as the cost of appointing new trustees or of bringing legal proceedings, are payable out of capital.

Where an audit takes place, however, the trustees may apportion the cost of this between capital and income in such proportions as they think fit.[79]

VI. EXCLUDING APPORTIONMENTS

The apportionment rules are designed to achieve fairness and in most cases it is easy to see the logic behind them. Nevertheless, it is becoming increasingly common for them to be expressly excluded. This is partly due to taxation considerations but in the main it is because the calculations which have to be made under some of the rules are so complicated that it is far simpler from an administrative point of view for apportionments to be excluded. Ironically, then, the long-term effect of the rules has probably been the reverse of what equity intended.

---

[78] (1883) 24 Ch.D. 643; see *ante*, p. 580.
[79] Trustee Act 1925, s.22(4).

CHAPTER 19

INCOME FROM THE TRUST FUND

FIVE questions have to be considered about the income from a trust fund.

   (i) What is the relationship between income received by the trustees from the assets which comprise the trust fund and the income to which the beneficiaries are entitled?

  (ii) Which beneficial interests under the trust carry the right to income?

 (iii) Are the trustees entitled to retain income?

 (iv) How are the trustees to apply income where the beneficiary is an infant?

  (v) What are the taxation consequences of entitlement to income?

I. THE INCOME OF THE TRUST FUND

1. *The Accounting Period*

One of the fundamental elements in the concept of income is that of time; it is only possible to speak of the income of trustees, or indeed of any person, if the period of time which is to be considered is known. For taxation purposes, the period to be considered is, generally,[1] the year of assessment which ends on April 5. Where a trust is created otherwise than on April 6, the first accounting period for taxation purposes will be from the date of the creation of the trust until the following April 5, and the final accounting period is from April 6, to the date of termination of the trust.

There are, however, no corresponding statutory rules for the purposes of general trust administration. The legislature may have assumed that the basic period of account would be 12 months,[2] but the trustees can select any period which they wish.[3] In practice, most trustees adopt for the purposes of

---

[1] The general rule applies for income tax and capital gains tax.
[2] See, for example, Trustee Act 1925, s.22(4) authorising trustees to have the trust accounts audited once in every three "years".
[3] Unless the trust instrument itself prescribes the accounting period.

trust administration the same accounting period as that adopted for taxation.

2. *Gross and Net Income*

The trustees may derive income from a number of sources during an accounting period. For example, they may receive dividends, bank deposit interest, and rent. From this gross income there will be deducted the expenses of the management of the trust so far as applicable to income and any other payments which the trustees make in the exercise of administrative powers.

However, the net income will usually only be determined at some point of time after the end of an accounting period. This is because trustees have a reasonable time[4] within which to exercise powers and discretions and they will often wish to wait until the end of an accounting period so that they can see the amount of gross income received in the whole of that period.

3. *Trust Management Expenses*

Expenses of a recurrent nature are generally payable out of income, unless the trust instrument provides otherwise. Thus, out of income is paid council tax and rates on any land owned by the trust[5]; rent payable in respect of leasehold property owned by the trust[6]; income tax[7]; and the cost of preparation of annual accounts and income tax returns.[8] The expenses which are payable from capital are discussed later.[9]

Although, in general, expenses are payable either from income or from capital according to their nature, the trust instrument can direct how the expenses are to be borne[10] and, in certain instances, the trustees are given a discretion.

Thus, where the trustees require the trust accounts to be audited under the statutory power,[11] they have an absolute discretion to pay the fees of the auditor from income or from capital, or partly from income and partly from capital.

4. *Administrative Powers*

In *Pearson v. I.R.C.*[12] the House of Lords drew a distinction between administrative powers and dispositive powers. Where payments are made by the trustees out of income in the exercise of administrative powers, these payments are treated in the same way as trust management expenses, that is to

---

[4] See, for example, *Re Gulbenkian's Settlement Trusts (No.2); Stephens v. Maun* [1970] Ch. 408.
[5] *Fountaine v. Pellet* (1791) 1 Ves. Jun. 337 at 342.
[6] *Re Gjers* [1899] 2 Ch. 54; *Re Betty* [1899] 1 Ch. 821.
[7] *Re Cain's Settlement* [1919] 2 Ch. 364.
[8] See *Shore v. Shore* (1859) 4 Drew. 501.
[9] See *post*, p. 616.
[10] However, the court may override the direction in the trust instrument; *Re Tubbs* [1915] Ch. 137; *Re Hicklin* [1917] 2 Ch. 278.
[11] Trustee Act 1925, s.22(4).
[12] [1981] A.C. 753.

say they are deducted from the gross receipts in determining the amount of the net trust income. Payments which are made in the exercise of a dispositive power are applications of net trust income.

There is in many respects no clear authority as to precisely which powers are to be regarded as administrative and which as dispositive. In the absence of authority, the following classification is suggested for present purposes; however, as will be seen in a later Chapter,[13] different considerations, and therefore a slightly different classification as to which powers are and are not administrative, may be necessary when it has to be decided, as a matter of private international law, which of these powers are governed by the proper law of a trust and which are governed by a different law which has been specified as governing that trust's administration.[14]

The following are classified as administrative powers for all purposes:

(i) the power to engage and pay agents and professional advisers;

(ii) the power to have investments held in the name of a nominee or by a custodian and to pay the nominee or custodian;

(iii) the power to insure trust assets and to pay the premiums;

(iv) the power to insure the life of the settlor and to pay the premiums;

(v) the power to pay taxes and duties[15]; and

(vi) the power to use income to improve land.

The following can also be classified as administrative powers for present purposes, although they may not be for the purposes of private international law:

(i) the power to charge for services;

(ii) the power to retain commission, brokerage, and directors' fees; and

---

[13] See post, p. 754.

[14] The proper law of the trust will govern the nature of the interests of the beneficiaries and the duties of the trustees towards them (including any powers which they have to determine the manner in which the income and capital of the trust is distributed and their duties to convert and apportion the trust property) and also the construction of the trust instrument (unless this has been expressly reserved to the law of some other jurisdiction). The trustees' duties to provide accounts and to give information to the beneficiaries are purely administrative, as are their powers to appoint and remove trustees and all the powers listed in the first group of powers below in the text. But a number of other powers which are, for other purposes, often classified as administrative are capable of affecting directly or indirectly the interests of the beneficiaries in the event that the provisions of the proper law and of the law specified as governing administration differ as to their existence or scope. The presence or absence of a power for the trustees to remunerate themselves clearly affects the income and capital available for the beneficiaries. So does the presence or absence of powers of advancement, maintenance and accumulation in the event that they are exercised. So too, to a lesser extent, do the trustees' powers of investment.

[15] As to which see Pearson v. I.R.C. [1981] A.C. 753 itself.

    (iii) the power to advance capital[16];

The following can be classified as dispositive powers for present purposes although it is not inconceivable that they could be classified as administrative for the purposes of private international law.[17]

    (i) the power to accumulate income;

    (ii) the power to pay or apply income to or for the maintenance, education, or benefit of a beneficiary;

    (iii) the power to allow a beneficiary to use trust assets (even if on the exercise of that power an interest in possession in the assets is not created);

    (iv) the power to pay the premiums on a policy of assurance which is effected for the benefit of a beneficiary; and

    (v) the power to pay or apply income in securing the discharge of an obligation owed by a beneficiary or in guaranteeing the performance of an obligation by a beneficiary.

5. *Net Trust Income*

The net trust income in respect of an accounting period may, therefore, be said to be the aggregate of the gross income received[18] in that period from all the trust assets, less trust management expenses paid from income either by virtue of their nature or pursuant to a provision in the trust instrument, and less other payments made from income in the exercise of an administrative power.

In the remainder of this Chapter, the net trust income in this sense is referred to as the trust income.

II. GIFTS CARRYING INCOME

Once the amount of the trust income has been ascertained, it is then necessary to determine whether any beneficiary is entitled to it. If he is, his interest is said to carry the intermediate income. The possibilities are:

    (i) a beneficiary is entitled to the income without any further decision of the trustees being necessary (this will usually be the case where trustees hold a fund upon trust to pay the income to Adam for life, with remainder to Eve);

---

[16] In *Inglewood (Lord) v. I.R.C.* [1983] 1 W.L.R. 866, this power was treated as "similar" to an administrative power even though its exercise unquestionably affects beneficial entitlement.

[17] By analogy with the power to advance capital listed above.

[18] In many respects it is uncertain whether an amount, in order to be taken into account, must be received or whether it can merely be receivable.

(ii) no person is entitled, as where the trustees accumulate the income;

(iii) a beneficiary is entitled to the income, but only in the exercise of the trustees' discretion; and

(iv) the income has not been effectively dealt with and so is held on a resulting trust either for the settlor or, in the case of a will trust, for the testator's residuary beneficiaries or those entitled on his intestacy.

Vested gifts will carry the intermediate income unless the trust instrument provides either that it is to be paid to someone else or that it is to be accumulated and added to capital.[19]

The question of whether contingent gifts carry intermediate income is more complex. It is largely, but not entirely, governed by section 175 of the Law of Property Act 1925. This section, which applies only to wills coming into operation on or after January 1, 1926, provides that, except in so far as the testator has otherwise expressly disposed of his income, the following types of gift carry the intermediate income from the testator's death:

(i) contingent or future specific devises or bequests[20] of property, whether real or personal;

(ii) contingent residuary devises of freehold land;

(iii) specific or residuary devises of freehold land to trustees upon trust for persons whose interests are contingent or executory.

The position in relation to vested and contingent interests under trusts coming into force after 1925 is as follows:

(i) The directions of the settlor or testator always prevail. Accordingly, if the trust instrument directs that the income is to be accumulated, that direction will prevent the gift from carrying the income.[21] Likewise, even if the gift is vested and there is a direction for the payment of the income to another, that direction will prevail (an example would be if property was held in trust for a minor absolutely subject to a provision that, until he attained the age of majority, the income should be paid to his cousin). Again, if payment is expressly deferred until a future date, the gift will not carry the intermediate income.[22]

(ii) In the absence of express directions from the settlor or testator, a vested interest will carry the intermediate income subject to just

---

[19] *Re Stapleton* [1946] 1 All E.R. 323.
[20] A "devise" is a gift of realty by will; a "bequest" is a gift of personalty by will.
[21] *Re Turner's Will Trusts* [1967] Ch. 15; *Re Ransome* [1957] Ch. 348; *Re Reade-Revell* [1930] 1 Ch. 52.
[22] *Re Geering* [1964] Ch. 136.

one exception, the case of a testamentary gift of residuary personalty which is expressly deferred to a future date.[23]

(iii) In the absence of express directions from the settlor, a contingent interest arising under an *inter vivos* settlement carries the intermediate income provided the contingency is attaining the age of majority or the happening of some event before that age.

(iv) In the absence of express directions from the testator, a contingent interest arising under a will carries the intermediate income if it is:
  (a) of residuary personalty[24] but not if the interest is expressly deferred to a future date[25];
  (b) of residuary realty[26] but not if the interest is expressly deferred to a future date[27];
  (c) a specific gift of personalty, other than a pecuniary legacy,[28] or of realty[29] even if the interest is expressly deferred to a future date.[30]

(v) In the absence of express directions from the testator, a pecuniary legacy does not generally carry the intermediate income. To this general principle there are two exceptions, when the gift does carry the intermediate income, namely:
  (a) if the gift was by a parent of the infant, or by some other person who stood in loco parentis to him, and:
    (1) if the gift is contingent, the contingency is not the attaining of an age greater than 18,[31] and
    (2) there is no other fund set aside for the maintenance of the legatee.[32]
  (b) the testator directs the legacy to be set apart from the rest of his estate for the benefit of the legatee.[33]

It should be emphasised that, as has already been mentioned, where the intermediate income is not carried, it is undisposed of; consequently, it is held on resulting trust for the settlor or, in the case of a will trust, for the testator's residuary beneficiaries or those entitled on his intestacy.

---

[23] *Re Oliver* [1947] 2 All E.R. 162; *Re Gillett's Will Trusts* [1950] Ch. 102.
[24] *Re Adams* [1893] 1 Ch. 329; unaffected by the 1925 legislation.
[25] *Re Geering* [1964] Ch. 136.
[26] Law of Property Act 1925, s.175.
[27] This situation is not covered by Law of Property Act 1925, s.175.
[28] There is little logic in the distinction between contingent pecuniary legacies and other contingent gifts of personalty.
[29] Law of Property Act 1925, s.175.
[30] *Re McGeorge* [1963] Ch. 544.
[31] *Re Jones* [1932] 1 Ch. 642; Family Law Reform Act 1969, s.1.
[32] *Re West* [1913] 2 Ch. 245. This is the effect of the words in what is now section 31(3) of the Trustee Act that the section "applies to a future or contingent legacy by the parent of the legatee if and for such period as, under the general law, the legacy carries interest for the maintenance of the legatee".
[33] *Re Medlock* (1886) 55 L.J. Ch. 738.

III. THE RETENTION OF INCOME

Where trustees do not pay out or apply all the income, they will necessarily either have accumulated it or have retained it in its character as income.

1. *Accumulation*

Accumulation is the conversion of what was income into capital. It occurs at the moment at which the trustees decide to accumulate the income and, while no formality is required, it is desirable as a matter of practice for the decision to accumulate to be recorded carefully in the trust's minutes.

Income can only be accumulated if, first, there is a trust or power enabling this to be done; secondly, that trust or power is not for an excessive period; and, thirdly, the trustees decide to give effect to the trust or to exercise the power.

2. *A Trust or Power to Accumulate*

Trustees have no general power to accumulate income. In *Re Gourju's Will Trusts*,[34] trustees held a fund upon protective trusts[35]; the fixed interest of the principal beneficiary having come to an end,[36] the trustees sought to accumulate the income. However, Simonds J. said[37]:

"I come to the conclusion that the obligation of the trustees is to apply the trust income as and when they receive it for the purposes indicated in the subsection. ... Putting it in a negative way, they are not entitled, regardless of the needs of the beneficiaries, to retain in their hands the income of the trust estate."

The trust or power to accumulate may arise either by statute[38] in the case of income which is held for the benefit of an infant beneficiary, to the extent that that income is not used for his maintenance,[39] or by virtue of the provisions of the trust instrument.

3. *Excessive Powers*

Where the trust is subject to English law, a trust to accumulate can only be prescribed for a maximum of one of the following periods[40]:

---

[34] [1943] Ch. 24.
[35] Under Trustee Act 1925, s.33.
[36] See *ante*, p. 231.
[37] [1943] Ch. 24 at 34.
[38] Trustee Act 1925, s.31.
[39] See *post*, p. 605.
[40] Law of Property Act 1925, s.164; Perpetuities and Accumulations Act 1964, s.13. These periods do not apply where the settlor is a body corporate; *Re Dodwell & Co. Ltds Trust Deed* [1978] 3 All E.R. 738.

(i) the life of the settlor;

(ii) a period of 21 years from the death of the settlor;

(iii) the duration of the minority or respective minorities of any person or persons living or *en ventre sa mère* at the death of the settlor;

(iv) the duration of the minority or respective minorities of infant beneficiaries who, if of full age, would be entitled to the income;

(v) a term of 21 years from the creation of the settlement; and

(vi) the duration of the minority or respective minorities of any person or persons in being when the settlement is created, whether or not they are beneficiaries or have any other connection with the a settlement.

The period most commonly utilised is the term of 21 years from the creation of the settlement ((v) above). However, the Law Commission has recently proposed the substitution of all the above six possibilities by a period of 125 years (accumulation during the infancy of a beneficiary will obviously also continue to the possible).[41] It remains to be seen whether this wholly unexpected proposal is put into effect.

If, at the end of the prescribed period, the income is prima facie payable to a beneficiary who is an infant, then income can nevertheless still be accumulated, to the extent that it is not utilised for the infant's maintenance, under the statutory trust to accumulate.[42]

If a trust power prescribes accumulation for a period which is longer than that prescribed by statute, the provision is void only as to the excess.[43]

Where a settlor wishes income to be accumulated for a period longer than the maximum permitted by English law, this can be achieved by providing for the trust to have as its proper law the law of a jurisdiction which permits a longer period. An on-shore jurisdiction which is popular for this purpose is Northern Ireland, which permits accumulation for the entire perpetuity period[44]; virtually all off-shore jurisdictions have longer accumulation periods, usually fixed periods of years. However, no jurisdiction anywhere has an accumulation period longer than the 125 years recently proposed by the Law Commission.

4. *Exercise of Power*

Trustees must exercise any discretion within a reasonable time. What is reasonable depends on the facts of each case. In *Re Gulbenkian's Settlement Trusts (No.2)*[45] trustees learned in April 1957 of a decision[46] which cast doubt on the validity of a provision in the trust instrument and they then retained

---

[41] See *ante*, p. 223.

[42] Trustee Act 1925, s.31(2).

[43] *Re Joel's Will Trusts* [1967] Ch. 14.

[44] For an example of the use of trusts governed by the law of Northern Ireland for this purpose, see *Vestey v. I.R.C.* [1980] A.C. 1148.

[45] [1970] Ch. 408.

[46] *Re Gresham's Settlement* [1956] 1 W.L.R. 573, subsequently overruled.

the income in their hands as income without accumulating it. The doubt as to validity was not resolved until the decision of the House of Lords in *Re Gulbenkian's Settlement Trusts*[47] in October 1968. Plowman J. held that in the circumstances the trustees' retention of the income was not unreasonable and they were therefore still able to exercise their discretion in respect of all the income which had arisen since 1957. Thus, provided that they act reasonably, trustees can clearly retain income as income for a considerable time and then accumulate it.

If the trustees are under a specific duty to accumulate income, that duty is not extinguished by lapse of time. In such circumstances, the trustees can carry out their duty long after the income has actually arisen; further, if they do not do so, the court will issue a direction to this effect.[48] If, on the other hand, the trustees merely have a power to accumulate, that is a duty to consider whether to accumulate but without any duty to exercise the power, their power to accumulate will be lost if they do not act within a reasonable time.[49]

5. *The Fiscal Effect of Accumulation*

Trust instruments which impose a duty or confer a power to accumulate frequently also confer a power for payments from capital to be made to beneficiaries. The trustees may thus have both a power either to distribute income as it arises to members of a discretionary class or to accumulate it and a trust or power to distribute capital, including accumulated income, to the same persons. What difference does it make to the beneficiary whether he receives a distribution of income or capital? This is largely governed by fiscal considerations.

What is the position of trustees of a fund who receive a gross income of £1,000 per annum which they have a discretion either to distribute as income or to accumulate and are considering making some form of distribution to two of the discretionary objects, George who pays income tax at the basic rate[50] of 23 per cent.[51] and Harry who pays income tax at the top rate of 40 per cent? The trustees are themselves liable to pay income tax at a total rate of 34 per cent on any income capable of being accumulated.[52] Of the £1,000 received by them, they will therefore be required to pay £340 in tax.[53]

If they then distribute the net amount of £660 to one of the two potential beneficiaries as income without first accumulating it, the beneficiary is treated as having received a gross payment of £1,000, from which tax at 34 per cent has been deducted. In the case of George, his marginal rate of tax

---

[47] [1970] A.C. 508.

[48] *Re Locker's Settlement Trusts* [1977] 1 W.L.R. 1323; see *ante*, p. 495.

[49] *Re Gourju's Will Trusts* [1943] Ch. 24; *Re Wise* [1896] 1 Ch. 281; *Re Allen-Meyrick's Will Trusts* [1968] 1 W.L.R. 499.

[50] See *ante*, p. 522.

[51] These examples assume that the top tax rate will not be altered if the beneficiaries receive another £1,000 gross income.

[52] The provision also applies to income subject to a discretion. Income and Corporation Taxes Act 1988, s.686 (as amended by Finance Act 1993).

[53] In this example, the expenses of the trust are ignored. That part of the income which is applicable to the expenses of the trust payable out of income is not subject to the additional charge.

is 23 per cent so he will be able to make a claim for the repayment of the difference between the tax which he ought to have suffered on the £1,000, namely £230, and the £340 tax which the income has actually borne; in the final result, he will therefore receive £660 from the trustees and £110 by way of tax reclaim. On the other hand Harry, who is liable to tax at 40 per cent, will be required to pay to the Inland Revenue the difference between the tax which the income of £1,000 has already borne, namely £340, and the £400 which is appropriate to his own top rate. He will therefore receive £660 from the trustees, £60 of which he will have to pay to the Inland Revenue.

If the trustees instead accumulate the net income of £660 and then at some later stage distribute it as a capital payment, it is treated as capital for all purposes relating to income tax; consequently, no repayment claims can be made nor can any further liability arise. Thus, George will be worse off because he will not be able to recover the £110 from the Inland Revenue but Harry will be better off since he will not have to pay the additional tax of £60. However, such a distribution from capital which has been derived from accumulated income will be treated in the same way as any other distribution of capital and may therefore give rise to a liability to inheritance tax.[54]

6. Retained Income

As income can be converted into capital as a result of a decision by the trustees to accumulate it, as a matter of strict theory the income can never be accumulated in the absence of such a decision. However, if the trustees are under a duty to accumulate, the longer the period which elapses the greater will be the willingness of the courts to hold that there has been an accumulation in any event. Similarly, the courts will infer that a decision to accumulate has been made if the trustees act in a manner which indicates that income has been accumulated; this will be the case, for example, where trustees complete an income tax return for the trust showing the income as having been accumulated.

7. Beneficial Entitlement

Special rules apply where income has been accumulated during the minority of an infant beneficiary.[55] Apart from these special rules, and subject to any contrary provision in the trust instrument, income which has been accumulated will be added to capital and the beneficiary ultimately entitled to the capital will also become entitled to the accumulations. On the other hand, income which is retained by the trustees without being accumulated will belong to the beneficiary, if any, who is entitled to income.

---

[54] Inheritance Tax Act 1984, s.65. See *ante*, p. 530.
[55] See *post*, p. 608.

IV. THE MAINTENANCE OF INFANT BENEFICIARIES

1. *The Trust Instrument Prevails*

Section 31 of the Trustee Act 1925 confers upon trustees a power to apply income in the maintenance of infant beneficiaries.[56] However, it was decided in *Re Turner*[57] that all the provisions of this section, irrespective of whether they are expressed as powers or as duties, are in fact only "powers conferred by this Act" for the purposes of section 69(2) of the Act (this sub-section of course provides that "the powers conferred by this Act on trustees" apply only in so far as there is no intention expressed in the trust instrument that they should not apply). Although, therefore, the general principle is that the statutory powers are additional to any powers in the trust instrument, any of the statutory powers, including the power of maintenance, may be expressly excluded under section 69(2).

The statutory power of maintenance will be excluded: first, if and to the extent that the terms of an express power of maintenance are inconsistent with the statutory power; secondly, where any other provision in the trust instrument is inconsistent with the statutory power, such as a direction to accumulate the whole of the income; and, thirdly, where there is a provision expressly excluding the statutory power.

Re Erskine's Settlement Trusts[58] is an example of the second and third of these circumstances. The settlor created a settlement for the benefit of his grandson Richard, who became entitled to the capital of the fund upon attaining the age of 22. The question arose as to Richard's entitlement to income prior to attaining that age. The trust instrument provided that the income should be accumulated both during the lifetime of the settlor and thereafter until Richard reached the age of 22 and also provided that the statutory powers of maintenance and advancement should not apply. The provision for accumulation was in fact void[59] but Stamp J., following *Re Turner*,[60] held that the statutory power of maintenance was nevertheless effectively excluded. Consequently the income remained undisposed of until Richard reached the age of 22; it therefore belonged to the settlor's estate.

While it is therefore possible to exclude the statutory power, that power will only be excluded if there is a clear expression of intention to that effect. If the trust instrument is silent on the point, then the statutory power will apply.

2. *The Statutory Power*

The statutory power of maintenance is contained in section 31 of the Trustee Act 1925. This provides[61] that, where property is held upon trust for any

---

[56] There is no statutory power to maintain adult beneficiaries.
[57] [1937] Ch. 15.
[58] [1971] 1 W.L.R. 162.
[59] Because it was contrary to the Law of Property Act 1925, s.164.
[60] [1937] Ch. 15.
[61] Trustee Act 1925, s.31(1).

infant, then during the infancy of that person the trustees may, if in their discretion they think fit, pay the whole or part of the income to the parent or guardian of the infant beneficiary or otherwise apply it for or towards his maintenance, education, or benefit. The trustees are under a duty to accumulate the whole of the income which is not paid or applied in this way.[62]

It follows from what has been said earlier in this Chapter that the trustees will have a power to maintain an infant beneficiary unless the gift to the infant beneficiary does not carry the intermediate income[63] or the power has been excluded.[64] Where the statutory power arises, it has the following noteworthy features:

(i) The statutory power applies where the interest of the beneficiary is vested and to this extent overrides the apparent provisions of the trust instrument. Where trustees hold a fund upon trust for Cedric for life, remainder to Edmund, the terms of the trust instrument would suggest that Cedric is entitled to the whole of the income. However, the effect of the application of the statutory power of maintenance, assuming that it has not been excluded, is to deprive Cedric of any right to the income while he is under the age of 18 except to the extent that the trustees decide to pay or apply the whole or any part of it for his maintenance.

(ii) The statutory power also applies where the interest of the beneficiary is contingent. So where a fund is held upon trust for Fergus if he attains the age of 30, the trustees may use the whole or any part of the income for his maintenance while he is under the age of 18, provided that the gift carries the intermediate income.[65]

(iii) Although the statutory power refers to vested interests, it applies also to vested interests which are defeasible. Thus it applies where a fund is held upon trust for Solly but, if he dies under the age of 30, for Holly.

(iv) The statutory power only applies while the beneficiary is under the age of 18.[66]

(v) Where the statutory power has not been excluded, the trustees are under a duty to consider whether to exercise their power but are under no obligation to do so. In deciding whether, and, if so, to what extent, to exercise the power, the trustees are directed by section 31 to have regard, first, to the age of the infant; secondly, to what other income, if any, is available for his maintenance; thirdly,

---

[62] s.31(2).

[63] See *ante*, p. 598.

[64] See *ante*, p. 605.

[65] See *ante*, p. 598. If the gift does not carry the intermediate income, there will obviously be no income available for the trustees to use.

[66] Family Law Reform Act 1969, Sched. 3, para. 5. See *post*, p. 607, as to the position when the beneficiary reaches the age of 18.

to his requirements; and, fourthly, "generally to the circumstances of the case". If the trustees know that other income is available for the maintenance of the infant and the total amount available exceeds the needs of the infant, then so far as is practicable a proportionate part only of each fund should be paid or applied for his maintenance. The trustees may pay any money which they decide to use either to the infant's parent or guardian[67] or apply it directly for his maintenance, education or benefit.

(vi) The statutory power applies whatever the nature of the property.[68]

(vii) Where the statutory power is to be exercised, the trustees must exercise it positively and not merely pay out the money for the infant's maintenance without considering whether or not it is desirable for them to do so. Thus, where[69] trustees made automatic payments to an infant's father without exercising any discretion, the court ordered that the money had to be repaid to the trust fund. But as long as the trustees exercise their discretion in good faith, the court will not interfere with their decision.[70]

3. Accumulation of Surplus Income

All income which is not paid to the parent or guardian of the infant beneficiary or applied by the trustees for his maintenance, education, or benefit must be accumulated.[71] Despite the fact that, by being accumulated, the surplus income becomes capital, the trustees may nevertheless use the income accumulated in previous years as if it were the income of a later year, provided that the interest of the beneficiary in question actually continues in that later year.[72]

4. Income Arising After the Age of 18

There is no statutory power to maintain an adult beneficiary. The general principle is therefore that once the beneficiary has reached the age of 18, he is thereafter entitled either to the whole of the income[73] or to none of it. It is, however, possible for the trust instrument to confer an express power to maintain.[74]

---

[67] *Sowarsby v. Lacy* (1819) 4 Madd. 142.
[68] *Stanley v. I.R.C.* [1944] K.B. 255; *Re Baron Vestey* [1951] Ch. 209.
[69] *Wilson v. Turner* (1883) 22 Ch.D. 521 and see *ante*, p. 184.
[70] *Re Bryant* [1894] 1 Ch. 324; *Re Lofthouse* (1885) 29 Ch.D. 921.
[71] Trustee Act 1925, s.31(2). The manner in which the accumulations are dealt with is discussed *post*, p. 608.
[72] *ibid.*
[73] *Re Jones' Will Trusts* [1947] Ch. 48.
[74] *Re Turner* [1937] Ch. 15.

In *Re McGeorge*,[75] a testator devised land to his daughter but declared that the devise should not take effect until the death of his wife. It was held that this was a "future specific devise" within section 175 of the Law of Property Act and so prima facie carried the intermediate income. The daughter was over 18 and so claimed the income of the property. Her claim was unsuccessful. Cross J. held that the testator, by having deferred the enjoyment of the property until after the widow's death, had expressed the intention that the daughter should not in fact have the intermediate income; it therefore had to be accumulated.

Where, on attaining the age of 18, the beneficiary has only a contingent interest in the trust property, he would, in the absence of any other provision, have no entitlement to anything until he satisfied the contingency. However, section 31(1)(ii) has the effect of accelerating the beneficiary's interest. It provides that, once the beneficiary has attained the age of 18, the trustees shall[76] thereafter pay to the beneficiary the income from the trust fund and the income from any accumulations[77] until the contingency is either satisfied or fails.

5. *Accumulated Income at the Age of 18*

When the infant beneficiary attains the age of 18, the trustees will hold any the accumulations, including income from the accumulated fund which has itself been accumulated, in accordance with any provision of the trust instrument and, if there is no such provision, either for the beneficiary absolutely or as an accretion to the capital of the trust property.[78]

A beneficiary will become entitled to the accumulations in the following circumstances: (i) in any circumstances in which the trust instrument so provides; (ii) if during infancy his interest was according to the settlement vested and he attains the age of 18[79]; (iii) if he attains the age of 18 and is then entitled to capital.[80] For the latter purpose, a beneficiary is entitled to capital if the property is realty where he is entitled to a fee simple absolute, a determinable fee simple, or an entailed interest[81] or if the property is personalty, where he is entitled to the property absolutely or for an entailed interest.[82]

In any other case, the accumulations are added to the capital of the property from which they arose.[83] Where they arose from a share of a fund

---

[75] [1963] Ch. 544.
[76] Despite this apparently mandatory provision, the section can be excluded; *Re Turner* [1937] Ch. 15.
[77] Trustee Act 1925, s.31(1)(ii).
[78] *ibid.*, s.31(2).
[79] *ibid.* s.31(2)(i)(a). This also applies if he marries under the age of 18 and had a vested interest until marriage.
[80] *ibid.* s.31(2)(i)(b). This also applies if he marries under the age of 18.
[81] See *Re Sharp's Settlement Trusts* [1973] Ch. 331 at 338, *per* Pennycuick V.-C.
[82] *ibid.*.
[83] Trustee Act 1925, s.32(2)(ii).

and that share continued to exist as a separate share, the accumulations are an accretion to that share and not to the fund as a whole.[84] This is in contrast to the position where a beneficiary dies before attaining the age of 18 (or marrying under that age), in which case, subject to any provision in the trust instrument, the accumulations are an accretion to the fund as a whole.[85]

This latter point arose for consideration in *Re Sharp's Settlement Trusts*.[86] A settlement had conferred a power of appointment, exercisable during the perpetuity period, over the trust property, to which in default of appointment the children of the settlor were entitled in equal shares if they attained the age of 21. The settlor had three children: Penelope, who attained her majority in 1964; Russell, who attained his majority in 1967; and Joanne, who was at all material times an infant. Income had arisen under the settlement since 1966 and the trustees had appointed it to the three children equally; it obviously had to be paid out to any child who was of age. Between 1966 and the date when Russell attained his majority in 1967, his share of accumulated income amounted to about £5,000. Between 1966 and the date of the hearing, in May 1972, Joanne's share of accumulated income amounted to about £41,000 and accumulation was continuing. Did the accumulations of Russell's and of Joanne's shares of the income pass to them absolutely when each attained the age of 21 or did they instead form part of the settled fund, in which case they would still be subject to the future exercise of power of appointment? Since the fund was personalty, Pennycuick V.-C. held that Russell and Joanne were not absolutely entitled to the accumulations so that the accumulations were subject to the power of appointment (this is admittedly anomalous[87]; had the property been realty and the interest of the beneficiaries a determinable fee,[88] they would have been entitled to the accumulations). The further question then arose as to whether the accumulations were accretions to their individual shares or accretions to the fund as a whole. Penelope argued for the latter (because she would therefore potentially become entitled to part of the income from them). However, Pennycuick V.-C. took the opposite view; thus the accumulations from Russell's share were held, with that share itself, for Russell subject to any future exercise of the power of appointment, and Joanne's share was held in the same way, contingently on her reaching the age of 21. Russell was therefore immediately entitled to the income from his share, including the income produced by the accumulations.

The manner in which trustees deal with accumulations when a beneficiary reaches the age of 18 is illustrated by the following table. For the purposes of the table, "Conditions A" means that the beneficiary had a vested interest during infancy and attains the age of 18 and "Conditions B" means that the beneficiary attains the age of 18 and becomes entitled to the capital.

---

[84] *Re Sharp's Settlement Trusts* [1973] Ch. 331.
[85] See *Re Joel* [1967] Ch. 14; see *ante*, p. 586.
[86] *Re Sharp's Settlement Trusts* [1973] Ch. 331.
[87] See *ibid*., at 340, *per* Pennycuick V.-C.
[88] Although not a fee simple subject to a condition subsequent. As to the distinction, see Megarry and Wade, *The Law of Real Property* (5th ed., 1983), pp. 67 *et seq*.

Trust instrument provides for fund to be held for	Circumstances	Entitlement	Remarks
Andrew absolutely[89]	Andrew attains 18	Andrew	Conditions B
	Andrew dies under 18	Andrew's estate	The entitlement is by virtue of the original gift, not s.31
Brian for life	Brian attains 18	Brian	Conditions A
	Brian dies under 18	Added to capital	Neither Conditions satisfied
Charles for life if he attains 18	Charles attains 18	Added to capital	Charles' interest during infancy was contingent only; and he does not become entitled to the capital
	Charles dies under 18	Added to capital	Neither Conditions satisfied
Douglas if he attains 18	Douglas attains 18	Douglas	Conditions B
	Douglas dies under 18	Added to capital	Neither Conditions satisfied
Edward if he attains 30	Edward attains 18	Added to capital	Neither Conditions satisfied
	Edward dies under 18	Added to capital	Neither Conditions satisfied
Frank, but if he dies under 30, for George	Frank attains 18	Frank	Although Frank's interest was defeasible, it was vested, and Conditions A is satisfied
	Franks dies under 18	Added to capital	Neither Conditions satisfied
Henry, but if he dies under 18, for Ian	Henry attains 18	Henry	Conditions A
	Henry dies under 18	Added to capital	Neither Conditions satisfied

It will be seen from this table: first, that where the beneficiary dies under the age of 18, the accumulations will always be added to capital, except where the property was held for an infant beneficiary absolutely (as in the case of Andrew); secondly, that where the beneficiary has a life interest which is contingent on his attaining the age of 18, or some later age, then, notwithstanding the fact that he satisfies the contingency, the accumulations are added to capital (as in the case of Charles and Edward); and, thirdly, that the distinction between a contingent interest (as in the case of Charles and

---

[89] Andrew's infancy being the only reason why he could not call for the capital to be transferred to him.

Edward) and a vested interest which is defeasible (as in the case of Frank) is crucial.

V. Taxation Consequences

Section 31 and the actions taken by trustees thereunder can have a material effect on the fiscal position of the beneficiary. In considering these fiscal consequences, it is necessary to keep in mind, first, that section 31 can be excluded and, secondly, that where, according to the terms of the settlement, an infant beneficiary has a vested life interest, by section 31 that interest is converted into a life interest contingent on his attaining 18 in respect of any income which is accumulated (this happens because, notwithstanding the terms of the settlement, during the minority of the beneficiary the trustees will have a power to maintain and a trust to accumulate the remaining income and the beneficiary (or his estate) will only become entitled to the accumulations if he attains the age of 18).

The latter point can cause considerable confusion. In order to determine the destination of accumulations, then whether or not a beneficiary had during his infancy a vested interest regard is paid to the terms of the trust instrument. For all other purposes, however, the nature of the beneficiary's interest is determined by the terms of the trust instrument as modified by the section itself.

1. *Income Tax*

It has already been seen[90] that the trustees are liable to income tax at the basic rate[91] on all income which they receive, regardless of whether it is used for the payment of trust management expenses, paid to a beneficiary, or accumulated and that, if they have a discretion with regard to income or are directed to accumulate it, they are liable to income tax at the higher flat rate of 34 per cent.[92]

If section 31 applies, then, whether the beneficiary's interest is under the terms of the trust instrument is vested or contingent, the trustees have a discretion, in that they have a power to maintain; consequently, they are liable to the higher flat rate of 34 per cent.[93] However, there is no further liability on the beneficiary unless the income is actually paid out to him, or applied for his benefit.

---

[90] See *ante*, p. 522.
[91] At present (1998–1999) this is 23% except for company distributions and bank interest, which are taxed at 20%.
[92] The additional rate is not payable in respect of that part of the gross income which was paid out in trust management expenses, which have in the first instance to be set against income taxed at 20% and only subsequently against income taxed at 23%.
[93] On the income from company distributions and deposit interest, the trustees will have to pay only a further 14% tax so as to bring the total up to 34%.

There is, however, a further rule under which a beneficiary will be taxable on the whole of the net trust income if he has a vested interest in it. He is taxable according to the rate of income tax applicable to his own income but he is entitled to a credit in respect of the income tax already paid by the trustees on the trust income paid to him. Suppose, therefore, that Harry, the beneficiary of a trust, has income apart from the trust of £36,000; that the income of the trust fund is £2,000, all from company disbursements and deposit interest, on which tax of £400 has been retained, that £250 is used for trust management expenses and that £1,350 is paid to Harry. Harry's liability is as follows:

The trustees have received	£2,000	
on which tax at 20% has been retained	£400	
leaving	£1,600	
from which they have paid trust management expenses of	£ 250	
leaving net income paid to Harry of	£1,350	
This is treated as a gross sum of	£1,687.50	
from which income tax[94] has been deducted of	£337.50	
	£1,350.00	
So that Harry's trust income is:		
the amount paid to him	£1,350.00	
and the tax deducted	£337.50	
		£1,687.50
which is added to his other income of		£36,000.00
		£37,687.50
On the "slice" of income between £36,000 and £37,687.50 the present rate of income tax[95] is 40% to give a liability of (40% x £1,687.50)		£675.00
Harry suffered by deductions		£337.50
and has a further liability of		£337.50

---

[94] In effect, the £400 paid by the trustees is attributed: as to
      250/1600 x 400 = 62.50 to trust management expenses
    1350/1600 x 400 = 337.50 to income paid to Harry.
[95] For 1998–99.

Using the figures of this example:
(a) if the whole of the income is accumulated, the total
    liability will be that of the trustees, as follows:

Gross income		£2,000
less: tax retained at 20% as before	£400	
less: tax at the flat rate of 34%, discounting the 20% already retained on that part of the gross income of the trust £2,000 as is not used in the payment of trust management expenses		
	£250	£250
	£1,750	£1,750
that is: 14% x £1,750	£245	
so that the total tax paid is	£645	£645
and net amount accumulated is		£1,105
(b) if the whole of the income is treated as Harry's the total tax payable, as before is		£675
leaving the benefit[96]		£1,012.50

The income will be treated as that of Harry, during Harry's minority, first,
if he is absolutely entitled to both capital and income, so that his infancy is
the sole reason why he cannot call for the capital to be transferred to him,
and either he, if he lives, or his estate, if he does not, will be entitled to the
accumulations[97]; and, secondly, if, according to the terms of the trust instrument, Harry is entitled to the whole of the income, section 31 therefore being
excluded, so that the trustees do not have power to accumulate any part of
it.

In all other circumstances, only that income which is actually paid to
Harry or applied for his benefit, is treated as his for the purposes of income
tax.[98] The remainder of the income, which is accumulated, is taxable in the
hands of the trustees at the effective rate of 34 per cent.

2. *Inheritance Tax*

It has already been explained[99] that the tax legislation[1] divides settled
property into two main categories, according to whether or not there is, at

[96] The net income paid to Harry, £1,350, less the further tax payable by him in respect of it, £337.50
[97] *Roberts v. Hanks* (1926) 10 T.C. 351; *Edwardes-Jones v. Down* (1936) 20 T.C. 279.
[98] *Stanley v. I.R.C.* [1944] K.B. 255.
[99] See *ante*, p. 530.
[1] Finance (No.2) Act 1987.

the time being considered, an interest in possession in that property. A beneficiary has an interest in possession if he is entitled to the trust income without the need for any further decision of the trustees to that effect.[2] Subject to certain limited exceptions, a charge to tax arises whenever an interest in possession terminates.[3]

In general, if there is no interest in possession in settled property and one then arises, there is a charge to inheritance tax at that time.[4] However, special inheritance tax privileges are given to "accumulation and maintenance settlements". These are governed by section 71 of the Inheritance Tax Act 1984, which was drafted with section 31 of the Trustee Act in mind. Section 71 of the 1984 Act provides that a settlement is an accumulation and maintenance settlement at a given time if,[5] at that time, first there is no interest in possession thereunder; secondly, the income is applied for the maintenance, education or benefit of a beneficiary and, to the extent that it is not so applied, it is to be accumulated; and, thirdly, it can be said that one or more beneficiaries will, on attaining a specified age not exceeding 25, become beneficially entitled either to the settled property itself or to an interest in possession therein.

Where the conditions for an accumulation and maintenance settlement are satisfied, the trust is not subject to what would otherwise be a charge to tax on every tenth anniversary of the date of its creation[6] and there is no charge to tax when a beneficiary becomes entitled either to an interest in possession in the settled property or to the settled property itself.[7]

The following table[8] illustrates the interaction of section 31 of the Trustee Act and the inheritance tax provisions. In the table, "I.H.T." means Inheritance Tax, "Acc. & Mtce" means an accumulation and maintenance settlement, "I.I.P." means interest in possession, and "D.T." means a discretionary trust other than an accumulation and maintenance settlement.

---

[2] *Pearson v. I.R.C.* [1981] A.C. 753; see *ante*, p. 596.

[3] Inheritance Tax Act 1984, ss.51, 52.

[4] *ibid.*, s.65.

[5] Only the basic conditions are given in the text; certain further ancilliary conditions must also be satisfied. See Inheritance Tax Act 1984, s.65.

[6] By virtue of Inheritance Tax Act 1984, ss.64, 66.

[7] *ibid.*, s.65.

[8] There is no need to try to memorise this table. It is intended to show how it is necessary to consider, first, the terms of the trust instrument; secondly, whether the gift carries the intermediate income; and, thirdly, whether s.31 is or is not excluded.

Inter-action of Trustee Act 1925, s.31 and Inheritance tax provisions

Trust instrument provides for	Section 31 Applies			Section 31 Excluded		
	I.H.T. category during minority	Whether charge to tax on death under age 18	I.H.T. effect on attaining 18	I.H.T. category during minority	Whether charge to tax on death under age 18	I.H.T. effect on attaining 18
Andrew absolutely	Personal	Yes	Continues to be personal	Personal	Yes	Continues to be personal
Brian for life	Acc. & Mtce[1]	No	Brian becomes entitled to I.I.P	I.I.P.	Yes	I.I.P continues
Charles for life if he attains 18	Acc. & Mtce[2]	No	Charles becomes entitled to I.I.P.	(i) I.I.P. if gift carries intermediate income (ii) D.T. otherwise	Yes / No	I.I.P. continues — I.I.P. arises, if gift then carries intermediate income; and charge to tax
Douglas absolutely if he attains 18	Acc. & Mtce[3]	No	Personal	(i) I.I.P. if gift carries intermediate income (ii) D.T. otherwise	Yes / No	Personal No charge to tax Personal Charge to tax
Edward if he attains 30	(i) Acc. & Mtce[4] if gift carries intermediate income (ii) D.T. otherwise	No	(i) I.I.P. if gift carries intermediate income (ii) D.T. otherwise	(i) I.I.P. if gift carries intermediate income (ii) D.T. otherwise	Yes / No	I.I.P. if gift continues to carry the intermediate income (i) I.I.P. arises if gift begins to carry intermediate income. Charge to tax (ii) Otherwise D.T. continues
Frank, but if he dies under 30, for George	Acc. & Mtce if gift carries intermediate income	No	I.I.P. if gift carries intermediate income. No charge to tax	I.I.P. if gift carries intermediate income	Yes	If gift carries intermediate income, I.I.P. contines
Henry, but if he dies under 18, for Ian	Acc. & Mtce if gift carries intermediate income	No	Personal. No charge to tax	I.I.P. if gift carries intermediate income D.T. if gift does not carry intermediate income	Yes / No	Personal. No charge to tax if gift has carried intermediate income. Charge to tax

(1) The apparent interest in possession of Brian is removed by s.31.
(2) The conditions for an accumulation and maintenance settlement are prima facie satisfied because Charles will become entitled at an age not exceeding 25.
(3) Provided that the gift carries the intermediate income.
(4) The vested defeasible interest of Edward is converted by s.31.

CHAPTER 20

APPLICATIONS OF TRUST CAPITAL

In general, entitlement to capital will depend, in the case of a fixed trust, on the terms of the trust instrument or, in the case of a discretionary trust, on the decision of the trustees. However, as in the case of entitlement to income, the quantum of capital which is available for beneficiaries will be determined after the payment of those costs and expenses which are attributable to capital.[1] Further, even in the case of a fixed trust, the trustees may take decisions altering the time at which a beneficiary will take capital or affecting the quantum of his entitlement.

The main powers which affect the quantum of entitlement are the powers of *Advancement*, *Appointment*, and *Appropriation*. Appointments have already been considered. This Chapter will, after dealing with expenses payable from capital, be concerned primarily with the powers of Advancement and Appropriation.

I. Expenses from Capital

It has already been seen[2] that, in general, recurrent expenses are payable out of the income of the trust fund. This is partly because of the recurrent nature of these expenses and partly because such expenses are generally for the benefit primarily of the beneficiary who is entitled to income. The corollary is that, in principle, the capital of the trust fund has generally to bear expenses which constitute capital expenditure on one or more assets of the trust or apply to the trust as a whole and can, therefore, be said to be for the benefit of all beneficiaries.

Examples of expenses which are treated as capital expenditure on a trust asset are calls on shares which are partly paid,[3] sums applied in discharging mortgage debts,[4] and sums applied in improving land and buildings.[5] Where a building is purchased by the trustees in a derelict state, the cost of putting it into good condition at the outset will be treated as if it were part of the purchase price and so will be chargeable to capital.[6] On the other hand, ordinary repairs are, in principle, payable out of income but, where

---

[1] As to net income, see *ante*, p. 595.
[2] See *ante*, p. 595.
[3] *Todd v. Moorhouse* (1874) L.R. 19 Eq. 69; Trustee Act 1925, s.11(2).
[4] *Whitbread v. Smith* (1854) 3 De G.M. & G. 727; *Marshall v. Crowther* (1874) 2 Ch.D. 199.
[5] *Earl of Cowley v. Wellesley* (1866) L.R. 1 Eq. 656; *Re Walker's Settled Estate* [1894] 1 Ch. 189.
[6] *Re Courtier* (1886) Ch.D. 136.

the repairs can be said to be for the benefit of all beneficiaries, the court may direct that the whole or part of the cost is to be borne by capital.[7]

The second category of expenses which are borne by capital covers those items relating to the trust as a whole and which can be said to be for the benefit of all beneficiaries. Examples are the costs of the appointment of new trustees,[8] of making changes in investment, of obtaining legal advice as to the extent of the trustees' powers,[9] and of taking or defending court proceedings for the protection of trust assets.[10]

It has already been mentioned[11] that, in certain circumstances, by virtue of either statute or the trust instrument, trustees are given a discretion as to whether outgoings are to be paid from income or from capital. This power must be exercised in such a way that the particular outgoings will be borne equitably between the beneficiaries with different interests.[12]

II. ADVANCEMENTS

1. *The Concept*

An advancement consists in essence of the payment or the application of a capital sum in order to establish a person in life or to make permanent provision for him.[13] An advancement is often of an amount which, in the light of the circumstances of the recipient, is large and, where a payment is in this sense large, there is a presumption that it is made by way of advancement.[14]

It is not now generally necessary to consider in relation to the administration of trusts[15] whether a payment is, strictly, by way of advancement because either under the statutory power, which is considered below, or under an express power in the trust instrument, the trustees will usually have a power to apply capital for the advancement or other benefit of a beneficiary.

2. *The Statutory Power*

The statutory power is contained in section 32 of the Trustee Act 1925. This section gives trustees a power to pay or apply capital for the benefit of any beneficiary who is interested in the capital of the trust fund, whether his

---

[7] Under the Settled Land and Trustee Acts (Courts' General Powers) Act 1943 and Emergency Powers (Miscellaneous Provisions) Act 1953.

[8] *Re Fulham* (1850) 15 Jur. 69; *Re Fellows' Settlement* (1856) 2 Jur. (N.S.) 62.

[9] *Poole v. Pass* (1839) 1 Beav. 600.

[10] *Re Earl of Berkeley's Will Trusts* (1874) 10 Ch. App. 56; *Re Earl De La Warr's Estates* (1881) 16 Ch.D. 587; *Stott v. Milne* (1884) 25 Ch.D. 710.

[11] See *ante*, p. 505.

[12] *Re Lord De Tabley* (1896) 75 L.T. 328; *Re Earl of Stamford and Warrington* [1916] 1 Ch. 404.

[13] *Boyd v. Boyd* (1867) L.R. 4 Eq. 305; *Taylor v. Taylor* (1875) L.R. 20 Eq. 155; *Re Hayward* [1957] Ch. 528; *Hardy v. Shaw* [1975] 2 All E.R. 1052.

[14] *Taylor v. Taylor* (1875) L.R. 20 Eq. 155 at 157, *per* Jessel M.R.; *Hardy v. Shaw* [1975] 2 All E.R. 1052 at 1056, *per* Goff J.

[15] It is otherwise in the administration of estates; see Administration of Estates Act 1925, s.46(1).

interest is vested or contingent, and whether or not it is liable to be defeated by the exercise of a power. Exercise of the power always has one and may have two important effects.

First, the beneficiary who receives the advancement inevitably obtains a capital benefit from the trust earlier than he otherwise would have done. If trustees who hold a fund upon trust for Gerald for life, with remainder to Harry, pay part of the fund to Harry during the lifetime of Gerald,[16] Harry takes the benefit of that part at that time, rather than having to wait until the death of Gerald.

Secondly, the beneficiary who receives the advancement may well receive a capital benefit from the trust which he otherwise might not have received at all. If trustees who hold a fund upon trust for Ian if he attains the age of 30 but, if he dies under that age, for John pay part of the trust fund to Ian when he is aged 22, the subsequent death of Ian at the age of 25 means that he has obtained a capital benefit for which he never in fact qualified.

(A)   The Extent of the Statutory Power

The trustees can make payments by way of advancement or benefit to the same beneficiary on more than one occasion, provided that the total which is paid or applied does not exceed one half of the presumptive or vested share of the beneficiary.[17] It was decided in *The Marquess of Abergavenny v. Ram*[18] that where, at the time of the advancement, the trustees pay out the entire permissible half of the presumptive or vested share, then their power of advancement in favour of that beneficiary is exhausted and no further advancement can be made to him even if the value of the remaining trust assets subsequently appreciates.[19] If the trustees of a trust out of which there have been no previous advancements made an advancement of £25,000 in 1994 to its sole contingent beneficiary when the value of the trust fund was £50,000 but by 1999 the value of the unadvanced half has risen to £80,000, they will have fully exhausted their power in 1994 and can make no further advancement in 1999. If, however, they only advanced £24,000 in 1994, so that their power was not fully exhausted, in 1999 they could advance the further sum of £28,000[20] (although it would again be better to advance only (say) £27,000 so as to leave room for further advancements in the future).

---

[16] As to the need for Gerald to give his consent, see *post*, p. 619.

[17] Trustee Act 1925, s.32(1), proviso (a).

[18] [1981] 1 W.L.R. 843.

[19] The decision was on a provision of the Marquess of Abergavenny's Estate Act 1946 but it is equally applicable to s.32 of the Trustee Act 1925.

[20] The calculation is:

Value of fund in 1999	£80,000
Add: amount previously advanced	£24,000
	£104,000
One half thereof	£52,000
less: previously advanced	£24,000
Maximum further advance	£28,000

(B) Bringing Advancements into Account

If, after a beneficiary has received an advancement, he is or becomes absolutely and indefeasibly entitled to the trust property or to a share in it, he must bring into account the amount of his advancement.[21] If trustees who hold a fund upon trust for James and John in equal shares if and when they attain the age of 30 paid £20,000 by way of advancement to James when he was aged 26, then in the event that by the time when the fund is distributed to James and John it is worth £100,000 the amounts which they will receive are:

Value of fund		£100,000
Amount advanced		£20,000
Total		£120,000

Entitlement

	James	John
$\frac{1}{2}$ x £120,000	£60,000	£60,000
Less: advancement	£20,000	—
Net entitlement	£40,000	£60,000

When an advancement was not made in cash but *in specie*, the amount to be brought into account is the value of the asset at the time when the beneficiary becomes absolutely and indefeasibly entitled to his share.[22]

If the beneficiary who received the advancement had only a contingent or defeasible interest and never becomes absolutely and indefeasibly entitled, the amount advanced to him cannot be clawed-back. The trustees therefore can, by making an advancement to a contingent beneficiary, partially defeat the interests of other beneficiaries.

(C) The Possible Need for Consents

Where the making of an advancement will prejudice the interest of a prior beneficiary, the advance can only be made if that beneficiary is of full age and consents in writing to it. Thus if £10,000 is settled upon trust for Mary for life, with remainder to Derek, the trustees have a power to advance up to £5,000 to Derek but only if Mary consents. If Mary consents and an advancement of the full £5,000 is made, thereafter her income will be that produced by the remaining £5,000 and not, as previously, by £10,000. It should be noted that a person on whom property is settled on protective trusts will not normally forfeit his life interest by consenting to an advancement.[23]

---

[21] Trustee Act 1925, s.32(1), proviso (b). The Law Reform Committee (23rd Report, 1982) recommended that the amount to be brought into account should be increased by reference to movements in the Index of Retail Prices.

[22] See, *e.g. Hardy v. Shaw* [1975] 2 All E.R. 1052.

[23] See *ante*, p. 236.

(D) The Nature of Property which can be Advanced

The statutory power of advancement applies only to money or securities or to land which is the subject matter of a trust of land. It therefore does not apply to capital money arising under a settlement subject to the Settled Land Act 1925.[24]

3. Extensions and Exclusions of the Statutory Power

The statutory power will apply even where there is no mention of it in the trust instrument; however, the power is one which falls within the scope of section 69(2) of the Trustee Act 1925[25] and so may be excluded by the settlor or testator in the trust instrument. Thus, in *Re Evans's Settlement*[26] Stamp J. held that, where the trust instrument provided that the trustees could advance up to £5,000, this by implication excluded the statutory power of advancing up to one-half of the prospective interest. Further, in *I.R.C. v. Bernstein*,[27] where there was a direction to accumulate income during the settlor's lifetime, the Court of Appeal held that this was a sufficient indication that the settlor did not intend the statutory power of advancement to apply.

It is more likely, however, that the statutory power will be extended. The most usual extensions give the trustees a power to advance up to the whole and not merely half of the beneficiary's share, extend the power to the subject matter of settlements under the Settled Land Act 1925, and, in some cases, do away with the need to obtain the consent of beneficiaries with prior interests.

4. The Purpose of an Advancement

It has already been seen[28] that, originally, a power of advancement had to relate to some substantial preferment in life. Examples were the purchasing of a commission in the Army[29]—the modern equivalent would be purchasing a partnership in a business or practice, the purchasing or furnishing of a house,[30] or even establishing a husband in business.[31] It has also been seen that the need for a substantial preferment of this kind has been modified by the extension of the statutory power of advancement to payments which produce "benefit", which is a word of wide import. However, the trustees must still consider whether a particular advancement is for the benefit of the beneficiary in question. In *Lowther v. Bentinck*[32] it was held that the payment of his debts was not for the benefit of a beneficiary, though in special circumstances a payment to a beneficiary which enabled him to discharge

---

[24] Trustee Act 1925, s.32(2) (substituted by Trusts of Land and Appointment of Trustees Act 1996 Sched. 3, para. 3(8)). No further settlements under the Settled Land Act can now be created.
[25] See *ante*, p. 605.
[26] [1967] 1 W.L.R. 1294.
[27] [1960] Ch. 444.
[28] See *ante*, p. 617.
[29] *Lawrie v. Bankes* (1857) 4 Kay & J. 142.
[30] *Perry v. Perry* (1870) 18 W.R. 482.
[31] *Re Kershaw's Trust* (1868) L.R. 6 Eq. 322.
[32] (1875) L.R. 19 Eq. 166.

his debts might be a benefit for this purpose. And it is extremely clear that the trustees must not make an advancement which will benefit themselves. In *Molyneux v. Fletcher*,[33] the trustees made an advance to a beneficiary to enable her to pay the debts which her father owed to one of the trustees; this was held to be an improper exercise of the power of advancement.

In most cases the "benefit" for which an advancement is made is some form of material benefit. In some circumstances, however, the court will authorise an advancement to be made for the moral, and not necessarily material, benefit of the beneficiary. In *Re Clore*[34] a beneficiary who was entitled to an interest in a trust fund of considerable value felt a moral obligation to make payments to charity. Pennycuick J. authorised this on the apparent basis that, since the beneficiary felt that he was subject to this obligation, the payment by the trustees was only relieving him of a financial obligation which he would otherwise have sought to meet from his personal funds. The judge made it clear, however, that the beneficiary must genuinely feel the moral obligation himself; the trustees were not at liberty to make payments in satisfaction of what they considered to be the beneficiary's moral obligations if the beneficiary did not share their view. Further, with the possible exception of relatively small amounts, it is prudent for trustees to seek the prior sanction of the court before making advancements of this nature.

Just as trustees cannot properly make an advancement in order to benefit themselves,[35] they cannot make an advancement with a view to benefiting some other person. In *Re Pauling's Settlement Trusts*[36] the bankers Coutts & Co. were trustees of a fund for a wife for her life, with remainder on her death to her children. The trust instrument contained an express power for the trustees to advance to the children up to one-half of their share with the consent of the wife. The husband of the life tenant, who was the father of the children, regularly lived beyond his means and therefore sought to obtain part of the trust moneys. A series of advancements were made, nominally to the children, but the money advanced was used for the benefit of the father or the family in general; the proceeds of one advancement were used to purchase a house for the father in the Isle of Man and the proceeds of another advancement to discharge a loan incurred by the mother. Counsel had advised the trustees that, so far as they were concerned, they were advancing the money to the children for their own absolute use and that what the latter then did with the money was not the trustees' concern. This view was unanimously rejected by the Court of Appeal, who considered that:

"the power [of advancement] can be exercised only if it is for the benefit of the child or remoter issue to be advanced or, as was said during argument, it is thought to be 'a good thing' for the advanced person to have a share of capital before his or her due time. . . . [A] power of advancement [can] be exercised only if there is some good reason for it. That good reason must be

---

[33] [1898] 1 Q.B. 648.
[34] [1966] 1 W.L.R. 955.
[35] *Molyneux v. Fletcher* [1898] 1 Q.B. 648.
[36] [1964] Ch. 303.

beneficial to the person to be advanced; [the power] cannot be exercised capriciously or with some other benefit in view."[37]

In their consideration of the circumstances in which an advancement could properly be made, the Court of Appeal drew a distinction between the situation where the beneficiary applies for an advancement for a particular purpose and the situation where the trustees themselves stipulate the purpose to which the advancement is to be put. As Willmer L.J. said:

"if the trustees make the advance for a particular purpose which they state, they can quite properly pay it over to the advancee if they reasonably think they can trust him or her to carry out the prescribed purpose. What they cannot do is to prescribe a particular purpose and then raise and pay the money over to the advancee, leaving him or her entirely free, legally and morally, to apply it for that purpose or to spend it in any way he or she chooses. . . . This much is plain, that if such misapplication [of the money advanced] came to [the trustees'] notice, they could not safely make further advances for particular purposes without making sure that the money was in fact applied to that purpose, since the advancee would have shown him or herself quite irresponsible."[38]

The court expressly left open the question whether, in the event that money advanced for a particular purpose was used for something quite different, that money could be recovered by the trustees. This possibility apart, the trustees certainly have no legal control over the money once they have paid it to the beneficiary; consequently, they must ensure that the beneficiary is under a moral obligation to apply the money to the purpose intended.

5. Adult beneficiaries

While, as has already been seen,[39] the statutory power of maintenance applies only to infant beneficiaries, the statutory power of advancement can be exercised in favour of beneficiaries of any age.[40]

6. Fiscal Considerations

Where an advancement is made, there is a potential liability to both capital gains tax and inheritance tax.

If the advancement is made in cash, there can be no liability to capital gains tax in respect of the advancement itself although, if the trustees disposed of chargeable assets in order to produce funds with which to make the advancement, a liability to capital gains tax in respect of that disposal may have arisen according to general principles.[41] If, however, the advancement is made in specie then, at the time when the trustees decide to make the

[37] ibid., at 333.
[38] [1964] Ch. 303 at 334, 335.
[39] See ante, p. 605.
[40] In Hardy v. Shaw [1975] 2 All E.R. 1052 there was an advancement, in the strict sense, in favour of persons who were middle-aged.
[41] See ante, p. 526.

advancement, they will be deemed to have disposed of the asset at its market value at that time and then immediately to have re-acquired it at that value as nominees for the beneficiary.[42] If the asset has risen in value since it was acquired, the same capital gains tax will be payable as if the asset had actually been sold for that value. However, provided that the beneficiary is resident in the United Kingdom, the trustees and the beneficiary can elect that "hold-over" relief shall apply if the assets settled comprise business property[43] or if the creation of the trust involves a chargeable transfer for the purposes of inheritance tax.[44]

With regard to inheritance tax, if the advancement is to a beneficiary who immediately before the advancement had an interest in possession, there will be no liability to inheritance tax by virtue of the advancement.[45] In every other case there will be a liability,[46] although in the case of small advancements, this liability may be reduced by the use of the annual exemption[47] of the beneficiary who has the interest in possession.

III. ADVANCEMENTS INTO SETTLEMENT

1. *Generally*

Originally, an advancement necessarily consisted of an outright payment of money or the transfer of an asset to a beneficiary but during this century[48] it has become established that a power of advancement can, in principle, be exercised so that the money or property is not transferred outright but becomes held on new trusts for the benefit of the beneficiary in question.[49]

This is usually done in one of three ways. First, if the beneficiary is *sui juris*, the trustees might make an outright payment to him, thereby putting him in the position of creating a new settlement.[50] Secondly, the trustees might exercise a power given to them in the trust instrument by declaring that thenceforth they will hold a part of trust fund on separate trusts for the benefit of one or more of the beneficiaries.[51] Or, thirdly, a new settlement might be created, either by the trustees or by some other person, usually with a nominal sum of money, so that a convenient "vehicle" can be

---

[42] Taxation of Chargeable Gains Act 1992, s.71(1).

[43] *ibid.*, s.165.

[44] See *ante*, p. 530.

[45] Finance Act 1975, Sched. 5, para. 4(3).

[46] *ibid.*, para.4(2).

[47] For 1998–99, this is £3,000. There will be no tax payable if the taxpayer has not used his seven year nil rate band.

[48] Following certain decisions at the end of the last century.

[49] The principle has long been established. See *Re Halstead's Will Trusts* [1937] 2 All E.R. 570; *Re Moxon's Will Trusts* [1958] 1 W.L.R. 165; *Re Ropner's Settlement Trusts* [1956] 1 W.L.R. 902; *Re Wills' Will Trusts* [1959] Ch. 1; *Re Abraham's Will Trusts* [1969] 1 Ch. 463; *Re Hastings-Bass (dec'd.)* [1975] Ch. 25; *Pilkington v. I.R.C.* [1964] A.C. 612.

[50] In *Roper-Curzon v. Roper-Curzon* (1871) L.R. 11 Eq. 452, where it was necessary for the court to give its sanction to an advancement; it refused to give that sanction unless the beneficiary resettled the amount to be advanced.

[51] See, *e.g. Hoare Trustees v. Gardner* [1978] 1 All E.R. 791.

established. The trustees of the existing settlement then transfer the amount to be advanced to the trustees of the new settlement as an addition to the funds of that settlement to be held on the trusts declared by it.[52]

It follows that the trustees of the original settlement may, but not necessarily will, be the trustees of the advanced fund.

Whichever method is used, whether by way of resettlement, appointment, or transfer to a new settlement, this Chapter clearly needs to consider some aspects of the passing of funds from an existing settlement into a new settlement. A number of questions arise which will be considered in turn.

2. Is the Proposed Advance for the Benefit of the Beneficiary?

Any advancement, whether outright or into settlement, must be for the benefit of the beneficiary to be advanced. The following principles are established by the authorities.

In general, "benefit" means direct financial benefit, so that it is unlikely that there will have been a valid exercise of the power of advancement if the quantum of the beneficiary's interest is reduced. This point is most likely to arise where the trustees wish to make a settled advance on protective trusts for the beneficiary in question. In Re Morris[53] Jenkins L.J. laid down the principle that a "power of advancement is a purely ancillary power, enabling the trustee to anticipate by means of an advance under it the date of actual enjoyment by a beneficiary and it can only affect the destination of the fund indirectly in the event of the person advanced failing to attain a vested interest". He therefore held that advancement into settlement on protective trusts was not valid because it altered the beneficial interests. However,[54] some advancements on protective trusts can nevertheless be held to be for the direct financial benefit of the beneficiary, provided that they comply with the remaining requirements.

An advancement on settlement will be for the benefit of the beneficiary if a fiscal liability which would otherwise arise in respect of the funds held for the beneficiary is mitigated.[55] The position was summarised by Viscount Radcliffe in Pilkington v. I.R.C.[56] when he said[57] that "if the advantage of preserving the funds of a beneficiary from the incidence of [tax][58] is not an advantage personal to that beneficiary, I do not see what is". If, in order to effect the fiscal mitigation, it is necessary for the beneficiary not to take any, or any direct, financial interest in the advanced fund, the advancement may still be proper. Re Clore's Settlement Trusts,[59] which has been mentioned,[60] concerned a transfer of funds into a charitable settlement under which the beneficiary took no beneficial interest.[61]

---

[52] See, e.g. Hart v. Briscoe [1978] 1 All E.R. 791; Pilkington v. I.R.C. [1964] A.C. 612.
[53] [1951] 2 All E.R. 528.
[54] See post, infra.
[55] Re Ropner's Settlement Trusts [1956] 3 All E.R. 332; Re Meux [1958] Ch. 154; Re Wills' Will Trusts [1959] Ch. 1.
[56] [1964] A.C. 612.
[57] ibid. at 640.
[58] The tax in question was estate duty.
[59] [1966] 1 W.L.R. 955.
[60] See ante, p. 621.
[61] The decision may depend on its particular facts.

In determining whether an advancement into settlement is for the benefit of a beneficiary, all the terms of the instrument which constitutes the new settlement, not merely those under which the trustees are in practice likely to act, must be considered. In *Re Hunter's Will Trusts*,[62] a testator settled property upon trust for his sister for life, with remainder to her children with "such provision for their respective advancement maintenance and education" as the sister should by will appoint; one of the sister's sons was financially unstable and in fact became bankrupt shortly after she made her will. In an attempt to enable her son to enjoy the benefit of part of the trust property, she purported to appoint that property upon protective trusts for him. Cross J. held the trust invalid, following the dictum of Jenkins L.J. in *Re Morris*[63] that protective trusts should not be regarded

"merely as a device to enable a forfeiting life-tenant to enjoy the income notwithstanding purported alienation and so forth or the event of his or her bankruptcy, and that the discretionary trust should be regarded merely as machinery to that end and not as really designed to confer any beneficial interest on the issue nominally included in it. The validity or otherwise of the discretionary trust declared in the event of forfeiture must, in my view, be determined by reference to what the trustees are empowered to do under such a trust, and not by reference to what they would in fact be likely to do, or be expected to do, under it."

A beneficiary may derive a benefit from knowing that financial provision is being made for his wife and children. So, in *Re Halsted's Will Trusts*,[64] Farwell J. held that trustees could in the exercise of a power of advancement for a beneficiary properly settle funds on trust for the beneficiary, his wife and his children. Nor is there any necessary connection between "benefit" and "need". Thus, an advancement of funds may be valid if the trustees consider that it is for the benefit of the beneficiary, irrespective of his needs.[65]

3. *The Benefit of the Other Beneficiaries under the Advancement*

Property will only be settled if at least one person other than the beneficiary receiving the advancement has some interest therein, either vested or contingent. The fact that one or more other persons will or might benefit does not in itself make an advancement into settlement defective. This is one of the several points which the House of Lords decided in *Pilkington v. I.R.C.*[66]

A testator set up a will trust under which the trustees were directed to hold the trust fund upon trust, broadly, for the benefit of the testator's

---

[62] [1963] Ch. 372.

[63] [1951] 2 All E.R. 528.

[64] [1937] 2 All E.R. 570.

[65] In *Re Pilkington's Will Trusts* [1961] Ch. 466 the Court of Appeal had held that there could only be a valid advancement into settlement where the benefit to be conferred was related to the real or personal needs of the beneficiary. This was rejected by the House of Lords in *Pilkington v. I.R.C.* [1964] A.C. 612.

[66] [1964] A.C. 612.

nephew Richard for life, with remainder to such of his children as he should appoint, or, in default of appointment, for all of his children in equal shares. Richard had three children, all born after the death of the testator, one of whom was his daughter Penelope. When Penelope was still very young, the trustees wished to advance funds into a new settlement for her benefit. Accordingly, her grandfather proposed the creation of a settlement under which the income would be accumulated or used for Penelope's main- tenance until she reached the age of 21. Penelope was to be entitled to income on attaining that age and to the capital on attaining the age of 30; if she died under the age of 30, other members of the family were to benefit. The trustees of the original settlement proposed to transfer one half of Penelope's share under that settlement to the trustees of the proposed new settlement. The House of Lords held that, in principle,[67] this would be within the trustees' power of advancement, notwithstanding the fact that other members of the family might benefit.

4. Can Dispositive Discretions be Conferred under the New Settlement?

In *Re Wills' Will Trusts*[68] Upjohn J. said[69] that "a settlement created in exercise of the power of advancement cannot in general delegate any pow- ers or discretions, at any rate in relation to beneficial interests, to any trustees or other persons, and in so far as the settlement purports to do so, it is *pro tanto* invalid". These remarks have given rise to the view that an advance into a discretionary settlement would be unauthorised; they have also given rise to the the view that, if there is an effective advancement into a settlement on protective trusts, the discretionary trusts which would normally arise on the termination of the principal beneficiary's life interest would also be ineffective. Both the dictum of Upjohn J. and the views to which it has given rise follow the *maxim delegatus non potest delegare*.

However, the better view seems to be that discretions can be conferred on the trustees of the new settlement. In the first place, in *Pilkington v. I.R.C.*[70] Viscount Radcliffe said[71]:

"I am unconvinced by the argument that the trustees would be improperly delegating their trust by allowing the money raised to pass over to new trustees under a settlement conferring new powers on the latter. In fact I think the whole issue of delegation is here beside the mark. The law is not that trustees cannot delegate: it is that trustees cannot delegate unless they have authority to do so. If the power of advancement which they possess is so read as to allow them to raise money for the purpose of having it settled[72] then they do have the necessary authority to let the money pass out of the old settlement into the new trusts. No question of delegation of their powers or trust arises."

---

[67] The actual appointment was void because it contravened the rule against perpetuities.
[68] [1959] Ch. 1.
[69] *ibid.* at 13.
[70] [1964] A.C. 612.
[71] *ibid.* at 639.
[72] Which was how the power was read by the House of Lords.

This seems to mean that, provided that the power in the original settlement is sufficiently wide, the advancement can properly be made into a new settlement which does confer dispositive powers on the trustees and that the statutory power, or an express power to the like effect, will be construed as being sufficiently wide.

Secondly, where there is an advancement into settlement, the principle of *delegatus non potest delegare* will rarely be observed in its entirety. It is clear that the new settlement may itself include powers of advancement.[73] While in concept a power of advancement may be a power merely to bring forward the date at which a beneficiary would otherwise enjoy the trust property,[74] it has already been seen[75] that the exercise of such a power may well alter the beneficial entitlement to the funds advanced.

Thirdly, if in appropriate circumstances[76] there can be a valid advancement into a settlement under which the beneficiary to be advanced takes no beneficial interest, it is absurd if there cannot be a valid advance into a settlement under which he is a discretionary beneficiary.[77]

While it is therefore thought that there is no fundamental objection to a new settlement conferring dispositive powers on its trustees, it is still necessary in any particular case to show that that is for the benefit of the beneficiary who is being advanced.

5. *What Perpetuity Period Applies to the New Settlement?*

Where the trustees of an existing settlement make an advance into a new settlement, for the purposes of the rules against perpetuities the trustees are treated as if they had exercised a special power of appointment. Accordingly, the interests limited by the new settlement, when read back into the original settlement, must comply with the perpetuity rule. It was on this ground that the House of Lords held that the proposed appointment in *Pilkington v. I.R.C.*[78] would have been void.

The Perpetuities and Accumulations Act 1964 will therefore only apply to the advancement if the original settlement itself was made after July 15, 1964[79]; thus the pre-existing rules must still even today govern many advancements. Where, however, the 1964 Act does apply, the interests under the new settlement will be treated as valid until, if at all, it becomes established that they will in fact vest outside the perpetuity period.[80]

If some of the interests purportedly created by the new settlement will not vest within the perpetuity period, the result of the advancement will depend on whether the effective provisions of the new settlement, when taken by

---

[73] *Re Mewburn* [1934] Ch. 112; *Re Morris* [1951] 2 All E.R. 528; *Re Hunter's Will Trusts* [1963] Ch. 372.

[74] *Re Morris* [1951] 2 All E.R. 528; see *ante*, p. 624.

[75] See *ante*, p. 617.

[76] As in *Re Clore's Settlement Trust* [1966] 1 W.L.R. 955; see *ante*, p. 621.

[77] Although the issues of benefit and delegation are separate, much greater tax mitigation may be achieved by using discretionary, rather than fixed, trusts.

[78] [1964] A.C. 612; see *ante*, p. 625.

[79] s.15(4) will apply to exclude the Act in the case of original settlements made before that date.

[80] s.3; see *ante*, p. 213.

themselves, will be for the benefit of the beneficiary to be advanced, and will not be totally different in effect from what the trustees intended. This is shown by the decision in *Re Hastings-Bass (deceased)*,[81] where trustees transferred from an existing settlement the sum of £50,000 to be held upon the trusts of a new settlement, intending that transfer to be an advancement for the primary benefit of a beneficiary, William. The trustees misunderstood the effect of the new settlement, under which William took a valid life interest but all of whose remaining provisions were void for perpetuity.

The first question was whether the statutory power of advancement could be exercised where its effect was to give the advanced beneficiary, in this case William, only an interest in income and no interest in capital. The court held that this was a sufficient "application" of the funds and that the appointment was not necessarily defective on that ground.

The second question was of more general application. Was the purported exercise of the power effective when the trustees did not fully appreciate the effects of the new settlement and so could not take into account all the relevant circumstances? The court held that, where trustees purport to exercise a power in good faith, then, even if the effect of that purported exercise is different from that intended by the trustees, the court would only interfere with the purported exercise in two circumstances. First, the court would interfere if the result actually achieved was not authorised by the trustees' power. Secondly, the court would interfere if it was clear that the trustees would not have acted as they did had they not taken into account considerations which they ought not to have taken into account or if they had not failed to take into account considerations which they ought to have taken into account. In this case, the effect of conferring upon William an effective life interest was to achieve a substantial saving of estate duty.[82] It was likely, therefore, that the trustees would have acted broadly as they did even if they had appreciated the true effect of the advancement; consequently, the court held that the exercise of their power was valid. If, however, the trustees would not have acted as they did had they appreciated the true effect of the advancement, their purported exercise of their power would have been void.[83]

6. *Fiscal Considerations*

Just as a liability to capital gains tax may arise in the case of an ordinary advancement,[84] so it may arise in the case of an advance into settlement. The capital gains tax legislation treats most settlements as if they are each separate legal persons. Thus, if an asset is transferred from one settlement to another settlement, that asset is deemed to have been disposed of by the trustees of the transferring settlement and to have been acquired by the trustees of the acquiring settlement. However, the capital gains tax legislation does not actually prescribe any rules for determining precisely what

---

[81] [1975] Ch. 25.
[82] The inheritance tax rules are different; no tax would be saved if the facts recurred at the present time.
[83] *Re Abraham's Will Trust* [1969] 1 Ch. 463.
[84] See *ante*, p. 622.

constitutes a separate settlement. Particular difficulties arise where the trustees of a settlement declare that they will themselves henceforth by way of advancement hold part of the trust fund on separate trusts for the benefit of one of the beneficiaries; when will that part of the trust fund become subject to a new settlement and when will it remain within the original settlement? In *Roome v. Edwards*[85] Lord Wilberforce said[86] "Since 'settlement' and 'trusts' are legal terms, which are also used by businessmen or laymen in a business or practical sense, I think that the question whether a particular set of facts amounts to a settlement should be approached by asking what a person, with a knowledge of the legal context of the word under established doctrine and applying this knowledge in a practical and commonsense manner to the facts under examination, would conclude."

If the resettlement occurs only as the result of the exercise by the trustees of their powers under the original settlement, it seems that the exercise of a special power of appointment will not amount to a resettlement so that there will be no consequential deemed disposal of the property in question[87]; on the other hand, while the exercise of a wider power, such as a power of advancement, will not necessarily amount to a resettlement, it will have this effect if the new settlement is complete in itself and is sufficiently separate to require no further reference back for any purpose to the original settlement.[88] If there is such a resettlement, the trustees of the original settlement are deemed to dispose of all the assets which become subject to the new settlement at their market value at the time and the assets are then reacquired at that value. However, if the acquiring settlement is resident in the United Kingdom, hold-over relief is available if the assets comprise business property[89] or if the creation of the new settlement involves a chargeable transfer for the purposes of inheritance tax.[90]

There may also be a liability to inheritance tax if there was an interest in possession under the original settlement and the same beneficiary does not have an immediate interest in possession under the new settlement.[91] There will not usually be a liability if there was no interest in possession either under the original or the new settlement[92] but in other cases there usually will be.

IV. OTHER APPLICATIONS OF CAPITAL

In some cases, the power of maintenance and advancement contained in the trust instrument, or the statutory powers, will not be sufficient for a beneficiary's needs. Where this is the case, there are four other possibilities: (i) maintenance out of capital; (ii) an application to the court under section 53

---

[85] [1981] 1 All E.R. 736.
[86] *ibid.* at 739.
[87] *Roome v. Edwards* [1981] 1 All E.R. 736; *Bond v. Pickford* [1983] S.T.C. 517.
[88] *Swires v. Renton* [1991] S.T.C. 490.
[89] Taxation of Chargeable Gains Act 1992, s.165.
[90] See *ante*, p. 530.
[91] Inheritance Tax Act 1984, ss.51, 52.
[92] *ibid.*, s.81; however, for tax purposes the property remains comprised in the first settlement.

of the Trustee Act 1925; (iii) an application to the court under its inherent jurisdiction; and (iv) an application to the court to vary the trust (this is considered in Chapter 23).

1. *Maintenance out of Capital*

Although, in principle, income is to be used for the maintenance of a beneficiary,[93] it is just about possible that the trustees can use capital for this purpose.

Section 31 of the Trustee Act 1925 clearly envisages that only income will be used for maintenance and in a note to the old case of *Barlow v. Grant*[94] it was said that "the court will not permit executors and trustees to break in upon the capital of infants' legacies without the sanction of the court, and the court itself, though it will break in upon the capital for the purpose of advancement, will rarely do so for maintenance". But, however rarely a court may exercise its power to use capital for an infant's maintenance, it undoubtedly does have such a power. Lord Alvanley L.C. said in *Lee v. Brown*[95] that "[t]he principle is now established that if an executor does without application what the court would have approved, he shall not be called to account, and forced to undo that merely because it was done without application". The precise extent of this dictum—the case actually concerned an advancement—is not entirely clear but it is just about possible that a trustee who had maintained out of capital would not be called upon to make good the capital if the court would itself have ordered maintenance out of capital.

However, quite apart from the doubtful legality of such a course of conduct, there would today be fiscal disadvantages in following it; in respect of every £1 taken out of capital for this purpose, the trustees would today have to deduct income tax at the basic rate and pay it over to the Revenue.[96] In contrast, no income tax is payable where an advancement of capital is made; thus, by making an advancement, the same result as a purported maintenance out of capital can be achieved more advantageously.

2. *Section 53 of the Trustee Act 1925*

This section provides that, where an infant is beneficially entitled to any property, the court may, "with a view to the application of the capital or income thereof for the maintenance, education, or benefit of the infant", make an order appointing a person to convey the infant's interest on his behalf. This section is chiefly used where the infant's interest is small and produces very little income and where, if the interest were sold, the proceeds could be used for the infant's maintenance or benefit.[97] It was however pointed out in *Re Meux*[98] that this section does not give the court power to

---

[93] See *ante*, p. 595.
[94] (1684) 1 Vern. 255.
[95] (1798) 4 Ves. 362.
[96] See *ante*, p. 522.
[97] *Ex parte Green* (1820) 1 Jac. & W. 253; *Ex parte Chambers* (1829) 1 Russ. & M. 577; *Ex parte Swift* (1828) 1 Russ. & M. 575.
[98] [1958] Ch. 154.

dispose of the infant's interest whenever it is merely for the infant's benefit; there must be "a view to the application" of the capital or income for the maintenance, education or benefit of the infant. It therefore seems that it must be intended to apply the capital or income in some way for the benefit of the infant. In *Re Heyworth's Contingent Reversionary Interest*[99] the court refused to give its consent under section 53 to a proposal merely to sell the infant's interest and hand over a cash sum without there being any clear idea as to what was to happen to that money thereafter. On the other hand, where what is proposed is to resettle the money and the transaction as a whole is for the infant's benefit, the court has held that the fact that there was to be a resettlement was a sufficient "application" to come within this section.[1]

An example of the use of this power can be seen in *Re Bristol's Settled Estates*.[2] There were two tenants in fee tail of settled land, the Marquess of Bath and his infant son, Lord Jermyn. The estate was a large one and in order to save estate duty it was, in essence, proposed that the existing settlement should be terminated, part of the property paid absolutely to the Marquess of Bath, and the remaining part resettled. Provided the Marquess lived for a period of five years (and an insurance policy was to be taken out to cover the possibility of him failing to do so), both he and the ultimate beneficiaries would gain by the arrangement, the only loser being the Inland Revenue. Before the scheme could be put into operation, it was necessary for the estates in fee tail to be "barred" by being converted into estates in fee simple. The Marquess of Bath was entitled to carry out this process in respect of his own estate in fee tail and, had Lord Jermyn not been a minor, he could have done the same with the consent of his father, who was (in the original sense of the expression) the protector of the settlement.[3] The court made an order under section 53 appointing a named person to execute with the consent of the Marquess of Bath an assurance on behalf of Lord Jermyn "barring" his estate in fee tail; that way the capital and income could, under the proposed scheme, be appointed for his benefit.[4]

Schemes for raising money for the education of an infant, or to provide him with a house, or to purchase a share in a partnership for him clearly also fall within the terms of section 53 of the Trustee Act 1925.[5]

3. *The Inherent Jurisdiction of the Court*

In limited circumstances the court has an inherent jurisdiction (quite apart from the Variation of Trusts Act 1958)[6] to modify the terms of the trust. One of the occasions in which it will do so is where a settlor or testator has made some provision for a family but has postponed the enjoyment, for example, by directing accumulation of the income for a set period. Where this has been done, the trustees cannot themselves use the income to maintain an

---

[99] [1956] Ch. 364.
[1] *Re Meux* [1958] Ch. 154.
[2] [1965] 1 W.L.R. 469.
[3] For the original and the modern sense of this expression, see *ante*, pp. 165, 166, n. 15.
[4] See also *Re Lansdowne's Will Trusts* [1967] Ch. 603.
[5] *Re Baron Vestey's Settlement* [1951] Ch. 209.
[6] See *post*, p. 656, as to the circumstances in which the court may vary beneficial interests in this and other cases.

infant but the court will assume from the fact that the settlor has made
provision for the family that he did not intend to leave the children inadequately provided for. The court has, therefore, in some cases directed that
the income (or some part of it) is not to be accumulated but is instead to be
used for the maintenance of the infant.[7]

V. APPROPRIATION

Appropriation occurs when trustees effectively set aside part of the trust
property and earmark it for a specific purpose. For the purposes of trust law
generally, the effect of appropriation is that beneficiaries who have an
interest in the appropriated fund have no rights in respect of the non-
appropriated property, and the beneficiaries of the non-appropriated property have no rights in respect of the appropriated fund. The position is,
generally speaking, as follows:

  (i) trustees do not have any general power to appropriate.[8]

 (ii) the trust instrument may direct appropriation or confer on the
      trustees a power to appropriate.

(iii) if the trust instrument directs that different property to be held on
      different trusts, that will be treated as an implied direction to
      appropriate.[9] If, therefore, the trust instrument directs one quarter
      of the trust property to be held on trust for Pinky for life, with
      remainder to her issue, and the other three quarters to be held on
      trust for Perky for life with remainder to her issue, then separate
      funds should be appropriated.

 (iv) it seems that, if property is held on express trust for sale, the
      trustees have an implied power to appropriate unless there is a
      direction to the contrary in the trust instrument[10].

  (v) a mere power to appropriate, whether express or implied, will
      require the consent of any adult beneficiaries affected, although not
      of infant or unborn beneficiaries. However, the power may go
      beyond one merely to appropriate, in which case it will be a power
      to appropriate without any consent being required. In any event,
      consents are not required where the trust instrument directs
      appropriation.

 (vi) personal representatives are given a statutory power of appropria-
      tion,[11] but this does not apply to trustees.

---

[7] *Havelock v. Havelock* (1881) 17 Ch.D. 807; *Re Collins* (1886) 32 Ch.D. 229; *Revel v. Watkinson*
(1748) 1 Ves. Sen. 93; *Re Walker* [1901] 1 Ch. 879; *Greenwell v. Greenwell* (1800) 5 Ves. 194;
Cavendish v. Mercer (1776) 5 Ves. 195; *Errat v. Barlow* (1807) 14 Ves. 202.
[8] The Law Reform Committee (23rd Report, 1982) recommended that trustees should be given
a statutory power of appropriation.
[9] *Fraser v. Murdoch* (1881) 6 App. Cas. 855; *Re Walker* (1890) 62 L.T. 449; *Re Nicholson* [1939] 3 All
E.R. 832.
[10] *Re Nickels* [1898] 1 Ch. 630; *Re Brooks* (1897) 76 L.T. 771.
[11] By Administration of Estates Act 1925, s.41.

CHAPTER 21

THE POSITION OF A BENEFICIARY UNDER A TRUST

In general terms, as long as a trust is being properly administered and is continuing, a beneficiary has no right to interfere in its administration but has passively to wait to receive the benefit appropriate to him under the trust. If, however, the trust is not being properly administered, the beneficiary can take steps to compel its proper administration, and in any case may take certain action to preserve his position. Ultimately, however, the destiny of the trust may lie in his hands for, if various conditions are fulfilled, he can bring the trust to an end even if this appears contrary to the wording of the trust instrument.

I. The Control of Trustees' Discretions

Two fundamental principles govern the control of trustees by beneficiaries. First, so long as the trust continues, decisions which have to be made in the administration of the trust are to be made by the trustees alone. Secondly, all the beneficiaries under the trust, if *sui juris* and between them absolutely entitled, may bring the trust to an end.[1]

The court is jealous to preserve the trustees' powers, largely because the main function of trustees is to control the trust as a whole, and the right to exercise all the decisions necessary goes to the root of trusteeship. Thus, even where it has power to do so under the Variation of Trusts Act 1958, the court will not approve an arrangement which could override the discretionary powers which the trustees intend to exercise.[2] The leading case on the subject is *Re Brockbank*,[3] although the actual decision in that case has been abrogated by statute. It was seen in an earlier Chapter[4] that, where no person is named in a trust instrument as having a power to appoint new trustees, then the existing trustee or trustees are given that power by section 36 of the Trustee Act 1925. In *Re Brockbank*, the beneficiaries, all *sui juris* and between them absolutely entitled to the whole of the beneficial interest under the trust, wished to appoint a person as a new trustee, against the wishes of the existing trustee. It was held that the appointment of new trustees was a power given to the existing trustees and this power could not be exercised by the beneficiaries. This principle survives in relation to

---

[1] See *post*, p. 637.
[2] *Re Steed's Will Trusts* [1960] Ch. 407, also discussed *post*, p. 666.
[3] [1948] Ch. 206.
[4] See *ante*, p. 462.

powers in general; however, where section 19 of the Trusts of Land and Appointment of Trustees Act 1996 applies to the trust in question (which it will do unless it has been excluded by the settlor), beneficiaries who are *sui juris* and between them absolutely entitled to the whole of the beneficial interest under the trust are now entitled to require the trustees to retire and appoint new trustees.

It has also been suggested,[5] probably correctly, that while the beneficiaries cannot generally speaking cut down the trustees' powers, they can add to them. It is important to stress that this right, if it exists, is only to add to the trustees' powers, not to their duties; their discretion is therefore preserved intact but is enlarged.

The main areas in which beneficiaries are likely to seek to control the trustees' discretions are with regard to investments and in respect of the exercise of their discretions under discretionary trusts. In both respects the trustees' position is essentially the same. They must take note of any representations made to them, for these representations may properly affect the exercise of their discretion. Thus, if one of the beneficiaries passes to the trustees confidential information that shares in a particular company are likely to improve rapidly, the trustees must give full consideration to that information in reaching their decision as to whether or not to buy. But the decision must be theirs, for they are the persons who can best judge the interests of all the beneficiaries and it will be them, not the beneficiary in question, who will be ultimately answerable for the decision reached.

To the general rule that the trustees should listen, but must alone make the decisions, there are certain exceptions.

  (i) The trustees' discretions may be limited by contract; thus, where a person acts as nominee for another, the terms of the arrangement between them may require the trustee-nominee to act in accordance with the directions of the beneficiary.
 (ii) The trustees' discretions may be limited by the terms of the trust instrument itself; the usual form of this limitation is to require the consent of a beneficiary or other person to the sale of a particular asset but there is no reason in principle why their discretions should not be restricted in some other way.
(iii) There is a further exception of somewhat uncertain extent, which arises from the decision of the Court of Appeal in *Butt v. Kelson*.[6] The trustees of a trust held a large proportion of the shares in a private limited company, of which they were also directors by virtue of their trust shareholding. The question arose how far the beneficiaries could control the votes of the trustees both as directors and as shareholders. It was held that the trustees' votes as directors could not be controlled by the beneficiaries, while their votes as shareholders could be controlled. The apparent inconsistency of this curious result may be explained by the fact that under company law directors have duties to all the shareholders,

---

[5] Underhill & Hayton: *Law of Trusts and Trustees* (15th ed., 1995), p. 665.
[6] [1952] Ch. 197.

not only to those shareholders, if any, whom they represent; it would therefore have been inconsistent with this obligation if the trustees had been compelled to vote as directors solely in accordance with the wishes of the beneficiaries. On the other hand, their votes as shareholders were not subject to this conflict of duty. That does not alter the fact that at first sight it seems that the manner in which the voting power was to be exercised should have been a matter for the trustees' discretion, exercisable by them free from any interference by the beneficiaries. *Butt v. Kelson* was on this ground criticised by Upjohn J. in *Re Whichelow*[7] as being inconsistent with the principle laid down in *Re Brockbank*. It is, however, possible to regard a right to vote in a company as a property right and for special considerations to apply to such votes. Nevertheless, *Butt v. Kelson* is probably incorrect in so far as it allows beneficiaries to control the votes of trustee-shareholders and should not be extended.

II. THE RIGHT TO COMPEL DUE ADMINISTRATION

Whether or not a beneficiary suspects that there has been any improper conduct on the part of the trustees, he may nevertheless insist that the accounts of the trust are audited by any solicitor or accountant who is acceptable to the trustees. If agreement cannot be reached as to the identity of the auditor, the audit is carried out by the Public Trustee. Unless special circumstances exist, the audit cannot be carried out more than once in every three years; a beneficiary who does require more frequent audits will therefore be ordered personally to pay the costs.[8] Although this is not particularly relevant for present purposes, the position is exactly the same where the trustee requires an audit to be carried out.

Where the beneficiary thinks that the trust is not being properly administered, where there is some point of doubt relating to the administration of the trust, and in certain other circumstances, he may make an application to the court.[9] There are two types of application: first, an application by way of summons for the determination of a specific question or questions; and, secondly, an action for the general administration of the trust. It is desirable that the former method should used whenever possible, because it is cheaper, quicker and simpler than the latter.

The following are examples of the circumstances in which it may be appropriate to apply to the court by way of summons.

(i) The court may be asked to approve a specific transaction for which permission is not given by the general law or by the trust instrument but which is thought to be in the interests of the beneficiaries

---

[7] [1954] 1 W.L.R. 5.
[8] Trustee Act 1925, s.22(4); Public Trustee Act 1906, s.13(5). The Law Reform Committee (23rd Report, 1982) recommended that s.13 of the 1906 Act should be repealed.
[9] For the comparable circumstances in which the trustee might wish to make an application to the court, see *ante*, p. 501.

as a whole.[10] In most cases, of course, this type of application will be made by the trustees.[11]

(ii) The court may be asked to direct the trustees to do a particular act which they ought to do or to refrain from doing a particular act which they ought not to do. The act referred to must be one which the trustees are under a definite obligation to do or not to do; it is not appropriate for a beneficiary to question by this means an act in respect of which the trustees have a discretion.[12]

(iii) The court may be asked to direct the payment of money in the hands of the trustees into court.[13]

(iv) The court may be asked to construe the provisions of the trust instrument or to ascertain the class(es) of beneficiaries.

(v) The court may be asked to determine any other specific question which arises in the course of the administration of a trust.

It is not generally appropriate to apply to the court by way of summons where the subject-matter of the proposed application will involve third parties or in any action against trustees for breach of trust where the facts are in dispute.

It will be seen that almost all the specific questions which arise in the administration of a trust can be dealt with by way of summons in this manner. An action for the general administration of a trust, that is an action where the court itself is to become responsible for the whole administration of the trust, will accordingly usually only be necessary where there have been constant disputes between the trustees, where the circumstances of the trust give rise to recurring difficulties which would require frequent single applications to the court, and where clear prima facie doubts exist as to the bona fides of the trustees.

III. THE RIGHT TO ENFORCE CLAIMS

As part of his right to compel the due administration of the trust, a beneficiary can apply to the court if the trustees fail to take any action necessary to preserve the trust property.[14] A cause of action against a third party can itself be an item of trust property. The court may direct the trustees to enforce that claim or it may allow the beneficiary to sue directly for the benefit of the trust, where necessary using the name of the trustees.[15] Alternatively, a beneficiary can sue the trustees, making those who are alleged to be under obligations to the trust co-defendants.

---

[10] See *Boardman v. Phipps* [1967] 2 A.C. 46 (which was, at least in the opinion of the court, an example of the circumstances where an application should have been made); see *ante*, p. 501.

[11] See *ante*, p. 501.

[12] *Syffolk v. Lawrence* (1884) 32 W.R. 899.

[13] As to the circumstances in which money is payable into court, see Trustee Act. 1925, s.63.

[14] *Fletcher v. Fletcher* (1844) 4 Hare 67.

[15] As in *Foley v. Burnell* (1783) 1 Bro. C.C. 274, a case of trespass to trust land.

In *Wills v. Cooke*[16] the trust property included a farm which was subject to a tenancy. The trustees had retained solicitors to advise them with regard to the administration of the trust but, it was alleged, the solicitors had failed to advise the trustees to take action to increase the rent in accordance with the Agricultural Holdings Act 1948. One of the beneficiaries sued the solicitors directly, claiming that the trustees had a right of action against them and that that right was an item of trust property. On an interlocutory application, Slade J. held that that right might be an item of trust property and that the statement of claim should not be struck out. He also said, however, that the right would not have been an item of trust property if the trustees had entered into the contract with the solicitors solely for their own protection and benefit.

IV. THE RIGHT TO TERMINATE A TRUST

If there is only one beneficiary under a trust who is *sui juris*, or if there are two or more beneficiaries and they are all *sui juris* and they are all in agreement, he or they can bring the trust to an end irrespective of the wishes of the trustees or of the creator of the trust. This is what is known as the Rule in *Saunders v. Vautier*[17] and has two underlying bases. First, equity regards the role of the trustees as primarily that of holding the balance between various beneficiaries with conflicting interests; where all the beneficiaries are of the same mind, the basic reason for the trustees' existence has therefore disappeared. On the other hand, if the beneficiaries still want the trust to continue, it has already been seen that they cannot generally speaking control the trustees' discretions; either the trust must be terminated or the trustees must be allowed to carry on with their task. Secondly, a voluntary trust is in equity the equivalent of a gift at common law[18] so that as a general principle, once a trust has been created, the settlor has no longer any control over it; after all, if he had made instead an outright gift of property to the beneficiaries, he would thereafter have had no control over what his donees subsequently did with that property. Thus, if all the beneficiaries are *sui juris* and between them entitled to the whole of the beneficial interest in the trust property, the settlor's provisions as expressed in the trust instrument will not prevent those beneficiaries from bringing the trust to an end.

In *Saunders v. Vautier* itself, a trustee held a sum of money upon trust to accumulate the income until a specified date, and then to pay it to a beneficiary. The beneficiary reached the age of 21, and so became *sui juris*, before the date specified for distribution. He successfully claimed that the capital and accumulated income to date should be paid over to him. If, however, the trust instrument had instead provided that the beneficiary did not obtain a vested interest unless and until he survived to the specified

---

[16] (1979) Law Soc.Gaz., July 11, 1979.
[17] (1841) Cr. & Ph. 240. See also *Josselyn v. Josselyn* (1837) 9 Sim. 63; *Gosling v. Gosling* (1859) Johns. 265; *Wharton v. Masterman* [1895] A.C. 186; *Re Johnston* [1894] 3 Ch. 204; *Re Smith* [1928] Ch. 915; *Re Lord Nunburnholme* [1911] 2 Ch. 510; *Berry v. Green* [1938] A.C. 575.
[18] *Re Bowden* [1936] Ch. 71.

date, then he would not have been able to invoke the rule without the concurrence of the person entitled in default of his attaining that age.[19]

If a beneficial interest under a trust is sold, the purchaser stands in the same position as the vendor and, if the vendor could have brought the trust to an end, the purchaser will be able to do so if he is *sui juris*. However, if the beneficial interest is question is merely mortgaged, the mortgagee cannot bring the trust to an end for so long as the beneficiary still has a right under the mortgage to have his beneficial interest redeemed upon payment of the amount secured.[20]

The rule also applies where beneficiaries are entitled by way of succession. So if property is held upon trust for Andrew for life, with remainder to Brian for life, with remainder to Charles, the three of them can bring the trust to an end if they are all alive and *sui juris* and they all join in. Whenever a trust is brought to an end in this way, the beneficiaries can compel the trustees to convey the property to whomsoever they direct[21] and, if the trustees refuse, they will personally have to pay the cost of the beneficiaries' application to the court for a direction to this effect.

Use may also be made of the Rule in *Saunders v. Vautier* to overcome the actual decision in *Re Brockbank*[22]; the beneficiaries can bring the trust to an end and compel the trustees to transfer the property to their own chosen trustees on the same trusts, although this potentially involves the payment of *ad valorem* stamp duty but at present only in the relatively unlikely case that consideration in money or money's worth is furnished.[23] However, as has already been seen,[24] use of the Rule in *Saunders v. Vautier* for this purpose will now only be necessary if the settlor has excluded section 19 of the Trusts of Land and Appointment of Trustees Act 1996.

More generally, it should, be noted that bringing a trust to an end may have other negative fiscal consequences since on the termination of a trust there will often be a liability both to capital gains tax and to inheritance tax.

If a trust is terminated and the trustees sell the investments comprising the trust fund, they will be liable to capital gains tax on any increase in value which has accrued while the investments have been subject to the trust. If they instead distribute the assets *in specie*, the beneficiaries will become absolutely entitled to the assets as against the trustees,[25] and, in principle, a liability to capital gains tax will again arise as if the trustees had disposed of the assets on the open market for their full value at the time when the beneficiaries became entitled.[26] However, if the beneficiaries are resident in the United Kingdom, they can claim holdover relief if the assets in question comprise business property[27] or if the vesting of the property in the beneficiaries involves a chargeable transfer for the purposes of inheritance tax.

---

[19] *Gosling v. Gosling* (1859) Johns. 265; *Re Lord Nunburnholme* [1912] 1 Ch. 489.
[20] This is the conclusion derived from *Re Bell* [1896] 1 Ch. 1.
[21] *Re Marshall* [1914] 1 Ch. 192; *Re Sandeman's Will Trusts* [1937] 1 All E.R. 368.
[22] [1948] Ch. 206; see *ante*, p. 633.
[23] See *ante*, p. 517.
[24] See *ante*, p. 633.
[25] This concept was considered *ante*, p. 526.
[26] Taxation of Chargeable Gains Act, s.71(1).
[27] *ibid.*, s.165.

Under this relief the beneficiaries are treated for capital gains[28] tax purposes as acquiring the assets at their base cost to the trustees. By claiming this relief, the liability for the tax is deferred until the beneficiaries actually dispose of the assets themselves.

The position with regard to inheritance tax is more complicated. Suppose that a fund of £100,000 is held upon trust for Elizabeth for life with remainder to Angela and it is agreed to bring the trust to an end by paying £40,000 to Elizabeth and £60,000 to Angela. It has already been seen[29] that, where a beneficiary has an interest in possession in settled property, he is treated for inheritance tax purposes as if he was beneficially entitled to the settled property itself.[30] Accordingly, immediately before the termination Elizabeth would be treated for inheritance tax purposes as being beneficially entitled to £100,000, whereas after the termination she would only be entitled to the actual sum of £40,000 paid to her. There would, therefore, be a potentially exempt transfer by Elizabeth of £60,000.[31] So far as Angela is concerned, she has given up a reversionary interest in a fund of £100,000 in order to obtain an immediate outright payment of £60,000. However, there will be no liability to inheritance tax on her because usually[32] no inheritance tax is payable where a person disposes of a reversionary interest.[33]

---

[28] See *ante*, p. 526.
[29] See *ante*, p. 530.
[30] Inheritance Tax Act 1984, s.49.
[31] No inheritance tax would be payable if Elizabeth survived for a further seven years. If she failed to do so, the tax payable would be calculated by reference to her lifetime transfers.
[32] This rule does not apply where the person disposing of the reversionary interest acquired it for value, or was himself the settlor: Inheritance Tax Act 1984, s.48(1).
[33] *ibid.*, ss.47, 48(1).

CHAPTER 22

TRUSTEES' REMUNERATION AND BENEFITS

THE fundamental rule is that the office of trustee is gratuitous, that is to say that its duties must be performed by the trustee without remuneration or profit. The development of this rule was due in part to the fact that trustees were often members of the family and persons of substance, who were prepared to act as trustees as part of the general obligations of kinship. In more recent years, however, it has come to be recognised that the management of money and assets is an activity which requires skill, aptitude, and often considerable technical support. Accordingly, it is now very common for trustees to be either professional advisers, such as solicitors and accountants, who act as part of their ordinary professional practice, or banks and similar trust companies. Such trustees are generally prepared to act only if given adequate recompense.

I. MODERN COMMERCIAL REMUNERATION TERMS

Throughout this Chapter, it will be helpful to keep in mind what types of remuneration a professional trustee or a commercial trust company may wish to obtain. The main items are: first, fees for acting as a trustee, including the actual day to day administration of the trust; secondly, fees for acting as a director where the trust property includes shares in a company and the trustees act as directors of that company; thirdly, commissions customarily paid by third parties in respect of business transacted on behalf of the trust (insurance companies and brokers both habitually pay commission to those who place business with them); and, fourthly, profits made by the trustee from services performed for the trust as its customer (a banker trustee will wish to retain for itself its ordinary commercial profit derived from acting as banker). The remainder of this Chapter considers the extent to which a trustee can achieve these objectives.

II. FEES: THE GENERAL RULE

As has already been seen, the general rule is that a trustee is not entitled to claim any salary or remuneration for carrying out his trusteeship[1]; this is the case even where the trustee in question devotes a considerable amount of

---

[1] *Robinson v. Pett* (1734) 3 P. Wms. 249; *Re Thorpe* [1891] 2 Ch. 360; *Re Barker* (1886) 34 Ch.D. 77.

time and trouble to managing a business belonging to the trust. In *Barrett v. Hartley*,[2] a trustee had managed a business for six years with such success that a large profit accrued to the beneficiaries; however, his subsequent claim for remuneration was unsuccessful on the grounds that his efforts were merely part of the duties imposed upon him as a result of his acceptance of the trusteeship. The stringency of the rule is illustrated by the facts of *Re Gates*,[3] in which it was held that, where a solicitor-trustee employed his own firm to act as solicitors to the trust, the firm was not entitled to charge for its services, despite the fact that the solicitor-trustee had agreed with his partner that he himself would receive no part of the fee. (Where, contrary to the general rule, a trustee-solicitor can charge because of the presence of a charging clause, the remuneration is not however regarded as mere bounty so the solicitor is entitled to treat it as earned income for fiscal purposes.[4])

The rule has always been harsh; it is now also illogical. It has already been seen in Chapter 15 that, even in the absence of any provision in the trust instrument, a trustee has wide powers under section 23 of the Trustee Act 1925 to appoint agents to carry out most of the work (although not actually to take the decisions) on his behalf and to pay them out of the trust funds for so doing. Nevertheless, if he instead does the work himself, as the settlor presumably intended at the time of his appointment, then in the absence of a charging clause he cannot be paid. The general rule denying remuneration was established in the eighteenth century, a time when agents could be employed only in very limited circumstances. It is arguable that both rules should have been changed at the same time; certainly the prohibition on the payment of trustees now requires revision. This is now the view of the Law Commission. It has already been seen[5] that in its recent Consultation Paper on Trustees' Powers and Duties[6] the Law Commission proposed extended powers of delegation. It is therefore entirely logical that it should also have proposed an implied statutory charging clause applicable in the absence of a direction to the contrary in the trust instrument in question[7]; this charging clause would permit any trustee or personal representative who is also engaged in a profession or business to charge and be paid out of the trust property for any business or act done, advice given, or time expended in connection with the trust, whether or not the matter was one which a non-professional trustee could have undertaken.[8] This proposal is most welcome and it is greatly to be hoped that it is enacted.

Whatever the position regarding remuneration, however, a trustee is always entitled to reimburse himself for actual payments which he has properly made in connection with his trusteeship; this extends to the costs

---

[2] [1866] L.R. 2 Eq. 789.
[3] [1933] Ch. 913, followed in *Re Hill* [1934] Ch. 623 and *Re French Protestant Hospital* [1951] Ch. 567.
[4] *Dale v. I.R.C.* [1954] A.C. 11.
[5] See *ante*, p. 515.
[6] Published in June 1997.
[7] Consultation Paper on Trustees' Powers and Duties (June 1997), para. 10.26. The implied statutory charging clause will be excluded where some other benefit or remuneration is provided by the trust instrument; this may cause difficulties where fixed remuneration provided is totally inadequate.
[8] *ibid.*, para. 10.27.

of taking or defending proceedings where he has acted reasonably in so doing.[9] This right to reimbursement is contractual.[10]

III. Fees: Exceptions to the General Rule

There are a number of exceptions[11] to the general rule denying any remuneration.

1. *Charging Clauses in the Trust Instrument*

(A) The Nature and Effect of Charging Clauses
The creator of any trust can authorise the trustees to be paid for their services and it is in practice obviously very common for this to be done where a professional person is appointed as trustee. Provisions to this effect are at present construed strictly against the trustee, although the Law Commission has understandably proposed that this should cease to be the case if its proposal for an implied statutory charging clause is enacted.[12] However, at least for the moment, a very wide charging clause is necessary if a solicitor-trustee is to be entitled to charge for work done by him in the administration of a trust which could have been done by someone who is not a solicitor.[13] Accordingly, charging clauses are usually expressed in something like the following form:

"Any trustee for the time being hereof being a solicitor accountant or other person engaged in any profession shall be entitled to charge and be paid all usual professional or other charges for business transacted, time expended and acts done by him or any partner of his in connection with the trusts hereof including business and acts which a trustee not being engaged in a profession or business could have done personally."

Provided that the charging clause is sufficiently wide, a trustee is entitled to engage a company which he controls to carry out on behalf of the trust and to pay that company for so doing. In *Re Orwell's Will Trusts*,[14] George Orwell's will contained a clause authorising the trustee[15] of a trust created thereby to charge for services performed by him or by his company.[16] Vinelott J. held that the company could be paid and that the trustee need not

---

[9] Where the trustee acts in a manner hostile to the beneficiaries, no costs will be recoverable; see *Holding and Management v. Property Holding and Investment Trust* [1989] 1 W.L.R. 1313.

[10] *Re Spurling's Will Trusts* [1966] 1 W.L.R. 920.

[11] In *Tito v. Waddell* (No.2) [1977] Ch. 106: see *ante*, p. 17, there may be thought to have been a clear conflict of interest but the type of "trust" under consideration in that case is outside the scope of this work.

[12] Consultation Paper on Trustees' Powers and Duties (June 1997), para. 10.32.

[13] *Harbin v. Darby* (1860) 28 Beav. 325; *Re Chapple* (1884) 27 Ch.D. 584.

[14] [1982] 1 W.L.R. 1337.

[15] The case concerned the literary executor of the will who, for the purposes of remuneration, was held to be in the same position as a trustee.

[16] The clause authorised the trustee to charge for work done by him "or his firm". Although the expression "firm" generally denotes an unincorporated partnership, the court held that for the purposes of this clause the expression extended to a private company.

account to the trust for the remuneration which he himself received from the company.[17]

Under this form of charging clause, the trustee cannot charge exactly what he likes but only what is reasonable. Where he is a solicitor, the beneficiaries can insist on having his charges taxed, that is assessed by an officer of the court. A solicitor will normally charge by the hour. However, professionals other than solicitors generally charge on the basis of the value of the assets being administered or dealt with; the *ad valorem* fees charged by the Public Trustee are set out below.[18] Provided that such fees are the normal charges of the professional in question, they will be within the type of charging clause set out above. However, whether or not a trustee is a solicitor, if he takes from the trust fund an amount in excess of what the beneficiaries consider is reasonable, they may bring an action against him for breach of trust,[19] although this is obviously more difficult where his charges are on *ad valorem* basis.

However, the remuneration payable need not actually be the trustee's normal professional charges (although it will quite rightly have to be under the Law Commission's proposed implied statutory charging clause). It may be expressed to be a fixed amount (the position where trustees who have agreed a fixed level of remuneration subsequently wish to increase it is considered below[20]). Less commonly, it may be expressed to be the income from some proportion or part of the estate[21] or even part of the capital by virtue of the exercise of a power of appointment.[22] Since this is what the trust instrument has provided, there seems no reason why the beneficiaries should be able to object to this, provided of course that the trustee actually fulfils his functions as such.

(B) The Risks of Charging Clauses

Charging clauses in an *inter vivos trust* are normally effective; the only possible risk for a professional trustee is the relatively unlikely possibility of the trust being set aside for one of the reasons discussed in Chapter 7, in which case there will of course be no trust property out of which his fees can be paid. This risk is very much more substantial in relation to charging clauses in a will because of the possibility of the will being void or the estate having insufficient funds to pay the remuneration.

If the will turns out to be void, the charging clause will obviously be void as well; a professional executor who has begun to administer the estate under the impression that he is to receive his normal fees will not be able to charge and will have to return any fees which he has already been paid. Thus in *Gray v. Richards Butler*,[23] what was thought to be the testatrix's last will nominated as executor one of the partners in the defendant firm of solicitors. Pursuant to a charging clause he paid his firm more than £25,000 for work done in the administration of the estate. When the will was

---

[17] Compare *Re Gee* [1948] 1 All E.R. 498; see *post*, p. 652.
[18] See *post*, p. 644.
[19] *Re Wells* [1962] 1 W.L.R. 784.
[20] See *post*, p. 646.
[21] *Public Trustee v. I.R.C.* [1960] A.C. 398.
[22] *Re Beatty's Will Trusts* [1990] 1 W.L.R. 1503.
[23] (1996), The Times, July 23, 1996.

subsequently held to be void because the two witnesses had not both witnessed it at the same time, the plaintiff, who had been nominated as executor under the testatrix's previous will, successfully claimed that the defendant had to repay this sum to the estate.

Further, even when the will is valid, a charging clause ranks only as a pecuniary legacy; consequently, if the estate in question is insolvent or is exhausted by specific gifts, there will be no assets available out of which the remuneration can be paid, while if the estate is insufficient to pay all the pecuniary legacies the fees payable will abate in the same proportions as those legacies. These rather startling propositions emerge from the decision of the Court of Appeal in *Re White*[24] and of course mean that a professional executor who has administered the estate under the impression that he is to receive his normal fees may find himself deprived of some or all of them because the estate turns out to be subject to some unexpected claim which has priority over his. The existence of this trap for professional trustees has been consistently criticised and the Law Commission has recently[25] adopted a proposal originally made by the Law Reform Committee in 1982[26] that a charging clause should no longer be regarded as either a conditional gift or a legacy but as remuneration and as such an expense of administering the estate or trust in question.[27] The enactment of this proposal would also be most welcome.

(C)   The Ad Valorem Fees Charged by the Public Trustee

As an illustration of fees charged on an *ad valorem* basis, the following fees are what the Public Trustee is at present charging.[28]

(1)   Executorship fee

When the Public Trustee act as an executor or administrator under a will or intestacy, an Executorship fee is charged calculated on the gross capital value of the estate and covers all work done during the executorship or administration period except for the same Activity Fees as those mentioned in (2)(c) below.

On the first £50,000	5.5 per cent
On the excess over £50,000 up to £75,000	4.0 per cent
On the excess over £75,000 up to £100,000	2.0 per cent
On the excess over £100,000	1 per cent
Minimum fee £550	

---

[24] [1898] 2 Ch. 217.
[25] In its Consultation Paper on Trustees' Powers and Duties (June 1997).
[26] In its 23rd Report, (1982) Cmnd. 8733.
[27] Consultation Paper on Trustees' Powers and Duties (June 1997), para. 10.30.
[28] As at April 1, 1997. The basic legislation is the Public Trustee (Fees) Act 1957; Public Trustee (Fees) Orders are made from time to time thereunder, the current one being the Public Trustee (Fees) Order 1985 (S.I. 1985 No. 373), since amended by a series of Public Trustee (Fees) (Amendment) Orders, at present those of 1992 (S.I. 1992 No. 724), 1993 (S.I. 1993 No. 619) and 1994 (S.I. 1994 No. 714).

(2)   Trusts

(a)   **Acceptance fee.** This is due when the Public Trustee is appointed as
original trustee of a new settlement or as trustee of an existing will or
settlement. The fee is one half of the rate shown in the table above with the
same minimum fee of £550.

However, when the Public Trustee is appointed under a declaration of
trust to carry out investment portfolio management or by the Supreme
Court under a Standard Trusts Order or as trustee of an infant's legacy, the
fee is lower: 1.25 per cent on the first £50,000 and 0.5 per cent on any excess
over £50,000, the minimum fee being £175.

(b)   **Administration fee.** This is due annually on April 1 each year on the
net capital value of funds under administration: the valuation date is whichever of the following dates most recently precedes the date on which the fee
is payable: July 1, 1987, in the case of any estate or trust in which the Public
Trustee was acting on that day; September 30, 1991, in the case of any estate
or trust in which the Public Trustee was acting on that day; and, in any other
case, the date of the acceptance of the trust by the Public Trustee or such
convenient date as he may select.

On the first £30,000	1.65 per cent
On the excess over £30,000 up to £150,000	1.38 per cent
On the excess over £150,000 up to £375,000	0.825 per cent
On the excess over £375,000 up to £2,500,000	0.55 per cent
On any excess over £2,500,000	0.22 per cent
Minimum fee £30	

(c)   **Activity fees.** An income collection fee is charged of 3.5 per cent on
the gross income actually received by the Public Trustee. There is no fee on
income paid direct from source to a beneficiary.

A reasonable additional fee may be charged according to the work
involved for various matters including: dealing with a business, dealing
with assets outside the United Kingdom, dealing with freehold or leasehold
property or a mortgage, and for duties of an unusual, complex or exacting
nature. When acting as a tax agent, the charges are commensurate with the
work involved.

(d)   **Withdrawal fee.** This is due on the distribution or withdrawal of
trust property or on the retirement from the trusteeship of the Public Trustee
at a percentage rate 6.5 times the effective rate of the administration fee due
on April 1 prior to the distribution, withdrawal or retirement with a maximum percentage rate of 7.5 per cent. No withdrawal fee is charged where
the Public Trustee retires and the total value of the trust does not exceed
£10,000.

When the Public Trustee is appointed under a declaration of trust to carry
out investment portfolio management or by the Supreme Court under a
Standard Trusts Order or as trustee of an infant's legacy, there is no maximum percentage rate but no withdrawal fee is charged where funds are

withdrawn for transfer to an executorship or to a new trust accepted by the
Public Trustee.

2. *Authorisation from the Court*

The second exception to the general rule is that the court may, under its
inherent jurisdiction, first, authorise a trustee to be remunerated where there
is no charging clause[29]; secondly, authorise a trustee to retain remuneration
which he has already received[30]; and,thirdly, authorise a trustee to charge in
excess of what he agreed to receive when accepting appointment.[31]

In some of the older cases, the court was not averse to allowing the trustee
reasonable remuneration. In *Brown v. Litton*,[32] the captain of a merchant ship
took with him on a voyage a sum of money to use in trade. During the
voyage he died and his mate, on assuming command of the vessel, took
possession of the money and with it made considerable profits in trade. The
mate was ordered to account for his profits but Harcourt L.K. nevertheless
held him entitled to a fair remuneration, which was to be fixed by the court,
for his trouble.

More recently, the court has instead adopted the policy of only authorising the receipt of remuneration by a trustee where his services have been of
exceptional benefit to the trust.[33] Thus remuneration or increased remuneration in respect of future work will only be ordered if the court considers that,
having regard to the nature of the trust, the experience and skill of a
particular trustee is of great importance for the interests of the beneficiaries,
while such orders will only be made in respect of work already done if the
work in question was wholly outside what could have been anticipated at
the time of appointment. In *Foster v. Spencer*,[34] substantial remuneration for
their past work was awarded to two of the trustees of a moribund cricket
club who had over a twenty year period had to engage in repeated administrative procedures and various types of legal proceedings in order successfully to bring about a sale of the club's ground[35]; however, it was held that
the remaining task of determining the beneficial interests and dealing with
the proceeds of sale was insufficiently onerous to justify an order for future
remuneration. On the other hand, future remuneration was ordered in *Re
Duke of Norfolk's Settlement Trusts*,[36] where a trust company accepted the
trusteeship of a discretionary trust on the basis that it would receive a low,

---

[29] *Bainbridge v. Blair* (1845) 8 Beav. 558; *Re Freeman's Settlement Trusts* (1887) 37 Ch.D. 148; *Re Masters* [1953] 1 All E.R. 19; *Re Worthington (dec'd)* [1954] 1 All E.R. 677.

[30] *Forster v. Ridley* (1864) 4 De G.J. & Sm. 452.

[31] *Re Duke of Norfolk's Settlement Trusts* [1982] Ch. 61.

[32] (1711) 1 P.Wms. 140.

[33] See, for example, *Protheroe v. Protheroe* [1968] 1 W.L.R. 519, *ante* p. 309, where the trustee was only entitled to reimbursement of his actual expenses.

[34] [1996] 2 All E.R. 672.

[35] One of the trustees, a chartered surveyor who had been principally engaged in dealing with the planning authorities and the prospective purchasers, was awarded 5 per cent commission on the purchase price while the other, who lived near the ground and had had to bear the brunt of dealing with squatters, the neighbours and the municipal authorities, was awarded £5,000 per annum for the most crucial 10 year period.

[36] [1982] Ch. 61.

fixed, annual fee. It became involved in an extensive re-development pro-gramme in the Strand and applied both for special remuneration in respect of the re-development, which was granted,[37] and for an increase in the ordinary standard of remuneration. The Court of Appeal held that it could authorise an increase in the agreed level of remuneration, but it would only do so if the experience and skill of the trustee made it in the interest of the beneficiaries to do so. The Court of Appeal also held that it was relevant to take into account remuneration charged by other trust companies although it is not yet clear how much reliance can actually be placed on that.

The inherent jurisdiction has also been used to award remuneration to those guilty of a breach of fiduciary duty or of undue influence where their conduct has produced a substantial benefit for the other party. In *Boardman v. Phipps*,[37a] Boardman was the solicitor to the trustees of a will, who held among other assets 8,000 out of an issued 30,000 shares in a private com-pany. Boardman, thinking there was considerable scope for making a profit, considered with the trustees whether they should acquire the remaining shares in the company but the trustees refused, partly because under the terms of the trust instrument they had no power to acquire additional shares in the company.[38] Boardman, by using knowledge which he had gained as a solicitor to the trust, then fought a takeover battle for control of the company on behalf of himself and one of the beneficiaries. As Wilberforce J. observed at first instance, "it is interesting, and at times fascinating to watch, through the long correspondence that has been put in [evidence], the man-ner in which [Boardman] drives [the chairman of the company] from one prepared position to another until the fruit is ready to drop into his hand."[39] Eventually the fruit did indeed drop. Boardman acquired virtually all the shares in the company other than those held by the trust and, having gained control of the company, he was able to dispose of some of the assets and to make a capital distribution to all the shareholders, obviously including the trust. The trust benefitted to the tune of £47,000 and Boardman and his associate obtained £75,000, which the beneficiaries subsequently claimed. It was held on the facts that Boardman would not have been able to have conducted these negotiations without the knowledge which he had gained as solicitor to the trust and, controversially, that he and his associate became constructive trustees and so were liable to account for their profit. The Court of Appeal and the House of Lords[40] however considered that Boardman was "a man of conspicuous ability, of great energy, clarity of mind and persis-tence with a flair for negotiation" and, although he and his associate were nevertheless made to disgorge their profit, he was allowed "generous remu-neration". He was allowed remuneration because he had exceptional abili-ties in this respect, and had exercised them for the benefit of the trust. In other words, the average trustee, and even the average professional trustee, would not have been able to have achieved the results which Boardman achieved. In this case, remuneration was awarded even though Boardman

---

[37] At first instance ([1979] Ch. 37), and not reversed by the Court of Appeal.
[37a] [1967] 2 A.C. 46: see *ante*, p. 314.
[38] The Court of Appeal said that application should have been made to the court for permission to purchase these shares.
[39] [1965] Ch. 922 at 1014.
[40] Upholding Wilberforce J.

had committed a breach of fiduciary duty. In *O'Sullivan v. Management Agency and Music*,[41] remuneration was ordered even in favour of a fiduciary who had been guilty of undue influence. A fiduciary agent, whose contract with a performer was set aside for undue influence, was held to be entitled to remuneration, together with a reasonable sum by way of profit, on the basis that he had contributed significantly to the performer's success. On the other hand, in *Guinness v. Saunders*,[42] a claim for remuneration by a director who had acted in good faith but in a situation where there was a clear conflict between his interest and his duty was denied by the House of Lords—in fact the House of Lords doubted whether such remuneration would ever be ordered in favour of a director. Lord Goff[43] felt that the jurisdiction could not be exercised where it would encourage trustees to put themselves into a conflict situation—however, in this respect, the authorities are not consistent.

3. *Agreement with All Beneficiaries*

The third exception to the general rule is that, if the beneficiaries are all *sui juris* and between them absolutely entitled to the whole of the beneficial interest under the trust, they can validly agree with the trustees that they shall be paid. Such agreements are construed strictly, in the same way as provisions for payment in the trust instrument.[44] Where all the beneficiaries do not agree, or some are not *sui juris*, individual beneficiaries can agree with a trustee for his remuneration but that agreement obviously binds only the individual beneficiary on a personal basis and not the trust property as such.

4. *Judicial Trustees*

A judicial trustee may always charge for his services.[45]

5. *Custodian Trustees*

A custodian trustee is entitled to charge fees equivalent to those which the Public Trustee could charge for acting as a custodian trustee.[46] However, this only enables the custodian trustee to charge for the services which he performs in that capacity. In *Forster v. Williams Deacon's Bank*[47] an attempt was made to use the device of custodian trusteeship to overcome the absence of a charging clause in the trust instrument. In that case Williams Deacon's Bank had been appointed both managing trustee and custodian

---

[41] [1985] Q.B. 428.

[42] [1990] 2 A.C. 663.

[43] On the grounds that this would constitute interference by the court in the administration of the company's affairs.

[44] It seems that the agreement has to be concluded with the beneficiaries before the trustee takes up his office; *Douglas v. Archbutt* (1858) 2 De G. & J. 148; *Re Sherwood* (1840) 3 Beav. 338. This appears to be contrary to principle.

[45] Judicial Trustees Act 1896, ss.1(5), 4(1).

[46] Public Trustee Act 1906, s.4.

[47] [1935] Ch. 359.

trustee. It was appreciated that the bank could not charge as managing trustee, but it was anticipated that it could derive its remuneration from its capacity as a custodian trustee. The Court of Appeal rejected the device, however, holding that the deed merely constituted the bank the sole trustee and so the inability to charge remained. A similar attempt in a later case was held to be totally ineffective.[48]

Nor does the fact that a validly appointed custodian trustee may always charge for his services entitle him to profit in other ways from the trust. Thus in *Re Brooke Bond*[49] an insurance company was a custodian trustee under the trust deed securing the pension scheme of Brooke Bond & Co. Under the terms of the trust deed the managing trustees were entitled to effect with any insurance company a policy assuring the payment of the pensions under the scheme. The managing trustees proposed to effect the policy with the custodian trustee. Cross J. held that the custodian trustee could not without the authority of the court contract with the managing trustee for its own benefit but, application having been made to the court, the learned judge authorised the managing trustees to effect the policy with the cus-todian trustee on the basis that the latter need not account for its profit, on condition that the terms of the policy were approved by an independent actuary.

6. *The Public Trustee*

The Public Trustee is always entitled to charge for his services.[50] Details of some of the fees which he currently charges have been given previously.[51]

7. *Trust Corporations*

As has already been seen,[52] the court has a power to appoint a trustee and will do so principally where one cannot be appointed without the assistance of the court. When the court does so, it has power to authorise the trustee to be paid and, where it appoints a trust corporation to be a trustee, it will almost invariably authorise that corporation to be paid. That does not alter the fact that in principle a trust corporation is in exactly the same position as an individual trustee as regards remuneration—it is certainly not entitled to charge merely because it is a trust corporation.[53] However, it may well be that the court will nevertheless approve the payment of fees according to the trust corporation's ordinary scale of fees, particularly where the benefici-aries do not object.[54]

Once a trustee has been appointed by the court, he will generally have no further connection with the court thereafter. However, the court may also, on the application of any person interested in the trust, appoint someone to

---

[48] *Arning v. James* [1936] Ch. 158.
[49] [1963] Ch. 357.
[50] Public Trustee Act 1906, s.9; Administration of Justice Act 1965, s.2; Public Trustees (Fees) Act 1957.
[51] See *ante*, p. 644.
[52] See *ante*, p. 477.
[53] See also *Re Barbour's Settlement* [1974] 1 W.L.R. 1198.
[54] *Re Codd's Will Trust* [1975] 1 W.L.R. 1139.

be a judicial trustee. A judicial trustee, who is usually either the Public Trustee, or the Official Solicitor, or a trust corporation, becomes for the purpose an officer of the court and as such he is able at any time to obtain the directions of the court without formality. Unless there has been mismanagement, the court will only in exceptional circumstances appoint a judicial trustee where suitable private persons are willing to act as trustees.[55] As has already been seen, a judicial trustee may always charge for his services.[56]

8. *The Rule in Cradock v. Piper*

The so-called Rule in *Cradock v. Piper*[57] is a curious exception to the principle that a solicitor trustee, like any other trustee, may not pay either himself or another member of his firm for work done for the trust[58] (in the absence of authorisation by the trust instrument or by the court) save where he can properly employ an outside solicitor in which case he may employ and pay another member of his firm provided that it has been expressly agreed that the solicitor-trustee will not take any share in the profits.[59] The effect of this rule is that, where a solicitor-trustee acts as a solicitor for himself and his co-trustees in litigation relating to the trust and the costs of acting for both of them do not exceed the expense which would have been incurred if he had been acting for the co-trustees alone, then he may be paid his usual costs.

The Rule in *Cradock v. Piper* is firmly established[60] but it is quite illogical. If it is proper for a solicitor to be paid his usual fees for litigation, why is it not proper for him to be paid his usual fees for non-litigious work? In *Re Corsellis*[61] Cotton L.J. made a feeble attempt to justify the difference: "There may be this reason for it, that in an action, although costs are not always hostily taxed, yet there may be a taxation where parties other than the trustee-solicitor may appear and test the propriety of the costs, and the court can disallow altogether the costs of any proceedings which may appear to be vexatious or improperly taken." There is, however, little merit in this explanation. In the first place, even where there is the usual charging clause, or remuneration for non-contentious business is authorised by the court, this will not authorise payment for acts which are not properly done. Further, where there is an express power for a solicitor-trustee to charge, a beneficiary can always insist that a solicitor-trustee's bill of costs be taxed[62]; it has even been decided that where the beneficiaries are dissatisfied with a bill, it is the solicitor-trustee's duty to inform the beneficiaries of their right to have it taxed.[63] There remains, therefore, no logic in the distinction between court proceedings and other business for this purpose. But the rule is firm. It will,

---

[55] *Re Chisholm* (1898) 43 S.J. 43.
[56] Judicial Trustees Act 1896, s.1.
[57] (1850) 1 Mac. & G. 664.
[58] *Christophers v. White* (1847) 10 Beav. 523.
[59] *Clack v. Carton* (1866) 30 L.J. Ch. 639.
[60] *Broughton v. Broughton* (1855) 5 De G.M. & G. 160; *Lincoln v. Windsor* (1851) 9 Hare 158; *Re Baker* (1886) 24 Ch.D. 77.
[61] (1887) 34 Ch.D. 675 at 682.
[62] *Re Fish* [1893] 2 Ch. 413.
[63] *Re Webb* [1894] 1 Ch. 73.

however, be abrogated on the grounds of redundancy if the recent proposals of the Law Commission to which reference has already been made are enacted.[64]

9. *Trust Property Abroad*

Where the trust property is situated abroad and the law of the country where the property is situated allows payment, the trustees appear to be entitled to retain their emoluments. In *Re Northcote*[65] English executors had to get in assets of the deceased in America. To do so they had to obtain a grant of probate in the State of New York, under the law of which they were entitled to a commission on the value of the assets. They deducted this for themselves and the English court held they need not account for it to the trust.

IV. DIRECTORS' FEES

The second type of remuneration which a trustee may seek to retain is fees paid to him as a director of a company in which the trust fund is invested. Three questions arise: first, whether the trustee-director is in principle liable to account for his director's fees; secondly, whether there are any exceptions to the basic principle; and, thirdly, if the trustee-director does have to account, how the fees should be treated in the administration of the trust.

1. *Liability in Principle to Account*

There are two preliminary points. First, in the case of private companies, the articles of association often endeavour to prevent the directors from acting contrary to the interests of shareholders by providing that any person who becomes a director must himself hold, or must within a short specified time acquire, a number of shares in that company. In this way it is hoped that, as the director will wish to advance the value of his own shares, he will also be acting in the interests of the other shareholders. Secondly, by section 360 of the Companies Act 1985,[66] a company is not allowed to take notice of the fact that shares might be held upon trust and, as far as the company is concerned, it deals with trustees who are registered holders of shares in exactly the same way as shareholders who are beneficially entitled. It will therefore be apparent that directors can use shares which they hold as trustees as their share qualification; if they do so, will they be allowed to keep their directors' fees?

---

[64] This is specifically proposed in para. 10.31 of the Consultation Paper on Trustees' Powers and Duties (June 1997).
[65] [1949] 1 All E.R. 442.
[66] Replacing provisions of previous Acts.

In *Re Francis*,[67] under the articles of association of a company, the holders of a specified number of shares were entitled to vote themselves into directorships. Trustees held sufficient shares on behalf of their trust and duly procured their appointment as directors. Kekewich J., following the general principle that a trustee cannot profit from his trusteeship, held that they had to account to the trust for their fees. This case, however, was not even cited in *Re Dover Coalfield Extension*,[68] which introduced new considerations. The company Dover Coalfield Extension held shares in the Consolidated Kent Collieries Corporation, with whom they did business. In order to protect the interests of the former company, one of its directors was appointed a director of the latter company; as such, he had a contract which governed the services which he was to perform and also regulated his remuneration. However, all directors were required to acquire 1,000 shares within one month of appointment. Dover Coalfield Extension therefore transferred to him this number of shares, which he held upon trust for the Dover company. It was not disputed that he had to account to the Dover company for the dividends on those shares and he did in fact do so; however, he claimed that he did not have to account for his directors' fees. The Court of Appeal held that, even though he could not have continued in office without the shares, he could retain his fees; he had been appointed a director by an independent board of directors before he had acquired the shares and his directorship did not therefore automatically flow from his trusteeship.

In *Re Macadam*,[69] following *Re Francis*,[70] trustees who by virtue of the trust shareholding were able to elect themselves directorships and did in fact do so were held liable to account for their fees. However, this decision was distinguished in *Re Gee*,[71] where Harman J. said that in some circumstances, even where a trustee is able through his voting rights to compel his appointment as director, he is nevertheless entitled to retain his fees, if his appointment was in fact independent of his trust shareholding. He reviewed the previous cases and concluded that the test was whether the trustee has used powers vested in him as trustee to procure his appointment as a director. To be liable to account the trustee therefore, first, must have powers vested in him as trustee and, secondly, must have utilised those powers to procure his appointment as director.

If any of these elements is missing, the trustee-director may retain his fees—as in *Re Dover Coalfield Extension*, where the trustee has his directorship first and, although he has powers as trustee, does not use those powers to procure his appointment as a director. Similarly, if the trustee-director has a majority shareholding in a company beneficially, as well as a minority holding as trustee, and votes himself into a directorship, his directorship will be the result of his beneficial voting power and not his voting power as trustee. Similarly, where others hold the majority shareholding, the trustee has a minority shareholding, and he is appointed a director by the votes of the others, although he has powers as trustee he will not have used those

[67] (1905) 74 L.J.Ch. 198.
[68] [1908] 1 Ch. 65.
[69] [1946] Ch. 73.
[70] (1905) 74 L.J.Ch. 198.
[71] [1948] Ch. 284.

powers to procure his appointment. The court will consider all the circumstances to see whether or not the appointment was truly independent of the
voting powers held as trustee.

In *Re Orwell's Will Trusts*,[72] the facts of which have already been considered,[73] Vinelott J. distinguished *Re Gee*. He held that, while the general
rule is that a trustee must account for any benefit, such as remuneration,
which he obtains from a company as a result of his position as a trustee, this
rule does not apply if the company was properly entitled to be paid from the
trust fund and there is no other nexus between the company with which the
trustee is connected and the trust fund.

2. *Exceptions to the Basic Principle*

Where a trustee-director is, in principle, not entitled to retain his director's
fees, there are two circumstances in which, nevertheless, he may do so.

(i) The settlor can include an effective power in the trust instrument
authorising the retention of directors' fees. This power may be
express or implied. So in *Re Llewellin*,[74] where the testator had
expressly provided that the trustees could use the trust shares to
acquire directorships, it was held that he had also impliedly
authorised them to retain their directors' fees.

(ii) The court can authorise a trustee-director to retain his director's
fees. In deciding whether to exercise this power, it will consider the
extent of the skill and effort which has been applied. The general
rule is that a trustee is expected to exercise in the discharge of his
trusteeship the effort and skill which a prudent man of business
would in general undertake in the management of his own investments. A trustee-director is expected to exercise the same standard
when acting as a director. So, in *Re Keeler's Settlement Trusts*[75] the
court directed that an inquiry should be held as to the extent to
which trustee-directors had exerted effort and skill above that
standard and held that they could retain their directors' fees, but to
that extent only.

3. *The Manner in which Forfeited Fees should be Applied*

Where a trustee-director is obliged to account for his directors' fees and does
so, it seems that, notwithstanding the revenue character of those sums so far
as the company is concerned, in the administration of the trust they are to be
treated as an addition to the settled property and added to capital.[76]

---

[72] [1982] 1 W.L.R. 1337.
[73] See *ante*, p. 642.
[74] [1949] Ch. 225.
[75] [1981] Ch. 156.
[76] *Re Francis* (1905) 74 L.J. Ch. 198.

V. COMMISSIONS

The third category of payment which a trustee may seek to retain is commissions paid by third parties.

1. *The General Rule*

The general rule is that the trustee is accountable for commissions which he receives in respect of trust business.[77] The test is not whether the trust has suffered a loss but whether the trustee has made a profit. Thus, in *Williams v. Barton*[78] the trustee was a stockbrokers' clerk who was paid commission earned on business introduced by him to his firm. He arranged for his firm to value the trust assets and was duly paid his commission. It was held that he had to account for that commission. There was no suggestion that the valuation of the trust assets was improper or unnecessary but nevertheless the trustee was not entitled to make a profit from it. Had this not been the case, the trustee might have been tempted to have the assets valued more frequently than was in fact necessary.

2. *Exceptions*

The trust instrument can, and often does, empower trustees to retain commissions. The court undoubtedly also has power to authorise this but there does not seem to be any reported case in which it has exercised this power.

Furthermore, the rule does not apply where the recipient of the commission is discharging a duty imposed by statute and in so doing does not act harshly or oppressively. So in *Swain v. The Law Society*[79] the House of Lords held that The Law Society was entitled to retain the equivalent of commission paid in respect of the compulsory insurance against negligence which solicitors are obliged to maintain.[80] The Law Society was required to apply that commission for the benefit of the profession as a whole.

VI. COMMERCIAL PROFITS

The last category of benefit which, in ordinary circumstances, a trustee may seek to keep is profits derived by him in carrying on a business, where the trust is a customer of that business.

1. *The General Rule*

As in the case of commissions, it seems that the trustee is liable to account for his profit.[81]

---

[77] This question is discussed more fully: see *ante*, p. 289.
[78] [1927] 2 Ch. 9.
[79] [1983] A.C. 598: see *ante*, p. 21.
[80] Solicitors Act 1974, s.37.
[81] *Re Sykes* [1909] 2 Ch. 241.

2. *Exceptions*

The trust instrument can empower trustees to retain their profit. So, in *Re Sykes*[82] two brothers who were wine merchants were appointed the trustees of a will under which one of the assets of the trust was a public house. Under the terms of the will, they were authorised to supply wine to the public house and they were held entitled to their usual profit for doing so. Similarly, in *Space Investments v. Canadian Imperial Bank of Commerce*,[83] a bank trustee was entitled under a settlement to deposit trust funds with itself on a normal commercial basis; no breach of trust was committed by the bank in so doing and the position of the trust was no better than any other depositor or general creditor, even when the bank went into liquidation.

The court also has power to authorise trustees to retain a commercial profit.

VII. OTHER FINANCIAL BENEFITS

Finally, quite apart from the specific examples already considered, there is anyway a general rule that a trustee is not to be entitled to profit in any way from his trusteeship unless he is authorised to do so by the trust instrument or by the court.

An extreme, if unusual, example is *Sugden v. Crossland*,[84] where a person was anxious to become a trustee of a will. He therefore paid the existing trustee £75 to retire and to appoint him in his place. It was held that the retirement and appointment was ineffective and also that the £75 so paid belonged to the trust. Similarly in *Webb v. Earl of Shaftesbury*,[85] Lord Eldon held that trustees were not entitled to exercise sporting rights over land held by them as trustees. He held that either the rights should be let for the benefit of the beneficiaries or, if they could not be let, should be held for the heirs of the settlor on a resulting trust. The trustees could not themselves derive any benefit.

In view of the above, it hardly needs to be said that, quite apart from the rules relating to investments,[86] a trustee must not use trust moneys in his own trade or business. If he does so, he will be liable to account for the profit he makes or, at the beneficiaries' option, compound interest.[87] The rule applies not only to profits which are made at the expense of the trust but also to profits which are made without any loss to the trust at all but which are derived by virtue of the trusteeship. This principle has already been considered in Chapter 10.[88]

---

[82] *ibid.*
[83] [1986] 1 W.L.R. 1072.
[84] (1856) 3 Sm. & G. 192.
[85] (1802) 7 Ves. 480.
[86] See *ante*, pp. 540 *et seq.*
[87] See *post*, pp. 688 *et seq.*
[88] See *ante*, p. 304.

CHAPTER 23

VARIATION OF TRUSTS

IF all the beneficiaries of a trust are *sui juris* and absolutely entitled they can, if they think fit, terminate the trust and if they so choose, set up new trusts in respect of the trust property.[1] But if they are not all so qualified, it is necessary for an application to be made to the court for a variation of the trusts. It is important to make a distinction for this purpose between two classes of variation by the court: first, variations concerned with the management or administration of the trusts and, secondly, variation of the beneficial interests arising under the trusts.

I. MANAGEMENT AND ADMINISTRATIVE VARIATIONS

1. *The Inherent Jurisdiction of the Court*

The court has always had an inherent jurisdiction to sanction a departure from the terms of a trust but it is now clearly established that this jurisdiction applies only to the management or administration of the trust. It therefore does not apply to any rearrangement of the rights of the beneficiaries to the beneficial interests themselves,[2] with the sole exceptions of cases of "maintenance"[3] and "compromise",[4] assuming that the latter amounts to a variation in the true sense of the word.[5]

The inherent jurisdiction, although still somewhat nebulous, was defined by Romer L.J. in *Re New*[6] to cover an "emergency" which has arisen in the administration of the trust, that is to say something for which no provision is made in the trust and which could not have been foreseen or anticipated by the settlor of the trust. The inherent jurisdiction is, therefore, of distinctly limited scope. In *Re New* itself the trustees of shares in a company were authorised by the court as a matter of emergency to concur in a scheme under which shares were to be exchanged for more realisable shares in a new company. The sanction of the court was required because the trustees

---

[1] See *ante*, p. 637.
[2] *Chapman v. Chapman* [1954] A.C. 428 at 454, 455.
[3] See *post*, p. 660.
[4] See *post*, p. 660.
[5] This is perhaps doubtful because it seems that the court's sanction to a compromise of disputed rights (which is what "compromise" in this context means) does not result in a variation of the beneficial trusts but only brings to an end any dispute about them. See *post*, p. 660, for further discussion of "compromise" in this sense.
[6] [1910] 2 Ch. 524.

had no power of investment in the new shares under the terms of the trust instrument. This was in the circumstances a transaction analogous to the "salvage" of the trust property.[7]

2. Section 57 of the Trustee Act 1925

One of the reasons why the inherent jurisdiction is so nebulous is that it has been largely superseded by section 57 of the Trustee Act 1925, which is based on a concept wider than that of "emergency". The basis of the section is rather expediency. It provides in effect that the court may empower trustees (but not trustees under the Settled Land Act 1925)[8] to perform any act relating to the management or administration of the trust property which is not authorised by the trust instrument when in the opinion of the court it is expedient. The ambit of the section was considered by the Court of Appeal in the conjoined appeals in *Re Downshire's Settled Estates, Re Chapman's Settlement Trusts* and *Re Blackwell's Settlement Trusts.*[9] According to Lord Evershed M.R. and Romer L.J. in a joint judgment:

"The object of section 57 was to secure that trust property should be managed as advantageously as possible in the interests of the beneficiaries, and, with that object in view, to authorise specific dealings with the property which the court might have felt itself unable to sanction under the inherent jurisdiction, either because there was no actual 'emergency' or because of inability to show that the position which called for intervention was one which the creator of the trust could not reasonably have foreseen but it was no part of the legislative aim to disturb the rule that the court will not rewrite a trust."[10]

Moreover, the court must be satisfied that the proposed transaction is for the benefit of the trust as a whole and not simply for one of its beneficiaries.[11]

The section does not, therefore, confer on the court any general jurisdiction to vary beneficial interests; it is limited to the managerial supervision and control of trust property by the trustees and cannot be stretched further than that.

Subject to this decisive limitation, however, it is an overriding provision which is to be read into every trust.[12] And it has been used for a number of purposes: to authorise the partitioning of land where the necessary consent could not be obtained[13]; to authorise the sale of a reversionary interest which

---

[7] The principle was applied in *Re Tollemache* [1903] 1 Ch. 955.
[8] Trustee Act 1925, s.57(4).
[9] [1953] Ch. 218; Denning L.J. dissented. On appeal to the House of Lords *sub nom. Chapman v. Chapman* [1954] A.C. 429, it was conceded that s.57 did not apply. In the House of Lords, the statement of law in the Court of Appeal regarding s.57 was neither approved or disapproved and, therefore, is still good law.
[10] *ibid.*
[11] *Re Craven's Estate (No. 2)* [1937] Ch. 431.
[12] *Re Mair* [1935] Ch. 562.
[13] *Re Thomas* [1930] 1 Ch. 194.

the trustees had no power to sell until it fell into possession[14]; and to blend two charitable funds into one.[15] The section has also been used to extend trustees' investment powers,[16] most recently in *Mason v. Farbrother*[17] and *Anker-Petersen v. Anker-Petersen*.[18] It used to be thought that applications for this purpose were better made under the Variation of Trusts Act 1958.[19] However, *Anker-Petersen v. Anker-Petersen* has now established that, provided the beneficial interests are not also affected by the proposed extension of the trustees' investment powers, section 57 should be used in preference to the Variation of Trusts Act 1958.

II. VARIATION OF BENEFICIAL INTERESTS

It has been seen that the rules already discussed relate only to variations relating to the management and administration of the trust. Variation of the beneficial interests of a trust obviously involves a much more drastic rewriting of its provisions.

1. *Section 64 of the Settled Land Act 1925*

This section provides that the court may sanction any transaction affecting or concerning the settled land or any part thereof or any other land (not being a transaction otherwise authorised by the Settled Land Act 1925 or by the terms of the settlement) which in the opinion of the court would be for the benefit of the settled land, or any part thereof, or the persons interested under the settlement.[20] Furthermore, the word "transaction" is widely defined so as to include a "compromise or other dealing or other arrangement".[21] It is now clear that, as the majority of the Court of Appeal held in *Re Downshire's Settled Estates*,[22] the section confers a more ample jurisdiction than that conferred by section 57 of the Trustee Act 1925.[23] It is not in any sense restricted to steps of a purely administrative character and therefore enables the beneficial interests under the settlement to be remoulded.[24]

A relatively recent example of the utilisation of this jurisdiction, which is likely to become progressively less significant now that the Trusts of Land

---

[14] *Re Cockerell's Settlement Trusts* [1956] Ch. 372; compare *Re Heyworth's Contingent Reversionary Interest* [1956] Ch. 364.
[15] *Re Shipwrecked Fishermen and Mariners' Benevolent Fund* [1959] Ch. 220.
[16] *Re Brassey's Settlement* [1955] 1 W.L.R. 192; *Re Shipwrecked Fishermen and Mariners' Benevolent Fund* [1959] Ch. 220, not following *Re Royal Society's Charitable Trusts* [1956] Ch. 87.
[17] [1983] 2 All E.R. 1078.
[18] [1991] 88/16 Law Soc. Gaz. 32.
[19] See *post*, p. 662 and *Re Coates' Will Trusts* [1959] 1 W.L.R. 375; *Re Byng's Will Trusts* [1959] 2 All E.R. 54 at 57. In *Mason v. Farbrother* [1983] 2 All E.R. 1078 it was held that this was not possible because the parties were not fully representative.
[20] s.64(1). The powers have been extended by the Settled Land and Trustee Acts (Court's General Powers) Act 1943, s.1 as amended by the Emergency Laws (Miscellaneous Provisions) Act 1953, s.9.
[21] s.64(2); *Raikes v. Lygon* [1988] 1 W.L.R. 281.
[22] [1953] Ch. 218.
[23] See *ante*, p. 657.
[24] *Raikes v. Lygon* [1988] 1 W.L.R. 281.

and Appointment of Trustees Act 1996[25] has prohibited the creation of any more settlements under the Settled Land Act 1925, is *Hambro v. Duke of Marlborough*.[26] The Blenheim Estate is held by the successive Dukes of Marlborough for an estate in fee tail which is, by Act of Parliament, "unbarrable", that is to say incapable of being converted into an estate in fee simple. The Duke and the trustees of what was then a settlement under the Settled Land Act 1925 considered that the Duke's heir apparent, the Marquess of Blandford, would be incapable of managing the estate if and when he succeeded his father because of what were referred to as his "unbusinesslike habits and the lack of responsibility shown by him". They proposed to seek approval for the Duke to convey the estate to the trustees of a new settlement on trust for sale[27] to pay the income to the Duke for life, subject thereto for the Marquess of Blandford on protective trusts, and subject thereto on the trusts of the pre-existing settlement. The matter came before Morritt J. on the preliminary issue as to whether such a conveyance, which would clearly vary the Marquess of Blandford's existing beneficial interest, would be a "transaction" which the court could sanction under section 64. This question was answered in the affirmative and approval was subsequently given.[28]

The section used also to apply to land held on trust for sale,[29] but this is now no longer the case following the Trusts of Land and Appointment of Trustees Act 1996.

2. *Section 24 of the Matrimonial Causes Act 1973*

Under this Act, replacing earlier longstanding legislation, the Family Division of the High Court has a wide jurisdiction, after pronouncing a decree of divorce or nullity of marriage, to vary the trusts contained in any ante-nuptial or post-nuptial settlement which has been made for the benefit of the parties to the marriage or the children of that marriage.[30] It is clearly established that the jurisdiction extends to a rearrangement of beneficial interests and the fact that a saving of inheritance tax or other taxes will result will have no bearing on the exercise of this jurisdiction.[31] A recent extremely significant application of this jurisdiction is the decision of the House of Lords in *Brooks v. Brooks*[32] that a pension scheme of which a former husband was the sole member could be varied to provide an immediate annuity and

---

[25] s.2(1). Existing settlements will continue only for as long as any land or heirlooms remain subject thereto.

[26] [1994] Ch. 158.

[27] Thus bringing to an end the settlement under the Settled Land Act 1925 pursuant to s.1(7) thereof. The new settlement, to which the estate was presumably conveyed following the subsequent approval of the scheme, must now be a trust of land as a result of Trusts of Land and Appointment of Trustees Act 1996, s.1(2)(a).

[28] See *The Times*, July 23, 1994.

[29] Danckwerts J. so interpreted Law of Property Act 1925, s.28 in *Re Simmons* [1956] Ch. 125 but this section has now been repealed by Trusts of Land and Appointment of Trustees Act 1996, Sched. 4.

[30] Matrimonial Causes Act 1973, s.24.

[31] See *Thomson v. Thomson and Whitmee* [1956] P. 384.

[32] [1996] 1 A.C. 375.

an eventual pension for the former wife. This decision has already been considered in detail in the Chapter on Pension Trusts.[33]

3. *Section 96(3) of the Mental Health Act 1983*

This provision gives the Court of Protection power to make a settlement of the property of the patient and subsequently to vary it if any material fact was not initially disclosed, or there has been a substantial change in circumstances.

4. *Maintenance*

The position here is and has long been that where a testator or settlor has made a settlement in such a way, which is particularly capable of occurring where the trusts provide primarily for income to be accumulated, that the immediate beneficiaries have no funds out of which they can be maintained, the court will assume that the intention to provide sensibly for the family is so paramount that it will order maintenance in disregard of the trusts.[34] Any such order for maintenance will obviously result in a variation of the beneficial interests. Moreover, the jurisdiction is not restricted to cases of "emergency",[35] nor is it dependent on the beneficiaries in question being infants.[36]

5. *Compromise*

It has long been clearly established that the court may sanction on behalf of an infant or unborn person a "compromise" proposed by those persons beneficially interested in the trusts who are *sui juris*, thus protecting the trustees from subsequent liability to the infant or unborn person. This is, like the power to award maintenance,[37] part of the inherent jurisdiction of the court and, where applicable, clearly also enables beneficial interests to be varied.

In conjoined appeals in *Re Downshire Settled Estates, Re Chapman's Settlement Trusts* and *Re Blackwell's Settlement Trusts*,[38] the Court of Appeal had to consider the important question of what amounts to a "compromise" for this purpose. The majority of the court, Lord Evershed M.R. and Romer L.J., held that the word "compromise" should not be construed narrowly so as to be confined to a compromise of disputed rights but covered any arrangement between a tenant for life and the remaindermen. The arrangements proposed in *Re Downshire Settled Estates* and *Re Blackwell's Settlement Trusts* were duly held to be in the nature of a compromise in this wider sense of the word and were accordingly sanctioned. But the majority refused to sanction

---

[33] See *ante*, p. 460.
[34] *Re Downshire Settled Estates* [1953] Ch. 218 at 238, *per* Evershed M.R. and Romer L.J., considered in *Chapman v. Chapman* [1954] A.C. 429 at 445, 455–457, 469, 471: see *ante*, p. 630. See also *Re Collins* (1886) 32 Ch.D. 229 at 232; *Havelock v. Havelock* (1881) 17 Ch.D. 807.
[35] See *ante*, p. 656 and *Hayley v. Bannister* (1820) 4 Madd. 275.
[36] *Revel v. Watkinson* (1748) 1 Ves.Sen. 93.
[37] See *ante*, p. 656.
[38] [1953] Ch. 218.

the arrangement proposed in *Re Chapman's Settlement Trusts* because they involved no compromise even in this extended sense; the court was merely being asked to destroy trusts which had been expressly created. Denning L.J. however dissented on the basis of a broad principle that the court had the power to deal with the property and interests of infants or other persons under disability in a manner not authorised by the trust whenever the court was satisfied that what was proposed was most advantageous for them, provided that everyone of full age also agreed. He was therefore prepared to give the inherent jurisdiction of the Court a very wide scope indeed.

However, when an appeal from the decision of the Court of Appeal was taken to the House of Lords in *Chapman v. Chapman*,[39] the House of Lords not only unanimously affirmed the decision of the Court of Appeal but, by a majority, adopted a considerably narrower meaning of "compromise" than that adopted by Lord Evershed M.R. and Romer L.J. The latter had shown that the inherent jurisdiction was limited to some degree by holding that the word "compromise", however widely construed, would not cover every kind of arrangement. But the majority of the House of Lords (Lord Simonds, Lord Morton and Lord Asquith) stated that the power of the court to sanction a compromise in a suit to which a person, such as an infant or unborn person, was not a party did not extend to cases where there was no real dispute between the parties. Lord Cohen alone was prepared to accept that the jurisdiction of the court extended to "compromises" in the wider sense accepted by the majority of the Court of Appeal. This decision clearly established that a "compromise" means a compromise of a disputed right and this is as far as the inherent jurisdiction of the court goes.[40] This decision led directly to the enactment of the Variation of Trusts Act 1958.[41]

It was therefore clear that in *Re Downshire Settled Estates* and *Re Blackwell's Settlement Trusts* the Court of Appeal had gone too far in giving the word "compromise" an unnatural meaning, although that did not mean that those cases had actually been wrongly decided.[42] However, a number of schemes had been approved in the Chancery Division prior to the decision of the House of Lords on the basis of the wider principle upheld by the majority of the Court of Appeal which could not possibly be so justified and the orders made therein had accordingly been made without any jurisdiction.[43] Further, it immediately became fashionable to scrutinise settlements with a view to finding a provision of sufficient ambiguity or uncertainty in its effect on the beneficial interests to form a peg on which to hand a compromise of a "genuine" dispute, a clearly undesirable development susceptible of bringing the law into disrepute.

---

[39] [1954] A.C. 429.
[40] It was subsequently held not to include a compromise of a simulated dispute (*Re Powell-Cotton's Resettlement* [1956] 1 W.L.R. 23) or a variation of the existing investment powers (*Mason v. Farbrother* [1983] 2 All E.R. 1078).
[41] See *post*, p. 662.
[42] They could probably have been justified under Settled Land Act 1925, s.64: see *ante*, p. 658.
[43] See, *e.g. Re Leeds (Duke) and Re The Coal Acts 1938 to 1943* [1947] Ch. 525. *Re Downshire Settled Estates* and *Re Blackwell's Settlements Trusts* [1953] Ch. 218 may also be taken to be overruled on this point, although these decisions could probably be justified under Settled Land Act 1925, s.64; see *ante*, p. 658.

This bizarre situation clearly could not long continue so the Law Reform Committee was invited in 1957 to consider the position. They reached the conclusion that the result produced by *Chapman v. Chapman* was most unsatisfactory. It was pointed out that on the grant of a decree of divorce or nullity the court had the power to sanction variations in the marriage settlement even if these were designed to produce a saving in estate duty or tax. The Committee fairly inquired why an infant whose parents were happily married should be in a worse position than an infant whose parents had just divorced. The recommendations of the Committee were accordingly given legislative effect in the Variation of Trusts Act 1958.

6. *The Variation of Trusts Act 1958*[44]

The principal motive for the invocation of the inherent jurisdiction of the court to vary beneficial interests on the basis of a "compromise" was in order to minimise fiscal liabilities which would be incurred if the trust remained unaltered. The old-fashioned settlement with its succession of limited interests had, in particular, fallen out of favour because on the death of each limited owner estate duty (the predecessor of inheritance tax) was leviable on the value of the whole settled funds. A great deal of ingenuity had been and for that matter still is devoted to the formulation of schemes dividing up the trust funds between those interested in capital and income respectively in such a way that such fiscal liabilities were minimised.

(A) Permissible Motives[45]
These schemes formerly presented to the court for its sanction under the head of "compromise" are therefore now presented to the court under the Variation of Trusts Act 1958. Although Lord Morton said in *Chapman v. Chapman*[46] that, if the court had power to approve and did approve schemes for the purpose of avoiding taxation, "the way would be open for a most undignified game of chess between the Chancery Division and the legislature", the plain fact remains that very many applications under the Act have been made successfully for this very purpose alone.[47]

Yet despite these realities, echoes of judicial repugnance towards tax avoidance can still occasionally be heard and it is arguable, if only faintly, as a result of the controversial decision in *Re Weston's Settlements*,[48] that certain forms of tax avoidance may still be regarded as illegitimate. In this case the applicants applied for an order for approval of an arrangement by which property settled on English trusts should be freed from those trusts and settled on a Jersey settlement. The purpose of the exercise was to avoid a heavy liability to capital gains tax and estate duty.[49] Stamp J. said at first instance: "I am not persuaded that this application represents more than a

---

[44] For a detailed discussion of the relevant case law, see Harris (1969) 33 Conv. (N.S.) 113, 183.
[45] See also *post*, p. 775.
[46] See *ante*, p. 661.
[47] See, *e.g. Re Norfolk's Will Trusts* (1966), *The Times*, March 23, 1966 (the purpose was to reduce duty on estates worth £3 million).
[48] [1969] 1 Ch. 223; see *post*, p. 777 for further discussion of this decision.
[49] Approximately £160,000.

cheap exercise in tax avoidance which I ought not to sanction, as distinct from a legitimate avoidance of liability to taxation."[50] The Court of Appeal, however, tended to place emphasis on other factors (not that Stamp J. ignored them). As is shown in a later Chapter,[51] the primary basis of the Court of Appeal decision appears to have been that no administrative benefits would accrue in transferring the settlement to Jersey because the family had been living in Jersey for only a few months and probably would not stay there. There was also doubt as to the competence of the Jersey courts to administer trusts.[52] And finally the element of moral or social benefit was stressed. In the words of Lord Denning M.R.:

"There are many things in life more worthwhile than money. One of these things is to be brought up in this our England which is still 'the envy of less happier lands'. I do not believe that it is for the benefit of children to be uprooted from England and transported to another country simply to avoid tax. Children are like trees: they grow stronger with firm roots."[53]

The result of this case can be justified on the grounds just mentioned. But to introduce notions of "legitimate" and "illegitimate" tax avoidance seems to be not only uncontrollably vague but also wholly unworkable.[54]

(B) The General Scheme of the Act

The Variation of Trusts Act 1958, which came into force on July 23, 1958, applies to trusts of real and personal property, whether the trusts arise before or after the passing of the Act, under any will, settlement or other disposition.[55] The court may, if it thinks fit, by order approve an arrangement varying or revoking all or any of the trusts, or enlarging the powers of the trustees to manage or administer any of the trust property, on behalf of four classes of beneficiaries or potential beneficiaries. These are as follows:

(i) by virtue of section 1(1)(a), persons having, directly or indirectly, a vested or contingent interest who by reason of infancy or other incapacity are incapable of assenting;

(ii) by virtue of section 1(1)(b), persons, whether ascertained or not, who may become, directly or indirectly, entitled to an interest at a future date or on the happening of a future event, if they then answer a specified description or qualify as members of a specified

---

[50] [1969] 1 Ch. 223 at 234.

[51] See *post*, p. 777.

[52] [1969] 1 Ch. 223 at 223, *per* Stamp J. (Chancery Division), at 247, *per* Harman L.J. (Court of Appeal); this doubt has certainly since been favourably resolved, see *post*, p. 776.

[53] [1969] 1 Ch. 223 at 245; see *post*, p. 777.

[54] The scheme was one of "tax avoidance", not "tax evasion". The latter amounts to a criminal offence and clearly a scheme which "evaded" tax could not be sanctioned. But to take advantage of the existing tax laws for a person's own benefit and thereby "avoid" tax is generally regarded as a legitimate exercise; see also Bretten [1968] 32 Conv. (N.S.) 194; Harris [1969] 33 Conv. (N.S.) 183 at 191 *et seq*.

[55] s.1(1).

class, but not including such persons if the future event had happened at the date of application to the court[56];

(iii) by virtue of section 1(1)(c), persons unborn;

(iv) by virtue of section 1(1)(d), persons who will be interested as
discretionary beneficiaries under protective trusts[57] if the interest
of the principal beneficiary thereunder should fail or determine.[58]

The court can only approve the arrangement on behalf of the persons
listed in the first three classes if it is for their benefit. But the potential benefit
of the persons listed in the final class does not need to be considered.[59]
Further, if a beneficiary falls both within this final class and within one of the
other classes, then because the four classes are alternatives it is only necessary to apply for approval on the basis of his membership of the final class
and so no benefit needs to be established.[60]

The Act thus largely gives to the court the jurisdiction for which Denning
L.J. had contended in *Re Chapman's Settlement Trust*.[61] It has commendably
done away with the hair-splitting technicalities involved in the precise
nature of a "compromise" and has attracted a great many applications to the
court since it was passed. However, it must be emphasised that, although
the jurisdiction is wide in many respects, it is nevertheless limited in that it
only empowers the court to authorise arrangements on behalf of the persons
designated in the Act, as if they were all ascertained and *sui juris*. It does not
enable the court to override any objection, no matter how unreasonable, or
dispense with the consent, even if unreasonably withheld, of any beneficiary
who is in fact ascertained and *sui juris*. In such circumstances, the Act simply
cannot be invoked.

(C)   The Trusts to which the Act Applies

While, by virtue of section 1(1), the Act applies where "property, whether
real or personal, is held on trusts arising under any will, settlement or other

---

[56] For decisions on the meaning of this paragraph, see *Re Suffert's Settlement* [1961] Ch. 1; *Re Moncrieff's Settlement Trusts* [1962] 1 W.L.R. 1344. Briefly, if the class in question is, for example, the statutory next-of-kin of a living propositus, then the latter is treated as having died at the date of application to the court and the next-of-kin consequently become notion-ally ascertainable. Since the "future event", the death of the propositus, has notionally happened, a member of the class of next-of-kin who is in existence cannot be bound by an order for variation without his consent (see *Re Suffert's Settlement* [1961] Ch. 1). Further, persons who have contingent interests, however remote, are already entitled; they are not persons who "may become entitled". Consequently, in *Knocker v. Youille* [1986] 1 W.L.R. 934, it was held that consent could not be given on behalf of a very numerous class of contingently entitled beneficiaries, whose approval it was not practical to obtain.

[57] See *ante*, p. 231.

[58] s.1(1); see also s.1(2), which defines "protective trusts" as the trusts specified in Trustee Act 1925, s.33(1)(i), (ii) or "any like trusts". For the meaning of this last expression, see *Re Wallace's Settlement* [1968] 1 W.L.R. 711 at 716, *per* Megarry J.: "The word 'like' requires not identity but similarity and similarity in substance suffices without the need for similarity in form or detail or wording." See also *Gibbon v. Mitchell* [1990] 1 W.L.R. 1304.

[59] s.1(1), proviso; see also *post*, p. 669.

[60] *Re Turner's Will Trusts* [1960] Ch. 122.

[61] [1953] Ch. 218. In *Re Chapman's Settlement Trusts (No. 2)* [1959] 1 W.L.R. 372, an application to create substantially the same scheme was granted under the Variation of Trusts Act 1958.

disposition", it nevertheless does not apply to every type of trust. *Allen v. Distillers Co. (Biochemicals)*[62] arose as a sequel to proceedings which had been commenced on behalf of children who were alleged to have been born with physical deformities as a result of their mothers having taken the drug thalidomide during pregnancy. These proceedings had been settled on the basis that the manufacturers of the drug paid into court nearly £6 million on terms that various sums should be paid out or applied "in such manner as the judge may direct to or for the benefit of each [deformed] child". An application was consequently made under the Variation of Trusts Act 1958 for the payment of money out of court to be held by trustees on the terms of a draft which was submitted to the court for approval. Under the terms on which the original proceedings had been settled, each child was entitled to payment on attaining the age of majority, whereas under the proposed draft, the trustees were to be empowered to defer the date upon which the child would be entitled. The court held that it had no jurisdiction under the Act to approve the "variation" of the terms upon which the money had been paid into court. Eveleigh J.[63] said[64] that the terms upon which the money had been paid into court was not

"a trust of the kind referred to in the 1958 Act. The Act contemplates a situation where a beneficial interest is created which did not previously exist and probably one which is related to at least one other beneficial interest."

Similarly in *Mason v. Farbrother*[65] an application under the 1958 Act for the variation of the existing investment powers of a pension fund was not pursued because of doubts about whether the parties were truly representative of the classes of beneficiaries whom they purported to represent.

The jurisdiction conferred by the Act may also now be confined to trusts governed by English law. Prior to the enactment of the Recognition of Trusts Act 1987, the English courts asserted jurisdiction to vary trusts governed by any law provided, of course, that they had jurisdiction over their trustees. Thus, in *Re Ker's Settlement Trusts*[66] the court made an order varying the trusts of a settlement whose proper law was that of Northern Ireland and a similar order was made in *Re Paget's Settlement*[67] in respect of a settlement whose proper law was believed to be that of New York. However, as will be seen in Chapter 25,[68] the Hague Convention on the Law applicable to Trusts and their Recognition confers exclusive jurisdiction to vary trusts on the courts of the jurisdiction of their proper law. Now that this convention has been incorporated into English law by the Recognition of Trusts Act 1987, it is therefore considered unlikely that English courts still have any jurisdiction to make orders under the Variation of Trusts Act 1958 varying any trust

---

[62] [1974] 2 All E.R. 365.
[63] As he said in the judgment, "a common lawyer with this problem" of what constitutes a trust.
[64] [1974] 2 All E.R. 365 at 374.
[65] [1983] 2 All E.R. 1078.
[66] [1963] Ch. 553.
[67] [1965] 1 W.L.R. 1046.
[68] See *post*, p. 752.

whose proper law is not English law; this seems to be the case even if the trustees of such a trust are personally susceptible to the jurisdiction of the English courts.

(D) Specific Considerations for the Court

(1) Benefit

The only essential guidance specifically provided in the Act as to the principles on which the exercise of the jurisdiction is based is that, with the exception of discretionary beneficiaries under protective trusts, the arrangement proposed should be for the benefit of the persons designated in the Act[69] on whose behalf its approval is sought. A definite benefit, even if it is not purely financial, must be conferred on such persons. In *Re Van Gruisen's Will Trusts*[70] it was shown that the provisions for infants and unborn persons were from an actuarial point of view more beneficial to them under the proposed arrangement than under the trusts of the will. The arrangement was therefore approved but Ungoed-Thomas J. sounded a warning note by saying:

"The court is not merely concerned with the actuarial calculation . . . the court is also concerned whether the arrangement as a whole in all the circumstances, is such that it is proper to approve it. The court's concern involves, *inter alia*, a practical and businesslike consideration of the arrangement, including the total amount of the advantages which the various parties obtain and their bargaining strength."

Similar reasoning was applied in the earlier decision of *Re Clitheroe's Settlement Trusts*,[71] where the arrangement was designed to exclude any future wife from the class of objects of an immediate discretionary trust[72] but in compensation gave her the benefit of a covenant by the settlor to pay the trustees an annual sum for her benefit. Danckwerts J. sanctioned the arrangements in principle but required evidence to show that it was in fact for the benefit of a future wife.

The rule that a "benefit" is all-important has caused some, though admittedly very few, applications to fail. Thus in *Re Steed's Will Trusts*,[73] the Court of Appeal refused to sanction a variation sought by the beneficiary enabling her to take the whole beneficial interest because it did not take sufficient account of a "spectral spouse" whom the trusts were also designed to benefit and whom the beneficiary in question might conceivably marry.

---

[69] s.1(1), proviso.

[70] [1964] 1 W.L.R. 449.

[71] [1959] 1 W.L.R. 1159.

[72] It was not a protective trust, so the proviso to s.1(1) did not apply.

[73] [1960] Ch. 407. See also *Re Cohen's Settlement Trusts* [1965] 1 W.L.R. 1229 (it was proposed to substitute June 14, 1973 in lieu of the applicant's death as the date when the persons to take were to receive the capital of the settled funds; Stamp J. refused the application on behalf of unborn beneficiaries because it could happen (even if it was a remote eventuality) that the applicant might survive the proposed date and under the arrangement such persons would have no interest in the fund, whereas they would have under the original settlement).

Again, in *Re Tinker's Settlement*,[74] Russell J. declined to accept the argument that it was for the benefit of unborn persons as members of a family viewed as a whole that something should be done which, although reasonable and fair, was to their financial detriment.

The same test was applied in *Re T.'s Settlement Trusts*[75] although in this case this does not appear to have been the primary reason for the decision of Wilberforce J. to refuse to approve a proposed arrangement to transfer an infant female's share of settled funds to trustees to hold on protective trusts for her lifetime, with remainders over. The infant would otherwise have become absolutely entitled in possession to the funds on attaining 21 and the arrangement had been devised because she had shown herself to be irresponsible in matters of money. A secondary reason for this refusal was that the proposals were not confined simply to dealing in a beneficial way with the special requirements of the infant. Another proposal for variation was later approved; this was to the effect that the infant's right to capital should be deferred for a time, she being given a protected life interest in the meantime.

It must, however, be admitted that these authorities do not appear to be entirely consistent with the decision of Danckwerts J. in *Re Cohen's Will Trusts*.[76] It was contended that in the admittedly unlikely event of one of the testator's children predeceasing his widow, who was then aged nearly 80, the proposed arrangement would not be advantageous to his grandchildren, some of whom were infants. However, Danckwerts J. held that risk of some kind was inherent in every application under the Act and, since this risk was one which it would be reasonable for an adult to run, the court would run it on behalf of the infants.

This sort of attitude is clearly sound when a risk is non-existent. Indeed in such cases it may not even be necessary to apply to the court. Thus it has been held[77] that trustees can properly and with complete safety deal with their funds on the basis that a woman of 70 will not have a further child and in such circumstances an application under the Act is inappropriate; "the Act is concerned to vary trusts applicable in events which will or may happen and not to cover impossible contingencies".[78] But where there is an identifiable risk, the more general attitude is to require it to be covered by insurance. This is particularly appropriate if the risk is that a beneficiary will die within a short time of the variation being made. In such circumstances, when the proposed variation is, when viewed broadly, for the financial benefit of the beneficiaries, the court will generally require the life of that beneficiary to be insured, even if the premiums have to be paid for out of income and are in that sense at the expense of an infant beneficiary.[79]

---

[74] [1960] 1 W.L.R. 1011.

[75] [1964] Ch. 158. The primary ground for the decision of Wilberforce J. is discussed *post*, p. 672.

[76] [1959] 1 W.L.R. 865; compare *Re Cohen's Settlement Trusts* [1965] 1 W.L.R. 1229 (which concerned a completely different family), see *ante*, n. 73).

[77] *Re Pettifor's Will Trusts* [1966] Ch. 257.

[78] *ibid.* at 260, 261, *per* Pennycuick J. See also *Re Westminster Bank Ltd's Declaration of Trust* [1963] 1 W.L.R. 820, where an order was made under the Variation of Trusts Act 1958 in respect of a woman aged 50.

[79] For an example, see *Re Robinson's Settlement Trusts* [1976] 3 All E.R. 61.

Finally, it should be emphasised that the wishes of the settlor or testator do not prevent the court from concluding that an arrangement confers benefit. In *Goulding v. James*,[80] the testatrix left her residuary estate to her daughter for life, remainder to her 32 year old grandson at the age of 40 absolutely, remainder to any of her great-grandchildren living at her grandson's death. An arrangement was proposed whereby 45 per cent was to be held for each of the daughter and the grandson absolutely, with the remaining 10 per cent held for the as yet unborn grandchildren, who even if born obviously only had a somewhat limited chance of receiving anything under the existing trusts.[81] Laddie J. refused to approve this on the grounds that the testatrix had, on the evidence, wished to prevent her daughter from having any access to capital because she did not trust her son-in-law and wished to defer her grandson's interest until the age of 40 because he had not yet "settled down".[82] This decision was reversed by the Court of Appeal. Mummery L.J. held that "the intentions and wishes of [the testatrix], expressed externally to her will in relation to the adult beneficiaries and an adult non-beneficiary, had little, if any, relevance or weight to the issue of approval on behalf of the future unborn great grandchildren, whose interest in residue was multiplied five-fold under the proposed arrangement".[83] Sir Ralph Gibson went even further, saying that it was not clear to him "why evidence of the intention of the testator can be of any relevance whatever if it does no more than explain why the testator gave the interests set out in the will and the nature and degree of feeling with which such provisions were selected".[84]

The authorities considered thus far have, like the immense majority of all applications under the Act, been concerned exclusively with financial benefit; this is a mundane consideration admitting of reasonable proof. But it has been clearly established that this is not necessarily the only consideration to be taken into account by the court. Thus in *Re T.'s Settlement Trusts*[85] the judge approved the alternative scheme of variation because on the special facts of the case the evidence showed that the infant beneficiary was irresponsible and immature; "there appears to me to be a definite benefit for this infant for a period during which it is to be hoped that independence may bring her into maturity and responsibility to be protected against creditors".[86] This decision was followed by Megarry J. in *Re Holt's Settlement*[87] where he said in relation to an arrangement postponing the vesting of interests in children from the age of 21 to 30: "The word 'benefit' in the proviso to section 1 of the Act of 1958 is plainly not confined to financial benefit, but may extend to moral or social benefit".[88] This approach was

---

[80] [1997] 2 All E.R. 239.
[81] The actuarial valuation of their contingent interest was only 1.85 per cent.
[82] [1996] 4 All E.R. 853.
[83] [1997] 2 All E.R. 239 at 251–252.
[84] *ibid.* at 252.
[85] [1964] Ch. 158.
[86] *ibid.* at 162.
[87] [1969] 1 Ch. 100.
[88] *ibid.* at 121.

confirmed by the decision of the Court of Appeal in *Re Weston's Settlement*,[89] where it was decided that it was for the benefit of children to be educated in England rather than in Jersey.

An even broader view of "benefit" in this context was taken in *Re Remnant's Settlement Trusts*,[90] where Pennycuick J. approved an arrangement deleting forfeiture clauses depriving certain children of their interests if they practised Roman Catholicism or married a Roman Catholic. This appears to have been on the basis that such provisions might operate as a deterrent to them in the selection of a husband and might also be a source of possible family dissension.

It is also clear that an arrangement which results in improvement in the general administration of the trust may also be a "benefit" within the meaning of the Act. As will be seen in a later Chapter,[91] it is on this ground that the courts have approved applications for the export of trusts to countries abroad where the beneficiaries are resident.

(2) The position of discretionary beneficiaries under protective trusts

It has already been stated that it is unnecessary to establish that an arrangement confers any benefit on discretionary beneficiaries under protective trusts.[92] Nevertheless, their interests cannot be simply ignored. As Wilberforce J. held in *Re Burney's Settlement Trusts*,[93] in approving an arrangement varying discretionary trusts, the discretionary power conferred on the court has still to be judicially exercised and it is incumbent on the applicant to make out a case for interfering with protective trusts. Indeed, the basic principle had been stated earlier, more generally, by Lord Evershed M.R. in *Re Steed's Will Trusts*,[94] where he said that "the court is bound to look at the scheme as a whole and when it does so, to consider, as surely it must, what really was the intention of the benefactor". The requirements were spelt out in *Re Baker's Settlement Trusts*,[95] where Ungoed-Thomas J. said that where property was held on protective trusts for the benefit of the applicant and an application was made to vary those trusts, evidence (including in this case that of the financial position of the applicant and her husband) should be laid before the court to show to what extent the protective trusts continued to serve any useful purpose.

(3) Fraud and public policy

Obviously a variation which is fraudulent or contrary to public policy will not be sanctioned.

Fraud has only arisen in connection with the doctrine of fraud on a power. In *Re Robertson's Will Trusts*,[96] the applicant had exercised a special power of

---

[89] [1969] 1 Ch. 223; for further discussion of this case, see *post*, p. 777. See also *Re C.L.* [1969] 1 Ch. 587 (mental patient surrendered his protected life interest and contingent interest in remainder; Cross J. held that it was for the patient's benefit because in all probability it was what he would have done if of sound mind).

[90] [1970] Ch. 560; compare *Re Tinker's Settlement* [1960] 1 W.L.R. 1011.

[91] See *post*, p. 775.

[92] s.1(1), proviso.

[93] [1961] 1 W.L.R. 545.

[94] [1960] Ch. 407 at 421.

[95] [1964] 1 W.L.R. 336.

[96] [1960] 1 W.L.R. 1050.

appointment in favour of his children as a preliminary to the proposed arrangement. His purpose and intention in making the appointment was to benefit his children and not himself. Later he was advised that his financial position would in fact be improved if the appointment were made and the scheme approved. But Russell J. held that to suppose his original purpose and intention had been changed or added to was unjustified. It followed that there was no fraud on the power, though, if there had been, the court would not have been able to approve the scheme.

However, subsequent case law appears to indicate a certain conflict as to the precise principles to be applied. In *Re Wallace's Settlement*[97] Megarry J. said that the fact that protected life tenants had executed appointments in favour of their children in itself raised a case for inquiry because the life tenants benefited by the arrangement; however, on the evidence he was satisfied that there was no fraud on the power because the benefit to the life tenants was not substantial and they had intended to make the appointment before the arrangement was approved. On the other hand, in *Re Brook's Settlement*[98] Stamp J. adopted a rather different approach. He held that the exercise of a special power of appointment amounted to a fraud on the power and he was unable to approve the variation. Here one of the purposes of the appointment (by a protected life tenant in favour of his children from which he would also benefit from a division of the capital) was to enable the life tenant to obtain what he could not otherwise get, namely capital rather than income. This was enough to invalidate the appointment. The important feature of *Re Brook's Settlement* is that the judge emphasised that the question is whether the purpose of the appointment amounted to a fraud, not, as was apparently suggested in *Re Wallace's Settlement*, the effect of the appointment on the financial position of the appointor. It is thought that *Re Brook's Settlement* applies the correct principle.

The difficulties that may thus arise as a result of a fraud on the power, however inadvertent, may in some circumstances be avoided by releasing the power. For no question of a fraud on a power can arise on a mere release. And it has been held that, provided that the power in question can be released,[99] the court will approve an arrangement varying a settlement even though the objects of the power are ignored.[1] There appears to be some doubt as to whether the release should be effected by deed, or whether it can be inferred from the facts. The latter would seem to be sufficient.[2]

Even if the power cannot be released (if, for example, it was given to the donee as trustee)[3] it still seems possible to apply to the court for an arrangement extinguishing the power because this amounts to varying or revoking a trust within section 1 of the Act. But because the power is not of itself

---

[97] [1968] 1 W.L.R. 711.

[98] [1968] 1 W.L.R. 1661.

[99] See *Re Will's Trust Deeds* [1964] Ch. 219; see *ante*, p. 197, and see Hawkins (1968) 84 L.Q.R. 64.

[1] *Re Christie-Miller's Settlement* [1961] 1 W.L.R. 462; *Re Courtland's Settlement* [1965] 1 W.L.R. 1385; *Re Ball's Settlement* [1968] 1 W.L.R. 899.

[2] In *Re Ball's Settlement* [1968] 1 W.L.R. 462 Megarry J. insisted on a formal release but in *Re Christie-Miller's Settlement* [1965] 1 W.L.R. 462 and *Re Courtland's Settlement* [1965] 1 W.L.R. 1385 an inferred release was regarded as sufficient.

[3] See *ante*, p. 198.

capable of release, the court is likely to impose conditions on the release. Thus in *Re Drewe's Settlement*[4] Stamp J. in approving an arrangement insisted that such a power could only be effected by deed and with the consent of the trustees.

The only reported case in which considerations of public policy have arisen is *Re Michelham's Will Trusts*,[5] where they were neatly sidestepped by Buckley J. Approval was sought to an arrangement whereby trust property was transferred to the applicants absolutely. The efficacy of the scheme depended on their continuing to remain unmarried. Insurance policies were therefore to be effected which would ensure that, if either did in fact marry, certain sums would become available to replace the funds thus transferred. The policies included a stipulation that the insurers should be indemnified by a Swiss bank if the policy moneys became payable. The bank proposed to give the indemnity on terms that it, in turn, should be indemnified by one or other of the applicants if the moneys became payable. The judge, in approving the arrangement, held that, although the counter-indemnities given by the applicants to the bank ought to be regarded as tending to discourage the applicants from marrying, that would not affect its validity. This was so because if the counter-indemnities were unenforceable by the bank on grounds of public policy, something which was a question of Swiss law, that fact alone would not relieve the bank from its obligation to indemnify the insurers.

(4) Perpetuity

The Perpetuities and Accumulations Act 1964[6] applies only to instruments taking effect after the commencement of the Act.[7] The question is how far this provision affects variations made under the Act of 1958. In *Re Holt's Settlement*[8] Megarry J. held that an arrangement (taken with the court order)[9] as an "instrument" for this purpose, with the result that provisions deriving their validity from the 1964 Act might be included in the arrangement and that this would apply not only to trusts created since the commencement of the 1964 Act but also to those created before this date.[10]

However, the difficulty does remain as to whether the instrument must take effect as a "disposition". The 1964 Act tends to suggest that this is necessary.[11] The point did not arise in *Re Holt's Settlement* because the applicant there surrendered a life interest and this clearly amounted to a "disposition". It seems, however, that if the arrangement does not involve a disposition, then the benefits of the 1964 Act cannot be utilised in respect of subsequent variations of the original trusts.[12]

---

[4] [1966] 1 W.L.R. 1518.
[5] [1964] Ch. 550.
[6] See *ante*, p. 208.
[7] s.15(5).
[8] [1969] 1 Ch. 100.
[9] See *post*, p. 674.
[10] The same principle was applied but no reasons were given in *Re Lloyd's Settlement* [1967] 2 W.L.R. 1078 in relation to s.13 and to the accumulation periods.
[11] See ss.1, 3(5).
[12] See *Re Holmden's Settlement* [1968] A.C. 685, where it was suggested that a mere alteration of the period for which discretionary trusts should continue was not a "disposition".

(5) The precise meaning of "arrangement"

There is no doubt that this term has been widely construed to cover many classes of variation. As Lord Evershed M.R. said in *Re Steed's Will Trusts*,[13] "it is deliberately used in the widest possible sense to cover any proposal which any person may put forward for varying or revoking trusts". It need not, therefore, necessarily be *inter partes*. Views of the trustees are relevant but not conclusive and, if necessary, will be overridden.[14]

The wide meaning thus attached to an arrangement was, however, modified in *Re T.'s Settlement Trusts*,[15] whose facts have already been considered. Here Wilberforce J. refused, as the primary ground for his decision, to sanction the arrangement initially proposed because it amounted to a completely new settlement and that was beyond the jurisdiction conferred by the Act. If this represents the true position there are limits to the conception of an "arrangement", although this does appear to be an unjustified abridgment of the court's jurisdiction.

Nevertheless subsequent case law does seem to have accepted the distinction between "variation" and "resettlement". In *Re Ball's Settlement*[16] Megarry J. laid down the following test:

"If an arrangement changes the whole substratum of the trust, it may well be that it cannot be regarded as merely varying that trust. But if an arrangement, while leaving the substratum effectuates the purpose by other means, it may still be possible to regard that arrangement as merely varying the original trusts, even though the means employed are wholly different and even though the form is completely changed."

However, he actually held that, although the arrangement sought rescinded all beneficial and administrative trusts of the settlement and substituted new provisions, he could approve it because it preserved the "general drift" of the old trusts. The fact remains that a pedantic distinction has grown up between "variation" and "resettlement" for which there appears to be neither any sanction in the words of the Act nor any practical justification.

(E) The Trustee Investments Act 1961

The Trustee Investments Act 1961[17] expressly preserves the discretion of the court under the Variation of Trusts Act 1958 to extend the trustees' powers of investment. And many applications have been made under the Variation of Trusts Act 1958 to extend the trustees' investment powers as well as to vary the beneficial trusts. The question, however, is whether the trustees are entitled under the Act of 1958 to obtain investment powers greater than those conferred by the Act of 1961. The answer in most of the reported cases was originally negative. Thus, in *Re Cooper's Settlement*,[18] Buckley J. held that the court must be satisfied that there are "special circumstances" in which the trustees should be given wider powers than the "normally appropriate"

---

[13] [1960] Ch. 407 at 419.
[14] *ibid.* at 420.
[15] [1964] Ch. 158; see *ante*, p. 667.
[16] [1968] 1 W.L.R. 899. See also *Re Holt's Settlement* [1969] 1 Ch. 100 at 117, *per* Megarry J.
[17] s.15, see *ante*, p. 554.
[18] [1962] Ch. 826.

powers indicated by the Act of 1961. The fact that the extension of investment powers proposed was part of an arrangement to vary beneficial interests was specifically rejected as amounting to a special circumstance
justifying a departure from the scope of the statutory scheme. Likewise in *Re
Kolb's Will Trusts*,[19] where the settlor clearly wished to invest the whole fund
in equities and it was only because of the wording of the instrument that the
trustees did not have the power to do so, Cross J. doubted whether this fact
alone constituted such special circumstances as to justify an extension of the
powers of investment conferred by the Act of 1961. Further, in *Re Clarke's
Will Trusts*[20] Russell J. was only prepared to go so far as to substitute the
requirements of the dividend history demanded of wider-range securities,
in place of those provided for in the trust instrument.

Only in one reported case from this period were "special circumstances"
justifying an extension found. This was in *Re University of London Charitable
Trusts*,[21] which as its name suggests related to charitable trusts. Wilberforce
J. held, *inter alia*,[22] that he was entitled to extend the range of investment
beyond that permitted by the Act of 1961 because, if he did not, the benefits
of a proposed combined investment pool which would arise from the saving
of administrative expenses, convenience of administration and the practica-
bility of dividing the combined pool into parts would be frustrated. However, the courts have now accepted that the Trustee Investments Act 1961
has become outdated and are now once again prepared to authorise extensions of investment powers. Thus in *Trustees of the British Museum v.
Attorney-General*[23] Megarry V.-C. took the view that the principle laid down
in *Re Kolb's Will Trusts* should no longer be followed. However, as has
already been seen, it has now been held[24] that, provided the beneficial
interests are not affected by the proposed extension of investment powers,
section 57 of the Trustee Act 1925 should be used in preference to the
Variation of Trusts Act 1958.

(F) Procedure and Formalities

(1) Form of application

An application should normally be made by a life-tenant or other person
entitled to the income of the trust funds. It should only be made by the
trustees, as Russell J. said in *Re Druce's Settlement Trusts*,[25] where "they are
satisfied that the proposals are beneficial to the persons interested and have
a good prospect of being approved by the court, and further, that if they do
not make the application no one else will". As these principles were satisfied
in this case, the application by the trustees was held to be proper.

In the ordinary way the trustees will be respondents, as will be all the
existing beneficiaries, adult and infant and the Attorney-General[26] if the

---

[19] [1962] Ch. 531.
[20] [1961] 1 W.L.R. 1471.
[21] [1964] Ch. 282.
[22] See also *ante*, p. 436.
[23] [1984] 1 W.L.R. 418.
[24] In *Anker-Petersen v. Anker-Petersen* (1991) 88/16 Law Soc. Gaz. 32.
[25] [1962] 1 W.L.R. 363.
[26] See *Re Longman's Settlement Trusts* [1962] 1 W.L.R. 455.

existing settlement contains a charitable trust. It is, moreover, the duty of persons appointed guardians *ad litem* for an infant to take proper legal advice and apprise themselves fully of the nature of the application and the manner in which the beneficial interest of the infant is proposed to be affected.[27] At the same time it is recognised that there is a limit to the necessity for joinder of parties. So it seems unnecessary, for reasons of practicality and expense, to join persons who are merely potential members of a class. Thus, it has been held that it is unnecessary to join persons who are only interested as the objects of a power which may never be exercised.[28] And the same view has been applied to persons interested under protective trusts which it is proposed to vary; as Wilberforce J. said in *Re Munro's Settlement Trusts*,[29] the court looks prima facie to the trustees as watchdogs to see that interested parties' interests are protected.

(2) Combined applications

Under section 53 of the Trustee Act 1925,[30] the court has power to make vesting orders in relation to an infant's beneficial interest. In some cases it may prove necessary to combine an application under this section with one under the Variation of Trusts Act 1958. This happened in *Re Bristol's Settled Estates*,[31] where Buckley J. authorised the execution of a disentailing assurance on behalf of an infant tenant in tail in remainder so that the property could be dealt with for his benefit under a proposed "arrangement" which the judge also approved.

(3) The effect of a variation

It now seems to be established that it is the arrangement itself and not the order of the court which effects the variation.[32] But it seems necessary to regard the order of the court and the arrangement as having been made at the same time.[33] The arrangement will, however, be embodied in, or referred to in, the order and, where this causes a disposition of beneficial interests, stamp duty was formerly payable (such voluntary dispositions are no longer subject thereto). In *Thorn v. I.R.C.*,[34] Walton J. had to consider the nature of the disposition affected. A trust fund was held upon protective trusts for the settlor's wife for life, with remainder to the settlor's daughter for life, and ultimately for the children and remoter issue of the daughter. An order had been made under the Act approving a variation on behalf of the unborn and unascertained issue of the daughter. The trustees contended that in giving its approval the court, in effect, dealt with the interest of each

---

[27] *Re Whittall* [1973] 1 W.L.R. 1027.

[28] *Re Christie-Miller's Settlement* [1961] 1 W.L.R. 462.

[29] [1963] 1 W.L.R. 145; compare *Re Courtland's Settlement* [1965] 1 W.L.R. 1385.

[30] See *ante*, p. 630.

[31] [1965] 1 W.L.R. 469; see also *Re Lansdowne's Will Trusts* [1967] Ch. 603.

[32] *Re Holt's Settlement* [1969] 1 Ch. 100. See also *Re Holmden's Settlement* [1968] A.C. 685 at 701, 705, 713; *Spens v. I.R.C.* [1970] 1 W.L.R. 1173 at 1183, 1184. Megarry J. in *Re Holt's Settlement* followed *Re Joseph's Will Trusts* [1959] 1 W.L.R. 1019, not *Re Hambledon's Will Trusts* [1960] 1 W.L.R. 82, which had held that the court order effected the variation.

[33] *Re Holt's Settlement* [1969] 1 Ch. 100 at 115. The main reason for this requirement seems to be that decisions made on the basis of *Re Hambledon's Will Trusts* [1960] 1 W.L.R. 82 would have been made without jurisdiction.

[34] [1976] 2 All E.R. 622.

unborn or unascertained person. Each interest, looked at separately, would have had almost no value. However, Walton J. held that the order affected the disposition of the totality of the separate interests which therefore fell to be valued as a composite whole. This decision will once again become important if *ad valorem* duty is ever reimposed on voluntary dispositions.

A further question is whether the trusts are effectively varied by the arrangement when the court order is made even though the arrangement does not comply with section 53(1)(c) of the Law of Property Act 1925. This requires that the disposition of an equitable interest should be in writing.[35] In *Re Holt's Settlement*[36] Megarry J. answered this question in the affirmative. In coming to this conclusion, he relied on *Oughtred v. I.R.C.*,[37] on the basis that the arrangement amounted to a specifically enforceable oral contract and so gave rise to a constructive trust; this meant that the requirements of section 53(1)(c) could therefore be ignored because of section 53(2) which exempts constructive trusts from them. In the House of Lords in *Oughtred v. I.R.C.*, this view was in fact adopted only by Lord Radcliffe, who was dissenting on the main issue, to which this point was, in the view of the majority, irrelevant.[38] However, Lord Radcliffe's view has since been expressly confirmed by the Court of Appeal in *Neville v. Wilson*,[39] so that the decision of Megarry J. now clearly constitutes the law. However, a variation will only take effect without formality on this basis where the subject matter of the trusts which have been varied is entirely pure personalty because all contracts for the sale of land are now required to be in writing.[40]

---

[35] For further discussion of this section and the authorities, see *ante*, p. 46.
[36] [1969] 1 Ch. 100.
[37] [1960] A.C. 206; see *ante*, p. 59.
[38] See *ante*, ibid.
[39] [1997] Ch. 144; see *ante*, p. 61.
[40] Under the Law of Property (Miscellaneous Provisions) Act 1989, s.2.

CHAPTER 24

BREACH OF TRUST

A breach of trust occurs if a trustee does any act which he ought not to do, or fails to do any act which he ought to do with regard to the administration of the trust, or with regard to the beneficial interests arising under the trust. It would be undesirable to attempt an exhaustive list of circumstances in which a breach of trust can be committed, but the following are examples:

(i) investment of trust moneys in unauthorised investments;

(ii) taking a profit from the trust not authorised by the trust instrument or by the court;

(iii) manipulating the investments to benefit one beneficiary at the expense of another;

(iv) negligently allowing trust property to remain under the control of one trustee only;

(v) paying trust property to the wrong person;

(vi) purchasing trust property without authority;

(vii) failing to exercise a proper discretion with regard to trust decisions.

Where there is an allegation of breach of trust, the following questions have to be considered:

(i) Has a breach of trust been committed?

(ii) If so, is the proposed defendant liable?

(iii) If so, what is the prima facie measure of liability?

(iv) Is there any right to contribution or indemnity?

(v) Is the proposed plaintiff in time to sue?

(vi) May the proposed defendant be relieved from liability by the court or otherwise?

If these questions are applied to alleged breaches of trust, they should be adequate to ensure that no relevant point is overlooked when looking at the position from the point of view of the trustee. If the matter is being looked at from the point of view of the beneficiary, it is also necessary to ask whether the beneficiary can take any other action if sufficient redress cannot be obtained from the trustees. This question is the subject of the last part of this Chapter.

I. THE LIABILITY OF A TRUSTEE FOR HIS OWN ACTS

There will usually be little difficulty in ascertaining whether a breach of trust has been committed by a trustee during his trusteeship. Complications sometimes arise, however, in respect of acts done at the beginning and end of a trusteeship.

On appointment, a trustee should take certain steps. He should inspect the trust instrument to ascertain the terms of the trust and to see whether any notices have been indorsed on it. He should ensure that all the trust property is transferred into his name jointly with the other trustees, for he may be liable if he allows the property to remain in the hands of another.[1] He may wish to go through the trust papers in order to familiarise himself with the circumstances of the trust. If in doing so, or in any other way, he learns that a breach of trust has been committed, he must obtain satisfaction from the person responsible. Should the new trustee not do so, he will himself be liable for breach of trust for his own omission. The only exception to this principle is if he is reasonably satisfied that it would be useless to institute proceedings because, for example, the former trustee cannot be found, or is destitute.[2]

On the other hand, unless he has knowledge that a breach of trust has been committed, or there are suspicious circumstances, a new trustee may assume that there has been no breach of trust.[3]

When a trustee retires from a trust, in principle he remains liable for breaches of trust committed during his trusteeship and his estate will be held liable if he is dead. He is only relieved from liability if and to the extent that he may have been released by the continuing trustees or by the beneficiaries provided that the latter were in possession of the relevant facts at the time.

It may sometimes happen that a breach of trust may occur shortly after one trustee retires. The retiring trustee will be liable if he contemplated that a breach of trust would occur and he retired with the intention of facilitating it or, believing that it would occur, he retired to avoid being involved in it. In such circumstances, he is liable because his motive in retiring was to enable the breach of trust to occur. If he merely realised that his retirement would facilitate the breach of trust, he will not be liable just for that reason[4] but he will be liable if, in addition to realising that his retirement would facilitate the breach, he foresaw, or ought reasonably to have foreseen, that such a breach would in fact take place. In this case he will have failed in his duty to prevent a breach of trust occurring. It follows that, if the retiring

---

[1] He will only be liable if loss is caused as a result of the property being left in the hands of others; *Re Miller's Deed Trusts* (1978) Law Society Gazette, May 3, 1978.

[2] *Re Forest of Dean Coal Co.* [1878] 10 Ch.D. 450.

[3] *Re Stratham* [1856] 8 De G.M. & G. 291.

[4] *Head v. Gould* [1898] 2 Ch. 250.

trustee did not foresee what would happen and the remaining trustees have simply taken advantage of his absence to perpetrate the breach, he will not himself have failed in any of his duties and will not be liable.[5]

Apart from this, a trustee is not liable for breaches of trust which occur after his retirement.

II. THE LIABILITY OF A TRUSTEE FOR THE ACTS OF HIS CO-TRUSTEES

A trustee can never be liable for the acts of his co-trustees as such but in certain circumstances he will be liable where a breach of trust is committed by his co-trustees if he himself has been in some way at fault. The position is governed by section 30 of the Trustee Act 1925, which has already been considered,[6] as interpreted in Re Vickery,[7] in which Maugham J. applied Re City Equitable Fire Insurance Co.[8]

The general intention of section 30 is clear, namely that a person is responsible for his own acts, neglects and defaults, and not for loss caused through the acts, neglects or defaults of any other person, including co-trustees and agents, unless the loss occurs "through his own wilful default".

It will be recalled that the difficulty arises from the meaning of the words "wilful default". It has already been explained[9] that the interpretation of "wilful default" made in Re Vickery and in Re City Equitable Fire Insurance Co. has been criticised by several writers because it does not represent the pre–1926 position. Section 30 of the Trustee Act 1925 replaced the now repealed section 31 of the Law of Property Amendment Act 1859, which itself merely incorporated the indemnity clause which it was then the usual practice to insert in trust instruments.[10] Cases decided on that indemnity clause and on the 1859 Act show clearly that the form of words purporting to exclude liability for loss unless it occurred through the wilful default of the trustee did not exclude liability even for purely passive and innocent breaches of trust.[11] It was thus formerly the law that a trustee would be liable for a breach of trust arising through the act or default of his co-trustee if he merely left a matter in the hands of his co-trustee without inquiry. The majority of pre-1926 cases fall into the following categories:

(i) where the trustee leaves a matter in the hands of his co-trustee without inquiry[12];

---

[5] ibid.
[6] See ante, p. 511.
[7] [1931] 1 Ch. 572.
[8] [1925] Ch. 407.
[9] See ante, p. 511.
[10] See Re Brier (1884) 26 Ch.D. 238 at 243, per Lord Selborne.
[11] Chambers v. Minchin (1802) 7 Ves. 186; Shipbrook v. Hinchinbrook (1810) 16 Ves. 477; Hanbury v. Kirkland (1829) 3 Sim. 265; Broadhurst v. Balguy (1841) 1 Y. & C.C.C. 16; Thompson v. Finch (1865) 8 De G.M. & G. 560; Mendes v. Guedalla (1862) 8 Jur. 878; Hale v. Adams (1873) 21 W.R. 400; Wynee v. Tempest (1897) 13 T.L.R. 360; Re Second East Dulwich Building Society (1899) 68 L.J.Ch. 196.
[12] See the authorities cited ante, n. 11.

    (ii) where he stands by while a breach of trust of which he is aware is being committed[13];

    (iii) where he allows trust funds to remain in the sole control of his co-trustee[14];

    (iv) where, on becoming aware of a breach of trust committed or contemplated by his co-trustee, he takes no steps to obtain redress.[15]

These rules sometimes operated inequitably in the case of passive breaches of trust. Thus, in *Underwood v. Stevens*[16] a trustee in good faith allowed trust funds to remain in the hands of his co-trustee and, when he made inquiries of his co-trustee as to certain transactions with those funds, the co-trustee gave false information. The trustee was held liable, however, notwithstanding the fact that the trust instrument provided that trustees should not be liable for loss unless it occurred through their wilful default. The effect of the indemnity clause was, therefore, markedly different from the prima facie meaning of the words used. The effect of the decision in *Re Vickery*[17] has, in effect, been to modify the third of the rules stated above, in interpreting "wilful default" as a consciousness of negligence or a recklessness in the performance of a duty.

Section 30(1) of the Trustee Act 1925 specifically exempts trustees from liability for signing receipts for the sake of conformity, unless they have actually received the trust money or securities. As all trustees have, as a general principle, to sign receipts, it will be appreciated that these documents frequently circulate among trustees prior to a transaction so that all the necessary signatures are obtained by the time that the transaction is to be completed. A trustee is not liable if any breach of trust occurs merely as a result of his having signed such a receipt, though of course if, for example, having signed it he allows his co-trustee to obtain money with the document and to retain that money for an unreasonable time, he will thereby have acted recklessly and will accordingly make himself liable.

The circumstances in which a trustee is liable for the acts of his agents have been considered in Chapter 15.

III. THE MEASURE OF LIABILITY

What is the measure of liability of a trustee who has committed a breach of trust? Leaving on one side the situation where the beneficiary seeks the

---

[13] In *Styles v. Guy* (1849) 1 Mac. & G. 422 at 433, Lord Cottenham stated that it is the duty of executors and trustees "to watch over, and if necessary, to correct, the conduct of each other". See also *Booth v. Booth* (1838) 1 Beav. 125; *Gough v. Smith* [1872] W.N. 18.

[14] *English v. Willats* (1831) 1 L.J.Ch. 84; *Ex parte Booth* (1831) Mont. 248; *Child v. Giblett* (1834) 3 L.J.Ch. 124; *Hewitt v. Foster* (1843) 6 Beav. 259; *Wiglesworth v. Wiglesworth* (1852) 16 Beav. 269; *Byass v. Gates* (1854) 2 W.R. 487; *Trutch v. Lamprell* (1855) 20 Beav. 116; *Cowell v. Gatcombe* (1859) 27 Beav. 568; *William v. Higgins* (1868) 17 L.T. 525; *Rodbard v. Cooke* (1877) 25 W.R. 555; *Lewis v. Nobbs* (1878) 8 Ch.D. 591.

[15] *Boadman v. Mosman* (1779) 1 Bro.C.C. 68; *Wilkins v. Hogg* (1861) 8 Jur.(N.S.) 25 at 26, *per* Lord Westbury.

[16] (1816) 1 Mer. 712.

[17] [1931] 1 Ch. 572; however compare *Re Lucking's Will Trusts* [1968] 1 W.L.R. 866.

imposition of a constructive trust on property which the trustee has himself obtained as a result of his breach of trust,[18] what the beneficiary will be seeking is an award of equitable compensation under *Nocton v. Lord Ashburton*[19]; the effect of that decision is that equitable compensation is available whether or not there has been a misappropriation of trust property.[20]

The primary means by which a beneficiary who is the victim of a breach of trust can obtain equitable compensation therefor is by requiring the trustee to comply with his obligation to account for his stewardship.[21] This involves the trustee rendering an account of what he has done with the trust property which has been in his hands. If the beneficiary is dissatisfied with what the trustee has done, then he has the right to "surcharge" or "falsify" the account rendered. If the trustee has negligently failed to obtain all the income or capital that he should have done for the benefit of the trust, the beneficiary will surcharge the account, in other words claim a sum additional to the amount which the trustee actually obtained; in these circumstances the excess is calculated on what is known as a footing of wilful default, in other words by reference to the specific amount of the loss occasioned by the trustee's lack of skill and care. If, on the other hand, the trustee has made an unauthorised disbursement, the beneficiary has the option of falsifying the account in that respect, in other words of disallowing the expenditure in question; in that case the trustee will then be treated as if he was still holding on trust the sum paid away and, once the account has been taken,[22] will be obliged to reimburse that sum to the trust.[23] However, where the disbursement was an unauthorised investment which has subsequently appreciated in value, it will not be in the interests of the beneficiary to falsify the account; he will therefore instead normally accept the unauthorised investment as part of the trust property and, in such circumstances, he is said to affirm or adopt the transaction. Whenever an account is surcharged or falsified, "the obligation of a defaulting trustee [to compensate the trust fund for such a loss] is essentially one of effecting restitution to the estate. The obligation is of a personal character and its extent is not to be limited by common law principles governing the remoteness of damage."[24]

---

[18] This type of claim was considered in Chap. 10.
[19] [1914] A.C. 932, discussed in detail *ante*, p. 288.
[20] Equitable compensation had always been available when there had been a misappropriation of trust property and in this respect the House of Lords did no more than reaffirm the continued existence of equity's jurisdiction to award it, then thought in some quarters to have been extinguished due to the very wide interpretation which was being given to *Derry v. Peek* (1889) 14 App.Cas. 337. However, the House of Lords went considerably further than this and upheld the existence of the same jurisdiction when there had been no misappropriation of trust property but merely a breach of fiduciary duty (in that case the fact that the defendant solicitor had failed adequately to disclose a conflict of interest).
[21] See Sir Peter Millett, writing extrajudicially: (1998) 114 L.Q.R. 214.
[22] The obligation to reimburse the trust does not arise as soon as the unauthorised disbursement has been made but only when the beneficiary elects to falsify it; until then, the trustee does not know whether or not he will choose to do so.
[23] *Clough v. Bond* (1838) 3 My. & Cr. 490 at 496–497, *per* Lord Cottenham L.C.
[24] *Re Dawson* [1966] 2 N.S.W.L.R. 211 at 214 (Supreme Court of New South Wales).

However, the taking of an account will not necessarily or usually be appropriate where there has been neither a failure to obtain nor a misapplication of trust property, where for example the breach of trust complained of is the failure of the trustee adequately to disclose a conflict of interest and duty.[25] In such circumstances, there will normally be nothing that can be surcharged or falsified and the quantum of recovery will therefore have to be established in some other way. Exactly how is a matter of considerable debate since, as one commentator has put it, "in many of the cases involving losses which stem from a fiduciary breach, courts jump straight from a finding of breach to a conclusion that the plaintiff must be completely restored to the position he was in before breach."[26] However, the general view is that in these circumstances it is appropriate to apply common law principles of remoteness of damages to the assessment of equitable compensation. This was the approach adopted by Lord Browne-Wilkinson in *Target Holdings v. Redferns*[27] when he applied the "but for" test of causation to the assessment of equitable compensation; although, as will be seen later on,[28] this was a case in which an account could appropriately have been taken, the beneficiary did not seek such an account. Lord Browne-Wilkinson's decision and the Commonwealth authorities on which he relied[29] were subsequently applied by Hobhouse L.J. in *Swindle v. Harrison*[30] and are therefore clearly applicable to any case in which an account is not taken.

It should be added that equitable compensation is not awarded in order to punish the trustee; however, if he has been fraudulent or has otherwise behaved particularly badly, the court will reflect its displeasure by increasing the amount of interest payable by the trustee above that which he would otherwise have been ordered to pay.[31]

The following examples illustrate these principles. All are concerned with the prima facie liability of the trustee and do not take into account the possibility of some protection or relief being given to the trustee in the manner which will be discussed later on.[32]

1. *Payments to the Wrong Person*

Where the trustees pay trust money to the wrong person, the beneficiaries are clearly entitled to falsify the disbursement made; consequently, the trustees are clearly liable to make good to the trust fund that amount, so

---

[25] Such a breach of fiduciary duty had been found in *Nocton v. Lord Ashburton* itself and equitable compensation was awarded. It was also held to have arisen in *Swindle v. Harrison* [1997] 4 All E.R. 705 where a solicitor failed to disclose all the facts of a loan transaction between him and his client; however, the client had suffered no loss as a result of the solicitor's breach of duty so no equitable compensation was actually awarded in that case.

[26] J. D. Davies in *Equity, Fiduciaries and Trusts 1993* (ed. Waters, 1993) 279 at p. 302.

[27] [1996] 1 A.C. 421.

[28] See *post*, p. 682.

[29] *Re Dawson* [1966] N.S.W.L.R. 211 (Supreme Court of New South Wales); *Canson Enterprises v. Boughton & Co.* (1991) 85 D.L.R.(4th) 129 (Supreme Court of Canada).

[30] [1997] 4 All E.R. 705 at 727–728.

[31] See *post*, pp. 688–690.

[32] See *post*, pp. 699–704.

that the income or capital sum wrongly paid, together with interest thereon,[33] can be paid out to the correct beneficiary.

An unusual recent illustration of the operation of this principle is provided by *Target Holdings v. Redferns*.[34] The plaintiff had agreed to lend £1,525,000 on the security of two properties which were in fact being acquired for £775,000 but, as a result of the interposition of two intermediate purchasers, appeared to be being purchased for £2,000,000. The defendant solicitors, who were acting in the normal way both for the purchasers and for the plaintiff mortgagee, were holding the mortgage advance on trust for the plaintiff with authority to release it to the vendor only upon receipt of the duly executed conveyances and mortgages of the properties. However, they released the funds to the intermediate purchasers several days before the execution of these documents. The plaintiff nevertheless obtained, admittedly after the release of the funds, the mortgage securities which it had instructed the defendants to obtain. However, those securities proved to be insufficient and the plaintiff failed to recover more than £1,000,000 of the sum advanced; this loss would of course have been incurred even if the defendants had complied with their instructions.

The plaintiff sought reconstitution of the trust fund. On an application for summary judgment, the Court of Appeal[35] held that the obligation of a trustee who had committed a breach of trust was to put the trust fund in the same position as it would have been if no breach had taken place and that, where the breach consisted in the wrongful payment of trust moneys to a stranger, there was an immediate loss which the trustee was immediately liable to reimburse; it was not necessary for there to be any inquiry as to whether the loss would have occurred if there had been no breach of trust. Summary judgment was therefore ordered. However, this decision was reversed by the House of Lords. Lord Browne-Wilkinson held that there was only any obligation to reimburse the trust fund at all when the trust in question was ongoing rather than where the beneficiary was, like the plaintiff, absolutely entitled; further, even when such an obligation arose, it was not possible to "stop the clock" at the moment when the wrongful payment occurred and ignore all subsequent events. He therefore held that the liability of a trustee to pay equitable compensation was subject to a "but for" test of causation. The defendants would consequently only be liable if it could be shown that the transaction would not have proceeded and the plaintiff's loss would therefore not have been incurred but for the payment by the defendants to the intermediate purchasers in breach of trust.[36] The defendants were therefore given leave to defend the action; however, because of the high probability that the test of causation would be satisfied, they were ordered to pay £1,000,000 into Court as a condition of being allowed to do so.

---

[33] For the rate of interest, see *post*, pp. 688–690.

[34] [1996] 1 A.C. 421. This case is analysed in detail in *Trends in Contemporary Trust Law* (ed. Oakley, 1996), p. 217.

[35] [1994] 1 W.L.R. 1089.

[36] This had been able to be shown in *Alliance & Leicester Buidling Society v. Edgestop* (1991), unreported.

It has been contended[37] that this case would have been more appropriately decided on the basis of the defendant trustees' obligation to account. The plaintiff had authorised a payment only in exchange for the mortgage securities; consequently, it was entitled to "falsify" the defendants' account in respect of the payments to the intermediate purchasers since those mortgages had not yet been executed. Had an account been taken at that stage, the plaintiff would undoubtedly have been entitled to reimbursement of the whole sum paid away and could clearly have obtained summary judgment therefor. However, the defendants had subsequently complied with their instructions by obtaining the mortgage securities, something which they were at that stage still authorised to do; this transformed their unauthorised payment into an authorised one. Consequently, nothing would be found to be due to the plaintiff on any subsequent taking of an account. The taking of an account would thus have produced exactly the same result as that arrived at by the House of Lords. This analysis cannot be faulted but that does not alter the fact that no account was actually sought in the proceedings. This was because the plaintiff initially brought only proceedings for professional negligence; it was only in the course of the trial at first instance that the plaintiff became aware of the payment to the intermediate purchasers and the consequential breach of trust. The decision of the House of Lords therefore remains a perfectly acceptable authority on the measure of equitable compensation available where no account is taken. However, the taking of an account is obviously the more appropriate method by which to proceed when trust funds have been paid to the wrong person. It is therefore inevitable that an account will normally be the means by which beneficiaries proceed in cases of this kind.

2. *The Making of Unauthorised Investments*

Where trustees invest the trust funds in unauthorised investments, the beneficiaries have the right to falsify the disbursement and require the trustees to replace the funds wrongfully invested. In such circumstances, the trustees will in effect have to sell the unauthorised investments and make good whatever loss results.[38] On the other hand, where the unauthorised investment has made a profit, it will not be in the interests of the beneficiaries to falsify the account and, provided that they are all ascertained and *sui juris*, they will therefore be able to adopt the unauthorised investment and take the profit. Where they do so, they clearly should not be entitled also to claim the difference between the value of the improper investment and any higher amount that would have been obtained by an authorised investment. However, there is in fact a conflict of authority on this point.[39] Where the trust is for persons by way of succession, an unauthorised investment which yields a very high income will have benefited the

---

[37] By Sir Peter Millett in (1998) L.Q.R. 214.

[38] *Re Salmon* (1889) 42 Ch.D. 351.

[39] The conclusion suggested in the text was adopted in *Thornton v. Stokill* (1855) 1 Jur. 151 but in *Re Lake* [1903] 1 K.B. 439 the beneficiaries were held to be entitled to the additional amount as well.

income beneficiary at the expense of the remaindermen. Consequently, whether the investment is falsified or adopted, it will be necessary for the income actually obtained to be apportioned between the income beneficiary and the remaindermen; the income beneficiary will be entitled to interest at the ordinary rate and the balance of the income will then be added to the trust fund as capital.[40]

In one unusual case, the unauthorised investment consisted of an unauthorised improvement to other trust property; in such circumstances, the beneficiaries will in effect have no option but to adopt the investment. In *Vyse v. Foster*,[41] trustees held land and money upon a common trust. Without authority, they expended some of the money on erecting a bungalow on the land at a cost of £1,600; this benefited the trust by more than the £1,600 expended. An attempt was made to say that not only were the trustees liable to reimburse the £1,600 because this expenditure was unauthorised but the beneficiaries were also entitled to the benefit of the bungalow because it was an accretion to the trust property. The Court of Appeal and House of Lords rejected this argument and it is only surprising that it was accepted at first instance. However, had the erection of the bungalow benefited the trust by less than the cost of erecting it, the beneficiaries could undoubtedly have surcharged the disbursement and recovered the difference.

A special rule governs losses on mortgage securities. As has been seen, when an unauthorised investment is made which results in loss, the trustees are generally liable for the whole of that loss. But in the case of investments on the security of mortgages, section 9 of the Trustee Act 1925 provides that where trust moneys are invested on "mortgage security which would at the time of the investment be a proper investment in all respects for a smaller sum" the trustee will only be liable for the excess over that smaller sum, although that may not represent the loss to the estate. A trustee will not, however, be protected by this section where he ought not to have invested on the security of mortgages at all.[42]

3. *Sales of Authorised Investments for Improper Purposes*

If trustees sell an authorised investment and reinvest the proceeds in an unauthorised one, the beneficiaries have the same choice as to whether to falsify or to adopt the unauthorised investment. If it is falsified, that is likely to be because it has resulted in a loss. In such circumstances, the beneficiaries have a further choice. They can compel the trustees either to make good the difference between the sale price of the authorised investment and the proceeds of sale of the unauthorised investment, or to repurchase for the trust the authorised security, taking credit for the proceeds of sale of the unauthorised security. Suppose, therefore, that the trustees hold sell 400 shares in I.C.I. plc (an investment which is authorised by the Trustee Investments Act 1961) for £1,000 and reinvest that £1,000 in the purchase of shares in the Uranium Exploration Co. Ltd (an unauthorised investment because the latter is a private company). If a year later the shares are sold at a loss

---

[40] *Re Emmet's Estate* (1881) 17 Ch.D. 142. As to the "ordinary" rate of interest, see *post*, p. 688.
[41] (1872) L.R. 8 Ch. 309, affirmed (1874) L.R. 7 H.L. 318.
[42] *Re Walker* (1809) 59 L.J. Ch. 386; see *ante*, p. 567.

for £200, the beneficiaries have a choice. They can compel the trustees to pay to the trust fund £1,000, the proceeds of the I.C.I. plc shares, less the £200 which they have paid in from the sale of the Uranium Exploration Co. Ltd shares. Alternatively, they can compel the trustees to purchase for the trust 400 I.C.I. shares, however much they might then cost; if shares in I.C.I. plc have doubled in price, the trustees will therefore have to pay £2,000 for them, less the £200 received from the sale of the unauthorised investments.

This principle was taken a stage further in Re Massingberd.[43] In that case the trustees sold Consols and reinvested in an unauthorised security. The unauthorised security was in due course sold without loss but by this time the price of Consols had risen. The court held that the trustees should place the beneficiaries in the same position as they would have been had no sale taken place with the result that they had themselves to pay the increase in the price of the Consols.

Where an unauthorised investment is falsified, the trustees are not entitled to take into account any loss which would have been sustained if they had strictly performed the trust.[44] Suppose, therefore, trustees are directed to invest in one particular investment. They improperly sell that investment for £1,000 and invest that sum in another investment. The latter declines in value and is sold for £800, but the investment which the trustees were directed to make has also declined and its market price is £700. If the beneficiaries falsify the account, the trustees are liable to make good, at the option of the beneficiaries, the difference between £800 and £1,000 and they are not excused from liability by virtue of the fact that, if the investment which they had been directed to make had been retained, the holding would have been worth only £700. This is because the effect of falsifying the investment is that the trustees are treated as having held £1,000 on trust for the beneficiaries at all times.

4. Failure to Invest the Trust Property Properly

Section 11(1) of the Trustee Act 1925 gives trustees the power to pay trust money into a bank while an investment is being sought. However, there seems no reason why this should affect the cases decided before 1926 to the effect that moneys must not be left uninvested for an unreasonable time.[45] On the basis that the old rules still apply, the beneficiaries will be entitled to the following equitable compensation (this will not be an appropriate case for the taking of an account). If the trustees ought to have invested in a range of investments, as will usually be the case, their liability is limited to making good the difference between any interest actually received and the rate of interest fixed by the court.[46] The trustees are not liable for any capital loss, because it is impossible to ascertain it.[47] If, on the other hand, the trustees

---

[43] (1890) 63 L.T. 296.
[44] Shepherd v. Mouls (1845) 4 Hare 500 at 504; Watts v. Girdlestone (1843) 6 Beav. 188; Byrchall v. Bradford (1822) 6 Madd. 235.
[45] Cann v. Cann (1884) 33 W.R. 40.
[46] As to which, see post, p. 688.
[47] Shepherd v. Mouls (1845) 4 Hare 500 at 504, per Wigram V.-C.

ought to have invested in one specified security only but did not do so, in the event of the price rising they can be compelled to purchase such an amount of that specified security as they could have purchased with the trust fund at the proper time.

Trustees may erroneously regard their investment powers as more limited than they actually are and, as a result invest in a more restricted range of investments than they were actually obliged to. This occurred in *Nestlé v. National Westminster Bank*.[48] The Court of Appeal held that a beneficiary who could prove that loss had been suffered thereby could obtain equitable compensation. However, save in extreme cases (the court used as an example the investment of the entire trust fund in fixed interest securities when the trustees had power to invest in equities), such a loss will be extremely difficult to prove and could not be established in that case.

5. *Use by Trustees of the Trust Funds for their Personal Purposes*

If the trustees use the trust money for their personal purposes, the beneficiaries will clearly be entitled to falsify these disbursements. The trustees will consequently be liable to pay back the amount used, or the value[49] of any property improperly sold to provide the funds which the trustees have used.

Special rules apply as to interest.[50] However, instead of receiving interest, the beneficiaries can instead require the trustees to pay over the actual profit which they have received.[51] Further, if a trustee has mixed the trust money with his own money and invested the whole in something which is still identifiable, the beneficiaries will normally be able to maintain an equitable proprietary claim and recover, at their election,[52] either the amount of the trust money invested or a proportional share of whatever profit has been made—they will obviously do the former if the investment has fallen in value and the latter if it has risen in value. However, their right to the profit has been held to be restricted to cases where that profit was actually enhanced by the use of the trust money[53]; it will clearly only be in extremely unusual circumstances that this will be held not to be the case.

6. *The Date at which Losses are to be Assessed*

Where a trustee improperly deals with an asset which thereby ceases to be under his control, it is necessary to determine the date at which the loss to

---

[48] [1993] 1 W.L.R. 1260.
[49] Ascertained as at the date of judgment.
[50] See *post*, p. 688.
[51] *Newman v. Bennett* (1784) 1 Bro.C.C. 359; *Ex parte Watson* (1814) 2 V. & B. 414; *Walker v. Woodward* (1826) 1 Russ. 107 at 111; *Att-Gen. v. Solly* (1829) 2 Sim 518; *Wedderburn v. Wedderburn* (1838) 4 My. & Cr. 41 at 46; *Jones v. Foxall* (1852) 15 Beav. 388; *Williams v. Powell* (1852) 15 Beav. 388; *Macdonald v. Richardson* (1858) 1 Giff. 81; *Townend v. Townend* (1859) 1 Giff. 201; *Re Davis* [1902] 2 Ch. 314.
[52] The existence of this election was upheld in *Foskett v. McKeown* [1998] 2 W.L.R. 298 at 310, *per* Scott V.-C., although no profit was in fact recoverable in that case. Profits were recovered in *Docker v. Somes* (1834) 2 My. & K. 655 and *Edinburgh Town Council v. Lord Advocate* (1879) 4 App.Cas. 823. Equitable proprietary claims are considered *post*, pp. 716–743.
[53] *Re Tilley's Will Trusts* [1967] Ch. 1179; see *post*, p. 732.

the trust fund is to be measured. Previously, when the values of many assets were more stable than at the present time, the loss was ascertained at the date when proceedings were commenced. Thus in *Re Massingberd*,[54] where trustees improperly sold Consols, the Court of Appeal ordered them to pay the cost of replacing the Consols as at the date of the writ. Much more recently, in *Re Bell's Indenture*,[55] Vinelott J. said[56] that this was incorrect, and that the general principle was that the loss should be ascertained at the date of judgment. Subsequently, in *Jaffray v. Marshall*,[57] it was held that this question had not actually had to be decided in either of these cases which were therefore of no assistance; however, the conclusion actually reached in this case, that where there had been a continuing breach of trust, the trustees were liable to compensate the trust at the highest intermediate value of the property between the date of breach and the date of judgment, was clearly inconsistent with the subsequent decision in *Target Holdings v. Redferns*[58] and the House of Lords duly held that *Jaffray v. Marshall* had been wrongly decided. The law is thus uncertain at present; however, the view of Vinelott J. seems preferable.

Whatever the general rule is, it is at least clear if the trustees improperly dispose of an asset which, had they not disposed of it then, would have been properly disposed of at a later date, the loss is to be ascertained at that later date and not at any date thereafter. In *Re Bell's Indenture*[59] the court was concerned with a marriage settlement made in 1907 and a voluntary settlement made in 1930, which had a common trustee who was also a common beneficiary. In 1947, the trustees of the marriage settlement improperly sold a farm for £8,200 to the trustees of the voluntary settlement. In 1949 the latter properly sold the farm to a third party for £12,400. If the trustees of the marriage settlement had not sold the farm in 1947, they would undoubtedly have done so when the trustees of the voluntary settlement did in 1949. Vinelott J. held that the liability of the trustees of the marriage settlement was to be limited to the value of the farm in 1949. He also held that no account should be taken of the fact that, if the trustees of the marriage settlement had sold in 1949, they would probably have reinvested the proceeds of sale in another farm, because it was impossible to determine how any such other farm would have appreciated or depreciated.

Where in other circumstances a defaulting trustee is liable to make a payment by way of restitution, that liability continues until restitution is actually made; this is the case even if the settlement has in the meantime come to an end. In *Bartlett v. Barclays Bank Trust Co. (No.1)*[60] trustees were held liable for permitting a company in which they had a controlling interest to engage in hazardous property speculation and for the loss which ensued from the fall in the value of the shares in the company. Three of the beneficiaries became absolutely entitled to their shares in 1974 but the trust company continued to hold the shares as nominees of the beneficiaries until

---

[54] (1890) 63 L.T. 296.
[55] (1980) 1 W.L.R. 1217.
[56] *ibid*. at 1233.
[57] [1993] 1 W.L.R. 1285.
[58] [1996] 1 A.C. 421.
[59] [1980] 1 W.L.R. 1217.
[60] [1980] Ch. 515.

September 1978, when the company disposed of all its speculative invest-ments and all the shares were sold. In *Bartlett v. Barclays Bank Trust Co. (No. 2)*[61] it was held that the loss suffered by the beneficiaries was to be assessed as at September 1978.

7. *The Absence of any Allowance in respect of Tax*

Where a trustee takes trust moneys and applies them for his own purposes, he is liable to restore the moneys which he has taken and is not allowed to benefit from any reduction in the liability to tax which ensues from the misapplication.[62] A further point which arose in *Re Bell's Indenture*[63] was that, if the trustees of the marriage settlement had not improperly sold the farm in 1947 but had instead retained it until 1949, sold it then, and rein-vested the proceeds of sale, the value of the trust fund would have been much greater than it actually was. This would in turn have given rise to greater liabilities to estate duty[64] on the deaths of the successive income beneficiaries. It was that the defaulting trustee was not entitled to reduce the amount which he had to pay to make good the breach of trust by the amount of that tax saving. This decision was followed in *Bartlett v. Barclays Bank Trust Co. (No. 2).*[65] Had the trustee in that case not permitted the company to engage in loss-making speculative property investments, the company would have made larger dividend payments. This would have increased the income and with it the income tax liability of the beneficiaries. Similarly, if the company had not sustained losses, the shares could have been sold for a higher price, which would probably have increased the liability of the beneficiaries to capital gains tax. Brightman J. however, held, that the trus-tees were liable to make good the gross loss and could not take into account the tax savings which had occurred, even though this produced "a some-what unjust bias"[66] against the trustees.

8. *The Incidence of Interest*

Where a trustee has misapplied trust funds, he is liable not only to replace those funds, but also to pay interest thereon. A trustee is similarly liable to pay interest where income is lost as a result of his failure to make an investment.[67] In such circumstances, two questions arise: first, at what rate is the interest to be calculated and, secondly, whether the interest to be simple or compounded and, if the latter, at what frequency.[68] The approach of the courts, particularly with regard to the rate of interest, has changed in recent years. The present position appears to be as follows.

---

[61] *ibid.*
[62] Thus, the rule in *British Transport Commission v. Gourley* [1956] A.C. 185 does not apply.
[63] [1980] 1 W.L.R. 1217; see *ante*, p. 687.
[64] The forerunner of inheritance tax.
[65] [1980] Ch. 515.
[66] *ibid.* at 538.
[67] *Stafford v. Fiddon* (1857) 23 Beav. 386.
[68] The differences are striking. On £10,000, 10% simple interest for 10 years will amount to £10,000, 10% interest compounded yearly will amount to £15,937 and 10% interest com-pounded half-yearly will amount to £16,533.

Although in the nineteenth century the ordinary interest rate was 4 per cent,[69] this is now accepted to be totally out of line with modern rates and the general rule is instead now broadly for the payment of the current commercial rate of interest. This has sometimes been taken to be 1 per cent above what used to be called the minimum lending rate (now rechristened the base rate).[70] However, an alternative practice[71] has been to take the rate allowed from time to time on the court's short term investment account.[72] This rate, which is generally in line with that offered on National Savings investments, is varied from time to time by statutory instrument. Changes are usually made towards the beginning of a calendar year and, because they are made much less frequently than changes in base rate, calculation of the interest payable is more straightforward. If a trustee uses trust money for his own purposes, he will be ordered to pay a higher rate where it can reasonably be concluded that he would have realised a higher rate.[73] This is the case even in the absence of any evidence that the trustee did in fact derive a higher rate.

Simple interest is the general rule in the absence of special circumstances.[74] However, the court has a discretion to order a trustee to pay compound interest. He will be ordered to pay interest compounded annually if he was under an obligation to accumulate the trust income.[75] If, however, he should have invested the fund in a specified investment and accumulated the income therefrom, then the interest must be compounded at the same intervals as interest or dividends would have been received on that investment.[76] A trustee will also be ordered to pay interest compounded annually if he has used trust money in his own business[77] or for his own commercial purposes but probably not if he has used it in his professional practice.[78] Although the purpose of ordering a trustee to pay compound rather than simple interest has been stated[79] not to be to punish the trustee,

---

[69] *Att.-Gen. v. Alford* (1855) 4 De G.M. & G. 843; *Fletcher v. Green* (1864) 33 Beav. 426.

[70] *Wallersteiner v. Moir (No. 2)* [1975] Q.B. 373; *Belmont Finance Corporation v. Williams Furniture (No. 2)* [1980] 1 All E.R. 393; *Guardian Ocean Cargoes v. Banco do Brasil (No. 3)* [1992] 2 Lloyd's Rep. 193.

[71] *Bartlett v. Barclays Bank Trust Co Ltd (No. 2)* [1980] Ch. 515; *Jaffray v. Marshall* [1993] 1 W.L.R. 1285 (overruled on other grounds by the House of Lords in *Target Holdings v. Redferns* [1996] 1 A.C. 421); *Mathew v. T. M. Sutton* [1994] 1 W.L.R. 1455.

[72] Established under s.6(1) of the Administration of Justice Act 1965. The rates payable from time to time are set out in The Rules of the Supreme Court (the "White Book").

[73] *Att.-Gen. v. Alford* (1855) De G.M. & G. 852; *Mathew v. T. M. Sutton* [1994] 1 W.L.R. 1455.

[74] *Stafford v. Fiddon* (1857) 23 Beav. 386; *Burdick v. Garrick* (1870) 5 Ch. App. 233; *Vyse v. Foster* (1874) L.R. 7 H.L. 318; *Belmont Finance Corporation v. Williams Furniture (No. 2)* [1970] 1 All E.R. 393. This was the basis on which the lower courts held the local authority liable to pay compound interest in *Westdeutsche Landesbank Girozentrale v. Islington L.B.C.* [1994] 4 All E.R. 890 (Hobhouse J.) [1994] 1 W.L.R. 938, CA. However, the House of Lords [1996] A.C. 669 held that the local authority was not a trustee and so this basis did not apply; the House also held, by a majority, that there was no equitable jurisdiction to order the payment of compound interest on a purely common law claim.

[75] *Raphael v. Boehm* (1805) 11 Ves. 92; *Re Barclay* [1899] 1 Ch. 674.

[76] *Re Emmet's Estate* (1881) 17 Ch.D. 142; *Gilroy v. Stephens* (1882) 30 W.R. 745.

[77] *Wallersteiner v. Moir (No. 2)* [1975] Q.B. 373; *Guardian Ocean Cargoes v. Banco do Brasil (No. 3)* [1992] 2 Lloyd's Rep. 193.

[78] *Burdick v. Garrick* (1870) 5 Ch. App. 233; *Hale v. Sheldrake* (1889) 60 L.T. 292.

[79] By Lord Hatherley in *Burdick v. Garrick* (1870) 5 Ch. App. 233.

compounding does appear to have been used for this purpose in certain cases of active and deliberate fraud or misconduct.[80]

Where a trustee pays interest, it seems that it is for the court to decide whether or not the income beneficiaries are entitled to receive the whole of that interest. In *Bartlett v. Barclays Bank Trust Co. (No. 2)*[81] Brightman J. said[82]: "To some extent the high interest rates payable on money lent reflect and compensate for the continual erosion in the value of money by reason of galloping inflation. It seems to me arguable, therefore, that if a high rate of interest is payable in such circumstances, a proportion of that interest should be added to capital in order to help maintain the value of the corpus of the trust estate. It may be, therefore, that there will have to be some adjustment as between life tenant and remainderman." This approach, which reflects that adopted where there is an unauthorised investment in a high income producing security, was applied in *Jaffray v. Marshall*,[83] in which judicial notice was taken of the fact that high rates of interest contain a large element which merely preserves capital values (which should belong to the remaindermen) while, in times when inflation was at a less high level, the rate of return needed to preserve capital was not as high. Since the period in question was of the latter kind, the interest (at the short term investment account rate) was apportioned equally between the tenant for life and the remainderman. It is to be hoped that the overruling of this decision on other grounds by the House of Lords in *Target Holdings v. Redferns*[84] does not prevent these helpful observations from being applied in future similar cases.

9. *The Right to Set-Off*

If a trustee commits more than one breach of trust, he cannot set off a gain made in one transaction against a loss suffered in another. However, each transaction is considered as a whole. In *Fletcher v. Green*[85] trustees made an authorised investment on mortgage. The property was in due course sold at a loss and the proceeds were paid into court. The court authorities invested the money in Consols, which rose in price. It was held that the trustees could offset the gain in the Consols against the loss on the mortgage as both were incidents in the same transaction. On the other hand, in *Dimes v. Scott*[86] trustees committed a breach of trust in that they ought to have sold an unauthorised investment and invested the proceeds in Consols. Much later on, part of the unauthorised investment was sold and the proceeds were then invested in Consols. By that time the market price of Consols had fallen considerably from the price at which they had been standing when the investment should have been made. The trustees sought to offset the gain made by virtue of the fact that they had thus been able to buy a larger quantity of Consols against the loss which had been suffered on the sale of

---

[80] Such as *Jones v. Foxall* (1852) 15 Beav. 388; *Gordon v. Gonda* [1955] 1 W.L.R. 885.
[81] [1980] Ch. 515.
[82] *ibid.* at 538.
[83] [1993] 1 W.L.R. 1285.
[84] [1996] 1 A.C. 421.
[85] (1864) 33 Beav. 426.
[86] (1828) 4 Russ. 195.

the unauthorised investment. It was held that they could not do so for these were two distinct transactions, not one. The breach of trust was in not realising the unauthorised investment. The gain arose from the authorised investment being at an unusually low figure. *Dimes v. Scott* was followed in *Wiles v. Gresham*,[87] where trustees of a marriage settlement committed a breach of trust by negligently failing to recover from the husband the sum of £2,000 which he had covenanted to pay to them. They then committed a further breach of trust by investing some of the other trust funds in the purchase of land without having any authority so to do. However, the husband improved the land considerably by the use of his own funds and it consequently became worth considerably more than the trustees had paid for it. When a claim was made against them for failure to recover the £2,000, the trustees sought to set off the profit which had fortuitously been made on their unauthorised investment in the land; they also were held to be unable to do so because the two transactions were distinct. Both decisions, particularly that in *Dimes v. Scott*, are on the harsh side and it may be that if similar facts recurred today the court might strive to reach different conclusions.

While the rule established by these authorities is entirely clear, namely that a gain can only be set off against a loss if both occur in the same transaction, it is not always easy to decide whether two or more events are stages in the same transaction or separate transactions. The test seems to be whether all the individual steps taken in pursuance of a common policy can be treated as one "transaction" for this purpose. Thus, in *Bartlett v. Barclays Bank Trust Co. (No. 1)*,[88] where the trustee allowed the company to embark on two speculative property developments as part of the company's policy of seeking to increase the cash funds available to it, the trustee was allowed to offset the profit from one development against the loss arising from the other.

IV. THE POSITION OF TRUSTEES INTER SE

Trustees are under a duty to act jointly; therefore they only have the authority to act individually if the trust instrument so provides. Decisions of trustees must usually be unanimous and with very limited exceptions there is no question of a vote of the majority binding them all.[89] They are also under an obligation to ensure that all the trust property and investments are placed in the names of all the trustees. In principle, each trustee therefore takes an equal part in the administration of the trust and has an equal say in what happens to the trust property. Thus, if a breach of trust has been committed, each trustee should be equally liable. However, the wronged beneficiary is not obliged to sue every single trustee; he can do so but is just as entitled to sue only one or two of them. For this reason the liability of trustees is joint and several.

---

[87] (1854) 2 Drew. 258 24 L.J.Ch. 264.
[88] [1980] Ch. 515. See also *ante*, p. 572.
[89] See *ante*, p. 492.

If an action is successfully brought against only one or some of the trustees, the general rule is that the trustee(s) sued have a right of contribution against his co-trustees so that in the end each trustee will have contributed equally to the compensation paid to the beneficiary. Despite the principle of contribution, the trustee(s) sued may sometimes be in a very difficult position. Suppose that there are three trustees, Timothy, Titus and Tom, who commit a breach of trust involving the loss of £30,000. A beneficiary who chooses to sue Timothy alone has the right to recover the entire £30,000 from Timothy, the latter's right of contribution being completely irrelevant. Timothy can of course claim £10,000 from each of Titus and Tom but, if Titus has disappeared and Tom has gone bankrupt, Timothy's claim will remain unsatisfied; he will thus have paid out £30,000 without recovering any of it, and will not have received anything. The basic rule providing for equal contribution between trustees jointly liable for a breach of trust was, however, somewhat relaxed by the Civil Liability (Contribution) Act 1978 in order to achieve a greater degree of flexibility and a more equitable result. Under this legislation where the loss occasioned by the breach of trust occurs after 1978[90] the court has power to award, in favour of one trustee against another, contribution of such amount as is found to be just and equitable, having regard to the extent of the responsibility of the other trustee for the loss.[91] However, there can be little doubt that the old rule that no right of contribution arises where the trustees have been guilty of fraud[92] has survived this legislation.

Under the old rules of equity which are now affected by the Civil Liability (Contribution) Act 1978,[93] there were three cases in which a trustee who was successfully sued could claim a complete indemnity from one or more of his co-trustees. These were, first, where the breach of trust was committed on the advice of a solicitor-trustee; secondly, where one trustee alone had benefited from the breach of trust; and, thirdly, where one of the trustees was also a beneficiary.

Where one of the trustees was a solicitor and the breach of trust was committed solely in reliance on his advice, then the solicitor-trustee was obliged to indemnify his co-trustees.[94] It was not sufficient to show merely that one of the trustees at the time of the breach was a solicitor: it had to be shown that the other trustees were relying entirely on his advice. Thus in *Head v. Gould*[95] Miss Head and a solicitor, Mr Gould, were the trustees of a settlement. They sold a house forming part of the trust property and, instead of reinvesting the proceeds, in breach of trust paid the proceeds to the life tenant, Miss Head's mother. Following a successful action by the remainderman against the two trustees, Miss Head unsuccessfully sought to be indemnified by Mr Gould. Kekewich J. found that she had not relied on Mr Gould but had actively urged him to commit the breach. Where the basic rule applied because the breach of trust was committed principally on the advice of the solicitor-trustee, in order successfully to resist a claim by his co-trustee

---

[90] ss.7(1), 10(1).
[91] ss.1(1), 2(1).
[92] *Bahin v. Hughes* (1886) 31 Ch.D. 390.
[93] s.2(2).
[94] *Lockhart v. Reilly* (1856) 25 L.J.Ch. 697.
[95] *Head v. Gould* [1898] 2 Ch. 250.

for indemnity it was for the solicitor-trustee to show that his co-trustee was in full possession of all the relevant facts and made an independent judgment. *Re Partington*[96] was a case involving improper investments. Stirling J. said: "I have got to consider the question, has [the solicitor] communicated what he did to [the co-trustee] in such a way as to enable her to exercise her judgment upon the investments, and to make them, really and in truth, her act as well as his own?" The judge found in favour of the co-trustee, who was therefore entitled to an indemnity.

The situation where one trustee alone has benefited from the breach was considered in *Bahin v. Hughes*.[97] Cotton L.J. refused to limit the circumstances in which an indemnity would be ordered, saying "I think it wrong to lay down any limitation of the circumstances under which one trustee would be held liable to the others for indemnity, both having been held liable to the *cestui que trust* but so far as cases have gone at present, relief has only been granted against a trustee who has himself got the benefit of the breach of trust, or between whom and his co-trustees there has existed a relation which will justify the court in treating him as solely liable for the breach of trust." In that case there were two trustees, one of whom was content to leave the administration of the trust to the other. The latter acted honestly but made an improper investment which resulted in a loss. The passive trustee unsuccessfully claimed an indemnity. It is obviously by no means clear how far this dictum of Cotton L.J. was intended to go.

The situation where a trustee is also a beneficiary was considered in *Chillingworth v. Chambers*.[98] It was held that a trustee who was also a beneficiary and who had participated in a breach of trust must indemnify his co-trustee to the extent of his beneficial interest. However, this only applied if the trustee-beneficiary had, as between himself and his co-trustees, exclusively benefited from the breach of trust. Suppose that Abraham and Ambrose were the trustees of a trust, in which Ambrose had a beneficial interest worth £2,000, but in which Abraham had no interest. If the trustees were to invest in unauthorised securities in order to obtain a higher income and Ambrose enjoyed the benefit of that higher income, something which Abraham obviously would not do, but the investment ultimately produced a capital loss of £4,000, Ambrose would be liable to indemnify Abraham to the extent of £2,000, leaving the remaining liability of £2,000 to be shared by them equally. It is not clear whether for the rule in *Chillingworth v. Chambers* to apply it was necessary for the trustee-beneficiary actually to receive a benefit from the breach, or whether it was sufficient if the breach was committed with the intention to give him a benefit; the latter view seems preferable.

The three situations which have just been considered are now regulated by the Civil Liability (Contribution) Act 1978. This provides[99] that, in proceedings where contribution is claimed, the court has power to exempt any person from liability to contribute, or to direct that the contribution to be recovered shall amount to a complete indemnity. However, it does not

---

[96] (1887) 57 L.T. 654.
[97] (1886) 31 Ch.D. 390.
[98] [1896] 1 Ch. 685.
[99] s.2(1).

appear likely that this provision will either modify or add materially to the cases in which indemnity was available under the pre-existing law.

V. LIMITATION OF ACTIONS

On the assumption that a breach of trust has been committed which has caused some loss, the further question arises as to whether the beneficiaries are in time to sue. The history of limitation of actions in respect of breaches of trust has been highly complicated; however the position is now governed by the Limitation Act 1980, coupled with the application in certain respects of the equitable doctrine of laches (laches occurs where a wronged person has delayed so long in bringing his action that he is deemed by his conduct to have waived his claim). Two distinct situations have to be considered.

(A) Where there is No Statutory Period of Limitation
Section 21(1) of the Limitation Act 1980 provides that there shall be no statutory period of limitation in respect of an action by a beneficiary under a trust if the action is one:

"(a) in respect of any fraud or fraudulent breach of trust to which the trustee was a party or privy, or

"(b) to recover from the trustee trust property or the proceeds thereof in the possession of the trustee, or previously received by the trustee and converted to his use."

Paragraph (a) has recently been considered in *Armitage v. Nurse*[1] where the Court of Appeal held that it "is limited to cases of fraud or fraudulent breach of trust properly so called, that is to say to cases involving dishonesty".[2] It follows that, whenever trustees have, in this sense, committed fraud or have retained any of the capital of the trust, there is no question of any defence under the statute. Thus, in *Re Howlett*[3] where a trustee occupied property belonging to the trust, he was held to be outside the scope of the Act. Likewise, in *Wassell v. Leggatt*,[4] where a husband forcibly took property belonging to his wife, thereby becoming a trustee of it for her, and kept it until his death, his executors were unable to plead limitation.

A question which has also recently been considered by the Court of Appeal, in *Paragon Finance v. D.B. Thakerar & Co.*,[5] is whether paragraph (a) is restricted to fraudulent breaches of existing trusts, as in *Wassell v. Leggatt*, or whether it also applies to situations where the fraudulent act in question is the reason for the existence of the trust, in other words where the trust in question is a constructive trust which has only arisen because of the fraud of the constructive trustee. The expression "trust" in the Limitation Act 1980

---

[1] [1998] Ch. 241.
[2] *ibid., per* Millett L.J. at 260.
[3] [1949] Ch. 767.
[4] [1896] 1 Ch. 554; see also *Re Tufnell* (1902) 18 T.L.R. 705; *Re Eyre-Williams* [1923] 2 Ch. 533.
[5] (1998), unreported.

extends to constructive trusts.[6] However, the Court of Appeal held that this does no more than apply paragraph (a) to fraudulent breaches of already existing constructive trusts. Consequently, paragraph (a) does not apply to situations where the fraudulent act in question is the reason for the existence of the trust. As Millett L.J. said:

"There is no logical basis for distinguishing between an action for damages for fraud at common law and the corresponding claim in equity for 'an account as constructive trustee' founded on the same fraud.".

Where there is no statutory period of limitation, however, the defence of laches may nevertheless be raised. To establish this defence, it is necessary to show that the beneficiary has known of the breach of trust for a substantial period of time and has acquiesced in it. There are no fixed rules as to the period of time which must elapse; it must in the particular case be sufficiently long to enable the court to impute acquiescence. Likewise, if the beneficiaries clearly acquiesce after only a fairly short time, that will be a sufficient defence. The essence of the defence is therefore acquiescence on the part of the beneficiary when he has full knowledge of the facts. Accordingly, it is generally considered that delay in taking action is merely evidence of acquiescence[7]; although it has also been suggested that mere delay may in itself constitute a separate defence quite apart from any acquiescence.[8]

(B) Where there is a Statutory Period of Limitation

(1) The General Position
Section 21(3) of the Limitation Act 1980, which applies both to express trustees[9] and to implied or constructive[10] trustees, provides that actions to recover trust property or in respect of breaches of trust must be brought within six years from the date on which the right of action accrued. In the case of breaches of trust, this is the date on which the breach in question occurred, not the date when the loss was sustained.[11] Suppose that a beneficiary knows that the trustees invest in unauthorised investments and that at first the investments do well but later lead to losses. Even though the losses may not be sustained for several years, the limitation period runs from when

---

[6] Because the definitions section of the Limitation Act 1980, (s.38) incorporates the definition of trust in the definitions section of the Trustee Act 1925 (s.68).

[7] *Morse v. Royal* (1806) 12 Ves. 355; *Life Association of Scotland v. Siddal* (1861) 3 De G.F. & J. 58.

[8] *Re Sharpe* [1892] 1 Ch. 154 at 168, *per* Lindley L.J. See also *Smith v. Clay* (1767) 3 Bro.C.C. 639n. Lacher was held to a defence in *Nelson v. Rye* [1996] 1 W.L.R. 1378.

[9] The section does not apply to an action by the Att.-Gen. against the trustee of charitable trusts which in this sense have no beneficiaries; *Att.-Gen. v. Cocke* [1988] Ch. 414.

[10] s.19(2) only applies where the action is against a "trustee", and not where the action is against someone who, although in a fiduciary capacity, is not a trustee. In *Tito v. Waddell (No. 2)* [1977] Ch. 106 (see *ante*, p. 17) the Crown was held not to be in a fiduciary position. However, Megarry V.-C. said (at 249) that, even if the Crown had been in a fiduciary position, it would not have been a trustee; consequently, the claim would not have been barred by s.19(2) of the Limitation Act 1939 (now re-enacted as s.21(3) of the Limitation Act 1980. Further, the doctrine of laches applied but was no bar in this case because it had not been pleaded.

[11] *Re Somerset* [1894] 1 Ch. 231.

the unauthorised investment was made. In *Re Swain*[12] trustees were under an obligation to convert the deceased's assets into authorised investments but in breach of trust continued to carry on the deceased's business until the youngest beneficiary attained the age of 21. When, eight years later, one of the other beneficiaries sought to make the trustees liable for the loss caused through carrying on the business, they were held entitled to plead limitation.

Although in general no statutory period will run where the trustee has himself received trust property, a special rule applies where the trustee is also a beneficiary. If the trustee distributed the trust fund honestly and reasonably, but made an over-distribution to himself, the statutory period applies to the extent of his own share, but the excess is subject only to the doctrine of laches.[13]

Section 21(3) contains a proviso that, where a beneficiary has a future interest, for the purposes of the Limitation Act 1980 the right of action is deemed not to have accrued until his interest falls into possession. This does not of course prevent the beneficiary from suing before this point if he wishes to do so. Consequently, a remainderman can take action in respect of a breach of trust at any time during the subsistence of a prior life interest, or within six years from becoming entitled to an interest in possession.

The Court of Appeal has recently had to consider the precise meaning of "future interest" in the context of this proviso in *Armitage v. Nurse*.[14] Trustees held income upon trust to accumulate it until the beneficiary in question reached the age of 25 subject to a power to pay it to her or apply it for her benefit.[15] The Court of Appeal held that while she was under the age of 25 she had a future interest for the purposes of the proviso, rejecting an argument by the trustees that the fact that she was entitled to see the trust documents was sufficient to give her an interest in possession thereunder. Millett L.J. held that the rationale of the proviso was that a beneficiary "should not be compelled to litigate (at considerable personal expense) in respect of an injury to an interest which he may never live to enjoy. Similar reasoning would apply to exclude a person who is merely the object of a discretionary trust or power which may never be exercised in his favour."[16] While it is clearly appropriate that a beneficiary of a fixed trust with a future interest should be able to impeach any breaches of trusts committed since the trust was created when his interest vests in possession, it is superficially rather startling that a discretionary beneficiary or the object of a power to whom no income is appointed until (say) 20 years after the creation of the trust may at that point maintain an action for any breach of trust which has occurred during the previous 20 years. However, there seems no way of avoiding this conclusion since the wording of the statute provides no obvious means of distinguishing between the two cases.

This rationale enunciated by Millett L.J. may be extremely significant when the as yet unanswered question of how this proviso operates in the

---

[12] [1891] 3 Ch. 233.
[13] Limitation Act 1980, s.21(2).
[14] [1998] Ch. 241.
[15] She then acquired an absolute interest in the income but did not become entitled to the capital until she reached the age of 40.
[16] [1998] Ch. 241 at 261.

case of pension trusts has to be decided. Is the interest of a beneficiary of a pension trust a future interest in this sense until he becomes entitled to receive his pension? He will obviously not live to enjoy his pension if he dies before retirement age; on the other hand, his death before that time will inevitably lead to the payment both of a lump sum death benefit and of a pension for his surviving spouse and other dependants so he certainly has an interest worth defending in the intervening period. The contention that his interest is indeed a future one until he becomes entitled to his pension has been pleaded in a number of pension trust cases but does not appear yet to have been argued in court. If it is upheld, then the liability of the trustees of pension trusts for breach of trust will be to all intents and purposes indefinite. However, in that event, they will obtain at least some protection from section 21(4), which is discussed below.

The way in which the proviso operates in practice is shown by *Re Pauling's Settlement Trusts*.[17] In that case improper advancements were made to beneficiaries and the trustees pleaded, among other defences, that the period of limitation ran in their favour from the time when the advancements were made. In rejecting this defence, the Court of Appeal held that the interests of the children to whom the advancements had been made were future interests within the terms of the proviso to section 21(3) and that, if an improper advancement was made while this was the case, that did not start the limitation period running. Since the advancements were improper, they did not bind the children at all. The latter could, therefore, sue at the time when they ought to have received the whole of their share, namely when their interests vested in possession.

As was indicated above, the operation of the proviso to section 21(3) is however restricted by section 21(4), which provides that, where limitation can be pleaded against any particular beneficiary, he cannot benefit from an action brought by a beneficiary against whom limitation cannot be pleaded.[18] Suppose that trustees who hold investments upon trust for Daphne for life, with remainder to Chloe, sell one of those investments and improperly hand over the proceeds to Daphne's daughter. In the absence of fraudulent concealment, Daphne will be debarred from suing after six years. Chloe is obviously entitled to wait until Daphne's death before suing but is not obliged to. If she does sue before then, she can compel the trustees to make good the capital loss. Assuming they do so, they can themselves retain the income from that property during the lifetime of Daphne; this is on the basis that Daphne, by not suing, has in effect consented to the breach of trust and so the trustees, having repaired the breach, are entitled to the income which she would otherwise have received.[19]

(2) Cases of Fraud

It has already been stated that there is no statutory period of limitation in respect of a fraudulent breach of trust. However, it is possible for a non-fraudulent breach of trust to have been committed which is subsequently concealed by fraud. Special provision is therefore made for actions based on

---

[17] [1964] Ch. 303.
[18] *Re Somerset* (1894) 1 Ch. 231.
[19] *Fletcher v. Collis* [1905] 2 Ch. 24.

fraud and for rights of actions concealed by fraud. Section 32 (which is of
general application and is not confined to actions for breach of trust) provides that, where an action is based upon the fraud of the defendant or his
agent and where a right of action is concealed by fraud, "the period of
limitation shall not begin to run until the plaintiff has discovered the fraud
... or could with reasonable diligence have discovered it". For the purposes of this section, "fraud" is wider than the type of conduct which would
give rise to an independent action; in *Beaman v. A.R.T.S.*[20] Lord Greene M.R.
pointed out that the fraudulent conduct "may acquire its character as such
from the very manner in which that act is performed".

The scope of section 32[21] was illustrated by *Eddis v. Chichester Constable*.[22]
One of the assets of the trust was a painting of St John the Baptist by
Caravaggio. The painting was normally hung in a stately home where the
life tenant lived but in 1950 he lent it for an exhibition at Burlington House.
During that exhibition, he sold it to a consortium of art dealers, who
subsequently sold it to an art gallery in Kansas City. The life tenant obviously had no title to the painting and, when the trustees discovered the loss
of painting in 1963, they brought an action for breach of trust against, *inter
alios*, the estate of the life tenant, who had by then died. In the course of his
judgment, Lord Denning M.R. said[23]:

"one thing is quite clear: the right of action was 'concealed by the fraud' of
the [life tenant]. I do not know that he did anything actively to deceive the
trustees, but that does not matter. His wrongful sale of the heirloom was
enough. It was a fraud and by saying nothing about it, he concealed the
fraud."

(C)   The Applicability of the Act to Actions for an Account

Section 23 of the Limitation Act 1980 provides that "an action for an account
shall not be brought after the expiration of any time limit under this Act
which is applicable to the claim which is the basis of the duty to account".
The section clearly prevents any action for an account being brought in
respect of a breach of trust which is already statute-barred, even though a
separate provision for this purpose hardly seems necessary; until recently it
was difficult to see what further purpose the section serves. In *Attorney-
General v. Cocke*[24] the Attorney-General brought an action against the executors and trustees of an estate held on charitable trusts, seeking inter alia
accounts and enquiries as to the estate. Section 21(3) of the Limitation Act
1980 was clearly inapplicable; first, because the action was being brought by
the Attorney-General and not by a beneficiary and, secondly, because the
claim was neither to recover trust property nor in respect of any breach of
trust. Harman J. held that all fiduciaries were under a permanent duty to

---

[20] [1949] 1 K.B. 550.
[21] The decision was on s.26 of the Limitation Act 1939, which corresponds with Limitation Act
    1980 s.32. The latter provision was considered in *Paragon Finance v. D. B. Thackerars Co.* (1998)
    unreported.
[22] [1969] 2 Ch. 345.
[23] *ibid.* at 356.
[24] [1988] Ch. 414. This decision was applied in *Nelson v. Rye* [1996] 1 W.L.R. 1378.

account arising out of their fiduciary relationships; such claims were not subject to any period of limitation under the Act and so there was no time limit to which section 23 could apply in respect of such a claim. However in *Paragon Finance v. D. B. Thackerars Co*[24a] Millett L.J. held that "an action for an account brought by a principal against his agent is more than a mere agent but is a trustee of the money which he received." Thus section 23 protects fiduiciaries who are not trustees from any additional liability to account.

VI. RELIEF OR EXEMPTION FROM PRIMA FACIE LIABILITY

Even if an action for breach of trust can prima facie be brought against a trustee, it may nevertheless be possible for him to claim total or partial relief. He may be able to do so first by virtue of a provision in the trust instrument; secondly, by means of an application to the court; thirdly, by virtue of an act of the beneficiaries, whether concurrence in or waiver of the breach; and, fourthly, by virtue of an indemnity obtainable from one or more of the beneficiaries.

(A) Provisions in Trust Instruments

It has already been seen that a trust instrument can authorise a large number of acts which a trustee would not otherwise be able to do. If the trustee takes advantage of such a provision, he is of course not guilty of a breach of trust.

However, even if a trustee is guilty of a breach of trust, the provisions of the trust instrument may nevertheless be effective to relieve him from liability. One clause in common use is:

"In the professional execution of the trusts hereof no trustee shall be liable for any loss to the trust property arising by reason of any improper investment made in good faith or by reason of any mistake or omission made in good faith by any trustee hereof or by reason of any other matter of thing except wilful and individual fraud or wrongdoing on the part of the trustee who is sought to be made liable."

The effect of such clauses has recently had to be considered by the Court of Appeal in *Armitage v. Nurse*,[25] where the clause in question was: "No trustee shall be liable for any loss or damage which may happen to [the] fund or any part therefor or the income thereof at any time or from any cause whatsoever unless such loss or damage shall be caused by his own actual fraud." The court construed this clause as excluding any liability for breach of trust in the absence of dishonesty, which was held to mean "at the minimum an intention on the part of the trustee to pursue a particular course of action, either knowing that it is contrary to the interests of the beneficiaries or being recklessly indifferent whether it is contrary to their interests or not".[26] (The longer clause set out above would clearly be interpreted in the same way.) The beneficiary contended that clauses of this type

---

[24a] (1998) Unreported. *Nelson v. Rye* [1996] 1 W.L.R. 1378 was overruled.
[25] [1998] Ch. 241.
[26] *ibid.* at 251.

were void, either for repugnancy or as contrary to public policy, in that they therefore excluded liability for gross negligence,[27] a position which has been adopted by the legislature in some other jurisdictions.[28] However, the court held that this proposition was not supported by any English authority and, further, that "English lawyers have always had a healthy disrespect" for the distinction between negligence and gross negligence,[29] a distinction which is of course a necessary consequence of not permitting liability for gross negligence to be excluded. Exemption clauses of this kind are therefore valid, at least for the moment. However, the court "acknowledged that the view is widely held that these clauses have gone too far"[30] but held that only Parliament could deny them effect; whether Parliament should do so is at present under consideration by the Trust Law Committee.

Statute does, however, already prohibit exclusion clauses from exempting from liability for negligence trustees of debentures,[31] managers or trustees of unit trusts,[32] and, in respect of investment functions only, trustees of pension trusts.[33]

(B) Applications to the Court

Before an act is actually carried out, the court has power over a wide field to sanction acts even if they would otherwise be a breach of trust.[34]

Where no such application has been made prior to the act being carried out, however, by virtue of section 61 of the Trustee Act 1925 the court has a discretion to grant relief. The section provides that if it appears to the court that a trustee is or may be personally liable for any breach of trust but has acted honestly and reasonably, and ought fairly to be excused for the breach of trust or for omitting to obtain the directions of the court in the matter in which he committed such breach, then the court may relieve him either wholly or partially for personal liability. Thus the trustee must, first, have acted honestly; secondly, have acted reasonably; and, thirdly, ought fairly to be excused.

"Honestly" here means in good faith. "Reasonably" is a question of fact which depends on the circumstances of each case. The courts have consistently refused to lay down any rules[35] but there have been numerous applications under the section, and under the provisions which it replaced. In *Re Kay*[36] the applicant was an executor and trustee of a will of a testator who left over £22,000 with apparent liabilities of only about £100. Before advertising for claims, the executor paid to the widow a legacy of £300 and only afterwards learned of liabilities which exceeded the value of the estate. It was held that it was reasonable for the executor to assume that with an

---

[27] This view is taken by P. Matthews [1989] Conv. 42.
[28] In Jersey and Guernsey. The Turks and Caicos Islands have gone even further and do not permit liability even for negligence to be excluded.
[29] [1998] Ch. 241 at 254.
[30] *ibid.* at 256.
[31] Companies Act 1985, s.192.
[32] Financial Services Act 1986, s.84.
[33] Pensions Act 1995, s.33.
[34] See *ante*, p. 501.
[35] *Re Turner* [1897] 1 Ch. 536, *per* Byrne J.; *Re Kay* [1897] 2 Ch. 518 at 524, *per* Romer J.
[36] [1897] 2 Ch. 518.

estate of this size liabilities would not approach the value of the estate, so that he could safely pay the legacy. The court therefore granted him relief.

Difficulties sometimes arise when a trustee has taken legal advice which turns out to be wrong. Although it is hard on the trustee, the fact that he has taken and has followed legal advice does not automatically excuse him from liability. In *National Trustee Co. of Australia v. General Finance Co. of Australia*,[37] trustees followed the wrong advice given by their solicitors. It was held in the special circumstances that they should not be granted relief. One of the factors to be taken into account is the size of the trust property. If the property is of low value, trustees would probably be reasonable in taking merely the advice of a solicitor, whereas if the trust fund were very large, the advice of a Queen's Counsel might well be warranted.

Two aspects of the section were considered by Plowman J. in *Re Rosenthal*.[38] The testator devised his house to his sister and left the remainder of his estate to his widow. The estate duty payable in respect of the house should have been paid by the sister, but the executors, who for this purpose were treated as trustees,[39] transferred the house to the sister without making any arrangements with her to secure the payment of the duty.[40] They paid £270 on account of the liability and a further £1,500 plus interest was still outstanding. One of the trustees, who was a solicitor and who was acting in connection with the administration of the estate, claimed to be entitled to rely on section 61. Plowman J. rejected this contention on two grounds. First, in respect of the £270 which had been paid, improperly, from residue, although the trustee had acted honestly, he had not acted reasonably and had not shown that he ought fairly to be excused. In this respect, Plowman J. took account of the fact that he was a professional trustee,[41] for which reason he appears to have adopted a more stringent approach. Secondly, in respect of the question of whether section 61 could apply to an anticipated breach of trust (the sum which was still to be paid had not been paid from residue so that no breach of trust had yet actually occurred in respect of it), the solicitor was in effect seeking a declaration that he was entitled to take this sum from residue. Plowman J. held that the section was incapable of giving relief in respect of a breach of trust which had not yet occurred.

It does not follow that, whenever it is shown that a trustee has acted honestly and reasonably, he will automatically be excused; it is only when these conditions are fulfilled that the court has a discretion to grant relief. It has been suggested that, where a trustee takes the wrong advice of his solicitor, he should basically sue his solicitor. Where he does not seek to recover the loss in this way (assuming the solicitor is in fact potentially liable for negligence), the court will probably not excuse the trustee.

---

[37] [1905] A.C. 373.

[38] *Re Rosenthal* [1972] 1 W.L.R. 1273.

[39] One of the persons appointed as an executor had purported to resign from his office by means of the appointment of new trustees. This was probably invalid but the so-called new trustees were treated by the judge as trustees for the purposes of the case.

[40] The liability of the sister arose under the Finance Act 1894, s.9(1). See *Re the Countess of Oxford* [1896] 1 Ch. 257.

[41] [1972] 1 W.L.R. 1273 at 1278.

It is clear that it is far more difficult for a paid trustee to obtain relief than it is for an unpaid trustee to do so. In *National Trustee Co. of Australia v. General Finance Co. of Australia* the court had in mind the fact that the trustees were paid. But in *Re Pauling's Settlement Trusts*[42] the Court of Appeal held that relief under section 61 can be granted to a paid trustee if the circumstances are appropriate and a degree of relief was indeed granted in that case to paid trustees who were bankers. However, in its judgment the Court of Appeal held that "Where a banker undertakes to act as a paid trustee of a settlement created by a customer, and so deliberately places itself in a position where its duty as trustee conflicts with its interest as a banker, we think that the court should be very slow to relieve such a trustee under the provisions of the section."[43]

If the court does decide to grant relief, it has a discretion to grant partial or total relief.

(C) Acts of the Beneficiaries

A beneficiary who has once agreed to, or concurred in, a breach of trust cannot afterwards sue the trustees in respect of it. This applies only if three conditions are satisfied: (i) that the beneficiary was of full and sound mind at the time when he agreed or concurred; (ii) that he had full knowledge of all relevant facts and of the legal effect of his agreement or concurrence; and, (iii) that he was an entirely free agent and was not under any undue influence.

A good example of the working of this rule is *Nail v. Punter*.[44] In that case trustees held stock upon trust for a married woman for life, with remainder to such person as she should by will appoint. During her lifetime, the woman's husband persuaded the trustees to sell the stock and pay him the proceeds. The wife then brought an action against the trustees but, before it was concluded, died, having by her will appointed the stock to her husband. The husband endeavoured to claim the same remedy as his wife had sought. But the husband, having become a beneficiary by virtue of the exercise of the power of appointment, could not succeed because he had been a party to the breach.

A trustee is also protected from action if the beneficiaries subsequently learn of the breach and either acquiesce in it or give the trustee a release. Again, the beneficiaries must be *sui juris*, have full knowledge of the relevant facts, and act as free agents. Often releases are granted formally by deed, but an informal release, if supported by consideration, will be effective. In *Ghost v. Waller*,[45] part of the trust property was lost through a breach

---

[42] [1964] Ch. 303.

[43] See also *Re Windsor Steam Coal Company* (1901) [1929] 1 Ch. 151 and *Re Waterman's Will Trusts* [1952] 2 All E.R. 1054. In *Re Cooper (No. 2)* (1978) 21 O.R. (2d) 579 (Ontario), the two trustees were the senior partner in a trustee law firm and one of his junior partners. The whole of the conduct of the administration was left in the hands of the senior partner, who stole Can.$180,000 and was sentenced to seven and a half years imprisonment. The court found that the junior partner had no reason to suspect the fraud of his senior partner, and that he had acted honestly and reasonably. It therefore granted him relief under the Ontario equivalent of s.61.

[44] (1832) 5 Sim. 555.

[45] (1846) 9 Beav. 497.

of trust. The beneficiary agreed through her solicitors by letter that in consideration of the trustees undertaking to assist in recovering part of the loss she would "give up all claims if she has any against her trustees for negligence". This was held to be an effective release.

Neither a formal nor an informal release will be effective if the beneficiary was not in full possession of the facts. In *Thompson v. Eastwood*[46] the beneficiary was entitled to a legacy under a will. The trustee denied the beneficiary's right to that legacy by virtue of alleged illegality and the dispute was settled on the payment by the trustee of a smaller sum than that to which the beneficiary was entitled. A formal deed of release was executed but when the beneficiary discovered the true position, he was held entitled to claim the full legacy, despite the deed of release, and despite an interval of over 25 years from the breach.

In *Re Pauling's Settlement Trusts*,[47] one of the defences put forward by the trustees was that the beneficiaries, when over 21 (then the age of majority), had consented to the improper advances being made. It is clear that, had those consents been effective, the beneficiaries could not afterwards have succeeded in an action against the trustees. It has, however, long been clearly established that, where an infant makes a gift in favour of his parent, there will be a presumption of undue influence on the part of the parent[48] and that this presumption will continue for a short time—the exact period is undefined and depends on the circumstances of each case—after the infant attains his majority.[49] This raised the question of what for the purposes of any liability of the trustees is the effect on an advancement which favours a parent and not a child of a consent given by that child which may be the result of undue influence. The Court of Appeal said: "Without expressing a final opinion, we think that the true view may be that a trustee carrying out a transaction in breach of trust may be liable if he knew, or ought to have known, that the beneficiary was acting under the undue influence of another, or may be presumed to have done so, but will not be liable if it cannot be established that he so knew or ought to have known." A trustee who is asked to commit a breach of trust for the benefit of a parent on the basis of consent by a beneficiary just turned 18 ought, therefore, to be reasonably sure that the child is emancipated from the parent.

(D) Indemnities Obtainable from Beneficiaries

It has already been shown that, subject to the conditions just mentioned, a beneficiary who with full knowledge concurs in a breach of trust cannot afterwards sue his trustees. This does not, however, affect the right of other beneficiaries to take action and if such action is taken the trustee may be able to claim an indemnity out of the beneficial interest of the beneficiary who is concerned in the breach. In particular, if the beneficiary who has concurred in the breach of trust is the tenant for life and the trustee repairs the breach at the behest of the remainderman, he is entitled to the income which the

---

[46] (1877) 2 App.Cas. 215 and see *Re Freeston's Charity* [1978] 1 W.L.R. 741 (no acquiescence in a breach of a charitable trust).
[47] [1964] Ch. 303, and see *ante*, p. 621.
[48] *Huguenin v. Baseley* (1807) 14 Ves. 273.
[49] See *Lancashire Looms v. Black* [1943] 1 K.B. 380.

tenant for life would otherwise have received during the remainder of his lifetime.[50] Outside this special situation, there are two rules which overlap:

(i) Under its inherent jurisdiction, the court has power to order a beneficiary to give the trustee an indemnity if he instigated[51] or requested[52] a breach of trust with the intention of obtaining a personal benefit (whether or not such personal benefit was in fact received) or if he concurred in a breach of trust and actually derived a personal benefit from it.[53]

(ii) Under section 62 of the Trustee Act 1925, the court may impound the interest of a beneficiary in the trust fund if he instigates or requests or consents in writing to a breach of trust by the trustee. Where the section applies, the court has a discretion whether to impound, and, if so, whether to impound the whole or only part of the beneficiary's interest.

Section 62 applies irrespective of personal benefit, or of a motive for personal benefit. On the other hand, it only applies in the case of mere consent to a breach of trust if such consent was in writing, whereas the general jurisdiction of the court operates whether or not the consent is in writing. The court will not exercise its power to impound the beneficiary's interest unless the trustee can show that the beneficiary fully appreciated that the proposed action would constitute a breach of trust.

As the result of a fairly robust construction, it was held in *Re Pauling's Settlement (No. 2)*[54] that the power under section 62 can be exercised in favour of a person who is not a trustee at the time when the breach of trust occurred. In coming to this decision, Wilberforce J. was clearly influenced by the consideration that, if the section only applied to persons who were trustees at the time of the application, the court might be loath to remove trustees before such application has been made, even if from the other circumstances of the case their removal was desirable.

Where a beneficiary unsuccessfully brings proceedings against a trustee alleging breach of trust, the trustee will be entitled to take his costs out of the trust fund and only if that is insufficient will an order be made against the beneficiary personally.[55]

VII. THE PERSONAL AND PROPRIETARY BASIS OF REMEDIES FOR BREACH OF TRUST

So far this Chapter has been concerned with the actions against trustees personally for breach of trust. So far as a beneficiary is concerned, this may

---

[50] *Fletcher v. Collis* [1905] 2 Ch. 24.
[51] *Trafford v. Boehm* (1746) 3 Atk. 440.
[52] *Fuller v. Knight* (1843) 6 Beav. 205.
[53] *Montford v. Cadogan* (1816) 19 Ves. 635.
[54] [1963] Ch. 576.
[55] *Re Spurling's Will Trusts* [1966] 1 W.L.R. 920.

be inadequate and clearly will be if the trustees are insolvent. In these circumstances the beneficiaries may seek either a personal remedy against persons who have wrongly received the trust property or a proprietary remedy operating against the trust property itself. Such circumstances involve considering the legal basis of remedies for breach of trust. In the leading case of *Re Diplock*,[56] Caleb Diplock by his will directed his executors to apply his residuary estate "for such charitable institution or institutions or other charitable or benevolent object or objects" as they should in their absolute discretion think fit. His executors distributed the residue, which amounted to over £200,000, among 139 charities. Subsequently, the testator's next-of-kin challenged the validity of the bequest. The House of Lords duly held (in *Chichester Diocesan Fund and Board of Finance v. Simpson*[57]) that the bequest was invalid. *Re Diplock* was concerned with the next-of-kin's claims to recover the money from the executors and the charities which had received it.

The claims of the next-of-kin against the executors were eventually compromised, with the approval of the court. But actions continued for the considerable balance of the funds distributed against the charities, who had used the money paid to them for diverse purposes. In the majority of cases, the cheques sent to them had been paid into their general accounts at the bank. Some of such accounts were in credit; some were overdrawn on either a secured or an unsecured basis. In a few cases payment had been made into a special account. In others it had been earmarked for some designated purpose. In yet others the money had been spent on altering or enlarging existing buildings owned by the charity. The next-of-kin based their claim to recover the money on both in *personam* and in *rem* claims. The in *personam* claim was against the charities personally by reason of the "equity" which the next-of-kin had to recover the money; they contended that any unpaid creditor, legatee or next-of-kin possessed such an "equity" as against an overpaid beneficiary or stranger to the estate. The in *rem* claim was to follow identifiable assets—whether unmixed or part of a mixed fund—into the hands of innocent volunteers, which the charities who had wrongly received the assets undoubtedly were. Both claims succeeded.

It should be noted that, although *Re Diplock* was concerned with claims against innocent volunteers who had received property from personal representatives, similar general principles apply where (as more usually happens) the claim is directly against trustees or persons in a fiduciary position. Furthermore, the proprietary remedy in *rem* is of more significance in the law of trusts than the claim in *personam* because, if it lies, it enables the beneficiaries to follow the trust money into the property acquired with it, in priority to the general creditors of the recipient if he is insolvent—this is because a trust or fiduciary obligation attaches to that property. However, it is nevertheless necessary to discuss the in *personam* claim as well. In this respect *Re Diplock* remains the principal authority governing claims in *personam* and discussion of them must focus almost entirely on that decision. This

---

[56] [1948] Ch. 465, affirmed by the House of Lords *sub nom. Ministry of Health v. Simpson* [1951] A.C. 251.

[57] [1944] A.C. 341 and see *ante*, p. 415.

is not the case for the claims *in rem*, in respect of which *Re Diplock* is only one of a number of leading authorities.

1. *Personal Claims*

(A) The Moral Claim of the Charities

It was argued for the charities that, notwithstanding the formal invalidity of the bequest, it should at any rate be presumed that Caleb Diplock intended them to enjoy the residuary estate in preference to his blood relations and that therefore it did not lie in the months of the next-of-kin to allege any "unconscientiousness" on the part of those whose claim was in accordance with the wishes of the testator, however ineffectually those wishes had been expressed. However, this argument, based as it was on the proposition that the conscience of the recipients should be in some degree affected by their retention of the moneys, was rejected by the court as wholly untenable: "it is impossible to contend that a disposition which according to the general law of the land is held to be entirely invalid can yet confer upon those who, *ex hypothesi*, have improperly participated under the disposition some moral or equitable right to retain what they have received against those whom the law declares to be properly entitled."[58]

(B) The Recipients' Notice of the Invalidity of the Gift

It was argued for the next-of-kin that by the terms of the letter which accompanied all the executors' payments, which, though not entirely accurately, set out the terms of the gift, the charities had been given notice of the invalidity of the trusts, or at least were put on enquiry as regards their validity. Therefore the charities were subjected to a constructive trust of the moneys received in favour of the next-of-kin. But this argument, although not without some attraction, was rejected. "Persons in the position of the [charities], themselves unversed in the law, are entitled in such circumstances as these to assume that the executors are properly administering the estate."[59]

(C) The Equitable Right of Recovery of the Next-of-Kin

This argument, which the Court of Appeal subjected to an exhaustive analysis, was to the effect that, in the words of the court: "Apart from any notice which the respondents may have had of the true effect of the testator's will, they had in truth no right to receive any of the moneys paid to them and that ... the unpaid next-of-kin had a direct claim, recognised and established by the courts of equity, to recovery from the respondents of the sums improperly paid to the respondents and properly belonging to the next-of-kin."

(1) Mistake of law

At first instance,[60] Wynn-Parry J. had come to the conclusion that an unpaid beneficiary could only sue the wrongly paid recipient in equity when

---

[58] [1948] Ch. 465 at 476.
[59] *ibid*. at 478–479.
[60] [1947] Ch. 716.

the payment had been made under a mistake of fact, whereas in this case the mistake was one of law.

The Court of Appeal acknowledged that the mistake was one of law and that, as Wynn-Parry J. had held, common law claims for money had and received would not lie where money had been paid under a mistake of law.[61] However, the Court of Appeal differed from him by holding that such common law claims were in no sense derived from equity but had a lineage altogether independent of it.[62] The court took the view that there was no "necessity in logic for the claim as being clothed, as it were, with all the attributes or limitations appropriate to the common law action for money had and received",[63] and went on to consider the relevant authorities dating back as far as the days of Bridgman L.K. and Finch L.K. (afterwards Lord Nottingham L.C.) to see what principles had been established by them.[64] Having done so, the court rejected the contention that in equity the mistake under which the payment is made must be one of fact. As Lord Simonds said[65] in the House of Lords, where the decision was affirmed:

"It would be a strange thing if the Court of Chancery having taken upon itself to see that the assets of a deceased person were duly administered was deterred from doing justice to the creditor, legatee or next-of-kin because the executor had done him wrong under a mistake of law. If in truth this were so, I think that the father of Equity would not recognise his own child."

Further, the underpaid creditor, legatee or next-of-kin will necessarily not himself be a party to the wrongful payment; only the executor will be responsible for that. As Lord Simonds said, it is therefore difficult to see what relevance the distinction between mistake of fact and law can have to such a situation.[66]

(2) Administration of the estate by the court

Wynn-Parry J. had also held that it was necessary that for there to be or have been administration by the court for the equitable remedy *in personam* to lie. However, the Court of Appeal, after analysing the authorities,[67] came to the

---

[61] This was certainly the law then but it may not be so for much longer following the decision of the House of Lords in *Woolwich Equitable Building Society v. I.R.C.* [1993] A.C. 70; judgment of the House of Lords on precisely this point in *Kleinwort Benson v. Birmingham City Council No. 2)* is awaited as this edition goes to press.

[62] [1948] Ch. 465 at 480.

[63] *ibid.* at 481.

[64] *ibid.* at 482. The cases cited and discussed at length included *Nelthrop v. Hill* (1669) 1 Ch.Cas. 135; *Grove v. Banson,* (1669) 1 Ch.Cas. 148 at p. 148; *Chamberlain v. Chamberlain* (1675) 1 Ch.Cas. 256; *Noel v. Robinson* (1682) 1 Vern. 90; *Anon.* (1682) 1 Vern. 162; *Newman v. Barton* (1690) 2 Vern. 205; *Anon.* (1718) 1 P.Wms. 495; *Orr v. Kaines* (1750) 2 Ves.Sen. 194; *Walcot v. Hall* (1788) 2 Bro.C.C. 304; *Gillespie v. Alexander* (1827) 3 Russ. 130; *Greig v. Somerville* (1830) 1 Russ. & My. 338; *David v. Frowd* (1833) 1 My. & K. 200; *Sawyer v. Birchmore* (1836) 1 Keen 391; *Thomas v. Griffith* (1860) 2 Giff. 504; *Fenwick v. Clarke* (1862) 4 De G.F. & J. 240; *Peterson v. Peterson* (1866) L.R. 3 Eq. 111; *Rogers v. Ingham* (1876) 3 Ch.D. 351; *Re Robinson* [1911] 1 Ch. 502; *Re Hatch* [1919] 1 Ch. 351; *Re Rivers* [1920] 1 Ch. 320; *Re Mason* [1928] Ch. 385, [1929] 1 Ch. 1; *Re Blake* [1932] 1 Ch. 54.

[65] *Ministry of Health v. Simpson* [1951] A.C. 251 at 270.

[66] *ibid.*

[67] See the authorities cited ante, n. 64.

conclusion that they wholly negatived any such requirement[68]; if the court had administered the estate, there would be every reason why equity should come to the rescue of an underpaid legatee if a wrong payment were made but there seemed no reason why such an administration should be essential.

(3) Strangers to the estate

The authorities already referred to[69] also established that it is irrelevant to the applicability of the remedy that the original recipient had no title at all and was a stranger to the estate.[70] Many of the cases were undoubtedly concerned with providing equality between the original recipient and other persons having a title similar to that of the recipient—such as next-of-kin—but that is not a reason why the remedy should not also be applied against a stranger even though the effect of the refund will be actually to dispossess him rather than to produce equality.

(4) The "conscience" of the recipient

It had been argued that the conscience of the recipient, on which equity must fasten, was not affected in circumstances such as these. But the Court of Appeal decided that it is prima facie at least a sufficient circumstance that the charities had received some share of the estate to which they were not entitled.[71] As Leach M.R. had said long before in *David v. Frowd*,[72] "a party claiming under such circumstances has no great reason to complain that he is called upon to replace what he has received against his right".

(5) The conditions for the application of the equitable remedy

The previous discussion has shown that *Re Diplock* established, first, that an equitable remedy is available equally to an underpaid creditor, legatee or next-of-kin, and secondly, that a claim by the next-of-kin will not be liable to be defeated merely either in the absence of administration by the court or because the mistake under which the original payment was made was one of law rather than fact or because the original recipient had no title at all and was a stranger to the estate.[73]

However, there is one important qualification that must be fulfilled before a claim by an underpaid beneficiary can succeed. This was stated by the Court of Appeal in *Re Diplock* in the following way[74]:

"Since the original wrong payment was attributable to the blunder of the personal representatives, the right of the unpaid beneficiary is in the first instance against the wrongdoing executor or administrator; and the beneficiary's direct claim in equity against those overpaid or wrongly paid should be limited to the amount which he cannot recover from the party responsible. In some cases the amount will be the whole amount of the payment

---

[68] [1948] Ch. 465 at 489.
[69] See the authorities cited *ante*, n. 64.
[70] [1948] Ch. 465 at 502.
[71] *ibid.* at 503.
[72] (1883) 1 My. & K 200 at 211.
[73] [1948] Ch. 465 at 502.
[74] *ibid.* at 503.

wrongly made, *e.g.* where the executor or administrator is shown to be wholly without assets or is protected from attack by having acted under an order of the court."[75]

In *Re Diplock* the claims of the next-of-kin against the executors or their estates had already been compromised. Accordingly it was held that the amount recovered from the executors should be apportioned among the charities in proportion to the money the latter had wrongly received. This meant that the maximum recoverable from an individual charity by the next-of-kin should be rateably reduced.[76]

(6) The absence of any liability for interest

The Court of Appeal established that the recipients were only liable for the principal sum claimed and not for any interest.[77]

(D) Possible Limitations of the Claim In Personam

Re Diplock was a claim in respect of the administration of an estate and was dealt with by the Court of Appeal and by the House of Lords[78] strictly on that basis. It is not, therefore, so clearly established that the principles laid down will apply with equal force between beneficiaries under an *inter vivos trust*, although there seems no cogent reason why they should not do. In *Butler v. Broadhead*,[79] the plaintiffs had purchased land from a company in the course of being wound up. Some years later, it transpired that the company had had no title to the land and so the plaintiffs attempted to utilise the *in personam* claim in *Re Diplock* in order to claim against the contributories of the company, to whom its surplus assets had been distributed. It was argued that such an *in personam* claim was limited to the administration of estates; however, Templeman J. did not dismiss the claim on this ground but rather on the ground that it was barred by the Companies Act 1948[80] (it was assumed that the plaintiffs had failed to respond to the liquidator's advertisement seeking claims by the creditors of the company). This decision suggests that there is no reason in principle why the *in personam* claim should not apply to *inter vivos trusts*. Subsequently, in *Re J. Leslie Engineers Company*,[81] Oliver J. accepted the theoretical availability of such a claim to the liquidator of a company who was attempting to recover payments made to a creditor by a director after the liquidation had commenced; however, he denied the claim because the creditor had given value and the liquidator had not exhausted his remedies against the director. These decisions suggest that in an appropriate case, the *in personam* claim could be applied at least to *inter vivos trusts* and possibly also to companies in liquidation.

---

[75] For early authority for this proposition, see *Orr v. Kaines* (1750) 2 Ves. Sen. 195; *Hodges v. Waddington* (1684) 2 Vent. 360.

[76] [1948] Ch. 465 at 506.

[77] The authority is *Gittins v. Steele* (1818) 1 Swanst. 200.

[78] *sub nom. Ministry of Health v. Simpson* [1951] A.C. 251.

[79] [1975] Ch. 97.

[80] New Companies Act 1985, s.557.

[81] [1976] 1 W.L.R. 292.

A further limitation of the remedy *in personam* has presumably been created by the recognition by the House of Lords in *Lipkin Gorman v. Karpnale*[82] of a general defence of change of position. In *Re Diplock* itself, the House of Lords had actually refused to recognise any such defence, a decision which produced very considerable hardship for those charities who had used the funds to improve their buildings and, consequently, provoked very considerable criticism. This defence will be considered in detail in the next section of this Chapter. However, now that it has been established, the *in personam* remedy will be able to operate in a much more reasonable manner. Consequently, there seems no reason whatever why it should not now be extended to *inter vivos trusts* and perhaps also to companies in liquidation.

2. *Proprietary Claims*[83]

In *Re Diplock* the Court of Appeal also subjected to an exhaustive analysis the question of the next-of-kin's proprietary rights to trace identifiable assets—whether unmixed or part of a mixed fund—into the hands of the charities. They did so primarily in case their decision as to the personal remedy of the next-of-kin was reversed by the House of Lords. However, in *Ministry of Health v. Simpson*[84] the House of Lords, in affirming the decision of the Court of Appeal as to the *in personam* claim, did not find it necessary to consider the question of proprietary rights. The Court of Appeal actually upheld the proprietary claim of the next-of-kin, subject to certain defences which will be considered later on. However, their analysis of proprietary rights of this kind constitutes merely one of a number of important judicial discussions of claims of this type. The totality of these authorities, rather than the decision in *Re Diplock* alone, will be considered in the discussion which follows.

Proprietary claims have an important advantage over any claim *in personam*. If the claimant can identify his property in the hands of the defendant, he will be entitled to recover that property in full in priority to the claims of the general creditors of the defendant.[85] He will also normally be able to take advantage of any increase in the value of the property[86] and will also be able to claim its income or fruits from the date when it reached the hands of the defendant (the earliest date from which the payment of interest will be awarded in a personal claim is from the date when the writ was issued[87] and, in many cases, the payment of interest will only be ordered as from the date of judgment).[88]

---

[82] [1991] 2 A.C. 548.
[83] The best short discussion of proprietary claims is found in Goff & Jones, *The Law of Restitution* (4th ed. 1993), pp. 73–102. See also Birks, *An Introduction to the Law of Restitution* (1989), pp. 358–401. Smith, *The Law of Tracing* (1997) is devoted entirely to this subject.
[84] [1951] A.C. 251.
[85] Insolvency Act 1986, s.283.
[86] *Re Tilley's Will Trusts* [1967] Ch. 1179; see *post*, p. 732.
[87] *Jaffray v. Marshall* [1993] 1 W.L.R. 1285 (overruled by the House of Lords on other grounds in *Target Holdings v. Redferns* [1996] 1 A.C. 421).
[88] *Re Diplock* [1948] Ch. 465.

The terminology of proprietary claims has been the subject of some controversy. Until relatively recently, there has been a tendency to utilise the expressions "proprietary claims" and "tracing claims" interchangeably. However, as Millett L.J. has pointed out, both judicially[89] and extra-judicially[90]:

"Tracing properly so-called, however, is neither a claim nor a remedy but a process. Moreover it is not confined to the case where the plaintiff seeks a proprietary remedy; it is equally necessary where he seeks a personal remedy against the knowing recipient or knowing assistant. It is the process by which the plaintiff traces what has happened to his property, identifies the persons who have handled or received it, and justifies his claim that the money which they handled or received (and, if necessary, which they still retain), can properly be regarded as representing his property."[91]

This Chapter will accordingly use the expression "proprietary claim" to denote the substantive claim being brought and "tracing" to denote the process by which the claimant's property is identified. However, it must be borne in mind that many of the authorities utilise the latter expression in both these senses.

The attitudes of the common law and of equity to proprietary claims are quite distinct. Indeed, while the proprietary claim in *Re Diplock* has accurately been referred to as a claim *in rem*, since like all successful equitable proprietary claims it conferred a right *in rem* on the next-of-kin, it is questionable how far most of the proprietary claims recognised by the common law confer any rights *in rem* whatever. For this and other reasons, it is therefore necessary to consider legal and equitable proprietary claims separately.

(A) Proprietary Claims at Common Law

A person who seeks to assert a proprietary claim at law will use the action appropriate to the type of property which he is claiming. If he is claiming land, he will use the action for the recovery of land; he merely needs to show a better title than the other party and, if he can do so, he will not be defeated by the defence of bona fide purchase for value without notice although his action may become statute-barred as a result of the other party's adverse possession. A successful claim will produce an order for the specific recovery of the land so that a legal proprietary right to land is indeed a right *in rem*. If the claim is instead for specific chattels, the claimant will use a tortious action for conversion under the Torts (Interference with Goods) Act 1977.[92] Bona fide purchase for value without notice will now[93] only be a defence to such a claim if the purchaser is protected by the provisions of the

---

[89] In *Boscawen v. Bajwa* [1996] 1 W.L.R. 328 at 334.
[90] (1998) 110 L.Q.R. 399.
[91] *Boscawen v. Bajwa* [1996] 1 W.L.R. 328 at 334.
[92] s.1.
[93] It was formerly also a defence if the property had been purchased in market overt but this defence was removed by Sale of Goods (Amendment) Act 1994, which repealed Sale of Goods Act 1979, s.22(1).

Sale of Goods Act 1979.[94] However, a successful plaintiff is not entitled to specific recovery of the chattel, although the court has a discretion to so order.[95] Thus a legal proprietary right to chattels will only rarely amount to a right *in rem*. Finally, if the claim is for a chose in action or money, the claimant will only be able to use the action for money had and received, which imposes only a personal liability on the defendant. Thus, a legal proprietary right to property of this type will never amount to a right *in rem*. However, all the legal proprietary rights mentioned are now presumably subject to the defence of change of position, which will be discussed in detail later in this section.

(1)   Who can bring a legal proprietary claim?
Only the legal owner of property is entitled to bring a proprietary claim at common law. This was specifically held by the Court of Appeal in *MCC Proceeds v. Lehman Brothers International (Europe)*[96] where they rejected a claim by the beneficiaries of a bare trust to bring an action of conversion in respect of share certificates which their trustee had in breach of trust pledged to the defendant. As in that case and in cases such as *Re Diplock*, this requirement will generally prevent the beneficiaries of a trust from taking advantage of any potential legal proprietary claim to the trust property; the legal owner of property subject to a trust is the trustees who in such cases will themselves have been responsible for the property reaching the hands of the defendant and so are prevented from reclaiming it by the principle of non-derogation from grant. It is only where the trustees have themselves been defrauded by the potential defendant to a legal proprietary claim that such a claim is likely to be available to a trust.

(2)   What property can be the subject matter of a legal proprietary claim?

(a)   Property in its original form. Where the property which is the subject matter of the claim remains in its original form, the legal owner will, subject to the defences mentioned above, be able to claim it as against anyone in the world and obtain the appropriate remedy.

Difficulties may arise, however, when chattels are intermingled with other chattels of the same nature so that it cannot precisely be ascertained which belong to the claimant.[97] In these circumstances, it seems that a tortious action will still be available despite the mixing. This follows from *Jackson v. Anderson*,[98] where it was held that an action of conversion could be maintained against someone who had mixed the plaintiff's gold coins in a barrelful of the same description. So far as ownership of the intermingled chattels is concerned, this has traditionally depended on whether the mixing was accidental or deliberate. If chattels are mixed accidentally so that they cannot be separated or identified, then the original owners are treated as tenants in common of the whole in proportion to their contributions. This

---

[94] s.23. See also Consumer Credit Act 1974, Sched. IV, Pt I, para. 22.
[95] Torts (Interference with Goods) Act 1977, s.3.
[96] (1998), *The Times*, January 14, 1998.
[97] See R. A. Pearce: 40 Conveyancer (N.S.) (1976) 277.
[98] (1811) 4 Taunt. 24.

was held in *Spence v. Union Marine Insurance Co.*,[99] where bales of wool belonging to different owners became indistinguishable as the result of a shipwreck. On the other hand, in the same case[1] it was suggested that, where a person deliberately mixed the property of another with his own, then the whole must be taken to be the property of the other unless and until the mixer unmixed the chattels. However, this rule has now been described as no longer appropriate given the availability of modern and sophisticated methods of measurement. This was in *Indian Oil Corp. v. Greenstone Shipping Co.*,[2] where the owners of a vessel had mixed with their own crude oil a cargo of crude oil which they were shipping. The owners of the cargo claimed the whole of the crude oil. However, since it was possible to determine exactly the amounts of oil belonging to each party, it was held that the mixture was held in common and that the owners of the cargo were entitled to receive a quantity of the mixed oil equal to that which had gone into the mixture, any doubts being resolved in their favour, together with damages for any loss which they had suffered. While this view seems more appropriate in modern conditions, it remains to be seen which way the conflict of authority thus produced is finally resolved.

Legal proprietary claims to money, on the other hand, suffer from the difficulty that money has no earmark (it is rare for a note to be taken of the numbers of banknotes and there is no way of doing so in the case of coins). Further, since money is the universal medium of exchange, the transferor of money normally makes that money the property of the transferee. However, if a claimant can identify money in the hands of another as belonging to him (as would be the case where bank notes of known serial numbers were stolen and found in the possession of the thief), then that money could be recovered by an action for money had and received.

(b) **Property after a change of form.** Can property be traced at law through a change of form? Can money which has been deposited with an agent or stolen by a thief be traced at law into any property which the money is used to purchase? The conventional answer to this question is that at law property can be traced into its product and anything into which it is turned can be recovered, provided only that the property or its product has at all times remained identifiable, *Jackson v. Anderson*,[3] *Spence v. Union Marine Insurance Co.*[4] and *Indian Oil Corp. v. Greenstone Shipping Co.*[5] still being applicable for this purpose. However, if the property or its product has at any time become unidentifiable by, for example, being mixed with other money in a bank account, then it will no longer be able to be traced at law. In *Taylor v. Plumer*,[6] the defendant had given his stockbroker a draft for £22,000 to be disbursed on Exchequer Bills. The stockbroker, having cashed the draft and used £6,500 for this purpose, paid for certain American securities which he had already agreed to purchase and also obtained some

---

[99] (1868) L.R. 3 C.P. 427.
[1] *ibid.*, at 437–438. This is the rule in equity—see *Lupton v. White* (1808) 15 Ves. 432.
[2] [1987] 2 Lloyd's Rep. 286.
[3] (1811) 4 Taunt. 24.
[4] (1868) L.R. 3 C.P. 427.
[5] [1987] 2 Lloyd's Rep. 286.
[6] (1815) 3 M. & S. 562.

bullion with a draft which he had exchanged for cash. He then attempted to flee the country but was intercepted at Falmouth, where he surrendered the securities and the bullion. His trustee in bankruptcy tried to recover these assets or their value from the defendant on the basis that the latter's title could not survive these transactions; had he succeeded, the defendant would have had to take his turn with the general creditors. However, Lord Ellenborough C.J. held that the defendant could at all times have traced the product of his draft into the hands of the stockbroker since his property was at all times completely identifiable; consequently, he could claim the assets in priority to the general creditors. His lordship stated that only when property was turned into money and mixed with other money did the right to trace it disappear.

Although it has been contended[7] that this decision is no authority for a legal proprietary claim surviving a change of form of the property unless the nature of the transaction by which the change of form occurs is such as to vest title in the new form of the property in the claimant, *Taylor v. Plumer* has been repeatedly followed. In *Re J. Leslie Engineers Co.*,[8] the liquidator of a company was held entitled to trace at law a cheque drawn on the company account to cash into the postal orders which had been purchased with the cash and sent to the defendant. Similarly, in *Lipkin Gorman v. Karpnale*,[9] the House of Lords held that the plaintiff firm of solicitors could trace at law its right of action against its bankers in respect of the credit balance of its client account into the funds drawn in cash from the account by one of its partners and exchanged for gaming chips at the defendant's casino. In *Trustee of the Property of F. C. Jones & Sons (a Firm) v. Jones*,[10] the Court of Appeal held that the trustee in bankruptcy of a partnership could trace cheques totalling £11,700 which one of the partners had after the act of bankruptcy drawn on the partnership account in favour of his wife who paid them into a new account which she opened with commodity brokers and then, having traded profitably with this account, paid the commodity broker's cheque for the profit into another new account with a bank; the trustee in bankruptcy had at all times been the legal owner of the money, had at all times been able to identify it, and so could claim not only the £11,700 and interest thereon but also the profit made with it.

Further, *Taylor v. Plumer* was, if anything, extended in *Banque Belge pour l'Etranger v. Hambrouck*,[11] where the Court of Appeal emphasised that it is not the mere payment of money into a bank account which matters but the identifiability of the property. The defendant had fraudulently obtained £6,000 from the plaintiff by drawing cheques on his employers in favour of himself. He paid these cheques into his own account with another bank, an

---

[7] By S. Khurshid & P. Matthews: (1979) 95 L.Q.R. 78, who argue that the references in *Taylor v. Plumer* to the right of the defendant to trace were to tracing in equity, rather than to tracing at law. This argument is convincing historically and there is much to be said for it as a matter of principle; however, it is inconsistent with the authorities in which *Taylor v. Plumer* has been applied.

[8] [1976] 1 W.L.R. 292.

[9] [1991] 2 A.C. 548 (in fact, only a personal claim was being pursued in the House of Lords).

[10] [1997] Ch. 159.

[11] [1921] 1 K.B. 321.

account into which no other substantial sums were ever paid. From this account, he drew out cash which he paid over to his mistress in consideration for the continuance of their relationship; she paid these sums into a deposit account, whose outstanding balance was successfully claimed by the plaintiff. The majority of the Court of Appeal[12] held that the plaintiff was entitled at law to trace the money through the defendant's bank account because it was possible to distinguish the money at every stage; the fact that, to all intents and purposes, no other sums had been paid into that account meant that the funds abstracted from the plaintiff had never lost their identity.[13]

However, where property or its product has been turned into money and mixed with other money, any legal proprietary claim will be lost. Payment into a mixed fund or through an inter-bank clearing system will clearly prevent a legal proprietary claim while, as *Banque Belge pour l'Etranger v. Hambrouck* clearly illustrates, payment into an unmixed bank account (other than through such a clearing system) will not. However, it is not at present entirely clear whether legal proprietary claims are limited to physical substitutions (where, as in all the cases discussed in the previous paragraph, cash is withdrawn from one bank account and used to acquire some other asset, including a credit balance in another bank account) or also extend to other forms of transfer, such as an electronic transfer from one bank account to another where the funds have not had to pass through an inter-bank clearing system.

In *Agip (Africa) v. Jackson*,[14] the name of the payee on a payment order issued by the plaintiff was fraudulently altered and the sum in question was transferred by the plaintiff's bank in Tunis through its correspondent bank in New York, and presumably then through the New York clearing system, to an account at Lloyds Bank in London in the name of a shell English company controlled by the defendants, a firm of accountants from the Isle of Man. The plaintiff subsequently claimed to be entitled to trace this payment through the account of the shell company into an account of the defendants in the Isle of Man, to which it had subsequently been transferred. The shell company's account had contained no other funds at the relevant time so there would have been no difficulty about tracing the funds from that account to the account of the defendants. However, Millett J. held that the funds could not be traced at law into the account of the shell company. Given that the money had been transmitted by telegraphic transfer and had almost certainly passed through the New York clearing system, "nothing passed between Tunisia and London but a stream of electrons. It is not possible to treat the money received by Lloyds Bank in London or its correspondent bank in New York as representing the proceeds of the payment order or of any other physical asset previously in its hands and delivered by it in exchange for the money."[15] Millett J. thus seems to have

---

[12] Bankes and Atkin L.JJ.; Scrutton L.J. held that the plaintiff was entitled only to trace in equity.

[13] Atkin L.J. went so far as to say that it was possible to trace at law even into a mixed fund. However, this view is generally regarded more as an expression of hope than as a statement of reality.

[14] [1990] Ch. 265.

[15] *ibid.*

restricted legal proprietary claims to cases of physical substitution; however, in the Court of Appeal,[16] Fox L.J., while affirming the judgment of Millett J., placed a greater emphasis on the clearing system limitation. The view of Millett J. was subsequently reiterated in *Bank Tejerat v. Hong Kong and Shanghai Building Corp.*,[17] where Tuckey J. refused a legal proprietary claim to funds which had been the subject of telex instructions.

These decisions emphasise the restrictions of proprietary claims at law. However, they do not necessarily mean that payments made by cheque can never be traced at law; indeed the decision in *Trustee of the Property of F.C. Jones & Sons (a Firm) v. Jones*,[18] where cheques were traced at law, suggests quite the opposite. Consequently, where both payer and payee have their accounts at the same branch, it will clearly be possible to trace the payment at law from one account to another and this will almost certainly also be possible where the accounts are at different branches of the same bank. However, it is obviously likely that the intervention of any inter-bank clearing system will cause the funds to lose their identity and be prevented from being traced at law despite the existence of the original cheque, simply because no funds may actually have been transferred from the payer's bank to the payee's bank on the day in question (this will depend on the overall balance of cleared transactions between the two banks on that day). Whether or not this is actually the case, these restrictions on legal proprietary claims are clearly highly inconvenient; however, the difficulties have been substantially alleviated by the intervention of equity.

(B) Proprietary Claims in Equity

A person who seeks to assert a proprietary claim in equity will be relying on the existence of an equitable proprietary interest in the property in question which he will be endeavouring to enforce against the defendant. However, no such claim will be able to be made against a defendant who is a bona fide purchaser for value of a legal estate in the property without notice of the interest of the claimant (such a person inevitably takes the property free of such an equitable proprietary interest) or against any defendant who is able to invoke the recently recognised defence of change of position; there are also a number of further defences open only to innocent volunteers.

What are the consequences of a successful equitable proprietary claim? Normally, the defendant will thereafter be bound by the equitable interest of the claimant and will therefore be treated as a trustee of the property in question for him. This trust is often said to be a constructive trust; this expression is not inaccurate but it is potentially confusing.[19] It does not mean that the defendant will automatically be regarded as having been subject to all the obligations of a trustee from the moment when he originally received the property in question; that will only be the case if he is also liable for "knowing receipt" under the rules which were discussed in Chapter 10.[20] However, he will certainly be subject to such obligations thereafter

---

[16] [1991] Ch. 547.
[17] [1995] 1 Lloyd's Rep. 239.
[18] [1997] Ch. 159,
[19] See Sir Peter Millett, (1998) 114 L.Q.R. 399.
[20] See, *ante*, p. 336.

and if he does not comply with them he will be liable for "inconsistent dealing".[21] If the claimant is able to show that any particular item of property in the hands of the defendant is, in equity, either entirely his own property or entirely the product of his own property, then he will obviously be able to call for that property to be transferred to him. If, on the other hand, he is able to show that any particular item of property in the hands of the defendant is only partially the product of his own property, then he will normally have a lien or charge over it for the amount of his contribution thereto or, if it has gone up in value, for a beneficial interest in proportion to his contribution thereto; in both cases, he will enjoy the rights appropriate to the holder of such an interest in the type of property in question.[22] In all cases, his equitable proprietary right will amount to a right *in rem*, provided of course that it is actually enforceable against the defendant in the first place.

However, treating the defendant as a trustee is not the only possible consequence of a successful equitable proprietary claim. The claimant can alternatively be subrogated to rights which the defendant has against a third party. This happened in *Boscawen v. Bajwa*.[23] The Abbey National Building Society had agreed to make a mortgage advance to fund the purchase of a property belonging to the defendant. The purchasers' solicitors, who were as usual acting both for the building society and for the purchasers, transferred the funds to the defendant's solicitors who used them to pay off the defendant's mortgage with the Halifax Building Society. However, although the defendant had executed an undated transfer in favour of the purchasers, a small outstanding balance of the price was never paid so this transfer was never dated or registered; the purchasers therefore never acquired legal title. To make matters worse, the contract between the defendant and the purchasers did not comply with the necessary formalities[24] and so was void; consequently, the purchasers had never acquired any equitable interest either. The Abbey National therefore had no valid mortgage over the defendant's property yet their money had been used to pay off his mortgage. Various creditors of the defendant then obtained a charging order over the house and sought an order for sale. The Abbey National was able to comply with the requirements for an equitable proprietary claim and was able to demonstrate that its funds had in fact been used to discharge the mortgage. The Court of Appeal said this[25]:

"If the plaintiff succeeds in tracing his property, whether in its original or in some changed form, into the hands of the defendant, and overcomes any defences which are put forward on the defendant's behalf, he is entitled to a remedy. The remedy will be fashioned to the circumstances. The plaintiff will generally be entitled to a personal remedy; if he seeks a proprietary remedy he must usually prove that the property to which he lays claim is

---

[21] See *ante*, p. 348. *Sheridan v. Joyce* [1844] 1 Jo. & Lat. 41 (Court of Chancery of Ireland).
[22] Thus if it is land he will enjoy the same rights as any other beneficiary under a trust of land (see Trusts of Land and Appointment of Trustees Act 1996)
[23] [1996] 1 W.L.R. 328
[24] For failure to comply with the Law of Property (Miscellaneous Provisions) Act 1989, s.2.
[25] [1996] 1 W.L.R. 328 at 334–335, *per* Millett L.J.. In this passage, the references to the plaintiff are to the claimant in an equitable proprietary claim, not to the plaintiffs in the action.

still in the ownership of the defendant. If he succeeds in doing this the court will treat the defendant as holding the property on a constructive trust for the plaintiff and will order the defendant to transfer it *in specie* to the plaintiff. But this is only one of the proprietary remedies which are available to a court of equity. If the plaintiff's money has been applied by the defendant, for example, not in the acquisition of a landed property but in its improvement, then the court may treat the land as charged with the payment to the plaintiff of a sum representing the amount by which the value of the defendant's land has been enhanced by the use of the plaintiff's money. And if the plaintiff's money has been used to discharge a mortgage on the defendant's land, then the court may achieve a similar result by treating the land as subject to a charge by way of subrogation in favour of the plaintiff."

The Abbey National was therefore held to be entitled to be subrogated to the mortgage security of the Halifax which had been paid off with its money and therefore enjoyed priority over the plaintiffs' charging order. The facts of this case were very peculiar and it is not often that a claimant will need to have recourse to subrogation in order to enforce an equitable proprietary claim. However, there seems no reason why he should not do so in the sort of circumstances which occurred in *Boscawen v. Bajwa*.

(1)   What are the prerequisites of an equitable proprietary claim?

   (a)   An equitable proprietary interest. It is hardly necessary to state that an equitable proprietary claim can only be pursued if the claimant has an equitable proprietary interest in the property in question Although it is generally said that a claimant is able to trace an equitable proprietary interest into its product only if he can point to the existence of a fiduciary relationship, the converse is not true. Thus the fact that funds have been deposited with a fiduciary agent pursuant to a contract of loan does not entitle the depositor to bring an equitable proprietary claim; he has retained no proprietary interest in the funds deposited.[26] Nor does an agent who is retained to collect rents or other moneys on behalf of his principal automatically become a trustee of them for the latter; this will only be the case if he did or should have segregated the sums.[27]

   (b)   A fiduciary relationship. As has already been mentioned, it is generally said that a claimant is able to trace an equitable proprietary interest into its product only if he can point to the existence of a fiduciary relationship. In *Agip (Africa) v. Jackson*,[28] Millett J. held that:

"the only restriction on the ability of equity to follow assets is the requirement that there must be some fiduciary relationship which permits the

---

[26] *Daly v. The Sydney Stock Exchange* (1986) 160 C.L.R. 371 (High Court of Australia).
[27] *Cohen v. Cohen* (1929) 42 C.L.R. 91. However, any failure to segregate means that no priority will be able to be obtained unless the whereabouts of the funds can actually be established.
[28] [1990] Ch. 265.

assistance of equity to be invoked. The requirement has been widely condemned and depends on authority rather than principle."

Historically there was no such requirement. In *Re Hallett's Estate*,[29] the defendant solicitor sold bonds belonging partly to his own marriage settlement and partly to a client and mixed the proceeds with his own funds in a bank account. The beneficiaries of the marriage settlement could clearly point to the existence of a fiduciary relationship but the client was also permitted to maintain an equitable proprietary claim on the basis that she was the legal and beneficial owner of the property which she had deposited with the defendant. Similarly, in *Banque Belge pour l'Etranger v. Hambrouck*,[30] Scrutton L.J. who had doubted the availability of a legal proprietary claim, held that the plaintiff had an equitable proprietary claim and both the other members of the court stated that, had they not held the plaintiff to have a legal proprietary claim, they also would have permitted an equitable proprietary claim. None of the members of the court stated any requirement for the existence of a fiduciary relationship as a prerequisite to an equitable proprietary claim. There is, of course, no doubt whatever that the necessary fiduciary relationship could have been found in both these cases had it been necessary. As Millett J. went on to say in *Agip (Africa) v. Jackson*,[31] "the requirement may be circumvented since it is not necessary that the fund to be traced should have been the subject of fiduciary obligations before it got into the wrong hands; it is sufficient that the payment to the defendant itself gives rise to a fiduciary relationship." Both the defaulting solicitor in *Re Hallett's Estate* and the fraudulent employee in *Banque Belge pour l'Etranger v. Hambrouck* could undoubtedly have been held to be constructive trustees of, respectively, the proceeds of the bonds and the proceeds of the cheques. The significant fact is that none of the judges felt it necessary to look for and find such a fiduciary relationship.

However, it is generally thought that in *Re Diplock*[32] the Court of Appeal interpreted the decision of the House of Lords in *Sinclair v. Brougham*[33] as establishing, in the words of Goulding J. in *Chase Manhattan Bank v. Israel-British Bank (London)*[34] "that an initial fiduciary relationship is a necessary foundation of the equitable right of tracing". It is questionable both whether this was really the opinion of the Court of Appeal in *Re Diplock* and whether *Sinclair v. Brougham* imposed any such requirement. As will be seen later on, the actual decision reached in the latter case has recently been overruled by the House of Lords in *Westdeutsche Landesbank Girozentrale v. Islington L.B.C.*[35] However, the House did not consider the fiduciary relationship requirement, Lord Browne-Wilkinson merely saying the House "should not

---

[29] (1880) 13 Ch.D. 696. See [1975] C.L.P. 64.
[30] [1921] 1 K.B. 321.
[31] [1990] Ch. 265.
[32] [1948] Ch. 465.
[33] [1914] A.C. 398.
[34] [1981] Ch. 105.
[35] [1996] A.C. 669.

be taken to be casting any doubt on the principles of tracing as established in *Re Diplock*".[36]

In *Sinclair v. Brougham*[37] the House of Lords had had to look for and find a fiduciary relationship, wrongfully as it has now been held, because that was the only way of establishing that the depositors in an *ultra vires* banking business had an equitable proprietary interest in the funds of the building society which had been running it. This does not, however, of itself necessarily mean that a fiduciary relationship is required where the claimant has a pre-existing equitable proprietary right. Indeed, in *Re Diplock*[38] the Court of Appeal did no more than state that "equity may operate on the conscience not merely of those who acquire a legal title in breach of some trust, express or constructive, or of some other fiduciary obligation, but of volunteers provided that as a result of what has gone before some equitable proprietary interest has been created and attaches to the property in the hands of the volunteer." It is not obvious that this passage has the effect of requiring a fiduciary relationship where the claimant already has a pre-existing equitable proprietary interest. However, that is the way in which it has always been subsequently interpreted, both at first instance[39] and in the Court of Appeal.[40]

Whether or not such a requirement exists is not purely a technical issue. Even though the courts have on occasions strained the concept of fiduciary relationship to its limits, if not well beyond them, in order to satisfy this requirement, an absolute legal and beneficial owner of property cannot possibly point to any such relationship and so, according to the present understanding of the law, is therefore apparently not entitled to maintain an equitable proprietary claim. Consequently, if the property of such a person is stolen and its product is mixed with other money in a bank account, the victim of the theft will prima facie not be entitled to maintain a proprietary trace either at law (because of the mixing) or in equity (because of the absence of a fiduciary relationship). This ridiculous anomaly can only be rectified in one of the following ways. The first possibility would obviously be to challenge the requirement for a fiduciary relationship, something which is much advocated but which is realistically only possible in the House of Lords, where it would be likely to be given short shrift. The second possibility would be to holding that a thief holds stolen property on resulting trust for his victim, thus providing both the fiduciary relationship and the equitable proprietary interest necessary for an equitable proprietary claim. Such a conclusion was reached by the High Court of Australia in *Black*

---

[36] *ibid.* at 714. This may well have been a reference to the mixed fund rules established in *Re Diplock* (see *post*, pp. 736–737) rather than to its supposed enunciation of a fiduciary relationship requirement.

[37] [1914] A.C. 398.

[38] [1948] Ch. 465 at 530.

[39] In *Agip (Africa) v. Jackson* [1990] Ch. 265 and in *Box v. Barclays Bank* (1998), *The Times*, May 4, 1998. In the latter case Ferris J. denied the plaintiffs an equitable proprietary claim specifically because there was no fiduciary relationship (they had deposited money with a person running an unlicensed deposit taking business, a transaction which was classified as creating nothing more than a debtor-creditor relationship).

[40] In *Aluminium Industrie Vaassen v. Romalpa Aluminium* [1976] 1 W.L.R. 676 and in *Agip (Africa) v. Jackson* [1991] Ch. 547.

v. S. Freeman & Co.,[41] a decision which was cited with approval by Lord Templeman in *Lipkin Gorman v. Karpnale*,[42] which did not of course concern an equitable proprietary claim. The difficulty about this view is that, since a thief does not acquire title to the stolen property, it is not easy to see what he would actually be holding on trust. The third possibility would be to hold, as Lord Browne-Wilkinson indicated in *Westdeutsche Landesbank Girozentrale v. Islington L.B.C.*,[43] that a constructive trust can be imposed on the thief as a result of his fraudulent conduct; while there obviously is no difficulty about imposing a constructive trust on this ground,[44] exactly the same difficulty arises as to exactly what he would be holding on trust. The fourth possibility would be to hold that that constructive trust arises not when the thief steals the property but only if and when he turns it into money which, being the universal medium of exchange, becomes his property and so can become the subject matter of a trust. It is suggested that this is how the matter should be dealt with unless and until the fiduciary relationship requirement is abolished.

(2) When will these prerequisites be satisfied?

(a) Express trusts. It is obvious that the requirement for a fiduciary relationship will be satisfied where the person against whom the equitable proprietary claim is being brought is an express trustee of the property in question and it was held in *Re Diplock*[45] that the requirement will also be satisfied where the property in question was originally subject to an express trust, even though the equitable proprietary claim is in fact being brought against a subsequent holder thereof.

(b) Resulting trusts. The requirement will equally be satisfied where the person against whom the equitable proprietary claim is being brought is a resulting trustee of any of the traditional types.[46]

(c) Constructive trusts. The requirement will equally be satisfied where, as in *Attorney-General for Hong Kong v. Reid*,[47] the person against whom the equitable proprietary claim is being brought has been held to be a constructive trustee of the property in question; this will clearly be the case even where, as in *Agip (Africa) v. Jackson*,[48] the property in question became subject to a constructive trust only as a result of an improper disposition thereof.

(d) Void, voidable or mistaken transactions. Whether the requirement is also satisfied in the case of a recipient of property transferred to him under a transaction which is void, voidable, or mistaken is more controversial. It

---

[41] [1910] 12 C.L.R. 105.
[42] [1992] 2 A.C. 548.
[43] [1996] A.C. 669 at 715–716.
[44] See *ante*, pp. 358 *et seq.*
[45] [1948] Ch. 465.
[46] See *ante*, Chap. 9.
[47] [1993] A.C. 713
[48] [1990] Ch. 265; [1991] Ch. 547.

has on occasion been held, or stated, that such a recipient holds that property on trust for the transferor, thus providing him with both the existing prerequisites of an equitable proprietary claim, namely an equitable proprietary interest and a fiduciary relationship.

Sinclair v. Brougham[49] concerned a void transaction. In the course of the liquidation of the Birkbeck Permanent Benefit Building Society, it became apparent that a banking business which the Society had been running was in fact *ultra vires*. A question of priorities therefore arose between the shareholders of the society and the depositors in the banking business (both had agreed that the outside creditors should be paid off first). A majority of the House of Lords subsequently held that the depositors did indeed have an equitable proprietary interest arising under a trust.[50] However, this decision was overruled by the majority of the House of Lords in *Westdeutsche Landesbank Girozentrale v. Islington L.B.C.*[51] The parties had entered into an interest rate swap agreement, under which each agreed to pay to the other during a period of five years at six-monthly intervals an amount calculated by reference to the interest which would have accrued over the previous six-monthly period on a notional principal sum, the interest rate being fixed in the case of the bank and floating in the case of the local authority. However, during the five year period, such agreements were held to be *ultra vires* local authorities and consequently void.[52] The bank sought to recover the sums which it had paid to the local authority. In the lower courts,[53] it succeeded both at common law under an action for money had and received and on the basis of an equitable proprietary claim in accordance with *Sinclair v. Brougham*. However, the House of Lords held that the transferor of property under a void transaction who intends to pass that property to the transferee retains no equitable proprietary interest therein either under a resulting or a constructive trust. Consequently, the bank was not entitled to an equitable proprietary claim.[54] This decision has established, hopefully once and for all, that no equitable proprietary claim is available to the transferor of property under a transaction which is void.

Whether such a claim was available to the transferor of property under a transaction which is merely voidable appeared to have been considered by Millett J. in *El Ajou v. Dollar Land Holdings*.[55] In this case, the plaintiffs had been induced to purchase shares by fraudulent misrepresentations and were seeking to impose liability for "knowing receipt" on the defendant, into whose hands the purchase moneys had come for value but, as the Court of

---

[49] [1914] A.C. 398.
[50] Viscount Haldane L.C. and Lord Atkinson held that the trust in question was "a resulting trust, not of an active character", while Lord Parker of Waddington held that it was a constructive trust. Lord Sumner did not indicate with which of these two views he agreed.
[51] [1996] A.C. 669.
[52] By the House of Lords in *Hazell v. Hammersmith and Fulham L.B.C.* [1992] A.C. 1.
[53] [1994] 4 All E.R. 890 (Hobhouse J.); [1994] 1 W.L.R. 938 (Court of Appeal).
[54] Consequently the bank was not entitled to compound interest on the sum, which the local authority accepted in the House of Lords that it was liable to repay at common law with simple interest thereon.
[55] [1993] 3 All E.R. 717, affirmed by the Court of Appeal without discussion of this particular point [1994] 2 All E.R. 685. See *ante*, p. 340.

Appeal subsequently held,[56] with sufficient knowledge of the fraud for the imposition of such liability. Millett J. held that the plaintiffs were "entitled to rescind the transaction and revest the equitable title to the purchase money in themselves, at least to the extent necessary to support an equitable tracing claim", stating that "the trust which is operating in these cases is not some new model remedial constructive trust, but an old fashioned institutional resulting trust".[57] No equitable proprietary claim was being brought in this case but on the face of things if the plaintiffs were able to trace the funds in equity for the purposes of the imposition of liability for "knowing receipt" they should also have been able to do so for the purposes of an equitable proprietary claim. However, Millett J. has since stated, extra-judicially,[58] that different considerations would have arisen in the case of an equitable proprietary claim. Although there is no obvious reason why the rules of tracing should differ depending on the nature of the claim being brought, this does at least indicate, contrary to what was thought immediately after this decision, that no equitable proprietary claim is available to the transferor of property under a transaction which is voidable either. It is much to be hoped that this conclusion is confirmed judicially.

However, the availability of an equitable proprietary claim to the transferor of property under a transaction which is mistaken was controversially upheld by Goulding J. in the much earlier decision in *Chase Manhattan Bank v. Israel-British Bank (London)*.[59] The plaintiff New York bank as the result of a clerical error made twice rather than once a payment of U.S.$2,000,000 to another New York bank for the credit of the defendant London bank, which subsequently became insolvent. The plaintiff duly proved in the liquidation in respect of the second payment made under a mistake of fact but this gave no priority over the other creditors of the defendant. The plaintiff therefore also claimed to be entitled to an equitable proprietary claim against the defendant. The legal effects of the mistaken payment had to be determined in accordance with the law of the State of New York, where a payment under a mistake of fact of money which the payee cannot conscientiously withhold gives rise to the imposition of a constructive trust. Goulding J. held, rather unexpectedly, that this was "also in accord with the general principles of equity as applied in England".[60] He justified this conclusion on the grounds that "a person who pays money to another under a factual mistake retains an equitable property in it and the conscience of that other is subjected to a fiduciary duty to respect his proprietary right."[61] This decision seems highly questionable. It is not obvious how either an equitable proprietary interest or a fiduciary duty could conceivably have arisen as the result of a payment made through a third party bank intended to be in settlement of a commercial debt.

The decision in *Chase Manhattan Bank v. Israel-British Bank (London)* was expressly applied in the Court of Appeal of New Zealand in *Liggett v.*

---

[56] [1994] 2 All E.R. 685, reversing Millett J. on this point.
[57] [1993] 3 All E.R. 717 at 734.
[58] (1998) 114 L.Q.R. 399.
[59] [1981] Ch. 105.
[60] *ibid.* at 118.
[61] *ibid.* at 119.

Kensington.[62] A gold-dealer had offered its purchasers the option of leaving their bullion in its custody on their behalf as "non-allocated bullion". Purchasers who did so were issued with a certificate of ownership and were entitled to take physical possession of their bullion on seven days' notice. The gold-dealer subsequently became insolvent and the question arose as to whether these purchasers were entitled to an equitable proprietary claim in priority not only to its general creditors but also to a debenture holder. As has already been mentioned,[63] the majority of the Court of Appeal of New Zealand (Cooke P. and Gault J.) held that the gold-dealer was in a fiduciary relationship with the purchasers, breach of which led to the imposition of a constructive trust and thus in turn to the purchasers having an equitable proprietary interest in the purchase moneys and their product, the remaining bullion. Cooke P., however, also held, applying *Chase Manhattan Bank v. Israel-British Bank (London)*, that the mistaken belief of the purchasers that they were acquiring gold, not merely contractual rights, meant that they had throughout retained an equitable proprietary interest in the purchase moneys. However, when this case reached the Privy Council under the name of *Re Goldcorp Exchange*,[64] this decision was reversed. Lord Mustill held that there was no fiduciary relationship between the gold-dealer and the purchasers so that no equitable proprietary interest could arise in that way. Further, in relation to the claim based on the retention by the purchasers of an equitable proprietary interest in the purchase money, Lord Mustill held that, whether this claim was based on mistake, misrepresentation or a total failure of consideration, the purchasers had at no time sought to rescind their contracts with the gold-dealer on any of these grounds but had, on the contrary, "throughout the proceedings asserted various forms of proprietary interest in the bullion, all of them derived in one way or another from the contracts of sale". This stance was "wholly inconsistent with the notion that the contracts were and are so ineffectual that the customers are entitled to get their money back".[65] This of course meant that the Board did not have to consider the validity of the principle enunciated by Goulding J. in *Chase Manhattan Bank v. Israel-British Bank*; but Lord Mustill declined to express an opinion as to whether or not that case was correctly decided.[66]

His clear doubts in this respect were confirmed by Lord Browne-Wilkinson in *Westdeutsche Landesbank Girozentale v. Islington L.B.C.*[67] He specifically held that he did not accept the reasoning of Goulding J. Unfortunately, however, he went on to say that *Chase Manhattan Bank v. Israel-British Bank (London)* nevertheless "may well have been rightly decided" on the basis that "although the mere receipt of the moneys, in ignorance of the mistake, gives rise to no trust, the retention of the moneys after the recipient bank learned of the mistake may well have given rise to a constructive trust".[68] Lord Browne-Wilkinson did not specify the basis of the imposition

---

[62] [1993] 1 N.Z.L.R. 257.
[63] See *ante*, pp. 284–285.
[64] [1995] 1 A.C. 74.
[65] *ibid.* at 102.
[66] *ibid.* at 103.
[67] [1996] A.C. 669.
[68] *ibid.*, at 715.

of such a constructive trust; it could presumably be either a remedial constructive trust of the type which he appeared to envisage later in his speech[69] or a constructive trust imposed for "inconsistent dealing".[70] It is suggested that neither of these grounds is acceptable and that *Chase Manhattan Bank v. Israel-British Bank (London)* was both wrongly reasoned and wrongly decided. However, it would be optimistic to suggest that this conclusion represents the law at present so, at the moment, an equitable proprietary claim may (but certainly should not) be available to the transferor of property under a transaction which is mistaken.

(3) What property can be the subject matter of an equitable proprietary claim?

From its earliest days, equity has always been prepared to permit a beneficiary of a trust to enforce that trust against every transferee of the trust property save where the latter can show that he is a bona fide purchaser of a legal estate therein for value without notice or, today, can make out a defence of change of position. There seems no reason why such a claim should ever have been confined to the trust property in its original form for, otherwise, any alteration in the form of the trust property would have defeated the interests of the beneficiaries. Thus, equity was prepared to allow a beneficiary to trace the trust property into its product.[71] However, at this stage equity, like the common law, only permitted an equitable proprietary claim so long as the property or its product remained identifiable; consequently, the payment of the property or its product into a mixed fund was at this stage as fatal to an equitable proprietary claim as it was (and still is) to a legal proprietary claim. However, in 1852 in *Pennell v. Deffell,*[72] the Court of Appeal in Chancery held that the fact that property had become unidentifiable in a mixed fund was no bar to an equitable proprietary claim. The fact that it is thus possible to trace in equity property which has been mixed with the property of another has made equitable proprietary claims attractive to the suppliers of goods to manufacturers. They have sought, by means of what are known as retention of title clauses, to ensure that title to the goods which they have supplied does not pass to the manufacturers until the goods have been paid for. This has meant that the rules of tracing property in equity have had to be applied in a commercial context very different from the trust context in which they were originally developed.

(a) **Property which has not been mixed.** Where the claimant has an equitable proprietary interest in property which has not been mixed, whether that property is still in its original form or has suffered a change of form, he will often be able to compel the holder of the legal title to bring a legal proprietary claim. Thus, if property is stolen from a trust, the trustee will have the right to trace that property at law and the beneficiary will have the right to trace that property in equity. In such circumstances, because of the absence of a defence of bona fide purchase for value without notice at

---

[69] *ibid.,* at 716. See *ante,* pp. 277–278.
[70] See *ante,* p. 348.
[71] See *Ryall v. Ryall* (1739) 1 Atk. 59 and the other authorities cited in [1975] C.L.P. 64.
[72] (1853) De M. & G. 372.

law, the beneficiary will be better advised to compel the trustee to trace the property or its product at law. However, this will not be possible where, as in *Re Diplock*,[73] the trustee has himself in breach of trust disposed of the property in question since he will be estopped from bringing a legal proprietary claim by the principle of non-derogation from grant. In such circumstances, the beneficiaries will have to trace the property or its product in equity. The only defence to such a claim will be bona fide purchase for value of a legal estate without notice or, now, change of position. A successful claimant will be entitled, according to Jessel M.R. in *Re Hallett's Estate*,[74] to elect between calling for the property or its product to be transferred to him or taking a charge thereon for the amount of his property which was laid out in its acquisition.

Claims of this kind are not confined to cases in which the beneficiaries of a trust recover the original trust property or its unmixed product from a third party into whose hands it has been transferred in breach of trust. They have also been made in many of the cases involving retention of title clauses. In *Aluminium Industrie Vaassen v. Romalpa Aluminium*,[75] a company selling aluminium foil was, under the terms of the contract of sale, expressed to remain the owner of the foil until such time as the purchaser had paid the purchase price in full (it was also provided that the vendor would become owner of any new objects made as a result of mixing the foil with other materials). This did not prevent the purchaser from giving a good title to third parties but, as between vendor and purchaser, the goods remained the property of the vendor. The purchaser went into liquidation owing substantial sums in respect of unpaid foil. The vendor claimed to be entitled to such foil as remained in the possession of the purchaser and to the proceeds of sale of unmixed foil sold to third parties which had been paid by them to the receiver and had been placed by him in a separate bank account. Once it had been held that the terms of the contract were indeed as has been stated (this was in fact disputed by the purchaser), the vendor was clearly entitled to the foil which was still in the possession of the purchaser (the nature of this claim was not discussed at all but the vendor, as legal owner thereof, was clearly entitled to recover this property at law). However the vendor's claim to the proceeds of sale of the unmixed foil sold to third parties was based on *Re Hallett's Estate*.[76] The Court of Appeal held that the purchaser held the foil as a fiduciary agent of the vendor. Consequently, the vendor was entitled to trace the foil in equity into its product, the proceeds of sale. Given that neither the foil nor its proceeds of sale had ever become unidentifiable by being mixed with other property, there seems no reason why the vendor should not equally have been able to trace the proceeds of sale at law. However, the decision clearly establishes that, provided the necessary fiduciary relationship can be established,[77] a vendor will be able to recover

---

[73] [1948] Ch. 465.

[74] (1880) 13 Ch.D. 676 at 709.

[75] [1976] 1 W.L.R. 676.

[76] (1880) 13 Ch.D. 696.

[77] This has not been possible in a number of subsequent cases concerning retention of title clauses. Consequently, the vendors have necessarily had to trace at law. See *Clough Mill v. Martin* [1985] 1 W.L.R. 111 and *Hendy Lennox (Industrial Engines) v. Grahame Puttick* [1984] 1 W.L.R. 485.

property subject to a retention of title clause by means of an equitable proprietary claim.

(b) Property which has been mixed. Where the claimant has an equitable proprietary interest in property which has been mixed, the mixing will usually have occurred as a result of the property or its product having been mixed with other money in a bank account. In such circumstances, if the mixed fund has subsequently remained intact, the claimant will clearly be entitled to a lien or charge on the mixed fund for the amount of his property and, presumably, in the event that any interest has been earned, to the part thereof paid in respect of his property.[78] (In practice, however, sums will inevitably have been withdrawn from the mixed fund, in which case the result depends on whether the mixing was authorised or unauthorised. If it was authorised, the claimant will inevitably be entitled to the appropriate proportion of the mixed fund or its product. If, on the other hand, the mixing was unauthorised, it is necessary to have recourse to a series of presumptions in order to establish whether such withdrawals have been made from the mixed funds rateably or from one or more of its component parts. These rules will be considered in detail later on.) In the same way, at least in principle, a claimant who can show that his property has been mixed with other property to form a new object should be entitled to trace his property in equity into its product, provided that he can show the necessary fiduciary relationship. This has indeed been attempted in a number of cases concerning retention of title clauses. If, as in *Aluminium Industrie Vaassen v. Romalpa Aluminium*,[79] such a claimant can show both the necessary fiduciary relationship and a clear intention that any such new objects should become the property of the vendor in whole or in part, such a claim should in principle be able to succeed (no such claim was in fact brought in that case but in *Bordon (U.K.) v. Scottish Timber Products*[80] the formulation used was described as "presumably effective" for this purpose). However, for a variety of reasons, such claims as have been brought have been unsuccessful. It has sometimes[81] been held that the terms of the contract have not had the effect of giving the vendor any proprietary interest in the new object, it has sometimes[82] been held that there has been no sufficient fiduciary relationship, and it has sometimes[83] been held that any interest created in the new object amounts to a charge which should have been registered under what is now the Companies Act 1985[84] and in default is consequently void for non-registration.

(i) *Identifiability.* A claim to trace property in equity into a mixed fund has traditionally presupposed that the claimant can actually identify his

---

[78] There is some uncertainty about the right of the claimant to increases in value in the mixed fund; see *post*, p. 732.

[79] [1976] 1 W.L.R. 676.

[80] [1981] Ch. 25.

[81] In *Borden (U.K.) v. Scottish Timber Products* [1981] Ch. 25 and *Re Peachdart* [1984] Ch. 131.

[82] In *Re Bond Worth* [1980] Ch. 228; *Re Andrabell* [1984] 3 All E.R. 407; *Hendy Lennox (Industrial Engines) v. Grahame Puttick* [1984] 1 W.L.R. 485.

[83] In *Re Bond Worth* [1980] Ch. 228; *Re Peachdart* [1984] Ch. 131; *Re Weldtech Equipment* [1991] B.C.C. 16; *Compaq Computer v. Abercorn Group* [1991] B.C.C. 484.

[84] ss.395–404.

property or its product in that fund, if necessary with the aid of the various rules and presumptions as to withdrawals to which reference has already been made. Thus, in *Re Hallett's Estate*,[85] the Court of Appeal held that the priority given to the claimants was limited to the extent that they were able to identify the product of their property in the mixed fund. However, in recent years, there have been some indications that the courts may be prepared to relax this requirement of identifiability.

In *Space Investments v. Canadian Imperial Bank of Commerce Trust Company*[86] a bank trustee, which was expressly authorised to deposit trust funds with itself, did so and subsequently went into liquidation. A person who deposits money with a bank normally[87] necessarily makes the bank absolute legal and beneficial owner thereof—were this not the case, the bank would have considerable difficulty in earning the interest payable to the depositor since it would be unable to utilise the funds other than in accordance with the rules governing trust investments and would certainly not be able to use the funds to make unsecured loans. The Privy Council therefore held that, since the mixing of the trust funds with the trustee's own funds had been entirely lawful, the beneficiaries had retained no proprietary interest in the funds deposited and so could not bring an equitable proprietary claim; they were therefore no more than general creditors of the bank. However, Lord Templeman emphasised that, if the mixing had been carried out without such an express authorisation, it would have been unlawful. In such circumstances, the beneficiaries would have been allowed "to trace the trust money to all the assets of the bank and to recover the trust money by an equitable charge over all the assets of the bank".[88] If this hypothetical situation, it is inconceivable that the trust would have been able to identify its own funds within the general assets of the bank. Consequently, if it would indeed have been entitled to trace, then the rights to persons entitled to trace property in equity into a mixed fund are considerably wider than has previously been held. Giving such a claimant an equitable charge over all the assets of the bank converts him to all intents and purposes into a debenture holder since he obtains priority over the general creditors even in respect of assets which were not the product of the mixed fund. This seems wholly unfair to the general creditors.[89]

Lord Templeman's remarks have been considered in two decisions concerning payments into funds which subsequently became overdrawn, something which has traditionally been fatal to the right to trace in equity. In *Re*

---

[85] (1880) 13 Ch.D. 696.

[86] [1986] 1 W.L.R. 1072.

[87] The depositors in an *ultra vires* banking business had of course been held to have an equitable proprietary interest in *Sinclair v. Brougham* [1914] A.C. 398, see *ante*, p. 722, a decision which, surprisingly, was not cited. However, this decision has now of course been overruled anyway.

[88] [1986] 1 W.L.R. 1072 at 1074.

[89] See R. M. Goode: (1987) 103 L.Q.R. 433. An equally unorthodox, but this time excessively narrow, view of equitable tracing claims of this type was taken in *Re Att.-Gen.'s Reference (No. 1) 1985* [1986] Q.B. 491. However, this view was based on *Lister & Co. v. Stubbs* (1890) 45 Ch.D. 1 and therefore presumably cannot survive the criticism of that decision by the Privy Council in *Att.-Gen. for Hong Kong v. Reid* [1994] 1 A.C. 324, see *ante*, p. 293.

Goldcorp Exchange,[90] the Court of Appeal of New Zealand[91] applied Lord Templeman's remarks to this situation but the Privy Council, having held that the purchasers had no equitable proprietary interest at all, did not need to consider them. Lord Mustill, having referred with approval to the traditional rule, expressed the view that "the law relating to the creation and tracing of equitable proprietary interests is still in a state of development"[92]; however, he concluded that it was not "necessary or appropriate to consider the scope and ambit of the observations in *Space Investments* or their application to trustees other than bank trustees".[93] A similar approach was taken by the Court of Appeal in *Bishopsgate Investment Management v. Homan*,[94] where it was argued that the traditional rule should, on the strength of Lord Templeman's remarks, be overruled. The Court of Appeal rejected this argument, classifying the remarks as dicta, and holding that their extension to this situation had been rejected in *Re Goldcorp Exchange*; the traditional rule was applied. In neither of these two decisions was a view expressed as to the situation specifically envisaged by Lord Templeman where a bank trustee has unlawfully deposited with itself trust funds which can no longer be identified. However, the reliance placed in both cases on the traditional rules governing mixed funds suggests that these rules are likely to be followed in preference to the view expressed by Lord Templeman. It is hoped that this proves to be the case.

(ii) *Authorised Mixing.* In the relatively unlikely situation where the mixing of trust property with the property of another has been authorised by the trust instrument, the beneficiaries will inevitably be entitled to the appropriate proportion of the mixed fund. This somewhat obvious proposition does not appear to have been the subject of any English authority but was upheld in New South Wales in *Hagan v. Waterhouse*.[95] Following the death of their father, three brothers carried on the family bookmaking business as general partners. One having died, the other two, who were his executors and trustees, continued the partnership and therefore necessarily mixed the assets of the estate with their own. Kearney J. held that this mixing had been authorised by the terms of the will and therefore, quite irrespective of the presumptions which apply where mixing is unauthorised, the estate was entitled to a one-third interest in the income of the bookmaking business and the substantial investments purchased therewith.

(iii) *Unauthorised mixing.* It is much more likely that any mixing which has occurred will have been unauthorised. Where this occurs and sums have subsequently been withdrawn from the mixed fund, it has traditionally been necessary to have recourse to a series of presumptions in order to establish whether such withdrawals have been made from the mixed funds rateably or from one or more of its component parts; the presumptions differ depending on whether the mixed fund consists of funds of the claimant and

---

[90] [1995] 1 A.C. 74. Lord Templeman was a member of the Board.
[91] [1993] 1 N.Z.L.R. 257.
[92] [1995] 1 A.C. 74 at 109.
[93] *ibid.* at 110.
[94] [1995] Ch. 211.
[95] (1991) 34 N.S.W.L.R. 308.

funds of a fiduciary, of funds of two claimants both entitled to trace in equity into the mixed fund, or of funds of the claimant and funds of an innocent volunteer (it is obviously also possible for a mixed fund to consist of the funds of two claimants and the funds of a fiduciary or of the funds of two claimants and the funds of an innocent volunteer; in these circumstances, the situation is resolved by treating the two claimants as one and ascertaining first what they together can recover out of the mixed fund and then what part of this sum can be recovered by each individual claimant).

(iv) *Unauthorised mixing of funds of the claimant and funds of a fiduciary.* The traditional rules governing tracing into an unauthorised mixed fund consisting of funds of the claimant and funds of a fiduciary are based on the decision of the Court of Appeal in *Re Hallett's Estate.*[96] The defendant solicitor sold bonds belonging partly to his own marriage settlement and partly to a client and mixed the proceeds with his own funds in a bank account. Subsequently, he made various withdrawals from the mixed fund, which on his death was insufficient to satisfy all the claims thereon. The Court of Appeal, having held unanimously that both the beneficiaries and the client were entitled to bring equitable proprietary claims,[97] held by a majority,[98] that the funds drawn out must be debited to Hallett's share of the mixed fund on the basis that, where a man does an act which may be rightfully performed, he cannot be heard to say that that act was intentionally and in fact done wrongfully. The balance left in the mixed fund was sufficient to satisfy both claims so that it was not necessary to decide any question of priorities as between them.[99] The presumption, therefore, is that a fiduciary draws his own funds out first and so any balance left in the mixed fund represents the property of the claimant. His claim thereto is of course limited to the amount of his funds which were originally mixed (together with, presumably, any interest which has been earned in respect of the part thereof which is his property). This principle is not limited to funds but also extends to other assets which are mixed such as shares.

However, the claimant cannot normally assert a proprietary claim to further sums or property which become part of the mixed assets after the original mixing. In *James Roscoe (Bolton) v. Winder,*[1] the balance of the mixed fund fell to £25 as a result of repeated dissipation by the fiduciary. However, at his death the fund contained a balance of £358. Sarjant J. held the beneficiaries entitled to trace only £25; the sums which had been paid in went to the general creditors, with whom the beneficiaries could of course

---

[96] (1880) 13 Ch.D. 696.

[97] See *ante*, p. 719.

[98] Thesiger L.J. dissented, holding that payments out of the mixed fund should, in accordance with the decision of the Court of Appeal in Chancery in *Pennell v. Deffell* (1853) De M. & G. 372, be governed by the Rule in *Devaynes v. Noble, Clayton's Case* (1816) 1 Mer. 572: (see *post*, p. 734.

[99] Had this not been the case, priorities as between the two claimants would have been determined by the Rule in *Devaynes v. Noble, Clayton's Case* (1816) 1 Mer. 572 (see *post*, p. 734), as had indeed been held by Fry J. at first instance.

[1] [1915] 1 Ch. 62.

prove for the residue of their claim. This conclusion was approved and applied both by the Privy Council in *Re Goldcorp Exchange*[2] and by the Court of Appeal in *Bishopsgate Investment Management v. Homan*,[3] both of which concerned mixed funds which subsequently became overdrawn, thus barring any equitable proprietary claim completely. However, in the latter case, Dillon L.J.,[4] but not Leggatt L.J.,[5] was prepared to envisage the possibility of tracing funds through an overdrawn account where misappropriated funds are paid into the account in order to reduce the overdraft and so make finance available within the overdraft limits for the purchase of some particular asset. Provided that the link between the reduction of the overdraft and this subsequent purchase can be genuinely established, there seems no reason why this limited modification of the basic rule should not be adopted.

If the balance of the mixed fund is insufficient fully to discharge the liability of the fiduciary to the claimant, the latter can nevertheless trace the withdrawals into any identifiable product thereof and claim an equitable charge therein. In *Re Oatway*,[6] a trustee, having mixed the trust money with his own, first withdrew sums which he invested and later withdrew and dissipated the remainder. His trustee in bankruptcy suggested that, according to *Re Hallett's Estate*, what he had first withdrawn was his own money; consequently, the investments belonged to him and it was the trust money which had been dissipated. This unmeritorious claim was predictably rejected; Joyce J. held that the beneficiaries were entitled to the investments on the basis that their claim must be satisfied from any identifiable part of the mixed fund or its product before the trustee could assert any claim thereto.

In *Bishopsgate Investment Management v. Homan*[7] Dillon L.J. was also prepared to countenance the possibility of what Vinelott J. at first instance had called "backwards tracing".[8] This novel concept envisages a situation where a fiduciary acquires an asset with borrowed money and it can be inferred that the borrowing was subsequently repaid by funds misappropriated from the claimant; in such circumstances, the claimant can apparently recover the asset even though it was acquired prior to the misappropriation in question. However, this seems contrary to the nature of proprietary claims; indeed Leggatt L.J. explicitly rejected "backwards tracing", holding that "there can be no equitable remedy against an asset acquired before misappropriation of money takes place, since *ex hypothesi* it cannot be followed into something which existed and so had been acquired before the money was received and therefore without its aid".[9] This view seems preferable. Indeed it was approved by two of the members of the Court of Appeal in *Foskett v.*

[2] [1995] 1 A.C. 74.
[3] [1995] Ch. 211.
[4] *ibid.* at 216–217.
[5] *ibid.* at 222.
[6] [1903] 2 Ch. 356.
[7] [1995] Ch. 211.
[8] *ibid.* at 216–217.
[9] *ibid.* at 221.

McKeown,[10] Hobhouse L.J.[11] and Morritt L.J.[12] However, Scott V.-C.[13] wished "to make it clear that I regard the point as still open and, in particular, that I do not regard the fact that an asset is paid for out of borrowed money with the borrowing subsequently repaid out of trust money as being necessarily fatal to an equitable tracing claim by the trust beneficiaries". The availability of "backwards tracing" therefore clearly still awaits definitive resolution.

The precise scope of this right to trace the withdrawals from the mixed fund into their product is not entirely clear. In *Re Hallett's Estate*[14] Jessel M.R. stated that, where a claimant was seeking to trace into property which was the product of a mixed fund containing funds of the claimant and funds of a fiduciary, the only remedy available to him was to take a charge thereon for the amount of his property which was laid out in its acquisition. If this is indeed the case, the claimant's right to trace will be limited to his original contribution to the purchase price of the property and will not extend to any increase in its value. This view was followed in *Re Oatway*, where Joyce J. held that the trust had a charge on the investments which had been purchased by the trustee and went on to say that, because this charge was for an amount superior to their value, the investments and their proceeds of sale belonged to the trust.[15]

On the other hand, a different view was expressed in *Re Tilley's Will Trusts*.[16] An executrix, who was also tenant for life, paid the estate's funds into her own bank account and used the mixed fund as part payment for two houses, the remainder of the purchase money being provided by extensive overdraft facilities. She continued to engage in property transactions of this kind until her death. The remaindermen claimed to be entitled to a rateable share of the proceeds of the two houses. It was conceded, contrary to the view expressed by Jessel M.R. in *Re Hallett's Estate*, that where property is the product of a mixed fund the claimant has the right to "require the asset to be treated as trust property with regard to that proportion of it which the trust moneys contributed to its purchase".[17] Ungoed-Thomas J. clearly accepted this proposition as good law. However, on the facts, he held that the trust funds had not in fact been invested in the two properties since the use by the tenant for life of the estate's funds had merely prevented her from having to use more extensive overdraft facilities, which were clearly available to her. Hence the remaindermen were entitled only to the funds of the estate which had been mixed together with interest thereon. It is questionable whether it should in fact be open to a fiduciary who has

---

[10] [1998] 2 W.L.R. 298. This was an appeal against an order for summary judgment so it was not possible to reach a conclusion on whether the facts necessary to give rise to the possibility of "backwards tracing" had actually occurred. The facts of this case are discussed *post*, p. 741.

[11] *ibid.* at 321 (one of the majority on the main issue).

[12] *ibid.* at 327 (dissenting on the main issue).

[13] *ibid.* at 315 (the other member of the majority on the main issue). Scott V.-C. referred to L. Smith: [1995] C.L.J. 290, who is in favour not just of "backwards tracing" but of general tracing into the payment of a debt.

[14] (1880) 13 Ch.D. 696 at 709.

[15] This remark is a potential cause of confusion; however, there is no doubt that Joyce J. followed *Re Hallett's Estate*.

[16] [1967] Ch. 1179.

[17] *ibid.* at 1189.

committed a clear breach of trust by mixing trust funds with his own successfully to contend that any profits so made were not actually due to the use of the trust funds. While *Re Tilley's Will Trusts* clearly establishes that such a contention is possible, the opposite view has been taken in other jurisdictions.[18]

In relation to the more general question as to whether the claimant's right to trace is limited to his original contribution to the purchase price of the property, the matter may turn out to have been resolved by *Foskett v. McKeown*,[19] where Scott V.-C. stated[20] that one of "a number of well established principles" was:

"if in purchasing the asset the trustee uses his own money as well as trust money, the beneficiaries can ... claim the restitutionary remedy of a charge over the asset to recover their money and interest. Alternatively, the beneficiaries can claim a proportionate interests in the asset, the proportion being that which their money bears to the total purchase price. This alternative will, obviously, be preferred if the asset has increased in value since its purchase."

According to this dictum, the claimant therefore has a choice between taking a charge on the property for the amount of his funds invested therein (to his advantage if its value has fallen) or claiming an interest in the property in proportion to his contribution thereto (to his advantage if its value has risen). This seems a wholly acceptable resolution of the previous conflict of authority. However, since Scott V.-C. referred only to *Re Tilley's Will Trusts*, it is possible that *Re Hallett's Estate* may not have been cited to him on this point. The view expressed in the latter case has been supported[21] on the grounds that the priority of the claimant over the general creditors of the fiduciary should be limited to whatever is necessary to enable him to recuperate his lost funds and should not extend to any profit made thereby; (this would protect the general creditors of the fiduciary without enabling the latter to profit personally since, if solvent, he would anyway be liable to account to his principal for any profit which he had made).[22] Consequently, while the dictum of Scott V.-C. that the claimant has a choice seems preferable, the definitive resolution of this matter must clearly await a formal decision on the point.

A further question, on which there is no direct authority, is whether a claimant can elect to recover an asset which is the product of the mixed fund rather than taking any balance of the mixed fund to which he is entitled. It will be of interest for him so to do if he is indeed entitled to any increase in the value of such an asset or if any part of the mixed fund to which he is prima facie entitled has subsequently been invested in some other asset which has fallen in value. This situation has never arisen in any of the authorities since in no case have there been both a credit balance in the

---

[18] In Australia in *Scott v. Scott* (1963) 36 A.L.J.R. 345 and in the United States of America in *Primeau v. Granfield* (1911) 184 Fed. 480.

[19] [1998] 2 W.L.R. 298.

[20] *ibid.* at 310.

[21] See G. H. Jones, (1988) 37 King's Counsel 15 at 16.

[22] Under the principles discussed in *ante*, pp. 304–319.

mixed fund and assets purchased with funds withdrawn from it. However, the observations of all the judges, particularly those of Jessel M.R. in *Re Hallett's Estate*, indicate the mixed fund as the recourse primarily available to the claimant. The interests of the claimant and of the general creditors of the fiduciary are very evenly balanced where any part of the mixed fund to which the claimant is prima facie entitled has subsequently been invested in some other asset which has fallen in value. However, on the grounds of simplicity and consistency, it is suggested that the claimant must take any balance of the mixed fund to which he is entitled before proceeding to follow the withdrawals from the mixed fund into their product.

Finally, it must be emphasised that all the rules which have been discussed are no more than presumptions. Consequently, these presumptions can be rebutted in any given case if either the claimant or the fiduciary is able to establish to the satisfaction of the court that any particular withdrawal was intended to be made from some specific part of the mixed fund or that any subsequent payment back into the mixed fund was intended to replace a previous withdrawal.

(v) *Unauthorised mixing of funds of two claimants.* Where an unauthorised mixed fund consists of the funds of two claimants, both of whom are entitled to trace in equity into the mixed fund, withdrawals from the mixed fund are presumed to be made rateably from the funds held by each claimant. Since each claimant necessarily has an equitable proprietary interest in his part of the funds which have been mixed, the attribution of profits and losses rateably between them is entirely in accordance with principle. However, in the event that the mixed fund in question is an active unbroken bank account (the only relevant example is a current, but not a deposit, account), then the presumption that withdrawals from the mixed fund are presumed to be made rateably is displaced by a principle enunciated by Grant M.R. in *Devaynes v. Noble, Clayton's Case*,[23] which is generally known as the Rule in *Clayton's Case*. In such an account,

"there is no room for any other appropriation than that which arises from the order in which the receipts and payments take place, and are carried into the account. Presumably, it is the sum first paid in, that is first drawn out. It is the first item on the debit side of the account, that is discharged, or reduced, by the first item on the credit side. The appropriation is made by the very act of setting the two items against each other. Upon that principle, all accounts current are settled, and particularly cash accounts."[24]

Devaynes v. Noble did not concern a tracing claim but rather a question as to the appropriation of payments. The Rule was, however, applied to equitable tracing claims in the first case in which tracing was permitted in equity into a mixed fund, *Pennell v. Deffell*[25] in 1852. As has already been seen, the Court of Appeal decided by a majority in *Re Hallett's Estate*[26] that the Rule

---

[23] (1817) 1 Mer. 572.
[24] *ibid.* at 608–609.
[25] (1853) De M. & G. 372.
[26] (1880) 13 Ch.D. 696.

should no longer apply to mixed funds containing funds of a claimant and funds of a fiduciary. However, had any question of priorities between the two claimants in *Re Hallett's Estate* had to be determined, there is no doubt that the Rule in *Clayton's Case* would have been applied for this purpose, as it had indeed been applied by Fry J. at first instance; this was expressly recognised by all three members of the court.[27] The same conclusion was reached in *Hancock v. Smith*.[28]

Recently, in *Barlow Clowes International v. Vaughan*,[29] the Court of Appeal confirmed that the Rule provided a convenient method of determining competing claims where the funds of several beneficiaries had been blended in one account and there was a deficiency or where there had been a wrongful mixing of different sums of trust money in a single account. However, where its application would be impracticable or would result in injustice between the investors, because a relatively small number of investors would obtain most of the funds, or would be contrary to the express or implied intention of the investors, the rule would not be applied if a preferable alternative method of distribution was available. The Court of Appeal held that there had been such a presumed intention as between the various subscribers to a collective investment scheme by which their money would be mixed together and invested through a common fund; consequently, the assets which remained available for distribution would be distributed rateably between them.

However, the Rule in *Clayton's Case* is just as capable of enabling a relatively small number of investors to obtain most of the funds when applied to mixed funds consisting of the funds of two claimants as when it is applied to common funds in collective investment schemes. Suppose that a trustee mixes the funds of two trusts in a current banking account, paying in £2,000 of the funds of Trust A on one day and £1,000 of the funds of Trust B on the following day. If on the third day he withdraws £2,000 from the mixed fund and invests it in securities, those securities will have been purchased entirely with the funds of Trust A. If on the fourth day he withdraws £700 from the mixed fund and loses this sum gambling at a casino, the entire loss will fall on Trust B, whose only right will be to the £300 left in the mixed fund. (Were, on the other hand, the mixed fund a deposit account, both profits and losses would be shared rateably Trust A and Trust B would respectively be entitled to two-thirds and one-third of the securities and £200 and £100 of the balance of the mixed fund.) Why is this result any more absurd than it would have been to have permitted the later investors in a collective investment scheme to have recovered almost all their investment and the earlier investors to have recovered almost none of theirs (the consequence of the application of the Rule in *Clayton's Case* which induced the Court of Appeal to find the implied intention necessary to displace it in *Barlow Clowes International v. Vaughan*)?

---

[27] Jessel M.R. and Baggallay L.J., who had held that the Rule in *Clayton's Case* did not apply to a mixed fund consisting of funds of a claimant and funds of a fiduciary, agreed with Thesiger L.J., who had taken the opposite view, that the Rule in *Clayton's Case* clearly applied to mixed funds consisting of funds of two claimants.

[28] (1889) 41 Ch.D. 456, *per* Lord Halsbury L.C. and Cotton L.J. (Fry L.J. did not deal with the point).

[29] [1992] 4 All E.R. 22.

The Rule in *Clayton's Case* was trenchantly condemned by Learned Hand J. in *Re Walter J. Schmidt*,[30] although he was nevertheless compelled by precedent to apply it. However, unless and until a court is prepared to recognise the absurdity of the illustration set out above, the Rule will continue to apply to mixed funds consisting of funds of two claimants who are both entitled to trace in equity and also, as will be seen in the next section, to mixed funds consisting of funds of the claimant and funds of an innocent volunteer.

(vi) *Unauthorised mixing of funds of the claimant and funds of an innocent volunteer.* Where an unauthorised mixed fund consists of the funds of a claimant and the funds of an innocent volunteer, withdrawals from the mixed fund are presumed to be made in exactly the same way as withdrawals from a mixed fund consisting of the funds of two claimants, that is to say rateably unless the mixed fund in question is an active unbroken bank account, in which case the Rule in *Clayton's Case* applies.[31]

However, while the attribution of profits and losses rateably is entirely in accordance with principle in the case of a mixed fund consisting of the funds of two claimants, both of whom have equitable proprietary interests therein, it is highly questionable in the case of a mixed fund consisting of the funds of a claimant and the funds of an innocent volunteer. The claimant necessarily has an equitable proprietary interest in the mixed fund; if he did not, he would not be entitled to trace in equity. How can an innocent volunteer resist a claim by the holder of an equitable proprietary interest to recover his property? What defence, other than the defence of change of position, can an innocent volunteer possibly have to an equitable proprietary claim? In principle, the claimant should be able to recover his funds in full out of the mixed fund quite irrelevant of what withdrawals have been made therefrom by the innocent volunteer.

However, this is clearly not the law. In *Re Diplock*[32] Lord Greene M.R. held that the positions of the claimant and the innocent volunteer were equivalent.

"This burden on the conscience of the volunteer is not such as to compel him to treat the claim of the equitable owner as paramount. That would be to treat the volunteer as strictly as if he himself stood in a fiduciary relationship to the equitable owner which *ex hypothesi* he does not. The volunteer is under no greater duty of conscience to recognise the interest of the equitable owner than that which lies upon a person having an equitable interest in one of two trust funds of 'money' which have become mixed towards the equitable owner of the other. Such a person is not in conscience bound to give precedence to the equitable owner of the other of the two funds."

He therefore relied on *Sinclair v. Brougham*[33] as authority for the attribution of profits and losses rateably in mixed funds consisting of funds of a claimant and funds of an innocent volunteer. However, the analogy with

---

[30] (1923) 298 Fed. 314 (Supreme Court of the United States of America).
[31] *Re Diplock* [1948] Ch. 465 (in respect of the claim against the National Institute for the Deaf).
[32] *ibid.* at 524.
[33] [1914] A.C. 398.

Sinclair v. Brougham (which has now of course been overruled anyway)[34] is in fact unsound. The House of Lords indeed held that the shareholders and the depositors in the *ultra vires* banking business should share the remaining assets rateably but the depositors were held to be entitled to trace in equity by virtue of the existence of a trust in their favour. Therefore both they and the shareholders in fact had proprietary interests. This was not the case in *Re Diplock*, where only the claimants had an equitable proprietary interest.

It is of course highly unlikely, given the decision in *Re Diplock*, that an innocent volunteer will ever be held liable for the whole of the losses suffered by a mixed fund. It seems generally to be accepted that, subject to the effect of the operation of the Rule in *Clayton's Case*, at present losses should be attributed rateably between the claimant and the innocent volunteer. Profits are also attributed rateably at present, subject to the defence of change of position, which operates in an exceptionally favourable way in favour of an innocent volunteer; both these propositions are demonstrated by the recent decision of the Court of Appeal in *Foskett v. McKeown*,[35] which will be considered later on. However, prior to this decision it had been suggested that, provided that the claimant was in a position to recover his original contribution to the mixed fund in full by means of a charge on the mixed fund or on the property which constituted its product, the innocent volunteer should be entitled to retain the benefit of any improvements which he had made or profits which he had obtained.[36] This suggestion is now unlikely to be taken up; what is surprising is the fact that it was ever made—depriving the holder of an equitable proprietary interest of profits while retaining his rateable liability for losses does not seem very consistent with the nature of an equitable proprietary claim. But suggestions of this type clearly demonstrate that the leniency shown at present towards innocent volunteers is more likely to be amplified than taken away.

(4) When will priority be lost?

No equitable proprietary claim can succeed if the property in question has simply disappeared as a result of dissipation. If, for example, funds which are susceptible of being traced are expended on a case of wine which is then consumed, no proprietary claim will be able to be brought against the person who has expended the funds (nor will any proprietary claim be able to be brought against the vendor of the wine, who will be a bona fide purchaser for value without notice). The disappearance of the property is not, formally, a defence to an equitable proprietary claim but its effect is the same as if it were a defence. Quite apart from this situation, there are of course a number of formal defences which can be made out to an equitable proprietary claim.

(a)   Where the property has reached the hands of a person who has taken free of the equitable proprietary interest of the claimant. It is, of course, axiomatic that no equitable proprietary interest can survive the bona

---

[34] By the House of Lords in *Westdeutsche Landesbank Girozentrale v. Islington L.B.C.* [1996] A.C. 669.

[35] [1998] 2 W.L.R. 298; see *post*, p. 741.

[36] See D. J. Hayton: (1990) 106 L.Q.R. 87 at 100.

fide purchase for value of a legal estate or interest in the property in question to a person who has no notice of any kind of the equitable proprietary interest in question (or, in the case of registered land, the bona fide purchase for value of any interest by virtue of a duly registered disposition). Thus, if trust property is sold by the trustees to a bona fide purchaser for value who has no notice of the interests of the beneficiaries, the latter cannot pursue any equitable proprietary claim against the purchaser; their only possible proprietary claim will be to attempt to trace into the proceeds of sale.

On the other hand, an equitable proprietary interest will normally enjoy priority over any subsequent holder of the property who has acquired only an equitable, rather than a legal interest therein. This is the case except that "where the merits are unequal and favour the later interest, as for instance where the owner of the later equitable interest is led by conduct on the part of the owner of the earlier interest to acquire the later interest in the belief or on the supposition that the earlier interest did not then exist, priority will be accorded to the later interest."[37] Save in the relatively unlikely event of this exception applying, there is no doubt whatever that a beneficiary of an express or resulting trust will, by virtue of this rule, enjoy priority over the holder of any later equitable interest in the property in question. So will a beneficiary of a constructive trust, once the existence of that trust has actually been upheld by the court in question. What is less clear is the position of a potential beneficiary of a constructive trust, someone who is entitled to seek the imposition of a constructive trust but who has not yet obtained the necessary court order; this depends on whether his interest prior to the court order is classified as a full equitable interest, in which case he will enjoy the same priority, or a mere equity, in which case a bona fide purchaser for value of any later equitable interest without notice will take free.[38] In principle, it is suggested that his interest should be classified as a full equitable interest, giving him the same priority, but the matter awaits decision.[39]

(b) Where there has been a change of position. English law has traditionally denied any general defence of change of position[40] although in *Re Diplock*[41] the Court of Appeal held that innocent volunteers could rely on two limited (and controversial) manifestations of this defence as against equitable proprietary claims. However, in *Lipkin Gorman v. Karpnale*[42] the

---

[37] *Heid v. Reliance Finance Corporation* (1983) 154 C.L.R. 326 at 339, *per* Mason & Deane JJ. (High Court of Australia). The facts of this case provided a good example of the operation of this exception.

[38] *Latec Investments v. Hotel Terrigal* (1965) 113 C.L.R. 265 (High Court of Australia).

[39] The only relevant authority is *Re Jonton* [1992] 1 Qd.R. 105 (Supreme Court of Queensland) where the conclusion suggested in the text was reached; however, this case cannot be regarded as decisive since the holder of the later interest would, if necessary, almost certainly have been held to have constructive notice anyway.

[40] See particularly *Ministry of Health v. Simpson* [1951] A.C. 251.

[41] [1948] Ch. 465 at 546–548.

[42] [1991] 2 A.C. 548.

House of Lords upheld for the first time the existence of such a defence. This case was, in the House of Lords, concerned principally with an action for money had and received; no equitable proprietary claim was being pursued. However, it is clear that the defence so enunciated is generally applicable and will therefore apply to both legal and equitable proprietary claims.

All the members of the House of Lords agreed that, on the facts, the defendant casino could invoke the defence of change of position against the claim by the plaintiff solicitors to recover funds which had been stolen from its client account and subsequently lost at the casino but only to the extent that the casino had paid out winnings to the gambler. However, the House took considerable care not to pre-empt the subsequent development of the defence. Lord Bridge stated[43] that "in expressly acknowledging the availability of this defence for the first time it would be unwise to attempt to define its scope in abstract terms". Lord Goff said this[44]:

"I am most anxious that, in recognising this defence to actions of restitution, nothing should be said at this stage to inhibit the development of the defence on a case by case basis, in the usual way. It is, of course, plain that the defence is not open to one who has changed his position in bad faith, as where the defendant has paid away the money with knowledge of the facts entitling the plaintiff to restitution and it is commonly accepted that the defence should not be open to a wrongdoer. These are matters which can, in due course, be considered in depth in cases where they arise for consideration. It is not appropriate in the present case to identify all those actions in restitution to which change of position may be a defence. At present I do not wish to state the principle any less broadly than this: that the defence is available to a person whose position has so changed that it would be inequitable in all the circumstances to require him to make restitution, or alternatively to make restitution in full. I wish to stress, however, that the mere fact that the defendant has spent the money, in whole or in part, does not of itself render it inequitable that he should be called upon to repay, because the expenditure might in any event have been incurred by him in the ordinary course of things.

I wish to add two further footnotes. The defence of change of position is akin to the defence of bona fide purchase but we cannot simply say that bona fide purchase is a species of change of position. This is because change of position will only avail a defendant to the extent that his position has been changed; whereas, where bona fide purchase is invoked, no inquiry is made (in most cases) into the adequacy of the consideration. Even so, the recognition of change of position as a defence should be doubly beneficial. It will enable a more generous approach to be taken of the recognition of the right of restitution, in the knowledge that the defence is, in appropriate cases, available; and, while recognising the different functions of property at law and in equity, there may also in due course develop a more consistent approach to tracing claims, in which common defences are recognised as available to such claims, whether advanced at law or in equity."

---

[43] *ibid.* at 558.
[44] *ibid.* at 579–580.

It is clear from the final passage of this quotation that Lord Goff envisaged the application of the defence of change of position to both legal and equitable proprietary claims and that he did not regard this defence as supplanting the defence of bona fide purchase for value without notice. Only Lord Templeman gave any further illustrations of circumstances in which the defence of change of position would be available. He envisaged a situation in which a donee of stolen money has expended it

"in reliance on the validity of the gift before he receives notice of the victim's claim for restitution. Thus if the donee spent £20,000 in the purchase of a motor car which he would not have purchased but for the gift, it seems to me that the donee has altered his position on the faith of the gift and has only been unjustly enriched to the extent of the secondhand value of the motor car at the date when the victim of the theft seeks restitution. If the donee spends the £20,000 on a trip round the world, which he would not have undertaken without the gift, it seems to me that the donee has altered his position on the faith of the gift and that he is not unjustly enriched when the victim of the faith seeks restitution."[45]

Applying the various observations of the members of the House of Lords to legal and equitable proprietary claims, it is clear that a defaulting fiduciary will never be able to utilise the defence of change of position since he cannot have acted in good faith. On the other hand, a person who has received property in good faith and subsequently engaged in some expenditure which he would not otherwise have made will be entitled to invoke the defence of change of position to the extent that he is worse off as a result of the transaction. At law, if a person purchases stolen property in good faith and subsequently sells it on at a loss, he will be entitled to invoke the defence of change of position to the extent of his loss on the sale and repurchase. In equity, if an innocent volunteer receives in good faith property transferred to him in breach of trust, he will be able to invoke the defence of change of position to the extent that he has spent the property or its product in ways which have provided no lasting benefit to him, provided that he would not have engaged in the expenditure in question in any event. Thus a charity which, as in *Re Diplock*, receives in good faith a payment which has been made in breach of trust, will be able to invoke the defence of change of position to the extent that it discharges unsecured debts[46] or spends the funds on improvements to its properties which increases their value by less than the amount expended. A private individual will additionally be able to invoke the defence to the extent that he has spent the sum received on some item of one-off expenditure, such as a holiday, which he would not otherwise have made.

It obviously remains to be seen how the defence of change of position is developed by the courts. However, its effect on proprietary claims seems likely to be confined to cases of resales at a loss and of one-off non-productive expenditure.

---

[45] *ibid*. at 560.
[46] Unless L. Smith: [1995] C.L.J. 290 is right in his contention that the proceeds of unsecured debts can be traced.

(c) **Where tracing would be inequitable.** In *Re Diplock*[47] the Court of Appeal held that it would be inequitable for a claimant to trace in equity where an innocent volunteer had used the claimant's property either to alter or improve his land or to pay off his debts. These defences must now have been subsumed within the general defence of change of position enunciated in *Lipkin Gorman v. Karpnale* to the extent that the expenditure has produced no lasting benefit for the innocent volunteer and would not have been engaged in but for the receipt of the claimant's property. However, the defences enunciated by the Court of Appeal are not limited to this situation. The court clearly envisaged that improvements made to land would constitute a complete defence whether or not the value of the land had thereby increased in value. If it has indeed increased in value, there seems no reason why the claimant should not be entitled to obtain a charge over the land for the amount by which its value has increased. Further, although it is of course axiomatic that the payment of unsecured debts prevents any subsequent equitable proprietary claim (because the discharged creditor will be a bona fide purchaser for value without notice), there seems no reason why secured debts should be treated in the same way. If secured debts of an innocent volunteer are discharged by the use of the funds of the claimant, why should the claimant not be subrogated to the security discharged with his money and be entitled to enforce that security against the innocent volunteer?[48]

Some of these aspects of the decision of the Court of Appeal in *Re Diplock* were approved and applied by the majority of the Court of Appeal in somewhat different circumstances in *Foskett v. McKeown*.[49] A trustee insured his life for £1,000,000 for the benefit, after a series of assignments, of his mother and his children. He paid at least the first two years' premiums (of £10,220 per annum) from his own resources and at least the fourth and fifth years' premiums from the trust assets (it was not entirely clear from what funds the third year's premium had been paid; this partially depended on whether or not "backwards tracing" is possible).[50] Following the dissipation of the whole of the trust fund of £2,645,000, the trustee died by his own hand. The beneficiaries sought to trace the trust funds into the proceeds of the policy, claiming either the entire £1,000,000 (on the basis that the policy would not have remained on foot at all without the use of those funds) or the proportion of it that their contributions to the premiums paid actually represented. Laddie J. gave them summary judgment for what he regarded as the appropriate proportion.[51] The Court of Appeal, allowing an appeal by the children,[52] agreed that the beneficiaries could trace into the proceeds of the policy but held, by a majority, that they were entitled to a charge on the

---

[47] [1948] Ch. 465 at 546–548.

[48] See Goff & Jones, *The Law of Restitution* (4th ed., 1993), p. 600.

[49] [1998] 2 W.L.R. 298.

[50] See *ante*, p. 731.

[51] He actually awarded them the proportion of the accumulated units of the policy which the trust funds had been used to acquire. The majority of the Court of Appeal did not have to decide this particular point but Morritt L.J., who dissented, would have awarded the beneficiaries a different measure, namely the proportion of the proceeds equivalent to the proportion of the premiums paid out of the trust funds.

[52] The mother had survived her son and had received her proportion of the proceeds; however, she had subsequently died and her personal representatives were not joined.

proceeds of the policy only for the amount of the trust funds expended on the premiums and interest thereon. The majority took the view that the policy had not been kept on foot by the expenditure of the trust funds (had the later premiums not been paid, the policy would have been converted into a paid-up policy); that expenditure had merely enhanced the number of accumulated units.[53] They held that this was not a case where the trust funds had been used to acquire an identifiable asset (had it been, all the members of the court agreed that the beneficiaries and the innocent volunteer would have shared any increase in its value rateably, in this respect confirming what had previously been thought to be the law). Instead, the trust funds had been used to enhance the value of an asset which was, at any rate by the time of the payment of the fourth and fifth years' premiums, already vested in innocent volunteers.[54] Consequently, in accordance with *Re Diplock*,[55] the beneficiaries could not trace their funds into the asset so improved. Scott V.-C. went further and held[56] that, even had the trustee himself still been entitled under the policy at the time when the trust funds were utilised (which would have been the case if those funds had been used to pay the third year's premium), the only benefit which he would have obtained thereby would have been the fact that he had not had to use his own funds for the purpose; that too would have given the beneficiaries no right to more than the return of the trust funds with interest. The dissentient, Morritt L.J., took a different view of the policy, holding that its proceeds were payable in consideration of all the premiums payable and paid; in such circumstances, the beneficiaries were clearly entitled to the proportion of the proceeds equivalent to the proportion of the premiums paid out of the trust funds.[57] The result thus seems to have been determined more by the different judicial perspectives of the nature of the policy rather than by different views of the law. What the decision does clearly establish, however, since all three judges took this view, is that the defences enunciated by the Court of Appeal in *Re Diplock* have survived the enunciation of the general defence of change of position and extend well beyond the scope of that general defence.

(d) **Where compensation has been recovered from the fiduciary who perpetrated the breach of trust in question.** It has already been seen[58] that any *in personam* claim available against an innocent volunteer will be reduced to the extent that compensation can be obtained from any fiduciary responsible for having made any relevant disposition of trust property in breach of trust. In *Re Diplock*,[59] the Court of Appeal took the view that "prima facie and subject to discussion" any equitable proprietary claim should similarly be reduced by any amounts which the claimant had recovered from any fiduciary responsible for having made such a disposition. The court did not actually suggest that it was necessary for the claimant to sue

---

[53] [1998] 2 W.L.R. 298 at 307, *per* Scott V.-C., at 323, *per* Hobhouse L.J.
[54] *ibid.* at 311, *per* Scott V.-C., at 321, *per* Hobhouse L.J.
[55] [1948] Ch. 465.
[56] [1998] 2 W.L.R. 298 at 313–314. Hobhouse L.J. did not consider this point specifically.
[57] *ibid.* at 332–333.
[58] See *ante*, p. 708.
[59] [1948] Ch. 465 at 556.

any such fiduciary prior to embarking on an equitable proprietary claim, merely that if any compensation had been recovered it should constitute a rateable bar to any such equitable proprietary claim.[60] It is, frankly, difficult to see why the existence of a personal liability should constitute a bar to a proprietary claim.[61] However, if it is ever held that it is in fact necessary for such a claimant to sue any fiduciary first, it is to be hoped that the fiduciary will be subrogated to that part of the claim "which represents the difference between the total of the sum recovered from the [fiduciary] and the volunteer and the loss suffered by [the claimant]".[62] It would in fact be preferable to require the claimant to proceed against the innocent volunteer before suing the fiduciary, who would then be liable only for any amount which cannot be recovered from the innocent volunteer; however, such a solution could only be imposed by statute.[63]

---

[60] *Re J. Leslie Engineers* [1976] 1 W.L.R. 292.
[61] The argument that it should was specifically rejected in *Hagan v. Waterhouse* (1991) 34 N.S.W.L.R. 308 at 369–370, *per* Kearney J. (Supreme Court of New South Wales).
[62] Goff & Jones, *op. cit.*, p. 92.
[63] As in New Zealand (Administration Act 1952, s.30B(5)) and in Western Australia (Trustee Act 1962, s.65(7)). However, Queensland has gone even further than the Court of Appeal in *Re Diplock* and prohibits, except by leave of the court, any claim against any transferee of trust property transferred in breach of trust until the claimant has exhausted his remedies against the fiduciary responsible (Trusts Act 1973, s.109(2); see W. A. Lee: (1981) 1 O.J.L.S. 414).

CHAPTER 25

TRUSTS IN THE CONFLICT OF LAWS

THE rules of the conflict of laws, often also known and described throughout this Chapter as the rules of private international law, determine the jurisdiction by whose laws any legal relationship is governed. Its rules are relevant whenever a legal relationship, be it a contract, a tort, a marriage, a trust or an inheritance, has an international element. Taking an admittedly artificial example from outside the law of trusts, if a Frenchman and a German make a contract for the sale and purchase of shares in a Spanish company on board a ship flying the Liberian flag which at that time happens to be moored in the Port of Amsterdam, the law of any one of five jurisdictions could govern that contract in the event that the parties do not expressly provide for it to be governed by the law of some particular jurisdiction, which needless to say does not have to be any of those five—many commercial contracts, particularly shipping contracts, provide that they are to be governed by English law even though none of the parties or the subject matter of the contract has ever had any connection with the United Kingdom. In the context of trust law, if an English settlor creates a trust whose trustees are a Jersey company and a Cayman Islands company, whose beneficiaries live either in Florida or in California, and whose assets consist of shares in companies constituted in various tax havens and land in other jurisdictions scattered around the world, there are an equally large number of possible jurisdictions by whose law that trust may be governed. On the other hand, procedural questions are always governed by the law of the forum, the law of the jurisdiction in which any proceedings are being brought.

An additional complication is that states often contain more than one jurisdiction. The United Kingdom has six: England and Wales,[1] Scotland, Northern Ireland, Guernsey, Jersey and the Isle of Man, to which have to be added the separate jurisdictions of each of its colonies such as Bermuda, The Cayman Islands, and Gibraltar (to mention three which are important tax havens and so are relevant to the law of trusts). Federal States, such as the United States of America, Australia and Canada, have as many jurisdictions as there are individual states, provinces or territories plus, in each case, an additional federal jurisdiction whose rules, which are admittedly unlikely to be applicable to many matters in which private international law is relevant, apply to the entire state in question. Even basically unitary states, such as Spain, have distinct rules governing such matters as matrimonial property

---

[1] Throughout this Chap. references to "England" and "English law" therefore mean "England and Wales" and "the law of England and Wales". This is in the interests of brevity and no disrespect is thereby intended to the inhabitants of the Principality of Wales.

regimes and inheritance which apply in different parts of the state in question.

The situation is complicated still further by the fact that the application of the rules of private international law of different jurisdictions not infrequently produces different answers to the question of which jurisdiction's laws govern the transaction in question. This is because the common law jurisdictions, such as England and its former Colonies, tend to determine the applicable law by the use of connecting factors which differ in almost every respect from those utilised by civil law jurisdictions such as those of mainland Europe. The common law jurisdictions tend to utilise connecting factors such as the domicile of the persons involved (a highly technical concept[2]) and the location of any relevant assets, whereas the civil law jurisdictions tend instead to utilise connecting factors such as habitual residence and nationality (in the case of a United Kingdom national, nationality presumably means the United Kingdom jurisdiction with which he has the closest connection).[3] Even worse, some but by no means all jurisdictions accept a reference back to their own law where the law which they regard as prima facie applicable so dictates and some common law jurisdictions also accept a reference on to the law of a third jurisdiction (both types of reference are technically known as "renvoi"). All this means that the law applicable to any given transaction is likely to differ depending on which jurisdiction's courts have to decide the question. Consequences of this type can only be avoided if the different rules adopted by the common law and the civil law jurisdictions can be synthesised in an international convention; this obviously involves both groups of jurisdictions giving way in substantial respects. The effect of such a convention will be that those states who sign and ratify it will then all apply the same rules to the same legal transaction.

Fortunately, the law of trusts is governed by such a convention, The Hague Convention on the Law Applicable to Trusts and their Recognition, which was incorporated into English law by the Recognition of Trusts Act

---

[2] Domicile has nothing to do with habitual residence. A person's domicile of origin is the jurisdiction in which one of his parents (usually his father) was domiciled at the time of his birth. He will only be held to have given up that domicile of origin in favour of a domicile of choice if he goes to another jurisdiction with the intention of remaining there permanently (this is a question of fact, often an extremely difficult one); however, once he has obtained a domicile of choice, he can give that up simply by leaving the jurisdiction in question. If his departure does not result in him obtaining a further domicile of choice elsewhere, his domicile of origin revives. See Collier, *Conflict of Laws* (2nd ed., 1994) pp. 40–63.

[3] This at least was what was held in the highly criticised but undoubtedly pragmatic decision in *Re O'Keefe* [1940] Ch. 124. This case is a good illustration what can actually happen in practice. The question was what law governed the intestate succession to the movable property of a U.K. national who had died with a domicile of choice in Italy. The English court initially applied Italian law on the grounds that the relevant connecting factor under English private international law was domicile. However, the relevant connecting factor under Italian private international law was nationality. The English court therefore accepted Italian law's reference back to U.K. law under the doctrine of *renvoi* (discussed in the next sentence of the text) and then decided that in this case United Kingdom law meant Irish law (which was duly applied) on the grounds that the deceased's domicile of origin had been what is now the Republic of Ireland (part of the U.K. at the time of her birth); it made no difference that she had only ever paid one short visit there. See Collier, *Conflict of Laws* (2nd ed., 1994) pp. 21–29.

1987. This now largely governs the question of the jurisdiction by whose
rules of trust law any particular trust is primarily governed. The law in
question is generally known as the proper law of the trust and it will
determine at the very least the interests of the beneficiaries under the trust
and the duties of the trustees to them (it is, however, possible for the trust
instrument to provide for other questions to be governed by the law of some
other jurisdiction). The incorporation of this Convention into English law
certainly means that it is no longer necessary (if indeed it ever was) for the
student of the law of trusts to master the intricacies of doctrines of private
international law such as domicile and *renvoi*. Nor need such a student try
to work out what would happen if proceedings were brought in the courts
of any jurisdiction other than England, although this is obviously relevant to
anyone setting up a trust governed by the law of some other jurisdiction.
This Chapter, after a brief discussion of the situations in which the rules of
private international law governing trusts may be relevant, therefore needs
to consider only two questions: first, in what circumstances an English court
has jurisdiction to hear trust proceedings and, secondly, which jurisdiction's
rules of law it will apply. It cannot be emphasised too often that these two
questions are wholly independent of one another[4] and must therefore
always be considered separately.

I. SITUATIONS WHERE PRIVATE INTERNATIONAL LAW IS RELEVANT

The most straightforward situation in which the rules of private international law governing trusts are relevant in the English courts is where the
beneficiaries of a trust which is not (or may not be) subject to English law
bring proceedings against their trustees for breach of trust in England on the
basis that either the trustees themselves or some part of the trust property
are physically present in this jurisdiction. An example is the leading case of
Chellaram v. Chellaram.[5] The settlors of the discretionary trusts in question
were almost certainly domiciled in India at the time of the settlements,
which were drawn up in India in English form and executed by them
respectively in Singapore and in Lagos. Two of the original trustees were
permanently resident in England and the third had a United Kingdom
passport and spent some months each year here in a house of his ownership.
The trust property was shares in Bermudan companies whose assets were
situated in many parts of the world but not in India. Some of the beneficiaries brought proceedings in England seeking the removal of the then
trustees, who were all born and domiciled in India but were not all resident
there and all of whom visited London on a regular basis. Even on the basis
that the trust was governed by Indian law, the English court was held to
have jurisdiction.

The rules of private international law can also be relevant where applications in relation to the assets of a trust which is not governed by English law
are made in the course of other proceedings in respect of which the English

---

[4] The distinction emerges clearly in *Macmillan v. Bishopsgate Trust (No. 3)* [1995] 1 W.L.R. 978 at
989, *per* Millett J..
[5] [1985] Ch. 409; see *post*, p. 755.

courts clearly have jurisdiction. Such applications usually occur in the course of proceedings for the reallocation of property following a divorce, when one of the former spouses claims to be entitled either to have taken into account or to receive assets to which the other former spouse is entitled under a trust governed by some law other than English law. Such applications have been successful in the past[6] and it seems likely that English courts will be held still to have jurisdiction to deal with them despite the Recognition of Trusts Act 1987[7] since otherwise putting assets in a foreign trust would be far too easy a way of protecting them from potential claims by former spouses.[8] Applications have in the past also been made under the Variation of Trusts Act 1958[9] in respect of foreign trusts but it is doubtful whether the English courts still have jurisdiction in such proceedings following the Recognition of Trusts Act 1987.[10]

Finally, the rules of private international law can also be relevant where the assets of trusts subject to English law have been disposed of in breach of trust to persons in other jurisdictions and the beneficiaries are trying to maintain equitable proprietary claims or to impose liability for "knowing receipt" or "dishonest assistance". There is no difficulty about the first two of these types of claim where they are being brought against the person to whom the property subject to the trust was directly transferred. Assuming that such a person is susceptible to the jurisdiction of the English courts in the first place, English law will clearly apply to the claims against him because he can be shown to have received the property in question.[11] Difficulties do however arise where either of these types of claims is being brought against someone to whom the original recipient has transferred the trust property on, the principal problem being that of determining by what law the second or subsequent transfer is governed. It is also far from clear what law governs the liability for "dishonest assistance" of both original and subsequent recipients. Every conceivable variety of this type of claim is at present the subject of major litigation in the Commercial Court and so a definitive statement of the relevant law can be confidently expected by the time the next edition of this work has to be prepared. At the moment, however, the position is somewhat uncertain.

---

[6] Claims to vary pre-nuptial or post-nuptial settlements of property abroad governed by foreign law with exclusively foreign trustees were successfully made in *Nunneley v. Nunneley* (1890) 15 P.D. 186; *Forsyth v. Forsyth* [1891] P. 363; and *Goff v. Goff* [1934] P. 107. More recently, claims for the reallocation of property on divorce were successfully made in *Browne v. Browne* [1989] 1 F.L.R. 291 (Jersey discretionary trust, Liechtenstein trust) and in *E v. E* (Financial Provision) [1990] 2 F.L.R. 233 (Guernsey discretionary trust); *T v. T* [1996] 2 F.L.R. 357 (Jersey discretionary trust); however, in these proceedings no reference was made to the Recognition of Trusts Act 1987.

[7] It has been argued in unreported proceedings that the English courts no longer have jurisdiction to make orders governing such trusts but such arguments have not yet been the subject of a reasoned judgment.

[8] This is the view taken by Dicey & Morris: *The Conflict of Laws* (12th ed., 1993), pp. 767–768 and it is certainly likely to be difficult to persuade an English court to adopt any other view.

[9] *Re Ker's Settlement* [1963] Ch. 553; *Re Paget's Settlement* [1965] 1 W.L.R. 1046.

[10] See *post*, p. 757.

[11] *Arab Monetary Fund v. Hashim (No. 8)* (1994), unreported (liability for "knowing receipt"). There are a number of unreported judgments in this interminable case; this one was handed down on June 13, 1994.

For the purposes of an equitable proprietary claim against a subsequent recipient of the trust property, it appears that the effect of a transfer of that property between persons who are both in a jurisdiction other than England will be governed by the law of that jurisdiction.[12] Consequently, such a claim will only be able to be maintained against the later recipient if under the law of that jurisdiction the equitable interests of the beneficiaries continue to affect the property transferred to him. If they do not,[13] then the beneficiaries will be unable to demonstrate that any of their property ever reached the hands of the recipient and so will not possibly be able to maintain an equitable proprietary claim in respect of it.

For identical reasons, the result ought to be exactly the same in the case of a claim to impose liability for "knowing receipt" against a subsequent recipient. However, the rules by which English law traces property into its product appear to be more flexible in cases of this kind,[14] although they certainly should not be! If such rules are classified as procedural rather than substantive (which they could conceivably be)[15] and so apply irrelevant of where any transfer took place, then the beneficiaries may nevertheless be able to demonstrate that the recipient actually received their property. It is to be hoped that this latter view is not adopted.

Precisely what rule of private international law governs liability for "dishonest assistance" is not certain either. The Court of Appeal has held that, for the purpose of service of proceedings out of the jurisdiction, this type of liability is not tortious.[16] It has also been held at first instance that it is not tortious for the purposes of the rules of private international law either.[17] The judge in question, Chadwick J., then stated that whether or not a person can be held liable for "dishonest assistance" "where the fault alleged lies wholly in things done or not done in a foreign jurisdiction . . . is a question to which the authorities provide no ready answer".[18] However, he went on to hold that the matter was governed by a rule of private international law which at one time used to govern liability for tort [19] but has long since

---

[12] *MacMillan v. Bishopsgate Trust (No. 3)* [1995] 1 W.L.R. 978 (Millett J.), [1996] 1 W.L.R. 387 (Court of Appeal). The conclusion in the text seems to follow from the statements in the Court of Appeal at 399 *per* Staughton L.J., at 410 *per* Auld L.J., and at 424 *per* Aldous L.J., each of whom held that the effect of such transfers was governed by the law of the place where it took place. At first instance, Millett J. reached the same conclusion for a different reason, namely that this was the place where the enrichment of the recipient took place.

[13] This would be the case once money had been transferred to a Swiss bank because under Swiss law deposits in banks become the property of the depositee and no proprietary interest of the depositor or anyone claiming through him can survive. See *Arab Monetary Fund v. Hashim (No. 8)* (1994), unreported (judgment of June 13, 1994) transcript at 316, *per* Chadwick J.

[14] *El Ajou v. Dollar Land Holdings* [1993] 3 All E.R. 717, *per* Millett J. at 736; see *ante*, p. 340.

[15] This point was left open by Millett J. (it did not have to be decided because in that case the property had been received here). The point also arose, and was again left open, in *Chase Manhattan Bank v. Israel-British Bank* (London) [1981] Ch. 105 at 127.

[16] *Metall & Rohstoff v. Donaldson Lufkin & Jenrette* [1990] 1 Q.B. 391 at 474.

[17] *Arab Monetary Fund v. Hashim (No. 9)* (1994), unreported (judgment of October 11, 1994) transcript at 22–23, *per* Chadwick J.

[18] *ibid.*, at 24.

[19] The principle enunciated in *The Halley* (1868) L.R. 2 P.C. 193 (a decision of the Privy Council but, because it was on appeal from the Court of Admiralty, an English precedent).

ceased to do so.[20] On this basis, liability depends, first, on whether the alleged accessory is liable under English law and, secondly, on whether he is exempted from liability under the law of the jurisdiction where the assistance took place. Only if he is both liable under English law and not exempted by the law of the other jurisdiction, will he be liable for "dishonest assistance". It seems scarcely satisfactory to reject the applicability of the rule of private international law governing liability in tort and then to return to and adopt as of general application an abrogated authority on tort which has long since been rejected by the House of Lords. This conclusion is at best an unsatisfactory half way house; fortunately, it is at present not even binding in the Chancery Division, never mind in the Court of Appeal. It is to be hoped that a more satisfactory rule emerges from the proceedings at present pending in the Commercial Court.

II. The Jurisdiction of the English Courts[21]

Most well-drawn trust instruments today contain a clause specifying the proper law of the trust, which will govern all questions concerning that trust unless any of them is stated to be governed by the law of some other jurisdiction. Where English law is specified as the proper law of a trust, there can be no doubt whatever that the English courts have jurisdiction over all questions concerning that trust (other of course than any which is stated to be governed by the law of another jurisdiction). Indeed, many trust instruments contain a further clause specifically conferring that jurisdiction on the courts in question. It is of course theoretically possible for a trust to contain both a clause specifying English law as the proper law of the trust and a clause giving jurisdiction over all questions concerning the trust to some other jurisdiction. The latter clause would presumably have to be upheld in proceedings between the trustees and the settlor, all of whom would obviously have agreed to it by executing the trust instrument. However, the most likely parties to any proceedings are the trustees and the beneficiaries, who are highly unlikely to have executed the trust instrument. In such circumstances, it is inconceivable that the English courts would decline jurisdiction to hear proceedings brought by any beneficiary of a trust who had not executed the trust instrument where English law was specified as the proper law.

As has just been indicated, a trust instrument can also specify that some questions concerning its trusts are to be governed by the law of some jurisdiction other than that of its proper law. The administration of a trust is what is most often excluded from the ambit of its proper law, although in this and all other cases it is usually prudent also to define extremely precisely exactly what has been so excluded. Many modern trust instruments

---

[20] It was rejected by the House of Lords in *Boys v. Chaplain* [1971] A.C. 356, where a different rule was adopted. This has in turn been replaced by yet a further rule contained in Private International Law (Miscellaneous Provisions) Act 1995.

[21] The remaining sections of this new Chap. have benefited enormously from the kindness of Prof. David Hayton and Prof. Paul Matthews, both of King's College, London, in permitting the author to attend their LL.M. Course on International and Comparative Trust Law, from which much of the material discussed in these sections is derived.

expressly envisage the possibility of the proper law and the law governing the administration of the trust being different by referring to them in separate clauses, even if both are initially to be governed by the law of the same jurisdiction (this is in order to enable the two to be separated later under the change of law clauses which such instruments tend also to contain). It is also not uncommon to specify that the trust instrument should be construed in accordance with the law of a particular jurisdiction, usually that of the jurisdiction in which it is being drawn up; this can be advantageous since it enables technical expressions such as "issue" to be given the meaning which the draftsman intended them to have and permits presumptions which the draftsman will consciously or unconsciously have had in mind to be carried into effect. If the law chosen to govern the construction of the trust instrument or the administration of the trust or anything else is English law, there is equally no doubt that the English courts have jurisdiction in that respect.

Where a trust instrument contains no clause specifying what law is to apply, the English courts will equally have jurisdiction where all the relevant parties and the relevant property are habitually physically within their jurisdiction; such trusts will inevitably be held to be subject to English law anyway. Further, in relation to proprietary claims, the English courts are likely to assume jurisdiction if only the property and none of the parties is within the jurisdiction in this sense. It is also possible for defendants outside the jurisdiction to submit to the jurisdiction of the English courts by giving someone within the jurisdiction authority to accept service on their behalf.[22] The crucial question is obviously in what other circumstances the English courts will assume jurisdiction.

The basic rule is that the physical presence of the defendant within the jurisdiction, no matter how fleeting it may be, is sufficient to confer jurisdiction on the English courts even if the proper law of the trust is not English law. In *Ewing v. Orr-Ewing*[23] an order was sought by an English infant beneficiary against English and Scottish executors, all of whom were regarded as having been properly served,[24] for the administration by the English court of both the English and Scottish assets of the estate of a Scottish domiciliary. Part of the assets had originally been within the jurisdiction but had been removed to Scotland by the time that the action commenced. The House of Lords made the order sought. In *Cook Industries v. Galligher*,[25] an order was sought by and granted to the plaintiff, a New York creditor under a New York judgment, for the inspection of a property in France which the defendant, an American who lived in England for approximately six months a year, was alleged to hold on trust for the plaintiff's judgment debtor. These, and other authorities not involving trusts, were relied on by Millett J. in *El Ajou v. Dollar Land Holdings*[26] in support of the proposition that liability for "knowing receipt" could be imposed on an English company in respect of assets which it had knowingly

---

[22] As some of the trustees had in *Chellaram v. Chellaram* [1985] Ch. 409.
[23] (1883) 9 App.Cas. 34.
[24] The Scottish executors seem to have been served in Scotland without any special leave of the court but no objection was taken.
[25] [1979] Ch. 439.
[26] [1993] 3 All E.R. 717 at 737.

received abroad.[27] Similarly, in *Chellaram v. Chellaram*,[28] whose facts have already been considered,[29] all the trustees had been served in England, some as a result of having submitted to the jurisdiction, so the English court clearly had jurisdiction.

Further, the leave of the court can be obtained[30] for service on defendants who are out of the jurisdiction in a number of circumstances, of which the most relevant for present purposes is where "the claim is brought to execute the trusts of a written instrument being trusts that ought to be executed according to English law and of which the person to be served with the writ is a trustee, or for any relief or remedy which might be obtained in any such action".[31]

However, even where an English court has jurisdiction under the rules set out above, it may nevertheless decline to hear the proceedings under the doctrine of *forum non conveniens* if it is satisfied that the courts of another jurisdiction constitute a more appropriate forum. This complicated doctrine[32] is beyond the scope of this Chapter but an example of a situation where an English court might well decline jurisdiction in proceedings involving a trust would be where the trustees had been served on a casual visit to this country and had no assets within the jurisdiction, none of the trust property was within the jurisdiction, and it was clear that the judgment of the English court would not be enforced in the jurisdiction(s) where the trustees and the trust property were physically present; in such circumstances, the latter jurisdiction(s) would clearly constitute a more appropriate forum.

The rules which have just been discussed do not, however, apply when the proceedings in question fall within the scope of what are known as the Brussels and Lugano Conventions, which govern jurisdiction and judgments within, respectively, the European Union and the European Free Trade Association. They were incorporated into English law by the Civil Jurisdiction and Judgments Acts of 1982 and 1991 respectively. The Conventions provide for the allocation of jurisdiction among the courts of the states who have signed them (all the member states of the European Union but not all the members of the European Free Trade Association) and for the automatic enforcement in all those states of the judgment of whatever court has been allocated jurisdiction.[33] The Conventions prohibit the exercise of jurisdiction on the basis of physical presence within the jurisdiction but permit service outside it in all cases allocated to that jurisdiction. No action can be stayed on the ground of *forum non conveniens* and actions can only be stayed

---

[27] This proposition does not form part of his ratio since the company had actually received the assets in England. Millett J. was using this proposition based on hypothetical facts in order to establish that, if the company was potentially liable for "knowing receipt" if the assets had been received abroad, it was *a fortiori* potentially liable if they had been received in England.

[28] [1985] Ch. 409.

[29] *ante*, p. 746.

[30] Under Ord. 11 of the Rules of the Supreme Court.

[31] Ord. 11, r. 1(1)(j).

[32] See Collier, *Conflict of Laws* (2nd ed., 1993) pp. 91–111.

[33] See *post*, p. 759.

or jurisdiction declined if proceedings have already validly been commenced in a court of another signatory state (this is possible because most of the provisions of the conventions do not confer exclusive jurisdiction).

The relevant provision of the Conventions for proceedings involving trusts is Article 5(6) which provides that a person with a domicile (which means a habitual residence, not the technical English private international law concept of domicile) in a signatory state may be sued in another signatory state if he is "settlor, trustee or beneficiary of a trust created by the operation of a statute, or by a written instrument, or created orally and evidenced in writing, in the courts of the [signatory state] in which the trust is domiciled". Because trusts do not have legal personality and so cannot really be said to have a habitual residence and because the United Kingdom is not a sole jurisdiction, specific provision has had to be made as to when and where a trust is domiciled in the United Kingdom; it is domiciled in the United Kingdom if it is domiciled in any part of the United Kingdom and is domiciled in a part of the United Kingdom "if and only if the system of law of that part is the system of law with which the trust has its closest and most real connection".[34] This system seems likely to be that of the proper law of the trust, even if neither the trustees nor the trust property are physically present in that jurisdiction. However, Article 5 is overridden by Article 17 where any jurisdiction has been the subject of a choice of law clause in a trust instrument; in this case Article 17 confers exclusive jurisdiction (something which Article 5 does not do) on the jurisdiction so selected. There are, however, two exceptions to both Article 5 and Article 17. Where proceedings relate to the title to immovable property or to a leasehold interest therein, the courts of the state where the immovable property is situated have, under Article 16(1), exclusive jurisdiction.[35] And the Conventions do not apply at all to trusts in favour of creditors, testamentary trusts and ante-nuptial settlements.[36]

III. WHAT LAW WILL THE ENGLISH COURTS APPLY?

As has already been mentioned, the rules of English law governing the proper law of trusts are now contained in The Hague Convention on the Law Applicable to Trusts and their Recognition ("the Convention"), incorporated into English law by the Recognition of Trusts Act 1987.[37] As the title of the Convention suggests, it actually had two broad purposes: that of determining the law by which different aspects of trusts are governed and of enabling the recognition of trusts in jurisdictions where the trust concept

---

[34] Civil Jurisdiction and Judgments Act 1982, s.45.

[35] This does not prevent the English courts from having jurisdiction over proceedings relating to the beneficial interests in such property. See *Webb v. Webb* [1994] Q.B. 696, where a father successfully claimed that his son held French land on resulting trust for him; these proceedings did not concern the legal title to the land and consequently the English court could exercise jurisdiction by virtue of the physical presence of the son in England.

[36] Art. 1(1).

[37] See D. J.Hayton, (1987) 36 I.C.L.Q. 260 (Prof. Hayton was the head of the U.K. delegation to the body which produced the convention and is therefore uniquely qualified to comment on its background and provisions).

is unknown; indeed it was the authorities of the latter jurisdictions who suggested to the Hague Secretariat that a Convention should be prepared. The sort of potential problems which the provision of such recognition was intended to resolve have already been considered in Chapter 1.[38] This Chapter is only concerned with the determination of the law by which trusts are governed.

It must first be made clear that preliminary issues concerning the question of whether a trust has actually been created are not governed by the proper law of that trust but by whatever system of law governs the capacity of the settlor to create the trust and the means by which the trust property is vested in the trustees. This is expressly provided by Article 4 of the Convention and would be the case even if the Convention contained no such provision (the Convention does not as such deal with trusts created by oral declaration (see Article 3) but it cannot seriously be contended that they would not be in the same position. Under English law an infant has the capacity neither to create a trust nor to transfer property to its trustees and, in the admittedly unlikely event that he purported to do so, the property would remain vested in whoever previously held it and no trust would have been created because it would not have become completely constituted; the fact that the trust instrument provided that it should be governed by the law of some jurisdiction where the law was in some way different[39] would have no effect whatever. Similarly, transfers of property to trustees can be set aside under the Insolvency Act 1986, the Matrimonial Causes Act 1973 and the Inheritance (Provision for Family and Dependants) Act 1975 notwithstanding the fact that the trust in question is expressed to be governed by some law other than English law. Settlors from other jurisdictions may also transfer property to trustees in breach of the rules of their matrimonial property regime or of that jurisdiction's forced heirship provisions (provisions which require a particular proportion of a person's lifetime assets to pass to his spouse and children on his death).[40]

Nor is the proper law of the trust likely to be applied if the trust created is contrary to English public policy. If English land were settled on a form of trust which is prohibited by English law but permitted by the law of the jurisdiction to whose law it is expressed to be subject, such as a trust for the settlor for life or until bankruptcy[41] or on trusts which can last for ever and so blatantly infringe the rule against perpetuities,[42] an English court would

---

[38] See *ante*, p. 13.

[39] Because the age of majority was lower there. It is difficult to think of any jurisdiction where this is the case; however, if a 19 year old person from Jersey (where the age of majority is 20) tried to create a trust, the fact that it was expressly subject to English law would not make it valid.

[40] The ability to impeach such transactions does of course depend on the property in question still being within the reach of those seeking to set the transfers aside. It will not be if it is in the control of trustees of another jurisdiction which does not recognise and enforce the judgments of courts in the jurisdiction where any such transfer is set aside; this is the case in many off shore trust jurisdictions.

[41] Permitted in, *e.g.* the Cook Islands.

[42] Permitted in, *e.g.* The Cayman Islands. However, it is unlikely that there would be any difficulty about perpetuity and accumulation periods which are merely longer than the maximum period permitted by English law; most off-shore trusts jurisdictions have such provisions and even Northern Ireland has a longer accumulation period.

be highly likely to apply English law and declare the trust to be void (it would of course have jurisdiction so to do because the subject matter was land within the jurisdiction). This would also be the case with movable property which was actually within the jurisdiction at the time of the proceedings. It is less certain how the English courts would react to the various types of purpose trusts which have recently become fashionable in many off-shore trust jurisdictions[43] which are contrary to the rules of English trust law because they have no beneficiaries or to the more extreme trusts (or so-called trusts) which deprive their beneficiaries of any right to enforce them.[44]

Once a trust has been completely constituted, however, it will normally be governed by whatever law has been specified. As has already been stated, the proper law of the trust will govern at the very least the nature of the interests of its beneficiaries and the duties of the trustees towards them; this was specifically stated in *Chellaram v. Chellaram.*[45] It will also govern all other questions concerning the trust other than any which has been stated to be governed by the law of some other jurisdiction, which will of course instead be governed by the law of that jurisdiction. However, unless the trust instrument has defined extremely precisely what is to be regarded as constituting whatever has been excluded from the ambit of its proper law, considerable difficulties can be encountered in determining precisely what is to be governed by the law of which jurisdiction.

It has already been stated that the construction of the trust instrument and the administration of the trust are what are most commonly excluded from the ambit of its proper law. There is no difficulty in defining the scope of the former exclusion but very considerable difficulties can be encountered in defining precisely what constitutes administration in the absence of an express definition. Prior to the enactment of the Recognition of Trusts Act 1987, the leading practitioners' text on the Conflict of Laws, Dicey & Morris,[46] drew a distinction between, on the one hand, the validity, interpretation and effect of a trust and, on the other hand, its administration; the former were said to be governed by its proper law and the latter was said to be governed by the law of its place of administration. This distinction was rejected by Scott J. in *Chellaram v. Chellaram,*[47] who expressed the view that all four were governed by its proper law (this view has been adopted by Dicey & Morris in its current edition).[48] However, that does not answer the question of what is to be regarded as administration when the settlor has stated that administration is to be governed by a law other than the proper law without defining what he means by administration.

It has already been stated that the proper law of the trust will at the very least govern the nature of the interests of the beneficiaries and the duties of the trustees towards them (the latter will clearly include any powers which they have to determine the manner in which the income and capital of the trust is distributed and their duties to convert and apportion the trust

---

[43] Pioneered by Bermuda but now relatively common.
[44] This is now permitted in The Cayman Islands.
[45] [1985] Ch. 409 at 432.
[46] Conflict of Laws (10th ed., 1980), Rules 120 & 121.
[47] [1985] Ch. 409 at 432.
[48] Conflict of Laws (12th ed., 1993), Rule 153.

property). The proper law will also undoubtedly govern the construction of the trust instrument if this has not been expressly reserved to the law of some other jurisdiction. At the other extreme, there can be no doubt that the trustees' duties to provide accounts and to give information to the beneficiaries are purely administrative; so are some of their powers, such as the power to appoint and remove trustees, to appoint agents, and to insure. But a number of other powers which are, for other purposes, often classified as administrative are capable of affecting directly or indirectly the interests of the beneficiaries in the event that the provisions of the proper law and of the law specified as governing administration differ as to their existence or scope. The presence or absence of a power for the trustees to remunerate themselves clearly affects the income and capital available for the beneficiaries. So does the presence or absence of powers of advancement, maintenance and accumulation in the event that they are exercised. So too, to a lesser extent, do the trustees' powers of investment. And where powers exercisable by persons other than the trustees, such as the settlor or the protector, fit in is anyone's guess; the law applicable will presumably (or at any rate should) be determined by the nature of the power in question. There therefore seems no sensible way of drawing a line in the absence of a precise definition in the trust instrument and it is consequently impossible to predict what would happen in the event that an English court had to decide by which law such powers were governed.

Such a situation would open the way for the court to ignore the provisions of the trust instrument completely and simply apply English law. Indeed, this is precisely what Scott J. did in *Chellaram v. Chellaram*,[49] which was admittedly decided before the enactment of the Recognition of Trusts Act 1987. In this case, the facts of which have already been considered, [50] the beneficiaries were seeking the removal and replacement of the trustees. Scott J. was prepared to apply the provisions of English law to this question even if both the proper law of the trust and the law under which it was being administered turned out to be Indian law. He said this[51]:

"The function of English courts in trust litigation is to enforce or protect the rights of the beneficiaries which bind the conscience of the trustee defendants. The identification and extent of those rights is a matter for the proper law of the settlement, but the manner of enforcement is, in my view, a matter of machinery which, under English domestic law, can be exercised by English courts where necessary in order to enable the rights of beneficiaries to be enforced or protected. . . . Accordingly, except where rights conferred by the settlement are under consideration, the removal of trustees and the appointment of new ones are not, in my judgment, a matter to be governed by the proper law of the settlement. Nor, in my opinion, is it a matter to be governed by the law of the place where the administration of the settlement has taken place. It is, in my judgment, a matter to be governed by the law of the country whose courts have assumed jurisdiction to administer the trusts of the settlement in question."

---

[49] [1985] Ch. 409.
[50] *ante*, p. 746.
[51] [1985] Ch. 409 at 432–433.

The last sentence of this passage suggests, without actually stating, that English law was applicable simply because it was the law of the forum. If English domestic law is indeed applicable whenever it is necessary to protect the interests of the beneficiaries, then the possibilities for its application are infinite. It is of course possible that this approach would be held no longer to be appropriate in the light of the subsequent enactment of the Recognition of Trusts Act 1987. But in the event that it is still applicable, the provisions of that Act could well turn out to be a dead letter in any proceedings brought by beneficiaries against trustees to enforce their interests in which the English courts have jurisdiction.

However, on any view, the proper law of the trust still has a substantial role to play. How then is it determined in the absence of a specific provision in the trust instrument?

The Convention refers to the proper law as "the applicable law". Having provided in Article 6 that a trust shall be governed by the law chosen by the settlor, so long as that law "provides for trusts or the category of trust involved",[52] it then provides in Article 7:

"Where no applicable law has been chosen, a trust shall be governed by the law with which it is most closely connected.

In ascertaining the law with which a trust is most closely connected reference shall be made in particular to—
(a)   the place of the administration of the trust designated by the settlor;
(b)   the situs of the assets of the trust;
(c)   the place of residence or business of the trustee;
(d)   the objects of the trust and the places where they are to be fulfilled."

The delegations negotiating the terms of the Convention decided to restrict themselves to these four factors. The need for both common law and civil law jurisdictions to make concessions meant the former had to accept the absence of domicile and the latter the absence of nationality, factors which are generally all important in these respective jurisdictions; these factors must presumably therefore be disregarded. However, as the wording of Article 7 itself recognises, the four factors actually listed do not constitute an exclusive list. The habitual residence of the testator is clearly a key factor in testamentary trusts, although the habitual residence of the settlor will obviously be less relevant in *inter vivos trusts* if different from that the place of residence or business of the trustee. The actual language of the trust instrument, and in particular any references which it may make to the statutory provisions of any particular jurisdiction, must also be highly significant. However, the extent to which the habitual residence of the beneficiaries should be relevant, if different from the place of residence or business of the trustee (which it always will be in an off-shore trust), is much more questionable.

If whatever factors are decided to be relevant in any given place point towards the law of two different jurisdictions, one under which the trust

---

[52] If it does not, then the choice is not effective and Art. 7 applies.

would be valid and one under which it would be void, English law at least would be likely to opt for the jurisdiction in which it is valid.[53]

Article 8 then goes on to provide that the applicable law shall govern "the validity of the trust, its construction, its effect, and the administration of the trust" (although this is subject to Article 9 which permits "a severable aspect of the trust, particularly matters of administration" to be governed by a different law). There then follows a non-exhaustive list of what the applicable law will govern. This contains nearly everything which could be expected. The only significant omission appears to be powers vested in persons other than the trustee such as the settlor or a protector. However, it cannot seriously be contended that these would not be governed by the proper law (unless, of course, their subject matter related to "a severable aspect . . . governed by a different law").

The inclusion in the list of what the applicable law will govern of "(h) the variation or termination of the trust" leads to the conclusion that, as has already been mentioned,[54] the English courts no longer have the jurisdiction which they have previously arrogated[55] to approve applications under the Variation of Trusts Act 1958[56] in respect of trusts whose proper law is not English law. This is theoretically also the position where property held under such trusts is the subject matter of an application for the reallocation of property following a divorce[57]; however, as has also already been mentioned,[58] it is not likely that an argument to this effect will find favour with the English courts since otherwise putting assets in a foreign trust would be far too easy a way of protecting them from potential claims by former spouses.[59]

Article 10 deals with changes of applicable (or other) law and provides that the question of whether such a change is possible shall be determined by "the law applicable to the validity of the trust". This presumably means the applicable law but it would be more helpful if the Convention actually said so specifically. Such changes, at least under English law, will require a clause expressly permitting this, the agreement of all the beneficiaries, or if any of the beneficiaries is not *sui juris*, the leave of the court under the

---

[53] In accordance with the decision of the majority of the Court of Appeal in *Re Baden's Deed Trusts* [1969] 2 Ch. 126, see *ante* p. 179, that, where the considerations were evenly balanced in arriving at one or other conclusion, the court was at liberty to lean towards the conclusion which might effectuate rather than frustrate the settlor's intentions (the point did not arise on the subsequent appeal to the House of Lords (*McPhail v. Doulton* [1971] A.C. 424)). This case concerned a private trust but the existence of a similar attitude towards charitable trusts was confirmed by the *House of Lords* in *I.R.C. v. McMullen* [1981] A.C. 1, see *ante* p. 380, although the House did not need to resort to it in that case.

[54] *ante*, p. 747.

[55] *Re Ker's Settlement* [1963] Ch. 553; *Re Paget's Settlement* [1965] 1 W.L.R. 1046.

[56] *ante*, p. 662.

[57] It has been argued in unreported proceedings that the English courts no longer have jurisdiction to make orders governing such trusts on applications of this type but such arguments have not yet been the subject of a reasoned judgment.

[58] *ante*, p. 747.

[59] This is the view taken by Dicey & Morris, *The Conflict of Laws* (12th ed., 1993), pp. 767–768 and it is certainly likely to be difficult to persuade an English court to adopt any other view. It is possible that Art. 15, *post* p. 758, could be relied on in support of the view of Dicey & Morris.

Variation of Trusts Act 1958.[60] However, the latter two methods would certainly involve a deemed disposal for the purposes of Capital Gains Tax because at least for a moment of time the beneficiaries would be absolutely entitled to the trust property[61] this could conceivably also be a consequence of a change pursuant to an express provision. Surprisingly, Article 10, unlike the provisions governing the originally applicable law, contains no restriction to jurisdictions which "provide for trusts or the category of trusts involved". A change to a jurisdiction which did not recognise trusts and so regarded the trust in question as either revocable by the settlor or in his favour could have disastrous fiscal consequences,[62] as could a change to a jurisdiction which recognised trusts but only of a type which English law regarded as void for public policy. Presumably, the Convention assumes that the trustees will be sensible! However, serious consideration should be given by draftsmen to restricting the scope of clauses permitting a change of law to, at the very least, jurisdictions which recognise trusts.

The only other provisions of the Convention which require comment are Articles 15 and 16, both of which are mandatory. Article 15 provides that those rules of the private international law of the forum which "cannot be derogated from by voluntary act" are applicable despite the provisions of the Convention, referring in particular to, among other things,[63] "(a) the protection of minors and incapable parties; (b) the personal and proprietary effects of marriage; . . . (e) the protection of creditors in matters of insolvency". These provisions might be an alternative method by which English law could justify the invalidity of trusts made by infants or in fraud of creditors, spouses, and dependants[64] and/or the continuation of the jurisdiction to order the reallocation, following divorce, of property held under a trust not subject to English law.[65] However, English courts might well be rather wary about declaring that any of the rules of English law "cannot be derogated from by voluntary act", since such declarations might have all sorts of implications in other situations. Article 16 (the second paragraph of which does not form part of English law) similarly provides that "those provisions of the law of the forum which must be applied even to international situations, irrespective of" its rules of private international law are also applicable despite the provisions of the Convention. The only obvious situation to which this would apply (and this is fairly far-fetched) would be if the trustees of a trust not subject to English law brought proceedings in an English court connected in some way with assets whose sale, purchase or ownership is prohibited by English law (examples are arms, drugs, classical

---

[60] See *ante*, p. 662.

[61] See *ante*, p. 526.

[62] Because the settlor would under English law be regarded as being beneficially entitled to the trust property and, if he was subject to English taxation, would therefore become liable to Income Tax and Capital Gains Tax on its assets. This would also stop any seven year period running for the purposes of Inheritance Tax.

[63] Those not listed are not relevant to English law, although "(d) the transfer of title title to property . . . " may well confirm the conclusions which have already been expressed (*ante*, p. 748) about the limitations on equitable proprietary claims and liability for "knowing receipt".

[64] See *ante*, p. 753.

[65] See *ante*, p. 757.

architectural artifacts and protected species) but is permitted by its proper law.

IV. THE ENFORCEMENT BY ENGLISH COURTS OF FOREIGN TRUSTS JUDGMENTS

Any judgment in proceedings involving a trust given by a court which has jurisdiction under the Brussels or Lugano Conventions[66] will be automatically recognised and enforced by the English courts[67] unless it falls foul of Article 27 of these Conventions for one of the following reasons: first, because it is contrary to public policy; secondly, because judgment was given in default of appearance in circumstances where the defendant was not properly served in sufficient time to prepare his defence; thirdly, if the judgment cannot be reconciled with a judgment already given by an English court in a dispute between the same parties; and, fourthly, if the judgment was given pursuant to a rule of private international law as to capacity, matrimonial property rights, or succession which produced a result different from that which would have been reached under English private international law.

Any judgment in proceedings not subject to these two Conventions will also be recognised and enforced if it is within any bilateral or multi-lateral convention for the enforcement of judgments between the state where the judgment was given and the United Kingdom and is duly registered in the High Court. If no such convention is applicable, then the foreign judgment will not be recognised or enforced by the English courts; it will merely create an obligation binding on the defendant which the successful plaintiff will have to enforce by bringing a separate action in the English courts.[68] This is still the position where a successful plaintiff in any of the jurisdictions of the United States of America seeks to enforce his judgment in the English courts.[69]

---

[66] See *ante*, p. 751.

[67] Arts 26 & 31.

[68] Since he will normally be able to obtain summary judgment, this is not usually any slower than the process of registering a judgment under a bilateral or multi-lateral convention.

[69] And of course vice-versa.

CHAPTER 26

EXPORTING TRUSTS

I. MOTIVES

A person may wish to create a new trust abroad or to export an existing trust for a variety of reasons. Generally, these are one or more of the following.

1. The beneficiaries or a majority of them are resident abroad or are intending to reside abroad and it will be most convenient for the trust to be administered in the country in which they are resident.[1]

2. There is a widespread fear that future United Kingdom legislation might aim to achieve a more even distribution of wealth among members of the community and that this can only be achieved by, in effect, confiscating part of the assets of those who are thought to be wealthy. A wealth tax is only one form which such legislation might take. It is not appropriate to comment here on the ethics or political wisdom of any such measures but man is an essentially greedy animal and, having acquired assets, will usually go to great lengths to retain them. Some people think, not always correctly, that if assets are transferred abroad and held by trustees, then they will be safe from the tax gatherer's prying eyes and preying hands, particularly if the present owner does not retain any legal entitlement to them.

3. From time to time, although admittedly not at present, there is an associated fear that, as a currency, sterling may not be stable and that the value and security of wealth may be enhanced if it is held abroad.

4. A settlor may occasionally wish to take advantage of foreign rules of law. Some of these rules have been considered in the previous Chapter. Although it is not "foreign" in this sense, a particular example is Northern Ireland where it is possible to direct accumulation for much longer than in England and Wales; many off-shore jurisdictions, which certainly are "foreign"in this sense, permit types of purpose trusts which are void under English law. However, advantage can only be taken of rules of these types if the proper law of the trust, determined in the manner also considered in the previous Chapter, is the law of the jurisdiction whose trust law contains

---

[1] This was the reason for the approval of the court given in *Re Seale's Marriage Settlement* [1961] Ch. 574 and in *Re Windeatt's Will Trusts* [1969] 1 W.L.R. 692. See *post*, p. 775. See also *Re Whitehead's Will Trusts* [1971] 1 W.L.R. 833, *post*, p. 778.

them. The settlor of a newly created trust can of course select whatever proper law he wishes. However, a pre-existing trust will only be
able to change its proper law to that of a foreign jurisdiction if the
trust instrument contains a clause expressly permitting this or all the
beneficiaries agree (which, if any of them is not *sui juris*, will require
the leave of the court under the Variation of Trusts Act 1958).

5. Lastly, and predominantly, settlors and beneficiaries wish to reduce
   their fiscal liabilities and to ensure so far as possible that funds are
   protected from the admittedly increasingly unlikely possibility of
   any re-introduction of United Kingdom exchange control.

This Chapter is concerned entirely with the extent to which this final
objective can effectively be achieved. It examines the main aspects of the law
which apply when a person resident in the United Kingdom wishes to create
a new trust abroad or when an existing United Kingdom trust is transferred
abroad (in this Chapter, trusts which are administered abroad are referred to
as "off-shore"[2] trusts).

II. THE LEGACY OF EXCHANGE CONTROL

United Kingdom exchange control legislation was suspended in 1979.[3] It
was intended, when enacted, to conserve the United Kingdom's gold and
foreign currency resources and to assist the balance of payments by restricting the outflow of funds from the United Kingdom. While the legislation
was in operation, very broadly a person resident in the United Kingdom[4]
who wished to purchase an investment or other asset abroad[5] had to do so
in one of three ways.

(i) With currency purchased through the official foreign exchange
market. This was controlled strictly by the Bank of England, acting
as the exchange control authority. In principle, the Bank of England
gave permission for the use of foreign currency purchased at the
official rate of exchange only where the investment was likely
directly to promote United Kingdom exports, or where it promised
an early benefit to the balance of payments. Permission was not
generally given for personal investment.

(ii) With "investment currency". After the introduction of exchange
control, persons who were resident in the United Kingdom and
who had foreign currency securities[6] were obliged, when they sold

---

[2] The expression includes anywhere outside Great Britain and Northern Ireland and so
includes the Channel Islands, the Isle of Man and all other colonies and dependencies of the
United Kingdom.

[3] With effect from October 24, 1979.

[4] Or in the other Scheduled Territories, namely the Channel Islands, the Isle of Man, the
Republic of Ireland and Gibraltar.

[5] That is, outside the Scheduled Territories. A special relaxation applied in the case of investment in other members of what was then known as the European Economic Community.

[6] That is securities denominated or payable in any currency other than sterling.

them, to sell them through controlled channels and receive the proceeds of sale in sterling. Those proceeds of sale, known as investment currency, were available for sale to other United Kingdom residents but, because of the shortage of investment currency, at a premium which was often in excess of 40 per cent. This applied even where an investor resident in the United Kingdom wished to sell one foreign currency security and to re-invest the proceeds in another such security.

(iii) With the proceeds of foreign currency borrowings. These were sums borrowed abroad in a currency other than sterling. Such foreign currency borrowing required the permission of the Bank of England, which was not generally granted to private investors.

A further restriction was that, whenever foreign currency securities were purchased, irrespective of the source of the funds, the certificates of the securities had to be held by depositories designated by the Bank of England.[7] Furthermore, there was a general prohibition on maintaining foreign currency bank accounts.

While exchange control was in force, an individual who wished to invest abroad was therefore subject to numerous restrictions and almost invariably substantial extra cost. Furthermore, there was always the risk that in acute national financial circumstances the Government would take action to compel the foreign currency securities held by the designated depositories to be realised.

In 1979 the legislation was suspended but not repealed.[8] The general view, admittedly not universally held, is that it could be brought back into operation again merely by the Treasury laying a Statutory Instrument before Parliament.[9] However, it has to be admitted that, even on the assumption that the legislation could be brought back into operation so easily, the chances of any reintroduction are negligible for both political and practical reasons. It would be politically impossible to impose exchange control between the United Kingdom and the other Member States of the European Union and no such reintroduction is really necessary anyway in the light of the ever-increasing facilities for the interchange of information between Member States; the Inland Revenue can find out about any assets held openly by any United Kingdom tax-payer in any other Member State. Further, although exchange control could certainly be reintroduced between the United Kingdom and non-Member States, far too many assets are far too long gone to have any chance of being discovered unless their owners wished voluntarily to repatriate them or to declare their existence; any legislation requiring them to do either of these things would, frankly, have about as much chance of success as the Prohibition Legislation in the United States of America earlier this century.

That does not alter the fact that since 1979, and particularly in the first decade thereafter, many individuals resident in the United Kingdom have

---

[7] Most banks and practising solicitors were so designated.
[8] By the Exchange Control (General Exemption) Order 1979 (S.I. 1979 No.1660) and the Exchange Control (Revocation) (No. 2) Direction 1979 (S.I. 1979 No.1162).
[9] Under the Exchange Control Act 1947.

created trusts with a view to enabling their funds to be free of any reintroduction of exchange control. The strategy was and is based on the premise
that, where the trustees are resident abroad and the investments are situated
abroad, the trustees will not themselves be subject to United Kingdom
exchange control legislation and the beneficiary, not having the power to
control the trustees, will himself not be able to procure that the funds are
brought within the scope of the control. In the jargon of the 1980s, such non-
resident trustees are said to be "non-compellable".

There can therefore be no doubt that the fear that exchange control might
be re-introduced has been and to a lesser extent still is a powerful stimulus
to the formation of new off-shore trusts.

Trusts which already existed during the period of exchange control were,
on the other hand, classified either as resident or as non-resident. Their
classification depended entirely on the residential status of the creator of the
trust at the time of its creation, the settlor in the case of an inter vivos trust
and the deceased at the date of his death in the case of a will trust. Where
a trust was resident, there was no restriction on the appointment of non-
resident trustees as such but the assets could only be transferred to them
with the consent of the Bank of England, which unsurprisingly was only
sparingly given. In general, permission was always refused unless it could
be shown that all the possible beneficiaries were themselves non-resident.
On the other hand, there were very few onerous restrictions on trusts which
had throughout their existence been non-resident or which had been made
non-resident before the original introduction of exchange control.[10] Accordingly, once exchange control had been suspended, there was considerable
and obvious motivation in favour of making existing trusts non-resident
and taking the assets abroad while there was no restriction on so doing.

III. TAXATION

1. *Taxation Generally*

In order to determine the taxation advantages of a trust which is for the time
being non-resident[11] it is necessary to consider the taxation liability of both
the settlor, the trustees and the beneficiaries.

2. *Income Tax*

(A) The Settlor
It is extremely unlikely that a resident settlor of a non-resident trust would
make himself a beneficiary of that trust but if he were to do so his position
would be the same as that of any other beneficiary. However if, as is
obviously more likely, his unmarried infant children are beneficiaries, then
in the highly unlikely event that any income is actually paid to and applied

---

[10] By the Defence (Finance) Regulations 1939, issued under the Emergency Powers (Defence)
Acts.
[11] For the sake of simplicity, in this Chap. the expression "non-resident" is used to mean both
non-resident in the strict sense and non-ordinarily resident.

for their benefit, that income will be treated as his income for the purposes of income tax.[12] This rule applies to all trusts, whether resident or non-resident; it is, however, hard to imagine that any settlor would be likely to set up a non-resident trust with a view to receiving income from it for his unmarried infant children.

(B) The Trustees

An underlying principle of United Kingdom income tax law is that a person is liable to income tax on his total world-wide income if he is resident here but, if he is not resident here, only on income which is derived from a source in the United Kingdom.

It therefore follows that non-resident trustees will not be liable in respect of income derived from sources outside the United Kingdom but will be liable in respect of income derived from sources within the United Kingdom to the same extent as trustees who are resident here. It has already been seen[13] that, in principle, this liability will be in the case of fixed trusts to income tax of 23 per cent (20 per cent in the case of company distributions and bank interest) and the case of accumulation and discretionary settlements to income tax of 34 per cent.[14]

Accordingly, non-resident trustees will be free of United Kingdom income tax if all the investments are made abroad.

(C) The Beneficiaries

(1) Actual income

Where a beneficiary is entitled to receive income from a foreign trust, he is liable to income tax on that income[15] whether or not he actually physically receives it.[16] This is so irrespective of the jurisdiction in which the trust assets are situated. No income tax saving is effected, therefore, where the beneficiary is actually entitled to the income.

(2) Other benefits from income

Were there no other provision, the beneficiaries would therefore escape liability if income were accumulated abroad and either retained abroad or subsequently paid to them as capital. To counter this, there are two far-reaching anti-avoidance provisions.

(a) **Section 739 of the Income and Corporation Taxes Act 1988.** This provision applies where all the following requirements are satisfed:

> (i) An asset[17] is transferred to a person abroad.[18] This requirement is satisfied even if the asset has not been transferred from the United

---

[12] Income and Corporation Taxes Act 1988, s.660B.

[13] See *ante*, p. 522.

[14] See *ante*, p. 523.

[15] Under Case V of Sched. D.

[16] Liability is deferred if it is impossible to remit the income to the U.K.; s.418. If the person entitled to the income is resident but not domiciled in the U.K., foreign income is only liable to U.K. income tax if remitted to the U.K.

[17] The expression includes money and property or rights of any kind.

[18] That is to say out of Great Britain and Northern Ireland.

Kingdom. So, if Andrew, a resident of, say, South Africa, offers to make a gift of R2,000 to Bertram, who is a United Kingdom resident, but Bertram directs Andrew to pay that sum to trustees on his behalf in Guernsey,[19] the payment of that sum will constitute a transfer of an asset for this purpose. In *I.R.C. v. Brackett*,[20] the taxpayer entered into a contract of employment with a Jersey company and was held to be caught by the section because the rights created by the contract were assets transferred to a person abroad.

(ii) By virtue of, or as a consequence of, that transfer, the income is either directly or indirectly[21] payable to a person or company resident abroad.[22] There is no requirement that that person should have been non-resident at the time of the transfer.[23]

(iii) Either the transferor or his spouse is a United Kingdom resident[24] and enjoys, or has power to enjoy, that income—the definition of "power to enjoy" is very wide indeed.[25]

(iv) In respect of income arising on or before November 25, 1996, either the transferor or his spouse was at the time of the transfer a United Kingdom resident[26] (in respect of income arising thereafter, it does

---

[19] Which is "abroad" for this purpose.

[20] [1986] S.T.C. 521.

[21] This follows from the application of the general principle to a transfer by "an associated operation". s.739 defines "associated operation" in relation to any transfer as "an operation of any kind effected by any person in relation to any of the assets transferred or any assets representing, whether directly or indirectly, any of the assets transferred, or to the income arising from any such assets, or to any assets representing, whether directly or indirectly, the accumulations of income arising from any such assets".

[22] For this purpose, "income" does not include director's remuneration.

[23] *Congreve v. I.R.C.* [1948] 1All E.R. 948.

[24] *Vestey v. I.R.C.* [1980] A.C. 1148.

[25] s.742(2) provides that for the purposes of the section an individual is deemed to have power to enjoy the income of a person resident or domiciled out of the U.K. if:

"(a) the income is in fact so dealt with by any person as to be calculated, at some point of time, and whether in the form of income or not, to enure for the benefit of the individual, or

(b) the receipt or accrual of the income operates to increase the value to the individual of any assets held by him for his benefit, or

(c) the individual receives or is entitled to receive, at any time, any benefit provided or to be provided out of that income or out of moneys which are or will be available for the purpose by reason of the effect or successive effects of the associated operations on that income and on any assets which directly or indirectly represent that income, or

(d) the individual has power, by means of the exercise of any power of appointment or power of revocation or otherwise, to obtain for himself, whether with or without the consent of any other person, the beneficial enjoyment of the income, or may, in the event of the exercise of any power vested in any other person, become entitled to the beneficial enjoyment of the income, or

(e) the individual is able in any manner whatsoever, and whether directly or indirectly, to control the application of the income."

Even this is extended by s.742(3).

[26] *I.R.C. v. Willoughby* [1997] 1 W.L.R. 1071.

not matter where the transferor or his spouse were resident at the time of the transfer).[27]

Where the section applies, the income arising abroad is treated for income tax purposes as the income of the United Kingdom resident with the power to enjoy it to the extent that the foreign resident does not actually distribute it to anyone else. Section 741 establishes two exceptions to this provision:

(i) Where the Board of Inland Revenue is satisfied that tax avoidance was not the purpose or one of the purposes for which the transfer was effected. The House of Lords has recently held that taking advantage of an offer of freedom from tax which the legislation has specifically made does not constitute tax avoidance for the purpose of this exception, stating that "tax avoidance within the meaning of section 741 is a course of action designed to conflict with or defeat the evident intention of Parliament".[28] This exception is therefore likely to prove much more useful than was previously thought.[29]

(ii) Where the transfer was part of a bona fide commercial transaction and not designed for the purpose of avoiding tax. The precise scope of the phrase "bona fide commercial" has been the subject of some dispute[30] and awaits a definitive interpretation.[31]

Nevertheless in most cases where a United Kingdom resident forms a trust abroad and places money or other assets in that trust under which he or his spouse is a beneficiary, section 739 will apply and there will be no saving of income tax. Indeed, the liability incurred can be greater than if the income had arisen within the United Kingdom. In *Lord Chetwode v. I.R.C.*,[32] Lord Chetwode created a settlement in the Bahamas, which owned the entire share capital of a Bahamian investment company. It was held that he was assessable on the whole[33] of the income of the investment company and that he could not even deduct the expenses of the management of that company in computing the amount of income to be brought into account for tax.

(b) Section 740 of the Income and Corporation Taxes Act 1988. The provision just considered, section 739, applies only where the transfer of assets was made by the taxpayer or his spouse. Section 740 applies where an individual who is resident in the United Kingdom can benefit under a foreign trust but was not a settlor in relation to it. If, therefore, Edward creates a non-resident discretionary settlement under which he and his son

[27] Finance Act 1997, s.81.
[28] *I.R.C. v. Willoughby* [1997] 1 W.L.R. 1071 at 1079, *per* Lord Nolan.
[29] Previous editions of this work have, clearly wrongly, described it as "more apparent than real" (5th ed., p. 431; 6th ed., p. 564). Precisely how the "evident intention" of Parliament will be established of course remains to be seen.
[30] See, in the context of a different statutory provision, *I.R.C. v. Goodwin* [1976] 1 W.L.R. 191.
[31] The point was specifically left open in *I.R.C. v. Willoughby* [1997] 1 W.L.R. 1071 at 1081, *per* Lord Nolan.
[32] [1977] 1 All E.R. 638.
[33] In practice, the Revenue do allow a very limited deduction from the gross income in respect of the costs of collecting that income.

Frank are discretionary beneficiaries and both are residents, during Edward's lifetime section 739 will apply. Frank will be liable on general principles to income tax on any income which he actually receives but, provided he took no part in setting up the arrangements, he will only be liable, if at all, under section 740 in respect of income which he does not actually receive. During Edward's lifetime, Frank will not be taxed under section 740 in respect of income on which Edward is taxed under section 739. But after Edward's death Frank is clearly potentially liable under section 740.

Under section 740, it is necessary to calculate all the income of a foreign trust which arose after March 9, 1981 directly or indirectly from a transfer of assets and which can be used for providing a benefit for an individual who is resident in the United Kingdom. Thus, in the example, income which is accumulated on which Edward is not taxed under section 739 is relevant income for this purpose because it is capable of providing a benefit for Frank at some time in the future. A running notional record is kept of this income but no liability arises at that stage. When, however, the individual receives a benefit from the trust which is not taxable as ordinary income, the value of that benefit is treated as forming part of his income for the year in which he actually receives it. Thus, if the trustees made a discretionary capital payment to Frank, he will be subject to income tax on it to the extent that it is covered by income which has already arisen to the trustees on which tax has not yet been paid.

In summary, therefore, the general position is that:

(i) a beneficiary resident in the United Kingdom will be liable to income tax on the actual income which he receives or to which he is entitled;

(ii) the settlor and his spouse[34] will, if resident in the United Kingdom, be liable to income tax on income retained within the trust unless it cannot be applied for his or her benefit, this liability being to tax when the income arises;

(iii) other beneficiaries resident in the United Kingdom will only be liable to income tax retained within the trust when they actually receive benefit from it.

Non-resident trusts are, therefore, a useful means by which the liability to income tax can be deferred.

3. *Capital Gains Tax*

For capital gains tax purposes, a trust will, in principle, only be regarded as non-resident if both the following conditions are fulfilled:

(i) The general administration of the trust is ordinarily carried on outside the United Kingdom. There is no definition of precisely what this means but the general administration of the trust is

---

[34] Which for this purpose includes his widow.

probably regarded as ordinarily carried on in the place where the trustees habitually meet or, if the trust is large enough to have its own secretariat, in the place where that secretariat is situated.

(ii) The majority of the trustees are not resident or ordinarily resident in the United Kingdom.[35]

These requirements can be satisfied despite the fact that the settlor was resident in the United Kingdom at the time when the trust was created.

However, a trust will also be regarded as non-resident if all the following three conditions are satisfied:

(i) all the trust property is derived from a person who is not domiciled or resident in the United Kingdom;

(ii) some or all of the trustees are individuals or companies whose business consists of or includes the management of trusts or of acting as trustees;

(iii) a majority of the trustees are either such persons, or persons who are actually non-resident.[36]

Trusts who satisfy these three requirements are regarded as being non-resident even if their general administration is actually carried on in the United Kingdom.

(A) The Settlor

A settlor of any non-resident trust who in any year is both domiciled and resident in the United Kingdom will be personally liable to capital gains tax on all gains realised by the trust which would have been taxable if the trust had been resident where a "defined person" benefits or will or may become entitled to a benefit in either the income or the capital of the trust.[37] A "defined person" is the settlor, the settlor's spouse, any child or the spouse of any child of either the settlor or the settlor's spouse, and companies controlled by any such person.[38] In the case of trusts which are created or receive further property or go "off-shore" on or after March 17, 1998, the list also includes any grandchild or the spouse of any grandchild of either the settlor or the settlor's spouse.[39] From the same date, this liability also applies to the settlors of trusts created before March 19, 1991,[40] which were formerly exempt.[41]

This is an absolutely lethal provision, particularly because it includes children and step-children (and now grandchildren and step-grandchildren) of any age. However, some alleviation is provided by the fact that it only

---

[35] Taxation of Chargeable Gains Act 1992, s.69(1).

[36] ibid., s.69(2).

[37] ibid., s.86.

[38] ibid., Sched. 5, para. 2(3).

[39] Finance Act 1998, s.130.

[40] ibid., s.132.

[41] Taxation of Chargeable Gains Act 1992, Sched. 5, para. 9. The subsequent addition of property or of a "defined person" as a beneficiary destroyed the exemption.

applies where the settlor is both domiciled and resident in the year in question. Settlors of off-shore trusts can therefore avoid liability by becoming non-resident themselves before substantial capital gains are realised or by leaving the trust property in the form of assets such as cash which are not liable to capital gains tax in the first place. Further, many trusts which are created, as distinct from transferred, off-shore are purportedly created by non-resident settlors who, for a consideration, settle a nominal amount of their own money; the real trust property then reaches the hands of the trustees by a route which can best be described as circuitous (this was admittedly easier to achieve when it was considerably more difficult to follow bank transfers than it has now become).[42] Settlements with genuine off-shore settlors are of course outside the scope of this provision altogether.

(B) The Trustees
In common with non-resident individuals, non-resident trustees are not chargeable to capital gains tax in respect of gains arising on the disposal of assets, even if the assets are situated in the United Kingdom.[43]

(C) The Beneficiaries
The liability of the beneficiaries of non-resident trusts to capital gains tax depended until March 16, 1998 on whether the trust in question was what was known[44] as a section 87 trust[45] and or a fully foreign trust.[46] However, in respect of capital gains arising on or after March 17, 1998 all non-resident trusts are subject to the regime which formerly applied only to section 87 trusts.

---

[42] For this reason the extension to formerly exempt trusts is unlikely to have much impact.

[43] Taxation of Chargeable Gains Act 1992, s.2(1). There is, however, a liability if the non-resident carries on a trade in the U.K. and disposes of trading assets (*ibid.*, s.10(1)).

[44] Colloquially, not by statute.

[45] "Section 87" trusts, that is trusts which were within section 87 of the Taxation of Chargeable Gains Act 1992, were trusts in which, during the year of assessment being considered:
  (i) the trustees were non-resident;
  (ii) if the trust was created *inter vivos*, and the settlor was still alive, the settlor
      (a) was domiciled and resident in the United Kingdom at the time when the settlement was created; or
      (b) was domiciled and resident in the United Kingdom in the year of assessment being considered; or
  (iii) if the settlement was created *inter vivos* and the settlor was dead, he was domiciled and resident in the United Kingdom when the settlement was created; or
  (iv) if the settlement was created by will, the testator was domiciled and resident in the United Kingdom at the date of his death.

[46] A "fully foreign trust" was one which was non-resident and which was outside the scope of s.87. No liability attached to beneficiaries, even if resident in the U.K., in respect of gains realised by the trustees of a fully non-resident trust. This was so whether or not the trustees made capital payments to the beneficiaries. However, where a beneficiary became absolutely entitled to assets as against the trustees of a fully foreign trust, he would in general be treated as acquiring those assets at a nil base cost and so he would be taxable on the whole of the proceeds of sale when he disposed of them. This regime does not apply to any capital gains realised by a non-resident trust on or after March 17, 1998. However, beneficiaries who became absolutely entitled to assets as against the trustees of a fully foreign trust before that date will still be taxable on the whole of the proceeds of sale when they dispose of them.

The provisions of section 87 of the Taxation of Chargeable Gains Act 1992, which now apply to all future capital gains realised by non-resident trusts, are similar to those of section 740 of the Income and Corporation Taxes Act 1988.[47] A notional record is maintained of all gains which accrue to the trustees after March 9, 1981. These are known as "trust gains". When the trustees make a capital payment to a beneficiary[48] that payment is treated as representing a capital gain to the extent of the available trust gains. Suppose, therefore, that the trustees realise the following gains, and make the following capital payments:

Year of assessment	Gains	Capital Payment
1995/1996	nil	£8,000 to Andrew
1996/1997	£20,000	nil
1997/1998	£20,000	£15,000 to Brian
1998/1999	£20,000	£50,000 to Charles
1999/2000	£20,000	nil

The trust gains for 1995/1996 are nil. Of the gains realised in 1996/1997, £8,000 are attributed to Andrew for 1996/97, and the balance of £12,000 is carried forward to 1997/1998. The trust gains for 1997/1998 are (a) the balance brought forward from 1996/1997, £12,000, and (b) the gains arising in the year, £20,000, less (c) £15,000 which is attributed to Brian. The balance of £17,000 is carried forward. In 1998/1999 the trust gains total £37,000[49] so that £37,000 is attributed to Charles for 1998/1999. The remaining £13,000 which he has received in that year will have the gains for 1999/2000 attributed to it. If any of Andrew, Brian or Charles is domiciled and resident in the United Kingdom in the year in which any of these gains is attributed to a capital payment made to him, he will have to pay the appropriate capital gains tax thereon in accordance with the normal rules; thus, he can deduct from the attributed gain any losses and his annual exemption and will be taxed on the balance at the same rate as that at which he pays income tax. However, no capital gains tax will be payable by any beneficiary who is not domiciled and resident in the United Kingdom in the year in question.

However, in addition to the basic capital gains tax payable in the manner illustrated in this example, beneficiaries who receive capital payments after April 5, 1992 and are liable to pay capital gains tax because they are domiciled and resident in the United Kingdom also have to pay a supplementary interest charge of 10 per cent per annum of the tax actually payable in respect of any period up to six years during which payment of capital gains tax has been deferred.[50] In the example above, the capital payment to Andrew is not liable to this interest charge because no capital gains tax was actually deferred. However, the capital payments made to Brian and Charles will be liable to this payment. Of the £15,000 attributed to Brian in

---

[47] See ante, p. 766.
[48] Whether resident or non-resident.
[49] That is to say £17,000 brought forward from 1997/1998 and the £20,000 which arises in 1999/2000.
[50] Taxation of Chargeable Gains Act 1992, ss.91–97.

1997/1998, £12,000 was brought forward from 1996/1997 if he is domiciled and resident in the United Kingdom in 1997/1998, he will therefore have to pay an extra 10 per cent of the tax due in respect of that £12,000 (no interest will be payable in respect of the other £3,000 since that gain arose in the year in which he received the capital payment). In the same way, Charles will, if domiciled and resident in the United Kingdom in 1998/1999, have to pay an extra 10 per cent of the tax due in respect of £17,000 of the £37,000 attributed to him in 1998/1999.

The provisions seem complicated but their effect is that no liability can attach to a resident beneficiary until he actually receives a capital payment. Accordingly, deferment of capital gains tax can be achieved merely by retaining all capital within the trust, although such deferment will of course now be liable to an interest payment of 10 per cent per annum of the tax due in respect of any gains during the six years prior to the receipt of a capital payment by a resident beneficiary.

(D) Exporting Trusts
Since March 19, 1991, the exportation of a trust has constituted a deemed disposal by the trustees[51] similar to that which occurs when a beneficiary becomes absolutely entitled to the whole or any part of the trust property.[52] The deemed disposal is said to take place immediately before the trustees cease to become resident in the United Kingdom. Consequently, it is the retiring United Kingdom trustees who make the disposal and become primarily liable for the tax. This obviously means that exporting a trust involves the payment of capital gains tax on all gains made prior to export. Subsequent capital gains realised before March 17, 1998 escaped tax to the extent that the trust when exported did not become a section 87 trust (which it usually would have anyway).[53] Otherwise capital gains tax will be payable if any capital payments are made to beneficiaries who are domiciled and resident in the United Kingdom. The introduction of this exit charge has made exporting trusts considerably less attractive than hitherto. Nevertheless, provided that the settlor does not himself become liable to tax on the capital gains realised by the trust, there is still some merit in hiving off and exporting those assets in a trust which are likely to make substantial capital gains in the future and there is everything to be said for hiving off and exporting those assets in a trust which are actually showing a capital loss.

4. *Inheritance Tax*

Where settled property is situated in the United Kingdom, inheritance tax will in any event be payable by the settlor, the trustees and the beneficiaries according to the ordinary rules already discussed, which depend on whether or not there is an interest in possession in that property.[54]

Where settled property is situated outside the United Kingdom, that property is "excluded property" for inheritance tax purposes if, but only if,

---

[51] *ibid.*, s.80(2).
[52] See *ante*, p. 526.
[53] Because of the domiciliary and residential status of the settlor; see *ante*, n. 45.
[54] See *ante*, pp. 530, 535.

the settlor was domiciled outside the United Kingdom at the time when the settlement was made.[55] If property is excluded property, there will be no liability upon the coming to an end of an interest in possession, or upon any of the occasions on which inheritance tax is normally payable in the case of a discretionary trust, such as the making of a capital distribution out of the settled property, or the decennial anniversaries of the creation of the settlement.

The settlor will be treated as being domiciled in some part of the United Kingdom at the time when the settlement was created if:

(i) he would be treated as so domiciled according to the general law; or

(ii) he would be treated as being so domiciled according to the general law within three years prior to the creation of the settlement[56]; or

(iii) he was resident in the United Kingdom for at least 17 out of the 20 years ending with that in which the settlement was made.[57]

The last two categories only have full application where the property became settled after December 9, 1974.

Where, at the time when a settlement was made, the settlor was domiciled in some part of the United Kingdom, that settlement will, in principle, be permanently within the purview of inheritance tax. Strictly, inheritance tax will be payable even if the settlor, trustees, and all possible beneficiaries are resident outside the United Kingdom, and all the settled property is situated outside the United Kingdom.

In some circumstances, where a settlement is being exported, the parties are content to rely on the rule that one state will not enforce the tax laws of another. In other words, although inheritance tax may be payable, the parties will so conduct themselves that the tax cannot be recovered.

In other circumstances it may be possible to rely on a specific exemption which applies to Government securities. Most United Kingdom Government securities issued before March 18, 1977[58] are exempt from all United Kingdom taxation, including inheritance tax,[59] while they are in the beneficial ownership of persons who are neither domiciled,[60] nor ordinarily resident in the United Kingdom. This exemption applies to settled property where a person who is neither domiciled nor resident in the United Kingdom has an interest in possession in the securities.[61] If there is no interest in possession in the securities, the exemption only applies if it can be shown that all known persons for whose benefit the settled property or income from it has been or might be applied are neither domiciled nor ordinarily

---

[55] Inheritance Tax Act 1984, s.6(1).

[56] ibid., s.267(1)(a).

[57] ibid., ss.6(2), 267(1)(b).

[58] ibid., s.6(2).

[59] But the requirements for the exemption in the inheritance tax legislation must be satisfied: Van Ernst & Cie S.A. v. I.R.C. [1980] 1 All E.R. 677.

[60] "Domiciled" here has its ordinary, and not its extended, meaning.

[61] Inheritance Tax Act 1984, s.48(4).

resident in the United Kingdom.[62] Anti-avoidance provisions prevent exempt securities from being channelled from a trust with resident discretionary beneficiaries to one without any.[63]

It follows that where, for example, a fund is held upon trust for Andrew for life, with remainder to Hamish, inheritance tax will be avoided if, at the death of Andrew, he is neither domiciled nor resident in the United Kingdom and the fund is invested in exempt Government securities.

However, the liability to inheritance tax does not generally depend on the residential status of the trust. If the settlement was created by a non-domiciled settlor, and the property is situated abroad, the excluded property rules apply whether the trust is resident or non-resident. If the trust property consists of exempt British Government securities, and the beneficiaries are non-domiciled and non-resident, the exemption will also apply whether the trust is resident or non-resident. Exporting a trust will, therefore, neither mitigate nor exacerbate the liability to inheritance tax.

5. *Taxation Summary*

The preceding parts of this Chapter have attempted briefly to describe the effect of highly complex legislation. It will have been seen that if a new non-resident trust is created, or if an existing resident trust is exported:

(i) there will be no income tax saving in respect of income received, or receivable by a resident beneficiary;

(ii) liability to income tax on accumulated or withheld income may be deferred until the benefit of it is received by a resident beneficiary;

(iii) provided that the settlor does not become liable to tax on the capital gains realised by the non-resident trust, the liability of a resident beneficiary to capital gains tax will be deferred until a capital payment is received subject to the payment of interest in respect of the period of deferment, but only after the exit charge has been paid, thus restricting benefit to subsequent capital gains;

(iv) liability to inheritance tax will be the same as if the trust had remained resident.

IV. HOW TRUSTS ARE EXPORTED

The incidence of the taxes to which the settlor, the trustees and the beneficiaries of a non-resident trust are potentially liable does not in any case depend on the identity of the proper law of the trust in question. The proper law of any newly-created non-resident trust will almost inevitably not be English law. However, it is highly likely that the proper law of any existing

---

[62] *ibid.*
[63] *ibid.*, s.48(5).

resident trust which is exported will be English law. Any change in that proper law will require either the existence of a clause in the trust instrument expressly permitting this, or the agreement of all the beneficiaries, or, if any of the beneficiaries is not *sui juris*, the leave of the court under the Variation of Trusts Act 1958.[64] But not only is such a change not necessary in order to export a trust; it will not of itself achieve the fiscal advantages which have already been considered. None of these can be obtained unless the trustees also become non-resident; further, capital gains tax advantages can only, generally speaking, be obtained if the general administration of the trust is thereafter ordinarily carried on outside the United Kingdom.[65]

A change in the proper law may be desirable for other reasons, such as a wish to take advantage of what are perceived as the more favourable provisions of the trust law of some other jurisdiction[66] or simply a wish to have the trust property administered in accordance with the trust law of the jurisdiction where it or the administration of the trust is to be situated.[67] More fundamental changes to the existing trust instrument may also be necessary to take account of differences between English trust law and the new proper law. Indeed, if a trust is to be exported to a jurisdiction which does not recognise trusts or does not recognise them in the form known to English law, the beneficial interests may have to be completely recast. Most modern trust deeds contain what are known as overriding powers of appointment, permitting the trustees and/or the settlor and/or the protector to revoke all the existing beneficial interests and declare new ones; however, the standard forms of this power can probably only be used to declare new "trusts" in the sense in which that term is understood by English law. It may be that wider powers including a provision to declare new beneficial interests as nearly as possible equating to trusts under English law may become common. In the absence of any such power, an application to the court will be necessary under the Variation of Trusts Act 1958 even if all the beneficiaries are *sui juris* and in agreement.[68]

Where a change of proper law or some more fundamental change to the existing trust instrument is either desirable or necessary for one of the reasons referred to in the previous paragraph, then whether or not that is possible will be determined by the provisions of the trust instrument and/or the agreement of the beneficiaries and/or the court. However, whether or not this is the case, it will undoubtedly be necessary for the trust to acquire non-resident trustees. Where no other changes are desirable and/or possible, this is all that will be necessary. In principle, and very much in theory, the existing trustees (or one or more of them) could themselves simply emigrate. This is obviously possible where the existing trustees include the settlor and/or the beneficiaries but is almost inconceivable in the case of professional trustees and corporate trustees who could not emigrate even if they wanted to. In practice, therefore, it is almost inevitable that it will be

---

[64] See *ante*, p. 757.
[65] See *ante*, p. 767.
[66] See *ante*, p. 760.
[67] *ibid.*
[68] See *ante*, p. 662.

necessary to replace at least some of the existing resident trustees by non-resident trustees.

Superficially, this process appears quite straightforward. Whoever has the power to appoint new trustees to the trust in question[69] can simply appoint new non-resident trustees and the existing trustees can then retire with the trust property being simultaneously transferred to the new trustees or being left to vest in them automatically.[70] Unfortunately, however, as the next two sections of this Chapter demonstrate, this apparently straightforward process is not always as simple as it seems.

V. When Non-Resident Trustees May be Appointed

There are no statutory provisions referring specifically to the appointment of non-resident, as distinct from resident, trustees, probably because the possibility would not even have occurred to anyone until the middle of the last century and certainly did not become at all common until long after the Trustee Act 1925 was enacted. Such rules as have been developed have therefore had to be developed by the courts.

The English courts undoubtedly have power to appoint non-resident trustees of a settlement whose proper law is English law[71] and also have power to approve an arrangement under the Variation of Trusts Act 1958 by which non-resident trustees are appointed and the trust is consequently exported.[72] This power will be exercised if the court considers that such an appointment is in the interest of the beneficiaries.

It will usually be in the interest of the beneficiaries for the trust to be administered and for the trustees to be resident in the same territory as that in which the beneficiaries, or a majority of them, reside. *Re Seale's Marriage Settlement*[73] was concerned with a marriage settlement made in 1931 at a time when the husband and wife were domiciled in England. The husband and wife subsequently emigrated to Canada with their children and at the date of the hearing in 1961 had been living in Canada for some years and were domiciled there. Buckley J. found as a fact that they intended to continue to reside there. They wanted to export the trust to Quebec in two stages: first, by the appointment of a Canadian trust corporation to be trustee of the marriage settlement with the consequential discharge of the English trustees and, secondly, by the property subject to the marriage settlement being transferred to the Canadian corporation as trustee of a new Quebec settlement. The new settlement followed as closely as possible the terms of the English settlement but could not include certain protective life interests which were not recognised by the law of Quebec. Buckley J. was satisfied that it was to the advantage of all the beneficiaries for the settlement to be exported and he approved the arrangements. This decision was

---

[69] See *ante*, p. 468.

[70] See *ante*, p. 482.

[71] *Meinertzhagen v. Davis* (1844) 1 Coll.N.C. 355; *Re Long's Settlement* (1869) 17 W.R. 218; *Re Seale's Marriage Settlement* [1961] Ch. 574; *Re Whitehead's Will Trusts* [1971] 1 W.L.R. 833.

[72] *Re Seale's Marriage Settlement* [1961] Ch. 574; *Re Windeatt's Will Trusts* [1969] 1 W.L.R. 692; *Re Whitehead's Will Trusts* [1971] 1 W.L.R. 833.

[73] [1961] Ch. 574.

followed in *Re Windeatt's Will Trusts*.[74] The testator, who died domiciled in England, created a will trust for the benefit principally of his daughter and her children. The daughter and her children had lived in Jersey for 19 years prior to the application and were held to be permanently resident there. Pennycuick J. approved an arrangement for two Jersey residents to be appointed as trustees and for the trust assets to be transferred to them.

In certain circumstances it will also be in the interests of the beneficiaries for non-resident trustees to be appointed even if the beneficiaries are resident in a jurisdiction different from that in which the trustees are resident. It may be in the interests of the beneficiaries for the trust to be exported from the United Kingdom so that it may cease to be liable to United Kingdom taxation but not appropriate for the trust to be exported to the jurisdiction in which the beneficiaries are resident if that jurisdiction does not recognise, or is not fully acquainted with, the concept of a trust; in such circumstances, it may clearly be appropriate for the trust to be exported to a territory which does recognise trusts. In *Re Chamberlain*[75] some of the beneficiaries of a trust subject to English law were resident in France and the others were resident in Indonesia; neither of these jurisdictions recognised trusts and so the court approved an arrangement to export the trust to Guernsey by the appointment of trustees resident there.

On the other hand, the court will not approve the appointment of non-resident trustees if they are resident in a territory which may be reluctant to enforce the trust. If all the trustees are non-resident and the assets are situated abroad, the court will be incapable of protecting the beneficiaries and it will therefore wish to be satisfied that, in the case of any maladministration, the beneficiaries will be given protection by the local law. This was a factor which influenced the Court of Appeal in *Re Weston's Settlement*[76] to refuse to appoint non-resident trustees, although, as will be seen later on, this was not the principal reason for their decision. The basis of this conclusion was the fact that there was no equivalent of the Trustee Act 1925 in Jersey and that no *inter vivos* settlement had at that time ever had to be enforced by the courts of Jersey. While this general principle is unquestionably sound, the particular objection to Jersey appears to have been misconceived and Pennycuick J. subsequently approved the exportation of trusts to Jersey in both *Re Windeatt's Will Trusts*[77] and *Re Whitehead's Will Trusts*.[78] It should be added that comprehensive trust legislation has now been enacted in Jersey.

Whether the court will approve exportation where the beneficiaries are all resident in England and the principal purpose is the mitigation of fiscal liabilities is much less clear. In principle, in view of the attitude which the court has taken in the case of applications to mitigate such liabilities in other circumstances,[79] there should be no insuperable objection to the export of a

[74] [1969] 1 W.L.R. 692.
[75] [1976] N.L.J. 1934.
[76] [1969] 1 Ch. 223, discussed in detail *ante* p. 662; *post*, p. 777.
[77] [1969] 1 W.L.R. 692; see *ante*, p. 775.
[78] [1971] 1 W.L.R. 833; see *post*, p. 778.
[79] See for example *Pilkington v. I.R.C.* [1964] A.C. 612; *ante*, p. 625 and decisions on the Variation of Trusts Act 1958, *ante*, pp. 662 *et seq.*

trust in these circumstances. However, some doubts were cast on this conclusion by the decision in *Re Weston's Settlements*,[80] where there were admittedly three different grounds on which approval was denied.

The settlor had in 1964 transferred a total of 500,000 shares in The Stanley Weston Group to the trustees of two settlements for the benefit of his two sons. In the very next year, the legislature introduced, for the very first time, a capital gains tax, something which neither the settlor nor his advisers had anticipated. The shares rose in value and, by the time of the hearing at first instance in 1968, were pregnant with a liability to capital gains tax of £163,000. The settlor lived in England until 1967. Having in the first half of that year made three visits of a few days each to Jersey, he then purchased a house there, in which he lived from August 1967. In November 1967 an application was made to the court for the appointment as trustees of the two settlements of two professional men in Jersey of impeccable standing and the approval of an arrangement under which the property subject to the settlements could be transferred to settlements in identical terms subject to the law of Jersey. It was hoped that the property subject to the settlements would thereby avoid capital gains tax[81] and also estate duty.[82]

Both Stamp J. and the Court of Appeal refused to sanction the arrangement. They were influenced by two main factors.[83] First, there was clearly some doubt whether the settlor and his children, the main beneficiaries, would live in Jersey permanently, particularly as they had only been there for a few months prior to the date of the hearing; that was insufficient to show any settled intention to remain and the court was clearly worried about the possibility that, following the approval of the arrangement and a sale of the shares free of capital gains tax, the beneficiaries would return to England.[84] Secondly, as has already been mentioned in a previous Chapter,[85] this was, according to Stamp J., "a cheap exercise in tax avoidance" which ought not to be sanctioned,[86] a view also taken in the Court of Appeal by Harman L.J., who described it as "an essay in tax avoidance naked and unashamed".[87]

It is, frankly, somewhat surprising that this seems to have disturbed the court in the light of the fact that numerous applications under the Variation of Trusts Act 1958 have had as their main, if not their only, motive the minimisation of fiscal liabilities.[88] It is impossible to avoid wondering whether the court was influenced by the feeling that the settlor, who was the son of a Russian immigré who had built up his fortune in England during the 1939–45 war, should not be permitted to escape the tax liabilities to which he would normally have been subject. With the benefit of hindsight,

---

[80] [1969] 1 Ch. 223; see also *ante*, p. 662.

[81] The exportation of the trust would now of course amount to a deemed disposal and so capital gains tax would be payable; see *ante*, p. 771.

[82] Now replaced by inheritance tax.

[83] [1969] 1 Ch. 223 at 245, 246, *per* Lord Denning M.R.

[84] A third one, whether the courts of Jersey would enforce the trust, has already been considered; see *ante*, p. 776.

[85] See *ante*, p. 662.

[86] [1969] 1 Ch. 223 at 234.

[87] *ibid.* at 246.

[88] See *ante*, p. 662.

it seems that the trustees were unfortunately advised and that the arrangement would have been approved if it had been made a few years later, when it could have been shown that the beneficiaries had genuinely settled in Jersey. However, in *Re Windeatt's Will Trusts*[89] Pennycuick J. expressed himself[90] to be "in the most complete agreement" with the decision in *Re Weston's Settlements* and in *Richard v. MacKay*[91] Millett J. said that the court was unlikely to appoint non-resident trustees "where the scheme is nothing more than a device to avoid tax and has no advantages of any kind". However, since neither of these decisions involved any tax avoidance whatever, it remains to be seen what view is adopted when the question actually has to be decided; facts such as those in *Re Weston's Settlements* are obviously unlikely to recur. Provided that the scheme is not entirely motivated by tax avoidance, the practical answer for trustees in this position is probably to make the appointment themselves, assuming of course that they have power to do so, in the way envisaged in *Re Beatty (deceased) (No. 2)*,[92] which is discussed below.[93]

The authorities considered so far have concerned the question of when the courts will appoint non-resident trustees. It is now necessary to consider whether, and if so when, resident trustees who have adequate powers for the purpose under the trust instrument or the Trustee Act 1925 can themselves do so.

It has long been clear that, where the court would itself be prepared to appoint non-resident trustees, resident trustees with the power to do so can make an effective appointment without the intervention of the court. In *Re Whitehead's Will Trusts*,[94] the main beneficiary had emigrated to Jersey in 1959 and was found to be permanently resident there.[95] In 1969 the trustees, who were resident in the United Kingdom, executed a deed under section 36 of the Trustee Act 1925[96] appointing persons resident in Jersey as new trustees and retiring from the trusts. However, since the resident trustees wished to be fully protected, the deed of retirement and appointment was made conditional upon the principal beneficiary obtaining from the court a declaration that the resident trustees were effectively discharged. Pennycuick V.-C. duly made the declaration sought.

However, two further questions arise: first, are the trustees only protected if a declaration of this sort is obtained and, secondly, can the trustees also exercise their own powers in circumstances where the courts would not themselves appoint non-resident trustees?

In *Re Whitehead's Will Trusts*,[97] where a declaration was of course obtained, Pennycuick V.-C. said[98]:

---

[89] [1969] 1 W.L.R. 692.
[90] *ibid*. at 696.
[91] (1987), unreported; see 11 Trust Law International 22–25 and *post*, p. 777.
[92] (1991), unreported; available on Lexis.
[93] See *post*, p. 780.
[94] [1971] 1 W.L.R. 833.
[95] *ibid*. at 838.
[96] See *ante*, p. 470.
[97] [1971] 1 W.L.R. 833.
[98] *ibid*. at 837.

"the law has been quite well established for upwards of a century that there is no absolute bar to the appointment of persons resident abroad as trustees of an English trust. I say 'no absolute bar', in the sense that such an appointment would be prohibited by law and would consequently be invalid. On the other hand, apart from exceptional circumstances, it is not proper to make such an appointment, that is to say, the court would not, apart from exceptional circumstances, make such an appointment, nor would it be right for the donees of the power to make such an appointment out of court. If they did, presumably the court would be likely to interfere at the instance of the beneficiaries. There do, however, exist exceptional circumstances in which such an appointment can properly be made. The most obvious exceptional circumstances are those [which actually occurred in that case] in which the beneficiaries have settled permanently in some country outside the United Kingdom and what is proposed to be done is to appoint new trustees in that country."

However, this view has subsequently been rejected in two unreported decisions. In *Richard v. MacKay*,[99] trustees sought a declaration that they were entitled to exercise a power undoubtedly vested in them to transfer about a quarter of the assets of an accumulation and maintenance trust for the benefit of the settlor's children to a new trust which the settlor proposed to create in Bermuda. The settlor, his Malaysian wife, and the children were all resident in the United Kingdom but they had substantial contacts with the Far East both of a financial and of a family nature and there was a real possibility that the children, and indeed their mother in the event of early widowhood, would decide to settle in the Far East. The trust's assets were invested all over the world and the principal motive was flexibility and diversification rather than any immediate tax advantage. Millett J. referred to the observations of Pennycuick V.-C. set out above and said:

"In my judgment, the language of Sir John Pennycuick, which is narrowly drawn, is too restrictive for the circumstances of the present day if, at least, it is intended to lay down any rule of practice. Nor, in my view, is it accurate to equate the approach that the court adopts in the exercise of its own discretion with the approach which it adopts when asked to authorise the trustees to exercise theirs.

Where the court is invited to exercise an original discretion of its own, . . . the court will require to be satisfied that the discretion should be exercised in the manner proposed. The applicants must make out a positive case for the exercise of the discretion, and the court is unlikely to assist them where the scheme is nothing more than a device to avoid tax and has no advantages of any kind.

Where, however, the transaction is proposed to be carried out by the trustees in exercise of their own discretion, entirely out of court, the trustees retaining their discretion and merely seeking the authorisation of the court for their own protection, then, in my judgment, the question that the court asks itself is quite different. It is concerned to ensure that the proposed exercise

---

[99] (1987), unreported; see 11 Trust Law International 22–25.

of the trustees' power is lawful and within the power and that it does not infringe the trustees' duty to act as ordinary, reasonable and prudent trustees might act, but it requires only to be satisfied that the trustees can properly form the view that the proposed transaction is for the benefit of beneficiaries or the trust estate.

... In my judgment, where the trustees retain their discretion, as they do in the present case, the court should need to be satisfied only that the proposed transaction is not so inappropriate that no reasonable trustee could entertain it."

He therefore made the declaration sought. His views were subsequently approved and applied by Vinelott J. in another unreported case, *Re Beatty (deceased) (No. 2)*,[1] where a similar declaration was sought by the trustees of the will of a testatrix who had died domiciled and resident in the United Kingdom; they wished to appoint replacement trustees resident in Jersey and transfer to them an absolutely enormous residuary estate, held in more or less equal shares for one resident beneficiary, one non-resident beneficiary, and one beneficiary who was about to become non-resident, in order to avoid a deemed disposal for the purposes of capital gains tax which would arise when the latter two obtained interests in possession.[2]

The trustees can therefore certainly exercise their own powers to appoint non-resident trustees in circumstances where the courts would not themselves do so provided that the proposed transaction is not so inappropriate that no reasonable trustee could entertain it. Given that this is now clearly the law, there cannot possibly be any formal need for them to go to the court for a declaration in every case, although they might well feel that it was prudent for them to do so in a case with facts as extreme as those in *Re Weston's Settlements*![3] However, where they do not seek a declaration, then for the reasons stated in the next section they may also be well-advised to seek adequate indemnities from the non-resident trustees or the beneficiaries.

VI. EXPORTING PART OF THE TRUST

Richard v. MacKay[4] was a case in which non-resident trustees were appointed of part, but not the whole, of the trust fund. Provided that the circumstances are appropriate for the appointment of non-resident trustees in the first place, there is obviously no fundamental objection to this. Indeed, section 37(1)(b) of the Trustee Act 1925 provides that a separate set of trustees may be appointed for any part of the trust property held on trusts distinct from those relating to any other part of the trust property; this provision clearly covers the situation where separate trustees are appointed even although there is no alteration to the trustees of the remainder of the trust fund.

---

[1] (1991), unreported; available on Lexis.
[2] Fortunately for them, judgment in this case was given just 19 days before the exportation itself became a deemed disposal; see *ante*, p. 771.
[3] [1969] 1 Ch. 223.
[4] (1987), unreported; see 11 Trust Law International 22–25.

However, as the trustees in *Roome v. Edwards*[5] found out, there are major risks in so doing. This case concerned a marriage settlement created in 1944. In 1955, a power of appointment was exercised in respect of a comparatively small part of the trust fund, whereby that part was thereafter to be held on trust to accumulate the income until a daughter of the marriage reached the age of 25 and then to transfer the capital of that part to her. The appointed fund was, from 1955 onwards, administered as if it were a trust separate from the main fund. One of the assets of the main trust appreciated very substantially in value and with a view to saving capital gains tax the main fund, but not the 1955 fund, was exported by means of the retirement of the resident trustees and the appointment of trustees resident in the Cayman Islands. The capital gain was realised shortly thereafter and the Inland Revenue claimed the capital gains tax from the trustees of the 1955 fund, who were still resident. The House of Lords held that the 1955 fund and the main fund still comprised only one settlement for the purposes of capital gains tax; consequently, the claim succeeded by virtue of the fact that, where part of the property comprised in a settlement is vested in one set of trustees and part in another, they are to be treated as together constituting and acting on behalf of a single body of trustees. The resident trustees of the 1955 fund were therefore liable to pay the tax on the gain realised by the non-resident trustees of the main fund. Lord Roskill gave a clear warning[6]:

"Persons, whether professional men or not, who accept appointment as trustees of settlements such as these are clearly at risk under the [1992] Act and have only themselves to blame if they accept the obligations of trustees in these circumstances without ensuring that they are sufficiently and effectively protected whether by their beneficiaries or otherwise for fiscal or other liabilities which may fall on them personally as a result of the obligations which they had felt able to assume."

Not only are there therefore particular risks in the export of part rather than the whole of a trust but the decision in *Roome v. Edwards* reinforces the view that, whenever resident trustees retire in favour of non-resident trustees without the intervention of the court, they should always seek adequate indemnities.

---

[5] [1981] 1 All E.R. 736.
[6] *ibid.* at 744.

INDEX

[All references are to page number]

783

INCOME OF TRUST FUND, 595–615
accounting period, 595–596
accumulation, 601
administrative powers, 596–598
dispositive powers, 596–598
generally, 595
gifts of, 598–600
gross income, 596
income tax, 611–613
inheritance tax, 613–614
intermediate, 599
maintenance of infant beneficiaries, *see*
MINORS.
management expenses, 596
net income, 596
net trust income, 598
retention of income,
accumulation, 601
excessive powers, 601–602
exercise of power, 602–603
generally, 601
trust or power to accumulate, 601
taxation,
generally, 611
income tax, 611–613
inheritance tax, 613–614
trust management expenses, 596
INCOMPLETE TRUSTS,
resulting trusts, 261–262
INCOMPLETELY CONSTITUTED TRUSTS,
completely constituted trusts and, 124–125
contractual remedies for, 150–162
after-acquired property, 151–152
contract to create trust,
common law, at, 152–153
equity, at, 152–153
covenant to create trust, 156–162
generally, 150–152
marriage settlements, 154–156
simple contract recognised only in
equity, 153–156
specialty contract,
action by trustees on covenant,
160–162
beneficiary party to the contract,
159–160
benefit of the covenant, 156–159
generally, 156–159
marriage settlements, 154–156
meaning, 39
principles of, 150–162
INCONSISTENT DEALING,
generally, 319–320
INDEMNITIES,
beneficiaries, from, 703–704
INFLATION ADJUSTED SECURITIES, 549
INHERITANCE TAX, 530–539
calculation, 532–534
chargeable transfers, 531–532
charitable trusts, 382–383
discretionary trusts, 536–538

INHERITANCE TAX—*cont.*
exempt transfers, 531–532
foreign trusts, 771–773
generally, 530–531
income of trust fund, 613–614
interest in possession settlements, 535–536
potentially exempt transfers, 531–532
rate, 530–531
settlements, liability of, 534–539
INSIDER DEALING, 573–574
INSOLVENCY OF DONEE,
discretionary trusts, 196
powers, 196
INTENTION, CERTAINTY OF, 82–87
changing attitude of courts, 82–83
effect of uncertainty, 86
modern rule, 82–85
sham trusts, 86–87
uncertainty, effect of, 86
INTEREST,
breach of trust, 688–690
INTEREST IN POSSESSION
SETTLEMENTS,
inheritance tax, 535–536
INTERMEDDLING BY STRANGERS,
319–349
agents, liability of, 335–336
corporate fraud, 321–322
dishonest assistance, liability for, 323–336
accessory to misfeasance or breach,
329–331
agents, liability of, 335
breach of trust, 327–329
dishonesty by accessory or person
assisting, 331–335
elements of liability, 325–335
existence of trust, 326–327
generally, 319, 320
invalidly appointed trustees, liability of
agents of, 335
misfeasance, existence of, 327–329
partners of persons liable, 335–336
suspicions of agents, action on, 336
terminology, 323–325
"with knowledge", liability imposed on
persons acting with, 331–335
distinguishing between types of liability,
320–321
elements of liability,
remedies available, 336–339
generally, 267–268
inconsistent dealing, 348–349
generally, 319–320
invalidly appointed trustees, liability of
agents of, 335
knowing assistance, 319
knowing receipt,
available remedies, 336–339
beneficial receipt of property, 340–341
disposition of property in breach of
trust, 339